# THE YEAR'S WORK IN
# MODERN LANGUAGE
# STUDIES

# THE
# YEAR'S WORK IN
# MODERN LANGUAGE
# STUDIES

GENERAL EDITOR
## STEPHEN PARKINSON

ASSISTANT EDITORS
## LISA BARBER

## JOHN ANDREW

SECTION EDITORS

LATIN, ROMANCE LINGUISTICS, FRENCH,
OCCITAN, SPANISH, CATALAN, PORTUGUESE,
GALICIAN, LATIN AMERICAN, SLAVONIC
## STEPHEN PARKINSON, M.A., PH.D.
*Lecturer in
Portuguese Language and Linguistics,
University of Oxford*

ITALIAN, ROMANIAN, RHETO-ROMANCE
## JOHN M. A. LINDON, M.A.
*Professor of Italian Studies,
University College London*

CELTIC
## DAVID A. THORNE, M.A., PH.D.
*Reader in Welsh,
University of Wales, Lampeter*

GERMANIC
## DAVID A. WELLS, M.A., PH.D.
*Professor of German,
Birkbeck College, University of London*

## VOLUME 61
# 1999

MANEY PUBLISHING
*for the*
MODERN HUMANITIES RESEARCH ASSOCIATION
2000

*The Year's Work in Modern Language Studies* may be ordered from the Hon. Treasurer, MHRA, King's College London, Strand, London WC2R 2LS, England.

ISBN 1 902653 35 1

ISSN 0084-4152

*Produced in Great Britain by*
MANEY PUBLISHING
HUDSON ROAD   LEEDS LS9 7DL   UK

# CONTENTS

PREFACE                                                         *page* xi

I   LATIN
    I    MEDIEVAL LATIN,                                         I
         *by* PROFESSOR C. J. MCDONOUGH, M.A., PH.D.

    II   NEO-LATIN, Postponed


2   ROMANCE LANGUAGES
    I    ROMANCE LINGUISTICS                                    13
         *by* PROFESSOR J. N. GREEN, M.A., D.PHIL.

    II   FRENCH STUDIES
         Language,                                              30
         *by* PROFESSOR GLANVILLE PRICE,
              M.A., DOCT. DE L'UNIV.
         Early Medieval Literature,                             50
         *by* SARA JAMES, B.A., M.A., PH.D.
         Late Medieval Literature,                              69
         *by* ROSALIND BROWN-GRANT, B.A., PH.D.
         The Sixteenth Century,                                 92
         *by* CATHERINE REUBEN, M.A., PH.D.
         The Seventeenth Century,                               119
         *by* JOHN TRETHEWEY, B.A., PH.D.
         *and* J. P. SHORT, B.A.
         The Eighteenth Century,                                151
         *by* PROFESSOR D. A. DESSERUD, M.A., PH.D.
         The Romantic Era,                                      153
         *by* JOHN WHITTAKER, B.A., PH.D.
         The Nineteenth Century (Post-Romantic), Postponed
         The Twentieth Century, 1900–1945, Postponed
         The Twentieth Century, since 1945,                     173
         *by* H. G. MCINTYRE, B.A., PH.D.
         French Canadian Literature,                            183
         *by* C. D. ROLFE, M.A.
         Caribbean Literature,                                  196
         *by* MARY GALLAGHER, M.A., PH.D.
         African and Maghreb Literature, Postponed

III OCCITAN STUDIES

Language,      200
*by* KATHRYN KLINGEBIEL, M.A., PH.D.

Literature,      213
*by* CATHERINE E. LÉGLU, B.A., M.A., PH.D.


IV SPANISH STUDIES

Language,      218
*by* PROFESSOR STEVEN DWORKIN, M.A., PH.D.
*and* AENGUS WARD, M.A., PH.D.

Medieval Literature,      232
*by* JANE E. CONNOLLY, PH.D.,
MARÍA MORRÁS, PH.D.,
*and* DOLORES PELÁEZ, PH.D.

Aljamiado Literature, Postponed

Literature, 1490–1700 (Prose and Poetry), Postponed

Literature, 1490–1700 (Drama), Postponed

Literature, 1700–1823,      253
*by* GABRIEL SÁNCHEZ ESPINOSA, D.PHIL.

Literature, 1823–1898, Postponed

Literature, 1898–1936,      259
*by* PROFESSOR K. M. SIBBALD, M.A., PH.D.

Literature, 1936 to the Present Day,      280
*by* OMAR A. GARCÍA-OBREGÓN
*and* IRENE MIZRAHI, M.A., PH.D.


V CATALAN STUDIES

Language,      297
*by* SÍLVIA LLACH

Medieval Literature,      301
*by* PROFESSOR LOLA BADIA, LLIC.FIL.
*and* MIRIAM CABRÉ, LLIC.FIL., PH.D.

Literature (Nineteenth and Twentieth Centuries), Postponed


VI PORTUGUESE STUDIES

Language,      309
*by* STEPHEN PARKINSON, M.A., PH.D.

Medieval Literature, Postponed

Literature, 1500 to the Present Day, Postponed

VII GALICIAN STUDIES

Language, 319
*by* PROFESSOR DAVID MACKENZIE, M.A., PH.D.,
FRANCISCO DUBERT GARCÍA, LIC.FIL., PH.D.
*and* XULIO SOUSA FERNÁNDEZ, LIC.FIL., PH.D.

Literature, 329
*by* DOLORES VILAVEDRA, PH.D.
*and* DEREK FLITTER, M.A., D.PHIL.

VIII LATIN AMERICAN STUDIES

Spanish-American Literature: The Colonial Period,
Postponed

The Nineteenth Century, 340
*by* ANNELLA MCDERMOTT, M.A.

The Twentieth Century, 344
*by* PROFESSOR D. L. SHAW, M.A., PH.D.

Brazilian Literature, 366
*by* MARK DINNEEN, M.A., PH.D.

IX ITALIAN STUDIES

Language, 373
*by* ADAM LEDGEWAY, M.A., PH.D.
*and* ALESSANDRA LOMBARDI, DOTT. LETT., M.A., PH.D.

Duecento and Trecento I (Dante), 394
*by* CATHERINE KEEN, M.A., PH.D.

Duecento and Trecento II (excluding Dante), Postponed

Humanism and the Renaissance, 423
*by* P. L. ROSSI, M.A.,
*and* GERALDINE MUIRHEAD, M.A.

Seicento, Postponed

Settecento, 454
*by* G. W. SLOWEY, M.A.

Ottocento, 468
*by* PROFESSOR J. M. A. LINDON, M.A.

Novecento, 497
*by* ROBERTO BERTONI, DOTT. LETT.,
*and* PROFESSOR CATHERINE O'BRIEN, M.A., DOTT. LETT.

X ROMANIAN STUDIES

Language, 527
*by* PROFESSOR MARTIN MAIDEN, M.A., M.PHIL., PH.D.

Literature, 541
*by* PROFESSOR MIRCEA ANGHELESCU, PH.D.

viii     *Contents*

  XI   RHETO-ROMANCE STUDIES     549
         *by* INGMAR SÖHRMAN, M.A., PH.D.

## 3  CELTIC LANGUAGES

   I   WELSH STUDIES

Language,     553
   *by* DAVID THORNE, M.A., PH.D.

Early and Medieval Literature,     556
   *by* JANE CARTWRIGHT, B.A., PH.D.

Literature since 1500,     561
   *by* A. CYNFAEL LAKE, M.A., PH.D.

   II   BRETON AND CORNISH STUDIES, Postponed

  III   IRISH STUDIES

Early Irish, Postponed

Modern Irish, Postponed

  IV   SCOTTISH GAELIC STUDIES, Postponed

## 4  GERMANIC LANGUAGES

   I   GERMAN STUDIES

Language,     567
   *by* CHARLES V. J. RUSS, M.A., M.LITT., PH.D.

Medieval Literature,     587
   *by* PROFESSOR DAVID A. WELLS, M.A., PH.D.

The Sixteenth Century,     637
   *by* MARK TAPLIN, B.A., M.LITT., PH.D.

The Seventeenth Century,     650
   *by* ANNA CARRDUS, B.A., PH.D.

The Classical Era,     659
   *by* JEFFREY MORRISON, M.A., D.PHIL.

The Romantic Era,     680
   *by* LAURA MARTIN, B.A., M.A., PH.D.

Literature, 1830–1880,     704
   *by* W. N. B. MULLAN, B.A., M.LITT.

Literature, 1880–1945, Postponed

Literature from 1945 to the Present Day,     752
   *by* OWEN EVANS, B.A., PH.D.

   II   DUTCH STUDIES

Language, Postponed

Literature, 776
*by* WIM HÜSKEN, DR.

III DANISH STUDIES
Language, 798
*by* TOM LUNDSKÆR-NIELSEN, M.PHIL., PH.D.
Literature, Postponed

IV NORWEGIAN STUDIES
Language, Postponed
Literature since the Reformation, 804
*by* ØYSTEN ROTTEM, CAND.PHILOL.

V SWEDISH STUDIES
Language, 810
*by* GUNILLA HALSIUS, M.A.
Literature, 821
*by* BIRGITTA THOMPSON, FIL.MAG., M.A., DIP.LIB.

5 SLAVONIC LANGUAGES
I CZECH STUDIES
Language, Postponed
Literature, Postponed

II SLOVAK STUDIES
Language, Postponed
Literature, Postponed

III POLISH STUDIES
Language, 845
*by* NIGEL GOTTERI, M.A.
Literature, 861
*by* JOHN MICHAEL BATES, B.A., M.PHIL., PH.D.

IV RUSSIAN STUDIES
Language, Postponed
Literature from the Beginning to 1700, Postponed
Literature, 1700–1820, Postponed
Literature, 1820–1880, Postponed
Literature, 1880–1917, Postponed
Literature from 1917 to the Present Day, Postponed

V UKRAINIAN STUDIES, Postponed

VI BELARUSIAN STUDIES, Postponed

x                    *Contents*

VII    SERBO-CROAT STUDIES
       Language, Postponed
       Literature, Postponed
VIII   BULGARIAN STUDIES, Postponed


ABBREVIATIONS

I    ACTA, FESTSCHRIFTEN AND OTHER                877
     COLLECTIVE AND GENERAL WORKS

II   GENERAL                                      885

III  PLACE NAMES                                  887

IV   PERIODICALS, INSTITUTIONS, PUBLISHERS        887


NAME INDEX                                        937

# PREFACE

This volume surveys work, published in 1999, unless otherwise stated, in the fields of Romance, Celtic, Germanic, and Slavonic languages and literatures. An asterisk before the title of a book or article indicates that the item in question has not been seen by the contributor.

The attention of users is drawn to the lists of abbreviations at the end of the volume, which are also available on-line on the MHRA's WWW site (http://www.mhra.org.uk/YWMLS). Also worthy of note is the new format adopted for the Name Index, making a clearer distinction between current scholars and authors or historical figures.

Many authors, editors and publishers supply review copies and offprints of their publications. To these we and our contributors are grateful, and we would invite others to follow their example, especially in the case of work issuing from unusual, unexpected, or inaccessible sources of publication. We would ask that, whenever possible, items for review be sent directly to the appropriate contributor; where no obvious recipient can be identified, as in the case of books or journal issues relating to a number of fields, the item should be sent to one of the editors, who will distribute the contents accordingly.

The compilation of a contribution to the volume, especially in the field of the major languages and periods of literature, is a substantial research task requiring wide-ranging and specialized knowledge of the subject besides a huge reading effort accompanied by the constant exercise of critical judgement. We are deeply grateful to the authors who have devoted significant amounts of increasingly precious research time to this enterprise. The measure of their task is indicated by the number of sections for which the editors have failed to find contributors; we encourage approaches from potential contributors or groups of contributors for future volumes.

We record with gratitude the contributions of two former General Editors, which come to an end with this volume. Peter Mayo has retired as Slavonic Editor, after a long association with the journal as contributor, Slavonic Editor, General Editor, and indexer. At the same time, our Germanic Editor David Wells contributes his last article on Medieval German Literature, closing an uninterrupted sequence going back to volume 30 (1968), and thus equalling the record of thirty-two successive contributions.

The completion of this volume would not have been possible without the contribution of Lisa Barber, Assistant Editor and compiler of the Index, who took over the General Editor's responsibilities during his recent convalescence. Thanks are also due to the other institutions and individuals who have contributed in one way or another to the making of the volume. They include, in particular, John Andrew, Assistant Editor for Slavonic contributions; the secretarial and administrative staff of the Faculty of Modern Languages, Oxford University; and our printers, Maney Publishing, particularly Michael Gallico and Liz Rosindale, whose expertise and patience have as ever ensured the smooth progress of this complex operation.

*5 December 2000*                                     S.R.P., J.M.A.L., D.A.T., D.A.W.

# 1

# LATIN

## I. MEDIEVAL LATIN

By CHRISTOPHER J. MCDONOUGH, *Professor of Classics, University of Toronto*

### 1. GENERAL

J. W. George, 'Venantius Fortunatus: the end game', *Eranos*, 96, 1998:32–43, examines the chronological order of the poems in Books 10 and 11, argues for a later dating of the last four poems, and shows how V. used the authority of the Latin literary tradition to advance the political and ecclesiastical interests of Tours and Poitiers. A. W. Astell, 'Cassiodorus's *Commentary on the Psalms* as an *ars rhetorica*', *Rhetorica*, 17:37–75, argues that the *Commentary* established the Bible as an alternative source to pagan theory and practice for the liberal arts and especially as a model for rhetorical imitation, as passages marked in the Psalter reveal. H. Fuhrmann, 'Pseudoisidor und die Bibel', *DAEM*, 55:183–91, considers the implications of several intertexts embedded in the preface to the pseudo-Isidorian Decretals. R. Jakobi, 'Adnoten zu den *Ioca monachorum*', *Eranos*, 96, 1998:72–74, solves several *aenigmata* through textual emendations. E. Poppe, 'Reconstructing medieval Irish literary theory: the lesson of *Airec Menman Uraird maic Coise*', *CMCS*, 37:33–54, discusses the terms *fabula*, *historia* and *delectatio* in the colophon to *Táin Bó Cuailnge* in assessing the balance between historical and allegorical interpretive modes for secular (pseudo-) historical narrative prose. M. Giovini, '"O admirabile Veneris ydolum": un carme d'amore paidico del X secolo e il mito di Deucalione', *SM*, 40:261–78, argues that the text's structure is organized around the themes of solid (stone)/liquid (water) and fixity and motion, before he discusses the classical sources, including Juvenal, Vergil, and Ovid. M. Giovini, '*Nel ventre della balena*: un'indagine sul mito di Giona (Letaldo di Micy (X. sec.)), Ariosto, Collodi, Montale', *Maia*, 51:111–22, demonstrates the Protean nature of the myth of Jonah by examining texts, including Hrotswitha's *Dulcitius*, from the 10th to the 20th century. A. E. Witte, 'De l'excrément à l'or: l'anthropologie des noms attribués aux ânes de l'époque romaine à William Shakespeare', *SM*, 40:249–59, surveys popular and medieval associations of the ass as a symbol of the body, flesh, sin, and impurity, before examining the character of Bottom in *A Midsummer Night's Dream* in relation to the doublet arse/ass in medieval and Renaissance texts. G. Binding, '*Architectus, magister operis, wercmeistere*: Baumeister oder Bauverwalter im Mittelalter', *MJ*, 34:7–28, traces how the concepts attaching to *architectus* and *architector* vary from author to author, and how the meaning of the former was influenced by Paul's first *Letter to the Corinthians*. T. Gärtner, 'Zur Eustachius-Vita "Ne mea segnicie"', *ib.*, 175–78, suggests two improvements to the martyr's verse life contained in Paris, BN, MS lat. 11341.

## 2.   ANGLO-SAXON ENGLAND

Mechthild Gretsch, *The Intellectual Foundations of the English Benedictine Reform*, CUP, xii + 471 pp., emphasizes that psalters, Aldhelm glosses, Aethelwold, and the Royal Psalter show a marked interest in the stylistic and intellectual refinement of the vernacular. M. B. Bedingfield, 'Reinventing the Gospel: Aelfric and the liturgy', *MAe*, 68:13–31, notes the pervasive influence of the *Visitatio sepulchri* on the perceptions of Christian history and illustrates the ways in which Aelfric reinvents the biblical narrative by means of additions and collation. M. Griffith, 'How much Latin did Aelfric's *magister* know?', *NQ*, 46:176–81, adduces historical and textual reasons to show that Aelfric's anecdotal reference to his teacher was intended to contrast his master's incomplete understanding of the allegorical meaning of Genesis and the ignorance of unlearned priests. M. J. Menzer, 'Aelfric's *Grammar*: solving the problem of the English-language text', *Neophilologus*, 83:637–52, reveals how Aelfric used the *Grammar* as a tool for understanding English and also discusses grammatical interpretation in the *Catholic Homilies*. G. Knappe, 'The rhetorical aspect of grammar teaching in Anglo-Saxon England', *Rhetorica*, 17:1–35, argues that instruction in *praeexercitamina*, a part of the grammatical curriculum, may have offered an alternative to the classical *ars rhetorica*. Id., 'Classical rhetoric in Anglo-Saxon England', *ASE*, 27, 1998:5–29, finds that the same rhetorical tradition within grammar, already present in Cassiodorus's *Expositio psalmorum*, was adapted to enable scholars to express themselves effectively. S. Hollis, 'The Minster-in-Thanet foundation story', *ib.*, 41–64, argues that the OE fragment in London, BL, MS Cotton Caligula A. xiv, fols 121ᵛ–124ᵛ, records a version of the Mildred legend about the origins of the Thanet lands that is closer to the common archetype than the three Latin lives. R. Marsden, '*Manus Bedae*: Bede's contribution to Ceolfrith's bibles', *ib.*, 65–85, uncovers three textual additions Bede made to the Vulgate bible pandect preserved in London, BL, MSS Add. 37777 and 45025; M. W. Herren, 'The transmission and reception of Graeco-Roman mythology in Anglo-Saxon England,

670–800', *ib.*, 87–103, assembles the available sources from which information about mythological figures was gleaned and gathered in glosses. D. A. Bullough, 'A neglected early-ninth-century manuscript of the Lindisfarne *Vita S. Cuthberti*', *ib.*, 105–37, collates Munich, Bayerische Staatsbibliothek, MS Clm. 15817, discusses the text, and suggests improvements to the 1940 edition of B. Colgrave. S. Gwara, 'The transmission of the "Digby" corpus of bilingual glosses to Aldhelm's *Prosa de virginitate*', *ib.*, 139–68, identifies Oxford, Bodleian Library, MS Digby 146 as the principal source of glossarial scholarship on Aldhelm, and discusses its relation with two other MSS. P. Lendinara, 'The battle of Brunanburh in later histories and romances', *Anglia*, 117:201–35, includes William of Malmesbury in tracing the story of the battle in Latin chronicles down to the 14th century.

### 3. CAROLINGIAN AND OTTONIAN

O. Bouzy, '*Spatha, framea, ensis*. Le vocabulaire de l'armement aux VIIIe-XIIe siècles', *MA*, 105:91–107, uses texts, ranging from Rabanus Maurus to Guibert of Nogent, and iconography to supplement the imprecise archaeological record to define each term. J. Story, 'Cathwulf, kingship, and the royal abbey of Saint-Denis', *Speculum*, 74:1–21, uses manuscript and textual evidence to date the composition of Cathwulf's *littera exhortatoria* to the same period as the dedication of the new basilica at Saint-Denis in 775, a connection with broad implications. C. Meyer, 'La théorie des *Symphoniae* selon Macrobe et sa diffusion', *Scriptorium*, 53:82–107, finds from analysing the MSS that the extract occurs in the framework of the theoretical teaching of music and was used as a compendium for teaching the mathematical foundations of the acoustic system. F. M. Casaretto, 'Sankt Gallen, Stiftsbibiothek 265: Ad Grimaldum abbatem?', *Maia*, 51:471–83, reconsiders the MS as a whole and adduces reasons to support the view that the letter of Ermenrich of Ellwangen is an apograph of the dedicatory copy that was first published in 866. S. Coates, 'Ceolfrid: history, hagiography and memory in seventh- and eighth-century Wearmouth-Jarrow', *JMH*, 25:69–86, examines the anonymous *Vita Ceolfridi*, Bede's *Historia abbatum* and the role that gifts made to the community played in constructing his memory, as well as the Gallic models, including the *Vita Honorati* by Hilary of Arles and the *Vita Caesarii* by Cyprianus of Toulon. K. H. Krüger, 'Neue Beobachtungen zur Datierung von Einhards Karlsvita', *FmSt*, 32, 1998:124–45, advances the date of the biography to the summer of 823. M. Gorman, 'The commentary on Genesis of Angelomus of

Luxeuil and biblical studies under Lothar', *SM*, 40:559–631, catalogues the most important differences between the two recensions and the use made of Ps. Bede's work, after describing the style, sources and exegetical method of Angelomus's commentary. A. Bisanti, 'Within il calvo', *ib.*, 843–56, argues that the theme of baldness in Letaldus's poem symbolizes purification and renewal. D. Zimpel, 'Zur Bedeutung des Essens in der "Relatio de legatione Constantinopolitana" des Liutprand von Cremona', *HZ*, 269:1–18, connects the theme of eating in the narrative to Liutprand's diplomatic refusal to dine with Nikephoros Phokas.

## 4. THE ELEVENTH CENTURY

A. Galloway, 'Word-play and political satire: solving the riddle of the text of *Jezebel*', *MAe*, 68:189–208, restores the graphic riddle of the fly and the bridle (*musca-camus*) to line 3, and uncovers additional logographic wordplay, before he argues that *Jezebel* and *Semiramis* may be read as a two-part satire against Cnut and the two women he was associated with, Aelgifu and Emma. Francis Newton, *The Scriptorium and Library at Monte Cassino, 1058–1105*, CUP, xxvi + 421 + 212 pls, describes the scriptorium under Abbot Theobald, its scribal practices, the classical, patristic and medieval MSS it owned, and the books that were presented to the abbey. E. D'Angelo, 'Hrotswitha's attitude towards homosexuality', *MJ*, 34:29–39, concludes from examining the hagiographic poem *Pelasgius* that Hrotswitha does not stigmatize homosexual desire as shameful or sinful. M. Kulikowski, '*Litterae, legati, nuntii*: communications in the *Historia Roderici*', *Latomus*, 57, 1998:900–08, suggests that the reasons for the Cid's failure to meet Alfonso and for his second exile are illumined by social history. J. Rubinstein, 'Liturgy against history: the competing visions of Lanfranc and Eadmer of Canterbury', *Speculum*, 74:279–309, emphasizes the conflicts present in the medieval sources concerning Lanfranc's treatment of English saints and Eadmer's perception of his conduct, and finds that the conflicts were drawn along lines of national identity. M. Otter, '1066: the moment of transition in two narratives of the Norman Conquest', *ib.*, 565–86, considers the use of indirect narration and metanarrative deployed in the anonymous *Vita Aedwardi Regis* and in William of Malmesbury's *Vita Wulfstani* to negotiate the issue of the transition to Norman rule. F. Lifshitz, 'La Normandie carolingienne, essai sur la continuité avec utilisation de sources négligées', *AnN*, 48, 1998:505–24, re-examines the beginnings of Norman power and the ways in which Frankish and Carolingian bishops worked to integrate the conquerors. H.-H. Kortüm, '*Gerbertus qui et Silvester*', *DAEM*, 55:29–62, investigates the meaning of Gerbert's choice of the name Silvester and connects it with the medieval portrait of Silvester as the pope who championed ecclesiastical autonomy vis-à-vis the power of the laity. H. Hoffmann, 'Die Historien Richers von Saint-Remi', *ib.*, 54, 1998:445–532, discusses the date and origin of the autograph MS, its literary, historical and political tendencies, style, language, and its reception, before he edits a previously unpublished letter of bishop Deraldus of Amiens on the selection of abbot Waltbert as bishop of Noyon. T. Haye, 'Rahewin als Dichter', *ib.*, 533–66, offers a first edition of a poem contained in Munich, Bayerische Staatsbibliothek, MS Clm 19488, which amalgamates the philosophic and allegorical mode of Boethius and Martianus Capella and the dialogue form of an eclogue. C. Fraïsse, 'Un traité des vertus et des vices illustré à Moissac dans la première moitié du XIe siècle', *CCMe*, 42:221–42, examines Paris, BN, MS lat 2077, an illustrated codex with a text similar to that in Paris, BN, MS lat. 2843, from Saint-Martial in Limoges.

## 5. The Twelfth Century

Constant J. Mews, *The Lost Love Letters of Heloise and Abelard. Perceptions of Dialogue in Twelfth-Century France*, NY, St. Martin's Press, xvii + 378 pp., argues that the anonymous letters copied at Clairvaux in the 15th c. were written by Abelard and Heloise early in their relationship and sets them in the wider context of relationships between educated men and women of the period; the correspondence is translated and briefly annotated. P. A. Hayward, 'The *Miracula inventionis beate Mylburge virginis* attributed to "the Lord Ato, Cardinal bishop of Ostia"', *EHR*, 114:543–73, demonstrates that the work, here edited from Lincoln Cathedral Library, MS 149, serves as a good example of saints' lives being used to legitimize the takeover of a church and its resources. Id., 'Saint Albans, Durham, and the cult of Saint Oswine, king and martyr', *Viator*, 30:105–144, concludes from examining hagiographic materials and miracle stories that the cult was constructed by St Albans to defend its title to Oswine's church at Tynemouth. R. M. Thomson, 'Serlo of Wilton and the schools of Oxford', *MAe*, 68:1–12, modifies R. W. Southern's thesis about the lack of evidence for a continuing academic tradition at Oxford by arguing that Serlo, among others, taught at Oxford, where the *trivium* formed part of the curriculum and advanced instruction was offered. G. E. Hood, 'Falcandus and Fulcaudus, "Epistola ad Petrum, Liber de regno Sicilie". Literary form and author's identity', *SM*, 40:1–41, identifies the author of the history and the prefatory letter with Hugues Foucaud, a Sicilian émigré who settled in France and later became abbot of Saint-Denis (1186–1197), on the basis of

Peter of Blois's letters and common stylistic traits between charters of
Hugues and the works of Hugo Falcandus. D. A. Lines, ' "Faciliter
edoceri": Niccolò Tignosi and the audience of Aristotle's 'Ethics' in
fifteenth-century Florence', *ib.*, 139–68, discusses the commentaries
of Agostino Favaroni da Roma, Guglielmo Becchi Fiorentino, and
that of Tignosi to reveal how the audience's level and their
expectations affected the teaching and presentation of the *Ethics*.
H. Linke, 'Beobachtungen zu den geistlichen Spielen im Codex
Buranus', *ZDA*, 128:185–93, discusses cruces in *CB* 26* and *CB* 13*.
M. Giovini, 'Il *De sompnio* tra elegia ed epica: una revisitazione onirica
del mito de Cerere e Fame', *Maia*, 51:279–93, explores the stylistic
complexity of a pseudo-Ovidian play and its relation to Ovid, *Amores*
3.5, and the significance of intertexts from Vergil and Lucan in
presenting the two myths. M. Goullet, 'Métamorphose d'Ovide: la
représentation du sentiment amoureux dans la "comédie élégiaque"
du XIIe siècle', *REL*, 76, 1998:241–69, studies the new ways of
describing love that were inspired by Ovid and connects them with
developments in contemporary vernacular works. P. G. Schmidt,
'Zwei Höflinge im Streit. Eine mittellateinische Versinvektive des 12.
Jahrhunderts', *Fest. Schupp*, 275–83, expands the genre of elegiac
comedy by editing from Metz, Bibliothèque-Médiathèque, MS 647,
which also contains a previously unknown witness of Bernardus
Silvestris's *Mathematicus*, a poem that probably emerged from the
circle of Matthew of Vendôme. C. Strijbosch, 'Himmel, Höllen und
Paradiese in Sanct Brandans "Reise" ', *ZDP*, 118:50–68, provides
the literary and theological context for the vernacular work and finds
that the notion of two paradises and three heavens owes nothing to
the works of Johannes Scotus Eriugena. W. G. East, 'Abelard's
allusive style', *MJ*, 34:41–49, uncovers a reference to Bede's sermon
on the Purification of the Virgin in Abelard's *Hymnary*. G. B. Winkler,
O. Cist., 'Die Kreuzzugsmotivation Bernhards von Clairvaux', *ib.*,
51–61, distinguishes four layers of motivation, and finds that the idea
of the Crusade as an historical mission plays almost no role in his
thinking. G. Lecuppre, 'L'empereur, l'imposteur et la rumeur: Henri
V ou l'échec d'une "rehabilitation" ', *CCMe*, 42:189–97, tracks the
growth of a story that Henry withdrew to a cloister in the narratives
of Roger of Hovedon, Walter Map, and Gerald of Wales, and
discusses why this fiction was invested with such significance. J.-G.
Gouttebroze, 'Deux modèles de sainteté royale. Édouard le Confes-
sseur et saint Louis', *ib.*, 243–58, suggests that Edward belongs to the
tradition of the providential saint, while Louis models an empirical
sainthood. M. Pastoureau, 'Le temps mis en couleurs. Des couleurs
liturgiques aux modes vestimentaires (XIIe-XIIIe siècles)', *BEC*,

157:111–35, studies the origins, diffusion, and the religious symbolism of colours, especially as manifested in the clothing of both rich and poor in daily life. M. Evans, 'An emended joke in Gerald of Wales', *JWCI*, 61, 1998[1999]:253–54, notes that the unique MS attests 'alleluia', not 'altera', in *Gemma ecclesiastica* Dist. II, cap. 25, and finds the humour to reside in a liturgical text, the antiphon to the *Benedictus* on the Wednesday after Easter. M. Schmitt, O.S.B., 'Hildegard of Bingen: *viriditas*, web of greening life-energy: II', *ABR*, 50:357–80, shows Hildegard's symbolic use of the term in the fields of theology, ethics and cosmology. T. Gärtner, 'Der Inzest des Amnon und sein ovidisches Vorbild. Zur Imitation klassischer Vorbilder in den Grossdichtungen des Laurentius von Durham', *Wiener Studien*, 112:153–73, explores the intertextual relationships between the story of Byblis and her brother as narrated in Ovid's *Metamorphoses* and the biblical story cited to illustrate the dangers of love in the *Hypognosticon*. C. Ratkowitsch, 'Astrologie und Selbstmord im *Mathematicus*. Zu einem Gedicht aus dem Umkreis des Bernardus Silvestris', *ib.*, 175–229, proposes that the author was not Hildebert, but an anonymous from the school at Tours, before she discusses the poem's meanings, its literary significance, and the possibility that an historical figure stands behind the figure of Patricida. S. Loutchitskaja, 'L'image des musulmans dans les chroniques des croisades', *MA*, 105:716–35, offers a semantic analysis of the terms and the sociocultural context to show how the criteria for constructing the Other were established. G. Borriero, 'Il tópos dell' ineffabile nella retorica medievale e nella lirica trobadorica', *MedRom*, 23:21–65, includes the treatment of the topic in rhetorical works ranging from Matthew of Vendôme's *Ars versificatoria* to John of Garland's *Parisiana poetria*.

## 6. THE THIRTEENTH CENTURY

*Clericus in Speculo. Studien zur lateinischen Verssatire des 12. und 13. Jahrhunderts und Erstedition des 'Speculum prelatorum'*, ed. Elisabeth Stein, Leiden, Brill, viii + 405 pp., discusses the aims and style of Gillebert's *De superfluitate clericorum*, Heinrich of Würzburg's *De statu curie Romane*, and Aegidius of Corbeil's *Hierapigra ad purgandos prelatos*, before she offers a first edition of the *Speculum prelatorum*, accompanied with a full introduction on the author, date, contents, structure, sources, style and description of the two MSS. *Oratio. Mittelalterliche Redekunst in lateinischer Sprache*, ed. Thomas Haye, Leiden, Brill, viii + 340 pp., contains 14 speeches, including those by Gerbert of Reims and by Bartholomäus of Capua, which illustrate the spectrum of medieval rhetoric; each sample is translated into German, followed by an

analysis of its structure and mode of argumentation. T. A.-P. Klein,
'Der "Liber Pictaleon" in der Tradition mittelalterlicher Sprichworts-
sammlungen', *SM*, 40:333–55, edits from three MSS a possibly
French collection of proverbs composed in leonine hexameters, with
a rich supply of sources. G. Cremascoli, 'I classici nella "Legenda
sancti Francisci versificata" di Enrico di Avranches', *ib.*, 523–34,
discusses the significance of intertexts from Ovid, Vergil, and Horace
in the saint's biography. R. Jakobi, 'Der "fehlerlose" frühe Arche-
typus. Adnoten zu Überlieferung und Quellen von Raoul von
Longchamps Anticlaudianus-Kommentar', *ib.*, 887–95, documents
textual errors common to the two classes of MSS that served as the
basis of the *editio princeps* in order to demonstrate that the archetype
was not supervised by the author. Charles F. Briggs, *Giles of Rome's De
regimine principum. Reading and Writing Politics at Court and University,
c. 1275 — c. 1525*, CUP, xiv + 207 pp., contains a full inventory of
Latin *De regimine* MSS of English and French origin and numerous
MSS containing translations of the work into French, with a full
discussion of the social, intellectual and historical implications of its
insular and continental dissemination. M. S. Hoffman, 'A forgotten
bestiary: St John's College, Cambridge, MS A. 15', *NQ*, 46:445–47,
describes the four separate volumes that comprise what was intended
to be an illustrated bestiary, lists the locations of the entries in the
MS, and discusses its provenance. C. R. Sneddon, 'The origins of the
"Old French Bible": the significance of Paris, BN, MS fr. 899', *SFr*,
127:1–13, concludes from examining the contents of the mutilated
fr. 899 that it represents the sole surviving copy of the complete OF
Bible, a finding which supports the view that the Bible was the result
of a single project. C. T. Maier, 'Kirche, Kreuz und Ritual: Eine
Kreuzzugspredigt in Basel im Jahr 1200', *DAEM*, 55:95–115, poses
a series of questions to a sermon of Martin, abbot of the Cistercian
cloister of Pairis, viewed as a complex act of communication, in an
attempt to recover its aims, methods, results, and the public's reaction
to it. H. Brall, 'Homosexualität als Thema mittelalterlicher Dichtung
und Chronistik', *ZDP*, 118:354–71, studies a case from the *Dialogus
miraculorum* of Caesarius of Heisterbach while examining the motives
and meanings of the opposition to homosexual relations.
M. Camargo, '*Tria sunt*: the long and the short of Geoffrey of
Vinsauf's *Documentum de modo et arte dictandi et versificandi*', *Speculum*,
74:935–55, dates the *Tria sunt* after 1216, argues that Geoffrey was
its author, and comments on the broader significance of the text's
association with Oxford. J. M. Powell. 'Patriarch Gerold and
Frederick II: the Matthew Paris letter', *JMH*, 25:19–26, explains the
origins and significance of the forged letter. G. Grassin, 'Le travail
des gemmes au XIIIe siècle dans la *Doctrina poliendi pretiosos lapides*',

*CCMe*, 42:111–37, edits Latin and OF versions of a technical work, and identifies material from Isidore and Albert the Great. C. Leyser, 'Vulnerability and power: the early Christian rhetoric of masculine authority', *BJR*, 80, 1998:159–73, traces the language of vulnerability deployed by medieval female mystics back to Augustine and Gregory the Great. Alexander Neckam, *Suppletio defectuum Book 1. Alexander Neckam on plants, birds and animals. A supplement to the Laus sapientie divine* edited from Paris B.N. lat. 11867, ed. Christopher J. McDonough, SISMEL, lxxxvi + 184 pp., presents a first edition of the herbal and bestiary lore added by Neckam to the poetic version of the *De naturis rerum*. D. Roth, 'Wahrheit und Aussagefunktion. Zu Engelberts von Admont Traktat "Utrum sapienti competat ducere uxorem" ', *FmSt*, 32, 1998:288–306, summarizes the reception of the so-called Theophrastus-fragment, before he analyses a serious treatment of the topic, which is formally cast as a learned treatise replete with authorities and logic. M. E. Crossnoe, 'Education and the care of souls: Pope Gregory IX, the order of St. Victor, and the University of Paris in 1237', *MedS*, 61:137–72, emphasizes the importance of the papal letter not only for the organization of pastoral ministry, but also for insight into the role of the Victorines in developing the University. F. delle Donne, 'Una disputa sulla nobiltà alla corte di Federico II di Svevia', *MedRom*, 23:3–20, discusses the treatment of this well-known theme in the elegiac comedy *De Paulino et Polla* by Riccardo of Venosa and in the *Contentio de nobilitate generis et probitate animi*, which is partially edited here.

7.   THE FOURTEENTH AND FIFTEENTH CENTURIES

K. Rivers, 'Memory and medieval preaching: mnemonic advice in the *Ars praedicandi* of Francesc Eiximenis (ca. 1327–1409)', *Viator*, 30:253–84, detects similarities between Francesc's mnemonic techniques and those recommended in the *Rhetorica ad Herennium*. F. Reichert, 'Odorico da Pordenone and the European perception of Chinese beauty in the Middle Ages', *JMH*, 25:339–55, recovers from the travel memoirs of a Franciscan, preserved in different Latin redactions and in the vernacular, an early account of the Chinese custom of foot-binding that embraces its historical, social and erotic aspects, and connects it with Pierre Bersuire's allegorical interpretation of the human foot as an expression of carnal lust. A. Ostrowitzki, 'Der "Liber dictaminum" des Abtes von Himmerod als Zeugnis für die *cura monialium* im spätmittelalterlichen Zisterzienserorden', *DAEM*, 55:157–81, points to the rich picture of social life in the convents depicted in the book. M. Aprile, 'Questioni relative alla fonte latina alla base del volgarizzamento della *Mulomedicina* di Vegezio condotto da Giovanni Brancati (cod. Vat. Ross. 531)', *ZRP*, 115:209–33, tracks the influence of Vegetius's work in Latin and vernacular treatises of animal medicine in Italy. G. D. Caie, 'Innocent III's "De miseria" as a gloss on "The Man of Law's Prologue" and "Tale"', *NMi*, 100:175–85, suggests that the five passages glossed in Latin serve to counterbalance the narrator's rhyme royal. P. Nobel, 'Le glossaire latin-français du MS. de Stockholm', *Romania*, 117:4–31, edits entries grouped under the letter C contained in Stockholm, Kungliga Biblioteket, MS N 78, a witness not as old as Montpellier, Bibliothèque Universitaire, MS H 110, and discovers its main interest to lie in the scribe's attempt to expand the number of French glosses. J. Summers, 'Gower's *Vox clamantis* and Usk's *Testament of Love*', *MAe*, 68:55–62, connects Usk's allegorical episode "Shippe of Traveyle" to Gower's opening *visio*, the dream allegory of the 1381 Peasants' Revolt, and suggests that the Margarite to whom Usk pledges loyalty represents on one level King Richard. F. N. M. Diekstra, '*The XII Lettyngis of Prayer*, Peraldus's *Summae virtutum ac vitiorum*, and the relation between *ÞE Holy Boke Gratia Dei*, *ÞE Pater Noster of Richard Ermyte* and *Book for a Simple and Devout Woman*', *ESt*, 80:106–45, edits *The XII Lettyngis of Prayer* and its Latin source, and concludes from an analysis of the intertextual relations of MSS HBGD and PN that the compilers drew their material on prayer not from each other, but from an English translation of Peraldus's work and the pseudo-Bernardine *Meditationes piissimae de cognitione humanae conditionis*. J. J. Murphy and M. Winterbottom, 'Raffaele Regio's 1492 *Quaestio* doubting Cicero's authorship of the *Rhetorica ad Herennium*: introduction and text', *Rhetorica*, 17:77–87, review Regio's arguments against Cicero's authorship but conclude that he left the question open. R.-H. Steinmetz, 'Die "Historij von Diocleciano." Eine eigenständige deutsche Version der "Sieben weisen Meister"', *ZDP*, 118:372–90, documents the unique features of an adaptation of the German Vulgate version of the *Historia septem sapientum*. C. S. Celenza, 'Pythagoras in the Renaissance: the case of Marsilio Ficino', *RQ*, 52:667–711, shows how Ficino came to view a period in the history of philosophical thought through the late antique lenses of the Pythagorean tradition. W. Hübner, 'Verse über den Tierkreis in einem Zodiologion aus Gerona', *MJ*, 34:77–99, offers a diplomatic text based on a more accurate examination of Gerona, Archivo del Catedral, MS 91, identifies sources and compares it with eight other known versions of the work. W. Röll, 'Nachlese zur Überlieferung der "Gesta Romanorum"', *BGDSL*, 121:103–08, identifies additional MSS of this popular work. A. Hudson, '*Accessus ad auctorem*: the case of John Wyclif', *Viator*, 30:323–44, examines the tools, among them summaries, indices, and lists of biblical passages, that were developed to ease access to Wyclif's numerous works, before she assesses their origins and models. E. Beltran, 'Un manuscrit autographe de la *Grammatice basis* de Guillaume Tardif', *BHR*, 61:495–508, edits a grammar that transmits Lorenzo Valla's teaching on the rules of language and the usage of the Latin authors. D. R. Carlson, 'The civic poetry of abbot John Whethamstede of St. Albans (+ 1465)', *MedS*, 61:205–42, discusses the poems' style and classicism with an emphasis on the Ciceronian ideal of eloquence directed at solving problems of state, before he explores John's association with the scholarly circle of Humfrey, duke of Gloucester. M. Tarayre, '*Miracula* et *mirabilia* chez Vincent de Beauvais. Étude de concepts (1)', *MA*, 105:367–413, differentiates the two terms, finding the latter mainly restricted to characterizing externals manifest in nature, whereas the former is most often linked with the divine. L. M. Eldredge, K. A. R. Schmidt, and M. B. Smith, 'Four medieval manuscripts with mathematical games', *MAe*, 68:209–17, edit mnemonic verses from Oxford, Bodleian Library, MS Bodley 496, that solve the puzzle of the so-called Josephus Problem, namely how to ensure the survival of Christians in an overcrowded boat at sea. N. Orme, 'Children and literature in medieval England', *ib.*, 218–46, discusses mainly English texts, but he also surveys school MSS, primers, and examples of narrative literature associated with children, such as the beast-fable, which circulated first in Latin.

## NEO-LATIN

POSTPONED

# 2

# ROMANCE LANGUAGES

## I. ROMANCE LINGUISTICS

By John N. Green, *University of Bradford*

### 1. Acta, Festschriften

*LSRL 28* and Treviño, *Semantic Issues*, the companion vol. to *LSRL 26*
(*YWMLS* 60 : 13), confirm and even accelerate a trend lamented more
than once in these pages: analyses of generally impeccable quality,
concentrating almost entirely on MIT-inspired syntactic topics (*LSRL
28* has only two items on phonology), most resolutely monolingual in
their actual data, but making sweeping claims of applicability across
'Romance'. Perhaps owing to limitations of the conference-paper
format, these more fundamental claims tend to be tested only in
explicit work on variant parameter setting, now on the margins of the
Minimalist mainstream. The trend is equally evident in two collections assembled by and for scholars long associated with the annual
Linguistic Symposia on Romance Languages: *Jaeggli Vol.* offers eight
essays on syntax, several Romance, commemorating the life and
pioneering work of its dedicatee in Chomsky's Principles and
Parameters (P&P) framework; while *Saltarelli Vol.* salutes a researcher
happily still very productive, with 15 essays akin to *LSRL* in concept
and appearance, judiciously focused around passives and clitics (see
sections 6 and 7 below).

*Koerner Vol.*, II, billed as a celebration of the scholar who has done
more than anyone to professionalize the historiography of linguistics
in the 20th c., contains a dedication, a bibliography of K.'s extensive
writings (xxix-lv), and 22 essays, including a subset on 'Latin and
comparative Romance linguistics', further discussed below. *Lloyd Vol.*,
a compact and fitting tribute by leading Hispanists, opens with 'A
scholarly portrait and bibliography' by S. N. Dworkin (1–11), moving
on to 15 essays ranging over Ibero-Romance and occasionally further
afield. *HR*, 67.4, contains a similar bibliography, together with
tributes and a fuller biography of 'Paul Max Lloyd', by J. M. Regueiro
(431–37). *RPh*, 52, revamped and newly transferred to the Belgian
publisher Brepols, opens with reminiscences and assessments of the
founding editor, 'Yakov Malkiel, 1914–1998', by J. R. Craddock and
fellow members of the editorial board (1–12), revealing highly
nuanced reactions to a great scholar and complex personality.

## 2. GENERAL ROMANCE AND LATIN

An unstuffy introduction for the hypothetical Romance globe-trotter needing reassurance on similarities and inherited patterns is offered by Sanda Reinheimer and Liliane Tasmowski, *Pratique des langues romanes*, Paris–Montréal, L'Harmattan, 1997, 285 pp.; but phonology, lexis and verbal morphology are treated more conventionally, and syntax is conspicuously absent (see A. Niculescu, *RLiR*, 63:256–63, and A. Gather, *VR*, 58:237–41). Useful and infuriating in almost equal measure, John Hewson's *Workbook for Historical Romance Linguistics*, Munich, LinCom Europa, 1998, x + 87 pp., combines a well-illustrated but idiosyncratic set of problems on vowel systems, diphthongization, the morphology of adjectives, verbs and personal pronouns, with the inevitable appendix of the parable of the lost son in the five Romance standards; but the references effectively stop in 1970, and some of the comments and analyses really have not advanced beyond Meyer-Lübke and Bourciez. S. N. Dworkin, 'Three new introductions to Romance linguistics', *RPh*, 52:119–31, covers E. Blasco Ferrer, *Linguistik für Romanisten* (Berlin, Schmidt, 1996, 240 pp.), J.-M. Klinkenberg, *Des Langues romanes* (*YWMLS*, 57:22, 58:16; 2nd ed. 1999), and R. Posner, *The Romance Languages* (*YWMLS*, 58:16), averring that only Posner achieves scholarly originality — an epithet common to other reviews, where it is not unalloyed praise (see, for instance, R. de Dardel, *VR*, 58:231–37, and A. Vàrvaro, *RF*, 111:444–48). Dissatisfied with the arid morphosyntactic correspondences used for the 'Classification des langues romanes', *ZRP*, 115:20–44, M. Gawełko challenges Romanists to seek the elusive *Sprachgeist*, manifest in criteria like economy versus maximal informativity, lexical autonomy, and degrees of abstraction.

Philip Baldi, *The Foundations of Latin*, Berlin–New York, Mouton de Gruyter, xxviii + 534 pp., eclipses earlier work in the comparative tradition by the sheer breadth of its documentation and erudition; excellent treatments of epigraphic evidence and the evolution of Latin phonetics and morphology baulk before syntax, acknowledged to be vast and treacherous. B.'s 'Observations on two recently discovered Latin inscriptions', *Koerner Vol.*, II, 165–74, deal with the Lapis Satricanus and the Garigliano Bowl, both dated to *c.* 500 BC. Michel Banniard, *\*Du Latin aux langues romanes*, Paris, Nathan, 1997, has been generally welcomed (see, for instance, B. Vance, *FR*, 72:948–49). *Latin vulgaire V*, a splendid collection of 53 papers from the 1997 Heidelberg colloquium, covers issues in Late Latin differentiation, internal structure, texts and documents, and technical registers and style. Rewarding are: J. Herman, 'La conscience linguistique de Grégoire de Tours' (31–39), proposing a spectrum of awareness, from Gregory's everyday speech to traditional written Latin, which he understood but lacked the erudition to imitate, with, in between, the flexible register of his own written medium, comprehensible when read aloud to his illiterate compatriots; H. Lüdtke, 'L'objectif visé par la réforme linguistique carolingienne' (41–48), limiting the aim to papal *rectitudo* in Church communications, and noting that the lack of phonetic terminology meant that the reform could only be spread by word of mouth, incidentally depriving us of records of the implementation; and R. Wright, 'Reading a will in twelfth-century Salamanca' (507–16), inferring, from the fact that the will of an important person was read aloud to a large group of witnesses who had to understand the contents, that the revised pronunciation of medieval Latin, officially adopted in León in 1080, was still only patchily implemented a century later. On related themes, W. also contributes: 'La inteligibilidad pan-Romance en el siglo IX', Aleza, *Estudios*, 273–85, on dialect continua and the probable intelligibility of the Strasbourg Oaths to a visitor from Al-Andalus; 'Expansión y divergencia: el latín en el viejo mundo, el español en el nuevo', *ALFAL 11*, 107–22, on the symbolic value of a unified orthography and the limited effects of bilingual contacts; 'Periodization and how to avoid it', *Lloyd Vol.*, 25–41, on temporal continuities and against hypostasized language labels; and 'Comparative, structural and sociolinguistic analyses of the history of the Romance languages', *Koerner Vol.*, ii, 175–88, on the nefarious effects of over-enthusiastic reconstruction, *à la* Hall and Dardel.

Nothing daunted, R. de Dardel continues to reconstruct ever more intricate layers of proto-Romance: 'Traits classiques résiduels en protoroman', *Latin vulgaire V*, 5–10, draws on toponymy to buttress his earlier work on the three-phase loss of the case system (*YWMLS*, 58 : 16, 59 : 24); and 'L'origine du génitif-datif', *VR*, 58 : 26–56, argues that an evolution akin to creolization and partial mesolectal decreolization saw the morphological merged case rebuilt, *after* the diffusion of the syntactic periphrasis that would eventually triumph. Moreover, Dardel and A. Zamboni, 'L'interfixe -i- dans les composés protoromans', *RLiR*, 63 : 439–69, reconstructing two phases and two zones of development for a persistent vowel that ought not to have survived syncope and other changes, show how a late western reanalysis could give rise to a productive, if non-etymological, model like GUARD-I- > *guardavalle*. Unconvinced, J. Kramer, 'Sind die romanischen Sprachen kreolisiertes Latein?', *ZRP*, 115 : 1–19, is sceptical about the woolly notion of semi-creole, reluctant to resort to creolization to explain morphological developments that fall within a well-attested spectrum of change, and dismissive of the alleged comparability of social conditions at the crucial period.

Commenting on changing attitudes and so-called 'new philology', G. Holtus and H. Völker, 'Editionskriterien in der romanischen Philologie', *ZRP*, 115:397–409, decide that adapting medieval writings to be accessible to modern readers destroys the very context that is essential to their understanding. An example of good practice, M. Aprile, 'Questioni relative alla fonte latina alla base del volgarizzamento della *Mulomedicina* di Vegezio', *ib.*, 209–33, strips away the accretions of popularizing translations to reconstruct at least part of this 5th-c. treatise on equine diseases.

## 3. HISTORY OF ROMANCE LINGUISTICS

P. Swiggers, 'Les débuts de la linguistique romane comparée', *CILL*, 24, 1998:41–52, calls attention to the work of Lorenz Diefenbach (1806–83), whose 1831 monograph, predating Diez, improved greatly on Reynouard in scientific rigour and brought a much-needed cultural anthropological slant to the emergent sub-branch of Indo-Germanic linguistics. P. Swiggers and H. Seldeslachts, 'Documenta linguistica', *Orbis*, 40, 1998[1999]:179–205, continue their earlier revelations about Schuchardt (*YWMLS*, 60:16), with evidence of an exchange on sound laws with L. Tobler (197–205), and three illustrations of S.'s contribution to debates about artificial auxiliary languages. Meanwhile, two items by J. del Valle explore the mutual reinforcement of state ideologies and standard languages, abetted — perhaps innocently — by scholars who give credibility to a 'standard' forged from diverse linguistic realities, leading directly to the subordination of those original variants: 'Lenguas imaginadas: Menéndez Pidal, la lingüística y la configuración del estándar', *BHS(L)*, 76:215–33; and 'Lingüística histórica e historia cultural', *Lloyd Vol.*, 173–87, an account of a 19th-c. polemic between R. J. Rufino and the Spanish novelist and diplomat Juan Valera, the latter defending the integrity (and hegemony, thinks del V.) of Spanish culture and language in South America against R.'s empirical evidence of divergence. More recent regional trends are amply chronicled by I. Vintilă-Rădulescu, 'Romanistica românească din ultimei două decenii', *SCL*, 47, 1996[1999]:247–72, covering both themes and specific languages.

I. Leroy-Turcan, 'Les sources de Gilles Ménage comparatiste des langues romanes', *TLP*, 37:91–108, draws on the inventory of M.'s personal library and his bibliographic acknowledgements, fuller than normal for the period, to pinpoint some of the influences in his dictionaries of French and Italian. P. Lauwers, 'Jules Gilliéron: contrainte et liberté dans le changement linguistique', *Orbis*, 40, 1998[1999]:63–95, is persuaded that a coherent theory of linguistic change underlies the series of 'therapeutic' articles G. wrote in collaboration with Jean Mongin and later Mario Roques between 1905 and 1910, though it remains implicit until 'healthy' words succumb to random impairments requiring cures which in turn disrupt etymological continuities. Taking a wider panorama of 'La géographie linguistique de Jules Gilliéron', *CFS*, 51, 1998[1999]: 113–32, P. Swiggers portrays G. as a gradualist in sound change, and too aware of language as a communicative tool and repository of traditions to be more than a reluctant structuralist. A fair and informative assessment of the life and work of one who did successfully combine these different perspectives is supplied by J. Albrecht, 'André Martinet (1908–1999)', *RF*, 111: 628–32.

## 4. PHONOLOGY

Hulst, *Prosodic Systems*, takes in both cross-linguistic themes and analyses of particular languages and families; Romance data can be found in E. Visch, 'The rhythmic organization of compounds and phrases' (161–231); in A. Lahiri et al., 'Diachronic prosody' (335–422); and in I. M. Roca, 'Stress in the Romance languages' (659–811), a virtual monograph, extraordinarily rich in detail, concluding that modern Romance shows a high degree of unity (puckered only partially by French) and uniform differentiation of nominal and verbal stress patterns — because Latin nominal stress has been preserved almost intact whereas verbal stress has been morphologized. More discourse phonetic in orientation, P. Martin, 'Prosodie des langues romanes', *RFP*, 15: 233–53, makes good use of WinPitch 96 software to locate the 'contour of modality' (essentially, declarative versus interrogative) on the last stressed syllable of the phonological phrase — in which Romance languages are astonishingly similar, except of course that the generalization leads to different phonetic outcomes in French, where the locus is coincidentally the last syllable of the phrase.

There are no stress shifts without restructuring of the underlying segmental pattern, according to W. Mańczak, 'Nature des déplacements de l'accent dans les langues romanes', *RRL*, 43, 1998[1999]: 21–24, who cites, but does not quite endorse, the century-old explanations of Vendryes (tempting analogies with frequent derivational suffixes) and Neumann (that apparent syncopes like *íntegrum* > *\*intégru* > Fr. *entier* disguise an epenthetic vowel that left them proparoxytones even after the shift). M. may be encouraged by a theoretical piece by E. M. Kaisse, 'Resyllabification precedes all segmental rules', *LSRL 28*, 197–210, here illustrated from Argentinian Spanish.

Hulst, *Syllable*, a valuable set of case studies rather spuriously corralled into theoretical approaches, includes 'The Romansh syllable' by J.-P. Montreuil (527–50), and 'The Latin syllable', by G. Marotta (285–310), the latter particularly good on phonemic quantity, minimal pairs, long segments (tautosyllabic if vowels, heterosyllabic if consonants) and the sharp divergence of diphthongal tendencies (always vowel + glide in Latin, always glide + vowel in later Romance). Fernando Sánchez Miret, *La diptongación en las lenguas románicas*, Munich, LinCom Europa, 340 pp., continues arguments adumbrated last year (*YWMLS*, 60:17): the search for a unitary explanation for Romance diphthongization is not futile, though Schürr was wrong to locate it in metaphonic attraction; instead, early Romance tonic vowels, led by /ĕ/ and /ŏ/, diphthongized in contexts that enhanced their length. Finding unexpected parallels between 'Systematic vowel shifting in Vulgar Latin and Middle English', *Lloyd Vol.*, 57–65, J. R. Craddock is also prompted to ask how the merger of short high and mid long vowels /ĭ + ē, ŭ + ō/, so plausible in free tonic syllables, could have been extended to the 'unpropitious' contexts of closed and unstressed syllables.

Rodney Sampson, *Nasal Vowel Evolution in Romance*, OUP, xvi + 413 pp., gives a comprehensive, fair, and theoretically neutral account of processes that have touched all Romance varieties but provoked radical change in only French and Portuguese (as Galician is now denasalizing quite rapidly); the factors favouring phonemic nasalization are identified as regressive assimilation, long vowels, and stress, with coronal /n/ (*pacē* Foley) acting as the strongest trigger by far. Developing earlier themes (*YWMLS*, 59:27), K. J. Wireback tests 'The relationship between lenition, the strong word boundary, and sonorant strengthening in Ibero-Romance', *Lloyd Vol.*, 155–72, but — stymied by incomplete patterns — cannot prove a direct correlation between the lenition of intervocalic obstruents and the fortition of word-initial sonorants; he does ascribe the gemination of /l-/, /r-/ and partially /n-/ to an Iberian version of *raddoppiamento sintattico* (see also C. Wiltshire and E. Maranzana's Optimality account of 'Geminates and clusters in Italian and Piedmontese', *LSRL 28*, 289–303). Finally, anyone tempted to regard assimilation as straightforward should consult M. Besse, 'Assimilationsprozesse in Schweizer Namenpaaren', *ZRP*, 115:65–78, whose corpus of bilingual place names offers a bewildering array of consonantal correspondences.

## 5. INFLECTIONAL MORPHOLOGY

Richard Laurent, *Past Participles from Latin to Romance* (UCPL, 133), Berkeley–Los Angeles, California U.P., xxvi + 574 pp., is a mine of

information, both tabular and sensibly discursive, covering phono-
tactics, morphological patterns, geographical variation, and the 'ebb
and flow' between true past participial and adjectival functions. A
complementary study by Michele Loporcaro, *Sintassi comparata dell'ac-
cordo participiale romanzo*, Turin, Rosenberg and Sellier, 1998,
xiv + 272 pp., tackles competitive variation in Italian and more
widely (see *YWMLS*, 60:363, and G. Holtus, *ZRP*, 115:719–20).
Proposing an implicational hierarchy of agreements, J. C. Smith,
'Markedness and morphosyntactic change revisited', *Koerner Vol.*, II,
203–15, doubts whether Andersen's revival of Bréal's notion of
markedness as an explanation in historical linguistics, despite a
certain discreet charm, can be defined rigorously enough to avoid
Procrusteanism or vacuity.

Vogeleer, *Modalité*, is an interesting collection of 15 papers, several
dealing with the nuances or reinterpretation of Romance tense forms.
Genericity and single event reading are constraints on the interpretation of tense in the complements of epistemic verbs, claims M. Ambar
in 'Inflected infinitives revisited', *CanJL*, 43, 1998[1999]:5–36, then
applying similar tests to 'Infinitives vs. participles', Treviño, *Semantic
Issues*, 1–20, this time to highlight differences in aspectual properties.
Inflectional bifunctionality also preoccupies M. Squartini: 'On the
semantics of the pluperfect', *Linguistic Typology*, 3:51–89, treats the
likely but not inevitable neutralization of perfect-in-the-past and past-
in-the-past (as happened to the present perfect); while 'Riferimento
temporale, aspetto e modalità', *VR*, 58:57–82, considers the atypical
Italian use of the conditional, reserved for epistemic and evidential
modality, with future-in-the-past temporality taken over by the
conditional perfect. Examining the implications of competing analytic
and synthetic forms of a single 'paradigm', M. Loporcaro, 'Il futuro
cantare-habeo nell'Italia meridionale', *AGI*, 84:67–114, draws on
comparative evidence to counter the traditional view that the synthetic
form must be a non-indigenous borrowing. Mapping 'Preterite decay
as a European areal phenomenon', *FoL*, 33:11–18, W. Abraham
locates northern Romance, including French, as typologically mid-
way between the fully functional preterite of Ibero-Romance, Basque
and Scandinavian, and its complete absence from Slavonic.

L. Gasperini unpicks the 'Diachrony and synchrony of the Latin
ablative', *Diachronica*, 16:37–66, showing that the three IE sources
are still discernible in Latin, especially the instrumental, though the
syncretic ambiguities are usually resolved by prepositions that were
highly innovative in Italic. Similarly, M. Iliescu, 'L'origine des
syntagmes *à/a* + SN (COI) dans les langues romanes', *Latin vulgaire
V*, 267–75, uses cliticization as a test of two types of dative: animate
complements of trivalent verbs, in which the dative case gave way to

the AD + accusative periphrasis, and other circumstantial complements originally with a range of exponents which, later, converged
on AD.

## 6. CLITICS

Oxymoronic, the mighty clitic has swept all before it. Riemsdijk,
*Clitics*, vast but well conceived and authoritative, opens with R.'s
'Clitics: a state-of-the-art report' (1–30), and juxtaposes theoretical
position papers, peer commentaries, and reliable documentation on
language families, including A. Cardinaletti's 'Pronouns in Germanic
and Romance languages' (33–82), contrasting Germanic opacity with
the characteristic twin pronoun series of Romance and the special
syntax required to account for their displacement, and R. Vos and
L. Veselovská's fascinating tabulation of the responses to a 'Clitic
questionnaire' (891–1009), this time showing Romance as uniform on
the major typological indicators, but fracturing into sub-patterns on
almost all questions of detail. The theoretical sections are led by
A. Cardinaletti and M. Starke, 'The typology of structural deficiency'
(145–233), which develops referential tests to validate a three-way
distinction of strong and weak pronouns and clitics, the latter capable
of acting as semantic dummies (a pattern that does not map exactly
onto M. Nespor's three-way proposal for 'The phonology of clitic
groups', (865–87); and J. Edmonds, 'How clitics license null phrases'
(291–367), which justifies the *in-situ* generation of clitics by adding two
minor derivational conventions and, crucially, by pinning down the
maximal structural distance between a clitic and the empty phrase it
licenses. Against this, the case for clitic movement and a landing site
within the $Agr^0$ projection is vigorously made by A. Belletti, 'Italian/
Romance clitics: structure and derivation' (543–79). More eclectic,
I. Roberts, 'Agreement marking in Welsh and Romance' (621–37),
accepts the theoretical possibility of base-generation and movement,
with both adjunction to host and merger by absorption of case
features; while C. Dobrovie-Sorin, 'Clitics across categories' (515–40),
dichotomizes affixes, which usurp morphologically subcategorized
positions, and clitics proper, which adjoin to Infl or to Spec-less IP, as
an explanation for differing positions in finite clauses and imperatives.

For Paola Monachesi, *A Lexical Approach to Italian Cliticization*,
Stanford, CSLI, xvi + 247 pp., Italian and other Romance clitics
exhibit too many overlaps with other categories and too little internal
consistency to be treated as a single category (*YWMLS*, 60:22, 356);
her brand of compositionality classifies most Romance object clitics
as affixes (with a few eccentric items like *loro*) and, she claims, explains
why Italian does not tolerate split clitic sequences. Anyone baffled by

the splintering of theoretical approaches, should read D. Sportiche, 'Pronominal clitic dependencies', Riemsdijk, *Clitics*, 679–708, which distinguishes sharply between lexicalist and syntactic, the latter subdivided into base-generated and movement [again divided, we may add, according to the precise node for attachment]; she believes Romance clitics should be treated as syntax with movement, though subject and object clitics will still show differences. On cue, S. extends her 1995 analysis of object clitics to cover 'Subject clitics in French and Romance complex inversion and clitic doubling', *Jaeggli Vol.*, 189–221, updating in the process Kayne's classic proposal that they be generated in twin form (e.g. *Jean-il*) with constraints on subsequent deletions. In similar vein, J.-Y. Pollock, 'On the syntax of subnominal clitics', *Syntax*, 1 : 300–30, extends Kayne's analysis of French *en*, refining the theory of topic operators. But A. Terzi, 'Clitic combinations, their hosts and their ordering', *NLLT*, 17 : 85–121, claims, against Kayne, that clitics are not hosted by $Agr^0$, but by $T^0$ when tense features are weak, and otherwise by place-holder heads.

Frank R. H. van der Leeuw, *Clitics: Prosodic Studies*, The Hague, HIGL, 1997, xvi + 210 pp., an Amsterdam PhD thesis, surveys types and distributions, postulating a special category of mesoclisis in European Portuguese — a notion that also figures in A. Rouveret, 'Clitics, subjects and tense', Riemsdijk, *Clitics*, 639–77, contending that the enclitic eccentricity of Portuguese is due to the weak valency of the V-feature of Tense (on which, see also E. Raposo, 'Directionality of cliticization in European Portuguese', *Saltarelli Vol.*, 219–32). For E. Mallén, both 'Cliticization in Old Spanish and Wackernagel's Law', *TL*, 25 : 1–14, have been correctly observed but misconceived: the process is not phonetic but syntactic, and accords well with Chomsky's Minimalism. Disregarding conventional chronology, M. A. Kato, 'Strong and weak pronominals in the null subject parameter', *Probus*, 11 : 1–37, directly attributes to Pro-drop parameter resetting the impoverishment of pronominal distinctions and evolution of weak pronouns; her Minimalist account allows her to drop empty *pro* altogether. In marked contrast to the bombast, D. Wanner, 'Clitic clusters in Romance: a modest account', *Saltarelli Vol.*, 257–77, programmatic and uncharacteristically bereft of data, appeals to 'invisible-hand' effects of standardization as a partial explanation for differing clitic orders.

## 7. SYNTAX AND SEMANTICS

Aiming to clarify two useful but ill-defined concepts with significant overlaps, *Reanalyse und Grammatikalisierung in den romanischen Sprachen*, ed. Jürgen Lang and Ingrid Neumann-Holzschuh (LA, 410), vii + 202 pp., brings together an overview and ten papers, covering metonymy, parameter changing, auxiliary and adverb formation, dislocated word orders, and the creation of grammatical categories in mature creoles. B. Lamiroy, 'Auxiliaires, langues romanes et grammaticalisation', *Langages*, 135:33–45, a rather flighty overview of auxiliarization and intermediate stages, concludes that French has again outstripped its neighbours. Interesting not least for its fusion of methods often seen as competitive, N. Vincent, 'The evolution of c-structure', *Linguistics*, 37:1111–53, traces Romance prepositions right back to Indo-European sentence particles, disavowing teleology, but accepting cumulative analogy as an important driver. R. S. Kayne, 'Prepositional complementizers as attractors', *Probus*, 11:39–73, suggests a technical account of the development of *de/di*, located higher in the derivation than the infinitives they serve to introduce.

A cluster of items deal with possessives, in various guises. M. Haspelmath, 'Explaining article-possessor complementarity', *Language*, 75:227–43, learns from an extensive cross-linguistic survey that possessed NPs are very likely to be definite, so that simple economy militates against co-specification; Italian exceptions are acknowledged, but may be transitional. M. D. Kliffer, 'The western Romance drift away from external dative possessors', *Word*, 50:155–75, claims that EDP, after millennia of coexistence with alternative exponents of possession, is now declining rapidly in peripheral areas, abetted in Brazilian Portuguese by reduced use of clitics. B. Lamiroy, 'On the relation between the possessive dative and the ethical dative', *RRL*, 42, 1997[1999]:223–47, establishes twin gradients for inalienability (starting with prototypical body-parts) and exponents of possession (accusative > dative > genitive), pointing out that Spanish and Romanian, the languages with the most generous interpretation of inalienability, are precisely the pair with prepositional accusatives. A complementary study by E. Magni of 'La significazione del possesso in latino', *AGI*, 84:44–66, concludes that the MIHI EST ALIQUID type, originally reserved for inalienables where possessor and possessed are in a stable relationship without obvious control of one by the other, should be treated as an instance of reduced transitivity.

*Verbum* (Nancy), 21.1, ed. B. Lamiroy and M. van Peteghem, assembles nine papers from a 1997 Ghent colloquium on 'Transitivité et langues romanes', including M. Herslund, 'Incorporation et transitivité' (37–47), which contrasts the low transitivity of bare objects with the 'supertransitivity' of individualized prepositional accusatives in Spanish and Romanian, while Italian and Old French operate on a simpler dichotomy of incorporated versus non-incorporated objects. In a well-documented study of 'Late Latin pleonastic reflexives and the unaccusative hypothesis', *TPS*, 97:103–50,

M. Cennamo examines the interaction of control and telicity with exponents of intransitivity, showing that *se*-reflexives are unergative (confined to state and mental process verbs) while *sibi* nexi, which grammaticalized earlier, are unaccusative (and confined to changes of state or location); a comparable analysis for Spanish can be found in M. Sanz, 'Aktionsart and transitive phrases', Treviño, *Semantic Issues*, 247–59. C.'s 'Inaccusatività tardo-latina', *ZRP*, 115:300–31, offers further examples, including reflexive forms of *essere* and *avere* in Old Neapolitan, which she regards as intimately linked to auxiliary selection and probably responsible for the longer term decline of *essere* as an auxiliary. Standing history on its head, H. Kurzová, 'Typology and diachrony of the middle voice', *Koerner Vol.*, II, 115–29, acknowledges that reflexives are the continuators of middles, but, since they both make poor substitutes for passives to signal marked voice, infers that those IE and later languages with a morphological passive in /-r-/, could not have developed it from earlier reflexives.

M. T. Espinal, 'On the semantic status of *n*-words in Catalan and Spanish', *RLFRU*, 18:49–60, establishes a strength hierarchy — negative quantifiers > minimizers > N-words > polarity items — with minimizers and N-words responsible for syntactic differences between Spanish and Catalan (see also E. Herberger, 'On the interpretation of Spanish n-words', Treviño, *Semantic Issues*, 89–104). Christopher Laenzlinger, *\*Comparative Studies in Word Order Variation*, Amsterdam, Benjamins, 1998, x + 371 pp., apparently concentrates on adverbs, pronouns and clause structure in Romance and Germanic, within a P&P framework. C. Cecchetto, 'A comparative analysis of left and right dislocation in Romance', *SL*, 53:40–67, argues that the two processes, though similar, are not mirror images: LD may be a form of double topicalization, whereas RD involves displacement into a VP-peripheral topic position. A. Eguzkitza and G. A. Kaiser defend the unaccusative hypothesis in accounting for 'Postverbal subjects in Romance and German', *Lingua*, 109:195–219; there is no need for Belletti's dubious recourse to partitive case, but one must recognize surface and language-specific conditions on verb order.

## 8. DISCOURSE AND PRAGMATICS

Ostensibly about the bleaching of aspectual value from the Latin perfectum, M. M. Manoliu, 'Changing culture — changing grammar', *BJL*, 12, 1998:103–27, proposes a much more ambitious programme of research, linking the new result-centred compound tenses, appropriate for expressing the rich temporal event hierarchies of medieval Romance oral discourse, with far-reaching changes to the voice system and even the category of gender, ascribing the loss of the neuter to a downgrading of the nominal feature [passive] from inherent to merely contextual. Agreements do matter: C. Faussart et al., 'Gender and number processing in spoken French and Spanish', *RivL*, 11:75–101, report on an empirical study of Det + N agreement mistakes, invariably leading to longer reaction times (on which, see also the more theoretical item by A. Hulk and C. Tellier, 'Conflictual agreement in Romance nominals', *LSRL 28*, 179–95). D. Varga, 'Discours indirect dans les langues romanes', *SRAZ*, 43, 1998:1–9, draws on a corpus of biblical translations to investigate sequence of tenses, finding that allegedly mandatory rules dissolve into a Romance prototype with a halo of variants. A slight misnomer, H. Bäckvall's 'Verbes déclaratifs en français et en espagnol', *RLiR*, 63:509–44, in fact deals with the choice of narrative verbs (termed '*vicariants*' of *dire*, and often elliptical, like *aulló* for *dijo aullando*); his corpus is surprisingly constant across the languages, except for Vargas Llosa, who rejoices in pushing the range to its limits. G. Fiorentino, 'Clausole relative romanze tra innovazione e conservazione', *RevR*, 34:25–60, draws on extensive corpora in Italian, French, and Spanish to argue for innovation along register lines: whereas formal processes of relativization have changed little since Latin, in so-called 'substandard' contexts, all three languages permit the generic relativizer {ke}, even with prepositions.

Ann-Kathrin Mälzer, *Methodische Überlegungen zur Adjektivstellung in den romanischen Sprachen*, Erlangen–Jena, Palm & Enke Vlg., 253 pp., after extensive review of the theoretical approaches, homes in on eight pairs of antonyms, located here on a cline of 'growing mass' to explain their relative position, incidentally showing up French as the furthest removed from Latin. J. Hilton, 'The role of discourse and lexical meaning', *Glotta*, 74, 1997–98[1999]:198–210, sees the spatial and metaphorical readings of INDE and its derivatives as a buttress against erosion, contrasting with IAM, NUNC and TUM, which were more easily grammaticalized into discourse markers. Broadly vindicating C. Kroon's assertion that neither ENIM/NAM nor UERO/AUTEM/SED are synonym sets, D. Langslow, 'Late Latin discourse particles', *Latin vulgaire V*, 169–82, tests their occurrences in technical and stylistically dry medical registers, but is unable to corroborate her further claim of a pragmatic subdivision in terms of internal text organization as opposed to interaction with the addressee.

## 9. LEXIS

Miguel Casas Gómez, *Las relaciones léxicas* (*ZRP*, Beiheft 299), Tübingen, Niemeyer, viii + 241 pp., is an essay on lexicographic method, with particular reference to synonymy, polysemy, and homonymy, laying the foundations for an eventual functional dictionary of Spanish. But lexical fields can be deceptive and L. Callebat, 'Observations sur le vocabulaire de l'habitat romain', *Latin vulgaire V*, 519–27, cautions against hasty inferences: although housing and architectural terms have survived well in technical registers, many of the etyma were vague and polysemous in Latin and there is no guarantee of continuity of referent. G. Colón, 'COPIA "traslado, reproducción de un escrito"', *RLiR*, 63:5–22, asks how 'abundance' — still a possible reading in high registers of Italian and Ibero-Romance — slipped to mundane 'copy', ingeniously pinpointing the shift to judicial/notarial copying houses, where *facere copiam scripturae* would originally have meant to give full account of the contents of a document, often achieved by making a generous excerpt or copy.

The late Raymond Arveiller's 25 valuable *Addenda au FEW XIX (Orientalia)*, contributed to *ZRP* between 1969 and 1996, are reissued with an updated bibliography by Max Pfister (*ZRP*, Beiheft 298), Tübingen, Niemeyer, xi + 645 pp. Surveying 'La lexicologie historique des langues romanes', *Latin vulgaire V*, 183–91, B. Müller praises the achievements of recent etymological dictionaries, lamenting the glaring lacunae they expose in Romanian and Ibero-Romance scholarship. Both pragmatist and defeatist over unresolved etymologies, M. Sala, 'Rom. *arăta*, Fr. *rêver*', *SCL*, 47, 1996[1999]:199–205, avers that we must acknowledge a small category of words that defy conventional evolutionary paths in both phonetics and semantics. Accepting the offer, C. Jordán-Cólera, 'De las teóricas evoluciones románicas del latín INSULA', *ZRP*, 115:45–55, queries whether an array like *iscla*, *isca* and *isla* can all arise phonetically from INSULA; instead, he derives them from one root, *ISOLA, meaning originally 'river island', with the -N- of the 'classical' form representing a popular etymology IN SALE, which is where most of them were!

Boldly tackling a problem that seems to have foxed even Malkiel, T. J. Walsh, 'The etymology of Sp./Port. *aterirse*', *Lloyd Vol.*, 223–36, rejects TERERE as the ultimate etymon of *aterirse*, *aterecerse*, *derretirse* since, despite plausible phonetics, no one has succeeded in accounting for the semantic leap from rubbing to melting; his own proposal of DĒRIGĒRE/DĒRIGĒSCERE 'to be/become stiff or numb with cold', works a dream on the semantics, but is less straightforward in its phonetics than W. cares to admit. Even more boldly stepping out where only Lanly and Mańczak dare to go, H. Petersmann, 'Der Einfluß des *sermo militaris* auf das Vulgärlatein', *Latin vulgaire V*, 529–37, finds unmistakable Greek attestations of the mysterious AMBITARE (as ἀμβιτεύειν) meaning 'march' in the barracks speech of

the eastern Empire, and points out that the small slippage 'march >
walk/go' would merely portend that of Fr. *marcher* centuries later.

O. Gsell, 'Von Windeiern und Weicheiern', *VR*, 58: 112–23, traces
the descendants of APALUS/(H)APALUS < Gk. ἀπαλός 'soft', applied
both to shell-less eggs and soft-boiled, in Central Romance, from
Picard in the north to Sardinian and Italian, but curiously with no
certain reflexes in *langue d'oïl* French. C. Stroh, 'MIT-Relationen in der
Romania', *STUF*, 52: 183–95, asks why the comitative, instrumental
and modal functions of CUM should have been differentially replaced
by APUD HOC in Catalan, Gascon, and French, with the latter
eccentric on most comparative criteria. G. Colón, 'De arabismos
interhispanos', *TLP*, 37: 131–39, questions the alleged lower frequency of Arabic items in Catalan, concluding that a large fund of
original Arabisms was available to all Hispanic varieties, but as part
of inherited stock rather than overt borrowings. Arabisms in Ibero-
Romance are also treated in linked articles by E. Grab-Kempf: 'Von
Juwelen, Perlen und Glasperlen', *ZRP*, 115: 155–62, argues that the
myriad terms linked to *lu'lu'*, *ḥabb*, *ḥabb al-lu'lu'*, *al-ǧauhar*, *ḥaǧar*,
betoken not random variation but a highly developed quality
assurance system for pearls; while 'Reflexe von ar. *ḥabb* (Koll.), *ḥabba*
(Nom. un.) als Bezeichnungen für Maße, Gewichte, Tribute, Bruch-
teile', *ib.*, 464–71, are widely distributed alongside *grano/grão* <
GRANU as a 'grain of gold', and thence 'any tiny measure', leading
eventually to interferences, as in OSp. *non valie una hava* — worthless
as a gold blend bean.

G. Bernhard, 'Formale Verfremdungstechniken', *RF*, 111: 567–86,
compares young people's speech in French, Spanish, and Italian,
finding broad derivational similarities in the creation of technical and
semi-secret registers. X. Blanco, 'Noms composés et traduction
français-espagnol', *LInv*, 21, 1997[1999]: 321–48, finds intriguing
structural mismatches between supposed equivalents, from a mere
preposition (*chasse aux sorcières* — *caza de brujas*) to wholesale replacement (*autocuiseur / marmite autoclave* — *olla a presión*). According to
A. Cuniţa, circumstantial complements like '"Sain de corps et
d'esprit": construction et interprétation dans les langues romanes',
*SCL*, 47, 1996[1999]: 79–87, probably can be traced back to Latin
forebears, but subsequent diversification casts doubt on the usefulness
of 'restructuring' as an explanation. F. Reiner, 'Italiano e latino
giuridico: il caso del prefisso *retro-*', *LN*, 60: 79–82, notes the great
vogue for *retro-* in medieval Latin (and more recently), but with a very
homogeneous group of verbs, all implying transaction, transfer, and
later physical movement. According to B. García-Hernández, 'La
reinterpretación de *sub(-)*, prefijo y preposición en latín tardío', *Latin
vulgaire V*, 223–33, involves semantic slippage from 'motion upwards'

to 'location beneath', a shift imperfectly understood by Latin grammarians and commentators. Sympathetic to the autonomy of morphology, M. Maiden, 'Romance historical morphology and empty affixes', *Koerner Vol.*, II, 189–202, advises modern practitioners to learn from the work of Malkiel and Menéndez Pidal on the analysis of complex affixation and apparently empty elements. M. further contributes 'Il ruolo dell'"idoneità" in morfologia diacronica', *RLiR*, 63:321–45, a case study of realignment to achieve a more transparent match of form and meaning. Reviewing recent approaches to 'Die morphologische Struktur verbaler Parasynthetika', *ZRP*, 115:79–116, A. Gather complains of fuzzy definitions and disagreement on the status of the infinitive, without which debates on circumfixing or serial affixation are pointless; if in doubt, be guided by economy and (semantic) explanatory adequacy. For A.-M. Di Sciullo, however, 'Verbal structures and variation', Treviño, *Semantic Issues*, 39–55, the formation of de-adjectival verbs (bare Fr. *blanchir* vs It. *imbiancare* with obligatory prefix) can be ascribed to differential outcomes of underspecification.

## 10. ONOMASTICS

A notable revival of interest in anthroponymy and onomastics more generally has been led by the magnificent *Namenforschung* (*YWMLS*, 57:29; vol. 2 and a full vol. of indexes both appeared in 1996, xxx + 979–1890, xxxii + 1891–2259 pp.), and by regular conference proceedings published by the indefatigable Dieter Kremer in the Patronymica Romanica series. Though many of the individual studies are inevitably local, more general patterns are emerging from the collocations. K.'s *Dictionnaire historique de l'anthropologie romane* (PatRom, 9), Tübingen, Niemeyer, 1997, cviii + 370 pp., is, for instance, warmly welcomed by G. Holtus, *ZRP*, 115:517–18. Further contributory work is catalogued in: *Dictionnaire historique des noms de famille romans [IX]. Actas del IX coloquio (Uviéu/Oviedo, 26–29 de octobre 1995)*, ed. Ana María Cano González (PatRom, 11), Tübingen, Niemeyer, xiv + 201 pp.; *Antroponimia medieval galega (ss VIII-XII)*, ed. Ana Isabel Boullón Agrelo (PatRom, 12), *ib.*, vii + 558 pp.; and *Onomastik. Akten des 18 internationalen Kongresses für Namenforschung, Trier 12–17 April 1993*, a projected six-vol. set of which two are now available: *Namensoziologie*, ed. Dieter Kremer and Friedhelm Debus (PatRom, 16), *ib.*, vii + 299 pp., and *Personennamen und Ortsnamen*, ed. Dieter Kremer and Thorsten Andersson (PatRom, 17), *ib.*, viii + 330 pp. But cobwebs get everywhere: V. Popovici's well-documented 'Propuneri pentru *Neo-REW*: REW 593b ARĀNEŌSUS, \*RŌNEŌSUS', *SCL*, 47, 1996[1999]:143–59, advocates a model for future etymological dictionaries based on Wartburg, but also taking account of medieval onomastics — likely to be the earliest attestations for many forms. A similar point is made by E. Nieto Ballester, whose 'Quelques notes sur les collectifs latins en -*ētum*, -*ēta*', *Latin vulgaire V*, 137–53, demonstrates a high frequency that could be overlooked but for the evidence of numerous toponyms.

## 11. SOCIOLINGUISTICS AND CONTACT

Reconstructing attitudes and language loyalty during the period of Graeco-Latin bilingualism, B. Rochette, '*Latinitas* — *peregrinitas*', *Orbis*, 40, 1998[1999]:97–110, considers that the original Latin antonyms were simple calques of the terms ἑλληνισμός — βαρβαρ-ισμός, but that after the Greek norm had shifted decisively to Athens, the preferred terms became ἀττικισμός — σολοικισμός, leading in turn to the replacement of *Latinitas* by *Romanitas*. Ž. Muljačić, 'Sulla formazione "decentralizzata" delle prime lingue romanze', *Baum Vol.*, 269–77, disputes whether the famous phrases *in rusticam Romanam linguam* or *lingua theotisca* would have had consistent interpretations in ninth-c. texts or in territories where numerous vernaculars were liable to rapid fluctuations of status. M. also dispenses with 'Un fantôme terminologique: la distance linguistique minimale', *Actes* (Barcelona), 34–37, criticizing the Klossian term as inadequately defined, and only ever appropriate to binary power relationships between language varieties, when in fact many are more complex. R. Penny, 'Standard versus dialect: linguistic (dis)continuity in the Iberian Peninsula', *Lloyd Vol.*, 43–55, attributes the unusual congruity of some Hispano-Romance phonological isoglosses to the standardizing effects of literacy induced by the 13th-c. cultural revolution. Nearer home, J. L. Blas Arroyo, ' "Buenas noches, *bona nit*" ', *Orbis*, 40, 1998[1999]: 111–34, treats Catalan-Spanish code-switching as functional, con-cluding that ambiguity, structural mismatch, and even humour can affect the moment and direction of change.

Two major collections challenge assumptions in creolistics and improve the data available for comparative typology. *Language Creation and Language Change. Creolization, Diachrony and Development*, ed. Michel DeGraff, Cambridge, Mass, MIT Press, x + 573 pp., focuses on discontinuous transmission and language acquisition under excep-tional circumstances; its 12 essays cover the bioprogram, learnability, cues, and parameter (re-)setting, with implications well beyond creoles (witness, R. A. Sprouse and B. S. Vance, 'An explanation for the decline of null pronouns in certain Germanic and Romance languages', 257–84). By contrast, the 26 papers from a 1996 Berlin colloquium, *Lenguas criollas de base lexical española y portuguesa*, ed. Klaus

Zimmermann, Frankfurt, Vervuert, 556 pp., largely steer clear of theory and offer a wealth of solid analytical data, with good coverage of neglected and disputed areas, such as the semi-creole status of Helvecian Portuguese.

# II. FRENCH STUDIES*

## LANGUAGE

By GLANVILLE PRICE,
*University of Wales Aberystwyth*

### 1. GENERAL AND BIBLIOGRAPHICAL

Haut Conseil de la Francophonie, *\*L'État de la francophonie dans le monde: données 1997–1998 et 6 études inédites*, Documentation française, 610 pp. Charles Durand, *\*La Langue française: atout ou obstacle*, Le Mirail-Toulouse U.P., 447 pp.

*TrL*, 38, is a thematic issue mainly devoted to 'Sémantique, interprétation et effets syntaxiques'. Five of the six articles grouped under this heading relate specifically to French: M. Barra-Jover, 'L'opposition abstrait/concret et les dimensions spatio-temporelles' (29–61); D. Van de Velde, 'La multiplication des sentiments' (63–87), concluding that one of the consequences of the type of analysis of certain types of predicative nouns proposed is that 'le même nom prédicatif, tout en restant un nom abstrait et aussi un nom de sentiment, semble attribuer à l'un de ses arguments un nouveau rôle thématique lorsqu'il s'emploie au pluriel'; L. Abouda, 'Les modes verbaux dans les phrases indépendantes, localisation syntaxique' (89–108); S. Kindt, '*En pleurs* vs. *en pleurant*: deux analyses irréconciliables?' (109–18).

*Wilmet Vol.* includes, in addition to 27 contributions classified under the overall headings 'Le syntagme nominal', 'Le système verbal' and 'Au-delà du syntagme' (see below), an appreciation of W.'s work by Robert Martin (9–20) and a biobibliography by A.-R. Delbart (21–30).

N. Spence reports on 'La querelle du "franglais" vue d'outre-Manche', *Linguistique*, 35.2:127–39. Jean Dutourd, *\*A la recherche du français perdu*, Plon, 250 pp. Thierry Leguay, *\*Les Poules du couvent couvent: les curiosités du français*, Mots et Cie, 121 pp. Claude Duneton, *\*La Mort du français*, Plon, 180 pp. *\*La Langue française à la croisée des chemins*, L'Harmattan, 144 pp.

Marzys, *Variation*, is a collection of twenty of his articles, conference papers, and lectures; many of them having been previously published only in journals or volumes that are not easily accessible, this collected edition is most welcome; for individual items, see below.

---

* The place of publication of books is Paris unless otherwise stated.

## 2. History of the Language

*Atti* (Palermo) includes C. Buridant, 'Vers une typologie holistique de l'ancien français', 1, 101–08. *Nouvelle histoire de la langue française*, ed. Jacques Chaurand, Seuil, 817 pp., has much to recommend it, complementing as it does (but not replacing) existing histories of the language. There is wide-ranging coverage of external history, with varying amounts of attention accorded to pronunciation, grammar, orthography and lexicon. Interspersed among seven chronologically differentiated sections, from 'Préhistoire, protohistoire et formation de l'ancien français' (R. Chaudenson) to two (by F. Gadet and É. Brunet respectively) on the 20th c., are others on 'Les français d'outre-mer' (R. Chaudenson), French in Belgium, Switzerland and Quebec (J.-M. Klinkenberg), and 'Le français et ses patois' (M.-R. Simoni-Aurembou). One notices a certain imbalance among sections in terms both of the range of topics covered and length: whereas the period from the 13th to the 15th centuries (S. Lusignan) has only 50 pages and the 16th c. (G. Clerico) has 78, the 19th c. (J.-P. Saint-Gérand) has 126, which is more than the 118 pages in which J.-P. Seguin has to cover the 17th and 18th cs together. Most (not all) sections have extensive and useful bibliographies (though works in languages other than French are seriously under-represented). Jean-Louis Tritter, *Histoire de la langue française*, Ellipses, 352 pp., attempts to cover too much ground in the available space: internal history (phonology, morphosyntax, lexicon, orthography), history of linguistic ideas (including grammars, dictionaries, and the teaching of French), registers, dialects, *la francophonie*, etc.; in consequence, though there is much in it of interest, it tends all too often either to superficiality or to be so concentrated as to risk not being readily accessible to the 'public large' for whom it is intended. Christiane Marchello-Nizia, *\*Le français en diachronie: douze siècles d'évolution*, Gap, Ophrys, 170 pp.

## 3. History of Grammar and of Linguistic Theory

Basing himself on Gilliéron's *Études de géographie linguistique* (1915), P. Lauwers, 'Jules Gilliéron: contrainte et liberté dans le changement linguistique', *Orbis*, 40, 1998[1999]:63–95, seeks to synthesize in a way in which G. never did himself 'l'aspect théorique de l'étymologie gilliéronienne'. J. Trabant, 'Die französische Sprache gegen ihr Genie verteidigen', *ZFSL*, 109:1–24, though prompted by H. Meschonnic's *De la langue française: essai sur une clarté obscure* (1987, see *YWMLS*, 59:35), is far more than a review article.

The greater part of *CFS*, 52, is devoted to 'Mélanges en hommage à Claudine Normand', ed. S. Bouquet, J.-L. Chiss and C. Puech; contributions include (together with six others falling outside the scope of *YWMLS*): the editors, 'Claudine Normand et le Groupe de Recherche en Histoire de la Linguistique' (3–19); M. Arrivé, 'Lacan grammairien. 1. Prémisses saussuriennes' (19–36); S. Bouquet, 'D'une théorie de la référence à une linguistique du texte: Saussure contre Saussure?' (37–42); M.-C. Capt-Artaud, 'Émetteur et récepteur ou la pertinence du sens' (43–55); P. Caussat, 'Pour Claudine Normand; contre le saussurisme ou d'une fidélité indocile' (57–67); J.-C. Chevalier, 'Albert Sechehaye, pédagogue et théoricien' (69–81); M. Décimo, 'Une petite famille de travailleurs autour de Georges Guieysse: le monde de la linguistique parisienne' (99–21); and A.-M. Frýba-Reber, 'Maurice Grammont (1866–1946) et l'école française de linguistique' (139–53).

Marzys, *Variation*, includes: 'Vaugelas ou l'indifférence à l'histoire' (37–53); 'La formation de la norme du français cultivé' (55–72); 'Norme et usage en français cultivé' (73–84); 'Pour une édition critique des *Remarques sur la langue françoise* de Vaugelas' (85–102); 'La langue littéraire du XVIe siècle dans l'opinion des fondateurs du "bon usage"' (103–11); 'L'archaïsme, Vaugelas, Littré et le *Petit Robert*' (137–47); 'Le burlesque et les fondateurs de la langue classique' (175–81); 'Vaugelas et la norme actuelle du français' (183–96); 'Molière et la langue classique' (197–210); 'Du raisonnable au rationnel: les avatars du bon usage' (211–22); 'Rabelais et la norme lexicale' (239–48); and 'La codification du français à l'époque de la Renaissance: une construction inachevée' (275–93).

### 4. Texts

*Atti* (Palermo), VI, includes: H. Böhmer, 'Grammaire générale et grammaires spécifiques des genres de texte: l'exemple des chartes médiévales' (27–36); V. Bubenicek, 'A propos des textes français copiés en Italie: le cas du roman de *Guiron le Courtois*' ([59–67]); P. F. Dembowski, 'Étude linguistique de la prose de Martin le Franc' (113–24); Y. Otaka, 'La langue du ms. inédit OUL 1 (olim Phillipps 23240). Histoire de Troye la grant' (365–82).

D. Trotter assesses 'L'importance lexicographique du *Traitier de cyrurgie* d'Albucasis en ancien français', *RLiR*, 63:23–53.

Marzys, *Variation*, includes: 'La place et l'expression du sujet dans le *Roman de Jehan de Paris* (fin du XVe siècle)' (11–18); and 'Commentaire philologique d'une page de Rabelais' (197–222).

The basis for K.-A. Arvidsson, 'Notes sur le vocabulaire argotique et populaire du *Père Peinard* (1889–1900)', *NMi*, 100:309–32, is a weekly journal published by the anarchist and trade-unionist, Émile Pouget.

## 5. PHONETICS AND PHONOLOGY

B. Post discusses 'Restructured phonological phrases in French: evidence from clash resolution', *Linguistics*, 37:41–63. F. J. Señalada Garcia, 'Le vocalisme de Rambaud: les voyelles de moyenne ouverture', *Atti* (Palermo), I, 385–92, is on a 1578 book by H. Rambaud. E. Schafroth, 'Zur Virtualität des [ə]. Forschungsbericht, Fragen und Ergebnissse zu einem bekannten Phänomen', *ZFSL*, 109:113–47, is a useful survey article. V. Delvaux, 'A propos des voyelles nasales du français', *Linguistique*, 35:3–23, adduces experimental evidence to oppose the view that nasal vowels tend to open. N. Armstrong and S. Unsworth, 'Sociolinguistic variation in southern French schwa', *Linguistics*, 37:127–56, looks into differential treatment by young male and female speakers. Mario Rossi, *\*L'Intonation, le système du français: description et modélisation*, Gap, Ophrys, 237 pp. A. Di Cristo, 'Vers une modélisation de l'accentuation du français', *JFLS*, 9:143–79, the first part of a major two-part study, deals with general problems relating to accentuation and surveys previous work on the accentuation of French.

## 6. ORTHOGRAPHY

L. Biedermann-Pasques reports on 'Un dictionnaire historique de l'orthographe française, le *DHOF*', *Atti* (Palermo), III, 65–75. *\*L'Ortografe? C'est pas ma faute*, ed. Renée Honvault, Condé-sur-Noireau, Corlet, 184 pp., is a special no. (42) of *Panoramiques*. *A qui appartient la ponctuation?*, ed. Jean-Marc Defays, Laurence Rosier and Françoise Tilkin, Louvain-la-Neuve, Duculot, 1998, 465 pp., publishes the proceedings of a colloquium held at Liège in March 1997; after an 'avant-propos' by Marc Wilmet (7–9) and two introductory items, L. Rosier, 'La ponctuation et ses acteurs' (15–30), reviewing the contents of the volume, and N. Catach, 'La ponctuation et les systèmes d'écriture: dedans ou dehors?' (31–43), presenting a brief historical overview, the contributions are grouped under three headings: section 1, 'Les écrivains, praticiens de la ponctuation', comprises: J. Lemaire, 'Un système de ponctuation original dans l'oeuvre d'un dramaturge français du XVIe siècle' (47–56), on Gérard de Vivre of Ghent; M. Watthée-Delmotte, 'Ponctuation et symbolisme de la voix: le cas de Villiers de l'Isle-Adam' (57–68); M. Colas-Blaise, 'Ponctuation et dynamique discursive. *La Modification* de Michel Butor' (69–85); J. Leblanc, 'La ponctuation face à la théorie de l'énonciation' (87–98), aiming to 'préciser dans quelle mesure les points de suspension et les blancs typographiques peuvent être traités comme une figure de réticence', with particular reference to G. La Roque's novel *Serge d'entre les morts* (Montreal, 1976); A. Grobet, 'Le rôle des ponctuants dans le marquage des unités périodiques, à la lumière d'un exemple tiré de *Fin de partie* de Samuel Beckett' (99–116); I. Serça, 'La parenthèse, troisième dimension du texte proustien' (117–29); J.-M. Defays, 'De l'usage du point d'exclamation dans les genres comiques, érotique et fantastique' (131–48), with special reference to Maupassant's *Contes fantastiques*; and S Montes and L. Taverna, 'M. Tournier, E. Boubat: l'écrit, l'image. La ponctuation comme système' (149–60). Section 2, 'Les "intermittents" de la ponctuation', includes (together with a few items falling outside the scope of *YWMLS*): M. Stasse, 'Retour aux sources: point final!' (179–89), on the *Eulalia*, the Strasbourg Oaths, and extracts from three other medieval texts; D. Blampain, 'L'*efficace*, l'*énergie* et l'*élégance* de la ponctuation selon Jean Bosquet, grammairien "belge" du XVIe siècle' (191–98); F. Tilkin, 'Ponctuation et récit de paroles dans les éditions originales des Contes de Voltaire' (199–210); G. Purnelle, 'Théorie et typographie: une synthèse des regles typographiques de la ponctuation' (211–21); C. Morinet, 'La ponctuation entre logique de l'oral et logique de l'écrit' (275–88); P. Schoentjes, 'Ponctuer l'ironie' (303–16); and F. Boch, 'La flèche, une marque (de ponctuation?) ignorée' (317–35). Section 3, 'De la réception à l'appropriation', includes: L. Rosier, 'Discours grammatical et ponctuation: l'exemple du discours rapporté' (353–64); A. Van Sevenant, 'L'architecture des guillemets dans l'oeuvre de Jacques Derrida' (365–72); J. Authier-Revuz, 'Le guillemet, un signe de "langue écrite" à part entière' (373–88); and items on the equivalent of punctuation in films, on Japanese punctuation, and on punctuation and computerization.

G. Parussa, 'Autographes et orthographe. Quelques considérations sur l'orthographe de Christine de Pizan', *Romania*, 117:143–59, is based on Christine's *Epistre Othea*, of which some 50 MSS are known, many of them believed to be in her own hand.

## 7. GRAMMAR

### OLD AND MIDDLE FRENCH

Marzys, *Variation*, includes 'Du moyen français au français moderne: quelques transformations syntaxiques fondamentales' (261–63) (see *YWMLS*, 57:37).

*Atti* (Palermo), II, includes: A. Abé, 'A propos du comparatif épistémique' (3–14): J. Carruthers, 'Surcomposé "général" et surcomposé "régional": deux formes distinctes?"' (143–54); P.Charles, 'Les tournures *riens moins que* et *rien de moins que*' (155–74); G. Chevalier, 'Nature de l'alternance entre la complétive [SN que P] et la relative complément de point de vue [SN selon REL]' (175–85); N. Delbecque, 'Les limites de la pronominalisation: les compléments directes' (205–15); P. Demarolle, 'L'emploi des formes verbales en français: valeur épistémologique des catégories de référence' (217–24); D. Gaatone, 'La notion de clitique en français' (351–56); Y. Haruki, 'Pronominal moyen et pronominal neutre en français moderne' (405–16); H. P. Helland, 'Éléments pour une analyse syntaxique et sémantique des structures *être + participe passé d'un verbe transitif* en français moderne' (429–42); K.Jonasson, 'La structure des SN complexes du type *Ma copine Blandine*' (495–501); L. R. Lorentzen, 'Quelques emplois du pronom *y* en français moderne' (577–87); H. Lüdke, 'La conjugaison en tant que module fonctionnel' (589–96); G. Manno, '*On applaudit!*: être péremptoire tout en sauvant la face de tout le monde' (605–17); C. Muller, '*Que*, la subordination et l'inversion complexe' (631–43); M. Pierrard, 'La valeur sémantique de *ce* introduisant une subordonnée' (663–72); F. Skutta, 'Points de vue pour le classement des conjonctions de coordination en français' (765–69); P. Sleeman and E. Verheugd, 'Deux types d'adjectifs postnominaux en français' (771–81); D. Van Raemdouck, 'L'adverbe existe: je l'ai rencontré! *ou*, La fonction adverbiale en question' (849–60); W. Zwanenburg, 'La distribution des catégories lexicales en morphologie française' (867–74); *ib.*, III, includes: S. Karolak, 'Sur la dépendance entre le sens du nom et la sélection de l'article' (363–71); S. Michels, 'La valeur confirmative de l'adverbe *bien*' (503–11); H. Nølke, 'Les adverbes paradigmatisants révisés: non sur tout mais surtout sur *surtout*' (629–39); A. Rodriguez Somolinos, 'De la cause à la concession: *portant, pourtant*' (767–76).

Monique L'Huillier, *Advanced French Grammar*, CUP, ix + 706 pp., is comprehensive and clearly planned, and written with the needs of the English-speaking learner in mind. The approach adopted in Philippe Monneret and René Rioul, *Questions de syntaxe française*, PUF, 297 pp., is commendably and rigorously practical. Each of the 21 chapters is devoted to a specific grammatical point studied on the basis of its use in a given literary passage or passage (e.g. adjectives in a page of Colette's *La Maison de Claudine*, 'L'inversion du sujet' in a page of Gide's *Thésée*, negation in Supervielle's poem 'Mouvement'). The analyses proposed are accompanied by references to the

*Grammaire méthodique du français* (see *YWMLS*, 56:43). Marc-Mariel
Friedemann, *\*Sujets syntaxiques. Positions, inversions et pro*, Berne, Lang,
1997, xii + 222 pp. A.-R. Rădulescu, 'Subiect morfologic /vs/
subiect semantic', *SCL*, 47, 1996[1999]:181–88, relates specifically
to French.

    M. A. Jones, 'Subject-clitic inversion and inflectional categories',
*JFLS*, 9:181–209, takes a Chomskyan approach. Paul Bessler, *\*Une
analyse morphosyntaxique de l'accord grammatical en français*, Sainte-Foy
(Quebec), Laval U.P., 152 pp. J. Guilford discusses 'L'attribution du
genre aux emprunts à l'anglais', *Linguistique*, 35:65–85.

    *Wilmet Vol.* includes under the heading 'Le syntagme nominal':
M. Pierrard, 'Syntagme nominal et pronoms: la grammaticalisation
des pronoms "essentiels" indéfinis' (33–46); N. Furukawa, 'Cet objet
curieux qu'on "appelle" l'article' (47–54); A. Henry, '*Tel/cel*: un
couple fumeux' (55–64), seeking to distinguish between two forms
which, in Middle French manuscripts, are easily confused;
M. Herslund, 'Le français, langue à classificateurs?' (65–73), claiming
that the French system of what he terms 'deux articles indéfinis' (one
being the 'soi-disant article partitif') has much in common with the
classifiers of 'exotic' languages such as Chinese; K. Jonasson, 'Ce
Marc nous fait bien bosser! Sur le rôle du démonstratif devant le nom
propre' (75–85); G. Kleiber, '*Tout* et ses domaines: sur la structure
*tout* + déterminant + N' (87–98); L. Melis, 'Réflexions sur la structure syntaxique du syntagme nominal' (99–123), and M. Tuţescu,
'Généricité, modalité et figurativité dans le groupe nominal'
(117–123), both of which stem from Wilmet's own work; R. Van
Deyck, 'La détermination nominale en ancien français' (125–36);
and D. Willems, 'Un petit rien sur *quelque chose*' (137–45). *\*LaF*, 122,
ed. Anne Daladier, is devoted to 'Le groupe nominal: contraintes
distributionnelles et hypothèses de descriptions'. H. Bonnard, 'Complément', *FM*, 67:125–32, would wish the notion of 'complément' to
include 'épithète' and 'apposition' but to exclude 'l'objet'.

    Observing that, more often than not, grammars either do not
define what they mean by 'adjective', or else do so in negative terms
(it is not a noun, not a verb . . .), Jan Goes, *L'adjectif: entre nom et verbe*
(Champs linguistiques), Louvain-la-Neuve, Duculot, 348 pp., here
offers a thoughtful and penetrating study of the status of the adjective.
A first chapter starts with the Classical, Medieval, and Renaissance
grammarians but concentrates on the views of the Port-Royal and
later French grammarians. A thoroughgoing survey of the morphological and syntactical characteristics of the adjective and of its
interrelationship with other parts of speech (the noun and the verb,
as referred to in the title, but also the determiner and the adverb)
leads to a definition of the prototypical adjective which, if valid for

French, is not necessarily so for all other languages and which cannot be adequately summarized in a few words; here, it must suffice to say that Goes attaches great importance to the fact that, in French, the adjective, though normally following its noun, can in certain circumstances precede it, and that he concludes that 'l'adjectif-prototype se présente [. . .] comme une partie du discours sémantiquement et syntaxiquement dépendante d'une base nominale, qu'il se trouve en fonction épithète ou en fonction attribut, qu'il soit antéposeé ou postposé'. Michèle Noailly, *L'Adjectif en français*, Gap, Ophrys, 168 pp.

Hervé Curat, *Les Déterminants dans la référence nominale et les conditions de leur absence. Essai de sémantique grammaticale*, II (Langue et cultures, 32), Geneva, Droz, 352 pp., is a follow-up to C.'s *Morphologie verbale et référence temporelle en français moderne* (1991; see *YWMLS*, 53:32–33) — indeed, the two volumes are described by the publishers as forming a diptych. Like the earlier volume, this one is theory-oriented but is documented with authentic examples throughout, drawn from such varied sources as literary texts from the 17th c. onwards, sociological works (C. Lévi-Strauss, M. Foucault), de Gaulle's memoirs, *Astérix*, and journalism. The basic thesis advanced is that 'le déterminant est un pronom dont le rôle est d'opérer la référence du syntagme nominal à un lieu spatial dans l'univers dont parle le locuteur, et que seules la classification et la dénomination de ce référent sont le fait du substantif'.

J.-M. Authier, 'On the issue of syntactic primacy: evidence from French', *Probus*, 11:165–67, is based on the demonstrative pronoun *ce*. C. Schnedecker, '*Autrui*: un pronom vraiment pas comme les autres', *JFLS*, 9:69–90, combats the view that *autrui* is 'une forme annexe et archaïque réservée à de purs emplois littéraires ou académiques'.

*TrL*, 39, a thematic issue devoted to 'Temps verbaux et relations discursives', includes: L. Gosselin, 'La cohérence temporelle: contraintes linguistiques et pragmatico-référentielles' (11–36); W. De Mulder and C. Vetters, 'Temps verbaux, anaphores (pro)nominales et relations discursives' (37–58); Co Vet, 'Temps verbaux, relations rhétoriques et chaînes topicales' (59–75); A. Molenduk and H. de Swart, 'L'ordre discursif inverse en français' (77–96), on sequence of tenses; and A. Le Draoulec, 'Subordonnées temporelles et cohérence discursive' (97–111). On a related topic, but not forming part of the main part of the volume, is Co Vet, 'Les temps verbaux comme expressions anaphoriques: chronique de la recherche', *ib.*, 113–30.

Vogeleer, *Temps*, and Vogeleer, *Modalité*, are both devoted to papers presented at the Second Chronos Colloquium, held at the Institut Libre Marie Haps (Brussels), in January 1997. Though some of the

papers (especially in *Modalité*) deal with general theoretical considerations or relate to languages other than French, the great majority of
those in each volume deal specifically or principally with French.
Excluding papers outside our scope, *Temps* includes: C. Vetters, 'Les
"temps" du verbe: Réflexions sur leur temporalité et comparaison
avec la référence (pro)nominale' (11–43), mainly on French but with
evidence also from English and Russian; J. Moeschler, 'Ordre
temporel, causalité et relations de discours: une approche pragmatique' (45–64); H. Irandoust, 'Le passé simple et les combinaisons
séquentielles' (65–78); B. Sthioul, 'Le passé composé: une approche
instructionelle' (79–94), drawing on D. Sperber and D. Wilson's
Relevance Theory and the work of, among others, G. Guillaume and
H. Reichenbach; L. de Saussure, 'La temporalité dans la négation
d'événements: problèmes d'ordre et d'encapsulation' (95–112); J.-M.
Luscher, 'Influence des connecteurs et des reprises pronominales sur
l'interprétation d'énoncés aux temps du passé' (113–29); A. Borillo,
'Les adverbes de référence temporelle comme connecteurs temporels
de discours' (131–45); J. Bres, 'Fluence du temps impliqué et
orientation: l'imparfait et le passé simple revisités' (157–70), concluding that 'les temps verbaux ont bien une valeur sémantique,
comptable des innombrables effets de sens en discours';
L. Tasmowski-De Ryck and W. De Mulder, 'L'imparfait est-il un
temps méronomique?' (171–89), takes up a distinction drawn by
G. Kleiber between the terms *méronomique* and *méronymique*, but
comprehension is not facilitated by the fact that, in their basic
definition of the two terms, *méronomique* is used not only for itself but
also, by an unfortunate misprint, for *méronymique*; M. Vuillaume, 'Le
discours indirect libre et le passé simple' (191–201); S. Mellet,
'Présent et présentification: un problème d'aspect' (203–13), arguing
(against Guillaume) that the present is 'parfaitement homogène'; and
A. Judge, 'Choix entre le présent narratif et le système multifocal
dans le contexte du récit écrit' (215–35); *Modalité* includes:
P. Dendale, '*Devoir* au conditionnel: valeur évidentio-modale et
origine du conditionnel' (7–28); L. Gosselin, 'Les valeurs de l'imparfait et du conditionnel dans les systèmes hypothétiques' (29–51);
P. Kreutz, ' "Ou": la disjonction et les modalités' (53–76); S. de
Vogüé, 'Ni temps, ni mode: le système flexionnel du verbe en français'
(93–114), arguing for a radically new interpretation, according to
which there would be a correlation 'entre structuration morpholo-
gique du système et structuration sémantique, les flexions morpho-
logiquement "thématiques" opérant une prédication d'existence,
tandis que les flexions strictement affixales relèvent d'une prédication
attributive'; P. Bourdin, '*Venir de* et la récence: un marqueur
typologiquement surdéterminé?' (203–31), contrasting the French

construction with comparable ones in a number of other languages; C. Marque-Pucheu, 'L'inchoatif: marques formelles et lexicales et interprétation logique' (233–57); É. Saunier, 'Contribution à une étude de l'inchoation: *se mettre à* + *inf[initif]*' (259–88), paying particular attention to the *effets de sens* and properties of the verb *mettre*; C. Schnedecker and M. Charolles, 'Référence et changement. Étude du prédicat *(se) transformer*' (289–308); and G. Achard-Bayle, 'Pour un traitement linguistique du problème de l'identité à travers le temps. Étude aspectuelle des prédicats transformateurs métamorphiques' (309–27). A. E. Nielsen, 'Quels topoï *permettre* permet-il?', *RevR*, 34:1–24, generalizes from her findings to conclude that 'la théorie des topoï est une des approches les plus intéressantes pour rendre compte de la signification des mots en contexte'.

Monika Sokol, \**Das Zusammenspiel der Verbalkategorien und die französische Futura* (LA, 409), ix + 218 pp. *Wilmet Vol.* includes under the heading 'Le système verbal': a preamble by L. Rosier, under the title ' "L'avenir dure longtemps" ' (149–61), constituting a further assessment of aspects of W.'s work; M. Bracops, ' "Cache ce nain que je ne sais plus voir". Contribution à l'analyse syntaxique et sémantique de *pouvoir* et *savoir* combinés avec l'infinitif' (163–74), arguing that the distinction between the two verbs in question is that between 'possibilité momentanée' and 'capacité fondamentale'; J. Bres and B. Verine, 'D'un zeugme verbo-temporel: l'appariement [PS *et* IP]' (175–85) – the abbreviations stand for '*passé simple*' and '*imparfait*'; M. Dominicy, 'Paradoxes "temporels" chez Baudelaire' (187–98); M. Forsgren, 'L'emploi du passé simple dans la langue d'aujourd'hui' (199–208), which is in part a contrastive study with Swedish and English; A. Jaubert, '*Praesens fingo*. Le présent des fictions' (209–18); S. Karolak, 'Remarques sur l'aspect des noms abstraits' (221–28); and B. Pottier, 'Le système verbal et les modalités discursives' (229–34). *CPr*, 32, is devoted to 'l'imparfait narratif', with contributions by L. Gosselin, S. de Vogüé, B. Kuszmider, J. Bres, A.-M. Berthonneau and G. Kleiber, L. de Saussure and B. Sthioul, and J.-C. Chevalier. J. Carruthers, 'A problem in sociolinguistic methodology: investigating a rare syntactic form', *JFLS*, 9:1–24, deals specifically with the *passé surcomposé* but is of considerably wider methodological importance. A. Martinet, 'Remarques sur l'usage oral du "passé simple" ', *Linguistique*, 35:87–95, reports on an unpublished survey dating from 1960. M. Larjavaara, 'Primarily transitive verbs without objects in modern French', *JFLS*, 9:105–11, discusses briefly the use of different types of 'transitive verbs with missing objects'. N. Rossi, 'Déplacement et mode d'action en français', *ib.*, 259–81, is inspired by the work of Z. Wendler and J. P. Boons. Marc Wilmet, *Le Participe passé autrement. Protocole d'accord,* *exercices et corrigés*, Louvain-la-Neuve, Duculot, 122 pp., ranges widely and thoroughly over the problem, starting from the principles that the participle is (1) both a verb and an adjective, and (2) 'l'apport (ou le "receveur d'accord") d'un support (le "donneur d'accord")'; there is good practical advice, the essentials of which are that, once the 'support' has been identified, various tests are to be applied, after which one has to ascertain that 'aucun blocage n'entrave le jeu normal de l'accord'. *\*LaF*, 135, ed. Hava Bat-Zeev Shyldkrot, is devoted to 'Les auxiliaires: délimitation, grammaticalisation et analyse'.

K. Hunnius, 'Der Konzessivsatz aus kognitiver Sicht. Überlegungen zur französischen Syntax', *ZFSL*, 99:241–55, tackles the problem of the use of the subjunctive in concessive clauses asserting a state of fact.

H. de Swart, 'Négation et concordance négative en français', *RLFRU*, 18:91–101, considers the semantics of the negative indefinites *personne, rien,* and *aucun*.

K. Peterson, '*Beaucoup de* partitif?', *FM*, 67:133–46, concludes that sometimes it is, sometimes not.

J. van Baardewijk, 'La positivité par contraste de *bien*', *RLFRU*, 18:13–22, seeks to define the role of *bien* as a discourse marker. A. Rabatel discusses '*Mais* dans les énoncés narratifs: un embrayeur du point de vue et un organisateur textuel', *FM*, 67:49–60. Whereas previous studies have attempted to identify what is common to the different uses of *mais*, T. Nyan, 'Vers un schéma de la différence: le cas de *mais*', *JFLS*, 9:211–38, starts from a common basis and seeks to account for the fact that, 'd'un cas à l'autre, certains traits et fonctions ne sont pas présents au même degré, ou même disparaissent'.

N. Thatcher, 'La coréférence lexicale', *ib.*, 91–104, examines the role of lexical anaphors in a journalistic piece. Catherine Schnedecker, *\*Les Corrélats anaphoriques*, Metz U.P., 192 pp. M. Velcic-Canivez discusses 'L'anaphorique *ils* et le contournement de l'acte de dénomination', *FM*, 67:147–64.

J. Goes, 'La relative attributive et les verbes de perception', *RRL*, 43, 1998[1999]:25–35, deals exclusively with French. H. L. Andersen, 'Propositions adverbiales non introduites en français parlé', *RevR*, 34:163–80, on constructions of the type *je serais au club avec les collègues je m'amuserais*, deals with temporal, conditional, iterative, consecutive, concessive and situational clauses. Anne-Élizabeth Dalcq et al., *Mettre de l'ordre dans ses idées: classification des articulations logiques pour structurer son texte*, Louvain-la-Neuve, Duculot, 107 pp., is, within the limits that are clearly indicated by its title, a clearly thought out and presented communicative grammar; a first part, 'Les objets du monde', is subdivided into 'L'espace', 'Le temps', and 'Les faits', while a brief second part, 'Le discours', deals with 'L'agencement du discours' and 'L'intervention du locuteur'. C. Muller, 'L'inversion du sujet clitique en français: hypothèse V dans C et diachronie', *LInv*, 20, 1997:75–96, is on the constructions *Quand est arrivée Marie?, Quand est-elle arrivée?* and *Quand Marie est-elle arrivée?* E. Havu offers 'Quelques observations sur le discours indirect introduit par *que*', *NMi*, 100:333–52.

*Wilmet Vol.* includes under the heading 'Au-delà du syntagme': D. Van Raemdonck, 'Sous mon arbre, volait un esthète' (237–52), which discusses the terms *extension* and *incidence* that W. had taken from Beauzée and Guillaume respectively; A. Boone, '*C'est une énigme que cette construction*: essai d'analyse d'un "gallicisme"' (253–66); A.-R. Delbart, 'Des comptages au conte ou les avatars d'une théorie' (267–78), a follow-up to W.'s articles on anteposition and postposition of the adjective in French; D. Droixhe, 'Aspects de la syntaxe et de son évolution dans *Les Voyages aux Indes orientales* de François Pyrard de la Val (1611, 1679)' (279–99); D. Gaatone, 'Réflexions sur un adjectif substantivé: la construction "l'important est d'agir"' (301–09); A. Joly, 'Du "strapontin basculant" au fauteuil d'orchestre: faire et refaire l'article' (311–29); J. Lago Garabatos, 'Quelques remarques sur le concept de translation en linguistique' (331–44); J.-M. Léard, 'Subordination, phrase, proposition: le choix sémantique' (345–54); and A. Vassant, 'De la théorie de l'incidence, encore' (355–68). It emerges clearly from the bibliography to Mylène Blasco-Dulbecco, *Les Dislocations en français contemporain: étude syntaxique*, Champion, 340 pp., that there has been no lack of attention to French dislocations in recent decades; this work, however, is a ground-breaking study that proposes a re-interpretation of the different types of dislocation on the basis of a shrewd analysis of an impressive corpus of some 2000 examples (three quarters of them from speech, the rest from written texts), introduced by a 60-page historical overview, 'La dislocation à travers les siècles', taking us back to early Old French; an admirable volume that can be recommended without reservation.

Florence Lefeuvre, *La Phrase averbale en français*, L'Harmattan, 352 pp.

## 8. LEXICOGRAPHY

*Atti* (Palermo), III, includes: J.-C. Boulanger and M. C. Cormier, 'Les noms propres dans l'espace dictionnairique'(99–110); F. Lagueunière, 'Le traitement de la variation diatopique en français moderne dans le *Französisches Etymologisches Wörterbuch*' (387–950; A. Thibault,

'Le dialogue entre lexicographie générale et lexicographie diffé-
rentielle illustré par l'exemple du *DFSR*' (893–905) (*DFSR* =
*Dictionnaire des particularités lexicales contemporaines du français en Suisse
romande*); R. Verbraeken, 'Pierre Richelet et André Félibien. Emprunts
et réminiscences' (941–49); T. R. Wooldridge, 'Le lexique français de
la Renaissance dans les textes et dans les dictionnaires' (969–81).

Kurt Baldinger's *Dictionnaire étymologique de l'ancien français*, Tübingen, Niemeyer, has reached *fasc. H3, HERBERGIER–HONTE,
96 pp.

E. Dawes, 'Le traitement des variantes dans le *Dictionnaire des
locutions en moyen français*', *ZRP*, 115:244–59, takes the expression
*trousser ses quilles* as the basis for a case-study and suggests far-reaching
structural reforms for any future edition.

A *CD-ROM edition of the first edition (1694) of the *Dictionnaire de
l'Académie française* has been published by Champion Électronique, in
both text-mode and facsimile.

*Dictionnaire explicatif et combinatoire du français contemporain: recherches
lexico-sémantiques 4*, ed. Igor Mel'cuk and André Clas, Montreal U.P.,
347 pp. Christian Lacour, *Dictionnaire français des mots oubliés: du XIIe
au XIXe siècle*, 2 vols, Nîmes, Lacour, 770 pp., is a straightforward
dictionary of head-words and definitions, based on a comparison of
Littré, Becherelle, the 1842 ed. of the *Dictionnaire de l'Académie*, and
others, with contemporary dictionaries; though it lacks etymologies
and datings, the fact that it claims to contain some 30,000 entries is,
in itself, enough to render it a useful reference work; the range of
entries can be illustrated by, for example, *Beau-sire-Dieu* 'cérémonie
en usage ches les abbesses de Remiremont', *caner* 'aller à la selle',
*opaler* 'remuer le sucre dans les formes avec un coteau', *royaliser*,
'rendre royaliste'. Jean-Paul Colin and Jean-Pierre Mével, *Dictionnaire de l'argot et de ses origines*, Larousse, 792 pp. Agnès Pierron,
*Dictionnaire des expressions populaires*, Marabout, 356 pp. Alfred Gilder,
*En vrai français dans le texte: dictionnaire franglais-français*, Cherche Midi,
376 pp. Maurice Rat, *Dictionnaire des expressions et locutions tradi-
tionnelles*, Larousse, 464 pp. Jean-Claude Bologne, *Dictionnaire com-
menté des expressions d'origine biblique*, Larousse, 288 pp. Alain Duchesne
and Thierry Leguay, *Dictionnaire des subtilités du français*, Larousse,
351 pp. Thérèse Moreau, *Le Nouveau Dictionnaire féminin-masculin des
professions, des titres et des fonctions*, Geneva, Metropolis, 184 pp., is 'une
version entièrement repensée' of a work that first appeared in 1991
but which somehow escaped mention in these pages (*mea culpa*). With
probably some 1400 entries, it is far more than a mere list of forms
and definitions, including as it does an introduction chronicling
changing attitudes to women particularly as reflected in language and
in different parts of *la francophonie*, and, in the body of the dictionary,

giving examples of women having exercised various professions or functions (e.g. Renée Guébriant, 1614–59, the first French *ambassadrice*, here meaning 'ambassador' not 'ambassador's wife'); the more recent terms listed range from the unsurprising (*footballeuse, professeure, une juge*) to others that are perhaps less predictable (*cheffe d'orchestre, une curée* '(hypothetical) woman Catholic priest').

## 9. LEXICOLOGY

*Atti* (Palermo) includes: F. Rainier, 'La réduplication française du type *fifille* d'un point de vue diachronique' (I, 279–89); B. Fradin, 'La dérivation à partir d'unités lexicales' (II, 325–28); M. Hug, 'Le témoignage d'une base de données sur la double nature du mot *donc*' (II, 467–81); J. A. Ahokas, 'Pour une autre étymologie du verbe *écraser*' (III, 3–6); M. Bonhomme, 'La néologie par téléscopage en français contemporain: le cas de la publicité' (III, 89–98); E. Dawes, 'Les variantes de la locution dans le système' (III, 201–11); R. Honvault, 'Les familles de mots, chaînes dérivatives, variations morphologiques et modifications sémantiques des radicaux français' (III, 349–61); O. Ozolina, 'Corrélation sémantique et fonctionnelle des latinismes et de leurs équivalents populaires dans les textes littéraires et documentaires du Moyen Âge' (VI, 383–90).

Jean H. Duffy, *Using French Vocabulary*, CUP, ix + 476 pp., consists of classified vocabularies with exercises. *La Linguistique*, 35.2, has two posthumous items by A. Martinet, 'Genre et sexe' (5–9), and 'Le synthème' (11–16), with a bibliography by Jeanne Martinet (17–21). *FrSoc*, 10, devoted to 'La féminisation des noms de métiers, fonctions, grades ou titres. Au Québec, en Suisse romande, en France et en Communauté française de Belgique', contains: P. Bouchard, N. Guilloton and P. Vachon-l'Heureux, 'La féminisation linguistique au Québec: vers l'âge mûr' (6–29); J.-F. De Pietro and M.-J. Béguelin, 'La Suisse romande. Le féminin dans la langue: un espace de variation et de réflexion' (30–44); M.-J. Mathieu, 'La France. La féminisation des noms de métiers, titres, grades et fonctions: un bilan encourageant' (45–64); and M.-L. Moreau, 'La féminisation des termes de professions en Belgique francophone' (65–80); the articles are accompanied by useful bibliographies. Annie Becquer, Bernard Cerquiglini et al., *\*Femme, j'écris ton nom: guide d'aide à la féminisation des noms de métiers, titres, grades et fonctions*, Documentation française, 124 pp. Anne-Marie Houdebine-Gravaud, *\*La Féminisation des noms de métiers en français et dans d'autres langues*, L'Harmattan, 1998, 198 pp. Jean Dubois and Françoise Dubois-Charlier, *\*La Dérivation suffixale en français*, Nathan, 303 pp. N. Rodriguez, 'Sur les oppositions sémiques des adjectifs dénominaux dans quelques séquences binaires', *CLe*,

74:29–51, deals with 18 types of pairs differing in their suffix, e.g. *dentaire* ∼ *dental*, *gaullien* ∼ *gaulliste*, *laiteux* ∼ *laitier*. P. Pupier, 'Le morphème est plus une unité de forme qu'une unité de signification. Le cas de -*on* en français', *ib.*, 53–60, concludes that -*on* in words such as *capuchon*, *dindon* is indeed a suffix which 'détermine le genre (masculin) pour le nom suffixal'. M. Plénat discusses the 'Morphophonologie des dérivés argotiques en -*ingue* et en -*if*', *Probus*, 11:101–32. N. Flaux, 'A propos des noms collectifs', *RLiR*, 63:471–99, is specifically on French. *TeN*, 20, is devoted to 'Nouveaux outils pour la néologie'.

C. Schmitt, 'Untersuchungen zu den Namen der französischen Feld- und Waldvögel. Ein Beitrag zur galloromanischen Etymologie und Lexikographie', *ZRP*, 115:410–63, is well documented and informative but would have been more user-friendly (both to linguists and to ornithologists) if it had been better laid out, with subheadings classifying the birds by species and giving their scientific names. J.-C. Boulanger and J. de Blois, 'Au nom du Père, du Fils, du Saint-Esprit et de la Vierge Marie', *CLe*, 74:149–70, studies the treatment of the nouns in questions and words derived from and expressions based on them in a number of French dictionaries. P. W. Brossman, \**The Rhine Franconian Element in Old French*, NY, Lang, 311 pp. W. Sayers, 'L'ancien judéo-français *étupé* "ayant un prépuce, incirconcis": glose biblique — et insulte religieuse?', *ZRP*, 115:234–43, speculates on a possible semantic evolution of a derivative of STUPPARE. L. Rossi discusses the origin and meaning of the word *flabel* 'fabliau', *Romania*, 117:342–62. F. Rainer notes an early attestation (1850) of the word *chèque*, *CLe*, 74:225–6, and Id. '*Bimétallique* et sa famille, origine française et diffusion européenne', *FM*, 67:165–68, reveals that the term was invented by H. Cernuschi in 1869; Id., 'Sur l'histoire de *inflation* et dérivés', *VR*, 57, 1998:172–75, finds an example dating from 1886 (33 years before the earliest attestation in the *TLF*) and traces the semantic evolution of the word. Charlotte Schapira, \**Les Stéréotypes en français: proverbes et autres formules*, Gap, Ophrys, 172 pp. M. Cucu, '*Coup*: action et évaluation (de la sémantique à la pragmatique', *SCL*, 47, 1996[1999]:67–77, is on locutions of the type *coup de feu*, *coup de main*.

10. SEMANTICS

*Atti* (Palermo), III, includes: P. Dendale and W. De Mulder, 'Sur *sur*. Réflexion sur l'emploi des ressemblances de famille en sémantique cognitive' (213–22); H. Geckeler, 'Synonymie, antonymie et champ lexical' (261–67); G. Hessler, 'Contexte thématique et explication du sens' (331–40); R. Landheer, 'L'interaction entre la sémantique lexicale et la sémantique textuelle. Un cas d'espèce: l'énoncé paradoxal' (397–404); M. Rinn, 'Approches de la sémantique lexicale de l'indicible' (741–54). Hans-Burkard Krause, *Lexikologische Beschreibungen zum konzeptuell-semantischen Netz 'intelligence' im heutigen Französisch*, Berne, Lang, 393 pp.

11. ONOMASTICS

Auguste Longnon, *Les Noms de lieu de la France. Leur origine, leur signification, leurs transformations* (preface by Jacques Chaurand), Champion, 864 pp., is a new edition by Paul Marichal and Léon Mirot of a work first published in 1920.

12. DIALECTS AND REGIONAL FRENCH

*Atti* (Palermo) includes: J. L. Léonard, 'Microdialectologie et syntaxe: aspects du pronom neutre poitevin' (II, 543–56); J. Herman, 'La situation linguistique dans la Gallia Narbonensis et les origines de la séparation du domaine français et du domaine provençal' (IV, 455–66); J. Kruijsen, 'Adaptation et permanence à la frontière linguistique en Hesbaye' (V, 411–23); P. Stein, 'La première enquête de géographie linguistique dans le domaine gallo-roman. La traduction des phrases de Wenker en patois alsacien, lorrain et wallon' (V, 659–71).

*Variétés géographiques du français de France aujourd'hui: approche lexicographique*, ed. Pierre Rézeau (Champs linguistiques), Louvain-la-Neuve, Duculot, 395 pp., arises from an awareness that, as compared with what had been accomplished in relation to French-speaking Belgium, Switzerland and Canada, the regional vocabulary of French itself had hitherto been the object of inadequate attention. What we have here is a dictionary of regionalisms, consisting of about 140 articles (the longer of them running to several pages), providing definitions, examples, geographical, historical and etymological notes, and references to such sources as the *FEW*, the *TLF* and other dictionaries (including regional dictionaries), dialectal monographs, linguistic atlases, etc.; there is also an extensive bibliography. J. Serme, 'Le lexique français commun comme source de régionalismes: le phénomène de survivance et ses avatars', *FM*, 67: 169–97, distinguishes four categories of what have been classified, sometimes rightly sometimes wrongly, as 'survivals'.

*Les Dialectes de Wallonie*, *23–24 (1995–96[1997]), publishes the proceedings of a 1996 colloquium marking the 50th anniversary of the death of Jean Haust. Marguerite and Henri Blanquaert, *Dictionnaire encyclopédique du patois lillois*, Lille, Publi-Nord, 1998, 551 pp. René Lepelley, *La Normandie dialectale*, Caen U.P., 176 pp., is an excellent introduction to the subject; introductory chapters on the definition of dialectology and the place of French within the Romance-speaking world are followed by a chapter usefully tracing the history of Norman dialectology, others characterizing admirably the lexical, phonetic and morpho-syntactic features of the Norman dialects, and surveys of the regional French of Normandy, Norman onomastics (personal names as well as place-names), and 'la littérature patoisante'; there is also a good selective bibliography. Bonneton's series of dictionaries of regional French on which we have frequently commented (see, most recently, *YWMLS*, 60:45, and references thereat) continues with Philippe Blanchet and Henriette Walter, *Le Français régional de Haute-Bretagne: de Vannes à Saint-Malo, de Nantes à Saint-Brieuc*, 157 pp., which draws on research by the authors and includes, in addition to a dictionary of 538 entries, an introduction incorporating four maps, annexes covering *inter alia* pronunciation and grammatical features, a brief selection of texts, and a bibliography. \*Langues et parlers de l'Ouest: pratiques langagières en Bretagne et Normandie, ed. Francis Manzano, Rennes U.P., 1997, 188 pp. Jean-Pierre Chambon, \*Études sur les régionalismes du français, en Auvergne et ailleurs, Klincksieck, 282 pp.

Y. Kawaguchi, '*Éclair* dans les dialectes du nord-est de la France', *VR*, 57, 1998:138–55, identifies five different terms in use and concludes that the distribution of the term *éclair* demonstrates 'l'existence vraisemblable de voies d'extension du français de l'Île-de-France'.

The interest of N. C. W. Spence, ' "Conservatism" versus "innovation" in Jèrriais', *ABSJ*, 27:448–56, is wider than the title suggests, providing as it does a useful summary of sources of information on Jèrriais as well as of conservative and innovative features of the language as compared with French.

Marzys, *Variation*, includes: 'Les emprunts au français dans les patois' (19–35); 'De la *scripta* au patois littéraire: à propos de la langue des textes francoprovençaux antérieurs au XIXe siècle' (113–35); 'Les pronoms personnels sujets dans le parler francoprovençal de Faeto et Celle' (149–61); 'La description des faits grammaticaux dans un dictionnaire multidialectal' (163–73); and 'Une charte jurassienne inédite du début du XIVe siècle' (249–60).

### 13. ANGLO-NORMAN

W. Rothwell, 'Sugar and spice and all things nice: from Oriental bazar to English cloister in Anglo-French', *MLR*, 94:647–59, draws attention to the hitherto underrated extent to which French was used in England in the 14th and early 15th cs 'not as a social grace or literary ornament but as a mundane tool in the world of work', and again highlights the need for the publication of more non-literary documents (which exist in abundance) from this period.

## 14. FRENCH IN NORTH AMERICA

S. Poplack and D. Turpin, 'Does the *Futur* have a future in (Canadian) French?', *Probus*, 11 : 133–64, find that it seems to be on the way out but 'cannot predict with certainty whether it will go to completion'. J. Auger, 'Le redoublement des sujets en français informel québécois', *CanJL*, 43, 1998:37–63, argues for a conception of linguistic competence allowing for morphosyntactic variation. M.-T. Vinet, 'Contrastive focus, French *n*-words and variation', *ib.*, 121–41, contrasts the syntax of *personne, rien*, etc., in Quebec French and in Standard French.

Gaston Dulong, *Dictionnaire des canadianismes* (nouvelle édition revue et augmentée), Sillery (Quebec), Septentrion, xix + 549 pp. Yves Cormier, *Dictionnaire du français acadien*, Saint-Laurent (Quebec), 440 pp. C. Lyche, 'Le mot phonologique en cadien', *JFLS*, 9 : 25–38, stresses the importance of the phonological word in Cajun which is, she concludes, 'une langue dont le rythme a une base syllabique'; this is perhaps to be attributed to the influence of American English of which, however, it is not a systematic calque.

## 15. FRENCH IN AFRICA

*Le français langue africaine: enjeux et atouts pour la francophonie*, ed. Gervais Mendo Ze, Publisud, 383 pp.

## 16. CREOLES

Claire Lefebvre, *Creole Genesis and the Acquisition of Grammar*, CUP, 480 pp. *French and Creole in Louisiana*, ed. Albert Valdman, NY–London, Plenum, 1997, 359 pp. Pierre Pinalie and Jean Bernabé, *Grammaire du créole martiniquais en 50 leçons*, L'Harmattan, 224 pp. Robert Damoiseau, *Éléments de grammaire comparée français–créole martiniquais*, Petit-Bourg (Guadeloupe), Ibis rouge, 174 pp. E. Nikiema, 'De la variation du déterminant /la/ dans les créoles haïtien et st-lucien', *Lingua*, 107 : 69–93, is on a postposed determiner, e.g. /livla/ 'le livre'.

## 17. SOCIOLINGUISTICS

C. S. Dukiens, 'La "Bataille du français" en Suisse romande durant l'Entre-deux-guerres: le purisme linguistique dans les chroniques de langage de la presse romande', *VR*, 57, 1998:156–71, identifies feelings of linguistic and political insecurity on the part of the chroniclers in question and their readers.

### 18. SPECIAL REGISTERS

On the strength of a questionnaire-based survey of people's perceptions, A. Lodge, 'Colloquial vocabulary and politeness in French', *MLR*, 94:355–65, looks at the functioning of French colloquial vocabulary from sociolinguistic and pragmatic standpoints, raising the problem of the definition of such terms as *argot*, *vulgaire*, *populaire* and *familier*, and taking issue with some of the views of P. Guiraud. Marcel Schwob, *\*Études sur l'argot français et le jargon de la coquille*, Alia, 160 pp.

### 19. PRAGMATICS AND DISCOURSE ANALYSIS

*Atti* (Palermo) includes: J. M. Coletta, 'A propos de la modalisation en français oral' (IV, 65–80); M. Drescher, 'Les manifestations de l'expressivité en français parlé: le cas de l'interjection' (IV, 101–09); M. Laforest and G. Martel, 'L'usage spontané de l'argument d'autorité' (IV, 163–74); F. Mougeon, 'Étude de plusieurs marqueurs discursifs dans deux corpus du français parlé' (IV, 193–201); E. Sonntag, 'La fonction modale de l'intonation' (IV, 269–79); A. Vanderheyden, 'Les arrêts de conversation: l'insertion du monologue rapporté dans le texte médiéval' (VI, 495–504).

In a contribution 'hors thème', D. Flament-Boistrancourt and G. Cornette, 'Bon français ou vrai français?', *TrL*, 38:119–152, attempt an in-depth analysis of the act of questioning on the basis of an extract from the *Lancom* corpus, with the purpose of discovering what is central to the way of speaking of native speakers, and concluding that more than purely informational purposes are served by the act of questioning. B. Peeters, '*Salut! Ça va? Vous avez passé un bon weekend?*', *JFLS*, 9:239–57, aims to show 'the pragmatic differences between "health enquiries" and "weekend routines" in French and (Australian) English'. G. Manno, 'Le remerciement prospectif, ou la condensation de l'échange directif. Pour une conception plus dialogale des actes de discours', *CFS*, 52:203–35, is illustrated largely from French but with some consideration of English.

### 20. CONTRASTIVE STUDIES

Morris Salkoff, *\*A French-English Grammar: A Contrastive Grammar on Translational Principles*, Amsterdam, Benjamins, xvi + 342 pp., is described by the publishers as a comparative grammar for translators. Barbara Kuszmider, *Aspect, temporalité et modalité en français et en polonais*, Gap, Ophrys, 294 pp. Sibylle Kurt, *Erlebte Rede aus linguistischer Sicht: Der Ausdruck von Temporalität im Französischen und Russischen*, Berne, Lang, 661 pp. A. Moustaki, 'Analyse constrastive des formes *être Prép X* en grec moderne et en français', *LInv*, 20, 1997:19–73. Man-Ghyu Pak, 'Les relations causales directes en français et en coréen', *ib.*, 139–62.

# EARLY MEDIEVAL LITERATURE

By SARA I. JAMES

## I. GENERAL

Douglas Kelly, *The Conspiracy of Allusion: Description, Rewriting, and Authorship from Macrobius to Medieval Romance*, Leiden, Brill, xiv + 313 pp., studies the influence of the Latin tradition of *inventio*, *ordo* and *mutatio*, and its recasting in French vernacular texts, analysing description and narration in *Erec et Enide*, *Le Roman de Troie*, *Eneas*, *Le Bel Inconnu*, *Le Roman de la Violette*, *Le Roman du Châtelain de Coucy et de la Dame du Fayel* and Jean Renart's *Rose*. Sophie Marnette, *Narrateur et points de vue dans la littérature française médiévale*, Berne, Lang, 1998, 262 pp., uses linguistic analysis of epic, verse and prose romance, hagiography, and chronicle to examine both the notion of narrative point of view and the broader issue of generic classification. M. Accarie, 'Verité du récit ou récit de la vérité: le problème du réalisme dans la littérature médiévale', *Razo*, 15: 5–34, reflects on the distinction between 'real' and 'concrete' in medieval literature, further problematized by the notion of the *speculum* through which reality is perceived. D. Kelly, 'Forlorn hope: mutability *topoï* in some medieval narratives', *Nykrog Vol.*, 59–78, compares episodes from Chrétien de Troyes, Marie de France and Benoît de Sainte-Maure to explore how actions and speech lead to irrevocable ruptures or temporary rifts, depending upon the author's view of human relations. D. Poirion, 'Mask and allegorical personification', *YFS*, 95: 13–32, explores the seeming inconsistency in 13th-c. literature's fascination with both the distance between image and reality (parallel to metaphor and allegory), and the idea of image as reflection of reality. R. H. Bloch, 'Medieval French literature and its devices', *ib.*, 237–59, uses the *Privilège aux Bretons* (*c.*1230), a multi-generic parody, to study the liminal space of town meeting forest, nobles meeting commoners, as well as the importance accorded to writing itself within the text. M. A. Santina, *The Tournament and Literature: Literary Representations of the Medieval Tournament in Old French Works, 1150–1226*, Berne, Lang, 197 pp., studies the tournament in *L'Histoire de Guillaume le Maréchal*, Marie de France's *Milun*, *Guigemar*, *Le Laüstic*, *Le Fresne* and *Chaitivel*, *Eneas*, *Le Roman de Thèbes*, *L'Estoire de la guerre sainte* and the *Chronique de Guines et d'Ardre*; while Y. Ferroul, 'Le mythe du courage individuel et de l'exploit singulier', *Suard Vol.*, 251–72, cites (briefly and for the most part in footnotes) romances by Chrétien, Hue de Rotelande, Jean Renart and others in this sweeping overview of representations of tournaments in Classical literature, historical documents, and Old French texts. E. B. Vitz, *Orality and Performance in Early French Romance*, Woodbridge, D. S. Brewer, xiii + 314 pp., contends that throughout medieval verse romance, orality and literacy combined to reflect deliberately both minstrel and clerical traditions in the courtly milieu in which both originated and flourished. V. examines oral and literary aspects of the *Tristan* material, the *Roman de Thèbes*, and the works of Chrétien de Troyes, subsequently drawing conclusions regarding the influence of orality on the various authors. D. Poirion, 'Literature as memory: "Wo die Zeit wird Raum"', *YFS*, 95:33–46, focuses on the relationship between oral literature and memory, its representation in written works of the Middle Ages, and resulting perceptions of time and space. J. Enders, 'Memory, allegory and the romance of rhetoric', *ib.*, 49–64, muses on the rhetorical as opposed to the dialectical nature of the 'romantic' in romance, and on the question of whether there is a specific poetic of romantic romance. R. Dragonetti, 'L'inachevable', *PRIS-MA*, 15:173–85, uses brief reflections on methods of closure in Chrétien de Troyes, *Le Roman de la Rose, Galeran de Bretagne, L'Escoufle* and *Guillaume de Dole*. L. C. Brook, 'Rewards and punishments in the *De Amore* and kindred texts', *RMS*, 25:3–16, is of interest to French medievalists in its examination of the parallels between the *Lai du Trot* and *Li Consaus d'Amours*, compared with the *De Amore* and Heloise's *Art d'Amour*. K. Busby, ' "Plus acesmez qu'une popine": male cross-dressing in medieval French narrative', Taylor, *Gender Transgressions*, 45–59, examines examples of men dressing as women to further (humorously) their own goals, rather than as instances of social subversion, bringing to bear such texts as *Meraugis de Portlesguez, Claris et Laris*, the *Tristan en prose, Trubert* and *Wistasse le Moine*. On the same subject, M. Szkilnik, 'The grammar of the sexes in medieval French romance', *ib.*, 61–88, shows how certain male characters' cross-dressing is seen as evidence of their less-than-maleness by authors who refer to them as female (*Roman d'Ysaïe, Valentin et Orson, Roman de Silence, Cassidorus, Perceforest*). I. Garreau, 'Eustache et Guillaume ou les mutations littéraires d'une vie et d'un roman', *Médiévales*, 35:105–23, seeks to demonstrate the intertextuality of late 12th-c. genres through an analysis of *La vie de saint Eustache* and *Guillaume d'Angleterre*. D. S. King, 'Humor and holy crusade, *Eracle* and the *Pèlerinage de Charlemagne*', *ZFSL*, 109:148–55, argues for a re-evaluation of both works, which have been dismissed as inconsistent in register; K. asserts that a broader view of generic elements and seemingly contradictory tones within medieval works is needed to appreciate them fully.

## 2. EPIC

GENERAL. R. Lafont, 'Pour rendre à l'oc et aux Normands leur dû: genèse et premier développement de l'art épique gallo-roman', *CCMe*, 42 : 139–78, provides an offbeat but fascinating argument for Provençal origins of the *chanson de geste*, bringing to bear the Paris-Meyer debate of the late 19th c. (with its implications for definitions of the epic), the history of the South during Charlemagne's reign, and *La Chanson de sainte Foy* as evidence. J. Flori, ' "Les héros changés en saints . . . et les saints en héros". Sacralisation et béatification du guerrier dans l'épopée et les chroniques de la première croisade', *PRIS-MA*, 15 : 255–72, shows that just as heaven and earth, in medieval terms, were not two separate worlds, nor were men of war and men of God presumed to be two separate categories. Not only are holy men (e.g., Turpin) shown in support of Christian warriors, but the Crusades bring about a conflation of violence with penitence, and the notion of the 'just war'. Id., 'Des chroniques aux chansons de geste: l'usage des nombres comme élément de typologie', *Romania*, 117 : 396–422, re-evaluates the numbers given for both Crusader and enemy troops in 'fiction' (epic) and in 'historical document' (chronicle). F. holds that unrealistic estimates are not the exclusive preserve of epic, nor is epic consistently incredible. S. Marnette, '*Il le vos mande, ge sui qui le vos di*: les stratégies du dire dans les chansons de geste', *RLiR*, 63 : 251–52, provides another analysis of how reported discourse in a variety of forms contributes to our understanding of orality in the *chansons de geste*. J. Merceron, 'La voix problématique du messager dans les chansons de geste', *Olifant*, 19 : 207–22, studies the social, legal and narrative role played by the messenger.

ROLAND AND CHARLEMAGNE M. W. Morris, ' "The Other" as a reflection of Augustinianism in the *Chanson de Roland*', *MedP*, 14 : 166–76, sees Charlemagne as a divine force uniting the *communitas* (understood as Christian), with the Saracen enemy — among others — excluded, in a rather blatant oversimplification of the issue of epic alterity. J. Flori, 'La croix, la crosse et l'épée. La conversion des infidèles dans *La Chanson de Roland* et les chroniques de Croisade', *Suard Vol.*, 261–72, analyses the role of conversion in the *Roland*, as salutory for the converted as it is exculpatory for the Christians; the chroniclers (clerics, for the most part) focus more heavily on the liberation of Jerusalem and the Holy Sepulchre. B. Cazelles, 'Du visuel au sonore: les manifestations de la sainte perfection (*Alexis*) et de l'excellence héroïque (*Roland*)', *PRIS-MA*, 15 : 239–54, sees the two paragons — whose perfection is by definition abstract — through two opposing models of concretization. J. R. E. Bliese, 'Courage and honor, cowardice and shame: a motive appeal in battle orations in

*The Song of Roland* and in chronicles of the central Middle Ages', *Olifant*, 20:191–212, provides a much-needed analysis of what both epic and chronicle can reveal about psychologically potent rhetorical methods of motivating participants in battle. E. J. Mickel, 'The council scene in the Oxford *Roland*', *ib.*, 19:113–120, analyses the pivotal scene in the light of a similar episode recounted by Orderic Vitalis. R. A. Hall, ' "A Roland for an Oliver": their quarrel again', *ib.*, 20:109–44, uses a line-by-line reading of laisses 130–131 (Brault ed.) to attempt to come to a definitive interpretation of both heroes. H.-E. Keller, 'Une *Chanson de Roland* négligée du XVe siècle', *Suard Vol.*, 465–73, discusses the variants found in a decasyllabic poem (late 14th c.), a version in prose (c. 1460) and a printed version in prose (c. 1500). M. J. Ailes, 'The date of the chanson de geste *Fierabras*', *Olifant*, 19:245–71, gives a comprehensive overview of the evidence (MS tradition, literary references, language) to support a late 12th-c. date of composition. Id., 'Comprehension problems and their resolution in the Middle English verse translations of *Fierabras*', *FMLS*, 35:396–407, discusses the Middle English translation, c. 1200, of the Old French *chanson de geste*. G. Knott, 'Notes on reality and improbability in *Fierabras*', *Olifant*, 20:145–70, examines in greater detail some elements of A. de Mandach's *Geste de Fierabras* — *le jeu du réel et de l'invraisemblable* of 1987 (see *YWMLS*, 49:73).

GUILLAUME D'ORANGE AND THE GARIN CYCLE. M. Tyssens, 'Le Roman de Guillaume d'Orange: trois notes de lecture', *Suard Vol.*, 915–26, offers disparate observations on differences in language, style and character development between the verse and prose versions of *Guillaume d'Orange*. E. A. Heinemann, 'The art of repetition in the short cycle of *William of Orange* (the printed AB Version)', *Olifant*, 19:177–206, uses analysis of laisse length and structure to support an argument for the *Prise d'Orange*, *Le Charroi de Nîmes* and *Le Couronnement de Louis* surpassing the *Roland* on both technical and artistic grounds. C. A. Kent, 'Fidelity and treachery: thematic and dramatic structuring of the laisses in an episode of the *Couronnement de Louis* (laisses 43–54)', *ib.*, 223–38, studies the episode of Guillaume's defence of Louis against the rebel Acelin and its reinforcement of feudal devotion as a virtue. P. E. Bennett, 'Hétéroglossie et carnaval dans le cycle de Guillaume', *Fourquet Vol.*, 135–49, analyses the multiplicity of voices, genres and discourses present in *Le Charroi de Nîmes* and other texts of the cycle in the light of Bakhtin's observations. N. Clifton, 'Adolescent knights in the *Song of William*', *Olifant*, 20:213–33, shows how the prodigies that are Guillaume's nephews and brothers-in-law are portrayed as recognizably adolescent in thought, speech, and action. A. Labbé, 'Les "jeux d'orange": matériau onirique et illusion magique dans les *Enfances Guillaume*', *Sénéfiance*, 42:269–91, examines the complex nature of Orable's relationship with the supernatural: though her aims are laudable, she nevertheless incarnates alterity through both paganism and femaleness. C. Latrouitte Armstrong, 'D'Orable à Guibourc, ou l'évolution guidée de l'adorable supplément: une étude onomastique de l'héroïne de *La Prise d'Orange*', *Fourquet Vol.*, 301–12, studies in detail how the seemingly formulaic descriptions of Orable/Guibourc reveal her primary characteristics. N. Andrieux-Reix, 'La dernière main. Approche de fins cycliques', *ib.*, 109–20, reflects on the implicit *explicit*, or the different techniques of bringing a specific text or cycle to a close, using poems from the Guillaume cycle as examples. P. E. Bennett, 'Le jeu de l'intertextualité dans la *Chevalerie Vivien*', *Suard Vol.*, 57–68, scrutinizes episodes and recurring themes in the various poems of the *Aliscans* cycle in order to reconstitute their chronology and probable influence on each other. M. de Combarieu du Grès, 'De l'histoire à la légende: Narbonne dans le cycle d'Aymeri', *Fourquet Vol.*, 205–15, examines the historical and literary sources regarding both the city of Narbonne and the character of Aymeri. M.-G. Grossel, '"Ains por Forcon tant ne fist Anfelixe con ie per vos, amis, se vos ravoie [. . .]": composition et romanesque dans la *Chanson de Fouque de Candie*', *Suard Vol.*, 351–60, sees the author's constant evocation of themes and motifs from elsewhere in the Guillaume cycle as a means of adding substance to his tale. A. Moisan, 'De l'illusion à la magie dans la geste de Rainouard', *Sénéfiance*, 42 : 351–63, traces the encounters of Rainou-art, himself an almost supernatural force, with increasing degrees of Otherness, culminating in his voyage to Avalon.

EPICS OF REVOLT. W. Azzam, 'La geste interminable. *Raoul de Cambrai*: fins et suites', *PRIS-MA*, 15 : 17–29, defends the second part of the work against charges made by S. Kay et al. of its being influenced by epic and therefore less valid as epic; A. claims that the second part, while indeed leading critics to ask whether it is a worthy ending to the tale, raises crucial questions about its (now lost) sources. W. W. Kibler, '*Raoul de Cambrai* et la paix de Dieu', *Suard Vol.*, 483–90, holds that Bernier's actions, like Raoul's, reject any possibility of peace or compromise. M. de Combarieu du Grès, '" . . . et in hora mortis nostra": sur l'*aristeîa* de Raoul', *Littératures*, 41 : 5–31, offers comparisons between the episode of Raoul de Cambrai's asking forgiveness and *La Queste del saint Graal* and Hugo's *La Légende des siècles*, in a general reflection on the theme of *démesure*. Id., '*Iter Hierosolymitanum*: Renaut de Montauban en Terre Sainte (d'après les ms Douce et La Vallière)', *Suard Vol.*, 197–208, compares the theme of pilgrimage in a linear reading of two MSS. S. Baudelle-Michels, '*Renaut de Montauban* et *Les Quatre Fils Aymon*: Les avatars de la querelle aux échecs', *ib.*, 45–56, closely analyses the scene of Bertholet's murder by Renaud. D. Boutet, 'Au carrefour des cycles épiques: la chanson de *Doon de Mayence*', *ib.*, 102–09, argues that far from falling into the second of the famous three classifications of epic — cycle du roi, cycle des barons revoltés, cycle de Monglane — *Doon de Mayence* unifies significant aspects of all three.

OTHER EPICS. D. Kullmann, 'Gautier de Châtillon et les chansons de geste françaises', *Suard Vol.*, 491–501, argues that Gautier was influenced both linguistically and thematically by contemporary vernacular epic in his composition of the *Alexandreis*. *Les Enfances de Godefroi* and *Le Retour de Cornumarant*, ed. E. J. Mickel (Old French Crusade Cycle, 3), Tuscaloosa, Alabama U.P., 483 pp., comprises considerable introductory material on the MS tradition of the Crusade cycle, the popular history associated with the cycle, thematic analysis, appendices, variants, index of proper names and glossary. Id., 'The *Enfances Godefroi*: an epic in formation', *Romania*, 117:98–114, compares MSS to see how themes and episodes (e.g. role of Ida, voyage of Cornumarant) vary, while the Crusaders' characters are consistently portrayed to emphasize a destiny that is both noble and holy. C. Brucker, 'Vers une esthétique nouvelle: sensibilité et structure dans *Lion de Bourges* et dans *Herpin von Bourges*', *Fourquet Vol.*, 171–92, argues that a closer reading of *Lion de Bourges* in comparison with the German version reveals original traits such as the coexistence of realism with the fantastical, and psychological development. K. A. Campbell, 'Commemorative formulae in the *Geste des Loherens*', *Olifant*, 19:101–12, examines how repeated references to the heroic genealogy reinforce the cyclical nature of the epic itself and its notion of time. D. Ion, 'L'esprit généalogique comme stratégie littéraire dans le prologue de *Garin le Loheren*', *Suard Vol.*, 445–54, combines plot summary with reflections on the importance of genealogy and lineage in the cycle. C. M. Jones, 'L'enlèvement dans *Garin le Lorrain* et *Hervis de Metz*', *ib.*, 455–64, compares the epic narrative of violence towards women with that in romance. J.-C. Herbin, 'L'enchanteur Tulles dans *Anseÿs de Metz*', *Sénéfiance*, 42:209–32, studies the way in which *Anseÿs de Metz*, unlike other works of the Lorrain cycle, features a magician in a significant role. Id., 'L'Episode du crâne de Fromont dans *Gerbert de Metz*', *Suard Vol.*, 407–22, discusses the significance of Fromont's death and the subsequent use of his skull within the context of both ancient practice and the larger cycle. J. Subrenat, 'Les *Chétifs* et l'idée de croisade', *ib.*, 879–91, argues that the *Chétifs* provide evidence of not only an author but an audience who, in spite of the bloody siege of Jerusalem, were capable of attributing human qualities to the enemy Saracens. E. Hoyer-Poulain, 'Du bon usage du Sarrasin courtois: le personnage de Caraheu, des *Enfances Ogier* au remaniement en alexandrins',

*Fourquet Vol.*, 263–72, studies the valiant Saracen who remains the hero's closest friend though he never converts, thus technically remaining the enemy. F. Wolfzettel, 'Quelques réflexions sur le thème des enfants-cygnes et le status du conte populaire au Moyen Age', *Suard Vol.*, 1015–29, reviews much of the German scholarship on folklore from the 19th c. onwards, concluding that although Old French texts such as *Elioxe* and *Béatrix* confirm a theory of simultaneous development of folkloric themes, they give greater scope to their female characters than do proto-versions. F. E. Sinclair, 'Suppression, sacrifice, subversion: redefining the feminine in the *Naissance du Chevalier au Cygne*', *Olifant*, 20:33–61, traces the development of female characters within the *Cygne* poems, with reference to the original swan-children folk legend.

### 3. ROMANCE

GENERAL. F. Gingras, 'Les noces illusoires dans le récit médiéval (XIIe–XIIIe siècles)', *Sénéfiance*, 42:173–89, provides a survey of episodes, drawn mostly from Arthurian texts, Wace, and *Raoul de Cambrai*, in which sexual activity is accompanied by some form of illusion, from dreams to spells; G. also examines the role played by female characters and their presumed connection to the otherworldly. C. Alvarez, 'Gauvain et l'impossible dénouement romanesque', *PRIS-MA*, 15:1–15, somewhat diffusely addresses the extent to which marriage in romance both connects and alienates characters, while speech is capable of both deferring and formalizing the desire which is at the heart of the genre. F. Gingras, 'Le sang de l'amour dans le récit médiéval (XIIe–XIIIe siècles)', *CRISIMA 4*, 207–16, focuses on episodes from Béroul's *Tristan* and Chrétien's *Le Chevalier de la Charrette*, in which the lovers' meetings are marked with blood against a white background, an ambivalent image evoking both the taboo of menstruation (the blood of the Fall) and a positive sign of fertility (the blood of redemption). N. Grandperrin, 'Le roi, mari trahi: par sa femme, son imagination ou ses hommes? (Lais et romans arthuriens des XIIe et XIIIe siècles)', *BDBA*, 17:143–58, studies individual examples of adultery (real or potential) and its effects on the larger context of the court, in *Graelent*, *Guingamor*, *Lanval*, *Le Lai du Cor*, *Le Lai du Cort Mantel*, *La Vengeance Raguidel*, the *Perceval Continuations*, *Yder* and *La Mort le roi Artu*, concluding that with few exceptions, episodes of adultery — symbolic of feminine duplicity in general — constitute no more than a brief digression.

CHRÉTIEN DE TROYES. A.-L. Bucher, 'Féminité et purification du héros dans les romans de Chrétien de Troyes', *PRIS-MA*, 15:215–38, sees the hero as confronting and integrating the feminine in order to accede to a higher level of knowledge and perfection. D. Nelson, 'A woman is like . . .', *RoQ,* 46:67–73, argues that Chrétien, like Marie de France, compares women to animals, to the former's denigration. C. Noacco, '*Par nigromancie* et *par enchantement*: niveaux et nuances du magique dans les romans de Chrétien de Troyes', *Sénéfiance*, 42:383–406, offers a typology of both kinds of magic and of practitioners. K. B. Haas, 'Erec's ascent: the politics of wisdom in Chrétien's *Erec et Enide*', *RoQ,* 46:131–40, explores the possibility of the tale representing the getting of wisdom necessary to accede to kingship. H. sees the notion of the rite of passage to rule as stemming from the tradition of political theorists such as John of Salisbury and Macrobius; he also sees Enide as symbolic of Boethius's Lady Philosophy. P. Walter, 'Erec et le *cocadrille*. Note de philologie et de folklore médiéval', *ZRP*, 115:56–64, focuses on the origins of the word *cocadrille*, an animal depicted on Erec's throne, and the connotations of the animal in popular mythology. B. Burrichter, ' "Ici fenist li premiers vers" (*Erec et Enide*) - noch einmal zur Zweiteiling des Chrétienschen Artusromans', Wolfzettel, *Erzählstrukturen*, 87–98, analyses v. 1796 as an effective dividing line between the first and second parts of the narrative. R. N. Illingworth, 'Some observations on the structure of the Guiot *Charrete*', *NMi*, 100:127–41, argues that the *charrette* tale must be seen as tripartite in structure in order to gain full awareness of the parallels and contrasts between Parts 1 and 2 (together) and Part 3. N. Klassen, 'The lover's *largesce*: agency and selfhood in Chrétien's *Le Chevalier de la Charrette (Lancelot)*', *FrF*, 24:5–20, examines Chrétien's portrayal of the interaction between reason and morality, specifically in Lancelot's demonstrations of generosity, a virtue which Chrétien views as part of a functioning rational mind. K. J. Taylor, 'Desexualizing the stereotypes: techniques of gender reversal in Chrétien's *Chevalier au lion* and *Chevalier a la charrete*', Taylor, *Gender Transgressions*, 181–203, points to Gauvain, among others, as an example of how subversion of gender stereotypes is not exclusively modern. R. Allen, 'The roles of women and their homosocial context in *Le Chevalier au Lion*', *RoQ,* 46:141–54, rejects views of female characters as empowered or disempowered (which sees them in isolation); rather, A. studies relationships between women such as Lunete and Laudine, concluding that they must be studied as complementary halves of a whole. D. Hüe, 'De quelques transformations animales', *Sénéfiance*, 42:233–53, treats the subject broadly, but in particular wonders whether the medieval belief in lycanthropy could inform our reading of Yvain's madness. G. M. Armstrong, 'Questions of inheritance: *Le Chevalier au lion* and *La Queste del saint Graal*', *YFS*, 95:171–92, examines how episodes of the defence or release of disinherited or imprisoned women occur in both;

however, Chrétien's episodes show knights adhering to a temporal justice which has failed, while the *Queste* emphasizes a divine justice. E. Baumgartner, *Chrétien de Troyes: Le Conte du Graal*, PUF, 127 pp., provides a brief yet accessible overview of the MS tradition as well as conditions of composition and reception of the work, followed by analysis of various themes and a brief passage from the *Graal*; there is also a bibliography, which, like the rest of this study, will be of use to undergraduates. *Perceval: The Story of the Grail*, trans. Burton Raffel, New Haven, Yale U.P., x + 310 pp., is a faithful translation into English verse of Poirion's edition, with an afterword by J. Duggan. B. Guidot, '*Perceval ou le Conte du Graal*: quelques délicates attentions de l'écriture de Chrétien de Troyes', *Suard Vol.*, 361–72, maintains that, although incomplete, *Perceval* is Chrétien's masterwork, offering a series of lessons in medieval narrative technique at its peak. D. Kullmann, 'Frühe Formen der Parallelhandlung in Epos und Roman: Zu den Voraussetzungen von Chrétiens *Conte du Graal*', Wolfzettel, *Erzählstrukturen*, 23–45, argues that Chrétien innovates in his structuring of the *Conte du Graal*, using techniques drawn from both romance and epic to mark new passages. P. McCracken, 'The poetics of sacrifice: allegory and myth in the Grail quest', *YFS*, 95:152–68, studies the sacrificial and religious symbolism of Perceval's three drops of blood in the snow: not only does the blood evoke the theme of violence against women, but also that of lineage (blood) and its place in reinforcing the social order. B. Milland-Bove, 'Les orgueilleux dans le *Conte du Graal*', *Suard Vol.*, 617–27, sees these characters as symbolic of knights who must earn salvation through humility and penitence, as well as sources of conflict. L. J. Walters, 'Female figures in the illustrated manuscripts of *Le conte du Graal* and its *Continuations*: ladies, saints, spectators, mediators', *BJR*, 81.3:7–54, examines MS illustrations as evidence of how artists as 'active interpreters' of the text choose to portray women, especially in relation to sacred themes; women are allowed important secular roles, but not religious ones.

OTHER ARTHURIAN. F. Wolfzettel, 'Doppelweg und Biographie', Wolfzettel, *Erzählstrukturen*, 119–41, proposes seeing Arthurian romance as 'biographical romance' reminiscent of *enfances* narratives, with its emphasis on individual psychology and character development. C. F. C. Carreto, '*Ce est merveoille et deablie*: économie du désir et magie verbale dans quelques récits arthuriens en vers', *Sénéfiance*, 42:89–109, analyses the way in which the genre of romance parallels economic growth, in that both are based on mobility and exchange; C. uses examples of verbal exchange in *Yvain*, *Guillaume d'Angleterre* and the *Roman de Silence* to develop a compelling theory. C. R. Dover, 'Galehot and Lancelot: matters of the heart', *Nykrog Vol.*, 119–36, provides a close analysis of Galehot's character and actions in order to clarify his relationship with Lancelot, which is seen as a homoerotic one in the guise of idealized friendship. M. T. Bruckner, 'Knightly violence and Grail Quest endings: conflicting views from the Vulgate cycle to the *Perceval* Continuations', *MH*, 26:17–32, addresses the bipartite structure inherent in the presence of two heroes, Gauvain and Perceval; B. perceives a significant shift in the nature of the quest as the identity of the questers becomes multiple. The failure of Arthur's kingdom on both political and moral grounds moves the narrative focus to individual salvation. J.-R. Valette, 'Illusion diabolique et littéraire dans la *Queste del saint Graal* et dans le *Dialogus miraculorum* de Césaire de Heisterbach', *Sénéfiance*, 42:547–67, argues that the two works complement each other inversely: both are informed by the Cistercian movement and engage with the supernatural, the latter presents lessons from monk to novice that are then put into practice, while the *Queste* shows the heroes confronting various challenges, from which they then extract the meaning. N. F. Regalado, 'The medieval construction of the modern reader: Solomon's ship and the birth of Jean de Meun', *YFS*, 95:81–108, argues that a certain vision of the reader is implicit in the fiction, as with two works she studies: *La Queste del saint Graal*, in which it is clear that the future reader is counted on to interpret the text correctly, and Jean de Meun's *Roman de la Rose*, whose reading and eventual decoding are deferred in favour of the pursuit of love. J. O. Fichte, 'Telling the end: Arthur's death', Wolfzettel, *Erzählstrukturen*, 275–90, analyses the way in which the structure of the *Mort le roi Artu* and related texts diverges from previous Arthurian tales; the fact of the king's death means that the plot is linear, moving ineluctably towards fall rather than the usual cycle of adventure and growth. A. Berthelot, 'Merlin magicien?', *Sénéfiance*, 42:51–64, disputes the emphasis placed on Merlin's role as sorcerer; in looking closely at texts such as the *Suite-Vulgate*, *Merlin* and *Lancelot*, B. finds Merlin presented as prophet, royal and military councillor, and indeed as enchanter, but a far less active one than might be supposed. V. Bubenicek, 'Quelques figures de rois-chevaliers errants dans le roman en prose de *Guiron le Courtois*', *BDBA*, 17:49–61, analyses an Arthurian text which focuses exclusively on knighthood and its potential for conflict with kingship. A. Gier, 'Lästern, lügen, schweigen', Wolfzettel, *Erzählstrukturen*, 219–31, asserts that Girart d'Amiens's *Escanor* features characters who correspond to and yet confound Propp's typology of heroic functions.

TRISTAN AND ISEUT. G. J. Brault, 'Le personnage de Roald le Foitenant dans le *Tristan* de Thomas', *Suard Vol.*, 125–31, summarizes the prologue recounting Tristan's early history and examines the role played by Roald, marshal to Tristan's father Rivalen and protector of the young hero. T. Adams, ' "Pur vostre cor su jo em paine": the Augustinian subtext of Thomas's *Tristan*', *MAe*, 68:278–91, sees Tristan's lovesickness in theological terms, corresponding to the 12th-c. notion of the 'unruly will'. G. Milin, 'La Navigation de Caïphe: de *L'Estoire del Saint Graal* au *Tristan en prose*', *MA*, 105:643–66, examines the disovery of the exiled Caiaphus; the subsequent debate on the nature of his guilt transposes elements of Robert de Boron's work into the *Tristan en prose*. M. further studies the portrayal of Caiaphus in canonical, apocryphal and secular literature. B. Milland-Bove, '*La Dameisele [. . .] qui sa seror desheritoit*: enjeux d'une ré-écriture dans le Tristan en prose', *Romania*, 117:78–97, compares the incident of the *Noire Epine* maidens in both Chrétien de Troyes and in the prose in order to analyse opposing representations of secular justice within the Arthurian world. F. Plet, 'Le castel des destins croisés: sur une digression du *Tristan en prose*', *Suard Vol.*, 723–32, defines the relatively brief episode of the Castel Marin as unifying the major themes of the *Tristan*. S. Sasaki, 'Tristan et ses/les "brachets" dans le *Roman de Tristan en prose*', *ib.*, 821–30, studies the instances of hunting dogs owned by Tristan. D. James-Raoul, 'Rhétorique de l'entrelacement et art de régir la fin: le cas du *Tristan en prose* (MS. Vienne 2542)', *PRIS-MA*, 15:85–111, argues that the *Tristan en prose* continues a particular narrative technique begun in the *Lancelot-Graal*, in which various strands of the story are interwoven, not only referring back to the sources of legend which inspire them, but also deferring, through sheer volume and complexity of material, any resolution or definitive ending.

ROMANS D'ANTIQUITÉ. G. W. Carl, ' "Tu cuides que nos seions taus/Come autres femes comunaus" ', Taylor, *Gender Transgressions*, 107–27, uses the much-praised Amazons of the *Roman de Troie* to contrast modern views of medieval attitudes towards women with the 'surprising' open-mindedness attested by a variety of works. M. Thiry-Stassin, 'Personnages estompés dans le songe d'Andromaque du *Roman de Troie en prose* (version Bodmer)', *Suard Vol.*, 893–902, argues that, in comparison with Benoît de Sainte-Maure's vivid language, the prose author's muted vocabulary creates far less lively and touching characters, which leave the reader unmoved. J.-J. Vincensini, 'De la fondation de Carthage à celle de Lusignan: "engin" de femmes vs prouesse des hommes', *Sénéfiance*, 42:579–600, examines *Eneas* and *Mélusine*'s female characters, both of whom need the male hero to complement their own supernatural abilities in establishing new territory.

OTHER ROMANCES. F. Pomel, 'Les plaisirs du dénouement dans le *Roman de la Rose*: pratique sexuelle et pratique scripturale', *PRIS-MA*,

15:137–52, examines the manner in which Jean de Meun both replicates and remedies Guillaume de Lorris's temporary abandonment of the Lover's quest; Jean de Meun's technique furthers the action while deferring the eventual possession of the Rose through elaborate digressions, constantly reinforcing the theme of sexual tension heightened by delay. E. Hicks, '*Donner à voir*: Guillaume de Lorris or the impossible romance', *YFS*, 95:65–80, examines the stylistics of Guillaume de Lorris's writing in reference to the naming of allegorical figures, and their representation as static or tautologically fluid (active). H. also studies the extent to which these representations contribute to the reader's understanding of the allegorized topos. E. L. Friedrich, 'When a rose is not a rose: homoerotic emblems in the *Roman de la Rose*', Taylor, *Gender Transgressions*, 21–43, argues that the identification of Rose as female in Guillaume de Lorris's text ignores the homosexual aspect of Bel Accueil's loss and the Lover's explicit appeal to him. E. J. Burns, 'Speculum of the courtly lady: women, love, and clothes', *JMEMS*, 29:253–92, studies how representations of women's clothing (in Provençal works and in the *Roman de la Rose*) imply women's status as visual object; however, this becomes more complex depending upon whether the woman is observed by a man, or observing herself. Philippe de Remi, *Le Roman de la Manekine*, ed. B. N. Sargent-Baur, Amsterdam, Rodopi, iii + 675 pp., is an edition of BNF fr. 1588 with facing-page translation in English verse and comprehensive introductory material. P. Eley and P. Simons, '*Partonopeus de Blois* and Chrétien de Troyes: a re-assessment', *Romania*, 117:316–41, argue that *Partonopeus de Blois* could well pre-date and have influenced Chrétien, establishing the conventions that Chrétien then subverted. The issue of date is examined both thematically and historically. C. Gaullier-Bougassas, 'L'Orient troyen des originies, l'Orient byzantin de Mélior et l'Occident français dans *Partonopeu de Blois*', Suard Vol., 295–304, examines representations of the East in *Partonopeu* as revelatory not only of references to contemporary texts and received ideas, but also of the author's originality. P. Simons and P. Eley, 'Male beauty and sexual orientation in *Partonopeus de Blois*', *RoS*, 17:41–56, examine the rhetoric of the hero's blazon and various ways in which his physique complicates a traditionally heterosexual male view of appearance in romance. M. T. Bruckner, 'Romancing history and rewriting the game of fiction: Jean Renart's *Rose* through the looking glass of *Partonopeu de Blois*', Nykrog Vol., 93–118, insists that the latter (and nowadays less well known) work must be studied in order to understand better the former, closely analysing characters, themes and plot to support this argument. R. Wolf-Bonvin, 'Amadas, Ydoine et les *faés* de la dort-veille', *Sénéfiance*, 42:601–16, agrees with A. Micha that *Amadas et Ydoine* is indeed a revised *Cligès*, but one in which the lovers' guilt is less, mitigated by their minimal recourse to the supernatural and by their own suffering. S. L. Burch, 'The lady, the lords and the priests: the making and unmaking of marriage in *Amadas et Ydoine*', *RMS*, 25:17–31, examines the representation of marriage and adultery in the text, comparing it with both Chrétien's *Cligès* and contemporary practice. F. Dubost, 'L'enchanteur et son double, Mabon et Evrain: thématique de la dualité dans *Le Bel Inconnu*', *Sénéfiance*, 42:123–41, argues that the seeming superfluity of Evrain as a second, less than active, magician in *Le Bel Inconnu* functions both as a symbol of duality and to reinforce the ambiguous nature of the text. M.-L. Chênerie, 'Dénomination et anthroponymie dans les romans de Hue de Rotelande', *LR*, 52:203–34, studies the use of specific names in *Ipomedon* and *Protheselaüs* in situating individuals within a familiar mythical framework. R. L. A. Clark, 'A heroine's sexual itinerary: incest, transvestism, and same-sex marriage in *Yde et Olive*', Taylor, *Gender Transgressions*, 89–105, rejects a Freudian emphasis on the incest theme in order to read Yde as an anti-Manekine, actively controlling her destiny and finally, in C.'s words, 'rewarded with a phallus'. P. McCaffrey, 'Sexual identity in *Floire et Blancheflor* and *Ami et Amile*', *ib.*, 129–51, examines the theme of 'paradoxical identity', in which lovers share attributes. E. Derrien, '*Blancandrin* ou l'apprentissage de la royauté', *BDBA*, 17:91–101, examines the way in which royalty, lineage and knighthood interact. R. Stuip, '*Blancandrin et l'Orgueilleuse d'Amour*: nouveaux fragments', *Suard Vol.*, 861–69, offers an edition of newly-discovered fragments to support the case for an oral stage of the text's transmission. E. Gaucher, 'Les influences épiques dans le roman de *Robert le Diable* (à propos du manuscrit B.N. fr. 25516)', *Suard Vol.*, 285–94, situates the romance within an epic framework not only on account of the neighbouring texts in the MS (*Beuves de Hanstone*, *Elie de saint-Gilles*, *Aiol*), but also because of recurrent epic themes. Id., 'Sang vermeil, merveille du *sen*: à propos de *Robert le Diable*', *CRISIMA 4*, 217–26, argues that the role of blood in *Robert le Diable* parallels its contradict-ory significance in Christianity, sign of both sin and expiation. C. Lucken, 'Le suicide des amants et l'*Enseignement* des lettres: *Piramus et Tisbé* ou les métamorphoses de l'amour', *Romania*, 117:363–95, reflects on incidents in *Piramus et Tisbé* as revelatory not only of deeper sexual meaning within the text but also of the author's views on the nature of literary creation. D. Maddox, ' "Courtois" d'Aupais: l'ombre du prodigue dans *Gautier d'Aupais*', *Suard Vol.*, 561–78, studies this brief 13th-c. tale in comparison with the *Courtois d'Arras*. S. D. White, 'Imaginary justice: the end of the ordeal and the survival of the duel', *MedP*, 13, 1998:32–55, looks at the representations of trial by ordeal and its variants in the *Roman de la Violette*.

LAIS.  M. Griffin, 'Gender and authority in the medieval French lai', *FMLS*, 35:42–56, uses the uncertainty of Marie de France's identity as author to show the reader's need to assign gendered authorial voice to works, which genders the works themselves. V. Krause and C. Martin, 'Topoï et utopie de l'amour dans les *Lais de Marie de France*', *DFS*, 42:3–15, offers a typology of relationships in Marie's works, concluding that the fundamental instability of love contributes to a pessimistic dominant view. R. T. Pickens, 'Marie de France et la culture de la cour anglo-normande: corrélations entre les *Lais* et les *Fables*', *Suard Vol.*, 713–22, rejects the view that the *Lais* and the *Fables* were produced for two different audiences, arguing instead that both were produced for an aristocratic Anglo-Norman court, drawing on the *matières* Marie professed to reject in order to create her own. R. H. Bloch, 'Other worlds and other words in the works of Marie de France', *Nykrog Vol.*, 39–58, casts doubt upon the stereotypically feminine attributes (e.g. warmth, simplicity, sincerity) which critics have traditionally assigned to Marie. In a compelling article, B. argues that speech acts such as lying, promising, saying too much or too little, are in fact at the centre of the *lais* and *fables*. Furthermore, the *Espurgatoire* shows its protagonist in need of a Latinist, paralleling Marie's own quest to place her female, vernacular voice within a male, Latin tradition. I. De Pourcq, 'La fable dans la deuxième moitié du XIIe siècle, un genre sans frontières? Le cas de Marie de France', *Reinardus*, 12:139–49, argues for broadening the boundaries of generic definition through establishing a continuum for each aspect (form, tropes and themes) found in a genre such as Marie's *Fables*. N. Cottille-Foley, 'The structuring of feminine empowerment: gender and triangular relationships in Marie de France', Taylor, *Gender Transgressions*, 153–80, asserts that Marie subverts the traditional view of women and turns potentially problematic triangular relationships into models of harmony. P. Whitfield, 'Power plays: relationships in Marie de France's *Lanval* and *Eliduc*', *MedP*, 14:242–54, claims that whereas the fairy lover of *Lanval* represents Marie's vision of future possibilities for female autonomy, Guildeluec exemplifies medieval woman in her self-sacrifice. P. Walter, 'Yonec, fils de l'ogre: recherches sur les origines mythiques d'un lai de Marie de France', *Suard Vol.*, 993–1000, retraces various possible lines of inquiry into Irish and Indian mythology, seeking similar motifs and structures to those in *Yonec*. C. Bouillot, 'Quand l'homme se fait animal, deux cas de métamorphose chez Marie de France: Yonec et Bisclavret', *Sénéfiance*, 42:65–78, examines both the manner in which metamorphosis takes place and the folkloric sources of such tales. D. B. Leshock,

'The knight of the werewolf: *Bisclavret* and the shape-shifting meta-phor', *RoQ*, 46: 155–66, disputes the assumption that the knight-werewolf in Marie's tale is a sympathetic character; rather, the tale is critical of the medieval knight who, like the wolf, is a greedy, highly skilled killer. B. McCreesh, 'Translation and adaptation in *Lay le Freine*', *FMLS*, 35: 386–95, discusses the Middle English reworking of Marie de France's *Fresne*. J. H. McCash, 'The lady in *Le Chaitivel*: villainous or vilified?', *MedP*, 14: 140–51, argues against condemna-tion of the lady, who, far from being cold-hearted, values her independence and does not wish to encourage lightly any one of the four suitors without serious intentions. A. Sobczyk, 'Le lai de *Tydorel* ou la magie du silence', *Sénéfiance*, 42: 507–18, shows how the two conflicting worlds of real and supernatural are reconciled through language. R. Dubuis, 'Le jeu de la vérité dans les lais bretons anonymes', *Razo*, 15: 45–58, states that the literary technique of the medieval *conteur* is to be found within the *lai* itself; he further analyses the relationship between 'realism' and fantasy within the rules governing the genre itself.

## 4. Religious Writings

D. Boutet, 'L'approche des figures royales et de la royauté dans la *Vie de saint Thomas Becket* de Guernes de Pont-Sainte-Maxence', *BDBA*, 17: 35–48, explores the complications inherent in a text that is both hagiography and historiography; the representation of the king is a particularly delicate matter. K. Ashley and P. Sheingorn, *Writing Faith: Text, Sign and History in the Miracles of Sainte Foy*, Chicago U.P., x + 205 pp., examine how changing narratives of one saint's life and miracles reveal corresponding changes in the culture producing the narratives. Y. Foehr-Janssens, 'L'antihéroïne est la sainte: à propos de la *Vie de sainte Marie l'Egyptienne*, I', *PRIS-MA*, 15: 273–81, argues that the character of Marie as prostitute-penitent conflicts with the model of the desert ascete, usually male or desexualized female. J. Zatta, 'The *Vie Seinte Osith*: hagiography and politics in Anglo-Norman England', *SP*, 96: 367–93, gives a brief overview of the main historical and fictional points of a little-known saint's life; based on a Latin original, there is one MS dating from the 13th century. A. P. Tudor, 'Sexe et salut dans la première *Vie des pères*', *Reinardus*, 12: 189–204, gives a vivid and convincing analysis of the conflict between sexuality, whether potential or realized, and 'holy space'; nevertheless, the conflict — and its eventual, pious resolution — is an essential step towards salvation. M.-G. Grossel, 'L'illusion diabolique dans les *Vies des pères* dédiées à Blanche de Champagne (Lyon, MS 0868)', *Sénéfiance*, 42: 191–207, examines the varied and lively portrayal of the devil in the saints' lives offered to the pious Blanche. D. M. Hayes, 'Birth, flesh and bodies: the construction of sacred space in *The Miracles of Our Lady of Chartres*', *MedP*, 14:98–114, considers the miracles as an 'advertising brief' to raise the profile of Chartres through its association with the Virgin. M. Zink, 'L'expression de la contemplation dans le *Mirour de Seinte Eglyse* de saint Edmond d'Abingdon', *Suard Vol.*, 1031–40, insists that not only does the *Mirour* influence other religious writings, but also seemingly secular works of the same period; dating from the early 12th c., it shows considerable Cistercian influence, while ostensibly addressing lay men and women in their everyday roles. L. Spetia, '. . . un faus franceis sai d'Angleterre', *CN*, 59:129–48, provides an overview of the structure, MS tradition, language and some thematic aspects of the Old French life of Edward the Confessor. E. B. Vitz, 'Gender and martyrdom', *MH*, 26:79–99, argues that female martyrdom must be understood in a Christian context, one that does not see female martyrs as exemplars of female victimhood, but rather, like their male counterparts, as victors.

## 5. OTHER GENRES

LYRIC. W. C. Jordan, 'The representation of the crusades in the songs attributed to Thibaud, Count Palatine of Champagne', *JMH*, 25:27–34, argues that Thibaud's poetry serves as effective crusader propaganda; furthermore, the repeated references to love convince the author that, as J. Riley-Smith stated, crusading was 'an act of love'. E. Doss-Quinby, '*Rolan, de ceu ke m'avez/parti dirai mon semblant*: the feminine voice in the Old French *jeu-parti*', *Neophilologus*, 83:497–516, provides a thorough examination of the poetry associated with female authors, and representations of the female voice as active judge and interlocutor. R. Pensom, *Aucassin et Nicolete: The Poetry of Gender and Growing Up in the French Middle Ages*, Berne, Lang, 160 pp., is a brief yet thorough introduction to the celebrated *chantefable*, presumably for undergraduates. Each episode is given in English translation, followed by Pensom's analysis of both action and characters, which draws on Freudian analysis, post-structural literary theory and narratology to elaborate on certain points. C. Roussel, 'Mots d'emprunt et jeux de dupes dans *Aucassin et Nicolette*', *Romania*, 117:423–47, surveys existing scholarship on the commonly recognized intertextual parody of the text.

ROMAN DE RENART. *Le Roman de Renart (Branche XX et dernière): Renart Empereur*, ed. F. Lecoy (CFMA, 132), Champion, xi + 153 pp., is an edition of the text from MS B (de Cangé, BNF fr. 371), vv. 18876–22202, complete with critical notes and variants, a table of proper nouns, and glossary. E. B. Vitz, 'La liturgie, *Le Roman de Renart*, et le problème du blasphème dans la vie littéraire au Moyen Age, ou les bêtes peuvent-elles blasphémer?', *Reinardus*, 12:205–225, argues that Renart's irreligious speech and actions can only be found blasphemous in a literal sense, but that the medieval definition of blasphemy was both more fluid and more complex than is supposed. R. Bellon, 'Comment en finir avec Renart? Quelques remarques sur la clôture romanesque dans le *Roman de Renart*,' *PRIS-MA*, 15:31–52, demonstrates that the serial nature of the *Renart* poses particular problems for the author wishing to show definitive closure. B. concludes that the motive for action in most texts — Renart's adventures typically start with his quest for food or justice — provides consistent internal structure, with each individual episode ending satisfactorily, while leaving open the possibility of future adventures. R. Bellon, 'Quand Renart se fait magicien: à propos de *l'art d'enchantement* dans l'unité 24 du manuscrit M du *Roman de Renart*', *Sénéfiance*, 42:35–49, analyses the way in which Renart's knowledge of magic (acquired when captured by a magician of Toledo) is put to the fox's usual nefarious ends, consistent with the work as a whole. M. Bonafin, 'Osservazioni sul testo e sulla tecnica narrativa della *Branche* 2 del *Roman de Renart*', *MedRom*, 23:66–94, manages to discuss oral elements in the text, the role of the prologue, intertextual references and internal structure in a relatively brief article.

FABLIAUX. L. Rossi, 'Observations sur l'origine et la signification du mot *flabel*', *Romania*, 117:342–62, goes beyond the purely lexical study indicated in the title, to examine the extent to which the word indicated a degree of realism in narration. The author concludes that the pre-12th-c. usage generally indicated an entertaining tale, with the restricted meaning of *fabliau* developing subsequently. B. J. Levy, 'Malades et maladies dans les fabliaux', *Reinardus*, 12:81–93, shows how themes of real and pretended illnesses, patients and doctors meld into the *fabliau* world of deceit and overt sexuality. B. Nolan, 'Turning over the leaves of medieval fabliau anthologies: the case of BNF MS fr. 2173', *MedP*, 13, 1998:1–31, questions received ideas about the role of MSS in fabliau composition and dissemination; N. disputes the idea that they were purely oral, and points to their coexistence in MSS with other works as evidence of sophisticated intertextual reading and interpretation. A. Smets, 'De la maille à la livre et de l'amour au commerce: le rôle de l'argent dans les fabliaux', *Reinardus*, 12:173–88, analyses the variety of situations in which money and exchange play a significant role; S. finds that over 50% of texts feature money, usually towards dishonest ends. R. Brusegan, 'Cocuce: la troisième voie de Rutebeuf dans *Le Pet au vilain*', *Suard Vol.*, 133–40, uses a parallel reading of *Audigier* combined with a variety of lexical, social, and historical associations (not all of which are fully developed) to delve deeper into Rutebeuf's meaning.

MORAL, DIDACTIC, AND ALLEGORICAL WORKS. L. Evodokimova, 'Vers et prose au début du XIIIe siècle: le *Joseph* de Robert de Boron', *Romania*, 117:448–73, concludes that while Robert's prose text was closely followed by the anonymous rhymer, important differences exist, e.g. in characterization of Joseph; the prose version both reinforces and undermines the ideal of sacred truth. A. Strubel, 'L'allégorie épique: la *Psychomachia*, de Prudence à Huon de Méry', *Suard Vol.*, 853–60, argues that the Manicheism inherent in epic parallels that found in allegorical works such as the *Tornoiemenz Antecrit*. M. Possamaï-Perez, 'Les "mutacions des fables": illusion et tromperie dans l'*Ovide moralisé*', *Sénéfiance*, 42:469–89, shows how the author uses the themes of metamorphosis and illusion to underscore the allegory of hidden truth, which the reader must unveil in order to find salvation.

HISTORICAL. P. Damian-Grint, 'Translation as *enarratio* and hermeneutic theory in twelfth-century vernacular learned literature', *Neophilologus*, 83:349–67, argues that vernacular historians adopted Jerome's hermeneutic of translation to endow their own renditions of learned texts with the authority that was attached to Latin works. Id., '*En nul leu nel truis escrit*: research and invention in Benoît de Sainte-Maure's *Chronique des ducs de Normandie*', *ANS*, 21:11–30, provides a close examination of Benoît's sources as well as of his highly literary style, juxtaposed with the 'orality' of Wace's work. *Wace's Roman de Brut: A History of the British*, ed. Judith Weiss, Exeter U.P., xxix + 385 pp., is an edition of the complete text with facing-page translation into English. Id., 'Two fragments from a newly discovered manuscript of Wace's *Brut*', *MAe*, 68:268–77, provides a codicological analysis and edition of the fragments. L. Mathey-Maille, 'La pratique de l'étymologie dans le *Roman de Brut* de Wace', *Suard Vol.*, 579–86, supports the claim that Wace was one of the first etymologists, his concern for the origins of words, and specifically place names, attesting to a larger interest in a science of language. P. Eley, 'History and romance in the *Chronique des ducs de Normandie*', *MAe*, 68:81–95, shows how Benoît de Sainte-Maure develops the action and motivation of his female historical characters in a way associated with romance. M.-G. Grossel, 'L'image du roi dans *L'Histoire de la guerre sainte* d'Ambroise (Richard Coeur de Lion et Philippe Auguste)', *BDBA*, 17:159–75, analyses Ambroise's adoring portrayal of Richard ('Richard le Magne', in an attempt to affiliate the king with Roland's emperor), represented as Crusade incarnate. S. Loutchitskaja, 'L'image des musulmans dans les chroniques des Croisades', *MA*, 105:717–36, provides an excellent overview of terminology for and representations of Islam in chronicles of the First Crusade, and the extent to which subsequent experience and contact modified them. P. Noble, 'Villehardouin, Robert de Clari and Henri de Valenciennes: their different approaches to the Fourth Crusade', Kooper, *Chronicle*, 202–11, compares the different accounts of the three writers to provide a brief overview of each one's proximity to key figures and events and the resulting objectivity (or lack thereof) in the texts. Id., 'L'influence de l'épopée sur la chronique de Henri de Valenciennes', *Suard Vol.*, 681–89, examines the chronicler's discriminating use of epic formulae and themes, drawing on the *chanson de geste* tradition while nevertheless developing a new generic style.

DRAMA. T. Revol, 'Charabias et magiciens dans le théâtre des XIIe–XIIIe siècles', *Sénéfiance*, 42:491–506, analyses three plays, two Latin, one Old French (*Le Miracle de Théophile*); Rutebeuf's work makes explicit the association between magic and dramatic representation through the roles of Théophile, dabbling in necromancy, and the miracle of the Virgin, or approved magic. J. Dufournet, 'L'intertextualité du *Jeu de Robin et Marion*: mise au point', *Suard Vol.*, 221–29, shows how Adam de la Halle dramatizes two lyrical genres, the *pastourelle* and the *bergerie*, while simultaneously acknowledging the influence of the *Jeu de saint Nicolas*.

# LATE MEDIEVAL LITERATURE

By ROSALIND BROWN-GRANT, *University of Leeds*

## 1. NARRATIVE GENRES

EPIC. D. Collomp, 'Hugues Capet: mystification ou mystique de la royauté?', *BDBA*, 17:63–75, argues that the favourable portrayal of this low-born king in the eponymous late medieval epic, compared to his negative depiction by authors such as Dante, is determined by contemporary political and social concerns; whereas J. E. Merceron, '*Ainsy disoit Huon*: le couplage discours-formule référentielle en vers d'intonation dans *Hugues Capet*', *Olifant*, 20, 1995–96 [1999]:249–79, sees the author's repeated use of the 'vers d'intonation' linking the hero's words to a description of his increasingly mature character as a key structuring element in this propagandistic text which attempts to legitimate the Valois dynasty by assocation with the Capetian king. C. Roussel, 'Les dernières chansons de geste et leur public', *Suard Vol.*, 809–20, examines the thematic and stylistic coherence of late medieval epic. I. Weill, 'Le rituel de la menace dans les chansons de geste tardives', *ib.*, 1001–14, shows how the formulation of threats as speech acts becomes gradually more prosaic and unimaginative in later epics compared to the *Chanson de Roland*. J.-L. Picherit, 'Chronologie et temps dans la chanson d'aventures', *Olifant*, 19, 1994–95 [1999]:19–36, contrasts the careful and coherent treatment of time and duration in *Lion de Bourges* with the more traditional *Tristan de Nanteuil* in which the same blocks of time are merely repeated from episode to episode. L. Z. Morgan, '*Berta ai piedi grandi*: historical figure and literary symbol', *ib.*, 37–56, argues that the symbolic depiction of the queen's foot-deformity as a moral flaw in this section of the *Geste Francor* puts the blame squarely on Berta for the tragedy which she brings upon Pipin and her own offspring. E. Hoyer-Poulain, 'Tradition/trahison? Scène de bataille dans *Les Enfances Ogier* d'Adenet le Roi', *Suard Vol.*, 435–44, re-evaluates A. as a writer of epic in terms of his supreme mastery of heroic rhetoric, extensive use of commentary to bring out the moral lesson of his text, and self-reflexivity. M.-G. Grossel, 'Tradition et renouvellement dans la *Chanson de Gaufrey*: les personnages de Grifon et Robastre', *Fourquet Vol.*, 217–30, points out the originality of this continuation of *Doon de Mayence* in its subtle portrait of the treacherous Grifon, and comic depiction of the half-supernatural hero Robastre. V. Naudet, 'Archefer aux marches de l'enfer: héros, pratiques magiques et rencontres diaboliques dans deux mises en prose du XVeme siècle', *Sénéfiance*, 42:365–81, reveals the ambivalent attitude towards magic and the role of the sorcerer in prose versions of *Renaut de Montauban* and the *Histoires de Charles Martel*. *Jourdain de Blaye en alexandrins*, ed. Takeshi Matsumura, 2 vols, Geneva, Droz, 584, 585–1162 pp., a new critical edition of this mid-15th-c. epic which is a massively expanded version of the original decasyllabic text, is based on the unique complete MS of the work preserved in Paris, Bibliothèque de l'Arsenal, 3144, using a modern copy of the destroyed MS of the Bibliothèque de la ville de Tournai, 102, and various other fragments as a control. T. Matsumura is also the author of 'Les proverbes dans *Jourdain de Blaye en alexandrins*', *TLP*, 37 : 171–215, in which he contrasts the large number of proverbs in this text (299) with the decasyllabic version (7), and classifies these proverbs by incipit; and '*Jourdain de Blaye en alexandrins* dans Godefroy', *ib.*, 217–49, in which he judges the great lexico-grapher to have been generally faithful to the meaning and context of items cited from the original text, compared to the rather less accurate *FEW*, which he deems to have frequently attributed items to the wrong version. P.-Y. Badel, 'La *Bataille d'Annezin*: une parodie de chanson de geste?', *Suard Vol.*, 35–44, offers a new edition of this short assonanced text by Thomas de Bailleul, based on British Library, Royal 20 A XVII, fols 176ᵛ–177ᵛ, and suggests that many of its key motifs are parodic echoes of the epic. C. Casanave, '*Huon de Bordeaux* au théâtre (le XVIe siècle)', *ib.*, 171–81, analyses the circumstances surrounding the two performances of this work in dramatic form when the Confrérie de la Passion was forbidden from putting on religious drama, and instead had to turn to more profane and historical subject matter; whilst J.-C. Vallecalle, 'Remarques sur le cycle en vers de *Huon de Bordeaux*', *ib.*, 927–35, argues for the coherence of the cycle as a whole due to the persistent recurrence of the theme of acts of treachery leading to the exile of the hero. D. Collomp, 'L'écho des bourgeois de Calais dans *Theseus de Cologne* et *Ciperis de Vignevaux*', *ib.*, 183–96, examines how the first of these texts links the length and ferocity of the siege of Cologne and the emotional trauma suffered by its inhabitants with that of Calais, whilst the second relates it to the siege of Canterbury by representing the same number of burgesses taken hostage as at Calais. V. Galent-Fasseur, 'Quand "je" devient un autre. Un processus de conversion dans *L'Entrée d'Espagne*', *ib.*, 273–83, analyses the process undergone by Roland, Sansonnet and Sanson as that of a conversion whereby each sheds his original identity to become the opposite of his former self in order that he might be reintegrated into the ranks of Christian knighthood; whilst S. Sturm-Maddox, 'Roland épigone d'Alexandre dans l'*Entrée d'Espagne*', *ib.*, 871–8, detects the influence of the *Roman d'Alexandre* on this work in that Roland is largely shorn of his more ambiguous character traits, and presented like the eponymous hero of this romance as the living embodiment of all chivalric virtues. A. Negri, '"Or devons revenir dou livre a la matiere": Tracce di letteratura esemplare nel *Girart de Roussillon* del XIV secolo', *ib.*, 657–66, considers the 13 *exempla* of charitable conduct which are evoked by Girart and his wife Berthe to have been inserted by the author as a symbolic and didactic means of pricking the conscience of his dedicatee, John, Duke of Burgundy, into giving help and support to the writer's abbey of Pothières.

ROMANCE. Y. Foehr-Janssens, 'Dénouement contre conclusion: rhétorique et poétique dans la *Châtelaine de Vergy*', *PRIS-MA*, 15:69–83, deems the somewhat facile rhetorical conclusion of the epilogue to be at variance with a poetic dénouement that reveals the impossibility of *fin'amor* in late medieval courtly society. D. Quéruel, 'Lettres d'amour et art épistolaire dans le roman du *Castelain de Couci et de la Dame de Fayel*', *Suard Vol.*, 759–71, shows how the love letters in this romance both advance the narrative and reveal the same intensity of the protagonists' emotions as the sections of lyric poetry inserted elsewhere in the text. C. M. Jones, 'Rape, redemption, and the Grateful Dead: *Richars li biaus*', Taylor, *Gender Transgressions*, 3–19, argues that the motif of the indebted dead knight restores both symbolic purity to the hero's origins as well as material and moral balance to his community; whilst L. M. Rouillard, 'Rape and marriage in *Richars li biaus*', *MedP*, 13, 1998:121–35, examines how rape becomes a dilemma for the offspring rather than for the violated mother, and marriage between the rapist and his victim serves mainly to resolve the identity crisis of the son. J.-J. Vincensini, 'De l'alliance à l'hostilité. Dons contraints et troubles de l'idylle dans le *Roman d'Eredus et de Serene*', *Suard Vol.*, 975–91, attempts to rehabilitate this long-neglected 14th-c. verse romance by highlighting its skilful and complex interrogation of the conflicting demands of spiritual and blood kinship. C. Ferlampin-Acher, '*Artus de Bretagne*: une histoire sans fin', *PRIS-MA*, 15:53–68, contrasts the sophistication of the suspended ending of the original version of this work in BNF fr. 761, which depicts the clerkly figure of Estienne ending the tournament in which Artus is dubiously engaged, with the more loosely-structured conclusion of the longer version preserved in BNF fr. 12549. *Perceforest. Deuxième partie*, ed. Gilles Roussineau, 1, Geneva, Droz, lxxvii + 701 pp., is the latest volume in his edition of this monumental text, based on BNF fr. 346, being the section which covers Gadiffer's wounding by a wild boar and Perceforest's incapacitation following his shock at hearing of the death of Alexandre. M. Szkilnik, 'Les morts et l'histoire dans le *Roman de Perceforest*', *MA*, 105:9–30, argues that the text's attempts to consign the ghosts of knights who haunt its pages to a final resting place is integral to its staging of the struggle between good and evil; whilst in her 'Le clerc et le ménestrel: prose historique et discours versifié dans le *Perceforest*', *CRM*, 5, 1998:87–105, Szkilnik contends that the verse elements of this work underpin its historical veracity by introducing a divinely-sanctioned causality which is missing from the prose sections. A. Martineau, 'Récit, croyance et vérité: la conception du Bossu de Suave', *Razo*, 15, 1998:81–91, analyses the question of truth-telling in this episode of *Perceforest*, in which a hunchback recounts how he was born deformed because his mother glanced at a misshapen dwarf hidden in her bedchamber at the crucial moment of his conception; whereas A. Berthelot, 'D'Alexandre à Arthur: épopée et roman au XIVe siècle', *Fourquet Vol.*, 151–58, examines how later romances such as *Perceforest* revive the figure of Alexander as a hero but in the diluted form of a series of descendants, many of whom are marked by a certain supernatural alterity through this connection. C. Gaullier-Bougassas, 'Jean Wauquelin et Vasque de Lucène: le "roman familial" d'Alexandre et l'écriture de l'histoire au XVe siècle', *CRM*, 5, 1998:125–38, notes how, though following different historiographical agendas, these two authors refute the traditional account of Alexander's illegitimacy in order to present him as an exemplary hero. David LaGuardia, *The Iconography of Power: The French Nouvelle at the end of the Middle Ages*, Newark, Delaware U.P., 178 pp., argues against reading these texts as realist and instead sees the anonymous *Cent Nouvelles Nouvelles* as a set of homoerotic fantasies, Philippe de Vigneulles' collection as tales which undermine the homosocial hierarchy, and the *Heptaméron* as a depiction of the double bind of female characters who are constricted within and yet forced to defend male-imposed notions of feminine virtue; whilst D. A. Fein, 'The dangerous sex: representations of the female body in the *Cent Nouvelles Nouvelles*', *RoN*, 39:195–202, examines how these texts represent the female body as having the power to thwart and preclude male sexual desire. D. Quéruel, 'Mariage: promotion ou mésalliance? La vie conjugale dans la littérature narrative des XIVe et XVe siècles', *Actes* (Spa), 225–47, surveys the portrayal of married life from the satirical images of the *Quinze Joyes* to the more sympathetic representation of the *Ménagier de Paris*. M. Marsh Heywood, '*Monstre de Nature*: la vieille entre discours médical et tradition littéraire', *MoyFr*, 39–41, 1996–97:357–68, demonstrates Jean Le Fèvre's use of medical and literary tradition in his portrait of the hideous old woman who tricks the narrator into sleeping with her in *La Vieille ou les dernières amours d'Ovide*. J.-J. Vincensini, 'Désordre de l'abjection et ordre de la courtoisie: le corps abject dans *Paris et Vienne* de Pierre de la Cépède', *MAe*, 68:292–304, questions the traditional view of this romance as sentimental by showing how social order in the text is reaffirmed only through the physical abjection of the foul-smelling Vienne and the geographical alienation of the racially-disguised Paris. L. Borràs Castanyer, 'El hijo de Tristán, *Ysaïe le Triste*, o la locura como reescritura original', *RLMed*, 11 : 165–78, suggests that the protracted bout of madness which Ysaïe suffers is less a necessary part of his role as a long-suffering lover than an important rite of passage from which he will mature into a knight fit to undertake a holy war; whilst P. Victorin, 'La fin des illusions dans *Ysaïe le Triste* ou Quand la magie n'est plus qu'illusion', *Sénéfiance*, 42 : 569–78, notes here how sorcery is replaced by trickery and illusion becomes a feature of story-telling itself. M. Colombo Timelli, 'De l'*Erec* de Chrétien de Troyes à la prose du XVe siècle: le traitement des proverbes', *MoyFr*, 42, 1998 : 87–113, reveals how the Burgundian *prosateur* omits many of C.'s proverbs in his desire to rid the text of what he deemed to be superfluous elements or linguistic terms no longer comprehensible to his contemporary audience. C. J. Harvey, 'Jehan Wauquelin "translateur" de *La Manekine*', *ib.*, 39–41, 1996–97 : 345–56, argues that this 15th-c. *mise en prose* is at once less courtly and folkloric but more religious and historical in tone than the original, and that it plays down the verse text's criticisms of the aristocracy possibly due to the author's wish to flatter his first patron, Jean de Croy; whilst Y. Foehr-Janssens, 'La *Manekine* en prose de Jean Wauquelin, ou la littérature au risque du remaniement', *CRM*, 5, 1998 : 107–23, stresses that, in making the text into an historical account of one individual's experiences, it eliminates the multiple intertextual allusions contained in the original 13th-c. verse romance. E. Gaucher, '*La vie du terrible Robert le dyable*: un exemple de la mise en prose (1496)', *ib.*, 153–64, similarly sees this late prose reworking of an earlier verse work as being more concerned with the historical and psychological reality of the main character. R. Dubuis, 'Un "petit roman philosophique" au XVe siècle: *Jehan de Paris*', *Suard Vol.*, 209–19, argues against seeing this work as simply either an amusing tale or a *roman à clé* about the marriage of Charles VIII and Anne of Brittany and instead shows that, beneath its humorous surface, the text puts forward radical ideas on marriage, peace and war which would not be out of place in a treatise of the Enlightenment. F. Bouchet, 'Les éléments épiques dans *Floriant et Florete*', *ib.*, 87–100, compares the 13th-c. verse and 15th-c. prose versions of this little-studied text for their treatment of various epic motifs such as the description of fight scenes, the evocation of Christian values in combat, and their use of gory and bloody details in battle; whereas in ' "Au temps du roy Jehan . . .", entre histoire et roman: le personnage de Jean le Bon dans *Jehan de Saintré*', *BDBA*, 17 : 23–33, Bouchet reveals that, compared to how Froissart and Christine de Pizan emphasize this king's role in the Hundred Years

War, the author of *Saintré* omits all mention of the war, and offers instead a rather ambivalent portrait of a benign but ineffectual ruler, especially in matters of love. C. Galderisi, ' "La femme et le pantin": la statue de cire du *Jehan de Saintré*, entre pratique pieuse et réification magique', *Sénéfiance*, 42 : 159–72, claims that the wax model which the heroine makes as a double of the hero symbolizes the impossibility of the narrative adequately to represent reality. G. Polizzi, 'Le crépuscule des magiciens: topiques de l'enchantement dans le *Livre du Cuer et les Amadis* français', *ib.*, 453–67, examines the decline of the use of magic as a motif and structuring device in these two works. J. H. M. Taylor, 'Le *Chevalier des dames du Dolent Fortuné*: image and text, manuscript and print', *BJR*, 81 : 153–76, argues that, unlike in other versions of this late 15th-c. allegorical romance, the illuminator of BNF fr. 1692 devises his/her miniatures as a way of making the text's structure easier to follow, rather than adhering to any mimetic principle of illustration.

## 2. POETRY

Opening up the works of Eustache Deschamps to long-overdue critical scrutiny are two important collections of articles, the first of which is *Eustache Deschamps, French Courtier-Poet: His Work and His World*, ed. Deborah M. Sinnreich-Levi, NY, AMS Press, 1998, 281 pp., in which I. S. Laurie offers a biography of D. (1–72); W. Calin reads D.'s 'Ballade to Chaucer' as evidence for the personal contacts which underpinned European court culture of the time (73–83); G. T. Diller notes the originality and dexterity of D.'s *rondeaux* of love, and in particular his creation of a distinct female voice (85–95); I. S. Laurie detects the presence of verbal polyphony and discordance in the poem 'Sui je belle' (97–107); E. J. Richards sees Christine de Pizan's *Epistre a Eustace Morel* as a parting shot in the 'Querelle de la *Rose*' which is heavily indebted to Dante and Petrarch (109–22); D. M. Sinnreich-Levi identifies a surprisingly sympathetic attitude towards women in D.'s poems in female voices (123–30), S. Huot reads the *Miroir de mariage* as a text which reiterates in more straightforward form the moral lessons of the *Rose* (131–44); whilst M. Stoneburner re-interprets this same text by D. as an attempt to use misogyny to comment on the political and social ills of the time (145–62); C. A. Jewers re-assesses the place of D. in the medieval poetic tradition (163–79); M. Lacassagne examines the *Art de dictier* in the context of the history of poetics (181–93); F. Canadé Sautman reveals D. to be the first true 'poet-folklorist' of French literature (195–207); K. Becker examines how D.'s medical poetry offers advice to his readers on how to keep healthy (209–27); R. Magnan discusses

D.'s status as a 'cartographer of the course of life' (229–44); and finally, T. Scully reveals D. to be a knowledgeable if sober-minded and under-provisioned gourmet (245–52). The second of these volumes is *Autour d'Eustache Deschamps. Actes du Colloque du Centre d'Etudes Médiévales de l'Université de Picardie-Jules Verne. Amiens, 5–8 Novembre 1998*, ed. Danielle Buschinger (Collection Médiévales, 2), Université de Picardie-Jules Verne Amiens, Presses du 'Centre d'Etudes Médiévales', x + 276 pp. In this collection, which would have benefited from closer proofreading and a unified house-style for references, J. Batany analyses the various types of nomenclature used by D. in his attempt to conceptualize the different strata of society (1–14); S. Bliggenstorfer examines how D.'s fictive dialogues exploit the device of using different personae in order to mask his criticisms of society (15–26); J.-P. Boudet shows how D.'s ambivalence towards astrology as a science leads him to reject astral determinism in favour of free will as the main motor of human existence (27–35); A. Crépin argues that although D. and Chaucer share the ideal of the writer as 'chevalier-poète', they nonetheless differ significantly in terms of their style and intended audience (37–43); A. d'Esneval characterizes D.'s late poetry as betraying an acute sense of apprehension and anxiety at the deteriorating state of French society (45–55); J. Devaux notes how D. vacillates between exalting the ideals of chivalric prowess and condemning the actual horrors and suffering of war in his poems about Charles VI's military campaigns in Flanders (57–71); G. Duchet-Suchaux perceives a 'pre-national' identity in D.'s verse (73–77); L. Dulac shows how Christine de Pizan both expands on many of D.'s ideas in her complex personification of France as an abandoned and suffering woman and also diverges from him in adopting a more optimistic outlook on the fate of the country (79–92); L. Evdokimova discusses D.'s debt to Cicero, Quintilian, St Augustine, and Cassiodorus for his conception of rhetoric as an oratorical and moral art (93–102); M.-G. Grossel reveals that Philippe de Mézières's *Livre de la vertu du sacrement de mariage* and D.'s *Miroir de mariage* both downgrade temporal marriage in favour of spiritual union (103–14); M. Lacassagne observes that D. develops the stylistic and rhetorical topos of 'médiocrité' into a veritable ethics of moderation as his response to the uncertainties and instabilities of his times (115–26); J. Laidlaw examines how D. innovates on the formal lyrical tradition bequeathed by Machaut in his use of *envois* and refrains in both his *ballades* and *chansons royales* (127–40); T. Lassabatere argues that D.'s animal symbolism is indebted both to heraldic and emblematic devices and to the prophetic allegory of Henri de Ferrières (141–52); D. Lechat notes how D.'s *Traité de Geta et Amphitrion* greatly expands the theme of metamorphosis compared to his source, the *Geta* of Vital de Blois, in order to create a kind of anti-art of poetry (153–60); J. V. Molle argues that D.'s *Trubert* should be reclassified as a *dit* and not a farce, given the scarcity of dramatic literature at the end of the 14th c. (161–70); J.-C. Mühlethaler analyses how, in his satirical *ballades*, D. adopts different masks and varies his tone of condemnation from the ludic to invective (171–84); A. Planche outlines the differences between D. and Charles d'Orléans in terms of their personal circumstances, origins, temperament and tone (185–98); F. Poplin analyses the place of hares and rabbits in D.'s taxonomy of animals (199–212); J. Quillet reads D.'s *Fiction du Lion* as an effusive but ultimately pessimistic evocation of the golden age of the reign of Charles V (213–19); C. Scollen-Jimack adds a further 12 fables to the corpus of 13 identified by G. Parussa, and reveals D.'s stylistic and rhetorical originality compared to his sources (221–32); A. Sobczyk argues that D.'s hesitations as to where to place himself in relation to the rest of the world paradoxically guarantee his status as teller of the truth (233–43); A.-K. Stanislaw-Kemenah examines how D. fluctuates between a factual, eyewitness objectivity and a more florid, glorificatory tone in his poems on war (245–60); and finally, in an odd article with which to end a volume on D., J. B. Williamson discusses Philippe de Mézières's debt to Albertus Magnus's *Book of Minerals* and other Christian lapidaries in his use of gemstone symbolism in the *Songe du vieil pelerin* and *Epistre au roi Richart* (261–76). Other studies on D. include S. Bliggenstorfer, ' "Une chose longue et malaisiee a faire et a trouver"; remarques sur le Lay de Verité d'E. D.', *MoyFr*, 39–41, 1996–97: 39–51, which reveals D.'s varied use in this work of *rimes riches*, antithesis, metaphor and alliteration in order to reinforce his satirical message against the venality of the times; and 'Les poèmes de supplication d'E. D.', *Actes* (Spa), 49–75, in which Bliggenstorfer examines the material circumstances behind D.'s request poems; I. Black, 'Beyond dietetics: the use of language of food and drink in the allegorical battles of E. D.', *DFS*, 48:3–18, which analyses the alimentary allusions in his *Dit des IIII offices* and *Contre le carême*; and M. Lacassagne, 'E. D.: "demonstration" contre "sortilèges" ', *Sénéfiance*, 42:293–305, which examines D.'s ambivalent attitude towards astrology and sorcery in this prose text. M. Jeay, 'Les poèmes énumératifs du XIIIe au XVIe siècle comme répertoires terminologiques', *MoyFr*, 39–41, 1996–97:297–315, argues that Rabelais' taste for lists in his works is indebted to a long tradition of texts based on the accumulation of insults, curses, household objects, and cures, from the *dits énumératifs* through the poetry of Deschamps to certain *sermons joyeux*. J.-F. Kosta-Théfaine, 'Du chant d'amour au chant du désespoir ou l'écriture d'une poétique de la tristesse dans la lyrique d'Othon de Grandson', *RZLG*,

23:297–310, shows hów this lesser-studied poet's insistence on writing of his suffering in love leads to a veritable poetics of unhappiness and despair. G. L. Smith, 'Christine de Pizan's *Dit de la pastoure* — a feminization of the pastourelle', *RoN*, 39:285–94, argues that C. transforms this genre by investing her shepherdess with an autonomous and surprisingly clerkly voice. J. T. E. Thomas, 'Lecture de la chanson R805, de Richard de Fournival', *Suard Vol.*, 903–13, reproduces this poem from P. Zarifopol and Y. G. Lepage's editions, with slight editorial changes, and examines how the poet compares himself here to Echo and the disdainful beloved to Narcissus, but none the less ends on a note of hope rather than of despair. A. Planche, 'Récit et vérité dans deux *Dits* de Jean Froissart: *L'Espinette amoureuse* et *Le Joli Buisson de Jeunesse*', *Razo*, 15, 1998:59–69, is a somewhat descriptive account of what these two texts reveal about F.'s life and times; whilst S. Ménégaldo, 'L'exemple chevaleresque dans la poésie de Jean Froissart', *CRM*, 6:149–66, compares F.'s use of romance and mythological figures in his *dits narratifs*, where the former are cited largely for their rhetorical and didactic import as examples either to be rejected or emulated, whereas the latter are more developed and thus exploited for a multiplicity of interpretations. Guillaume de Machaut, *Le Livre du Voir Dit*, ed. Paul Imbs (Lettres Gothiques), Livre de Poche, 829 pp, is an accessible version of this text, complete with facing-page Modern French translation and a short introduction to the MS tradition. M. J. Ehrhart, 'Machaut's allegorical narratives and the *Roman de la Rose*', *RMS*, 25:33–58, explores the nature of M.'s debt to the *Rose* which ranges from static allegory in the *Vergier*, *Remede* and *Behaingne* to the more dynamic allegory of the *Lyon* and *Alerion*, and culminates in typological allegory in the *Fonteinne amoureuse*. F. Ferrand, 'Doux Penser, Plaisance et Espérance chez Guillaume de Machaut et Charles d'Orléans: un nouvel art d'aimer', *Suard Vol.*, 241–50, detects a new conception of love in these two poets, in which love, though linked to separation, absence and exile, leads not to the suffering characteristic of the *trouvère* lyric but to joy and happiness. M. Arn, 'A "lost" poem by Charles de Nevers recorded by Charles d'Orléans', *NQ*, 46:185–86, supplies a diplomatic transcription of the important *rondeau* 'En la forest de longue actente' from BNF fr. 25458, omitted by P. Champion in his 1927 edition of C.'s poetry, which Charles de Nevers wrote as payment for the hospitality he had received at the French court after 1440; whilst A. Rodriguez, ' "A ce jour de Saint Valentin", les objectivations lyriques de l'affectivité chez Charles d'Orléans', *MoyFr*, 42, 1998:7–18, rejects a biographical or circumstantial reading of the poet's Valentine *rondeaux* in favour of seeing the texts as objectivized allegories of the emotions of the lyric 'I' with which C.'s audience could more readily empathize. D. F. Hult, 'The allegoresis of everyday life', *YFS*, 95:212–33, argues that Alain Chartier's ambivalence in the *Belle dame sans merci* towards making a clear distinction between the real and the allegorical, the particular and the universal, the individual and the exemplary, signals an innovatory attempt to prevent the text from being read as yet another stereotyped disquisition on the roles men and women should play in the scenario of courtly love; whilst G. E. Sansone, '*La Belle Dame Sans Merci* et le langage courtois', *MoyFr*, 39–41, 1996–97:513–26, sees the text as a critique of courtly values, as evidenced by the contrast between the linguistic rules of courtliness and the Lady's unequivocal language of refusal as she makes her bid for sexual autonomy. A. Berthelot, 'De Gautier de Coinci aux Rhétoriqueurs: glossalie et poésie mariale', *ib.*, 25–67, notes that whilst G. revels in the phonetic and semantic repetitions possible in the French language in his praise of the Virgin, the Rhétoriqueur poets instead downgrade the vernacular by using it simply as a signifier masking the signified of a prayer in Latin. P. Verhuyck, 'Jean Molinet et les étapes de la vieillesse. *Du bas mestier les plus grans coups sont oultre*', *Actes* (Spa), 421–50, reads this work as a moving account of the poet's decline and proposes new dates for events in his life such as the onset of his impotence and loss of sight in one eye. S. Korfanty, 'Edition et glossaire de trois textes d'Andrieu de la Vigne contenus dans le *Jardin de Plaisance et Fleur de Rethorique*', *ib.*, 29–69, offers a more user-friendly version of three works originally reproduced in A. Piaget's 1909 facsimile of A. Vérard's 1501 edition of this anthology of works by various Grands Rhétoriqueurs (respect-ively ,'Ne m'escrips plus homme eloquent', 'Prevoiant la cachineuse lecture de ma present epistre', and 'O mort detestable et acreuse'). C. J. Brown, 'De "La Louange à la tresglorieuse Vierge" aux *Chansons georgines*: la transformation d'une oeuvre de Georges Chastellain', *MoyFr*, 39–41, 1996–97:65–80, analyses the changes undergone by C.'s text from MS to printed form, which involve a different title, a shift in describing the author as an *escripteur* rather than an *orateur*, and the loss of textual coherence through the omission of rubrics which were designed to guide the reader through the work. S. Crane, 'Maytime in late medieval courts', *NML* 2, 159–79, discusses the depiction of Maying in French and English courtly poems as a ritual which both reaffirms the social status of the nobility and propounds sexual restraint in its audience by sublimating sexual desire through the fetishization of women as flowers. *Villon at Oxford: The Drama of the Text. Proceedings of the Conference Held at St. Hilda's College Oxford March 1996*, ed. Michael Freeman and Jane H. M. Taylor (Faux Titre, 165), Amsterdam, Rodopi, 391 pp., is an important new collection of studies in which D. Mus calls for a reassessment of the place of V. in

French literary history in relation both to the Grands Rhétoriqueurs and to later poets such as Du Bellay (1–34); J. H. M. Taylor reads the 'Ballade des seigneurs du temps jadis' (T, 357–84) as symptomatic of V.'s refusal to limit himself to single, coherent meanings (35–50); A. Armstrong questions the traditional critical distinction between V. and the Grands Rhétoriqueurs by arguing that the author's formal sophistication in his *Poésies diverses* equals and even surpasses that of a Molinet or a Meschinot (51–84); R. Cooper examines the literary legacy of V.'s *Testament* up to the 17th c., which ranges from serious moral works to others in a more typically humourous Villonesque vein such as those recording the last wishes of goslings (85–128); J. Koopmans re-interprets the lines devoted to Catherine de Vaucelles (T, 657–64) as referring to a leprous infection which V. had caught from his former lover and which had caused much of his hair to fall out and his scalp to be covered in unsightly red patches ('groseilles') (129–49); T. Hunt sees the concluding stanzas of the *Testament* as a deliberately ironic reversal of the *Lais* in that V. presents himself here as a thoroughly depoeticized martyr to lust rather than as a victim of love in his earlier work (150–58); R. Pensom analyses the hidden structuring patterns of repetition of commonplaces that underpin and guarantee the integrity of the *Testament* as a whole (159–69); E. Birge Vitz argues that the different types of prayer and liturgical elements in the *Testament* should be read as serious indicators of V.'s concern with eschatology, despite the irony and sarcasm found elsewhere in the text (170–94); K. Varty identifies a clear affinity between artist and author as marginalized outsider figures in the two series of images by A. Paul Weber which accompanied editions of V.'s work produced in the 1930s and 40s (195–224); B. N. Sargent-Baur examines how V. depicts Fortune as the main antagonist and cause of misfortune in his turbulent life (225–37); J.-C. Mühlethaler argues that the doubts expressed by Adam de la Halle, Charles d'Orléans, and V. about their own poetic authority and the adequacy of language itself paradoxically ensure their fascination for the modern reader (238–81); N. Freeman Regalado reveals V.'s debt to the medieval genre of *altercatio* between a wise man and a fool in his staging of a dialogue between high and low forms of wisdom (282–311); G. Roellenbleck demonstrates how V. uses the devices of retrospection, anticipation, and anecdote to structure the self and the *Testament* as a whole (312–30); R. Peckham gives details of key web sites and pages devoted to editions and critical commentary of V.'s works (331–42); and finally, P. Verhuyck proposes that the source for V.'s representation of a pug-nosed seneschal who 'shoes geese' in *huitain* 170 of the *Testament* may be the *Sottie du Magnificat* contained in the *Recueil Trepperel* and staged in 1455 (343–79). Other studies on Villon include: J. Ribard, 'Le didactisme dans l'oeuvre de F. V.', *Suard Vol.*, 773–79, which identifies V. as an intellectual in his discussion of issues such as determinism and free will using scholastic devices such as dispute and debate; J. H. M. Taylor, 'Metonymy, montage and death in F. V.'s *Testament*', *NML 2*, 133–58, which argues that the readers of this disjointed text are meant to fill in the referential gaps in V.'s interior monologue with their knowledge of the socially-levelling images of death portrayed in the *Danse macabré* series at the Cimetière des Innocents in Paris; R. Van Deyck, 'Création verbale et valorisation sémique dans le *Testament* de F. V.', *MoyFr*, 39–41, 1996–97:637–48, which examines how V.'s entire text is semantic-ally patterned around the themes of opposition to servility and refusal to pray; G. Gros, 'La vieille femme dans le *Testament Villon*. Etude sur un caractère', *Actes* (Spa), 105–22, which sees V.'s portrait of the old woman as innovatory in breaking with the traditional topos of linking old age with wisdom by showing her regret at not selling her favours at a higher price when younger and still desirable; N. J. Lacy, 'In defense of V.'s *Lais*', *FR*, 72:1000–09, which reads this work as an autonomous creation that differs from the *Testament* in terms of the author/narrator's trickster persona, his ludic references to scholasti-cism as a masturbatory activity and distrust of both the courtly and scholastic registers of language. Jacqueline Cerquiglini-Toulet, *L'écri-ture testamentaire à la fin du Moyen Age: Identité, dispersion, trace* (Legenda Special Lecture Series 3), Oxford, EHRC, 25 pp., argues that the 'testament' genre is characteristic of the late medieval obsession with melancholic forms of expression and 'arts de mourir', yet displays great verbal inventiveness and satirical coloration in the hands of poets such as Deschamps, Villon and Molinet. Jehan Marot, *Les Deux Recueils*, ed. Gérard Defaux and Thierry Mantovani, Geneva, Droz, ccxxvi + 603 pp., contains two important collections of M.'s com-plete verse, the first of which is based on BNF Rés. p. Ye. 432, an edition of his works produced by his son Clément and published in Paris by the widow of Pierre Roffet around 1533–34, whilst the second is a modern invention by the editors which brings together other works contained in a wide variety of separate MSS and printed editions. A. Armstrong, 'Jean Marot's rebus-rondeau: sense and space', *MoyFr*, 42, 1998:19–27, reproduces a facsimile of this text and examines the interaction of its layout and thematic and formal elements.

## 3. DRAMA

*Farces françaises de la fin du moyen âge. Transcription en français moderne*, ed. André Tissier, Geneva, Droz, 321 pp., is the fourth volume in this series and offers Modern French versions of the original 15th- and 16th-c. works contained in vols X, XI, and XII of the *Recueil de farces* collection by the same editor. Texts transcribed here include *Le Pet, La Cornette, Les Trois Amoureux de la Croiz, L'Abbesse et Soeur Fessue, Les Deux Savetiers, La Pipée* and the *Farce des Oiseaux*. J. Koopmans, 'Pathelin patarin: archéologies d'un monstre sacré', *RLaR*, 103 : 101–18, takes up W. W. Field's suggestion that the term 'patarin', which originally designated certain 11th-c. Italian heretics, is the origin of P.'s name in that his jargon-ridden speech renders him suspect to his contemporaries; whilst in 'Les démunis mis en scène: satire ou utopie, répression ou contestation', *Actes* (Spa), 123–39, Koopmans asks whether the depiction of poverty as inevitably following on from prosperity is meant to be read as satirical or sympathetic in a range of farces from the *Recueil Cohen*. O. A. Dull, ' "Escumer le latin": statut et fonctions de la barbarolexie dans le théâtre comique du XVe siècle; enjeux théoriques', *MoyFr*, 39–41, 1996–97 : 205–24, examines the parodic and satirical use of different languages in texts such as *Pathelin* and the *Sottie des coppieurs et des lardeurs*. Graham Runnalls, *Les mystères français imprimés: une étude sur les rapports entre le théâtre religieux et l'imprimerie à la fin du Moyen Age français, suivie d'un Répertoire complet des mystères français imprimés (ouvrages, éditions, exemplaires) 1484–1630* (Bibliothèque du XVe siècle, 61), Champion, 198 pp., which is accompanied by a complete inventory of all printed editions of French mystery plays, argues that printing slowed down the decline of the genre as it allowed texts to be disseminated all over French-speaking countries and thus ensured their consumption in written form even after prohibitions against actually performing them came into force in the mid-16th century. R. L. A. Clark and C. Sponsler, 'Othered bodies: racial cross-dressing in the *Mistere de la Sainte Hostie* and the Croxton *Play of the Sacrament*', *JMEMS*, 29 : 61–87, compares how these two plays of Host desecration betray ambivalent attitudes towards the Jew whose 'otherness' both menaces and reinforces the integrity of the hegemonic Christian community. P. Dumont, 'Andrieu de la Vigne l'enchanteur: magie dramatique et illusion temporelle dans le *Mystère de Saint Martin* (1496)', *Sénéfiance*, 42 : 143–57, examines the dramatic techniques by which the author creates the illusion of telling the story of a whole life in three days. *Drama and Community: People and Plays in Medieval Europe*, ed. Alan Hindley (Medieval Texts and Cultures of Northern Europe, 1), Turnhout, Brepols, xi + 294 pp., is a collection of 16 essays by leading scholars in the field which covers an impressively wide geographical and chronological range of different dramatic forms, and reveals the close involvement of urban communities in play performance. A. Hindley is also the author of 'Preaching and plays:

the sermon and the late medieval French *Moralités*', *MoyFr*, 42, 1998:71–85, in which he argues for the influence of sermons and preaching techniques on plays in this genre, whether in the form of dramatization of a sermon text, the delivery of a sermon within a play, or other devices taken from the *artes praedicandi* such as *amplificatio*. J.-P. Bordier, 'La grâce et la justification dans la *Passion* de Jean Michel', *Suard Vol.*, 73–86, highlights how M.'s work is indebted to Ockhamist doctrine for its depiction of the various stages towards conversion and salvation of characters such as Mary Magdalene, the Centurion and Lazarus. J. Subrenat, 'La vie quotidienne des "petites gens" et sa représentation dans les *Passions* du XVe siècle', *Actes* (Spa), 317–39, discusses the realistic portrayal of daily life in these works which present biblical characters in a range of social circumstances. Jody Enders, *The Medieval Theater of Cruelty: Rhetoric, Memory, Violence*, Ithaca–London, Cornell U.P., xvii + 268 pp., is a thought-provoking exploration of the interplay between rhetoric and torture as a mode of truth-telling in drama of the 15th and 16th centuries. R. K. Emmerson, 'Visualizing performance: the miniatures of the Besançon MS 579 *Jour de Jugement*', *Exemplaria*, 11:245–84, argues that this deluxe MS is a record of a lost theatrical performance in that the imagery of the miniatures appears to be inspired by the staging of the play rather than by earlier iconographical models.

4. HISTORICAL AND POLITICAL LITERATURE

C. Lachet, 'Les traits épiques dans *La Vie de Saint Louis* de Joinville', *Suard Vol.*, 515–26, identifies the influence of the epic on J.'s depiction of his subject as a warrior-king through such devices as oral address to the audience in the prologue, and links between parallel *laisses*; whilst M. Plouzeau, 'Joinville au programme!', *ib.*, 733–42, highlights the difficulties faced by students studying this text on the current *agrégation* programme owing to the editorial errors and inconsistencies contained in the version produced by Jacques Monfrin in 1995 and its supposedly identical reprint of 1997; and C. Croizy-Naquet, 'Le roi Richard dans *La Vie de saint Louis* de Joinville', *BDBA*, 17:77–89, argues that it portrays the crusader-king Richard as a paragon of chivalric prowess whose failure in his campaigns only serves to highlight more clearly the true saintliness and kingliness of Louis IX. Alain Bouchart, *Grandes Chroniques de Bretaigne*, ed. Marie-Louise Augier and Bernard Guenée, vol. 3, CNRS, 1998, 392 pp., is the third and final volume of their edition of this work, which introduces the text with an essay on the life and work of B. and a concordance of his sources. G. Labory, 'Les manuscrits de la *Grande Chronique de Normandie* du XIVe et du XVe siècle', *RHTe*, 28, 1998:183–233, supplements her introductory article on this text published in vol. 27 (1997) of the same journal, by providing a detailed inventory of the extant MSS of the work, preceded by a brief list of the 19th-c. bibliographical sources which she used to compile it. C. Raynaud, 'La reine dans les *Grandes Chroniques de France*', Kooper, *Chronicle*, 226–39, argues that its cycle of illuminations emphasizes the reproductive and dynastic function of the queen at the expense of her involvement in the exercising of political and juridical power. *Froissart across the genres*, ed. Donald Maddox and Sara Sturm-Maddox, Gainesville, Florida U.P., 1998, 257 pp., provides an important overview of F.'s works in which P. F. Ainsworth examines patterns of transmission in the *Chroniques* (15–39); C. T. Wood analyses F.'s personal view of the Peasants' Revolt of 1381 (40–9); G. T. Diller argues for the centrality of F.'s 1389 Journey to Béarn to his historiographical and narrative enterprise as a whole in Book 3 of his chronicle (50–60); W. W. Kibler shows how F. offers a critique of courtly culture in *Le joli buisson de Jonece* as the narrator undergoes a midlife crisis (63–80); K. Busby discusses images of enclosure and imprisonment in F.'s narrative poetry (81–100); D. Kelly reveals F.'s use of the exemplary mode in these same texts (101–18); R. T. Pickens re-evaluates the *Dit dou bleu chevalier* as a self-reflexive and multi-faceted work in F.'s poetic output (119–52); M. Zink reinterprets the *Meliador* as a harbinger of a new poetic sensibility (155–75); E. Kennedy contrasts F.'s portrayal of chivalry with that in the *Prose Lancelot* and the work of Geoffroy de Charny (179–94); J. M. Fyler compares F. and Chaucer as commentators on their age (195–218); and L. Harf-Lancner explains how the miniatures function as vehicles for political ideology in MSS of Book 1 of the *Chroniques*. Other studies on F. include P. Ainsworth, 'Heralds, heraldry and the colour blue in the *Chronicles* of Jean Froissart', Kooper, *Chronicle*, 40–55, which analyses F.'s debt to various heralds for key eye-witness accounts, his evocation of heraldic notation for the purposes of commenting on military events, and his ironic use of the colour blue in coats of arms (usually signifying loyalty) to criticize certain acts of treachery and brutality; whereas in 'A Parisian in New York: Pierpont Morgan Library MS M.804 revisited', *BJR*, 81 : 127–51, Ainsworth employs an integrated approach combining art history, codicology, philology, and textual analysis to study this MS of Books I and II of Froissart's *Chroniques*; and N. Chareyron, 'Le sang des martyrs de Nicopolis (1396)', *CRISIMA 4*, 321–30, which traces the different representations of this massacre in various contemporary chronicles, ranging from F. and the Boucicaut biographer's depiction of the victims as holy martyrs, to Philippe de Mézières's call for a new crusade and to the Religieux de Saint Denis's interpretation of the event as an act of divine vengeance on the corrupt and debauched knighthood of France. D. B. Tyson, 'Authors, patrons and soldiers — some thoughts on four Old French soldiers' *Lives*', *NMS*, 42, 1998:105–20, is a somewhat descriptive account of aspects of authorship, audience, and narrative style in *La prise d'Alexandrie, La Vie de Bertrand du Guesclin, La Vie du Prince Noir*, and *Le livre des fais du bon Messire Jehan le Maingre dit Boucicaut.* Christine de Pizan, *The Book of the Deeds of Arms and of Chivalry*, trans. Sumner Willard, ed. Charity Cannon Willard, Pennsylvania State U.P., 223 pp., is a highly accessible Modern English version of C.'s *Livre des Faits d'Armes et de Chevalerie* (1410), with a short but trenchant introduction in which the editor argues that the text is more original in its use of previous sources, such as Vegetius, than scholars have generally maintained. B. A. Carroll, 'C. de P. and the origins of peace theory', pp. 22–39 of *Women Writers and the Early Modern British Political Tradition*, ed. Hilda L. Smith, CUP, similarly shows the originality of C.'s political thought in offering a systematic analysis of the legitimate and illegitimate causes of war, stressing the need to educate both the prince and the people on the need for peace, and sidelining the authority of the church by refusing to legitimate late-medieval calls for crusade; whereas R. Blumenfeld-Kosinski, '"Enemies within/ enemies without": threats to the Body Politic in C. de P.', *MH*, 26:1–16, analyses how, from the *Avision-Christine* onwards, C. begins to attack France's internal enemies through a series of striking bodily metaphors representing the country's self-mutilation through the disintegration of the social order; and O. Matteoni, 'L'image du duc Louis II de Bourbon dans la littérature du temps de Charles VI', *Guenée Vol.*, 145–56, compares C.'s portrayal of this duke in mainly chivalric and courtly terms in her biography of Charles V with that given by Froissart and Michel Pintoin. A. Tarnowski, 'Unity and the *Epistre au roi Richart*', *MH*, 26:63–77, shows how Philippe de Mézières uses a variety of metaphors such as that of healing in order to argue that national differences between France and England should be subsumed through peace and inter-marriage. C. J. Brown, 'Allegorical design and image-making in fifteenth-century France: Alain Chartier's Joan of Arc', *FS*, 53:385–404, suggests that the interplay of text and image in C.'s *Quadrilogue invectif* and *Livre de l'Esperance* helps construct an image of Joan in his Latin text as both an allegorized figure of France and the three estates and the miraculous embodiment of Faith and Hope. F. Duval, 'Jean Tinctor, auteur et traducteur des *Invectives contre la secte de Vauderie*, *Romania*, 117:186–217, compares the polemical tone which the author uses in the French version of this demonological text of *c.*1460 when exhorting his Burgundian patron to persecute witches with the more reasoned theological arguments which he employs in his Latin version when addressing a clerical audience. C. Allmand, 'Entre honneur et bien commun: le témoignage du *Jouvencel* au XVe siècle', *RHis*, 301:463–81, argues that, far from being simply the story of the career of Jean de Bueil, this text highlights the growing disparity between chivalric ideology and military practice as part of its critique of changes in social, political and military conduct in the course of the Hundred Years War; whereas M.-Th. de Médeiros, 'Défense et illustration de la guerre: *Le Jouvencel* de Jean de Bueil', *CRM*, 5, 1998:139–52, maintains that this celebration of the deeds of war betrays none of the uncertainties about society characteristic of other works written at that time. J. Dufournet, 'Les *Mémoires* de Commynes, ou comment remédier à la faiblesse des princes?', *BDBA*, 17:103–18, shows how C.'s realistic and uncompromising treatment of princes whose worst excesses can only be remedied through good counsellors and proper consultation with the estates general, fits in with his pessimistic vision of the instability of humankind; whilst J. Blanchard, 'Commynes et la "nouvelle politique"', *Guenée Vol.*, 547–61, argues that C.'s experiences as a diplomat and a defector mark his political thought which, in its emphasis on pragmatism, anticipates that of Machiavelli. J.-C. Herbin, 'Un manuscrit inconnu du *Recoeil des Histoires de Troyes* de Raoul Lefèvre', *Fourquet Vol.*, 255–61, suggests that Metz, Bibliothèque-Médiathèque 403, which contains a copy of this work written for Philippe le Bon in 1464–5, could be used to clarify certain faulty passages in M. Aeschbach's recent edition of the text, and should be designated as W[2] in his stemma. P. Lewis, ' "Des humanistes en mal d'écrire". Réflexions sur la motivation et sur la réception de la polémique, en France, à la fin du Moyen Age', *Guenée Vol.*, 637–46, argues that Pierre Choinet's *Rosier des guerres*, written for the dauphin at the behest of Louis XI, is typical of its time in terms of its heavy reliance on sources and intentionally limited audience. G. Labory, 'Une généalogie des rois de France se terminant à Henri VI roi "de France" et d'Angleterre', *ib.*, 521–36, offers a transcription and brief discussion of this anonymous and somewhat idiosyncratic text contained in BNF fr. 10468, fols 105–110[v] and copied around 1436 for Robert Jolivet, abbot of Mont-Saint-Michel.

## 5. Religious, Moral, and Didactic Literature

Rosalind Brown-Grant, *Christine de Pizan and the Moral Defence of Women: Reading beyond Gender* (Cambridge Studies in Medieval Literature, 40), CUP, xiv + 224 pp., contends that C. tailored her critique of misogyny according to the genre in which she was writing and the audience she was addressing in each of her specific texts in defence of

women. R. Brown-Grant is also responsible for a new translation of
C.'s *Book of the City of Ladies* (Penguin Classics), Harmondsworth,
Penguin, xl + 284 pp., which differs from E. J. Richards' recently
revised version in being less literal in style, and featuring an
introductory essay situating the work in its historical and intellectual
context, as well as an extensive glossary to the characters, places and
books mentioned in the text. Christine de Pizan, *L'Epistre Othea*, ed.
Gabriella Parussa, Geneva, Droz, 539 pp., is a critical edition of this
work which has previously only been available in a facsimile of an
American PhD dissertation or in a Middle English translation. Based
on London, BL, Harley 4431, using BNF fr. 606 and fr. 848 as well as
Chantilly, Condé ms 492 as controls, the text is preceded by an
extensive introduction which discusses the works' sources, the MSS
in which it is contained, and the iconographical programme accompanying the work. G. Parussa is also the author of 'Autographes et
orthographe. Quelques considérations sur l'orthographe de C. de P.',
*Romania*, 117 : 143–59, a diachronic study of three MSS of the *Epistre
Othea* which reveals a distinct trend on C.'s part towards standardizing
her spelling but also questions whether Chantilly, Condé ms 492 is in
fact an autograph, given its orthographical divergence from Harley
4431. Other studies on C. include: D. Hubbard Nelson, 'Silent
women', *RoN*, 40 : 13–24, which contrasts how Marie de France in
her *Lais* shows women escaping into fantasy in order to compensate
for their disempowered state with the works of Christine de Pizan and
the 16th-c. mother and daughter Madeleine and Catherine des
Roches who sought to create autonomy for themselves through their
writings and thereby defy society's attempt to reduce women to
silence; H. Arden, 'Women's history and the rhetoric of persuasion in
C. de P.'s *Cité des Dames*', *MoyFr*, 39–41, 1996–97 : 7–17, which shows
how C. uses rhetorical questions, proverbs, hyperbole, repetition and
semantic doubling in order to reinforce her anti-misogynist argument
in this text; M. B. Mirabella, 'Feminist self-fashioning: C. de P. and
*The Treasure of the City of Ladies*', *EJWS*, 6 : 9–20, which argues that
C. constructs herself as a figure of authority against the misogynist
'Other' and empowers her female readers to do the same by
encouraging them to renegotiate for their own ends the precepts of
chastity, virtue and restraint traditionally preached by misogynist
authors in the interests of social control; M. Jeay, 'Traversée par le
verbe: l'écriture de soi comme geste prophétique chez C. de P.', *DFS*,
47 : 7–27, which reveals the links between C.'s self-presentation across
her works and the mystical and prophetic writings of other medieval
women such as Constance de Rabastens and Marie Robine; E. J.
Richards, '*Glossa Aurelianensis est quae destruit textum*: medieval rhetoric,
Thomism and humanism in C. de P.'s critique of the *Roman de la*

*Rose*', *CRM*, 5, 1998:247–63, which sees C.'s universalism and emphasis on the necessary moral and didactic role of literature as a response to what she perceived to be Jean de Meun's proto-nationalism and rhetorical sophistry; H. Solterer, 'Fiction versus defamation: the Quarrel over *The Romance of the Rose*', *MHJ*, 2:111–41, which examines the Roman rhetorical roots of the debate which involved accusations and counter-accusations of blame and blasphemy, and culminated in C.'s being accused of an act tanta-mount to *lèse-majesté* in her attack on the *Rose*; and 'States of siege: violence, place, gender: Paris around 1400', *NML* 2, 95–132, in which Solterer analyses the gender implications of the architectural tropes used by C. to express her position in the debate, which range from that of a besieged city to a monastic enclave, and from a humanist cell to a castle stronghold; L. Dulac, 'Bon et mauvais langage chez C. de P.', *CRM*, 6:169–85, which traces the evolution of this theme from C.'s lyric poetry, in which she delivers a cautionary lesson against the damage done by tale-bearing and boastful lovers to women's good name, to her political and didactic texts, in which C. explains how defamatory talk constitutes a form of sedition when directed against the prince; N. Margolis, ' "Où celestiel chimphonye chante . . .": voyage encyclopédique d'un terme musical devenu moral de Macrobe à C. de P.', *ib.*, 187–203, which demonstrates how C.'s use of Greek musical terminology to conceptualize the divine harmony of the spheres is indebted to a wide range of authorities from Macrobius and Boethius to Dante and Guillaume de Deguile-ville; E. Schulze-Busacker, 'C. de P., *Les Enseignemens Moraux*', *Suard Vol.*, 831–44, which notes C.'s debt to her three main sources — the *Disticha Catonis* and two versions of the *Facetus* — but also reveals the personal tone with which the author offers moral advice to her son; and J. J. Thompson, 'Medea in C. de P.'s *Mutacion de Fortune*, or How to be a better mother', *FMLS*, 35:158–74, which reads C.'s transformation into a man as both a counter-example to that of Medea who, as a mother, also took control of her family on the death of her husband, and as an allegorical model of how to perfect oneself spiritually in order to resemble Christ; whereas C. Gaullier-Bou-gassas, 'La vie d'Alexandre le Grand dans *Renart le Contrefait* et le *Livre de la Mutacion de Fortune*', *BDBA*, 17:119–30, argues that, whilst in the former text the story of Alexander is subverted as he is made to resemble the foxy narrator himself, in the latter work C. eliminates any details which detract from her depiction of A. as Fortune's most illustrious yet hapless and unlucky victim. Finally, Joël Blanchard and Michel Quéreuil, *Lexique de Christine de Pizan* (Matériaux pour le *Dictionnaire du Moyen Français* (*DMF*)–5), Klincksieck, v + 401 pp., is an invaluable if not exhaustive lexicon of C.'s vocabulary, compiled with particular reference to the *Mutacion de Fortune*, which will form part of the collated entries for the forthcoming *DMF* to be published by the CNRS. M. T. McMunn, 'Reconstructing a missing manuscript of the *Roman de la Rose*: the Jersey manuscript', *Scriptorium*, 53:31–62, pls 3–15, argues that this MS stolen in 1955 from the Public Library in St Helier, Jersey, belongs to E. Langlois' N family of MSS, and compares the miniatures reproduced from negatives made in 1929 with those in other *Rose* MSS; whilst K. Brownlee, 'Pygmalion, mimesis, and the multiple endings of the *Roman de la Rose*', *YFS*, 95:193–211, contends that the three different endings of the text do not simply effect narrative closure of Guillaume de Lorris's suspended erotic quest by representing the fulfilment of desire but also reveal Jean de Meun's authorial meditation on the problems of mimetic art itself; and S. Gaunt, 'Bel Acueil and the improper allegory of the *Romance of the Rose*', *NML 2*, 65–93, argues that the ambivalent textual and visual representation of the relationship between Bel Acueil and Amant undermines the text's supposed heteronormativity and suggests that Jean de Meun should be seen as a 'queer author' in the sense of playfully subverting the idea of 'straight' or unequivocal writing through his ambiguous use of allegory. G. Raimondi, '*Les Eschés amoureux*: studio preparatorio ed edizione (I: vv.1–3662)', *Pluteus*, 8–9, 1990–98:67–241, is a new critical edition of the first part of this 30,000–line octosyllabic poem which reworks the *Rose* and dates from 1370–80, the base MS being Venice, Biblioteca Nazionale Marciana, fr, app. XXIII, and the control Dresden, Sächsische Landesbibliothek, oc. 66. F. Féry-Hue, 'Un *Evangile aux femmes* inédit, conservé en rouleau', *ib.*, 5–18, offers a transcription of this anonymous 14th-c. satirical text preserved in scroll-form and held in a private collection, complete with an analysis of the MS and of the versification and language of the work. D. Lagorgette, 'Tabourets de diable ou crédules innocentes? *Les Evangiles des Quenouilles* dans la France de l'Inquisition', *Sénéfiance*, 42:307–21, reads this work as an attempt to rehabilitate as harmless superstitions beliefs which had been viewed by regular clergy of the time as tantamount to witchcraft. K. Pratt, 'Translating misogamy: the authority of the intertext in the *Lamentationes Matheoluli* and its Middle French translation by Jean Le Fèvre', *FMLS*, 35:421–35, argues that Le F.'s version of Matheolus's Latin text follows a more unequivocally anti-marriage agenda than the original, in that he largely replaces M.'s political and anticlerical concerns with arguments, examples, and analogies derived from the *Rose*. C. J. Brown, 'Textual and iconographical ambivalence in the late medieval representation of women', *BJR*, 81:205–39, analyses the interplay between writer and patron, text and image in male-authored depictions of female sovereignty in Antoine Dufour's *Vie des femmes célèbres* written for Anne of Brittany, and Michele Ricci's *Changement de Fortune en toute prospérité* commissioned by Margaret of Austria. A. Bengtsson, 'La réduplication synonymique dans le ms. Queen's College 305 (Oxford)', *MoyFr*, 39–41, 1996–97 : 19–24, compares his recent edition of the *Vie de sainte Bathilde* with P. Dembowski's edition of the *Vie de sainte Marie l'Egyptienne*, which both used this MS as their control, and suggests that the high number of verbal synonyms used in it shows the scribe to be an inventive and meticulous philologist of the period. Margaret Porette, *The Mirror of Simple Souls*, trans. Edmund Colledge, J. C. Marler, and Judith Grant (Notre Dame Texts in Medieval Culture, 6), Notre Dame, Indiana U.P., lxxxvii + 209 pp., is a translation based on Chantilly, Condé F xiv26, and other versions of the text, accompanied by an extensive introductory interpretative essay setting out the intellectual and doctrinal context of M.'s ground-breaking work. M. Boulton, 'Le langage de la dévotion affective en moyen français', *MoyFr*, 39–41, 1996–97 : 53–63, reveals how highly emotive devotional texts such as the *Contemplacioun de la Passion, Passion Isabeau*, and the translation of Ludolphe de Saxe's *Vie du Christ*, encourage their audience to identify directly with Christ on reading about his sufferings on the cross. A. Saunier, 'Présence et sens du sang dans *Le Livre de Vie Active de l'Hôtel-Dieu de Paris*', *CRISIMA 4*, 77–85, analyses the mentions of blood in this didactic work designed to encourage young women to serve as nuns in the Hôtel-Dieu hospital at a time of a crisis in recruitment. J.-P. Perrot, 'Du sang au lait: l'imaginaire du sang et ses logiques dans les Passions de martyrs', *ib.*, 459–70, examines how the symbolic representation of the martyrs' blood as an impure liquid evoking death is frequently replaced with milk as a more positive symbol of nourishment and everlasting life in a range of 13th- and 14th-c. prose saints' lives. M. Rus, 'Un récit fantastique de la fin du Moyen Age: *L'Excursion aux îles Lipari* d'Antoine de la Sale', *Poétique*, 118 : 157–67, argues that, in this passage in *La Salade* in which the narrator has a seemingly inexplicable encounter with a demon which is later rationalized, the text appears to anticipate the Enlightenment's emphasis on how human reason can explain all supernatural phenomena. M. J. Freeman, 'A fringueur fringueur et demi: création verbale et phénomènes de société dans le Paris de Guillaume Coquillart', *MoyFr*, 39–41, 1996–97 : 249–68, analyses how C. produces rich lexical variations on the term *fringuer* in his *Plaidoié d'entre la Simple et la Rusée* and *Les Droitz nouveaulz* in order to paint a satirical portrait of the exhibitionistic and fashion-obsessed bourgeoisie of late-15th-c. Paris. P. Ménard, 'Un reflet de la vie quotidienne: le Dit des *Crieries de Paris*', *Suard Vol.*, 607–16, dates this compilation of 130 cries from vendors in the streets of Paris contained uniquely in BNF fr. 837, fols 246–7, as c. 1265, and discusses the insight which it gives into common types of food and drink consumed by people in the Middle Ages. C. Thiry, 'Les catégories sociales revues (et corrigées) dans quelques sources littéraires françaises des XIVe et XVe siècles', *Actes* (Spa), 341–68, outlines the difficulties in extracting any reliable information on the cost of living in works by authors ranging from Gilles li Muisis to Villon; whilst S. Thonon, 'Une société dans tous ses états: le tableau du *Livre de la Deablerie* (1508) d'Éloy d'Amerval', *ib.*, 369–94, reveals how this text divides humans into spendthrifts and misers and discusses the destabilizing effects on society of these two types of sinner. M. Lecco, 'Le metamorfosi di Fauvel', *Reinardus*, 12:67–79, argues that the miniatures accompanying Chaillou de Pestain's version of the *Roman de Fauvel* which depict F. as a man with a horse's head should be read as a grotesque and carnivalesque parody of the mass which was probably inspired by similar scenes in certain branches of the *Roman de Renart*. Two important critical editions of works by Martin Le Franc which have been largely inaccessible to scholars hitherto are: *Le Champion des Dames*, ed. Robert Deschaux, 5 vols, Champion, 173, 271, 153, 238, 242 pp., a key text in the late medieval 'querelle des femmes' which stages arguments for and against women, and is based on a transcription of the version contained in Brussels, Bibliothèque Royale, 9466; and *L'Estrif de Fortune et Vertu*, ed. Peter F. Dembowski, Geneva, Droz, lx + 400 pp., a *prosimetrum* which takes the form of an allegorical debate between these two personified figures on the issue of determinism and human responsibility, and has been established using Brussels, Bibliothèque Royale ms. 9573, and Arras, Bibliothèque municipale ms. 748, and Chantilly, Condé, ms. 296 for variants. Jacques de Cessole, *Le Jeu des eschaz moralisé, traduction de Jean Ferron (1347)*, ed. Alain Collet, Champion, 277 pp., is a new critical edition of this important mid-14th-c. translation of C.'s *Liber super ludum scacchorum*, a collection of moralized *exempla* for preachers which use pieces on a chessboard to symbolize prescribed forms of behaviour for the different estates in society, and is based on Dijon, Bibliothèque municipale ms. 525, and using BNF fr. 19115 and Dijon, Bibliothèque municipale ms. 268 as controls. M. J. Walkley, 'Jean Gerson's use of the Bible in his *Exemplaires des petis enfans*', *NZJFS*, 20:5–18, notes how G. generally simplifies, compresses and conflates the Biblical elements on which he draws for his examples in order to make the story more understandable for his young audience. F. Guichard-Tesson and M. Felberg-Levitt, '*Heloys du Paraclit*: le défi d'éditer une traduction du XVe siècle', *MoyFr*, 39–41, 1996–97:269–95, a preliminary study for their forthcoming edition of this translation of the first book of Andreas Capellanus' *De Amore*, examines problems such as identifying which version of the Latin text the translator was using and understanding what his principles of translation might have been.

## 6. MISCELLANEOUS

B. Ribémont, 'Jean Corbechon, un traducteur encyclopédiste au XIVe siècle', *CRM*, 6:75–97, argues that C.'s omissions, corrections and explications to his translation of Bartholemeus Anglicanus' *De proprietatibus rerum* are in keeping with the intellectual climate of Charles V's court which valued an encyclopedia more as a political building-block in the formation of a cultured prince than simply as a repository of scientific knowledge.

## THE SIXTEENTH CENTURY

By CATHERINE REUBEN, *Kingston University*

### 1. GENERAL

Table 1 shows the number of mentions in titles of articles and reviews of various 16th-c. literary figures (source: ISI, 1 January 1999–1 April 1999) and books, counted manually, compared with 1998 totals (*YWMLS*, 60:87).

Table 1:  16th-c. French authors in titles of 1999 publications (1998 figures in parentheses)

|  | Articles/Reviews | Books |
|---|---|---|
| Montaigne | 87 (100) | 6 (10) |
| Rabelais | 48 (45) | 2 (5) |
| Ronsard | 15 (17) | 1 (3) |
| Marot | 14 (14) | 2 (2) |
| Labé | 12 (10) | |
| Marguerite de Navarre | 10 (11) | 1 (0) |
| d'Aubigné | 9 (7) | 4 (1) |
| Budé | 8 (5) | |
| Baïf | 5 (4) | 1 (0) |
| Palissy | 4 (9) | |
| Du Bellay | 4 (15) | |
| La Boétie | 4 (2) | 1 (0) |
| Scève | 3 (5) | |
| Du Bartas | 2 (1) | 2 (1) |

About 10% fewer articles appeared in 1999 but, otherwise, the balance of research has remained astonishingly constant.

#### HUMANISM AND IDEAS

In an eminently readable book, George Huppert, *The Style of Paris: Renaissance Origins of the French Enlightenment*, Bloomington, Indiana U.P., 146 pp., describes a 'group of young men who called themselves *philosophes* and whose outlook I choose to call that of the style of Paris [. . .] after the new and fashionable college curriculum which was at the centre of their philosophical stance'. He describes several of the forerunners of Enlightenment thought, notably Pierre Belon, Jean Brinon, Estienne Pasquier, François Garasse, and La Boétie. Pierre Belon (1517–64) was an apothecary and naturalist with sharp views on freedom of thought, social equality, and religious toleration. In his professional work, he spent time in Turkey where his colleagues were mainly Jews, and he returned to France to maintain that the Jews did not bleed on Christian holy days, nor did they have any need for Christian blood in their religious practices. He was roundly denounced for this heresy by the Protestant theologian Luther and the Catholic theologian Eck. In spite of his tolerance, he complained bitterly that the Turks ate salads without vinaigrette.

J. Mosley, 'Originality and the Ancients in late 16th century French biography: some "reclothings" of Charles IX', *FS*, 53 : 142–52, claims that history and biography were not properly distinguished in the 16th century. Biography as we know it today seems not to have existed. Authors looked to classical models such as Plutarch and Suetonius. Whilst pointing out a lack of individualism, or what today one might term psychological interest, M. examines the three lives of Charles IX, written in the period directly following the appearance of Plutarch's *Vies*, by Belleforest, Masson, and Sorbin. Belleforest is writing for Charles IX, who is both protagonist and reader, and 'the reigning King appears to receive ubiquitous praise while remaining inscrutable'. Masson's *Vita* appeared after Charles' death, and opinion is divided as to whether it is objective or venomous. The King is compared to Suetonius's portrait of Nero, which has obvious echoes for the Huguenots after the St Bartholomew's massacre. On the other hand, Sorbin's *Vie* endorses the Regency of Catherine de Medici and attacks the Hugenots as traitors to a King whom the biography makes into a Catholic symbol. M. concludes that Belleforest is a Christianized Plutarch, Masson restores Suetonian biography to its pristine state, and Sorbin weaves a patchwork of ancient pieces held together by a central thread.

The second volume of a four-volume series on memory disorders in literature has appeared. *Usages de l'oubli*, 2, ed. F. Lestringant (*RSH*, 256), 11–157, covers the 16th to 18th centuries. G. H. Tucker writes of Du Bellay turning his back on Olympus and plunging into the river Lethe in order to forget. Therein lies true eternity; the spirit can only survive at the expense of this loss. The example is given of Rome, who remains, wretched among the living, surrounded by the ruins of her empire. Other articles are by I. A. R. de Smet, A. Tarrête, F. Lestringant, F. Pawyza, M. Rappoport, M. Bombart, and M. Delon.

The 16th c. was a time of European exploration of the New World. The explorers of the time, although their writings could only marginally be described as literature, had a seminal influence on the writers of the time such as Montaigne (see p. 101) and on the intellectual climate. *La France-Amérique, XVIe–XVIIIe siècles. Actes du

*XXXVe colloque international d'études humanistes*, ed. Frank Lestringant, Champion, 616 pp., covers three centuries, and L. has also himself published work on one of the leading explorers, *Jean de Lery ou l'invention du sauvage: essai sur l'histoire d'un voyage faict en la terre du Brésil*, Champion, 221 pp.

POETRY

The *Vénus d'Amboise*, which was given to François Ier in 1530, was the subject of epigrams by various poets, such as Germain de Brie and Clément Marot, even including the King himself. P. Galand-Hallyn, 'Autour de la Vénus d'Amboise (1530): une refloraison du genre de l'*Ekphrasis*', *BHR*, 51 : 345–74, points out that, in the early years of the 16th c., France did not accord the same status as the Italians to the visual arts, so poetry describing a statue is all the more valuable. There is a discussion about the provenance of the statue, whether or not it was clothed and whether it is in the Louvre; also the poetry — how the myth of Venus fits in with the idea that the poets would like François I to embody the qualities they are prescribing.

Floyd Gray, *Anthologie de la poésie française du seizième siècle*, Virginia, Rookwood, 558 pp., says he has tried to be comprehensive and include as wide a range of poetry as possible in one volume. The wish to use integral texts has meant deciding which 'livre' of Héroët's *Parfaicte Amye*, which 'jour' of Du Bartas' *Semaine* and which 'livre' of d'Aubigné's *Tragiques* to include. Gray's criteria are poems which are particularly good, or which shed light on the author's life or times, or which show a variation on a Renaissance theme or *topos*. Meanwhile, the choice is broad including not only the obvious names but also Remy Belleau, Olivier de Magny, and Jacques Grevin, who may not be well known to non-specialist readers. There is also a section on the *rhétoriqueurs*, Jean Molinet, Guillaume Cretin, and Jean Lemaire de Belges, who are coming back into fashion. A notable omission is Jean Marot, father of the more famous Clément (see p. 108).

*Poésie encyclopédique et kabbala chrétienne: onze études sur Guy Le Fèvre de la Borderie*, ed. François Roudaut, Champion, 266 pp., consists of the papers from a 1995 conference in Rouen. Le Fèvre de la Borderie's work combined scientific interests with biblical studies. He was a Catholic and, in his *Hymnes ecclésiastiques*, he was trying to rival the Protestant successes such as Marot's Psalms. He was much influenced by the *Kabbala* and makes many references to the *Zohar*, written in Spain by Moses de León in 1280–86. He would have been involved in the intellectual ferment surrounding the emergence of the Lurianic Kabbala in the 16th century. Conference contributors were Y. Bellenger, J.-P. Brach, J. Dauphiné, M.-L. Demonet, M.-M.

Fragonard, F. Giacone, R. Gorris, N. Lombart, J.-F. Maillard, K. Meerhoff, and J. Miernowski. *Poésie et Bible de la Renaissance à l'âge classique 1550–1680, Actes du Colloque de Besançon, 1997,* ed. Pascale Blum and Anne Mantero, Champion, 294 pp., is another collection showing the interest in biblical subjects. B. comments in her introduction that these poems with a biblical intertext are a new form of literary output, inspired by the Holy Ghost rather than the usual poetic fury. Contributors on the 16th c. were Y. Bellenger, M. Clément, S. Lardon, J.-R. Fanlo, A. Blanc, G. Polizzi, M.-M. Fragonard, and E. Berriot-Salvadore.

ARCHITECTURE, GRAPHIC ARTS AND ORTHOGRAPHY

Architecture has been a significant theme this year as in J. Balsamo, ' "Dire le Paradis d'Anet": les poètes de la génération de 1550 et l'architecture', *Adirel,* 12:339–49 (see also p. 115). Just as Ronsard seemed to turn to the ancients rather than the discoveries of science in his ideas of creation, so too with architecture. Ronsard, Du Bellay, and their contemporaries appear to refer to idealized buildings rather than stone châteaux such as that of Anet built by Henry II for Diane de Poitiers. B. mentions that Henry II was more interested in architecture than in poetry, and thus poets wanting his patronage were obliged to praise both Anet and Diane de Poitiers. It was apparently 'de ton' to praise the liberality of the owner. Thus in Du Bellay's poem of 1558 for Diane, the 'belle architecture' was a metonymy which meant 'son artifice et despence admirable'. As for Ronsard, his bitterness towards architecture and architects is based on his dislike and jealousy of Philibert de l'Orme who was a favourite at court.

Another recurrent theme in this year's work has been the visual and graphic arts. M. Vasselin, 'Des fastes de Bacchus aux beuveries flamandes: l'iconographie du vin de la fin du XVe siècle à la fin du XVIIe siècle', *NRSS,* 17:219–51, discusses graphic art with reference to Bacchus and wine. She points out the range of images covered by the theme of wine, from the classical gods to the Old Testament, the 'wine which gladdens the heart of man', and the mystical wine of the blood of Christ in the mass. V. traces the differences in these themes under headings such as 'Cortèges, bacchanales et fêtes du vin', 'Vin, péché et tromperie: les conséquences de l'ivresse dans les scènes de l'Ancien Testament', 'Le vin eucharistique: la vigne, le vin et le Salut dans les Evangiles', et 'Amour et connaissance du vin dans les portraits individuels'. V. concludes this beautifully illustrated article by pointing out that glasses, bottles, and carafes in paintings reflect the contemporary fashions, 'mais peu importe le flacon pourvu qu'on ait l'ivresse'.

Alison Adams, *A Bibliography of French Emblem Books of the Sixteenth and Seventeenth Centuries*, Geneva, Droz, 670 pp., is but the first volume of the bibliography, covering the letters A to K. Quite apart from the importance of these books as a reflection of European graphic art, it is fascinating to see the famous names who contributed, such as Théodore de Bèze and Barthélemy Aneau, and the number of books produced by a single person. For example, Andrea Alciato's emblems 'not only constitute the first emblem book, but are also the most frequently printed' and appear to have been translated for popular consumption into French, German, Italian, and Spanish, whilst also appearing as 'an extremely learned and lengthy work in which the actual emblems are dwarfed by learned communications'. Both specialists and lay readers will eagerly await the second volume.

*NRSS*, 17.1, *L'écriture du français à la Renaissance: Orthographe, ponctuation, systèmes scriptuaires*, ed. J.-C. Monferran, is a special issue of the *Revue* dedicated to a single theme. M. points out in his introduction the difference in attitude between Du Bellay, who was not really interested in the way words were written and felt that the 'lecteur sçavant [. . .] ne s'arrestera à si petites choses', and Thomas Sébillet to whom the question was of great importance. M. feels that the way words were spelled and punctuated is of interest generally, not only to the specialist: the 'rules' in the 16th c. were slowly evolving during the upheaval and perceived need for consistency generated by the spread of printing. Contributors to the volume are O. Rosenthal (11–22), M. Huchon (23–36), G. Freyssinet (37–54), J.-M. Colard (55–66), J.-C. Monferran (67–84), Y.-C. Morin (85–106), G. Clérico (107–46), A. Tournon (147–60), and S. Baddeley (161–76).

COLLECTIONS, CONFERENCES AND WORKS OF REFERENCE

Terence Cave, whose seminal Cornucopian text was translated into French last year (*YWMLS* 60:91), has produced the first volume in a series edited by M. Jeanneret and M. Engammare and displays, as one might expect, an impressive breadth of scholarship. *Pré-histoires: textes troublés au seuil de la modernité*, Geneva, Droz, 200 pp., is based on a series of articles, conference papers, and lectures. C. points out that by definition a literary text is 'un objet culturel portant des signes de sa provenance'. It should therefore be studied from both historical and anthropological viewpoints. He feels that it is precisely the historical aspect — how things were perceived at the time they were written — that the modern reader misses: 'les ouvrages de cette époque sont profondément et très visiblement marqués de leur appartenance à l'histoire sociale, politique, religieuse et événementielle qui se déploie autour d'eux'. The 'textes troublés', by their very nature, may show aspects of life such as a religious subtext that were problematic at the time and therefore help the modern reader to 'ésquisser une topographie — toujours provisoire, toujours partielle — de ce pays étrange qu'est le passé'. Part I covers 'Troubles épistémologiques', 'Frontières de la croyance' and 'La zone médiane'; part II covers 'Fragments d'un moi futur: de Pascal à Montaigne', 'Pour une pré-histoire du suspens', and 'Fragments d'un moi futur: le récit et son sujet'.

Malcolm Smith, *Renaissance Studies: Articles 1966–1994*, ed. R. Calder, Geneva, Droz, xviii + 374 pp., are articles written over nearly 30 years by S., who died at the tragically young age of 52. Affectionate forewords by M. A. Screech and Michael Heath give an insight into his personality and breadth of scholarship.

There have been a number of publications focusing on women. *The Feminist Encyclopedia of French Literature*, ed. Eva Sartori, Connecticut, Greenwood, 636 pp., describes the life and works of prominent female authors such as Christine de Pisan 'the first woman in Europe to earn a living by her pen'. It also gives a woman's perspective on subjects such as the Bible. Marguerite Soulié writes about the involvement of three great noblewomen in the Reform movement and their relation to the Bible, namely Marguerite de Navarre, her daughter Jeanne d'Albret, and Charlotte Arbaleste, a survivor of the St Bartholomew's Massacre, who later married Philippe de Mornay. Each article is accompanied by a bibliography for further reading divided into primary and secondary sources. *Dans les miroirs de l'écriture: la réflexivité chez les femmes écrivains d'ancien régime*, ed. Jean-Philippe Beaulieu and Diane Desrosiers-Bonin, Montreal U.P., 171 pp., discusses the ways in which 14 female writers from the 15th to the 18th cs reflect and are themselves reflected in their works, in texts that vary from allegorical dreams to letters, from poetry to memoirs. Reflexivity is thus seen by the reader as a historical as well as a generic movement, 'une transitivité par laquelle le sujet feminin se désigne lui-même en dessinant les figures du même et de l'autre'. Apart from the introduction by the editors, seven 16th-c. writers are included. Contributors are: J. Rieu, C. Yandell, A. Larsen, D. E. Polachek, E. Viennot, F. Villemur, and M.-T. Noiset. Anne Larsen has edited a volume related to her chapter, Madeleine and Catherine des Roches, *Les missives*, Geneva, Droz, 456 pp. It includes an adaptation of Claudian's epic poem, *De raptu Prosperinae* and numerous elogia in the ladies' honour published during the 'Ancien régime'. *Des Femmes et des livres: France et Espagne, XIVe–XVIIe siècle*, ed. Dominique de Courcelles and Carmen val Julián, Geneva, Droz, 176 pp., is the proceedings of a day of study at Fontenay-St-Cloud in 1998. It considers the question of books being appropriated by women. Sociological analyses, considering books as cultural products according to the social and 'generic' identity of their readers, are contrasted with studies whose object is to judge the meaning of the books through their literary and linguistic function.

*Royaume de Fémynie: pouvoir, contraintes, espaces de liberté des femmes, de la Renaissance à la Fronde,* ed. Kathleen Wilson-Chevalier and Eliane Viennot, Champion, 299 pp., is the outcome of a conference in Blois in 1995. Women influenced government during the Renaissance through patronage, literature, religion, and at court. This book deals with more or less well-known women under the headings *Espaces de liberté, Exercices du pouvoir, Equivoque de l'imaginaire,* and *Royaume de Fémynie.* Articles include M. Lazard, 'Jacquette de Montbron, une bâtisseuse humaniste', M. B. McKinley, 'Louise de Savoie et le pouvoir du livre', M. Orth, 'Les fortunes précaires de Marie Dentière aux XVIe et XIXe siècles', G. Johnson, 'Marie de Médicis: mariée, mère, méduse', E. Nicholson, ' "Victoire aux femmes!" L'anarchie morale dans les farces conjugales: femmes d'esprit et maris ridicules (1470–1550)', and Frédérique Villemur, 'Eros et Androgyne: la femme comme un autre "soy-mesme"?'.

In her preface to *Entre la lumière et les ténèbres: aspects du Moyen Age et de la Renaissance dans la culture des XIXe et XXe siècles. Actes du congrès de Montréal, 1995,* ed. Brenda Dunn-Lardeau, Champion, 258 pp., D.-L. mentions G. Lanson's critique of Christine de Pisan and 'Cherchez la femme, oubliez l'écrivain' with reference to Marguerite de Navarre and Marguerite de Valois. Titles include K. A. Roberts, 'De l'autoportrait de Marguerite de Valois dans ses *Mémoires* à sa représentation romanesque dans *La Reine Margot* d'Alexandre Dumas père'; O. A. Dull, 'Le culte de l'esprit rabelaisien et de l'art de la Grande Rhétorique à la fin du siècle: avatars "Incoherents" du mot d'esprit'; and D. Smoje, 'L'héritage médiéval dans la musique de notre temps'.

*Littératures classiques,* special issue 37: *De l'utilité de la littérature,* ed. Alain Viala et al., Champion, 261 pp., contains the proceedings of a 1997 Paris conference, with two 16th-c. articles: A.-P. Pouey-Mounou, 'L'absolu et le libre plaisir dans l'*Elégie à Loïs des Masures* du "talentueux" Ronsard'; and A. Tarrête, 'Le stoïcisme de Guillaume du Vair, ou de l'utilité de la "philosophie par gros temps" '.

*Par la vue et par l'ouïe: littérature du Moyen Age et de la Renaissance,* ed. Michèle Gally and Michel Jourde, ENS Ophys, 203 pp., is the fruits of a seminar at Fontenay-St Cloud on how mediaeval and Renaissance poetry, narrative, and theatre posed the question of seeing and hearing. In what way was the discourse on these senses also a discourse on poetic creation, and to what extent was the ensuing literature affected by sentiments involving questions of theology, aesthetics, rhetoric, or politics? Papers on poetry, 'entre chant et image', are contributed by C. Lucken, M. Gally, J.-C. Monferran, and V. Denizot; on theatre, 'La parole et le corps: célébrations et interdits', by V. Dominguez and B. Louvat; and on narration, 'Vérités et troubles des sens', by I. Hersant and M. Jourde.

*Bibliographie de la littérature française XVIe–XXe siècles*, PUF, 318 pp., covers four centuries — a large proportion of French literature. Three new volumes in the *Bibliographie des écrivains français* series have been published by Memini: Yves Quenot, *Jean de la Ceppède*, 109 pp.; Jean Vignes, *Jean-Antoine de Baïf*, 254 pp.; Yves Bellenger and Jean-Claude Ternaux, *Du Bartas*, 163 pp. The excellent *Dictionnaire encyclopédique de la littérature française*, Laffont, 1097 pp., first published in 1997, has been reissued in small print in a portable form.

## 2. MONTAIGNE

Title of the Year award for 1999 goes to R. Bowers' short story, 'Montaigne and Me at Forty', *QQ*, 106:461–71, in which the narrator's shame at his voyeuristic lusting is contrasted with M.'s more measured aphorisms, with their ambivalence as to M.'s personal feelings. S. Meshkinfam covers the same theme more academically in ' "Merveilleuse" et "sotte" honte: meting out the paradoxes of shame in Montaigne', *EsC*, 39:150–60, the only 16th-c. contribution in an issue devoted to the topic of shame, pointing out that in 'Sur les vers de Virgile', M. criticizes contemporary youth for lacking a sense of sexual timidity, which he himself admires. He has the will but not the desire because of 'sotte honte'. He believes that this shame is linked to desire and helps him to articulate it. Shame moves one towards courtly love, but imagination is the domain of erotic love. On the question of female desire, M. argues against those who believe that all that is needed to be chaste is 'Just say no'.

The current interest in sexual ambiguity apparently had its equivalent in the 16th century. V. Groebner, 'Körpergeschichte politisch: Montaigne und die Ordnungen der Natur in den französischen Religionskriegen 1572–1592', *HZ*, 269:281–304, has taken two stories from M.'s *Essais*, one about a woman who pretended to be a man and married another woman, and the other about a woman who acquired male genitalia and a beard, and was rechristened *Germain*. A theory prevalent in the 16th c. was that women had all the characteristics of men, but they were inside their bodies, not sufficiently cooked to be men, as G. nicely puts it. As far as politics is concerned, there is scorn for unmanly behaviour such as cross-dressing, whether it was sexually based or for fun. D'Aubigné said that the French were worse off than the Romans, because they were slaves to a man/woman — Catherine de Medici — and a woman/man — Henry III. Propagandists on both sides of the religious divide used sexual imagery in their attacks on each other. According to Machiavelli, politicians in the 16th c. had to be both fox and lion, and G. says that the arts of change, simulation, and deception are some of the most important themes of political literature in the 16th c., and that M.'s essays should be read in this light.

Yves Delègue, *Montaigne et la mauvaise foi: l'écriture de la vérité*, Champion, 245 pp., accuses M. of not being honest with his readers, starting with his famous phrase, 'C'est icy un livre de bonne foy, lecteur'. In quoting authors such as Rousseau, who have questioned this statement, D. tries to discover what lies behind the apparent untruth, what hostile forces could have been involved, and what could have made M. so pessimistic.

The motif of the horse recurs in Daniel Martin, *Montaigne et son cheval ou les sept couleurs du discours: de la servitude volontaire*, Nizet, 116 pp. It is a brightly coloured book with the days of the week in different colours, in the middle formed into an 'M' for Montaigne, with a big yellow sun for Sunday. Martin too claims that M. is not being honest in his essays, and that he wrote *De la servitude volontaire* himself. Martin includes a modern French translation of the work in question. The second half of the book explains why M. was writing the way he did, through 'mnemotechnie'. Martin refers the reader to Frances Yates, *The Art of Memory* (1966), and insists that it has nothing to do with the occult but is merely a system of classifying texts. The horse in the title, incidentally, is the Trojan horse introduced, perhaps, into the citadel of M.'s supposed virtue.

J. Balsamo, 'Montaigne, le style (du) cavalier, et ses modèles italiens', *NRSS*, 17:253–67, has taken the metaphor of the horse in M's *Essais* and points out that, at the time of its publication, France lacked horsemanship just as it was searching for a literary style. Italians were at the forefront of the equestrian arts, and they taught the French at home or in Italy. They led in horsebreeding, dressage, and treatises on horsemanship. M. discusses the equestrian arts (1, xlviii) and praises, in particular, le prince de Sulmone and his 'fermeté de l'assiette'. Later the French would learn their art of horsemanship in the theatre of war, and this would show up the artificial side of the Italians, 'reposant sur un dressage finalisé du cheval et non pas sur la maîtrise de l'homme', as Balsamo puts it. M. preferred the French riders, 'bon homme à cheval, à l'usage de nostre parler, semble plus regarder au courage qu'à l'adresse'. This also applied to written style, and M. 'voulait adapter un style cavalier, également nourri de l'Italie et de son modèle équestre, et d'une certaine manière contre la leçon italienne [. . .] c'était le style de la conversation civile dans une époque troublée, [. . .] d'une "saison tumultuère qui n'est pas capable d'une bride courte et reglée" '. If M. perhaps exaggerated his own good faith, he may have been too modest about his linguistic ability. The publication by M. A. Screech of M.'s annotated Lucretius (*YWMLS*, 60:96) has induced A. Legros, 'La main grecque de Montaigne', *BHR*, 51:461–78, to reconsider M.'s statements as to his knowledge of Greek. M. wrote 'Je n'entens rien au Grec', and 'Je ne prens guiere [. . .] aux Grecs, par ce que mon jugement ne sçait pas faire ses besouignes d'une puerile et aprantisse intelligence'. M. always insists 'Qui veut guerir de l'ignorance, il faut la confesser'. Therefore, for him to be an 'apprentice' in Greek, as in theology or philosophy, could well be a positive attribute. Also, M. needed to avoid being thought a pedant if he wished to remain a 'gentilhomme' and be an author of works in French. L. reproduces various samples of M.'s use of Greek and suggests that he enjoyed writing it. Its importance for him was its precise meaning.

   M. was fascinated by the accounts of the New World brought back by Francisco López de Gómara, André Thevet, and Jean de Léry and produced two essays 'Des Cannibales' (I, xxi) and 'Des Coches' (III, vi) based on them. D. N. Losse, 'Montaigne recounts New World ethnography', *Neophilologus*, 83:517–28, examines Todorov's assertion that M. 'uses the Indians to illustrate his theses concerning our own society rather than seeking to know [Indian culture]'. For example, Thevet condemns outright cannibalistic practices of the native Brazilians, whereas M. claims that they were no more barbarous than certain European methods of torture. Polygamy leads to no jealousy on the part of Brazilian women; the jealousy of French wives is the major obstacle to a happy marriage. L. concludes that M. is both concerned with telling a good story and with seeing the basic qualities in the 'noble savages' that were once found in the people of Europe before avarice and intolerance drove them to dreams of world conquest. Given that the scale of genocide by the Conquistadores was unmatched until the 20th c. (not to mention the wars of religion and the Inquisition in Europe) it is hard to see how M. was able to maintain any level of detachment at all. Two seminal works on M. from the turn of the 19th c. have been reissued: Emil Faguet, *\*Autour de Montaigne*, Champion, 290 pp.; and Ferdinand Brunetière, *\*Etudes sur Montaigne*, Champion, 156 pp. Both are introduced by Antoine Compagnon.

## 3. RABELAIS

A. Frisch, 'Quod vidimus testamur: testimony, narrative agency and the world in Pantagruel's mouth', *FrF*, 24:261–83, discusses the world within the mouth of the giant in *Pantagruel*. The idea of a sleeping giant goes back at least as far as the Cyclops, Polyphemus, and the separate buccal world occurs in many mediaeval *chroniques gargantuines* (and, one might add, in the London Millennium Dome!). Alcofribas Nasier has a dual role as an eye-witness reporter and an omniscient narrator. F. maintains that this duality would be impossible if the narrator were physically present. It arises therefore from the textual medium that serves as its mode of transmission. Thus *Pantagruel* is as much a book as it is a story and is an example of the impact of the expansion of printing on literary form.

Luther's critique of the Catholic theology of salvation by works (see p. 103) used forceful images of monastic gluttony and lechery. Yvan Loskoutoff, 'Les appétits du ventre: évangélisme luthérien et satire du monachisme dans l'oeuvre de Rabelais', *RHRel*, 216:299–343, argues that R. uses the images of revelry and debauchery in his books to the same ends. Because they have not attained evangelical perfection, the giants are prey to these sins and, according to L., their excesses are not to be praised but rather to show 'l'esclavage du péché dont nulle créature n'est indemne'. Paradoxically, therefore, the monks who engage in these excesses are more open to redemption than their colleagues who *know* that they have found the truth. L. makes a strong case that flies in the face of nearly all modern critics.

*\*Le Tiers Livre, Actes du colloque international de Rome, 1996*, ed. Franco Giacone, Champion, 144 pp., is the report of a round table discussion of two earlier editions of the *Tiers Livre* edited by Mireille Huchon and Jean Céard. Panellists were J. Dupèbe, R. Cooper, G. Ferroni, M. L. Demonet, M.-M. Fragonard, and D. Ménager. A year after the round table, E. M. Duval, *Design of Rabelais' Tiers Livre de Pantagruel*, Geneva, Droz, 1997, 247 pp., was published and now a further study of the *Tiers livre* has appeared: Oumbelbanine Zhiri, *L'extase et ses paradoxes: essai sur la structure narrative du Tiers livre*, Champion, 271 pp. Duval and Zhiri both face the central problem of the *Tiers Livre* that, while *Pantagruel* is perfectly teleological with a beginning, middle, and end, the *Tiers Livre* begins with an ending, ends with a beginning, and contains a poorly specified and possibly pointless quest. Duval tries to impose a pattern for which he is criticised by Defaux (see p. 109). Z. quotes Barbara Bowen to the effect that 'The Renaissance writer had been brought up on paradox, educated by means of it and entertained by reading it'. Screech's view that, apart from moral questions such as freedom and will, the *Tiers Livre* deals with the

related subject of language and how it is conceived, used, and interpreted is appositely mentioned. Z. discusses the way these different elements develop in the text as it unfolds to the reader, at the same time as they are subverting the text and imposing on it different forms of logic. Z. wants the reader to take part in this amazing literary and philosophical game, together with the characters themselves.

V. Krause, 'Idle works in Rabelais' *Quart Livre*: the case of the *gastrolatres*', *SCJ*, 30:47–60, sees Pantagruel's visit to Gaster's isle in the *Quart Livre* as a parody of the increasingly popular travelogue (see p. 93). At first, the *gastrolatres* appear idle, and their land, as in so many of the travelogues, an earthly Eden. But Pantagruel's party have a hard climb to reach the top of Areté (virtue) and the Gasters turn out to be forced to work and to be slaves to both *penie* (poverty) and *gaster* (stomach). R. uses the travelogue to challenge Catholicism's 'salvation through faith and works in cooperation with God' with the Calvinist 'salvation through faith alone'. Work is justified as submission and discipline but not as cooperation.

In 'Philibert De L'Orme rabelaisien?', *Adirel*, 12:25–35, Y. Pauwels asks how great was the friendship between R. and the great French architect. Anthony Blunt's appealing theory that the Abbaye de Thélème was the fruit of their conversations has long been disproved. P. points out that R. and De L'Orme are not of the same generation, and that R. came from a more learned background; he questions whether, despite Thélème, R. was really interested in architecture. De L'Orme comes closest to R. in his architectural discourse when he, like the writer, enriched the French language with new vocabulary on two fronts: that of stone-cutting with great virtuosity and extraordinary results, and of composition. De L'Orme used hybrids in architecture — mixtures of different styles such as Ionic and Corinthian — as R. mixed different registers and dialects of French. P. even manages to find irony in De L'Orme's ornamentation of the château of Anet and imagines how Panurge would greet this freedom and inventiveness.

L. Marsh, 'Monks in the kitchen: reading one of Rabelais's curious combinations', *RN*, 40:25–31, discusses the question in *Quart Livre* 11: 'Que signifie [. . .] et que veult dire que tous-jours vous trouvez moines en cuysines, jamais n'y trouvez roys, papes ne empereurs?' He suggests that there is a paradigm of equivalence equating the kitchen, the Church and the cosmos. Thus frère Jean sees the kitchen in terms of the grandiose harmony of the cosmos, and Epistémon sees the Church in terms of the magnificent structure of the kitchen. The 'moine à l'envers', Lardon, sees the churches of Florence as incomparable to the numerous and sumptuous food shops of Amiens. The kitchen is the Church and scriptorium, written in culinary rather than religious code, whereas kings, popes, and emperors are in touch with earthly considerations such as power and status.

The Italian writer, Annibal Caro, is linked with R. in Franco Giacone, 'Rabelais et Annibal Caro: traditions, filiations et traductions littéraires', *RHLF*, 99:963–73. Caro's essay, *Nasea*, was probably composed in 1538; a verse form was translated into French in 1556. It concerns the importance of large noses, a theme dear to mediaeval burlesques. Caro invokes the authority of the Persians, who could not find a successor to King Cyrus with a nose sufficiently large; 'Na-bucco-de-nasor', Charles Quint, and François I owed their authority to their large noses and mouths. Absence of nose (les hommes 'ennasés') — would we say denasalized? — means dishonour. Of course, the hidden meaning is that nose = member, and Caro is perpetuating a tradition that a large nose means a large penis. The parallels with 'Maister Alcofrybas Nasier', as R. signed his first book, are many and have been pointed out by various critics including Michel Jeanneret. After comparing translations into French of Caro's *Nasea* and *Lettera*, G. concludes that Caro and R. share a style of writing 'tout un milieu littéraire qui se concrétise en Italie par les Académies poétiques'.

## 4. RONSARD

Y. Bellenger, 'Sur la poésie amoureuse de Ronsard avant *Les Amours* et sur les personnages de Janne et de Cassandre', *BHR*, 61:399–414, claims that, despite Laumonier's comments, the name Cassandre appears for the first time in R.'s poetry in 1550. There is a list of other loves, including Janne, a lady both 'impitoiable' and 'cruelle'; not a real person supposes B., but the name is 'associé à l'inconstance, "Janne" est parfois un peu sorcière ou tout bonnement vieille putain'. Who is Cassandre? It could be that only with the *Amours* of 1552 does Cassandre become a real person.

J. Della Neva, 'Teaching Du Bellay a lesson: Ronsard's rewriting of Ariosto's sonnets', *FrF*, 24:285–301, criticizes the received view that 'in a courtly gesture of deference to textual priority, R. avoided a direct confrontation with Du Bellay by choosing to use only texts not already imitated in the *Olive*' as a model for his sonnets. D. demonstrates that in fact R. sometimes reworked identical texts. He even appears on occasion to be giving Du Bellay a number of lessons in what he sees as an acceptable mode of literary imitation. D. suggests that R.'s rivalry in this field provoked the exiled Du Bellay to retaliate with *Les Regrets*.

M. Quainton, 'The liminary texts of Ronsard's *Amours de Cassandre* (1552): poetics, erotics, semiotics', *FS*, 53:257–78, discusses the opening four pages of R.'s 1552 edition. They consist of a title-page, facing profile portraits of R. and Cassandre, and a *voeu*. These pages reflect the respective roles of author and printer/publisher/compositor in the production process. Q. points out that R.'s name on the title page is in larger print than the actual book title, and he analyses the connotations of the adjective *vandemoys*, attached to the author's name. Q. maintains the facing mirror image portraits 'are the first of a multitude of references throughout the sonnets to a lexicon of engraving, portraiture, and the visual arts which underpins the entire collection and gives it structural coherence'. Through these texts, the many themes of the sonnets can be traced.

F. Bouchet, 'L'intertexte oublié: Ronsard et Chartier', *NRSS*, 17:205–18, draws a parallel between R. and Alain Chartier (1385?–1430?) who wrote the *Quadrilogue invectif* in 1422 during the Hundred Years War. R. composed the *Discours des misères de ce temps* in 1562–1563 during the first of the wars of religion. Chartier calls for national mobilisation after the debacle of the treaty of Troyes (1420) which made Henry V of England heir to the throne of France. R. sided with the King and the Catholics against the Protestant Reformation, which threatened the power of the King. Both authors were officially in the royal service and had a similar mission, the one in prose the other in poetry, to rouse the people and convince them of the validity of their cause. B. aims to show to what extent R. was inspired by Chartier as well as by classical sources. Whilst not denying the obvious differences between Chartier and R., B. maintains that borrowings would have been obvious to a cultivated French reader in the 1560s. They show that the 14th and 15th cs should not be written off as the dark ages, but rather seen as a period that was a productive transition between the 'Moyen Age central' and the 16th century.

Sara Sturm-Maddox, *Ronsard, Petrarch and the Amours*, Gainesville, Florida U.P., 208 pp., considers R.'s poetry in the light of the title given to him by Olivier Magny of 'Pétrarche Vandomois'. Whilst pointing out that it was fashionable to compare poets to their classical counterparts (e.g. Macrin, the 'French Horace', Marot, the 'Virgile françois') S.-M. feels that the case of R. and P. is singular; unlike other imitators, R. is not writing *like* P. but writing *as* P. 'This reappraisal seeks [. . .] not to contest many of the contrasts to the Petrarchan model often identified as constitutive of R.'s newness, but rather to reposition his originality as love poet in terms of his dialogue with P. S.-M. concludes with further evidence, in revisions in the successive collected editions of R.'s *Oeuvres*, of the enduring formative

imprint of the story of the *Rime sparse* for his self-definition as both
poet and lover.

The only 16th-c. piece in Jean Orizet, *Les aventures du regard: des
poètes et de la poésie*, Loire, J.-P. Huguet, 397 pp., is 'Pierre de Ronsard:
poète et gentilhomme vendômois'. It consists of a selection of articles
and thumbnail sketches written for various publications, particularly
the *Revue des Deux Mondes*, between 1984 and 1998.

John Nassichuk, 'Ronsard lecteur de Flaminio: note sur quelques
vers de *Hylas*' *BHR*, 61:729–36, compares R.'s version of *Hylas* with
that of the earlier Flaminio in 1529. He notes that both poets use an
image from Lucretius, that of a cow crying for her lost calf, to express
the distress felt by Hercules on the death of Hylas. The same image is
to be found in Ovid's *Fastes* to describe the despair of Ceres at the
rape of Proserpine. Other poets, such as Bereau, have treated the
subject using the lion's roar and altering the emphasis of the episode.
N. thinks that more work needs to be done on the possible influence
of Flaminio on R.

S. Lardon, 'Ronsard, "Pareil j'égale au soleil que j'adore [. . .]"',
commentaire du sonnet 5 des *Amours*', *SFr*, 43:87–96, finds, beside
various *topoi* of Petrarchism — the symbolism of the heart of stone
and the precious stone, fire, and ice; the relationship between
microcosm and macrocosm; the lady who is beautiful but cruel and
the poet who suffers in love — elements of Christian neo-platonism:
the lady's physical beauty reflects the beauty of her soul, hence her
chastity, which is a reflection of the beauty of the angels (not in this
sonnet, but in others) and of God, in this case the gods, graces, and
the whole universe. It thus follows that the lover can attain divine
perfection through his love for the lady, as is seen in the reference to
the crucifixion in the final line: 'De clous de feu sus le froid de sa
glace'.

R.'s *Hynnes* on the Creation are based on book learning and
exemplarity at a time when advances in astronomy and, in particular,
the discoveries of Galileo were throwing doubts on classical wisdom.
J. Dauphiné, 'L'architecture des origines dans les *Hynnes* de Ronsard',
*Adirel*, 12:255–60, argues that R.'s approach follows the recommendations of the Pléiade, who said that the good poet, as opposed
to 'l'ignorant versificateur', used poetry as a dialectic, venerating the
knowledge of the classics. Thus, in the *Hynne de l'Eternité* vv. 1–4, it is
through Apollo and Orpheus that R. is seeking the secrets of nature
and the heavens. R.'s sense of order includes precise details of a
classical rather than a scientific nature. In the light of Borges and
Eco, D. feels that Du Bartas exploited R.'s analogy between book and
architecture, and the world and a library. He points to a 'logique
culturelle' of the 16th c. that the architecture of the creation of the

world depends on the world of books. This reassuring universe shows little development, despite being directly threatened by scientific advances.

## 5. DU BELLAY

M. Bizer, 'Letters from home: the epistolary aspects of Joachim Du Bellay's *Les regrets*', *RQ*, 52:140–79, aims to show that Du B.'s addressing of the sonnets in *Les regrets* to friends in Italy and France was not merely a word play or dedicatory gesture; instead he perceived the sonnets as verse epistles specifically intended for their addressees. He sees his verse as a reliable secretarial confidant who sympathetically records his troubles in Rome. The Pléiade poets distanced themselves from Marot but Du B. nonetheless draws on his tailoring of the epistle to match the poetic persona and its experiences, and also on his use of familiar language resembling speech. The epistolary form permitted Du B. to reflect in a way possible in an essay, and with the advantage of a distinct addressee, but also distances the author to some extent from its recipient. In a sense, Du B. writes letters 'home from abroad' to express his sense of exile. In Rome, though at home with his cultural heritage, he yearns for the chimney smoke of his little village. Once he returns there, he writes to the humanist Dorat 'Adieu donques je suis encor Romain'.

C. Mouchard, 'Deguy, Du Bellay et le temps de la poésie', *Littérature*, 144:68–81, claims that, in looking back to Du B. and his *Regrets*, Michel Deguy is trying to find the essence of poetry. This is even though Du B. saw himself as overshadowed by Ronsard, 'une oeuvre travaillée par un sentiment d'inaccomplissement', as M. puts it. In this challenging and rather abstract article, Deguy claims that from Du B. he can receive the sense of poetry for itself, a raw poetry without exterior or prior legitimization, and suggests that this gift comes despite himself from Du B.'s situation as a poet, and that it is up to the poet of today to receive it and offer it in a new form to the dead poet — through his *Tombeau*. He feels that, through his suffering, Du B. has taken the simple idea of regret and transformed it into 'celle du Regret de ce qui a toujours (été) manqué et manquera toujours: entraînant ainsi la poésie vers la terre sans terre de la dépossession et de la déception, Waste Land "moderne"'. Through his constant theme of regret, Du B. has touched the very existence of poetry itself, its position in time and its work as affected by time. Deguy heralds the era of a poetry without any inherited glory, ritual, or hierarchy. Poetry can only be in search of itself through all that it comes across, ceaselessly creating and unravelling its own image.

## 6. Marot

The Marot event of the year was the republication by Slatkine, Geneva, of volumes 1 to 5 of the late C. A. Mayer's complete critical edition of M.'s work. They are: *1: Les Epîtres; 2: Oeuvres satiriques; 3: Oeuvres lyriques; 4: Oeuvres diverses; 5: Les Epigrammes. 6: Les Traductions* is still in print.

D. Brancher, ' "En la maison de son cler père alla" autour du "rondeau parfaict" de Clément Marot', *BHR*, 61:429–59, takes up the theme of the *rondeaux*, which appear to have been the invention of Marot *père et fils*, and argues that in his 'rondeau parfaict' Clément is breaking loose not only from prison but from his father's influence. B. also posits that this marks a change from the cult of Mary and Catholicism to that of Christ and a more evangelical view. This also ties in with the new edition of Jean Marot (p. 114) and Hüe's article last year (*YWMLS*, 60:105) on the Marots at the Puy de Rouen.

S. Lardon, 'Étude du Psaume Premier de Marot: traduction et création poétique', *SFr*, 128:313–24, sets out the problems of finding a definitive text for Psalm 1. She uses the Defaux text based on Mayer Bibl. 116, and also Defaux's theory that by 'hebraica veritas' M. was referring to the Hebrew Vulgate. However, the basic Latin text with which she compares early and late variants in M.'s translation as well as those of Olivetan, Lefèvre d'Etaples, Campensis, and Bucer, is the Gallic and Roman Vulgate, not the Hebraicam, as can be seen by the final line of v. 1, which shows the variant 'et in cathedra pestilentiae non sedit'. The enthusiasm L. shows for M.'s Psalm translation is symptomatic of the current interest in this work. B. Roussel, ' "Laisse gemir, et braire les Payens": Clément Marot et le Psaume 6', *Rivista Trimestrale Pubblicata della Facoltà Valdese Protestantesimo*, 54:256–72, brings the point of view of a theologian and expert on the Christian hebraists of the Reformation to M.'s translation of Psalm 6, 'Domine, ne in furore arguas me', composed between 1527 and 1531. He asks to what extent the poet personalized this well-known psalm, bearing in mind that he was not a biblical scholar. R. points out that it was the 'Gallican' version of St Jerome's Latin Vulgate that was best known, and thus M. might have been expected to follow the lessons of Lefèvre d'Etaple's *Quincuplex* (1509) or his translation of the Bible into French (1530). R. points to the probable use of Lefèvre, along with Martin Bucer (Aretius Felinus) and Campensis, although his *Paraphrases* were published after M.'s original Psalm 6. Any resemblance to Vatable, the first Professor of Hebrew at the *Collège des Lecteurs Royaux*, is probably through Bucer. Whilst admitting the influence of the Christian hebraists, R. concludes that M. has changed the Psalm, so that it is no longer of David or of Christ, but a 'Chant de Marot'.

## 7. Marguerite de Navarre

Marguerite de Navarre, *L'Heptaméron*, ed. Gisèle Matthieu-Castellani, Librairie Générale Française, 756 pp., has been issued as a paperback. In considering Day 1 of the *Heptaméron*, G. Defaux, 'Marguerite de Navarre et la guerre des sexes: Heptaméron, première journée', *FrF*, 24:133–61, feels that discourse on gender is not in itself a sufficient critical guide to the text, and that M. de N. is saying to both camps, 'Judge not that ye be not judged', especially in the light of her evangelical views. D. quotes from the text to point out that 'le vice est commun aux femmes et aux hommes' and that in both cases 'toute vertu vient de Dieu' and 'pour faire conclusion du cueur de l'un et de l'autre, le meilleur des deux n'en vault rien'. In a footnote, D. challenges both Edwin Duval and Michel Jeanneret, the former for always seeing an 'overall design' and the latter for seeing discontinuity everywhere. On the whole, D. sides with Duval who, he says, mentions Jeanneret's views, whereas he accuses Jeanneret of ignoring Duval. L. Petris, 'Morale religieuse et transgression dans la XXXe Nouvelle de l'*Heptaméron*', *SFr*, 43:14–29, points out that the stories in the *Heptaméron* do not have the fatal time element of the 1001 nights but are rather, like the *Decameron* (1352) or the *Canterbury Tales* (1385), intended to divert the participants. The tale of incest in Nouvelle xxx is analysed by M. de N. from a point of view both religious (evangelical) and psychological. The problem is that of the origin of evil — does it come about because the occasion to sin presents itself or because of man's inherently sinful nature since the Fall? The triple incest (mother/son, brother/sister, father/daughter) in this case came about because the mother would not admit her fault and confess to God, but rather sent her son away, with the consequence that he married their daughter unawares. For the evangelicals, it was a question of justification by faith rather than works, and M. de N., influenced by Lefèvre d'Etaples, Briçonnet and the groupe de Meaux, claims that hoping to conquer one's baser instincts without the help of God is mere foolish pride. N. Cazauran, 'Au marges de *l'Heptaméron*: l'ombre du chevalier de la Tour Landry', *NRSS*, 17:195–204, compares various episodes in M. de N.'s *Heptaméron* with the *livre* which Geoffroy de La Tour Landry wrote in 1371 for the 'education' of his daughters. She considers it likely that the Queen had read the book, which was in the royal library at Blois. Some of the episodes are strikingly similar, for example the errant husband who returns to his wife after consorting with low women. In both books, the wife does not reproach her husband, merely bringing him a towel and water to wash in, remarking that it is good to wash when one has been in dirty places. In the end, in both stories, the husband repents. Maybe the Queen was influenced by the moral instructions from the Knight for his daughters, which were taken not only from the Bible but from his experience of everyday life.

The old woman has been a staple character in literature since antiquity. B. Dunn-Lardeau, 'La vieille femme chez Marguerite de Navarre', *BHR*, 61 : 375–98, describes how she is given a new role in the works of M. de N., which also reflects the life of the Queen herself as an old woman. Amongst the innovations is the woman who preaches (Oisille in l'*Heptaméron*) who seems also to represent the evangelicals. D.-L. suggests that improvements in hygiene meant that more women survived childbirth and there were therefore more aristocratic old women at court and elsewhere. M. de N. herself miscarried at 51. This is a complex issue. On the one hand, Ambroise Paré arrived at the court of François I in 1529 and demonstrated podalic version (grasping the feet of an unborn child and turning it into the correct position to be born). On the other hand, this reduced infant rather than maternal mortality. Like Pierre Belon (see p. 92) Paré wrote in the vernacular, which angered the medical establishment. Peter Chambellan, the son of another Huguenot physician, invented obstetrical forceps, but too late to benefit M. de N. or her entourage.

Forgetting has been a popular theme this year and is taken up by G. Banderier, 'L'oubli de Dieu et l'honneur des hommes: fonctions et usages de l'oubli dans l'*Heptaméron* de Marguerite de Navarre', *SN*, 70:221–29. He reminds us that the muses were daughters of Mnemosyne, so that literature could be seen as an immense effort to snatch the author as well as the work from oblivion. The high frequency of the word 'oublier' has been shown statistically and B. composes a sort of syllogism on the lines of: 1. 'Oublier' is a frequently used term, proving the fragility of man. 2. The writing of stories is in opposition to 'l'oubli'. 3. Therefore 'oublier' is linked to human frailty and 'mémoire' to narrative composition. Noting that 'oublier' meant exactly the same in the 16th c. as now, B. compares the use of memory and forgetting in the Bible and the *Heptaméron*. In the *Heptaméron*, forgetting is seen in a negative light, but memory means that one tale can recall another. In the Bible, forgetting can be a condition of pardon, both divine and human. In the *Heptaméron*, the husband discovers his wife *in flagrante*. He kills the lover and makes his wife drink from the skull, but finally he forgives and forgets and they have many children.

Marguerite de Navarre, *The Coach* and *the Triumph of the Lamb*, ed. Hilda Dale, Exeter, Elm Bank, 142 pp., is a paraphrase into English of two poems — one secular, one religious — by M. de N. In *The Coach*, she shows the effects on the hearts and minds of two women of their (courtly) lovers' infidelities and the consequences of that betrayal for a third, who is perfectly happy with her faithful lover but feels she must leave him and support her friends. The original poem was in rhymed decasyllables. The rhyme schemes varied between the three women, so that each one had an individual voice. By translating into blank verse, D. has lost this subtlety, especially as her lines contain an excess of monosyllables. On the other hand she has certainly succeeded in making M. de N.'s poems accessible to the anglophone reader. In the second poem, *The Triumph of the Lamb*, the metaphor of the classical triumph is used as an image for Christ in glory as the victorious hero, as evoked in *Revelations*. M. de N. is one of three authors discussed in L. D. Gates' book (see p. 114).

## 8. LABÉ

Louise Labé wrote Petrarchan sonnets in French in the mid-16th century. Mary Wroth (1586?–1640?), niece of Sir Philip Sidney and daughter of Sir Robert Sidney, wrote in a similar format in English in 1621. R. Kuin compares the two sets of work in 'More I still undoe: Louise Labé, Mary Wroth, and the Petrarchan discourse', *CLS*, 36:146–61. In attempting the Petrarchan format, both were trying to intrude into what had traditionally been a masculine verse form expressing a male lover's condition. The male always desired and the female was the object of desire. Labé's work was characterized by much greater confidence and boldness than that of Wroth. K. finds two reasons. First, French is a gender-specific language — it is usually apparent after a few lines of a poem if the author is female — whereas English permits indeterminacy. Second, Wroth came after the Petrarchan sonnet had been 'deconstructed' by Shakespeare and the tradition was ending, whilst Labé wrote during its heyday. K. does not wholly prove his case. After all, gender specificity might well discourage publication altogether. The Brontës and George Eliot wrote as men. On the other hand, K.'s case is at least better than the Marxist view that Labé could permit herself liberties because she was a *bourgeoise* of some standing in Lyon. Labé was, after all, the wife and daughter of ropemakers, whereas Wroth was further up the social scale with the title 'Lady'.

## 9. AGRIPPA D'AUBIGNÉ

Last year saw an article by Fanlo (*YWMLS*, 60:107) on the Tronchin collection of d'Aubigné's papers. In G. Banderier, 'L'*Advis au Roy de la Grande Bretagne*: un texte inédit d'Agrippa d'Aubigné', *BHR*, 61:509–14, another unpublished work is reviewed, this time from the

Yelverton collection, which the British Museum acquired in 1953. The *Advis* is a plea to Charles I to ally himself with France against Austria. The obvious secrecy had to do with remarks about the untrustworthiness of Cardinal Richelieu, who had strong links with both Rome and Spain; '[. . .] le secret des affaires consiste à ruyner ledit Cardinal, il reste maintenant à trouver les moyens'. It is clear why d'A. did not keep a copy. B. has worked out by a process of elimination that, although the letter is only from 'Monsieur d'Aubigny à Geneve', it is indeed from Agrippa and not his son Constant. *Monluc, d'Aubigné, deux epées, deux plumes: actes du colloque Montluc, d'Aubigné, les événements en Aquitaine après 1560*, Agen, Centre Matteo Bandello d'Agen, 296 pp., is a series of papers about two soldiers who were also writers. One was Catholic, the other Protestant and both felt they had God on their side. Their exploits are seen against the background of the 'Agenais', which both men loved. Contributors are A.-M. Cocula, M. Cassan, M. Seguin, A. A. Morello, M. Lazard, J.-J. Supple, R. Knecht, C.-G. Dubois, J.-C. Sournia, B. de Monluc, A. Thierry, G. Schrenck, P. Tachouzin, J. Clémens, and N. Kuperty-Tsur.

The final volume of the critical edition of Agrippa d'Aubigné, *Histoire universelle*, x (1620–22), ed. André Thierry, Geneva, Droz, 304 pp., has appeared, as has *Poétiques d'Aubigné, Actes du colloque de Genève, 1996*, ed. Olivier Pot, Geneva, Droz, 304 pp., with contributions from most of the leading d'Aubigné scholars.

## 10. MINOR WRITERS

### PROSE

David Graham, 'Emblème et "vécriture" chez Georgette de Montenay', *DFS*, 47:29–60, starts by explaining Jacques Godbout's definition of 'vécrire', a combination of 'vivre' and 'écrire' made some 30 years ago. He contrasts this idea that there is an autobiographical element in good writing with Barthes's theory that the writer must 'supporter la littérature comme *un engagement manqué*'. It is to test these theories that Graham has studied the *Emblèmes ou devises chrestiennes* of Georgette de Montenay, a Protestant writer who frequented the court of Jeanne d'Albret, the daughter of Marguerite de Navarre and mother of the future Henry IV. G. feels that, despite problems of definition, the 'emblème' is closer to the fable than is the 'devise', which is attached to a person. G. shows that the 'emblème' has a far more general moral to offer (see p. 96). G. shows various 'emblèmes' and their illustrations, which have a moral use in persuading sinners to repent. They hold up a mirror to human foibles and thus have an active role in the evangelical process. One of the special aspects of the work is the appearance of 'emblèmes' representing Christian women who are virtuous but active, rather than passive. The Queen herself was a veritable Protestant heroine. G. feels that this concept of the heroic woman is central to the understanding of the book.

Marguerite de Valois, *Mémoires et autres récits, 1574–1614*, ed. Eliane Viennot, Champion, 364 pp., were widely read in their time and cover such seminal events as the St Bartholemew's Massacre. 'La reine Margot' was writing to her old friend Brantôme from 1594 onwards, in order to explain happenings and point out errors in the *Discours*, which he dedicated to her. The volume also includes the *Mémoire justicatif pour Henri de Bourbon* (1574), the *Discours docte et subtil* (1614) and her poetry, which exhibits a wide range of forms. Towards the end of her life, she was interested in the 'Querelle des femmes' and appears really to have enjoyed the battle. V. provides an in-depth commentary.

Gabrielle de Bourbon is another royal writer whose work, *Oeuvres spirituelles 1510–1516*, ed. E. Berriot-Salvadore, Champion, 352 pp., throws light upon the woman's role in the 16th c. and enlarges current views of life at the time. Her husband was the Jean II de la Trémoille mentioned by Jean Bouchet in his *Epîtres familières* (1547) as the 'chevalier sans reproche'.

S. Charles, 'La Boétie, le peuple et les "gens de bien"', *NRSS*, 17:269–86, argues that, in the *Discours de la servitude volontaire*, La Boétie was addressing the 'gens de bien' not the common people. Over the centuries, this discourse has been appropriated by many people with differing political views, starting with the Huguenots who printed it in 1574 even before Montaigne, and saw it as incitement to rebellion after the St Bartholomew's massacre. At the end of the 18th c., it was seen as a 'manifeste politique préconisant l'opposition au pouvoir gouvernemental'; in the 19th c. as republican, and in the 20th c. as revolutionary. It was even banned in occupied Belgium during World War II. C. however, argues that La B. never addressed himself to the common people and regarded them as irrational, credulous, and prone to rebellion, rather like children whom he saw it as his task to look after and if necessary correct. His judgement was that of an aristocratic magistrate rather than a democrat. His *Discours* actually addresses the 'gens de bien' who, like him, love the concepts of liberty, honour, and virtue, dear to the humanists.

Laura Doyle Gates, *Soubz umbrage de passetemps: Women's Storytelling in the 'Evangiles des Quenouilles', the 'Comptes amoureux de Jeanne Flore' and the 'Heptaméron'*, Montreal, Inedita et Rara, 146 pp., asks if the game of storytelling, including the rehearsal of erotico-humorous material, is a release from societal constraints or a clever trap for women players. Freud suggested that the passive presence of women during a session of 'dirty' jokes increases the company's pleasure. G. bases her inquiry into the poetics of the 'conte feminin' on women's freedom, responsibility, and choices in narrative activity. Her aim is to discover the usefulness of the positing of feminine subjectivity through the structure of the storytelling game. Is this subjectivity set up to be undermined, as in the *Evangiles*, used and found superfluous as in *Comptes amoureux*, or problematized as in the *Heptaméron?*

## POETS

In Jean Marot, *Les deux recueils Jehan Marot de Caen, poete et escripvain de la royne Anne de Bretagne, et depuis valet de chambre du treschrestien roy François premier*, ed. Gerard Defaux and Thierry Mantovani, Geneva, Droz, ccxxv + 603 pp., the editors have extended current interest in the works of Clément Marot to include the works of his father, Jean. The poetry of both has been neglected thanks to the criticism of the Pléiade school, and notably Du Bellay in his *Deffence et illustration de la langue françoyse* of 1549. The first selection of Jean's poetry was published and corrected by Clément between 1533 and 1534. The rest of poems have been compiled from manuscripts in various libraries all over Europe. There is thus the opportunity of measuring the son against the father, whom Clément rejected after his death. There is a poignant present-day analogy with Amis *père et fils*.

Whereas it was previously thought by many critics that Ronsard was the first poet to consider how his poems should be set out for posterity (see p. 105), O. Rosenthal, 'L'auteur devant son oeuvre: l'exemple de Jean Lemaire de Belges', *NRSS*, 17:181–93, mentions that Marot also had definite views on how, in particular, l'*Adolescence Clementine* should be organized. R. takes as her example Jean Lemaire de Belges, the court poet whose work circulated in both manuscript and printed form. Although, according to Jacques Abelard, the first complete works of L. de B. were published in 1524, after the author's death, R. maintains that he had a role in organizing them. He wished to reconcile two possible representations of the work and its public, the one political, destined for a particular reader such as Marguerite d'Autriche or Anne de Bretagne, the other poetic and addressing an anonymous reader through an exactly organised and set out poetic work. 'La pensée de l'oeuvre complète est donc à l'horizon du travail de Lemaire, mais cette pensée ne paraît pas encore fondatrice de l'oeuvre [. . .]'.

Six of Baïf's Poemes, in *Euvres en rime* (1573) are based on stories from Ovid's *Metamorphoses*. E. Vinestock, 'Ovid metamorphosed: Ovidian techniques transposed in Baïf's L'*Hippocrene*', *RS*, 13:63–72, has taken another of the poems and argues that in this case it is the *dispositio* that is influenced by Ovid, rather than the *inventio*. Both poets, however, share the theme of metamorphosis. The story is that of the Hippocrene fountain, 'formed from the hoof print of the winged horse Pegasus, who sprang from the blood of Medusa after she was decapitated by Perseus'. Baïf's poem, which focuses on poetic inspiration rather than, as Ovid, on the story of the hero Perseus, 'is autoreferential in a way that Ovid's poem is not'. Baïf thus alters the emphasis of the story from the decapitation of Medusa, which is dismissed in one-and-a-half lines, to the 'creation of the new fountain, which is sacred to the muses, and access to which is reserved for an elite of true poets'. Baïf's poem has 354 lines as opposed to the approximately 12,000 of the *Metamorphoses*.

T. Peach, 'Un poéte champenois retrouvé: Jules-César Le Besgue, quelques sonnets heroïques et autres poésies (1586)', *BHR*, 69:23–39, points out that the sonnets are heroic not only in their use of the alexandrine but also because they deal with classical heroes and heroines who recount their stories after their deaths. P. quotes lines from 'Bajazeth Hildrin, Empereur des Turcs', which have a positively Ozymandias-like quality. The remaining poetry deals with events closer in time such as the French civil war. P. notes that Le Besgue was 'avocat du roi au bailliage et siège présidial de Vitry-Le-François', and through him we perceive the literary taste of the 'gens du roi' in the French provinces towards the end of the 16th c.

Claude-Enoch Virey, *Vers itineraires: Allant de France en Italie 1592; Allant de Venise à Rome 1593*, ed. Anna Bettoni, Klincksieck, 264 pp., is a critical edition of the work of C. E. Virey who was 'avocat, homme de lettres, secrétaire d'Henri II de Condé, maire de sa ville natale (Chalon-sur-Saône) à plusieurs reprises entre 1627 et 1634'. Remy Belleau, *Oeuvres poétiques* III, ed. Guy Demerson, Champion, 219 pp., presents a critical edition of the *Oeuvres diverses* published from 1565 to 1572 as well as the *Ode* at Nogent and the 'poème macaronique', *Dictamen metreficium de Bello Hugenotico*. Isaac Habert, *Amours et Baisers*, ed. Nathalie Mahé, Geneva, Droz, 344 pp., is a critical edition of Habert's poetry.

G. Schrenck, 'Le Temple de Salomon dans *La Magnificence* de Du Bartas', *Adirel*, 12:261–74, continues the architectural theme (see p. 95). Du B. had his own architectural preoccupations in improving his château and was therefore aware of the appropriate terms for God, the architect, creating heaven and earth in *La Sepmaine*, and Solomon building his Temple. He did not lack sources, whether from the Bible, Josephus, or contemporary works on architecture. The *dédicace finale* links the person of Solomon to James I of England, with whom Du B. shared a literary friendship. Du B. has shortened the monotonous descriptions of the materials used for building the Temple, but he presents Solomon, the architect, as a painter, uniting the talents 'de Miron, de Phidie, et d'Apolle'. The King thus acquired the status of the 'génie artistique, de l'artiste total', which was the Renaissance ideal. Du B. also saw the book as a sort of temple to the glory of God. The Temple is the reverse of the Tower of Babel, and Du B. emphasises its tripartite nature, corresponding to the three stages of creation and also the three books of Solomon (Proverbs, Ecclesiastes, and the Song of Songs). Another aspect of Du B. concerns his influence on the Occitan poets. Philip Gardy, a specialist in Occitan literature, considers this in *La leçon de Nérac: Du Bartas et les poètes occitans (1550–1660)*, Bordeaux U.P., 237 pp. G. notes that '[. . .] leur attachement linguistique particulier les a poussés à cultiver à leur manière [. . .] le versant du langage dont la nymphe du lieu les avait invités à s'éprendre d'un étrange et assez singulier amour'. G. has organized the poets under three headings: first, 'Avant Du Bartas: la place de l'Occitan' with Gratianauld de Saint-Sever, Bernard du Poey, and Pierre de Nogerolles; second, 'La leçon de Nérac', with Du Bartas, Pey de Garros (see *YWMLS*, 60: 111), Auger Gaillard, Guilhem Ader, Larade, De Pérez, and Du Pré; and finally 'Narcisse écrivain: Pierre Godolin', with the eponymous poet and Jean-Guiraud Dastros.

### THEATRE AND RHETORIC

*Les Farces, Moyen Âge et Renaissance*, II: *Dupés et trompeurs*, ed. and trad. Bernard Faivre, Imprimerie nationale, 553 pp., is the second volume of the series, vol. 1 having been *La guerre des sexes*. F. points out that farce is not politically correct, as it depends on a person's being deceived, and that that person is necessarily weak, if not in some way handicapped, for example blind. Thus the farce is not politically correct. An example of the victim or *badin* is Mahuet in 'Mahuet qui donne ses oeufs au prix du marché', who is tricked into giving away his eggs. Interestingly, the woman involved is not satisfied with having played a trick on Mahuet but feels that he should be taught a lesson, yet through trying to be too clever, the man who got the eggs for nothing also suffers. F. referring also to the other plays in this volume comments, 'Nombreux sont les trompeurs qui basculent ainsi brutalement dans le camp des vaincus, pour avoir voulu trop en faire'. The other farces are: 'George le Veau', 'Trois Galants et Philpot', 'Le Pourpoint rétréci', 'Le Savetier et le Moine', 'Le Pâté et le Tarte', and 'Le Poulailler'. *Farces françaises de la fin du moyen âge*, ed. and trad. André Tissier, 2 vols, Geneva, Droz, 356, 313 pp., are two further volumes of farces translated into modern French. An example in vol. 1 is *Le*

*Savetier Calbain*. The introduction to the play notes that shoemakers often appear in farces, because they sing while they work. Calbain sings contemporary songs, some of which are still known today, or makes up words to well-known tunes. There is here a forerunner of the future *opéra comique*, in which song is mixed with the spoken word. Champion have published three further volumes of the tragedies of Robert Garnier: *Porcie*, ed. Jean-Claude Ternaux, 198 pp., *La Troade*, ed. Jean-Dominique Beaudin, 258 pp., and *Les Juifves*, ed. Sabine Lardon, 266 pp. These critical editions are minutely referenced, e.g. Lardon has a detailed introduction, but also notes on the text, biblical, classical and philosophical references, a concordance with G.'s other works, a glossary, a plan of the text, an index of images, a bibliography, and a biographical table with G.'s life and works, and the contemporary historical events.

Bernard Jolibert, *La Commedia dell'arte et son influence en France du XVIe au XVIIIe siècle*, L'Harmattan, 126 pp., points to two problems in trying to deal with this subject: first, the vastness of its area of influence and, second, how to explain the improvisations that were so much a part of the *Commedia dell'arte*, most of which have been lost. The book aims to give the reader a flavour of this rich and fertile form of theatre and to show its influence on various dramatists, notably Molière, Lesage, Marivaux, and Beaumarchais. Famous names and types are discussed such as Arlequin, Polichinelle, Pierrot, the doctor, and the lovers. The history is divided into ancient times, medieval, 16th, 17th, and 18th centuries.

Jean-Pierre Bordier, *Le jeu de la passion: le message chrétien et le théâtre français (XIIIe–XVIe siècles)*, Champion, 862 pp., is an enormous book, essential for enthusiasts of the mystery plays as well as those interested in religious controversy, and how it is personified. Daniel Poirion, in his preface, notes that these plays were for the people, and the people participated in them as audience. This is why the mystery plays, like the *fabliaux* and sermons in the vernacular, were regarded as subversive by the authorities, who liked to control all artistic and cultural activities. Bordier shows how the polemic of the Church Triumphant versus the Synagogue is changed during the Reformation, to suggest the new faith versus the old Catholic Church. For Agrippa d'Aubigné, of Isaac's twin sons, Esau was Catholicism. 'Les protestants reprochent aux catholiques de judaïser. Ils leur contestent l'election divine, l'espoir du triomphe et la certitude du salut. Les mystères de la Passion ne sont plus joués. Ils tombent peu à peu dans l'oubli'. The book is minutely referenced with a wide bibliography, and indexes of subjects, principal characters, authors and works, and passages from the Bible.

Ullrich Langer, \*Vertu du discours, discours de la vertu: littérature et philosophie morale au XVIe siècle en France, Geneva, Droz, 208 pp., provides a link between the rhetoric of praise, the theory of the virtues, and the representation of human behaviour in the literature of the French Renaissance. Rhetoric and literature themselves define what it means to live well.

Michael Hawcroft, *Rhetoric: Readings in French Literature*, OUP, 268 pp., aims to promote the use of rhetoric as a critical tool for the close reading of French literary texts. H. uses 16th-c. examples in his sections on Poetry (Protestant rhetoric in d'Aubigné's *Les tragiques*) and the self ('A rhetoric of mutability: Montaigne's *Essais*').

## THE SEVENTEENTH CENTURY

ByJ. TRETHEWEY, *University of Wales, Aberystwyth*, andJ. P. SHORT,*formerly Senior Lecturer in French at the University of Sheffield*

### 1. GENERAL

M. M. Bolovan, '*Surfing le dix-septième*: accessing French literature on the World Wide Web', *PFSCL*, 26: 301–08, examines availability and connectivity, and is pleased to find 'valuable resources both in terms of teaching and research', 'on-line or partially on-line courses', many forms of hypertext, and much material made accessible for the first time, but also 'clutter', and 'labyrinths' of 'redundancy and useless information'.

Fumaroli, *Rhétorique*, contains contributions with a European dimension, each with its own extensive bibliography, but those relevant to 17th-c. France are: F. Vuilleumier, 'Les conceptismes' (517–37); B. Beugnot, 'La précellence du style moyen (1625–1650)' (539–99); F. Hallyn 'Dialectique et rhétorique devant la "nouvelle science" du XVIIe siècle' (601–28); G. Declercq, 'La rhétorique classique entre évidence et sublime (1650–1675)' (629–706); V. Kapp, 'L'apogée de l'atticisme français ou l'éloquence qui se moque de la rhétorique (1675–1700)' (707–86); P.-J. Salazar, 'La voix au XVIIe siècle' (787–821).

*SCFS*, 21, prints conference papers on *Orthodoxy and Subversion*: P. Bayley, 'What was Quietism subversive of?' (195–204), recalls 'the celebrated row between Fénelon and Bossuet with Madame Guyon in the middle' and includes in his list of things subverted 'academic theology', the Gallican Church's cherished views on 'gender and authority', its assumptions on class and its xenophobia; L. F. Norman, 'Subversive Ancients? The *Querelle* revisited' (227–38), claims that the writings of the ancients were viewed at that time, 'not as a supporting foundation for contemporary moral and political arrangements, but [. . .] as a potent challenge to them, indeed, as a force of subversion' likely to 'disturb the current social order'. (See also under individual authors.)

*DSS*, 51.4, contains articles on *l'amitié*:J.-M. Constant, 'L'amitié: le moteur de la mobilisation politique dans la noblesse de la première moitié du XVIIe siècle' (593–608), consults the memoirs of La Châtre, Montrésor, Beauvais Nangis, Henri de Campion and La Rochefoucauld;J. Lesaulnier, 'Jean Chapelain et Antoine Le Maistre: histoire d'une amitié contrariée' (609–32), recalls Le M.'s decision to withdraw from society to live in pious solitude, and the reactions of C. and others; E. Méchoulan, 'Le métier d'ami' (633–56), compares

Charron, François de Sales and Malebranche; H. Merlin, 'L'amitié entre le même et l'autre ou quand l'hétérogène devient principe constitutif de société' (657–78), looks at the Cercle Conrart and the creation of the Académie française, Guez de Balzac's *De la conversation des Romains*, the views about friendship expressed by various of Corneille's characters, and finally, by way of contrast, at 17th-c. attitudes to 'les vertus civiles de l'inimitié'; U. Langer, 'De l'amitié à la complaisance: réflexions autour d'une "conversation" de Madeleine de Scudéry' (679–86), uses a passage drawn from *Clélie* as a starting and finishing point for a review of ideas on 'complaisance', its advantages and drawbacks, from classical authors (Aristotle, Cicero), via early Christians (St. Jerome, Aquinas) to Castiglione and 17th-c. France; S. Requemora, 'L'amitié dans les *Maximes* de La Rochefoucauld' (687–728), pieces together the relevant maxims in an attempt to 'cerner la définition toujours fuyante de l'amitié de celui qui pourtant se faisait appeler "La Franchise"'; she finds La R. to be 'plus psychologue que moraliste', seeking to define unconscious as well as conscious motivations; E. Bury, 'L'amitié savante, ferment de la République des lettres' (729–47), makes a general survey of the notion of *sodalitas* going back to classical times, before returning to Jean Le Clerc, Huet, and other 17th-c. examples.

Heyndels, *L'Autre*, prints colloquium *actes*: R. M. Wilkin, 'L'Algonquin par abjection: une mystique aborde le Nouveau Monde' (31–46), claims that the Ursuline missionary Marie de l'Incarnation 'aborde l'altérité du Nouveau Monde tout d'abord en tant que *mystique*', displaying her own feminine brand of mysticism; C. Rizza, 'La notion d'*autre* chez quelques écrivains libertins' (205–11), looks at Théophile, Sorel, Molière, Cyrano, and others; P.-J. Salazar, 'Des aristotéliciens de l'*autre*: Corneille et Mme de Lafayette' (213–22), analyses passages from *Polyeucte* and *La Princesse de Clèves*; M. Alcover, 'Un gay trio: Cyrano, Chapelle, Dassoucy' (265–75), finds it impossible to guess 'comment ils ont vécu leur différence' and must be content to 'analyser comment ils l'ont publiquement gérée'; P. Sellier, ' "Se tirer du commun des femmes": la constellation précieuse' (313–29), summarises the findings of a 'séminaire de recherches sur la préciosité', and reopens the question: 'qu'est-ce qu'être précieuse?' S. Houdard, 'Quand l'autre ressemble au même: le traître dissimulé' (357–66), is concerned with 17th-c. attitudes to heresy and hypocrisy, and points to situations (as in *Tartuffe*) where '*trop d'apparaître* dévot est égal à un *manque d'apparaître* dévot'.

P. Anis, 'L'Eros dans la littérature populaire de la première moitié du XVIIe siècle: vers une codification du comportement amoureux', *PFSCL*, 26:39–50, notes the predominantly didactic and edifying nature of these, for the most part, cautionary publications. J. Tansey and K. Gounaridou, 'The Fouquet Affair: the politics of patronage in theatre and painting under Louis XIV', *SCN*, 57:1–9, discuss the nature of the crises, personal and financial, that a variety of famous artists and writers, friends or protégés of F., experienced on his arrest. J. Charnley, 'L'image de l'Extrême-Orient dans deux journaux du dix-septième siècle', *DFS* 43, 1998:7–21, lists and analyses the numerous references to Japan, China and Siam in the journals of two protestant exiles, Henri Basnage de Beauval and Jean Le Clerc. F. Jacob, 'Extrême Orient ou Orient des extrêmes?', *ib.*, 23–44, cites a number of travellers' tales about China from the late 17th c. to the early 18th c., which inspired many artists to produce works and artefacts of fine quality that nevertheless betrayed utter confusion about the real nature of the country. R. M. Wilkin, 'Les mots et les choses "aux Hurons": l'archéologie d'une rencontre', pp. 55–75 of *Religion and French Literature*, ed. Buford Norman (*FLS*, 25), Amsterdam–Atlanta, GA, Rodopi, 1998, 219 pp., surveys the attitudes of missionaries Gabriel Sagard, Marc Lescarbot, Paul Le Jeune, Chrestien LeClercq, and Jean de Brébeuf to Native American languages, their ultimate aim being to create 'une Nouvelle France francophone'.

*LitC*, 37, prints papers under the title *De l'"utilité" de la littérature*: A. Viala, 'La fonctionnalité du littéraire: problèmes et perspectives' (7–20), discusses various 16th-18th c. French interpretations of Aristotle's *Poetics*, in particular those parts concerning imitation and *plaire et instruire*; B. Parmentier, 'Arts de parler, arts de faire, arts de plaire. La publication des normes éthiques au XVIIe siècle' (141–54), examines an extensive range of titles containing the word 'art' published between 1600 and 1699, in order to 'donner une vue globale des normes par lesquelles les lecteurs sont invités à transformer leurs conduites'; S. van Damme, 'Le collège, la cité et les livres: stratégies éducatives jésuites et culture imprimée à Lyon (1640–1730)' (169–83), studies school textbooks, their production, their aims, and their 'contexte local'. (See also individual authors under PROSE.)

Richard Crescenzo, *Peintures d'instruction: la postérité littéraire des Images de Philostrate en France de Blaise de Vigenère à l'époque classique*, Geneva, Droz, 366 pp., notes the influence of the *Images* on Artus Thomas, on Etienne Binet's *Essay des merveilles de nature*, on the *Cabinet de Monsieur de Scudéry*, on Antoine Godeau's *Tableaux de la pénitence* and on Pierre Le Moyne's *Peintures morales*, among others.

On demonic possession: K. Sauge-Roth, 'Médiations, figures et expériences de *l'autre vie*: Jean-Joseph Surin à la rencontre du démoniaque', Heyndels, *L'Autre*, 375–84, looks at S.'s account of the Loudun affair in his *Triomphe de l'amour divin* . . ., and the relations between Mère Jeanne des Anges and S., whose job it was to exorcise her; N. Paige, 'Je, l'Autre et la possession; ou, pourquoi l'autobiographie démoniaque n'a jamais constitué un genre', *ib.*, 385–92, examines the two known examples of this non-genre, by Jeanne des Anges (1644) and Madeleine Bavent (1652).

*LitC*, 36, prints papers on *Le Baroque en question(s)*: M. Kronegger, 'Introduction au Baroque' (17–22), defines it first by contrasting it with the classicism to follow, then by a series of images designed to underline its spirit of paradox and antithesis; C.-G. Dubois, 'Le Baroque: méthodes d'investigation et essais de définition' (23–40), considers its relationship to mannerism, ending by claiming French classicism to be a 'forme [. . .] étatisée, régulée, centralisée, du baroque européen'; J.-P. Chauveau, 'La France et le Baroque' (143–52), examines 'les causes de cette espèce de frilosité qui a régné et règne encore en France à l'égard du baroque', and picks out 'spécificités ou plus modestement encore, des particularités françaises' in baroque poetry and prose fiction. Kronegger, *Esthétique*, prints conference papers covering art and literature: E. Leonardy, 'La Figure du labyrinthe dans quelques jeux et divertissements du XVIIe siècle' (53–79), cites mazes from several countries, but examines particularly that at Versailles devised by André Le Nôtre, Charles Le Brun, and Charles Perrault, and notes its relationship to La Fontaine's *Fables*; A. Baccar, 'Interférences littéraires et picturales à l'époque baroque en France' (101–10), quotes sea evocations from Gomberville, Tristan, Mlle de Scudéry and Bouhours, but makes only one direct comparison with a contemporary painter (Le Lorrain, with a passage from S.'s *Artamène*).

José Manuel Losada Goya, *Bibliographie critique de la littérature espagnole en France au XVIIe siècle: présence et influence*, Geneva, Droz, 671 pp., gives 441 numbered and annotated 'notices' in alphabetical order of Spanish authors and works, each with the 17th-c. French translation or adaptation. An 'appendice' follows ('notices' 442–517) of French 'ouvrages divers sans source précise' and other works showing a Spanish interest, all similarly annotated. There are many items in this invaluable work which were hitherto unknown or unappreciated. Jean Jenny, \**Répertoire bibliographique des livres imprimés en France au XVIIe siècle*, XXIV, *Bourges* (Bibliographia Aureliana, 172), Koerner, 214 pp.

## 2. POETRY

LA FONTAINE.   Fanny Népote-Desmarres, *La Fontaine: Fables*, PUF, 124 pp., is a dense and stimulating approach to La F. which eschews the usual attitudes in order to penetrate more profoundly into the sources of the fables to be found in La F. himself, showing how his own experience helped to fashion his view of the world. It concludes that 'il apparaît que l'homme s'accomplit à la conjonction de deux modèles: dans l'ordre de l'action, celui du roi "soliveau" et dans l'ordre du verbe celui du "menteur" à la manière d'Ésope et d'Homère, le fabuliste'. D. L. Rubin, 'Translation and atavism; rewriting La F.', *Eustis Vol.*, 199–210, is a subtle and entertaining analysis of the pitfalls which lie in wait for those who would translate the *Fables*. It is almost impossible to do La F. justice as his range is far above that of those who try to translate him.

SAINT-AMANT. N. Négroni, 'Poète, poésie et altérité dans l'oeuvre de Saint-Amant', Heyndels, *L'Autre*, 402–23, is a very detailed investigation of the nature of the poet's identity in the works of St-A. Through a close and thoroughly argued analysis of many of his poems the difficulty of defining his identity is explored and the conclusion is reached that it is 'sans cesse alimentée par ses aspects polymorphes, que son essence provient de l'altérité'. S. K. Silver, 'Questioning taste: St-A. and the poetic grotesque', *PFSCL*, 26:159–73, is a very detailed analysis of two poems of St-A., *Le Fromage* and *Le Melon*, which examines questions of taste, both physical taste, because the poems deal with food and aesthetic taste because of the language that is used. For a period when the French language was being 'stripped of all that was *rude et barbare*, St-A.'s texts actively incorporated the grammarians' cast-offs.'

SCUDÉRY. C. Bernazzoli, 'Voyage réel, voyage imaginaire, voyage initiatique dans le pays de l'Autre: l'itinéraire du héros dans *Alaric ou Rome vaincue*', Heyndels, *L'Autre*, 57–67, describes the journey of Alaric from Sweden to Rome which can be seen as a metaphor for the education of a man as the hero has to conquer himself and change through self-knowledge thanks to this long and perilous journey.

THÉOPHILE DE VIAU. Théophile de Viau, *Oeuvres complètes*, III, ed. Guido Saba, Champion, 416 pp., is the final volume of the complete works of T. in this edition and contains texts attributed to him but which were not published in his lifetime including some *lettres françaises et lettres recueillies par Jean Mairet (1641)*. There are translations of the Latin texts and a chronology of his life. Id., *Théophile de Viau: un poète rebelle*, PUF, xix + 232 pp., studies in detail all the works, beginning with a summary of his ideas on literature. S. naturally devotes most space to the poetry, but he follows this up with close appraisal of *Pyrame et Thisbé*, the *Traité de l'immortalité de l'âme,* the narrative prose, pamphlets and letters. The conclusion underlines the modernity of his political, social and religious thought, particularly his desire for tolerance in all these domains.

TRISTAN L'HERMITE. I. Du Ryer, 'Deux Sonnets pour Monsieur Tristan', présentation de Marcel Israel, *CTH*, 21 : 57–60. These are two sonnets written by Isaac Du Ryer (father of Pierre) in which he praises the young T.'s verses. Isaac Du Ryer was a *douanier* but what his relationship with T. was is not known. The two sonnets, published in 1633 when Du Ryer was 65 and T. 35, are written by the older man in homage to the younger. The poetic talent of T. is recognized and praised by the older poet as he feels his own talent slipping away.

## 3.  DRAMA

Jan Clarke, *The Guénégaud Theatre in Paris (1673–1680)*, 1, Lampeter, Mellen, 1998, 399 pp., is a very full account of the history of the Guénégaud theatre. This volume deals with the foundation of the theatre in 1673 and discusses, among other things, its design and the way the theatre was administered. The description of the interior of the theatre is very interesting as it shows the way the stage was extended, boxes built, and an amphitheatre created. The stage was so designed that it was able to accommodate machine plays. The volume throws much light on a theatre less well known than the Hôtel de Bourgogne and is thorough in its approach based as it is on the author's painstaking researches in the archives of the Comédie-Française. J. Clarke, 'Illuminating the Guénégaud stage: some seventeenth-century lighting effects', *FS*, 53 : 1–15, is a description of the methods of lighting used at the Guénégaud theatre with a discussion of lighting effects in machine plays which gradually became more elaborate. Bruno Clément, *La Tragédie classique*, Seuil, 96 pp., is a very useful little handbook which covers competently and in a readable form all the main aspects of 17th-c. tragedy. However as it is conventional in its approach it does not hint at the richness of the debate which now surrounds the subject. Jane Conroy, *Terres tragiques. L'Angleterre et l'Écosse dans la tragédie française du XVIIe siècle* (Biblio 17, 114), Tübingen, Narr, 508 pp., treats a series of tragedies on topics of recent Scottish and English history written by French authors with a French bias. Mary Stuart and the Earl of Essex are favourite subjects (5 plays between them) but also treated are *Jeanne, Reine d'Angleterre* by La Calprenède which deals with the short reign of the tragic Lady Jane Grey, *Thomas Morus* by Puget de la Serre, and a play on Charles Stuart written in 1660 by one E. Aigrot. The plays are analysed and details are given of performances and editions, and sources and characters discussed from a psychological and moral point of view. The volume also contains informative appendices. N. Ekstein, 'Staging the tyrant on the 17th-c. French stage'. *PFSCL*, 26 : 111–29, examines the role of the tyrant mainly from the point of view of a tyrant's ability to exercise immoderate power and the consequences this has in creating disorder and unbalance in a dramatic situation. P. Gethner, 'La Métamorphose, métaphore de la mimésis théâtrale', Heyndels, *L'Autre*, 145–52, explores the many different kinds of metamorphosis to be found in *tragédies à machines* and *tragédies lyriques*, the reasons for its use and the effect it has on the way it is developed. Id., 'Challenges to royal authority in French classical comedy', *SCFS*, 21:85–90, looks at four comedies (including *Les Amants Magnifiques*) in which royal authority is challenged, unusually, as comedies do not normally feature kings. C. J. Gossip, 'Émulation et insuffisance: la quête de l'autre dans la tragédie classique', Heyndels, *L'Autre*, 163–70, examines references to parents and children in the tragedies of Racine and Corneille. The characters are, as it were, doubled and seek in 'another' the inadequacy they feel in themselves. Pierre Nicole, *Traité de la comédie et autres pièces d'un procès du théâtre*, ed. L. Thirouin, Champion, 1998, 318 pp., is a very useful compendium for following the *querelle du théâtre* of the 1660s. As well as the *Traité de la Comédie* there are other texts relevant to the affair including a hitherto unpublished letter of Singlin, the *Traité* of the Prince de Conti and the texts of Racine's quarrel with Port-Royal, as well as texts relating to *Tartuffe*. There is an excellent introduction. P. Scott, 'Resistance theories, orthodoxy and subversion drama in early modern France', *SCFS*, 21:57–73, examines attitudes towards regicide and their relevance to martyr plays where authority is defied by the martyr. An appendix gives the first list of martyr plays for the period 1596–1675. A. Soare, 'Subversion tragique et orthodoxie tragi-comique: la querelle des genres dans le deuxième tiers du Grand Siècle', *ib.*, 43–55, investigates and teases out the complicated relationship of tragedy and tragi-comedy in the 30s and 40s. The latter uses the former but it is simply a trompe-l'oeil because real suffering is not in question. G. Spielmann, 'Acteur, personnage, *persona*: modes de l'individualité et de l'altérité dans la comédie classique', Heyndels, *L'Autre*, 117–32, examines the relationship between the actor and the personage he is playing and explores the difficult questions which this relationship provokes about identity and reality. Valerie Worth-Stylianou, *Confidential strategies: the evolving role of the 'confident' in French tragic drama (1635–1670)*, Geneva, Droz, 247 pp., traces the history of the role of the *confident* from *Médée* to the *querelle de Sophonisbe* and shows how new strategies were developed from what was originally a dramaturgical device. Between 1660 and 1670 the *confident*'s role becomes less important as it is replaced by monologues and conflictual exchanges but Racine revives the role and the *confident* gradually evolves into a *conseiller* although characters, not called *confidents*, assume that role. This is a very full account of a vital aspect of 17th-c. dramaturgy.

CORNEILLE.    C. J. Gossip, *Corneille: Cinna*, CGFT, 1998, 98 pp., is an excellent addition to this series. G. covers much ground in his discussion of *Cinna* giving chapters on: structure and rhythms; the play in performance; conspirators; victims; tragedy; sources and background. This allows him to provide a great deal of useful information without weighing down the text while at the same time suggesting interesting interpretations of the many aspects of *Cinna* which demand discussion including the everlastingly fascinating clemency question. L. A. Gregorio, 'Their mean task: women and the classical ideal in Corneille's theater', *PFSCL*, 26:371–87, puts forward the view that Aristotle's notion of the mean is more appropriate to the female heroic characters of C. while Plato's ideas of an ideal are more suited to heroes. G. argues that women are more likely to be models of moderation than men in the plays of C. and thus more in keeping with the classical ideal of the mean. M. R. Margitic, 'Mythe, parodie et subversion chez C.', *SCFS*, 21:75–83, discusses the presentation of heroism and heroic action in C. and argues that it can often be seen as a parody of itself. There is much in common between Matamore and Rodrigue, and even Auguste seems at times to be a parody of absolute monarchy. J. Trethewey, 'Chimène's dissembling and its consequences', *RoS*, 17:105–14, provides powerful support for the view that *Le Cid* is really a tragedy by putting forward reasons, based on an analysis of her dissembling throughout the play, why it is improbable that Chimène will ever consent to marry Rodrigue.

MOLIÈRE.    *Le Festin de Pierre (Dom Juan)*, ed. Joan DeJean, Geneva, Droz, 317 pp., is an edition that reproduces for the first time since the 17th c. the 1683 Amsterdam text, the only one not subject to French censorship. The introduction traces the fortunes of *Le Festin de Pierre* (as it was known) showing where the text was censored in the 1682 edition of M.'s works and also discusses the difference which a knowledge of this 1683 Amsterdam edition makes to the understanding of the text. *Le Mariage Forcé*, ed. J. Prest, Exeter U.P., xxxiv + 60 pp., gives the text of the *livret* of the *Comédie-ballet* of 1664, describes the evolution of the text and gives that of the first edition of 1668. This is a very useful edition of an important text. Claude Bourqui, *Les Sources de Molière* (Questions de littérature), SEDES, 480 pp., is a very thorough examination of all the possible sources that M. might have used. These are subjected to a rigorous examination, and only the most reliable ones are presented as being veritable sources. All the relevant details of every work examined whether accepted or rejected are given so that it is possible to build up a very wide view of M.'s knowledge. Some interesting conclusions are reached. There is a spectacular interaction between M.'s plays and the dramatic and narrative literature of the period, and there is frequent recourse to situation patterns found in Italian and Spanish literature. This is not a study of sources as such but really an attempt to provide material in order to be able to 'décrire l'oeuvre dans ses substrats (les strates de choix qui ont abouti au résultat que nous connaissons)'. S. Chaouche, 'L'*actio* 'naturelle' prônée par M.', *RHLF*, 99 : 1169–90, is a study of declamation as understood in the 17th c., and the problems associated with M.'s 'natural' declamation. R. Goodkin, 'Dévier de soi: l'écart spirituel des *Femmes Savantes*', *Eustis Vol.*, 17–31, claims that the comedy is one of the most complex of M.'s and that Philaminte is an intelligent woman who is able to use irony for her purposes. M.-O. Sweetser, 'Reprises, variations et réécriture sur un thème comique chez M.', *ib.*, 33–51, traces the history of the theme of the jealous husband/would-be husband and the woman who loves elsewhere as it develops in Molière's comedies. J. D. Hubert, 'Command and obedience: an additional performative approach to M.'s theater', *ib.*, 53–62, examines those situations in M. where characters though proclaiming their authority and superiority nevertheless meet with defeat, and the comedy they provide. C. Abraham, 'M. and the reality of the *Fête*', *ib.*, 63–71, discusses the clashing worlds of reality and fantasy in *Le Bourgeois Gentilhomme* and *Le Malade Imaginaire*, and questions conventional interpretations of these comedies. J. F. Gaines, '*Le Malade Imaginaire* et le paradoxe de la mort', *ib.*, 73–83, discusses the significance of simulated deaths in *Le M.I.* and goes on to explore how these relate to M.'s view of the world. M. Greenberg, 'Molière: *Corpus Politicum*', *ib.*, 84–100, analyses, with the help of Freud, those aspects of Argan and Harpagon which display their concern with their bodies and their bodily functions which in turn throw light on their relationships with themselves, their families, and the world. C. J. Spencer, '*Dom Juan*: le rendez-vous de Samarkande', *ib.*, 101–13, juggles with great dexterity with questions of truth and non-truth in the play showing how impossible it is for the characters to know the truth or indeed what truth is as it is constantly subverted by Dom Juan, the arch-liar and his equally lying servant Sganarelle. W. O. Goode, 'Reflections in a bourgeois eye: noble essence in *Le Bourgeois Gentilhomme*', *RoN*, 39 : 163–69, looks at the role of Dorante and the way M. presents him as representing the nobility and argues it is not necessarily a negative view. J. Serroy, '*Tartuffe* ou l'autre', Heyndels, *L'Autre*, 153–62, argues that Tartuffe represents *l'autre* in various ways which make Orgon and the other members of this family reveal aspects of their personality which would otherwise not appear. He is a disturbing presence, representing something from outside which threatens the unity not only of the family but of society. S. Zebouni, '*L'Amphitryon* de M. ou l'autre du sujet', *ib.*, 347–55, examines identity and the expression of *moi-non moi* in the personages of Amphitryon/Jupiter and Sosie/Sosie. H. Melehy, 'M. and the value of image: *Le Bourgeois Gentilhomme*', *PFSCL*, 26:29–38, discusses the relationship between the *noblesse d'épée* and the bourgeoisie, arguing that the play shows the way the bourgeoisie is already moving in order to constitute itself as the ruling class. J. F. Gaines, 'Dandin on the big screen of history', *ib.*, 309–317, is an account of Roger Planchon's film of *George Dandin*. L. Chae-Kwang, 'Du texte écrit au texte joué. Réception scénique comme valorisation de la logique du caractère chez M. à travers *L'École des femmes*', *ib.*, 389–404, is an examination of the necessity of comparing and contrasting the text as written and the text as performed if a full understanding of the play is to be reached. L. W. Riggs, 'Dom Juan and Harpagon: M.'s symbiotic twin archetypes of modernity', *ib.*, 405–23, makes an unusual comparison between these two characters. D. Shaw, 'Legal elements in *Le Misanthrope*', *NFS*, 38:1–11, is an interesting analysis of *Le Misanthrope* using the legal background which erupts so frequently into the play to throw light on the character of Alceste. S. Simkova, '*Tartuffe*. Les Liaisons dangereuses', *RHT*, 215–32, studies various productions of *Tartuffe* in Slovakia and at the Prague National Theatre in the 80s. The productions were linked to the political background of Slovakia of the period and exploited, almost to a grotesque extent, possible interpretations of the text.

QUINAULT. Quinault, *Livrets d'Opéra*, ed. Buford Norman, 2 vols, Toulouse, Société de Littératures Classiques, 282, 318 pp., is an edition of eleven *livrets* written by Q. for the operas of Lully produced in the period 1673–1686. There is a very useful introduction which provides information about Q.'s career and the development of the opera in this period. Each *livret* has a very full notice giving the dates of the first performance of the opera and other details. This is a welcome edition as these texts are not easily available.

RACINE. Racine, *Théâtre-Poésie*, ed. Georges Forestier, Gallimard–NRF, 1801 pp., is Vol. 1 of the new Pléiade Racine replacing that of Raymond Picard and is a very worthy successor to that edition. Although the introduction does not cover much new ground, the section called 'Lire Racine' recognizes the importance of speech in R. and looks at, among other aspects, the pronunciation of the time. The texts printed are, unlike those of most modern editions, the first editions of the plays and the lines are numbered (unlike Picard's edition), but an ingenious device allows references from editions with different line numbering to be easily identified. Each play is followed by a section called 'autour de' which prints contemporary texts that the production of each play provoked and this is exceptionally useful. The works, plays and poems, are presented in chronological order and the poetic works are not separated from the plays but are found at their date. The *Notices* are placed at the end and are full, informative and stimulating. The notes are extremely useful. Vol. II is expected in a few years time. Jean-Pierre Battesti and Jean-Charles Chauvet, *Tout Racine*, introd. Christian Biet, Larousse, 663 pp., is a compendium which is rather more than a work of reference, and it gives very full pointers to all aspects of R.'s life and work. Inevitably the section dealing with criticism is too brief to be of much use but for a quick overview of a very vast field this can be helpful and save time. Jean Emelina, *Racine infiniment*, SEDES, 207 pp., is an eminently readable survey of R. and approaches to his tragedies at the end of the 20th century. Chapters cover the ways in which R. is appreciated today, the enigma of R.'s life, R. as a writer of tragedy and his treatment of the passions. The attempt is made to pin down what is meant by Racinian tragedy and concludes that its ambiguity will always defeat definition. Volker Schröder, *La Tragédie du sang d'Auguste. Politique et intertextualité dans 'Britannicus'* (Biblio 17, 119), Tübingen, Narr, 327 pp., is far more than a discussion of *Britannicus*. S. covers a whole range of issues illustrating as he does much of the complexity and diversity of Racinian tragedy. By looking in detail at aspects of intertextuality in *Britannicus* he opens perspectives which are original and profound not only on this tragedy but on the whole of R.'s *oeuvre*. Amy Wygant, *Towards a Cultural Philology. 'Phèdre' and the Construction of 'Racine'* (Legenda Research Monographs in French Studies, 4), Oxford, EHRC, 158 pp., discusses *Phèdre* under four headings: music, design, garden, and sublime, probing the layers of meaning which are revealed when these are examined. W. draws on art and musical history as well as the history of the formal garden to arrive at a concept of 'Racine' as distinct from Racine. *DFS*, 49, is a special issue devoted to Racine introduced by R.-L. Barnett and includes: J. F. Gaines, 'New world order: R. and the *Translatio Imperii*' (4–14), an investigation into new world order in various Racinian tragedies; R. E. Goodkin, 'Gender reversal in R.'s historical and mythological tragedies' (15–27), aims to show that R., in his historical tragedies, manipulates gender roles so as to heighten the power of female characters and lessen the power of male heroes. The opposite is the case in the mythological tragedies; A. Niderst, 'Les harmonies raciniennes' (28–37), argues that Greek tragedy does not have a direct influence on Racinian tragedy but rather leaves echoes; L. W. Riggs, 'In the labyrinth of discourse' (38–52), sees the major issues in R.'s plays as the difference between the constative-objective, merely noting what is, and the performative, willing certain things to be; for

C. Venesoen, 'Réflexions sur le péché d'adultère dans le théâtre de R.' (53–62), adultery in R. is seen as an irreparable fault which brings shame but it is painted with some ambiguity so as not to offend Louis XIV; R. Racevskis, 'Generational transition in *Andromaque*' (63–72), examines the presentation of the past and the future in the tragedy; T. J. Reiss, 'Between sovereignty and tyranny: *Britannicus*' (73–89), looks at the meaning and legitimacy of sovereign authority with special reference to Tacitus; H. T. Barnwell, '*Bérénice*: drama and elegy of self-deception' (90–102), demonstrates that it is possible for drama and elegy to be integrated parts of a dramatic action; J. Campbell, '*Bajazet* and Racinian tragedy: expectations and difference' (103–18), points to the inconsistencies of plotting and characterisation and asks whether, if a Racinian form of tragedy exists, this play fits into it; W. D. Howarth, 'The nature of tragedy in *Iphigénie*: a comparative approach' (119–31), illustrates those aspects of *Iphigénie* which make it tragic; L. K. Horowitz, 'R.'s laws' (132–44), investigates the significance of 'law' and 'legality' in *Phèdre* with regard to the political background and personal relationships; A. Soare, '*Phèdre* et les métaphores du labyrinthe: les tracés et les formes' (145–57), shows that in *Phèdre* words which express movement without progress echo and re-echo; R.-L. Barnett, 'The pathology of refraction: R.'s inbound enactments' (158–66), argues that 'the imperilled representation of refractive musings of inwardly propelled leaps and bounds is not a Racinian contrivance'; B. R. Woshinsky, '*Tombeau de "Phèdre"*: repression, confession and métissage in R. and Claire de Duras' (167–81), compares *Phèdre* and the early 19th-c. novel *Ourika*; M. J. Muratore, 'R.'s *Athalie* or the power of precedent' (182–92), argues that the tragedy is more about the effectiveness of neo-classical imperatives than about the legacy of the Old Testament; A. Maazaoui, 'Le R. de Proust' (193–202), shows in what ways Proust uses R. — he uses him to find ideas and recreates him in his own writing; J. Baetens, 'Vers classique et poésie contemporaine; pour introduire l'idée de R. dans un débat récent' (203–09), links R. to some modern approaches to poetry. *OC*, 24, a special issue devoted to R., has a wide range of articles. E. Bury, 'Les antiquités de R.' (29–48), examines antique sources of R. showing that it is essential to keep in mind the Latin sources as well as the Greek; M. Hawcroft, 'Le langage racinien' (49–74), is a very thorough analysis of the elements which go to make R.'s verse unique and inimitable; F. Sick, 'Dramaturgie et tragique de l'amour dans le théâtre de R.' (75–94), uses dramaturgy to suggest that, in R., what is a fault does not necessarily relate to a moral order; J. Emelina, 'La tragédie de R. et le mal' (95–114), is a long examination of the meaning of 'mal' and how it relates to what is tragic in R.; S. M. Guénon, 'La passion R. —

sous le lierre de la psychologie et la résistance à la psychanalyse'
(115–35), is a dense survey of attempts made to define and understand
what is meant by passion in the tragedies of R.; P. Ronzeaud, 'R.
et la politique: la perplexité et la critique' (136–58), presents an
overview of the role of politics in R., but politics defined in different
ways; B. Chédozeau, 'La dimension religieuse dans quelques tragédies
de R.; où fuir?' (159–80), argues that violence in R. comes from the
sacred: the Racinian universe is one where 'l'homme éperdu de sacré
ne peut se retrouver que sans raison'; C. J. Spencer, 'Impasse du
discours: R., Port-Royal et les signes' (181–92), is a discussion of the
significance of signs using *Bajazet* as the text to illustrate the argument;
M.-O. Sweetser, 'Les femmes dans la vie et l'oeuvre de R.' (193–215),
surveys the female characters and brings out their individual contribution to a general picture of how R. envisaged his woman characters;
C. Mazouer, 'R. et la comédie' (216–32), discusses the genesis of *Les
Plaideurs* and makes the point that even in comedy 'R. reste assez
profondément pessimiste'; C. Rizza, 'Fortunes et infortunes de R. en
Italie' (233–47), discusses R.'s fortunes in Italy; P. France, 'R.
britannicus' (248–63), is an overview of English and Scottish
translations of R. from the 17th c. to the present day; F. Nies, 'Le
"premier poète moderne" ravalé au rang de "farce bigarrée"?
Prolégomènes à un R. allemand' (264–80), shows that R. was
frequently misunderstood in Germany; M. P. Schmitt, 'L'hyperclas-
sique (R. à l'école)' (281–90), shows that although R. figures widely
on school programmes he is not always appreciated; F. Lagarde,
'1939, année racinienne' (293–314), is a fascinating survey of the way
the tercentenary of R.'s birth celebrated in 1939 but concludes:
'l'année racinienne ou beaucoup de bruit pour rien'. *RLC*, 73, is
devoted to articles concerning translations of R. into other languages.
The translations discussed are in English, Dutch, German, Italian,
modern Greek, Russian, Spanish, Swedish, and Hungarian. J. Dubu,
'*Mithridate*, pourquoi?', *RHLF*, 99: 17–40, is a long, subtle analysis of
the play taking into account many aspects such as rhyme, historical
background, interpretation of relationships, and character. M. Reilly,
'R.'s visions of violence: the case of *Bajazet*, *Britannicus* and *Bérénice*',
*NFS*, 38: 12–23, argues very clearly that violence although physically
absent from R.'s tragedies is nevertheless everywhere. J. Campbell,
'R. and the Augustinian inheritance: the case of *Andromaque*', *FS*,
53:279–91, is a very penetrating and well-argued article using an
analysis of *Andromaque* to continue the debate on the influence of
Jansenism on Racine. M. Reilly, 'Confessional discourse in *Britannicus*,
*Bérénice* and *Phèdre*: R.'s dark epiphany', *SCFS*, 21:91–99, examines
the role of confession in these three tragedies and shows how
confession is used as a means of manipulating others rather than as a

means of revealing the truth about oneself. E. R. Koch, 'Deferred acts: *Bajazet*, untimeliness and tragic orthodoxy', *ib.*, 101–11, looks at the role of time and space in *Bajazet* and concludes that the intensely interrelated use of these in this play means it 'should [. . .] come to occupy the place of orthodox model of tragic plot and temporality in the Racinian *oeuvre*'. R. Calder, 'Contrition, casuistry and Phèdre's sense of sin', *ib.*, 113–22, is a sequel to the author's article in *SCFS*, 20 (see *YWMLS*, 60: 133). It examines the question of Phèdre's view of her guilt in the light of contemporary Jesuit and Jansenist attitudes. F. Jaouen, '*Esther/Athalie*: histoire sacrée, histoire exemplaire', *ib.*, 123–31, argues that the sacred tragedies are bound to present a different concept of history, one based on 'un schéma providentiel' which shows history 'en perpétuel devenir' as distinct from the 'vision statique de l'histoire' in the profane tragedies. F. Sick, 'Étranger et aimé: l'autre dans les tragédies de R.', Heyndels, *L'Autre*, 425–39, investigates the relationship of lovers in R. and shows that the 'otherness' of the loved one (where love is not reciprocated) is the source of a new kind of tragic in the plays. S. Maslan, 'Féminité juive et le problème de la représentation au dix-septième siècle', *ib.*, 305–12, discusses the question of the morality of the theatre as seen by Jansenists, and the role of Esther in proving it possible to represent Christian virtues on the stage. M. Reilly, 'Racinian words of power', *AUMLA*, 91 : 13–25, examines, with examples, the different uses of the words *pouvoir* and *puissance* and comes to the conclusion that R.'s words of power uncover an astonishingly negative vision of man's will to power and the impossibility of his altering it. H. Ogura, 'Transgression du "naturel": du langage tragique des pièces mythologiques de R. - de *La Thébaïde* à *Andromaque*', *ELLF*, 74 : 3–16, discusses the use of language in these plays with emphasis on the expression of themes and motifs, and argues that the essential function of the poetic language of R. is to bring out the tragic sense of the play. K. Nagamori, 'Essai de définition du tragique racinien', *ib.*, 17–32. It would be difficult for an article to live up to this title. This one makes a brave attempt and concludes that the blindness of the characters is an important factor, because, coming into conflict as it does with a lucid awareness, it leads to ultimate despair.

ROTROU. R. Pirson, 'Du champ de la perception à la fracture du doute: la représentation de l'autre dans *Le véritable Saint-Genest*', Heyndels, *L'Autre*, 339–45, is mainly a discussion of perspective in the play and how that is relevant to the questions of *feinte* and *vérité*, and concludes that the representation on the stage of the conversion of Genest reflects the hidden face of a doubt which ran through the 17th century. Rotrou, *L'Hypocondriaque ou le Mort amoureux*, ed. J.-C.

Vuillemin, Geneva, Droz, 242 pp. This text is of particular interest because it contains dramatic elements that will recur in R.'s theatre. TRISTAN L'HERMITE. Tristan L'Hermite, *Oeuvres complètes*, vol. 5, sous la diréction de Roger Guichemerre avec la collaboration de Daniela Dalla Valle et Anne Tournon, Champion, 502 pp. This volume completes the publication of all T.'s works in this edition, which makes texts easily available which previously were not so. This volume contains three plays: *La Folie du Sage*, *Amarillis*, and *Le Parasite*, followed by the very interesting *plaidoyers historiques*.

### 4. PROSE

Debaisieux, *Violence*, prints conference papers covering the 16th-19th cs: N. Ferrand, 'Histoires de Peaux d'Âne, d'Apulée à Sade, ou les métamorphoses de la violence' (449–55), refers in passing to Scarron's *Roman comique*, Molière's *Le Malade imaginaire*, and Perrault's *Contes*. See also individual authors below. T. Pech, ' "Enfants de la mort": l'altérité criminelle dans les Histoires tragiques du premier XVIIe siècle', Heyndels, *L'Autre*, 95–115, examines collections by Belleforest, Rosset, and Camus. C. Hogg, 'Strong women, illustrious men: constructing history and civic virtue in the Grand Siècle', *PFSCL*, 26:19–27, compares two collections of 'illustrious lives', Mlle de Scudéry's *Les Femmes illustres ou Les Harangues héroïques* and Perrault's *Les Hommes illustres qui ont paru en France pendant ce siècle*. C. L. Chappell, ' "The pains I took to save my/his family": escape accounts by a Huguenot mother and daughter after the Revocation of the Edict of Nantes', *FHS*, 22:1–64, compares two accounts of separate departures, reproducing both in appendices.

G. Dotoli, 'L'Autre du moraliste', Heyndels, *L'Autre*, 171–84, takes up yet again the question: 'qu'est-ce qu'un moraliste?' in order to 'contribuer à une définition plus claire' suggesting that 'la connotation principale du moraliste est l'observation' in a scientific, analytical sense, his principal example being La Bruyère. Dagen, *Épicure*, prints papers on *la pensée morale* in the 16th-18th cs: P. Zoberman, 'Le lieu de l'altérité dans l'éloquence d'apparat' (223–35), points out various ways in which *altérité* is used to underline the uniqueness and perfection attributed to Louis XIV. F. Wild, 'Anecdote et réflexion morale dans les ana' (267–85), examines 'les premiers ana, réellement recueillis des conversations savantes, et les ana savants qui leur succèdent', and describes their contents and their evolution; A. Larue, 'Théâtre du monde et théâtralité des supplices' (289–315), writes of 16th- and 17th-c. 'théâtres' which 'n'ont de théâtral que leur titre', and which are 'recueils d'emblèmes ou d'exempla: un sous-genre à l'intérieur de la vaste pratique de la compilation'; E. Bury, 'L'écriture à l'épreuve de la pensée: essais, maximes et aphorismes à l'âge baroque', *LitC*, 36:307–25, cites Montaigne, Du Vair, and Guez de Balzac among others.

Edwige Keller, *Poétique de la mort dans la nouvelle classique (1660–1680)*, Champion, 544 pp., bases her study of 107 *nouvelles* on extensive tables and statistics, and finds that, despite profound changes in public taste, there is much continuity in the treatment of death between the *romans* of the previous generation and the *nouvelles*. D. Riou, 'Sorel et Scarron à l'aube du roman moderne: métadiscours et crise de la représentation', Pfersmann, *Fondements*, 35–43, examines the nature of the *métadiscours* in *Le Berger extravagant* and *Le Roman comique*, finding that there is a change from the seriousness of Sorel in the days of Richelieu, when 'l'âge héroïque croyait maîtriser la condition humaine', to the flippancy of Scarron during the 'période de déflation idéologique qui accompagne le ministère de Mazarin'. Nathalie Grande, *Stratégies de romancières: de 'Clélie' à 'La Princesse de Clèves' (1654–1678)* (Lumière classique, 20), Champion, 497 pp., has written 'une étude sociopoétique du roman féminin au milieu du XVIIe siècle'. G. asserts of her novelists that 'les découvrir, c'est découvrir à travers elles un peu de ce "continent perdu" qu'est le roman du XVIIe siècle, mais c'est aussi prendre conscience des lois non-écrites qui gouvernent le champ littéraire'. F. Assaf, 'Le corps baroque dans les histoires comiques', *LitC*, 36:79–94, cites many novels and stories in which 'le corps prime l'esprit et le dirige', from *La Vie généreuse des mercelots, gueuz et boesmiens* (1596) to Préfontaine's *L'Orphelin infortuné* (1660). Harold Neemann, *Piercing the Magic Veil Toward a Theory of the 'Conte'* (Biblio 17, 116), Tübingen, Narr, 187 pp., picks out the particular features of narrative structure and style in the *conte merveilleux* that distinguish it from other literary and folkloric forms, enumerating its 'diverse functions in the production of meanings within French society, culture and literature', and surveying the various approaches — historical, linguistic, and psychoanalytical — that have been made to it. G. Haroche-Bouzinac, 'La lettre à l'âge classique, genre mineur?', *RHLF*, 99:183–203, discusses the genre, its definitions, its fluctuations in respectability, and its gradual *minorisation* between the 1620s and the 1780s. L. Plazenet-Haut, 'D'un roman baroque', *LitC*, 36:293–305, defines a European form of the novel, prevalent between 1580 and 1660, and deriving largely from the 'Éthiopiques' (Heliodorus *et al*).

AULNOY. *Contes II: Contes nouveaux ou Les Fées à la mode*, ed. Jacques Barchilon and Philippe Hourcade, STFM, 1998, 577 pp., contains, besides 12 *contes*, a 'Glossaire', a 'Supplément bibliographique', and the 'Table des matières' for this and vol. 1 (see *YWMLS*, 59:139). Anne Defrance, *Les contes de fées et les nouvelles de Madame d'Aulnoy*

*(1690–1698): l'imaginaire féminin à rebours de la tradition,* Geneva, Droz, 1998, 361 pp., while not neglecting 'l'analyse des fonctions et des motifs', prefers to *'questionner l'origine du plaisir* qu'ils [les contes] produisent, examiner les raisons de cette fascination propre au genre [...] et *examiner les enjeux culturels et sociaux* qui les soutendent' (D.'s italics). C. Marin, 'Plaisir et violence dans les contes de fées de Madame d'Aulnoy', Debaisieux, *Violence,* 263–72, lists 18 forms of violence upon which A. rings the changes, then looks at the pleasure derived from violence by the perpetrators and spectators, and finally at 'le plaisir et la violence du point de vue de la victime'. M.-A. Thirard, 'Le meccano des contes de Madame d'Aulnoy', *PFSCL,* 26: 175–93, makes an inventory of five techniques employed by A. to resolve narrative problems presented by oral material from popular sources to be turned into sophisticated literature. A. L. Birberick, 'Fatal curiosity: d'Aulnoy's "Le Serpentin vert"', *ib.,* 283–88, points out that this *conte* retells the story of Psyche and Cupid with vital modifications in theme and structure which 'open up another level of didactic meaning in the tale', one less unflattering to women than is the case in the original.

BALZAC. M. Bombart, 'Représenter la distinction: comédie et urbanité chez Guez de Balzac', *LitC,* 37: 117–40, compares two essays from B.'s 1644 *Oeuvres diverses,* his *Réponse à deux questions, ou du caractère et de l'instruction de la comédie* and his *De la conversation des Romains,* and finds in them 'une étrange proximité de thèmes et d'objets'. Id., 'Guez de Balzac et Rome: oubli, trace, réminiscence', *RSH,* 256: 115–40, looks at *De la conversation des Romains* and asks why B., an admirer of ancient Rome, here doubts the continuing value of its written history as a 'modèle susceptible de fournir aux contemporains des exemples de vie et d'action'.

CAMUS. E. Henein, 'Le coeur mangé ... ruminé', Debaisieux, *Violence,* 77–88, picks the story, 'Le coeur mangé', from C.'s *Les spectacles d'horreur* (1630) as an example of the graphic style and didactic purpose of his *histoires tragiques,* and reproduces it in its entirety in an appendix. M. Vernet, 'Jean-Pierre Camus: prière pour demander à Dieu le bon usage de la violence', *ib.,* 89–98, quotes examples of violence from the fictions of C., and explains them by the violence of his times, and by his aim to inspire his readers with models of singular courage in adversity — an aim for the success of which C. inserts a prayer in the preface to *Les Evenemens singuliers* (1628).

CHALLE. A. de Sola, 'Héroïsme et vraisemblance romanesque: le cas des *Illustres Françaises*', *NFS,* 37.2, 1998: 12–25, accounts for the popularity of this work at the time of its publication by the fact 'qu'il a probablement été senti comme actuel ou contemporain pour ses lecteurs', and that C.'s version of *vraisemblance* in the depiction of his heroines contributed much to this sense of immediacy.

CHAPELAIN. *De la lecture des vieux romans*, ed. Jean-Pierre Cavaillé, Paris-Zanzibar, 89 pp., is accompanied by a 'Présentation' which reprints the editor's article, 'Galanterie et histoire de "l'antiquité moderne"', *DSS*, 50, 1998:387–415 (see *YWMLS*, 60:116). D. Blocker, 'Jean Chapelain et *les lumières de Padoue*: l'héritage italien dans les débats français sur l'utilité du théâtre (1585–1640)', *LitC*, 37:97–116, discusses the repercussions in early 17th-c. France of the Italian 'querelle du *Pastor Fido*', and in this context 'les déplacements que la notion d'utilité subit en France par l'intermédiaire de Jean Chapelain'. J. Peters, 'Ideology, culture and the threat of allegory in Chapelain's theory of *La Vraisemblance*', *RR*, 89, 1998:491–505, looks at C.'s preface to Marino's epic *Adonis* (1623).

CHOISY. N. Hammond, 'All dressed up . . .: L'abbé de Choisy and the theatricality of subversion', *SCFS*, 21:165–72, notes the associations with theatre made by C. in his references to cross-dressing, and his awareness of the 'destabilising effect' of the practice on spectators, whether in a theatre or in the outside world.

CHORIER. *L'Académie des dames ou La Philosophie dans le boudoir du Grand Siècle*, ed. Jean-Pierre Dubost, Arles, Picquier, 317 pp., is a critical edition of the French version (1680) of these erotic dialogues first published in Latin in about 1660.

CONRART. N. Schapira, 'Les enjeux d'une correspondance instructive: les lettres de Valentin Conrart à Lorenzo Magalotti', *LitC*, 37:155–68, takes these letters as examples to show why C. was considered by his contemporaries to be a perfect 'représentant de l'idéal social et culturel de l'honnête homme'.

CYRANO DE BERGERAC. P. Harry, 'L'altérité cyranienne: le jeu de cache-cache esthético-idéologique d'un marginal fiéffé', Heyndels, *L'Autre*, 441–51, finds in C.'s novels and *Lettres* the expression of one who wishes to 'revendiquer le droit d'être contre, dans tous ses aspects', who 'se veut exclu de tout système de domination'.

DESMARETS DE SAINT-SORLIN. M. Laugaa, 'Violence et représentation dans l'*Ariane* de Desmarets', Debaisieux, *Violence*, 195–205, surveys with examples the 'relations coupables que nouent ensemble, dans l'enceinte du roman de Desmarets, violence et représentation'.

SIMON DUCROS. M.-C. Canova-Green, 'La grâce, ou les derniers jours d'un révolté: *L'Histoire de la vie de Henry, dernier duc de Montmorency*', *SCFS*, 21:133–43, introduces this 1643 work by a former protégé of the duke which reacts to official versions of events leading up to his execution.

DU PÉRIER. E. Méchoulan, 'Noces ou funérailles? Ce que déflorer veut dire dans *Les Amours de Pistion et de Fortunie* d'Antoine du Périer',

Debaisieux, *Violence*, 165–74, shows the use to which this author puts *topoi* as preambles to his narrations which recount physical violence (by men) and verbal violence (by women).

FÉNELON. R. Morel, 'Sight unseen: Fénelon and the myth of invisibility', *NFS*, 37.2, 1998: 1–11, considers 'L'anneau de Gygès' and other stories from the *Fables et opuscules pédagogiques* (1690) to be tales with predictable moral conclusions, but which exploit the motif of *le merveilleux* to intriguing effect. C. Noille-Clauzade, 'La morale du *Télémaque*: pour une poétique platonicienne de la fable', *RSH*, 254:85–106, demonstrates that F.'s work does not meet Aristotle's definition of an epic, and asks why F. labelled thus a work in which 'il y a absence d'action, de système des faits', but which does have a structure 'fondée sur trois cycles éthiques', each with its utopia which 'vient figurer la perfection *ad hoc* de l'argumentation'. *Correspondance*, ed. Jean Orcibal, Jacques Le Brun, and Irénée Noye, XVI: *Les dernières années (1712–1715), texte* (HICL, 397), 464 pp.; XVII: *Les dernières années (1712–1715), commentaire* (HICL, 398), 398 pp.

FOIGNY. B. Knauff, 'The curious traveler in Foigny's *La Terre australe connue* (1676)', *PFSCL*, 26:273–82, describes Sadeur the narrator as being 'curious' in both senses of the word - an oddity who is desirous to learn.

GOMBERVILLE. M. Bertaud, 'Le *Polexandre* de Gomberville, quel procès de la violence?', Debaisieux, *Violence*, 185–94, writes of 'violence *blanche*' (legitimate, justified) and 'violence *noire*' (the reverse) and their manifestation in this novel among Christians, Moslems, and pagans, and reveals thereby G.'s prejudices and those of his time.

LA FAYETTE. *La Princesse de Clèves*, ed. Philippe Sellier (Le Livre de Poche classique), Librairie Générale Française, 253 pp., replaces Béatrice Didier's edition of 1972. Françoise Gevrey, *L'Esthétique de Madame de Lafayette*, SEDES, 1997, 250 pp., studies all the works attributed to L., but with *La Princesse de Clèves* as the centre of attention. Kim Sung, *Les Récits dans 'La Princesse de Clèves': tentative d'analyse structurale*, Saint-Genouph, Nizet, 1997, 282 pp., relies on narrative categories defined by Benveniste, and Bourneuf and Ouellet, in her analysis of the various récits, to chart the passage of time in the novel. Janet Letts, *Legendary Lives in 'La Princesse de Clèves'*, Charlottesville, Rookwood, 1998, 286 pp., is concerned with the novel's historical figures, present either in the action or in *récits* by characters. She concentrates on three figures in particular, Diane de Poitiers, Catherine de Médicis, and the Reine-Dauphine. André Brink, *The Novel: Language and Narrative from Cervantes to Calvino*, Basingstoke, Macmillan, 1998, 373 pp., devotes a chapter to *La Princesse de Clèves* (46–64), in which he concentrates on the theme of 'language-as-dissimulation'. *Approaches to Teaching Lafayette's 'La Princesse de Clèves'*, ed. Faith E. Beasley and Katharine Ann Jensen, NY, MLA, 1998, 211 pp., is a series of 23 essays covering reception, themes and narrative. F. Denis, '*La Princesse de Clèves*: Lafayette et Cocteau, deux versions', *FR* 72:285–96, compares the novel with the film scenario and (surprisingly?) prefers the first. C. Cartmill and R. Colborne, 'Qui a peur de la princesse de Clèves? ou Qu'est-ce que la critique féministe peut nous dire sur le classicisme?', *DFS*, 48:19–33, look at recent feminist interpreters of classicism and of this novel and conclude firstly that 'la critique a souvent beaucoup plus à dire sur nous-mêmes que sur les oeuvres', and then that there is need for 'un modèle éclaté' which would 'repenser la différence sexuelle, non pas comme partage en sujet et objet, mais comme élément structurant du texte'.

LA MOUSSAYE. *Correspondance du Marquis et de la Marquise de La Moussaye (1619–1630)*, ed. Jean-Luc Tulot, pref. Janine Garrisson, Champion, 440 pp., contains letters on both domestic and state subjects by these two high-ranking protestants from their estates in Britanny to family and a wide circle of distinguished acquaintances.

LA ROCHEFOUCAULD. *LitC*, 35, contains conference papers on the *Maximes et Réflexions diverses*: J. Rohou, 'La Rochefoucauld, témoin d'un tournant de la condition humaine' (7–35), writes first of La R.'s analysis of 'amour-propre', of the influence of Augustinianism on him, then defines at length the nature of the above-mentioned 'tournant'; L. van Delft, 'La Rochefoucauld et l'anatomie de tous les replis du coeur' (37–62), dwells on the word 'anatomie' and its significance to La R., seeing him as an 'homme de science' comparable to Galen; H. Merlin, 'Raisons historiques d'un genre: maximes (politiques) et amour-propre' (63–92), sets out her views on the words 'maxime', 'politique', 'amour-propre' and 'intérêt'; L. Thirouin, 'Réflexions sur un titre' (93–108), reflects on the title *Réflexions ou Sentences et Maximes morales* which he does not like, preferring posterity's simplification, but then asks about the author's intention: 'n'est-ce pas le signe que, pour lui, les trois termes ne se recouvraient pas exactement?'; M. Escola, ' "Ce désordre a ses grâces": effets de série, raison des effets dans la deuxième édition des *Maximes*' (111–51), ponders on the changes, additions, suppressions to be found in the five successive editions between 1664 and 1678 'et tout particulièrement [les] opérations qui intéressent la deuxième'; C. Noille-Clauzade, 'Les *Maximes* à l'oeuvre: le Livre de Sable' (153–74), dwells on the possibility or impossibility of in any way improving on the collection; G. Ferreyrolles, 'La Rochefoucauld devant la paresse' (175–94), searches for 'ce que représente existentiellement la paresse pour La Rochefoucauld, puis le rapport de celle-ci à la morale tel qu'il ressort des *Maximes* et *Réflexions diverses*' and finally attempts an 'esquisse d'une métaphysique de la paresse'. R. Hodgson, 'Délicatesse, justesse, politesse: qualités intellectuelles, morales et esthétiques dans les *Maximes* et les *Réflexions diverses* de La Rochefoucauld' (195–206), looks at the various contexts where these 'qualités de l'esprit' appear, especially in the *Réflexions diverses*, and asserts that, for La R., the three notions 'ne sont pas seulement des qualités intellectuelles, mais aussi des qualités morales et esthétiques qui se trouvent au coeur même de sa pensée morale'. O. Roth, 'La morale de la retraite: le cas La Rochefoucauld', Dagen, *Morale*, 61–72, compares two of La R.'s *Réflexions diverses*: II, 'De la société' and XVII, 'De la retraite', and shows that, despite superficial differences, they treat the same subject - *l'honnêteté* - and that 'leurs schémas d'argumentation se ressemblent' like 'deux faces d'un diptyque'. Three articles appear in *Littérature*, 39, 1998: B. Guion, ' "Cette obscure clarté": des secrets et de leur dévoilement dans les *Maximes*' (45–62); A. A. Morello, 'Des *Maximes* aux modernes' (73–85); P. Moret, 'Les *Maximes* et la question de la réflexivité' (63–71). P. Campion, 'La maxime dans la lumière de la mort', *Poétique*, 118:197–207, dwells, in the company of Hegel and others, on La R.'s assertion concerning 'la fausseté du mépris de la mort'. R. G. Hodgson, 'Le "commerce des honnêtes gens": le Moi, l'Autre et les autres chez La Rochefoucauld', Heyndels, *L'Autre*, 185–92, reflects on the variety of relationships that the moralist experiences with 'l'autre', 'les autres', 'autrui', 'le prochain', etc. Pierre Campion, *Lectures de La Rochefoucauld*, Rennes U.P., 1998, 159 pp., is an anthology of reactions.

LAMBERT. R. Marchal, 'Grandeur et servitude de l'officier d'après les écrits de Madame de Lambert', *Hipp Vol.*, 41–48, considers her *Lettre d'une dame à son fils. Sur la vraye gloire*, and contrasts its disenchantment with earlier letters by Mlle de Scudéry full of an 'official' enthusiasm for the exploits of Louis XIV's armies.

LENCLOS. L. Hinds, 'The critique of the "Philosophes de Ruelles" in Ninon de Lenclos's *La Coquette vengée*', *SCFS*, 21:173–82, surveys the details of L.'s attack on 'vulgarisers of Scholastic philosophy and writers of misogynist satires', and particularly on Louis de Lesclache's manual, *La Philosophie expliquée en tables*.

MARANA. R. Howells, 'The secret life: Marana's *Espion du Grand-Seigneur* (1684–86)', *FS*, 53:153–66, examines this late 17th-c. edition, 'progenitor' of the better known 18th-c. version, and reveals its 'hidden Enlightenment characteristics'. H. then discusses 'the secret' as a 'central topos in the narrative writing' of the time.

MÉRÉ. S. Guellouz, 'Souci de l'autre et culte de soi: l'honnêteté selon le chevalier de Méré', Heyndels, *L'Autre*, 193–203, discusses the forms used by M. in his moralistic writings, concentrating on the *Conversations* (1668–69) in which it is '*par* et *pour* l'autre que vit cet honnête homme dont le moraliste ne cesse, de texte en texte, de peaufiner le portrait.'

MONTPENSIER. M. Bertaud, 'Grandeur et servitude princière: l'exemple de Mademoiselle de Montpensier d'après ses *Mémoires*', *Hipp Vol.*, 5–14, treats three aspects of her life in the light of this double theme: her experiences as a courtier, the marriage plans which came to nothing, and her disgrace after the Fronde.

MME PALATINE. C. M. Probes, 'La Subversion au sein de la famille royale: les *Lettres françaises* de Madame Palatine', *SCFS*, 21 : 157–64, studies various of the Princess's letters in which she defends herself against charges of 'sottises', 'ordures' and 'galanteries', and particularly of medical unorthodoxy.

PERRAULT. J. Morgan Zarucchi, 'Perrault's titular subversions: tapestries, tales and medals', *SCFS*, 21 : 239–46, considers three curiously arranged title pages. M. Escola, 'Brèves histoires de loups', *RSH*, 254:63–83, analyses *Le Petit Chaperon rouge* for disturbing innuendos, then goes on to suggest that 'l'on peut produire le *Petit Chaperon rouge* à partir de la fable, "Le loup, la chèvre et le chevreau"' by La Fontaine.

PRÉFONTAINE. F. Assaf, 'Thésée sans fil d'Ariane ou l'orphelin dans le labyrinthe', *Eustis Vol.*, 187–98, following up suggestions from Louis Marin's *Utopiques*, interprets P.'s picaresque *Orphelin infortuné* as a dystopia, and its hero as a 'Thésée à l'envers' seeking to outwit its 'minotaure multiforme' consisting of 'autorité abusive, violence, faim'.

RETZ. S. Vance, 'Retz and his Memoirs: the question of orthodoxy and subversion', *SCFS*, 21 : 145–55, shows how R. defends his political aims during the Fronde. M. Marchal, 'Gondi dans une porte coincé. Le point de vue du mémorialiste', *Hipp Vol.*, 15–21, compares three accounts of R.'s embarrassing adventure in the Parlement de Paris on 21 August, 1651. M. Pernot, 'Le cardinal de Retz, archevêque de Paris (1654–1662): grandeur et servitude d'un prélat opposant à la monarchie absolue', *ib.*, 35–40, recounts the vain struggle of R. to defend his rights and fulfil his duties as archbishop. L. Desjardins, 'Du regard de l'autre à l'image de soi: mouvements intimes et lectures du corps', Heyndels, *L'Autre*, 245–54, draws mainly on R.'s *Mémoires* for examples of 'la lecture des signes que les passions impriment sur le corps'.

ROSSET. S. Poli, 'Violence et mythe dans l'histoire tragique: un exemple de François de Rosset', Debaisieux, *Violence*, 55–62, takes the *histoires tragiques* as examples of 'le schéma de la transgression suivie d'une répression obligatoire' which is what renders them 'exemplaires'. A. de Vaucher Gravili, 'Violence représentée, violence exorcisée: François de Rosset et la peinture de son temps', *ib.*, 63–76, chooses R. to represent a tendency: that of writers who like to 'stage' their narratives 'comme des pièces de théâtre ou des tableaux qui "piquent" le regard autant que l'ouïe'. G. cites Caravaggio, Artemisia Gentileschi, and Pietro Danini as comparable to R. in 'intensité brutale'.

SAINT-ÉVREMOND. Quentin M. Hope, *Saint-Evremond and his Friends* (Travaux du Grand Siècle, 13), Geneva, Droz, 490 pp., is a genial, readable study of the life and works of this engaging Epicurean who valued friendship and conversation more than 'the solitary activities of reading and writing'. Joseph M. Levine, *Between the Ancients and the Moderns: Baroque Culture in Restoration England*, New Haven–London, Yale U.P., xiv + 279 pp., studies St.-E. as one of four important figures in the period (the others being Evelyn, Dryden and Christopher Wren), and shows that all four start out as sympathetic to the Modern position before evolving towards *ancienneté*. J.-P. Sermain, 'Figures du sens: Saint-Évremond et le paradigme de la fiction au XVIIIe siècle', *RSH*, 254: 13–22, studies the *Lettre au maréchal de Crequi* in which St.-E. reveals the six authors — Montaigne, Malherbe, Corneille, Voiture, Bossuet, and, above all, Cervantes for his *Don Quixote* — whom he finds always re-readable. His reasons for choosing this last go some way to explaining how it retained its popularity throughout the Ancien Régime. D. Bensoussan, 'Saint-Evremond: le style du moraliste', Dagen, *Épicure*, 383–401, has, in addition, the running title, 'L'Otium de l'honnête homme', and concludes that 'de fait, c'est toute une gnoséologie épicuro-gassendienne parfaitement assimilée qui soutient discrètement le travail d'écriture morale de Saint-Evremond'.

SAINT-SIMON. M. Stefanovska, 'Un *voyeux* à la cour de Louis XIV: curiosité et écriture dans les *Mémoires* de Saint-Simon', *PFSCL*, 26:289–98, notes S.-S.'s predilection for viewing the French court and its inhabitants, as far as possible, anonymously, exempt from all 'règles de l'étiquette' and able therefore to 'dédier toute son énergie à l'observation et à l'interprétation de son objet'.

SCARRON. D. Riou, 'La violence comme "disgrâce" et comme "épreuve" dans *Le Roman comique* de Paul Scarron', Debaisieux, *Violence*, 207–16, examines 'les violences subies par Le Destin et par Ragotin', the first representing the heroic strain ('épreuve'), the second the burlesque ('disgrâce'). A. Wood, 'Abduction and irony in the *Roman comique*', *ib.*, 217–25, reviews the eight abduction episodes in the novel, and notes the 'ambivalent, ironic presentation of these actions' which S. is able to integrate more effectively and make more interesting than do the authors of *romans héroïques* of the time. M. Debaisieux, '*Le Roman comique*, ou la mise en scène du dé(voile)ment', *Eustis Vol.*, 171–85, seeks to 'définir la fonction textuelle du personnage du fou' who appears in two parallel episodes in Part II of S.'s novel. D. links the madman's role to the 'rapport établi par Bakhtine entre la culture populaire et la folie'.

SCUDÉRY, GEORGES DE. A. Arrigoni, 'Itinéraire géographique, itinéraire métaphorique dans l'*Ibrahim* de Georges de Scudéry', Heyndels, *L'Autre*, 47–56, analyses 'les déplacements d'Ibrahim/ Justinien' which amount to 'une cartographie "réelle" d'un voyage imaginaire de l'Europe au pays du Levant'.

SCUDÉRY, MADELEINE DE. H. Goldwyn, 'Désir, fantasme et violence: les enlèvements de Mandane dans *Le Grand Cyrus* de Mlle de Scudéry', Debaisieux, *Violence*, 227–35, notes how these 'rapts' stem from the fact that 'les rivaux de Cyrus choisissent le désir de Cyrus en élisant le même objet'. A. Niderst, 'Sade dans *Cyrus* et *Clélie*', *ib.*, 237–44, finds in these novels 'des malheurs et bien des supplices', which do not dominate but are nevertheless noticeable, and one description which is, he suggests, 'franchement sadique ou presque pasolinienne'. R. Nunn, 'The Rape of Lucretia in Madeleine de Scudéry's *Clélie*', *ib.*, 245–49, points to S.'s alterations to Livy's account which defer to 'l'usage du siècle'.

SÉVIGNÉ. R. Racevskis, 'Dynamics of time and postal communication in Mme de Sévigné's letters', *PFSCL*, 26:51–59, picks out some of Louvois's reforms to France's postal system 'in order to generate a historical context for a reading of textual time structures in the Sévigné letters'. C. R. Montfort and R. Lanning, 'Les "méchancetés" de Madame de Sévigné', *ib.*, 131–58, points out that S. frequently calls herself 'méchante', especially to her daughter, and gives examples of 'traits de raillerie' and wrong actions that she attributes to herself in her letters.

TALLEMANT DES RÉAUX. F. Wild, 'La morale des *Historiettes* de Tallemant des Réaux', Dagen, *Morale*, 73–83, could not justify the choice of T. as a moralist were it not for the fact that he is 'un penseur et écrivain d'esprit libertin'.

THÉMISEUL DE SAINT-HYACINTHE. C. Lelouch, 'Le péritexte au service de la formation des esprits: l'exemple du *Chef-d'oeuvre d'un inconnu* de Saint-Hyacinthe (1714),', *LitC*, 37:185–202, demonstrates that the *péritexte* of this mock 'ouvrage d'érudition' is as important as the text itself in ridiculing pedants, 'les parleurs de Phoebus et de Galimatias, and also 'les partisans des Anciens'.

TRISTAN L'HERMITE. *CTH*, 21, has the following: C. Thiollet, 'Variations sur la disgrâce dans *Le Page disgracié* de Tristan L'Hermite' (7–15), describes the novel's narrator as affecting to 'ignorer les causes [of his disgraces] sinon celle d'une prédestination vague, pseudo-scientifique, mélangeant astrologie et physiologie'; E. Desiles, 'La dimension métalangagière du *Page disgracié*' (17–24), shows T.'s concern for 'une adéquation la plus stricte possible entre les mots et les choses'; B. Bray, 'Tristan L'Hermite écrivain par lettres' (26–36), reviews approvingly two of the five sections of the *Lettres meslées*: the 'lettres amoureuses' and the 'lettres héroïques', and points to one principal theme: that of the 'décevant rapport qu'entretient l'écrivain avec les Grands dont il tente de gagner les faveurs'; S. Berregard, 'Le Caractère autobiographique des *Lettres meslées*' (37–45), provides a general survey of the collection, noting that in it (as in *Le Page disgracié*) T. oscillates 'entre le réel et l'imaginaire', and that 'la frontière entre fiction et autobiographie n'est pas toujours nette', though we do have a clear notion of his preoccupations: 'la souffrance physique, l'amitié, l'affection de proches', and his unhappiness with the system of 'clientélisme'; A. Tournon, 'La conception tristanienne de la justice dans les *Plaidoyers historiques*' (47–55), finds that these undervalued pieces show T.'s awareness of the complexity of justice, of the vast distance in this field between ideal and reality. B. Parmentier, 'L'espérance dans *Le Page disgracié*: une "fable incertaine"', *RSH*, 254:23–31, concentrates on the strange, ambiguously presented episode of the magician 'qu'on peut lire précisément comme une mise en fable du problème moral de l'espérance'. A. F. Garréta, '*Le Page disgracié*: problèmes de l'autobiographie baroque', Kronegger, *Baroque*, 81–98, claims that the novel's distortions of various sorts, 'la curieuse déformation et dispersion du sujet', make it typical of baroque. *\*Oeuvres complètes, 1, Prose*, ed. Jean Serroy (Sources classiques, 20), Champion, 450 pp., contains the *Lettres meslées, Le Page disgracié*, and T.'s *Discours de réception à l'Académie française*.

URFÉ. F. Lavocat, 'Théorie du roman et roman du moi: quelques lectures de *L'Astrée* au XVIIe siècle', Pfersmann, *Fondements*, 19–34, notes that readers such as J.-P. Camus, Patru, and Huet explain their love for this work, not so much by its capacity to supply 'le plaisir et l'instruction' but because it is, in their view, 'une oeuvre à clef', a work of autobiography. T. Meding, 'Epistles, epigraphs, and the subversion of writing in *L'Astrée*', *SCFS*, 21:29–41, points out how U. 'creates, within his romance, structures of textual orthodoxy and authority in order better to undermine them'. Id., 'Pastoral palimpsest: writing the laws of love in *L'Astrée*', *RQ*, 51:1087–117, dwells on the paradoxical interplay between constancy and inconstancy and follows the travels of the Laws of Love, their removal and falsification (by Hylas) and their final revision and restoration. M. Teixeira Anacleto, 'La violence dans la "bergerie": sens et/ou contre-sens d'un "scénario" *étrange*', Debaisieux, *Violence*, 175–84, considers moments of 'désarticulation', of 'transgression esthétique', and descriptions of disfiguring illness which disturb the natural order of Forez, and compares them to similar disturbances in Montemayor's

*Diana.* J.-P. van Elslande, 'L'altérité arcadienne', Heyndels, *L'Autre*, 393–401, sees *L'Astrée* as 'une pastorale qui a son mot à dire' about the politics of the time, by presenting a form of the society openly chosen and consented by its citizens.

VILLEDIEU. D. Kuizenga, 'Violences et silences dans l'oeuvre de Mme de Villedieu', Debaisieux, *Violence*, 251–62, counts some 360 examples of about 50 *topoi* associated with violence in V.'s prose works, but is on the whole more interested in the boundaries between what is 'légitime' and what 'illégitime', and in the separate roles of the sexes in the mayhem.

5. THOUGHT

Francis Mariner, *Histoires et autobiographies spirituelles: les mémoires de Fontaine, Lancelot et Du Fossé* (Biblio 17, 109), Tübingen, Narr, 1998, 182 pp., surveys the memoirs of three 17th-c. Jansenists who, at a time of persecution, separately recorded the reactions and other activities of Port-Royal. Alexander Sedgwick, *The Travails of Conscience: the Arnauld family and the Ancien Régime*, Cambridge, Mass., Harvard U.P., 1998, 297 pp. Thierry Wanegffelen, *Une difficile fidélité: catholiques malgré le Concile en France, XVIe–XVIIe siècle*, PUF, 256 pp., recounts the problems of the Jansenists, among others, in a post-Tridentine Church which linked 'fidélité' with 'soumission inconditionnelle'. O. Chaline, 'De la gloire', *LitC*, 36:95–108, considers the 'rencontre conflictuelle entre les deux aspects de la notion de gloire, théologique (petitesse de l'homme face à la grandeur de Dieu), politique (soumission du sujet au roi, source de toute gloire)', both characteristic of the prime-ministry of Richelieu. B. Chédozeau, 'D'une religion baroque? Une religion de la confiance naïve et flamboyante', *ib.*, 109–25, looks at Molinism followed by Augustinianism, the former *ultramontain*, 'optimiste et certainement humaniste' and, in C.'s view, the more baroque, the latter 'une religion du soupçon et de la *gravitas*'. F. Lestringant, 'Machines d'oubli (XVIe–XVIIe siècles)' *RSH*, 256:11–33, provides two examples of such *machines*, the first being the effort of the Church to wipe the Reformation out of history, 'une machination montée de toutes pièces pour offusquer la vérité', citing Antoine Arnauld and Pierre Nicole among others as contributors to the effort, and the second Marc Lescarbot's desire, expressed in his *Histoire de la Nouvelle France* (1609), to make Native Americans into French Christians; A. Tarrête, 'Entre mémoire et oubli: la citation chez trois lecteurs de Montaigne (Du Vair, Camus, Guez de Balzac)' *ib.*, 99–113, studies three writers who were sensitive, each in his own way, to Montaigne's 'critique de la vaine érudition'.

Michel Bouvier, *La morale classique*, Champion, 749 pp., covers the period 1659–88 and 'les petits moralistes', wishing to attempt 'une redécouverte du climat dans lequel s'épanouissaient les esprits du temps de Louis XIV', and believing 'qu'il ne pouvait pas se trouver de guides plus sûrs que ces auteurs parfaitement protégés par l'oubli'. B. considers his subject under the headings 'L'homme', and 'La société'. *DSS*, 51.1, prints articles presenting *Les Moralistes: nouvelles tendances de la recherche*: M. Bourgeois-Courtois, 'Réflexion morale et culture mondaine (matériaux pour une synthèse)' (9–19), opines that 'il n'existe pas, pour l'heure, de travail d'ensemble qui s'impose', but defines areas where valuable work has been done; M. Bouvier, 'Les *minores*' (21–26), picks out useful recent pioneering studies and editions; E. Bury, 'le moraliste classique et ses modèles antiques' (27–35), proposes 'trois niveaux différents pour poser le problème des modèles', to which *niveaux* he attaches the familiar terms, *inventio*, *dispositio*, and *elocutio*; D. Denis, 'Le discours moraliste: du style à l'inscription langagière' (55–65), suggests useful 'outils de travail empruntés au vaste domaine des sciences du langage'; G. Dotoli, 'Réflexion morale et sociologie' (67–73), claims that 'le moraliste est un sociologue avant la lettre', and cites methods adopted by moralists comparable to those of present-day social scientists; B. Guion, 'De l'anthropologie des moralistes classiques' (75–88), points to parallels between anthropology and 17th-c. works 'nées de l'augustinisme littéraire'; V. Kapp, 'Les moralistes et la rhétorique' (89–99), referring particularly to La Rochefoucauld, Pascal, Le Moyne, and La Bruyère, reviews recent studies of collections of maxims and other forms of 'discours discontinu' which seek to show what makes unified works of them; J.-F. Lecoq, 'Morales classiques et philosophies contemporaines' (101–18), surveys work on Hobbes, Locke, Gassendi, and Descartes; J. Leerssen, 'Caractères des nations et imagologie' (119–23), deals briefly with national stereotypes and with manifestations of 'relativisme culturel'; B. Papàsogli, 'L'espace intérieur et l'anatomie de l'âme' (125–34), draws our attention to recent work on moralists and writers on religion which have tried to 'restituer cette "culture de l'intériorité", cette invention d'un "monde intérieur" où l'anthropologie classique exprime certains de ses aspects les plus surprenants, parfois les plus modernes'; B. Parmentier, 'Entre l'écrit et l'oral' (135–46), notes that 'toute une série d'études consacrées à la parole rhétorique ont mis en relief la voix par opposition au texte', and herself underlines the importance of 'conversation' to moralists; A. Pons, 'Réflexion moraliste et sources italiennes' (147–56), reviews recent work on the influence in 17th-c. France of 16th-c. Italian *trattatistica sul comportamento*, notably those of Castiglione, Della Casa, and Guazzo; B. Roukhomovsky and L. van Delft, 'La question du fragment' (157–67), lists 93 studies on fragments, sententiae, 'pensées détachées' and other forms of 'discontinu'; A.-E. Spica, 'Moralistes et emblématique' (169–80), looks for recent signs that links have been sought between the two genres and, finding hardly any, makes some useful observations of her own; L. Thirouin, 'Littérature morale et spiritualité' (181–92), seeks to answer the question: 'en quoi la composante spirituelle est-elle un élément significatif pour l'appréciation littéraire des oeuvres morales?'.

Dagen, *Morale*, prints conference papers: J. Dagen, 'De la morale latine aux moralistes français' (21–31), cites neo-Latin as well as ancient influences on Montaigne, Descartes, Méré, Pascal, La Rochefoucauld, Vauvenargues, Montesquieu, and Rousseau; E. Bury, 'Humanisme et anti-humanisme dans les morales du Grand Siècle' (47–59), claims that 'l'arrière-plan métaphysique et anthropologique de ces différentes morales ne se laisse [. . .] pas traiter selon des oppositions claires et des jeux de rupture nets', and warns of the limitations of a too clear-cut distinction; B. Beugnot, 'La philosophie morale au Parnasse' (85–93), notes a link between 'la constitution d'une littérature de moralistes et la ruine du cosmos aristotélicien', and after considering the 16th-c. breakdown of the medieval world-picture, moves on to Montaigne, Pascal, and La Bruyère with side glances at Descartes, La Rochefoucauld, and Fontenelle; P. Sellier, 'Les tulipes et la peinture: "Vanités" littéraires et humus augustinien' (139–48), notes an evolution of the *Vanités* genre from being 'organiquement lié à la réflexion chrétienne' in the baroque period, to a situation where 'toute coloration religieuse' has disappeared, leading to denunciations from Pascal and Senault; J.-F. Lecoq, 'Le romancier moraliste' (155–74), wonders 'dans quelle mesure certaines aspirations, certaines tendances, présentes dans les livres de piété jusqu'à la fin du XVIIe siècle, se retrouvent dans les romans de Fénelon, de Challe, de Marivaux ou de Prévost'; H. Coulet, 'De La Rochefoucauld à Sade, la morale d'un immoraliste' (207–19), looks at the way in which Marivaux, Rousseau, Helvétius, Sénac de Meilhan and, of course, Sade, misunderstand, misuse or misquote La R.

Yves Charles Zarka, *Philosophie et politique à l'âge classique*, PUF, 1998, 296 pp., covers Europe from the late-16th to the late-18th cs, and is mainly concerned with the elaborators of two framing concepts: 'le concept de raison d'Etat et celui de tolérance'. The French thinkers incorporated are Jean Bodin (on 'l'idée de république'), Descartes ('l'étant et la représentation'), Jean Domat and Pascal ('théologie, politique et droit'), and Rousseau ('fiction et réalité' and 'tolérance et liberté'). P. Dumont, 'Est-il pertinent de parler d'une philosophie baroque?', *LitC*, 36:63–77, contrasts Descartes and Leibniz.

ARNAULD. M. van Meerbeeck, 'Un manuscrit important pour la correspondance d'Arnauld', *DSS*, 51:549–56, reveals the existence of a MS of over 250 unpublished letters by A. covering the period 1682–90 in the Cabinet des Manuscrits of the Bibliothèque Royale in Brussels (Manuscrits, 11.039). M. gives a brief history of the MS and promises a study.

BAYLE. Joy Charnley, *Pierre Bayle Reader of Travel Literature*, Bern, Lang, 1998, 202 pp., shows how B. drew on travel writing, exploiting it more fully and more frequently than his contemporaries, thus revealing its significance to his successors the *philosophes*. A. Niderst, 'Scepticisme ou fidéisme de Bayle?', *SCFS*, 21:205–14, concludes that B. 'fut un bon protestant [. . .]. Mais ce bon protestant est un augustinien, un hyper-augustinien [. . .]. Il lui paraît impossible de situer la vraie foi ni la morale chrétienne dans le monde'. E. D. James, 'Pierre Bayle on *évidence* and philosophical disputes', *FSB*, 73:8–10, reviews B.'s struggles with the concept and the problems it poses in various of his writings, particularly the *Commentaires philosophiques* of 1687–88. *Correspondance de Pierre Bayle. 1, 1662–1674, lettres 1–65*, ed. Elisabeth Labrousse et al., Oxford, Voltaire Foundation, 476 pp.

CHALLE. O. Hovasse, 'La notion de conscience dans les *Difficultés sur la religion proposées au père Malebranche* de Robert Challe', *Hipp Vol.*, 87–95, sees this work as more personal than the reference to M. suggests. He pronounces C. a deist and describes how he 'met à nu les structures de l'esprit — la conscience, la raison et le sentiment — afin d'élaborer sa propre théorie de la connaissance'.

CHANUT. Jean-François de Raymond, *\*Pierre Chanut, ami de Descartes* (Bibliothèque des archives de philosophie, 64), Beauchesne, 264 pp., is a biography of this philosopher-diplomat, intermediary between Descartes and Queen Christina of Sweden.

CHARRON. T. M. Carr, 'La perte de l'autre et l'autoconsolation', Heyndels, *L'Autre*, 367–73, finds in C. two 17th-c. sorts of consolation: the stoic and the Christian, both marked by the idea that 'le chagrin provoqué par le deuil est lui-même un autre'.

DESCARTES. G. Leyenberger, 'Métaphore, fiction et vérité chez Descartes', *Littérature*, 109, 1998:20–37, notes the predominance of 'métaphores architecturales, du cheminement et de la noyade comme mouvement vers le fond', creating the sense of 'un vide abyssal', and asserts that 'c'est pour faire face à ce vide, pour atteindre le fond à partir duquel une autre vérité pourra être construite ou façonnée, que Descartes a recours à la fiction'. J. D. Lyons, 'Descartes and the modern imagination', *PLit*, 23:302–12, examines the *Discours* and the *Méditations* and emphasizes D.'s proposal of 'an *active* use of imagination', recommending that we 'initiate the imaginative process rather

than suffer it passively', its useful place being 'obvious and indisput-
able in Descartes's primary purpose of practical and useful understanding of the material world'. R. W. Tobin, 'Descartes terre à terre:
la quête du *Discours de la méthode*', *Eustis Vol.*, 125–32, notes D.'s use of
imagery — of journeying, of light, of architecture — as means of
persuasion. E.-J. Bas, 'Descartes's *Lettre apologétique aux Magistrats
d'Utrecht*: new facts and materials', *JHP*, 37:415–33, proposes a new
date of publication and a new textual history. M. Rozemond,
'Descartes on mind-body interaction: what's the problem?', *ib.*,
435–67, gives a general survey of this 'relatively unproblematic' issue.
J.-L. Cornille, 'Le Solitaire et la Minerve', *PFSCL*, 26:359–70,
meditates on the rarity of names in D.'s published works, on his
fondness for the word 'car', on his superstitious regard for the date 11
November, and on other intriguing oddities. Stephen Mann, *Descartes
and Augustine*, CUP, 1998, xvi + 415 pp., re-examines the influence of
Augustinianism on D.'s *Méditations* and finds it more profound than is
usually suggested. B. D. Dutton, 'Physics and Metaphysics in
Descartes and Galileo', *JHP*, 37:49–71. P. Hoffman, 'Cartesian
Composites', *ib.*, 251–70. *Feminist Interpretations of René Descartes*, ed.
Susan Bordo, University Park, Pennsylvania State U.P.,
xii + 348 pp., collects essays, some new, some previously published.
The editor, in her 'Introduction' (1–25), claims that the aim of this
collection is to cover the 'representation of those areas [of the
Cartesian corpus] that have inspired response in the way of gender
analysis'. D. Boyle, 'Descartes' natural light reconsidered', *JHP*,
37:601–12, asserts that for D. 'natural light' is a purely passive
feature of the intellect. André Robinet, *\*Descartes, la lumière naturelle:
intuition, disposition, complexion* (De Pétrarque à Descartes, 67), Vrin,
448 pp.

FONTAINE.    P. Mengotti-Thouvenin, '*Non mihi, si linguae centum sint,
oraque centum ferrea vox*: la prison chez Nicolas Fontaine', *Hipp Vol.*,
59–71, surveys F.'s views and experiences, and his talents as a writer
in his *Relation de la prison de M. de Sacy*, and his *Mémoires*.

FONTPERTUIS.    F. Ellen Weaver, *Madame de Fontpertuis, une dévote
janséniste, amie et gérante d'Antoine Arnauld et de Port-Royal*, Klincksieck,
1998, 431 pp., is a biography of this talented 'femme d'affaires'
(serving at once the interests of herself, her family, and Port-Royal)
and friend and correspondent with Arnauld, Angélique de Saint-
Jean, and other notable Jansenists.

FRANÇOIS DE SALES.    Viviane Mellinghoff-Bourgerie, *François de
Sales (1567–1622), un homme de lettres spirituelles: culture, tradition,
épistolarité* (THR, 330), 535 pp., deals with his Savoyard origins and
'attaches culturelles', examines the spiritual influences upon him,
particularly of St. Bernard, and analyses the *Introduction à la vie dévote*

and the *Traité de l'amour de Dieu*. His letters, too, are reviewed, distinctions being made between private letters and *circulaires* destined for communal consumption, and between letters concerned with spiritual direction and those treating of *civilité*. Comparisons are made with contemporary and later letter-writers such as Mme de Sévigné (but not, surprisingly, Jeanne de Chantal). B. Teyssandier, 'L'exhortation au "combat spirituel" et sa mise en images dans l'*Introduction à la vie dévote*', Dagen, *Épicure*, 241–66, looks into the Bible, Loyola and Lorenzo Scupoli for precedents for the theme of combat, before turning to the 'cartographie morale' and the 'stratégie de combat' of the *Introduction*. J. Hennequin, 'L'amitié dans la correspondance de François de Sales', *Hipp Vol.*, 51–57, defines the saint's notion of friendship, examines 'ce qu'il dit dans sa correspondance de l'amitié pour soi-même, pour le prochain et pour Dieu' and goes on to 'montrer comment cette correspondance est elle-même une manifestation de cette amitié'.

GASSENDI. J.-C. Darmon, 'Gassendi et la logique des apparences: pour une théorie expérimentale du signe', Dagen, *Épicure*, 17–63.

LA MOTHE LE VAYER. D. Wetsel, 'La Mothe le Vayer and the subversion of Christian belief', *SCFS*, 21:183–93, reacts to Peter Gay's dismissal of 17th-c. *libertins érudits* by rescuing Le V. and indicating the various attacks on Christianity in his *Dialogues*.

MALEBRANCHE. *DSS*, 51.2, prints conference papers on *L'occasionnalisme de Malebranche*: V. Carraud, 'Malebranche: état présent des recherches' (313–16); P. Desoche, 'Malebranche et l'inconcevable existence' (317–33), considers M.'s views on 'la connaissance de l'existence', more particularly on the 'impossibilité de saisir conjointement l'essence et l'existence d'une même chose'; S. Nadler, 'Connaissance et causalité chez Malebranche et Geulincx: esquisse d'une histoire' (335–45), seeks to reconcile the views of M. and G., and compare them with those of medieval Islamic theologians; J.-C. Bardout, 'Y a-t-il une théorie occasionnaliste des passions?' (347–66), asserts that M. is obliged to counter 'la crise de la causalité ouverte par l'occasionnalisme' by going back to the doctrine of 'la vision en Dieu'; C. Trottmann, 'Malebranche, de la vision béatifique à la syndérèse ... et retour' (367–84). Jean-Christophe Bardout, *Malebranche et la métaphysique*, PUF, 315 pp., surveys first 'l'idée de la métaphysique', then examines its 'définition malebranchiste', highlights its important role in his philosophy, and finally sums up the contribution of M. to the evolution of the discipline of metaphysics during the French classical period.

NAUDÉ. A. Kupiec, 'La bibliothèque politique de Gabriel Naudé', pp. 11–29 of *Ecrire aux tournants de notre histoire*, ed. Mohammed Berrada et al. (*Tumultes*, 12), Kimé, 227 pp., finds N.'s all-embracing views on what a library should contain difficult to reconcile with his support for political absolutism.

NICOLE. B. Guion, 'Conscient et non-conscient dans la pensée morale de Pierre Nicole', Dagen, *Épicure*, 179–203, notes the development of N.'s theories on the unconscious in his theological writings (where 'pensées imperceptibles' are first mooted) and in his *Essais de morale*.

PASCAL. D. Wetsel, 'Pascal on death', *PFSCL*, 26: 195–203, begins with a commentary on P.'s letter to his sister on the occasion of their father's death, then examines particularly fr. 681 of the *Pensées* (Sellier ed.) for the implication of this approach for unbelieving or doubting readers. Vlad Alexandrescu, *Le paradoxe chez Blaise Pascal*, Bern, Lang, 1997, 262 pp., compares this aspect of P. to 'la notion générale de paradoxe' in Montaigne and Descartes. Bruno Clément, *Le Lecteur et son modèle: Voltaire, Pascal, Hugo, Shakespeare, Sartre, Flaubert*, PUF, 273 pp., contains the essay ' " . . . mon semblable, mon frère" (Voltaire lecteur de Blaise Pascal)' (25–100), which illustrates the lifelong interest of V. in the *Pensées*.

PIERRE POIRET. *La Paix des bonnes âmes*, ed. Marjolaine Chevallier (TLF, 486), 1998, 332 pp., gives the 1687 Amsterdam edition of this protestant polemical work, and includes Jurieu's *Critique* and Anne Bourignon's letters.

# THE EIGHTEENTH CENTURY

By D. A. DESSERUD, *Associate Professor of Politics,
University of New Brunswick at Saint John*

## MONTESQUIEU

THOUGHT AND INTELLECTUAL RELATIONSHIPS. Bertrand Binoche, *Introduction à 'De l'esprit des lois' de Montesquieu*, PUF, 1998, xi + 381 pp. B. provides an intelligent and detailed reading of M.'s *EL*, organized around two axes: one theoretical, one practical. The first consists of M.'s theories on government and society; the second his attempts to provide guarantees against despotism and in favour of liberty. Jean-Patrice Courtois, *Inflexions de la rationalité dans 'L'Esprit des lois': écriture et pensée chez Montesquieu*, PUF, 320 pp., is a detailed examination of Book I of the *EL*, in which M.'s metaphysics is reconciled with the practical applications found in the remainder of the text. Christopher Sparks, *Montesquieu's Vision of Uncertainty and Modernity in Political Philosophy*, Lewiston, Mellen, xlix + 239 pp., juxtaposes the postmodernist concept of uncertainty with M.'s social and political theory. While S. seems to spend more time discussing postmodern theory than he does M., he nevertheless provides some new and interesting readings.

N. Vazsonyi, 'Montesquieu, Friedrich Carl von Moser, and the "National Spirit Debate" in Germany, 1765-1767', *GSR*, 22:225–46, looks at M.'s influence on some German writers and the 'perceived absence of national pride' in mid-18th-c. Germany. M. Richter, 'Montesquieu and the concept of civil society', *The European Legacy*, 3, 1998:33–41, analyses how M., one of the first to distinguish between 'civil society' and the 'state', worked to explain the 'numerous and complex ways in which civil society may and should interact with the state', which in turn should provide valuable insights to those today concerned with the rise of new representative democracies. B. Parekh, 'Vico and Montesquieu: limits of pluralist imagination', pp. 55–78 of *Civilization and Oppression*, ed. Catherine Wilson (*CanJP*, supp. 25), discusses how M. and V. are praised by their readers for their critiques of 'moral monism', but both fail to overcome their own cultural myopia. M. in particular, argues P., remained 'eurocentric', assuming that the European institutions and practices which with he was familiar were necessarily the norms by which other cultures should be judged. Therefore, while M.'s thought might well provide space for a 'wide variety of customs and practices', it provided 'little or none for moral and cultural pluralism'. This will come as a surprise to M. scholars, given (as P. acknowledges) that M. argued repeatedly that his (European) readers could and should not judge the moral practices of others, including incest, polygamy and homosexuality, by their own values. S. Krause, 'The politics of distinction and disobedience: honor and defense of liberty in Montesquieu', *Polity*, 31 : 469–99. Although the role played by commerce is surprisingly absent in this interesting analysis (and perhaps plays a more prominent role in her thesis, upon which this article is based), K. nevertheless makes a compelling case for reconsidering M.'s concept of honour and its role in liberal democracy.

*1748, L'année de L'Esprit des lois*, ed. Catherine Larrère and Catherine Volpilhac-Auger, Champion, 191 pp., is a collection of essays concerning the state of M.'s world in the year he published *EL* and includes: C. Cave and D. Reynaud, 'L'année 1748 dans la *Gazette de France*' (19–30); S. Cornand, 'La fin de la guerre de succession d'Autriche: le témoignage de Barbier' (31–40); C. Volpilhac-Auger, 'Lire en 1748: l'année merveilleuse?' (47–60); J.-N. Pascal, 'L'année 1748 au théâtre' (61–70); J.-L. Jam, 'La musique en 1748' (71–78); V. Costa, 'La peinture en 1748' (79–104); L. Desgraves, 'Montesquieu en 1748' (111–16); C. Spector, 'Des *Lettres persanes* à *L'Esprit des lois*: Montesquieu, parcours d'une oeuvre' (117–40); C. Larrère, '*L'Esprit des lois*, tradition et modernité' (141–62).

*RMon*, 3, contains: G. Benrekassa, 'Montesquieu An 2000. Bilans, problèmes, perspectives' (5–40); C. Larrère, 'Le civique et le civil. De le citoyenneté chez Montesquieu' (41–62); G. Dessons, 'Le pluriel des manières' (63–78); J.-P. Seguin, 'Points, phrases et style dans le texte de *L'Esprit des lois*' (79–98); J. Ehrard, 'Montesquieu dans *Le Monde* en 1998' (99–110); C. Volpilhac-Auger, 'Du bon usage des *Geographica*' (169–78); C. Bustarret, 'Les papiers de Montesquieu. Une approche codicologique du fonds de La Brède' (179–86); C. Volpilhac-Auger, 'Du bon usage de la fessée' (187–90); J. Ehrard, 'Sur les origines berrichonnes des Secondat' (191–92); N. Masson, 'Les livres de Montesquieu' (192); J. Ehrard, 'À propos du *Voyage à Paphos*' (192–93).

Marc Régaldo, \**Montesquieu et la religion*, Bordeaux, Académie Montesquieu, 1998, 127 pp. Catherine Larrère, \**Actualité de Montesquieu*, Fondation nationale des sciences politiques, 133 pp. Annie Becq, \**Lettres persanes de Montesquieu*, Gallimard, 176 pp. P. Stewart, \*'Toujours Usbek', *ECF*, 11 : 141–50. M. W. Ghachem, \*'Montesquieu in the Caribbean: the colonial enlightenment between *Code Noir* and *Code Civil*', *HRef*, 25 : 183–210.

## THE ROMANTIC ERA

By JOHN WHITTAKER, *University of Hull*
(This survey covers the years 1998 and 1999)

### 1. GENERAL

R. J. Goldstein, 'Fighting French censorship, 1815–1881', *FR*, 71, 1998:785–96, describes an intense struggle, and the remarkable resourcefulness of authors, journalists, and dramatists, in their efforts to overcome the censors' restrictions. J. Herman, 'Ouverture: *Don Giovanni* en sept récitals', *RBPH*, 76:649–66, suggests that the Romantics reduced the potency of the Don Juan figure by relegating him to the ranks of ordinary human beings. S. Scott, 'L'ascendance rationaliste du moi romantique', *AJFS*, 35, 1998:156–77, shows that Romantic thought is firmly anchored in 18th-c. sensualism and rationalism, and indicates evidence which supports a view of Romanticism as evolution rather than revolution. Madeleine Ambrière, *Au Soleil du Romantisme: quelques voyageurs de l'infini*, PUF, 1998, viii + 418 pp., is a resolute and effective attempt at a definition of Romantic creativity, following the words which Baudelaire used to describe a picture by Delacroix: 'l'infini dans le fini'. The first part is devoted to Vigny and, in particular, the insights which may be gained from his correspondance. The third part is concerned with Balzac and the importance of his changing perceptions of science and history. Between the two, chapters are devoted to the contributions of Aloysius Bertrand, Charles Lassailly, Samuel-Henri Berthoud, and Caroline Valchère. Jean-Pierre Guillerm, *Vieille Rome: Stendhal, Goncourt, Taine, Zola et la Rome Baroque*, Villeneuve d'Ascq, Septentrion U.P., 1998, 165 pp., observes that, for 19th-c. intellectuals, visiting Rome was no longer a religious pilgrimage, but a form of tourism in which the pursuit of pleasure was paramount. For Stendhal, in *Promenades dans Rome*, it was associated with the search for self and otherness; for Taine, in *Voyage en Italie*, it coincides with the abandonment of didacticism; for the Goncourt brothers, in *Madame Gervaisis*, surprisingly to many readers including Zola, a temporary escape into the religious life of former times. Anne Martin-Fugier, *Les Romantiques: figures de l'artiste 1820–1848*, Hachette Littératures, 1998, 420 pp., is an historian's appraisal of Romanticism, concluding that the collapse of the artist's social identity and exalted mission, following the revolution of 1848, results in the decline of art into professionalism. *Cultural Interactions in the Romantic Age*, ed. Gregory Maertz, Albany, NY U.P., 1998, x + 258 pp., includes essays by F. Burwick, 'Romantic madness, Hölderlin, Nerval, Clare' (29–51), focusing on the 'insensé sublime' of 'Le Christ aux Oliviers', and by L. R. Furst, 'The salons of Germaine de Staël and Rahel Varnhagen' (95–103), comparing the gatherings in Coppet from 1804 to 1810 with those in Berlin from 1790 to 1806, and noting that the two ladies met in 1804.

## 2. CONSULATE WRITERS

CHATEAUBRIAND. *RHLF*, 98.6, 1998, is devoted to C. and contains: A. Michel, 'La beauté de Dieu dans la première partie du *Génie du Christianisme*' (1035–46), which refutes any suggestion that C. lacked religious commitment, and demonstrates his perception of God as a supreme artist; M. Delon, ' "L'orgue de Chateaubriand" ' (1047–53), on the instrument's symbolic and poetic importance in the *Génie*; J.-P. Clément, 'L'utilisation du mythe de Saint-Louis par Chateaubriand dans les controverses politiques de l'Empire et de la Restauration' (1059–72), on C.'s profound attachment to this mediaeval figure, whom he had intended as the hero of his third tragedy; E. Tabet, 'Chateaubriand et Bossuet orateur' (1073–86), on his appreciation of B. as the representative of his century, and the blending of the voices of the old and of the new; J.-C. Cavallin, 'Chateaubriand mythographe. Autobiographie et injonction du mythe dans les *Mémoires d'outre-tombe*' (1087–98), on the prevalent influence of Homer, Virgil, Ovid, and the Bible, and the way in which C. used these sources to construct an image of a 19th-c. hero; F. Bercegol, 'Chateaubriand et l'art de la conversation dans les *Mémoires d'outre-tombe*' (1099–1124), finding that C. used conversation as a proving-ground for his style, drawing from it the aesthetic values which underpin his writing; T. Weber-Maillot, 'La scène médiévale dans l'oeuvre de Chateaubriand' (1125–36), suggesting that C., having discovered the Middle Ages, felt himself to be better attuned to them than to his own period but that, in describing them, he distorted them to the point where they became alien; S. Menant, 'La Vie de Rancé dans le débat philosophique' (1137–46), showing how C. overcame his natural repugnance to treat the subject of his last work. Bertrand Aureau, *Chateaubriand, ADPF-Publications, 1998, 77 pp. Bruno Chaouat, *Je meurs par morceaux: Chateaubriand*, Villeneuve d'Ascq, Septentrion U.P., 1998, 176 pp., dwells on the circumstances surrounding C.'s last years, when he was no longer able to write and felt an increasing alienation from the society of the time. Béatrice Didier, *Chateaubriand*, Ellipses-Marketing, 119 pp. *Chateaubriand et les arts*, ed. Marc Fumaroli, de Fallois, 256 pp. Philippe Moisan, *Les Natchez de Chateaubriand: l'utopie, l'abîme et le feu*, Champion, 186 pp. Christophe Penot, *Chateaubriand aujourd'hui*, Saint-Malo, Cristel, 1998, 256 pp. *Vie de Napoléon*, ed. Marc Fumaroli, de Fallois, 446 pp. Juliette

Hoffenburg, *L'Enchanteur malgré lui: poétique de Chateaubriand*, L'Harmattan, 1998, 202 pp., considers the stages of C.'s life, which he claimed to fall into very different careers: as a soldier and traveller until 1800; a brief literary career from 1800–14; a political career during the Restoration years; retirement and writing his memoirs after the July Revolution. The conclusion is that both his life and his style are a mixture of diverse elements. When we consider his writing, we find in his poetics the fundamental basis for coherence in such diversity. MME DE STAËL. S. M. Riordan, 'Politics and Romanticism: Germaine de Staël's forgotten influence on nineteenth-century Sweden', *AJFS*, 35, 1998:209–25, investigates a number of documents connected with S.'s visit to Stockholm in 1812–13, and finds that Swedes were aware of her considerable influence on them, but that she was more often resented than appreciated. Pierre H. Dubé, *Bibliographie de la critique sur Madame de Staël, 1789–1994*, Geneva, Droz, 1998, 427 pp., is thorough and an extremely useful research tool. It lists 2742 items in 17 languages, with a brief summary of the content of most, and a translation of titles where necessary. The statistical analyses in the introduction are interesting, giving a measure of the extent of S.'s influence. Laure Lévêque, *\*Corinne ou l'Italie de Madame de Staël: poétique et politique*, Temps, 192 pp. Hubert de Phalèse, *\*Corinne à la page: analyse du roman de Mme de Staël*, Saint-Genouph, Nizet, 161 pp. *\*De la Littérature considérée dans ses rapports avec les institutions sociales*, ed. Axel Blaeschke, InfoMédia Communication, 1998, cxxii + 632 pp.

3. POETRY

GAUTIER. *Relire Théophile Gautier*, ed. Freeman G. Henry, Amsterdam–Atlanta, Rodopi, 1998, 263 pp., includes: P. Whyte, 'État présent des études sur Théophile Gautier' (11–34), giving evidence that G. continues to attract new readers, and drawing attention to the web pages devoted to him; C. Lacoste, 'De la contestation à l'autodiscipline ou le parcours d'un révolutionnaire' (35–48), following the trajectory of G.'s aesthetic career from fiery beginnings to mature control of writing; P. Berthier, 'Gautier journaliste' (49–71), suggesting that, despite the low points, a good number of articles on many different subjects should be considered as part of his literary output; M. Voisin, 'La pensée de Théophile Gautier' (73–89), underlining the breadth and the influence of G.'s thought and identifying him as one of the first to introduce the notion of the multicultural society; L. C. Hamrick, 'Gautier et l'anarchie de l'Art' (91–117), on his theory of multiple voices and the power of creativity which gradually crystallized as that of 'l'Art pour l'art';

P. Whyte, ' "L'Art" de Gautier: genèse et sens' (119–39), on the poem's origin in an odelette by Banville and its subsequent development; M. Delporte, 'Un poète à l'opéra, ce petit monde où l'on marche sur les nuages' (141–63), showing G.'s sound critical judgement and appreciation in his opera reviews in *La Presse*; M. Brix, 'Gautier, Nerval et le platonisme' (165–78), defining a shared idealism as part of the Romantic tradition; B. Schlossman, 'Mademoiselle de Maupin en noir et blanc: le deuil, la mélancholie et le cygne' (179–206), part of a study on Baudelaire and Walter Benjamin which goes some way to explain the dedication of *Les Fleurs du Mal*; R. Lloyd, 'Le prisme du désir dans les romans de Gautier' (207–20), comparing *Mademoiselle de Maupin* and *Le Capitaine Fracasse*, and finding in both a writer taking the utmost pleasure as an accomplished wordsmith; C. F. Sánchez, 'L'autre testament de Spirite ou le triomphe de Charbonneau: fantastique et humour en habit noir' (221–42), showing continuity of theme and structure in this and other stories by G., as well as his judicious deployment of black humour; C. G. Schick, 'Le donner à voir de Gautier ou pour un Candaule' (243–63), suggesting that the complexities in *Le Roi Candaule*, however disconcerting, represent an inherent feature of the author's skill as a writer.

HUGO. F. Laurent, 'La question du grand homme dans l'oeuvre de Victor Hugo', *Romantisme*, 100, 1998:63–89, identifies this as a vital thread running through all of H.'s work, the notion of greatness undergoing a profound change and affecting his aesthetic, historical, political and psychological viewpoints. M.-C. Pasquier, 'Hugo et la traduction', *ib.*, 106:21–30, brings together H.'s observations on the procedures involved in translation and explains its importance in his work, also the reasons why his son undertook the translation of Shakespeare. E. Pich, 'Le monochrome hugolien', *AJFS*, 36:280–92, considers the status of description in *Les Rayons et les Ombres*, noting that visual imagery suppresses colour in favour of clarity of line and gradation. Ludmila Charles-Wurtz, *Poétique du sujet lyrique dans l'oeuvre de Victor Hugo*, Champion, 1998, 727 pp., examines the bases, the form and the development of H.'s lyricism, from *Les Orientales* to *Les Chansons des rues et des bois*. Though the perspective has some limitations, depending to a certain extent on the selection of representative poems from the collections, the conclusion is no less valid: lyricism gave H. the means to speak about the people before exile, to the people during exile, and with the people after the Commune, presenting a different conception of the Republic and a new vision of poetry as the ally of democracy. John Andrew Frey, *A Victor Hugo Encyclopedia*, Westport–London, Greenwood Press, xxii + 305 pp., adopts the format of Van Tieghem's dictionary, while dismissing it as having about it 'the odor of 19th-c. positivism'. The orientation is different, aimed at the English-speaking community, including those with no knowledge of French. Its declared intent, of providing an interpretation of H.'s works and of debatable or questionable aspects of his personality, is adequately fulfilled, though posthumous publication has prevented the correction of certain contradictions. For example, we learn on p. 110 that 'Eugène did not go completely mad the day after Victor Hugo's marriage to Adèle', whereas on p. 137 we are told that 'During the night [he was] seized with total madness'. Claude Retat, *X ou le divin dans la poésie de Victor Hugo à partir de l'exil*, CNRS, 222 pp.

LAMARTINE. Gérard Calmettes, *Lamartine, voix de la République*, Précy-sous-Thil, L'Armançon, 1998, 144 pp., is an interesting account of the poet's political ideas and activity. He supported the abolition of slavery, freedom of expression, the defence of workers' rights, and assistance for the unemployed. His part in proclaiming the Second Republic was motivated by a desire for new solutions to social problems. Gérard Unger, *Lamartine, poète et homme d'état*, Flammarion, 1998, 540 pp., aimed mainly at the general reader, is a biography which stresses L.'s political thought and his role in public life.

MUSSET. Bernardette Chovelon, *Dans Venise la Rouge, les amours de George Sand et Musset*, Payot, 192 pp. Frank Lestringant, *Alfred de Musset*, Flammarion, 750 pp., undertakes the difficult task of bringing together the poet's life and work. The life story is full and detailed, yet sufficiently accessible for the general reader. In the strictly chronological progression, considerable attention is given to the poetry and the plays. The overall perspective shows M. attempting to replace literature with life or, unsuccessfully, endeavouring to make the two interact.

NERVAL. J. Fornasiero, 'Nerval vers 1850: éléments d'une bio-graphie politique', *AJFS*, 36:293–305, examines evidence of N.'s political orientation in the years 1848–51 and takes issue with the suggestion that he had lost interest in politics. Lucien Giraudo, *Nerval*, Nathan, 1998, 127 pp. Pierre Campion, *Nerval: une crise dans la pensée*, PUF, 1998, 120 pp.

SAINTE-BEUVE. Marie-Catherine Huet-Brichard, *La Poésie de Sainte-Beuve: un imaginaire de l'échec*, Clermont Ferrand, CRRR, 253 pp.

TASTU. Afifa Marzouki, *Amable Tastu, une poétesse à l'époque romantique*, Tunis, La Manouba U.P., 1997, 484 pp.

VIGNY. J. McLeman-Carnie, 'Monologue: a dramatic strategy in Alfred de Vigny's rhetoric', *NCFS*, 26:253–65, gives particular attention to 'Moïse', 'La Maison du berger', 'La Colère de Samson', and 'Le Mont des Oliviers', suggesting that the monologues, in the absence of narrator intervention, are essentially the theatrical device of persuading an audience towards a particular conclusion by means of vivid imagery and elevated rhetoric. *RHLF*, 98.3, 1998, publishes the papers of a conference held at the Sorbonne on the occasion of the bicentenary of V.'s birth, 22 November 1997. It contains: M. Ambrière, 'Alfred de Vigny connu, méconnu, inconnu' (357–65), on the critical response to V.'s writing in his own time, and the reasons why he addressed his work to posterity; A. Jarry, 'La femme dans l'oeuvre de Vigny' (367–74), undertaking what is acknowledged to be an enormous subject, including the consideration that the women whom V. portrays are often quite fearsome, but concluding that this is probably due to the ideology of the time; A. Pohorsky, 'Vigny et la malédiction du poète' (375–84), examining the frequent theme of the 'poète maudit', particularly in *Stello*, the preface to *Chatterton*, *Daphné*, 'Les Destinées', and 'La Maison du berger'; S. Marchal, 'Les salons et le clientélisme littéraire' (385–401), dealing with patronage and the literary world of V.'s time; L. Chotard, 'Vigny lecteur de Corneille' (403–15), on changes in V.'s appreciation of C., from admiration to disdain, and then to eventual reconciliation; G. Chamarat-Malandain, 'Le Christ aux Oliviers: Vigny et Nerval' (417–28), on similarities and differences between the two poems on the same subject, published in close chronological proximity; P. Bénichou, 'Un Gethsémani romantique: "Le Mont des Oliviers" de Vigny' (429–36), on V.'s handling of the New Testament sources and the question of whether 'Le Silence' is a denial of the existence of God; L. Sabourin, 'Vigny et l'homme de lettres' (437–50), on his classification of literary personae and his conception of the role of the poet; J.-P. Saint-Gérand, 'Alfred de Vigny: dessein du langage et amour de la langue' (451–72), a retrospective analysis of V. criticism, concluding that his distinctive style must be the real focus of his work, and including an interesting rendering of line 8 of 'L'Esprit pur'; J.-M. Bailbé, 'Vigny et "l'orchestre intérieur": poésie et musique' (473–84), on V.'s concern for the musicality of his poetry, his remarkable achievements in that direction, and his appreciation of the work of certain contemporary composers such as Berlioz; E. Sala, 'Vigny source de l'opéra romantique italien: le cas de *La Maréchale d'Ancre*' (485–94), on the highly successful adaptation by Giovanni Prati and Alessandro Nini, *La Marescialla d'Ancre*; R. Tanaka, 'Alfred de Vigny au Japon' (495–500), on the critical reception of V.'s work in Japan, the Japanese translations which are available, and the apparent decline in the amount of scholarly work done on him. André Jarry, *Alfred de Vigny: Étapes et sens du geste littéraire*, 2 vols, Geneva, Droz, 1998, viii + 537, 539–1036 pp., is a revised version of the doctoral thesis defended in 1992, applying Freudian psychoanalysis to V.'s writing. Stylistic analysis and textual psychoanalysis are combined, proceeding chronologically through the poetry and prose. The general conclusion is that descriptions such as that in 'Moïse' give evidence of a manic-depressive oscillation resulting from anxieties at the oral stage, and that V.'s literary career follows the three Lacanian stages of imaginary, symbolic and real. The symbolic stage is to be observed from Stello to 'Le Mont des Oliviers' and reality is dominant after 'La Maison du berger'. *Papiers académiques inédits*, ed. Lise Sabourin, Champion, 1998, 374 pp., present a certain amount of new material, coming mainly from three sources: the *Archives Jean Sagnier*, for items not published in the *Mémoires inédits* of 1958; the *fonds Vigny* of the Bibliothèque Nationale, partially published with deletions and insertions by Guillemin; the 'Carnet académique' of 1861–63, kept in the Archives de l'Institut and, though mentioned by Barrès in his *Cahiers*, hitherto unpublished, apart from the passage on Baudelaire's visit in 1861. These texts help us to gain a clearer picture of the man, the poet, the society in which he lived, and his role in the Académie. Id., *Alfred de Vigny et l'Académie Française: Vie de l'Institution (1830–1870)*, Champion, 1998, 1008 pp., completes the story and goes some way to dispel the myth of the poet's isolation in an ivory tower. Here we have a guide to the extent of his literary friendships, and the support he offered to other poets, as well as his reaction to the literary fashions of the time.

## 4. THE NOVEL

Florian Bratu, \**Le Réalisme français: essai sur Balzac et Stendhal*, Écrivains, 148 pp. Jacques Dürrenmatt, *Bien coupé mal cousu: de la ponctuation et de la division du texte romantique*, Saint-Denis, Vincennes U.P., 189 pp., is an informative exploration of the use of full stops, commas, *points de suspension* and representations of silence, italics and the division of novels into chapters. It includes discussion of why punctuation exists in the first place, and concludes that the Romantics used it as a further means of self-expression, in order to turn their text into an organic entity in which divisions would appear to be the work of nature.

### BALZAC

K. A. Comfort, 'Floral emblems of health in Balzac's *Le Lys dans la vallée*', *DFS*, 44, 1998:31–38, shows how images of flowers are used to constitute a separate narrative displaying Madame de Mortsauf's illness and untimely death. L. E. Dickinson, 'Pariah and parasite: la claque and historicity in Balzac's *La Comédie humaine*', *FS*, 52, 1998:305–15, finds that B.'s representations of the activities of the claque in novels dealing with the period 1820–30 are based on personal experience, and serve as a further means to present his views on the inevitable link between money and artistic success. B. L. Knapp, 'Balzac's *La Peau de Chagrin*: the gambler's quest for power', *NCFS*, 27 : 1–15, examines the comparison of chance in gambling and in life which is part of the framework of the novel. M. Lathers, ' "Tué par un excès d'amour": Raphael, Balzac, Ingres', *FR*, 71, 1998 : 550–64, finds that the story of Raphael and his mistress La Fornarina was well known in the 19th c., and a subject of considerable debate, to which *La Peau de chagrin* was intended as a contribution. E. C. Smith III, 'Honoré de Balzac and the "genius" of Walter Scott: debt and denial', *CLS*, 36 : 209–25, is concerned with the considerable debt which B. acknowledged to Scott, and shows how *La Comédie humaine* could be considered an 'unavowed continuation' of the *Waverley Novels*. S. Vachon, ' "Je lui passerai ma plume au travers du corps": Sainte-Beuve et Balzac', *RHLF*, 99 : 1191–1208, begins with B.'s reaction to S.-B.'s first article on him in the *Revue des Deux Mondes* and goes on to describe various stages of the literary and theoretical enmity between the two writers. S. Yates, 'Women in the discourse of Balzac's Horace Bianchon', *AJFS*, 36 : 172–87, suggests that one of the character's major roles is to allow B. to express his beliefs about women, whether as a biased male observer, or showing sympathy for women's social condition, as a reluctant seducer or as a misogynist. *ABa*, n.s., 19, 451 pp., includes: H. Robert, 'Louis-Philippe dans l'oeuvre de Balzac' (7–27), which shows that, despite B.'s general antipathy to the July Monarchy, he had a clear and novel perspective of the King's political role; R.-A. Courteix, 'La vision de l'Église catholique dans *Une Ténébreuse Affaire*' (29–38), concerned mainly with the figure of the abbé Goujet as an accurate representation of the Church in a changing society; J.-P. Chaline, 'L'élection en province vue par Balzac dans les "Scènes de la vie politique" ' (39–47), showing that B.'s view of provincial democracy was fundamentally pessimistic; M. Andréoli, 'Aristocratie et médiocratie dans les "Scènes de la vie politique" ' (49–61), finding in B.'s decriptions of different social strata evidence of progressive tendencies supported by his abiding faith in humanity; A. Lorant, 'Sources iconographiques des romans de jeunesse de Balzac' (65–79), on the influence of paintings, and not least those of Girodet; A.-M. Lefebvre, 'L'image du médecin dans le "cycle Hubert" ' (81–106), on the early elaboration of medical characters in the three novels of 1821; M. Ménard, '*Le Vicaire des Ardennes*: un roman de la curiosité' (107–20), using this motif as evidence of the writer's uneasy search for an identity; S. Vachon, 'Du nouveau sur Balzac: l'écho des romans de jeunesse' (121–54), which examines 66 documents dated from 1822 to 1826 in search of information on the impact and circulation figures of the novels signed

R'hoone and Saint-Aubin; M. Bongiovanni-Bertini, '*Antony* d'Alexandre Dumas dans *Le Rendez-vous* de Balzac' (157–76), showing that certain of B.'s dramatic scenes reproduce key moments in the play; P. Havard de la Montagne, ' "Enmalusons-nous!"': Balzac, les Malus et les Mabile' (177–212), suggesting that close members of the B. family may be the source of several characters in the novels, and even of Goriot; A. Besson-Morel, 'Presse enfantine et courrier des lecteurs à l'époque de Balzac' (213–24), on the remarkable development of children's newspapers in the years 1830–50; M. Delon, 'Le boudoir balzacien' (227–45), on the way in which *La Fille aux yeux d'or* was shaped by 18th-c. references and the philosophy of de Sade; A.-M. Lefebvre, 'Le rouge et le noir dans *La Peau de chagrin*' (247–60), showing, with reference to Stendhal, that a more exact title of B.'s novel might have been "Le noir ou le rouge"; J.-D. Ebguy, 'Le récit comme vision: Balzac voyant dans *Facino Cane*' (261–83), a re-examination of B.'s distinctive visionary realism and the notion of the power of language found in the narrative; P. Berthier, 'Le voile de Véronique' (285–301), on the composition and readings of *Le Curé de village*, with particular reference to the heroine; C. Dédéyan, 'Écriture et architecture: une question de langue' (303–29), on B.'s frequent use of technical terms in *La Comédie humaine*, and the rather tenuous link between his descriptions and architectural reality. The two volumes which follow are collections of papers published by the Groupe International de Recherches Balzaciennes. *Balzac et le style*, ed. Anne Herschberg-Pierrot, SEDES, 1998, 192 pp., contains: C. Mouchard, 'Volonté de style' (17–27), on the link between style and will, particularly in *Théorie de la démarche*; M. Sandras, 'Les tensions de la prose balzacienne' (29–33), on the poetic nature of B.'s style and the emergence of a new ideal for writers of prose; J. Grange, 'La prose comme institution du monde moderne' (35–45), suggesting that the prose of *La Comédie humaine* is not literature, but a means of enquiry into the lack of permanence or system in 19th-c. society; J. Neefs, 'Figurez-vous . . .' (41–45), on the formidable dramatic and analytical powers of B.'s writing; J.-P. Saint-Gérand, 'Balzac, rhétorique, prose et style' (49–65), on the ideas on style expressed in dictionaries and literary studies published during B.'s lifetime; J.-L. Diaz, 'Balzac stylisticien' (77–92), on B.'s ideas on style, as expressed in his critical analyses of the work of others; S. Vachon, ' "Se plonger dans les écuries d'Augias de mon style" (revue critique 1829–1850)' (95–111), on the origins of the idea that B. wrote badly; E. Bordas, 'Balzac, "Grand romancier sans être grand écrivain"?: du style et des préjugés' (113–31), on the history of the critical response to B., and the comparatively recent recognition of 'le style balzacien'; H. Mitterand, 'Un "bel artiste" ' (135–44), a redefinition of the aesthetic merits of B.'s style, as the basis of the continuity and integrity of his work; M. Léonard, 'Le style comme dramaturgie du sens' (145–56), an analysis of B.'s use of certain demonstratives; L. Finas, 'Balzac *est* style' (157–72), a critical appreciation of the three stages of development of B.'s style, as represented by *Le Curé de Tours*, *Théorie de la démarche*, and *Adventures administratives d'une idée heureuse*. *Balzac ou la tentation de l'impossible*, ed. Raymond Mahieu and Franc Schuerewegen, SEDES, 202 pp., includes: F. Schuerewegen, 'Scories ou pourquoi il y a une oeuvre là-dessus' (9–16), on B.'s reaction to the appearance in Russia of a pirated version of *Le Lys dans la vallée*; J.-L. Diaz, 'La stratégie de l'effraction' (19–28), on B.'s negative perception of boundaries, and the boundless domain of his imagination; B. Diaz, 'Sans limites' (29–35), suggesting that, nevertheless, the concept of social divisions and the ability to transcend them provide the essential structure of *La Comédie humaine*; A. Vanoncini, 'Balzac, Tocqueville, Michelet: du roman à l'histoire' (37–46), showing that the style of *Les Paysans*, turning aside from linear narrative in favour of observation and analysis, is the forerunner of that of modern historical discourse; F. Terrasse-Riou, 'Les enjeux de la représentation d'un seuil: l'hôtel de Chaulieu' (47–55), on flashback and the threshold effect in the *Mémoires de deux jeunes mariés*; D. Maleuvre, 'A la limite, la peinture: le chef d'oeuvre inconnu' (57–65), suggesting that Frenhofer's painting both acknowledges and negates dialectic boundaries; M. Milner, 'L'agonie' (67–75), on a frequent motif which is linked to the uncertain nature of the human condition; A. Del Lungo, 'Lettres, hiéroglyphes, arabesques' (79–87), on the use of epigraphs both to captivate the reader and to mark a textual boundary; G. Jacques, 'A la limite du roman et de la nouvelle' (89–96), on the transformation of *Même histoire* into *La femme de trente ans*; J. Gleize, '"Immenses détails". Le détail balzacien et son lecteur' (97–106), on the use of apparently superfluous and excessive detail to open up opportunities for interpretation of the text; D. F. Bell, 'Marque, trace, pistes: Balzac à la recherche d'une science des indices' (107–12), on the significance and the implications of Vautrin's branding as a criminal; C. Nez, 'Quand les mots ne suffisent plus . . .' (113–19), on the interjections and silences of B.'s female characters; F. Gaillard, 'Aux limites du genre: *Melmoth réconcilié*' (121–32), on the elaboration in the novel of B.'s prefatory remark to the effect that, in modern society, money had replaced honour; L. Schehr, 'Homo-diégèse' (135–41), on possible representations of homosexuality in *La Comédie humaine*; C. Nesci, 'L'oeuvre de la mort' (135–41), examining ideas on death and the boundless nature of art in *La Peau de chagrin* and *Ferragus*; A. Mura, 'Aux frontières du dicible' (153–58), concerned with the novella *Adieu*; A.-M. Baron, 'Entre la toise du savant et le délire du fou' (159–65), on B.'s evident search for an identity and a vocation in his early philosophical writings, and the subsequent evolution of his notion of genius; E. Bordas, 'Au commencement était l'impossible: la *Physiologie du mariage*' (167–78), suggesting that this earliest text of *La Comédie humaine* is a crucial landmark in the development of B.'s realist style; S. Vachon, 'La robe et les armes' (179–90), on the period 1832–34, B.'s early meetings with Mme Hanska in Geneva, his gifts of manuscripts, and a vital stage in the evolution of his status as a writer; R. Mahieu, 'Balzac, Vidocq, Gozlan' (193–97), a reflection on a meeting between the three in September 1844 and the story of a counterfeit coin, which could well be a symbol of narrative fiction. Max Andréoli, *Lectures et mythes: Les Chouans et Les Paysans d'Honoré de Balzac*, Champion, 384 pp. Pierre Barbéris, *Le Monde de Balzac*, Kimé, 640 pp. Anne-Marie Baron, *Balzac ou l'auguste mensonge*, Nathan, 1998, 239 pp., is concerned with B.'s view of the novel as a work of fiction which nevertheless had to present the truth in its detail, and which only by so doing could permit the creative flight of the imagination. Philippe Berthier, *La Vie quotidienne dans 'La Comédie humaine' de Balzac*, Hachette, 1998, 300 pp., demonstrates how the 2472 characters are aptly presented as representatives of the distinctive and exceptional features of the society of the time. Attention is given to housing and places to live, family life, working practices, high living, food and drink, and spare-time activities. Juliette Frølich, *Des Hommes, des femmes et des choses: langages de l'objet dans le roman de Balzac à Proust*, Saint-Denis, Vincennes U.P., 1997, 166 pp., begins with a quotation from *Une Fille d'Ève* in which B. refers to 'les choses qui parlent', and suggests the need for an object-oriented critique of the work of later writers. Evidence is used from the Parisian narratives of Flaubert and Proust. Jérôme Godeau, *Splendeurs et misères de l'écrivain: une lecture de 'La Comédie Humaine'*, Horay, 96 pp. Philippe Maxence, *Petit Voyage en Balzacie*, Bouère, Dominique Martin Morin, 110 pp. John Homayoun Mazaheri, *Myth and Guilt-Consciousness in Balzac's 'La Femme de trente ans'*, Lewiston, Mellen, iii + 112 pp. Isabelle Mimouni, *Balzac illusionniste: les arts dans l'oeuvre du romancier*, A. Biro, 144 pp. Roger Pierrot, *Ève de Balzac*, Stock, xiv + 551 pp., is a biography of Eve Rzewuska, later Hanska, the lady who, though she was only married to B. for a few weeks, kept his name for the remaining 32 years of her life.

EDITIONS. *La Comédie humaine*, ed. Anne-Simone and Pierre Dufief, vols 3 and 4, 1152, 1088 pp. *Le Cabinet des antiques*, ed. Nadine Satiat, Gallimard, 308 pp. *Le Colonel Chabert*, ed. Patrick Berthier, Gallimard, 192 pp. *La Duchesse de Langeais*, ed. Constance Cagnat-Deboeuf, LGF, 1998, 252 pp. *Eugénie Grandet*, ed. Samuel S. de Sacy, Gallimard, 275 pp. *La Maison du chat qui pelote*, ed. Patrick Berthier,

Garnier Flammarion, 96 pp. *Le Médecin de campagne*, ed. Pierre Barbéris, Garnier Flammarion, 383 pp. *Le Père Goriot*, ed. Thierry Boudin, Gallimard, 436 pp. *Ferragus*, ed. Catherine Defigier, Gallimard-Éducation, 1998, 288 pp. *Premiers Romans*, ed. André Lorant, vol. I, Laffont, 1170 pp. *Une Ténébreuse Affaire*, ed. Rose Fortassier, Garnier Flammarion, 409 pp.

## STENDHAL

L. G. Algazi, 'Throw away the key: the prison as maternal space in the Stendhalian novel', *NCFS*, 26 : 286–94, treats the familiar territory of the prisons in *Le Rouge et le Noir* and *La Chartreuse de Parme* as havens where Julien and Fabrice may return to their maternal mistresses, while demonstrating that this preverbal space constitutes a refuge from the language and culture of patriarchal society. P. Jousset, 'Le mari est d'argent, mais le silence est d'or', *Romantisme*, 103 : 79–96, describes and explains the links between money, love and art, which form the basis for *Feder ou le mari d'argent*, and the potential problems which they create for the would-be artist. C. Perry, 'Paysages du souvenir et du rêve dans la chasse au bonheur chez Stendhal', *NCFS*, 26 : 266–85, is concerned with the autobiographical element in certain passages from *La Vie de Henry Brulard* and *La Chartreuse de Parme*, which suggest that S. used literary reminiscences as a point of mediation between fiction and personal objectives. R. Servoise, 'Le merveilleux dans *La Chartreuse de Parme*', *RHLF*, 99 : 1191–1208, makes use of the deciphered *marginalia*, the hasty notes which S. scribbled to himself, in order to shed light on a number of issues including the possible origins of the story in the author's relationship with Mathilde Viscontini-Dembowski. Paul Désalmand, *Cher Stendhal: un pari sur la gloire*, Charenton, Presses de Valmy, 288 pp., is an essay of which the apparatus criticus is only available through the internet at <http://www.alpes-net.fr/~reysset/dossier.htm>. Edgar Pich, *Racine et Stendhal: de l'action au processus*, Lyon, ALDRUI, 1998, 170 pp.

EDITIONS.    *Correspondance générale*, ed. Victor Del Litto et al., vol. III, Champion, xiv + 891 pp., covers the important period from 1817 to 1830, which begins with Henri Beyle changing his name to S. and ends with the publication of *Le Rouge et le Noir*. Like the preceding volumes, it is extremely thorough and opens up new perspectives for those involved in S. studies. *Vol. II, Champion, 1998, xx + 806 pp., covers the period 1810–16.

## OTHER WRITERS

DUMAS PÈRE.    Daniel Compère, *Le Comte de Monte Cristo d'Alexandre Dumas: Lecture des textes*, Amiens, Encrage, 1998, 115 pp. Dominique

Fernandez, *Les Douze Muses d'Alexandre Dumas*, Grasset, 325 pp., analyses the nature of the multiple sources of inspiration in D.'s work: historical, ethnological, lyrical, and also that derived from both Parisian and provincial settings. Gilles Henry, *Les Dumas, le secret de Monte Cristo*, France-Empire, 320 pp., suggests that the story was D.'s attempt to come to terms with his own family's history, and with the racism from which he suffered, by seeking to explain his origins.

GAUTIER.   J.-M. Roulin, 'Confusion des sexes, mélange des genres et quête de sens dans *Mademoiselle de Maupin*', *Romantisme*, 100, 1998:31–40, shows how the figure of the androgyne is used to explore the erotic, the aesthetic, but also the nature of the novelist's technique, the reader being required to take a fuller part in interpretation than would be the case in an allegory.

HUGO.   K. M. Grossman, 'Trading places: public and private transport in Hugo's *Les Travailleurs de la mer*', *NCFS*, 26:295–307, examines motifs and metaphors of movement and displacement in the novel, which are used to define the boundaries of the human condition and the creative energy which can be used to transcend them. D. Peyrache-Leborgne, 'L'érotique hugolienne dans *L'Homme qui rit*', *Romantisme*, 103:19–29, draws attention to H.'s innovation in a direct approach to matters of a sexual nature, and the significance of the erotic bipolarity of the two main female characters. Myriam Roman, \**Victor Hugo et le roman philosophique: du drame dans les faits au drame dans les idées*, Champion, 832 pp. E. Noetinger, 'La sinistre beauté du masque: étude de *L'Homme qui rit* de Victor Hugo', *FS*, 53:405–16, celebrates the skill with which H. blends the aesthetics of beauty and the grotesque, and concludes that Gwyneplaine's expressionless grin is a powerful metaphor and stimulus for reflection.

MÉRIMÉE.   *Prosper Mérimée, écrivain, archéologue, historien*, ed. Antonia Fonyi, Geneva, Droz, xiii + 266 pp., is a collection of papers dealing with M.'s various occupations. It contains: F. Bercé, 'Les enjeux et les contradictions de l'archéologie et de la politique sous la Monarchie de Juillet et le Second Empire' (3–14); G. Poisson, 'Prosper Mérimée et les monuments historiques de Paris et d'Île de France' (15–26); O. Poisson, '*La Vénus d'Ille* entre archéologie et littérature en 1834' (27–38); V.-A. Deshoulières, 'Les métamorphoses de Pygmalion depuis Mérimée' (39–50); Y.-M. Bercé, 'Le roi caché: *Les Faux Démétrius*' (53–61); S. Carpenter, '*Les Faux Démétrius*: les ratés de l'histoire' (63–73); '*Histoire de don Pèdre Ier, roi de Castille*: sorcière et frères ennemis' (75–85); C. Millet, 'Le légendaire de Mérimée: le Mémorial de la Barbarie' (89–97); L. Charles-Wurtz, 'Le lyrisme de *La Guzla*' (99–110); D. Charles, '*Mosaïque: Les Orientales* de Mérimée' (111–12); P. Petitier, 'De la fable au fantastique: l'animalité dans *La Jaquerie*' (123–34); P. Brunel, 'Rue du Serpent' (137–48), in *Carmen*, and its possible original in the *calle de las Sierpes* in Madrid; T. Ozwald, 'Le récit endiablé de Mérimée' (149–58); D.-H. Pageaux, 'Figures du voyageur, ou Mérimée Protée voyageur' (159–66); M. Cadot, 'Mérimée ou la découverte de la littérature russe' (167–77); A.-M. Reboul, '*Carmen*: la rêverie de Prosper Mérimée' (179–89); A. Clancier, 'Mérimée et le travestissement' (191–96); A. Fonyi, 'La passion pour l'archè' (197–207); F. Marcoin, 'Mérimée, entre Voltaire et Shakespeare' (211–22); I. Gabolde, 'Altérité et structure cognitive dans la nouvelle mériméenne' (223–34); G. Ponnau, '*La Vénus d'Ille*: texte palimpseste?' (235–45); J. Gilles, 'Mérimée, Manet et Cie, la fin du modèle grec' (247–54); M. Sandras, 'Le style de personne' (255–64). Xavier Darcos, *Mérimée*, Flammarion, 1998, 539 pp., is an accessible and widely acclaimed biography which seeks to place M. within the context of his time and fill in the often unconsidered background of his life. The main focus nevertheless remains his literary production and, though the target audience is principally that of the 'general reader', the account is detailed and thorough.

MUSSET. H. Servaes, '*Emmeline* d'Alfred de Musset, un pré(-)texte musical', *RBPH*, 76:679–85, addresses the importance in the novella of the performances of Don Giovanni, and shows that they represent a three-stage semiotic hierarchy, of music, speech and writing, which complicates the relationship between signifier and signified.

SAND. E. Cosset, '*Consuelo*: nature et fonction de l'espace', *NCFS*, 27:51–61, is concerned with the function of different categories of space and the novel's equation of travel with an initiation into hidden truths. P. Dayan, 'Who is the narrator in *Indiana*?', *FS*, 52, 1998:152–61, suggests that Ralph is the true narrator, and that the novel, as the story of his acquisition of a voice, must place him in the third person until he gains the capacity to establish his personality in language. P. De Meo, ' "Ce que j'éprouve ressemble à la désorganisation": George Sand écrit la maladie', *DFS*, 47:87–92, finds that characters dying of a broken heart may not be merely a literary convention, but that there is strong evidence of a causal link between happiness and health in S.'s correspondance and life writing. M. Trouille, 'Towards a new appreciation of Mme de Genlis: the influence of *Les Battuécas* on George Sand's political and social thought', *FR*, 71, 1998:565–76, notes S.'s recollection, in *Histoire de ma vie*, of the immense enthusiasm with which, at the age of 16–17, she read this startlingly modern novel, and goes on to evaluate its lasting influence on her, both as a novelist and as an advocate for social reform. C. Van Den Broek, '*Le Château des Désertes* de George Sand, cours de jeu dramatique', *RBPH*, 76:687–708, compares S.'s negative representation of the Don Juan figure in *Lélia*, demonstrating the abuse of power over women, with the reworked intertextuality of this short novel, which uses the figure as the embodiment of her ideas on the theatre and the cult of the star. *Le Siècle de George Sand*, ed. David A. Powell, Amsterdam–Atlanta, Rodopi, 1998, xii + 373 pp., contains the proceedings of a conference held at Hofstra University in November 1996. It includes: F.-P. Bowman, 'The pleasures and pitfalls of reading literature in a historical context' (3–16); S. Vierne, 'George Sand: politique, le mot et la chose' (19–28), emphasizing the modernity of S.'s views; K. Biermann, 'George Sand et Victor Hugo — deux visions "parallèles" de la Révolution' (29–34); L. Frappier-Mazur, 'Ambiguïtés du politique: la musique populaire dans *Consuelo* et *Les Maîtres Sonneurs*' (35–43), on an art form which could be an indicator of nationalism, but which S. interpreted as a manifestation of universal human progress; A. M. Rea, '*La Filleule*: an a-political Sand' (45–54), concluding that she could never be so described; M. Hecquet, 'Sand: du socialisme à son abandon' (55–61), showing that, although S. did not remain in contact with socialist thinkers in the second half of the 19th c., she never abandoned the most fundamental socialist principles; S. Charron, '*Claudie* de George Sand (1851): vision prolétaire et féministe' (63–71), on a play with a new social and aesthetic message; S. Malkin, 'Between the Bastille and the Madeleine: Sand's theatre politics (1832–1848)' (73–83); T. Wilkerson, ' "Ton vengeur veille": *La Cause* de George Sand' (85–93), on the performance of April 1848 marking the last moment when S. could envisage the realization of a dream to improve the lot of the working classes; M. Rice-Defosse, 'The woman writer and the worker: social mobility and solidarity in *La Ville Noire*' (95–102), on a novel which transcends the binary thinking of the dominant culture of 1859; C. Betensky, 'When the people are not the people: populist paradoxes in Sand and Michelet' (103–09), comparing S.'s *Le Compagnon du tour de France* and M.'s *Le Peuple*; E. Sourian, 'George Sand et le coup d'état de Louis-Napoléon Bonaparte' (111–19); N.E. Rogers, 'He said/she said in *Horace*' (121–28), on how the female voice in the novel often represents authority; S. Van Dijk, 'George Sand et les mouvements d'émancipation féminine' (131–45); L. A. Minot, ' "Like a prostituted queen": refiguring revolutionary misogyny in 1830s France' (147–56), showing that the work of S. and the Saint-Simonians suggest ways in which the gendered metaphors of the Revolution still informed popular discourse; C. Fernandez, 'George Sand's "La Marquise": feminism and Romantic idealism' (157–64); C. Bertrand-Jennings, 'Déconstruction du genre et intertexte de l'androgyne: *Gabriel*' (165–77), on how the sexual ambiguity of the protagonist presents a universal feminine character; G. Seybert, 'George Sand: *Le Dernier Amour* and its sexual politics' (179–84); N. Harkness, 'Sand, Lamennais et le féminisme: le cas des

*Lettres à Marcie*' (185–92); J. M. Wright, ' "Une mauvaise copie de Monsieur de Wolmar: Sand's subversion of Rousseau's masculinities' (193–201); D. Laporte, 'La figure de l'actrice et la réflexivité du discours romanesque dans *Lucrezia Floriani*' (203–11); M. D. Garval, 'Visions of the great woman writer: imagining George Sand through word and image' (213–20); H. Hoogenboom, 'Wlademir Karénine and her biography of George Sand: one Russian woman writer responds to Sand' (225–35); M. I. Crummy, 'George Sand and her *Sage-femmes* as an inspiration for Jules Michelet's *La Sorcière*' (237–46); E. Cocke, 'Corinne and Consuelo: women artists in dialogue with the world' (247–52); R. C. Capasso, 'The Empress Eugénie in *Malgrétout*' (253–59); J. Goldin, 'Aurore directeur de conscience' (263–79); R. McGinnis, 'Sand and Baudelaire: the politics of charity' (281–91); K. McLean, 'George and Sigmund take tea: George Sand's *Lélia* as a philosophical contribution to the pre-psychoanalytic tradition' (293–300); D. J. Mickelsen, 'Building on Sand: from narrative zoos to imagined communities' (301–08); B. Diaz, 'Portrait de l'artiste en maçon: la correspondance entre George Sand et Charles Poncy (1842–1856)' (309–19); B. Diaz, ' "Music conducive to dream": Sand and the musical fantastic' (321–33); J.-M. Bailbé, 'Le regard de l'artiste sur la société chez G. Sand, après 1851' (335–41); B. M. Waldinger, 'George Sand's search for the heart of Faust' (343–48); T. Jurgrau, 'Antisemitism as revealed in George Sand's letters' (349–56); E. Gould, 'Sand's forgotten Bohemia' (357–65), which is concerned with *La Dernière Aldini*; M. Lukacher, 'Entre femmes: Sand/Colet et la question de *Lui*' (367–73). Béatrice Didier, *George Sand écrivain: "un grand fleuve d'Amérique"*, PUF, 1998, 839 pp., taking its subtitle from one of Flaubert's letters to S., goes on to celebrate the characteristics which F. identified in her work: 'énormité et douceur'. They are manifested by a remarkable diversity of subjects, settings, and characters. We are shown that, following the publication of S.'s complete correspondence, we are able to perceive more fully her manner of writing. This in turn enables a new perspective of her work, though we are warned that she does not fall easily into the category of the 'Woman Writer'. Janet Hiddleston, *George Sand and Autobiography*, Oxford, Legenda, 107 pp., considers the *Histoire de ma vie* from different points of view, relating to the formation of the autobiographical project, the complexity of S.'s family relationships, the structure of the work and the changing narrative voice. Particular attention is given to S.'s confused and ambivalent attitude to gender, leaving a text in which the contradictions are shown to be largely unresolved. *Sand-Barbès, correspondance d'une amitié républicaine*, ed. Michelle Perrot, Lectoure, Le Capucin, 193 pp.

TRISTAN. F. Gabaude, '*Les Pérégrinations d'une paria*: initiation, observation, révélation', *FR*, 71, 1998:809–17, shows how this account of T.'s journey to Peru, in 1833, represents a three-stage transition in her feelings, the first as neophyte, the second when she travels to a number of places which are classified as masculine, feminine or preliminary, and the third when she becomes aware of her true place in society. J. M. Kabulis, 'Why the novel?: toward a reconsideration of *Le Romanesque* in Flora Tristan's *Méphis ou le prolétaire*', *NCFS*, 27:38–50, begins with the paradox that T., having inveighed against the status of fiction in the preface to *Pérégrinations d'une paria*, proceeded to write this novel of 1838. This 'meta novel' is shown to be not only an exploration of the reasons for what she considers to be the novel's decline, but also a statement of the feminine experience and the complexity of its representation.

5. DRAMA

DUMAS PÈRE. B. T. Cooper, 'Rewriting *Antony*', *NCFS*, 27:251–61, suggests that the one-act *L'Honneur est satisfait* of 1858 may be read as a rewriting of the celebrated drama of 1831.

DUMAS FILS. *A Critical Edition of 'La Route de Thèbes' by Alexandre Dumas Fils*, ed. H. D. Lewis, Lewiston, Mellen, 1998, xiv + 284 pp., is an unfinished, previously unpublished play discovered by the editor in D.'s papers in the Bibliothèque Nationale. The introduction fills in the background of major trends in 19th-c. theatre and D.'s life story before turning to religion and science, women and their role, love, marriage and adultery, the play's structure and stagecraft, and the nature and location of the three manuscripts.

LAMARTINE. *Toussaint Louverture*, ed. Léon-François Hoffmann, Exeter U.P., 1998, xliii + 163 pp., is an edition of a play which tends to be dismissed by modern critics, and to which the Pléiade *Oeuvres poétiques complètes* gave comparatively little attention. This edition is much more informative, dealing with the play's historical background, its ideological stance, and its critical reception. It is shown to be part of L.'s active campaign for the abolition of slavery. Thorough attention is given to L.'s additions and deletions for stage performances.

HUGO. Nicole Mallet, \**Victor Hugo, bibliographie commentée de William Shakespeare 1864–1995*, Lettres Modernes, 82 pp.

MUSSET. \**Lorenzaccio*, ed. Derek F. Connon, London, Bristol Classical Press, 1998, xxxviii + 144 pp.

## 6. WRITERS IN OTHER GENRES

W. Guentner, 'The inscription of the sketch in the 19th-c. French journal: Michelet, Delacroix and the Goncourt Brothers', *NCFS*, 27:276–89, shows how two traditionally private modes of self-expression move into the public domain during the Romantic Era. L. Chotard, 'Les grands hommes du jour', *Romantisme*, 100, 1998:105–14, explains the surge of biographical activity in the years from 1815 onwards as the result of social, economic and political change. A. Gérard, 'Le grand homme et la conception de l'histoire au XIXe siècle', *ib.*, 31–48, traces the evolution of the notion of greatness with reference to Guizot, Comte, Michelet and Fustel. J. Noiray, 'Figures du savant', *ib.*, 143–58, considers the two very different images of the scientist in 19th-c. literature: as a defender of positivist ideology and as a comic figure: absent-minded, angry, grotesque, and sometimes evil. Alain Kerlan, *La Science n'éduquera pas*, Berne, Lang, 342 pp., addresses the paradox which positivism presents relating to the position of science in education.

BALLANCHE. J.-F. Marquet, 'Ballanche et l'épopée romantique d'*Orphée*', *RLC*, 452–70, is concerned with the prose work of 1829. Initiation, albeit premature and leading to catastrophe, is shown to be the key theme, with Orpheus himself presented as a mythological prefiguration of Christ. Alan J. L. Busst, *\*L'Orphée de Ballanche: genèse et signification: contribution à l'étude du rayonnement de la pensée de Giambattista Vico*, Berne, Lang, 343 pp. Arthur McCalla, *A Romantic Historiosophy: The Philosophy of History of Pierre-Simon Ballanche*, Leiden, Brill, 1998, xii + 464 pp., is a detailed analysis of B.'s work and thought, and of their impact on the 19th-c. history of ideas. Not least, we are shown B.'s position in a broad perspective which includes predecessors, such as Saint-Simon, and contemporaries, such as Hugo, Lamartine, Lamennais, and Quinet.

COLET. *Lettres inédites de Louise Colet à Honoré Clair, 1839–1871*, ed. Annalisa Aruta Stampacchia, Clermont-Ferrand, CRRR, 360 pp., contains a total of 135 letters, the replies to which have been lost, on such subjects as motherhood, feminine emancipation, Paris, travel, and literary composition.

COMTE. Angèle Kremer-Marietti, *\*L'Anthropologie positiviste d'Auguste Comte: entre le signe et l'histoire*, L'Harmattan, 264 pp.

FOURIER. Simone Debout, *L'Utopie de Charles Fourier*, Presses du Réel, 1998, 269 pp., describes F.'s fundamental influence on the processes of social organization, also his contribution to the emancipation of women.

GAUTIER. L. Stock, 'Gautier et le réalisme', *AJFS*, 36:306–26, finds that the 'Salons' published in *La Presse* reveal more of G.'s true feelings on new developments in the visual arts than his equivalent contributions to the *Moniteur universel.*

GUIZOT. J.-F. Jacouty, 'Le "Grand Homme" selon Guizot', *Romantisme,* 100, 1998:49–55, shows how G. drew from history examples of leaders with the necessary intellect, political expertise and moral conscience to guide their peoples into the future, in the belief that France now needed such a person and that he could aspire to the role.

HUGO. Nicole Savy, *Victor Hugo voyageur de l'Europe,* Brussels, Labor, 1997, 189 pp., is an account based on H.'s travel writings, and the descriptions of his family and others, of the many varied journeys he made in his lifetime. In later years he was drawn increasingly to the Rhine, to Belgium, and to French-speaking Switzerland, though when younger he also travelled through northern France, the Netherlands, Germany, Luxembourg, Italy, and Spain.

LEROUX. B. Viard, 'Les grands hommes dans la doctrine de l'humanité de Pierre Leroux', *Romantisme,* 100, 1998:57–62, examines L.'s evaluation of the relative importance of great leaders and the sovereignty of the people, and concludes that he suggested an inextricable link between greatness and humanity.

MICHELET. V. Kogan, 'Paradoxical pedagogy: Michelet, education and social mobility', *NCFS,* 27:262–75, is on the contrast between M.'s discourse of inclusivity, consistent with his personal experience of progression from an artisanal background to bourgeois status, and his more conservative views, more in keeping with the prevalent discourses of his time. Simone Bernard-Griffiths, *\*Variétés sur Michelet,* Clermont-Ferrand, Université Blaise-Pascal, Centre de Recherches Révolutionnaires et Romantiques, 1998, 198 pp. Chakè Matossian, *Fils d'Arachné, les tableaux de Michelet,* Brussels, Part de l'Oeil, 1998, 270 pp., assesses the importance of works of art in M.'s writing. Arthur Mitzman, *Michelet ou la subversion du passé,* Boutique de l'histoire, 214 pp., is based on the four lectures given by the author at the Collège de France in 1998, dealing with M.'s life and work, his intellectual and political development, and his historical methodology. Olivier Remaud, *\*Michelet, la magistrature de l'histoire,* Michalon, 1998, 128 pp. Paul Viallaneix, *Michelet, les travaux et les jours 1798–1874,* Gallimard, 1998, 591 pp., is a close examination of the historian's life and work. In the bicentenary year of M.'s birth, it represents no less than an attempt to reconstruct the 'Livre des livres', the personal account which M. envisaged but never wrote. Proceeding year by year, and sometimes almost day by day, it is very thorough and detailed, and reveals more than simply M. the historian.

NERVAL. S. L. F. Richards, 'The occidental tourist: Nerval's *Le Voyage en Orient* as pseudo-documentary', *PhilP,* 44:65–72, examines

N.'s contribution to the Romantic paradigm shift which transforms the meaning of the title from a documentary narrative to an exploration of personal geography, though without mention of a significant precedent in Hugo's *Les Orientales*. Meryl Tyers, *Critical Fictions: Nerval's 'Les Illuminés'*, Oxford, Legenda, 1998, xvi + 122 pp., urges us to set aside the tangled publishing history of the individual narratives, and questions relating to their originality, instead considering the whole as a work of art. As the first significant study of *Les Illuminés*, its purpose is that of drawing together disparate facts and details in order to construct a complete picture. Particular attention is given to N.'s preface, 'La Bibliothèque de mon oncle'.

NODIER.   J.-F. Jeandillou, 'Le tribunal des lettres: Nodier et les *Questions de la littérature légale*', *RHLF*, 99:57–74, reveals in what N. described as his 'doctes bagatelles' an acute theoretical awareness and innovative ideas on textual and poetic analysis.

QUINET.   *\*Lettres à sa mère*, ed. Simone Bernard-Griffiths and Gérard Peylet, vol. II, Champion, 1998, 326 pp., continues the edition from the time of his arrival in Paris in 1820 to his discovery of Herder's *Idées sur la philosophie de l'histoire de l'humanité*.

SAINTE-BEUVE.   J.-L. Diaz, 'Portrait de Sainte-Beuve en "meneur de spectres"', *RHLF*, 99:215–31, accounts for S.-B.'s defence of 'minor' writers, such as Senancour, Victorien Fabre, Horace, and Vauvenargues, as part of his reaction against what he termed the 'grandhomie' of the Romantic period.

# THE NINETEENTH CENTURY (POST-ROMANTIC)
## POSTPONED

# THE TWENTIETH CENTURY, 1900–1945
## POSTPONED

# THE TWENTIETH CENTURY SINCE 1945

By H. G. McIntyre, *Lecturer in French at the University of Strathclyde*

## 1. GENERAL

G. D. Chaitin, 'From the Third Republic to postmodernism: language, freedom and the politics of the contingent', *MLN*, 114:780–815, advances on a broad front but, in the process, offers a number of useful sections on Sartre and *La Nausée*, on contingency and Sartre's political thinking and on Sartre's relationship with the dissident student movement and the non-Communist left, as well as Bergson and *La Nausée*, all of which will be of interest to the literary scholar. E. Kushner, 'La survivance du mythe d'Orphée au XXe siècle', *RLC*, 73:615–29, makes reference to a number of modern adaptations of the Orpheus myth by Segalen, Cocteau, Anouilh, and Pierre Emmanuel.

## 2. AUTHORS

BATAILLE. R. M. Pyrczak, 'Les espaces du sacré: le vide, le bord, le seuil, le renversement et la relation au sacré dans la fiction de G. B.', *DFS*, 48:115–26, considers assorted motifs in B., principally in *Le bleu du ciel*, among which are living 'au bord des choses' or examples of *renversement*, actual or physical as well as semantic. These various motifs are related to *le sacré* in B. or are to be seen as manifestations of the desire to *désacraliser*; eye-opening stuff in places, particularly in its exploration of the erotic in B.

BEAUVOIR. J. Hardwick, 'Keeping it together and falling apart in S. de B.'s *La Femme rompue*', *EFL*, 35–36:165–77, offers a post-modernist rereading of the novella intended to counter the tendencies to view de B.'s writing as merely philosophical or straightforwardly realist. In particular, self-reference in *La Femme rompue* undermines the realist assumption of coherence or wholeness normally associated with diary-type fiction. Margaret A. Simons, *Beauvoir and 'The Second Sex': Feminism, Race and the Origins of Existentialism*, Lanham–Oxford, Rowman & Littlefield, xx + 262 pp., is not primarily a literary study but a philosopher's attempt to set the text in the broad context of the history and politics of the feminist movement, de Beauvoir's own ideas, her personal relationship with Sartre, her philosophical differences with him, and the influence of his thinking on the book. There are transcripts of two interviews with de B., conducted in 1979 and 1982. J.-A. Pilardi, *Simone de Beauvoir, Writing the Self: Philosophy becomes Autobiography*, Westport, CT, Greenwood–Praeger, 135 pp.

M. Fraser, *Identity without Selfhood: Simone de Beauvoir and Bisexuality*, CUP, x + 216 pp.

BECKETT. S. E. Cant, 'In search of 'lessness': translation and minimalism in B.'s theatre', *FMLS*, 35:138–57, defines lessness as 'the lowest common denominator of stage and word in which meaning is redefined through a process of reduction', and examines B.'s pursuit of the analogous goals of self-translation and minimalism in three plays: *En attendant Godot, La dernière bande* and *Pas moi*. The breadth of reference is broader than this, in fact, but only serves to underline the ultimate irony that, even in the search for 'style-lessness', the pursuit of reduction and estrangement creates a new form of style. S. E. Gontarski, 'Revising himself: performance as text in S. B.'s theatre', *JML*, 22:131–46, sets out to correct the bias towards the written text in B. criticism by charting B.'s evolution from playwright to theatre artist, from writer to director. It demonstrates how B.'s growing expertise and confidence as director of his own work led to constant revision of his existing texts and increased the importance of rehearsal and performance in determining the shape of new work. The consequent headaches for his publishers anxious to print a 'definitive' text are illustrated by examples of continual revision from e.g. *Play, Come and Go* and *Footfalls*. X. Garnier, 'Les personnages gigognes de S. B.', *Poétique*, 117:47–56, divides the characters of the trilogy into the M series (Molloy, Malone, Mahood etc.) and the W series (Worm, Watt) and distinguishes between mobile and immobile individuals. Having no particular axe to grind, it lingers on such incidentals as the significance of *le bâton*, represented by Malone's stick or even Molloy's crutches. G. Gasarian, 'Poésie et poétique chez B.', *ib.*, 119:317–42, addresses the apparent paradox of B.'s 'austère économie', 'dépouillement extrême' and flight from 'style' on the one hand and the extraordinary poetic power of his writing on the other. The bulk of reference is to *En attendant Godot* but the article ranges widely from B.'s 'manie crépuscule', via 'drame et dialogue' to 'les voix du sujet et du silence'.

BONNEFOY. A. Pearre, 'Le bouddhisme et la poésie contemporaine: Y. B.' *DFS*, 46:167–78, points to the interest in Zen Buddhism which can be discerned throughout B.'s work and which may have been sparked off by his discovery of the Japanese poet Bashô, translated by René Sieffert in 1968. The main attraction of Buddhism for B. would seem to lie not so much in the temptation to anti-rationalism as in the 'harmonie des contraires' it proposes.

BUTOR. F. Cox, 'A modern day Aeneas: Virgil's journey through B.'s *La Modification*', Cox, *Virgil*, 132–58, covers already well-documented ground but concentrates on establishing parallels between the doomed love of Dido and Aeneas and Delmont's relations with his wife and mistress. The discussion subsequently increases in breadth and interest to encompass parallels with Dante and Beatrice, Delmont's personal vision of Rome, and his views of history and Fascism while not losing sight of *La Modification* as a *nouveau roman* and as a 'lesson in how to read and how to write'. B. Valette, *Etude sur Michel Butor: La Modification* (Coll. Résonances), Ellipses-Marketing, 94 pp.

CAMUS. N. Harrison, 'C., *écriture blanche* and the reader, between Said and Barthes', *NFS*, 38:55–66, is essentially a study of *L'Etranger*, sandwiched between the conflicting views of Barthes and Said as to whether the text is neutral and innocent (Barthes) or guilty of concealment of and complicity in the colonial situation in Algeria (Said). The key to gauging the extent of C.'s *engagement* is the degree to which he invites the reader to identify with Meursault. While in theory the text creates various obstacles to this process of identification, there are ways in which the two divergent views can be at least partially reconciled in practice. *L'Etat de siège*, ed. P.-L. Rey (Coll. Folio Théâtre), Gallimard, 1998, 225 pp. S. E. Bronner, *Camus: portrait of a moralist*, Minnesota U.P., xii + 179 pp.

CARDINAL. E. Hoft-March, 'Clytemnestra's desire: M. C. and the mythical maternal', *DFS*, 48:155–64, considers C.'s exploration of the maternal, which raises questions unasked or unanswered by Freud's Oedipal analysis, and her gravitation towards the Clytemnestra myth, principally in *Les mots pour le dire* and *Le passé empiété*.

CIXOUS. M. Noonan, 'Performing the voice of writing in the in-between: H. C.'s *La Ville Parjure*', *NFS*, 38:67–79, analyses the play as a preamble to asking in what ways it represents an evolutionary step in C.'s project for a 'feminine' theatre as set out in 1977. Instead of the playful reworking of language we find in C.'s earlier fiction and the undermining of theatrical convention in earlier plays, we have a more traditional reliance on the power of metaphor and a number of striking images. What *La Ville Parjure* dramatizes is the tension between C.'s public vocation to engage her audience in reflection on contemporary socio-political conditions and her private or personal vocation as a poet to give expression to her own unconscious self. L. A. Jacobus and R. Barreca, *Hélène Cixous: Critical Impressions*, Amsterdam, Gordon & Breach, xv + 333 pp.

DEGUY. *Littérature*, 114, is a special number to mark D.'s departure from the Department of French Literature in Paris VIII. It contains a range of contributions of varying complexions from the personal and self-indulgent to more structured studies. Among the more interesting contributions are: C. Monchard, 'Deguy aujourd'hui' (5–16), which provides a useful initial survey of man and work; L. Finas, 'Le vent, c'est beaucoup plus que le vent' (35–41), which provides a similarly informative introduction to D.'s most recent work, *L'énergie du désespoir*, while J.-M. Rey, 'La rhétorique profanée' (42–53), is a more in-depth look at the same work, emphasising the recurring idea or motif that D.'s poetry is haunted by a *mouvement de fond* which he defines as 'une profanation des figures'; H. Meschonnic, 'Le rythme dans la figure ou il faut soigner ce rhume' (56–63), is a collection of random, general reflections on rhythm; C. Monchard, 'Deguy, Du Bellay et le temps de la poésie' (64–81), considers the relationship between the two poets with the help of D.'s *Tombeau de Du Bellay*; B. Clement, 'La colonie préliminaire' (82–92), discusses *La Machine matrimoniale ou Marivaux* in which D. sketches a kind of *ars poetica* not so much for the writer as for the reader; C. Elson, 'Anthropomorphose: l'humanisme dans la poétique de M. D.' (93–106), explores approaches to defining humanism in D.'s work and that anthropomorphism which is one of the 'sens principaux' of his writing.

DURAS. M.-C. Barnet, 'Ecrire, disent-elles: la vocation littéraire dans *L'Amant* de Duras et *L'Enfance* de Sarraute', *DFS*, 48:101–14, shows how the two *romans-récits* in question evoke, in a mixture of fact and fiction, the awakening of a literary vocation in their respective authors. It looks beneath the surface dissimilarities between the 'écolière modèle' (Sarraute) and the 'petite délurée' (Duras) and finds a similar 'ambiguité absolue' in both writers' approaches to writing about writing. C. Blot-Labarrère, *Dix heures et demie du soir en été de Marguerite Duras* (Coll. Foliothèque), Gallimard, 206 pp.

ERNAUX. N. Morello, 'Faire pour la mère ce qu'elle [n']avait [pas] fait pour le père: étude comparative du projet autobiographique dans *La Place et Une Femme* d'Annie Ernaux', *NFS*, 38:80–92, centres on two novels from the eighties in which E. explores her relationship with her father and mother respectively. Both books seem to serve a similar therapeutic purpose for E. since she attempts to *expliquer* and *disculper* her mother in *Une Femme* by placing her in her socio-cultural context as she had done already for her father in the earlier *La Place*. L. Day, '*Ce qu'ils disent ou rien* in Annie Ernaux's trajectory as a writer', *EFL*, 35–36:178–205, concentrates on this middle panel of the early triptych comprising also *Les Armoires vides* and *La Femme gelée* which precedes *La Place*. Anne's adolescent reading and first attempts at writing reflect E.'s natural concerns as developing writer and the subtext of the novel addresses fundamental questions of form and technique which preoccupied E. in the 70s and may not have been resolved by the 90s. This broad and detailed study concludes that *Ce qu'ils disent ou rien* 'argues the need for a kind of writing which it does not itself deliver'. L. D. Kritzman, 'Ernaux's testimony of shame', *EsC*, 39.4:139–49, is devoted to an analysis of *La Honte* in which E. seeks to come to terms with feelings of shame and guilt occasioned by a traumatic childhood event in June 1952: witnessing a scene of domestic violence between her father and mother. While this attempt to translate trauma into words helps E. confront her feelings, it also reveals the impossibility of achieving true cognition. N. C. Cottille-Foley, 'Abortion and contamination of the social order in Annie Ernaux's *Les Armoires vides*', *FR*, 72:886–96, not only regards abortion as a powerful expression of social alienation but argues that using the womb as a mode of representation and creating various associations allows E. to reverse common dichotomies and transgress binary oppositions.

GENET. V. Kocay, 'Language and truth: Sartre, Bataille, Derrida on Genet', *DFS*, 48:127–45, undertakes a comparison of three very different approaches to G.: Sartre's monumental study, Bataille's (partial) reply, and Derrida's enigmatic *Glas*. Least space is given to the most substantial of these, on the grounds that it is already the most familiar; Bataille's *Genet* is analysed more as a reading of Sartre than G.; and there is a commendable and welcome attempt to shed some light on *Glas*. F. Ekotto, 'Shamelessness as a creative mechanism in Jean Genet's *Notre-Dame des Fleurs* and Dany Laferrière's *Comment faire l'amour avec un Nègre sans se fatiguer*', *EsC*, 39.4:80–89, compares two novels which deal with the shame of exclusion, symbolized for the subjects by containment within confined spaces. Both writers use shamelessness as a mechanism to deflect the stigma of shame but this analysis distinguishes between the reactive or weak shamelessness felt by L.'s characters and G.'s exploration of a strong 'shame-lessness' which tries to transcend the binary opposition of the shameful and the shameless.

GRACQ. C. J. Murphy, 'Gracq, lecteur de Poirier', *FR*, 72:696–708, confronts the writer-critic J. G. and his *alter ego*, the history-geography teacher Louis Poirier, finding unsurprisingly themes and preoccupations familiar in G. in his other self e.g. the same attitude to the relationship between man and his environment. The most interesting section is that on 'Gracq autographe' which notes the feminization of certain spaces in G.'s texts and suggests that geographical space and autobiographical space in G. both centre on 'un espace qui figure le maternel'.

LE CLÉZIO. J. L. Dutton, 'Du paradis à l'utopie: ou le rêve atavique de Le Clézio' *EFL*, 35–36:206–17, acknowledges the well-documented prominence of the *paradis* theme in Le C. but makes a distinction between that and the less obvious utopia theme. She uses this idea to construct a *grille de lecture* which is applied to two works, *Chercheur d'or* and *Voyage à Rodrigues*. These are already 'un ensemble indissociable' on autobiographical grounds, but charting the progression from *paradis* to *utopie* suggests a more nuanced and less obvious complementarity between them. M. Salles, *Etude sur J. M. G. Le Clezio:* *Désert* (Coll. Résonances), Ellipses-Marketing, 96 pp.

LEDUC.    C. Viollet, 'Violette Leduc, une sincérité intrépide?', *DFS*, 47 : 133–42, calls into question the autobiographical assumption made by many about L.'s work and initially fostered by Simone de Beauvoir. The article offers some fascinating background glimpses into L.'s successive reworkings, transpositions, and emendations of biographical materials which demonstrate that here is a permeable membrane separating fact from fiction in her writing. S. Marson, *Le Temps de l'autobiographie: Violette Leduc*, Vincennes U.P., 1998, 259 pp., considers the ambiguities implicit in the autobiographical enterprise and those factors which contribute to blurring the distinction between autobiography and *récit*, principally the ambivalent position of the author as narrator and character. It is an informative and thought-provoking mixture of detailed comment on L. and issues of wider relevance. C. Jansiti, *Violette Leduc: biographie*, Grasset, 488 pp.

MICHAUT.    *Littérature*, 115, is a special number devoted to Michaut. J. P. Martin, 'Les nés-fatigués me comprendront' (3–13), considers different definitions of the idea of fatigue in M.'s writing. J.-C. Mathieu, 'Portrait des *Meidosems*' (14–30), is a close look at the series of lithographs and texts making up the collection. R. Bellour, '400 hommes en croix' (31–41), examines the image of the crucified Christ. V. Metzger, 'Poèmes et prose: quelques réécritures', (42–7), emphasizes, with the aid of some examples, the importance of those 'quelques moments de rencontre' when M.'s prose reinterprets or rewrites his verse. G. Dessons, 'Lire la peinture' (48–54), tackles the relationship between the written and the pictorial and how the 'reading' of one complements the other. Dong Qiang, 'Acérer la plume, "lacérer le vide"' (55–69), is a reading of *Idéogrammes en Chine* but can be hard going without an inside appreciation of Chinese calligraphy. J. Roger, 'Ponge, lecteur de Michaut: un différend sans merci' (70–86), examines, in a detailed and wide-ranging fashion, the enigmatic relationship between these two contemporaries and the clash of 'deux poétiques inconciliables'.

MODIANO.    G. Neumann, 'Aux carrefours de la vie: le chien dans les romans de Patrick Modiano', *AJFS*, 37 : 246–64, concentrates initially on identifying canine references, allusions and images in *Villa Triste* in order to illuminate neglected aspects of this particular novel but, using the insights gained thereby, the article develops into an interesting survey of a number of other texts up to the most recent *Dora Bruder*. There is ample illustration which confirms the existence of a surprising wealth of themes associated with the discrete but significant presence of man's best friend in M.

OBEY.  C. Turrettes, 'Ambiguïté d'une Iphigénie moderne: une fille pour du vent d'André Obey', *RHT*, 99:171-81, points out the ambiguous mixture of ancient borrowing and modern addition and emendations in O.'s treatment of the Iphigenia myth. It is argued that O.'s distortion, indeed inversion, of the story is not merely ludic in nature but is intended to raise questions in his contemporary postwar audience about pacifism, ambition, and the lust for power.

PINGET.  F. Cox, 'The good shepherd: Virgil in the novels of Robert Pinget', Cox, *Virgil*, 189-214, examines the presence of the *Bucolics* in two novels, *L'Apocryphe* and *Théo ou le Temps neuf*, analysing how the Virgilian intertext is exploited to convey a characteristic *nouveau roman* sense of textual instability and of the instability of the world in general.

PONGE.  D. Sears, 'The prose poem and Ponge's *Proême*', *EsC*, 39.1:60-70, begins with some observations and speculations on the origins and significance of the term *proême*, then tackles two texts 'on the limits of prose and poetry': *Strophe* and *De la modification des choses par la parole*. A detailed contrastive textual analysis of both illustrates how the conflict of poetic and prosaic codes in P. results in the creation of a hybrid genre. *Francis Ponge et Jean Tortel: Correspondance 1944-81*, ed. B. Beugnot and B. Veck, Stock, 322 pp.

ROBBE-GRILLET.  B. Stoltzfus, '*La Belle Captive*: Magritte, Robbe-Grillet et le Surréalisme', *FR*, 72:709-18, argues that the inclusion of 77 pictures by Magritte in *La Belle Captive* suggests links between Surrealist aesthetics and those of the *nouveau roman*. The dual character of *La Belle Captive* as commentary on both the mystery and ludic structures of Magritte's painting and also the processes of the *nouveau roman* leads the reader into the same 'jeu' as making sense of the *nouveau roman* narrative. The article also suggests a number of specific links between the book and the 1938 edition of the *Oeuvres complètes* de Lautréamont, introduced by Breton and illustrated by Magritte and others, and the 1948 edition of *Les Chants de Maldoror*, illustrated by Magritte alone. R. Ramsey, 'Visual generators as pre-texts in Robbe-Grillet's new novels', *AJFS*, 36:229-45, examines the relationship between text and images in a variety of R.-G. works, in particular the use, repetition, and transformation of pictorial sources. The discussion is interesting for its range of detailed, specific references.

SALACROU.  Hyo Suk Jo, 'Les formes de la mort dans le théâtre d'Armand Salacrou', *RHT*, 99:21-40, is a clear and orderly survey of the obsessive theme of death in S. under various headings: physical death represented by suicide and heroic self-sacrifice for a noble cause, spiritual death, and 'la mort de l'avenir' i.e. old age.

SARRAUTE.  M. L. Lee, 'L'écriture et la vie: Nathalie Sarraute', *DFS*, 47:143-54, reflects on the long creative career of S. and asks what is the relationship between life and writing for her, what writing means for her and if the passing years have changed this relationship. After some biographical details and observations on her preferred place and methods of working, the answer emerges as a paradox. It is the separation of life and writing, in a sense the *manque de moi* in S.'s writing, which is the key to understanding her work. J. Rothenberg, 'Gender in question in the theatre of Nathalie Sarraute', *FMLS*, 35:311–20, tests S.'s claims not to be concerned with gender issues against the evidence of her plays, finding in them an evolution in the treatment of gender and character from *Le Silence* (1964) to *Pour un oui ou pour un non* (1982). This does not reflect the evolution discernible in her non-theatrical writing since it is less easy in the theatre to blur the distinction among the gendered relationships and stereotypes of the conventional bourgeois society she portrays. J. S. Gjerden, 'Le portrait selon Nathalie Sarraute. Configuration du sujet moderne dans *Portrait d'un inconnu* et *Ici*', *RevR*, 34:265–84, draws a parallel between S.'s interest in Arcimboldo's portraits in her late 1995 text *Ici* and her original project in *Portrait d'un inconnu* to create a series of original configurations of the modern subject. The comparison becomes threefold since the replacement of the *sujet autonome* by a new *sujet ouvert*, defining itself solely by virtue of its 'ouverture à l'autre' suggests an unexpected parallel with Levinas. A.-C. Gignoux, 'Nathalie Sarraute, une leçon de rhétorique', *LR*, 53:137–43, regards *Ouvrez* as a kind of treatise on rhetoric or 'réflexion métalinguistique' and therefore a departure from S.'s usual preoccupations with *tropismes* in favour of words or *personnages-mots*. The argument identifies in *Ouvrez* the five divisions of rhetorc and the analysis is structured under these headings: *invention, élocution, disposition, mémoire,* and *action*. V. Minogue, 'Nathalie Sarraute (1900–1999): a tribute', *RoS*, 17.2:iii–vi, records the death of N. S. on 10 October 1999 and offers in homage an overview of her major works and achievement.

SIMON. F. Cox, 'La Bataille de la phrase: Virgil in the novels of Claude Simon', Cox, *Virgil*, 159–88, despite the title, deals mainly with *La Bataille de Pharsale* and *Les Géorgiques*. On the other hand, it draws not only Virgil but also Lucan, Caesar, and others into the intertextual discussion. In *La Bataille de Pharsale*, the proliferation of sources and the discrepancies between them, plus the role of memory, contribute to the polyvalence of meaning basic to the *nouveau roman*. In the relatively more harmonious and accessible *Les Géorgiques*, the debatable degree of Virgilian influence and the predominance of the Orpheus myth are assessed. L. Fraisse, 'La lentille convexe de Claude Simon', *Poétique*, 117:27–46, examines, principally in *La Route des Flandres* and via the various implications of the convex lens motif, aspects of spatial representation and dislocation. There is much reference to Proust and some allusion to other of S.'s novels. J. H. Duffy, 'Artistic biographies and aesthetic coherence in Claude Simon's *Jardin des plantes*', *FMLS*, 35:175–92, notes a shift of focus in S.'s latest novel away from the paintings and sculpture on which he draws in earlier fiction and towards the biographies of the artists themselves, in this instance Novelli and Picasso. Despite this change of focus, however, the analysis sets out to demonstrate that S.'s reservations about biography or the biographical approach to literature have not altered and *Le Jardin des plantes* is based on the same compositional or creative principles as his earlier fiction.

SOLLERS.   P. Forest, 'Le Roman, divine autofiction: sur *Lettres aux années de nostalgie* de Kenzaburô Oé et *Le Coeur absolu* de Philippe Sollers', *RLC*, 73:47–61, chooses two novels 'd'une étonnante proximité' but without suggesting any mutual influence between them since the S. novel was published in 1987 and the Japanese novel not translated until 1993. Any similarity derives from their common exploitation of Dante's *Divine Comedy*, but a sustained comparison under a variety of headings e.g. space and time, the narrator and his double, Ulysses in Paradise, etc., makes for an interesting and readable study.

TOURNIER.   V. Tumanov, 'Black and white: Michel Tournier, Anatole France and Genesis', *OL*, 54:301–14, is a hypo/hypertextual exploration of the first chapter of *Gaspard, Melchior et Balthazar* which details points of correspondence between the T. hypertext and its hypotext, Anatole France's short story *Balthasar* (1889), as well as T.'s apparent use of the sister-wife hoax motif which occurs three times in Genesis. C. Anderson, *Michel Tournier's Children: Myth, Intertext, Initiation*, NY, Lang, 1998, 145 pp., attributes T.'s marginality in relation to major literary trends to his straddling two seemingly incompatible genres: children's literature and serious high quality fiction. This study explores T.'s 'myth' of adult-child relations, one of initiation and growth, of mentorship and partnership between child and adult, drawing our attention in particular to the thematic and textual roles of childhood in T. and the role of the author/narrator as a guide to childhood reading. The book is divided into two major sections 'Children as agents' and 'Children as readers' and is well structured and readable throughout. A. Bouillaguet, 'De Defoe à Tournier: le destin ou le désordre des choses. Sur trois incipit', *EF*, 35:55–64, considers the relationship between what the author terms 'le désordre des choses' and the workings of the forces of destiny in three texts, *Robinson Crusoe* and *Vendredi ou les limbes du pacifique* in its two versions, the original and *La Vie sauvage*. The gist of the argument is that destiny is present and has manifested itself already in *Vendredi* in the form of tarot cards whereas the world of things is less sinister or worrying in

*La Vie sauvage* since the tarot cards have been replaced by ordinary cards. J.-P. Zarader, *Robinson philosophe: Vendredi ou la vie sauvage de Michel Tournier, un parcours philosophique* (Coll. Philo-essais), Ellipses-Marketing, 207 pp.

YOURCENAR. J. S. Alesch, '*Le Cours des devises* in Marguérite Yourcenar's *Mémoires d'Hadrian*', *FR*, 72:877–85, draws attention to the dual function of narration in *Mémoires d'Hadrian* via the conflict between the 'narrative' of his life and reign which Hadrian constructs in official formulas and the existence of a hidden alternative 'narrative' version of his life, crystallised in the suicide of Antinoüs which Hadrian cannot understand or come to terms with.

## FRENCH CANADIAN LITERATURE

By CHRISTOPHER ROLFE, *Senior Lecturer in French, University of Leicester*
(This survey covers the years 1998 and 1999)

### 1. GENERAL

The issue of censorship is, of course, of prime significance in the Quebec context. Pierre Hébert, *Censure et littéraire au Québec. Le livre crucifié 1625–1919,* Montreal, Fides, 1997, 294 pp., is a well-organized, well-documented overview of this crucial issue. The volume is divided into three sections: 'L'Eglise souffrante, l'ère pré-censoriale', 'L'Eglise militante: grandeurs et misères de la censure proscriptive (1840–1910)', and 'L'Eglise triomphante. Le virage prescriptif: du cas Laurent-Olivier David à l'action positive (1896–1919)'. Theatre — which has been well covered elsewhere — is not included here. *VI,* 23.2, 1998, has an excellent dossier, 'La censure 1920–1960', which complements H.'s volume. The years in question are especially significant since they witnessed a transition from Church control to more disparate forms of censorship. Typical of the scholarship and insight on offer is E. Salaün, 'Erotisme littéraire et censure: la révolution cachée' (297–313) which examines how the Church, unable itself to prevent the distribution of erotic literature, was obliged to appeal to civil justice, which led to the 1959 Fulton Act.

*Les Soirées du Château de Ramezay de l'Ecole littéraire de Montréal,* ed. Micheline Cambron and François Hébert, Montreal, Fides, 351 pp., is an important edition of the 1900 publication, a forerunner of *Le Nigog* and *La Relève,* which gives us a glimpse of the stirrings of a literature far removed from the ideological literature advocated at the time. Pierre Rajotte, *Le Récit de voyage. Aux frontières du littéraire,* Montreal, Triptique, 1997, 282 pp., is a wide-ranging discussion of the genre. The essay on 'Les récits de voyageuses' (177–207) is particularly welcome. *VI,* 23.3, 1998, has a dossier on 'Le récit littéraire des années quatre-vingt et quatre-vingt-dix' (437–525). In addition to articles discussing the whys and wherefores of this extraordinary phenomenon (over 200 récits have been published in Quebec since 1980) three explore specific texts. *Le Rébus des revues. Petites revues et vie littéraire au Québec,* ed. Jacques Beaudry, Sainte-Foy, Laval U.P., 1998, 174 pp., is a collection of studies tracing the destiny of a dozen minor literary journals between the years 1930–1970.

* The author of this report gratefully acknowledges the support of the University of Leicester in granting him study leave for the second semester of 1998–99.

Particularly valuable for the light it sheds on the origins of *La Relève*, *La Barre du jour*, and the early career of G. Miron. Michel Biron and Corinne Larochelle, *Les Revues littéraires de langue française du Québec et du Canada des origines à 1995. Essai de répertoire*, Montreal, UQAM, 95 pp., lists over 400 journals and is a most useful research tool. *Le Journal 'Le Canadien'. Littérature, espace publique et utopie 1836–1845*, ed. Micheline Cambron, Montreal, Fides, 421 pp., is a series of essays that discuss the role of *Le Canadien* in the literary, political, and social world of early 19th-c. Quebec and, in particular, its role in the promotion of a Utopian ethos. Jean-Cléo Godin and Dominique Lafon, *Dramaturgies québécoises des années quatre-vingt*, Montreal, Leméac, 264 pp., contains important sections on the avant-garde and on four major playwrights of the period: M. Bouchard, N. Chaurette, R.-D. Dubois, and M. Laberge. *Les Littératures d'expression française d'Amérique du Nord et le carnavalesque*, ed. Denis Bourque and Anne Brown, Moncton, Editions d'Acadie, 1998, 348 pp., is a collection of essays that discuss the concept of the *carnavalesque* in francophone literature other than that of Quebec. Pierre Nepveu, *Intérieurs du nouveau monde*, Montreal, Boréal, 1998, 278 pp., presents some 15 essays on North American writers who posit 'une Amérique non pas embrassée à corps perdu et vécue comme une aventure exaltante et même extatique, mais éprouvée à partir d'une subjectivité fragile, souvent repliée sur elle-même et sur son univers intime'. Quebec authors studied include Marie de l'Incarnation, L. Conan, A. Grandbois, A. Hébert and Saint-Denys Garneau. Excellent stuff. *Les Abeilles pillotent. Mélanges offerts à René LeBlanc*, ed. Edouard Langille and Glenn Moulaison, Pointe-de-l'Eglise, Revue de l'Université Ste-Anne, 1998, xiv + 353 pp., is a collection of essays on Acadian society, history and literature. Not surprisingly, the literature section leans heavily towards Antonine Maillet. However, L. Lavoie, 'Les violences physiques et morales dans *Le Djibou* de Laval Goupil et dans *Les Belles-Sœurs* de Michel Tremblay', is a stimulating comparison of the New Brunswick writer and the Quebec writer. The volume as a whole is highly recommended: many of the non-literary pieces (e.g. L. C. Stanley-Blackwell, 'The mysterious stranger and the Acadian Good Samaritan: leprosy folklore in 19th-century New Brunswick') are extremely enlightening for the literature specialist. Robert Dion, *Le Moment critique de la fiction. Les interprétations de la littérature que proposent les fictions québécoises contemporaines*, Quebec, Nuit blanche, 1997, 212 pp., tackles intertextuality in key texts by J. Brault, M. LaRue, N. Brossard, N. Chaurette, V.-L. Beaulieu, G. Bessette, and R. Racine. A stimulating, sophisticated volume. Josef Kwaterko, *Le Roman québécois et ses (inter)discours*, Quebec, Nota bene, 1998, 224 pp., addresses *interdiscursivité* in texts by J. Ferron, H. Aquin, R. Carrier,

R. Ducharme, J. Godbout, G. Bessette, and R. Robin. The excellent pages on the way Lord Durham's infamous words about Quebec's lack of a literature have been exploited by novelists are typical of the study as a whole. Catherine Pont-Hubert, *Littérature du Québec*, Paris, Nathan, 1998, 126 pp., is a *manuel d'étudiant* that usefully covers the whole spectrum from J. Cartier's writings to the immigrant literature of recent years. *Littérature*, 113, has a first-rate dossier entitled 'La littérature au Québec' which includes articles on R. Ducharme, G. Roy, and J. Poulin. Paul-Emile Roy, *Lectures québécoises et indépendance*, Montreal, Méridien, 203 pp., is a spirited polemic that brings R.'s own *séparatisme* to bear on a series of literary figures and themes. Great fun but extremely crass in places as when he castigates Gabrielle Roy for believing in a *Canadian* nationalism. *Cultural Identities in Canadian Literature*, ed. Bénédicte Mauguière, NY, Lang, 1998, 230 pp., is a challenging collection of essays addressing gender, language, race, nationalism and ethnicity from a postcolonial perspective. Of those essays dealing with French Canadian writers the following are likely to be of most interest: R. L. Dufault, 'Marie Laberge's feminist existentialism' (65–71); B. Mauguière, 'Fictions et réalités du territoire dans *L'Herbe et le varech* d'Hélène Ouvrard' (111–21); P. Nepveu, 'Vers une nouvelle subjectivité' (123–29), which discusses Elise Turcotte's *Le Bruit des choses vivantes*; and H. Servin, 'Passions dévorantes et satisfactions alimentaires dans *Une Liaison parisienne* de Marie-Claire Blais' (143–50). *Parcs, places et jardins. Représentations québécoises et canadiennes anglophones*, ed. Marie-Lyne Piccione and Bernadette Rigal Cellard, Talence, MSHA, 1998, 140 pp., contains the papers given at an international conference at Bordeaux III in 1997. Amongst the authors discussed are Y. Beauchemin, R. Ducharme, M. Tremblay, G. Roy, A. Hébert, S. Paradis, and L. Bissonnette. *Echanges culturels entre les 'Deux solitudes'*, ed. Marie-Andrée Beaudet, Sainte-Foy, Laval U.P., 220 pp., presents a dozen somewhat eclectic pieces — there are several on literary themes — that coalesce into a vital study of something of a taboo subject. *VI*, 24.3, has a dossier on 'La littérature québécoise sous le regard de l'autre', which presents four essays on different aspects of Anglo-Canadian reception of Québécois literature. Of particular note is B. Godard, 'Une littérature en devenir, la réécriture textuelle et le dynamisme du champ littéraire. Les écrivaines québécoises au Canada' (495–527) which lucidly demonstrates how the works of G. Roy, A. Hébert, and M.-C. Blais, the most translated of Quebec's writers, have been dehistoricized in favour of an emphasis on universal archetypes. Marie Vautier, *New World Myth: Postmodernism and Postcolonialism in Canadian Fiction*, Montreal, McGill U.P.–Kingston, Queens U.P., 1998, 339 pp., examines six works of fiction that oppose traditional conceptions of myth through the use of irony, parody, and intertextuality. J. Godbout's *Les Têtes à Papineau*, J. Marchessault's *Comme une enfant de la terre*, and F. Barcelo's *La Tribu* are the Francophone texts studied. J. Allard, 'Le roman du Québec', *Iapétus*, 3:109–22, is an introductory overview whose several engagingly sharp observations and stimulating perspectives would, ironically, be lost on the neophyte. *Littératures francophones*. II. Les Amériques. Haïti, Antilles-Guyane, Québec, ed. Jack Corzani, Léon-François Hoffmann, and Marie-Lyne Piccione, Paris, Belin, 1998, 320 pp. The section on Quebec (185–288) is solid and comprehensive, its coverage of less obvious writers good. Ultimately, however, its tendency towards potted abstracts palls.

Bénédicte Mauguière, *Traversée des idéologies et exploration des identités dans les écritures de femmes au Québec (1970–1980)*, NY, Lang, 1997, 385 pp., adopts a sociological approach to discuss the ideologies that marked women's writing, its production and reception during the seventies. A lucid, intelligent study that encompasses much more than its title would suggest. *Women by Women: The Treatment of Female Characters by Women Writers of Fiction in Quebec since 1980*, ed. Roseanna Lewis Dufault, Madison, Fairleigh Dickinson U.P., 1997, 270 pp., is a collection of important essays inspired by feminist theory. Lucie Joubert, *Le Carquois de velours: l'ironie au féminin dans la littérature québécoise, 1960–1980*, Montreal, L'Hexagone, 1998, 225 pp., is an excellent study of women writers from G. Roy to Y. Villemaire, from M. Ferron to S. Jacob, from Andrée Maillet to Y. Naubert that concludes that women's irony is much more subversive than men's. See also Joubert's 'L'église et ses émissaires: la cible privilégiée de l'ironie au féminin dans la littérature québécoise (1960–1980)', *QuS*, 25, 1998:46–57, which concentrates on women writers' use of irony in attacking a clergy reluctant to adapt to social change. J. Levasseur, 'Le féminisme québécois et la littérature sexuelle', *FR*, 71, 1998:971–84, is a useful overview of the topic. B. Mauguière, 'L'homo/textualité dans les écritures de femmes au Québec', *ib.*, 1036–47, is perhaps particularly valuable for its comments on Louise Maheux-Forcier and Hélène Ouvrard. R. Koski, 'A voice of one's own: women's writing in Quebec since 1960', pp. 105–23 of *Francophone Voices*, ed. Kamal Salhi, Exeter, Elm Bank, 248 pp., is a fairly useful but bland overview. I. Boisclair, 'Roman national ou récit féminin? La littérature des femmes pendant la Révolution tranquille', *Globe*, 2:97–115, claims that while male authors sought to assert Quebec's specificity during the Quiet Revolution, women writers sought to assert a feminine specificity and to free themselves from patriarchy. F. Bordeleau, 'L'écriture féminine existe-t-elle?', *LQu*, 92, 1998:14–18.

*Les Romantiques québécois,* ed. Claude Beausoleil, Montreal, Les herbes rouges, 1997, 310 pp., is an anthology of poems which appeared between 1832 and 1934. A solid introduction brings out the specific characteristics of Québécois romanticism whilst contextualizing it within the more universal tradition. *Le Nordir. Dix ans de création et de réflexion en Ontario français, 1988–1998,* ed. Robert Yergau, Ottawa, Le Nordir, 1998, 148 pp., is an anthology of Franco-Ontarian writers celebrating 10 years of publishing by *Le Nordir.* *Les Grands poèmes de la poésie québécoise: anthologie,* ed. Joseph Bonenfant, Alain Horic, and France Théoret, Montreal, L'Hexagone, 348 pp.

2. INDIVIDUAL AUTHORS

AQUIN. Hubert Aquin, *Confession d'un héros. Le Choix des armes. La Toile d'araignée,* ed. Jean Cléo Godin, Montreal, Leméac, 1997, is a welcome publication bringing together three plays written for Radio-Canada. Manon Dumais and Jacinthe Martel, *Répertoire Hubert Aquin. Bibliographie analytique 1947–1997,* Montreal, Quebec U.P., 1998, 470 pp. This comprehensive bibliography is all the more precious in that each reference is followed by an evaluation. Hubert Aquin, *Récits et nouvelles. Tout est miroir,* ed. François Poisson et al, Montreal, Bibliothèque québécoise, 1998, 324 pp., is an excellent critical edition of some 20 early pieces by Aquin. A. Leblanc, '*Neige noire* et la quête de l'identité', *Tribune,* 10:71–81, explores to good effect why A. chose to set his novel in Norway. M. Randall, 'L'homme et l'œuvre: biolectographie d'Hubert Aquin', *VI,* 23, 1998:558–79, proposes a rereading of *Trou de mémoire* as a kind of coded autobiography.

BEAUCHEMIN. A. Cassanello, 'L'enfance dans l'oeuvre d'Yves Beauchemin: lieux et cheminement d'un thème', *Tribune,* 10:27–37.

BEAUGRAND. J.-F. Chassay, 'Le progrès en question. Beaugrand et Simon face aux Etats-Unis', *VI,* 24:168–79, illustrates how in B.'s *Jeanne la fileuse* and S.'s *L'Ecrin disparu,* the idea of progress (epitomized by the train and the car) defines the authors ideologically vis-à-vis the USA. C. Gosselin Schick, '*Jeanne la fileuse* et le rapatriement des émigrés', *FR,* 71, 1998:1007–17, is an interesting attempt to rehabilitate B.'s unjustly marginalized novel.

BEAULIEU. A. E. Cliche, 'Jusqu'à la fin de tous les temps ou le souvenir d'enfance (*Satan Belhumeur* de Victor-Lévy Beaulieu)', *VI,* 25:36–59.

BÉLAND. V.-L. Tremblay, 'L'intertexte de l'homosexualité dans *L'Orage sur mon corps* d'André Béland', *CanL,* 159, 1998:141–60, argues that B.'s novel, in addition to accepting homosexuality, 'bien avant les écrivains de la décennie 1960 [...] a amorcé le discours bariolé du baroque et du grotesque pour désigner le réel québécois.'

BESSETTE. M.-L. Piccione, 'Bal masqué chez Freud: *Le Semestre* de Gérard Bessette', pp. 95–101 of *Masques et Mascarades dans la littérature nord-américaine*, Talence, MSHA, 1997, contends that distancing and deceiving are the rule in B.'s novel. A series of masked portraits of contemporary intellectuals fails to conceal B.'s own anguished sense of exile.

BLAIS. D. Bourque, 'Héloïse ou La voix du silence dans *Une Saison dans la vie d'Emmanuel*', *VI*, 23, 1998: 329–45, examines the part played in relation to that of the protagonist by this little discussed female character. *QuS*, 25, 1998, has two pieces on Blais: K. S. McPherson, 'Archaeologies of an uncertain future in the novels of Marie-Claire Blais' (80–96), and K. L. Gould, 'Geographies of death and dreams in Marie-Claire Blais's *Soifs*' (97–104). Irène Oore and Oriel C. L. MacLennan, *Marie-Claire Blais. An Annotated Bibliography*, Toronto, ECW Press, 1998, 159 pp., comprehensively covers the works and criticism of B., rising well to the challenge posed by the breadth and diversity of the works and their reception and interpretation. Broadcast and audiovisual material are included, plus a representative selection of reviews. Altogether an essential research tool.

BOUCHETTE. Alain Lacombe, *Errol Bouchette 1862–1912. Un intellectuel*, Montreal, Fides, 1997, 240 pp., seeks to rehabilitate this neglected essayist, novelist, and journalist. Chapter 6 assesses his *roman à thèse, Robert Lozé*. The volume as a whole constitutes a valuable portrait of the writer's era.

BRAULT. Luc Bouvier, *'Je' et son histoire. L'analyse des personnages dans la poésie de Jacques Brault*, Orléans, David, 1998, 153 pp., analyses four of B.'s collections with a view to laying bare the structure of each. Hard-going.

CARRIER. G. Snaith, 'Roch Carrier's *La Guerre, yes sir!*: a Carnival of Truths', Rolfe, *Quebec*, 14–25, shows how C. uses the *carnavalesque* to express truths about Canada in 1968 and 'truths about human beings of any time.' G. Dorion, '*Petit Homme Tornade* de Roch Carrier: le métissage des mythes et des cultures', *VI*, 25: 176–89, is a reading of C.'s latest novel from the viewpoint of the confrontation between Amerindian and American myths.

CHAURETTE. Pascal Riendeau, *La Cohérence fautive. L'hybridité textuelle dans l'œuvre de Normand Chaurette*, Quebec, Nuit blanche, 1997, 164 pp., is an excellent critical study of *Provincetown Playhouse, juillet 1919, j'avais 19 ans*, and *Scènes d'enfants*. S. Nutting, 'L'écologie du tragique: *Fragments d'une lettre d'adieu lus par des géologues* de Normand Chaurette', *FR*, 71, 1998: 949–60, concludes that the tragic dimension of C.'s play derives not from the hero's death but from the failure of the geologists to give it any value or meaning.

CHOQUETTE. C. D. Rolfe, 'A collaborative (ad)venture: *Metropolitan Museum*', *BJCS*, 13, 1998:1–16, explores the input of both C. and Edwin Holgate to this major *livre d'artiste*.

CONAN. K. Roberts, 'Découvrir, fonder, survivre, les romans historiques de Laure Conan', *VI*, 24:351–71, offers a feminist and a narratological scrutiny of C.'s historical novels and the theme of French Canadian colonisation. T. M. Carr, Jr, 'Consolation and the work of mourning in *Angéline de Montbrun*', *FR*, 71, 1998:997–1006, seeks to do justice to the centrality of mourning and consolation in C.'s canonical novel.

DUBÉ. Michel Laurin, *Etude de 'Un Simple soldat' de Marcel Dubé*, Laval, Beauchemin, 1997, 93 pp., is a useful introduction.

DUBOIS. S. Huffman, 'Draguer l'identité: le *camp* dans *26 bis, impasse du Colonel Foisy* et *Ne blâmez jamais les Bédouins* de René-Daniel Dubois', *VI*, 24:558–72, examines camp discourse in the plays as a destabilising, subversive strategy.

DUCHARME. J. Przychodzen, 'La dialectique du paradoxe et du paroxysme dans *Dévadé* de Réjean Ducharme', *VI*, 23, 1998:346–59, discusses the intertexts that structure the novel and that shape Bottom's metamorphosis. A. R. Vianna Neto, 'La représentation de l'*ethos underground* et l'inscription de la pluralité dans l'œuvre de Réjean Ducharme', *Globe*, 2:57–74, considers, *inter alia*, the development in *L'Avalée des avalés* of a pluricultural aesthetic as a reaction to orthodoxy of meaning

FERRON. Marcel Olscamp, *Le Fils du notaire. Jacques Ferron 1921–1949. Genèse intellectuelle d'un écrivain*, Montreal, Fides, 1997, 428 pp. This biography and intellectual contextualisation of the young F. is particularly valuable given the massive presence of autobiographical elements in his work. Jacques Ferron and Pierre L'Hérault, *Par la porte d'en arrière. Entretiens*, Outremont, Lanctot, 1997, 319 pp., is also very valuable, not only for the views expressed but also for the typical humour and irony that emerge. Jacques Ferron, *Laisse courir ta plume … Lettres à ses sœurs 1933–1945*, ed. Marcel Olscamp, Outremont, Lanctot, 1998, 128 pp., presents F.'s correspondence to his sisters during the years of his studies at the Collège Jean-de-Brébeuf and Laval University, and provides plenty of insight into his literary apprenticeship and tastes, and his emerging style. Complements the correspondence with his father to be found in the important *Jacques Ferron, Papiers intimes. Fragments d'un roman familial: lettres, historiettes et autres textes*, ed. Ginette Michaud and Patrick Poirier, Outremont, Lanctot, 1997, 444 pp. Andrée Mercier, *L'Incertitude narrative dans quatre contes de Jacques Ferron. Etude sémiotique*, Montreal, Nota bene, 1998, 171 pp., discusses the ambiguity of the narrative discourse so evident in 'Bêtes et mari', 'L'été', 'Le Petit

William', and *Gaspé-Mattempa*. Not always an easy read but it does repay persistence. M. Velguth, 'La nuit dans un sac: étude des *Confitures de coings* de Jacques Ferron', *QuS*, 25, 1998:68–79, is a stimulating if not totally convincing reading of the work as a nationalist 'diptych'. G. Lafrance, 'Au seuil de la mémoire: le récit de naissance dans *La Créance* de Jacques Ferron', *VI*, 24:151–67, examines the ambiguous nature of autobiographical memory. A. Lamontagne, 'Relire l'enfance: le fantasme intertextuel dans *L'Amélanchier* de Jacques Ferron', *ib.*, 25:126–43, shows fantasy to be not an escape mechanism but a way of constructing identity.

GARNEAU, F.-X. *François-Xavier Garneau. Une figure nationale*, ed. Gilles Gallichan, Kenneth Landry, and Denis Saint-Jacques, Quebec, Nota bene, 1998, 400 pp., is a collection of some 18 essays that provide valuable new insight into the writer, his *milieu, and his œuvre*, particularly his *Histoire du Canada*.

GARNEAU, ST-D. Stéphanie Wells, *La Crise dans la correspondance des années trente. Lecture sociocritique des lettres d'Alfred DesRochers, Alain Grandbois et Saint-Denys Garneau*, Montreal U.P., 1998, 157 pp., discusses the extent to which the Depression impinges on the correspondence of the three writers and what this tells us about the links between 'discours épistolier et rumeur sociale' and the writers themselves. The chapter on G. is particularly interesting in that his letters are largely devoid of social comment and 'c'est sur le mode de l'intime que se déploie un discours sur la société qui l'entoure.' G. Montbertrand, 'Expansion et réductions dans l'oeuvre de Saint-Denys Garneau', *FR*, 71, 1998:1018–35, reveals and explores two contrasting tendencies in the poet's work. R. Melançon, 'Lire, cette pratique . . . Lecture de "Un bon coup de guillotine" de Saint-Denys Garneau', *VI*, 24:289–300, brings out the 'impersonalisation' of G.'s poetry as opposed to the autobiographical nature of his *Journal*.

GIRARD. S. Kevra, 'Indigestible stew and holy piss. The politics of food in Rodolphe Girard's *Marie Calumet*', *QuS*, 27:5–23.

GRANDBOIS. François Gallays and Yves Laliberté, *Alain Grandbois, prosateur et poète*, Orleans, Ontario, Editions David, 1997, 221 pp., is a collection of eight essays which bring out, amongst other things, the significant influence of the Bible on G. and also, intriguingly, that of romanticism.

GUEVREMONT. Yvan Lepage, *Germaine Guèvremont: la tentation auto-biographique*, Ottawa U.P., 1998, 205 pp. R. Baillie, '*Le Survenant*', *lecture d'une passion*, Montreal, XYZ, 183 pp., offers nothing startlingly new but is nevertheless a lucid, comprehensive study of the novel.

GURIK. M. Klementowicz, 'Robert Gurik's *Le Pendu*: allegory for a "Quiet Revolution"', *IJCS*, 1, 1998:83–92, certainly draws some stimulating parallels but also begs a number of questions.

## French Canadian Literature 191

GUYARD. Marie-Florine Bruneau, *Women Mystics Confront the Modern World: Marie de l'Incarnation (1599–1672) and Madame Guyon (1648–1717)*, Albany, SUNY U.P., 1998, 279 pp., is a thoughtful and readable study of the impact of the shift in epistemology upon the lives and works of the two women. B.'s analysis of M. de l'I. brings out how, although restricted to accepted formulae, she managed to record a woman's view of life in the New World. Françoise Deroy-Pineau, *Marie de l'Incarnation. Marie Guyard femme d'affaires, mystique, mère de la Nouvelle France 1599–1672*, Montreal, Fides, 299 pp., is a straightforward biography which has little to say about her important correspondence or her *Ecrits spirituels et historiques*. C. Zecher, 'Life on the French-Canadian hyphen: nation and narration in the correspondence of Marie de L'Incarnation', *QuS*, 26:38–51, concludes that M. de l'I.'s letters are a narrative of and a counter-narrative to 17th-c. French colonialism.

HAMELIN. P. Ruggeri, '*Cowboy* de Louis Hamelin. Le *Far West* québécois ou la redéfinition des frontières nordiques', *Globe*, 1, 1998:9–27.

HÉBERT. Kelton W. Knight, *Anne Hébert. In Search of the First Garden*, NY, Lang, 1998, 122 pp., examines how H. utilises memory to reconstruct the past. Although insightful, the study adopts the laboured strategy of going through the texts in their chronological order and spends much time paraphrasing. Z. Kassim, 'Une lecture pragmatique de *Kamouraska*. Un roman de "stream of consciousness"', *Etudes littéraires. Théories, analyses et débats*, 31.1:119–31, is a close study of the novel's complex linkages and their narrative function. G. Marcotte, 'Anne Hébert: "Un bruit de soie"', *VI*, 24:301–09, argues that the poem resists the received eschatological interpretation of *Tombeau des rois*. A.-M. Picard, 'L'enfant du *Torrent* ou le sujet de l'œuvre en puissance', *ib.*, 25:102–25, analyses the redemptive dimension of writing as it seeks to divest itself of a mother's omnipotence. H. S. Krognes, 'Une voix organisatrice dans *Les Fous de Bassan* d'Anne Hébert', *Tribune*, 10:83–99, emphasises how H. plays with the narrative 'ce qui rend le roman énigmatique pour un lecteur qui s'attend à un système narratif stable et univoque'. R. Chapman, 'Sites of the past in the Québécois novel', Rolfe, *Quebec*, 26–36, examines the ways *Kamouraska* and Madeleine Ouellette-Michalska's *La Maison Trestler* make use of historical subject matter.

HÉNAULT. M. Biron, 'Au-delà de la rupture: "Bestiaire" de Gilles Hénault', *VI*, 24:310–23, develops the idea of a poem that does not seek to revolutionize but rather to integrate old and new. S. Joachim, 'Eros le cri et l'anaphore: *Signaux pour les voyants* de Gilles Hénault', *QuS*, 27:70–79, argues that H.'s collection involves its readers in a paradoxical reflection on language since these poems use language to disparage language.

JACOB. M. Barbance, 'De parole et de liberté', *Nuit blanche*, 72, 1998:4–8, presents an interview from 1997 with the writer. A. Brochu, 'The unaccountable Rhizome', *ellipse*, 61:11–22, is a sympathetic discussion of *La Part de feu*.

LAFERRIÈRE. P. De Souza, 'Comment écrire un roman sans se fatiguer: stratégies perlocutoires d'un best-seller chez Dany Laferrière', *QuS*, 27:62–69.

LAPOINTE. Paul-Marie Lapointe, *Le Vierge incendié* suivi de *Nuit du 15 au 26 novembre 1948*, Montreal, Typo, 1998, 177 pp., is an excellent edition of L.'s extraordinary volume with a short but useful preface by Pierre Nepveu.

LASNIER. E. Nardout-Lafarge, 'Les "parnasses houleux" de Rina Lasnier', *VI*, 24:324–36, analyses 'Naissance obscure du poème' and suggests that poetic creation is linked to the poet's submission to the experience of a *loss* of meaning.

LEJEUNE. P. Berthiaume, 'Paul Lejeune ou le missionaire possédé', *VI*, 23, 1998:529–43, examines L.' s *récit* in which he reveals his defeat by the shaman Carigonan, and argues that L.' s failure may have owed something to the similarities between 17th-c. inquisitorial procedures and the discursive basis of shamanism.

LESCARBOT. Marc Lescarbot, *Les Muses de la Nouvelle-France*, ed. Jean-Marc Desgent, Montreal, Les herbes rouges, 1998, 94 pp., is a competent edition of this (historically) important poem.

LORANGER. P. Nepveu, 'Jean-Aubert Loranger: contours de la conscience', *VI*, 24:277–88, discusses 'Moments' as a discourse on a fragmented subjectivity, shaped by emptiness and silence.

MAILLET. S. Knutson, 'From Marichette to Rosealba and *La Sagouine*. A genealogy *au féminin* for Acadian theatre', *CanL*, 157, 1998:36–53, seeks to show that M.'s Sagouine develops a long established popular theatrical tradition.

MARTIN. I. Boisclair, 'Claire Martin, tous genres confondus', *QuS*, 26:52–61, examines the impact of mixed genres on both the formal and symbolic aspects of M.'s work.

MIRON. *Poésie*, 81, 1997, has a dossier entitled 'Hommage à Gaston Miron' (23–59) with uneven contributions from, amongst others, P. Ouellet and J. Royer. Wilbrod Michel Bujold, *L'Antimiron, l'hommage plus que manifeste*, Montreal, Varia, 1998, 189 pp., is a self-indulgent attempt to 'explain' M. whilst emulating his style of discourse (notably his orthographic and syntactical licence). Lise Gauvin, *L'Ecrivain francophone à la croisée des langues. Entretiens*, Paris, Karthala, 1997, 183 pp., presents extremely valuable interviews that discuss the creative tensions of language(s) in a multilingual context with M. (49–69) and Antonine Maillet (97–112). The same interview is also to be found in a dossier on M. included in *Jungle. Poésie internationale*, 19. *\*Dossier Gaston Miron*, Bordeaux, Le Castor astral, 158 pp. *EF*, 35.2–3, is a double volume devoted entirely to the poet and brings together some 30 very different pieces under the title 'Gaston Miron: un poète dans la cité'. Essential reading.

MONETTE. A. Boivin, '*Le Double suspect* ou la recherche de soi par l'autre', *QuF*, 108, 1998:88–91. *Relectures de Madeleine Monette*, ed. Janine Ricouart, Birmingham Al., Summa Publications, 249 pp., is an impressive collection of critical essays. Not surprisingly, *Le Double suspect* and *Armandes et melon* are the focus of many of the pieces.

NELLIGAN. Pascal Brissette, *Nelligan dans tous ses états. Un mythe nationale*, Montreal, Fides, 1998, 225 pp., does not so much seek to deconstruct the myth of N. as — moving from Louis Danton to Michel Tremblay and André Gagnon — to *understand* it. Gabriel Landry, *Poésies d'Emile Nelligan*, Montreal, Hurtubise HMH, 1998, 96 pp., is a readable introduction intended for students whose comments on style are especially useful. J. Blais, 'Décadence chez Nelligan: le cas du poème "[Je veux m'éluder]" ', *VI*, 24:264–76, identifies traces of decadence in the sonnet's several anomalies. C. Beausoleil, 'Emile Nelligan et le temps', *Nuit blanche*, 74:28–33. See also F. Couture, 'La liberté niche-t-elle ailleurs? L'Ecole littéraire de Montréal, *Le Terroir* de 1909 et le régionalisme', *VI*, 24:573–85, which argues that post 1900 the members of the Ecole might have been more daring than is generally thought.

OLLIVIER. Louise Gauthier, *La Mémoire sans frontières. Emile Ollivier, Naïm Kattan et les écrivains migrants au Québec*, Sainte-Foy, Laval U.P., 1997, 143 pp., is a lucid study that examines several important issues raised by the emergence of a so-called 'écriture migrante' in Quebec. Close readings of O.'s *Passages* and K.'s *La Fiancée promise* support the argumentation. E. Ollivier, 'Et me voilà otage et protagoniste', *Les Ecrits*, 95:161–73, is the writer's contribution to the 26th *Rencontre québécoise internationale des écrivains* on '*Ecritures, identités et cultures*' and usefully illuminates his concept of 'migrance' and the place of immigrant writing in Quebec. See also N. Kattan, 'L'identité en mouvement', *ib.*, 141–46. Further useful pieces on immigrant writers are M. L. Longo, 'Un "pastiche" de genres: *Laurence* de Yves E. Arnau', *Iapétus*, 1, 1998:65–8, which briefly discusses the borrowings from Poe in this *polar*, and F. Bordeleau, 'Ying Chen: la dame de Shanghai', *LQu*, 89, 1998:9–10.

POULIN. Pierre Hébert, *Jacques Poulin. La création d'un espace amoureux*, Ottawa U.P., 1997, 205 pp., analyses each of P.'s novels in turn with a view to presenting the novelist's *éthique* and *esthétique* of love. L. Saint-Martin, 'L'androgynie, la peur de l'autre et les impasses de l'amour: *La Tournée d'automne* de Jacques Poulin', *VI*, 24:541–57, disputes the received reading of the novel as one which, exceptionally for P., gives us a successful love affair and a happy ending. K. Kvia, 'Apprendre le bonheur. Une étude sur *La Tournée d'automne* de Jacques Poulin', *Tribune*, 10:39–55.

ROY. *Féminisme et forme littéraire. Lectures au féminin de l'œuvre de Gabrielle Roy*, ed. Lori Saint-Martin, Montreal, UQAM, 1998, 111 pp., offers four studies whose aim is to 'saisir, chez Gabrielle Roy, les rapports entre forme textuelle et pensée féministe'. Of particular note perhaps is K. Roberts' 'Le droit à la ville: Florentine et l'errance au féminin' which offers a feminist analysis of the city in *Bonheur d'occasion* and concludes that 'c'est justement la présence de Florentine en ville qui fait de ce texte un des livres-phares de la littérature québécoise'. S. Montreuil, 'Petite histoire de la nouvelle "Un jardin au bout du monde" de Gabrielle Roy', *VI*, 23, 1998:360–81, examines the creative process (there were at least five draft texts including a screenplay) that led to the short story. J.-G. Hudon, 'Gabrielle Roy et Germaine Guèvremont, 1945–1996', *Nuit blanche*, 71, 1998:8–12, usefully, if somewhat tenuously, links the two writers. Ismène Toussaint, *Les Chemins secrets de Gabrielle Roy. Témoins d'occasions*, Montreal, Stanké, 289 pp, is a collection of interviews, some of more consequence and interest than others, made with people who knew R. *'Bonheur d'occasion' au pluriel. Lectures et approches critiques*, ed. Marie-Andrée Beaudet, Quebec, Nota bene, 264 pp., is a collection of papers presented at a seminar on R. at the University of Laval in 1996. Usefully reassesses the novel in the light of contemporary methodologies. C. Wiktorowicz, 'Gabrielle Roy: cohérence du parcours littéraire et espace autobiographique', *QuS*, 27:46–61.

THÉORET. B. Havercroft, 'Quand écrire, c'est agir: stratégies narratives d'agentivité féministe dans *Journal pour mémoire* de France Théoret', *DFS*, 47:93–113, sheds further light on T.'s autobiographical project.

THÉRIAULT. C. Gagnon, 'De la Belle à la Bête. La décadence du couple chez Yves Thériault', *QuF*, 113:80–82, is an illuminating reading of *La Fille laide*.

TREMBLAY. Louise Vigeant, *Une Etude de 'A toi pour toujours, ta Marie-Lou'*, Montreal, Boreal, 1998, 129 pp., and Yves Jubinville, *Une Etude de 'Les Belles-Sœurs'*, Montreal, Boreal, 1998, 115 pp., are useful *manuels* that not only supply analysis and comment but attempt to encourage response and real understanding. M. Cardy, 'Varieties of anger in some early plays of Michel Tremblay', *RoS*, 31, 1998:5–17, explores, with clarity and insight, *Les Belles-Soeurs*, *A toi pour toujours, ta Marie-Lou*, and *Sainte Carmen de la Main*.. C. Robinson, 'Transvestism, identity and textuality in the work of Michel Tremblay', *RoS*, 32,

1998 : 69–77, offers lucid, fresh comment on some old themes. Robert Verrault, *L'Autre côté du monde, Le passage à l'âge adulte chez Michel Tremblay, Réjean Ducharme, Anne Hébert et Marie-Claire Blais*, Montreal, Liber, 1998, 167 pp., takes a significant recurrent theme in Québécois literature, one which looms particularly large in these four authors. Although more often than not the rite of passage is a disaster (the adolescent clings to an Edenic childhood and refuses adulthood), sometimes the figure of the writer emerges and perpetuates the dream and innocence. A fascinating, highly recommended study. F. Rochon, 'Fatalisme et merveilleux chez Michel Tremblay. Une lecture des *Chroniques du Plateau Mont-Royal*', VI, 24 : 372–95, is a multi-layered analysis that repays careful reading. J. Cardinal, 'L'abîme du rêve. Enfants de la folie et de l'écriture chez Michel Tremblay', *ib.*, 25 : 74–101, discusses the origins of Marcel's madness that ends the *Chroniques* cycle.

VIGNEAULT. Gilles Vigneault, *Comme un arbre en voyage. Entretiens avec François-Régis Barbry and Jean Royer*, Edipresse, 239 pp., presents two sets of interviews with the singer-poet carried out some 20 years apart.

## CARIBBEAN LITERATURE

By MARY GALLAGHER, *University College Dublin*

### I. GENERAL

Chris Bongie, *Islands and Exiles: The Creole Identities of Post/Colonial Literatures*, Stanford U.P., 1998, 543 pp., is a richly-textured and lively exploration of a complex yet clear central thesis, conducted through astute readings of a variety of 'colonial' and 'post-colonial' texts: notably *Robinson Crusoe, Paul et Virginie, Bug Jargal* and several works by Carpentier, Glissant, and Maximin, in addition to Faulkner's *Absalom, Absalom*, Hulmes's *The Bone People*, and Coetzee's *Foe*. For Bongie, 'the language of identity politics that our increasing awareness of creolization so rightly warns us against is not something we can simply transcend'. He shows how essentialist claims to or about identity are necessarily entangled with the poetics of creolization that is held to challenge or to deny them. The slash between 'post' and 'colonial' in Bongie's subtitle thus refers to the ambivalent, but endlessly complicit link between these two competing, yet mutually inseparable representations. Crosta, *Récits*, contains close criticism of writing in this genre by Capécia, Zobel, Schwarz-Bart, Chamoiseau, and Confiant. Much of the originality of the study derives from its valuable attempt to relate literary explorations of childhood both to the negotiation between Caribbean past, present, and future, and to reflection and discourse on Caribbean identity. The title of J. Michael Dash's *The Other America: Caribbean Literature in a New World Context*, Charlottesville, Virginia U.P., 1998, 197 pp., is based on an expression defined by Glissant as early as 1956. Dash argues the need for a 'synthesizing account of Caribbean literature' which would highlight the entire Caribbean as an interlectal and intertextual space. His premise is the paradigmatic centrality of the Caribbean not just to New World experience, but also to contemporary culture in general. Insofar as it focuses on particular spaces, the book privileges Haiti and Martinique, since it devotes a chapter to each. The study follows the course of modernist and post-modern phases in the (self-)construction of the Caribbean: first as prelapsarian paradise; then as an experiment (in Haiti) in modernist politics; thirdly as a series of attempts, via négritude, Marxism and Indigenism, to return to an 'ideal heterocosmic space' and also, via an image of the Mediterranean, to ground 'the archipelago in its hemispheric context'; fourthly, as site of the undoing of all systematizing ideology, a phase in which 'post-modern play predominates'. The book closes with a study of the articulation within Martinican culture of a 'strategy of resistance' used by the 'marginalized within a culture of consent'. Haigh, *Caribbean Francophone Writing*, is a ground-breaking English publication which includes, in addition to timely studies on individual authors, important chapters on more general topics, such as B. Jones on theatre and resistance in the French Caribbean (83–100); B. Ormerod on the representation of women in French Caribbean fiction (101–17); and an illuminating chapter by C. Zimra on the writing of Lacrosil, Manicom and Maximin, all three of whom realign issues of race and gender in an intertextual salute to the seminal importance of Fanon's reading of Capécia (177–94). Lydie Moudileno, *L'Ecrivain antillais au miroir de sa littérature: mises en scène et mise en abyme du roman antillais*, Karthala, 1997, 214 pp., explores elegantly and persuasively the significance of the diverse ways in which the figure of the writer is mobilized in five self-reflexive novels (by Confiant, Chamoiseau, Glissant, Condé, and Maximin). S. Haigh, 'Voix féminines/Voix féministes'? Women's writing from the Francophone Caribbean', pp. 141–55 of *Francophone Voices*, ed. Kamal Salhi, Exeter, Elm Bank, 248 pp., reviews the gradual development of a tradition of writing by women (Maryse Condé, especially) which counters the androcentric discourse of négritude, yet which can only problematically be regarded as feminist. *CEA*, 148, 1997, contains three articles of note: C. Chivallon, 'Du territoire au réseau: comment penser l'identité antillaise' (767–94), offers a sophisticated and cogent critique of binary (and exclusive) models of identity which only allow for either a territorial or a rhizomatic relation to space; M. Giraud, 'La créolité: une rupture en trompe-l'oeil' (795–811), outlines some contradictions inherent in the ideology of the créolité movement whose fundamentally (and fundamentalist) political discourse of authenticity masquerades as a purely cultural one; M.-J. Jolivet, 'Libres, marrons et créoles ou les Amériques noires revisitées' (993–1003), usefully compares the lesser or greater focus on slavery and African origins underlying several different constructions of black New World identity. T. C. Spear, 'L'enfance créole: la nouvelle autobiographie antillaise', Crosta, *Récits*, 143–67, is a wide-ranging comparative study showing how three 'Creole' texts relate to various Metropolitan works (by Sartre, Céline, and Sarraute) and how all three raise in different ways issues of race, gender, genre, narratology, family structure, urban space, and violence.

## 2. INDIVIDUAL AUTHORS

CÉSAIRE. A. Chambers, 'Critical approaches to the literatures of decolonization: C.'s *Cahier d'un retour au pays natal*', Haigh, *Caribbean Francophone Writing*, 35–50, follows the fortunes of Césaire's text.

CAPÉCIA.    Christiane P. Makward, *Mayotte Capécia, ou l'aliénation selon Fanon*, Karthala, 230 pp., with a preface by Jack Corzani, is an engaging piece of literary detective work and demystification. The trajectory of the maligned author and the complex genesis and complicated authorship of her texts are skilfully reconstructed in a generous and genuinely illuminating study, which, given C.'s pivotal position as putative archetype of alienation, will constitute henceforth a central reference in French Caribbean studies.

CHAUVET.    J. Dayan, 'Women, history and the gods: reflections on Mayotte Capécia and Marie Chauvet', Haigh, *Caribbean Francophone Writing*, 69–82, wonders what is so threatening about these two writers' 'visions of colour, class and sexuality' that their works cannot be accommodated in the 'liberal compact of cultural, feminist or African-American studies'.

CONDÉ.    M.-A. Sourieau, 'Entretien avec Maryse Condé: de l'identité culturelle', *FR*, 72:1091–98, concentrates on the identity quest in C.'s work and on how it relates to issues of location. L. Moudileno, 'Maryse Condé and the fight against prejudice: making room for the Haitian neighbour', *Thamyris*, 5, 1998:239–53, is a study of three works by C.: *Haïti Chérie, La Colonie du Nouveau monde*, and *Traversée de la mangrove*. All three are shown to challenge the myth of créolité which proves to be exclusive rather than accommodating of diversity. The Haitian, ostracized in Martinique and Guadeloupe, is shown to be créolité's Caribbean other, serving to 'consolidate a local Creoleness, as opposed to a trans-Caribbean Creoleness which doesn't have any political reality'.

CONFIANT.    R. Chandler Caldwell Jr, 'Créolité and postcoloniality in Raphaël Confiant's *L'Allée des soupirs*', *FR*, 73:301–11, explores how C.'s novel, despite its foregrounding of non-Western cultural elements, underlines the 'conflicted Westernism' at the heart of Martinican culture and thereby the problematic postcoloniality of the créolité programme which the novel actualizes.

FANON.    P. Williams, 'Frantz Fanon: The routes of writing', Haigh, *Caribbean Francophone Writing*, 51–68, examines F. as a 'black Atlantic writer, beginning in the Caribbean but becoming something else' because of his geographical trajectory and also because of the deliberate 're-routeing' of his writing from Caribbean social psychology to the politics of decolonization.

GLISSANT.    Celia M. Britton, *Edouard Glissant and Postcolonial Theory: Strategies of Language and Resistance*, Virginia U.P., 224 pp., is an important and compelling study which situates G.'s thought and writing (specifically, the essays and the novels) both in relation to each other and to postcolonial theory (in particular, Fanon, Spivak, Bhabha, and Gates). G.'s mapping of subjectivity within language is studied as a strategy of cultural resistance. Examined diachronically, this strategic mapping associates language first of all with lack (in that it belongs to the Other), then with subordination, subsequently with delirium, then camouflage, and finally, with relation or relay. C. Britton, 'Collective narrative voice in three novels by Glissant', Haigh, *Caribbean Francophone Writing*, 135–48, discusses *Malemort, La Case du commandeur,* and *Mahagony,* using G.'s vision of relation (as relay or as link) to show how narrative voice gradually evolves in these three novels into an ever closer approximation of G.'s ideal: the creation of a 'dynamic, internally differentiated consciousness'. S. Niang, 'Particularités orales des récits de vie dans *Le Quatrième Siècle* et *Tout-Monde* d'Edouard Glissant', Crosta, *Récits,* 129–41, is illuminating.

SAINT-JOHN PERSE. Mireille Sacotte, *'Eloges' et 'La Gloire des Rois'*, Foliothèque, Gallimard, 231 pp., is a very welcome, clear, yet appropriately subtle guide to one of the landmark texts of the Caribbean imagination. M. Gallagher, 'Seminal praise: the poetry of Saint-John Perse', Haigh, *Caribbean Francophone Writing*, 17–34, outlines the poet's importance as a key point of (intertextual) reference for contemporary Caribbean literature.

PINEAU. K. Gyssels, 'L'exil selon Pineau, récit de vie et autobiographie', Crosta, *Récits,* 169–87, studies various aspects of P.'s work of autofiction, *L'Exil selon Julia,* most notably, the representation of language, exile, childhood, and the gender divide, arguing that the text is given particular depth by P.'s bifocal generational perspective (i.e. her treatment of the grandaughter/grandmother relationship).

ZOBEL. S. Crosta, 'Birago Diop et Joseph Zobel: confluences éthiques et pérégrinations esthétiques', Crosta, *Récits,* 101–20, comments on how Zobel's taste for Japanese floral art marks his autobiography (*D'amour et de silence,* Editions Prosveta, 1994).

# III. OCCITAN STUDIES

## LANGUAGE

By KATHRYN KLINGEBIEL, *Associate Professor of French,*
*University of Hawaii at Mānoa*

### 1. BIBLIOGRAPHICAL AND GENERAL

C. Bonnet, 'Occitan Language', *MLAIntBibl*, 1997[1998], III, 200–02; and *ib.*, 1998[1999], III, 200–02. For 1996, K. Klingebiel compiles 'Current Studies in Occitan Linguistics', *CRLN*, 46.2, 1997:29–42 and for 1997, *ib.*, 47.2, 1998:29–40. These are followed by M. Westmoreland, 'Current Studies in Occitan Linguistics [1998]', *ib.*, 48.2:38–42. In the survey year, K. Klingebiel has also published 'Occitan Linguistic Bibliography for 1997–1998', *Tenso*, 14:164–250, and *Bibliographie linguistique (1983–1997) de l'ancien occitan* (AIEO 8), Birmingham U.P.–AIEO, iii + 296 pp., with more than 3,000 items. F. Pic, 'Catalogue d'une cinquantaine de manuscrits de dictionnaires et glossaires occitans. Complément à la *Bibliographie des dictionnaires patois gallo-romans*', *RLiR*, 63:201–14. Jean Fourié, *Bibliographie des ouvrages, oeuvres, études et articles en langue d'oc ou intéressant la langue et la littérature d'oc, publiés en 1997* (*Lou Félibrige*, 228, supp.), 1998, 56 pp. (see also *YWMLS*, 59:257). G. Nariòo welcomes 'Lo CIRDOC, ostau d'Occitania', *PG*, 191:13; this brand-new library of Occitania in Béziers houses 46,000 volumes, 1,700 periodicals, 3,400 records and cassettes, plus videos, posters, and images.

P.-H. Billy, 'De l'onomastique en France: principales publications (1992–1995)' has appeared only on the internet <http://fuzzy.arts. kuleuven.ac.be/icosweb/ F92_95.htm>. Electronic sources for Occitan are reviewed by the creator of OccitaNet: M. Van Den Bossche, in *PN*, 82:19–23. Id. provides Occitan addresses and terms, e.g. *teleranha occitana, espaci uèb*: 'Desvelopament deu hialat occitan', *PGA*, 57, 1998:12–22. P. Swiggers, 'Okzitanisch und Romanisch / L'occitan et les langues romanes', article 461 [in French], Holtus, *Lexikon*, VII, 67–82, traces the history of contacts with French and with other Romance languages. P. V. Davies provides succinct descriptions of Gascon and Occitan in Price, *Encyclopedia*, 190–92 and 343–48, respectively. D. Pfeiffer, *\*'La okcitana lingvo'*, *Esperanto*, 91.2, 1998:29–30. G. Bazalgues, *\*'L'Occitan: de la scripta médiévale au patois'*, *QR*, 87, 1997:42–46.

J. Delmas, 'Bilan des actions 98 du BELRM', *AqAq*, 132:6, describes the double focus of the independent Bureau Européen pour les Langues moins répandues: the 'Convention-Cadre pour la protection des minorités nationales', and the 'Charte européenne des langues régionales'. T. Dupuy, 'Adiéu la Charto Euroupenco di lengo regiounalo', *PrA*, 109, 1997:2, is less optimistic than E. Ros, 'Las lengas regionalas de mai en mai d'actualitat', *PN*, 81, 1998:1–3. Both discuss the report made by Bernard Poignant to Prime Minister Jospin, June 1998, on French regional languages and the Charte européenne; *Les Langues de France et la République* (*LDGM*, special no., 5), 1998, 8 pp., presents the full text. A. Gaquin, *FR*, 73:94–107, notes that France remains the sole EC member whose constitution specifies a single official language. M. Braç examines the 'Carta del Comitat Republican per la modificacion de l'article 2', *Occitans!*, 84, 1998:11. Article 2 ('La langue de la République est le français') has attracted much attention in the Occitan press, e.g. 'Comitat Republican de Lengadòc. Cambiar l'article 2', *Occitans!*, 87, 1998:4–5. The Occitan movement today appears to be counting on the construction of a new Europe to deconstruct the French centralist/anti-federalist model. See, for example, N. Lafont, 'L'ensenhament de l'occitan dins lo Cantal', *Lo Convise*, 23, 1998:1, pointing out possible support for the Occitan dialects: 'uèi, la regionalizacion marcha ambe l'Euròpa'.

## 2. Medieval Period (to 1500)

MORPHOSYNTAX. Rosa María Medina Granda, *Polaridad negativa en Occitano Antiguo. Elementos de comparación con otros romances medievales*, Oviedo U.P., 404 pp. Two companion pieces by the same author have also appeared: 'A propósito del comportamiento distribucional del occitanico antiguo *ge(n)s*. Elementos de comparación con el francés y el catalán antiguos *g(i)ens* y *gens*', *RFR*, 15, 1998:77–119, which examines how OPr. *ge(n)s* behaved like similar syntactic TPNs ('término de polaridad negativa') in Old French and Old Catalan, developing negative value through pronominal usage. Id., 'Occitano antiguo *pas* y *miga* (*mija, mi[c]a*): análisis del comportamiento distribucional de estos términos', *Tenso*, 14:111–54.

LEXIS AND LEXICOLOGY. Kurt Baldinger has produced Fasc. 9 of the *DAG*, 1998, 80 pp. Under the direction of Wolf-Dieter Stempel, Fasc. 2 of the *DOM*, 80 pp., appeared in 1998 (see also *YWMLS*, 59:259).

PARTICULAR SEMANTIC FIELDS. J. Santano Moreno, 'Oficios en documentos occitanos de Navarra y Aragón', *NRO*, 33–34:159–90, lists 151 Old Occitan names for professionals, tradesmen, artisans, ecclesiastics, and administrative workers, with an appendix (183–86) devoted to 'La familia *baldrés* ~ *baldragas* y la ciudad de *Bagdad*'. R. M. Medina Granda, '*No·m sofranhera hiera* (Raimbaut de Vaqueiras, descort plurilingüe, IV, 8). Propuesta de reanálisis de *hiera*', pp. 601–18 of *Corona Spicea. In Memoriam Cristóbal Rodríguez Alonso*, Oviedo U.P., 824 pp. M. G. considers *hiera* adverbial ('not at all') rather than nominal ('buckle').

ONOMASTICS. \*'Les Voies romaines en Gaule', *L'Archéologue. Archéologie nouvelle*, 28, 1997:7–40. Of interest for the Midi is C. Landes, 'La Voie Domitienne' (36–40). B. Boyrie-Fénié highlights the link between place names and the realia they represent in 'Patrimoine archéologique et toponymie: l'exemple des Landes', pp. 53–70 of *La Toponymie, un patrimoine à préserver. En Inde, en Gascogne, en Alsace, vers une politique de réhabilitation des anciens toponymes?*, ed. Solange Wydmusch, L'Harmattan, 1998, 176 pp. P.-H. Billy, 'Les Noms de rue au bas Moyen Age: essai de typologie', *NRO*, 33–34:261–69, arranges examples into functional descriptions (e.g. *Carrera Balneorum*, 1335 Toulouse) and the social, historical, geographical, and natural universes. J.-P. Chambon, \*'Méthodes en anthroponymie historique: à propos du nom de famille *Dental* et congénères et de l'article DENTALE du *Dictionnaire historique des noms de famille romans* (PatRom)', pp. 65–81 of *Dictionnaire historique des noms de famille romans, 9. Actas del IX Coloquio (Uviéu/Oviedo), 26–29 de octubre 1995*, ed. Ana María Cano González, Tübingen, Niemeyer, 1998, xiv + 201 pp. F. Rigaud, 'Leis illas de Provènça (*Liber insularum Provinciae*), assai sus la toponimia insulara, sègles XIIen-Xven', *EOc*, 22, 1997:2–14, studies small islands off Marseilles and La Ciotat. S. Thiolier-Méjean, 'Ganges et son troubadour Arnaut Peire', *FL*, 126, 1998:193–207, reviews etymologies for *Ganges/Agange* (Hérault).

HISTORICAL SOCIOLINGUISTICS. U. Mölk, 'Plan- und Kunstsprachen auf romanischer Basis. II Altokzitanisch / *Langues artificielles à base romane*. II *L'ancien occitan*', article 492 [in German], Holtus, *Lexikon*, VII, 687–98, examines the development of troubadour language. J.-P. Chambon, \*'Sur la répartition des toponymes en –ANU et –ANICU et les courants de romanisation de la Gaule méridionale', *TLP*, 37:141–61. Study of both large-scale and small-scale maps yields a clearer picture of the distribution of rural settlements, as well as the diffusion of these suffixes. Id., 'L'agencement spatial et fonctionnel des vicairies carolingiennes dans le midi de la Gaule: une approche linguistique', *RLiR*, 63:55–174. Detailed examination, with maps, of sites in Ardèche, Cantal, Aveyron, Corrèze, and Haute-Vienne. N. Coulet, 'Relations de transhumance entre Aix et Barcelonnette au milieu du XVe siècle', *PrH*, 191, 1998:100–06, edits a letter written by a notary for a certain Jean Guiramand.

TEXTS. Rogièr Teulat, *Sermons de Sant-Marçal (sègle 12)*, Orlhac, Lo Convise, 64 pp. (see also *YWMLS*, 59:262). Jean-Pierre Barraqué, \**Le Martinet d'Orthez. Textes médiévaux inédits: violence, pactes et pouvoir* *judiciaire en Béarn à la fin du Moyen âge*, Biarritz, Atlantica, 309 pp. A. Cauhapé winds down his long-running series 'Sexualité et vie conjugale ... autrefois': (26), *PG*, 184, 1998:6–7; (27), *ib.*, 185, 1998:9–10; (28), *ib.*, 186, 1998:5–6, the last concerning Gaston Fébus. M. Selig, *'Zu den Anfangen der altokzitanischen Urkundenschriftlichkeit', *LiLi*, 27, 1997:24–44. Latin and Old Occitan texts of a 12th-c. *rouergat* charter of donation to the Knights Templar are compared within the pragmatic context of their sociocultural traditions. X. Ravier, 'Remarques sur la charte de Nizezius', *NRO*, 33–34:111–42, takes a new look at the toponyms found in this 7th-c. document from Moissac. A text from the Rouergue is described by M. Vaissière, 'Le Temporel de l'Abbaye de Comberoumal', *RRou* 57:113–23; fiefs are classified, Occitan names provided. D. Iancu-Agou, 'Un juif de Marseille à la veille de l'expulsion', pp. 297–304 of *De Provence et d'ailleurs. Mélanges offerts à Noël Coulet* (*PrH*, 195–96), edits MS 351 E 570, folio 29, Fonds Laget-Maria, Archives Départementales des Bouches-du-Rhône; books sold by Manuel Levi to Jacob Salves in 1492 are listed in Latin and translated. M. R. Bonnet, 'Une transaction en langue provençale concernant le couvent des religieuses de St Césaire d'Arles en 1499', *PrH*, 191, 1998:69–99, edits and translates MS 17 F 74, Archives Départementales des Bouches-du-Rhône. J. Vesòla, *'Un bocin d'un terrièr de la fin del XVe s.', *Lo Convise*, 26:9, edits two folios of a 1474 *cens* (tax declaration) from MS E suppl., dossier 49, chemise Laroche-Lambert, Archives Départementales du Cantal.

### DIALECTS

PROVENÇAL. M. Hébert, 'Latin et vernaculaire: quelles langues écrit-on en Provence à la fin du Moyen Age?', *PrH*, 188, 1997:281–99. Random mixing of languages in medieval documents masks a logic that may remain uncoverable today.

LIMOUSIN. J. Becquet edits the 'Actes du Vicomte Adémar et de l'évêque de Limoges (1107) en faveur de Cublac (Corrèze)', *Lemouzi*, 141, 1997:95–98. R. Joudoux and T. Pataki, 'Acte de partage des biens de feu Jacques Brossard entre ses enfants, notamment de La Chapoulie, près de la cathédrale, en latin et en langue limousine (1481)', *ib.*, 144, 1997:85–107, edit the Occitan text of MS J1950/2, Archives Départementales de la Corrèze. R. Joudoux provides notes and commentary in *ib.*, 148, 1998:85–117. J. and E. Roux, *Remembransa sia ... Textes occitans du 'Livre Noir' de Périgueux (1360–1450). I. Les Subsistances à Périgueux au temps de la Guerre de Cent Ans. Commerce, aumônes publiques, vols et brigandage...* (*PN*, n.s. 76), 1997, 28 pp., offers sample texts from the consular register of Périgueux.

AUVERGNAT. P.-H. Billy, *'La Société bas-auvergnate au prisme de la nomination (XIV-XVe s.)', *Onoma*, 34:45–58.

### 3. POST-MEDIEVAL

GENERAL. The September 1999 congress of the AIEO, sixth of its kind, is described in glowing detail by E. Tourtet, 'Viena a l'ora occitana', *AqAq*, 137:8–9; several of the 100 communications are described briefly. A. Viaut, 'L'Occitan et les langues d'oïl', *BIO*, 15: 2–3 and *ib.*, 16: 2–3, contrasts the natural grouping of the Occitan dialects under *un même toit occitan* with the centrifugal nature of northern dialect differentiation. Id., 'Le Concept du sud et l'occitan', *Garona*, 14, 1997:33–47, examines changing perceptions that underlie the terms *sud, midi, austral, domaine occitan*, and now *Grand Sud*. P. Giroussens asks *'L'occitan est-il une discipline?', *Lengas*, 46:7–20. *Actes de l'Université d'Eté 1996*, ed. Georges Péladan, Nîmes, MAR-POC, 1997, 247 pp., includes two titles of general interest here: J.-P. Tardiu, 'L'Escrivaire e la causida de la lenga' (203–04); and G. Kremnitz, 'Le plurilinguisme en littérature' (173–202), the latter with a sociolinguistic approach. M. C. Alén and H. Boyer, *'L'Occitan sur Internet: signe des temps, champ du cygne ou pied de nez?', *Lengas*, 46:21–32.

ORTHOGRAPHY. 'Brèva presentacion de las preconizacions graficas del Conselh de la lenga occitana, Tolosa junh de 1997–Nîmes agost de 1997', *EOc*, 22, 1997:38–39, outlines 17 points of change vis-à-vis Alibert's norms (*Gramatica Occitana*). J. Lafitte and F. Beigbeder, *'Lo Conselh de la Lenga Occitana e las soas purmèras "preconizacions"', *LDGM*, 11, 1998:39–45. In August 1997, 47 specific rules for Provençal subdialects were provided by the Conseu de la Lenga Occitana and the Sector de Lingüistica, CREO Provence, in 'Convencion sus lo provençau, l'aupenc e lo niçard' and outlined by D. Sumien, *Occitans!*, 84, 1998:18–19. Summarized in *CIL*, 127:26, additional recommendations dating from December 1998 cover graphic accentuation of verbs, borrowings, neologisms, and learned words; orthography of /s/. All these texts can be found in full at < http://www.geocities7156/CLO.html >. J. Lafitte, *'Preconizacions 2 (lenga) e lo gascon', *LDGM*, 14:12–16. R. Toscano, 'Grafia dau Provençau e dau Niçard', *Occitans!* special no. 85–86, 1998:15–16, comments on several of the 'preconisacions' for *nissart*. In an interview with C. Laux, 'Quin ròtle jogarà lo Conselh de la lenga occitana?', *L'Occitan*, 130, 1997:4–5, J. Taupiac, head of the IEO Sector Lingüistica, explains the decision to allow double spellings in certain cases, e.g. *consí/cossí, la fonccion/foncion, paralizar/paralisar*. R. Teulat, 'Accentuacion de las P3', *Lo Convise*, 25:19–20, discusses choices available for third-person plural verb forms, and agrees with the IEO's decision: 'L'accentuacion de *càntan, cantaran*', *GS*, 33:296–300. Id., *\*'Vocalas finalas dels mots de manlèu'* (1), *Lo Convise*, 27:7–8, and (2), *ib.*, 18–19. D. Sumien sounds a warning note in 'Per la qualitat e la credibilitat de l'IEO', *EOc*, 22, 1997:47–50. The IEO must respect its own orthographic norms if it wishes to regain and retain its credibility. J. Ubaud, 'Problèmas de nòrma', *LPO*, 33, 1998:3–28, offers a general presentation of the GIDILOc and its conception, as she reviews use of the grave accent and other problem areas that await further attention. M.-L. Gourdon, *\*'La Quête de la "bonne graphie".* Les motivations de choix graphiques en Pays d'Oc au XIXe siècle', *Lengas*, 45:7–52.

LEXIS. Louis Alibert, *Dictionnaire occitan-français selon les parlers languedociens* (6th edn), Toulouse, IEO, 1997, 699 pp. Cristian Rapin has published the third volume of his *Diccionari francés-occitan*, covering *E-F-G*, Puylaurens, IEO, 404 pp.; *A-B* appeared in 1991, *C-D* in 1994. Louis Boucoiran, *Dictionnaire analogique et étymologique des idiomes méridionaux qui sont parlés depuis Nice jusqu'à Bayonne et depuis les Pyrénées jusqu'au centre de la France [...]*, originally published in parts, Nîmes, 1875–76, has been reprinted in 3 vols as *Dictionnaire des idiomes méridionaux*, Nîmes, Lacour, 1997, 1348 pp. Pierre Trinquier, *\*Les Herbes d'Oc et leurs vertus. Les principales espèces végétales méridionales sous leurs divers noms occitans & quelques-unes de leurs propriétés médicinales ou autres*, Nîmes, Lacour, 1997, 413 pp. J.-L. Fossat, 'Néologie dialectale et implantation en socioterminologie spatiale', *TeN*, 16, 1997:7–32. A two-pronged model of lexical status is proposed to cover the disparity between controlled and uncontrolled usage of terminology; existing dialect vocabulary tends to prevent the implantation of French terms.

PARTICULAR SEMANTIC FIELDS. I. Villebrun, 'Genèse d'une terminologie au XVIIIe siècle: L'exemple des forges à la Catalane', *TeN*, 16:55–62. J. Grzega, *\*'Die galloromanischen Bezeichnungen der Lakritze: Zu den Bereichen Etymologie, Onomasiologie und Bezeichnungswandel unter besonderer Berucksichtigung der Volksetymologie', *GLS*, 1998, 49:13–28, details 20 form types for 'licorice'.

ONOMASTICS. J. Chaurand, *'La Bédoire, La Bétoire*: deux traitements, deux aires d'extension', *NRO*, 31–32, 1998:4–10 (<BIBITORIUM, -ORIA 'abreuvoir'). J.-C. Bouvier, 'Odonymes d'agglomération entre l'écrit et l'oral', *NRO*, 33–34:303–10. Old names are being pressed into new service, e.g. *carriero de la Masso*.

SOCIOLINGUISTICS. The full text of the 'Declaracion universala de dreches lingüistics', as approved at the June 1996 Barcelona convention, is provided in *RevO*, 6, 1997:120–39 (see also *YWMLS*, 59:264–65). H. Boyer, 'Regards sur la situation sociolinguistique de l'espace occitan. Fin de substitution?', *Plurilinguismes*, 17:133–55, fears for Occitan, despite promises and legislative actions taken to protect it in recent years. E. Ros, 'Enquesta lingüistica sus l'occitana en Aquitània', *Occitans!*, 85/86, 1998:8–10, is also concerned for the future of Occitan, even though 60–70% of those questioned during the 1997 survey voiced their support of the language. Id., 'L'Enquesta linguistica sus l'Occitan en Aquitania', *PN*, 80, 1998:1–3, draws conclusions from the foregoing. 'Une enquête linguistique en Aquitaine', *PGA*, 55, 1998:2–3, publishes the second round of results from this survey. *L'occitan dins lo mond/Occitan in the World/ L'Occitan dans le monde*, Toulouse, Conservatoire Occitan, 1997, 15 pp. (see also *YWMLS*, 60:195). Gérard Tautil et al., *Chemins d'occitanie/Camins d'occitania: espace, territoires, identité, démocratie ... (politique occitane, 974–2000)*, L'Harmattan, 1997, 302 pp. J. Delmas, 'TV-Oc, per doman?', *AqAq*, 133–134:8–9, notes reduced presence of Occitan on television. C. Laux, 'Occitan e catalan a France-Inter', *L'Occitan*, 142:6, discussing a half-hour program that aired on 18 July 1999, points out that Occitan is one of the few 'parlars locals o lengas' of France that still provide a 'lenga de comunicacion'. J. Green, *'Language: Polari'*, *CQ*, 39, 1997:127–31. Occitan-based Polari (or Parlyaree), in use around the Mediterreanean, consists solely of lexical items. P. Gardy, *'Nommer l'occitan? A propos d'un récit mythique de nomination (Joseph Delteil, La Deltheillerie)'*, pp. 251–70 of *Le Nom des langues*, 1, *Les Enjeux de la nomination des langues*, ed. Andrée Tabouret-Keller, Louvain-la-Neuve, Peeters, 1997, 274 pp., studies the sociolinguistic dimensions of Delteil's idiosyncratic *franco-patois*. R. Merle, *'Quelques remarques sur l'usage de la langue d'oc dans la propagande démocrate-socialiste sous la Seconde République'*, *Lengas*, 46:33–44. L. Fornés, 'L'occitanòfila valenciana Euphemia Llorente', *PdO*, 2, 1998:9–32, describes Llorente's little-known proposal for a joint linguistic codification of Valencian, Catalan, and Occitan.

## 4. GASCON AND BÉARNAIS

GENERAL. J. Lafitte continues to insist on language status for Gascon: 'Gascon, occitan et langue d'oc', *EOc*, 22, 1997:15–22, describing his brochure *Lenga d'òc, morta o viva? Ont n'èm? Qué har?* (2nd edn, 1996) and its French version (see *YWMLS*, 59:266 for both), revised and reprinted as *Le Gascon, langue à part entière, et le béarnais, âme du gascon. Suivi de la 'Lettre aux Gascons' d'Yves Gourgaud, professeur d'occitan* (*LDGM*, special no. 4), 56 pp. In rebuttal, J. Sibille, 'Gascon, occitan: per n'acabar', *EOc*, 22, 1997:31–38 concludes: 'lo gascon es un dialecte occitan perqué los gascons son occitans'. B. F. Bassetto introduces Gascon to a Brazilian audience as \*'Uma língua românica em ascensão', *ELin*, 26, 1997:395–400. Halip Lartiga, \**Les Racines de la langue gasconne: identité culturelle, limites linguistiques*, Belin-Beliet, Princi Negre, 1998, 52 pp.

ORTHOGRAPHY. J. Lafita, 'Sus la grafia de *Reclams*', *LDGM*, 12, 1998:36–39, finds contradictions between usage in *Reclams* and the 1984 *Petit Dictionnaire français-occitan (Béarn)* published by Per Noste/ *La Civada*. Id. further justifies his one-man effort to revise Gascon spelling, in 'Toponimes gascons', *LDGM*, 12,1998:42–48 and *ib.*, 14:22–30. Reactions vary. J. Taupiac argues against Lafitte's introduction of 'x' into Gascon spelling, since 'sh' suffices elsewhere in Occitan: 'Deishatz lo peish gascon dins l'aiga occitana!', *ib.*, 12, 1998:20–24.

MORPHOSYNTAX. In his series 'Parler plan', G. Narzòo studies the Gascon concessive: '*Per mei que forcèssi*' ('j'avais beau forcer'), *PG*, 178, 1997:14. Id., 'A prepaus de la plaça deu complement de un grop verbau', *ib.*, 179, 1997:15 (*que la pòdes véser* rather than \**pòdes véser-la*). Id. argues for lack of past participle agreement in '*Las poesias que m'as enviat*', *ib.*, 180, 1997:16. Id., '*Que la s'a bastida eth*', *ib.*, 181, 1997:14 ('he built it [*la maison*] for himself'). Id. argues against use of *dont* in phrases such as *lo vesin, la molhèr deu quau ei anglesa* (*ib.*, 182/183, 1997:12). Id., 'Mantengam l'expressivitat de la nosta lenga: Un vilatjòt qu'ei un vilatge petit . . .', *ib.*, 189, 1998:10, explains his reasons — usage, context, euphony — for choosing between synthetic and analytic forms.

ONOMASTICS. M. Grosclaude, '*Francés* ou *Francesc?*', *PG*, 178, 1997:15; by AD 1000, a series of Gascon names from the lexical field of 'franchise, affranchissement' are attested: *Franc(a), (H)ranquina*, etc. G.-J. Néel, \*'Note à propos de l'origine de *Biarritz*', *NRO* 31–32, 1998:281–82. Jean Bonnemaison, \**Noms de rue gascons de Bordeaux*, Belin-Beliet, Princi Negre, 1997, 116 pp. R. Aymard, \*'Anciens noms de famille du Nestés', *BSR*, 1998:43–70, is reviewed by P.-H. Billy, 'Note de lecture', *NRO*, 33–34:360; B. has reservations about several recent tendencies in onomastic research, notably attempts to 'expliquer le passé par le présent'. J. L. Lizundia, \*'Questions relatives à l'onomastique dans les zones actuellement non-bascophones du Pays Basque', *ICOS 19*, 1, 196–200.

SUBDIALECTS. Joan-Edoard Fauche, \**Estudi gramaticau de la lenga gascona (parlar de Tonens), par un felibre de l'Escòla de Gensemin*, introd. Christian Rapin (*La Mémoire du fleuve*, special no.), Tonens, p.p., 1998. Jean-Pierre Laurent and Paul Pedoya, \**Dictionnaire occitan-français et grammaire du parler de Montseron (Ariège)*, [Montreuil], p.p., 1997, 83 pp. Jean-Pierre Laurent, \**Etude grammaticale et lexicale des parlers du castillonnais: Bethmalais, Bellongue, Biroussan, Castillon*, [Montseron], p.p., xxiv + 42 pp. Id. and René Pons, *Parler du Haut-Massatois de la Vallée du Port: étude grammaticale et lexicale; suivi de 'Un troc de vida als Ourtrigous'*, [Montseron], p.p., xxii + 36 + xii pp. The Comitat dera Lengua has produced a dictionary of *bigourdan*: *Atau que's ditz! Dictionnaire français-occitan (Gascon des Hautes-Pyrénées)*, Tarbes, Conseil général des Hautes-Pyrénées, 1998, 151 pp. Anon., 'Era Val d'Aran', *L'Occitan*, 128, 1997:7. A thumbnail history of this Pyrenean valley, its 7,000 inhabitants, and their three official languages. J. Lafitte provides several short pieces on *aranes*: *'La Vath d'Arann e los aranés', LDGM, 13:3–4. Id., *'Sinòpsi de las nòrmas oficiaux (gascon de França/aranés)', *ib.*, 13:4–17. Id., *'Las nòrmas ortograficas aranesas — Teoria e pratica', *ib.*, 13:18–32. Id., *'Nòtas filologicas sus l'aranés', *ib.*, 14:7–10. SOCIOLINGUISTICS. L. Alèxis, 'Front National e lengas "regionaus"', *RBG*, 1998.3:16–28: local cultural identity is seen as a window onto the future. Bruno Rigal, *Enfants de migrants à l'école bilingue: français-occitan*, Bordeaux, Univ. Bordeaux-2, Psychologie scolaire, 1998, situates his study in an elementary school in Villefranche-de-Rouergue (Aveyron).

TEXTS. A. Cauhapé, 'Sexualité et vie conjugale ... autrefois', presents modern texts in *PG*, 178, 1997:7–8; 179, 1997:7–8; 180, 1997:9–10; 181, 1997:6–7; and 182/183, 1997:5–6.

5. SOUTHERN OCCITAN

LANGUEDOCIEN

GENERAL. Ernest Nègre has prepared the 5th edition of Joseph Salvat's *Gramatica Occitana dels parlars lengadocians*, Toulouse, Collège d'Occitania, 1998, iii + 187 pp.

LEXIS AND LEXICOLOGY. Charles Mouly, *Dictionnaire de la Catinou*, Portet-sur-Garonne, Loubatières, 1997, 208 pp.

ONOMASTICS. C. Laux studies the spread of 'Le nom de famille *Carayon*', *RT*, 78, 1998:629–33, via listings on the Minitel; responding with a 'Note de lecture', *NRO*, 33–34:359, P.-H. Billy identifies the etymon of this name as CARAGONUS. F. R. Hamlin and J. Gulsoy, '*Montpellier* en Languedoc et *Montpeller* en Catalogne', *NRO*, 33–34:143–57; both derive independently from PISULUM '(wild) pea'. C. Marichy, *'Toponymie vécue et cadastre: l'exemple de l'Hérault', *NRO*, 31–32, 1998:61–82. G. Costa, *'Evolution du panorama patronymique des Pyrénées-Orientales (1841–1931)', *ICOS 19*, III, 93–105. P. Fabre, *'Les Noms propres dans les poèmes de La Fare-Alais, poète languedocien du XIXe s.: les avatars de la fonction référentielle', Billy, *Onomastique*, 355–62. Referential function intersects with symbolism in the work of this precursor of the renaissance of Oc.

SUBDIALECTS. Louis Breysse, *Le Patois bourguesan: œuvre posthume*, Bourg-St-Andeol, Lou Caleu, 1997, 123 pp.

SOCIOLINGUISTICS. J.-F. Courouau, 'L'occitan, lenga de normalitat', *RBG*, 4, 1997:42–44, describes the inauguration of bilingual road signs in Gabian (Lengadoc-Rosselhon). Zefir Bòsc, *Les Gabarriers du Lot, lorsque la haute vallée d'Olt était naviguée*, Rodez, Grelh Roërgàs, 1997, 218 pp. (see also *YWMLS*, 59:272).

PAREMIOLOGY. Louis Alibert, *Proverbes de l'Aude*. Classés et mis en orthographe occitane par Raymond Chabbert, Enèrgas, Vent Terral, 1998, 250 pp., publishes for the first time some 2,000 proverbs arranged by theme, with another 1,000 sayings and expressions. Pierre Trinquier has edited Anne de Rulman's *Inventaire alphabétique des proverbes du Languedoc: qui marquent la fécondité du langage populaire, la gentillesse de l'esprit & la solidité du jugement des habitants du pays (1626)*, Nimes, Lacour, 157 pp. René Domergue, with Nelly Chapotte, *Des platanes, on les entendait cascailler: vivre et parler dans un village du Midi*, Aix-en-Provence, Edisud, 189 pp.

## PROVENÇAL

GENERAL. Guy Martin and Bernat Moulin have edited a major new grammar produced by the Comitat Sestian d'Estudis Occitans (IEO Provence), *Grammaire provençale et cartes linguistiques*, La Calade, CREO Provence, 1998, 224 pp. Reviewers to date have either welcomed or rejected the use of non-Mistralien *graphie originelle* as well as the authors' insistence on Provençal as a dialect of Oc. Reinat Toscano applies this same classic graphy to his *Gramàtica niçarda*, Belin-Beliet, Princi Negre, 1998, 161 pp. N. Simian-Seisson, 'Dóu prouvençau dins soun raport is àutri lengo roumano', *PE*, 6, 1998:19–27. An informal introduction to comparative Romance linguistics, with exercises contrasting Latin, Spanish, Portuguese, Italian, French and Provençal.

LEXIS AND LEXICOLOGY. Jùli Coupier, *Pichot diciounàri francés-prouvençau*, La Calade, Edisud, 1998, 360 pp. An attractively priced shorter version, with 13,000 words, of the major work of 1995 (see also *YWMLS*, 57:280). Alan and Jaque Michel-Bechet, *Tiero de referènci binouminalo dis aucèu de Prouvènço*, Draguignan, Mantenènço de Prouvènço dóu Felibrige, 1998, 73 pp. Jean-Claude Rey, *Les Mots de chez nous*, Marseilles, Autres Temps, 265 pp.

ONOMASTICS. Céline Magrini, *'De Fournigueto à l'Angloro: l'héroïne du Pouème dou Rose'*, Billy, *Onomastique*, 371–77, charts the changes of names of the central character in Mistral's hymn to the Rhône.

SUBDIALECTS.   Jean-Louis Caserio has edited the work of Stéphane Vilarem and Barthélémy Ciravegna, *Le Lexique français-
roquebrunois, avec textes, documents, proverbes et chansons* (Annales de la
Société d'Art et d'Histoire du Mentonnais), Menton, *ASAHM*, 1998,
151 pp. A separate article introduces this project undertaken 'sans
aucune prétension universitaire' in the 1980s and revised for publication after the death of the authors, with texts, proverbs, and a
bibliography. Id., 'Le Lexique français-roquebrunois', *OPM*, 87,
1998:24. Jean-Luc Domenge, *Grammaire du provençal varois*, I. *Morphologie*, La Farlède: AVEP, 1998, 232 pp., has a preface by the late
Charles Rostaing. R. Gasiglia, 'Avem pas perdut lou nouostre latin',
*LSPS*, 136:26–27, sketches surviving evidence of Latin tenses and
syntax. Under the rubric 'Gràmatica', J. Chirio studies groups of two
pronouns in *nissart*: 'Les pronoms personnels compléments de
groupe', *ib.*, 124, 1996:44 and *ib.*, 125, 1997:44. Id. discusses various
details of *nissart* noun and verb morphology in 'Du danger de calquer
le niçois sur le français', *ib.*, 131, 1998:53; *ib.*, 132, 1998:53; *ib.*, 134,
1998:49. J. Pastour and M.-T. Imbert, 'Expressions et proverbes',
*ib.*, 133, 1998:27, provides a page of *nissart* wine-related lexicon and
20 pithy proverbs. L.-J. Calvet, 'Du côté de Marseille', *FMon*, 287,
1997:22. Marseilles youth are now drawing on Old Provençal,
Italian, Arabic, even Armenian to enrich their everyday vocabulary.
*Le Parler de Clans*, ed. James Dauphine et al., Mont de Marsan, Ed.
InterUniversitaires–SPEC, 170 pp. (Clans, Alpes-Maritimes).
   SOCIOLINGUISTICS.   J.-Y. Casanova, *'Le triangle des langues en
Provence aux XVIe et XVIIe siècles'*, pp. 203–30 of *Contacts culturels
et échanges linguistiques au XVIIe s. en France*, PFSCL, 1997, 310 pp.
Maria Carmen Alén Garabato, *Quand le 'patois' était politiquement utile.
L'usage propagandistique de l'imprimé occitan à Toulouse durant la période
révolutionnaire*, L'Harmattan, 198 pp. *Paroles et musiques à Marseille: les
voix d'une ville*, ed. Médéric Gasquet-Cyrus, Guillaume Kosmicki, and
Cécile Van den Avenne, L'Harmattan, 208 pp., includes the following: C. Barsotti, 'Un siècle de chansons marseillaises d'expression
occitane' (31–56); L.-J. Calvet, 'L'Endogène, l'exogène et la néologie:
le lexique marseillais' (57–71); Y. Tochard and C. Van den Avenne,
'Langue, discours et identité dans les chansons de Massilia Sound
System' (149–69). G. Chanut, 'Au Lazaret du port de Nice', *LSPS*,
128, 1997:8–9, describes this maritime leprosarium.
   TEXTS.   A. Wanono, 'Où l'on reparle de la reine Esther: essai
d'interprétation lexicologique à partir d'une parodie hébraïco-
provençale de Crescas du Caylar (c. 1327)', *FL*, 128:126–56, presents
the author's doctoral work at the CEROC, a new edition of a 16th-c.
Judeo-Provençal fragment of Crescas du Caylar's parody of the book
of *Esther*, with a tableau of Provençal graphemes transliterated into

Hebrew. Philippe Blanchet and Roger Gensollen edit, translate, and study the 'Recueil de diversos pessos en vers prouvencaux' of Pierre Chabert (1630?–1720?) in *Vivre en pays toulonnais au XVIIème siècle*, Marseille, Autres temps, 1997, 341 pp. R. Teulat completes his edition of *'Teodòr Aubanèl: Lo Libre de l'Amor (11–14)', *Lo Convise* 21, 1998:4–7; (15–18), *ib.*, 23, 1998:2–5; and (19–20), *ib.*, 24, 1998:2–4 (see also *YWMLS*, 60:201).

## 6. NORTHERN OCCITAN

### LIMOUSIN

LEXIS AND LEXICOLOGY.    Yves Lavalade, *Dictionnaire occitan-français. Limousin-Marche-Périgord. Etymologies occitanes*, ed. Lucien Souny, Le Puy Fraud, 240 pp., with 10,000 entries, complements L.'s 1997 *Dictionnaire français-occitan: dialecte limousin* (see *YWMLS*, 59:277).

ONOMASTICS.    Y. Lavalade interviews local inhabitants to inventory and transcribe place names, with French equivalents and notes. Studied are: Peyrelevade (Corrèze), *ClL*, 123, 1998:17–20; Genouillac (Charente occitane), *ib.*, 125, 1998:20–21; and St-Marin-la-Méanne (Corrèze)', *ib.*, 125, 1998:22–23. C. Bisson and B. Lesfargues, 'Entau s'apelen nòstras comunas', *BP*, 1998.4:18–25. Sixth and final instalment of Limousin place names arranged by arrondissement and commune; the full series is reviewed by Y. Lavalade, who offers corrections and additions in *BP*, no.1:25–27.

SUBDIALECTS.    N. Quint, 'Aperçu d'un parler occitan de frontière: le marchois', *ClL*, 118, 1997:1–10. J.-P. Baldit, 'A propos du dialecte marchois', *ib.*, 121, 1998:20–23. Id., 'La perception du dialecte marchois dans la Creuse (1)', *ib.*, 123, 1998:10–12. The 17th and 18th centuries already perceived this subdialect as intermediary between *oïl* and *oc*.

SOCIOLINGUISTICS.    M. Duverneuil, *'A perpaus de nòstre parlar', *BP*, 1:22–24, presents a speech on 'Les parlers périgordins' by Gaston Guillaumie during festivities honouring the 1937 centenary of Eugene Le Roy. I. Balès, *ClL*, 123, 1998:9, looks at the influence of Occitan on local French (francitan), e.g. *t'a tombé ton stylo* (*as tombat ton estilò*) 'tu as laissé tomber ton stylo'.

### AUVERGNAT

GENERAL.    J. Fay is interviewed by N. Lafont in 'Occitania: 15 ans d'émissions', *Lo Convise*, 22, 1998:5–10, as they discuss F.'s years of service to Occitan radio.

LEXIS AND LEXICOLOGY.    Pierre Bonnaud, *Nouveau dictionnaire général français-auvergnat*, Nonette, Créer, 780 pp. A treasure trove of more than 40,000 French entries with 200,000 Auvergnat words and expressions, covering Basse-Auvergne, Velay, southern Bourbonnais, and north Cantal. This is the revised and corrected edition of B.'s *Grand Dictionnaire français-Auvergnat* (3 vols, Beaumont, Auvernhà, Tarà d'Oc, 1978–80). Joannès Dufaud, *\*Dictionnaire français-nord-occitan (Vivarais et Velay)*, ed. J.-P. Huguet, with preface by Georges Massot, St Julien-Molin-Molette, 1998, 336 pp., covers Ardèche, Haute-Loire, Vivarais, and Velay.

ONOMASTICS.   Pierre-Henri Billy and Marie-Renée Sauvadet, *\*Dictionnaire historique des noms de famille du Puy-de-Dôme*, I, Clermont-Ferrand, Assoc. de Recherches Généalogiques et Historiques d'Auvergne, 1998, iii + 283 pp. This first volume studies some 7,000 names; a second volume is promised.

SUBDIALECTS.   H. Stroh, 'Pau Gayraud e la sintaxa occitana', *Lo Convise*, 25:5–8, contributes various rectifications to Gayraud's *Sintaxa Milhaguesa*, Rodez, Subervie, 1986, 100 pp. Francés de Murat (1766–1838), 'Vocabulaire du parler de la région de Sainte-Eulalie (1)', *La Cabreta*, 148, 1997:5–15, lists *a-m*, in normalized graphy; *n-y* continues in (2), *ib.*, 150, 1998:2–9. N. Lafont, 'Lo parler auvernhat d'a Chailada', *Lo Convise*, 20, 1997:9–13.

## 7.  PROVENÇAL ALPIN

ONOMASTICS.   P. Peyre, 'Dins lo corrent deis aigas', *AqAq*, 127–28, 1998:7. Terms for 'valada' and 'corrent d'aiga'. Id., 'A l'estiva ambe lei fedas', *ib.*, 7 (*pasquier, bramafan*, etc.). André Faure, *Noms de lieux et noms de familles des Hautes-Alpes*, Gap, Espaci Occitan, 1998, xxx + 412 pp., includes 6,000 entries.

SUBDIALECTS.   Nicolas Quint, *\*Le Parler occitan ardéchois d'Albon. Canton de Saint-Pierreville, Ardèche. Description d'un parler alpin vivaro-vellave du boutiérot moyen*, L'Harmattan, 162 pp. Description of a mixed *parler* from central Ardèche, with numerous proverbs and expressions. S. Arneodo, 'La Provenza alpina. L'etnia e la lingua provenzale', *Coumboscuro*, 318, 1998:4, describes briefly the birthplace of *Coumboscuro*.

TEXTS.   S. Garnero, 'Val Mairo. La memorio de nosto lengo (1): "Couro la Val Mairo couentavo"', *Coumboscuro*, 315–16, 1998:4–5, offers 'leggende e immaginario collettivo nella cultura orale'.

# LITERATURE

By CATHERINE LÉGLU, *Lecturer in French, University of Bristol*

## 1. MEDIEVAL PERIOD

*The Troubadours: An Introduction*, ed. Simon Gaunt and Sarah Kay, CUP, xii + 330 pp. This introductory volume presents essays by an international group of contributors, covering the major aspects of current research trends in troubadour literature (issues of language and linguistics are not covered). Contributions comprise: R. Harvey on courtly culture (8–27), L. Paterson on *fin'amors* and the *canso* (28–46), C. Léglu on the satirical repertoire (47–65), S. G. Nichols on the early troubadours (66–82), G. Gouiran on the 'classical' period of *c.*1160 to *c.*1200 (83–98) and M. Routledge on the later troubadours (99–112). The *trobairitz* are presented by T. Sankovitch (113–26), Italian and Catalan troubadours by M. Cabré (127–40). M. Switten presents music and versification (141–63), S. Spence rhetoric and hermeneutics (164–80), M.-L. Meneghetti intertextuality (181–96), D. Monson parody (197–211). S. Kay on desire and subjectivity (212–27), S. Gaunt on orality and literacy (228–45), W. Burgwinkle on the *chansonniers* (246–62) and S. Huot on the connections with Old French narrative (263–78). The book also has three appendices (names and dates of troubadours, a glossary and research apparatus), plus a full bibliography. Miriam Cabré, *Cerverí de Girona and his Poetic Traditions*, Woodbridge, Boydell and Brewer, 224 pp. This wide-ranging study of the later Catalan troubadour includes examinations of Cerverí's learning and use of preaching techniques, as well as his aesthetics and didactic style. Olivia Holmes, *Assembling the Lyric Self: Authorship from Troubadour Song to Italian Poetry Book*, Minneapolis, Minnesota U.P., 240 pp. This study of how manuscript transmission moulded the construction of the author places the troubadour *chansonniers* in the context of medieval Italian poetic and book culture, and challenges the methodological opposition between Medieval and Renaissance concepts of authorship. Jean-Claude Marol, *L'Amour libérée, ou l'érotique initiale des troubadours*, Dervy, 1998, 198 pp. A monograph on the life and works of Guilhem IX, featuring his poetic corpus with facing-page translations, probably aimed at the general reader. Nikki Kaltenbach Markey, *Le Roman de Jaufre: A Jungian Analysis* (StH, 30), NY, Lang, 1998, 143 pp. A systematic Jungian reading of the romance as a quest for individuation. New editions include: *La Passion catalane-occitane, édition, traduction et notes*, ed. Aileen Ann MacDonald, TLF, 368 pp. A useful edition of this linguistically hybrid play, which includes a thorough discussion of the language, manuscript tradition, and possible cultural context of the text (13–59). Appendix 1 gives all the relevant Biblical citations; a glossary is provided. Appendix 2 contains the fragments, including two actors' scripts, of plays connected to the text. *Raimon Vidal. Il 'Castia-Gilos' e i testi lirici*, ed. Giuseppe Tavani, Milan, Luni, 152 pp. *Le Poesie di Folchetto di Marsiglia*, ed. Paolo Squillacioti, Pisa, Pacini, xii + 500 pp. *Rolando a Saragozza*, ed. Gian Carlo Belletti, Alessandria, Edizioni dell'Orso, 1998, 127 pp., contains an introduction (5–26) and text with facing-page translation into Italian. Sergio Vatteroni, *\*'Falsa clercia'. La poesia anticlericale dei trovatori*, Alessandria, Edizioni dell'Orso. Under the direction of Anna Ferrari, the first volume has appeared of the project *Intavulare: tavole di canzonieri romanzi*, I, *Canzonieri provenzali*, ed. Antonella Lombardi and Maria Careri (Studi e testi, 387), Vatican City, Biblioteca Apostolica Vaticana. This volume contains tables of MSS *A* (Vat. lat 5232), *F* (Chig. 50.4.106), *L* (Vat. lat. 3206), *O* (Vat. lat. 3208) and *H* (Vat. lat. 3207). This project intends to tabulate all extant Romance lyric *chansonniers*. *Literature of the French and Occitan Middle Ages: Eleventh to Fifteenth Centuries*, ed. Deborah Sennrich-Levi and Ian S. Laurie (The *Dictionary of Literary Biography*, 208) Detroit–London, Gale Group, xxi + 440p., provides a useful reference base. A number of anthologies have also appeared: Emmanuel-Yves Monin, *Le Grand Chant des troubadours, trouvères et autres fidèles d'amour*, Y. Monin, 277 pp. *Le Livre d'Or des troubadours: XIIe–XIVe siècle: anthologie*, ed. Gérard Zucchetto and Jorn Gruber, Editions de Paris, 1998, 310 pp. This volume provides three songs for each troubadour included, two of the texts in bilingual format, and one in translation only. See also Gérard Zucchetto, *Terre des troubadours*, Montpellier, Les Presses Multimédia, 1998, CD-ROM, which is aimed at the general public. *A Bilingual Edition of the Love Songs of the Troubadour Bernart de Ventadorn in Occitan and English: Sugar and Salt*, trans. Ronnie Apter with Michael Herman, Lewiston–Lampeter, Mellen, xvii + 307p., with CD. This original volume presents Bernart's 43 attributed songs with two translations into English, one literal and one poetic. The texts are accompanied by transcriptions of 18 melodies, five with performable text. Dietmar Rieger, *Chanter et dire: études sur la littérature du moyen âge*, Champion, 1997, 293 pp. A collection of articles that includes the following: 'Guillaume IX d'Aquitaine et l'idéologie troubadouresque. Remarque sur l'emploi des noms propres chez le 'premier' troubadour' (3–17), '*Lop es nomnat lo pes e lop no es. Un devinalh sans solution*?' (19–30), 'Audition et lecture dans le domaine de la poésie troubadouresque. Quelques réflexions sur la philologie provençale de demain'(31–44), and '*Chantar et faire*. Remarques sur le problème de l'improvisation chez les troubadours' (45–58). Jean-Charles Huchet, 'L'entropie lyrique chez les troubadours', pp. 85–107 of Id., *Essai de clinique littéraire du texte médiéval,* Orléans, Paradigme, 1998, 211 pp. Among articles this year *RlaR,* 103.1, 'Présence juive en Occitanie médiévale', includes: A. Schippers, 'Les poètes juifs en Occitanie au Moyen Age: le catalogue d'Abraham de Béziers' (1–20), discussing the interaction of Occitan Jewish poets with troubadours as well as Hispano-Arabic poets (see also *YWMLS,* 59:282); C. P. Hershon and P. T. Ricketts, 'Les textes hébraïques du *Breviari d'Amor* de Matfre Ermengaud' (55–97), analysing the script, transmission and intended readership of the Hebrew sections in the text, setting the work in the historical context of Béziers between *c.*1280 and *c.*1320. Includes texts with commentary. C. P. Hershon, 'Isaac de Lattes et the *Kiryat Sefer.* Etude d'une source historique occitane' (27–53), reconstructs the cultural and intellectual context of the text composed in Lattes, *c.*1372. See also Cyril P. Hershon, *Faith and Controversy: The Jews of Medieval Languedoc,* AIEO–Birmingham U.P., 418 pp., a historical study of the main medieval Jewish communities of the Languedoc, focusing on intellectual history and the importance of poetry (173–91). V. Galent-Fasseur, 'La Dame de l'arbre: Rôle de la "vue" structurale dans le *Bréviaire d'Amour* de Matfré Ermengau', *Romania,* 117:32–50, describes and analyses the allegorical image, in relation to the *Breviari* as a whole. S. Guida, 'Cartulari e trovatori. 1. Arnaut Guilhem de Marsan 2. Amanieu de la Broquiera 3. Guilhem Peire de Cazals 4. Amanieu de Sescas', *CN,* 59:71–129, examines documentary evidence for identification and dating of these authors. G. Borriero, 'Il tópos dell'ineffabile nella retorica medievale e nella lirica trobadorica', *MedRom,* 23:21–65, attributes the topos to *laus et descriptio* tropes, and focuses on the phrase 'non puosc'. R. Lafont reconsiders the case for the Occitan origins of the *chanson de geste* in 'Pour rendre à l'oc et aux Normans leur dû: genèse et premier développement de l'art épique gallo-roman', *CCMe,* 42:139–78. J. Alturo i Perucho, 'Restes codicologiques del més antic manuscrit de *Jaufré* amb algunes consideracions sobre aquesta novella provençal', *BRABLB,* 46, 1997–98:9–22, proposes a dating *c.*1200–25 of the oldest (fragmentary) MS of the text. G. R. Mermier, 'The diaspora of the Occitan troubadours: influence of Occitan troubadour lyrics on the poetry of Galician-Portuguese trovadores', *Mediterranean Studies,* 7, 1998[1999]:67–91. D. W. Lacroix, 'Les caractères du chant chez les troubadours du XIIe siècle', *Chant et enchantement,* 189–204. D. A. Trotter, 'Arabic surgery in Eastern France and the Midi: the Old French and Occitan versions of the *Chirurgerie d'Albucasis*', *FMLS,* 35:358–71, examines a 14th-c. Occ. translation of chapter 30 of the 10th-c. treatise *al-Tasrif,* and examines the use of loanwords from Arabic and Latin. R. Harvey, 'A propos de la date de la première "chanson de croisade": *Emperaire, per* *mi mezeis* de Marcabru (PC 293, 22)', *CCMe*, 42:55–60. Using new documentary evidence in her work on a new edition of the poem, H. analyses the two tornadas of this song to establish a firm dating in 1137. H. Jeanjean, '*Flamenca*: a wake for a dying civilisation?', *Parergon*, 16, 1998:19–30, proposes to read the romance as a politically determined and potentially heretical text. L. Verdon, 'La femme en Roussillon aux XIIe et XIIIe siècles: statut juridique et économique', *AMid*, 111:293–309, examines documents specific to this region. E. J. Burns, 'Speculum of the courtly lady: women, love and clothes', *JMEMS*, 29:253–92, examines how description of women's clothes may alter the subject-object relation of *fin'amors*, by reversing the direction of the visual gaze. W. D. Paden, 'The troubadour's lady as seen through thick history', *Exemplaria*, 11:221–44, analyses the 19th-c. construction of *fin'amors*, with reference to the intellectual influences on Alfred Jeanroy and Gaston Paris. S. Neumeister, 'Vier Stationen des Selbstkonstitution weiblicher Subjektivität in der höfischen Lyrik: Na Castelloza — Christine de Pisan — Gaspara Stampa — Sor Juana Inés de la Cruz', Haug, *Mittelalter*, 100–27. N.'s comparative analysis of four women poets addresses the construction of Castelloza as an active participant in courtship. P. Uhl, 'Contribution à la typologie d'un genre provençal du XIVe siècle: le *Reversari*', *SN*, 70, 1998:89–100, distinguishes between this minor genre and other forms of nonsense or paradoxical poetry, suggesting that it may have existed as early as the 12th c. C. Bowser-Nott, 'Trobar clus: a category of critical poetry', *Parergon*, 15, 1997:21–40. The first volume of *\*Rivista di Studi Testuali*, ed. Luciana Borghi-Cedrini, Alessandria, Edizioni dell'Orso, includes the following articles: P. Allegretti, '*Parva componere magnis*. Una stropha inedita di Bernart de Ventadorn (BdT 70, 33) e due schede per BdT 461, 127'; A. Fassò, 'Sulle tracce del trovatore'; L. Lazzerini, 'Il nome della dama del *corn*'; S. Melani, 'Aimeric de Belenoi, Thibaut de Champagne e le crociate'; W. Meliga, 'La sezione delle tenzoni nelle canzionieri provenzali IK'; P. T. Ricketts, 'Venguz soi a bon/mal port: a metaphor for pleasure and pain in the lyrics of the troubadours'. M. Tomaryn Bruckner, 'Mathematical bodies and fuzzy logic in the couplings of troubadour lyric', *Tenso*, 14:1–22, presents the alternating assertion/non-assertion of bodies and ideas in *cansos*, *tensos* and Guilhem IX's *vers de dreit nien*. J. Tasker Grimbert, 'Diminishing the *trobairitz*, excluding the women trouvères', *ib.*, 23–38, takes Pierre Bec to task for proposing a male-authored genre, the *chanson de femme*, which has suppressed the existence of women poets; M. Wolterbeck, ' "De Gimel . . . per Niol": geographic space and placenames in Song One of William of Aquitaine', *ib.*, 39–52, examines the role of Confolens in the song and as a frontier between Poitiers and

Limousin; identifies Niol as Nieul-sur-l'Autise; W. Pfeffer, 'Bibliography of Occitan literature for 1996–1997', *ib.*, 56–104. *Filologia romanza e cultura medievale. Studi in onore di Elio Melli*, ed. Andrea Fassò, Luciano Formisano, and Mario Mancini, 2 vols, Alessandria, Edizioni dell'Orso, 1998, xxii + 916 pp., includes articles by D. Barca on the terms *canso* and *fin'amors* in the *novas* (25–44), M. M. Cocco on Uc de Saint-Circ's relationship with ecclesiastical authorities (217–61), M. Fumagalli on a Vaudois text on the Macchabees (333–52), D. Kullmann on *Girart de Roussillon* and clerical learning (403–17), M. Mancini on dreams and visions in Flamenca (451–69), M. C. Marinoni on the Occ. versions of Ramon Llull's *Doctrina Pueril* (509–23), E. Muratori on the biography of Guilhem de Saint-Didier (555–73), and G. Noto on intertextuality in Guilhem IX (595–62). Two instances of the 20th-c. reception of troubadour lyric have been studied by R. Rosenstein, 'A medieval troubadour mobilised by the Resistance', *JHI*, 59, 1998:499–522, and S. Levarie, 'Henry Adams, avant-gardist in early music', *American Music*, 15, 1997:429–45, on the first performances of medieval music in the USA.

## 2. FROM 1500 ONWARDS

Annie Charnay, *Paroles de voleurs: gens de sac et de corde en pays toulousain au début du XVIe siècle*, Champion, 1998, 423 pp. This analysis of trial documents from the *commanderie* at Caignac reveals the Occ. spoken by the poorest classes in the 1520s; with a glossary of Occ. terms and an introduction by Françoise Hildesheimer. Another analysis of the social function of Occ. is by M. Carmen Alen Garabato, *Quand le patois était politiquement utile: l'usage propagandiste de l'imprimé occitan à Toulouse durant la période révolutionnaire*, L'Harmattan, 189 pp. P. Gardy, '*L'oeuvre au noir* de Pey de Garros', *RlaR*, 103:261–76, examines the Eclogues published as *Poesias gasconas* in 1567. F. Pic, '*Ourdenansas & Coustumas del Libre Blanc . . ., Nompareilhas receptas . . ., Requeste faicte & baillée par les Dames de la ville de Tolose . . .*: Les tribulations de trois textes toulousains du XVIe siècle, ou un cas notoire d'inaccessibilité de la littérature occitane moderne', *ib.*, 317–45, discusses a series of satirical texts analysed in more detail in the third chapter of Philippe Gardy, *La Leçon de Nérac: Du Bartas et les poètes occitans (1550–1650)*, Bordeaux U.P., 1998, 240 pp. Alain Viaut, *Écrire pour parler: Los Tradinaires: présentation d'une expérience d'écriture en occitan en Médoc*, Talence, Maison des sciences de l'homme en Aquitaine, 1998, 331 pp. *Écritures occitanes d'aujourd'hui*, ed. Philippe Gardy, is a special issue of the periodical *Berenice: rivista quadrimestale di studi comparati e ricerche sulle avanguardie*, 17.

## IV. SPANISH STUDIES

### LANGUAGE

By Steven Dworkin, *University of Michigan*, and
Aengus Ward, *University of Birmingham*
(This article covers the period 1998–99, for the areas of Diachronic Studies,
Sociolinguistics, and Dialectology only.)

### 1. Diachronic Studies

#### General

Studies by two of the great masters of Spanish historical linguistics
have been made available. R. Menéndez Pidal's 1963 essay 'El
lenguaje español en tiempo de Felipe II', is reprinted in *Moenia*
5:3–32. R. Lapesa's 1931 doctoral dissertation appears in print for
the first time: *El dialecto asturiano occidental en la Edad Media*, Seville
U.P., 163 pp. R. Penny offers useful observations on the role of
linguistic variation in Spanish language history in '¿En qué consiste
una historia del castellano?', *CIHLE 4*, ii, 583–94. Broad philosophical and epistemological questions concerning the practice of Spanish
historical linguistics and grammar are raised by P. M. Lloyd, 'La
historia y la gramática histórica', *ib.*, i, 77–90, and A. Varvaro, 'La
historia de la lengua española modelo para la lingüística histórica',
*ib.*, 149–62. Mercedes Quilís Merín, *Orígenes históricos de la lengua
española*, Valencia U.P., 374 pp., presents a critical overview of
knowledge concerning the early history of Spanish, the 'período de
orígenes del español'. The appearance of the first Romance texts is
treated by R. Harris-Northall, 'Official use of the vernacular in the
thirteenth century: medieval Spanish language policy?', Gutiérrez-
Rexach, *Advances*, 152–65, who describes the gradual use of Romance
instead of Latin in royal chancellery documents during the reign of
Fernando III (1217–1252), and F. J. Hernández, 'Sobre los orígenes
del español escrito', *VLet*, 10:133–66, who studies the historical
background of the Castilian chancellery and the first written texts in
Romance. R. Wright, 'Reading a will in twelfth-century Salamanca',
Petersmann, *Latin vulgaire V*, 505–16, shows how a 12th-c. 'Late Latin'
document can be read as a Romance text. Id., 'Periodization and
how to avoid it', *Lloyd Vol.*, 25–41, calls into question periodization
based on external and internal criteria in the linguistic history of
Spanish. R. Penny, 'Standard versus dialect: linguistic (dis)continuity
in the Iberian Peninsula', *ib.*, 43–55. aims to examine the effects of
the creation of standard literary languages starting in the 13th c. upon
the geographic distribution of linguistic features in the Iberian

Peninsula. Non-linguistic factors in language history are discussed in J. R. Lodares, 'Consideraciones sobre la historia económica y política de la lengua española', *ZRP*, 115:117–54; see also Id., 'Lengua y economía en la Castilla medieval', *CIHLE 4*, II, 507–12. F. González Ollé, 'Intereses comerciales y económicos en la protección de la lengua española (1549–1801)', *Alarcos Vol.*, 57–70, describes the background to several royal decrees giving preference to Castilian over regional varieties. F. Marcos Marín, 'Romance andalusí y mozárabe: dos términos no sinónimos', *Colón Vol.*, 335–41, recommends, as have other specialists, *romance andalusí* rather than *mozárabe* as a linguistic label.

DIACHRONIC PHONOLOGY

D. E. Holt, 'The moraic status of consonants from Latin to Hispano-Romance: the case of obstruents', Gutiérrez-Rexach, *Advances*, 166–81, claims that the reduction of obstruent geminates is directly related to the vocalization of syllable-final velar consonants and that both phenomena are a consequence of the loss of vowel length in late spoken Latin. D. L. Ranson, 'Variation in voicing in Spanish syncopated forms', *Lloyd Vol.*, 125–54, studies 149 Spanish forms in an effort to identify the factors which affect variable voicing in syncopated forms. K. J. Wireback, 'The relationship between lenition, the strong word boundary, and sonorant strengthening in Ibero-Romance', *ib.*, 155–72, seeks to link word-initial sonorant strengthening in Ibero-Romance to the effects of an obstruent strength pattern. C. Pensado, 'El artículo *ell* y otras formas con *–ll* final en castellano medieval', *BRAE*, 79:377–406, discusses several issues concerned with OSp. forms displaying *–ll*. The aspiration of /s/ is examined in two papers. J. M. Chamorro, 'Nuevos testimonios de aspiración de /s/ implosiva en los albores y finales del siglo XVII granadino', *RFE*, 78, 1998:195–208, offers data, while J. A. Pascual, 'El revolucionario conservadurismo del español norteño. A propósito de la evolución de la *s* implosiva', *Colón Vol.*, 387–400, raises the possibility of aspiration of *–s* in late medieval northern Spain. E. Martínez Celdrán, 'Explicación fonética de los cambios que implican el paso por una aspiración', *CIHLE 4*, I, 251–62, presents instrumental phonetic evidence on the nature of such changes as /f-/ > /h-/ and /-s/ > /-h/. B. Miranda Hidalgo, 'A vueltas sobre el paso /š/ > /X/', *ib.*, 262–71, discusses details of that change, while D. L. Ranson treats in broader and comparative terms sound shifts involving velarization and backing in 'Velarización y posteriorización: variantes paralelos, y mecanismo del cambio', *ib.*, 279–87. P. Sánchez Prieto-Borja, 'Para una historia de la escritura castellana', *ib.*, 289–301, discusses the relationship between the study of paleography, graphemics, and historical phonology. R. Pellen, 'Variation et régularité dans l'espagnol de la première moitié du XIIIe siècle. Contribution de la linguistique à l'édition des textes', *CLHM*, 22 : 33–49, studies variation in the use of apocope in the manuscripts of Berceo. The evolution of Spanish orthography and the letter-sound relationship has been the subject of many papers. M. Ariza, 'Fernando III y el castellano alfonsí', *Colón Vol.*, 71–84, demonstrates (as have several other scholars) that the so-called Alfonsine spelling system was already the norm in documents from the reign of Fernando III. Blecua, *Grafémática*, contains a number of important studies. G. Clavería Nadal, 'Grafías cultas en las variantes del *Rimado de Palacio* de P. López de Ayala y de los *Soliloquios* de Fr. P. Fernández Pecha' (49–64), studies the use of Latinizing orthographies in the manuscript traditions of these late 14th-c. works. R. J. Penny, 'La grafía de los textos notariales castellanos de la Alta Edad Media; ¿sistema logográfico o fonológico?' (211–23), examines a document from 1100 AD to determine whether its spelling system is logographic or phonology-based and whether the language of the text can be characterized as Latin or Romance. Comments on individual points appear in C. Cabrera, 'Reflexiones sobre el sistema gráfico avulgarado de los textos primitivos leoneses' (9–23); R. Ciérbide, 'Notas gráfico-fonéticas sobre la documentación medieval Navarra' (37–47); P. Díez de Revenga Torres, 'Algunos problemas gráficos en documentos murcianos' (65–74). F. Gimeno Menéndez, 'Grafemática y sociolingüística histórica: a propósito del *Libro de los Primitivos Privilegios de Alicante*' (123–33), seeks to analyse medieval orthographic practices from the perspective of historical sociolinguistics. Different aspects of the graphic representation of medieval sibilants are examined in A. Líbano Zumalacárregui, 'Diacronía de las alternancias gráficas navarro-aragonesas: las sibilantes medievales' (135–48); M. J. Mancho, 'Sobre las grafías correspondientes a los resultados de *ty* y *ky* en los *Documentos lingüísticos de España*' (149–68); and C. Osés Marcaida, 'Sibilantes en la documentación medieval guipuzcoana' (199–209). Other papers include J. R. Morala Rodríguez, 'Norma gráfica y variedades orales en el leonés medieval' (169–87); M. Morreale, 'La (orto)grafía como tropiezo' (189–97); C. Pensado, 'Sobre los límites de la mala ortografía en romance. ¿Por qué el inglés *fish* no se escribe *ghoti* después de todo?' (225–42); R. Santiago, 'Apuntes para la historia de la puntuación en los siglos XVII y XVII' (243–80); J. Terrado Pablo, 'Grafías y fonética en manuscritos turolenses medievales (siglos XIII-XV)' (281–92); M. Torreblanca, 'Sobre la representación gráfica de los diptongos *ie, ue* en el español antiguo' (292–301).

DIACHRONIC MORPHOLOGY

J. Rini has contributed an impressive number of studies in this area. His book *Exploring the Role of Morphology in the Evolution of Spanish*, Amsterdam, Benjamins, 187 pp., examines a series of changes in Old Spanish verbal roots and suffixes. Among the problems studied are diphthongization in the stems of *dormir* and *morir*, the shift *o* > *u* in preterit stems (e.g., *ove, tove, estove* > *hube, tuve, estuve*, the shift *e* > *i* in *recebir, escrevir, bevir* > *recibir, escribir, vivir*, the change *veer* > *ver*, the history of the verb endings *–ades, -edes, -ides*, the *–y* of *hay*, and the genesis of *eres*. Id., 'The "clinching factor" in the addition of *–y* in Spanish *doy, estoy, soy, voy*', *JHR*, 4 : 1–11, seeks to explain the *-y* by invoking leftward palatal extension before stressed /-ó/ in syntagms such as /so jo/, /do jo/. In Id., 'The formation of Old Spanish *buey(s), bueyes, grey(s), greyes, ley(s), leyes, rey(s), reyes*: a morphophonological analysis'. *HR*, 66, 1998 : 1–19, R. claims that the singular forms arose as back formations from the plurals in *–es*. OSp. plurals such as *bueys*, etc. represent a restructuring based on the back-formed singulars *buey*, etc. Id., 'The rise and fall of Old Spanish "y all": *vos todos* vs *vos otros*', *Lloyd Vol.*, 209–21, offers explanation for the triumph of *vos otros* over *vos todos* as second person plural subject pronoun in Spanish, and notes the typological parallel with American English *you all* > *y'all*.

Verbal morphology has received a great deal of attention. Javier Elvira, *El cambio analógico*, M, Gredos, 1998, 255 pp., is a critical examination based on changes in OSp. verbal morphology of laws of analogy proposed by Kuryłowicz and Mańczak. María Jesús López Bobo, *El vocalismo radical átono en la conjugación castellana. Etapa medieval y clásica*, Oviedo, Departamento de Filología Española, 1998, 316 pp., studies vowel alternation patterns in Spanish verb stems, with emphasis on the preterite. The same scholar examines related issues in '¡Quién lo vido y quién lo vee!', *Moenia*, 5 : 321–65.

E. Bustos Guisbert, 'Algunas alternativas a la analogía. A propósito de las alternancias vocálicas en el sistema verbal', *BRAE*, 78, 1998 : 349–90, offers an inconclusive discussion of whether verb-stem alternations result from interaction of rules, rule inversion, or reanalysis. B. Imhoff, 'On the chronology and recession of the Old Spanish *–ie* imperfect', *La corónica* 26.2, 1998 : 243–55, shows that a chronological comparative analysis of manuscript variation reveals that *–ié* ∼ *-ía* alternation was a feature of Spanish prose up to the end of the 15th century. R. Harris-Northall, 'Morphological shift in Old Spanish: the paradigmatic relationship between *–ecer* and *–ir* verbs', *Lloyd Vol.*, 111–23, seeks to explain why *–ecer* ceased to be productive after the late 13th century. E. Ridruejo 'La inserción de -*g*- en el

222     *Spanish Studies*

presente de *caigo, oigo, traigo*', *CIHLE 4*, I, 725–34, seeks to identify the
conditions underlying the analogical insertion of the velar in the verbs
at issue.

Little work has been done in diachronic derivational morphology.
D. Pharies, 'Additional evidence of template formation in Spanish',
*Lloyd Vol.*, 95–110, continues his work on the role of templates in
Spanish word formation. The same scholar links the suffix *-ucho* to
Lat. *-usculus* in his 'Origin of the Hispano-Romance suffix *-ucho*',
*Iberoromania*, 49 : 1–25. On the borderline between derivational mor-
phology and etymology is Id., 'El origen de *chisgarabís* "hombrecillo
de poca sustancia"', mequetrefe', *NMi*, 99, 1998 : 113–23, in which
the author seeks to demonstrate on semantic and phonetic grounds
that *chisgarabís* derives from *chirivía* 'parsnip'.

Outside the realm of verbal morphology we note M. J. Martínez
Alcalde, 'Cuestiones morfológicas en torno a la evolución de los
posesivos en español medieval', *Atti* (Palermo), I, 207–20. Adela
García Valle, *La variación nominal en los orígenes del español*, M, CSIC,
1998, 351 pp., describes variation in noun morphology observable in
early documents. J. L. Girón Alconchel, 'Sobre el reajuste morfológ-
ico de los demostrativos en el español clásico', *CIHLE 4*, I, 493–502,
traces in Golden Age grammars the demise of the long forms of the
demonstrative (*aqueste, aquesse*).

DIACHRONIC SYNTAX

Syntax is clearly the growth field in Spanish historical linguistics. The
period surveyed has seen the publication of the following books (for
the most part based on doctoral dissertations): Angeles Romero
Cambrón, *Historia sintáctica de las construcciones comparativas de desigual-
dad*, Cuenca, Universidad Castilla-La Mancha, 1998, 197 pp.; Mercedes Suárez Fernández, *El complemento predicativo en castellano medieval
(época prealfonsí) (Verba*, anexo 42), Santiago de Compostela U.P.,
1996, 251 pp.; Elena Rivas and María José Rodríguez Espiñeira, *La
cláusula en castellano medieval: constituyentes funcionales*. Santiago de
Compostela U.P.; Milagros Alfonso Vegas, *Construcciones causativas en
el español medieval*, Mexico City, UNAM–Colegio de México, 1998,
258 pp.; María Jesús Martín González, *La evolución de los adverbios de
lugar y tiempo a través de la documentación notarial leonesa*, Valladolid U.P.,
244 pp.; Manuel Mosteiro Louzao, *Las conjunciones de causa en castellano
medieval. Origen, evolución y otros usos (Verba*, anexo, 45), Santiago de
Compostela U.P., 277 pp.; Inmaculada C. Baez Montero, *La construcción con predicativo del complemento directo en castellano medieval*, Vigo U.P.,
1998, 206 pp.; A. Thibault, *Perfecto simple y perfecto compuesto en español
preclásico. Estudio de los perfectos de indicativo en La Celestina, el teatro de*

*Encina y el Diálogo de la lengua* (*ZRP*, Beiheft 301), Tübingen, Niemeyer, 239 pp. D. Wanner, 'Toward a historical syntax of Castilian', *Lloyd Vol.*, 189–207, outlines a possible collaborative project for an historical syntax of Castilian. B. Horcajada Diezma and P. Sánchez Prieto-Borja, 'La reduplicación distributiva del numeral y el arabismo morfosintáctico en el romance hispánico medieval', *ZRP*, 115:280–99, argue that this OSp. construction is of Arabic origin. M. Davies, 'The evolution of Spanish clitic climbing: a corpus-based approach', *SN*, 69, 1998:251–63, illustrates the need for using a large corpus of data to study such syntactic shifts as clitic climbing; R. J. Granberg, 'Clitic position in thirteenth-century Spanish: sentences with preverbal subjects', *La corónica* 27.2, 89–113, claims that preverbal or postverbal placement of clitic pronouns in sentences with preverbal subjects is conditioned by the presence or absence of prosodic stress on the subject; a postscript by S. N. Dworkin (114–18), updates this posthumously published article. F. J. Herrero Ruiz de Loizaga, 'Las oraciones causales en el siglo XV', *BRAE*, 78, 1998:199–273, deals with the conjunctions which introduce *oraciones causales* in the 15th c., a moment of transition in choice of conjunction. A. Veiga, '¿Condicionales en *si tuviera* o usos subjuntivos de *cantara* en el *Poema de Fernán González?*', *Moenia*, 5:271–306, denies the presence of subjunctive forms in *–ra* in the lost 13th-c. original of the poem at issue. R. Cano Aguilar, 'La construcción del discurso en el siglo XIII: diálogo y narración en Berceo y el *Alexandre*', *ib.*, 257–69, argues for the presence of hypotaxis in the construction of discourse from the time of the earliest texts. A. Ward, 'The *–ra* verb form in the conditional sentences of the *Estoria de Espanna*', *Verba*, 25, 1998:127–41; M. Porcar Miralles, 'La negación en la estructura comparativa. *mas que non* en castellano medieval', *ib.*, 165–96. C. Company and A. Medina Urrea, 'Sintaxis motivada pragmáticamente. Futuros analíticos y futuros sintéticos en español medieval', *RFE*, 79:65–100, seek to prove that the use of the synthetic future with an intercalated postverbal object pronoun is controlled by pragmatic features related to emphasis in the discourse. I. Andrés-Suárez, '*Estar* + participio pasado en *El Libro de Alexandre*', *Colón Vol.*, 53–69, exemplifies and discusses the construction at issue. C. J. Pountain, 'Person and voice in the Spanish infinitive', *BHS*, 75, 1998:393–410, stresses the importance of pragmatic factors in the historical development of the Spanish infinitive. Id., 'Learnèd syntax and the Romance languages: the "accusative and infinitive" construction with declarative verbs in Castilian', *TPS*, 96, 1998:159–201, examines the role of syntactic constructions borrowed from Classical Latin in the history of the syntax of Castilian declarative verbs.

M. Mosteiro Louzao, 'Sobre la construcción ". . . tanto avién el dolor" y otras afines', *Moenia*, 5:367–86; M. Suárez Fernández, 'El adjetivo destacado en castellano medieval y clásico: su funcionamiento en la cláusula', *AEF*, 21, 1998:383–406, and Id., 'El adjetivo destacado en castellano medieval y clásico: su funcionamiento en la frase', *Moenia*, 5:307–19.
Several relevant papers have appeared in *Atti* (Palermo), 1: C. Sánchez Lancis, 'Una reflexión sobre el cambio gramatical en el español preclásico' (349–60), surveys selected syntactic changes which culminated in the second half of the 15th century. Also worthy of note are B. Arias-Alvarez, 'Particularidades sintácticas del participio en la lengua española' (25–33); A. Arias Cabal, 'Diacronía del incontable o "neutro de materia" en asturiano' (35–49); I. Pujol Payet, 'Evolución de la estructura de SN que integra formas numerales en el español del siglo XII al XVI' (267–77); A. Ricós, 'Estudio contrastivo de la evolución de las construcciones pasivas en español y catalán' (291–305). Over 30 papers dealing with various aspects of Spanish diachronic syntax appear in *CIHLE 4*, 1, 321–910.

LEXIS

Bodo Müller's valuable *Diccionario del español medieval*, continues to appear slowly but regularly. The project has reached fasc. 19, ending with the entry for *alabar*. The Spanish Academy's *Diccionario histórico de la lengua española* has reached *apasanca* in the volume devoted to the letter *A* and *bajoca* in the volume devoted to *B*. Yolanda González Aranda, *Forma y estructura de un campo semántico*, Almeria U.P., 1998, 272 pp., offers a diachronic semantic study of selected verbs of movement in Spanish. Some papers examine specific issues of lexical loss and replacement. The incorporation of *fácil* and *difícil* in late medieval Spanish is described in R. Eberenz, 'Dos campos semánticos del español preclásico: *fácil* y *difícil*', *Colón Vol.*, 167–83. S. N. Dworkin, 'Lexical loss and neologisms in late medieval Spanish: two case studies', *BHS*, 75, 1998:1–11, studies the replacement of *mañero* 'sterile' and *gafo* 'leprous' in late Medieval Spanish by the Latinisms *estéril* and *leproso*. Id., 'Cambio semántico y pérdida léxica: la suerte del español antiguo *luengo* "largo"', *CIHLE 4*, 11, 99–107, claims that restructuring of the semantic field 'dimension' played a major role in the loss of OSp. *luengo* and its replacement by *largo*, originally 'wide' (cf. *La corónica* 26.1, 1997:53–65). Important observations on Latinisms appear in R. Harris-Northall, 'Re-latinization of Castilian lexis in the early sixteenth century', *BHS*, 76:1–12, who demonstrates that latinization is part of the standardization process. J. A. Frago Gracia, 'Unidad y diversidad en el léxico español del Siglo de Oro', *Alarcos*

*Vol.*, 71–90, offers a series of observations on the regional diversity of the Spanish lexicon of the Golden Age.

T. J. Walsh proposes new solutions to longstanding etymological cruxes. In 'Flawed definitions, neglected sound changes, and the development of Spanish *atinar*', Gutiérrez-Rexach, *Advances*, 278–90, he argues that the basic meaning of *atinar* is 'to guess' and that *atinar* and *adivinar* both derive from Latin ADDIUINARE. In Id., 'The etymology of Sp./Port. *aterirse* "to be stiff or numb with cold"', *aterecerse* "to become stiff or numb with cold", and Sp. *derretirse*, Port. *derreterse* "to melt, thaw"', *Lloyd Vol.*, 223–36, W. seeks to link these items to the family of Lat. RIGESCERE. J. L. Pensado, 'Notas etimológicas', *BRAE, 78*, 1998: 121–30, comments on the semantics of *fuente, periquete, tatamaco*. The semantic scope of OSp. *tornar* and the syntactic constructions into which it entered have attracted the attention of R. Eberenz, '*Tornar/volver* y *descender/bajar*: orígenes de dos relevos léxicos', *CIHLE 4*, II, 109–25, and M. Suárez Fernández, 'Valores semántico-sintácticos de un verbo muy productivo en la lengua medieval: *tornar*', *Verba*, 26: 311–25.

Other studies pertaining to individual items or semantic fields include M. Alvar, 'La formación del léxico psiquiátrico del español', *RFE, 78*, 1998: 5–25; G. Colón, 'Filología y sífilis: Sobre el mal de simiente o mal de sement', *ib.*, 275–308. F. de B. Marcos Alvarez, '*Cucaña* en el *Libro de buen amor* y otras menciones medievales', *Colón Vol.*, 301–34. J. Gómez de Enterría, 'Terminología científico-técnico en el español del siglo XVIII', *BRAE, 78*, 1998: 275–301, discusses problems of creating appropriate Spanish scientific terminology in the translation of French Enlightenment scientific works. M. T. Herrera lists and discusses 'Nombres de instrumentos quirúrgicos en textos médicos medievales', *Colón Vol.*, 217–27. I. D'Ors, '*Rematar, remate*: una etimología más que dudosa', *ib.*, 141–66, questions on semantic grounds the traditional derivation from *matar*. J. R. Carriazo Ruiz, 'El término *fragata* en el paso del español clásico al moderno', *RLex, 5*: 33–44, traces the semantic history of the Italianism *fragata* in Spanish from the 16th to 18th centuries. E. Jiménez Ríos, 'Los galicismos en el *Diccionario de Autoridades*, en el diccionario de Terreros y en la primera edición del *DRAE*', *AEF, 21*, 1998: 141–59, studies vocabulary of French origin in three major 18th-c. Spanish dictionaries. Also worthy of note are the following papers, all found in *CIHLE 4*, II: R. Gavara Gomis, 'Algunas precisiones acerca de *antojo* y *anteojo*' (191–207); M. T. Herrera del Castillo, 'De *acordar* "poner de acuerdo" a *acordar* "despertar, volver en sí": historia de un cambio semasiológico en el español medieval' (231–39); E. Montero Cartelle, 'El léxico erótico en el castellano medieval: claves para su estudio' (307–20); I. Pujol Payet, 'De *quattuor* a *cuadra* y *cuarta*: reflexiones lexicológicas y lexicográficas desde una perspectiva diacrónica' (349–58); L. A. Santos Domínguez, 'Pragmática y cambio semántico: los adjetivos *justo, puro,* y *mero*' (359–64). Arabisms continue to be of interest. J. García González analyses Arabisms by semantic fields in 'Clases de arabismos en los textos alfonsíes', *CIHLE 4*, II, 127–36. M. Morera, 'El arabismo español *hasta*: su evolución formal y semántica', *Verba*, 26:81–95, studies the semantic development of *hasta* vis-à-vis its Arabic etymon and its rivalry with terms of Latin, and discusses the source of the *-s-* of *hasta*. J. M. Fradejas Rueda, 'Unos pocos arabismos más del siglo XIII', *RLex*, 5:45–68, offers vignettes of 29 Arabisms found in *El libro de los animales que cazan*, a 1250 translation of an Arabic source. F. Corriente, *Diccionario de arabismos y voces afines en iberorromance*, M, Gredos, 592 pp., is a valuable etymological dictionary prepared by an expert.

2.   SOCIOLINGUISTICS AND DIALECTOLOGY

A number of important works relating to both sociolinguistics and dialectology have been re-edited or greatly expanded in the period in question. Among these are Emilio Lorenzo, *Anglicismos hispánicos*, M, Gredos, 1996, 710 pp., which gathers in one volume a theme covered in numerous works over the course of no less than 40 years; and Marius Sala, *Lenguas en contacto*, M, Gredos, 1996, 423 pp., which expands on the 1986 edition and which includes an extra chapter on language death. The bibliography in particular is as extensive as could be hoped for.

DIALECTOLOGY

Undoubtedly the most notable work in the field of Hispanic dialectology in the period that concerns us is *Manual de dialectología hispánica*, ed. Manuel Alvar, 2 vols, I: *El español de España*, II: *El español de América*, B, Ariel, 1996, 394, 254 pp., The editor provides some introductory chapters of a theoretical nature, but the principal focus is that of linguistic analysis of individual dialects. There is a rather uneven division between the two volumes as the first is, strangely, considerably more extensive than the second. Alvar has managed to unite a wide range of specialists to contribute articles by region (in Spain) and by country (in America). The strength of the work lies in the individual chapters, amongst which the obvious candidates such as Aragonés (263–92) and Andaluz (233–58), both compiled by Alvar, are supplemented by useful contributions on lesser-known varieties, amongst which María Rosa Fort Cañellas and María

Antonia Martín Zorraquino's description of 'la frontera catalano-aragonesa' stands out (293–304). The focus is explicitly linguistic, thus most identified varieties are analysed in terms of phonology, morphology, syntax, and lexis. This may appear somewhat strange, given the resolutely geographical and political nature of the chapter divisions. Some recognition of extra-linguistic factors beyond the most cursory might also have helped. Despite the rather absolute nature of some of the statements made, for example 'No hay lingüista con un mínimo de solvencia que no lo repita hasta el agotamiento, no hay más que un español' (II, 3) with all the consequences that so sweeping a statement brings in its wake, there is no doubt that the *Manual* will be of significant use to a wide range of specialists for some time. Also of special note is *La Torre*, nos. 7–8, 1998, devoted to the theme of dialectology. Two articles in particular take a theoretical stance. A. López-García, 'El concepto de lengua y dialecto a la luz de la teoría de prototipos' (7–19), attempts to approach an ever-thorny issue with a rather greater deal of awareness of complexity than that of the *Manual*. Part of the conclusion is an insistence on the necessity 'de tratar simultáneamente del dato y de la conciencia del dato'. R. Caravedo, 'Dialectología y sociolingüística, una propuesta integredora' (75–87), is an attempt to reconcile the two and to provide a theoretical framework within which both can function in harmony. As might be expected there is a wide range of works specifically dedicated to individual dialects, some of which have great difficulty in recognising the object of their attention as such. Amongst these is the contribution of Antonio Narbona et al., *El español hablado en Andalucía*, B, Ariel, 1998, 256 pp., which provides a detailed linguistic analysis of Andalucía, and the title of which gives more than sufficient indication of its theoretical stance. Elsewhere, Veronica Orazi, *El dialecto leonés antiguo*, M, Univ. Europea, 1997, 470 pp., is a traditional, detailed study of the origins of Leonese as exemplified by one medieval text and whose conclusion is that it is a mistake to view Leonese as a transition dialect between Castilian and Galician/Portuguese. Pablo Grosschmid, *Diccionario de regionalismos de la lengua española*, B, Juventud, 1998, 618 pp., is sadly lacking in detail and in essence provides no more than a very basic word list of dubious utility. There have also been published many works dealing with the linguistic varieties of the peninsula, amongst which María Luisa Arnal Purroy, *El habla de la baja Ribagorza occidental*, Zaragoza, Inst. Felipe el Católico, 1998, 492 pp., and María del Carmen Pérez Gago, *El habla de Luna*, Salamanca, Tesitex, 1997, 655 pp., stand out. Meanwhile Javier Medina López et al., *El español de Canarias hoy: análisis y perspectivas*, M, Iberoamericana, 1996, 304 pp., continue to ensure that Canario remains the object of significant interest. The relationship across the Atlantic is also catered for in J. J. de Bustos-Tovar, 'Variedades linguisticas diatópicas. A proposito del andaluz y del español de América', *La Torre*, 3, 1998:273–96, in which the question of language and dialect once more arises, and which is dealt with by means of a thoughtful ten-point summary. American Spanish is covered by a number of significant monographs and various shorter studies. María Vaquero de Ramírez, *El español de América*, I: *Pronunciación*, II: *Morfosintaxis*, M, Arco, 1996, 72, 72 pp., is a rather breathless overview of 500 years of linguistic history and is most useful as a pointer to other works. The first two volumes of a promised ten deal with pronunciation and morphosyntax in a large number of very dense sections. A useful bibliography omits, however, the work of Lipski. The remaining volumes will deal with geographical variations. A horse of a slightly different colour is Carmen Saralegui, *El español americano: teoría y textos*, Pamplona, Univ. de Navarra, 1997, 116 pp., which though as short as Vaquero's work aims to provide a general introduction to the topic for the students rather than the specialist. It contains a useful, if necessarily brief, survey of previous works and a traditional breakdown of the linguistic characteristics of Latin American varieties. Of particular note is the mention of the difference between the terms 'español de América/español en América'. Humberto López Morales, *La aventura del español en América*, M, Espasa Calpe, 1998, 272 pp., is aimed at a non-specialist market and ends with the rather plaintive cry that 'toda es una'; a cursory bibliography does at least refer to Lipski, although not without orthographic error. Of particular note is S. G. Armistead, 'Sobre el dialecto bruli de Luisiana', *La Torre*, 3, 1998:465–76, a wide-ranging short piece on a variety on the verge of extinction. The author makes special mention of the work of Holloway, for which see below. Elsewhere, G. Guitarte, 'El concepto de la filología hispanoamericana, La "base" del español en América', *ib.*, 417–34, also raises general questions with respect to the topic.

Judeo-español is dealt with in a number of ways. Ladino, Judeoespañol de Marruecos, and Judeo-español balcánico are the objects of chapters in the *Manual de dialectología hispánica* at the hands of Alvar (the first two) and Marius Sala. Otherwise the most significant contribution to the field comes in the shape of *Sephardica: Hommage à Haim Sephiha*, ed. Winfried Busse and Marie-Christine Varol-Bornes, Berne, Lang, 1996, 646 pp. Of the chapters devoted specifically to the language(s) a number stand out. M. Ariza, 'El judeoespañol' (155–74), is an analysis of the phonological system of Judeo-español, with an eye on that of 15th-c. Castilian. The author notes the importance of regional variations, and provides a catalogue of phonological information that will be of value to future studies of judeo-español, not to mention diachronic and synchronic studies of peninsular Romance. M. Gini de Barnatan, 'En defensa de la lengua judeo-española' (629–38), takes a rather more political than academic approach, and amongst measures suggested is the establishment of an academy of the language. Similarly political in outlook is M. Shaul, 'La ensenyansa del djudeo-espanyol en muestros dias' (617–28), which addresses the problems inherent in education, principally the lack of suitable teachers and a standardised spelling system. A slight tendency to exhortation converts the piece into something approximating to a manifesto. Rather more anecdotal in nature is C. Guigui-Grabli, 'Sefardisme: la transmission est-elle encore possible?' (373–84); while W. Busse, 'Le Judeo-espagnol: un jargon?' (239–45), reinforces the proselytising tone of the volume with statements such as 'il faudrait donc avant tout amener les Séphardes à changer d'attitude à l'égard de leur propre patrimoine linguistique'. A rather more focused linguistic approach is taken by M.-C. Varol-Bornes whose 'Influencia del turco en el judeoespañol de Turquía' (213–37), attempts an outline of precisely what is expressed in the title.

SOCIOLINGUISTICS

The Ariel publishing house has also been busy in other areas of linguistics, among these the area of sociolinguistics is served by Francisco Fernández Moreno, *Principios de sociolinguística y sociología del lenguaje*, B, Ariel, 1998, 400 pp. Described as 'una suerte de manual introductorio' the work claims no greater aim for itself than the distinguishing of sociolinguistics and sociology and provides a clear and authoritative text with an extensive bibliography and useful glossary. The work has a distinct 'anglo-sajón' feel to it, and it will no doubt serve to broaden access to other approaches for sociolinguistics researchers in Spanish-speaking countries, and it succeeds in covering all the major areas expected of a manual of this type. Edited by the same author is *Trabajos de sociolinguística hispánica*, ed. Francisco Fernández Moreno, Alcalá U.P., 1997, 178 pp., although this is rather more a work of original research whose object is to 'acercar la sociolingüística hispánica a la anglosajona', thereby giving the possibility of influence both ways. Seven papers deal with a range of issues, including language contact and euphemism. Of particular interest is the editor's contribution to the meeting of matters theoretical and practical, 'Metodología del Proyecto para el Estudio Sociolingüístico del Español de España y de América'. A similar attempt to gather the work of various researchers in the field of sociolinguistics is provided by *Estudios de sociolingüística: sincronía y diacronía*, ed. Pilar Díez de Revenga Torres et al., Murcia, DM, 1996,

253 pp., which gathers together 15 studies ranging from the theoretical to the very practical. The uniting factor is an admirable attempt to avoid compartmentalization in the field of linguistics and therefore to encourage the deployment of a wide range of theoretical tools in the production of sociolinguistic works. Of particular note are the efforts of a number of scholars, for example those of M. Abad Merino, Díez de Revenga Torres, and Fradrejas Rueda, to apply sociolinguistic methods to historical texts. A work with a more solid base in sociology of language is Dolors Mayoral i Marqué, *El lenguaje: diferencias culturales y desigualdades sociales*, Lleida, Pagés, 1998, 176 pp. Basing herself on the works of Bourdieu and Bernstein, the author proposes to explore power relations, sociology, and language, with a view to exploring why social inequality persists despite avowed ongoing efforts to eradicate it. Of related outlook is María José Serrano, *Cambio sintáctico y prestigio lingüístico*, M, Iberoamericana, 1996, 96 pp., the theoretical introduction to which is of interest on its own, and which is followed up with an exploration of the concept of prestige. The author makes the point that linguistic change and social change are not the same thing, and that the inter-relation of factors chosen in sociolinguistic studies is extremely complex. The final salutary reminder that none of the said factors can usefully be treated in isolation from the others is of especial interest.

Questions of bilingualism and languages in contact with each other provide the focus for a range of significant works. One such is José Luis Blas Arroyo, *Las comunidades de habla bilingues: temas de sociolingüística española*, Zaragoza, Pórtico, 1998, 320 pp., which despite its wide-ranging title concentrates almost exclusively on Valencia. Issues of language contact, mutual interference, code-switching, and attitudes to language, amongst others, are raised in a series of studies, most of which have already seen the light of day elsewhere, but which have a certain thematic unity gathered in this fashion. Although the standards of production occasionally leave something to be desired, there is a useful specialist focus and the work is of undoubted value. Language contact and bilingualism are covered in a range of works. Amongst these is *Spanish in Four Continents: Studies in Language Contact and Bilingualism*, ed. Carmen Silva-Corvalán, Washington, Georgetown U.P., 1995, 304 pp., being selected papers from a conference on the topic. As such, coverage is necessarily varied, but there are a number of important works, A. Elizaincín's continued efforts on the relationship between Spanish and Portuguese in Uruguay (117–31) providing one such. M. Sala also broaches related topics in his 'Lenguas en contacto en el ámbito hispánico', *Actas* (Birmingham), 1, 27–40. The subject matter is broadly in line with the monograph referred to above, although the outlook is more explicitly Hispanic, as the title would indicate. The question of the numerous and varied linguistic influences on the Spanish of the Canary islands is raised by D. Corbella Díaz, 'Contacto de lenguas e interferencias lingüísticas, el caso del español de Canarias', *ib.*, 106–16, the principal concern of which is with lexis, and which provides an extensive list of borrowings from other languages alongside some indication of origin. The influence of English on contemporary Spanish is the object of A. G. Ramírez, 'Lenguas en contacto, el español frente al inglés' *La Torre*, 3, 1998:399–413. The title of J. M. Lope Blanch's article 'La norma linguistica y la lengua literaria', *Actas* (Birmingham), 1, 240–46, is self-explanatory. Specific studies of the relationship between linguistic phenomena and social reality, of which J. A. Moya Corral and E. García Wiederman, 'La "ch" fricativa en Granada, un sonido del habla masculina', *ib.*, 270–83, is a fine example, have also seen the light of day in the period.

Elsewhere, amongst a host of works dealing with sociolinguistic topics, Charles Holloway, *Dialect Death: The Case of Brule Spanish*, Philadelphia, Benjamins, 1997, 220 pp., is a masterpiece of enquiry into a variety on the verge of extinction. In addition to his observations on the history of Brule Spanish and its links to Canary Spanish, the author also makes some important theoretical observations on the nature of dialect death and the attempts to define the category of 'semi-speaker' in particular are worthy of attention. His comments on the importance of phonetic transcriptions are also well made. Michael Clyne and Sandra Kipp, *Pluricentric Languages in an Immigrant Context*, Berlin, de Gruyter, 360 pp., while not solely concerned with Spanish, conduct an interesting empirical study of Spanish speakers in Australia. Meanwhile the *Asociación de Hispanistas Alemanes* publishes the fruits of one of their conferences in *Lenguaje y comunicación intercultural en el mundo hispánico*, Frankfurt, Vervuert, Iberoamericana, 1997, 216 pp., in which K. Henze investigates the importance of codeswitching in 'Comunicación intercultural y code switching' (87–104); S. Steckbauer examines the relationship between languages in Lima (147–67); and E. Boix studies the use of languages by parents in Barcelona in 'Ideologías lingüísticas en familias lingüísticamente mixtas (catalán-castellano) en la región metropolitana de Barcelona' (169–90). Linguistic choices in Cataluña are also explored in Francisco Báez de Aguilar González, *El conflicto lingüístico de los emigrantes castellanohablantes en Barcelona*, Málaga U.P., 1997, 229 pp., which, when focused on the object of study, is a well-crafted empirical study of an andaluz community in Barcelona, and is a model of transparency in its methodology.

## MEDIEVAL LITERATURE

By JANE E. CONNOLLY, *University of Miami*, MARÍA MORRÁS, *Universitat Pompeu Fabra, Barcelona*, and M. DOLORES PELÁEZ BENÍTEZ, *Simmons College*

### 1. GENERAL

Martin J. Duffell, *Modern Metrical Theory and the 'verso de arte mayor'* (PMHRS, 10), 104 pp., first reviews comparative metrics, with special attention to the parametric theory of K. Hanson and P. Kiparsky. He then applies linguistics and statistical analysis to discern patterns of Romance verse, with special attention given to *arte mayor* and Juan de Mena's *Laberinto de Fortuna*. Id., 'The metric cleansing of Hispanic verse', *BHS(L)*, 76:151–68, argues that syllabic verse is not a natural development for Iberian languages, and that much apparently isosyllabic verse is the product of 'metric cleansing', i.e., the elimination of unwanted exceptions through editorial intervention. P. Canettieri, 'La metrica romanza', Boitani, *Produzione*, 493–554, considers the metrics of medieval Hispanic texts. Marcelino Menéndez Pelayo, *Menéndez Pelayo digital*, M, Digibis Publicaciones Digitales, CD-ROM, is the complete collection of the author's publications in electronic form with a bibliography of his work registering over 3000 items. G. Orduna, 'Nuevos enfoques para una historia de la literatura medieval española', *Studia Hispanica Medievalia IV*, 7–15, emphasizes three basic concepts for the realization of a new history of medieval literature: 'oral community', 'literary community' and 'textual community'. The concept of orality is essential for a literary history, and the Castilian Middle Ages are particularly marked by three textual communities: Palencia, Toledo, the Catholic Kings. Pedro Sánchez-Prieto Borja, *Cómo editar los textos medievales. Criterios para su presentación gráfica*, M, Arco Libros, 1998, 263 pp., reviews fundamental concepts for current textual criticism, offering criteria for the transcription of medieval texts based on the status of knowledge of medieval phonetics and phonology. J. M. García Martín, 'Función primaria de las variantes textuales para un historiador de la lengua', *CLHM*, 22:7–16, argues for the synoptic edition of texts as a better approach to the linguistic reality of medieval texts. C. Mencé-Caster, 'L'édition des textes médiévaux espagnols: quels critères pour quels lecteurs?', *ib.*, 17–31, proposes criteria for minimal editorial intervention. M. Morreale, 'El texto como fin y la filología como medio (en la propuesta universitaria)', *Studia Hispanica Medievalia IV*, 16–33, defends the so-called 'old philology' and shows how its knowledge is useful even for the study of 20th-c. poets like Machado and García Lorca; she argues that philology ought to be used to make old texts come alive as read (or recited) beings. P. Díaz-Mas, 'Influencias judías en la literatura castellana medieval', *RDTP*, 54:129–44, focuses on some aspects that reveal mutual influence between Jewish poetry and Christian poetry: the diffusion and use of Jewish poems among a Christian audience; possible Jewish influences in *Ay, Jerusalem;* the adoption of formal recourses particular to Semitic poetry in Christian poetry; and metrical features of Christian poetry in Jewish poetry. J. Ferro, 'El concepto de "mesura"': una cuestión de analogía', *Studia Hispanica Medievalia IV*, 124–31, follows its meaning in rhetoric, and in the courtly and moral spheres, giving abundant examples. M. J. Lacarra, ' "De la disculpa en el reír": santos y diablos ante la risa', *Santiago-Otero Vol.*, 1, 377–91, traces the origins of the religious rejection of laughter using doctrinal sources, and observes its application in Romance texts, noting that moderate or silent laughter is a sign of intelligence and humanity while roaring laughter or disproportionate gesturing characterize the sinner and the devil. E. Pardo de Guevara, 'Presencia de la materia genealógica en la literatura histórica medieval. La conformación de un género histórico', *ib.*, 393–403, examines genealogical material in Peninsular chronicles, from early Latin chronicles to lineage books; he considers the *Genealogía de los reyes de España* by Alfonso de Cartagena to be a hybrid, with influences from the *Liber regum* and the *Crónica de 1344*. Valeria Bertolucci, Carlos Alvar, and Stefano Asperto, *Storia delle Letterature Medievali Romanze. L'area iberica*, directed by M. Luisa Meneghetti, Bari, Laterza, 379 pp., includes 'La letteratura castigliana medievale' (99–324) by Alvar, which covers Spanish literature from its origins (principally the epic) to the autumn of the Middle Ages. *Brujas, demonios y fantasmas en la literatura fantástica hispánica*, ed. J. Pont, Lérida U.P., 367 pp.

2. EPIC, BALLADS

EPIC

E. Lacarra Lanz, 'Political discourse and the construction and representation of gender in *Mocedades de Rodrigo*', *HR*, 67:467–91, through an analysis of the poem centred on the genealogical narrative of its introduction, argues that the construction of masculinity is predicated on the marginalization of women, whose femininity, against historical records, is exclusively represented as an object of exchange circulating among men. M. Bailey, 'El diablo como protagonista en el *Poema de Fernán González*: un concepto clerical de la historia', *Olifant*, 20:171–89, is an analysis of the figurative and metaphorical language in the poem showing how, contrary to its prosification in the chronicle tradition, the clerical author chooses to present evil as one of the main reasons for the Christian's defeat, and therefore conveys a new interpretation of history in which the battle between God and Evil becomes the leading force.

### POEMA DE MIO CID

*Poema de Mio Cid, Manuscrito de Per Abbat. Cantar de Mío Cid* (Colección Tesoros de la Biblioteca Nacional), M, Biblioteca Nacional-Ministerio de Cultura, 1998, CD-ROM, contains a MS facsimile, its transcription (with a program that allows the creation of a hyper-textual concordance), its recitation, a map of the Cid's Spain and an audio-visual journey through same. Alberto Montaner, *El Cid en Aragón*, Zaragoza, Caja de Ahorros de la Inmaculada, 1998, 110 pp., studies the relation of the historic Cid with Aragón (with Zaragoza and the conflicts of Graus, Almenar, Rueda and Tévar, as well as the Morella campaign) and its reflection in the *Cantar* and in the Cid legends. Irene Zaderenko, *Problemas de autoría, de estructura y de fuentes en el 'Poema de mío Cid'*, Alcalá de Henares U.P., 1998, 206 pp., argues that the second *cantar* was composed by a learned author based on the *Historia Roderici* and documents on the Cid; a second learned author may have written the first *cantar*, using fictional elements but with a basis in reality; and, the third *cantar* could have been the product of a third author, who composed it after 1207, centring it on the juridical problem of the *riepto* as codified at the end of the 13th century. P. Rochwert, 'Recherches sur la mise en prose des poèmes héroïques dans l'*Histoire d'Espagne. Le Cantar primero* du *Poème du Cid* dans la *Chronique de vingt rois*', *CLHM*, 22:131–60, claims to have identified 'les mécanismes de mise en prose qui permettent la dissimulation de la nature du texte-source et la récupération monarchique du discours'. S. Luongo, 'Dal verso alla prosa', Boitani, *Produzione*, 613–46, treats the relationship between the *Cid* and *Estoria de España*.

### BALLADS

Louise O. Vasvari, *The Heterotextual Body of the 'Mora Morilla'* (PMHRS, 12), 115 pp., is an extensive study of the ballad, locating it within the pan-European folk tradition of the Moorish/dark girl, finding analogies in eight languages. She gives special attention to the ballad's sexual suggestiveness and argues that it may have been a wedding song. *Romancero*, ed. Pedro M. Piñero, M, Biblioteca Nueva, 278 pp., has an extensive preliminary study of the history of the *romance* texts (medieval ballad, 16th-c. editions, the 17th- and 18th-c. tradition, modern ballads), the theories and work of R. Menéndez Pidal, and literary aspects of the ballad. *Romancero de Palacio (siglo XVI)*, ed. José

J. Labrador Herraiz, Ralph A. DiFranco, and Lori A. Bernard, prol. Juan Fernández Jiménez, Ohio U.P., 411 pp., is an edition of Biblioteca de Palacio MS II-996, a rich collection of ballads that reflect the literary fashion of the last years of the 16th c. and includes the *romance viejo;* there is a detailed MS study. G. Di Stefano, 'Consideraciones sobre la clasificación de los romances', *Romanceiro Ibérico*, 1 : 13–27, quickly reviews the classifications by Martín Nucio, Agustín Durán, Ferdinand Joseph Wolf, and the *Catálogo General del Romancero* by Diego Catalán and the Seminario Menéndez Pidal; he does not share the classification of 'literary' ballads made by the latter, although he agrees with the need for an ethnographic focus. A. Valenciano, 'El trasvase de romances en la frontera hispano-portuguesa', *ib*., 29–51, comments on the mode of transmission of traditional ballads from Galicia and the borders of Zamora, Salamanca and Extremadura with Portugal; the Galician ballads are almost always transmitted orally and textually in Spanish, even though the received versions have Galician colloquialisms; the Hispano-Portuguese ballads mix the two languages. S. G. Armistead, 'El romancero sefardí: medievo y diáspora', *ib*., 53–69, cites several *romances* (*El rey Fernando en Francia, Almerique de Narbona, Roncesvalles, Las bodas de París*) as examples of the medievalism of Sephardic ballads and of the latency and independence of the modern oral *romancero* with respect to the printed 16th-c. texts. E. Baltanás, 'Ropaje carolingio, realidad vulgar: *Conde Claros en hábito de fraile* en la tradición moderna', pp. 73–82 of *Romances y canciones en la tradición andaluza*, ed. P. M. Piñero, E. Baltanás, and A. J. Pérez Castellano, Seville, Fundación Machado, 290 pp., analyses the theme and fable of the Andalusian versions of this pseudo-Carolingian ballad. E. Boretz, 'In Filomena's domain: the realm of the *romance*', *La corónica*, 27.2 : 75–88, believes that the speech of the severed tongue effects justice for a dual violation: the rape of Filomena and the invasion of her '*amiga*'s kingdom' (orality). V. Infantes, 'El Abad don Juan de Montemayor: la historia de un *cantar*', *AHLM* 7, II, 255–71, deals with the interest that the prodigious adventures of Don Juan de Montemayor have held for medieval studies.

## 3. THIRTEENTH AND FOURTEENTH CENTURIES

Juan Casas Rigall, *La materia de Troya en las letras romances del siglo XIII hispano*, Santiago de Compostela U.P., 297 pp., is a detailed study of the sources of the Troy material in 13th-c. Iberia. The first chapter is a synthetic panorama of the Trojan cycle from its origins to the 13th c.; C.R. then dedicates individual chapters to *Libro de Alexandre*, *Libro de las generaciones*, Alphonsine historiography, *General estoria*, and *Historia troyana polimétrica.* The appendices complement the analysis of the Alphonsine case, giving a complete catalogue of Trojan sources of Parts 2–3 of *General estoria.*

POETRY

CUADERNA VÍA VERSE. J. K. Walsh, 'Obras perdidas del mester de clerecía', ed. and introd. A. Deyermond, *La corónica,* 28.1 : 147–66, reviews questions related to the creation and dissemination of *cuaderna vía* texts, noting that a large number of poems were long lost and only discovered relatively recently, and offers a catalogue of lost texts with supporting evidence for their existence. M. G. Capusso, 'El vestido y el disfraz en el *Libro de Apolonio*: valores socio-culturales, origen literario y simbolismo religioso', *AHLM* 7, I, 431–46, studies the treatment of garments.

LIBRO DE ALEXANDRE. F. Baños Vallejo, 'La estatua de sal o la metamorfosis verdadera: *Libro de Alexandre,* 2387–2393', *La corónica,* 28.1 : 13–24, analyses in particular 2393, seeing in it one of many instances of the cleric's *maestría.* M. J. Lacarra, 'Los vicios capitales en el arrabal del infierno: *Libro de Alexandre,* 2345–2411', *ib.,* 71–81, examines the seven deadly sins within a medieval context. D. Nelson, 'El *Libro de Alexandre* y Gonzalo de Berceo: un problema filológico', *ib.,* 93–136, offers extensive lexical and grammatical evidence in support of Berceo's authorship of the *Libro de Alexandre.* J. Casas, 'Sobre la adaptación de *Ilias Latina* en el *Libro de Alexandre* y cuestiones conexas (de Dictis y Dares a Alfonso X)', *AHLM* 7, II, 39–53, considering the *Ilias Latina* as the main source for the passage on the Trojan war in *Libro de Alexandre,* analyses some of the most striking deviations in the Spanish poem from the Latin source. Amaia Arizaleta, *\*La translation d'Alexandre. Recherches sur la genèse et signification du 'Libro de Alexandre',* Paris, Klincksieck–Séminaire d'Études Hispaniques de l'Université Paris XIII, 367 pp.

BERCEO. N. A. Lugones, ' "En cabo do se souo, ali a de tornar' ': El *Physiologus* en el *Sacrificio de la misa', Berceo,* 13 : 15–31, finds the source for strophes 48–53, narrating the priest's movement from the right to the left of the altar, in the chapter about the *charadrius* (a type of bird) of the *Physiologus,* perhaps by way of the *Bestiaire* by Philippe de Thaun, which tells how this bird signals at a sick man's bed if he will die (moving toward the left) or survive (looking straight at him); the former also signifies the Jews' rejection of Christ. F. Baños Vallejo, 'Innovaciones en la edición de *Los Milagros de Nuestra Señora* de Berceo', *AHLM* 7, I, 293–304, contributes some examples of the innovations found in his edition of Berceo's *Milagros de Nuestra Señora,* referring to three aspects: the establishment of the text, its interpretation and the publication of a copy closer to the source. E. Franchini, 'Gonzalo de Berceo y el otro latino: *Vida de Santo Domingo*, 2c', *La corónica*, 28.1 : 25–34, renders 2c as 'puesto que no so tan estudiado como para escribir ningún latín'. I. Uría Maqua, ' "En dubda nos paramos en cuál empeçaremos": *Vida de Santo Domingo de Silos*, 351c', *ib.*, 137–45, arguing that 351 is linguistically and logically anomalous and noting the brisk introduction of the saint's miracle at 289–90, suggests that the miracle of the saint's captivity is misplaced and was meant to be the first in the series of the life miracles. F. Marcos Marín, 'GVNDISALVVS INFORMATICVS. Acceso y tratamientos electrónicos de la obra de Gonzalo de Berceo', *ib.*, 83–92, reviews digital sources of information for the study of Berceo.

   *LIBRO DE BUEN AMOR.* L. Rorchi, 'Trotaconventos, Doña Garoça and the dynamics of dialectical reasoning in the *Libro de buen amor*', *BHS(L)*, 76 : 21–33, believes that the debate between Trotaconventos and Doña Garoça reflects a knowledge of the techniques of disputation of Islamic scholasticism. G. Orduna, 'La versión del autor y la tradición manuscrita e impresa de la literatura medieval', *AHLM 7*, III, 115–26, considers the problematic created for the legitimacy of a text by the existence of a popularized and accepted form of the text (*textus receptus*), which does not correspond to the original version established by MS witnesses and philological study; he focuses on the concrete case of the *Libro del Arcipreste de Hita* previously studied by the author (see *YWMLS*, 50 : 292), re-emphasizing the necessity of distinguishing between the so-called *Libro de buen amor* and *Libro del Arcipreste de Hita. Arciprete di Hita. Libro del buon amore*, ed., introd., and notes Giuseppe Di Stefano, trans. Vincenzo La Gioia, Milan, Rizzoli, 739 pp., includes a faithful metrical and rhythmic translation of the original (using the text established by A. Blecua as the base). M. Garcia, 'Le *Livre de Bon Amour* avant Tomás Antonio Sánchez', *CLHM*, 22 : 53–81, beginning with the reading of the text by 18th-c. scholars, reflects on the current conception of the edition of medieval texts, concluding that we should value and study MSS *G* and *T* not merely as witnesses of a work of which they are fragments but as identifiable and coherent texts with interesting codicological and textual characteristics interesting in and of themselves. F. Gómez Redondo, ' "E busca mensajera de unas negras *patas*": *Libro de buen amor* 441a. La parodia del derecho canónico', *ib.*, 161–75, proposes that we read the line presenting Trotaconventos as 'mensajera de unas negras patas' and not 'pecas': 'por oposición a las blancas "calças de lino" de los mensajeros de paz que han de ser los sacerdotes'; the key to this interpretation is found in Alphonsine legislative texts. P. Payán Sotomayor, 'Las *Canticas de loores de Santa María* de Juan Ruiz', *AHLM 7*, III, 145–55, is a metrical and lexicographic study of the *canticas de loores de Santa María*. L. M. V. García, 'La astrología en el *Libro de buen amor*. Fuentes y problemas sobre el uso de conceptos astrológicos en la literatura medieval española', *RLit*, 61:333–48, follows the echoes of astrological theory found in *LBA*. S. D. Kirby, 'La función estética de la rima consecutiva en el *Libro de buen amor*', *RFE*, 89:101–21, maintains that this rhyme represents the poet's conscious effort to reinforce the moral of the strophes where it occurs, to call attention to the poetic expression found in them, or to emphasize the transition between episodes.

OTHER POETRY. L. Peláez, 'La *Historia Troyana Polimétrica*: una nueva tentativa de renovación de la épica culta', *Olifant*, 20:235–48, studies the metric and lyrical motifs in the *Polimétrica*'s octosyllabic verse to present them as an example of the 'new epic' developed in the 14th c. that had been identified by M. Vaquero in the *Poema de Alfonso XI*. *Proverbios morales de Sem Tob de Carrión*, ed. Paloma Díaz-Mas and Carlos Mota, M, Cátedra, 1998, 306 pp., includes an extensive preliminary study examining the MS tradition and the transmission of the poem, the author and the most relevant aspects of the text (metrics, rhyme, style, structure, themes, language), and its relation to the Hispano-Judaic and Sephardic traditions.

PROSE

Fernando Gómez Redondo, *Historia de la prosa medieval castellana. II. El desarrollo de los géneros. La ficción caballeresca y el orden religioso*, vol. 2, M, Cátedra, 1221–2076 pp., like the first volume (*YWMLS*, 60:209), is exhaustive in its presentation of information and bibliography. This volume deals with the 14th c., and covers the chronicles from Fernando IV to Pero López de Ayala, as well as *Zifar*, the primitive *Amadís*, didactic literature, sermons, translations and reworkings of foreign texts.

ALFONSO X EL SABIO. M. Calderón Calderón, 'Para la edición crítica de la *Crónica de Alfonso X*: cuestiones liminares', *AHLM* 7, I, 411–20, examines those aspects of the text's history (witnesses of the *Crónica*, its transmission and versions, external *collatio* and *textus receptus*) that the author believes need to be revised to undertake the kind of definitive editions of the Alphonsine work that should be done. *Textos y concordancias electrónicos de documentos castellanos de Alfonso X*, ed. María Teresa Herrera, María Nieves Sánchez, and María Estela González, Madison, HSMS, CD-ROM.

DIDACTIC LITERATURE. J. M. Lucía Megías, 'Hacia la edición crítica de *Flores de Filosofía*: la *collatio externa* y los modelos de compilación sapiencial', *AHLM* 7, II, 353–73, analyses the extant codices of *Flores de filosofía*, and remarks on the importance of studying the history of a text in order to edit it. M. Garcia, 'Acercamiento filológico al *Calila e Dimna*', *ib*., I, 71–82, considers the techniques employed by the translator of the Castilian version by studying the term *sávana*, and analyses the possible reasons for the differences in Dimna's complaint in the Arabic and Castilian versions. A. E. Ramadori, 'Estructura y estilo de las plegarias en *Barlaam e Josafat*', *Studia Hispanica Medievalia IV*, 153–61, studies a body of 15 prayers to establish their typology. L. Funes, 'El surgimiento de la prosa narrativa en Castilla: un enfoque histórico-cultural', *ib*., 162–71, analyses the theme from two basic concepts: prose as a discursive practice, and the literary and cultural evolution as a struggle between discursive practices; he illustrates the concepts through the consideration of two primary examples of short and long narrative, *Calila e Dimna* and *Estoria de España*. C. E. Armijo Canto, 'La predicación en el *Libro de los gatos*', *ib*., 132–42, argues that the translator of *Libro de los gatos* belonged to the Cistercian Order and used preaching to caution bad clergy. G. Rossarolli de Brevedan, 'Recreación de relatos bíblicos en el *Barlaam e Josafat*', *ib*., 143–52, concludes that the text's originality is in the selection and arrangement of the parable rather than in their adaptation. H. Ó. Bizzarri, 'La representación de la vida cotidiana en *Castigos e documentos* del Rey don Sancho IV', *ib*., 190–99, offers a characterization of the work's style, finding it possesses an erudition lacking in the *speculum principis*, and a marked rationalist character; he concludes that through the application of wisdom to daily life through its use of the *exemplum*, *similitudo*, dialogue, refrains, and the recreation of scenes from everyday life, *Castigos e documentos* took sententious discourse to a new level.

DON JUAN MANUEL. F. Degiovanni, 'Retórica de la predicación e ideología dominica en la quinta parte de *El Conde Lucanor*', *BH*, 101:5–17, finds that the *ars praedicandi* and Dominican ideology are the rhetorical and theological underpinnings of the fifth part, which D. views as an essential element of the tripartite organisation of the work and of Don Juan Manuel's triumvirate of concerns: the political, the literary, the religious. J. England, ' "Los que son muy cuerdos entienden la cosa por algunas sennales": learning the lessons of *El Conde Lucanor*', *BHS(G)*, 76:345–64, contests the argument by Laurence de Looze (see *YWMLS*, 57:311) that *CL* is as fundamentally ambiguous as the *Libro de buen amor*. E. Caldera, 'Árabes y judíos en la perspectiva cristiana de Juan Manuel', *Salina*, 13:37–40, sees an accepting and sympathetic attitude toward Jews and Muslims in Don Juan Manuel's oeuvre, noting that he is only critical or pejorative in his treatment of the latter when dealing with matters relating to the Reconquest. B. Taylor, 'El hígado de don Juan Manuel: una imagen de placer y provecho en *El Conde Lucanor*', *AHLM* 7, III, 447–58, nuances the reading of the text through a consideration of the significance of the liver and placing the text within the topos of the sweet and the useful. A. Lunadei, 'Don Juan Manuel y su gira proselitista en el *Conde Lucanor*', *Studia Hispanica Medievalia IV*, 172–79, attempts to determine the 'ideal reader' of *Conde Lucanor*, conjecturing that Juan Manuel directs it to young second-born noblemen as a means of forming his political party by offering them an educational programme of conduct. G. Olivetto, 'De las maneras de la amistad en el *Libro infinido* de Don Juan Manuel', *ib.*, 180–89, based on the work of Carlos Heusch, proposes a reading of the 'Maneras del amor' in the Manuelian work through a reconsideration of the concepts of friendship in the fourth *Partida*.

LIBRO DEL CAVALLERO ZIFAR. J. M. Cacho Blecua, 'El género del *Cifar* (Cromberger, 1512)', Canavaggio, *Novela*, 85–105, is an interesting contribution that argues that editors intervene between a text and its audience to condition directly or indirectly the work's reading; he cites the case of the *Zifar*, noting that in 1512 the editorial mediation and prologue by Jacobo Cromberger supposed a different horizon of expectations than that of the original text. M. L. Cuesta Torre, 'En torno al tema de la guerra en el *Libro del caballero Zifar*', *AHLM* 7, II, 113–24, offers an interesting study of the art of war and the typology of war situations in *Zifar*. G. Olivetto, ' "Punaredes de ganar amigos e en guardar e retener los que ouistes ganado" (Apuntes al cap. 156 del *Libro del Cavallero*)', *ib.*, III, 91–102, examines a section of 'Castigos del rey Mentón' in relation to *amicitia* and the protection from lovers, as well as a new claim of the relation of *Flores de filosofía* and *Zifar*. A. Varvaro, 'Il testo letterario', Boitani, *Produzione*, 387–422, is a study of the MS tradition of the *Zifar*. *La corónica*, 27.3, is dedicated to the *Zifar* and includes the following studies: V. Barletta, ' "Por ende deuemos *a* creer": knowledge and social practice in the *Libro del Cauallero de Dios*' (13–34), which applies philological, historical, and hermeneutical techniques to establish the *Zifar*'s understanding of socially contextualized knowledge. J. E. Burke, 'The *Libro del Cavallero Zifar* and the fashioning of the self' (35–44), analyses the *Zifar* as a mirror of princes, based on medieval concepts of personality. J. M. Cacho Blecua , 'Del *Liber consolationis et consilii* al *Libro del cavallero Zifar*' (45–66), proposes as a possible author of the *Zifar* the royal advisor and bishop of Cartagena Pedro Gómez Barroso. Id., 'Bibliografía del *Libro del Cavallero Zifar*' (227–50). I. Corfis, 'The fantastic in *Cavallero Zifar*' (67–86), observes that we find ourselves before one of the most fantastic books of medieval Spanish literature; she concludes that the main fantastic episodes are directly related to the reality represented in the work through the moral and political readings. M. Gerli, '*Zifar Redivivus*: patronage, politics, and the Paris manuscript of the *Libro del Cavallero Zifar*' (87–103), based on an analysis of the Paris MS, concludes that the interest of the patron (Enrique IV) in the story of Zifar is derived from his personal circumstances; in this sense it is a mirror of princes. F. Gómez Redondo, 'El *Zifar* y la *Crónica de Fernando IV*' (105–24), observes that both works share a common ideological stance, 'Molinismo' (for the queen regent María de Molina), that can be summarized in three points: never despair when faced with obstacles, place God first, act guided by innate intelligence. M. Harney, 'Law and order in the *Libro del Cavallero Zifar*' (125–44), emphasizes that law resides in the monarch, who is sovereign not so much by virtue of his lineage as by his exercise of virtue; H. believes that the book was intended for an urban audience, and thus the knights are not particularly favoured and the text does not have the escapist character of later chivalresque romances, but instead 'it gratifies the utopic yearnings of a bourgeoisie eager for greater security in its quest for economic prosperity'. J. M. Lucía Megías, 'Los castigos del rey de Mentón a la luz de *Flores de Filosofía*: límites y posibilidades del uso del modelo subyacente' (145–65), analyses *Flores de Filosofía* as a source for *Zifar* and its influence in the elaboration of a critical text of the latter. J. D. Rodríguez Velasco, 'El *Libro del cavallero Zifar* en la edad de la virtud' (167–85), refutes the theory that conceives *Zifar* as a work concerned with social mobility through a review of ruling political ideals; the second part of the study is dedicated to the figure of the *ribaldo*. W. Smith, 'Marital canon-law dilemmas in the *Libro del Cavallero Zifar*' (187–206), provides an in-depth analysis of the legal ramifications of the two marriages in the novel. J. M. Viña Liste, 'Variaciones sobre el motivo o tópico del llanto en el *Libro del cavallero Zifar*' (207–26), analyses mourning as a rhetorical motif in *Zifar* and its variations in the work.

PERO LÓPEZ DE AYALA. J. L. Moure, 'Pero López de Ayala y la integración de la *Crónica de los Reyes de Castilla*', *Studia Hispanica Medievalia IV*, 200–07, hypothesizes that the MS tradition of the *Crónicas*, and more precisely their integration as a corpus, was not Ayala's responsibility. M. C. Pastor Cuevas, 'Principios políticos en la *Crónica de Pedro I* de Pero López de Ayala', *AHLM 7*, III, 133–43, reveals the political principles derived from Ayala's historiographic production. L. N. Uriarte, 'Inés de Castro, mártir y mito', Botta, *Inês*, 27–34, examines, among other aspects, the echoes of the myth of the *Crónicas de los Reyes de Castilla* by Ayala (chs. 14 and 26) and various 15th-c. Portuguese chronicles.

OTHER PROSE WRITERS. A. M. Huélamo Santamaría, 'Tres huellas de Juan de Gales en castellano', *AHLM 7*, II, 245–53, attempts to elucidate traces of the *Communiloquium* in Castilian letters. *Textos clásicos de cetrería, montería y caza*, ed. José Manuel Fradejas Rueda, M,

Fundación Histórica Tavera, CD-ROM, includes 20 texts, both MS and printed texts from the 13th to 19th centuries. Of particular interest are: MS Biblioteca Nacional Madrid Res. 270 of *Moamín*, BNM 21549 of *Libro de cetrería* by Evangelista, the editions of *Libro de la montería* by López de Ayala in Bibliófilos Españoles, and by Argote de Molina. P. Díez de Revenga, 'La *Historia de la Doncella Teodor*: variaciones sobre un mismo tema', *CLHM*, 22 : 105–18, confirms the correctness of MS Biblioteca de Salamanca 1886, Escorial h.II.6, Biblioteca Nacional 17822 and 17822, which attest to 'una fidelidad bastante aceptable para lo que era usual en aquella época'. L. Funes, 'Historia, ficción, relato: invención del pasado en el discurso histórico de mediados del siglo XIV', *AHLM* 7, II, 175–86, examines a specific aspect of narrative through which different writers of history looked at the recent past, i.e. mid-14th-c. Castile. J. M. Cacho, 'La *ordinatio* del *Rams de flores* de Juan Fernández de Heredia', *ib.*, I, 397–409, studies the composition of this work in Escorial MS Z-I-2 and tries to discern the system of work in the *scriptorium* to which it belongs. M. Sanz Julián, 'Las rúbricas en la *Crónica Troyana* de Juan Fernández de Heredia', *ib.*, III, 372–83, is a study of the function and significance of the rubrics. A. Pérez Martín, 'La obra jurídica de Jacobo de las Leyes: las *Flores del Derecho*', *CLHM*, 22 : 247–70, studies the work's content, development and sources, and its connection with Alphonsine legal texts; he proposes the succession *Fuero real-Doctrinal-Partidas-Flores*, rejecting Galo Sánchez's view that *Flores* initiated the series. \**The Aragonese Version of the Secreto secretorum (from the Unique Escorial Ms.Z.I.2)*, ed. Lloyd Kasten, Madison, HSMS, x + 149 pp. \**Electronic Texts and Concordances of Andalusian Documents (1324–1500) Selected from the Collection of The Hispanic Society of America*, ed. Cynthia J. Kauffeld, Madison, HSMS, CD-ROM. \**Textos y concordancias electrónicos del 'Fuero general de Navarra'*, ed. Franklin M. Waltman, Madison, HSMS, CD-ROM.

## 4.   FIFTEENTH CENTURY
### GENERAL, BIBLIOGRAPHY, EARLY PRINTING

Á. Alcalá and J. Sanz, *Vida y muerte del príncipe don Juan. Historia y literatura*, Valladolid, Junta de Castilla y León, 372 pp., consists of two parts: a full biographical account of the prince's life and death is given and a compilation of literary texts on his death. L. M. Brocato, ' "Tened por espejo su fin". Mapping gender and sex in fifteenth- and sixteenth-century Spain', Blackmore, *Queer Iberia*, 325–65, focuses on the *Laberinto de Fortuna, Celestina*, and *Carajicomedia* to confirm that the elaboration of moral and social vision and cultural identity around sex was a main concern of the period. C. Faulhaber, 'Las bibliotecas medievales españolas', *Santiago-Otero Vol.*, I, 785–800, offers a general view on owners and books in medieval libraries. *Des femmes et des livres: France et Espagnes, XIVe–XVIIe siècle. Actes de la journée d'étude, Paris, 30 avril 1998*, ed. D. de Courcelles and C. Val, Paris, École National des Chartes–École Normale Supérieure de Fontenay/Saint-Cloud, 175 pp., includes two outstanding studies: P. Cátedra, 'Lectura femenina en el claustro (España, siglos XIV-XVI)' (7–53), comments on the presence of the book in religious communities at the end of the Middle Ages; A. Guillaume-Alonso, 'Des bibliothèques féminines en Espagne (XVIe–XVII siècles). Quelques examples' (61–75), in spite of the title, studies among others, Isabel la Católica's library and that of the mother of Garcilaso de la Vega. Á. Gómez Moreno, 'El reflejo literario', pp. 315–39 of *Orígenes de la monarquía hispánica: Propaganda y legitimación (ca. 1400–1520)*, ed. J. M. Nieto Soria, M, Dykinson, 607 pp., draws a general overview of genres and authors ordered around the themes of propaganda and royal power.

POETRY

CANCIONEROS. A. M. Gómez Bravo, 'Cantar decires y decir cantares: génro y lectura de la poesía cuatrocentista castellana', *BHS(L)*, 76:169–87, calls for a re-evaluation of the traditional generic designations *cantiga/canción* and *decir*, arguing that the differences between the two do not reside in the mode of reception or delivery but in metrics and rhetoric. J. C. Conde and V. Infantes, 'Un nuevo fragmento del *Cancionero de Barrantes*', *RLMed*, 11:209–15, identify MS 6584 from the Biblioteca Nacional de Madrid, which includes the *Vergel de Príncipes* by Rodrigo Sánchez de Arévalo, as one of the manuscripts that originally was part of the *Cancionero de Barrantes*. For V. Beltrán, 'Copistas y cancioneros', *Actas* (Corunna), I, 17–40, the study of the *Cancionero de Juan Fernández de Híjar* allows the reconstruction of the procedures of making *cancioneros* by additions from previous ones. Id., 'Tipología y génesis de los cancioneros. La organización de los materiales', Parrilla, *Estudios*, 9–54, fixes the main recurrent elements in the composition of Castilian *cancioneros*. A. Deyermond, 'La edición de cancioneros', *Actas* (Corunna), I, 41–70, raises in general terms the problems of each type of edition (by author, by *cancionero*, etc.). C. Alvar, 'Il dibattito nella poesia dei *cancioneros*', pp. 355–62 of *Il genere 'tenzone' nelle letterature romanze delle Origini (Atti del Convegno internazionale, Losanna 13–15 novembre 1997)*, ed. M. Pedroni and A. Stäube, Ravenna, Longo, 533 pp., establishes that the debate's strophic structure and rhetorical style relates it to the *tensó* and *partimen*, while it inherits from the epistle its dialogic form and the variety in the subject. P. Botta, 'Dos tipos de léxico frente a frente:

poesía cortés, poesía tradicional', *Studia Hispanica Medievalia IV*, 208–19, compares the vocabulary of traditional lyric with that used in the *cancioneros* and observes divergences and common elements. M. L. Cuesta, 'Personajes artúricos en la poesía de cancionero', Parrilla, *Estudios*, 71–112, shows that the characters most frequently mentioned are Merlin and Tristan, while Arthur is the least frequent; they appear especially in PN1 and MH1, and the poets who most often quote them are Villasandino, Pero Ferrús, and Juan de Dueñas.

SANTILLANA. *Poesía lírica*, ed. M. Á. Pérez Priego, M, Cátedra, 256 pp., is a critical edition with full notes of 70 lyrical poems (the sonnets are excluded) and an introduction; the most notable aspect is the textual study.

JUAN DE MENA. C. Mota, 'El condestable en su laberinto: memoria literaria de Ruy López Dávalos', *AHLM* 7, I, 49–62, deals with the heroic biography of this figure and examines its literary reflections, especially in Mena.

JUAN DEL ENCINA. F. Maurizi, 'Juan del Encina, Garci Sánchez de Badajoz, Jorge Manrique y Cartagena: acerca de unas coplas y de sus variantes', *AHLM* 7, II, 461–70, considers authorial problems. Juan del Encina's centenary is commemorated in Guijarro, *Humanismo*. D. Capra, 'E. frente a los clásicos (con un escorzo agustiniano)' (317–24), emphasizes the importance of St Augustine's influence on the poetic theory of this poet, especially in his ennobling of the rustic and of the *sermo humilis*. C. Salinas, 'Antiguos y modernos en el *Arte de poesía castellana* de Juan del Encina' (431–38), points out that, although E. defends the dignity of poetry on the *sapientia vetorum*, he realises that only the modern (Mena, Manrique, or Íñigo de Mendoza) write poetry according to his *Arte*. R. Senabre, 'Poesía y poética en Juan del Encina' (205–16), casts some light on the rhetorical figures included in his *Arte de poesía castellana*. J. Weiss, 'Tiempo y materia en la poética de Juan del Encina' (241–57), underlines the social character that E. attributes to poetry, which is able to transform human beings. J. Lawrance, 'La tradición pastoril antes de 1530: imitación clásica e hibridación romancista en la *Traslación de las Bucólicas de Virgilio*, de Juan del Encina' (101–21), observes how the 15th-c. tradition of satire on political themes and the first Italian essays to imitate the classical bucolic converge in Encina. J. San José, 'Juan del Encina y los modelos exegéticos en la poesía religiosa del primer Renacimiento' (183–204), maintains that the poet behaves at the same time as a humanist in search of fame and a medieval author, proud of his art; hence his use of allegory. D. Ynduráin, 'Juan del Encina y el Humanismo' (259–80), considers the poet a humanist, a fact reflected in the conversational tone of his poetry, in the way it is conceived as a re-elaboration of traditional or classical texts, and in its intimate relationship with its circumstance. M. Á. Ferrer and J. F. de Dios, 'Aproximación metodológica al análisis musical de la obra enciniana' (335–43), propose a methodology which includes the consideration of the relation between music and lyrics, rhythm, melody, voices, etc. M. J. Vega, 'La teoría musical humanista y la poética del Renacimiento' (217–40), relates musical theory and philological recovery of the past in the Renaissance. A. Deyermond, 'La Biblia en la poesía de Juan del Encina' (55–68), studies biblical and typological elements in *Égloga II* and *Égloga IX*. C. Domínguez, 'El factor testimonial en los relatos de peregrinación: el caso de la *Tribagia* de Juan del Encina' (325–44), centres his attention on two devices to infuse the account with verisimilitude: the chronological order in the narrative and the use of eyewitnesses. L. Rodríguez Cacho, 'El viaje de Juan del Encina con el Marqués: otra lectura de la *Tribagia*' (163–82), focuses on the relationship between the Marquis of Tarifa and the poet during their journey. M. I. Hernández, 'El viaje y el descubrimiento: hacia una lectura devocional de la *Tribagia* de Juan del Encina' (367–78), follows E.'s spiritual experience. A. Beresford, ' "¿Quién es ésse que me llama? ¡váyase en hora buena!"': sobre las *Coplas de la muerte* atribuidas a Juan del Encina' (281–91), comments on its content, which is related to current ideas on death. M. Calderón, 'Los villancicos de Juan del Encina' (293–316), is a formal and thematic analysis. C. Parrilla, 'Encina y la ficción sentimental' (123–37), thinks that E. has taken certain elements from sentimental fiction to characterize psychologically the protagonists in the *Égloga de Fileno y Cardonio*. A. del Río, 'Figuras al margen: algunas notas sobre ermitaños, salvajes y pastores en tiempos de Juan del Encina' (147–56), shows how these types, who personify social vices, are a negative re-elaboration of other outcast figures, such as *santeros*, madmen, and courtly jesters. J. Sanz, ' "No venían mal unas coplas de buen palo, en estilo y metro de Juan del Encina". Reminiscencias de E. en unas *solemnes fiestas celebradas en honra de los santos mártires* (Salaman -ca, 1745)' (439–46), examines E.'s image as a semi-folkloric and festive poet. V. Infantes, 'Hacia la poesía impresa. Los pliegos sueltos poéticos de Juan del Encina: entre el cancionero manuscrito y el pliego impreso' (83–101), makes a complete inventory of E.'s work in *pliegos sueltos*; the relationship between the author and the editors suggests that E. took part in their diffusion.

OTHER POETS. B. Campos, 'La poesía de Diego de Soria: problemas de edición', *Actas* (Corunna), I, 145–52, carries out a codicological and textual study of the four poems by this author. Id., 'Escollos en la atribución de dos poemas satíricos: Rodrigo Manrique frente a Pedro Manrique', Parrilla, *Estudios*, 55–70, cannot resolve the attribution of them due to lack of data. J. Gutiérrez Carou, 'Dante en la poesía de Diego de Burgos', *AHLM* 7, II, 209–21, traces Dante's influence through the uses of vocabulary and of allegory. A. Chas, 'Notas a la edición de una serie poética desencuadernada en el manuscrito 2653 de la Biblioteca Universitaria de Salamanca', *Actas* (Corunna), I, 207–14, makes some metrical and textual observations on a series of five answers belonging to a truncated dialogue in S7. V. Blay, ' "Sin sentir nadie la mía": el discurso sordo de la mujer poeta en el ocaso de la Edad Media', *AHLM* 7, I, 353–71, takes as a starting point Florencia Pinar in order to explore female poetic discourse. A. López Castro, 'La vena satírica de Gil Vicente', *ib.*, II, 315–25, points out the poet's nostalgic character, which reveals a permanent desire for order. J. C. López Nieto, 'Estructura y significado del *dezir que fizo Juan Alfonso de Baena*', *ib.*, I, 327–39, is a detailed analysis of the complex structure of this interesting poem. L. Simó, 'Un olvidado poeta de cancionero: Diego del Castillo', *ib.*, III, 397–411, focuses on his elegy for Alfonso V of Aragon. M. Moreno, 'La autoría como problema en la edición de la obra poética de Nicolás Núñez, poeta del *Cancionero General* (Valencia, 1511)', *Actas* (Corunna), I, 463–78, hesitates to rely on the rubrics of the British Library MS (the so-called *Cancionero de Rennert*), of which he gives a *status questionis*. Id. 'Las variantes en el Ms. Add. 10431 de la British Library *(LB1)*', *AHLM* 7, I, 37–48, discusses MS variants. C. Tato, 'Reflexiones sobre PN8 a partir de la edición de IDO145 "Alto rey pues conoscemos" ', *Actas* (Corunna), I, 677–92, studies two copies of this poem by Pedro de Santa Fe and concludes that one derives from the other. The same author, 'Pedro de Santa Fe: ¿poeta en catalán?', Parrilla, *Estudios*, 113–35, thinks it reasonable to attribute to him the poem in SA7, 'Non siau tal pus conoixeu'. M. Pampín, 'Una traducción al francés del *Triunfo de las donas* de Juan Rodríguez del Padrón', *Actas* (Corunna), I, 509–19, discusses the three copies of the *Le Triumphe des dames*, dedicated to Philip the Good.

PROSE

CHIVALRESQUE AND SENTIMENTAL FICTION. Regula Rohland de Langbehn, *La unidad genérica de la novela sentimental española de los siglos XV y XVI* (PMHRS, 17), 111 pp., summarizes the findings of her previous studies, tracing the characteristics that define the sentimental romance. C. Alvar and J. M. Lucía Megías, 'Hacia el códice del *Tristán de Leonís* (cincuenta y nueve fragmentos manuscritos en la Biblioteca Nacional de Madrid)', *RLMed*, 11:9–135, is a description and a paleographic and critical edition of the 59 fragments of the Castilian *Tristán* in MS 22.644 located in the cover of MS Biblioteca

Nacional Madrid 12.915. J. M. Lucía, 'La edición de libros de caballerías castellanos: defensa de la puntuación original', *Actas* (Corunna), I, 402–14, defends maintaining the original punctuation, which he views as meaningful. E. Sales, 'Garci-Rodríguez de Montalvo, regidor de la noble villa de Medina del Campo', *RFE*, 79:123–58, analyses Montalvo's biography and locates several historical reference in his work. C. Rubio, 'Mares frente a Tristán: del triángulo amoroso al enfrentamiento caballeresco', *AHLM* 7, III, 311–18, investigates the differences between the Spanish version and its source. *Schiavo d'amore (Siervo libre de amor)*, ed. C. De Nigris, Milan–Trento, Luni, 211 pp., is a new edition with an Italian translation and an exhaustive bibliography. M. Pampín, 'La función de los caballos en la *Estoria de dos amadores* de Juan Rodríguez del Padrón', *AHLM* 7, III, 115–24, underlines the symbolic character of horses in the story. G. Pérez Barcala, 'La *Fábula do rossynhol* y la novela sentimental castellana', *ib.*, I, 157–68, comments on the influence of the *Divina commedia* and sentimental fiction on Duarte de Brito. A. Rivas, 'Juegos de ficción y realidad en el *Breve tratado de Grimalte y Gradissa*', Guijarro, *Humanismo*, 423–30, follows the interweaving of both levels in the novel. R. Rohland, 'Materiales sapienciales y emblemáticos en *Penitencia de amor*, de Pedro Manuel Giménez de Urrea', *Studia Hispanica Medievalia IV*, 262–71, argues against M. R. Lida that it is a didactic work. F. Carmona, 'Tradición poética e inserciones líricas en la novela sentimental', *AHLM* 7, II, 11–29, studies the inserted poems considering their medieval provenance.

AMADÍS DE GAULA. P. Gracia, 'Sobre el espíritu del primer *Amadís de Gaula*', *RLMed*, 11:247–253, believes with M. R. Lida in the existence of only one '*Amadís* primitivo' that ended with Amadís's death at the hands of Esplandián, while rejecting the existence of an '*Amadís* cortés', and argues that Amadís's death is the result of the fatalism inherited from the Arthurian cycle that circulated in the Peninsula and originated *Amadís*. R. Ramos, 'La transmisión textual del *Amadís de Gaula*', *AHLM* 7, III, 199–212, comments on editorial problems. E. Sales, 'Algunos aspectos de lo maravilloso en la tradición del *Amadís de Gaula*: serpientes, naos y otros prodigios', *ib.*, 345–60, studies their role in the narrative. A. Suárez, 'Gwynedd en el *Amadís de Gaula*', *Studia Hispanica Medievalia IV*, 272–84, thinks it is futile to search for Arthurian material in the novel because the names can be traced to Gaelic sources.

DIEGO DE SAN PEDRO. J. Gilkison, 'Utterings and mutterings in the prison of love: What can a fifteenth-century Spanish sentimental romance tell us about language attitudes?', *BHS(L)*, 76:315–25, finds that *Cárcel de Amor* examines the power of language through its consideration of the importance of written and spoken language and its juxtaposition of language and action, while attempting to discover new ways of viewing language through two conceptual metaphors ('language as war' and 'language as a container').

ALFONSO DE CARTAGENA. M. Campos Souto, 'Notas para una edición del *Memorial de Virtudes*', *Santiago-Otero Vol.*, I, 153–62, summarizes the content of Escorial MS 4–III-11, the only copy of the Spanish text of this work by Alfonso de Cartagena.

SERMONS

*Un sermonario castellano medieval*, introd. and ed. M. A. Sánchez, Salamanca U.P., 2 vols, 293 + 745 pp., provides us with the sermons from Biblioteca Universitaria Salamanca MS 1854 with a full study on medieval preaching dealing with the cultural, religious, and social milieu in which the sermons were composed. P. Cátedra, 'El taller del predicador. A propósito de un sermón castellano para el Domingo de Ramos (RAE, MS 294)', *Santiago-Otero Vol.*, I, 291–320, infers the elements on which the preacher built up a mnemotechnic net for the *pronunciatio* from the marginal glosses of a sermon. M. I. Toro, 'La transmisión impresa de los sermones castellanos de San Vicente Ferrer', *Actas* (Corunna), I, 719–30, constructs a *stemma* on the data provided by ten editions, and chooses *T* as *codex optimus*. R. Muñoz, 'Estrategias de persuasión y oyentes judíos en dos sermones de san Vicente Ferrer', *El Olivo*, 33:25–43, focuses on two sermons by Vicente Ferrer and the way they appeal to Jews. J. Guadalajara, 'La edad del Anticristo y el año del fin del mundo, según fray Vicente Ferrer', *Santiago-Otero Vol.*, I, 321–42, traces the saint's obsession with the Antichrist to a revelation by a hermit during a visit to Italy. Martín Martínez de Ampiés, *Libro del Anticristo. Declaración del sermón de San Vicente (1496)*, ed. F. Gilbert, Pamplona, Eunsa, 186 pp., edits these two texts according to the 1496 edition with a thorough study of their sources.

TRANSLATION

R. Recio, 'La evolución de las ideas sobre traducción y traductor en Castilla: la introducción del *Infierno* de Villegas', *AHLM* 7, I, 213–20, summarizes ideas about translation in 15th-c. Spain. G. Avenoza, 'El manuscrito catalán de la *Visión deleitable* de A. de la Torre', *ib.*, 275–91, gives notice of a Catalan translation kept in the Biblioteca Lambert Mata (Reus), and inserts it in the *stemma* proposed by J. García López. C. Wittlin, 'Traducciones medievales: Tito Livio. Resumen y complementos', *ib.*, 233–40, comments on several aspects of the Romance translations. M. L. Cuesta, 'Problemas para la edición de las "traducciones" medievales de la "materia de Bretaña', *Actas* (Corunna), I, 193–205, finds that the most intricate problem for the editor is to decide whether the text is a translation or an adaptation with its own independent artistic value. M. L. Antonaya, 'La literatura *adversus iudæos*: obras de polémica religiosa (un manuscrito del siglo XV)', *ib.*, 97–102, gives notice of BNM MS 10276, that contains a Castilian treatise by Jerónimo de Santa Fe, whose sources are *Ad convincentum perfidiam iudæorum* and *De Iudaicis erroribus ex Talmut*. S. Fellous, 'La Biblia de Alba. Traduction et exégèse', *Santiago-Otero Vol.*, II, 1601–25, centres her attention on the preliminaries, where the translator proposes a philosophical and moral reading of the Bible so that it could became a meeting point for Christian and Jewish thought alike.

HISTORIOGRAPHY

J. L. Fuertes, 'Filosofía de la historia y utopía en el XV. Una aproximación al *Speculum vitae humanae* (1468) de Rodrigo Sánchez de Arévalo', *Santiago-Otero Vol.*, II, 1317–46, is a detailed examination of its content. B. Tate, 'Poles apart. Two official historians of the Catholic monarchs — Alfonso de Palencia and Fernando del Pulgar', *ib.*, I, 439–63, traces a fascinating and clarifying parallel between both royal historians. G. S. Hutcheson, 'Desperately seeking Sodom: queerness in the chronicles of Álvaro de Luna', Blackmore, *Queer Iberia*, 222–49, argues that Luna was not so much queered by texts and contexts as he was himself the source of queerness, the destabilizer even of those works intent on reinscribing him as the locus of normativity. B. Weissberger, '¡A tierra, puto! Alfonso de Palencia's discourse of effeminacy', *ib.*, 291–324, comments on the well-known references of the historian to Enrique IV's homosexuality, which are interpreted as an ideological weapon in favour of Isabel I. M. M. López Valero, 'La representación del hecho histórico y la estrategia dramática del discurso. Una aproximación a las crónicas medievales', *AHLM* 7, II, 339–41, examines the narrative elements in relation with the chronicler's interests. M. Á. Pallarés, 'La *Crónica de Aragón*, de Gauberto Fabricio de Vagad, una cuestión de Estado. Sobre el encargo de su redacción y de los problemas para ser impresa', Guijarro, *Humanismo*, 409–22, deals with the economic aspects of the original edition (1496–1499). J. M. Nieto Soria, 'La *Avisación de la dignidad real* (1445) en el contexto de la confrontación política de su tiempo', *Santiago-Otero Vol.*, I, 404–37, rejects the dating of H. O. Bizzarri who places the text at the end of the 14th c., and relates the *Avisación* to the Cortes de Olmedo.

OTHER PROSE WRITERS

Pedro de Chincilla, *Libro de la Historia Troyana*, ed. María Dolores
Peláez Benítez, M, Complutense, 413 pp., includes an ample intro-
duction that considers the presence of the Troy legend in medieval
Italy, France, and Spain, studies the *Historia* within its cultural and
literary contexts, and examines the MS language. S. Miguel-Prendes,
*El espejo y el piélago. La 'Eneida' castellana de Enrique de Villena*, Kassel,
Reichenberger, 1998, 306 pp., considers its gloss from the perspective
of the scholarly tradition. C. Brown, 'Queer representation in the
Arçipreste de Talavera, or *The Maldezir de mugeres* is a drag',
Blackmore, *Queer Iberia*, 73–103, offers a new reading of Talavera
based on the analysis of female representations and the reconstruction
of their voices. J. Fradejas Lebrero, 'Bibliografía crítica de fray
Hernando de Talavera', *Santiago-Otero Vol.*, II, 1347–58, also offers
some short commentaries. Á. Alonso, 'Rodríguez del Padrón, Inés de
Castro y la materia de Bretaña', Botta, *Inês*, 35–44, uncovers in the
lover's death in the *Estoria de dos amadores* an account based on the
murder of Inés. Id., 'El duelo de Persio y Leriano en *Cárcel de Amor*',
*Studia Hispanica Medievalia IV*, 255–61, cites a new source for Leriano's
combat against Persion in the duel between Hector des Mares and
Marigart in the *Prose Lancelot*. L. Simó, 'Un ejemplo de anotación a
dos citas legales contenidas en el *Tratado de las armas* de Diego de
Varela', *Actas* (Corunna), I, 649–65, establishes that two quotations
from the *Séptima Partida* do not follow the 1491 edition of Alfonso X's
legislative work. F. López Estrada, 'La "Embajada a Tamorlán"
castellana como libro de relación entre occidente y oriente en la Edad
Media', pp. 73–80 of *Mélanges María Soledad Carrasco Urgoiti*, ed.
E. Abdeljelil Temimi, Zaghouan, Fondation Temimi pour la Recherche Scientifique et l'Information, I, examines how otherness is
perceived in this travel account, which he edits with a lengthy
introduction and taking into account a new MS. J. M. Martínez
Torrejón, 'Neither/nor: dialogue in Juan de Lucena's *Libro de vida
beata*', *MLN*, 114:211–22, compares it with its sources and studies the
adaptation of the dialogue to the author's society. C. Salinas, 'La
*Epístola a los valientes letrados de España* del Príncipe de Viana', *AHLM 7*,
III, 361–71, is an interesting study on its form and content in relation
to Humanism. M. Amasuno, 'El *regimen sanitatis* en el pseudo
aristotélico *Secreto de los secretos*', *ib.*, I, 263–73, reviews the *ars medica* in
Castile at the end of the 15th c. and the sorry state of health during
that period, and offers a critical presentation of the doctrinal content
of the *regimen sanitatis* inserted in the *Secreto*. *\*Electronic Text and
Concordances of Alfonso Fernández de Palencia's 1492 Spanish Translation of
Flavius Josephus' "Guerra Judáica"*, ed. L. Fernando Tejedo-Herrero,

Pablo Ancos García, and Kyle T. Kendall, Madison, HSMS, CD-ROM. *Electronic Text and Concordances of Juan Alfonso de Zamora's Spanish Translation of 'Los nueve libros de Valerio Maximo' as contained in BNM MS. 2208*, ed. Stephen D. Johnson, Madison, HSMS, CD-ROM.

## THEATRE

C. Stern, 'Recovering the theater of medieval Spain (and Europe): the Islamic evidence', *La corónica*, 27.2 : 119–53, drawing especially on the work of Shmuel Moreh, considers the evidence of Islamic theatre in medieval Iberia (comic actors, mimetic dances, agon-dance drama, pageants and processions, puppet theatre, etc.), showing that that the commonly held view that Islam exerted no influence on indigenous and Roman forms of theatre is unfounded. F. J. Flores Arroyuelo, 'Teatro en el palacio medieval', *AHLM* 7, II, 155–65, analyses passages from the *Crónica de Juan II de Castilla* that reveal theatrical elements of the period. G. Hilty, 'El *Auto de los Reyes Magos*, ¿enigma literario y lingüístico?', *ib.*, II, 235–44, deals with the author's linguistic and cultural background. A. M. Álvarez Pellitero, 'Tradición y modernidad en el teatro de Juan del Encina', Guijarro, *Humanismo*, 15–26, comments on traditional elements found in Encina's modernization of his theatre. M. García-Bermejo, 'La Pasión según Juan del Encina', *ib.*, 345–55, tries to explain his religious representations in relation to rhetorical means such as *ekphrasis* or *descriptio* and *enargeia* or *evidentia*, and to spiritual works called *contemplaciones*. M. Á. Pérez Priego, 'Juan del Encina y el teatro de su tiempo', *ib.*, 139–45, observes in Encina's innovations the transmission of dramatic pieces, ordered temporally and by plot in a Cancionero; the initiation of the dramatic *égloga*; the presence of the *pastor confidente*, pastoral dialogue, and rustic language. F. Maurizi, 'Aproximación a la escritura teatral de Juan del Encina', *Studia Hispanica Medievalia IV*, 314–24, reflects on Encina's so-called 'segunda producción dramática', noting that the said period has nothing to do with his time in Italy. A. López Castro, 'Gil Vicente y su actitud ante la muerte', Guijarro, *Humanismo*, 385–98, comments on two aspects related to death in Vicente's theatre: the eschatological rite of passage and the treatment of the figure of Death. *Historia de los espectáculos en España*, ed. A. Amorós and J. M. Díez Borque, M, Castalia, 575 pp., includes: M. J. Ruiz Mayordomo, 'Espectáculos de baile y danza. Edad Media' (273–318), dealing with the Middle Ages (especially at pp. 275–87), and looking at the religious and liturgical realm and the role of the court. C. Alvar, 'Espectáculos de la fiesta. Edad Media' (177–206), shows the difficulty in the Middle Ages of separating spectacle, festival, and liturgy, and divides his study into two parts: festivals of the liturgical calendar, and civil celebrations. E. Lacarra, 'Espectáculos de la voz y la palabra. Juglares y afines' (405–18), offers an overall view of the theme: moral valuation, legislation of the profession, social condition, education, and activities of troubadours and *juglares*. J. González Cuenca, 'Espectáculos nobiliarios de riesgo: el torneo y sus variantes' (487–506), deals with the activities of knighthood when it found itself beyond war: the *riebto*, participation on stages, etc. A. M. Álvarez Pellitero, 'Espectáculos teatrales. Edad Media' (19–36), is an overall view of medieval Spanish theatre, with a section on the principal works.

## ALJAMIADO LITERATURE
POSTPONED

## LITERATURE, 1490–1700
## (PROSE AND POETRY)
POSTPONED

## LITERATURE, 1490–1700 (DRAMA)
POSTPONED

# LITERATURE, 1700–1823

By GABRIEL SÁNCHEZ ESPINOSA, *Lecturer in Hispanic Studies,*
*The Queen's University of Belfast*

## I. BIBLIOGRAPHY AND PRINTING

BIBLIOGRAPHY. F. Aguilar Piñal, *Bibliografía de Autores Españoles del
siglo XVIII. vol.* IX: anónimos I, M, CSIC, contains some 6,352 entries
alphabetically ordered according to their first significant word. This
long awaited tool for *dieciochistas*, that includes some extremely useful
indexes — of names, subjects, printers and topographical — will soon
be followed by volume X, the last of the series, that will be devoted to
legal and normative texts, chronologically ordered.

BOOKS AND PRINTING. F. Aguilar Piñal has also published *La
biblioteca y el monetario del académico Cándido María Trigueros (1798),*
Seville U.P., 154 pp., a study and edition of the posthumous
manuscript inventory of the collection of books and coins of the
Enlightenment writer and antiquarian, who died in 1798, and
donated his books to the *Reales Estudios de San Isidro*, where he had
been librarian. 60% of this collection of 1,073 books are works in
Latin; 18th-c. books make up nearly 49%; only 21% of the works are
Spanish printed works. This painstaking study by Aguilar Piñal
rounds off his earlier works dedicated to the life and works of this
man of letters. A. Megged, '*Revalorando* las luces en el mundo hispano:
la primera y única librería de Agustín Dhervé a mediados del siglo
XVIII en la ciudad de México', *BH*, 101 : 147–73, taking as its base
the inventory diligently sent to the Santo Oficio in May of 1759 (that
is to say, before the enthronement of Charles III) in accordance with
the regulations imposed by the printing commissioner J. Curiel, this
study evaluates the stocks of this bookshop that had family and
commercial links with Seville. *Los libros de Francisco de Bruna en el Palacio
del Rey*, ed. M.-L. López-Vidriero, Seville, Patrimonio Nacional–
Fundación El Monte, 652 pp., is a meticulous catalogue of the 225
printed works and 35 manuscripts that were added to the private
library of Charles IV in December 1807, after the death of F. de
Bruna, the uncompromising judge of the *Audiencia* of Seville, fre-
quenter of the *tertulia* held by the Peruvian Pablo de Olavide, and
member of the *Sociedad Patriótica Sevillana* from its foundation in 1775,
who brought together in Seville a library containing some 3,500
books and also a renowned cabinet of antiquities and curiosities.

## 2. THOUGHT AND THE ENLIGHTENMENT

R. Fernández Durán, *Gerónimo de Uztáriz (1670–1732): una política económica para Felipe V*, M, Minerva, 441 pp. J. Huerta Calvo and E. Palacios Fernández, *Al margen de la Ilustración: cultura popular, arte y literatura en la España del siglo XVIII*, Amsterdam, Rodopi, 1998, 245 pp., considers 'popular' figures (*bandoleros, majos*), texts (*comedias de bandidos, comedias de magia*), and practices (carnival) on the margins of 'elitist' enlightened discourse. The following articles stand out amongst those included: M.-C. García de Enterría, 'Magos y santos en la literatura popular (superstición y devoción en el Siglo de las Luces)' (53–76); J. Álvarez Barrientos, 'Teatro y espectáculo a costa de santos y magos' (77–95); E. Huertas Vázquez, 'Los majos madrileños y sus barrios en el teatro popular' (117–43) and N. Glendinning, 'Motivos carnavalescos en la obra de Goya' (207–18).

E. Lluch, 'La España vencida del siglo XVIII. El cameralismo, la Corona de Aragón y el "partido aragonés" o 'militar"', pp. 129–62 of Id., *Las Españas vencidas del siglo XVIII. Claroscuros de la Ilustración*, B, Crítica, 252 pp., ponders the influence of the figure of Frederick II of Prussia and Prussian cameralism (Bielefeld) on Spanish reformist literature and ideas in the second half of the 18th century. Ll. takes as an example of this Prussian influence the figure of the Count of Aranda and his continuous social prestige. It is interesting to note, in the same book by Ll., the article 'Contrapuntos de la Corona de Castilla: Sarmiento, Campomanes y Jovellanos' (163–215), that gives a global vision of their economic stance. Ll. emphasizes the influence of Sarmiento in Campomanes and calls into question Jovellanos's free trade image, underlining his protectionist proposals. J. Pérez Magallón, 'Lo francés en España, entre el Barroco y la Ilustración', *RLit*, 122:389–425, attempts to revise the received opinion that sees the beginning of French cultural influence in Spain in the change of dynasty brought about by the death of Charles II in 1700. Pérez Magallón, however, observes a continuity of attitude and interests of the social and intellectual elites in the decades preceding 1700. F. Sánchez-Blanco, *La mentalidad ilustrada*, M, Taurus, 386 pp., is a controversial reflection, from the perspective of the history of ideas, centred on the modes of implantation of the Enlightenment in Spain under Philip V and Ferdinand VI, periods that are looked down upon by those who place the real Enlightenment in the final third of the 18th century. S.-B. situates the true Enlightenment more on the side of the *novatores* and Feijoo, than on the eclectic current of thought headed by the erudite Valencian Mayans. The social and cultural implications of the *novator* movement lead directly to "enlightened" attitudes by the mid-18th c. especially during the government of the Marquis of Ensenada, and S.-B. observes a crisis in enlightened thought in the first years of the reign of Charles III. S.-B. judges it absurd to identify *las luces* with Charles III's technocratic realisations and despotism. The controversy arising from this solid work and the responses it will generate, will no doubt help to clarify our understanding of the significance of this cultural movement in Spain after a period of undoubted critical abuse of the application of the terms *Ilustración* and *ilustrado*. S.-B. promises a future study, along the same lines, dedicated to the reigns of Charles III and Charles IV.

## 3. LITERARY HISTORY

GENERAL. J. Álvarez Barrientos, 'La República de las Letras se representa', *Salina*, 13:41–50, examines the changes that take place in 18th-c. Spain with regard to the portrayal of the writer in paintings and prints: gradually the traditional iconographic signs that identified the writer as a member of the *República literaria* disapear, being replaced by those that signal the social class of the person portrayed. A. Amorós, *Siglo XVIII. Antología comentada de la Literatura española*, M, Castalia, 303 pp., despite its title, is more a history of literature than a true anthology of individually commented literary texts. The ensuing result is a hybrid mix of theoretical discussion, anthology of literary texts, and an unupdated selection of critical works. Bearing in mind that it aims at the university reader, it competes poorly against rigorous 18th-c. literary histories with such diverse focuses as those of G. Carnero and F. Aguilar Piñal, as well as against anthologies as original as that dedicated to the 18th-c. Spanish essay by F. Sánchez-Blanco. P. Deacon, 'El autor esquivo en la cultura española del siglo XVIII: apuntes sobre decoro, estrategias y juegos', *Dieciocho*, 22:213–36, classifies and comments on the diversity of stratagems and disguises used in 18th-c. texts in order to hide true authorship. The causes of this phenomenon vary from fear at the possible harmful repercussions brought on by expressing proscribed ideas through literature, to personal inhibition and reticence. F. López, 'Los *Quijotes* de la Ilustración', *ib.*, 247–64, studies the changes in the position of the *Quijote* and Cervantes in the literary canon of 18th-c. Spain. L. sees a political motivation behind the edition of the *Quijote* produced by Lord Carteret: to attract the then indecisive and neutral Spain to English positions. R. Schmidt, *The Canonization of Don Quixote through Illustrated Editions of the Eighteenth Century*, Montreal, McGill-Queen's U.P., 248 pp.

PERIODICAL LITERATURE. E. Larriba, *Le Public de la presse en Espagne à la fin du XVIIIe siècle (1781–1808)*, Paris, Champion, 1998,

403 pp., analyses a collection of 15,000 subscriptions to 18 periodical publications, taken out by a total of 8,526 different individuals. L. clarifies the overwhelming preponderance of Madrid in the consumption of publications, in view of their widespread diffusion in outlying areas of Spain. She points out the dominance of the middle class within the reading public and identifies a reduced, but enthusiastic, group of women readers that the periodical writers make great efforts to capture.

4. INDIVIDUAL AUTHORS

ARTEAGA. E. de Arteaga, *Investigaciones filosóficas sobre la belleza ideal*, ed. F. Molina, M, Tecnos, 293 pp., is a new edition of this work, originally published in Spain in 1789, re-edited now alongside the *Carta a don Antonio Ponz sobre la filosofía de Píndaro, Virgilio y Lucano*, that also appeared the same year. This publication, adequately annotated, once again puts at the reader's disposal two texts fundamental to the study of the intense debate concerning the idea of beauty and its presence in works of art that took place in neo-classical Spain.

BLANCO WHITE. A.-G. Loureiro, '*The Examination of Blanco by White*', *REH*, 33 : 3–40, edits Blanco's first autobiographical account written between December 1818 and the end of the summer of 1819, according to the unpublished manuscript kept in the University of Liverpool Library. In this text, in the form of an interrogation, L. sees the recent convert to Anglicanism trying to confront his erotic inclinations, and his relapse into atheism during the last years of his life in Spain.

CADALSO. J. Cadalso, *Los eruditos a la violeta y Suplemento*, 2 vols, Seville, Alfar, 68, 82 pp., is a facsimile edition of the first editions of these works originally published in Madrid in 1772 by the printer A. de Sancha. E. Scarlett, 'Mapping out the *Cartas Marruecas*: geographical, cultural, and gender coordinates', *REH*, 33 : 65–83, focuses on the tension between the goal of Europeanization and the strong criticism of Eurocentrism as unsuited to the Spanish national identity revealed in Cadalso's work through the masks of the Moroccan correspondents.

CIENFUEGOS. P. Álvarez de Miranda, 'Unas cartas desconocidas entre Nicasio Álvarez de Cienfuegos y el misterioso Florián Coetanfao: nuevos datos sobre una intensa amistad', *Dieciocho*, 22 : 177–212, edits and annotates the letters exchanged between the poet and the French botanist and mineralogist in May 1791. This correspondence, fascinating in that it gives us the opportunity to gain knowledge about the character and poetic formation of C., is also an excellent document for studying the value and intensity of friendship between enlightened men.

ISLA.  J.-F. de Isla, *Historia de la expulsión de los jesuitas (memorial de las cuatro provincias de España de la Compañía de Jesús desterradas del Reino a S.M. el rey don Carlos III)*, ed. E. Giménez López, Alicante, Instituto de cultura Juan Gil-Albert, 245 pp., presents a text somewhere between the factual account and the apology written by Father Isla in Corsica during the months immediately after the expulsion of the Jesuits from Spain. The editor situates this text in the context of the 'combat' literature written in defence of the Company of Jesus, produced in Italy by the exiled Spanish Jesuits, in which Isla participated significantly despite his age and ailments.

MÁRQUEZ.  A. Romani, 'Pedro José Márquez (1741–1820) e l'immagine del Messico antico nella sua opera sulla architettura precolombiana', *AHSJ*, 67, 1998:131–60, studies the efforts of this exiled Mexican Jesuit to spread and defend the culture and architecture of the ancient Mexicans in neoclassical Italy. Whilst in Rome, M. moved in the circles frequented by J.-N. de Azara and dedicated his time to the study of classical architecture.

TORRES VILLARROEL.  *Revisión de Torres Villarroel*, ed. M.-M. Pérez López and E. Martínez Mata, Salamanca U.P., 1998, 216 pp., brings together works produced for the *I encuentro sobre Torres Villaroel y su tiempo*, which took place in October 1995 in the University of Salamanca. The purpose of this collection of studies, of diverse perspectives and conclusions, is to open the controversy surrounding this unique author's position within 18th-c. Spanish literature and the Enlightenment. M-M. Pérez López (14–35), endeavours to dismantle common opinions and critical judgements that place T. in the Baroque, counter-reformist world, and that consider him distant from the newly-formed modernity; E. Martínez Mata (93–102), sees in T. the renovator of a genre until then insipid, the *almanaques*, that would create his popularity and bring him not insignificant economic benefits; P. Álvarez de Miranda (79–91), studies the well-known episode, which took place in 1723, of ghosts in the house of the Countess of los Arcos, told by T. in the '*Trozo tercero*' of his *Vida*, and previously outlined in his *Anatomía de todo lo visible e invisible* in 1738. Álvarez de Miranda has discovered a third version, a direct product of T.'s oral testimony, in the second part of Mañer's *Anti-Theatro Crítico* of 1731. Miranda indicates the ambiguous position held by T., between superstitious fear and a certain scepticism that cannot be termed enlightened. L. Fernández Cifuentes (155–71), focuses on the problematic '*Trozo quinto*' of the *Vida*, almost entirely dedicated to the account of a grave and unknown illness, in accordance with the Foucaultian understanding of illness as an 'individual experience'. He sets the vision of the illness of T.'s autobiography — an entirely 18th-c. outlook — in opposition to that of Blanco White — characteristically romantic. J.-M. Sala Valldaura, 'Talía juguetona o el teatro de Torres Villarroel', *RLit*, 122:427–47, offers a panoramic view of his *teatro de circunstancias*, written to be performed in private homes. He judges T.'s *teatro breve*, distanced as it is from contemporary reality, as being unrelated to the *sainetes* by Ramón de la Cruz unlike the *entremeses* of L. Quiñones de Benavente. VARGAS PONCE. *Había bajado de Saturno. Diez calas en la obra de José Vargas Ponce, seguidas de un opúsculo inédito del mismo autor*, ed. F. Durán López and A. Romero Ferrer, Cadiz U.P.–Instituto Feijoo de Estudios del Siglo XVIII, 237 pp., is a collection of studies of the widely dispersed work of this enlightened naval officer and writer. The following articles stand out amongst those included: J. Álvarez Barrientos, ' "Había bajado de Saturno." José de Vargas Ponce en la República de las Letras' (55–98); G. Espigado Tocino, 'El pensamiento pedagógico de José Vargas Ponce' (133–67).

## LITERATURE, 1823–1898

POSTPONED

# LITERATURE, 1898–1936

By K. M. SIBBALD, *McGill University*

## I. GENERAL

BIBLIOGRAPHY. C. Byrne, 'Review of miscellanies', *BHS(G)*, 76:727–36, lists items not recorded here on Baroja, Juan Ramón Jiménez, and Unamuno. More limited in scope, J. E. Serrano, 'Los estudios sobre la literatura en Aragón del siglo XX', *Jornadas de Filología Aragonesa*, Zaragoza, Institución 'Fernando el Católico', 129–61, has much bibliographical information on the *Revista de Aragón* and *Noreste*, José García Mercadal, Ramón J. Sender, Benjamín Jarnés, Luis Buñuel, and vanguard writing.

LITERARY AND CULTURAL HISTORY. José Esteban and Anthony N. Zahareas, *Los proletarios del arte. Introducción a la Bohemia*, M, Celeste, 1998, 235 pp., initiate a *Biblioteca de la Bohemia* and reflect on the intellectual significance of those like Julio Camba, Ernesto Bark, Ramón Pérez de Ayala, Cansinos-Assens, Joaquín Dicenta, and Alejandro Sawa who figure in this anthology of testimonies, *manifiestos*, self-portraits, and contemporary critiques. R. Alarcón Sierra, 'La ciudad y el domingo; el poeta y la muchedumbre. (De Baudelaire a Manuel Machado)', *ALEC*, 24:35–64, is a long *flânerie* through *El País*, *Juventud*, *La Ilustración Artística*, *ABC*, and *Los lunes de El Imparcial*, that takes in the changing visions of the aesthetic experience of urban life from Baudelaire's Paris through the turn of the century and on to *El mal poema*, with general comments on Baroja and Blasco Ibáñez, the Madrid School of Pedro de Répide, Emiliano Ramírez, Andrés González Blanco, Antonio de Hoyos, and Alberto Insúa, by way of Mauricio Bacarisse, Tomás Morales, Moreno Villa, Ramón Basterra, Gómez de la Serna, Gerardo Diego, and Juan Larrea. P. V. Greene, 'Utopías y utopistas en la España finisecular', *REH*, 33:325–36, quotes Unamuno to define the former as 'la sal de la vida' and the latter as both 'caballos de carrera' and 'la casta de los utilísimos pensadores de silla', so justifying a quick gallop through *La Revista Blanca* from 1885 on. Attention continues to focus on the Generation of 1898. M. A. Salgado, 'Rubén Darío y la Generación del 98. Personas, personajes y máscaras del fin del siglo español', *His(US)*, 82:725–32, studies Darío's *semblanzas* of the Generation that moulded both their vision of themselves and that of their readers; while C. Álvarez-Ude, 'Entre dos 98: *bestsellers*, crítica literaria, medios de communicación y otros apuntes', *ALEC*, 24:275–95, is a general overview of the 20th c. with particular comments on Unamuno, Ortega, Valle-Inclán, and Pedro Salinas.

The centenary celebration continues in print and quite typical are the following collections: *CA*, 74, highlights the American perspective and of interest here are: E. Zuleta Álvarez, 'España y América en el pensamiento de Ramiro de Maeztu' (36–49), M. Andueza, 'Miguel de Unamuno y la literatura hispanoamericana' (50–62), and L. Quintana Tejera, 'La Generación del 98 y el modernismo literario latinoamericano como expresión de la forma hispana de una crisis universal de valores' (114–23). *La independencia de las últimas colonias españolas y su impacto nacional e internacional*, ed. José María Ruano de la Haza, Ottawa, Dovehouse, 373 pp., ranges over accounts of the Spanish American War in the press of Argentina, Uruguay, and Canada, comments on the *Maine* episode, and summations of the after effects in Cuba, Puerto Rico, and the US, but of particular relevance here is the section dedicated to the Spanish writers of the turn of the century and after: L. Iglesias Feijoo, 'La generación del 98: tradición y modernidad' (193–211); E. I. Fox, 'El trasfondo intelectual del 98' (212–27); J. Pérez-Magallón and J. L. Suárez, 'Política e ironía en las *Cartas finlandesas* de Ángel Ganivet' (228–44); R. de la Fuente Ballesteros, 'Mundo fenoménico / mundo nouménico: una clave finisecular (Unamuno / Ganivet / Baroja)' (245–60); M. J. Valdés, 'Salamanca 1898: Unamuno en la hoguera' (261–78); F. Florit Durán, 'La recuperación de la literatura del Siglo de Oro en algunos ensayos del 98' (279–96); F. J. Díez de Revenga, 'Poesía del 98 y compromiso (decadencia, caciquismo, pobreza y emigración en Vicente Medina)' (297–321); A. Bagués, 'Donjuanes de la España finisecular' (322–31); A. Percival, '*Reposo*, novela de un intelectual noventayochista. Rafael Altamira' (332–40); J. Rubiera Fernández, 'Ortega y Gasset y la Generación del 98' (341–53); and A. Madroñal Durán, 'El 98 visto por el teatro simbolista: *Tiempo de 98* de Juan Antonio Castro' (354–72). *RILCE*, 15, appears as *Del 98 al 98. Literatura e historia en el siglo XX hispánico*, ed. Víctor García Ruiz, Rosa Fernández Urtasun, and David K. Herzberger, Pamplona, Universidad de Navarra–SSSAS, Univ. of Connecticut, 386 pp., the proceedings of rather uneven quality of the May 1998 Conference, of which of interest here are: L. Iglesias Feijoo, 'Sobre la invención del 98' (3–12), advocating an inclusive grouping of writers born with modernity; A. Carreño, 'Los silencios críticos de una recepción: Lope de Vega' (141–55), documenting parallel lines of interest in both Góngora and Lope in the 20th c., with comments on Alberti, Antonio Machado, Azorín, Miguel Hernández, Gerardo Diego, Aleixandre, and José Hierro; and A. Sinclair, 'Unamuno y Baroja ante el debate arte / ciencia' (159–69), taking as examples *El árbol de la ciencia* and *Abel Sánchez* to illustrate a debate at once impassioned but never resolved as Baroja deconstructs the traditional difference while

Unamuno stands it on its head. The junket for the 'other' centenaries celebrated in 1998 continues and J. Cano Ballester, 'Tres voces (airadas) de una generación: Federico García Lorca, Vicente Aleixandre y Dámaso Alonso', Díez de Revenga, *Tres poetas*, 9–32, provides a good summing-up for the *homenajes* reviewed below under the individual authors. Moving on, interest quickens in the Roaring Twenties and the *avant-garde: Nuevos caminos en la investigación de los años en España*, ed. Harald Wentzlaff-Eggebert, Tübingen, Niemeyer, 1998, 161 pp., turns away from the usual definitions in order to concentrate on attempts in Spain at renovation and radical chic as portrayed in sport, jazz, the silent cinema, and a nascent feminism, and contains much useful bibliography and some helpful pointers for new research in the following essays: J. Mecke, 'Literatura española y literatura europea — aspectos historiográficos y estéticos de una relación problemática' (1–17), which cites Valle-Inclán's *esperpentos*, Antonio Machado's *apócrifos*, and Unamuno's *agonismo* as literary practices that constitute a refraction of European modernity in Spain; F. Wolfzettel, 'Mitologización de lo propio e identidad nacional — la Generación del 98 y los mitos literarios' (19–25), which points up a peculiar *alteridad* in Spanish literature whose myths have a precise collective dimension and reviews with substantial bibliography the treatment of Don Quixote, Don Juan, La Celestina, and El Cid in this regard; M. Rössner, 'Jardiel Poncela — el café como taller de la estética vanguardista' (27–35), proposing the microcosmos of café society as the site of vanguard humour in Spain; S. Salaün, 'Vanguardias estéticas en España' (37–46), which argues cogently for the re-definition of the vanguard, within a revised time frame and with due consideration of the phenomena of cosmopolitanism and cultural interchange, that would update the literary criticism of the 1940s and 1950s and permit new textual readings; H. Wentzlaff-Eggebert, 'Literatura, arte y vida en las vanguardias españoles' (47–53), which outlines fruitful options for future research on the links between art and literature in, particularly, 'la generación unipersonal de Ramón Gómez de la Serna', and the mixing of media as in the case of music in Gerardo Diego, literature, and Buñuel, and the art and poetry of Moreno Villa, Juan Larrea, and Rafael Alberti; M. Scholz-Hänsel, 'El surrealismo español (1924–51) y la necesidad de una perspectiva intercultural en la historia del arte' (55–69), which deplores the absence of serious monographs on the writings of Salvador Dalí and Maruja Mallo and posits a true connection from 1924 to the 1950s (this despite the usual cut-off at the Civil War) by using reception theory to research both the Madrid and Barcelona Schools and their various artists; C. Serrano, 'Continuidad y recuperación de los mitos literarios — Don Juan y el teatro en España durante los años 20' (71–76), which follows on from his earlier collection of *Don Juanes* (see *YWMLS*, 60:266) with comments on Federico Oliver's *Han matado a Don Juan* (1929); U. Fetten, 'El discurso onírico e internacional en la obra de Federico García Lorca' (77–81), pressing for a homoerotic study that does not fall into the Freudian trap; V. Roloff, 'Literatura y cine en los años 20 en España — procesos intermediales en el surrealismo' (83–90), which lobbies for greater attention to be paid to the surrealists' literary efforts in a proper multimedia approach; J. Heymann, 'La imagen literizada de la vanguardia y el cine. Ramón — Ayala — Jardiel' (91–105), moving from *Cinelandia* (1923), *via* the writings of Ayala and Jarnés to Jardiel Poncela's four novels, *Amor se escribe sin hache* (1929), *Espérame en Siberia, vida mía* (1929), *Pero . . .¿hubo alguna vez once mil vírgenes?* (1931), and *La tournée de Dios* (1932), to reflect deeply on film theory and the word-image phenomenon; D. Miglos, 'Huellas ramonianas en *Estación. Ida y vuelta* o en busca de una prosa vanguardista' (107–13), which is a brief analysis of some Chacelian images that display a certain *estilo greguerístico*, echo Jiménez's *Diario de un poeta reciencasado*, and hint at parallels with Max Ernst; M. Albert, 'La prosa narrativa de vanguardia y su viraje político' (115–26), outlining a plan of action to recoup vanguard novelists like Valentín Andrés Álvarez, Felipe Ximénez de Sandoval, and Francisco Guillén Salaya among others; M. Prudon, 'De un manifiesto a otro — aproximacion(es) textual(es)' (127–37), comparing the *Manifest Groc*, signed by Lluís Montanyà, Sebastià Gasch, and Dalì on 28 March 1928, and the manifesto of the ADLAN Group (Los Amigos de las Artes Nuevos), signed by Luis Blanco Soler, Norah Borges de Torre, Ángel Ferrant, José Moreno Villa, Gustavo Pittaluga, and Guillermo de Torre in 1932; M. C. Zimmermann, 'Ruptura, creación y vanguardia en la poesía española de los años 20. Estudio comparativo sincrónico de J. R. Jiménez, A. Machado, F. García Lorca, R. Alberti y G. Diego' (139–50), which takes *Piedra y cielo*, *Canciones*, *Libro de poemas*, *Marinero en tierra*, and *Manual de espuma* as key texts forming a theoretical *isocentro* that explains the close and disparate nature of writers of the vanguard; while C. Rodick, 'Las antologías del 27 — enfoques y (des)ajustes' (151–61), indicates Diego's now classic anthology of 1932 as the model generally followed but prefers Díez de Revenga's 1987 *Panorama* of the group (see *YWMLS*, 49:354), notes that before 1980 Guillén and Aleixandre share top honours that after 1980 go to García Lorca exclusively, and makes some interesting observations about how anthologies composed inside and outside Spain differ in conception and purpose; M. F. Vilches de Frutos, 'La otra vanguardia histórica: cambios sociopolíticos en la narrativa y el teatro español de preguerra (1926–1936)', *ALEC*, 24:243–74, explains in a mass of detail how history becomes the stuff of literature in the key period by paying particular reference to the 'Generación del Nuevo Romanticismo' and the theatre companies of Margarita Xirgu and Lola Membrives in reviews of work by García Lorca, Alberti, and Valle-Inclán and the more politically identified authors César Garfias, Julio G. Miranda, Ricardo Gómez, and Manuel Ovejero; while *Naciendo el hombre nuevo . . . Fundir literatura, artes y vida como práctica de las vanguardias en el Mundo Ibérico*, ed. Harald Wentzlaff-Eggebert, Frankfurt, Vervuert — M, Iberoamericana, 299 pp., illus., takes in both Spain and Latin America with the following essays falling in our period: as an introduction to the collection, H. Wentzlaff-Eggebert, 'Literatura y artes, arte y vida' (9–16), underlining the capacity to 'anarquizar, oxigenar, liberalizar' of the writers and artists dealt with here, even if, traditionally, they have been seen only as minor figures; C. Nicolás, 'Surrealismo y provocación. La navaja en el ojo: una imagen literaria, pictórica y fílmica' (17–56), tracing an impressive pedigree for the notorious opening image of *Un chien andalou* (1929), that begins with Homer and Sophocles and runs through Lautréamont, Gómez de la Serna, Wagner, Nietzsche, Juan Larrea, bull-fighter Manuel Granero, Georges Bataille, Victor Brauner, Max Ernst, and René Magritte as intertexts for a complex image of rupture; D. Wansch, 'José Moreno Villa: pintor-poeta de la vanguardia española' (122–36), provides the background to an 'intrapersonal' reading of *Jacinta la pelirroja* (1929) as a 'poema en poemas y dibujos'; R. J. Díaz, 'Poesía y pintura en Juan Ismael' (137–50), documents vanguard activity in the Canary Islands in the context of the 1920s and 1930s in reviews like *La Rosa de los Vientos, Gaceta de Arte*, and *Cartones*, the ADLAN group and *postismo* in the 1940s, and the *pinturas-escrituras* of the 1970s and 1980s; while S. Klengel, 'Tupí or not Tupí' (151–71), concentrates on Eugenio F. Granell as a second generation surrealist; and, finally, I. Mizrahi, 'La agenda de *El surrealismo entre viejo y nuevo mundo* de Juan Larrea', *ALEC*, 24 : 121–34, explicates how emigration to the Americas after the Civil War confirms the 'myth of the New World' after the 'death of the West' in the surrealist power play. A. M. Aguirre, 'Sofía Casanova, la primera mujer gallega nominada para el Premio Nobel de Literatura', *La Torre*, 3, 1998 : 751–68, fleshes out the portrait of the 1925 nominee with reference to her long and distinguished career as journalist, feminist, poet, war-correspondent, cultural ambassador, and pacifist. K. M. Sibbald, 'La imagen de España en *The Criterion* de T. S. Eliot', *Ouimette Vol.*, 195–204, documents Cambridge Hispanist J. B. Trend's efforts to bring Spanish literature and music to life for the English reading public in much the same way as Antonio Marichalar did for his Spanish counterparts (see also *YWMLS*, 60:251); and *\*Literatura comparada. Relaciones* *literarias hispano-inglesas (siglo XX)*, ed. Emilio Barón, Almería U.P., 138 pp. A special issue compiled by Nigel Dennis on 'Spanish writers in exile: Mexico, 1939–1947', *RoQ*, 46, does not fall quite in our period, nevertheless, of interest here: J. Valender, 'Manuel Altolaguirre y su presente de la lírica mexicana (1946)' (15–24); M. Aznar Soler, 'El polémico regreso de Juan Gil-Albert a España en 1947' (35–44); G. Sheridan, 'Dos disputas literarias del exilio: Bergamín, Salinas y el rechazo mexicano' (25–34); and N. Alba, 'José Herrera Petere: España y los españoles vistos desde México' (45–57). R. S. Lubar (230–38) characterizes Salvador Dalì as 'Modernism's Counter-Muse' in an entertaining and informative piece. From a special issue on 'Sound on vision: studies in Spanish cinema', *BHS(G)*, 76, comes V. Molina Foix, '98 y 27: dos generaciones ante el cine. (Baroja y Lorca como guionistas)' (157–71), signalling the former as exceptional in his essentially logocentric generation, and the latter as typical of those in his interested in the eye behind the lens; while C. Perriam, '*A un dios desconocido*: resurrecting a queer identity under Lorca's spell' (77–91), indicates how, by quotation from García Lorca's 'Oda a Walt Whitman' and the opening shots of Granada in July 1936, the 1977 film constructs a new (homosexual) discourse of desire for a modern, cosmopolitan Spain after the severe repression of the Francoist years. A useful adjunct to cultural studies, *The Cambridge Companion to Modern Spanish Cultura*, ed. David T. Gies, CUP, 327 pp., spans two centuries on the axis 1868–1936–1975 and incorporates commentary on Castilian, Basque, and Catalan culture in 23 separate but complementary essays that include, notably, E. I. Fox on nationalism and national identity (see also Id., 'El siglo XX español y el discurso de la identidad nacional', *Ouimette Vol.*, 71–78), José Álvarez Junco's historical overview 1875–1936, Roberta Johnson on culture and prose, Thomas Mermall on the essay, Richard A. Cardwell on poetry, Dru Dougherty on the theatre, J. Martín Martínez on painting and sculpture, Kathleen N. Vernon on the cinema, Luis Fernández Galiano on architecture, Roger Tinnell on Spanish music, and Laura Fumen on dance.

2.   POETRY

Emilio Miró introduces and annotates *Antología de poetisas del 27*, M, Castalia, 284 pp., making long overdue amends in recognizing the other half of this hitherto male-only grouping. Pilar Gómez Bedate, *\*Poetas españoles del siglo veinte*, M, Huerga y Fierro, 314 pp.; Juventino Caminero, *\*Poesía española siglo XX. Capítulos esenciales*, Kassel, Reichenberger, 1998, 291 pp.; and Ricardo Senabre, *\*Claves de la poesía contemporánea. (De Bécquer a Brines)*, Salamanca, Almar, 380 pp.

*La metáfora en la poesía hispánica (1885–1936)*, ed. Hans Lauge Jansen and Julio Jensen, Seville, Alfar, 1997, 272 pp., contains papers from the 1996 Copenhagen symposium with short studies on Aleixandre, Antonio Machado, Juan Ramón, Alberti, León Felipe, and Cernuda among others. *\*Ludismo e intertextualidad en la lírica española moderna*, ed. Trevor J. Dadson and Derek W. Flitter, Birmingham U.P., 1998, xiv + 172 pp. Derek Harris, *Metal Butterflies and Poisonous Lights: The Language of Surrealism in Lorca, Alberti, Cernuda and Aleixandre*, Anstruther, Fife, La Sirena, 246 pp., directs our attention to 'linguistic strategies' and by some sharp analyses dispels the many obfuscations surrounding surrealist writing. C. E. López, '*La rueda del destino*: obra en verso de Rafael Cansinos-Assens', *BFFGL*, 24, 1998:99–120, takes a new look at some overlooked verse. Emilio Prados, *\*Tiempo. Canciones del farero*, ed. Francisco Javier Díez de Revenga, M, Biblioteca Nueva, 232 pp. V. Hartfield-Méndez, 'Mirrors and Pedro Salinas' "doubled you"', *BHS(G)*, 76:415–31, reflects the profound ambiguity in the special specular relationship of mirrors and language that marks both Salinas's actual participation in symbolist modernism and the way he anticipated postmodern writing.

### INDIVIDUAL POETS

ALBERTI.  José María Balcells introduces *Marinero en tierra (1924)*, B, Losada, 1998, 174 pp.; and Gregorio Torres Nebrera adds the critical apparatus to *Retornos de lo vivo lejano. Ora marítima*, M, Cátedra, 310 pp. *RCEH*, 24, is a 'Homenaje a un escritor del siglo' introduced by editor Nigel Dennis (3–4), as a 'figura clave *colosal*' of the 20th c., containing: T. McMullan, 'Fallen angels: Arthur Rimbaud and Rafael Alberti's *Sobre los ángeles*' (5–23), which documents in detail a coincidence in imagery and diction that shows how A. exploited Rimbaud's revolutionary legacy to illustrate the problematical nature of identity in a brand of surrealism that owes little or nothing to André Breton and his fellow travellers; C. B. Morris, 'The cryptic telegrams of Alberti's *Yo era un tonto y lo que he visto me ha hecho dos tontos*' (23–36), that analyses the rhetoric of oddity and the early cinema in the only partly decipherable cryptograms dedicated to Luisa Fazenda, Harry Langdon, and Larry Semon; D. Harris, '*Sermones y moradas*: "el hueco de la herida"' (37–49), which resuscitates interest in an often overlooked work; G. Mazzocchi, '*Santa Casilda*: algunas reflexiones sobre lo imaginario católico en el joven Alberti' (51–62), tracing connections between this theatre piece, composed in 1930–31 but made available only in 1990, and A.'s more famous *auto sacramental*, *El hombre deshabitado*; J. C. Wilcox, 'Juan Ramón Jiménez as intertext in Rafael Alberti's collected poetry' (63–86), which examines numerous direct references, the use of Jiménez's early paradigmatic metaphors in A.'s nostalgic vision of Spain, and the more diffuse impact of 'poesía desnuda' on A.'s own poetry of exile, to indicate A.'s always positive memories of the older man and master poet; R. Fasey, 'The "shock of recognition": Alberti's indebtedness to Russian writing' (87–104), noting more than a vague kinship with the Soviets in the real affinity between A. and both Dostoevskii's *Notes from Underground* (1864) and Andreyev's *Sashka Zhegulev* (1911); to be read together, J. R. López, 'Otredad y conciencia ideológica: Rafael Alberti y la vanguardia política' (105–22), which concentrates on *De un momento a otro* written in 1937–38, as does I. Rubio, 'En torno al teatro político de Rafael Alberti' (123–38), that documents this Spaniard's response to the call for a revolutionary European theatre as envisioned by Piscator and Brecht; using Lacan and Ricoeur, S. J. Fajardo, 'Art, ideology, poetry in Alberti's *La arboleda perdida*' (139–51), pinpoints the role of the father in A.'s artistic development; while K. M. Sibbald, 'Rafael Alberti's *La arboleda perdida*: autobiography as social situation' (153–70), concentrates upon audience, selfhood, and the public story in the various editions of A.'s presentation of his past (but for a contrary point of view, see also, C. B. Morris, 'Más allá de la autobiografía: el viaje de *Sobre los ángeles*', *ALEC*, 24:297–316, that argues that the poetry teaches us more about the man than the man writing his life story); P. Guerrero Ruiz, 'Recuerdos del Prado: *A la pintura*, de Rafael Alberti' (171–90), taking a long look at the indissoluble links between painting and poetry throughout A.'s double career; on the personal level, N. Dennis, ' "X a X": la correspondencia en verso entre Rafael Alberti y José Bergamín' (191–206), outlines the historical context of the 'morir interminable' of the 'sapo pardesco' in 17 letters in verse exchanged between 1971 and 1977 containing complementary comments on A.'s exile in Rome and Bergamín's lonely life in Madrid during Franco's last years, while E. Fermín Partido, 'En la fustiga transición: re-visiones en el retorno de Alberti' (207–20), situates A. in the post-Franco years of the transition to democracy in the press of the time, and M. Aznar Soler, 'Exilio republicano y escena dramática española: el estreno de *El adefesio* en Madrid (1976)' (221–35), recounts a particular political event, if not a great theatre experience, in María Casares's triumph that, ironically, author A. could not attend since the Communist Party had not yet achieved legal status in Spain; F. J. Díez de Revenga, 'Erotismo y poesía de senectud: en torno a *Golfo de sombras*, de Rafael Alberti' (237–47), which provides a close reading of A.'s representation of the female sex that provoked such uproar in 1986; and, last but not least, D. Gagen, ' "De mar a mar": Alberti's symbolic sea voyage' (249–61), studies the sonnet, presented as a lithograph to the Association of Hispanists of Great Britain and Ireland in 1992, in which A. identified as 'un navegar, fiel, permanente' his passage through Spanish literature. A.'s theatre sparks interest: J. Monleón, 'Alberti, un grande del teatro alternativo', *PrA*, 281:8–10, makes only general comments; while H. Laurenson, 'Furias, diosas y transvestidas: women in Rafael Alberti's *El adefesio*', *BHS(L)*, 76:337–47, correlates early lyricism with later dramatic form as she touches on female suicide, a complex network of sociocultural assumptions about women, the blurring of gender boundaries, and sexual repression in the 1944 play. E. Cueto-Asín, 'Travestismo, deshumanización y perversidad en *El adefesio* de Rafael Alberti', *REH*, 33:563–80, uses Judith Butler's research on performative arts and gender constitution to make some interesting, if not altogether convincing, parallels between José de Ribera's painting *Magdalena Ventura* of 1631, witchcraft, and Lady Macbeth.

ALEIXANDRE. G. V. García, '(Anti)platonismo en *La destrucción o el amor*', *His(US)*, 82:733–39, compares and contrasts A.'s work with the theorizing in *Ion* and *The Republic* to assert that A.'s aim to reveal the truth is very different from Platonic 'lies' that distract or amuse. As part of the tripartite centenary celebration collected in Díez de Revenga, *Tres poetas*, J. L. Bernal Salgado, 'Aleixandre y la experiencia de la vanguardia' (33–48), comments on A.'s *avant garde* pre-history as recorded in the early poems of *Álbum*, *Grecia*, *Diálogo de la Lengua*, and *Carmen*; A. Duque Amusco, 'Vicente Aleixandre: el imposible exilio' (49–63), reproduces letters dated 23 February 1938 to María Zambrano, from Dámaso Alonso in 1937 to the *Ministerio de Instrucción Pública*, and A.'s response dated 2 April 1938, all concerning A.'s failure to get permission to leave Spain on humanitarian grounds despite his long medical history of ill health; F. J. Díaz de Castro, ' "este que aquí miráis": los retratos líricos de Vicente Aleixandre' (65–97), is a long wander through A.'s portrait gallery, to be read with J. M. Pozuelo Yvancos, 'Retrato, historia y crítica literaria en *Los encuentros* de Vicente Aleixandre' (99–114), pointing up the significance of the anthology, and A. A. Gómez Yebra, '*Los encuentros* de Vicente Aleixandre en su tercera fase' (115–34), elucidating the autobiographical mosaic to be found in this testimony to friendship.

ALONSO. Also celebrating the 1998 centenary come: *Poesía y otros textos literarios*, ed. Valentín García Yebra, prol. Víctor García de la Concha, M, Gredos, 1998, xxxvii + 747 pp., an excellent compilation of the early texts and books of poetry with important information about the dating and first versions of the texts that will be of most use to the *gnoscenti*. *BFFGL*, 24, 1998, contains the 'Homenaje a Dámaso Alonso en su centenario' with: S. Salinas de Marichal, ' "La saca de los cuidados" y otros recuerdos' (11–14); J. Marichal, 'España en la poesía de Dámaso Alonso' (15–18); A. Carreira, 'Góngora después de Dámaso Alonso' (19–44), paying tribute to the scholarly achievement; and A. Salas, '*Hijos de la ira*: el grito necesario' (45–49), emphasizing the historical moment. In similar vein Díez de Revenga, *Tres poetas*, contains: E. Bou, 'Dámaso Alonso y Pedro Salinas desde el exilio' (257–74), exploring the epistolary relationship between Don Dámaso and Don Pedro in the long years of separation during and after the Civil War; M. Cruz Giráldez, 'La poesía de Dámaso Alonso' (275–87), painstakingly highlights the new aesthetic supposed by the publication of *Los hijos de la ira* in 1944; while F. J. Díez de Revenga, 'Dámaso Alonso en *Los hijos de la ira*: innovación y revolución' (289–312), considers the novel and the provocative nature of the publication; F. Florit Durán, 'Doce reseñas de Dámaso Alonso (1926–1932): amistad y filología' (313–29), unearths some forgotten reviews in *Revista de Filología* on criticism by George Northrup and Arturo Farinelli, and editions of work by Quevedo, Calderón, Góngora, and Meléndez Valdés, that underscore the common literary tradition of A. and his generation; while K. M. Sibbald, 'Dámaso Alonso, ¿crítico de la Generación del 27?' (331–46), re-reads the now classic essay first published in 1948 as an exercise in solidarity, construing it as the 'crítica oficiosa' of the 'Capitán Aranda' of his generation, whose poetic achievement has much in common with that of a notable Spanish contemporary, Jorge Guillén, as well as European and North American counterparts in the Modernist movement. A. S. Pérez-Bustamante Mourier, 'Voz con alcuza (sobre la imaginación simbólica en la poesía de Dámaso Alonso)', *Salina*, 13:145–70, painstakingly analyses all five books of poetry to discover a religious element throughout that speaks to A.'s on-going belief in Christian morality if not his faith in Christian theology; and Luis Vázquez Fernández, \**El humanismo religioso de Dámaso Alonso. Ensayos concéntricos*, M, Revista Estudios, 456 pp.

CERNUDA. (Auto)biography continues to excite critical commentary: M. A. Naval, 'Quince cartas de Luis Cernuda a Gerardo Diego (1925–1959)', *CHA*, 594:89–119, reproduces some unedited letters from the period 1925–33 and one from 1959 which tell of C.'s concerns about poetry and publishing; and A. Lumsden-Kouvel, H. Mathews, and I. L. McClelland, 'Awaiting the dawn in Glasgow', *BHS(G)*, 249–61, which comes complete with reproductions of Gregorio Prieto's 1927 drawing of C. and C.'s letter to Ivy McClelland dated 25 October 1948 in a three part commentary with general musings by Audrey Lumsden-Kouvel on C.'s very mixed feelings towards the University of Glasgow and the interior conflict between personal disappointment and creativity evident in *Como quien espera el alba*; I. L. McClelland, 'Cernuda's local source of inspiration for his poem "Los espinos"' (259–61), which tells of both the flowering hawthorns in the public gardens at the end of University Avenue, along which C. walked regularly on his way to class, and the windy stretch thereabouts, that figure in C.'s poem; while H. Mathews, '"Ni Glasgow ni Escocia me resultaban agradables": Luis Cernuda as university teacher' (253–57), in which a former student describes how C.'s poor communication skills, deficient English, too soft a voice, and little enthusiasm for the job itself made him unable to cope with the demands of teaching Spanish. D. Ródenas de Moya, 'Huellas del tránsito de *Cielo sin dueño* a *Un río, un amor* de Luis Cernuda', *HR*, 67:509–33, documents well the change in original title, the variants, and the editorial history of this series of 34 poems, including details on Cansinos-Assens, the 'leviatán de la C.I.A.P.', and that editorial's demise, intertextualities between C., Nerval, Gide, and Paul Éluard, and, most importantly, a close textual comparison between the two versions.

DIEGO. For the *aficionado*, Andrés Amorós edits with useful commentary *La suerte o la muerte. Poema del toreo*, M, Biblioteca Nueva, 323 pp., which includes illustrations by Molina Sánchez. S. Rivera, 'Gerardo Diego: conservador del museo lingüístico y terrorista literario', *ALEC*, 24:149–66, exploits the apparent contradiction that characterizes the 1927 Generation's complementary desire for tradition and novelty to focus on how D.'s 'poesía absoluta' best exemplifies this in his attempt to re-read the poetry of the past in order to obtain in full measure the possibilities of *creacionismo* and thereby ensure the *avant garde* an afterlife in postmodernism. F. J. Díez de Revenga, 'Gerardo Diego y los pintores de la vanguardia. Poesía y crítica', *Salina*, 13:137–44, takes a hard look at the significance of D.'s criticism of art and artists in *28 pintores españoles contemporáneos vistos por un poeta* (1975), to extract comments on the Paris Left Bank in the 1920s and, particularly, Pierre Reverdy's *Nord-Sud*, and Spaniards like Juan Gris, Picasso, Gutiérrez Solana, Francisco Gutiérrez Cossío, Benjamín Palencia, Gregorio Prieto, and Salvador Dalí. (See also pp. 261–63 above).

GARCÍA LORCA. As always, useful information impossible to cover here, with particular reference to the many special issues, anthologies, collections and editions celebrating the centenary, is contained in A. A. Anderson, 'Bibliografía lorquiana reciente', *BFFGL*, 24, 1998:151–56, and *ib.*, 25:141–55. Leslie Stainton, *Lorca. A Dream of Life*, NY, Farrar, Straus and Giroux, viii + 579 pp., an immensely readable biography that draws on unpublished letters, exclusive interviews with G.L.'s friends, family and acquaintances, and newly discovered archival material, is particularly good on G.L.'s theatre and his attempts at innovation in that medium. It will probably

become the standard one-volume work on the poet in English, but
should be read together with Ian Gibson's pioneering work (see
*YWMLS*, 47:379 and 49:357) and C. B. Morris's more recent
appraisal of the poetry (see *YWMLS*, 59:338). Travelling around
G.L.'s world: G. Siebenmann, 'Federico García Lorcas Amerika-
Erfahrungen', *Iberoromania*, 48, 1998:1–15, takes a look at G.L.'s
journeys in the New World; while A. A. Anderson, 'Federico García
Lorca en los fondos de la Biblioteca Nacional José Martí de la
Habana', *BFFGL*, 25:129–40, digs up new information on G.L. in
Cuba; and M. M. Campos Fernández-Figueroa, 'Lorca en Yugosla-
via', *ib.*, 107–26, adds to the European bibliography. Matching
biographical factors with known traits, A. A. Anderson, 'Was García
Lorca dyslexic (like W. B. Yeats)?', *MLR*, 94:700–17, scrutinizes
misspellings and transpositions in G.L.'s secondary school examinations to suggest most plausibly that G.L. might join, along with Hans
Christian Andersen, Balzac, Flaubert, Churchill, John Irving, and
W. B. Yeats, a select group for whom the trials and tribulations
associated with academic discipline were all too familiar. J. Salazar
Rincón, 'Ramos, coronas, guirnaldas: símbolos de amor y muerte en
la obra de Federico García Lorca', *RLit*, 61:495–519, documents the
vegetable empire as it translates references to sex and death. The
centenary celebrations spill over into print: Díez de Revenga, *Tres
poetas*, contains: I. Gibson, 'Federico García Lorca y el amor
imposible' (135–60), eloquently describing how much of a role gay-
bashing has played in any consideration of G.L.'s work from 1921
until the centenary year itself; C. de Paepe, ' "Un morir en el vivir":
resonancias de San Juan de la Cruz en la poesía de Federico García
Lorca' (161–80), privileges G.L.'s relationship with the mystic; but
J. Pérez Bazo, 'Agudeza y concepto en la "Soledad insegura" de
Federico García Lorca' (181–203), prefers to concentrate on G.L.'s
admiration for Góngora, and A. Soria Olmedo, ' "Me lastima el
corazón": Federico García Lorca y Federico Nietzsche' (205–23),
leaves the Golden Age to seek out the 'daimon' or 'duende' common
to Andalusia and 19th-c. Germany; V. Serrano and M. de Paco,
'García Lorca y el teatro' (225–38), explore *lo dramático* in both G.L.'s
poetry and theatre; while C. Oliva, 'La práctica escénica lorquiana'
(239–55), elucidates how G.L.'s technical metalanguage makes
possible some sort of fusion between popular and abstract theatre;
while *Recuerdos y homenaje a Federico García Lorca en su centenario
1898–1998*, ed. Gladys Granata de Egües, Mendoza, Fundar,
263 pp., is a mixed bag containing essays on various aspects of the
poetry and drama, relations with Guillermo de Torre, Góngora, and
the review *Claridad*, and specific comments on *Los sonetos del amor
oscuro, Mariana Pineda, Lola la comedianta, Así que pasen cinco años, Yerma*,

and *Tierra y Luna*. On the poetry: R. Stone, 'Misticismo y lujuria: the sacred and the profane in *Poema del cante jondo*', *ALEC*, 24:213–42, analyses the complex interplay of the Catholic religion and deep song with G.L.'s own brand of existential anguish and sexual dilemma; while E. Southworth, 'On Lorca's "San Rafael (Córdoba)" and some other texts', *MLR*, 94:87–102, is a close reading that elucidates the ancient *topos* of Heraclitus's paradox of continuity and change as seen in Cordoba's specific past and echoed in Mantegna's *St. Sebastian*, homosexuality, Mérimée, and Dalì. *BFFGL*, 25:9–44, contains a 'Homenaje a la Barraca durante la guerra civil' that is of relevance here with E. Haro Tecglen, 'Cuando la cultura era la libertad' (13–14); a recorded conversation between Carmen Rasine, Efrén and Luis Giménez-Cacho (15–38); poetry by M. Hernández, ' "Llamo a la juventud" ' (39–42); and personal reminiscing in J. Gil-Albert, 'La Barraca' (43–44). Concentrating on the theatre: P. Ambrosi, 'El prólogo en la concepción dramática lorquiana', *ALEC*, 24:389–409, documents this distinctive feature of G.L.'s dramatic production from the intimate and traditional approach in the early works to the complex, modernized texts that form part of a metatheatrical development of themes particularly dear to the author; S. J. Poeta, 'La metafísica de una moral: una visión kantiana de la tragedia lorquiana', *CG*, 20, 1998:88–98, dismisses Aristotelian influence to depict the trilogy as modern tragedy that is essentially metaphysical and Christian, while G. S. Basterra, 'Destino, responsabilidad y creación en el escenario trágico de Lorca', *ALEC*, 24:411–31, reads the same tragedies as showing the incapacity of the protagonists to act or react within their particular society, which makes necessary alternative modes of behaviour and creativity; and S. J. Poeta, 'Poetic and social patterns of symmetry and contrast in Lorca's *La casa de Bernarda Alba*', *His(US)*, 82:740–49, constructs a dialectic between poetic form and contextual history to illustrate the provocative nature of the work; documenting actual performances of G.L.'s plays, M. F. Vilches de Frutos, 'La presentación en España del teatro de Federico García Lorca durante la década de los sesenta', *BFFGL*, 25:81–106, sets the stage for both L. F. Higuera Estremera, 'El primer estreno comercial de García Lorca en la posguerra española (*Yerma*, Teatro Eslava, 1960)', *ALEC*, 24:571–92, which details family authorizations, censorship, and musical settings, the presentation at the Spoletto Festival, Luis Escobar's major role as director, as well as the response from both the theatre-going public and the professional reviewers; and G. Edwards, '*Yerma* on stage', *ib.*, 433–532, with comments on Víctor García's famous 'trampoline' production of 1971, and that of the National Theatre in London in 1987; while, finally, in comparative vein, G. Trautmann, 'Following the Lorquian model: parallels and divergences between *La casa de Bernarda Alba* and *António Marinheiro*', *Gestos*, 26, 1998:57–65, records striking parallels between the texts by G.L. and Bernardo Santareno in that both are the expression of a political message in the demand for change from dictatorship and strict censorship, M. T. García-Abad García, 'Lorca / Spielberg ¿la casa de Schindler o la lista de Bernarda?', *BFFGL*, 24, 1998:123–34, and E. Vallaba, 'García Lorca en Sam Sheppard', *ib.*, 135–47, which finds parallels between G.L.'s 'teatro bajo la arena' and Sheppard's Off Broadway productions. (See also p. 278 below).

MACHADO, ANTONIO.  Elisa Rosales Juega, *Comportamiento ético en la poesía de Antonio Machado*, Newark, Delaware, Juan de la Cuesta, 1998, 128 pp., studies the formal aspects of M.'s poetry to find an ethical position in his defence of art as a builder of moral conscience. C. S. (Newton) Gala, 'Iconografías machadianas: ejemplos de una dialéctica lírica', *Salina*, 13:129–36, concentrates on 'Fantasía iconográfica', 'A un viejo y distinguido señor', 'Un loco', 'Un criminal', 'La mujer manchega', and 'Llanto de las virtudes y coplas por la muerte de Don Guido', to discern the 'impulso epistemológico y regeneracionista del 98' in M.'s programme for change. P. G. Johnston, 'From palimpsest to print: the shaping of a sonnet (Machado's "Esta luz de Sevilla ...")', *Gallagher Vol.*, 126–34, outlines the three stages in the genesis of mature and polished verse, using as his example the 19-line poem dated 13 March 1916 entitled 'En el tiempo / 1882, 1890, 1892 / mi padre', the transcription made between 2 and 8 November 1924, and the fourth of five sonnets first published in *Alfar* in 1925 and added to the second edition of *Nuevas canciones* in 1928, one of the most accomplished texts in modern Spanish poetry. J. A. Ascunce, 'Sistemas de creación en Antonio Machado, Ramón Gómez de la Serna y Juan Ramón Jiménez. Búsqueda de una originalidad estética', *Ouimette Vol.*, 27–38, scans the evolution of Spanish poetry in the early decades of the 20th c. for examples of a new poetic creativity through *depuración* on to universality. Worthy of attention, J. A. Masoliver Ródenas, 'Antonio Machado: las voces traicionadas', *CHA*, 583:63–70 and 585:79–89, is a serious essay in two parts. J. M. Millanes, 'El otro irreductible de Juan de Mairena', *ib.*, 594:71–86; and M. A. Olmos, '*Juan de Mairena* y el pensamiento griego: una mixtificación', *RLit*, 61:467–93, defend M.'s choice of Plato as model instead of repeating the usual characterization of him as a modern day Socrates.

3. PROSE

Domingo Ródenas de Moya, *\*Los espejos del novelista. Modernismo y autorreferencia en la novela vanguardista española*, B, Península, 1998,

# Literature, 1898–1936    273

287 pp. *Spanish Women Writers and the Essay*, ed. Kathleen Glenn and Mercedes Mazquiarán de Rodríguez, Columbia, Missouri U.P., 1998, lx + 294 pp., collects essays of interest here on Carmen de Burgos, María Martínez de la Sierra, Margarita Nelken, Rosa Chacel, and María Zambrano. *\*A Further Range. Studies in Modern Spanish Literature from Galdós to Unamuno*, ed. Anthony H. Clarke, Exeter U.P., 290 pp. Zeroing in on civil war experiences and after, R. Espejo-Saavedra, 'Historia y traición: *Campo cerrado*, de Max Aub', *RCEH*, 23:239–54, using Hans Magnus Enzenberger and Jacques Rancière as springboards, examines how Aub breaks with the typical thesis novel in order to analyse the intimate relationship between language and power at both the individual and the collective levels; F. Degiovanni, 'El amanuense de los campos de concentración: literatura e historia en Max Aub', *CA*, 77:206–21; and *\*Diario de Djelfa*, ed. Xelo Candel Vila, V, Denes, 1998, 138 pp., adds six interesting photographs to the text. T. R. Franz, 'Un caso de la ambivalencia barojiana: *El árbol de la ciencia* y *Doña Perfecta*', *Revista Horizontes* (Puerto Rico), 79, 1998:73–90. J. L. Molina Martínez, 'Cartas inéditas de Blasco Ibáñez a Antón del Olmet', *CHA*, 592:111–20, first contextualizes (111–12) and then reproduces (113–20) the letters dated between 1924–26 from novelist to diplomat that tell of reading habits, travel plans, exile in Menton, and the politics involved in the Nobel Prize nomination. E. D. Myers, 'Epiphany on the road of life: Rosa Chacel's "En la carretera" ', *HisJ*, 19, 1998:61–73, reads the short story closely to pinpoint the epiphanic moment when the conventional male linear plot becomes a female *Bildung* characterized by circularity and tension in Chacel's special use of metaphor and allusion to describe protagonist Berta. C. d'Ors Führer, 'Para un diccionario filosófico de Eugenio d'Ors', *CHA*, 589–90:7–46, gives some sample entries; while J. R. Resina, 'Modernism of the essay in Eugeni d'Ors', *RoQ*, 46:216–29, is well constructed. Worth reading, D. Ródenas de Moya, '*El novelista* de Ramón Gómez de la Serna en la impugnación del modelo narrativo realista', *RHM*, 52:77–95; and J. S. Squires, 'Ramón Gómez de la Serna's *El incongruente* and Rafael Sánchez Ferlosio's *Industrias y andanzas de Alfanhuí*: an example of literary influence?', *Gallagher Vol.*, 184–90, indicates Gómez de la Serna as a forebear but stops short of making a full-blown case for direct influence. A. Sotelo Vázquez, 'Benjamín Jarnés en *La Vanguardia* (1931–1936)', *CHA*, 594:47–53, gives the context for the transcription of the 'Cinco artículos', *ib.*, 55–68, that follows; and Domingo Ródenas (de Moya) edits in handy fashion *El profesor inútil*, M, Espasa Calpe, 301 pp. Thomas Mermall introduces and annotates most usefully José Ortega y Gasset, *La rebelión de las masas*, M, Clásicos Castalia, 1998, 375 pp.

274     *Spanish Studies*

INDIVIDUAL WRITERS

AZORÍN.   Gayana Jurkevich, *In Pursuit of the Natural Sign. Azorín and the
Poetics of Ekphrasis*, Lewisburg, Bucknell U.P., 259 pp., discerns
parallels between the rise of landscape Impressionism in France and
the national reconstruction after 1898 by Spanish writers and painters
through a celebration of the Castilian landscape, and then goes on to
consider A.'s career as a literary landscapist fascinated by the word-
image dichotomy; lavish illustrations in both black and white and
colour make known the work of Aureliano de Beruete, Darío de
Regoyos, Santiago Ruisiñol, and Joaquim Mir (see comments on
work previously published in *YWMLS*, 56:383; 57:352; and 58:361).
Establishing anew the canon: D. Ródenas de Moya, 'La forma
transgresiva en las "Nuevas obras" de Azorín', *ALEC*, 24:167–91,
rescues from critical oblivion two novels first published in 1928–29 as
*Félix Vargas* and *Superrealismo* that reappeared later as *El caballero
inactual* and *El libro de Levante*, respectively, and indicates their original
structure and curious use of metalepsis; M. A. Lozano (Marco), 'Un
peculiar manifiesto: "Confesión de un autor". Azorín y el "nuevo
arte"', *Ouimette Vol.*, 107–12, uses the 1905 article to highlight the use
of the pseudonym and present the new style consolidated in *Los
pueblos*; R. F. Llorens, 'Aproximación al Azorín viajero', *ib.*, 113–25,
describes A.'s considerable contribution to Spanish travel literature
and appends a useful bibliography of 'Guías, libros y folletos de viajes
y de geografías', held in the library of the *Casa-Museo Azorín de
Monóvar*; while I. Soldevila Durante, 'Azorín y el canon', *ib.*, 205–11,
gives A.'s own list of the hundred great books from the 1941 article
'Leer y leer' in *Escorial* which contains some obvious choices and not
a few surprises. In comparative vein: J. L. Bernal Muñoz, 'Azorín y el
retrato de Cervantes', *CHA*, 583:79–102; L. Robles, 'Azorín y Giner
de los Ríos', *Ouimette Vol.*, 153–79, which sifts through A.'s correspondance to reproduce from the archives of the *Real Academia de la
Historia* three letters dated 7 July 1909, 13 April 1910, and 24 March
1912, respectively, obituaries from 1916, and some review articles
from 1920, 1930 and 1931, respectively; and D. F. Urey, 'Historias
inalcanzables en Azorín y Galdós', *REH*, 33:301–24, tracing A.'s
praise for the 'marvellous' novels of the last series of the *Episodios
nacionales* in the intertextual dialogue between *Cánovas* (1912) and
*Doña Inés* (1925). *Anales Azorinianos*, 7, celebrates 15 years of publishing
activity with a useful index to the previous issues (355–68) and papers
given at the 1998 international symposium in Alicante containing:
E. I. Fox, 'Azorín y la nueva manera de mirar las cosas' (11–22);
S. Riopérez y Milá, 'Azorín: vocación y destino de escritor' (23–39);
P. Caro Baroja, 'Recuerdos sobre Azorín y Baroja' (41–44); M. A.

Lozano Marco, 'Los valores literarios de clásicos y de modernos' (45–57); H. Laitenberger, 'Azorín y Lope de Vega' (59–76); A. Sotelo, 'Azorín, lector y crítico de Quevedo' (77–98); J. Pérez-Magallón, 'Azorín en la configuración del canon diechiochesco' (99–128); J. Escobar, 'Azorín y Larra: sátira y crítica, escepticismo y certidumbre en los primeros escritos de J. Martínez Ruiz' (129–56); E. Rubio Cremades, 'Azorín y los épigonos del naturalismo español' (157–69); J. Payá Bernabé, 'Blasco Ibáñez en Azorín' (171–85); J. M. Martínez Cachero, 'Los libros políticos de Azorín' (187–209); F. J. Díez de Revenga, 'Azorín poeta, Azorín lector de poesía' (211–34); R. Johnson, 'Azorín, los clásicos castellanos y el matrimonio' (235–451); A. Díez Mediavilla, 'Una lectura azoriniana del teatro finisecular' (247–61); C. Oliva, '*Lo invisible*, auténtica inovación en el teatro azoriniano' (263–70); M. de Paco, 'Azorín y Pirandello: un cuadro suprimido de *Judit*' (271–83); J. Montero Padilla, 'Azorín, comediógrafo (lejanas memorias)' (285–94); R. Conte, 'Azorín o el crítico' (295–302); E. Ruiz-Fornells, 'Azorín y la crítica norteamericana: una perspectiva literaria' (303–17); A. L. Prieto de Paula, 'Azorín confutador de Nietzsche: sobre el fracaso y la moral compasiva' (319–33); C. Manso, '*Charivari*. En casa de Martínez Ruiz' (335–46); M. Ruiz Babero, 'Azorín en la Biblioteca Nacional" (347–52).

GANIVET.   Gonzalo Sobejano prologues a centenary edition of Francisco García Lorca, *\*Ángel Ganivet. Su idea del hombre*, Granada, Diputación Provincial-Fundación Caja de Granada, 1997, 381 pp. *Siglo diecinueve (Literatura hispánica)* (Valladolid), 4, 1998, features 'Ángel Ganivet: *Cartas finlandesas* y un centenario (1898–1998)' and selected papers from the Montreal symposium among which: J. Pérez-Magallón, 'Entre Marruecos y Finlandia: Cadalso y Ganivet en sus *Cartas*' (8–23), establishes some interesting parallels; K. M. Sibbald, '*Cherchez la femme*, desde Andalucía a Helsinki' (25–35), pursues some real women in G.'s life in Finland to flesh out the polarity between Mascha Diakoffsky and Amelia Roldán, together with an interesting parallel between the eponymous protagonist of Juan Valera's *Pepita Jiménez* and G.'s ever ambivalent attitude towards 'la hija de Eva'; J. L. Suárez, 'Ironía y estilo en las *Cartas finlandesas* de Ángel Ganivet' (37–50), finds connections with Socrates, Kant, Hume, and Kierkegaard to explain G.'s modernity; N. Santiáñez, 'Nuevas lecturas, nuevas escrituras: Carlyle, Ganivet y el modernismo español' (51–66), traces the many intertextualities between G. and 'el gran autor de *Hero Worship* y *The French Revolution*' to elucidate well the particular commonality between *Sartor Resartus* and *Los trabajos del infatigable creador Pío Cid*; E. Rubio Cremades, 'Anotaciones y acotaciones azorinianas a lo textos de Ganivet' (67–74), documents both the holdings in the *Casa-Museo Azorín* and Azorín's close readings of, particularly, the *Epistolario de Ganivet*; while R. de la Fuente Ballesteros, 'Patología y regeneración: en torno al héroe ganivetiano' (75–91), indicates most eloquently how G. might be included in the end of the century decadent pose of 'sickness' and 'degeneration' as defined by Paul Nisard, B. A. Morel, Lombroso, and Max Nordau among others. Diagnosing 'el mal del siglo' even further, J. G. Ardila and Á. Ganivet V., 'Diagnóstico de los españoles y tratamiento para España: Ganivet, la historia y el siglo XX', *RHM*, 52:245–63; and M. P. del Maestro, 'Failed reform and lost Utopia in *Los trabajos del infatigable creador Pío Cid*', *Hispanófila*, 127:19–26, records G.'s attempts to combat Spain's *abulia*.

UNAMUNO.   Francisco Caudet usefully edits with full critical apparatus *Paz en la guerra*, M, Cátedra, 511 pp. Francisco La Rubia-Prado, *\*Unamuno y la vida como ficción*, M, Gredos, 271 pp. R. de la Fuente Ballesteros, 'Un autógrafo de *El otro* de Unamuno', *Ouimette Vol.*, 79–84, suggests that future editions of the tragedy should take into consideration MS 22323(13) in the *Biblioteca Nacional* and notes the variants to the text. Alejandro Martínez, *Lenguaje y dialogía en la obra de Unamuno*, M, Pliegos, 1998, 173 pp., deals with U.'s untiring attempts at communication with the self and other(s), with separate chapters on discursive practices in the prose, drama, and poetry. Revising previous criticism: F. J. Arias Santos, 'Una nueva visión de Unamuno', *CHA*, 589–90:179–90; A. Kennedy, 'Juan Goytisolo, Miguel de Unamuno and Spanish literary theory', *Gallagher Vol.*, 135–52, uses Hans Robert Jauss to go beyond mere intertextualities to find in a shared interest in Cervantes and a common 'openness' of writing a curious similarity in how both manipulated the balance between literature and the national culture in the dynamics of forming the canon; while J. Navarro, 'Tres facetas del pensamiento de Unamuno en el *Espejo de la muerte*: intrahistoria, fenomenología de la existencia y teoría de la creación poética', *Explicación de Textos Literarios*, 27, 1998–99:14–25, highlights U.'s Calderonian vision of existence as life as a dream and literature as the affirmation of this chimaera. On specific texts: F. J. Higuero, 'Configuraciones textuales del eterno presente en *Cómo se hace una novela*', *ib.*, 26, 1997–98:44–62, foregrounds an interpretation of the work as 'una reflexión metatextual, agujereada de vitalidad agónica y de un contundente desenfado discursivo' by making frequent references to earlier criticism; A. Rueda, '*La novela de Don Sandalio*: un tablero epistolar para jugar con Unamuno', *REH*, 33:539–61, documents the 'quiet move' in chess and, by way of Woody Allen, Lewis Carroll, and various chess masters, gives the heart *vs* intellect debate a new twist; while E. Amann, 'Restyling history through image: Unamuno's *Cancionero*', *RHM*, 52:46–59, re-considers the poetry.

VALLE-INCLÁN.    More texts are unearthed: A. Gago Rodó, 'Valle-Inclán ante la escena. La lectura de *Voces de gesta* en Pamplona (1912)', *ALEC*, 24:533–55, records the troubled relationship between V.-I. and the theatre company of Díaz de Mendoza and María Guerrero in references to inedited texts of the time; while J. Rodríguez, 'Valle-Inclán en 1925: una entrevista olvidada', *ib.*, 193–211, reproduces V.-I.'s comments on Proust as 'la exageración, la deformación, lo morboso', praise for Sarmiento and his *Facundo*, and admiration for 'el primer modelo de literatura de masas' that was *War and Peace*. Catalina Míguez Vilas, *Valle-Inclán y la novela popular: 'La cara de Dios'*, Santiago de Compostela U.P., 1998, 159 pp., details the genesis of V.-I.'s first long novel, pointing up its structural, aesthetic and ideological aspects by reference to cutting edge scholarship on semiotics and narratology; while R. Warner, 'Co-operative contexts: dialogue mode in the late novels and plays of Ramón del Valle-Inclán', *Gallagher Vol.*, 203–13, suggests that a fundamental concern of V.-I. was the range of possibilities afforded in contextualized dialogue. C. Feal, 'Bradomín después de las *Sonatas*', *RHM*, 52:35–45, is well researched; but S. I. Cardona, 'Utopía en las guerras de Valle-Inclán', *La Torre*, 3, 1998:731–50, finds, unsurprisingly, a use of irony in *La guerra carlista* which prefigures the *esperpentos*. Francisco Umbral, *Valle-Inclán: los botines blancos de piqué*, B, Planeta, 1998, 275 pp., is a provocative piece of 'creative' criticism which is of little use to the serious scholar.

ZAMBRANO.    J. Pérez, '*La razón de la sinrazón*: Unamuno, Machado, and Ortega in the thought of María Zambrano', *His(US)*, 82:56–67, is a sensitive influence study with a difference in that proper attention is paid to Z.'s idiosyncratic philosophical personality wherein her theological dimension, interest in dream states, and passionate love of Spain differentiate her from Ortega and place her closer to the Generation of 1898 and the philosopher-poet model epitomized by Unamuno and Antonio Machado. *Delirium and Destiny. A Spaniard in Her Twenties*, trans. Carol Maier, Albany, SUNY Press, viii + 265 pp., is an excellent translation of Z.'s memoir, written as an entry for a literary prize awarded in 1950 for a work concerned with European culture and biography but only reworked by the author for publication in 1988. It is accompanied by two explanatory studies, R. Johnson, 'The context and achievement of *Delirium and Destiny*' (215–35), which records the life and times narrated here and also gives a basic introduction to Z.'s work; and C. Maier, 'From *Delirio y destino* to *Delirium and Destiny*' (237–48), which recounts the genesis of the translation and the principles governing certain choices about the use of punctuation in English, the mainly literal renditions of Z.'s philosophical terminology, and the construing of Z.'s very personal and highly associative usage of *razón poética*, all complemented by a valuable 'Glossary' (249–65), which gives basic information on authors, works, place-names, and literary and philosophical currents mentioned in the text.

## 4. THEATRE

Critical work on the drama of the period is also noted above under ALBERTI, AUB, GARCÍA LORCA, UNAMUNO, and VALLE-INCLÁN. Items not recorded here on Max Aub, García Lorca, Concha Méndez, Unamuno, and Valle-Inclán may be found in P. Sheppard, C. Costello, and M. Dodaro, 'Modern drama studies: an annual bibliography', *MoD*, 42:59–170, see particularly section E: Hispanic (108–18). Fernando López Serrano, *\*Madrid, figuras y sombras. De los teatros de títeres a los salones de cine*, M, Universidad Complutense, 288 pp. Mariano Martín Rodríguez, *El teatro francés en Madrid (1918–1936)*, Boulder, Colorado, SSSAS, 476 pp., is full of information about the French repertoire that spanned all periods from Medieval, through Classical (particularly Molière), Romantic (where favourites were Mérimée, Musset, and Hugo), and Realist, on through examples of the 'Belle époque' and the 'Boulevard' to the Vanguard, all adding up to a solid presence on the Madrid stage. In the opposite direction, P. W. O'Connor, 'La universalidad del teatro español del siglo XX y la aventura norteamericana', *RLit*, 61:119–31, insists that political savvy and good marketing skills were the keys to getting plays put on even Off Off Broadway and cites Spain's poor record in this regard with only the very relative success in New York of playwrights like Benavente, Martínez Sierra, García Lorca, and Valle-Inclán, as compared to the smash hits enjoyed by the *Comédie française* and the Moscow Art Theatre. J. Rubio Jiménez, 'Goya y el teatro español contemporáneo. De Valle-Inclán a Alberti y Buero Vallejo', *ALEC*, 24:593–619, examines the long shadow of the master of satire, caricature, and the grotesque cast as far as the *esperpentos*, *Noche de guerra en el Museo del Prado*, and *El sueño de la razón*; while, in totally modern vein, C. Herrero Vecino, 'Teatro radiofónico en España: *Ondas* (1925–1936)', *ib.*, 557–70, examines the official organ of Union Radio as the ideal instrument to study the genesis and development of a new dramatic sub-genre and the connections between radio, theatre, and the cinema fostered by Azorín, Gómez de la Serna, and Tomás Borrás among others. Alejandro Casona, *\*La dama del alba*, ed. Fernando Doménech Rico, M, Castalia, 136 pp. G. Torres Nebrera, '*En Flandes se ha puesto el sol*: teatralidad, contexto histórico y parodia', *Salina*, 13:111–28, rather longwindedly examines Marquina's play act by act to establish, first, a connection in

1910 between his Flanders and Catalonia, *semana trágica*, and the disastrous campaign in North Africa, and then consider the parody *Yo puse una pica en Flandes* by Luis Gabaldón and Rafael Santa Ana, which used bull-fighting terms and imagery to poke fun. Julio Enrique Checa Puerta, *Los teatros de Gregorio Martínez Sierra*, M, FUE, 1998, 530 pp., is a comprehensive overview of the director, impresario, playwright in conjunction with wife María de la O. Lejárraga, and Hollywood script writer, and contains a particularly interesting recopilation of 143 letters sent from husband to wife over 30 years. Emilio de Miguel Martínez, *El teatro de Miguel Mihura*, Salamanca U.P., 1997, 320 pp. B. Ciplijauskaité, 'El Claudio de la Torre de los años 20', *HR*, 67 : 305–18, pursues parallels between the author of *En la vida del Señor Alegre* and *Tic-tac* and his contemporaries Maeterlinck, Somerset Maugham, Jean Sarment, and Henri-René Lenormand.

## LITERATURE, 1936 TO THE PRESENT DAY

By Omar García-Obregón, *Queen Mary and Westfield College, University of London*, and Irene Mizrahi, *Boston College*

### 1. General

*Paragraph*, 22.1, a special issue on 'New British Hispanisms', edited and introduced by Chris Perriam, is an important sign to remind us that the newer fields of Hispanism require appropriate inclusion in the sections of this volume, yet important areas of Spanish cultural studies that do not specifically fall under the area of literature continue to be excluded by the titles of the sections themselves, albeit adding 'culture' could, in the words of Jo Labanyi, 'make explicit [...] that language and literature will be studied in isolation from cultural processes', but whilst literature involves culture, culture is not limited to literature. P. J. Smith, 'Towards a cultural studies of the Spanish State' (6–13), discusses current trends in Anglo-American and Spanish Hispanisms and argues that 'cultural studies (and more particularly the work of sociologist Pierre Bourdieu) offers a future common ground or lingua franca for Hispanists in Spain and abroad'. R. Cleminson, 'Male homosexuality in contemporary Spain: signposts for a sociological analysis' (35–54), contributes to the history of male homosexuality in Spain, and specifically refers to the attack on Alfonso Hernández-Catá's *El ángel de Sodoma* in the earlier half of the 20th century. V. Knights, 'Taking a leap beyond epistemological boundaries: Spanish fantasy/science fiction and feminist identity politics' (76–94), uses Paloma Díaz-Mas's *El rapto del Santo Grial*, Rosa Montero's *Temblor*, and Elia Barceló's *Consecuencias naturales* as paradigms of a genre that allows women to explore emergent subjectivities outside patriarchal structures, in a 'transmodern feminism which combines the postmodern interrogation of fixed positions with an emancipatory, critical theory of agency'. J. Labanyi, 'Gramsci and Spanish cultural studies' (95–113), stands out; at the same time as she opens new areas of research, L. examines the productive aspects of Gramsci's works, already used by Latin Americanists, and proposes a much needed re-reading of Spanish culture in the light of Gramsci's theories, which can help us view Spain 'as a paradigmatic case of the importance of popular and mass culture in negotiating viable forms of cultural identity'.

*LPen*, 11.1, 1998, is a special issue on 'Voces y textos de la Guerra Civil Española' to mark the 10th anniversary of the journal (1988–98). J. Amor y Vázquez, 'Recuperaciones: antifranquismo neoyorquino: las Sociedades Hispanas Confederadas y sus *Bombas de mano*' (9–66), is an account of New York's Sociedades Hispanas Confederadas at the time of the Spanish Civil War and the group's publication of the satirical text *Bombas de mano* in 1938, representative of popular culture during the anti-fascist struggle; the next article (10–26), offers specific annotations to the facsimile reproduction that follows (27–66). M. Ugarte, 'Women and exile: the Civil War autobiographies of Constancia de la Mora and María Teresa León' (207–22), calls attention to M.'s *Doble esplendor* and L.'s *Memoria de la melancolía*. M. A. Stewart, 'Poet wives María Teresa León and Anna Murià tell their stories in alternative texts' (223–37), considers two writers in their own right overshadowed by their husbands; S. examines L.'s *Memoria de la melancolía* and M.'s *Crònica de la vida d'Agustí Bartra*; the latter is M.'s biography of her husband, where she 'tells her own story without ever directly acknowledging that project'. C. S. Gala, 'Hacia una sociología del signo poético: el *Romancero* de la guerra española' (247–61), analyses the relevance of the war in fostering collective works that rely on the popular *romance* for their communicative enterprise; the study is based on *Romancero de la guerra civil española* (ed. Gonzalo Santonja); *Romancero de la tierra* (ed. Serge Salaün); and *Romancero General de la guerra de España* (both the Ediciones Españolas edition and that of Alberti). A. Matilla Rivas, 'El archivo de Alfredo Matilla Jimeno y un testimonio inédito de la Guerra Civil y el exilio' (337–66), gives information on the unpublished work still available in Puerto Rico in the archives of the Matilla family, documenting their exile, and including poems, dramas, and novels, some by M.J. and some by his father, Aurelio Matilla García del Barrio, plus the recently found *Recuerdos de mi hermano Alfredo*, written by his brother Aurelio Matilla Jimeno. J. C. Mainer, 'El otoño del miedo: la imagen fílmica y literaria de Franco' (387–412), explores several texts that make evident their reception of the Franco period; M. criticizes the position of 'yoes disueltos' adopted by J. Goytisolo and J. A. Valente, whilst praising the angry responses of Carlos Sahagún, Manuel Vázquez Montalbán, and Ramón Irigoyen. Two sections are devoted to the reaction of Spanish film makers between 1970 and 1985, with special attention to metaphoric discourse, and a last section gives attention to Francisco Umbral's novel *La leyenda del César Visionario*, and to Vázquez Montalbán's *Autobiografía del General Franco*; in agreement with the latter's views about not letting the dictatorship years fall into collective oblivion, M. agrees that 'el antifranquismo, como todo antifascismo, como quizá otros muchos *antis* de la historia, no son empecinamientos irracionales e intolerantes sino fuente integral e inalienable de nuestra dignidad.' V. A. Chamberlain, 'Horsing around in Spanish literature: women writers and the erotic equine', *LPen*, 11:823–39, traces equine imagery with erotic connotations in women's writing back to the 13th century. Of relevance here are the inclusion of Ana María Matute, Carmen Laforet, Mercè Rodoreda, Concha Alós, Carmen Martín Gaite, Amparo Amorós, Esther Tusquets, Ana María Moix, Ana Rossetti, Clara Janés, and Almudena Grandes, whilst establishing connections with works by Jaime Siles and Luis Goytisolo. C. concludes that 'even during the era of Francoist repression and censorship, erotic imagery continued to be employed by women writers, although it often reflected negative qualities of violence and fear. Then, after the end of the Fascist dictatorship, it became again associated with joyous activity. And in the present time [...] the erotic equine is expressed by means of daring innovations and a perspective of sexual frankness.'

E. Bou, 'Ligeros de equipaje: exilio y viaje en la España peregrina (1936–1969)', *RHM*, 52:96–109, examines how exile shapes the experience of the journey, and takes as a starting point Edward Said's lead expressed in *Culture and Imperialism*; B. concentrates on Pedro Salinas and Max Aub, and concludes that 'el viajero no avanza, no se mueve, y si lo hace es para situarse no en un nuevo espacio real, sino para inventar uno imaginario, mental, que le traslada al tiempo anterior al exilio'. F. Caudet, 'Narrar el exilio', *RoQ*, 46:5–14, highlights the conflicts faced by exiled writers in general in their adopted places of residence, and in so doing tries to demystify claims such as José Gaos's and Claudio Guillén's, who refer to the integration of *transterrados*, a term C. rejects for the Republican exiles. M. Aznar Soler, 'El polémico regreso de Juan Gil-Albert a España en 1947', *ib.*, 35–44, documents the controversy caused by G.A.'s return to Franco's Spain, an act seen by his exiled contemporaries as a betrayal of the Republican cause. A.S., with the benefit of hindsight, calls attention to the fallibility of this interpretation of an author who chose inner exile, as manifested in his works. N. Alba, 'José Herrera Petere: España y los españoles vistos desde México', *ib.*, 45–57, rescues two books never published in Spain, H.P.'s poetry collection *Rimado de Madrid* (Mexico, 1946) and his novel *Niebla de cuernos* (Mexico, 1942), and analyses the importance of both in the light of the first exile literature. I. Ayestarán Uriz, 'El tirano hidráulico de Franco a Benet', *La Torre*, no. 11, 21–52, is an original article that attempts to elucidate the politics of Spanish governments post-Spanish Civil War until today in the field of hydrology, through the writings of those who have shown an interest in the environmental theme of water, be it for or against 'las grandes obras hidráulicas en los ríos de la Península Ibérica'. They are: Jesús López Pacheco's *Central eléctrica*; Ana María Matute's *El río*; Juan Benet's articles on the subject; Julio Llamazares's *El río del olvido* and *Retrato de un bañista*;

Miguel Delibes's *Mis amigas las truchas*, the article 'Los ríos moribundos' (in *He dicho*) and *La naturaleza amenazada*; Manuel Rivas's *Un millón de vacas*, the poems 'La memoria del agua' and 'Agua en la mano'; and Bernardo Atxaga's *Dos hermanos, Cuando la serpiente mira al pájaro, Obabakoak*, and the poem 'El erizo' (in *Poemas & híbridos*).

## 2. PROSE

### GENERAL

Juli Highfill, *Portraits of Excess: Reading Character in the Modern Spanish Novel*, SSSAS, 184 pp., aims to demonstrate how 'our interpretations of characters in life and in literature mutually inform each other' through a presentation of four case studies of 'excessive fictional beings': Galdos's usurer from *Torquemada en la hoguera* (ch. 1), Benjamín Jarnés's seductress from 'Andrómeda' (ch. 2), Miguel Delibes's domineering Carmen from *Cinco horas con Mario* (ch. 3), and Lourdes Ortiz's 'unreadable' characters from *Luz de la memoria* (ch. 4). H.'s study includes a clear and concise Introduction, in which she presents the theoretical parameters of her analysis, and a Conclusion, in which she tries to answer the question: 'Would it be possible to entirely "do away" with character, to erase those too-rigid models, paradigms, and structures engraved in our consciousness, and replace character with a fluid, plural subjectivity?'. María Pilar Rodríguez, *Vidas im/propias. Transformaciones del sujeto femenino en la narrativa española contemporánea*, West Lafayette, IN, Purdue Studies in Romance Literatures, 222 pp., is an excellent exploration of the evolution of prose fiction by and about women within the contexts offered by a number of schools of criticism from classics such as Lacan and Barthes to various schools of thought, such as feminism, queer studies, *Bildungsroman*, autobiographical works, and revisions of the canon. R. proposes a new concept of feminine development and emphasizes the importance of the voicing of women's sentiments, passions, desires, and opinions that have not been expressed before in the literature of Spain. R. includes six Spanish books, one for each decade from the 1940s to the present: Carmen Laforet's *Nada* , Elena Soriano's *La playa de los locos*, Merce Rodoreda's *La plaça del Diamant*, Carme Riera's two stories from *Te dejo el mar*, Carmen Gómez Ojea's *Los perros de Hecate*, and Luisa Etxenike's *Efectos secundarios*. R. shows how these texts deconstruct the image of women produced by official hegemonic discourses, which present their roles as wives and mothers as the most desirable possibilities of realization and development, and how they offer a multitude of vital, affective, and sexual options that highlight the diversity of the feminine experiences in the 20th c. and encourage us to question models of development that are monolithic.

A. I. Briones, 'Novela policiaca española y postmodernismo historicista en los años ochenta', *ALEC*, 24:65–83, focuses mainly on Manuel Vázquez Montalbán's *Asesinato en el Comité Central*, but includes the study of other novels of the 80s that make an ironic use of the *género policiaco* in order to revise recent historical events, the years of dictatorship in particular: Fernando Savater's *Caronte Aguarda*, Antonio Muñoz Molina's *Beltenebros*, Jorge Martínez Reverte's *Gálvez en Euskadi*, and Pedro Casals's *¿Quién mató a Felipe?*

J. Gilkison, 'From taboos to transgressions: textual strategies in woman-authored Spanish erotic fiction', *MLR*, 94:718–30, examines the importance of metaphor in Ana Rossetti's short story 'Del diablo y sus hazañas', claiming that 'the interplay of metaphors helps a feminist project, since it removes the currency of erotica [. . .] from the dominating conventions of phallocentrism by allowing an alternative, gynocentric reading'; the second part of the article examines the use of irony in women's writing, using as an example Mercedes Abad's short story 'Ligeros libertinajes sabáticos'. Both metaphor and irony are presented as textual strategies that reveal 'the practical difficulties women encounter when they attempt to take up the pen'. B. R. Cook, 'Division, duplicity, and duality: the nature of the double in three works by contemporary Spanish women writers', *LPen*, 11, 1998:657–77, through a feminist approach focuses on Ana María Moix's *Julia*, Concha Alós's 'La otra bestia', and Carmen Conde's *Creció espesa la yerba*, and claims that in all three the 'protagonists and texts are fragmented because disintegration and paradox describe the experience of women'.

## INDIVIDUAL AUTHORS

AMAT. I. Ballesteros, 'Intimidad y mestizaje literario: una entrevista con Nuria Amat', *LPen*, 11, 1998:679–89, poses intelligent questions that elicit revealing responses from this bilingual Catalan author who has chosen to write in Spanish.

AUB. R. Espejo Saavedra, 'Historia y traición: *Campo cerrado*, de Max Aub', *RCEH*, 23:239–54, sees a concern for the forms and logic of treason in A.'s historical novel and studies this concern in the light of the investigations of Hans Magnus Enzensberger and Jacques Rancière, who define treason as a concept constitutive of both political power and its representation by professional historians.

CASTILLO PUCHE. J. Belmonte-Serrano, 'José Luis Castillo-Puche cuenta la guerra a los niños: *El perro loco*', *LPen*, 11, 1998:327–36, contextualizes C.-P.'s 1965 novel, dedicated to his son, in the body of his other works on the subject of the Spanish Civil War.

DELIBES. A. Davies, 'Who is the model reader of Delibes's *Cinco horas con Mario?*', *MLR*, 94: 1000–08, reads beyond the usual critical divide surrounding this novel, of liberal vs conservative and women vs men in Franco's Spain. Using Carmen as a possible model reader, following Eco's concept corresponding 'to a preferred way of interpreting a text', D. analyses Carmen's subversion of her own marginalization through the act of reading, thus exposing 'the ideological nature of Mario's penchant for literature and, indeed, the ideological nature of literature itself'. J. Lowe, ' "¿Cómo quieres que te lo diga?"': devalued words in Miguel Delibes's *Cinco horas con Mario*', *Neophilologus*, 83: 543–57, focuses on 'the climactic section of Carmen's monologue' to examine the character through repeated key terms such as *confesar, jurar, prometer*, and *perdonar*, amongst others, which lead L. to conclude that Carmen's 'tarnished words, so often imprisoned in their previous contexts, have proved to be incapable of her confessional needs'.

DÍAZ-MAS. C. Henseler, 'The sixth chapter of *El sueño de Venecia*: vision and truth in Paloma Díaz-Mas', *RHM*, 52: 180–92, proposes to read 'through a character's eye' by working backwards — from the epigraph and the fifth chapter to the first — in an attempt to uncover the enlightening 'blind spots' of the painting, 'the site where sight creates meanings, versions, and distortions as the visual is reduced to language' in the novel, in which the 'postmodern "meta"-narrative irony emphasizes the deceiving power of the visual and the textual and points to the awareness of an always incomplete artificiality.'

GARCÍA MORALES. A. Tsuchiya, 'Family plots and romances: discourses of desire in Adelaida García Morales's narrative fiction', *BHS(L)*, 76: 91–108, deals with how, through group psychodynamics, novels such as *El sur, Bene* and *La lógica del vampiro* analyse the mechanism of power in contemporary Spanish society. According to T., these novels' exploration 'evokes a society of automaton-like beings in collective denial, willing victims of a symbolic authority figure', while suggesting at the same time that, to some degree, everyone participates 'in the structures of power that pervade every point of the social body'.

GOYTISOLO. D. Vilaseca, 'Juan Goytisolo's queer (be)hindsight: homosexuality, epistemology, and the "extimacy" of the subject in *Coto vedado* and *En los reinos de Taifa*', *MLR*, 94: 426–37, uses Lee Edelman's rereading of Freud's hypothesis of the 'primal scene' concerning the Wolf Man and his view of psychoanalysis's role *a tergo* (from behind), and Lacan's concept of 'extimacy' to analyse G.'s autobiographical volumes, concluding that 'it is impossible to distinguish in Goytisolo's uses of subjectivity what is "inside" and what is "outside" his own symbolic inscription, what comes "before" and

what "after", what belongs to the Symbolic, what to the Real.'
D. Vilaseca, ' "Waiting for the earthquake": homosexuality, disaster
movies and the "Message from the Other" in Juan Goytisolo's
autobiography', *Paragraph*, 22.1, 55–75, uses Lacanian intersubject-
ivity and Slavoj Žižek's critique of identity, to refocus on G.'s
autobiographical volumes, *Coto vedado* and *En los reinos de taifa*,
including the odd paragraph with, at times, verbatim recycling from
the article above.
JIMÉNEZ LOZANO. F. J. Higuero, 'Huellas diseminadoras del
silencio intempestivo en *Un dedo en los labios* de Jiménez Lozano', *LPen*,
11, 1998:551–67, examines the subversive role of a polysemous
silence in José Jiménez Lozano's collection of short stories.
LARREA. I. Mizrahi, 'La agenda de *El Surrealismo entre Viejo y Nuevo
Mundo* de Juan Larrea', *ALEC*, 24:121–34, shows how, in this essay
published in 1944, Larrea deconstructs Surrealism in order to reassert
the identity of Spanish Republicans in Mexican exile after the
Spanish Civil War.
LEÓN. M. Mazquiarán de Rodríguez, 'Protagonismo y testimonio
en dos "docu-memorias" de María Teresa León', *LPen*, 11:805–21,
is on the protective role of memory in two of L.'s texts written in
exile, *La historia tiene la palabra. (Noticia sobre el salvamento del tesoro
artístico)* (1944) and *Memorias de la melancolía* (1970).
MARÍAS. C. J. García, 'La resistencia a saber y *Corazón tan blanco*,
de Javier Marías', *ALEC*, 24:103–20, employs speech act theory —
in particular, the concept of the rhetoric of performativity — to
explore the dynamic of the desire for knowledge in M.'s novel.
M. González de Ávila, 'La faute et la parole: J. Marías, *Corazón tan
blanco*', *BH*, 101:199–217, studies the criticism of language as a
dominant theme in this novel. G.A. demonstrates how the narrator
reproduces the language that he himself deconstructs, thus using a
mechanism of defense against the power of language. K. M.
Simonsen, '*Corazón tan blanco* — a post-postmodern novel by Javier
Marías', *RHM*, 52:193–212, convincingly suggests that the novel can
be read as an 'ethical *Bildungsroman*' that constitutes a break with the
postmodern tradition from which it takes a certain number of traits,
but 'these are reduced to being preliminary'.
MARSÉ. S. Wykes, 'The rewriting of Marsé's *Si te dicen que caí*',
*BHS(L)*, 76:75–90, examines the changes made to the 1976 original
edition of M.'s novel in the 1989 'versión corregida y definitiva',
arguing that the latter constitutes 'the production of a new text',
despite M.'s affirmation, in his 'Nota a la nueva edición', that these
modifications do not alter drastically the readers' relation to the work.
In the new version, according to W., M. sought to adapt his original
text to a model of textual production similar to the one Roland

Barthes defines as the 'classical realist' model, 'thus producing a text that is not only different but less experimental, less complex and, ultimately, less thought-provoking'. A. Lee Six, 'La oscura historia del primo Paco/Francesc: code-switching in Juan Marsé's *La oscura historia de la prima Montse*', *ib.*, 359–66, uses sociolinguistic research to establish the relevance of code-switching (to French and Catalan) to reveal Paco not only as someone with a mixed identity (Catalan/Andalusian) but also as 'a ruthless and cynical player of power-games whose obsession with his unfortunate cousin speaks more of self-absorption in his own problems of identity than of altruistic concern for Catalonia-crossed lovers'.

MARTÍN GAITE. P. P. Garlinger, 'Lost lesbian love letters? Epistolary erasure and queer readers in Martín Gaite's *El cuarto de atrás*', *BHS(G)* 76:513–33, challenges the critics who see a total absence of lesbianism in the novel, claiming that, 'by unwriting compulsory heterosexuality, *El cuarto de atrás* allows for the possibility of desire among women in epistolary correspondence', despite the fact that the narrator, C., does not seem to present ambiguities concerning the masculine gender of her interlocutor. C. Uxó González, 'La recuperación de la memoria en *La reina de las nieves* de Carmen Martín Gaite', *Donaire*, 13:39–46, focuses on the issue of remembrance in this novel, which establishes intertextual links with Hans Christian Andersen's short story of the same title, and inserts it with M.G.'s other texts on the subject of memory, namely: *Entre visillos*, *Ritmo lento*, *Retahílas*, *El cuarto de atrás*, *Fragmentos de interior*, *Nubosidad variable*, *Las ataduras*, and *Lo raro es vivir*.

MATUTE. M. Sotelo Vázquez, '*Primera memoria* de Ana María Matute: la vida es una infancia repetida', *Salina*, 13:171–78, analyses the novel in the context of M.'s literary trajectory, focusing particularly on the double narrative perspective of the protagonist, Matía, whose process of development — in the tradition of the *Bildungsroman* — suggests that, for M., 'la vida es una infancia repetida'.

MERINO. Y. Agawu-Kakraba, 'Perspectivism, dreams, mirrors, and the act of literary creation: José María Merino's *La orilla oscura*', *JILAS*, 5.2:129–43, attempts to show how M. 'makes his readers skeptics in regard to the correct interpretation of his novel', through an examination of the novel's perspectivism, its manifestation through dream, fantasy, irreality, and memory, and its relationship with M.'s act of literary creation.

MILLÁS. Y. Agawu-Kakraba, 'Desire, psychoanalysis, and violence: Juan José Millás's *El desorden de tu nombre*', *ALEC*, 24:17–34, argues that M.'s work can be seen as a sophisticated elaboration of René Girard's postulates on the question of desire and violence.

MONTERO, ROSA.  J. Escudero, '*Bella y oscura*, de Rosa Montero: entre el resplandor y la muerte', *ALEC*, 24:85–101, aims to show how the metaphysical dimension has replaced the feminist preoccupation previously present in M.'s work through a detailed study of several important aspects of this novel: the thematic relations that exist between Baba's narration and Airelai's stories, a series of key images that vertebrate the work, and the function of genres such as the *Bildungsroman*, the *roman noir*, and the fantastic that are used in the book's composition.

MUÑOZ MOLINA.  N. Pérez García, 'El fantasma del estilo: la voz del autor en *Beltenebros*, de Antonio Muñoz Molina', *CILH*: 141–48, illustrates how this novel is the best example of M.M.'s stylistic skill. C. Larrea, 'Bridging the divide: film, popular culture and high culture in Antonio Muñoz Molina's *El invierno en Lisboa*', *Donaire*, 13:21–26, presents M.M.'s novel as a postmodern hybrid influenced by popular culture (American *film noir* and jazz) and high culture (music and painting), whilst affirming that paradoxically M.M. 'ultimately attempts to involve the reader in a traditional reading experience' and 'the final product is a curiously traditional, old fashioned novel'.

ORTIZ.  E. T. Gurski, '*Urraca*: metahistory and self-discovery', *RHM*, 52:171–79, employs Hayden White's methodology — as outlined in *Metahistory: The Historical Imagination in Nineteenth-Century Europe* — to analyze Urraca's ambivalence about the nature of history and her own role in it, concluding that the protagonist's 'metahistorical musings function structurally and thematically as a metaphor for her personal quest for self-discovery'.

RIERA.  N. Valis, 'True confessions: Carme Riera's *Cuestión de amor propio*', *RCEH*, 23:311–27, is a clever study of several key aspects of R.'s novel, among them the exploration of authority and its relation to the situation of a writer as a woman. In V.'s view, such exploration is realized through self-reflexive confession as well as through intertexts such as Leopoldo Alas's *La Regenta* and the 16th-c. text *Question de amor*.

ROIG.  C. Dupláa, 'Testimony and cultural memory in Hispanic narratives: the case of Montserrat Roig's *Els catalans als camps nazis*', *BHS(L)*, 76:235–43, describes the theory of testimony elaborated by Latin Americanists and brilliantly adapts and applies it to this novel, in which, in D.'s words, R. 'attempts to recover the voice of those who are forced to live in silence because otherwise she cannot participate in a liberating project for her culture'.

SENDER.  E. E. Merino, 'Trama y deseo en una lectura de *El fugitivo*, de Ramón J. Sender', *LPen*, 11:841–62, is on M.'s reception of S.'s novel; M. explores the difficulties in the pleasure of reading a text with a fragmented plot that betrays our expectations.

TOMEO. N. L. Molinaro, 'Writing masculinity double: paranoia, parafiction and Javier Tomeo's *La agonía de Proserpina*', *ALEC*, 24:135–48, argues that, in this novel, T. departs from his previous vision of human relationships, in which women were often cast in roles of absent antagonist or ancillary, by suggesting that the protagonist's self-construction and authorial capacities are compromised by women's participation and that paranoid texts may result from unequal distribution of agency between genders.

TORRENTE BALLESTER. A. L. Walsh, 'Belief and disbelief as part of narrative: Gonzalo Torrente Ballester's *Don Juan*, a road less travelled', *BHS(L)*, 76:349–58, examines 'the constant need to question the boundaries of fictional verisimilitude' in T.B.'s novel, in line with 'a trend in modern Hispanic fiction which requires readers to maintain their disbelief in what they are reading'.

### 3. POETRY

#### GENERAL

At the end of the millennium, we are threatened with yet another so-called 'generation', adding a finishing touch that takes us back to reassess the last 100 years of Spanish literary history, which have been plagued with the restrictive and canonical concept of generations. José Luis García Martín, *La generación del 99*, Oviedo, Ediciones Nobel, 493 pp., takes us to what by now is a popular hybrid of critical study (7–30; 469–85), with a creative selection and introduction per poet (65–468). Although G.M. affirms 'hago de indiscreto enredador, de compulsivo antólogo sectario'; expresses his belief in 'generaciones como comunidades de edad', where each writer is a product of his or her time; and states that the title does not intend to define a poetic generation but to bring attention to what in his opinion are the most noteworthy poets, it might be useful to recall Barthes's reference to the fact that 'language is never innocent'. The poets included are: Benjamín Prado, Jesús Aguado, Aurora Luque, Amalia Bautista, José Antonio Mesa Toré, Vicente Gallego, José Manuel Benítez Ariza, José Mateos, Juan Manuel Villalba, Juan Antonio González Iglesias, Ángela Vallvey, Álvaro García, Eduardo García, Luis Muñoz, José Luis Piquero, Pelayo Fueyo, Antonio Manilla, Lorenzo Oliván, Javier Almuzara, Javier Rodríguez Marcos, Ana Merino, Marcos Tramón, Pablo García Casado, Silvia Ugidos, Carlos Martínez Aguirre, Martín López-Vega, Andrés Neuman, and Carmen Jodra Davó.

J. Mayhew, 'The avant-garde and its discontents: aesthetic conservatism in recent Spanish poetry', *HR*, 67:347–63, discusses the conservatism of poets such as Luis García Montero and Felipe Benítez Reyes, who denigrate the avant-garde 'excesses' of the *novísimos* and subscribe to the idea of 'un arte sensato' produced by 'personas que se consideran individuos normales y no quieren refugiarse en la extravagancia'. F. J. Ávila, 'Poesía última española (1997–1998): pocas sorpresas y algunas esperanzas', *RHM*, 52 : 227–44, reflects on contemporary Spanish poetry taking into consideration several poetry collections published by both established and new authors approximately from June 1997 to February 1998, finding few innovations and some promising possibilities in the following books: Manuel Caballero Bonald's *Diario de Argónida*, Manuel Rico's *La densidad de los espejos*, Antonio Carvajal's *Alma región luciente*, María Victoria Atencia's *Las contemplaciones*, Ana Merino's *Días gemelos*, José Luis Jover's *Sólo tienes que pensarlo*, Manuel Padorno's *Para mayor gloria*, García Montero's *Completamente viernes*, Jorge Riechmann's *El día que dejé de leer 'El País'*, Fermín Herrero's *Echarse al monte*, Carlos Martínez Aguirre's *La camarera del cine Doré y otros poemas*, Juan Cobos Wilkins's *Llama de clausura*, José Luis Puertos's *Señales*, Angel Luis Luján Atienza's *El silencio del mar*, Dionisio Cañas's *El gran criminal*, and José Fernández de la Sota's *Todos los santos*.

C. Dreymüller, 'El canon de las mujeres: a propósito de la poesía de Ana María Fagundo, Cristina Peri Rossi y Ana Rosetti', *Alaluz*, 31 : 7–16, claims that these poets were influenced by a literary canon much more diversified than the Spanish canon — one that includes more works created by women — and that this influence explains the fusion between artistic creation and erotic celebration present in their work not only as a more or less intentional rebellion, but also as 'una autoconciencia distinta, confirmada por lecturas entre comillas "distintas"'.

G. Pulido Tirado, 'La poesía de la experiencia y la crítica literaria en algunas antologías: hacia la fijación de un canon poético', *Salina*, 13 : 179–84, is on the relevance of the hybridity of Spanish anthologies, including the critical and the creative, in the historiography of Spanish poetry, especially in the latter half of the 20th c., and particularly in the last two decades, which have been dominated by the *poesía de la experiencia*, canonized by the anthologies of the period.

J. Pérez, 'Voces poéticas femeninas de la guerra civil española', *LPen*, 11, 1998 : 263–79, focuses on the poetry of Clementina Arderiu, Rosa Chacel, Ernestina de Champourcín, Carmen Conde, Ángela Figuera, Gloria Fuertes, Concha Méndez, Pilar Valderrama, and Concha Zardoya, and claims that 'la lírica femenina de la guerra civil española adquiere en momentos un carácter de lamento, elegía, protesta o denuncia ausentes en la narrativa, que participa más de la naturaleza de crónica, testimonio, análisis'. A. Medina, ' "Nada me pertenece sino aquello que perdí": infancia y guerra en la generación poética del 50', *ib.*, 427–53, first explores the child's experience of war in the poetry of Gil de Biedma, Barral, and Valente; then focuses on memory and the individual as social subject in the postwar context, paying particular attention to the poetry of Carlos Sahagún and José Manuel Caballero Bonald; and finally studies the different stance of women poets, Gloria Calvo Nava, Concha Lagos, Cristina Lacasa, Aurora de Albornoz, and María Beneyto, whose texts privilege memory and display a period of recuperation of a maternal discourse after a time of loss and severance inflicted by the war.

### INDIVIDUAL AUTHORS

ALBORNOZ.   S. Keefe Ugalde, 'The poetry of Aurora de Albornoz and gendered poetic traditions', *LPen*, 11, 1998:569–83, participates in bringing attention to an often neglected poet, contextualizing her poetry in the canon of 20th-c. poetry, and affirming that A. 'enables female poetic traditions to move [. . .] to a place where dualities [. . .] dissolve'.

ATENCIA.   S. Keefe-Ugalde, 'Masks of canvas and stone in the poetry of María Victoria Atencia', *ALEC*, 24:227–42, analyses A.'s ekphrastic poems, whose referents are paintings and sculptures from the 19th and 20th c., and argues that these texts pay attention to the particular experience of women (e.g. they present a dichotomy between women as historical subjects and women as products of hegemonic discourses) while at the same time communicating universal questions such as fiction versus reality and the epiphany and transcendence of art.

BOUSOÑO.   M. Peluse di Giulio, 'A propósito de *El martillo en el yunque*, de Carlos Bousoño', *RLit*, 61:133–76, inquires into B.'s reworkings of *Invasión de la realidad*, *Oda en la ceniza*, *Las monedas contra la losa*, *Metáfora del desafuero*, and *El ojo de la aguja* in *El martillo en el yunque*, and claims that most poems are structurally in tune with the latest Spanish poetry. P.G. points out that this collection, in the tradition of Blas de Otero, more than being a mere anthology constitutes a new book.

FAGUNDO.   S. Rolle-Risseto, 'La riqueza metafórica del cuerpo femenino en la obra de Ana María Fagundo', *CILH*:245–59, studies the feminine body in F.'s poetry, proposing that it functions as a vehicle of knowledge and as an incarnation of the mystery of being. S. Rolle-Risseto, '*El sol, la sombra, en el instante*, de Ana María Fagundo: una sinfonía de luz y de sombra o su canto a la creación', *LetD*, 84:245–55, studies F.'s poetry as bridging the gap between discovery and communication, and examines the creative power of the *logos*, placing the poem as birth, whilst paying attention to the ontological questions raised in F.'s poetry.

GIMFERRER. R. Cole Heinowitz, '*Arde el mar*: "reformulating" the romantic symbol, a project in the present progressive', *RHM*, 52:477–86, emphasizes the act of discovery and argues that G.'s collection offers 'a complete reformulation' of Romantic poetics by establishing a connection between the universal and the particular, and claims that the text 'succeeds in releasing language from its contract to define and allowing it performative agency'. HIERRO. G. McNeer, 'José Hierro's *Cuaderno en Nueva York*. Strangers in a strange land: a case for mistaken identity and poetry translations', *LPen*, 11, 1998:487–549, claims this collection 'has all the trappings of postmodernism' and 'it stands as a poetic icon for future spiritual visitors to this cultural mecca of the mind'; the first ten poems of the collection are translated into English (498–549).

## 4. DRAMA

### GENERAL

Spanish Hispanists in particular continue the recent trend to focus on theatre practice rather than on textual analysis, at the same time as the factual element is retained by the emphasis on a methodology that favours the history of theatre. M. F. Vilches de Frutos, 'La temporada teatral española 1996–1997', *ALEC*, 24:621–77, provides an excellent panoramic view, including the representations of Spanish works (from the classics to the post-war period) and foreign works in the areas of Madrid, Catalonia, and the autonomous communities. E. J. Doll, 'Entrevista a cuatro dramaturgas españolas: Romero, Pedrero, Falcón y Pombo', *Gestos*, 28:149–57, focuses on questions such as the description of the period of ·democratic transition in relation to Spanish theatre, women's particular role in the theatrical movements of the transition period, differences between the theatre of the transition period and that of 1983, difficulty in representing a new play in the mid 1990s, and women's future in Spanish theatre. E. J. Doll, 'El teatro madrileño de los 90: una encuesta', *Estreno*, 25.2:12–19, includes interviews with Fermín Cabal, Concha Romero, Jerónimo López Mozo, José Luis Alonso de Santos, Lidia Falcón, Pilar Pombo, and Paloma Pedrero on questions such as new theatre tendencies, young playwrights' possibilities of representing new pieces, the effectiveness of alternative theatres, the impact of politics in Spanish theatre, and the future of Spanish drama. P. W. O'Connor, 'La universalidad del teatro español del siglo XX y la aventura norteamericana', *RLit*, 61:119–31, highlights the unhealthy state of affairs concerning representations of Spanish plays in Broadway, Off Broadway, and Off Off Broadway during the 20th c., and calls for an end to seeing Spanish culture as inferior; but, unfortunately, to achieve it she severs it from the term 'Hispanic' which would apparently remain reserved for the *latinos*; O. revealingly states: 'los españoles son europeos y blancos, proceden de un país desarrollado' whilst ' "hispánico" [. . .] connota minoría étnica pobre'. Ó. Cornago Bernal, 'Claves formales de la renovación del teatro en España (1960–1975)', *ib.*, 177–212, is a well-informed study of a documentary nature on the history of theatre in the 15 years embraced in the title. In line with more recent trends on the subject, it centres on drama 'no ya como género literario, sino como espectáculo escénico' and claims that 'los discursos teatrales y críticos que configuran el actual panorama teatral adquirieron sus trazos definitivos' in the 1960s. There is a short section dedicated to the transition from realism to the rejection of the mimetic (182–85), whilst more attention is devoted to the section 'Líneas de evolución formal' (185–205), where the following bipolarity is presented: 'jerarquización/dinamismo, transparencia/opacidad, representación/presentación, dramaticidad/narratividad y continuidad/fragmentación', finding in the 1960s the period of consolidation of simultaneity in line with current theories of postmodern theatre as opposed to claims of chronological evolution. C. Santolaria Solano, 'Hacia una caracterización del teatro independiente', *ib.*, 521–35, is an overview of the *Teatro independiente* which corroborates its own claim that critical attention has focused on the independent theatre of the 1960s and 1970s after the 1980s showed that the main theatre practitioners evolved from that group, which set the standards for the democratic period. S. Trancón, 'El teatro español de fin de siglo', *CHA*, 592:7–19, is a general overview that somehow idealizes the role of theatre for the new millennium, and highlights theatrical practices in the democratic period. J. L. Alonso de Santos, 'El autor español en el fin de siglo', *ib.*, 21–28, is of particular relevance for those interested in A.S.'s theatre and his own views as an author who, along with Francisco Nieva, Juan José Alonso Millán, Santiago Moncada, Jaime Salom, Albert Boadella, and José Sanchis Sinisterra, is one of the dramatists who has been able to stage a large number of plays during the last six years. Whilst acknowledging the heterogeneity of theatre practices, A.S. also provides a 'Decálogo orientador' (25–26), with his opinions on the characteristics of recent theatre trends. J. A. Hormigón, 'La dirección de escena en España', *ib.*, 29–39, is an excellent account of the state of affairs concerning stage directors in Spain. H., a director himself of the group of the 1960s, emphasizes the lateness of the stage director as a profession in Spanish theatre compared with the rest of Europe, mentioning that 'Lo dominante durante los primeros cuarenta años de nuestro siglo fue que las escenificaciones bastante simples y rutinarias que se hacían, corrieran a cargo del primer actor o la primera actriz y, en ocasiones, del propio autor.' He sharply criticizes those who continue to view themselves or others as directors without the appropriate methodology to back them up, and pinpoints the importance of the *Asociación de Directores de Escena de España* (ADE), created in 1982, in changing attitudes on the subject. E. Galán, 'El público y lo público en el teatro español: una política de promoción y difusión teatral', *ib.*, 41–47, is on the current institutionalized support for theatre in Spain. G. refers to the dramatic decrease in theatre-goers in 1996, in the light of which the *Instituto Nacional de Artes Escénicas y de la Música* (INAEM), of which he is deputy director, established a plan to improve the situation by promoting theatre, which has had a positive effect, and can report that 1998 marked in Madrid the highest number of spectators since the arrival of democracy. Ó. Cornago Bernal, 'Origen, forma y función del ritual grotesco en la escena española contemporánea: Miguel Romero Esteo, Luis Riaza y Alfonso Jiménez Romero', *Estreno*, 25.2, 48–54, is faithful to the title, and pays particular attention to R.E.'s *Paraphernalia de la olla podrida, la misericordia y la mucha consolación* and *Pasodoble*, R.'s *El desván de los machos y el sótano de las hembras*, and J.R.'s *El inmortal*, following C.B.'s by now characteristic approach, that of theatrical history.

INDIVIDUAL AUTHORS

BENET I JORNET.   S. G. Feldman, ' "Un agujero sin límites": la mirada fenomenológica de Josep M. Benet I Jornet', *ALEC*, 24:473–91, studies the literary trajectory of this Catalan author, arguing that his theatre makes evident a phenomenological orientation similar to the one present in the work of contemporary dramatists such as Richard Foreman, Harold Pinter, Peter Handke, Bernard-Marie Koltés, David Mamet, and Robert Wilson. F. claims that this orientation culminates in B.J.'s latest pieces — *Desig* (1989), *Fugac* (1992), and *Testament* (1995), in which space and time are constituted as exterior projections of subjective, fluctuating, and disturbing landscapes.

BUERO VALLEJO.   J. Rubio Jiménez, 'Goya y el teatro español contemporáneo. De Valle-Inclán a Alberti y Buero Vallejo', *ALEC*, 24:593–619, analyses the importance of Goya in the work of these three authors. Of relevance to this section is the study of *El sueño de la razón* (613–16), in which R.J. shows how B.V. employs the figure of a grotesque Goya in particular as an instrument both to reveal Spanish conflicts during Franco's regime and to move the audience to reflect on their own liberty and its limits at the time. M. P. Holt, 'Buero Vallejo's fifty years on stage: the neglected performance history',

*Estreno*, 25.1:42–49, is the first study indeed to pay attention to 'a performance history that is more than dates and names and which considers the relationship of scenic realization to the critical and audience perceptions of his plays both individually and as a total body of dramatic writing.'

LÓPEZ MOZO. D. K. Herzberger, '*El engaño a los ojos*: the theatrics of theatrical history', *Estreno*, 25.2:20–21, is an excellent critical review — followed by the script (22–42) — of L.M.'s play. According to H., this piece serves the dual end of embodying L.M.'s 'perception of how theater ought to be written [. . .] and of delineating the historical filiations of such theater beginning with Cervantes in the seventeenth century'. M. F. Vilches de Frutos, 'El compromiso del hombre con la historia: *Eloídes* (1992) y *Ahlán* (1996), de Jerónimo López Mozo', *Estreno*, 25.2:43–47, analyses L.M.'s critical view of two problems of contemporary society dramatized in these plays: unemployment and xenophobia.

MIRAS. M. de Paco, 'Historia y drama: *El libro de Salomón*, de Domingo Miras', *Estreno*, 25.1:50–53, argues that this play, as also the rest of M.'s dramatic production, is loyal to historical facts, while at the same time recreating characters and circumstances that did not exist necessarily in the way in which they are described. M.P. analyses the differences between historically documented and dramatized events particularly in relation to the characters.

NIEVA. F. Komla Aggor, 'Francisco Nieva's *Pelo de Tormenta* and the politics of eroticism', *Hispanófila*, 127:37–52, examines 'the symbolic ways in which the playwright dramatizes institutional repression and the contradictions that mark it', arguing that N.'s parody of official codification of sexuality acts 'as a mechanism for celebrating *el pueblo*, the ordinary people, through their exaltation of Eros as a vital force'. F. Komla Aggor, 'Ceremony in Francisco Nieva's *La carroza de plomo candente*', *Estreno*, 25.1:36–41, studies the function of the multiple layers of ceremony in this one-act play with the intention of underscoring N.'s 'use of ceremony as a political instrument employed to undermine heterosexual culture and traditional Catholic rituals'.

ONETTI. P. J. Hodge, 'Pictures in motion: images and socio-theatrical energy in *Madre Caballo* by Antonio Onetti', *Gestos*, 27:43–60, takes into consideration the theories of Christopher Balme and Stephen Greenblatt regarding theatre, and examines 'how images in theater intersect with contemporary social issues and [. . .] how they manifest a particular theatrical practice or tradition'.

POMBO. H. Cazorla, 'Conversación con Pilar Pombo', *Estreno*, 25.2:9–11, is a brief interview with this distinguished playwright, who passed away on 26 April 1999, on questions such as her beginnings as an author, her pieces, her influences, her talent, and her ideas about the Spanish theatre of the last twenty years. SANCHIS SINISTERRA. W. Floeck, 'Historia, posmodernidad e interculturalidad en la *Trilogía americana* de José Sanchis Sinisterra', *ALEC*, 24:493–532, discusses the metahistorical and intercultural themes as well as the techniques of deconstruction present in this postmodern trilogy published in 1992, emphasizing the ethical commitment and the search for a historical and actual extraliterary reality that these themes and techniques reveal.

# IV. CATALAN STUDIES

## LANGUAGE

By Sílvia Llach, *Universitat de Girona*

### 1. General

M. W. Wheeler, A. Yates, and N. Dols, *Catalan: A Comprehensive Grammar*, London, Routledge, 638 pp., is an exhaustive and definitive grammar of Catalan, valuable for the study of Catalan by native speakers or foreign learners. L. López del Castillo, *Gramàtica del català actual: sintaxi i morfologia* (El Cangur, 272), B, Edicions 62, 299 pp., is a manual of grammar that focuses on syntactic and morphological compounds. P. Verdaguer, *Grammaire de la langue catalane, 1. Les origines de la langue*, B, Curial, 389 pp., is the first volume of V.'s grammar; the topic dealt with here is the historical origins of the Catalan language.

### 2. Phonetics and Phonology

J. Carrera, A. M. Fernández, and J. Matas, 'Estudi contrastiu de vocals mitjanes del català oriental central i nord-occidental', pp. 143–49 of *Actes del I Congrés de Fonètica Experimental, Tarragona, 22, 23 i 24 de febrer de 1999*, B, Univ. Rovira i Virgili–Univ. de B, 323 pp., offers the acoustically significant differences of openness between the mid vowels of the anterior and posterior series of two Catalan dialects: 'barceloní' and 'lleidatà'. S. M. Cortés, 'Production and perception of English sounds by Catalan/Spanish speakers', *ib.*, 165–70, deals with the acquisition of the voiced labiodental fricative by Catalan/Spanish speakers since this sound is neither present in Spanish nor Catalan. The results showed that these speakers do produce /v/ significantly, by correlation with a good perception of this sound. I. Creus, 'Els enllaços vocàlics en lleidatà a partir de l'estructura conversacional', *ib.*, 171–78, proposes a descriptive study of vocalic contacts in adjacent words as a case of linguistic variation. N. Cuartero, 'Voicing assimilation in Catalan and English', *ib.*, 179–85, analyses the direction and temporal extent of voicing assimilation in Catalan and English voiceless–voiced stop sequences. The data obtained reveal that the processes are different in the two languages, involving categorical operation in Catalan and much more variability in the case of English. S. Llach, 'La neutralització de la sonoritat en els grups consonàntics finals de les formes verbals sense terminació del mallorquí', *ib.*, 241–48, shows that there are phonetic differences in voicing in phonologically neutralized segments. Differences remain in the best contexts from the point of view of perception and production. S. Oliva et al., 'Manifestació acústica de la resolució de xocs accentuals en català', *ib.*, 249–55, examine the production and perception processes involved in cases of clash. The perception experiment shows a high level of confusion. The production experiment reveals that the $F_0$ contour seems to be the main correlate of destressing in clash contexts. M. Riera, 'Definició d'una unitat d'àmbit local per a la generació automàtica de l'entonació en català', *ib.*, 295–301, looks for an intonational unit of local scope to describe and generate Catalan intonation for a text-to-speech system. The results suggest that the left stress group is the best unit for this purpose. D. Recasens, 'Theoretical and methodological issues on coarticulation', *ib.*, 67–75, shows that C-to-C coarticulatory effects are more prominent than V-to-C effects, due to the constraints involved in consonantal production. The experiment focuses on the dark /l/ and the alveolopalatal nasal of Catalan. Another issue dealt with in this paper is the direction of coarticulation. J. Jiménez, *L'estructura sil·làbica del català* (Biblioteca Sanchis Guarner, 49), V, IIFV — B, PAM, 268 pp., presents an analysis of Catalan syllabic phenomena (in the Valencian dialect) on the basis of Optimality Theory. D. Recasens and M. D. Pallarès, 'A study of /ɾ/ and /r/ in the light of the "DAC" coarticulation model', *JPh*, 27:143–69, present an electropalatographic and acoustic study of the production and coarticulatory characteristics of these sounds in CVC sequences, demonstrating articulatory and coarticulatory differences and suggesting that the trill is not a geminate counterpart of the tap. *Aplicació al català dels principis de transcripció de l'Associació Fonètica Internacional*, ed. J. Rafel, B, IEC, 16 pp., presents the normative adaptation of the norms and symbols of the IPA to the sounds and phonemes of Catalan.

### 3. Lexis and Morphology

M. P. Perea, *Complements a la flexió verbal en els dialectes catalans. Dotze quaderns de camp d'Antoni M. Alcover* (Textos i Estudis de Cultura Catalana), B, PAM, 291 pp., publishes dialectal and historical data about verbal flexion, including original lexical, phonological and morphological comments. E. Gelpí, *Mesures d'avaluació lexicogràfica de diccionaris bilingües* (Tesis doctorals microfitxades, 3415), Univ. de B, microfiche, focuses on the evaluation criteria applied in the field of bilingual dictionaries. M. Barri, *Aportació a l'estudi dels gal·licismes del català* (Biblioteca Filològica, 39), B, IEC, 623 pp., presents an exhaustive study of the presence and influence of gallicisms in the

Catalan lexicon. X. Favà, *Etimologia i variació dels ceps, raïms i vins: un lèxic d'ampelonímia catalana* (Tesis doctorals microfitxades, 3445), Univ. de B, microfiche, provides historical and variation data on the lexicon of vine growing. Joan Ferrer, Josep Ferrer, and J. Pujadas, 'L'"Onomasticon Cataloniae" de Joan Coromines. Història i metodologia', *RevCat*, 142:97–118, includes all data about the history and methodology of one of the major works on place names and etymology of Catalan. A. Bel Gaya, *Teoria lingüística i adquisició del llenguatge: anàlisi comparada dels trets morfològics en català i castellà*, Univ. Autònoma de B, 2 microfiches, presents a comparison between the acquisition of morphological features in Catalan and Castilian. A. Moll, 'El "Diccionari" de l'Institut. Aproximació a una altra aproximació (I–IV)', *RevCat*, 143:116–54, 144:157–72, 145:96–131, 146:84–105, replies to a previous study on the *Diccionari de l'Institut d'Estudis Catalans*, systematically analysing the criticism of dictionary criteria in the study mentioned.

4. SYNTAX, SEMANTICS, AND PRAGMATICS

L. Casanova, 'El sujeto en el catalán coloquial', *REL*, 29.1:105–31, analyses the presence or absence of the subject and its position in the phrase in oral Catalan sentences, from the relation between syntax and pragmatics. J. Solà, *Parlem-ne. Converses lingüístiques* (Proa La Mirada), B, Enciclopèdia Catalana, 328 pp., consists of a series of articles on certain controversial aspects of various topics, among others: fashionable words, the rhetoric of publicity, Castilian expressions, and the role that correctors of Catalan should play in the present. P. Sancho, *Introducció a la fraseologia. Aplicació al valencià col·loquial*, V, Denes, 184 pp., presents a general introduction to phraseology as the science that studies idiomatic expressions, focusing especially on the Valencian colloquial dialect. The study is based on cognitive grammar and its assumption that phraseology plays an important role in the knowledge and the use of a language. J. Ginebra and A. Montserrat, *Diccionari d'ús dels verbs catalans: règim verbal i canvi i caiguda de preposicions*, B, Edicions 62, 489 pp., is a dictionary of the correct use of verbs and prepositions. The book focuses on controversial features of current Catalan, which is influenced by language shift and foreign languages.

5. SOCIOLINGUISTICS

STANDARDIZATION. J. Armangué, 'La "Proposta per a una normalització del català de l'Alguer"(1992–1998)', *RCat*, 139:60–79, presents all data on the relationship between the group responsible for the introduction of Algueresian aspects in standard Catalan and the normative institution, the Institut d'Estudis Catalans.

## 6. DIALECTOLOGY

J. Colomina, *Dialectologia catalana. Introducció i guia bibliogràfica* (Biblioteca de Filologia Catalana, 7), Univ. d'Alacant, 353 pp., updates bibliographical data and references, with much information on studies of the Valencian dialect. J. Viaplana, *Entre la dialectologia i la lingüística. La distància lingüística entre les varietats del català nord-occidental*, B, PAM, 391 pp., aims to describe the present situation of various north-western dialects of Catalan. V. emphasizes evolutionary aspects, and includes the morphological differences that have been observed.

## MEDIEVAL LITERATURE

By LOLA BADIA, *Professor of Catalan Literature at the Universitat de Girona* and
MIRIAM CABRÉ, *Researcher at the Universitat de Girona*

### 1. GENERAL

BIBLIOGRAPHY. *BBAHLM*, 12:1–53, assembles the studies on medi-
eval Catalan in 1998. *Qüern*, 3, covers the years 1997–98. *L'AILLC*,
PAM, 256 pp., offers a detailed table of publications since 1968. S.
Asperti, 'La letteratura catalana medievale', pp. 327–410 of *Storia
delle letterature medievali romanze: L'area iberica*, ed. M. L. Meneghetti,
Bari, Laterza, 519 pp., surveys Catalan literature up to the 14th c.,
with an updated bibliography.
  COLLECTED ESSAYS AND HISTORICAL CONTEXT. X. Renedo, 'Joan
Coromines, editor de textos catalans i occitans', pp. 145–54 of *L'obra
de Joan Corominas: cicle d'estudi i d'homenatge*, ed. J. Solà et al., Sabadell,
Fundació Caixa de Sabadell, 313 pp., examines emblematic editions
by the late philologist. J. Sanchis Sivera, *Estudis d'Història Cultural*, ed.
M. Rodrigo Lizondo et al., *IIFV*–PAM, 255 pp., includes works on
biblical studies, Vicent Ferrer and drama. A. Mundó, *Obres Completes*,
vol. 1 : *Catalunya: 1. De la romanitat a la sobirania*, Curial–PAM, 1998,
629 pp., gathers his studies on Catalan culture up to the 12th century.
The collected works of M. Colom Mateu, *Cuestiones lulianas*, Inca, Illes
Balears U.P.–Ajuntament d'Inca, 1998, 174 pp., include unpublished
material. M. de Riquer, *Caballeros medievales y sus armas*, M, Instituto
Universitario 'General Gutiérrez Mellado', UNED, 308 pp., illustrates medieval knighthood and war with literary examples. The
innovative synthesis in D. Abulafia, *The Western Mediterranean Kingdoms
1200–1500: The Struggle for Dominion*, London, Longman, 1997,
300 pp., refers to figures such as Ramon Llull and the cabalist
Abraham Abulafia.
  ARCHIVAL RESEARCH AND READERSHIP. I. Padrosa Gorgot, 'Catà-
leg dels manuscrits catalans de la Biblioteca del Palau de Perelada',
*Annals de l'Institut d'Estudis Gironins*, 39, 1998:395–458, and J. de Puig,
'Manuscrits eimericians de la Biblioteca Capitular y Colombina de
Sevilla provinents de Girona', *ATCA*, 17, 1998:295–380, study two
library collections. See also G. Mele, 'Tradizioni codicologiche e
cultura tra Sardegna e Catalogna nel Medioevo. Note per un primo
bilancio', Maninchedda, *Sardegna*, 236–315, on Iberian MSS known
in Sardinia (8th-16th c.); and G. Avenoza, 'El manuscrito catalán de
la *Visión deleitable* de A. de la Torre', *AHLM* 7, 1, 192–275, on a new
MS witness. V. J. Escartí, 'Encara sobre escriptors i lectors a la
València del segle XV', *Atti* (Palermo), VI, 135–45; and A. Ferrando

and J. V. Escartín, 'Impremta i vida literària a València en el pas del segle XV al XVI', *BSCC*, 72, 1998[1999]: 161–78, deal with some aspects of Valencian readership.

## 2. LYRIC AND NARRATIVE VERSE

### AUSIÀS MARCH

New publications on M. have included a number of monographic volumes such as *Canelobre*, 39–40, and *Ausiàs March (Madrid, Biblioteca Nacional, 13 mayo-27 junio 1999)*, V, Generalitat Valenciana, 333 pp. Articles in *Ausiàs March i el món cultural del segle XV*, ed. R. Alemany, Alacant, *IIFV*, 376 pp., deal with a variety of 15th-c. topics, some specifically on M.: J. J. Chiner Gimeno, '1997, any March?: noves dades sobre el naixement d'Ausiàs' (13–45), suggests a new birthdate *c.* 1400–01; C. Di Girolamo, 'Il *canzoniere* di Ausiàs March' (45–58); V. J. Escartí, 'Encara sobre València i Ausiàs March al segle XVI' (173–97), documents 16th-c. interest in M.; and A. Espadaler, 'El concepte de *vergonya* en l'obra d'Ausiàs March' (77–93), analyses poem 42. The French translation *Chants de mort*, ed. D. de Courcelles, Paris, Corti, 156 pp., has an interpretative introduction. Two studies on M.'s reception: A. M. Compagna Perrone Capano, 'Il sogno marchiano di Joan Pujol', *Atti* (Milan), 319–26; and G. Colón, 'El manuscrit fantasma d'Ausiàs March', *BSCC*, 72, 1998[1999]: 341–44. J. J Chiner Gimeno, ' "En vós està fer con cas flach o fort" (107,9): correccions d'impremta, correccions d'autor a *Ausiàs March i la València del s. XV (1400–1459)*', *LlLi*, 10:361–84, gives a full list of corrections to the previous publication. It is worth highlighting J. Turró, 'Ausiàs March no va viure en temps d'Ovidi', Rafanell, *Estudis*, 176–99, on M.'s Ovidian background and its acquisition via grammar school.

### OTHER LYRICAL AND NARRATIVE POETRY

M. Cabré, *Cerverí de Girona and his Poetic Traditions*, London, Tamesis, 224 pp., outlines the cultural milieu of the royal court to analyse the 13th-c. troubadour, and her 'Italian and Catalan Troubadours', pp. 127–40 of *The Troubadours. An Introduction*, ed. S. Gaunt and S. Kay, CUP, 330 pp., gives a historical background to the overview of troubadour activity in Catalonia. J. Pujol, '*Jo viu lo Ray ab la nobla Leuzeta*. Ressons d'una *razo* a la literatura catalana del segle XV', *ASolP*, 4, 1998:93–100, corrects the typographical errors of the text in *ib.*, 3. J. J. Chiner Gimeno, 'Noves dades arxivístiques sobre la mort de Jordi de Sant Jordi', *AHLM* 7, 1, 67–70, gives 18 June 1424 as the date of the poet's death. Two studies describing MS songbooks:

V. Beltran, 'Tipologia i gènesi del cançoner J, ms. esp. 225 de la Bibliothèque Nationale de Paris', *ib.*, 337–52; and S. Martí, 'Fonts i problemes del Cançoner del Marquès de Barberà (S¹/BN1)', *Atti* (Palermo), VI, 311–24. On Jaume Roig's *Espill*: J. Ainaud Escudero, 'De Jaume Roig a Stephen Sondheim: canibalisme i misogínia', *AHLM* 7, I, 243–54, relates R.'s cannibalist episode to hagiographic iconography; and G. Grilli, 'Racconto, discorso e sogno nello *Spill* di J. Roig', *Atti* (Milan), 305–17, sets *Espill* in the context of 15th-c. Valencia.

## 3. Doctrinal and Religious Prose

### RAMON LLULL AND LULLISM

The annotated edition of L.'s *Ars brevis. Lateinisch-Deutsch*, ed. A. Fidora, Hamburg, Meiner, xlv + 146 pp., also has a German translation and an interpretative introduction. G. Pomaro and M. Pereira, 'Notizia di due manoscritti lulliani a Firenze', *SLu*, 38, 1998:63–83, describe two new MSS containing three of L.'s scientific treatises. Several articles touch on specific Lullian issues: T. Sales, 'La informàtica moderna, hereva intel·lectual directa del pensament de Llull', *ib.*, 51–61, uses computer science to explain ten of L.'s logical and mathematical ideas; A. Soler, 'Espiritualitat i cultura: els laics i l'accés al saber a final del segle XIII a la Corona d'Aragó', *ib.*, 3–26, relates L. and Arnau de Vilanova to the emergence of lay culture; F. Domínguez, 'Der Religionsdialog bei Raimundus Lullus. Apologetische Prämissen und kontemplative Grundlage', pp. 263–90 of *Gespräche lesen. Philosophische Dialoge im Mittelalter*, ed. K. Jacobi, Tübingen, Narr, 523 pp., typifies dialogue in L., with reference to the Dominican tradition; L. Badia, 'La literatura alternativa de Ramon Llull: tres mostres', *AHLM* 7, I, 11–32, explores L.'s use of literature with scientific contents as an ideological vehicle; and her 'La caiguda dels greus i la digestió dels remugants: variacions lul·lianes sobre l'experiència del coneixement', Rafanell, *Estudis*, 153–73, deals with L.'s use of scientific analogies.

### ARNAU DE VILANOVA AND OTHER SCIENTIFIC TEXTS

J. Ziegler, *Medicine and Religion c. 1300: The Case of Arnau de Vilanova*, Oxford, Clarendon Press, 1998, 342 pp., studies V. as a mystic and a physician within the context of the contemporary medical discipline. J. Mensa Valls, 'Comparació entre les regles i els principis d'interpretació bíblica de les obres autèntiques d'Arnau de Vilanova i les de l'*Expositio apocalypsis* i de l'*Expositio super vigesimum quartum capitulum Matthaei*', *ATCA*, 17, 1998:221–94, discusses V.'s exegetical theory.

L. Cifuentes, 'Vernacularization as an intellectual and social bridge: the Catalan translation of Teodorico's *Chirurgia* and of Arnau de Vilanova's *Regimen Sanitatis*', *Early Science and Medicine*, 4.2:127–48, deals with the circulation of these texts and the use of Catalan in scientific works. See also D. Guixeras, '*L'amor hereos* segons la glossa al *Viaticum* de Gil de Santarém (Arxiu Capitular de la Catedral de Girona, ms. 75)', Rafanell, *Estudis*, 129–51, on a scholastic definition of lovesickness and its cure. Two titles on alchemy: M. Pereira and B. Spaggiari, *Il 'Testamentum' alchemico attribuito a Raimondo Lullo*, Florence, Tavarnuzze–Galluzzo, Sismel, 631 pp.; and M. Pereira, 'Alchemy and the use of vernacular language in the late Middle Ages', *Speculum*, 74:336–56, which surveys Catalan alchemy texts and discusses their role in the spread of the vernacular.

### VICENT FERRER, FRANCESC EIXIMENIS, AND OTHER MORAL WRITERS

M. T. Ferrer Mallol, 'Frontera, convivencia y proselitismo entre cristianos y moros en los textos de Francesc Eiximenis y de san Vicente Ferrer', *Santiago-Otero Vol.* II, 1579–1600, analyses the attitude of F. and E. towards Islam. P. Cátedra, 'Fray Vicente Ferrer y la predicación antijudaica en la campaña castellana (1411–1412)', pp. 19–46 of '*Qu'un sang impur*' . . . *Les Conversos et le pouvoir en Espagne à la fin du moyen âge. Actes du 2ᵉ Colloque d'Aix-en-Provence (1994)*, Aix-en-Provence, Provence U.P., 1997, shows F.'s sermons as symptomatic in the issue of Castilian *conversos*. F. M. Gimeno Blay, 'Las *Schedulae sermonum* de San Vicente Ferrer en San Domenico de Perugia', *Anales valentinos*, 24, 1998[1999]:371–77, describes an unpublished sermon collection. There is also an edition of F.'s *Tractat de la vida espiritual*. *Sermons*, ed. A. Robles, B, Proa, 1998, 199 pp., and *ATCA*, 18, contains several articles on F. by J. Perarnau, some describing MS sources. On Eiximenis: J. J. Chiner Gimeno, 'Notes sobre el *Bellum iustum* en el *Dotzè* del *Chrestià* d'Eiximenis', *ASolP*, 4, 1998:57–74, studies E.'s treatment of war; A. Hauf, 'Corrientes espirituales valencianas en la baja Edad Media (s. XIV-XV)', *Anales valentinos*, 24, 1998[1999]:261–302, discusses E., Canals and Isabel de Villena; B. Taylor, 'The fables of Eiximenis: norm and abnormality', *MLR*, 94:409–14, analyses E.'s use of fables; and J.-A. Ysern Lagarda, 'Notes sobre la creativitat literària de Francesc Eiximenis en l'ús d'*exempla*', *ELLC*, 39:5–37, his use of *exempla*. On this genre, see also his 'Estudi i edició dels *exempla* esparsos del ms. Santes Creus 49 — *olim* 23 — pertanyent a la Biblioteca Pública de Tarragona', *ZK*, 12:49–82. M. Conca and J. Guia, 'El *Franselm*, un llibre dels bons amonestaments per a la Mediterrània catalana', Maninchedda,

*Sardegna*, 167–81, classify Turmeda's proverbs. J. J. Chiner Gimeno, 'Noves dades sobre Jeroni Fuster, autor de l'*Omelia sobre los Psalm "De profundis"*', *ELLC*, 39:83–92, draws data from the wills of Fuster and his father. R. J. Puchades Bataller, *Als ulls de Déu, als ulls dels homes: estereotips morals i percepció social d'algunes figures professionals en la societat medieval valenciana*, Valencia U.P., 222 pp., outlines the image of some professions in moral literature. Blackmore, *Queer Iberia*, contains three articles on Catalan moral texts.

4. HISTORICAL AND ARTISTIC PROSE, NOVEL

HISTORIOGRAPHY

A. Hauf, *La Littérature historiographique des origines à 1500*, GRLM, 11, 2, 1993:167–306, lists Catalan historiographic works within an Iberian context. On the chronicle of James I, J. Bruguera, *El vocabulari del «Llibre dels fets» del rei en Jaume, IIFV*–PAM, 226 pp., is a lexical study, with a list of corrections to the ENC edition; and J. Alturo Perucho, 'Un altre manuscrit del *Llibre dels fets* del rei Jaume I', *ATCA*, 17, 1998:490–506, presents a new fragmentary witness. On Muntaner's chronicle: V. Orazi, 'Il *Sermó* nella *Crònica* di Ramon Muntaner: la confluenza della voce dell'individuo nell'espressione corale di un popolo', Maninchedda, *Sardegna*, 406–18, analyses Muntaner's harangue. On later chronicles: M. Batlle, *Patriotisme i modernitat a la 'Fi del comte d'Urgell'*, Curial–PAM, 142 pp., proposes a late 16th-c. date following philological and legal analysis; and in Pere Antoni Beuter, *Primera part de la Història de València*. ed. V. J. Escartí, Valencia U.P., 1998, 212 pp., the section up to the 12th c. is edited and studied.

BERNAT METGE

Bernat Metge, *Lo somni*, ed. L. Badia, B, Quaderns Crema, 267 pp., is an annotated edition with a useful prologue. S. M. Cingolani, '*Lo somni* de Bernat Metge: prolegòmens per a una nova edició', *LlLi*, 10:245–78, outlines the main features of his edition in progress, new sources, and the emerging picture of M. as intellectual. J. E. Rubio, 'La fe raonada en una summa en vulgar del XV: el *Memorial de la fe catòlica* de Pertusa', pp. 361–76 of *Ausiàs March i el món cultural* (see p. 302), connects this apologetic work with M. and *Tirant*.

TIRANT LO BLANC AND CURIAL E GÜELFA

R. Beltrán and J. Izquierdo, 'Edicions i estudis sobre el *Tirant lo Blanc* (1995–1997)', *LlLi*, 10:387–401, is a monographic bibliography. A great many publications have appeared in this field. The monographic issue *Caplletra*, 23, 1997[1999], is mainly concerned with modern translations of *T.*, but also includes J. Butinyà, 'Sobre la font d'una font del *Tirant lo Blanc* i la modernitat de la novel·la' (57–74), on the notion of Fortune; and R. M. Mérida, 'La fortuna del *Tirant lo Blanch* entre alguns lectors hispànics dels segles XVI al XIX' (75–89). *Tirant lo Blanc: New Approaches*, ed. Arthur Terry, London, Tamesis, 139 pp. contains R. Beltran, 'Comedy and performance in *Tirant lo Blanc*' (15–28); T. R. Hart, 'Language and intimacy in *Tirant lo Blanc*' (83–90); A. Hauf, 'The eschatological framework of Tirant's African adventure' (69–82), on the image of Islam; J. Guia and C. Wittlin, 'Nine problem areas concerning *Tirant lo Blanc*' (109–26), on the authorship of *T.*; J. Lawrance, 'Death in *Tirant lo Blanc*' (91–107), on the suitability of labelling *T.* as a medieval novel; M. Piera, '*Tirant lo Blanc*: rehistoricizing the "other" Reconquista' (46–58), on comparative features with Muntaner's chronicle; J. Pujol, ' "Poets and historians" in *Tirant lo Blanc*: Joanot Martorell's models and the cultural space of chivalresque fiction' (29–43), on the role of historiographic sources; J. D. Rodríguez Velasco, "The chivalresque worlds in *Tirant lo Blanc*" (1–14), on ideas of knighthood as a narrative drive; and M. J. Rubiera Mata, '*Tirant lo Blanc* and the Muslim world in the fifteenth century' (59–67). *El arte de la seducción en el mundo románico medieval y renacentista*, ed. E. Real Ramos, Valencia U.P., 1995, 358 pp., has two articles on *T.*: R. Beltran, 'Tres magas en el arte de la seducción: Trotaconventos, Plaerdemavida y Celestina' (29–38); and A. Hauf, 'Seducció i anti-seducció: d'Ovidi a l'*Heptamerón*, passant pel *Tirant lo Blanch*' (119–44). P. Limorti, *Tirant lo Blanc i la historiografia catalana medieval*, Alacant, GV–Institut de Cultura Juan Gil-Albert, 154 pp., analyses historiographic sources in *T* as a narrative device. A. Hauf, ' "Sinó per la fe de Jhesucrist" (*Tirant lo Blanch, c.* 403)', *BSCC*, 72, 1998[1999]:49–75, discusses a sermon included in *T.* J. M. Perujo Melgar, 'L'obra de Guido delle Colonne reutilitzada en el *Tirant lo Blanch*', Maninchedda, *Sardegna*, 462–72, typifies the use of this source. T. Martínez Romero, '*Funus triumpho simillimum*? Consideracions al voltant de la mort i del dol per Tirant lo Blanch', *BSCC*, 72, 1998[1999]:23–48, discusses the use of Seneca and the meaning of the novel's ending. J. M. Manzanaro Blasco, *Fortuna en el 'Tirant lo Blanch' i en el 'Curial e Güelfa'*, Alacant U.P., 1998, 164 pp. includes *T.* and *C.* in his discussion on Fortune and supplies an updated bibliography. Two items specifically focus on *C.*: M. Piera, '*Curial y Güelfa' y las novelas de caballerías españolas*, M, Pliegos, 1998. 187 pp.; and A. M. Saludes Amat, 'I sogni nel *Curial e Güelfa*', *Atti* (Milan), 273–87, on the echo of Dante in *C.*'s visions.

JOAN ROÍS DE CORELLA

L. Badia, 'L'ascensió irresistible de l'astre literari de Joan Roís de Corella: cinc anys de bibliografia (1993–1997)', *LlLi*, 10:402–16, is a monographic bibliography on C. Research on this author has been remarkably abundant. *Estudis sobre Joan Roís de Corella*, ed. V. Martines, Alcoi, Marfil, 329 pp., includes R. Alemany, 'El mite d'Orfeu en Bernat Metge i en Joan Roís de Corella: lectura comparativa' (41–54); A. Annichiarico, 'Presenza e presenza-assenza di madonna Fiammetta e di Corella nel *Tirant lo Blanc*' (55–69); E. Casanova, 'La llengua de Joan Roís de Corella (1435–1497)' (89–105); S. M. Cingolani, 'Anticavalleria com a anticlassicisme a l'obra de Joan Roís de Corella' (107–23); A. Ferrando, 'L'anònim *Pròleg d'una no poc devota adoració de Jesús crucificat*: una mostra de la prosa artitzada de les darreries del segle XV' (133–56), who edits an incunable on a devotional topic; and T. Martínez Romero, 'Per a una interpretació de la *Balada de la garsa i l'esmerla*' (265–81), on the motif of spring birdsong, with a full bibliography. The monographic *Caplletra*, 24, 1998[1999], contains several articles relating C. to contemporary writers and their cultural milieu: A. Annicchiarico, '*Voglia di pathos* e un'altra *connexió*: Fiammetta e Corella nel *Tirant lo Blanc*' (25–44); A. Hauf, 'Possibles ressons de les *Tusculanes* en el poema XXXVII d'Ausiàs March?' (105–15), on Stoic notions in March's poem 37; T. Martínez Romero, 'Variacions sobre el tema *Corella i els contemporanis valencians*' (45–66), on relationships between Valencian writers; C. Miralles, 'Corella i el *Tirant*: qüestions d'intertextualitat' (67–80), on the use of orally transmitted works by C. in *Tirant*; J. Romeu Figueras, '*Tragèdia de Caldesa*, de Joan Roís de Corella: una aproximació textual' (81–92), who edits C.'s text and interprets it as autobiographically inspired; C. Wittlin, 'La biblioteca de la família Mercader de València l'any 1489' (93–104), on the Mercaders as a cultural point of reference in 15th-c. Valencia. J. L. Martos, 'El *Cançoner de Maians* (BUV MS 728): un cançoner d'autor de Joan Roís de Corella', *ELLC*, 39:93–113, offers a codicological description.

5. TRANSLATIONS AND OTHER GENRES AND TEXTS

J. Perarnau Espelt, 'La traducció catalana medieval del *Liber secretorum eventuum* de Joan de Rocatalhada', *ATCA*, 17, 1998:7–219, is an annotated edition. C. Wittlin, 'La traducció catalana del *Speculum Ecclesiae* d'Hug de Saint-Cher, impresa a Càller l'any 1493', Maninchedda, *Sardegna*, 447–61, is a study and partial edition of this incunable. M. M. López Casas, 'Una altra traducció al català de la *Carta de Lèntul al Senat de Roma*', *Actas* (Corunna), I, 361–70, presents a

1524 edition containing also a Catalan *Legenda aurea*; see also her 'Versions hispàniques de la *Carta de Pilat a Tiberi*', *AHLM* 7, II, 303–14; G. Navarro, 'Faula, història i exemplaritat: dues compilacions catalanes de la *Histoire ancienne jusqu'à César*', *ib.*, III, 79–90, analyses translation methodology; and J. Samsó, 'Traducciones científicas árabo-romances en la península ibérica', *ib.*, 199–232, includes a survey of Catalan translations. T. M. Capuano, 'The agricultural texts appended to the 14th-c. Iberian translations of Palladius', *Manuscripta*, 38, 1994:253–63, suggests that these texts were written in Barcelona and Valencia. Several articles deal with 15th-c. theoretical discussions and also with Italian influences: A. M. Badia Margarit, *Les 'Regles de esquivar vocables' i la 'qüestió de la llengua'*, B, IEC, 512 pp., edits the first formulation on the Catalan language; S. Miguel Prendes, *El espejo y el piélago. La 'Eneida' castellana de Enrique de Villena*, Kassel, Reichenberger, 1998, 306 pp., discusses 15th-c. literary ideas, using Villena's commentary as a starting point; V. Orazi, 'Il *somni recitant lo procés d'una qüestió enamorada* di Francesc Alegre: cornice onirica per un'allegoria di sapore umanistico nella Barcellona della fine del XV sec.', *Atti* (Milan), 289–304, searches for rhetorical and cultural models; M. Vilallonga, 'El viatge dels catalans a Roma durant el segle XV', Rafanell, *Estudis*, 201–21, explores the impact of Rome on Margarit and Jeroni Pau; and T. Cirillio Sirri, 'Pere Miquel Carbonell e i fratelli Geraldini', Maninchedda, *Sardegna*, 154–66, studies the presence of the Geraldini in one of Carbonell's MSS.

6. DRAMA

*La teatralidad medieval y su supervivencia. Actas del Seminario celebrado con motivo del III Festival d'Elx de Teatre i Música Medieval*, Elx, Ajuntament d'Elx–Institut de Cultura Juan Gil-Albert, 1998, 203 pp, includes some articles on the historical background of the *Misteri d'Elx*.

LITERATURE (NINETEENTH AND TWENTIETH CENTURIES)

POSTPONED

# VI. PORTUGUESE STUDIES

## LANGUAGE

By STEPHEN PARKINSON, *Lecturer in Portuguese Language and Linguistics,*
*University of Oxford*

### 1. GENERAL

M. F. Gonçalves, 'Grammaires portugaises et brésiliennes', pp.
381–415 of *Corpus representatif des grammaires et des traditions linguistiques*
(*HEL*, hors-série, 2) SHESL, 1998, gives bibliographical and analytical entries for 20 Ptg. grammars from Oliveira and Barros to
Torrinha and Sequeira. M. Q. Leite, 'A contribuição modernista
para a fixação da norma lingüística brasileira', *RANPOLL*, 4,
1998:221–47, focuses metalinguistic texts by Manuel Bandeira and
Rubem Braga. Cristina Altman, *A pesquisa lingüística no Brasil*
*(1968–1988)*, SPo, Humanitas, 1998, 379 pp., surveys the formative
years of Brazilian linguistics, with close analysis of the contents of key
journals. Divergence (between *linguistas* and *filólogos*; *linguistas do texto*
and *linguistas da sentença*) has been stronger than convergence, despite
the unifying role of studies of spoken BPtg. *Padrões sociolinguísticos*, ed.
Gisele Machline de Oliveira e Silva and Maria Marta Pereira
Scherre, Rio de Janeiro, Tempo Brasileiro–UFRJ, 1996, 395 pp.,
provides a series of paired articles on six well-known variables, each
one being discussed first from the point of view of linguistic variables
and subsequently in terms of sociolinguistic variation. Of the editors,
Scherre covers *concordância nominal,* and Silva the replacement of *seu*
by *dele* and the occurrence of articles with possessives; M. C. M.
Mollica compares *ir a, ir para,* and *ir em*; N. P. de Omena returns to
*nós* and *a gente*; and M. C. A. Paiva studies the monophthongization
of /ei ou/. Ataliba Teixeira de Castilho, *A língua falada no ensino do*
*português*, SPo, Contexto, 1998, 158 pp., argues convincingly for
mother-tongue language teaching centred on discourse structures
and spoken language, giving rich examples of both. *Análise de textos*
*orais*, ed. Dino Preti (Projetos paralelos–NURC/SP, 1), 4th edn, SPo,
Humanitas, 236 pp., sets the tone of the series by focusing on
discourse and spoken language as evidenced in NURC materials. In
similar vein, *O discurso oral culto*, ed. Dino Preti (Projetos paralelos–
NURC/SP, 2), SPo, Humanitas, 1997, 173 pp., has articles on
general features of the *norma urbana culta,* including D. Preti, 'A
propósito do conceito de discurso urbano oral culto: a língua e as
transformações sociais' (17–27); D. L. P. Barros, 'A propósito do
conceito de discurso oral culto: definições e imagens', (29–43);

B. Brait, 'Imagens da norma culta, interação e constituição do texto oral' (45–69); M. Q. Leite, 'Purismo no discurso oral culto' (63–90); and H. Urbano, 'A expressividade na língua falada de pessoas cultas' (91–110). On discourse strategies, L. L. Fávero, 'Processos de formulação do texto falado: a correção e a hesitação nas elocuções formais' (111–24); I. M. Alves, 'Marcas do discurso de divulgação na linguagem falada culta' (125–33); and P. T. Galembeck, 'Preservação da face e manifestação de opiniões: um caso de jogo duplo' (135–50). Z. M. Zapparolli, 'Considerações sobre a utilização de novas tecnologias na análise do léxico do português falado culto de São Paulo' (151–73), uses Camlong's STABLEX program to distinguish *vocabulário preferencial* from high- and low-frequency *vocabulário básico*. Similar contributors and themes return in *Estudos de língua falada: variações e confrontos*, ed. Dino Preti (Projetos paralelos – NURC/SP, 3), SPo, Humanitas, 1998, 234 pp.: L. A. Marcuschi, 'Atividades de compreensão na interação verbal' (15–45); D. L. P. Barros, 'Procedimentos e recursos discursivos na conversação' (47–69); D. Preti, 'Tipos de *frame* e falantes cultos' (71–86); B. Brait, 'Elocução formal: o dinamismo da oralidade e as formalidades da escrita' (87–108); L. A. Silva, 'Polidez na interação professor/aluno' (109–30), looks at face-threatening verbal behaviour by students, and teachers' responses; H. Urbano, 'Variedades de planejamento no texto falado e escrito' (131–51); L. L. Fávero and M. L. Andrade, 'Os processos de representação da imagem pública nas entrevistas' (153–77); M. Q. Leite, 'Língua falada: *uso* e *norma*' (179–28), looks at competing constructions such as *chamar (de), ir a/para/em; assistir (a)*; P. T. Galembeck, 'O emprego do subjuntivo e de formas alternativas na fala culta' (209–34).

P. Teyssier, 'A diferenciação linguística entre Portugal e Brasil', *(Pré)Publications*, 168:4–11, shows the appreciation of differences between EPtg. and BPtg. emerging in late 18th-c. grammars and theatre. C. Martins, 'O padrão e a variante brasileira na expressão oral: uma questão de ensino', *ib.*, 43–55, gives a sample of useful quotations from the debates on the independence of BPtg.

2. History of Portuguese

TEXTS. A. Emiliano, 'O mais antigo documento latino-português (882 a.D) — edição e estudo grafémico', *Verba*, 26:7–42, gives a new edition of the 882 *Carta de fundação da igreja de Lardosa*, in an exemplary conservative paleographical transcription with extensive critical apparatus. The orthography of the text is conservative but still allows a Romance phonological base to be deduced, which E. represents in a speculative IPA transcription. *Chancelarias Portuguesas. D. Duarte*, ed.

João José Alves Dias, L, Centro de Estudos Históricos, Univ. Nova de Lisboa, 1998, 517 pp., adds to the store of administrative texts, though the transcription leaves much to be desired. Antônio Geraldo da Cunha, César Nardelli Cambraia, and Heitor Megale, *A carta de Pero Vaz de Caminha*, (Série Diachronica, 1), SPo, Humanitas, 89 pp., give a fascimile and transcription (based on Cunha 1964) of this emblematic text.

On orthography and textual editing, *SFLP 1* contains: C. N. Cambraia, 'Subsídios para uma proposta de normas de edição de textos antigos para estudos lingüísticos' (13–23); J. A. de Santana Neto, 'Critérios propostos para dupla leitura do tratado ascético-místico "Castelo Perigoso"' (25–39); F. O. Rodrigues, 'As histórias de Trancoso: um projeto de texto crítico' (41–53); S. A. Toledo Neto, 'Aspectos da variação gráfica no português arcaico: as variantes consonantais no *Livro de José de Arimatéia* (cod. ANTT 643)' (55–63).

PHONOLOGY. Rodney Sampson, *Nasal Vowel Evolution in Romance*, OUP, xvi + 413 pp., has an extensive chapter on Portuguese, recapitulating his 1983 views on the nasal endings (*YWMLS*, 45 : 396) and rejecting suggestions of resyllabification of intervocalic nasals prior to nasalization. G. Massini-Cagliari, 'Lingüística histórica e fonologia não-linear', *SFLP 1*, 121–38, gives a modern theoretical interpretation to philological data, presenting competing patterns of accentuation (assuming different types of versification to represent different systems) as divergent implementations of a metrical phonology based on the moraic trochee. The analysis is developed at greater length (but with differences of detail) in her *Do poético ao lingüístico no ritmo dos trovadores: três momentos da história do acento*, Araraquara–SPo, UNESP–Cultura Acadêmica, 207 pp.; her 'A paragoge rítmica na lírica profana galego-portuguesa', *APL 14*, II, 169–82, shows paragogy to be a predictable effect of word-stress based on the moraic trochee.

SYNTAX. M. E. Davies, 'The diachronic interplay of finite and non-finite verbal constructions in Spanish and Portuguese', *BHS(G)*, 73, 1996:137–58, continues his corpus-based studies (*YWMLS*, 58:410), showing an increase in the use of V + inf causative constructions leading to an increase in the frequency of finite complement structures in non-causative contexts from O Ptg. to Modern Ptg. M. C. V. Silva, *APL 14*, II, 431–41, compares infinitive complements in Portuguese-Latin and O Ptg. texts.

SEMANTICS. N. Nunes, 'Inquéritos lexicais sobre a produção açucareira na ilha da Madeira', *APL 14*, II, 287–95, compares modern surveys with 15th- and 16th-c. documents. C. A. A. Murakawa, 'Mudanças semânticas no vocabulário do Português Fundamental: um estudo sobre o substantivo', *ib.*, 265–72, gives some bland quantitative results from a comparative study of classic dictionaries. C. Rocha, 'A distribuição de "conhecer" num corpus do português medieval', *ib.*, 375–90, shows *conhecer* to have a wider range of complements in OPtg. than in Modern Ptg. (see *YWMLS*, 58:402, 60:305).

## 3. PHONETICS AND PHONOLOGY

Thais Cristófaro Silva, *Fonética e fonologia do português*, SPo, Contexto, 254 pp., is a practical textbook focusing almost entirely on BPtg. phonemes and allophones. M. Cruz-Ferreira, 'Portuguese (European)', pp. 126–30 of *Handbook of the International Phonetic Association*, CUP, 204 pp., is a great improvement on previous illustrations, despite the provocative choice of [ɯ] in place of [ə] as the symbol for unstressed *e*: the absence of a full-length study of Ptg. phonetics stands out more starkly. Luiz Carlos Cagliari, *Fonologia do português* II, Campinas, the author, 156 pp., adds to his earlier survey *Fonologia do português* I (*YWMLS*, 59:384; now in a revised 2nd edn, 1998, 153 pp.), with sections on recent feature theory, /R/, /l/, and a number of morphological cases including -*mente* and -*zinho* (and other cases of affixes with consonantal augments). Id., *Acento em português*, Campinas, the author, 96 pp., tries to cover a survey of accentual phonology, and a full account of Ptg. prosody and metrics; inevitably there is much simplification. M. H. M. Mateus, 'Investigação em fonologia do português', *APL 14*, II, gives a bibliography of work by Portuguese research groups and a very sketchy list of foreign (including Brazilian) publications. S. Parkinson, 'Once a problem always a problem: the phonology of Portuguese "closed a"', *OUWPLL 4*, 117–26, shows that the derived contrast of /a/ and /ɐ/ corresponds to two different subversions of the basic vowel pattern, and proposes an underlying potential contrast which is only activated in the preterite forms in -*ámos*. D. J. Silva, 'Vowel lenition in São Miguel Portuguese', *His(US)*, 81, 1998:166–78, distinguishes devoicing and deletion of unstressed vowels, the former influenced by context and the latter by vowel quality. (See also Id., *'The variable deletion of unstressed vowels in Faiense Portuguese', *LVC*, 9, 1997:1–15.)

PROSODY. *Estudos de Prosódia*, ed. Ester Mirian Scarpa, Campinas, Unicamp, 327 pp., combines phonetic and phonological contributions on a range of topics related to prosodic structure: P. A. Barbosa (21–52) explores how to generate rhythmic structure and segmental length in speech synthesis; J. A. Moraes (69–84) measures vowel duration with a view to factoring out quality- and stress-related length variation; E. C. Albano et al. (85–109) develop a phonologically orientated notation for synthesis; G. Massini-Cagliari (141–87) reprises her analysis of Gal-Ptg. stress (see p. 311); E. M. Scarpa (253–84) looks at fillers and hesitation sounds; M. B. M. Abaurre, C. Galves, and E. M. Scarpa (285–323) lean heavily on some improbably categorical data to claim direct influence of syntactic structure on the blocking of interverbal contraction. *RANPOLL*, 6–7, contains a section on 'Ritmo, entoação e rima', which includes a preliminary study by A. R. M. Simões (131–40) arguing against duration as a cue for BPtg. stress, and P. Martin, 'L'intonation du français et du portugais: phonétique et phonologie' (255–59).

## 4. Morphology

MORPHOLOGY. Antônio Sandmann, *Morfologia lexical*, SPo, Contexto, 1997, 82 pp., is a concise but data-rich introduction to word formation and lexical expansion. R. Laurent, 'Resultados en las lenguas romances de adjetivos con desinencias derivadas de -UTUM', *RFE*, 78, 1998:27–48, lists forms in -*udo* and finds an interplay between augmentative and pejorative values. C. V. Rodrigues, *APL 14*, II, 391–96, sorts spatio-temporal prefixes (*pré-, pós-*, etc.). M. C. F. Gouveia, 'A propósito do masculino genérico em português', *ib.*, 21–28, finds some trivial exceptions to the often overstated general principle that (only) masculine forms can refer to both genders.

## 5. Syntax

GENERAL. A. M. Brito, 'Português europeu / português brasileiro: algumas diferenças sintácticas', *(Pré)Publications*, 168:12–34, gives an excellent summary of syntactic differences, and a synthesis in which they are attributed (cautiously) to a move in spoken BPtg. towards weakening of the Agr (*Concordância*) component and eventual change of the null subject parameter. Such an explanation for the reduction in subject-verb inversion is contested by A. J. Naro and S. J. Votre, 'Discourse motivations for linguistic regularities: verb/subject order in spoken Brazilian Portuguese', *Probus*, 11:75–100, who argue from extensive speech samples that the distribution of SV and VS orders in informal spoken BPtg. is neither grammatically constrained nor simple stylistic variation, but is governed by a discourse principle by which 'the use of VS order indicates a low level of communicative tension: the subject is not presented as topical and the clause is not situated on the central line of referent/information flow.'

GB SYNTAX. Carlos Mioto, Maria Cristina Figueiredo Silva, and Ruth Elisabeth Vasconcellos Lopes, *Manual de sintaxe*, Florianópolis, Insular, 208 pp., fill a major gap with a simple introduction to GB syntax, introducing many recent developments in the direction of functional categories, but still leaving many basic points unclear. S. H. L. Nascimento, 'Português brasileiro e Kaingáng: estrutura sentencial e marcação casual', *APL 14*, II, 273–85, compares word order and case marking in BPtg. (head-first, nominative) and the indigenous language Kaingáng (head second, split ergative). G. Matos, 'Negação frásica e concordância negativa em português europeu', *ib.*, 197–218, defends negative absorption as the principle for semantic intepretation of multiple negatives; the ungrammaticality of (e.g.) *Ninguém não* . . . results from a conflict of scope between the two negative particles, which denies absorption the single syntactic domain it requires. A. L. Santos, 'A ordem de palavras nas construções de particípio absoluto', *ib.*, 397–411, tries to resolve problems of Case assignment raised by word order variation in 'participial absolute' constructions. C. Schmitt, 'Lack of iteration: accusative clitic doubling, participial absolutes and have + agreeing participles', *Probus*, 10, 1998:243–300, treats the participial absolutes (together with a number of superficially unrelated constructions in Sp. and Ptg.) as 'identificational small clauses', and draws conclusions for the nature of Ptg. DPs. M. Âmbar, \*'Inflected infinitives revisited', *CanJL*, 43, 1998[1999]:5–36, and 'Infinitives vs participles', Treviño, *Semantic Issues*, 1–20, starting from the assumption of two Tense elements in syntactic structure, spells out the checking mechanisms determining temporal and aspectual readings of non-finite complement clauses. S. L. Waichel, 'O estatuto das interrogativas-wh no português europeu e no português brasileiro', *APL 14*, II, 613–23, analyses well-known EPtg.-BPtg. divergences in terms of Rizzi's WH-criterion. M. P. Machado, 'Algumas questões sobre a sintaxe dos advérbios de modo em português', *ib.*, 103–12, explores a range of analyses for *bem*, including its occurrence as complement of verbs like *comer, portar-se*. F. Martinho, 'Nomes nulos e adjectivos discretos: condições de legitimação e identificação', *ib.*, 149–67, looks at nounless NPs as cases of DP with elliptical pro. M. Maia, 'A formal explanation for a case of variation between European Portuguese and Brazilian Portuguese' *RANPOLL*, 3, 1997:135–64, returns to the comparison of the BPtg. preference for null objects (analysed as null epithets) and the EPtg. tendency for null subjects.

CLITICS. A. Rouveret, 'Clitics, subject and tense in European Portuguese', Riemsdijk, *Clitics*, 639–77, analyses clitics as 'visible D-morphemes', with enclisis resulting from a 'weak valency of V-features of Tense' which affects the site to which tensed verbs can raise. E. Raposo, 'Direction of cliticization in European Portuguese', *Saltarelli Vol.*, 219–32, characterizes the EPtg. alternation of enclisis and proclisis as 'psychotic', and proposes that the clitic is essentially proclitic but that its landing site, the functional category F, is itself a clitic, and is enclitic. M. Vigário, 'Cliticização no português europeu: uma operação pós-lexical', *APL 14*, II, 577–98, gives obvious data implying that cliticization follows word-level inflectional morphology, except in lexicalized mesoclisis; clitic-related allomorphy is 'precompiled' rather than derived by phonological rule. (See ROMANCE LINGUISTICS, pp. 20–21, for further references). VERBS. T. S. Silva, 'A alternância entre o pretérito imperfeito e o futuro do pretérito na fala de Florianópolis', *APL 14*, II, 459–71, studies syntactic factors on the choice of conditional and imperfect tense forms to indicate the future in the past, from a corpus heavily weighted towards conditional constructions. T. S. Pimpão, 'O estatuto do modo verbal na marcação da categoria modalidade', *ib.*, 321–32, looks at the grammaticalization of the use of the subjunctive in terms of the low referentiality of the *irrealis* modality determined by main clauses. V. L. P. Silva, 'A variação na referência à segunda pessoa do singular na fala do Rio de Janeiro', *ib.*, 473–83, studies plays from the period 1845–1992 to document the return of morphological 2nd person pronoun and verb forms. E. M. Gorski, 'Infinitivo pessoal no português falado no sul do Brasil: o preenchimento do sujeito em orações substantivas', *ib.*, 7–20, shows variable use of overt subjects with personal infinitives, with the highest occurrence in subject clauses. ADJECTIVES. S. G. C. Pereira, 'Predicados adjectivais: propriedades semânticas e aspectuais', *APL 14*, II, 309–20, shows how the aspectual value of adjectives (reflected in their co-occurrence with *ser* or *estar*) determines their possible interpretation as predicates (see also *YWMLS*, 60:307). NOUNS. A. L. Müller has two articles on possessives: 'A lógica subjacente à variação entre as formas possessivas de terceira pessoa: *seu* versus *dele*', *RANPOLL*, 3, 1997:11–32, argues that *seu* is a pronominal with a bound variable while *dele* is a free pronominal; 'Significado da ordem dos pronomes possessivos no sintagma nominal', *ib.*, 4, 1998:11–37, observes uncontroversially that preposed possessives are definiteness markers ('sujeito do sintagma nominal') while postposed possessives are adjuncts, functioning predicatively. DISCOURSE (see also GENERAL above). *SFLP 1*, contains: M. L. Braga, 'As orações de tempo sob uma perspectiva funcionalista' (97–108); L. A. Marcuschi, 'Marcas de interatividade no processo de textualização na escrita' (139–56); M. H. M. Neves, 'Articulação de orações: a questão dos estados de coisas' (83–96); E. G. Pezatti, 'Gramática e funcionalismo: a disjunção entre orações' (65–81). T. Móia, *APL 14*, II, 219–38, laboriously analyses the semantics of expressions of time based on *há . . .* and *desde há . . ..* B. Moreira, 'Para a caracterização enunciativa do marcador *por pouco*', *APL 14*, II, 253–63, notes the ambiguity of *por pouco não*, whose interpretation depends on the implications of success or failure conveyed by its context. M. T. F. Oliveira, 'Para uma descrição enunciativa do marcador "quem"', *APL 14*, II, 309–20, gives a Culiolian account of the semantics of *quem*. M. A. Tavares. 'Um estudo de *aí, daí* e *então* como conectores no discurso oral', *ib.*, 531–43, places them in a predictable sequence of grammaticalization from spatial to temporal and thence to textual functions.

### 6. Lexicon

I. Castro and P. E. L. Mendes, 'O *Dicionário de Regionalismos e Arcaismos* (DRA) de Leite de Vasconcellos', *RevL*, 16, 1997:91–117, report on the preparation of L. de V.'s dictionary for publication, giving sample entries AA-AB and examples of edited and unedited entries. D. Messner, 'O "Dicionário da Lingoa Portugueza" de 1793 e as suas fontes', *ArCCP*, 38,:363–71, shows its sources to include the *Encyclopédie*, 18th-c. scientific treatises, and Covarrubias. A. Villalva gives a 'Comentário linguístico à *Classificação Nacional das Profissões*', *APL 14*, II, 599–612. E. Faustich, 'A função social da terminologia', *SFLP 1*, 167–83. C. Augusto, 'Dos frades tonsurados aos frades fedorentos: a densidade semântica da palavra "frade"', *RLFRU*, 18:1–11, reflects on the wide range of expressions incorporating a word whose principal referent had disappeared from Ptg. society by 1850.

ETYMOLOGY. H. Schwertck, 'Portugiesisch *saraiva* "Hagel"', *RF*, 111:225–29, suggests a Celtic etymon *\*sparagma*.

### 7. Sociolinguistics

BRAZIL. S. A. M. Cardoso provides 'Remarques sur la division dialectale du Brésil', pp. 323–35 of *Languages in Time and Space, Studies in Honour of Wolfgang Viereck on the Ocasion of his 60th Birthday*, ed. Heinrich Romisch and Kenneth Wynne, Stuttgart, Steiner, 1997, xlviii + 510 pp. D. da Hora and F. S. Silva, 'Processo de monotongação em João Pessoa', *APL 14*, II, 79–93, find /ou/ invariably realised as /o/, and /ei/ preferentially monophthongized before /r/ and palatals, and never in verb endings; /a(i)/ is a different case, being part of a phonetic process of diphthongization in palatal contexts. H. G. Vieira, 'Variantes da língua portuguesa falada em Santa Catarina — Brasil', *ib.*, 565–75, studies the palatalization of final *-s*, which appears well established in all communities and social groups in coastal regions, and is closely associated with the diphthongization of the preceding vowel. M. A. Cohen reports on 'Remanescentes do judeu-espanhol na comunidade de Belo Horizonte', *Revista de Estudos Judaicos*, 1, 1998:30–36. M. M. Taddoni Petter, 'Línguas especiais, línguas secretas: na África e no Brasil', *RANPOLL*, 4, 1998:185–201, compares the *cupópia* of Cafundó with a Central African secret language. AFRICA. A major project to describe Mozambican Ptg. begins to produce results, in *Panorama do Português oral de Maputo*, ed. and introd. Christopher Stroud and Perpétua Gonçalves (Cadernos de pesquisa, 22, 24, 27), 3 vols, Maputo, Instituto nacional do desenvolvimento da educação, 1997, 167, 126, 167 pp. Vol. I, *Objectivos e métodos*, contains: C. Stroud on the state of Mozambican Ptg., and sociolinguistic factors in variation (26–42); P. Gonçalves on data collection (47–73); A. Tuzine on social networks (75–100); S. Monteiro and F. Martins on transcription conventions for oral language samples (101–24); A. Moreno on problems of textual analysis using Micro-OCP (125–47) and some sample transcriptions (153–67); in vol. II, *A construção de um banco de 'erros'*, P. Gonçalves, 'Tipologia de "erros" do português oral de Maputo: um primeiro diagnóstico' (37–70), illustrates features from a range of linguistic components; A. Moreno and A. Tuzine, 'Distribuição social de variáveis linguísticas no português oral de Maputo' (7–91), select three variables (the use of an invariant reflexive *se*; lack of standard patterns of nominal and verbal concord) to show somewhat predictably that profession and level of education correlate with closeness to EPtg. norms. Vol. III, *Estruturas gramaticais do português: problemas e exercícios*, identifies divergences relevant to the teaching of Portuguese, without going so far as to advocate teaching a distinctive Mozambican Ptg. standard.

## 8. CREOLES

Luigi Scantamburlo, *Dicionário do Guineense*, I, *Introdução e notas gramaticais*, Lisbon–Bubaque, Colibri–FASPEBI, 218 pp. + 3 maps, gives preparatory material for his dictionary, including an introduction to the language situation in Guiné-Bissau, notes on a corpus of spoken and written Guineense, and a well-illustrated summary account of phonology, morphology, and syntax.

T. Hagemeijer, 'Serialização e gramaticalização em são-tomense', *APL 14*, II, 65–78, attempts to distinguish serial verb constructions from other verbal complexes, and finds some intermediate cases.

J. Ladhams, 'The Pernambuco connection?: an examination of the nature and origins of the Portuguese elements in the Surinam creoles', pp. 209–40 of *Spreading the Word*, ed. Magnus Huber and Makael Parkvall, Univ. of Westminster Press, documents the Ptg. component of Saramaccan and tests and convincingly rejects all the sociohistorical links in the 'Jewish slave' hypothesis, under which Ptg. elements in Saramaccan were brought from Brazil by African slaves speaking a Brazilian Portuguese Creole, in the household of Portuguese Jews leaving Pernambuco after the fall of the Dutch colony in 1654; Id., 'Response to Norval Smith', ib., 299–304, defends his creativist hypothesis against N. Smith, 'Pernambuco to Surinam 1654–1665? The Jewish slave controversy', ib., 251–98, who insists that pidgin-like properties must have an origin in a pidgin, and that the only candidate is the Brazilian Portuguese Creole controversially assumed to underlie modern colloquial BPtg., a view rejected once more by H. H. Couto, 'The question of (prior) creolization in Brazil', ib., 177–94. J. Arends, 'The origin of the Portuguese element in the Surinam creoles', ib., 195–208, examines sociohistorical evidence for an alternative theory, of the transfer of a Portuguese pidgin by slaves brought from Africa.

# MEDIEVAL LITERATURE
## POSTPONED

# LITERATURE, 1500 TO THE PRESENT DAY
## POSTPONED

# VII. GALICIAN STUDIES

## LANGUAGE

By Francisco Dubert García, *Universidade de Santiago de Compostela*, David Mackenzie, *University College, Cork*, and Xulio Sousa Fernández, *Universidade de Santiago de Compostela*

(This survey covers the years 1997–99)

### 1. Bibliographical and General

*Atlas lingüístico galego*, III, *Fonética*, ed. M. González González, Corunna, ILG–Fundación Pedro Barrié de la Maza, 517 pp., with 423 maps, continues this excellent enterprise, to the same high standard as that of the previous volumes. The organization of the volume is based on etymological and diachronic criteria, and the data are divided under three broad heads: stress shift; reflexes of Latin vowels; and the evolution of consonants. The presentation of the maps is first class, bearing witness no doubt to the intervention of the computer, and there are complete indices both of maps and, most usefully, of word-forms. M. González González, R. Losada Soto, and E. Fernández Rei, 'O galego e as tecnoloxías da fala: o caso do sintetizador de voz', *CIEG* 5, II, 703–16, describe their voice synthesizer, called COTOVÍA, and the technical and linguistic problems encountered in setting it up. H. Monteagudo, *Historia social da lingua galega*, Vigo, Galaxia, 555 pp., is a thoughtful and useful work, basically a sociolinguistic history of the Galician language and its vicissitudes. C. García et al., *Diccionario da Real Academia Galega*, Corunna, RAG, 1998, xx + 1241 pp., represents another step in the long march of Galician lexicography. It contains some 25,000 entries, and each definition is supplemented by an example of usage, some of which are said to be drawn from a corpus of Modern Galician, but unfortunately there is no indication of this, so that we do not know which examples are invented and which authentic. Galician still lacks the full-size monolingual dictionary it should be the duty of the Academy to produce.

### 2. Historical and Dialectology

M. Fernández Rodríguez, 'Las primeras propuestas de "selección de norma" para el gallego: del Padre Sarmiento a fines del siglo XIX', *HistL*, 24, 1997: 139–57, distinguishes three main trends in the 18th and 19th cs: the adoption of the language of the people; the elaboration of an archaizing norm; and an adaptation of Portuguese.

The authors studied show a preference for the first. In complementary articles, A. Santamarina, 'O Padre Sarmiento, precursor dos estudios románicos', *Sarmiento*, ii, 31–65, and H. Monteagudo, 'Martín Sarmiento e o idioma galego no contexto ideolóxico e histórico-lingüístico', *Verba*, 24, 1997:7–43, reveal how advanced the Enlightenment scholar S. was in his views on language, with abundant references to his works. M. Ferreiro Fernández, *Gramática histórica galega* ii. *Lexicoloxía*, SC, Laiovento, 1997, 409 pp. is an account of word-formation in Galician, but even the undergraduate audience at which it seems to be aimed will bridle at its *longueurs*. The work is divided into more than 400 sections, most of which are furnished with examples: *eza*, for instance, has thirteen, thus *pobreza (< pobre + eza)*. The odd derivations noted in vol. i (*YWMLS*, 57:398) surface here also on occasion: ABHORRESCERE > *avorrecer* > *aborrecer*. R. Mariño Paz, *Historia da lingua galega*, SC, Sotelo Blanco, 1998, 582 pp., is a much more solid external history of the Galician language from the earliest times to the present. R. Varela Cabezas, 'Galeguismos en *La madre naturaleza*, de Emilia Pardo Bazán', *CadL*, 16, 1997:103–29, classifies the Galician words and phrases he finds in the novel, levels severe and well-deserved criticism at the editor of the 1992 edition (I. J. López) for his often crass attempts to elucidate these elements, and finishes with a useful listing of all the terms. M. S. López Martínez, 'Algunhas expresións denominativas na lingua medieval', *Flores Vol.*, i, 194–205, describes verb phrases formed with *chamar* and two verbal locutions with denominative value (*aver nome* and *poer nome*), and studies their syntax and semantics. X. Maure Rivas, 'A perda do galego instrumental: dous documentos notariais de Baiona (1518 e 1522)', *Alonso Montero Vol.*, i, 677–89, studies contamination between Galician and Castilian in two documents of the 16th c., one Galician, the other Castilian: Castilian interference in the Galician document is on morphology and phonetics, while that of Galician in the Castilian document is mostly lexical, which is precisely what one would have expected. B. Real Pérez, ' "Conversacións". Diálogos inéditos en lingua galega recompilados por Louis Lucien Bonaparte', *CadL*, 20:29–64, highlights the linguistic interest of this text, and suggests that it is in fact a translation of a method for learning French compiled by José Sánchez de Santa María. M. D. Sánchez Palomino, 'A postura de Cuveiro ante o diccionario e a lingua', *Alonso Montero Vol.*, i, 933–48, considers this Galician lexicographer a successor of F. J. Rodríguez, who, despite seeing his work as helping to raise a monument to Galician literature, and as a manual for Castilian speakers, held the view that Galician presented such a confusion of forms that the confection of a grammar and a complete dictionary was impossible. Along similar lines, Id., 'Ideas que sustentan a elaboración do diccionario de Valladares', *CadL*, 20:5–28, undertakes a detailed study of V.'s dictionary, concluding that, although he too was moved by patriotic views, his lexicographical criteria were more sound than those of his predecessors, both in the choice of entries and in their elaboration. X. Sousa Fernández, 'O verbo *enviar* en construccións con infinitivo nos textos medievais galegos', *Alonso Montero Vol.*, 1, 979–88, studies the use and function of the sintagm *enviar* + infinitive in a corpus of medieval texts, and shows that it behaves as a periphrastic phrase with modal function 'facer a través dun intermediario'. He further supports his grammaticalization hypothesis by pointing to the fixed order of the constituents and the loss on the part of *enviar* of any government function. J. A. Souto Cabo, 'A língua de Rui Vasques (*c.*1435–*c.*1495). Umha nova ediçom da crónica de Íria', Touriñán, *Interculturalidad*, II, 511–29, presents, in odd orthography, a worrying proposal in that he seems to be unaware of recent work on this chronicle. F. R. Tato Plaza, *Libro de notas de Álvaro Pérez, notario da terra de Rianxo e Postmarcos*, SC, Consello da Cultura Galega, 758 pp., produces a careful edition, an interesting, copiously illustrated codicological study, and a full linguistic study of this text of 1457; there is a complete glossary which provides, in addition to the usual definition and variant forms, the etymology and the occurrences of each word in other texts of the medieval period. X. H. Costas González, 'Ás voltas co enxordecemento das sibilantes sonoras no galego medieval', *APL 14*, I, 433–45, in a complementary article to that of Lorenzo (*YWMLS*, 57:398), suggests that the phonemic distinction between voiced and voiceless coronal fricatives had disappeared by the 13th c., and that perhaps it had been lost even earlier. A. S. Alonso Núñez, 'Os sufixos nominais diminutivos *-iñ-o / -iñ-a, -it-o / -it-a* e *-ic-o / -ic-a* na fala do concello de Castrelo do Val', *CadL*, 20:127–43, is a workmanlike piece of fieldwork. F. Dubert García, *Aspectos do galego de Santiago de Compostela* (*Verba*, Anexo 44), Santiago de Compostela U.P., 249 pp., in a groundbreaking work both in its approach and in its treatment of a large urban area, undertakes what he terms a geolinguistic study of the spoken Galician of the capital city, establishing both variation rules and categorization rules and attempting thereby to integrate linguistic variation into a grammar of the language. R. Mariño Paz, 'O tratamento do grupo consonántico heterosilábico /kt/ no galego medieval', *APL 14*, II, 113–34, and Id., 'Os reflexos do grupo consonántico latino /ks/ no galego medieval', *Verba*, 26:43–79, studies the medieval reflexes of two Latin consonant groups. H. Monteagudo, 'Castelao e os problemas da elaboración da lingua', *Flores Vol.*, I, 206–25, looks at orthographic and morphological evolution in C.'s written code. E. M. Moscoso Mato, '*Aver*, verbo de posesión na Idade Media', *Alonso Montero Vol.*, i, 739–49, and Id., 'O verbo "ter" como non auxiliar na lírica profana medieval galego-portuguesa', *Flores Vol.*, i, 226–38, studies the semantics of non-auxiliary uses of the verbs *haber* and *ter* in medieval secular lyric poetry. F. Fernández Rei, *Ramón Cabanillas, Manuel Antonio e o mar da Arousa. Dúas singraduras na construcción dun idioma para unha patria*, Corunna, RAG, 146 pp., studies the construction of an elaborated code in C.'s and M.A.'s works. X. H. Costas González, 'Valverdeiro, lagarteiro e mañego: o "galego" do Val do Río Ellas (Cáceres)', Fernández, *Estudios*, 83–106, studies the language of three municipalities in Cáceres where Galician is allegedly spoken. X. Varela Barreiro, 'As locucións prepositivas en galego nos Séculos Escuros', *Flores Vol.*, i, 350–70, discusses the meaning and structure of prepositional phrases in the early modern period. Id., 'A evolución do radical dos pretéritos irregulares sigmáticos', *Alonso Montero Vol.*, i, 1047–72, examines the evolution of the stem vowel of *dicir, facer, traer, pór, poñer* and *querer*. M. S. López Martínez, 'A preposición *a* co complemento directo no galego e no castelán medievais', *Lorenzo Vol.*, 633–47, attempts to explain the difference between Castilian and Galician in the use of preposition *a* as object-marker, using examples taken from two medieval texts. X. L. Regueira, 'A construcción causativa *fazer + infinitivo* na prosa medieval galega', *ib.*, 649–59, compares the use of the construction in the medieval and the modern language, and concludes that modern Galician is closer to the medieval construction than modern Portuguese. X. C. Sousa Fernández, 'Esquemas sintácticos do verbo *preguntar* no galego medieval', *ib.*, 687–96, studies phrases in the medieval language in which the verb functions as predicate.

### 3. GRAMMAR

R. Álvarez, 'O complemento de solidariedade: a complicidade entre os interlocutores', *CIEG 4*, 37–53, in a study of the ethic dative in Galician, assesses its vitality in the modern language, and studies its syntax and its position in the sequence of atonic pronouns. X. Varela Barreiro, 'A existencia de dúas expresións clíticas de segunda persoa singular en galego', *ib.*, 319–42, analyses the reasons for the existence of two pronouns for P2, distinguished by function, makes a comparison with the Portuguese situation, and suggests that the survival of two forms in Galician is due to the use of the ethic dative. X. Rosales Sequeiros, 'Presuppositional effects in English and Galician', *GalR*, i, 1997: 13–26 is a contrastive analysis of differences between the two languages in the areas of intonation and word-order. V. Longa, G. Lorenzo, and G. Rigau, 'Subject clitics and clitic recycling:

locative sentences in some Iberian Romance languages', *JL*, 34, 1998: 125–64, is a study of locative constructions and pronominal clitics functioning as subject in Galician, Asturian, Catalan, and certain dialects of Spanish; for Galician, the authors suggest that object clitics undergo a transformation which allows them to assume a subject function. F. A. Cidrás Escáneo, 'Marcaxe preposicional de obxecto en galego. Emerxencia e vicisitudes dun proceso de gramaticalización sintáctica', *Lorenzo Vol.*, 569–80, analyses the prepositions used in Galician as object-markers, and considers that the preference for *a* is evidence for the grammaticalization of one of the prepositional forms. C. Silva Domínguez, 'A alternancia e coexistencia de artigo e posesivo en frases nominais de carácter "Inalienable" do galego contemporáneo', *ib.*, 661–85, shows that the semantics of the referent determine the presence or absence of the article. R. Álvarez, '*Entre min e ti*', *Flores Vol.*, I, 117–41, is a study of the forms of the P1 personal pronoun after *entre*, in which A. concludes, after a detailed analysis of the situation in the other languages of NW Spain as well as in medieval and modern Galician, that the use of the nominative after preposition is autochthonous, not Castilian. She notes also that the P1 always comes first (*eu e ti*). A. also produces a good, serious linguistic study, 'Porque non todos somos iguais. Achega ó estudio do tratamento en galego', *Alonso Montero Vol.*, I, 207–28, of the forms of address used by the protagonists of popular tales collected in SW Galicia. M. Álvarez de la Granja, 'A formación de locucións verbais. Estudio sintáctico-funcional', *ib.*, 229–47, analyses the syntax of almost 1,000 verbal locutions and discovers that the most frequent are the simplest and that their structure is that of the basic verb phrase. She also has an interesting study of 'A manipulación das unidades fraseolóxicas', *Madrygal,* 2 : 31–40, which deals with verbal phrases with *double entendre*, and concludes that this is a frequent phenomenon in both written and spoken Galician. F. A. Cidrás Escáneo, 'Non todo se pode dicir por activa e por pasiva', *Alonso Montero Vol.*, I, 307–23, studies the potential for passivity of various classes of verbs, and suggests that all phrases with stative or modal value lack this option. R. Álvarez, 'A posición do pronome átono en construccións de infinitivo e xerundio en galego antigo', *Actas* (APL 1996), II, 7–29, undertakes a detailed descriptive study of the position of the pronominal clitic in contexts in which the infinitive and the gerund function as predicate, and compares use in old texts with that of modern Galician and Portuguese. X. M. Sánchez Rei, 'Repercusións gramaticais do uso da interpolación pronominal en galego', *CadL*, 19 : 85–110, studies the syntactic context in which the clitic is separated from the verb by a tonic particle, and gives frequency of occurrence; unfortunately he uses the texts of his corpus indiscriminately and allows himself in his conclusions to be bemused by prescriptivist criteria. V. M. Longa, 'Teoría da optimalidade e ordenación das restriccións universais: presentación e tratamento dos infinitivos conxugados', *Alonso Montero Vol.*, i, 533–50, expounds the principles of OT, and shows the problems it has in dealing with certain areas of syntax: his examples are case designation and the Galician conjugated infinitive. M. S. López Martínez, 'O emprego de *a* + CD na lingua galega falada', *ib.*, 551–63, attempts to analyse the extent to which determinacy and animacy affect the use of the preposition before a direct object: her data from the spoken language lead her to conclude that the use of the preposition in this context is not grammaticalized for the most part, and that the two features are insufficient on their own for a full explanation of all occurrences. T. Moure, 'Aspectos da sintaxe do galego desde a perspectiva tipolóxica', *ib.*, 751–66, takes three elements of the syntax of Galician — ergative and antipassive constructions and the direct object with preposition *en* — and uses them to demonstrate that features which are often presented as peculiar to a language become less so when approached from a typological perspective. E. X. González Seoane, 'A derivación verbal isocategorial en galego', *ib.*, 473–500, studies verbs formed on verbs, looking at the affixes used and the resultant changes in meaning. X. Rosales Sequeiros, ' "Disque" e "seica" ', *CIEG* 5, ii, 717–26, examines the semantic and pragmatic differences between the adverb pairs *quizais/acaso* and *disque/seica*, concluding that the latter are contingent, rather than modal.

4. LEXIS AND SEMANTICS

D. X. Cabana, 'Modios e moios. Nota sobre metroloxía galega medieval', *ATO*, 30, 1997:11–33, points out the inaccurate interpretation of the medieval unit of measurement, the *modio*, in modern editions and studies. T. Vidal Figueiroa, 'Presuntos "falsos amigos" entre portugués e galego. ii', *Viceversa*, 3, 1997:67–74, and X. A. Fernández Salgado and X. M. Gómez Clemente, 'Un problema de comparación de linguas: falsos amigos en galego e portugués', *CIEG* 4, 375–90, note the difficulty translators have with certain Portuguese words because of Galician cognates or homographs with different semantics. A. Santamarina, 'Galego *boliga, apoupar*. Castelán *boñiga, apopar*. Sobre dúas palabras galegas e a representación do galego no DCECH', *Lorenzo Vol.*, 949–63, uses two examples to show how a better knowledge of Galician lexicography would have helped Corominas to solve some of his etymological difficulties. M. A.

Kuchenreuther, ' "Tocar" en galego e en alemán', *CIEG* 5, ii, 739–53, analyses verbs of affective contact in Galician and Castilian, and notes that such verbs in German, unlike those in Galician and Castilian, always have in their origins the feature [+physical]. J. L. Pensado Tomé, 'Notas etimológicas gallegas', *Alonso Montero Vol.*, i, 809–23, studies *arbela, antigoo, arsedo, cantolrrom, duya, gameito, mazarico,* forms discovered by him in documents and published works of different periods, and examines their treatment in the dictionaries, making suggestions for better definitions.

5. ETYMOLOGY, ONOMASTICS, AND TOPONYMY

D. Kremer, 'O *Onomástico* de Fr. Martín de Sarmiento e a onomástica galega', *Sarmiento*, ii, 15–30, takes S.'s pioneering *Onomástico etimológico de la lengua gallega* (Tuy, 1923) as the starting-point for his own list of proposals of work to be done in Galician onomastics. A. I. Boullón Agrelo, 'Procesos de castelanización nos apelidos galegos', *CIEG* 4, 195–219, using the 1980 census, offers a detailed study of the Castilianization of certain Galician surnames. She also studies 'A influencia franca na onomástica medieval galega', *Lorenzo Vol.*, 867–901, using medieval MS sources, and concludes that motivation is mixed, being politico-economic, religious, and literary. With F. R. Tato Plaza, B.A. looks at 'Personal names in Galicia as a sign of cultural identification: historical scope and current situation', *Onoma*, 34, 1998:15–44, using a sociolinguistic perspective to examine Galician onomastics since the middle ages, noting a current revival of the use of Galician names. M. C. Díaz y Díaz, 'Propuesta etimológica para el topónimo Arzúa', *Lorenzo Vol.*, 923–27, suggests *argiola < ARGIA, which would describe the scrubland characterizing the area. U. Hafner, 'Beodachtungen zu *Iria* als weiblichem Vornamen', *ib.*, 915–21, reviews earlier studies of the etymology of the place-name *Iria*, and inclines to the view that it should be considered a derivation of *María*. G. Navaza Blanco, 'Algúns antrotopónimos do concello de Lalín', *ib.*, 903–14, studies the etymologies of 24 place names which derive from Latin Christian personal names. H. J. Wolf, 'Galicien und die spanischen Ortsnamen auf -'ara(s)', *ib.*, 929–41, looks at the distribution of Galician and Castilian toponyms with the atonic ending *-ara(s)*, and considers that they could have been brought to Galicia by the Celts. A. I. Boullón Agrelo, *Antroponimia medieval galega (séculos VIII-XII)*, Tübingen, Niemeyer, 558 pp., studies personal names and their evolution over time, using a corpus of texts: there are over 2,000 entries, with full etymological and semantic details, plus a complete bibliography. M. González González, 'Estudio xeolingüístico dos nomes da píntega en galego', *Alonso Montero Vol.*, i,

455–72, considers the various names for the salamander in Galician, their etymologies, and their geographical distribution. G. Navaza Blanco, 'Quelques noms de personne dans les noms d'endroits de la Galice méridionnale', *ICOS 18*, IV, 281–304, studies the etymologies of 112 personal names which became used as toponyms, pointing out that these latter preserve anthroponyms which are no longer used as such, and those substituted by a Castilianized form. Id. and A. Palacio Sánchez, 'Toponimia de Ventosela', *Alonso Montero Vol.*, I, 767–74, offer an etymological analysis of the place names of this parish in Ourense province, with some documentary evidence. R. Mariño Paz helpfully provides 'Apuntamentos histórico-etimolóxicos sobre algúns dos "Bocablos gallegos escuros" glosados polo bacharel Olea (ca. 1536)', *ib.*, 629–53.

6. PHONETICS AND PHONOLOGY

E. Fernández Rei, 'Contribución ó estudio da entoación das cláusulas interrogativas totais e parciais en galego', *CIEG 4*, I, 241–53, provides a useful acoustic description of the two basic types of interrogative intonation — partial and total — and compares these patterns with that of declarative intonation. M. González González and M. González, 'Algunhas consideracións ó redor do [ŋ] en galego', *ib.*, 291–308, argue that the intervocalic velar nasal segment in the indefinites *unha, algunha, ningunha* forms the coda of the syllable having [u] as its nucleus, whereas F. Dubert García 'Reflexións sobre o silabeo de *unha, algunha* e *ningunha*', *Verba* 25, 1997:143–63, maintains that the velar nasal occupies the onset position at the lexical level. F. Martínez-Gil, 'Word-final epenthesis in Galician', Martínez-Gil, *Issues*, 269–340, examines the Galician paragogic /e/, situates it in the post-lexical component, and distinguishes it from other kinds of epenthetic /e/ in the lexicon. C. Martínez Mayo, 'Análise acústica descritiva da pronunciación masculina e feminina nos ditongos galegos tónicos', *CadL*, 16, 1997:35–70, shows the values of $F_1$, $F_2$ and $F_3$ in vowel + glide and glide + vowel strings in Galician. X. A. Méndez, 'Noun stress in Galician: an OT perspective', *CIEG 4*, I, 255–80, attempts to show the utility of Optimality Theory in the explanation of problems of stress placement in Galician substantives. R. Posner, 'Galician within Romance and Europe', *ib.*, 23–36, reflects on the changes wrought on Galician and other 'minority' languages by globalization and the construction of Europe. X. L. Regueira, 'Elementos para a definición dun modelo fonético estándar da lingua galega', *ib.*, 178–94, offers a series of contrastive acoustic analyses which provide empirical proof that the language of many TV and radio presenters is indeed as unnatural as frequently alleged. T. Vidal

Figueiroa, 'Estructuras fonéticas de tres dialectos de Vigo', *Verba*, 24, 1997:313–32, describes in articulatory terms three distinct sociolects of Galician in Vigo: one traditional Galician, another slightly Castilianized, and the last having completely Castilian phonetics. F. Dubert García, 'Máis sobre o rotacismo de /s/ en galego', *Alonso Montero Vol.*, i, 367–87, analyses the change of syllable-final /s/ > /r/ in certain contexts, using feature underspecification, and syllabification and redundancy rules. S. Labraña Barrero, 'Estudio comparativo cos valores do VOT nos sons oclusivos do catalán, castelán e inglés', *CIEG 5*, ii, 683–702, in addition to comparing voice onset times in Galician and the other languages, attempts to show that in Galician these VOT values serve to distinguish voiced and voiceless occlusive obstruent segments. M. A. Sobrino Pérez, 'A entoación do galego do Baixo Miño. Aproximación descritiva', *CadL*, 20:97–125, gives a brief theoretical introduction, followed by a description of the acoustics of declarative, interrogative, imperative, and exclamatory sequences found in data from the lower Miño region.

7. SOCIOLINGUISTICS AND PSYCHOLINGUISTICS

H. Monteagudo, 'Modelos de lingua. Consideracións teóricas ó fío do debate sobre a estandarización do galego', *CadL*, 16, 1997:5–33, looks at the application of the concepts of language, history of the language, and standard language to the Galician situation. J. Kabatek, 'Strengthening identity: differentiation and change in contemporary Galician', pp. 185–99 of *Taming the Vernacular*, ed. J. Cheshire and D. Stein, London, Longman, 1997, vii + 261 pp., perceives what he calls 'koineization' in the development of Galician, whereby a new, urban Galician has evolved combining elements from the proposed standard (the ILG/RAG *Normas*), from dialect varieties, and from Castilian, in a complex process of selection or rejection of possibilities. He illustrates his thesis using three case studies — the conjugated infinitive, the position of clitics, and the use of the ethic dative ('pronome de solidariedade') — in which the first two are losing ground in normal speech, but are becoming fashionable in the elaborated and written codes as markers of elevated style. The ethic dative is less useful for his purposes, given its essentially oral nature, and he seems to avoid the obvious conclusion that the absence of this feature in new urban Galician speech might have to do with social class factors. Id., '*Dime cómo hablas y te diré quién eres*. Mezcla de lenguas y posicionamiento social', *RASoc*, 6, 1997:215–36, considers the theoretical implications of linguistic variation, and shows, using examples from Galician, how the correlation of linguistic varieties and social groups is signalled. S. R. Roseman, 'Lenguas de solidaridad en el medio rural: el mantenimiento del gallego vernáculo', Lorenzo, *Dinamización*, 105–22, uses speech accommodation theory to examine the linguistic behaviour of rural speakers. F. Fernández Rei, 'Espagnol-galicien', Goebl, *Kontaktlinguistik*, II, 1285–96, provides a brief description of the current sociolinguistic situation in Galicia, and then examines the linguistic consequences of contact with Castilian: interference and code-switching. B. García Turnes, 'A situación do galego entre 1875 e 1916. Perspectiva sociolingüística', *CIEG 5*, II, 799–815, outlines the situation of Galician in the period, and points out that the shift towards Castilian that took place affected the middle and lower classes in the towns. Id., 'Cultivo e elaboración da lingua galega no período da restauración (1875–1916)', *Alonso Montero Vol.*, I, 435–54, uses a Klossian analysis to show that, on the other hand, the Galician texts produced during the same period would indicate that this language was experiencing a period of consolidation and advance. A. Iglesias Álvarez, 'O poder explicativo e predictivo das actitudes lingüísticas', *Verba*, 26:273–307, reviews studies dealing with the mismatch between expressed attitude and actual linguistic behaviour, and suggests ways of making sociolinguistic surveys more reliable. S. Labraña Barrero, 'Prexuízos lingüísticos e identificación social', *Alonso Montero Vol.*, I, 519–32, is a serious sociolinguistic study of the attitudes of Galician emigrants in Barcelona towards Castilian, Catalan, and Galician. F. Fernández Rei, 'A situación do galego en Galicia e no Occidente de Asturias, de León e de Zamora', Fernández, *Estudios*, 27–81, is a useful sociolinguistic overview of the Galician-speaking area, both within and outwith Galicia proper. X. L. Regueira, 'Estándar oral e variación social da lingua galega', *Alonso Montero Vol.*, I, 855–75, considers the construction of a standard oral Galician over time, and the interaction between Castilian, colloquial Galician, standard Galician, and what he terms 'new urban Galician'. E. M. Parga Valiña, 'A interferencia lingüística no galego oral', *ib.*, 789–808, classifies the different kinds of borrowing from Castilian in the spoken language.

# LITERATURE

By DOLORES VILAVEDRA, *Departamento de Filoloxía Galega, Universidade de Santiago de Compostela* and DEREK FLITTER, *Senior Lecturer in Modern Spanish Language and Literature, University of Birmingham*

## 1. GENERAL

Dolores Vilavedra, *Historia da literatura galega*, Vigo, Galaxia, 370 pp. L. Tato, *Historia do teatro galego. Das orixes a 1936*, Vigo, Promocións Culturais Galegas, 167 pp., furnishes a wealth of information in an admirably documented historical study. I. Seoane, 'A primeira historia de literatura galega escrita en galego', *Alonso Montero Vol.*, II, 1421–35, examines the fourth chapter, dedicated to literary history, of Florencio Vaamonde's *Resume da historia de Galicia* of 1899. L. Villalta, *Ó outro lado da música, a poesía. Relación entre ambas artes na historia da literatura galega*, Vigo, A Nosa Terra, 155 pp., is an interdisciplinary study investigating historical connections. J. Santos Simões, 'Os rostos e a alma', *Alonso Montero Vol.*, II, 1451–58, recounts literary journeys across the Galician landscape. A. Varela Suanzes-Carpegna, 'Un achegamento ao estudio das antoloxías literarias do primeiro tercio do século XX: a *Antoloxía comentada* de Filgueira Valverde e *A pequena antoloxía lírica* da F.M.G.', *ib.*, 1535–41, briefly contextualizes the subject. M. X. Lama, 'A cultura galega dende México, poderosas brazadas de náufrago', Axeitos, *Exilio*, 201–12, surveys the contribution to Galician literature made by writers exiled in México. X. L. Axeitos, 'A revista *Cabalgata*, outra publicación do exilio galego', *Alonso Montero Vol.*, II, 153–59, deals with a cultural journal first appearing in Buenos Aires in 1946.

## 2. POPULAR LITERATURE

D. Blanco, 'Do refrán á cantiga', *Alonso Montero Vol.*, II, 203–33, supplies a closely researched historical overview of the relationship, based principally upon 18th- and 19th-c. *cancioneiros*. C. Lamela Villaravid, 'A morena no cancioneiro popular galego: a rosa das rosas', *ib.*, 755–70, takes a wide-ranging look at a commonplace figure in popular verse collections. M. Quintáns Suárez, ' "Sucedido" do cura de S. Mamede. O mito das "lavandeiras da noite" na cultura popular galega', *ib.*, 1205–28, investigates the sources, symbolism, and cultural resonance of a celebrated folkloric tradition.

## 3. POETRY

F. Lillo Redonet, 'A cultura grega antiga como fonte de inspiración dos poetas galegos', *Alonso Montero Vol.*, II, 781–93, supplies a panoramic survey of Greek influences. T. López, 'María Balteira, señora do tempo pasado', *ib.* 795–811, examines the presence of this figure, addressee of numerous mediæval *cantigas*, in a range of 20th-c. Galician verse. X. Xove Ferreiro, 'Noticia da colaboración galega na coroa de Azara', *ib.*, 1631–49, details the literary tributes paid to the Aragonese diplomat José Nicolás de Azara y Perera, and in particular the poems in Galician included in the *Glorias del caballero Azara en el siglo XIX* of 1852. J. Ventura, 'Uns poemas galegos no xornal *El Día de Terrassa* (1921)', *ib.*, 1553–61, considers these poems — by Risco, Cabanillas, Manoel Antonio, and Gonzalo López Abente — as part of an ongoing cultural exchange between Catalan and Galician nationalists. F. Villares Mouteira, 'Crecente Vega e a escola poética do Seminario de Mondoñedo', *ib.*, 1603–12, examines the work of a writer felt to be representative, in terms of theme and vision, of the poetic production of the 'Mondoñedo school'. M. X. Nogueira, 'Do *fonema* á *paisaxe*. O discurso metalingüístico na poesía galega dos noventa', *ib.*, 1061–77, assesses diverse trends in contemporary Galician lyric, relating them to questions of sociolinguistics, normalization and bilingualism. H. González, 'Poesía: dos poemarios e modelos diversos', *AELG*, 1998:261–70, provides an appraisal of the year's new poetry.

## 4. NARRATIVE

S. Gaspar Porras, 'Unha cala á literatura fantástica do século XIX: o tema do xuramento', *Alonso Montero Vol.*, II, 643–54, pursues the theme in a cluster of works from the last two decades of the century. T. López, 'Arredor da Nova Narrativa', *ATO*, 37:37–58, locates the Galician movement in a 20th-c. European context. D. Vilavedra, 'Algunhas calas no discurso metaliterario galego nos 80 e nos 90', *Alonso Montero Vol.*, II, 1563–75, considers recent progress towards a Galician discourse of literary autonomy. Id., 'Narrativa do 98: polos vieiros rozados', *AELG*, 1998:255–60, is a critical evaluation of the year's novelistic production.

## 5. THEATRE

L. Tato, 'Unha cala no medio rural: o teatro na comarca de Ortigueira', *Alonso Montero Vol.*, II, 1475–87, is an amply documented account dealing principally with the early decades of the 20th century.

J. M. Paz Gago, 'Teatro da subversión. As tradicións do Antroido no teatro galego contemporáneo', *ib.*, 1125–38, makes a Bakhtinian assessment of the carnivalesque in Galician theatre from the 'Xeración *Nós*' to the 'Grupo Abrente'. N. Pazó, 'Panorámica da literatura dramática: o ano de R. Vidal Bolaño', *AELG*, 1998: 271–76, appraises the year's theatre, with special attention given to the author mentioned.

## 6. TRANSLATION

C. Noia, 'Novas anotacións á traducción ó galego do *Ulises* de J. Joyce', *Alonso Montero Vol.*, II, 1079–91, argues closely that Otero Pedrayo's Galician translation of fragments of Joyce's text were made from the French of Valéry Larbaud rather than from the English original. N. Pazó González, 'A traducción no teatro galego: 1960–1978', *ib.*, 1139–55, looks at the role of translation in this aspect of Galician cultural revival and consolidation. G. Constenla, 'Traducción literaria: sen rumbo fixo', *AELG*, 1998: 277–86, assesses works in Galician translation published in the course of the year.

## 7. MEDIEVAL LITERATURE

Y. Frateschi, *\*En cas dona Maior. Os trovadores na corte señorial galega no século XIII*, SC, Laiovento, 171 pp. C. P. Martínez Pereiro, *A indócil liberdade de nomear (por volta da "Interpretatio nominis" na literatura trovadoresca*, Corunna, Espiral Maior, 226 pp., is an erudite study of naming in the mediæval ballads. A. Resende, 'Galicia trobadoresca', *AELG*, 1998: 207–32, furnishes a fresh approach to the issue of the Galician contribution — that is, from within Galicia — to the mediæval Galician-Portuguese lyric. M. Brea, 'Coita do mar, coita de amor', *Alonso Montero Vol.*, II, 235–48, takes a detailed look at forms of poetic complaint. M. P. Ferreira, 'Codax revisitado', *AELG*, 1998: 157–68, revises the same writer's earlier seminal study *O Som de Martin Codax*. M. Arbor Aldea, 'Don Afonso Sanchez e Vaasco Martîiz de Resende: a *tensó* como xogo de corte', *Alonso Montero Vol.*, II, 109–36, provides a densely documented historical study and edition of the *cantiga* addressed by the Portuguese troubadour to his poetic rival, emphasizing the ludic qualities of courtly verse. E. Corral Díaz, 'As *bestas* de Fernand'Esquio', *ib.*, 347–64, contextualizes, edits, and analyses the poem 'Dis[s]e hum infante ante sa companha'. P. Lorenzo Gradín, 'O mosteiro de Arouca e a madeira nova', *ib.*, 877–97, studies and edits Don Afonso Lopez de Baian's *cantiga* 'En Arouca unha casa faria'. S. Parkinson, 'As *Cantigas de Santa María*: estado das cuestións textuais', *AELG*, 1998: 179–205, from one of the most prominent international specialists in the field, provides an overview of current work on authorship, manuscripts, metre, language and structure, and editing. M. O'Neill, 'Oral and literate processes in Galician-Portuguese song', *GalR*, 3–4:8–18, traces processes of interaction between oral and literate culture in the *Cantigas de Santa María*. E. Fidalgo, ' "Joculatores qui cantant gesta principum et vitas sanctorum": as *Cantigas de Santa María*, entre a lírica e a épica', *Flores Vol.*, ii, 318–34, once more demonstrates the eclecticism of the collection. Id., 'As prosificacións castelás de dúas cantigas de *loor* alfonsinas', *Alonso Montero Vol.*, ii, 575–87, considers the Castilian prose versions of *cantigas* 10 and 20 found in the *Códice Rico*. G. Avenoza, 'El deán y el villano: un poema de Alfonso el Sabio y una canción tradicional', *Madrygal*, 133–38, elucidates the imprint of a traditional *cantiga* upon a poem by Alfonso the Wise. R. Lorenzo and X. L. Couceiro, 'Correccións á edición da *General Estoria* de Ramón Martínez López (ii)', *Flores Vol.*, ii, 209–33, is a continuation of the authors' earlier study. J. L. Rodríguez, 'De castelhano para galego-português: as traduções medievais', *Alonso Montero Vol.*, ii, 1285–99, specifies mediaeval translations within processes of cultural exchange.

## 8. Individual Authors

ALONSO MONTERO. C. Mejía Ruiz, 'Xesús Alonso Montero e os seus *Versos satíricos*', *Alonso Montero Vol.*, ii, 935–45, examines the satirical uses of literary models in A.M.'s 1998 verse collection. X. M. Salgado, 'O poeta Alonso Montero', *ib.*, 1379–87, makes a broad survey.

BLANCO TORRES. The honorand of the *Día das Letras Galegas 1999* attracted the customary critical attention, although the relative paucity of his work in Galician meant that the volume of publications was less than in most preceding years; the following are some of the highlights. In *R. Blanco Torres. Xornadas de alerta e agonía*, Vigo, Xerais, 109 pp., R. Nicolás, 'A obra literaria de Blanco Torres e a súa fortuna crítica' (57–84), provides an historical survey of the reception of B.T.'s work, while M. Valcárcel, 'Roberto Blanco Torres no xornalismo galego' (85–104), furnishes a detailed appraisal of the place of B.T. within Galician journalism of the period. In *Roberto Blanco Torres. O combate incesante*, *A nosa cultura*, 20, M. Bascoy and M. Romero, 'A musa alemana' (52–56), take a rare look at B.T.'s translation of German poems by F. Hebbel, while X. M. Millán, '*Orballo de media noite*: unha poética persoal' (57–62), examines B.T.'s idiosyncratic assimilation of the poetic avant-garde. In *Roberto Blanco Torres. Vida e obra. Actas das Xornadas de Cuntis*, Vigo, Xerais, are the especially interesting literary studies by A. López-Casanova, 'Blanco Torres e a poesía do seu tempo' (69–77), a rigorous contextualization of the author and his work, and X. L. Méndez Ferrín, 'Os escritores galegos na 2a República: Blanco Torres' (15–21). CABANILLAS. F. Fernández Rei, 'Consideracións sobre a lingua de *A noite estrelecida'*, *Flores Vol.*, II, 303–17, evaluates the contribution of C.'s collection to the development of Galician literary language. A. X. Pociña López, 'Ramón Cabanillas e Teixeira de Pascoaes: dúas formas de ve-la saudade', *Alonso Montero Vol.*, II, 1163–78, details points of convergence. CASTRO. V. Álvarez, 'A primeira carta en prosa en galego moderno: Camilo Álvarez de Castro escribe a Rosalía sobre *Cantares gallegos* (1863)', *Grial*, 143:453–74, provides a glimpse into the reception of Rosalía's collection in the year of its publication. The same writer's 'Sobre as orixes de Rosalía', *ATO*, 39:29–55, is an important documentary contribution to the clarification of Rosalía's obscure family background. M. C. Ríos, 'A orixe popular de *Contos da miña terra (Conto gallego)*, obra atribuida a R. de Castro', *Flores Vol.*, II, 606–25, searches for the origins of the tale in popular literature. L. Fontoira, 'Os pre-textos de *Follas novas'*, *Alonso Montero Vol.*, II, 603–28, details changes — of metre, orthography, grammar, and arrangement — made to many of the poems appearing in literary journals before publication in the volume of 1880. J. Wilcox, 'Rosalía de Castro', *ATO*, 40:11–40, analyses the place of specific images and metaphors in Rosalía's poetic cosmology. A. López and A. Pociña, 'Sobre as traduccións feitas por Rosalía', *Alonso Montero Vol.*, II, 813–27, examines Rosalía's Castilian versions of her own Galician poems and her Galician versions of poems by other Spanish writers. J. M. González Herrán, 'Rosalía de Castro en la literatura española de su tiempo: cien años de recepción crítica (1864–1960)', *ib.*, 665–76, chronicles periods of 'crítica coetánea', 'rescate noventay-ochista', 'consagración', and 'interpretación y valoración crítica'. X. Alonso, 'O nome e a obra de R. de Castro no exilio exterior e no exilio interior no ano do seu centenario (1937)', Axeitos, *Exilio*, 125–41, follows the historical trail of Rosalía in Galician literature one hundred years after her birth. A. Alonso Nogueira, 'A invención do escritor nacional. Rosalía de Castro: a poeta e a súa patria', *Alonso Montero Vol.*, II, 41–64, examines Murguía's preparation of the 1909 *Obras completas* edition of *En las orillas del Sar*, scrutinizing issues of textual editing and elucidating Murguía's ongoing figuration and projection of Rosalía within discourses of nationhood and the sacred. S. Fox, 'De literata a literata. Anne Marie Morris canta a Rosalía de Castro en inglés', *AELG*, 1998:277–86, evaluates the English translations of Rosalía's poems made by Morris, concentrating on two specific examples. X. M. Dasilva, 'Una tradução de Rosalía para português', *Alonso Montero Vol.*, II, 381–401, takes a wide-ranging look at literary translation as an affirmation of imaginative relationships between Galicia and Portugal. See also POZO GARZA.

CORTEZÓN.   A. Abuín, 'A traxectoria teatral de D. Cortezón: cara a unha poética do drama histórico galego', is a preliminary study (pp. 78–119) included in the Centro Dramático Galego's edition of *Xelmírez ou a gloria de Compostela*, SC, IGAEM, 363 pp.

CUNQUEIRO.   X. Carro, 'A viaxe imaxinaria', *Alonso Montero Vol.*, II, 305–13, surveys *Se o vello Sinbad volvese ás illas*. C. Criado, 'Cunqueiro ante el incesto en Elsinor', *ib.*, 365–80, considers the location of *Don Hamlet* within a mythical tradition ranging from Sophocles and Aeschylus via Shakespeare to the Galician author. X. M. Paz Gago's 'O teatro de A. Cunqueiro' provides an introduction (pp. 55–110) to the Centro Dramático Galego's edition of their production of *Se o vello Sinbad volvese ás illas*, SC, IGAEM, 177 pp. R. Rodríguez Vega, 'A tendencia á hipercorrección do escritor bilingüe. O caso das autotraduccións ó castelán de Álvaro Cunqueiro', *Alonso Montero Vol.*, II, 1355–71, is a rigorously argued assessment of C.'s translations of his own work.

CURROS ENRÍQUEZ.   E. López furnishes an extensive 'Introducción' (pp. 85–306) to *A poesía galega de M. Curros Enríquez*, 2 vols, Corunna, Deputación, 1012, 1969 pp., a mammoth edition with notes and appendices that includes also C.E.'s poetry in Castilian Spanish, his surviving letters, reviews, and other archive material. A. M. Aguirre, 'A note on Manuel Curros Enríquez and the Galician *Rexurdimento*', *GalR*, 3–4 : 34–40, supplies a broad assessment of C.E.'s life and work. E. López Varela, 'Os dous procesos a Curros', *Alonso Montero Vol.*, II, 861–76, closely chronicles the circumstances of C.E.'s dual persecution on the grounds of politics and religion. J. J. Moralejo, 'Mundo clásico en Curros', *ib.*, 997–1016, ranges widely with ample citation and produces succinct conclusions.

DANS.   X. M. Fernández Castro, 'De Raúl Dans a *Lugar*', introduces (pp. 51–138) the Centro Dramático Galego's edition of their production of *Lugar*, SC, IGAEM, 203 pp.

DELGADO GURRIARÁN.   R. Gurriarán, *F. Delgado Gurriarán. Vida e obra dun poeta valdeorrés, republicano e galeguista*, Sada, O Castro, takes a broad overview. M. X. Lama López, 'Un caso de mestixaxe cultural na literatura galega do exilio: os poemas mexicanos de F. Delgado Gurriarán', *Alonso Montero Vol.*, II, 739–53, reads the poems as a form of convergence between the absence of Galicia and dynamic presence of Mexico.

DÍAZ CASTRO.   A. Requeixo, 'A poesía de Xosé María Díaz Castro: prehistoria de *Nimbos*', *Alonso Montero Vol.*, II, 1247–59, examines the gestation of the collection by investigating the prior appearance of versions of some of the poems in newspapers and magazines.

DIESTE. C. A. Molina, 'Os *Arquivos* de R. Dieste', pp. 13–28 of *Xornadas sobre R. Dieste*, SC, Xunta. From the same volume, D. Vilavedra's 'Achegas para unha revalorización do Dieste dramaturgo' (99–104), provide broad-based commentary. O. Rodríguez, 'Rafael Dieste e "O neno suicida". A narración do tempo ás avesas', *Madrygal*, 127–32, documents other literary instances of backward-flowing time, including those found in Ramón Gómez de la Serna and Pedro Salinas. E. Irizarry, 'El idioma del corazón: el uso del gallego en el *Félix Muriel* de Rafael Dieste', *Alonso Montero Vol.*, II, 727–37, argues that D. used his native tongue both as a vehicle for collective values and affective reliance and as a linguistic stimulus to interest in Galicia in the wider diaspora.

FERREIRO. E. Río, 'A visión do exiliado en *A fronteira infinda* de C.E. Ferreiro', Axeitos, *Exilio*, 125–41, analyses F.'s poetic configuration of the exile. A. López-Casanova, 'Sistema epocal e poética de razón histórica. (Sobre a situación de Celso Emilio Ferreiro na lírica galega)', *Alonso Montero Vol.*, II, 829–43, considers the applicability or otherwise of chronological or aesthetic categories, concluding that F. in *O soño sulagado* and *Longa noite de pedra* represents and defines the vital sensibilities of the historical moment. E. Río Conde, 'Analoxías entre *El Señor presidente* de Miguel Ángel Asturias e "A caza de bruxas" (*A fronteira infinda*) de Celso Emilio Ferreiro', *ib.*, 1275–84, draws suggestive parallels. E. J. Torres Feijó, 'O galego Esteban: a estratégia para a configuraçom dum herói', *ib.*, 1489–1510, makes a mythological reading of F.'s tale and its central character.

FILGUEIRA VALVERDE. L. Méndez Fernández, 'Algunhas notas sobre Filgueira Valverde e o neotrobadorismo', *Alonso Montero Vol.*, II, 947–55, assesses F.V.'s little-known *6 Canciones de mar 'in modo antico'*, the texts themselves appearing together for the first time since their publication in 1941.

FOLE. X. A. García, 'O teatro de Ánxel Fole', *Dorna*, 25:141–52, seeks to locate F.'s theatre by pursuing its relationship with a wider Galician context.

GARCÍA ACUÑA. X. A. Míguez, 'A colección de *Orballeiras* de Fernando García Acuña', *Alonso Montero Vol.*, II, 973–81, assesses, with due contextualization, the verse collection first published in 1887.

GARCÍA BARROS. X. R. Freixeiro provides a wide-ranging introduction (pp. 9–60) to G.B.'s life, work and thought in the volume of previously unpublished material *Cos pés na Terra. Personalidade e obra inédita ou esquecida de Manuel García Barros*, A Estrada, Fouce, 199 pp.

GARCÍA-BODAÑO. A. Tarrío, 'Breve achegamento á poesía de S. García-Bodaño', *Flores Vol.*, II, 670–85, is, as the title implies, a broad survey.

LAMAS CARVAJAL. X. Alonso provides an introduction (pp. 3–35) to the facsimile edition of *Espiñas, follas e frores (ramiño primeiro)*, SC, Xunta, 104 pp.

LEIRAS PULPEIRO. X. Alvilares, 'M. Leiras Pulpeiro e a crítica do cristianismo', *Alonso Montero Vol.*, II, 83–94, briefly contextualizes L.P.'s 19th-c. anti-clericalism.

LENCE-SANTAR. X. Freyre and A. Requeixo supply a contextualizing introduction (pp. 13–55) to the new annotated edition *Poesía galega*, SC, Libros da Frouma, 103 pp.

LÓPEZ-CASANOVA. R. Raña's annotated edition of *Mesteres*, Vigo, Xerais, 135 pp., contains a broad introduction (pp. 11–50).

MANOEL ANTONIO. J. M. Ribera Llopis and O. Rodríguez González, 'Joan Salvat-Papasseit e Manuel Antonio: o mar como espacio poético da aventura', *Alonso Montero Vol.*, II, 1261–73, compares imaginative projections of the sea within the two writers' experience of the avant-garde.

MÉNDEZ FERRÍN. A. Angueira includes a thoroughgoing introduction (pp. 11–70) to the critical edition *Poesía enteira de Heriberto Bens*, Vigo, Xerais, 133 pp. J. J. Moralejo, 'Mundo clásico en *O fin dun canto* de X. L. Méndez Ferrín', *Flores Vol.*, II, 518–31, examines the volume's Graeco-Roman influences. F. Cabo Aseguinolaza, 'Temporalidade interna e autocomunicación: a propósito dun conto de Méndez Ferrín', *Alonso Montero Vol.*, II, 261–70, theoretically anchored in Lotman and Segre, analyses the tale 'Medias azuis' from *Arraianos*. I. Cochón Otero, 'Poesía, ideoloxía e manifesto: a "Homenaxe a Fidel Castro" de X. L. Méndez Ferrín', *ib.*, 329–45, makes an efficient structure-based study of M.F.'s poem.

MURGUÍA. H. Rabunhal, *Manuel Murguía*, SC, Laiovento, 146 pp., supplies a new intellectual biography of the 19th-c. writer.

NAVAZA. A. S. Alonso Núñez, 'O lector modelo, crítico e inxenuo, en *Erros e Tánatos*', *Alonso Montero Vol.*, II, 65–81, schematically examines questions of narratology and the implied reader in the cited 1996 collection of short stories.

OTERO PEDRAYO. A. Solla González, ' "Os pañales de luar", un conto recuperado de Otero Pedrayo', *Alonso Montero Vol.*, II, 1459–67, reproduces, with commentary, a tale published in *El Pueblo Gallego* in April 1931. M. Outeiriño, 'Sobre as baladas líricas de Otero Pedrayo', *ATO*, 40:139–51, is an edition with commentary of three ballads by the writer. C. Patterson, 'North and south and *The Decline of the West*: Galicia, Spengler and Otero Pedrayo', *GalR*, 3–4:52–76, analyses O.P.'s personal reworking, with application to Galicia, of Spenglerian concepts of time and history. D. Flitter, 'Romantismo vivencial e estructura vangardista en *Devalar*, de Ramón Otero Pedrayo', *Alonso Montero Vol.*, II, 589–601, examines O.P.'s text as cumulative imaginative projection of Galician identity. M. Fernández Rodríguez, 'Virginia Woolf from Galicia: hyperborean dream and cosmopolitan symphony', *GalR*, 3–4:41–51, examines Galician representations of the English writer in O.P.'s *Devalar* and Claudio Rodríguez Fer's short story 'Mórbida mole'. X. M. Salgado, 'Rousseau estivo en Ourense', *Flores Vol.*, II, 645–54, detects the presence of the French writer in O.P.'s work. M. F. Vieites, 'R. Otero Pedrayo, J. Joyce e o *Ulysses*. Creación dramática, identidade e construcción nacional. Algunhas anotacións para un estudio', *AELG*, 1998:75–116, seeks to resolve some of the questions raised by O.P.'s drama in the light of his prior knowledge of the great Irish writer.

PAZ LESTÓN.    M. Villar, 'X. Paz Lestón (1898–1977), paradigma do compromiso dun poeta emigrante co exilio e coa súa literatura', Axeitos, *Exilio*, 67–82, undertakes a thorough survey of P.L.'s literary activity in exile.

PEREIRO.    C. Pérez Varela, 'Nerval na *Poesía última* de Lois Pereiro', *Alonso Montero Vol.*, II, 1157–61, centres on the poetic treatment of death.

PÉREZ BALLESTEROS.    J. L. Forneiro Pérez, 'José Pérez Ballesteros e o romanceiro tradicional galego', *Alonso Montero Vol.*, II, 629–42, examines P.B.'s work as collector and editor in the *Cancionero popular gallego* of 1885–1886.

PIMENTEL.    L. Pozo Garza, ' "Palabras" de Luís Pimentel', *Alonso Montero Vol.*, II, 1195–1204, via intertextual references, examines the necessary 'mixtilingüismo' of P.'s poem.

PINTOS.    X. Xove, 'O primeiro texto galego coñecido de J. M. Pintos', *Flores Vol.*, II, 731–42, provides an edition with commentary of P.'s first Galician poem of 1843.

PONDAL.    X. R. Baixeras introduces (pp. 9–64) an annotated edition of *O divino sainete*, Vigo, Xerais, 143 pp. X. R. Pena, 'Pondal desde *Os Eoas*', *ATO*, 37:13–26, reaffirms the centrality of this work to the overall understanding and significance of the recuperation of features of Galician identity. M. T. Amado Rodríguez, 'Os gregos e Pondal', *Alonso Montero Vol.*, II, 95–107, examines P.'s translation and imitation of specific Classical Greek texts. M. Ferreiro, ' "Terra verde": un poema inédito de Eduardo Pondal', *ib.*, 511–27, reproduces the autograph manuscript located in the library of the Real Academia Galega and provides an edited version with fulsome notes.

POZO GARZA.    C. Blanco, 'Luz Pozo Garza falando a Rosalía: escribir con tinta da nai', *Alonso Montero Vol.*, II, 185–201, examines the critical and creative dialogue between the two poets.

QUEIZÁN. A. Acuña and C. Mejía, 'O amor na obra de M. X. Queizán, *Madrygal*, 11–20, surveys one of Q.'s salient themes.
RODRÍGUEZ CASTELAO. M. Rei, *Arte e verdade (a obra literaria de Daniel Castelao)*, Vilaboa, Cumio, 155 pp., is a monograph dedicated to the consideration of its subject's work from a socio-historical perspective, a study rather distorted by its own author's ideological emphasis. J. C. Rodríguez, 'Castelao e a literatura', *Alonso Montero Vol.*, II, 1301–19, is a series of personal reflections with the obligatory final reference to Lenin. E. Vázquez Souza, 'Unha lectura de "Sabela" de Castelao', *ib.*, 1543–51, contextualizes *Retrincos*.
RODRÍGUEZ FER. See OTERO PEDRAYO.
SEOANE. H. González Fernández, 'Figuras femininas na obra literaria de Luís Seoane', *Alonso Montero Vol.*, II, 655–64, looks at S.'s figurations of the feminine: mythical, popular, legendary and historical. I. Ogando, 'Sobre a(s) traducción(s) e edición(s) de *A soldadeira* de L. Seoane', Axeitos, *Exilio*, 91–108, is a rigorous comparative study which seeks to prove that the text was originally written in Galician. The same writer's '*A soldadeira* de Luís Seoane: ¿teatro histórico?', *Alonso Montero Vol.*, II, 1093–1105, analyses the play's utilization of history in its projection of meaning.
SIGÜENZA. X. M. Dobarro, 'Xulio Sigüenza, nacionalista e poeta galego en Cuba: trece poemas galegos', *Alonso Montero Vol.*, II, 429–50, closely details S.'s literary activity in Havana and reproduces the poems written between 1918 and 1920.
TORO, SUSO DE. P. Fallon, 'Sobre a construcción do corpo político galego en *Tic-tac* de Suso de Toro', *AELG*, 1998: 141–56, analyses the novel as an invitation to its reader to imagine, via its post-modern conception of the body politic, the Galician nation.
VAAMONDE. M. T. Amado, 'Ecos clásicos na lírica de F. Vaamonde', *AELG*, 1998: 11–41, provides a repertory of the diverse dialogues with Greek and Latin authors found in V.'s poetry.
VARELA, LORENZO. X. R. Brea, 'Lorenzo Varela: a voz solidaria do exilio', Axeitos, *Exilio*, 19–34, examines V.'s relationship with the Misiones Pedagógicas and with the magazine *Hora de España*. X. G. Ferreiro Fente, 'A poesía de guerra de Lorenzo Varela', *Alonso Montero Vol.*, II, 529–54, details the circumstances of composition and publication of 14 poems, all subsequently reproduced with notes. C. Rodríguez Fer, 'Escritos de combate de Lorenzo Varela', *ib.*, 1321–43, deals with the same poems, reproducing also V.'s creative and critical prose writing from the same period.
VILLAR PONTE. C. Fernández, 'Na orixe da nova dramaturxia e do teatro galego moderno: *A Patria do Labrego* (1905), de A. Villar Ponte', *Alonso Montero Vol.*, II, 457–82, makes a detailed study of the play.

ZAPATA GARCÍA. M. Villar, 'Do "secuestro" á censura. A intrincada historia editorial do libro *A roseira da soidade* de Antón Zapata García', *Alonso Montero Vol.*, II, 1589–1601, is a fascinating piece of literary detective work.

## VIII. LATIN AMERICAN STUDIES

### SPANISH AMERICAN LITERATURE
### THE COLONIAL PERIOD
POSTPONED

### THE NINETEENTH CENTURY

By ANNELLA McDERMOTT, *Department of Hispanic, Portuguese and Latin American Studies, University of Bristol*

1. GENERAL

J. Castillo, 'El "sublime Niágara" y los abismos de la modernidad en la poesía hispanoamericana decimonónica', *BHS(L)*, 76:245–60, examines the treatment of the Niagara Falls as an emblem of the sublime in poems by José María de Heredia, Gertrudis Gómez de Avellaneda, Rafael Pombo, and Juan Antonio Pérez Bonalde. S. M. Hart, 'Signs of the subaltern: notes on nineteenth-century Spanish American literature', *JILAS*, 5:27–35, deals with the use of the Inca Emperor Huayna Capac as narrator of much of *La victoria de Junín*, by José Joaquín de Olmedo, and with the figure of the black slave who commits suicide by swallowing his own tongue in Cirilo Villaverde's *Cecilia Valdés*. E. Jaramillo-Zuluaga, 'Artes de la lectura en la ciudad del águila negra: la lectura en voz alta y la recitación en Santafé de Bogotá a fines del siglo XIX', *RevIb*, 64, 1998:471–84. K. Lehman, 'Geography and gender in the narrative of Argentinean national origin: the pampa as chronotype', *REH*, 32, 1998:3–28, pays particular attention to Sarmiento's *Facundo*, Hernández's *Martín Fierro*, and Martínez Estrada's *Radiografía de la Pampa*. M. Meléndez, 'Obreras del pensamiento y educadoras de la nación: el sujeto femenino en la ensayística feminina decimonónica de transición', *RevIb*, 64, 1998:573–89, looks at views on the education of women and their role in society in essays by Gertrudis Gómez de Avellaneda, Juana Manuela Gorriti, Clorinda Matto de Turner, and Adela Samudio. K. Niemeyer, ' "Este es un pueblo que se desarrolla de golpe" — la (re)presentación de la modernidad en las novelas argentinas del "ciclo de la bolsa" ', *RCLL*, 47, 1998:123–46, looks at the vision of modernity in Julián Martel's *La Bolsa* and Segundo I. Villafañe's *Quilito* and *Horas de Fiebre*. M. del R. Oviedo y Pérez de Toledo, 'Encrucijada del 98: Larreta y Rodó o el nacionalismo en el Río de la Plata', *CMHLB*, 70, 1998:221–34, suggests that despite differences in the Spanish and Latin American visions of 98, there were similarities in the ideologies of identity and nationhood embraced on the one hand by Spanish writers of the Generation of 98 and Latin American writers such as Larreta and Rodó. C. Pera, 'De *viajeros* y *turistas*: reflexiones sobre el turismo en la literatura hispanoamericana', *RevIb*, 64, 1998: 507–28, has an emphasis on the 19th century. D. Sobrevilla, 'El surgimiento de la idea de Nuestra América en los ensayistas latinoamericanos deimonónicos', *RCLL*, 50: 147–63, refers to texts by Bolívar, José Cecilio del Valle, José Victorino Lastarria, and Francisco Bilbao.

INDIVIDUAL AUTHORS

DARÍO, RUBÉN. C. Giudicelli, 'Rubén Darío et Manuel González Prada, deux écrivains latino-américains face a "1898"', *CMHLB*, 70, 1998: 205–20, deals with two articles, D.'s 'El triunfo de Calibán' and González Prada's 'Españoles y yankees'. C. Jauregui, 'Calibán, ícono del 98. A propósito de un artículo de Rubén Darío', *RevIb*, 64, 1998: 441–50, also deals with 'El triunfo de Calibán'. C. Pailler, 'L'envoyé spécial de *La Nación* de Buenos Aires: Rubén Darío à Madrid, 1898', *CMHLB*, 70, 1998: 221–34, analyses D.'s articles from this period. M. A. Salgado, 'Rubén Darío y la generación del 98: personas, personajes y máscaras del fin de siglo español', *His(US)*, 82: 725–32, looks at pen-portraits of themselves and other writers by D. and members of the Spanish Generation of 98, and notes the influence of these portraits on subsequent comments on the writers portrayed. F. Solares-Larrave, 'A harmony of whims: towards a discourse of identity in Darío's *Palabras liminares*', *HR*, 66, 1998: 447–65, sees this prologue to the *Prosas profanas* as formulating a declaration of self-determination through the use of parody and carnivalesque devices. J. Torres-Pou, 'Un escritor centroamericano ante el 98: Rubén Darío cronista del fin-de-siglo', *BHS(L)*, 76: 261–66, examines D.'s comments on Spain's reactions to the loss of Cuba in articles written for the Argentinian newspaper *La Nación*.

ECHEVERRÍA, ESTEBAN. L. Skinner, 'Carnality in *El matadero*', *REH*, 33: 205–24, shows that the story points insistently to the rape of its young protagonist by the butchers in the slaughterhouse, yet elides the act of violence itself, and he proposes that this silence relates to E.'s reluctance to identify with the Unitarians, whom he considered divorced from Argentine reality.

FERNÁNDEZ DE LIZARDI, JOSÉ JOAQUÍN. J. P. Dabove, 'Espejos de la ciudad letrada: el "arrastraderito" y el juego como metáforas políticas en *El Perriquillo Sarniento*', *RevIb*, 65: 31–48, suggests that these metaphors express a certain questioning by the novelist of his own role as writer and intellectual. J.C. Ramírez-Pimienta, 'Picaresca mexicana: *El Periquillo Sarniento* en el tejido mental de la nación', *RHM*, 51, 1998:225–35, looks at how the writing and reading of this novel contributed to the formation of a sense of Mexican nationhood.

GÓMEZ DE AVELLANEDA, GERTRUDIS. Carolina Alzate Cadavid, *Desviación y verdad. La re-escritura en Arenas y la Avellaneda*, SSSAS, ix + 269 pp., analyses G. de A.'s *Guatimozín, último emperador de México* and *El cacique de Turmequé*. R. Pagés-Rangel, 'Para una sociología del escándalo: la edición y publicación de las cartas privadas de Gertrudis Gómez de Avellaneda', *RHM*, 50, 1997:22–36. A. Roselló Selimov, 'La verdad vence apariencias: hacia la ética de Gertrudis Gómez de Avellaneda a través de su prosa', *HR*, 67:215–41, examines the treatment in the novels and other prose writings of two contrasting ideas of virtue: one authentic, and arising from Nature, the other simply an appearance of virtue, based on hypocrisy and social convention. *REH*, 32, 1998, has a *Diálogo crítico* on G. de A., comprising S. I. Stein, 'Gertrudis Gómez de Avellaneda's bourgeois liberal *Sab* story' (153–70), which argues that the novel, far from being a radical text that promotes the possibility of real social transformation, is a conservative text which in fact protects the status quo. D. Sommer, 'A program of reading, not a reading for a programme' (171–74), argues that this is too schematic a reading, and suggests instead that the ambiguities and contradictions in the novel should be celebrated. W. Luis, 'How to read *Sab*' (175–85), argues that the novel should be understood, not in the context of present-day debates, but in the context of its time.

GUDIRI Y ALCÓCER, JOSÉ MIGUEL. B. de Alba-Koch, 'Los *Apuntes de la vida* de Gudiri y Alcócer: lo privado y lo público en una autobiografía novohispana', *BHS(G)*, 76:463–86, demonstrates that the text, while adding to our knowledge of social institutions such as the *tertulia*, also reveals the private sentiments of the writer.

GUTIÉRREZ, EDUARDO. S. Hart, 'Public execution and the body politic in the work of the Argentine *folletinista* Eduardo Gutiérrez', *BHS(G)*, 76:673–90, links the work of this writer, particularly the treatment of executions and duels, to the process of nation building.

LARRAÍNZAR, ENRIQUETA AND ERNESTINA. N. Araújo, 'Aceptar y escapar. Viajeras mexicanas en el siglo XIX', *CAm*, 217:29–39, places the book by these two sisters, *Viaje a varias partes de Europa [1880–82]*, in two contexts: the notion of nation-building and travel-writing as a genre.

LÓPEZ, VICENTE FIDEL. R. Ianes, 'Arquetipo narrativo, costumbrismo histórico y discurso nacionalizador en *La novia del hereje*', *HR*, 67:153–73, draws attention to the heterogeneous nature of the text, which is seen as typical of 19th-c. Latin American literature.

MÁRMOL, JOSÉ. I. A. D. Stewart, 'Two literary representations of "El Terror": the possible influence of Francisco Xavier de Achas's *Una víctima de Rosas* on José Mármol's *Amalia*', *BHS(G)*, 76:383–98, demonstrates thematic similarities between the play and the novel, and notes similarity in the evolution of the political ideas of the two authors. M. could not have seen the play performed in public, but he may have known it in printed form or by reputation.

MARTÍ, JOSÉ. J. Febles, 'Martí, el deporte y los Estados Unidos: el ludismo dialéctico como estrategia crítica en las *Escenas norteamericanas*', *RHM*, 51, 1998:273–90, analyses M.'s comments, which are mainly critical, on boxing, American football, baseball, marathon walking, tennis, badminton, and yachting regattas. M. Gomes, 'Modernidad y retórica: el motivo de la copa en dos textos martianos', *RevIb*, 64, 1998:457–70, looks at imagery of thirst, wine, and goblet in *Amor de ciudad grande* and in M.'s prologue to Juan Antonio Pérez Bonalde's *Poema del Niágara*. C. J. Morales, 'José Martí: poesía y revolución en *El presidio político en Cuba*', *CAm*, 214:90–104, argues that the text successfully combines ideological and aesthetic ends.

PALMA, CLEMENTE. G. Mora, 'Decadencia y vampirismo en el modernismo hispanoamericano: un cuento de Clemente Palma', *RCLL*, 46, 1997:191–98, draws attention to the use of transgressive themes and the absence of moralistic comment in the story *Vampiras*, from *Cuentos malévolos*.

VILLAVERDE, CIRILO. F. M. González, 'De lo invisible a lo espectacular en la creación de la mulata en la cultura cubana: *Cecilia Valdés* y *María Antonia*', *RevIb*, 64, 1998:543–58, compares the portrayal of the mulatto woman in the novel and Sergio Grial's film. D. Sommer, ' "No todo se ha de decir": Cecilia no sabe, *Beloved* no narra', *CAm*, 217:105–12, looks at the role of suppression of information in *Cecilia Valdés* and the novel by Toni Morrison.

# THE TWENTIETH CENTURY

By D. L. SHAW, *Brown-Forman Professor of Spanish American Literature in the University of Virginia*

## 1. GENERAL

General works include S. Hart, *\*A Companion to Spanish American Literature*, Woodbridge, U.K., Boydell & Brewer, 216 pp. See too his ' "El oficio de escribir." Some notes on literary print culture in Spanish America in the twentieth century', *Neophilologus*, 83: 387–409, on the massification of literature. J. Beverley, *\*Subalternity and Representation: Arguments in Cultural Theory*, Durham, Duke U.P., 224 pp. *\*Modernism and Its Margins: Reinscribing Cultural Modernity from Spain and Latin America*, ed. A. L. Geist and J. B. Monleón, NY, Garland, xxxv + 320 pp. *El debate de la postcolonialidad*, ed. A. de Toro and F. de Toro, M, Iberoamericana, 408 pp., has 20 essays in three languages on this hot topic. *\*El discurso crítico en América Latina*, ed. Z. Palermo, BA, Corregidor, 1997, 255 pp. M. Gomes, *\*Los géneros literarios en Hispanoamérica. Teoría e historia*, Pamplona, Eunsa, 1998, 244 pp. E. López Parada, *Una mirada al sesgo. Literatura desde los márgenes*, M, Iberoamericana, 200 pp., on the alleged collapse of traditional genres in contemporary Latin American literature. H. Costa, *\*Mar abierto. Ensayos sobre literatura brasileña, portuguesa e hispanoamericana*, Mexico D.F., FCE, 1998, 470 pp. *\*Al borde de mi fuego. Poética y poesía hispanoamericanas de los sesenta*, ed, J. Fornet, Alicante U.P., 1998, 195 pp. C. Reverte Bernal, *\*Fuentes europeas-vanguardia hispanoamericana*, M, Verbum, 1998, 156 pp. E. Chirinos, *\*La morada del silencio. Una reflexión sobre el silencio en la poesía a partir de las obras de E.A. Westphalen, G. Rojas, O. Orozco, J. Sologuren, J. E. Eielson y A. Pizarnik*, Lima, FCE, 1998, 259 pp. W. Seimens, *\*Mundos que renacen. El héroe en la novela hispanoamericana moderna*, Mexico D.F., FCE, 1998, 264 pp. V. Torres, *\*La novela bolero latinoamericana*, Mexico D.F., UNAM, 1998, 333 pp. S. M. Colombo and G. Tommasini, *\*Comprensión lectora y producción textual: minificción hispanoamericana*, Rosario, Fundación Ross, 1998, 279 pp. D. N. Cohn, *\*History and Memory in the Two Souths. Recent Southern and Spanish American Fiction*, Nashville, Vanderbilt U.P., 256 pp. I. Avelar, *\*The Untimely Present. Postdictatorial Latin American Fiction and the Task of Mourning*, Durham, Duke U.P., 272 pp. N. Gervassi-Navarro, *\*Pirate Novels: Fictions of Nation-Building in Spanish America*, Durham, Duke U.P., 256 pp. H. Geldrich-Leffman, *\*The Dialogue of Marriage in Contemporary German and Latin American Short Stories*, NY, Lang, 180 pp. M. Aronna, *\*Pueblos enfermos. The Discourse* *of Illness in Turn of the Century Spanish and Latin American Essays*, Chapel Hill, N. Carolina U.P., 160 pp.

POETRY. J. O. Jiménez, *Poetas contemporáneos de España y América*, M, Verbum, 1998, 351 pp. *CHA*, 588:7–66, has an important dossier on 'Aspectos de la poesía hispanoamericana' with five important essays on recent Colombian, Cuban, Peruvian, Costa Rican, and Argentine poetry, and one on the Venezuelan poet Rafael Cárdenas. R. Sarabia, *Poetas de la lengua hablada*, London, Támesis, 1997, 166 pp., covers Nicanor Parra, Rosario Castellanos, Ernesto Cardenal, Raúl González Tuñón, and Luisa Futoranski. J. Calzadilla, 'Mapa de las vanguardias poéticas en Latinoamérica', *Quimera*, 176:16–20 is superficial. *Las vanguardias literarias en Bolivia, Colombia, Ecuador, Peru. Bibliografía y antología crítica*, ed. H. Pöppel, M, Iberoamericana, 1998, 224 pp. H. Wentzlaff-Eggebert, *Fundir el hombre nuevo*, M, Iberoamericana, 400 pp., is on the new vision of creativity in vanguardist writing.

FICTION. R. L. Williams, *Postmodernidades latinoamericanas: la novela postmoderna en Colombia, Venezuela, Ecuador, Perú y Bolivia*, Bogotá, Univ. Central, 1998, 192 pp. D. L. Shaw, *Nueva narrativa hispanoamericana*, M, Cátedra, 408 pp., is a vastly amplified sixth edition of his 1981 book of the same name, now expanded to include the Postboom and Postmodernism. P. Sánchez López, 'La novela hispanoamericana en España y el debate sobre el realismo (1967–72)', *BHS(L)*, 76:57–73, examines journalistic reactions. R. de la Campa, 'Magical realism and world literature: a genre for the times?', *RCEH*, 23:205–19, examines it in relation to postmodernism. C. Fernández Prieto, *Historia y novela, Poética de la novela histórica*, Baranaín, Univ. de Navarra, 1998, 240 pp., includes some Latin American historical novels. F. Reati and G. Gómez Ocampo, 'Académicos y gringos malos: la universidad norteamericana y la barbarie cultural en la novela latinoamericana reciente', *RevIb*, 184–85, 1998:587–609, examine novels on U.S. academic life by José Agustín, M. T. Aguilera Sarramuño, E. Sosa, and J. Donoso. J. Jones, *A Common Place: The Representation of Paris in Spanish American Fiction*, Crombury, N.J., Buckland U.P. 1998, 136 pp. M. J. Daroquí, *(Dis)locaciones: narrativas híbridas del Caribe hispano*, Valencia, Tirant lo Blanc, 1998. *Hispanisms and Homosexualities*, ed. R. M. Irwin and S. Molloy, Durham, Duke U.P., 1998, 319 pp., includes a few items on Spanish American gay writers, especially V. Piñera, and Puerto Rican lesbian narrative. *Teorías sin disciplina, Latinoamericanismo, postcolonialidad y globalización en debate*, ed. S. Castro-Gómez and E. Mendieta, Mexico D.F., Porrúa, 1998, 294 pp. A. Joan-Elia, 'La teoría literaria postcolonial', *Quimera*, 174, 1998:30–35, is a handy survey with bibliography. *NTC*, 21–22, 1998, is on Latin American film, chiefly in Argentina, Brazil, and Mexico.

ON MORE THAN ONE AUTHOR. N. Burns, *\*Un vals en un montón de escombros. Poesía hispanoamericana entre la modernidad y la postmodernidad (Nicanor Parra, Enrique Lihn)*, Berne, Lang, 175 pp. M. R. Olivera-Williams, 'Retomando a Eros. Tres momentos en la poesía femenina hispanoamericana. Agustini, Mistral, Peri-Rossi', *RevIb*, 186: 117–33, is on the evolution of erotic poetry by these poets. *\*Asedios a textos literarios. Postestructuralismo / Semiótica / Desconstrucción*, ed. M. E. Blanco, M, Betania, 1997, 227 pp., apparently includes essays on Borges, Arenas, Carpentier, Rulfo, and others. K. Hargrave and G. Smith Seminet, 'De Macondo a McOndo. Nuevas voces en la literatura latinoamericana', *Chasqui*, 27.2, 1998: 14–26, interview Alberto Faguet, David Toscana, Rodrigo Fresnán, and Edmundo Paz-Soldán. *Sex and Sexuality in Latin America*, ed. D. Balderston and D. J. Guy, NY U.P. 1997, viii + 288 pp. includes essays bearing on Senel Paz and A. Pizarnik. D. Palaversich, 'Caught in the act: social stigma, homosexual panic and violence in Latin American writing', *Chasqui*, 28.2: 60–75, examines homosexual behaviour in works by Luis Zapata, José Donoso, Pedro Lemebel, and Jorge Marchant Lazcano. A. Kaminski, *After Exile: Writing the Latin American Diaspora*, Minneapolis, Minnesota U.P., 206 pp., includes essays on Benedetti, Donoso, Peri Rossi, Valenzuela, and others. S. González and L. Wilde, *Palabra crítica*, Mexico D.F., Univ. Autónoma, 1977, 488 pp., includes essays on Cortázar, Ribeyro, Rulfo, and others. P. González Rodas, *\*Premios Nobel latinoamericanos de literatura. Estudios sobre Mistral, Neruda, Asturias, García Márquez y Paz*, Zaragoza, Pórtico, 328 pp. A. E. Contreras, *\*Experiencia y narración. Vallejo, Arlt, [Pablo] Palacio y Felisberto Hernández*, Mérida (Venezuela), Univ. de los Andes, 1998, 220 pp. J. Manrique, *\*Eminent Maricones. Arenas, Lorca, Puig and Me*, Madison, Wisconsin U.P., 152 pp. P. Orgambide, *\*Poética de la política*, BA, Colihue, 1998, 221 pp., includes essays on Borges, Benedetti, Martínez Estrada, and others. C. J. Alonso, *The Burden of Modernity*, NY, OUP, 1998, x + 227 pp., includes study of the will to be modern in Quiroga, Vargas Llosa, García Márquez, Fuentes, and others.

THEATRE. D. W. Foster, *\*Espacio escénico y lenguaje*, BA, Galerna, 1998, 123 pp. *Théâtre et territoires. Espagne et Amérique Hispanique, 1950–1996*, ed. S. Bournardel and G. Champeau, Bordeaux, Maison des Pays Ibériques, 1998, 498 pp., has articles on plays by Jorge Díaz, E. Pavlovski, F. Sánchez, G. Reyes, J. Triana, and E. Buenaventura. F. de Toro, *Intersecciones: ensayos sobre teatro*, M, Iberoamericana, 230 pp., collects sundry earlier essays chiefly of a theoretical bent. In *Itinerario del autor dramático iberoamericano*, ed. F. Cabal, San Juan (Puerto Rico), Lea, 1997, 222 pp., six Spanish American dramatists discuss writing for the stage. *Performance, pathos, política de los sexos. Teatro postcolonial de autoras latinoamericanas*, ed. H. Adler and

K. Röttger, M, Iberoamericana, 242 pp., has 12 essays on modern transgressive drama by women writers. L. H. Quackenbush, *Devotas irreverencias: el auto en el teatro latinoamericano*, Mexico D.F., Univ. de Tlaxcala–Brigham Young Univ., 1998, 238 pp., discusses *autos* by J. Díaz, J. J. Arreola, J. Triana, V. Leñero, and A. Cuzzani. *Teatro, público, sociedad* ed. D. Meyran, Perpignan U.P., 1998, 559 pp., has many essays on *inter alia*, C. Gorostiza, M. A. de la Parra, M. Puig, R. Arlt, G. Gambaro, and E. Carballido.

GENDERED WRITING. *Poética de escritoras hispanoamericanas al alba del próximo milenio*. Miami, Universal, 1998, 244 pp., has essays and bibliography on contemporary women poets in Argentina, Mexico, Chile, Peru, Puerto Rico, and the Dominican Republic. *Estudios en honor de Janet Pérez, el sujeto femenino en escritoras hispánicas*, ed. S. Carvallo, Potomac, Maryland, Scripta Humanistica, 1998, xlviii + 320 pp., has a few essays on Spanish American women writers. M. Agosín, *\*Passion, Memory and Identity: Twentieth Century Latin American Jewish Women Writers*, Albuquerque, New Mexico U.P., 217 pp. L. Damjanova, 'Femina ludens — lexis ludens: creación poética femenina en Centroamérica', *Hispamérica*, 82:109–117, is based on work by Consuelo Tomás, Luz Méndez, and Gioconda Belli. J. A. Brown, 'Feminine anxiety of influence revisited: Alfonsina Storni and Delmira Agustini', *RCEH*, 23:191–203, is Bloomian. *Latin American Women Dramatists. Theatre, Texts and Theories*, ed. C. Larson and M. Vargas, Bloomington, Indiana U.P., 1998, 277 pp., includes essays on G. Gambaro, M. Villalta, E. Garro, C. Boullosa, and half a dozen more.

## 2. INDIVIDUAL COUNTRIES

### ARGENTINA

L. Pollmann, *La separación de los estilos: para la historia de la conciencia literaria argentina*, Frankfurt, Vervuert, 1998, 152 pp., discusses the difference between criollo and immigrant writing since 1880. M. K. Schäffauer, *\*ScriptOralität in der argentinischen Literatur (1890–1960)*, Frankfurt, Vervuert, 1998, 367 pp. B. Frederick, *\*Wily Modesty. Argentine Women Writers*, Tucson, ASU Center for Latin American Studies, 1998, 214 pp. M. Fernández de Perico, 'Lunario sentimental y el desprestigio de la luna romántica', *Thesaurus*, 49, 1994 [1999]:558–63, is inadequately researched. T. Barrera, *\*Baldomero Fernández Moreno (1915–1930)*, Lérida U.P., 1998, 140 pp. F. J. Rosenberg, 'Modernidad y arrepentimiento: Oliverio Girondo de los años 20 a *Campo nuestro*', *RCEH*, 23:255–69, is on his return to tradition. M. Grünfeld, 'Oliverio Girondo y el viaje de la vanguardia', *Hispamérica*, 82:11–34, is on his ambiguous vision of Europe. P. J.

Mendiola, 'Oliverio Girondo, la ciudad animada', Rovira, *Ciudad*, 93–110, is on his urban vision. L. Senkman, 'El aura de la palabra poética de Juanele', *Hispamérica*, 82 : 101–07, examines the poetry of Juan L. Ortiz. E. Crites, 'El universo maravilloso de *Pasión de la tribu* de Juan González', *SELA*, 42.4 : 43–53, is on his celebration of life. J. J. Bajarlía, \**Alejandra Pizarnik: anatomía de un recuerdo*, BA, Almagesta, 1998, 152 pp. M. Nicholson, 'From sybil to witch and beyond: female archetypes in the poetry of Olga Orozco', *Chasqui*, 27.1, 1998 : 11–22, is on her 'occult feminine figures'. \**José Isaacson, poeta crítico*, ed. Thorpe Running, BA, Grupo Editorial Latinoamericano, 169 pp. J. Kuhnheim, 'La promiscuidad del significado: Néstor Perlongher', *RevIb*, 187 : 281–92, is on his poetic neobaroque eroticism. A. Nuño interviews Arturo Carrera on his poetry in *Quimera*, 183 : 19–21, with interesting remarks. A. Apter-Cragnolino, \**Espejos naturalistas. Ideología y representación en la novela argentina (1884–1919)*, NY, Lang, x + 187 pp. S. Molloy, 'La violencia del género y la narrativa del exceso. Notas sobre mujer y relato en dos novelas argentinas de principios de siglo', *RevIb*, 184–85, 1998 : 520–42, discusses the presentation of women in *Borderland* (1907) and *La eterna angustia* (1908) by Atilio Chiáppori. R. Szmetan, '*Este pueblo necesita* (1934) de Manuel Gálvez, un libro olvidado por la crítica', *CA*, 73 : 226–42, is on Gálvez's ideology at the time. E. Thomas Dublé, 'Poética de la desesperación en el Mar del Plata: desmitologización y mitificación del lenguaje', *RCL*, 53, 1998 : 5–35, examines R. Arlt's *El amor brujo*, L. Marechal's *Adán Buenosaires* and A. Posse's *La reina del Plata*. A. Giordano, \**Razones de la crítica sobre literatura, ética y política*, BA, Colihue, 157 pp., has essays on Arlt, Borges, Bioy Casares, Luis Guzmán, and the Reviews *Sitio* and *Litoral*. E. Drucaroff, \**Arlt, profeta del miedo*, BA, Catálogos, 464 pp. D. L. Hernández, \**Los cuentos de Roberto Arlt*, Tenerife, La Laguna U.P., 1998, 160 pp. S. Saítta, 'Nuevos viajeros, otras miradas. Roberto Arlt en España', *Hispamérica*, 82 : 35–43, is on his prudent vision of the mother country. J. S. Kuhnheim, 'Arlt: masoquismo y Estado', *Hispamérica*, 83 : 117–24, is on masculinity and feminization in *Los siete locos*. B. Herrera, *Arlt, Borges y Cia, narrativa rioplatense de vanguardia*, San José de Costa Rica U.P., 1997, 245 pp., emphasizes the avant-garde context of their work in the 20s and 30s.

BORGES.    A. Albanowski, \**En el umbral del texto: la obra de Jorge Luis Borges*, Warsaw U.P. 1998. *Jorge Luis Borges y el saber en el siglo XX*, ed. A. de Toro and F. de Toro, M, Iberoamericana, 1998, 378 pp. (also published in English), concentrates on his significance outside purely literary studies. O. Ferrari, *En diálogo II*, BA, Sudamericana, 1998, 312 pp., is a second volume of his interviews with Borges. S. N. Barei, \**Borges y la crítica literaria*, Sta Cruz de Tenerife, Tauro, 181 pp. *CHA*, 585, has a dossier with five articles and an interview, of considerable interest. *Letras Libres* (Mexico) has seven commemorative essays. *Magazine Littéraire* has a dossier, with articles, an interview, and a little known 1922 article. *Quimera*, 183, has a dossier on Borges with four rather journalistic articles. *Theoria* (Univ. of Tucumán), special no., 1997, is a homage to Borges with sundry essays. *Variaciones Borges*, 7, has a dozen articles on Borges and Philosophy; *ib.*, 8, has ten articles on Borges and the city of Buenos Aires, and two interviews with D. Balderston, chiefly about Borges and R. L. Stevenson. *Hispamérica*, 83:33–54, has three short, reminiscent articles on Borges by J. E. Adoum, R. Fernandez Retamar, and S. Garmendia. A. Camp and F. Bouchardeau, *Jorge Luis Borges*, Paris, H.B. Editions, 171 pp., has an interview and nine essays. N. Helft, *\*Jorge Luis Borges, Bibliografía completa*, BA, FCE, 1997, 288 pp. R. Braceli, *\*Don Borges, saque su cuchillo porque . . . Vida, pasión y muerte del tercer Borges*, BA, Galerna, 1998, 271 pp. M. Couture, 'Empty words, vanity in the writings of Jorge Luis Borges', *RoN*, 39:265–311, is trifling. J. L. Suárez, 'Borges y el tercer hombre, o la necesidad del realismo', *ib.*, 303–13 is very cogent on Borges's vision(s) of poetry and reality. C. Bulacio and D. Grima, *Dos miradas sobre Borges*, BA–Tucuman, Tucuman U.P., Ediciones de Arte Guglianone, 1998, 173 pp., includes essays on well-worn themes: time, language, reality, the infinite, etc. R. Gutiérrez Girardot, *\*Jorge Luis Borges. El gusto de ser modesto*, Bogotá, Panamericana, 1998, 206 pp., contains seven earlier published essays. A. Hanke-Schaefer, *\*Jorge Luis Borges zur Einführung*, Hamburg, Junius, 190 pp., appears to be introductory for German readers. E. Volek, 'Borges total, paralelo y plural', *Chasqui*, 27.1, 1998:103–22, discusses his 'indeterminación ontológica'. C. A. Zito, *\*El Buenos Aires de Borges*, BA, Aguilar, 1998, appears to be descriptive and heavily illustrated. J. R. Navarro, 'El Buenos Aires de Borges', Rovira, *Ciudad*, 129–41, is rather thin. M. Charles, 'Le miroir d'encre en questions. Le travail créatif et son devenir à travers les fictions de Borges', in *Simbolisation et processus de création*, ed. B. Chauvier, Paris, Dunod, 1998, 216 pp. L. Block de Béjar, *\*Borges ou les gestes d'un voyant aveugle*, Paris, Champion, 1998, 224 pp., collects a group of earlier slightly excentric essays. E. de Olaso, *\*Jugar en serio. Aventuras de Borges*, Mexico D.F., Paidos, 160 pp. S. L. del Carril, *\*Borges en Sur*, BA, Emecé, 358 pp. K. B. Cowal Byrne, 'Inventing the New World. Finding the mythology of Jorge Luis Borges', *Hispanófila*, 126:67–83, declares him not to be postmodernist. J. Ortega, 'El Aleph y el lenguaje epifánico', *HR*, 67:453–67, is complex on referential and epiphanic language in this story. H. J. Brant, 'The queer use of communal women in Borges's "El muerto" and "La intrusa" ', *Hispanófila*, 125:37–50, is a queer-critical reading of both stories. J. C. Piñeyro, 'El rescate del traidor en "La forma de la espada" de Jorge Luis Borges', *SN*, 70, 1998:231–42, is on the 'redemption' of Moon. D. Laraway, 'Facciones: fictional identity and the face in Borges's "La Forma de la espada" ', *Symposium*, 53 : 151–63, is on the face as the site of identity. L. Sabrizi, 'Borges and Petrus Damiani — the question of time', *RHM*, 52 : 110–24, helpfully relates 'La otra muerte' to Peter Damian's ideas. P. Dove, 'Cultural margins in Borges's mimesis. Autobiography and catastrophe', *RCEH*, 23:41–60, is chiefly on 'El zahir'. M. Mínguez Arranz, 'Análisis semiótico de la representación del sujeto en *El Aleph* de J. L. Borges', *Thesaurus*, 49, 1994[1999]:245–74, deals with narratorial stance in four stories. E. Pennington, 'Death and denial in Borges's later prose', *Notes on Contemporary Literature*, 29.4 : 2–4, includes an interpretation of 'El disco'. M. Erdal Jordan, *La narrativa fantástica. Evolución del género y su relación con las concepciones del lenguaje*, M, Iberoamericana, 1998, 156 pp., has essays on Borges, Bioy, Macedonio Fernández, and Cortázar.

OTHER WRITERS. J. de Navascués. 'Una mapa de la destrucción: casas tomadas en la narrativa porteña', Rovira, *Ciudad*, 143–58, is a descriptive list of town mansions in sundry works. J. M. Camacho Delgado, 'Ulrico Schmidel y Mujica Láinez. Cronistas de la fundación de Buenos Aires', *RHM*, 52 : 125–34, is basically on Mujica's 'El hambre'. A. Iurilli, 'Lo legendario; a propósito de *El unicornio*', *StLI*, 32:73–79, is basically on irony in this novel by Mujica Láinez. P. N. Klingenber, *\*Fantasies of the Feminine: The Short Stories of Silvina Ocampo*, Cranbury, Bucknell U.P. E. Francomano, 'Escaping by a hair', *LF*, 25:65–77, examines Silvina Ocampo's short story 'Mi amada'. M. Goloboff, *\*Julio Cortázar: la biografía*, M, Seix Barral, 1998, 332 pp. D. Mesa Gancedo, *\*La aportación órfica: hacia el sentido de la poesía de Julio Cortázar*, Berne, Lang, 334 pp. J. D. Rohart, 'Notas sobre la moral de J. Cortázar en *Rayuela*', *LNL*, 309:39–45, is on involving the reader in a moral quest. G. González, 'Gender stereotypes in the treatment of the reader/receptor in Cortázar's "Las ménades" ', *RoN*, 39:337–44, is on his conflictive vision of the reader. U. K. Heise, *Chronoschisms: Time, Narrative and Postmodernism*, CUP, xii + 286 pp., includes a section on Cortázar. D. Sorensen, 'From diaspora to agora. Cortázar's reconfiguration of exile', *MLN*, 114:357–88, is rather general on his evolving outlook. P. McNab, 'Sexual silence and equine imagery in Valenzuela and Cortázar', *BHS(G)*, 76:263–79, is very cogent on Valenzuela's 'Cambio de armas' and 'De noche soy tu caballo' plus Cortázar's 'Cuello de gatito negro' and 'Verano'. J. Amícola, *\*Encuentro Internacional Manuel Puig*, La Plata, Orbis Tertius, 1998, 383 pp. G. Falery, *\*Personaje y lectura en cinco novelas de M. Puig*, Frankfurt, Vervuert, 1998, 286 pp. *Hispamérica*, 80–81, has a dossier on Puig with three articles on *El beso* . . . and a bibliographical item. A. Janquert 'Manuel Puig et la polyphonie: *Boquitas pintadas*

(1969)', *LNL*, 310:129–38, is superficial on its debt to the tango and the *novelón*. D. T. Frost, 'Transcription, invention and fraudulence. Simulated cinema in the epigraphs of *The Buenos Aires Affair*', *RHM*, 51, 1998:354–67, is on their contribution to the novel's artifice. E. E. Stern, 'Unravelling the web: power in Puig's *El beso de la mujer araña*', *MIFLIC Review*, 7:145–57, is on breaking free from stereotypes. G. Martí-Peña, '*Pubis angelical*: del texto a la imagen', *RCEH*, 23:61–84, analyses the text and the film version. J. Romero, 'Manuel Puig: del delito de la escritura al error gay', *RevIb*, 187:305–25, is biographical and documental. J. de Navascués, 'Marco Denevi: de la escritura a la representación', *CHA*, 586:113–17, is too general. C. Montes, 'Modalidad contrautópica y subjetividad lírica en *Una sombra ya pronto serás* de Osvaldo Soriano', *RCL*, 53, 1998:67–85, is clumsily written on its challenge to rationality. M. I. Zaldívar, 'El viaje triste, solitario y final del periodista argentino Osvaldo Soriano a la ciudad de Los Angels', *Hispamérica*, 83:17–31, is on modes of subversion in Soriano's 1973 novel. J. Fernández Vega, 'De la teología a la política: el problema del mal en la literatura policial de Rodolfo Walsh', *ib.*, 5–15, is on his need to go beyond the rational in this genre. C. Canaparo, *\*El artificio como cuestión. Conjeturas en torno a 'Respiración artificial' de Ricardo Piglia*, Rosario, Beatriz Viterbo, 1998, 87 pp. H. D. Fernández L'Hoeste, 'Between comic strips and literature. Fragmentation and identity in Ricardo Piglia's *La Argentina en pedazos*', *Secolas*, 30:52–59, is on his exploration of Argentine identity. S. Serrano and I. García, 'Entrevista con Abel Posse', *CHA*, 584:101–06, with useful declarations. J. L. Martínez interviews Juan José Saer in *CMar*, 148:53–55, with mordant remarks. E. Tomlinson, 'Rewriting fictions of power. The texts of Luisa Valenzuela and Marta Traba', *MLR*, 93, 1998:695–709, is chiefly on Valenzuela's *Como en la guerra*. S. Sauter, 'Liberación de y reencuentro con "lo otro" en *Cambio de armas*', *Chasqui*, 27.2, 1998:87–105, is Jungian on feminine self-liberation in the tales. L. A. Chesak, '*Film noir*, *Novela negra* and Luisa Valenzuela', *RoN*, 39:295–302, is on her re-writing of the 'thriller'. P. Swanson, 'Theory and the body: Luisa Valenzuela's *Novela negra con argentinos* as test case', *FMLS*, 35:95–106, is on its ludic approach to sexual difference. P. C. O'Connell, 'Historical memory, parody and the use of photography in Ana María Shua's *El libro de los recuerdos*', *WLT*, 73:77–87, is on their destabilization of historical order. B. S. Locklin, '"Qué triste es ser mujer." The Chinese microcosm of Reina Roffé's *Monte de Venus*', *REH*, 33:473–94, is on her critique of repression in Argentina. J. Corbatta, 'Lo que va de ayer a hoy', *Chasqui*, 28.2:78–88, is on her evolution towards banality. J. Weiss, 'Alicia Dujovne Ortiz', *Hispamérica*, 82:45–58, is an interview on her novels. P. L. O'Connell, 'Homecoming and identity in the autobiographical narrative of Tununa Mercado', *Chasqui*, 27.2, 1998:106–15. M. García Calderón, 'La escritura erótica y el poder en *Canon de alcoba* de Tununa Mercado', *RevIb*, 187:373–82, is (again) on the sexual content of this 1988 work. C. M. Tomkins, '*Pasos bajo el agua* y "Bosquejo de alturas" de Alicia Kozameh: tortura, resistencia y secuelas', *Chasqui*, 27.1, 1998:59–69, is on the effects of torture in these two testimonial works. \**Tradición, modernidad y posmodernidad. VI Congreso Internacional de Teatro Iberoamericano y Argentino*, ed. O. Pellettieri, BA, Galerna, 317 pp. See too his \**Inmigración italiana y teatro*, BA, Galerna, 148 pp., and his 'Peronismo y teatro', *CHA*, 588:91–99, chiefly on 'Teatro Independiente' and C. Gorostiza's *El puente*. \**Poéticas argentinas del siglo XX: literatura y teatro*, ed. J. Dubatti, BA, Belgrano 1998, appears to have several good essays on different dramatists. L. Borrás, *Reescribir la escena*, M, Fundación del Autor, 1998, 263 pp., includes a manifesto by Griselda Gambaro, and essays on three women playwrights: Leonor Manso, Lucía Laragione, and Cristina Escofit. M. Calderón Campos, \**Análisis lingüístico del género chico andaluz y rioplatense (1870–1920)*, Granada U.P., 1998, 545 pp. J. Tcherkaski, \**Habla Copi: homosexualidad y creación*, BA, Galerna, 1998, 160 pp. Jean Graham-Jones, '*Oficios útiles*: el teatro de Marcelo Ramos', *LATR*, 32.2:61–67, postulates his subversiveness. S. Pellarolo, *Sainete criollo. Democracia/representación. El caso de Nemesio Trejo*, BA, Corregidor, 1997, 237 pp., a wide-ranging contextualization and analysis of his playlets. G. Woodyard, 'Making America or making revolution: the theatre of Ricardo Halac in Argentina', pp. 177–98 of *Theatre Matters*, ed. R. Boon and J. Plastow, CUP, 1998. D. Altamiranda, 'Las armas y las letras: respuesta de los intelectuales a la guerra sucia', *Chasqui*, 27.1, 1998:23–32, is on essays by N. Jitrik, M. E. Walsh, and S. Kovadoff.

### BOLIVIA

E. Paz-Soldán, 'Nación (enferma) y narración: el discurso de degeneración en *Pueblo enfermo* de Alcides Arguedas', *RHM*, 52:60–76, is a slashing attack on this famous work.

### CHILE

X. Cortés Oñate, 'Volodia Teitelboim y la Generación del 39', *Atenea*, 478, 1998:207–14, is an interview on this literary group. L. Byre, 'The "Other" in the poetry of Gabriela Mistral', *SELA*, 41.1–2, 1997:46–58, is on her assumption of the stance of an outsider. E. Marchant, 'The professional outsider: Gabriela Mistral on motherhood and nation', *LALR*, 53:49–56, is on Mistral's *Lecturas para mujeres*

(1923). A. M. Cuneo, 'El mujerío en Gabriela Mistral: plenitud y diferencias', *RCL*, 53, 1998: 107–15, examines her view of femininity in her prose. S. Mulnich, ' "La fuga" de Gabriela Mistral', *Atenea*, 479: 203–19, is a *lecture expliquée* of the poem. K. Ellis, 'Vicente Huidobro y la Primera Guerra Mundial', *HR*, 67: 333–46, is a survey of his evolving attitude. C. J. Morales, 'Una versión ideal para el *Adán de Vicente Huidobro*', *StLI*, 32: 61–71, is a re-write of the poem! J. E. Albada, 'Mourning, melancholy and the millennium in Martin Juy, Julia Kristeva and Pablo Neruda', *Literature and Theology*, 13: 34–45, is on Neruda's 'Un perro ha muerto' and 'Celebración (del año 2000)'. F. Martínez Bonati, 'La poesía de Gonzalo Rojas y la agonía de la modernidad', *Atenea*, 479: 175–201, is rather too general on his outlook. C. Cisterna, '*Las cartas olvidadas del astronauta* de Javier Campos', *RCL*, 53, 1998: 87–105, interprets the sci-fi elements. C. de Zegher, *The Precarious. The Art and Poetry of Cecilia Vicuña*, Hanover, NH, Ediciones del Norte, 1998, 140 pp., includes an interview and four essays. T. R. Strojkov, 'Au delà du Temps des fièvres: Jorge Teiller', *Iris*, 99: 187–205, is general, based on his essay 'Sobre el mundo donde veradaderamente habito'. C. Duncan, 'Reading power: some observations on the construction of meaning and authority in María Luisa Bombal's *La última niebla*', *RHM*, 51, 1998: 304–15, offers a new reading. A. Ostrov, 'Espacio y sexualidad en *El lugar sin límites* de José Donoso', *RevIb*, 187: 341–48, is on sexuality and social hierarchy. Z. N. Martínez, '*Casa de Campo* de José Donoso', *Hispamérica*, 80–81, 1998: 5–16, is on demythifying fictionality. M. L. Friedman, 'The genesis of *La desesperada* by José Donoso', *STCL*, 23: 255–74, illuminatingly studies Donoso's notes for the novel. L. Pearson, 'Review essay: Donoso', *Chasqui*, 27.1, 1998: 123–42, usefully discusses his last works and recent criticism. *\*Nueva narrativa chilena. Actas del seminario*, ed. C. Alvarez, Santiago, LOM, 1997, 179 pp. K. Bergenthal, *\*Studien zum Mini-Boom der Nueva narrativa chilena. Literatur im Neo-Liberalismus*, Frankfurt, Vervuert, 301 pp. *\*Conversations with Isabel Allende*, ed. J. Rodden, Austin, Texas U.P., 466 pp. S. Henighan, 'The metaphor war and the proverb artillery. Language and power in Skármeta's *Ardiente paciencia*', *RoN*, 39: 177–83, analyses the linguistic presentation of the *pinochetazo*. C. Schwalb, ' "Fagocitos" posmodernos: el poder asimilador de las imágenes en la novela *Match Ball* de Antonio Skármeta', *RCL*, 53, 1998: 107–15, is on some of its tropes. L. Scholz interviews Skármeta in *Hispamérica*, 83: 61–66, with interesting remarks. G. García Corrales, 'Nostalgia y melancolía en la novela detectivesca del Chile de los noventa', *RevIb*, 186: 81–87, sees some of them as unhappy allegories. J. A. Epple, 'De piel a piel: el erotismo como escritura en la nueva narrativa femenina de Chile', *ib.*, 383–94, is on sexuality as rebellion and self-liberation. R. Cánovas, *Novela chilena, nuevas generaciones: el abordaje de los huérfanos*, Santiago de Chile, Univ. Católica, 1997, 207 pp., is on post-*golpe* writers in the 80s. I. Avelar, 'An anatomy of marginality: figures of the eternal return and the Apocalypse in Chilean post-dictatorial fiction', *STCL*, 23:211–37, elucidates much about Eltit's very difficult *Lumpérica* and *Los vigilantes*. C. M. Tompkins, 'Aporia: la vaca sagrada de Diamela Eltit', *ETL*, 27.1:50–61, is Derridean on the technique of *Vaca sagrada*. M. B. Tierney-Tello, 'Testimony, ethics and the aesthetic in Diamela Eltit', *PMLA*, 114:78–96, is on *El padre mío* and *El infarto del alma*. G. García Corrales, 'Entrevista con Diamela Eltit', *Chasqui*, 27.2, 1998:85–88, is on *El infarto del alma* and *Los vigilantes*. L. Cecilia Ojeda, '*Extraño estío de María Carolina Geel: hacia una reconfiguración de la Generación Chilena del 58*', *Hispanófila*, 126:53–65, is on her feminism. D. Eltit, 'Mujer, frontera y delito', *REH*, 33:227–35, examines critically M. C. Geel's *Cárcel de mujeres* (1956). L. Cecilia Ojeda, 'Entre simulacros y enmascaramientos: "Cuando Santiago está a oscuras" y "Cartas de inocencia" de Pía Barros', *RCEH*, 23:101–17, is on the subversiveness of these two 1994 stories. L. Guerra, '*Maldita yo entre las mujeres* de Mercedes Valdivieso', *RCL*, 53, 1998:47–65, is on her view of feminine identity. C. Rubio, 'Lo cómico-serio en "Maldito gato" de Juan Emar', *ib.*, 37–45, is on its parody of realism. R. M. Galindo, 'Modernidad y liberación femenina en *Antigua vida mía* de Marcela Serrano', *Chasqui*, 28.1:32–41, criticizes her middle-class outlook in this 1955 novel. A. Mateo del Pino, 'Chile, una loca geografía o las crónicas de Pedro Lemebel', *Hispamérica*, 80–81, 1998:17–28, is on his testimonial articles. J. A. Piña, *Veinte años de teatro chileno, 1976–96*, Santiago de Chile, Red Internacional del Libro, 1998, 261 pp., collects 66 reviews of plays. A. Vergara-Mery, 'El miedo en *Los invasores* de Egon Wolff', *Hispanófila*, 127:69–79, is too obvious. O. Lepeley, \*'Teatro y dictadura', *CRR*, 17, 1998:58–64. O. Lepeley, \*'El teatro chileno desafía a la dictadura', *RLA*, 9, 1998:567–72. *Gestos*, 26, 1998, has articles on and by M. A. de la Parra and on Juan Radigán among others. M. Moody, 'Marco Antonio de la Parra', *Hispamérica*, 82:59–70, is an interview on his plays and novels. E. Luengo, 'Poder, resistencia y reacción en "Hechos consumados" de Juan Radigán', *LATR*, 32.2:69–86, is on imagination versus the social power structure.

## COLOMBIA

I. Ulchur Collazos, *García Márquez, del humor y otros dominios*, Quito, Eskeletra, 1997, 255 pp., is a wide-ranging discussion of his humour. C. Bodtorf, \**A Synergy of Styles. Art and Artifact in Gabriel García Márquez*,

Lanham, Maryland, U.P. of America, iii + 147 pp. R. Ianes, 'Para leerte mejor: García Márquez y el regreso a la huérfana colonial', *RoN*, 39:345–56, is on his parody of the sentimental romance in *Del amor y otros demonios*. E. W. Hood, ' "La santa" de Gabriel García Márquez, del periódico al cine al cuento', *QIA*, 80, 1996[1999]:97–104, clarifies the origins of this story from *Doce cuentos peregrinos*. E. Houvenaghel, 'La doble retórica de lo verosímil en *Doce cuentos peregrinos*', *Neophilologus*, 83:59–71, is on their ambiguity. A. López-Mejía, 'Women who bleed to death: Gabriel García Márquez's "Sense of an ending" ', *RHM*, 82:135–50, is on Amaranta Ursula from *Cien años de soledad* and 'El rastro de tu sangre en la nieve' from *Doce Cuentos*. B. Weaver, 'Gabriel García Márquez attends the Courtly Love convention', *Notes on Contemporary Literature*, 29.4:10–12, associates courtly love with 'La bella durmiente' of *Doce cuentos*. L. Guerra-Cunningham, 'De Babel al Apocalipsis', *LF*, 25:9–26, is descriptive on the fiction of Albalucía Angel. M. Krakusin, 'Del romance a la realidad: erotismo irónico en *Señora de la miel* de F. Buitrago', *Thesaurus*, 49, 1994[1999]:273–84, is on Teodora's self-discovery. C. Bustillo, 'Álvaro Mutis. Parodia y antiparodia en *La mansión de Araucaíma*', *ib.*, 142–63, analyses this parody of the gothic novel. L. Correa Díaz, 'El grito colombino de "Tierra" en el relato de Pedro Gómez Valderrama', *ib.*, 92–109, is on its interpretation of the Discovery. L. E. Prescott, *\*Without Hatreds or Fears. Jorge Artel and the Struggle for Black Literary Expression in Colombia*, Gainesville, Florida U.P., 368 pp.

COSTA RICA

F. Herrera, *\*García Monge. Plenitud del escribir*, San José de Costa Rica, Univ. Estatal a Distancia. A. González, 'Fabián Dobles: memories of a Costa Rican novelist', *WLT*, 73:485–88, is on his *Los años, pequenos días* (1988). P. Ramsay, 'Quince Duncan's literary representation of the ethno-racial dynamics between *latinos* and Afro-Costa Ricans of West Indian descent', *AfHR*, 17.2, 1998:52–60, is entirely thematic. T. Wayne Edison, 'An interview with Afro-Costa Rican writer Quince Duncan', *ib.*, 18.1:29–33, is mainly on his current writing.

CUBA

I. Llorens, *\*Nacionalismo y literatura: constitución e institucionalización de la 'república de las letras cubanas'*, Lérida U.P. 1998, 283 pp. P. M. Smorkaloff, *\*Cuban Writers on and off the Island*, NY, Twayne, xxiii + 100 pp. V. Fowler Caleada, 'Literatura y homosexualidad ¿en Cuba? ¿hoy?', *QIA*, 80, 1996[1999]:61–70, is a gripping survey.

M. Elías, 'Nicolás Guillén and the "economy of the game"', *SELA*, 41.1–2, 1997: 26–37, is on transculturation in his poetry. S. J. Clark, 'Poesía, política y autobiografía. *La mala memoria* de Heberto Padilla', *Hispanófila*, 126: 85–99, is on his self-image. N. Araújo, 'Voz y voces de *Aquellos tiempos* . . . Memorias de Lola María [de Ximeno]', *RCEH*, 23: 23–40, is too simply factual on the memoires (1930) of this poetess. G. Price, 'Cosas, nombres y la dimensión espiritual en la poesía de Eliseo Diego', *RevIb*, 186: 89–102, contrasts his work with committed poetry. E. M. Martínez, 'Erotismo en la poesía de Magaly Alabau', *ib.*, 187: 395–404, is on its evolution. *AfHR*, 17.1, 1998, is a *homenaje* to the black Cuban poet Marcelino Arozarena. H. Habra, 'El negrero como personaje romántico en *Pedro Blanco, el negrero* de Lino Novás Calvo', *ib.*, 18.1: 46–52, is merely descriptive. A. M. Teja, '*Paradiso* y la cuestión del destino: tragedia, comedia, epifanía', *RHM*, 52: 151–70, is on the positive ending of J. Lezama Lima's novel. A. Beaupied, *Narciso hermético. Sor Juana Inés de la Cruz y José Lezama Lima*, Liverpool U.P., 1997, 241 pp., has much on Lezama's *Muerte de Narciso*. J. Miller Powell, 'The conflict of becoming: cultural hybridity and the representation of focalization in Caribbean literature', *LitP*, 45: 63–91, is basically on being Caribbean in Carpentier's *El reino de este mundo*. S. Arias, 'Tierra en espera, caribe prometido; la modernidad y la cuestión del espacio en *El siglo de las luces*', *SELA*, 42.2–3: 1–9, has nothing new. P. Tovar, 'Al compás de La Habana en la obras de Alejo Carpentier', Rovira, *Ciudad*, 229–58, is a descriptive survey of references to the city. W. Cancio Isla, 'Un asunto de decadencia', *RevIb*, 187: 349–57, reprints a brief article by Carpentier on transvestism. S. J. Clark, *Autobiografía y revolución en Cuba*, Barquisimeto (Venezuela), Río Cenizo, 145 pp., includes essays on G., Cabrera Infante, H. Padilla, C. Franqui, and R. Arenas. F. Soto, *\*Reinaldo Arenas*, NY, Twayne, 1998, xx + 185 pp. A Cacheiro, *Reinaldo Arenas, una apreciación política*, Boston, International Scholars Publications, 167 pp. C. Alzate, *\*Destrucción y verdad. La reescritura en Arenas y la Avellaneda*, Boulder, SSSAS, ix + 269 pp. S. Rosell, 'Cecilia Valdés de Villaverde a Arenas: la (re)creación del mito de la mulata', *AfHR*, 18.2: 15–21, is on Arenas's deconstruction and parody of the earlier novel. H. Pato, 'The power of abjection. Reinaldo Arenas in his *Palacio*', *RCEH*, 23: 144–53, is Kristevan on horror in *El palacio de las blancas mofetas*. L. D. Bertot, 'Autenticidad y opresión. La transformación madre-estado en el discurso subversivo de Reinaldo Arenas', *SELA*, 41.1–2, 1997: 9–17. H. J. López Cruz, 'Subversión en el discurso histórico de *El color del verano* de Reinaldo Arenas', *ib.*, 1–8, is on his parody of Cuban history. B. Schulz Cruz, '*Antes que anochezca*', *ib.*, 18–25, is on autobiography as exorcism. D. Nouhaud, 'De bruit et de fureur: "El Central (Leprosario)" de

Reinaldo Arenas', *LNL*, 310:155–82, is a rather obvious commentary on this poem of 1990. *Cubana. Contemporary Fiction by Cuban Women*, Boston, Beacon, 1998, xix + 213 pp., has a scholarly introduction and 2 articles on this topic. J. Weiss interviews Nivaria Tejera in *Quimera*, 183:8–13, on her exile fiction. V. Smith, 'La construcción de la héroe socialista: *Tonia, la guerrillera inolvidable*', *LF*, 25:27–37, introduces this testimonial text. C. Ortiz Ceberio, 'La narrativa de Zoe Valdés: hacia una reconfiguración de la na(rra)ción cubana', *Chasqui*, 22.2:116–27, is on the critical attitude to Cuba of this 'new' exile novelist. *De las dos orillas: teatro cubano*, ed. H. Adler and A. Herr, M, Iberoamericana, 223 pp., has a dozen essays on Cuban theatre of today both in and out of Cuba. F. Morín, *Por el amor al arte, memorias de un teatrista cubano 1940–1970*, Miami, Universal, 1998, 378 pp., has many useful insights. *Ollantay Theatre Magazine*, 6.10, 1998, has articles on J. Díaz, J. Triana, and F. Arriví. S. Millares, *'La subversión del logos en el teatro de Virgilio Piñera', *Teatro* (Alcalá), 11, 1997:235–45. W. Detjens-Montero, 'La negación de la ética cubana: *El no* de Virgilio Piñera', *LATR*, 32.2:105–15, is on the presentation of pre-revolutionary Cuban society. J. J. Barquet, 'Subversión desde el discurso no-verbal y verbal de *Los siete contra Tebas* de Antón Arrufat', *ib.*, 19–33, chiefly examines the play's non-verbal elements. N. Christoph, 'El teatro me ha dejado a mí: una entrevista con Antón Arrufat', *ib.*, 143–49, is on his abandonment of playwriting. *Ollantay Theatre Magazine*, 5.2, 1997, has an interview with Matías Montes Huidobro and an article on his *Oscuro total. Conjunto*, 109, 1998, is dedicated to contemporary Cuban theatre.

## DOMINICAN REPUBLIC

F. V. Holguín, *'En el tiempo de las mariposas* de Julia Alvarez: una reinterpretación de la historia', *Chasqui*, 27.1, 1998:92–102, is on a woman's view of the Trujillo regime.

## ECUADOR

S. Pacifici, 'La contrapartida del deseo', *LF*, 25:95–106, introduces this poetry collection by Luz Argentina Chiriboga. G. Geisdorfer Feal, 'The legacy of Ba-Lunda: black female subjectivity in Luz Argentina Chiriboga's *Jonatás y Manuela*', *AfHR*, 17.2, 1998:24–29, is on its picture of slavery. M. Handelsman, 'Las contradicciones ineludibles del no-racismo ecuatoriano: a propósito de *Junguyo* como artefacto de la diáspora afroamericano', *Chasqui*, 27.1, 1998:79–91, discusses the presentation of blacks in this 1943 novel by A. Ortiz.

EL SALVADOR

*Antipodas* 10, 1998, has 5 articles and an interview with Manlio Argueta.

GUATEMALA

R. K. Sitler, 'Miguel Angel Asturias "Gran Lengua" of the Mayas', *SELA*, 41.2–3, 1997: 1–8, examines critically his supposed Mayan identity. S. Henighan, 'El indígena y el alma nacional en *El problema social* de Asturias', *Hispamérica*, 80–81, 1998: 207–15, is on the early influence of Positivism. W. H. Corral, 'Carta de Estados Unidos. El negocio de Rigoberta Menchú', *CHA*, 587: 129–34, is on new developments à propos of her veracity.

HAITI

Y. Pérez Torres, 'Regresando a la Guinea. Historia, religión y mito en las novelas caribeñas de Mayra Montero', *RevIb*, 186: 103–16, is on her ambivalent vision of Haiti.

MEXICO

A. Stanton, *\*Inventores de tradición. Ensayos sobre poesía mexicana moderna*, Mexico D.F., FCE, 1998, 238 pp. M. Beneyto, 'Dossier: nueve poetas mexicanos', *Quimera*, 178: 24–45, is a quick panorama of the newest poetry. A. Chouciño, 'Poesía mexicana 1990–96', *RevIb*, 186: 135–48, is a highly positive survey. *CA*, 70.4, 1998: 11–70, has five commemorative essays on Paz. A. Pasten, *\*Octavio Paz. Crítico practicante en busca de una poética*, M, Pliegos, 232 pp. M. Ulacia, *\*El árbol milenario. un recorrido por la obra de Octavio Paz*, B, Galaxia Gutenberg, 410 pp. G. Wawerla, *\*Die Lyrik von Octavio Paz*, Frankfort, Lang, 192 pp. R. Medina, *\*Autor, autoridad y autorización: escritura y poeetica de Octavio Paz*, Mexico D.F., Colegio de Mexico, 252 pp. A. Picard, 'L'Espagne, intime fratrie d'Octavio Paz', *LNL*, 310: 139–53, is superficial on his relationship with Peninsular culture. C. Tomlinson, 'Conversación en Cambridge', *CHA*, 585: 105–24, has a fascinating interview with Paz. H. J. Verani, *\*Bibliografía crítica de Octavio Paz (1931–1996)*, Mexico D.F., El Colegio Nacional, 1997, 674 pp. M. Paúl, 'La novela de la revolución mexicana y la revolución en la novela', *RevIb*, 186: 49–57, is general and commonplace. B. Salvo Aguilera, 'La sombra de Martín Luis Guzmán', *CA*, 73: 213–25, is informative on the historical and biographical background to *La sombra del caudillo*. D. Laraway, 'Doctoring the revolution: medical discourse and interpretation in *Los de abajo* and *El águila y la serpiente*', *Hispanófila*, 127:53–65, sees the authors as 'diagnosing' the Revolution. \**Nocturno en que todo se oye*. *José Revueltas ante la crítica*, Mexico, Era, 330 pp. J. Durán, 'Apuntes sobre el grotesco en tres novelas de José Revueltas', *Chasqui*, 28.2:89–102, is on its evolution. F. Manzo-Robledo, 'El discurso homofóbico: el caso de *Los muros de agua* de José Revueltas', *ib.*, 27.2, 1998:27–37. M. L. Gili Iriarte, \**Testamento de Hecuba*. *Mujeres e indígenas en la obra de Rosario Castellanos*, Seville U.P., 336 pp. D. J. Mennel, 'El secreto de Romelia', *LF*, 25:49–63, examines the film version of Castellanos's *El viudo Román*. S. Seiber, 'The deconstruction of gender as archetype in Rosario Castellanos's *El eterno femenino*', *LF*, 25:39–48, is on negotiating the feminine. R. Irwin, 'La homosexualidad cósmica mexicana. Espejos de diferencia en Xavier Villaurrutia', *RevIb*, 187:293–304, is on inter-racial homosexuality in *La mulata de Córdoba*. L. Martínez Carrizales, \**Juan Rulfo, los caminos de la fama*. *Juan Rulfo ante la crítica literario-periodística de Mexico*, Mexico D.F., FCE, 1998, 163 pp. M. González Casillas, \**La sociedad en la obra de Juan Rulfo*, Guadalajara, Secretaría de Cultura, 1998, 166 pp. S. López Mena, \**Revisión crítica de la obra de Juan Rulfo*, Mexico D.F., Baxis, 1998, 172 pp. D. Bozt, 'Against the wall. Religious crosscurrents in Juan Rulfo', *Secolas*, 30:5–12, examines (ir)religious motifs in *El llano en llamas*. A. Hamman, 'A subject of desire: sexuality, creation and the (maternal) individual in Juan Rulfo's *Pedro Páramo*', *REH*, 33:441–71, foregrounds Susana. A. M. Hernández de López, 'Pedro Páramo y Artemio Cruz: dos personajes de la Revolución Mexicana', *CA*, 77:222–31, is painfully obvious on their reactionary roles. A. B. Caravaca, \**Juan José Arreola*, Valencia, Tirant Lo Blanc, 1998. M. Beneyto, 'Pasea por Granada: reflexiones de Juan José Arreola', *Quimera*, 174, 1998:6–12, has an interview with useful remarks. D. Nonhand, 'Mujer divina o la región más trasparente del texto', *LNL*, 307, 1998:5–29, is on the novel's levels of discourse. T. P. Waldemar, 'Lost and found in translation. Carlos Fuentes's "Las dos orillas"', *RoN*, 39:145–51, is on its interpretation of Mexican hybridism. L. Egan, 'Sor Juana and Carlos Fuentes, between times and lines', *RCEH*, 23:221–38, combs Fuentes for references to Sor Juana. I. M. López, 'El intelectual mexicano frente a las crisis sociales en dos novelas de los noventas', *Hispanófila*, 127:81–89, examines Fuentes's *Diana o la cazadora solitaria* and M. L. Puga's *La reina*. B. Vickers, 'Entrevista con Carlos Fuentes', *Quimera*, 175, 1998:18–21, is mainly on his latest novel *Los años con Laura Díaz*. E. Pfeiffer, 'El dilema entre el poder y la palabra: el encuentro con el otro en dos piezas teatrales de Carlos Fuentes', *Hispamérica*, 80–81, 1998:199–205, is under-researched. F. Solares-Larrave, 'De la ciencia y el relato, rasgos de la postmodernidad en *Noticias del Imperio*

360 *Latin American Studies*

de Fernando del Paso', *RevIb*, 186:13–30, is chiefly on orality. A. L. Calvillo, *\*José Agustín. Una biografía de perfil*, Mexico D.F., Sansores. 1998, 224 pp. R. J. Friis, 'A comala of the mind. José Emilio Pacheco's early theory of influence', *MIFLIC Review*, 7, 1997–98:127–36, examines his 'dialogue with the dead'. S. Yurkievich, 'El arte risueño de Augusto Monterroso', *Quimera*, 180:13–15, is just journalistic. F. Valerio-Holguín, 'Augusto Monterroso en la era de la poscrítica', *ETL*, 26.2, 1997–98[1999]:1–10, is on fictional criticism in *Lo demás es silencio*. See too his 'La perversión del texto en *Obras completas (y otros cuentos)* de Augusto Monterroso', *RoN*, 40:41–48, on subversion of narrative codes. G. E. González Centeno, 'Augusto Monterroso: el animal y la recreación paródica de una tradición literaria', *Chasqui*, 28.1:16–31, is on his animal fables. M. Westmorland, 'Postmodern depthlessness and finding pleasure in [Luis] Zapata's *Melodrama* [1983]', *MLS*, 28.2, 1998:103–16, examines shifting codes in this camp novel. B. Ruiz, 'Prostitución y homosexualidad. Interpelaciones desde el margen en *El vampiro de la colonia* de Luis Zapata', *RevIb*, 187:327–39, is on gay self-presentation. I. M. López, '*Las posibilidades del odio*: el doble perfil de un texto narrativo', *CH*, 20, 1998:68–76, is on the ambiguity of M. L. Puga's 1978 novel. L. H. Dowling, 'The erotic dimension of Elena Garro's "La culpa es de los Tlaxcaltecas"', *Chasqui*, 28.2:31–59, is on female sexuality and gender roles in this famous short story. I. M. López, 'Crónica de un desengaño: el México moderno en *Paseo de la Reforma* de Elena Poniatowska', *ib.*, 28.1:80–90, is on its historical revisionism. W. Pino-Ojeda, 'Literatura de mujeres, mercado y canon: una conversación con Elena Poniatowska', *RCL*, 53, 1998:145–56, has interesting remarks. *\*Acercamientos a Carmen Boullosa*, ed. B. Droscher and C. Rincón, Berlin, Tranvía, 276 pp. R. Roffé interviews Angeles Mastretta in *CHA*, 593:77–90, with revealing comments. R. García Bonilla interviews Rosa Beltrán and Bárbara Jacobs in *Hispamérica*, 80–81, 1998:147–58, and *ib.*, 159–69, with interesting remarks. K. Sugg, 'Paternal and patria-archal identifications: the fatherlands of Silvia Molina', *Chasqui*, 28.2:14–30, is on the role of Dorotea in *La familia vino del norte* (1987). A. Parada, 'Subjetividad femenina y alienación en "Me olvido de olvidarte" de María Luisa Mendoza', *ib.*, 3–13, examines female oppression in this 1985 short story. S. C. Fernández, *\*Gustavo Sainz. Postmodernism in the Mexican Novel*, NY, Lang, x + 151 pp. K. S. Salkjelsvik, 'El desvío como norma: la retórica de la receta en *Como agua para chocolate*', *RevIb*, 186:171–82, attributes subversiveness to the recipes. L. L. Romo, '*La ley del amor* de Laura Esquivel', *Secolas*, 30:44–51, is on reader reception of this 1995 novel. A. Charlon, 'Les investigations tous azimuts de Paco Ignacio Taibo II dans *Sombra de la sombra* et *La vida misma*', *LNL*, 307, 1998:31–43, is on his ambiguous vision of fiction and reality. M. Paúl and M. L. de la Garza, 'Alberto Ruy Sánchez, calígrafo del erotismo', *RevIb*, 187:359–71, introduces this new novelist via the sex-content of his work. A. Partida, *\*Dramaturgos mexicanos 1970–1990. Biobibliografía crítica*, Mexico D.F., Bellas Artes, 1998, 249 pp. E. Mijares, *\*La realidad virtual del teatro mexicano*, Mexico D.F., Ediciones de la Casa Juan Pablo, 150 pp. *\*Brecht en México a los cien años de su nacimiento*, ed. R. Johnson, Mexico D.F., UNAM, 1998, 155 pp. M. Del Río Reyes, 'Presencia de Alexandro Jodorowsky en el teatro mexicano de los sesenta', *LATR*, 33.1:55–72, is on his renovatory influence. F. Beverido, 'Espacio y tiempo: creatividad actoral en *La bufadora* de Hugo Salcedo', *ib.*, 32.2:35–52, analyses this 1992 play and its staging. *\*Theatre Forum*, 14, has an article by K. F. Nigro on 'The theatre of Sabina Berman'. N. Martínez de Olcoz, *\*Águila o sol* de Sabina Berman', *Teatro* (Alcalá), 11, 1997:219–34. S. A. Day, 'Berman's Pancho Villa versus neoliberal desire', *LATR*, 33.1:5–23, shows how she comments on current Mexican political ideologies. F. Dauster, *\*'Victor Hugo Rascón Banda y el nuevo realismo', *RLMexC*, 3, 1998:88–93. A. Gladheart, 'Monitoring Sor Juana: satire, technology and appropriation in Jemma Rodríguez's *Sor Juana en Almoloya'*, *RHM*, 52:213–26, is on the play's picture of modern Mexico. J. Bisset, 'La revolución y el papel de la mujer en el teatro de Consuelo de Castro y Pilar Campesino', *LATR*, 33.1:45–53, contains a feminist approach to Campesino's *Super Ocho* (1979). S. Wimmer, 'Existenzphilosophie und Essayistik in Mexico', *Iberoromania*, 48, 1998:97–123, is basically on the influence of Heidegger.

## NICARAGUA

M. A. Pastor Alonso, *La posía cósmica de Ernesto Cardenal*, Huelva, Diputación Provincial, 1998, 260 pp. R. K. Curry, 'Revolución y tradición en la poesía de Ernest Cardenal', *ETL*, 26.2, 1997–98:11–19, contains nothing new. J. M. Montero, 'The *Psalms* of Ernesto Cardenal', *SELA*, 42.4:1–7, is on their liberation theology. A. González, 'Historical (re)visions of the Conquest: Rosario Aguilar's *La niña blanca y los pájaros sin piés'*, *ib.*, 42.2–3:29–34, examines the quest for female identity in this 1992 historical novel.

## PANAMA

H. López Cruz, 'Transparencia social en la novelística de Rosa M. Britton', *MIFLIC Review*, 7, 1997–98:137–44, is on her social criticism.

PARAGUAY

A. Ostrov, 'En el nombre del Padre (lectura de *Hijo de hombre* de Augusto Roa Bastos)', *Hispamérica*, 83:125–31, is under-researched on the suppression of Guaraní culture. E. Geisler, 'Lenguaje, verdad, historia. La novela de Augusto Roa Bastos *Yo el Supremo* como réplica a Rousseau', *Iberoromania*, 48, 1998:77–96, examines Roa's ideas. R. Lefere, 'Sentidos y alcance de *Vigilia del Almirante* de Augusto Roa Bastos', *BHS(G)*, 76:535–55, examines its mythification process.

PERU

N. Villanova, \*Social Change and Literature in Peru, Lewiston, Mellen, 244 pp. B. Angvik, *La ausencia de la formada forma a la crítica que forma el canon literario peruano*, Lima, Univ. Católica, 432 pp., has essays on Vallejo, Vargas Llosa, José Diez Canseco, and others. L. Rojas-Trempe, \*Alumbramiento verbal en los 90. Escritoras peruanas: signos y pláticas, Lima, Arteida, 362 pp. \*A imagen y semejanza. Reflexiones de escritoras peruanas, ed. M. Robles, Lima, Tierra Firme, 1998, 152 pp. S. M. Hart, 'Vallejo's "Other": versions of otherness in the work of César Vallejo', *MLR*, 93, 1998:710–23, is on his ambiguous self-projection. W. Orrillo, \*César Vallejo. Periodista paradigmático, Lima San Marcos, 1998, 134 pp. C. López Degregori, \*Generación poética peruana del 60. Estudio y muestra, Lima U.P., 1998, 299 pp. H. Araújo, 'Entrevista a Américo Ferrari', *Quimera*, 181:6–10, has interesting declarations. *AfHR*, 18.1:25–28, has a useful compilation: 'Nicomedes Santa Cruz: cronología y bibliografía reciente'. M. A. Zapata, \*Metáfora de la experiencia. La poesía de Antonio Cisneros, Lima, Univ. Pontificia, 1998, 445 pp. G. Minardi interviews Carmen Ollé briefly in *Hispamérica*, 83:55–59, with useful declarations. W. Rowe, 'De los indigenismos en el Peru: examen de argumentos', *RevIb*, 186:191–97, attacks Vargas Llosa on Arguedas. C. A. Sandoval and S. M. Boschetto-Sandoval, \*José María Arguedas: Reconsiderations for Latin American Cultural Studies, Athens (Ohio), Center for International Studies, 1998, xlii + 312 pp. M. A. Arenas and M. I. Arenas, 'Identidad y presencia social del indio en dos novelas de Arguedas: *Yawar fiesta* y *Los ríos profundos*', *Thesaurus*, 49, 1994[1999]:519–26, is inadequately researched on his evolution. K. C. Dworkin y Méndez, 'Beyond Indigenism and Marxism', *SELA*, 42.1, 1998:1–12, is on the 'two voices' in *Los ríos profundos*. H. Morote, \*Vargas Llosa, tal cual, Lima, Campodónico, 1998, xxxiii + 272 pp. B. Angvik, \*A Novelist who Feeds on Social Carrion: Mario Vargas Llosa, San José, Porvenir, 1997, xi + 180 pp. V. Lavenia, 'Mario Vargas Llosa. Funzione della letteratura e ruolo sociale dello scrittore', *StLI*, 32:99–107, is too introductory. M. Esquerro, 'L'écriture ou la castration', *Los cachorros'*, *Imprévue*, 1–2, 1998:211–22, is inadequately researched. J. A. Portugal, 'Gótico, satírico, grotesco, Andes, revolución, utopia en la obra de Vargas Llosa', *Secolas*, 30:60–69, is enlightening on his inversion of the idealized vision of the Andes. R. Truth Goodman, 'Mario Vargas Llosa and the rape of Sebastiana', *LALR*, 53:81–107, is broadly on the symbolism of this episode in *La guerra del fin del mundo*. D. E. Marting, 'Concealing Peru in Mario Vargas Llosa's *Elogio de la madrastra*', *Chasqui*, 27.2, 1998:38–53, is turgid on the allegedly 'hidden Peru' in the novel. L. Valencia Assogna, 'El inasible', *Quimera*, 181:11–14, is a necrological tribute to Julio Ramón Ribeyro. E. M. Valero, 'La ciudad invisible en los cuentos de Julio Ramón Ribeyro', Rovira, *Ciudad*, 259–82, is on his hostile vision of Lima. E. Snaawaert, \**Crónica de una escritura inocente. La focalización implícita como base interpretativa de las novelas de Alfredo Bryce Echenique*, Louvain U.P. 1998, vii + 160 pp. M. Krakusin, 'El retorno del protagonista: mito y escritura en la novelística de Alfredo Bryce Echenique', *Hispanófila*, 125:75–85, is on the role of the Oedipus complex. J. L. de la Fuente, 'A través del espejo: la parodia en Alfredo Bryce Echenique', *HR*, 67:37–50, sees his works as 'inversiones irónicas de la narrativa sentimental'. I. Gallego, 'Alfredo Bryce Echenique en el fin de siglo', *RevIb*, 184–85, 1998:611–26, is on his vision of the past of Peru. See too Id., 'El otro lado de la comicidad', *StLI*, 32:109–29, on Bryce's *Permiso para vivir* (1993). M. B. Tierney-Tello, 'Through a child's eyes: narrative and social critique in Laura Riesco's *Ximena de dos caminos*', *REH*, 33:237–64, is on the narrator's growing awareness of injustice. C. Tisnado, '*Ximena de dos caminos*, self-representation and the power of language', *HR*, 67:535–47, is content-based, on autobiography without an 'I'. B. L. Lewis, 'Narratorial necessities: Aguirre's redemption in *Crónica de blasfemos* by Félix Alvarez Saenz', *RoN*, 40:103–09, is on the narratorial stance. P. D'Allemand, 'Las contribuciones de Mariátegui a la crítica latinoamericana', *Thesaurus*, 49, 1994[1999]:449–90, is too general. W. W. Stein, *Dance in the Cemetery: José Carlos Mariátegui and the Lima Scandal of 1997*, Maryland, U.P. of America, 1997, 271 pp., is on his early formation.

### PUERTO RICO

A. Díaz Quiñones, 'Orfeo en Guayama', *Quimera*, 176:6–10, is on the late poetry of Luis Palés Matos. C. M. Rivera Villegas, 'Sobreviviendo en la metrópoli. El multiculturalismo en la prosa de Julia de Burgos', *Bilingual Review*, 23, 1998:214–21, is on her view of national identity. C. A. Salgado, 'Archivos encontrados: Edgardo Rodríguez Juliá o los diablejos de la historiografía criolla', *CA*, 73:153–203, is on his historical trilogy. J. D. Perivolaris, 'Heroes, survivors and history: Edgardo Rodríguez Juliá and Puerto Rico's 1898', *MLR*, 94:691–99, is on his *El cruce de la Bahía de Guánica* (1984). G. B. Irizarry, 'El 98 en *La llegada* (1980) de José Luis González: las trampas de la historia', *RevIb*, 184–85, 1998:397–411, is on its ideology. C. A. Salgado, 'El entierro de González. Contrafiguraciones del 98 en la narrativa ochentista puertorriqueña', *ib.*, 397–411, examines reactions to González's ideas by other writers.

URUGUAY

García Pinto, 'El retrato de una artista joven. La musa de Delmira Agustini', *RevIb*, 184–85, 1998:559–71, is too discursive. J. L. Castillo, 'Delmira Agustini o el modernismo subversivo', *Chasqui*, 27.2, 1998:70–84, is not very new on her conquest of a feminine poetic space. D. Noemi, 'Entrevista a Cristina Cabral', *AfHR*, 18.2:50–55, has interesting remarks on black writing. \**Actas de las jornadas de homenaje a Horacio Quiroga*, ed. S. Lago and A. Torres, Montevideo, Univ. de la República, 1998, 221 pp. J. C. Mondragón, \**El misterioso Horacio Quiroga*, Montevideo, Cal y Canto, 1998, 308 pp. *Rio de la Plata*, 19, 1998, is a homage to Felisberto Hernández, with 30 essays of varying quality. N. Giraldi dei Cas, \**Felisberto Hernández, musique et littérature*, Paris, Indigo, 1998, 291 pp. J. A. Rosario-Andújar, \**Felisberto Hernández y el pensamiento filosófico*, NY, Lang, 160 pp. C. Singler, 'Matières à écrire. Le cinématographe et Felisberto Hernández', *Iberoromania*, 49:123–32, emphasizes visual and musical aspects of his work. \**Mario Benedetti: inventario cómplice*, ed. C. Alemany Bay, Alicante U.P., 1998, 620 pp. F. Rocco, 'Entrevista con Mario Benedetti', *StLI*, 32:81–98, with useful remarks. *Onetti and Others*, ed. G. San Román, Albany, SUNY Press, 191 pp., has 12 excellent comparative essays on Onetti and other Spanish American writers. P. T. Dejbord, \**Cristina Peri Rossi: escritora del exilio*, BA, Galerna, 1998, 268 pp. C. Arkinstall, 'Refiguring the blazón: the politics of empire building in Cristina Peri Rossi's *Descripción de un naufrago*', *RHM*, 51, 1998:423–40, sees the work as allegorical. F. Moreno Turner, 'Parodia, metahistoria y metaliteratura (en torno a *Maluco* de Napoleón Baccino Ponce de León)', *Hispamérica*, 82:3–20, is on its relativistic view of reality. \**Florencio Sánchez entre las dos orillas*, ed. O. Pelletieri and R. Mirza, BA, Galerna, 1998, 166 pp. H. Habra, 'Multiplicidad de juegos en *El apuntador* de Carlos Maggi', *Hispanófila*, 125:63–73, is on Maggi's perplexed view of reality. P. Bravo Elizondo, 'Teatro en Uruguay: conversación con Jorge Pignataro Calero', *LATR*, 33.1:153–60, is on post-dictatorship theatre.

VENEZUELA

M. E. Valero, \**El legado de Saturno en la obra de José Antonio Ramos Sucre*, Carabobo U.P., 1997, 105 pp. H. Jaimes, 'La historia y la autobiografía en los ensayos de Mariano Picón-Salas', *Hispanófila*, 125: 23–36, sees him as a representative figure. See too his 'Mariano Picón-Salas y el discurso de la historia', *RHM*, 51, 1998: 327–40, on his vision of historiography. J. Marbán, *La vigilia del vigía. Vida y obra de Arturo Uslar Pietri*, Caracas, Fondo Editorial, 1997, 383 pp., perceptively analyses his prose. W. Deaver, 'La aceleración, la inercia polar y lo escatológico en "La máquina de hacer ¡Pu! ¡Pu! ¡Puuu!" por Julio Garmendia', *ETL*, 27.1, 1998–9: 62–70, is on its critique of modern life. Z. Paternina, 'César Rengifo y el teatro venezolano', *LATR*, 32.2: 117–35, is chiefly on his staging devices. O. Obregón, 'Los soportes histórico y científico de la pieza *Humbolt y Bonpland taxidermistas* de Ibsen Martínez', *ib.*, 33.1: 25–43, is on the impact of European science on Latin America.

## BRAZILIAN LITERATURE

By MARK DINNEEN, *Spanish, Portuguese and Latin American Studies,*
*University of Southampton*

### 1. GENERAL

José Aderaldo Castello, *A literatura brasileira: origens e unidade*
*(1500–1960)*, SPo, USP, is a two-volume survey of Brazilian literature,
which, in mapping out its development, highlights the thematic and
ideological currents that have given a sense of unity to the process,
and the key attributes that have distinguished it. Volume 1, 463 pp.,
covers up to the 19th c., with particular emphasis on Romanticism,
whilst volume 2, 583 pp., deals with the 20th c., centring on
*modernismo*. Roberto Schwarz, *Sequências brasileiras, ensaios*, SPo, Com-
panhia das Letras, 249 pp., consists of 23 brief but wide-ranging
essays, covering prose, poetry, and drama, and discussing different
critical approaches. A. Johnson, 'Reading Roberto Schwarz: outside
out-of-place ideas', *JLACS*, 8.1:21–33, is a critique of S.'s studies of
the adaptation in Brazil of 19th-c. European liberal ideas. M. Silva,
'Pre-modernismo e historiografia literaria brasileira', *LALR*,
54:53–67, examines the establishment of the Brazilian literary canon,
arguing that the focus on the post-1922 modernist writers has led to
the neglect of important authors of the previous decades. Lúcia
Helena Vianna, *Cenas de amor e morte na ficção brasileira*, Niteroi, edUFF,
196 pp., discusses the presentation in Brazilian literature of male and
female roles and relationships. The analysis centres on key episodes
in works by Machado de Assis, Graciliano Ramos, Guimarães Rosa,
and Clarice Lispector. João Cezar de Castro Rocha, *Literatura e*
*cordialidade: o público e o privado na cultura brasileira*, R, EDUERJ, 1998,
251 pp., uses Sérgio Buarque de Holanda's concept of 'cordiality' as
a central characteristic of Brazilian cultural identity as the starting
point for an in-depth analysis of the nature of Brazil's literary
production. Antônio Paulo Graça, *Uma poética do genocídio*, R,
Topbooks, 1998, 172 pp., examines the different ways in which the
Indian has been represented in Brazilian literature, studying examples
by such writers as José de Alencar, Mário de Andrade, Darcy Ribeiro,
and Antônio Callado. Genocide is identified as the theme common to
their diverse approaches. M. Silva, 'O sorriso da sociedade: literatura
e academicismo no Brasil', *RCLL*, 49:145–76, discusses the role of
the Brazilian Academy of Letters, and the aesthetic values associated
with it, making particular reference to Coelho Neto. Guido Bilharinho, *Romances brasileiros: uma leitura direcionada*, Uberaba, Instituto
Trianguinho de Cultura, 1998, 208 pp., is a collection of short

articles, some in almost note form, sketching out the key features of major Brazilian novels written between 1870 and 1970. Flora Sussekind, *A voz e a série*, R, Sette Letras, 1998, 297 pp., gathers together 18 essays previously published in journals. It is a heterogeneous collection, dealing with diverse aspects of the work of such writers as Gerald Thomas, Bia Lessa, Melo Neto, João Gilberto Noll, and Augusto de Campos. Léo Schlafman, *A verdade e a mentira: novos caminhos para a literatura*, R, Civilização Brasileira, 1998, 224 pp., discusses the relationship between literature and social reality in a series of short essays referring to novels from different eras and different nations. Machado de Assis, Graciliano Ramos, Guimarães Rosa, Clarice Lispector, and Cornélio Penna are among the Brazilian writers covered.

## 2. COLONIAL

R. Wasserman, 'The theater of José de Anchieta and the definition of Brazilian literature', *LBR*, 36.1:71–85, considers the contrasting views of A.'s work — as either adhering closely to Portuguese models or as establishing the foundation for national expression — in a reassessment of A.'s position within the development of Brazilian literature. M. I. S. de Matos, 'Imagens perdidas no rio das Amazonas: conquista e gênero', *ib.*, 36.2:51–61, discusses the chronicles written by Frei Gaspar de Carvajal and Father Acuña on the basis of their Amazon expeditions, to show how their construction of male and female identity is linked to the relationship between the colonizer and the colonized. Thomas M. Cohen, *The Fire of Tongues: Antônio Vieira and the Missionary Church in Brazil*, Stanford U.P., 1998, 262 pp., is a well-researched study of V.'s beliefs and missionary work which provides valuable context for his writing.

## 3. THE NINETEENTH CENTURY

*Machado de Assis: Reflections on a Brazilian Master Writer*, ed. Richard Graham, Austin, Texas U.P., 134 pp., consists of four essays by well-known scholars, which, focusing particularly on *Dom Casmurro*, discuss whether M. is best understood as a realist or anti-realist writer. Marta de Senna, *O olhar oblíquo do bruxo: ensaios em torno de Machado de Assis*, R, Nova Fronteira, 1998, 147 pp., contains ten essays which adopt a comparative literary approach to discuss different aspects of M.'s work. Connections are drawn between his novels and the writing of such authors as Fielding, Sterne, and Borges. Valéria Jacó Monteiro, *Dom Casmuro: escritura e discurso, ensaio em literatura e psicanálise*, SPo, Hacker, 1997, 134 pp., analyses Machado's novel in the light of the theories of Lacan and Jakobson. Karin Volobuef, *Frestas e arestas: a prosa de ficção do romanticismo na Alemanha e no Brasil*, SPo, UNESP, 470 pp., highlights some of the peculiarities of Brazilian Romanticism in a comparative study of Romantic prose. Jean M. Carvalho França, *Literatura e sociedade no Rio de Janeiro oitocentista*, Lisbon, Imprensa Nacional, 276 pp., examines the conditions for literary production in Rio during the century, the role of literature, and the representation of Rio in the writing of the time. Sheldon C. Klock, *\*Themes in the Novels of Aluísio Azevedo*, Timonium, York Press, 72 pp. N. P. Naro, 'Onstage, offstage. Women and slaves in the theatre of protest', *PortSt*, 15:81–92, explores how women and slaves were presented in 19th-c. plays, and how they themselves used theatre and music to challenge dominant patriarchal values. E. Felinto de Oliveira, 'Uma história do mesmo: persistência do Naturalismo e exclusão do estético na canonização de *O cortiço*', *LALR*, 54:39–52, examines how Azevedo's novel became established within the Brazilian literary canon, and relates the process to the ideology and aesthetic values prevailing in the country at the close of the 19th c. A. Maggi, 'The "natural relationship": Qorop-Santo's plays and the liminal performance of morality', *LBR*, 36.2:1–12, argues that Q.'s works cannot be described as plays in any traditional sense, and that understanding of them has been limited because they have generally been analysed according to the criteria of conventional drama criticism. S. L. Prado Bellei, 'A virgem dos lábios sem mel', *ib.*, 63–80, analyses the inconsistencies in the plot of Alencar's *Iracema*, in order to highlight the ideology underlying the work. Cláudio Aguiar, *Franklin Távora e o seu tempo*, SPo, Ateliê, 1997, 380 pp., is the first major biography on T. It is a detailed and very readable study, which also contains an interesting discussion on the literary debates of the period. Cilaine Alves, *O belo e o disforme: Álvares de Azevedo e a ironia romântica*, EDUSP, 1998, 189 pp., seeks to challenge earlier studies of A.'s work with a detailed analysis of his poetry, emphasising his fusion of different styles. Beatriz Berrini, *Utopia, utopias*, SPo, Educ, 1997, 199 pp., discusses *Canção de exílio* by Gonçalves Dias, along with Manuel Bandeira's *Vou-me embora pra Pasárgada*, in the light of different concepts of utopia.

## 4. The Twentieth Century

### POETRY

Susana Vernieri, *O Capibaribe de João Cabral em 'O cão sem plumas' e 'O rio': duas aguas?*, SPo, Annablume, 195 pp., offers a detailed study of Melo Neto's two epic poems from the 1950s, focusing on the language used and the influence of Medieval Iberian poetry. Félix de Athayde,

*Ideias fixas de João Cabral de Melo Neto*, R, Nova Fronteira, 1998, 151 pp., collects extracts from interviews given by M.N., expressing his views on topics ranging from his own work and that of other poets, to wider social and cultural issues. S. Reckert, 'There and back again', *PortSt*, 15:162–77, includes reference to Manuel Bandeira and João Cabral de Melo Neto in a discussion of the theme of the journey in poetry, especially in terms of a search for one's roots. Marleine P. Marcondes e Ferreira de Toledo, *A voz das águas: uma interpretação do universo poético de Olga Savary*, L, Colibri, 119 pp., traces the development of S.'s poetry from the 1970s to the 1990s, giving particular prominence to her original use of the *haiku*. Maria Zilda Ferreira Cury, *Horizontes modernistas: o jovem Drummond e seu grupo em papel jornal*, Belo Horizonte, Autêntica, 1998, 240 pp., studies the emergence of *modernismo* in Belo Horizonte in the early 1920s, focusing on the poetry and other writing of Carlos Drummond de Andrade. Tereza Virginia de Almeida, *A ausência Lilás da Semana de Arte Moderna: o olhar pós-moderno*, Florianópolis, Letras Contemporâneas, 1998, 134 pp., rethinks Brazilian Modernism from a post-modernist perspective. See also Beatriz Berrini, under NINE-TEENTH CENTURY for a study of Manuel Bandeira's *Vou-me embora pra Pasárgada*. Maria Luzia dos Santos, *Da lira ao LUDUS: travessia. Leitura da poética de Gilberto Mendonça Teles*, SPo, Annablume, 1998, 229 pp., traces the development of M.T.'s poetry through three distinct stages, marked principally by increasing linguistic complexity.

DRAMA

Paulo Roberto Correia de Oliveira, *Aspectos do teatro brasileiro*, Curitiba, Juruá, 211 pp., is mainly useful as an introduction to the Brazilian theatre. It gives an overview of its evolution since the late 19th c. and identifies major phases, playwrights, and works. Sábato Magaldi, *Moderna dramaturgia brasileira*, SPo, Perspectiva, 1998, 323 pp., collects together a series of brief essays written over several decades, which review some of the major Brazilian plays of the 20th century. Among the dramatists discussed are Oswald de Andrade, Suassuna, Nelson Rodrigues, Jorge Andrade, and Dias Gomes. Eudinyr Fraga, *Nelson Rodrigues: Expressionista*, SPo, Ateliê, 1998, 214 pp., follows a lengthy discussion on expressionism with detailed studies of R.'s major plays, with the aim of demonstrating how they may be classified as expressionist works. G. Icle, 'Usina do trabalho do ator: um teatro canibal', *LATR*, 33.1:97–108, reports on how one Brazilian theatre group uses Oswald de Andrade's concept of *antropofagia* to explore Brazilian cultural identity. L. B. Ellis, 'In the jungle of the a*ntropófagos*: Brecht in Brazil', *ModD*, 42:269–79, discusses how the assimilation of Brecht's theories by Brazilian playwrights has produced original expressions of Brazilian cultural reality. A. Pereira Bezerra, 'Entretien avec Augusto Boal', *Caravelle*, 73:241–52, consists of extracts from talks given by B. in the 1990s, outlining and evaluating the development of his 'Theatre of the Oppressed'. Carmelina Guimarães, *Antunes Filho: um renovador do teatro brasileiro*, Campinas, UNICAMP, 1998, 183 pp.

PROSE

Piers Armstrong, *Third World Literary Fortunes*, Lewisburg, Bucknell U.P., 262 pp., considers the international reception of Brazilian literature, drawing comparisons with Spanish American writing of the 'boom'. It concludes that writers such as Guimarães Rosa and Mário de Andrade have suffered in terms of international readership because of the relative lack of recognizable national representation in their work. Jorge Amado is seen as the exception that proves the rule. Nancy T. Baden, *The Muffled Cries: The Writer and Literature in Authoritarian Brazil, 1964–1985*, Lanham, University Press of America, 272 pp., is a well researched historical study, analysing the effect on literature of the censorship imposed by the military dictatorship, and the experiments carried out by writers in order to express resistance. Marcelo Magalhães Bulhões, *Literatura em campo minado: a metalinguagem em Graciliano Ramos e a tradição literária brasileira*, SPo, Annablume, 172 pp., uses Bakhtin's literary theory to explore the role played by metalanguage in R.'s work, and seeks to show how that metalanguage is compatible with the author's social criticism. Hermenegilso Bastos, *Memórias de Cárcere, literatura e testemunho*, Brasília U.P., 1998, 169 pp., highlights links between Ramos's book of prison memoirs and his novels, and develops an interesting discussion on the relationship between fiction and testimony, and literature and psychoanalysis. On the same work, J. Courteau, '*Memórias do cárcere*: between history and imagination', *His(US)*, 82:46–55, analyses the narrative strategies which it employs. Regina Fátima de Almeida Conrado, *O mandacaru e a flor: a autobiografia 'Infância' e os modos de ser Graciliano*, SPo, Arte e Ciência, 1997, 208 pp., is a detailed study of the text, focusing on Ramos's use of irony in its construction. C. Ferreira-Pinto Bailey, 'Sonia Coutinho: desconstruindo mitos de feminilidade, beleza e juventude', *His(US)*, 82:713–24, discusses how C.'s female characters confront the social stigmatism attached to ageing. R. Igel, 'Brazilian Jewish women writers at the crossroads', pp. 59–84 of *Passion, Memory and Identity: Twentieth Century Latin American Jewish Women Writers*, ed. Marjorie Agosín, Albuquerque, New Mexico U.P., 216 pp., focuses on Elisa Lispector, Frida Alexander, Janette Fishenfeld, and Sara

Riwka Erlisch, examining their allegiance to and critical perspective on Judaism. N. H. Vieira, 'Clarice Lispector's Jewish universe', *ib.*, 85–113, considers the relationship between L.'s writing and the ethical teachings of Judaism. Regina Zilberman et al., *Clarice Lispector: a narração do indizível*, Porto Alegre, Artes e Ofícios, 1998, 144 pp., consists of nine essays by well-known experts on L.'s work, which vary widely in focus and in critical approach. J. L. Passos, 'A *figura*, o requiem e a cerveja: tres visões de um Brasil entre Darcy Ribeiro e Antônio Callado', *RCLL*, 49:217–30, compares the representation of indigenous cultures in R.'s *Maíra* and C.'s *Quarup* and *A Expedição de Montaigne*. F. Amory, 'Euclides da Cunha and Brazilian positivism', *LBR*, 36.1:87–94, seeks to show how evolutionism, rather then positivism, informs C.'s *Os sertões*. M. Chor Maio, 'Estoque semita: a presença dos judeus em *Casa grande e senzala*', *ib.*, 95–110, contends that Freyre's work, far from conveying an anti-semitic perspective, as claimed by some, in fact presents Jews as playing a positive role in Brazilian history. N. Lindstrom, 'The patterns of allusions in Clarice Lispector', *ib.*, 111–21, responds to the many studies recently published which highlight the manifestations of L.'s Jewish background in her writing, arguing that the sources that she assimilated were too diverse for her work to be considered as representing one particular cultural or religious tradition. A. Klobucka 'Quest and romance in Lispector's *Uma aprendizagem ou o livro dos prazeres*', *ib.*, 123–30, argues that ambiguity is the predominant characteristic of L.'s novel, often considered to be atypical of her work. F. Arenas, 'Writing after paradise and before a possible dream: Brazil's Caio Fernando Abreu', *ib.*, 36.2:13–21, discusses A.'s vision of modern Brazil by analysing the relationship between the global, the national, and the personal in his writing. C. Ferreira-Pinto, 'O desejo lesbiano no conto de escritores brasileiras contemporâneas', *RevIb*, 187:405–21, argues for a new reading of the stories of Elda Van Steen, Sonia Coutinho, Márcia Denser, Lygia Fagundes Telles, and Myriam Campello, in order to highlight the theme of lesbian desire implicit or explicit within them. Regina Abreu, *O enigma de 'Os sertões'*, R, Funarte–Rocco, 1998, 412 pp., is a sociological study of Da Cunha's masterpiece, which aims to explain exactly how and why it became such an influential and emblematic work. Ana Maria Roland, *Fronteiras da palavra: fronteiras da historia*, Brasília, UnB, 1997, 267 pp., discusses Da Cunha's *Os sertões* alongside Octavio Paz's *El laberinto de la soledad*, comparing the contribution of each to the debate on the formation of national cultures in Latin America. Antônio Hohlfeldt, *Trilogia da campanha: Ivan Pedro de Martins e o Rio Grande invisível*, Porto Alegre, Edipucrs, 1998, 317 pp., analyses three novels by M. from a sociological approach. Linking them to earlier naturalist and regionalist fiction, and using Lukács' theory of the novel, the study explores M.'s interpretation of social change in Rio Grande do Sul. Joaquim Alves de Aguiar, *Espaços da memória: um estudo sobre Pedro Nava*, SPo U.P., 1998, 218 pp., is a study of the six volumes of memoirs through which N. critically reflected on his life and times. *A liberdade de escrever: entrevistas de Érico Veríssimo*, ed. Sérgio Rodrigues, SPo, Globo, 210 pp., consists of 13 interviews given by V. in the 1960s and 70s, looking back on his career and reflecting upon the problems confronting the writer as a result of the military dictatorship of those decades. Dorine Cerqueira, *A ironia e a ironia trágica em 'A morte de Quincas Berro D'Agua'*, R, Razão Cultural, 1997, 166 pp., uses various theories of irony in order to shed light on Amado's novel. Juan Arias, *Confissões de Paulo Coelho*, L, Pergaminho, 211 pp., is a translation from the 1998 Spanish edition, in which, in a series of interviews, C. talks about intimate aspects of his life and writing. Maria Zenilda Grawunder, *Instituição literária: análise da legitimação da obra Dyonelio Machado*, Rio Grande do Sul, Edipucrs, 1997, 158 pp., examines the change of M.'s position within Brazilian literature, from marginalized writer during most of his career, to one of growing critical recognition today. *Leituras da psicanálise: estéticas da exclusão*, ed. Mário Eduardo Costa Pereira, Campinas, Mercado de Letras–ALB, 1998, 168 pp., gathers together six symposium papers focusing on the psychoanalytical study of literary works. Clarice Lispector, Modesto Carone, and João Guimarães Rosa are the Brazilian authors covered.

# IX. ITALIAN STUDIES

## LANGUAGE

By ADAM LEDGEWAY, *University Assistant Lecturer in Romance Philology, University of Cambridge*, and ALESSANDRA LOMBARDI, *Part-time Lecturer in Italian, University of Cambridge*

### 1. GENERAL

Alfredo Stussi, *Tra filologia e storia. Studi e testimonianze*, F, Olschki, 315 pp., is a fitting reminder of the author's considerable contribution to Italian philology over the last three decades, bringing together in a single volume 17 of his essays (three of them previously unpublished) tracing the development of Italian philology and linguistics as a discipline between the 19th and 20th c. Patrizia Tabossi, *Il linguaggio*, Bo, Il Mulino, 125 pp., provides a simple yet clear introduction to many general aspects of language, principally illustrated from Italian. Covering such topics as systems of communication, psycholinguistics, cognitive processes, language use, and the mind, this volume should prove a useful introductory tool for undergraduate linguistics courses. Of particular note are the *Atti* (Palermo), I-VI, which provide broad diachronic and synchronic coverage of Italian and the dialects on a range of topics. *Grande dizionario italiano dell'uso*, ed. Tullio De Mauro, 4 vols, T, UTET, 1169, 1183, 1173, 1211 pp., also available in CD-ROM, is a monumental work representing a must for all serious scholars of the language, bringing together in one source a rich collection of written and spoken Italian and setting particular store by diachronic, diastratic, diamesic, and diatopic variation. Benefiting from the collaboration of such renowned scholars as G. Lepschy, this work offers considerably more than the average dictionary by providing the user with a whole host of valuable and time-saving functions, including various options to create personalized searches or access detailed grammatical descriptions by lexical entry and subject matter, and the possibility of creating customized dictionaries.

### 2. HISTORY OF THE LANGUAGE, EARLY TEXTS, AND DIACHRONIC STUDIES

Rosa Casapullo, *Il medioevo*, Bo, Il Mulino, 476 pp., is an ideal companion to the other eight volumes in this series on the history of the language edited by Francesco Bruni. With the exception of 13th-c. Tuscan, which will form the sole topic of a separate volume already in preparation, this book undertakes a detailed examination of the vernacular traditions in 12th- and 13th-c. Italy through a wide selection of texts. The first of the sections into which the work is divided examines, in 12 chapters, the emergence of the vernacular and its wide-ranging use in texts of various styles and registers, while the second section brings together a rich anthology of texts organized according to their provenance and supplemented with detailed linguistic commentaries and translations. Gabriella Ronchi, *Il trattato de la spera. Volgarizzato da Zucchero Bencivenni*, F, Accademia della Crusca, 213 pp., is a critical edition of the Florentine Bencivenni's 14th-c. translation of Giovanni Sacrobosco's treatise on astronomy and cosmography *De sphaera*. Claudio Marazzini, \**Da Dante alla lingua selvaggia: sette secoli di dibattito sull'italiano*, Ro, Carocci, 268 pp. R. Coluccia, A. Cucurachi and A. Urso, 'Iberismi quattrocenteschi e storia della lingua italiana', *Atti* (Palermo), III, 127–36, reiterates the importance of a proper understanding of the extent of Iberian lexical interference on Campanian texts of the latter half of the 15th c. M. Pagano, 'La vita di S. Onofrio e qualche osservazione sulla *scripta* siciliana medievale: esiti di un sondaggio', *ib.*, VI, 391–401, draws on a comparison of the two manuscripts of the Sicilian *Vita di S. Onofrio* to remind us of some of the problems of editing early texts. Danilo Poggiogalli, *La sintassi nelle grammatiche del Cinquecento*, F, Crusca, 388 pp., will prove a valuable tool for those interested in both the external and internal histories of the language. Organized into eight chapters broadly coinciding with the traditional parts of speech, P. draws together the opinions of 16th-c. grammarians on a wide range of syntactic phenomena. Through detailed interpretations and comparisons of a large textual corpus consisting of 21 different sources, P. produces a clear and illuminating survey of prescriptive usage within the grammatical tradition of the time.

A. Espósito, 'Italian *niente* < NE INDE: an Aragonese analog', *Lloyd Vol.*, 237–52, takes a fresh look at the etymology of Italian *niente* in the light of comparative evidence culled from the medieval Aragonese corpus of Juan Fernández de Heredia, which would seem to support NE INDE as the most viable source for Italian *niente*. Textual evidence from the Heredian corpus reveals that reflexes of NE INDE (> *nin de*/ *ninde*), as well as NON INDE (> *non de*/*nonde*), occur only in preverbal position and increasingly in contexts where the *ende*/*inde* element lacks its original referential value, facts which point to the incipient reanalysis of the compound as a negative polarity item. Though accounting more satisfactorily for the semantic and syntactic development of *niente* than the competing etymologies NEC ENTE and NE GENTE, this explanation still suffers from a number of phonetic shortcomings which E. suggests may be resolved by appealing to southern dialect borrowing. M. Maiden, 'La tesi di Reichenkron e l'origine delle desinenze -*i* e -*e* nel romanzo "orientale"', *Atti* (Palermo), I, 173–86, reconsiders the question of the origin of final -*i* and -*e* in Eastern Romance, drawing on some convincing evidence from a number of Italian dialects, from Dalmatian, and from Rumanian which lend support to Reichenkron's phonetic explanation. Those interested in the morphosyntactic development of the Italian determiner system will find the following two contributions by L. Vanelli particularly enlightening: 'Sull'origine dell'articolo definito maschile plurale *i*', *ib.*, II, 827–38, and ' "Punti di crisi" nell'italiano contemporaneo', Cardinale, *Insegnare italiano*, 99–120, the latter exploring the precarious status of the semi-clitics *egli* and *loro* in relation to their respective 'popular' rivals *lui* and *gli*. Starting from a discussion of the ambivalent behaviour of the former pair in modern Italian, V. offers a very cogent explanation for their marginalization within the pronominal system which highlights the role of the normative grammatical tradition in arresting the spontaneous evolutionary tendencies of early Florentine. In particular, the incipient emergence of a series of subject clitics in early Florentine, leading to the increasingly restricted distribution of *egli* and the greater use of *lui* as a nominative pronoun, is claimed to have been blocked by the interventions of language arbiters of the puristic tradition, thereby giving rise to the semi-clitic status of modern Italian *egli*. On the other hand, the unique behaviour of *loro* within the pronominal system is explained as an historical residue of an earlier semi-clitic dative/genitive pronominal series, from which *loro* was carried over as a suppletive dative clitic to distinguish between the singular and plural functions previously syncretized in the clitic *gli*. M. Cennamo, 'Inaccusatività tardo-latina e suoi riflessi in testi italiani antichi centro–meridionali', *ZRP*, 115:300–31, explores the diachronic development of pleonastic reflexives as markers of Split Intransitivity, which are demonstrated to distinguish two different subclasses of intransitive verb (unergatives vs unaccusatives) in early central and southern texts and have important consequences on patterns of auxiliary choice and participial agreement. C. Robustelli, 'Nota su due costrutti della prosa di Bembo', *Atti* (Palermo), II, 718–25, considers the status of two apparently similar causative constructions *farsi a credere* and *fare a credere* in the writings of Bembo. Contrary to the traditional thesis, which views both constructions as simple variants of a single causative construction, R. presents evidence to demonstrate that in the reflexive variant the verb *fare* cannot be considered a causative but, rather, should be interpreted as an aspectual with ingressive value. R. Middleton, 'The formation of the Romance relative marker (*il quale, lequel, el cual etc.*): some suggestions',

*OUWPLPP 4*, 102–16, charts the principal stages in the grammaticalization of reflexes of (ILLE +) QUALIS as a relative marker in Italian and other Romance varieties. Still within a historical perspective is Giuliana Fiorentino, *Relativa debole. Sintassi, uso, storia in italiano*, Mi, FrancoAngeli, 201 pp., which explores the so-called 'weak' relative clause introduced by an invariable complementizer optionally followed by a clitic marked for case, for instance, *la signora che (ne) ho visto la figlia*. On the basis of both literary and spoken corpora, F. retraces the genesis and development of the weak relative, providing a clear exposition of its syntax and usage, and some insightful comparisons with analogous French and Spanish constructions. In contrast to the traditional view which sees the emergence of such structures as the consequence of a general tendency in the spoken language towards simplification, the author retraces the origin of the weak relative to Late Latin, charting its subsequent structural evolution in Western Romance and highlighting its compatibility with the general typological tendencies of Romance. This study is juxtaposed to a parallel diachronic investigation of the canonical relative clause (introduced by a relative pronoun), which F. demonstrates to have coexisted *ab antiquo* alongside of the weak relative.

3.   PHONETICS AND PHONOLOGY

Luciano Canepari, *Il dizionario di pronuncia italiana*, Bo, Zanichelli, 584 pp., is a rich and user-friendly reference work containing 60,000 entries, including proper nouns, surnames, Italian and foreign toponyms, and a large selection of foreign words and locutions in common use. In contrast to traditional works of this kind, C. is to be praised for his attention to diatopic, diastratic, and diaphasic variation, which provides, where relevant, a whole range of variant pronunciations classified accordingly as *pronunce* 'moderna' (superregional, neutral), 'tradizionale' (Tuscan), 'accettabile' (widespread within central Italy), 'tollerata' (regional within central Italy), 'trascurata' (uneducated, regional), 'intenzionale' (learnèd, affected) and 'aulica' (obsolescent). The criteria for such distinctions are discussed fully in a detailed introduction, which also includes a useful survey of the principal types of variation found within the peninsula, a detailed introduction to Italian phonetics, and a section dealing with the problems posed by particular graphemes. An ideal companion to this work is Id., *Manuale di pronuncia italiana*, Bo, Zanichelli, 2nd edn, viii + 575 pp. + two audiocassettes. This new edition, which contains many new additions, as well as benefiting from a considerable reworking of the original text, provides an extremely detailed treatment of all aspects of Italian phonetics, including detailed sections on regional and non-standard varieties, intonation, and exemplary audio material, an ideal reference work for undergraduate courses. F. Dovetto, 'Sprache, Stimme und Phonetik. Positionen einiger italienischer Theoretiker aus der zweiten Hälfte des 18. Jahrhunderts', pp. 101–15 of *Sprachdiskussion und Beschreibung von Sprachen im 17. und 18. Jahrhundert*, ed. H. Hassler and P. Schmitter, Münster, Nodus, 502 pp. P. Monachesi, 'Phonological phrases in Italian', *RLFRU*, 18:79–89, considers the problems for the syntax–phonology interface raised by the behaviour of infinitival complements to restructuring predicates which, though yielding two different syntactic structures, as witnessed by the behaviour of clitic placement (biclausal [*voglio*] + [*leggerlo*] vs monoclausal [*lo voglio leggere*]), correspond to a single prosodic configuration, as demonstrated by phonological rules of *raddoppiamento sintattico*, stress retraction, and final lengthening. To resolve such non-isomorphism between prosodic and syntactic constituency, M. advocates an algorithm for the mapping of syntactic and prosodic structures which is not driven wholly by syntactic principles. F. Albano Leoni, F. Cutugno, and R. Savy, 'Il vocalismo dell'italiano televisivo. Analisi acustica di un corpus', *Atti* (Palermo), IV, 3–16, reports on the results of a spectro-acoustic study of Italian vowels on the basis of a corpus of regional news programmes broadcast in Lombardy, Tuscany, Lazio, and Campania. Surprisingly, the findings demonstrate some significant divergences from the expected Italian vocalic model, including, for example, only a weak correlation between vowel length and syllable type, and a significant reduction in vowel quality and centralization of atonic vowels. M. D'Impero and S. Rosenthall, 'Phonetics and phonology of main stress in Italian', *Phonology*, 16:1–28, observing that the phonetic and phonological approaches (namely, shortening vs lengthening) to stressed vowel duration in Italian are diametrically opposed, maintain that lengthening of the stressed vowel is the correct characterization of the observed duration differences. Rather than proposing a single rule of stressed vowel lengthening, the authors argue for two types of lengthening, phonological lengthening which affects only the duration of penultimate vowels, and phonetic lengthening which accounts for the length of antepenultimate vowels. In this way, the differences between phonological and phonetic lengthening are shown to support the generalization that stressed penultimate syllables are heavy. The phonological causes of meta-phonetic raising in Italian dialects form the topic of discussion in A. Calabrese, 'Metaphony revisited', *RivL*, 10, 1998:7–68, and J. Cole, 'Deconstructing metaphony' (69–88). Calabrese's contribution focuses on the peculiar output of metaphony on [-ATR] mid-vowels, which are either diphthongized, tensed or raised to high

[+ATR] vowels in accordance with dialectal variation. These metaphonetic outcomes are interpreted by the author within a theory of phonological markedness, according to which the expected [+high, -ATR] configuration produced by metaphony acting on [-ATR] mid-vowels is, on account of its markedness value, eliminated by various repair strategies which yield the range of observed outcomes. Cole, on the other hand, contends that the set of vowel raisings that define metaphonic systems in Italian dialects do not result from a unified operation of height assimilation but, rather, are the product of a restricted assimilation of high–mid vowels and a subsequent vowel shift that conditions both the vowel raising and fronting. On this view, low and low–mid vowels raise to fill the gap created by assimilation of /e, o/ to /i, u/. M. Frascarelli, 'The prosody of focus in Italian (and the syntax–phonology interface)', *Probus*, 11 : 209–38, deals specifically with the prosodic domain of focus in Italian building on the theory of Prosodic Phonology. In particular, F. provides evidence for the influence of focus on the application of phonological rules in Italian, for which she proposes a theory capable of deriving prosodic constituency in narrow and wide focus sentences.

4. MORPHOLOGY

A. Thornton, 'Diagrammaticità, uniformità di codifica e morfomicità nella flessione verbale italiana', *SLI 31*, 483–502, contrasts and compares the merits of Natural Morphology and Arnoff's theory of *Morphology by itself* in accounting for Italian 3rd person plur. verb forms. L. Gaeta, 'Polisemia e lessicalizzazione: un approccio naturalista', *ItStudien*, 20 : 7–27, is a detailed study of Italian action nouns within the framework of Natural Morphology. F. Dovetto, A. Thornton, and C. Burani, 'Violazione di restrizioni sulla suffissazione e interpretabilità semantica', *SILTA*, 3, 1998 : 451–77, explore within the Lexical Morphology model the differing effects of violations of various restrictions operative on rules of Italian nominal suffixation. On the basis of an experiment in which Italian subjects were asked to assess the relative acceptability of a number of nonsense words forged through six productive denominal and deadjectival suffixes, it was demonstrated that pseudo-words violating the categorial restrictions of the base (e.g., *seppellaio*) were judged the least interpretable, whereas those only violating the inherent syntactico–semantic features of the base (e.g., *umoraio*) were amenable to a greater degree of interpretability. In turn, both of these classes of nonsense words were shown to exhibit a lesser degree of interpretability than those in which there were no such violations of the syntactic and semantic features of the base (e.g., *\*quadernaio*), which the authors interpret as confirming the validity of recognizing such restrictions and their relative weighting. E. Schafroth, 'Produttività e accettabilità dei verbi in *-icchiare, -acchiare, -ucchiare*', *Atti* (Palermo), III, 793–805, reports on the results of an investigation into the productivity of the iterative *-cchiare* verbal suffix which, though limited to a closed class of verbs in the written language, is argued to enjoy a greater degree of productivity in spontaneous speech production. A. Calabrese, 'I sincretismi fra i pronominali clitici nei dialetti italiani e sardi e la teoria della morfologia distribuita', *ib.*, II, 107–22, is an admirable attempt within the framework of Distributed Morphology to explain some otherwise puzzling, yet widespread, cases of syncretism in the clitic systems of many Sardinian and southern dialects, in which the 3rd person dative clitic, and/or 1st person plur. clitic, have been replaced by the genitive or locative clitic.

## 5. Syntax

L. Dezsö, 'Le reggenze dei verbi e degli aggettivi italiani (un approccio tipologico)', *Atti* (Palermo), II, 225–32. W. Dietrich, 'Funzione e sintassi dell'articolo partitivo dell'italiano e francese', *ib.*, 245–53, compares the use of the partitive article in Italian and French, pointing out a number of differences in its distribution according to syntactic context and register. P. Acquaviva, 'Negation and operator dependencies: evidence from Italian', *Lingua*, 108:137–74, contends that Italian indefinite NPs like *nessuno* and *alcunché* differ from familiar polarity items like English *anyone*, in that they are simultaneously subject to the distributional conditions on LF-movement and on polarity items, thereby exhibiting a behaviour quite distinct from that of both canonical LF–raising quantifiers and polarity items. Paola Monachesi, *A Lexical Approach to Italian Cliticization*, Stanford, CSLI, xv + 247 pp., explores various topics in Italian cliticization within the HPSG framework, seeking to demonstrate that Italian clitics are not syntactically independent elements, as is generally advocated within the generative tradition, but inflexional affixes. Individual chapters include discussion of the various uses of clitic *si*, argued to behave both as an argument (reflexive/reciprocal, impersonal) and non-argument (middle, ergative and inherent-reflexive), the status of *loro*, which is treated not as an affix but as a lexical item in order to account for its distinctive properties, and clitic climbing. Discussing the latter, M. challenges the idea that clitic climbing is incompatible with a lexical analysis of cliticization, proposing an alternative to the Feature Principle for long-distance dependencies which allows the subcategorization requirements of the embedded verb to be transferred to the verb triggering clitic climbing. R. Folli, 'Causative/Inchoative alternations in Italian', *OUWPLPP 4*, 33–49, questions the validity of traditional accounts of the causative/ inchoative alternation which take the inchoative variant to be derived from its corresponding causative pendant by means of a detransitiviz- ation process (spelt-out in the reflexive clitic *si*) applying to a prior transitive structure (e.g., *rompere* > *rompersi*). Capitalizing on the aspectual characteristics of such verbs, F. argues for a more nuanced analysis which recognizes three types of causative/inchoative alterna- tion, as witnessed by the availability or otherwise of the clitic *si* (e.g., *rompere/rompersi* vs *fondere/fonder(si)* vs *affondar(\*si)*). C. Cecchetto, 'A comparative analysis of left and right dislocation in Romance', *SL*, 53:40–67, disputes the traditional analysis of clitic left-dislocation (CLLD) and clitic right-dislocation (CLRD) as simple variants of a single operation. Though acknowledging undeniable pragmatic similarities between the two structures, C. draws on evidence from ECP effects and Aux-to-Comp to highlight a number of differences between CLLD and CLRD. Such facts lead to the proposal that right-dislocated XPs sit in a VP-peripheral position (both at Spell- Out and LF), whereas left-dislocated XPs occupy an IP-peripheral position. Maria Luisa Zubizarreta, *Prosody, Focus, and Word Order*, Cambridge, Mass., MIT Press, 213 pp., explores the interaction between prosody and syntax in Germanic and Romance, dedicating ample space to question of focus, prosody, and word order in Italian. Italian VOS orders, in which the subject carries narrow focus, are argued to be derived from an underlying SVO structure in which the subject is first moved to a Specifier position of a Focus Phrase to which the TP (containing VO) is subsequently left-adjoined. The latter operation, termed p(rosodically-motivated)-movement, is invoked to preclude a conflict between the output of a focus–promin- ence rule and that of a rule of assignment of non-contrastive phrasal prominence. M. Ippolito, 'Pseudo-relatives and existentials: a unified analysis', *OUWPLPP 4*, 50–69, advances a unified structural analysis of Italian pseudo-relatives and existentials, two apparently unrelated constructions both of which I. takes to involve a Larsonian double- object structure. R. Posner, 'The present form in English and Romance — a diachronic view', *ib.*, 127–40, provides some interes- ting remarks on the distribution of the so-called simple present and periphrastic progressive present forms in Italian and the dialects, noting, in particular, the growing use of the latter as the unmarked form in southern varieties. Guglielmo Cinque, *Adverbs and Functional Heads. A Cross-linguistic Perspective*, OUP, xii + 275 pp., draws on considerable data from Italian and northern dialects to argue for the existence of a finely articulated hierarchy of clausal functional projections. Based on the evidence of the possible positions occupied by adverb phrases of different classes in both finite and non-finite clauses, C. provides some convincing evidence that the number, type, and relative order of functional projections remains invariant across languages.

### 6. SEMANTICS

M. Mazzoleni, 'Il prototipo "cognitivo" ed il prototipo "linguistico": equivalenti o inconciliabili?', *LS*, 34:51–66, challenges the assumption that linguistic categories may be defined in terms of cognitive prototypes, pointing out significant differences between prototypes of the cognitive kind and those adopted to define linguistic categories, which lack the formal status of cognitive prototypes derived from personal experience in a sociocultural context. M. Vignolo, 'Proposizioni e indicali', *ib.*, 317–38, focuses on sentences containing indexicals in order to defend the Fregean theory of proposition, concluding with some suggestions for a reassessment of the Fregean notion of 'thought'. M. Prandi, 'Dall'analogia all'inferenza: la motivazione delle espressioni idiomatiche', *QS*, 20:131–45, constructs a typology of the conceptual factors underlying the processes whereby complex expressions acquire an idiomatic reading.

Various analyses and aspects of metaphor are discussed in *LS*, 34, including C. Bazzanella, 'La metafora tra mente e discorso: alcuni cenni' (150–58), which outlines some of the issues that characterize metaphor as a cognitive and textual–conversational device, concentrating on such issues as metaphor and non-literal meaning, metaphor as a cognitive process, functions of metaphor, and its linguistic forms; C. Cacciari, 'La metafora: un ponte tra il linguaggio e l'esperienza percettiva' (159–66), advocates that literal language is fundamentally inadequate to describe the perceptual and experiential complexity of the world and has to be used metaphorically to increase its descriptive and communicative force, thereby filling the gap between the complexity of the perceptual world and the limitations of the linguistic repertoire; F. Casadei, 'Alcuni pregi e limiti della teoria cognitivista della metafora' (167–80), outlines some of the merits and limits of the cognitivist approach to metaphor; M. Prandi, 'La metafora come costruzione linguistica: le forme interne del conflitto concettuale' (201–10), holds that, while the principal assumptions of cognitivist theories of metaphor account well for consistent metaphors, they are seriously challenged by inconsistent metaphors.

J. Trumper, M. Maddalon, M. T. Vigolo and N. Misiti, 'Il possibile ruolo della linguistica in rapporto ai saperi naturalistici', *QS*,

20:147–57, reaffirms the importance of the interdisciplinary relationship between linguistics, ethnoanthropology, and other related fields through an analysis of the botanical class of the *gramineae*. M. Maddalon, 'Biotassonomie e categorie cognitive. Proposte di analisi lessicale per il repertorio fitonimico', *Atti* (Palermo), III, 459–69. A. Nesi, 'Salamandra tra realtà e mito', *ib.*, 33–59, explores the distribution of *salamandra* in its different denominations throughout the Italian peninsula, with some hypotheses regarding the various influences underlying the observed variation. O. Lurati, 'Per un approccio pragmatico e semantico alle "voci eccentriche". Il caso *monello* e altri qualificativi per "ragazzo"', *ib.*, 445–58.

7. PRAGMATICS AND DISCOURSE

Rita Franceschini, *\*Riflettere sull'interazione. Un'introduzione alla metacomunicazione e all'analisi conversazionale*, Mi, FrancoAngeli, 1998, 220 pp. Anna De Marco, *\*Sociopragmatica dei diminutivi in italiano*, Rende, Università degli Studi della Calabria, xii + 212 pp. M. Berretta, 'Valori pragmatici diversi dell'ordine OV (OVS/OSV) nell'italiano contemporaneo', *Atti* (Palermo), II, 81–90, offers a clear exposition of the pragmatic functions of the principal types of OV sentences found in Italian, in which O variously functions as theme and rheme. A. Capone, 'Dilemmas and excogitations: considerations on modality, clitics and discourse', *OUWPLPP 4*, 18–32, investigates the semantics and pragmatics of the clitic *lo* in conjunction with verbs of propositional attitude, the effects of which are shown to allow certain presuppositions to survive in those sites where they are generally filtered out. For example, in the sentence *Giovanni ha detto che (lo) sa che Maria è a Parigi*, the presupposed truth of the most deeply embedded clause is not implied if the clitic *lo* is omitted. In contrast, when the clitic is in place, the speaker commits himself to the belief that Maria is in Paris and assumes that this belief is also shared by the hearer. C. Bazzanella, 'Corrispondenze funzionali di *well* in italiano: analisi di un testo letterario e problemi generali', *ER*, 42:99–110, explores the various Italian equivalents of the English discourse marker *well* through a comparison of an English novel and its Italian translation. By the same author is ' "Address inversion" and "teknonymy" as involvement markers in an Italian talk show', pp. 159–69 of *Dialogue Analysis and the Mass Media*, ed. Bernd Naumann, Tübingen, Niemeyer, 248 pp., a fascinating study of two non-standard forms of social deixis, address inversion (use of kin term to express the speaker's, and not the addressee's, role in the dyad) and teknonymy (use of a kin term appropriate to a different kin relation), on the basis of a corpus culled from an Italian talk show. The particular emotional setting of the latter is shown to favour the host's use of linguistic strategies such as address inversion and teknonymy to forge an empathetic bond between the guests, the host, and the audience. C. Bazzanella and R. Damiano, 'The interactional handling of misunderstanding in everyday conversations', *JP*, 31:817–36, examines the handling, within the conversational interaction, of linguistic misunderstanding on the basis of an Italian corpus. It is suggested that misunderstanding should not be considered a polar process (absence/presence of comprehension), but, rather, a continuum. The same authors follow up this topic in 'Coherence and misunderstanding in everyday conversations', pp. 175–87 of *Coherence in Spoken and Written Discourse*, ed. Wolfram Bublitz, Uta Lenk and Eija Ventola, Amsterdam, Benjamins, 300 pp. L. Anelli, M. Balconi, and R. Ciceri, 'Ulisse o Richelieu? Stili verbali della comunicazione menzognera', *LS*, 34:379–401, is a highly revealing analysis of the main communicative verbal styles and strategies used by speakers when lying under different contextual conditions. C. Bazzanella, G. Braiato, and M. Danieli, 'The functions of repetition in human-machine dialogue', pp. 64–77 of *Elaborazione del LN e riconoscimento del parlato*, ed. M. Danieli, Trento U.P., 122 pp., is an innovative study comparing the presence, forms, and functions of repetition in human-machine dialogue and human dialogue. The findings demonstrate that repetition is also exploited in human-machine dialogue, though with more limited functions than those found in human dialogue, namely confirmation and correction, but not disagreement, and that repetition in human-machine dialogue helps the comprehension process, albeit as a yes–no process rather than as a scalar process as in human dialogue.

8. LEXIS

Diego Marconi and Francesca Scrofani, \*La competenza lessicale, Ro–Bari, Laterza, x + 247 pp. Achille Lucarini, \*Dizionario delle parole straniere in uso nella lingua italiana, Ro, Editori Riuniti, x + 313 pp. O. Cristea, 'Peculiarità dei doppioni etimologici della lingua italiana', *Atti* (Palermo), III, 179–85, assumes an excessively restrictive definition of the term *doppione*, pointing out a number of apparent misuses of the term by other scholars. R. Kiesler, 'A proposito degli arabismi nella lingua italiana', *ib.*, IV, 467–75. S. Sgroi, 'Uno "squilibrio" etimologico di origine settentrionale', *QS*, 39:169–89. S. Spina, 'La nascita della terminologia linguistica in Italia: il lessico tecnico di Giovanni Flechia in alcuni inediti', *Atti* (Palermo), III, 829–44, provides a systematic analysis of the linguistic terminology used by a 19th-c. scholar as recorded in his unpublished lecture courses of

1872–73. A. Zangrandi, 'Il lessico del *Marco Visconti* di Tommaso Grossi nella prima edizione milanese', *LS*, 34:227–51, highlights the obsolete and literary lexical features of this 19th-c. novel, which show traces of the influence of the linguistic ideas that gave rise to the first edition of Manzoni's *Promessi sposi*. M. de Boer, '*Le cazzate* di Coliandro: osservazioni sintattiche, semantiche e pragmatiche sulle parolacce italiane', *RLFRU*, 18:35–48, offers an intriguing case study on the use of *cazzo* and its derivatives, and a number of other *parolacce* in a novel by the crime writer Carlo Lucarelli. Through a detailed study of the morphology, syntax, pragmatics, and semantics of such terms, de B. produces some interesting results on the frequency of individual *parolacce* and their semasiological functions. Z. Fábián and Á. Bencze, '*Lőrinc* nell'ungherese e *Lorenzo* nell'italiano', *Verbum*, 1:239–50, is a comparative onomastic study of the various outcomes of Lat. LAURENTIUS in Hungarian and Italo-Romance, documenting its diffusion as an anthroponym (first name and family name), toponym, common noun, and its use in idioms. F. Cabasino, 'Défigement et contraintes syntaxiques. Une analyse comparée des presses française et italienne', *CLe*, 74:99–147, compares the phenomenon of destructured set phrases in the French and Italian press over the last 15 years, identifying the morphosyntactic and semantic mechanisms operating in certain configurations of two related languages. M.-T. Greco, 'Un gergo del napoletano: *la parlèsia*', *Atti* (Palermo), III, 293–316, takes a rare look at the lexis of *parlèsia*, a Neapolitan-based *gergo* formerly employed exclusively by buskers making their living within the city of Naples, but now used extensively by musicians throughout the peninsula.

9. SOCIOLINGUISTICS

Fabio Rossi, \*Le parole dello schermo: analisi linguistica del parlato di sei film dal 1948 al 1957, Ro, Bulzoni, 548 pp. Elena Landoni, *Grammatica italiana: lavori in corso. Aggiornamenti sulle regole incerte della nostra lingua*, Mi, Mursia, 206 pp. B. Pasetto, 'Appunti per una definizione della varietà di italiano parlato a Mantova', *BALI*, 22 (1988):145–58, highlights the absence of a homogeneous regional variety character-istic of the city as a whole. A. Colonna Romano and G. Mammana, 'Italiano regionale in Sicilia in una prospettiva diatopica', *Atti* (Palermo), V, 129–41, identifies areas of diatopic variation in the regional Italian spoken in Sicily through an investigation of lexical variation. G. Tropea, 'Alcuni esempi del lessico degli studenti a Messina', *BALI* 22 (1988):43–51. G. Alfonzetti, 'Passato prossimo e passato remoto: dimensioni di variazione', *Atti* (Palermo), II, 27–37, reports on the use of the two past tense paradigms in the regional

Italian of Sicily, observing, in particular, that their distribution is not determined specifically by aspectual considerations but increasingly by sociolinguistic factors, with older speakers marking greater use of the *passato remoto* and younger speakers tending more towards the use of the *passato prossimo* in line with the (northern) Italian model. C. Schirru, 'Sulla lunghezza consonantica nell'italiano della Sardegna', *BALI* 22 (1988): 53–91. Ines Loi Corvetto, *Dai bressaglieri alla fantaria. Lettere dei soldati sardi nella grande guerra*, Nuoro, Ilisso Edizioni, 146 pp., represents a rich and valuable textual source of data of regional Italian from the province of Cagliari, bringing together just over 400 letters written between 1882 and 1923. In addition to the letters, this volumes offers informative introductory sections on plurilingualism, the linguistic varieties spoken in Sardinia, the value of epistolary evidence as a linguistic tool, and an in-depth discussion of the principal linguistic features of the regional Italian exhibited by this collection of letters. R. Rindler Schjerve, 'Sul cambiamento linguistico in situazione di bilinguismo instabile: aspetti del code-switching fra sardo e italiano', *Atti* (Palermo), v, 589–602, discusses evidence to support the claim that code-switching has now become an integral part of communication in Sardinia, a strategy which ensures the continued use of the dialect but which, at the same time, entails an ever-increasing degree of Italianization of the latter.

10. PSYCHOLINGUISTICS AND LANGUAGE ACQUISITION

*\*Processi comunicativi e linguistici nei bambini e negli adulti: prospettive evolutive e sociali*, ed. Alda Scopesi and Mirella Zanobini, Mi, FrancoAngeli, 1998, 457 pp. Donatella Antelmi, *La prima grammatica dell'italiano. Indagine longitudinale sull'acquisizione della morfosintassi italiana*, Bo, Il Mulino, 1997, 237 pp., is an impressive study based on an investigation of the development of phenomena such as verb inflection, nominal structures, and interrogatives, which are shown to lend substantial support to the Radfordian thesis that the major task of the child during the transitional period between the two-word stage and subsequent developmental stages lies in the acquisition of functional categories. The same topic within a comparative perspective is taken up by C. Caselli, P. Casadio, and E. Bates, 'A comparison of the transition from first words to grammar in English and Italian', *JCL*, 26:69–111, which reports on the results of a comparative study of English- and Italian-speaking children between one-and-a-half and two-and-a-half years old, investigating possible cross-linguistic differences in the acquisition of vocabulary within and across the age range and similar differences in the pace and shape of grammatical development, and its relation to vocabulary size. While no differences

were noted with regard to the first prediction, a comparison of the longest sentences produced demonstrated considerable cross-linguistic differences with regard to the amount of morphology acquired in relation to vocabulary size, with Italian children producing a greater amount of grammatical morphology and thus reflecting the greater morphological load they have to acquire. A. Devescovi, S. D'Amico, and P. Gentile, 'The development of sentence comprehension in Italian: a reaction time study', *First Language*, 19:129–63, compares sentence interpretation in Italian-speaking children aged between five and ten and young adults, focusing specifically on the contributions of morphological, syntactic, and semantic information to the assignment of agent–object roles. In contrast to previous research which holds that children have control over most aspects of word order and morphology by the age of four, the results of this study highlight that the process of language development is not complete until between ten and early adulthood. G. Vigliocco and J. Franck, 'When sex and syntax go hand in hand: gender agreement in language production', *JMemL*, 40:455–78, questions whether the language production system uses conceptual information regarding biological gender in the encoding of gender agreement between subject and predicate. P. Zoccolotti et al., 'Markers of developmental surface dyslexia in a language (Italian) with high grapheme–phoneme correspondence', *Applied Psycholinguistics*, 20:191–216, explores the reading performances of four Italian boys displaying severe slowness associated with reduced text comprehension. The results of the study indicate that parallel visual processing of words was impaired and that the patients analysed words sequentially, possibly through an orthographic–phonological conversion.

A. Giacalone Ramat, 'Functional typology and strategies of clause connection in second-language acquisition', *Linguistics*, 37:519–48, argues that typological generalizations based on the way languages encode the relationships between semantically connected clauses may shed light on the development of clause combining in the untutored acquisition of L2 by adult learners. Data collected from four learners of Italian reveal an ordering in the emergence of different types of clause linkage according to the following hierarchy: purpose > before > after, when > reality, condition, reason. In the coding of complement clauses, the relations situated at the left end of the hierarchy make use of 'deranked' verb forms, whereas those situated at the right end exploit 'balanced' verb forms. Important differences in the acquisition of deontic and epistemic modality in L2 are highlighted by the same author in 'Grammaticalization of modality in language acquisition', *StLa*, 23:377–402. Whereas deontic modality is shown to be immediately expressed through modal verbs, epistemic modality is achieved through various lexical, paralinguistic (hesitations, gestures), and intonational strategies. These results demonstrate that the acquisition of modality in L2 learners conforms to a common path of grammaticalization (implicit > lexical > grammatical) rooted in the semantics of modality. M. Chini, 'Riferimento personale e strutturazione di testi narrativi in italofoni e in apprendenti tedescofoni di italiano', pp. 213–43 of *Grammatik und Diskurs. Studien zum Erwerb des Deutschen und des Italienischen/Grammatica e discorso. Studi sull'acquisizione dell'italiano e del tedesco*, ed. Norbert Dittmar and Anna Giacalone Ramat, Tübingen, Stauffenburg, 298 pp., compares the acquisition and use of Italian linguistic means for reference to person by adult learners of Italian (L1 German) and by Italian native speakers. An analysis of their types, forms, and cohesive functions demonstrates that language-specific preferences as to anaphora, cohesive patterns, and information organization tend to be acquired later than the principal morphological forms.

11. DIALECTOLOGY

NORTHERN DIALECTS. S. Schmid, 'Tipi sillabici nei dialetti dell'Italia settentrionale', *Atti* (Palermo), v, 613–25, examines a number of aspects of the phonotactic structure of northern Italian dialects through a contrastive analysis of syllabic repertories in Genoese, Piedmontese, Milanese, Romagnol, Venetian, Feltrino, and Friulan.

PIEDMONT. Maurizio Cabella, *Vocabolario del dialetto tortonese*, Alessandria, Orso, xviii + 277 pp. *Tradizione popolare e linguaggio colto nell'Ottocento e Novecento musicale piemontese. Atti del convegno, Alessandria, 15–16 aprile 1997*, ed. Maurizio Benedetti and Maria Titli, T, Centro Studi Piemontesi, 256 pp. + one compact disc. M. Parry, '*It capîssesto quaicòsa ti?*. La costruzione interrogativa in piemontese', pp. 295–307 of *J'At dij XII e XIII Rëscontr antërnassional dë studi an sla lenga e la literatua piemontèisa*, ed. Gianrenzo Clivio, Dario Pasaero, and Censin Pich, Ivrea, Ferraro, 378 pp., retraces the development of (WH- and Yes/No) interrogative structures from the earliest Piedmontese texts to the present day. In this lucid and succinct treatment, P. charts the near demise of the original inversion structure (*Co fe-tu?*) and the concomitant increase in strategies that dispense with verb movement, namely WH- + COMP structures (*Còsa ch'it veuele?*), clefting (*é-lo da s'i ch'as passa?*), and intonation (*Còs it l'hai fàit? it l'has vëddù tò barba?*). S. Canobbio, 'Baccagliare a Torino. Appunti di lavoro sul linguaggio giovanile', *RID*, 22:195–208, presents the preliminary results of an investigation into the language of young people carried out between 1995 and 1998 on a group of students from Turin University. R. Bauer, 'Storia della copertura linguistica della Valle d'Aosta dal 1860 al 2000: un approccio sociolinguistico', *NCEFRW*, 39:76–96, explores the development of plurilingualism in the Valle d'Aosta since Italian Unification. In particular, B. follows the changing fates of French and Italian as *roofing languages* in the area and the effects of such changes on the status and use of Francoprovençal and Piedmontese. The contemporary sociolinguistic situation in the Valle d'Aosta is explored in some detail by the same author in 'Aspetti del plurilinguismo in Valle d'Aosta/Vallée d'Aoste', *Atti* (Palermo), v, 31–45, which presents the results of an investigation into the role and significance of context, education, age, and gender as parameters in the use of Francoprovençal, Italian, and French. While Francoprovençal is the predominant language employed in informal situations, especially among men, Italian is shown to be gaining ground in all situations, especially among young educated women, while French, though now limited to specific situations, is shown to be still widely spoken.

LIGURIA. F. Toso, 'La componente ligure nel lessico capraiese', *ZRP*, 115:472–501, presents the results of an investigation into the lexis of the dialect spoken on Capraia, which due to its location and history proves particularly significant both in establishing the extent of Genoese linguistic influences on the island and in defining lexical correspondences among the three surrounding areas of Tuscany, Corsica, and Liguria. Id., 'Lessicografia genovese del sec. XVIII', *BALI*, 22, 1988:93–119. L. Coveri and P. Landini, 'Tassonomia popolare nei nomi dei pesci nel dialetto di Camogli', *Atti* (Palermo), v 185–98. W. Forner, 'La coniugazione interrogativa nei dialetti liguri', *ib.*, 319–36, documents the development of interrogative clitic inversion in the dialects of Liguria, tracing its areal distribution and the factors which led to its ultimate demise in the modern dialects.

VENETO. Gianna Marcato and Flavia Ursini, *Dialetti veneti. Grammatica e storia*, Padua, Unipress, vi + VI + 470 pp., provides an excellent structural survey of the dialects spoken in the Veneto. Organized in five sections ('Dialetto, storia, oralità'; 'Nome, aggettivo, articolo'; 'Il pronome'; 'Il Verbo'; 'Avverbio, preposizione, congiunzione'), this volume brings together a wealth of data from the main dialect areas, highlighting diachronic developments and differences between individual dialects, and drawing interesting comparisons with dialects of other regions.

EMILIA-ROMAGNA. Adelmo Masotti, *Grammatica romagnola*, Ravenna, Girasole, vi + 140 pp., despite the misleading title, is a traditional-style grammar of the dialect spoken in Ravenna. Though lacking in in-depth grammatical description, this volume contains useful notes on phonetics and orthography, morphology, and sentence structure, supplemented with a number of illustrative texts.

F. Marri, 'La lingua italiana a Ferrara', *Atti dell'Accademia delle Scienze di Ferrara*, 75:69–131, documents the use of dialect and Italian in the city through a close examination of available texts. S. Lazard, 'Il verbo denominativo in romagnolo: la questione della regolarità semantica del sistema derivativo', *RID*, 22:59–90, examines 232 deverbatives (pairs of verbs derived from a single noun) from Romagnol in an attempt to determine to what extent the meaning of a derivative can be predicted by the meaning of its base. In contrast to the somewhat 'chaotic' view of derivation maintained by Anglo-American studies, L.'s findings demonstrate that the meaning of 76% of the verbal pairs could be predicted from the semantics of the base noun, confirming the high degree of readability observed elsewhere within Romance in analogous contexts.

CENTRAL AND SOUTHERN DIALECTS. F. Sánchez Miret, 'Aspectos de la metafonía en los dialectos italianos. ¿Hubo realmente diptongación de /ɛ, ɔ/ condicionada por (-*i*, -*u*)?, *Atti* (Palermo), I, 361–69, is an attack on the generally accepted traditional Schuchardt-Schürr hypothesis which views the diphthongization of the low mid-vowels before final -*i* and -*u*, as witnessed in central and southern dialects, as a result of metaphony. F. Avolio, 'A sud della linea Roma–Ancona. Contatti e reazioni linguistiche nell'Italia centro–meridionale', *ib.*, V, 15–29, draws on phonetic, morphological, and lexical evidence from the dialects spoken in and around L'Aquila and the transitional zone between Lazio, Abruzzo, Molise, and Campania to demonstrate the non-homogeneous nature of the dialects spoken below the Rome–Ancona isogloss. M. Loporcaro, 'Il futuro CANTARE-HABEO nell'Italia meridionale', *AGI*, 84:67–114, refutes traditional claims that reflexes of CANTARE-HA(BE)O never took root in the dialects of southern Italy. In this brilliantly argued piece, L. reconsiders and reinterprets the geolinguistic, phonetic, and morphological evidence to show beyond any doubt that the synthetic future in the dialects of southern Italy must be considered an indigenous formation. This conclusion is further supported by detailed early textual analysis highlighting the preponderance of the synthetic future over the rival analytic HABERE + AD/DE + AB + infinitive construction, an observation clearly incongruent with the traditional thesis which views the former as a Tuscan literary import and the latter as the future marker *ab origine* in the South. Instead, L. sees the analytic construction as a later development, the grammaticalization of which as a marker of future time ultimately led in most cases to the specialization of the synthetic paradigm as a marker of epistemic modality, paralleled by a frequent reduction of the synthetic paradigm to the 3rd persons. R. Sornicola, 'Tra tipologia e storia: i pronomi soggetto e le colonie gallo-italiche', *Atti* (Palermo), V, 639–58, contrasts the morphological and syntactic development of subject pronouns in the southern Gallo-Italian dialects of Faeto and Guardia Piemontese on the one hand and those spoken in Sicily on the other. Observed differences between the two groups are argued to follow from differing socio-historical conditions: the more conservative nature of the mainland dialects is attributed to their 'comunità chiuse', while the more innovative nature of the pronominal systems of the Sicilian dialects is claimed to be a result of their being spoken in 'comunità aperte' where they were exposed to the external influences of the surrounding indigenous Sicilian dialects.

TUSCANY. B. Pacini, 'Il processo di cambiamento dell'indebolimento consonantico a Cortona: studio sociolinguistico', *RID*, 22:15–57, presents a quantitative study focusing on the possible realizations of voiceless occlusives in intervocalic position in the speech of the city of Cortona. P. observes that the introduction and spread of Florentine–Sienese spirantization within the city carries strong social overtones and is limited by speakers' age, social class, and gender.

THE MARCHES. A. Harder, 'La declinazione dei verbi in un dialetto di transizione nelle Marche', *Atti* (Palermo), v, 389–99, offers a much-awaited synchronic description and diachronic explanation of a typologically unique development within Romance concerning the inflectional paradigm of the verb in the dialect of Ripatransone. In addition to the usual person/number agreement, the Ripiano verb also presents the possibility of gender agreement with the subject (e.g. [vedu] 'I (masculine) see' vs [vede] 'I (feminine) see') and with a preposed object (e.g. [ia vedu karlu] 'I see Carlo' vs [ia lu veda] 'I see him'), not to mention the possibility of agreement configurations in conjunction with so-called invariable parts of speech (e.g., [ndovu va] 'where you (masculine) go' vs [ndove va] 'where you (feminine) go').

LAZIO. Luigi Cimarra, *Il dialetto di Sant'Oreste*, Sant'Oreste, Aperion, 203 pp., provides a valuable description of the principal phonetic characteristics of Santorestese, with some, albeit brief, notes on morphology and syntax, and two texts in transcription. In addition to an Italian translation of the original manuscript by W. Elwert, this edition contains detailed, supplementary notes by C. and a glossary.

CAMPANIA. A. Ledgeway, 'La ristrutturazione in napoletano', *Atti* (Palermo), II, 529–41, explores the obligatory nature of Neapolitan restructuring in conjunction with modals, aspectuals, and subject control verbs. Id., 'Asyndetic complementation in Neapolitan dialect', *The Italianist*, 17, 1997[1999]: 231–73, outlines the syntax of a marked finite verb + finite verb complementation pattern in conjunction with the verbs *jì* (go) and *venì* (come), tracing its emergence to the reinterpretation of an original infinitival structure. An appendix offers useful comparisons with three apparently similar paratactic structures attested in a wide range of other Italian dialects. CALABRIA. J. Trumper and A. Lombardi, 'Il ruolo della morfologia verbale nella determinazione di eteroglosse calabresi significative (ed eventuali ipotesi storiche)', *Atti* (Palermo), II, 815–26, draws on considerable evidence from the verbal morphology of the dialects of Calabria to argue for a quadripartite dialectal division of the region, already supported by analogous classifications based on previous phonetic and lexical investigations. SICILY. N. Bernardi, 'Soprannomi in Sicilia', *Atti* (Palermo), V, 59–67. A. Michel, 'Ispanismi di Sicilia. Alcune nuove possibilità d'interpretazione', *ib.*, 425–37. B. Rocco, 'Il giudeo-arabo e il siciliano nei secoli XII–XV: influssi reciproci', *ib.*, IV, 539–45. S. Trovato, 'Ancora su *mafia*', *ib.*, III, 919–25, provides further evidence to support Avolio's original proposal which retraces *mafiuso* (> *mafia*) to Arabic origin. D. Bentley, 'Alcune osservazioni sulla modalità nell'area di Palermo', *ib.*, V, 47–58, investigates the sociolinguistic, morphosyntactic, and semantic distribution of a number of modal forms in the dialects and Italian varieties spoken in the province of Palermo. Examples from the sound system, the morphosyntax, and the lexicon form the focus of the same author's attention in 'Language and dialect in modern Sicily', *The Italianist*, 17, 1997[1999]:204–30, which investigates the continuum between standard Italian and dialect, providing a valuable insight into the current sociolinguistic situation of the island. Although the standard undoubtedly enjoys the greatest prestige, B. concludes that the dialect is still very strong, with the great majority of the island's population exhibiting a degree of competence in several varieties/codes. S. Sgroi, 'Diasistema e variabilità diatopica e diacronica dell'articolo indeterminativo nel siciliano', *Atti* (Palermo), V, 627–37, confirms through a study of the forms of the indefinite article a degree of morphological variation similar to that encountered at the phonetic and lexical levels. In particular, S. identifies as many as five basic morphological systems in use in the various Sicilian dialects, together with six multiple systems incorporating various combinations of the basic systems.

## 12. SARDINIAN

H. Wolf, 'L'ancien sarde *\*kidere* et la langue des *condakes*', *RLiR*, 63:189–200, questions the authenticity of the reconstructed Logudorese verb *\*kidere* 'to concede', generally accepted since first proposed by Meyer-Lübke on the basis of 1sg. forms *chido/kido* attested in such formulae as *EGO iudice Mariane de Laccon chido* ... Through some impressive philological rereading of the texts in question, W. demonstrates that forms such as *chido* should be interpreted, rather, as the sequence *chi* (relative) + *do* ('I give'). I. Loi Corvetto, 'La Sardegna plurilingue e la politica dei Savoia', Sala Di Felice, *Sardegna*, 45–70, examines the linguistic attitudes and policies of the House of Savoy directed towards Sardinia following its annexation to the Kingdom in 1720. This period of domination heralds the beginning of a long, slow process of Italianization of the island, characterized by a relaxed and tolerant linguistic policy towards its plurilinguistic character which is argued to reflect an earlier, analogous linguistic policy adopted by Savoy in tackling the linguistic diversity of Piedmont. A. Mura Porcu, 'Aspetti linguistici del *Giornale di Sardegna* (1795–96)', *ib.*, 71–104, concentrates predominantly on the lexical characteristics of the language used in this 18th-c. Italian-language newspaper, highlighting its notably literary Tuscan style, as well as the frequent use of neologisms, Gallicisms, and Sardinian regionalisms. A. Dettori, 'Terminologie sarde settoriali: categorie semantiche e tassonomiche', *Atti* (Palermo), V, 237–51, examines the extent of areal, generational, and social variation in ichthyofaunistic terminology in various Sardinian dialects. A work of particular merit for its chronological and areal breadth of coverage is Giovanni Spano, *Vocabolariu sardu–italianu. Vocabolario italiano–sardo*, ed. Giulio Paulis, 4 vols, Nuoro, Ilisso, 421, 477, 351, 415 pp. First published between 1851 and 1852 in two volumes, this new edition incorporates 5,000 new entries taken from one of S.'s previously unpublished manuscripts.

## 13.　Italian Abroad

Arnold Cassola, *L'italiano di Malta. Storia, testi e documenti*, Malta U. P., 1998, 143 pp., brings together seven of the author's previously published articles in a single volume, offering a succinct, yet detailed, account of the vicissitudes of the Italian language in Malta through a large selection of texts and documents ranging from the 15th-c. to the present day. The seven chapters deal with a wide range of topics, including the external history of the language, southern dialect interferences, register and style, and the use of Italian during the French and English periods of rule of the Island. J. Cremona, ' "*Acciocché ognuno le possa intendere*". The use of Italian as a *lingua franca* on the Barbary Coast of the seventeenth century: evidence from the English', *JAIS*, 5, 1997:52–69, brings together a sample of texts unearthed in the Tunisian consular archives involving English residents in Tunis. The texts show evidence of an imperfect form of Tuscanized chancery Italian and abundant traces of the influence of French, Spanish, Catalan, and the various dialects of Italy.

C. Bettoni, 'Italiano e dialetti italiani fuori d'Italia', *RID*, 22:393–404, provides a broad overview of research over the last ten years on Italian and the dialects spoken outside Italy, noting the buoyant state of the field, as well as some specific areas, notably the acquisition of Italian and dialect as L2 and detailed sociolinguistic studies of various Italian regional groups, which continue to be largely overlooked. J. Vizmuller-Zocco, 'L'italiano in Canada: ai margini o al centro del cambiamento linguistico?', *Atti* (Palermo), v, 731–39, challenges the traditional thesis that contemporary changes in the language are not generally replicated by Italian varieties spoken abroad. Putting aside the notable exception of lexical innovation, V.-Z. draws on morphosyntactic evidence from Italian speakers living in Toronto to demonstrate that their language shares many of the innovations characteristic of varieties of *italiano popolare* spoken within Italy. N. Misti, 'Dialetto, italiano e inglese: due generazioni a confronto nella comunità calabrese di Sydney', *ib.*, 439–52, documents and offers some hypotheses on the on-going demise of dialect and Italian among a sample of 70 Calabrian immigrants and their offspring living in Sydney. A. Mocciaro, 'Su alcuni aspetti del rapporto tra dialetto e lingua nazionale: analisi linguistica di lettere di emigrati siciliani', *ib.*, 453–74, is a valuable analysis of the *italiano regionale popolare* documented in 20 letters from Sicilian immigrants living in North America and Australia. J.-E. Jahn, 'Il gruppo nazionale italiano (GNI) nel contesto etnolinguistico istriano', *RID*, 22:91–114, reports on the ethno- and sociolinguistic situation of the Italian minority in Istria which, following the political and social upheavals of the last decade, has witnessed significant changes in the language attitudes of the area, leading to a reinforcement of the regional Istrian identity.

## DUECENTO AND TRECENTO I
## DANTE

By CATHERINE M. KEEN, *Lecturer in Italian, University of Leeds*

### 1. GENERAL

1999 has seen a number of publications on Dante that broach questions appropriately anticipating the themes of Jubilee and anniversary and the millenarian dimensions so much discussed in many spheres on the eve of the third millennium. Several studies have, for instance, turned to D.'s cosmology, and looked at the physics and/or the theology of his vision of the universe. A particularly interesting study is W. Egginton's 'On Dante, hyperspheres, and the curvature of the medieval cosmos', *JHI*, 60: 195–216, a stimulating and accessible outline of consonances between modern scientific understandings of our universe as a hypersphere, and the cosmology of Dante's Empyrean. Descriptions of the Empyrean in the closing canti of *Par.* as being 'at once finite and boundless' (200) reveal how pre-Newtonian cosmology had a capacity to imagine place and space in ways that would be abolished by the Scientific Revolution, but which arrive at understandings almost parallel to those of modern mathematics and physics. E. argues persuasively that we should be wary of believing the extension of scientific knowledge to be inevitably linear and progressive, urging that the forms of imagination taken by, for instance, D.'s cosmology, remind the modern age of a need for intellectual flexibility and of the importance of remembering that what seems unthinkable today may prove thinkable tomorrow, and may have been equally thinkable in the more distant, but not less intellectually sophisticated, medieval past. If E. outlines an interest in modern approaches to D.'s science of the universe, there is also strong interest in the post-Newtonian world's understanding of D.'s theological concerns. Brief mention of D. is made in R. Girard, 'Literature and Christianity: a personal view', *PLit*, 23: 32–43, on the position of Christianity and literature in the post-modern and post-Christian age. His remarks underline the importance of the theme of conversion in many Christian, but also in ostensibly a-religious, writers (for instance, Proust). In the case of D., he focuses on the role of Virgil and stresses how the narrative of a descent into Hell, both literally and through the vehicle of profane literature (the *Aeneid*), is presented as a profoundly transformative, i.e. conversional, experience for D.-character and D.-poet. C. Moevs, 'God's feet and hands (*Paradiso* 4.40–48): non-duality and non-false errors', *MLN*, 114: 1–13, is a relatively short but dense article that has implications for the *DC* as a whole, besides the passage from *Par.* referred to in the title. Promised as a foretaste of what should prove an absorbing larger study, the article engages with debates over metaphysics and over reading strategies that pertain to fundamental Dantean considerations about truth and fiction. M. reminds us that the post-Enlightenment outlook on reality is essentially dualist and materialist, whereas D.'s world-view sees reality as 'ultimately one, and ultimately spiritual' (1): in the deiform universe duality must ultimately give way to unity. M. returns to the well-worn issue of allegory and urges that D.'s poem dissolves the distinctions between *historia* and *fabula*. Instead, it exercises a continuity with Scriptural reality that is embodied in such 'non-false errors' as the attribution of hands and feet to God, communicating 'non-contingent self-awareness ("truth")' through the 'spatio-temporal contingencies' of fiction (9). Further reflections on D.'s relationship to the Scriptures, to theology, and to the wider question of textual practice in reading and writing, are addressed by Peter S. Hawkins in *Dante's Testaments: Essays in Scriptural Imagination*, Stanford U.P., xvii + 378 pp. The majority of the essays (ch. five excepted) have appeared elsewhere in earlier versions; they are linked by their common exploration of aspects of D.'s attitude to the medieval intellectual heritage, whether that of the Bible, of the classical authors, or of contemporary vernacular narratives by preachers or pilgrims. D.'s authentication of his own texts by allusion to *auctoritates* such as Virgil and Ovid, or St John and St Augustine, is investigated through a number of stimulating *lecturae* of particular sequences. The *DC* also of course makes strong claims to originality, and Hawkins shows how D. continually draws attention to the poem's novelty, which makes it a new 'testament' (in the words of the title) to the Scriptural truths in which he wholeheartedly, and creatively, believes. H. suggests that, in the case of D., the Kierkegaardian distinction between the *personae* of 'genius' and 'apostle' cannot be applied: and that it is this double awareness of authority and tradition on the one hand, and of originality and individuality on the other, that makes D.'s poem perennially intriguing.

Another area in which millenarian concerns seem perhaps to emerge is that of *interpretazione esoterica*, with several recent publications in a decidedly mystical key. A common debt to the theories of Luigi Valli indicates the kind of approach that such publications take: indeed, V.'s work has itself been re-issued, with selections from his studies put together to form a canto-by-canto commentary to the *DC* in Luigi Valli, *Lo schema segreto del poema sacro*, Foggia, Bastogi, 1998, 168 pp.: the excerpts highlight his perennial concern with the 'allegorical architecture' of the *DC* and its use of the symbols of the cross and the eagle. The volume is published under the auspices of the 'Biblioteca Massonica'; and Primo Contro, *Dante templare e alchimista. La pietra filosofale nella Divina Commedia: Inferno*, Foggia, Bastogi, 1998, 204 pp., also forms part of this series. The opening chapters outline C.'s interest in astrological and alchemical lore, and in the possible role of the Templars in transmitting Cabbalistic lore to Western Europe, perhaps using Gothic architecture as an allegorical medium. The book proceeds largely as a canto-by-canto *lettura* of *Inf.*, outlining a theory that the poem forms part of an 'alchemical' project, transforming not lead to gold, but carnal man to spiritual man. In similar vein is another 'mystical' study, Mirko Mangolini, *Dante et la quête de l'âme*, Paris, Lanore, 191 pp., a reading of the *DC* which makes heavy use of numerology, and of theories of symmetrical correspondence, to produce a series of interpretative schemes for the poem, liberally illustrated with diagrams. M. draws on Jung, the Tarot, and the Grail legends, as well as more conventional Biblical and Aristotelian sources, in his interpretation of the *DC*, which again shows heavy debts to Valli. Adriano Lanza, \**Dante all'"Inferno'. I misteri eretici della 'Commedia'*, Ro, Tre Editori, 220 pp. Anniversaries of a Dantean rather than millenarian variety provide the occasion for G. Savino, 'Dante addentato', *Mazzoni Vol.*, 283–98, a delightful 'saggio paradantesco' (298) on the paleographical and philological detective work surrounding the creation and identification of two forged documents purporting to record D.'s involvements in street brawls, as the author or recipient of a bite to the hand. Anniversaries and their politics are also brought to our attention in S. Bellomo, 'Le prime vicende del sepolcro di Dante', *LC*, 28:55–71, which investigates the lengthy historical struggles between Florence and Ravenna for custody of the poet's remains. The article is mainly an investigation of the very early remodellings of the tomb in the course of the Trecento, and the problem of epitaphs; it also outlines a possible chronology for the composition, inscription, and erasure of three of the earliest known epitaphs to be associated with the sepulchre. An engagingly disparate series of musings on Dantean themes appears in M. Martelli, 'Alagheriana minima adnotanda', *Mazzoni Vol.*, 199–210, mostly relating to questions of sources.

The figure of Beatrice, and the question of the poet's varying depictions of his *donna* are addressed in several studies. Corrado Bologna, *Il ritorno di Beatrice: simmetrie dantesche fra Vita Nova, 'Petrose' e Commedia*, Ro, Salerno, 1998, 147 pp., addresses the problem of B.'s apparent absence during a whole arc of D.'s writing, from the middle of the *VN* to the end of the *Purg.*, beyond a few very brief allusions. The study argues that this absence is illusory — B. remains an essential presence in D.'s works — and outlines a series of precise textual and structural allusions through which the female protagonist of the *VN* continually re-emerges and is re-invented. The author stresses D.'s obsession with patterns of circle, repetition, and return: numbers, anniversaries, and reappearances provide circularities of theme, while lexis, citation, and above all metrics (from sonnet to *sestina* to *terza rima*) maintain patterns of repetition in his formal practice. Repetition by its nature involves rewriting: and the tight philological and textual arguments of this study show how D.'s revisions of language and idea at each re-use sketch a constant process of poetic *ripensamento*. By the time that B. returns in the *Purg.*, D. has recast not only his personal but also his poetic autobiography through constant intertextual reference (not only to his own works, but also in particular to the Bible and to Occitan works); and throughout the writing of the *DC*, he is shown to accumulate new senses retrospectively around his original texts. D. De Vita, 'Il segno di maggior disio', *Belfagor*, 54:147–69, pursues her thesis that B. is *not* to be identified as Bice Portinari, but as a figure of rich allegorical significance whose historical analogue is to be found in the person of Piccarda Donati. The B. described in the *VN* offers clear points of similarity to P., the would-be nun dedicated to Franciscan principles of *imitatio Christi* (which De V. suggests would have particular appeal to a D. whom she believes to have at least toyed with a Franciscan vocation); while the book's constant concern with *Amore* is argued to reveal a Franciscan dedication to *charitas*. In the *DC*, the distinction between an allegorical B.-guide and the historical P.-*personaggio* encountered in *Par.* III, which might seem confusing, is in De V.'s view corroborative: the name of P. relates to the exemplary individual, but the name of B. refers to her reality *sub specie aeternitatis*, as typological reminder of spiritual concerns; when 'B.' is indicated as 'segno di maggior disio', D. invites the reader to realize that it is an allegorical *senhal*.

The relevance of D. to modern debates over the nature and purpose of literature and of literary criticism is emphasized in the lively article by G. Johnson, 'A tongue of one's own: Dante, Bloom and Gates', *DaSt*, 115, 1997[1999]:251–72. Taking Harold Bloom and Henry Louis Gates Jr. as representatives of what might be termed the opposing poles of the controversy, J. shows that both views can make a very convincing 'claim' on D. Bloom has placed him almost at the centre of the 'Western Canon' and made him a powerful example in his defence of the traditions of aesthetic criticism. But J. argues that, despite D.'s academic canonization, and his undeniable membership of the ranks of 'dead white European males', he is in many ways a writer who addresses concerns expressed by Gates vis-à-vis questions of black writing and black criticism. The article makes

the thought-provoking suggestion that, just as defence of the vernacular, a language of low literary status, and of marginalized and
disempowered political communities, is of central importance to
contemporary black (and Hispanic, female, working-class, etc.) critics
within the American academy, so it is to D. himself, whether writing
as critic in the *DVE*, self-commentator in the *Cvo*, or poet in the *DC*.
His linguistic theory and practice both reveal a 'public', i.e. political
and partisan, side to D.'s endeavour in the *DC*, however much we
may also recognize it to be a work whose inner and 'private' qualities
have qualified it for inclusion in B.'s canon of works to be addressed
via a depoliticized and aesthetic approach.

A number of interesting studies relating to questions of intertextuality and narrativity appear in the collection Picone, *Dante*, also
valuable because it reproduces the spoken responses to each of the
conference papers and the concluding round-table discussion
(421–39). A number of articles give consideration to aspects of D.'s
uses of classical myth. The opening contribution, M. Picone, 'Dante
e i miti' (21–32), offers a general survey of the manner in which
D. plays on classical legend and considers the implications this has
for his poetics. P. studies the consistency with which D. uses myth,
particularly the stories of Ovid's *Metamorphoses*, to provide 'allegorical'
or 'fictional' references for the spiritual truths that his own text
conveys, going well beyond standard medieval moralization. The
metamorphoses that D. describes are (at least according to the poem's
fiction) realized literally and historically in the experiences of the
protagonist, allowing his new text not merely to echo or reprise the
classical author, but almost typologically to complete meanings about
human experience that Ovid himself could approach only allegoric-
ally. Z. G. Barański, 'Notes on Dante and the myth of Orpheus'
(133–54), updates his study of the O. myth reviewed in last year's
*YWMLS* entry. P. Boitani, 'Dall'ombra di Ulisse all'ombra d'Argo'
(207–26), offers another of his stimulating reflections on the two great
seafaring myths in D.'s poem and on their D.-filtered appearance
elsewhere, notably in Joyce. He stresses the importance of the
questions about human nature raised by D.'s U. and shows how
obstacles to interpretation raised by the U. episode are resolved via
allusion to the myth of the Argonauts, which in *Par.* especially
provides a counterbalancing example of a divinely-sanctioned
exploration of the unknown. D. Clay, 'The metamorphosis of Ovid
in Dante's *Commedia*' (69–85), suggests that it is O., not Virgil, who
provides the inspiration for D.'s 'new' poetry in the *Purg.* and *Par.* The
prominent allusions in the opening cantos of these two *cantiche* to the
Ovidian myths of Calliope, Marsyas, and Glaucus are all concerned
with the transmutation of corporeal reality (whether negatively or

positively) through poetic activity, in ways that bear clear relation to D.'s claims about the transformative message that his own poem conveys. C. Kleinhenz, 'Mito e verità biblica in Dante' (367–89), investigates the way in which D. employs citations, references, and claims about his own creative activity to assert a Biblical and truthful textuality for his poem (as opposed to the allegorical veracities of profane literature). Thoughtful general observations are accompanied by more specialized discussions of D.'s readings of Scripture, which investigate his use of citation and allusion, and also his highly visual imagery, which often seems similarly to 'cite' the iconographic conventions of religious painting and sculpture. L. Pertile, 'L'albero che non esiste' (163–77), is an extract from *La puttana e il gigante*. K. Stierle, 'Mito, memoria e identità nella *Commedia*' (185–201), explores D.'s use of myth (especially classical and Biblical stories) in relation to his conception of history, paying especial attention to the interaction of the particular and the universal, or allegorical, in his approach to the legends of the past and the contemporary worlds. G. Güntert, 'Dante autobiografo: dal mito religioso al mito poetico' (117–26). J. Pépin, 'La théorie dantesque de l'allégorie, entre le *Convivio* et la *Lettera a Cangrande*' (51–64), offers a comparative reading of the apparently rather different understanding of the forms and functions of allegory (poetic/theological, double/quadruple) in the two texts. E. Pasquini, 'Il mito dell'amore: Dante fra i due Guidi' (283–95), looks at D.'s self-positioning with regard to the stylistic and thematic concerns of Guinizelli and Cavalcanti, and their doctrines of *Amore*. D.'s creation of mythology with a political emphasis receives distinguished attention. P. Armour, 'Il mito del paradiso terrestre: rinnovamento della società mondiale' (341–54), focuses on the myth of the Earthly Paradise and on the allegorical pageant of the *Purg.*'s closing sequence. Besides their anagogical or eschatological significance, regarding humanity's collective return to Edenic innocence, A. argues that, in the light of *Mon.* III.xv, they have terrestrial (philosophical and political) implications. The essay emphasizes D.'s combination of a sense of specific historical urgency about the need for regeneration in the contemporary world, with more abstract, almost a-historical conceptions of renewal based on the mythology of the Golden Age or New Jerusalem. J. Ferrante, 'History is myth, myth is history' (317–33), investigates what might be termed D.'s historiographic practice, placing it within the context of the many forms of historical writing and the many views about what constitutes historicity, prevalent in the medieval world. She examines the way in which veracity, or at any rate credibility, was constructed within various different forms of historiography, normally with a morally or politically didactic intent, and shows D. to share such concerns, making the question of sources and verification of only secondary importance to a poet who manipulates fact to his own creative ends. J. A. Scott, 'Il mito dell'imperatore negli scritti danteschi' (89–105), offers a stimulating study, which draws together passages from *Cvo*, the political letters, the *Mon.* and the *DC*, to stress the essential compatibility of the ideas presented in these chronologically and formally diverse texts. It underlines the consistency with which D. presents the emperor as *Christomimetes*, and sheds light on the 'political theology' (Kantorowicz, 1957) of several symbols associated with imperial issues in the *DC* (the *Veltro*, the Griffin, etc.). S. shows that the journey of the *DC* may be divided into two main stages, with the protagonist's guides representing the activities of empire and papacy defined in *Mon.* iii.xv: Virgil, often the mouthpiece of Aristotelian philosophy, takes D. to the Earthly Paradise, while Beatrice guides him on to the Empyrean.

Studies placing D. within the context of the culture of his own age always enrich our understanding of the poem's importance to the present day. A fine example of a detailed philological and historical study of both the letter and the spirit of Dante's texts is provided by Claudio Giunta, *La poesia italiana nell'età di Dante: la linea Bonagiunta-Guinizelli*, Bo, Il Mulino, 390 pp., which explores D.'s place on the poetic 'scene' of the late Duecento and early Trecento. G. engages with the persistent problems raised by D.'s categorizations, in the *DVE* and in *Purg.* xxiii-xxvi, of contemporary poetic practice. He argues that we should not treat these as sacrosanct, nor even necessarily reliable, and provides detailed surveys of B.'s and G.'s output which suggest that D.'s assignation of the two to separate and opposing 'schools' was either uninformed or deliberately misleading. The book, with its scholarly survey of B.'s and G.'s verse, makes an important contribution to the study not only of D. but of the early Italian lyric in general. Medieval rhetorical classifications are also explored by Z. G. Barański, in ' "'nfiata labbia" and "dolce stil novo"': a note on Dante, ethics, and the technical vocabulary of literature', *Mazzoni Vol.*, 17–35, a dense and stimulating study of D.'s employment of the technical vocabulary of literature and of its implications for the way in which the *DC* should be read. An initial brief survey of *Inf.* vii's description of Pluto's "'nfiata labbia' shows how D.'s terminology often makes connections between rhetorical and ethical categories. The main substance of the article deals with *Purg.* xxiv's designation of 'Donne ch'avete' as written in a 'dolce stil novo'. The survey of both this canto, and the relevant passages of the *VN*, suggests that the terms refer to the debate over *leu* ('dolce') vs *clos* ('aspro') styles, and may imply criticism of D.'s own practice at the time of the *canzone*'s composition, when over-rigid regard for the rules of the *genera dicendi* led him to obfuscate the moral status of his experiences. Only in the 'mixed' or 'comic' style(s) of the *DC* does D. achieve a correspondence between stylistic accessibility (*leu* or *dolce*) and moral veracity, and become a true scribe at the inspiration of *Amore* (God). G. Chiecchi, 'Dante e la *consolatio*', *AIV*, 157:91–122, explores D.'s deployment of the conventions of Christian *consolatio* to explore the relationship between sorrow and faith, especially in the *VN* and *Cvo*. Although less prominent in the *DC*, where destinies are immutable and hence outside the ambit of consolation, some interestingly parodic uses are identified in the *Inf.* in particular, which also suggest intertextual allusion to the *petrose*. G. Ledda, 'L'impossibile *convenientia*: topica dell'indicibilità e retorica dell'*aptum* in Dante', *LS*, 34:449–69, also explores the areas of rhetoric and genre, regarding D.'s observances of and divergences from the medieval rules of *convenientia* — including those he himself elaborates in the *DVE*. The article shows how the poem's 'mixed' style, and its reworkings of the ineffability topos in application to 'mixed' subjects, outline what may be seen as a new theory of *convenientia*, punctuated in turn by declarations of what L. calls *indicibilità retorica* (466), which indicates the limitations not of language itself but of the apt correspondence between style and subject that is prescribed even by the new poetics of the *DC*. D.'s poetics are also under discussion in J. A. Scott, ' "Veramente li teologi questo senso prendono altrimenti che li poeti" (*Convivio* II.i.5)', *Mazzoni Vol.*, 299–320, a sustained investigation of how D. understands theological versus poetic allegory to function.

D.'s position vis-à-vis medieval science and natural philosophy is explored in the work of S. Gilson, notably in his 'Dante and the science of "perspective": a reappraisal', *DaSt*, 115, 1997[1999]: 185–219. The 'reappraisal' takes as its point of departure Parronchi's long-canonical 1959 study of D.'s knowledge of contemporary *scientia perspectiva* and argues for a substantial revision of many of P.'s conclusions. It provides an impressively detailed survey of 13th-c. optical and *perspectiva* theory, covering both specialist works on natural philosophy, and on theology, and vulgarizations in the form of sermons or verse in the vernacular. Through close analysis of particular passages from the *Cvo* and *DC* in particular, G. shows that past estimates of D.'s scientific knowledge have exaggerated its technical and specialist quality. G. concludes that D. does not show specific awareness of the most up-to-date contemporary thinking and that his references may be plausibly explained as deriving from sources easily accessible to the layman: the innovative quality of D.'s optical observations lies less in their technical aspect and more in the poet's ever-ready linguistic and thematic inventiveness, the impressive scope of which emerges very strongly from this study.

## 2. FORTUNE

There have been numerous studies relating to the early reception. G. C. Alessio, 'Sul *Comentum* di Benvenuto da Imola', *LC*, 28:73–94, discusses the methods and intentions of B.'s commentary against the context of contemporary practice. The article investigates the vexed issue of B.'s Latinity (denounced by Salutati as an unworthy to accompany D.'s text), stressing that its deliberate (if to humanist eyes inelegant) closeness to the vernacular is dictated by choice, not incapacity, given the pragmatic demands of B.'s principal form of delivery, the university lecture, and is comparable to other Trecento university practice. N. Bianchi, 'Tasso lettore di Dante: teoresi retorica e prassi poetica', *MR*, 12, 1998[1999]:223–47, looks not only at *dantismi* in T., but at the nature of the process by which he selects and reflects upon these linguistic, stylistic, and rhetorical allusions; with some reflection on his engagement with D.'s theories of allegory. D. Delcorno Branca, 'Percorsi danteschi del Poliziano', *LItal*, 51:360–82, investigates both P.'s position in the 15th-c. debates over D.'s place in the literary tradition, and the significance of 'occorrenze dantesche' (whether explicit or unacknowledged) in P.'s own work. She traces patterns of allusion to *Purg.* and *Inf.* in particular, which suggest that P. treats the *DC* as an 'enciclopedia degli stili' (375) and an important source of imagery. She also investigates P.'s use of D. as both *auctor* and *auctoritas* in his work on classical literature in the Florentine Studium, which offers additional indications about the significance that P. was prepared to accord D. as poet and as philosopher. A. Mazzucchi, 'Da Benvenuto a Matteo Chiromono: riproduzione e rifacimento', *FC*, 24:3–32, returns to the question of the commentary tradition, showing that adaptations from B.'s *Comento* of the kind C. operates in his version reflect engagement with and esteem for the text at a fairly serious scholarly level, even in the age of humanism. P. Pasquino, 'Nuovi appunti sulla tradizione dell'*Ottimo Commento*', *MR*, 12, 1998[1999]: 121–41, investigates the philological questions raised by Ageno's (1982) revision of Rocca's (1891) account of the *OC*'s textual tradition, showing that the conclusions of both may be reconciled by hypothesizing two distinct traditions of transmission for the single original composition. L. C. Rossi, 'Il Commento dantesco di Graziolo Bambaglioli', *LC*, 28:43–54, is an informative contribution on the *Commento*, and the phases of its production. R. suggests that the commentary, which can seem simplistic and over-moralizing to the modern reader, offers insights into the nature of the *DC*'s early reception, and especially its status in the university milieu of B.'s native Bologna: and argues that its errors and omissions indicate, not defective understanding on B.'s part, but his eagerness to provide an *apologia* for an author then the subject of much controversy at Bologna over points of politics, of theological orthodoxy, and of scientific learning. A. Vallone, 'Carlo d'Aquino, traduttore di Dante', *Mazzoni Vol.*, 321–29, deals with the techniques d'A. typically adopted in his study of D.'s similes, and in his translation of the *DC* into Latin, noting how the demands of the translator's seventeenth-century Jesuit milieu constrain his rhetorical and thematic choices, despite the sensitivity to the complexities of D.'s language and metaphorical practice that V. finds in d'A.'s introductory comments to his works. C. Vasoli, 'Noterelle "ficiniane" su Trifone Gabriele', *ib.*, 331–44, traces a marked Ficinian influence over the Platonist strand in G.'s *Annotationi su Dante*.

For D.'s later *fortuna*: M. and U. Hollender, 'Die deutsche Dante-Rezeption 1933–1945 in Publizistik und Wissenschaft: Zwischen politischer Instrumentalisierung und menschlicher Integrität', *DDJ*, 74:13–84, examines the thorny issues of the extent and nature of the 'Fascistization' of D. criticism in Germany during the Nazi period. The article surveys the propagandist (and occasionally racist) readings of passages from D., both to bolster the Rome-Berlin accord, and to denigrate Germany's opponents, at a popular and a more intellectual level; and it shows a pattern of systematic 'Germanization' of D. and his political views in both journalistic and academic criticism. F. Salvadori, 'L'*Inferno* redento: William Blake interprete di Dante', *LItal* 51:567–92, argues for the importance of treating B.'s visual reception of D. on an equal footing with verbal criticism. She underlines the interpretative significance of many of B.'s artistic choices in the illustrations to the *DC* (for example, the depiction of D.-*personaggio* as an Everyman, rather than following the portrait tradition) and reveals at times unexpected affinities between two artists whose works set out universal and transcendent moral schemes, at times *lacunae* in sympathy and comprehension that make B. radically 're-write' D. through the production of new symbolic images to represent his own interpretations of the text.

COMPARATIVE STUDIES. Essays covering the Trecento to the early modern period: V. Branca, 'Consacrazioni e dissacrazioni dantesche nel *Decameron*: una lettera a Francesco Mazzoni', *Mazzoni Vol.*, 53–63, is a highly personal, almost conversational musing on Boccaccio's relationship to D. The essay first draws attention to B.'s use of irony in allusions to D., illustrated by a *lettura* of *Decam*. IV.2 as a parodically intertextual rewriting of D.'s exile lyrics for Lisetta, in which the use of Venetian dialect and allusions reinforces his textual subversions. The second point concerns changes in B.'s Dantean borrowings over time, describing how a comparative reading of the earliest with the later redactions of the *Decameron* show a steady diminution of textual *dantismi*. R. E. Edwards, 'The desolate palace and the solitary city: Chaucer, Boccaccio and Dante', *SP*, 96:394–416, looks at intertextual echoes of *Lamentations* in all three writers and at the chain of increasingly parodic intertextual references from D. to B. to C. With regard to D., the author focuses on the citations and imagery from Jeremiah in the *VN*, revealing its typological reading of *Lamentations* in tandem with the *Song of Songs*, whereby loss and desolation are accompanied by an assurance of future redemption. By inscribing these Christian typological concerns into narratives about erotic love, all three writers raise serious points about the nature and purpose of amorous relationships, and of profane literature. W. Franke, ' "Enditynges of worldly vanitees": truth and poetry in Chaucer as compared with Dante', *ChRev*, 34:87–106, investigates the different attitudes of C. and D. towards the truth-bearing qualities of fictional texts. He suggests that the gap between the two authors in generation and cultural milieu finds a dichotomy also in their capacity to see a synthesis between faith and reason: this is possible in the Thomist intellectual framework familiar to D., but not in C.'s skeptical, Ockhamite outlook. M. W. Musgrove, 'Cyclopean Latin: intertextual readings in Dante's *Eclogues* and Góngora's *Polifemo y Galatea*', *CML*, 18 (1998):125–36, reads the Polyphemus reference in D.'s *Ec.*s as alluding not, or not only, to political considerations, but as part of the linguistic and stylistic debate which forms the basis of his and Giovanni del Virgilio's exchanges. Playing on the two most famous classical references to P. that he knew (Virgil's violent ogre, Ovid's amorous but still menacing figure), D. uses his allusion to engage with questions about genre (epic, pastoral) and register (comic, tragic) that his classical *auctoritates* had also confronted. M.'s comparative reading of allusions to the same episode in G. provides consolidation for this argument; and she concludes that both poets use the reference to continue a classical debate over levels of style and genre, whilst also asserting the validity of modern, vernacular poetic enterprises. A. Villa, ' "Molto egli oprò con 'l senno e con la mano": esempi di ricontestualizzazioni dantesche nella *Gerusalemme Liberata*', *LItal*, 51:27–51.

Comparative studies for the nineteenth and twentieth centuries: E. C. Brown, 'Boyd's Dante, Coleridge's *Ancient Mariner*, and the pattern of infernal influence', *Studies in English Literature*, 38 (1998): 647–67, suggests that the Dantean presences in the *AM* may be more extensive and more carefully plotted than previously appreciated. In particular, he points out several correspondences between the Mariner and D.'s Ulysses and Charon figures, and suggests that his 'inhospitably' (in C.'s words) killing the albatross finds a punishment corresponding to that of D.'s traitors in Cocytus who abuse the laws of hospitality (*Inf.* xxxiii). The parallels in language and imagery to B.'s often un-Dantean translation are especially emphasized. F. Bruni, 'Dante e Byron: un incontro ravennate', *LC*, 28:95–153, is an article densely packed with information on B.'s activities, literary, amorous, and political, at Ravenna. The Dantean part focuses primarily on the composition, publication, and translation into Italian of *The Prophecy of Dante*, relating its composition to the context of early 19th-c. Italian political and literary events and debates. The notable edn George Byron, *La profezia di Dante. Testo inglese con le traduzioni di Michele Leoni e Lorenzo Da Ponte*, ed. Francesco Bruni and Loretta Innocenti, Ro, Salerno, 253 pp., has a substantial introductory essay. F. Bugliani-Knox, '*Galeotto fu il libro e chi lo scrisse*: nineteenth-century English translations, interpretations and reworkings of Dante's Paolo and Francesca', *DaSt*, 115, 1997[1999]:221–50, highlights the way in which 19th-c. cultural preoccupations — whether of Romantics, Victorians, or *fin-de-siècle* decadents — conditioned its reception, and shows how modern criticism finds reworkings of the episode (in painting, verse, drama, etc.) acceptable as autonomous products of their own cultural milieux, but is far less tolerant of 19th-c. attempts at its translation. The latter's typical shortcomings are surveyed via the example of the much-mistranslated *Galeotto* reference, frequently rendered with 'pander', or even 'Galahad'. The article closes with the commendation of two versions (Byron's and D. G. Rossetti's), where knowledge of Italian language and culture made for both accuracy and sensitivity. D. Caselli, '"L'andar su che porta?": Dante nel primo Beckett', *The Italianist*, 18, 1998[1999]:130–54, concentrates particularly on D.'s fluid and constantly shifting presence in two early works, the *Dream of Fair to Middling Women* and *More Pricks than Kicks*. Their *dantismi* reveal patterns of allusion between not only B.'s and D.'s works, but between and within B.'s own texts, which promote reflection upon the nature of authorship and of *auctoritas* in and through both writers' creative practices. F. O'Gorman, 'Ruskin's *The Art of England*, and Aeschylus', *NQ*, 244:479–80, argues that R.'s reference to A. as a guide in the *Inf.* is not the result of confusion, but reflects his knowledge of the Cary translation in which several Aeschylan parallels to Dantean passages and images are underlined. R. Preda, 'D. G. Rossetti and Ezra Pound as translators of Cavalcanti: poetic choices and the representation of women', *TrLit*, 8:217–34, whilst predominantly concerned with C., points out that the approaches of both translators are affected in turn by their estimation of D., R.'s interest being conditioned almost exclusively by his concern with D. and with the translation of the *VN*, P. instead urging C.'s primacy not simply amongst the *stilnovisti* in general, but also in relation to Dante. J. N. Serio, 'Frost's *Fire and Ice* and Dante's *Inferno*', *The Explicator*, 57:218–21, argues that the moral system outlined in F.'s lyric shows correspondences to that of D.'s Hell. M. S. Titone, 'Mario Luzi: Dante mio contemporaneo', *NA*, 583, provides the text of an engaging interview with L. in which he reflects on the importance of D. for his own poetic career, and on the place of D. in the developments of 20th-c. poetry, both inside and outside Italy.

## 3. Textual Tradition

A. Castellani, 'Sul codice Laurenziano Martelliano 12', *Mazzoni Vol.*, 85–97, presents a new thesis on the provenance of the MS, which contains texts from the *VN* and the *Rime*, assigning it Gubbian origins. D. De Robertis, 'Sul testo delle canzoni del *Convivio*', *ib.*, 105–12, examines the editorial problems raised by the multiple transmissions of the *canzoni*, identifying at least three different possible forms of textual tradition: as isolated lyric works, or as constituent texts of the *Cvo* — and in the latter case, either as the head-of-chapter transcriptions *in extenso*, or as the single lines quoted within the commentaries. De R. discusses the difficulties this presents for investigations of the relationship between citations of the *verba* (lyric text) and of their *sententiae* (commentary text) within MSS of the *Cvo* itself. D. Robey, 'Counting syllables in the *Divine Comedy*: a computer analysis', *MLR*, 94:61–86, investigates the principles of syllable scansion in the *DC*, examining the incidence of regularity versus irregularity within D.'s overall practice. The article provides an insight into the way that R. employs the resources of modern computer technology to provide a systematic definition of D.'s tendencies; and, in producing a very thorough survey of the incidence of *dieresi*, *dialefe*, *sinaresi*, and *sinalefe*, moves towards the longer-term aim of quantifying the stylistic effect that D.'s practice tends to produce, through the consideration of specific examples. Id., 'Rhythm and metre in the *Divine Comedy*', *Lepschy Vol.*, 100–16, addresses the problem of finding a systematic method of representing the *DC*'s accentual rhythm, with some reflections on problems relating to rhythmic variation around issues such as caesura, punctuation, and irregularity, especially in view of the varying requirements of computer analysis vs oral recitation. F. Sanguineti, 'Prolegomeni all'edizione critica della *Comedìa*', *Mazzoni Vol.*, 261–82, surveys the MSS used by himself and by Barbi in the preparation of critical editions of the *DC* and proposes a *stemma codicum* of the seven MSS he identifies as being free from the influence of the so-called 'tradizione ß'.

## 4. Minor Works

On the *VN*: G. Gorni, '*Vita nova*, libro delle "amistadi" e della "prima etade" di Dante', *ib.*, 113–27, argues that the 'nova" of the *VN*'s rubric refers not to religious-amorous 'renewal', but to the author's age during its principal events, corresponding to the 'prima etade' or 'adolescenza' period described in the *Cvo*. 'Adolescenza' is characterized as the age when friendships are formed, and G. identifies five important 'amistadi' described in the *VN*, all bearing on D.'s activities as both poet and lover of Beatrice. In conclusion, G. suggests that D. may have divided his other first-person narratives according to the ages they represent: D.'s remarks on the *Cvo*'s 'virile' style, and the *DC*'s reference to the 'mezzo del cammin', suggesting that they jointly represent first and second phases within the arc of 'gioventute'. P. Nasti, 'La memoria del *Canticum* e la *Vita nuova*: una nota preliminare', *The Italianist*, 18, 1998[1999]: 14–27, approaches the debate over possible sources or models for the *VN* with the argument that the *Song of Songs*, particularly in relation to its medieval exegesis, provides one of the text's 'modelli fondanti'. Like the *Song*, the letter of the *VN*'s amorous content is revealed via learned gloss and commentary to have higher, spiritual senses, and through comparisons with the allegorization of the *Song* by medieval theologians, N. outlines the way in which D. structures his book as a virtual rewriting of the Biblical text and gloss into a contemporary vernacular form. B. Porcelli, '*Vita nova* 18, 19, 20: il motivo della privazione e un passo controverso', *SPCT*, 58:83–87, focuses on the paragraphs describing the death of B. (numbering follows Gorni's new edn, reviewed last year), with their repeated allusions to solitude and deprivation and citations of Jeremiah. In relation to the question why describing B.'s death should make D. 'laudatore di me medesimo', P. refers to the episode's obsessive employment of calendrical references, and suggests that the cult of anniversaries and of number symbolism already established within the text creates a danger that the episode will become associated with Gemini, the birth-sign of D. himself, and so distract attention away from B., and from the Christological references outlined by Jerusalemic citations, to which all other allusions in the sequence are deliberately dedicated. Id, 'Numeri, strutture, errore e *conversio* nella *Vita Nova*', *FC*, 24:90–100, addresses similar concerns, again basing his arguments on the insights offered by Gorni's renumbering of paragraphs. Here he engages with the issue of numerology in the text as a whole. Besides the well-known association of B. with the number nine (and its square root three), he suggests that D. uses the number 10 to indicate himself and his work; and that the number four and its root two are used for themes of miscomprehension and disharmony (two screen-ladies, two premonitions of B.'s death, etc.). The article also explores issues of structure, and the careful balancing of episodes, focusing especially on the theme of pilgrimage, and the presentation of spirituality and conversion in the final paragraphs, between the 'Deh peregrini' and 'Oltre la spera' sonnets. G. E. Sansone, 'Appunti esegetici su *Donne ch'avete intelletto d'amore*', *La parola del testo*, 3:85–90, explores D.'s placing of the *canzone* within the love tradition, especially in relation to Occitanic literature. He points particularly to D.'s interest in B. as a *domna* figure (associated with *gentilezza* and banishing *villania*), and also explores the deployment of terms that had acquired key significance in the value system of the Provençal poets, arguing that this web of referents establishes the *intelletto d'amore* shared by the ladies D. addresses as a specific value system created and transmitted through literary texts.

On the *Rime*: E. Gragnani, 'La revisione della produzione guittoniana nelle rime dantesche', *EL*, 24.1:39–57, provides an intertextual exploration of the presence of G. in D.'s *Rime*, both in the *VN* and in the *canzoni* of the *Cvo* and the exile period. The article concentrates especially on the two poets' divergent stances over the moral status of love and love poetry, but finds evidence for respectful, as well as critical, receptions of Guittonian practice in D's lyric verse.

On the *Mon*: G. Padoan, ' "Alia utilia reipublice": la composizione della *Monarchia* di Dante', *LC*, 28:7–27, offers a series of arguments for the dating of the text to the very end of D.'s life (around 1320), using various types of evidence. He draws on considerations regarding political concerns expressed in other works, notably the *Cvo*, and a change of views traced within the *DC* between *Inf.* and *Par.*; on evidence regarding the nature and chronology of D.'s later writing from D.'s contemporaries, especially Giovanni del Virgilio and Boccaccio; and, especially, on historical references and the time-indicators of verb tenses, within the text of the *Mon.* itself.

On the *Epistles*: L. Pertile, 'Dante looks forward and back: political allegory in the Epistles', *DaSt*, 115, 1997[1999]:1–17, lucidly outlines the context within which the three political letters were composed, as regards both D.'s personal and political circumstances and the wider field of Italian politics, and demonstrates that the political views set out in the letters are in many ways ones that modern sensibility would have to regard as reactionary, intolerant, and highly unrealistic. But P. also recalls the pitfalls of such judgements, and provides illuminating readings of many of the letters' allegorical passages, which stress

D.'s tendency to treat all human events from an eschatological viewpoint, submitting Christian and classical texts alike to figural interpretation, so as to urge humanity towards 'the restoration of a totally Christian society' (16). P.'s lively study helps remind us that it is due to historical chance that D. was forced to pursue this goal in exile by means of the composition of the *DC*, rather than by a successful political career within the Ghibelline and reactionary Florence that the political letters wish to establish.

On the *Quaestio*: Z. G. Barański, 'The mystery of Dante's *Questio de aqua et terra*', *Lepschy Vol.*, 146–64, addresses the puzzle of why D. interrupted the composition of his professed masterwork, the *DC*, to address a minor, and apparently tangential, point of academic debate. The article argues that the treatise provides in fact supporting argument for the views expressed in the poem and is intended to be read in conjunction with the bigger project. This overturns recent critical suggestions that the *Quaestio* retracts the poem's cosmological proposals: in fact, B. argues that the treatise mounts a subtle and concise attack on those rationalist philosophers who refused to accept a miraculous explanation of phenomena within the created universe and draws together D.'s poetic and philosophical interests in an intellectual exposition of the cogency of arguments he elsewhere presented in poetic form.

On the *Fiore*: G. Breschi, 'Ancora sul *Fiore* CCXI 13', *Mazzoni Vol.*, 65–74, discusses one of the *Fiore*'s most famous textual *cruces*, and provides extensive philological discussion to back up a suggested emendation of the line's final word from 'dura' to 'nome'.

## 5. COMEDY

Marc Cogan, *The Design in the Wax: The Structure of the Divine Comedy and its Meaning*, Notre Dame U.P., xxiv + 396 pp., is a study of the poetic programme of the *DC* that is almost dauntingly vast in scope. The introduction assures us that no single episode of the *DC* can be rightly understood without consideration of its place within the tightly organized overall structure of D.'s afterworld, with its hierarchies of sin and virtue, and that this in turn requires a thorough investigation of medieval Aristotelianism (especially via Aquinas) to be understood. Fortunately, C. proves able to deliver such exposition clearly and engagingly, and to generate real excitement about the coherent intellectual and poetic scheme that he views as structuring the poem; although any return to questions over the extent and nature of D.'s epistemological debt to Aristotle and Aquinas risks causing controversy at some point. The detail and complexity of his arguments are punctilious, taking a case-by-case and *cantica*-by-*cantica* approach to the problems of defining and ordering human weaknesses and strengths, and of recognizing the failures in both intellect and will that need to be addressed in conversion. He suggests that poetry, prominent from the opening of the *DC* thanks to the figure of Virgil, as well as to the many reflections on the poetic act of D.-*poeta*, is valorized within this overall structure because of its capacity to provide the *dulcis* as well as the *utilis*, attracting will as well as reason to the truths presented in the text.

More student-oriented studies include: Riccardo Merlante, *Il Dizionario della 'Commedia'*, Bo, Zanichelli, 1999, 320 pp., a compact reference work, with an accessible series of entries that cover a wide range of possible avenues. Besides entries on the *DC*'s protagonists, its references to proper names (historical, geographical, mythological, etc.), and the structure of D.'s afterworld, it includes information on D.'s life, works, and place in the contemporary literary world, on the *DC*'s sources and antecedents, on much of its astronomical, scientific, philosophical, and rhetorical terminology, and on its principal commentators and illustrators. Whilst gaps can inevitably be found in such a relatively compact work, it provides a reliable (and easily portable!) point of basic reference; and its appendices, with graphic and tabular information on the *DC* and on the Middle Ages (bibliography, maps and plans, chronological tables, etc.) will prove particularly useful to students. Inos Biffi, *La poesia e la grazia nella Commedia di Dante*, Mi, Jaca Book, xxxii + 89 pp., is an accessible if somewhat *parti pris* study of D.'s relationship to theology and of the vexed question of what it may mean to label the poet *theologus Dante*. B. re-examines the question of D.'s relationship to Thomism and to the mystical theology represented by Sigier and by St Bernard; but he reminds us also that 'Dante è Dante' (xxviii) and that his relationship to theology is highly personal. The *DC*, in its narrative about conversion via direct intervention from heaven (and separate chapters consider each of D.-*personaggio*'s various guides), is argued to be structured theologically, according to the doctrine of grace; but also to retain an individual sense of the importance of aesthetic and imaginative qualities in representing theological truths to its readers. Another book that aims to introduce new readers to the complexities of D.'s poem is the essay collection *Dante*, ed. Jeremy Tambling, London, Longman, ix + 212 pp. It gathers together a selection of studies previously published in more specialist books and journals, to offer a varied selection of recent English-language criticism on the poem from ten distinguished scholars: Z. G. Barański, T. Barolini, P. Boitani, P. Dronke, K. Foster, J. Freccero, R. Jacoff, G. Mazzotta, R. J. Quinones, J. Tambling.

Aside from these book-form studies, articles which make general observations on the *DC* as a whole include: R. Baehr, ' "Suso in Italia bella giace un laco" '. Zwischen Realismus und Allegorie: zu Herkunft, Charakter und Funktion landschaftlicher Elemente in der *Divina Commedia*', *DDJ*, 74:85–104, which stresses the importance of the theme of landscape to the poetics of the *DC* as a whole, relating it to the fundamental question, raised from the outset by the allusions to journeying and place, of the text's reception as either an authentic spiritual vision, or as an epic and allegorical *fictio*. The essay explores ways in which 'realist' references to familiar topographies from the secular world (even if they in turn carry literary associations) assist the construction of literal and allegorical meanings within the poem. A. M. Costantini, 'Elementi cronachistici e sacre rappresentazioni nei due da Montefeltro', *LC*, 28:29–42, provides a comparative reading of the meetings with members of the Montefeltro family in *Inf.* XXVII and *Purg.* V, with reference also to the appearance of Guido in *Cvo* IV. L. De Poli, 'De la mélancolie à la jubilation, ou les limites de la mémoire dans la *Commedia*', *ChrI*, 55–56 (1998):101–31, investigates the theme and imagery of memory in the *DC*, with wide reference also to the *VN* and the *Rime*. Alongside allusions to memory's accuracy in D.'s narrative constructions of sincerity, the *DC* also, from *Inf.* I onwards, addresses the problem of failed or dysfunctional memory. De P. suggests that the portrayal of memorial dysfunction as a Medusan, petrifying, and negative experience, is typical of the melancholic temperament which D. suggests himself to possess, in his tendency to obsession by single, retrospective memories or ideas. Against this tendency, the positive processes of revelatory and testimonial memory are represented by the figure of Matelda, who releases D. from the petrification of doubt and regret, and frees his mind to receive the images which, in subsequent memory, will prompt the writing of the poem. S. Gilson, 'Light reflection, mirror metaphors and optical framing in D.'s *Comedy*: precedents and transformations', *Neophilologus*, 83:241–52, draws on the author's detailed knowledge of medieval optical theory to show D.'s capacity to synthesize and transform scientific concepts from different traditions in his poetry. The article proposes that the Pauline distinction between vision 'in a glass darkly' and 'face to face' (*I Cor.* 13:12) provides a fundamental point of intertextual reference to the *Par.* in particular. The concluding consideration of the conception of *homo viator* in the *DC* and in St Paul, with its proposals about the narrative and conceptual shifts between the two kinds of vision, is especially stimulating. W. Hirdt, 'Immagini del mondo e mondo delle immagini. Il "visibile parlare" in Dante', *Mazzoni Vol.*, 129–42, argues that D.'s use in the *DC* of simile in particular is motivated not only by the rules of literary *ornatus*, but by its *necessitas* to the discussion of spiritual matters. In conclusion, H. suggests that an almost painterly quality that he identifies in D.'s visual imagery explains his particular appeal for Michelangelo, discussing M.'s poetic and painterly *dantismi*, with especial reference to the Sistine's *Last Judgement*. R. Hollander, 'Dante as Uzzah? (*Purg.* x. 57 and *Ep.* xi. 9–12)', *ib.*, 143–51, provides an engaging consideration of the ways in which D. reflects on the enterprise of writing the *DC*, and at times reveals his awareness of the project's possibly presumptuous, even blasphemous, implications, as well as suggesting that it is a divinely sanctioned and prophetic text. Using evidence from the references to heuristic Uzzah in *Purg.* x and *Ep.* xi, H. shows that D. casts himself as a David-like mouthpiece of divine truths, whilst playfully acknowledging awareness of his moral audacity by alluding specifically to the Biblical episode of Uzzah's profanation of the vehicle of textual authority, the Ark of the Covenant. C. Honess, 'Communication and participation in Dante's *Commedia*', *Lepschy Vol.*, 127–45, offers a wide-ranging discussion of two themes which she shows to be closely linked in the *DC* and which bear on considerations about language and identity. The study makes specific allusion to several passages in the *DC* where the question of 'national' language (Latin, Occitan, Florentine, etc.) are of specific importance to D. and his protagonists. From the non-communicating non-community of Dis, up to the silencing of the most instinctive of language in *Par.* xxxiii, H. shows that the need to communicate, using appropriate and accessible language, is fundamental to D.'s project and to its 'comic', pluristylistic poetics. A. A. Iannucci, 'Il Limbo dei bambini', *Mazzoni Vol.*, 153–64, demonstrates that by establishing a single Limbo containing infants and adults alike, D. diverges from the mainstream of Scholastic thought. I. shows how this allows D. to introduce elements of theological and poetic surprise: initially in his valorization of the morally and intellectually dignified adult pagans of *Inf.* IV, later, in *Par.* xxxii, by his surprising return to the question of unbaptized infants, and the significance of the salvation of this anonymous group, after the expectations raised by the Limbo episode so much earlier in the poem. C. Kleinhenz, 'The land of the living and the land of the dead: burial, entombment, and cemeteries in Dante's *Divine Comedy*', *Religion and Literature*, 31.1:49–59. A. G. Meekins, 'The study of Dante, Bonaventure, and mysticism: notes on some problems of method', *Lepschy Vol.*, 83–99. L. Pertile, 'La *Comedìa* tra il dire e il fare', *Mazzoni Vol.*, 233–47, investigates the way in which D. manages his dual *personae* as narrator and protagonist of the *DC*, and the strategies he employs to persuade his readers of his text's veracity, or at least credibility. He explores the way in which D. presents the *dire* of the poem as a form of *fare*, discussing how the roles of *actor* and *scriptor* were addressed in Christian and classical tradition. The closing discussion of the *DC*'s rubric, 'Comedia Dantis Alagherii', offers the stimulating suggestion that it bears a double sense, as 'genitivo d'attore' (246) as well as 'd'autore', using the title itself to assert the autobiographical, eyewitness reliability of the story told in the *DC*. A. Stefanin, 'Etica cortese e "tópoi" cavallereschi: riflessioni su alcuni luoghi della *Commedia* di Dante', *MR*, 12, 1998 [1999]: 81–119, whilst considering several passages from the *DC* in brief (notably *Purg*. XIV-XVI, *Par*. XV-XVI), concentrates especially on the poem's two clearest references to the Lancelot story, in *Inf*. V and *Par*. XVI. S. investigates the Lancelot story's representation of virtue and guilt, from both religious and chivalric standpoints, and suggests that these double (if convergent) ethical strands also inform D.'s intertextual allusions to the romance. S. Vazzana, 'Il Giubileo del 1300 nel poema dantesco', *L'Alighieri*, 49:75–90, identifies some possible references to the Jubilee in the *Par*., as well as the two explicit ones in *Inf*. XVIII and *Purg*. II, and also recalls the general consciousness of the Jubilee suggested simply by the careful dating to Holy Week in 1300 of the *DC*'s narrative of pilgrimage and renewal.

INFERNO

An insight into the working practices of an important twentieth-century *dantista* is provided by Antonio Pagliaro, *Commento incompiuto all'"Inferno" di Dante: canti I–XXVI*, ed. Giovanni Lombardo, Ro, Herder, xxi + 645 pp., a traditional canto-by-canto commentary composed during the late '50s and early '60s. The detail of P.'s observations made the volume too unwieldy to use as a school textbook and the project was abandoned; the present volume thus reproduces a work-in-progress in which information varies considerably in quantity and nature from canto to canto. P.'s constant sensitivity to points of doctrine and rhetoric, and his ability to deal elegantly with the ancient and the modern commentary traditions, make this a valuable contribution. Perhaps especially interesting are the passages where P. suggests, with lucid supporting arguments, readings which diverge from his base text (the 1921/1960 *edizione nazionale*).

All other studies in this section relate to specific cantos. On *Inf*. I: M. Chiamenti, 'Un'altra *schedula* ferina: Dante, *Inf*. I 52', *LN*, 60:34–38. On *Inf*. II: M. Picone, '*Inferno* II: l'"altro viaggio"', *Mazzoni Vol*., pp. 249–60, provides stimulating reflections on the modes of allegory that appear at the beginning of the *DC*, arguing for a deliberate and significant shift between the modes of the first two cantos. Canto I employs traditional medieval poetic allegory, à la

*Roman de la Rose*; it is only in canto II, P. argues, that theological or typological allegory makes an appearance, and that the 'io' changes from quasi-personification to historical *agens*, whose experiences are narrated in a Biblical or epic mode. Similarly, Beatrice and Virgil are present in the canto as themselves, not as allegories; but also intertextually as protagonist and author of narratives that in turn may be interpreted typologically; and these considerations heighten the reader's awareness of D.'s narratological innovation in canto II, and in the *DC* as a whole, as compared to the apparently 'safer' poetics proposed in canto I. On *Inf.* III: A. Musumeci, 'Diacronia dei guai', *FoI*, 33 : 39–60, includes a brief mention of D.'s employment of the term 'guai' in ll. 22–28. G. Güntert, 'Von den Lauen und den Großgesinnten: Semiotische Betrachtungen zu *Inferno* III und IV', *DDJ*, 74 : 105–21, considers the peculiar status of the two cantos, falling between the Prologue sequence and the entry to Hell proper. G. outlines some stimulating parallels with the organization of the realm of Purgatory in the structure of this Hellgate-to-Limbo sequence from the peripheral area of the *sospesi* (*pusillanimi*/ contumacious) to a seven-tiered zone crowned by fire and containing a population of *magnanimi* from the worlds of nobility and intellectual endeavour. On *Inf.* v: Ignazio Baldelli, *Dante e Francesca*, F, Olschki, 93 pp., investigates questions relating, on the one hand, to the chronicling of the story of Paolo and F. and, on the other, to the literary allusions of the canto as a whole. After a detailed section-by-section *lectura* of the canto, B. passes on to a more general survey of the treatment of lust and love in the *DC*, investigating the case of P. and F.'s regional compatriot, the amorous but beatified Cunizza, and emphasizing D.'s continuous interest in the question of how reason controls choices and actions, and how doubtful he at times appears to be of his own capacity to exercise self-restraint. F. Adorno, 'Una riflessione sul rapporto anima-corpo-luce-tenebra-luce in Dante', *Mazzoni Vol.*, 3–9, uses the Paolo and Francesca episode to explore D.'s reflections on the spirit, isolating a Platonist strand in his thinking about the effects of misdirected love upon spiritual well-being and underlining his use of light imagery to refer to the state of the soul and to its varying liberation from or subordination to the body and its desires. P. Levine, 'Why Dante damned Francesca da Rimini', *PLit*, 23 : 334–50, returns to a perennial question and offers two possible, though perhaps conflicting, solutions. In the first, the episode finds D. 'thinking like a philosopher, suspicious of passion and narrative' (349); but the second solution is that he is less suspicious than careful: warning against literary cliché. F.'s lust is similar to D.'s in the youthful *VN*, obsessed by egoistic desire for the stereotypes of romance, whereas the *DC* finds D. re-reading his relation with

B. away from convention and towards a salvific acknowledgement of the importance of individual personality and circumstance, such as occurs in *Purg.* xxx. C. Villa, 'Tra affetto e pietà: per *Inferno* v', *LItal*, 51:513–41, outlines significant linguistic and thematic allusions to Virgil's portrayal of Dido in *Aeneid* IV as part of the intertextual scheme of the Paolo and Francesca episode. The insertion of Virgilian references alongside those to contemporary literature (Arthurian tales, Guinizelli, and D.'s own *VN* and *Petrose*) raises a number of issues pertaining to genre conventions: those of epic, 'tragedy', and 'comedy', and the rules for the vernacular lyric outlined in the *DVE*. It thus extends consideration of the status and purpose of love literature outside the realm of the intellectually new and poorly established vernacular, to embrace the most prestigious — classical Latin — literature and language, raising the standing of the former in the process. On Inf. ix: A. Iannucci, 'Virgil's Erichthean descent and the crisis of intertextuality', *FoI*, 33:13–26, provides an extensive and stimulating discussion of the intertextual implications of V.-character's revelation, in *Inf.* ix, of his previous descent into Lower Hell. Beyond the gates of Dis, D. and V. enter a realm equivalent to the classical Tartarus which V.'s Aeneas could not visit; and their temporary inability to pass those gates, with the accompanying revelation that V.'s previous entry was commanded by a character, Erichtho, from the 'dark' epic of Lucan, indicates D.-poet's need to extend the scope of his intertextual references to embrace the blacker registers of L. and Statius, alongside continuing Virgilian borrowings, in order to describe the deeper levels of the underworld. On *Inf.* x: J. A. Scott, 'Dante jottings', *Lepschy Vol.*, 117–26, addresses the question as to how the Middle Ages understood the quality of *magnanimitas*, in approaching a gloss of the line 'quell'altro magnan-imo' (73). Placed back into medieval context, the term is found to be less approbatory than we nowadays suppose, and a survey of the early commentaries further corroborates this. On *Inf.* xv: W. W. T. Pugh, 'Dante's poetics of corruption: cantos xv and xvi of the *Inferno*', *RoN*, 40:3–12, investigates possible homosexual referents in the two cantos. On *Inf.* xx: E. Esposito, '*Inferno* xx', *L'Alighieri*, 49:7–16. On *Inf.* xxvi: A. Deisser, 'Dante e le dernier voyage d'Ulysse', *ECla*, 67:21–41, looks at D.'s alterations to the canonical classical accounts of the end of U.'s journey, and outlines how this deliberate change inaugurates a series of innovative Ulyssean portrayals, from Tasso to Auden, based on D.'s new tradition. P. Grimaldi Pizzorno, '*Sic notus Ulixes?* Retorica sapienziale e retorica fraudolenta nel canto XXVI dell'*Inferno*', *StCrit*, 14:357–85, returns to this much-discussed canto with a reminder of how much the historical reception of D.'s U. has been affected by the critics' knowledge or ignorance of Homer, and in turn, how modern criticism is affected by a myriad of texts in which the story of U. — Dantean, Homeric, or otherwise narrated — is continuously reworked. The article attempts to return to the 'U. *di* D.' (360), and to investigate D.'s own intertextual and thematic programme. The pastoral simile of the opening lines is reintegrated with the U. episode, stressing the importance of the Virgilian intertext, whereby the implicit political element stresses the destructive consequences of false counsel to ancient and modern cities; whilst its specific allusion to a *villano* (in V., 'pastor') in quiet contemplation draws a philosophical separation between U.'s unreflecting vagabond instinct and the contemplative stance adopted by D.-*personaggio* in the sequence. This in turn adduces greater trust in the words of D.-poet, a *rhetor* in different mode to U.; and the article's survey of journey images suggests that U. has none of the heroism for D. that has been identified by modern criticism, but is rejected categorically as *folle* in word and deed. S. C. Hagedorn, 'A Statian model for Dante's Ulysses', *DaSt*, 115, 1997[1999]: 19–43, gives a stimulating reading of the episode which outlines a strong intertextual connection between the portrayal of U. in *Inf.* and in Statius's *Achilleid*. She stresses that both authors present U. as an accomplished but essentially fraudulent *rhetor*, and a donor of destructive gifts, whose seductive words and objects are alike intended to distract their recipients from moral obligations, especially from familial and social duty. Additional remarks on S. stress the intratextual reprises from the *Inf.* episode during the meeting with S.-character in *Purg.* XXI, while a final excursus presents evidence for her argument that D. casts himself as epic hero in the *DC* not only in the long-recognized moulds of *alter Aeneas* and *alter Ulixes*, but also as *alter Achilles*, in allusion to the Statian epic which enjoyed such high esteem in the Middle Ages. G. Padoan, 'Dante e gli Ulissidi dell'Atlantico', *LC*, 28: 155–69, is a two-part reflection on themes relating to D.'s Ulysses and to the moral condemnation he incurs. The first, and more properly Dantean part, examines the motives for this condemnation, placing it within the context of the Patristic and Scholastic distinction between *vera* and *vana sapientia*. The second part of the article is primarily historical, looking at the earliest explorations of the Atlantic by Italian and other European navigators, some reaching as far as Iceland and North America in their U.-like ventures beyond the confines of the Mediterranean. On *Inf.* XXVIII: D. Della Terza, 'Dante tra "quei che scommettendo acquistan carco": lettura del canto XXVIII dell'*Inferno*', *La parola del testo*, 3:91–101. On *Inf.* XXIX: M. Pereira, 'Alchemy and the use of vernacular languages in the late Middle Ages', *Speculum*, 74:336–56, mentions D.'s infernal alchemists Griffolino and Capocchio among her survey of vernacular references to alchemy. On *Inf.*

xxx: F. Salsano, '*Inferno* XXX', *L'Alighieri*, 49:17–27. On *Inf.* xxxi: F. Tateo, 'L'immobilità dei giganti e la premura di Anteo: note per l'interpretazione di *Inferno* xxxi', *La parola del testo*, 3:103–112, claims pivotal significance for the canto, both via reflection on its numerical position in the structure of the cantica, and via the symbolism of its giant protagonists. The giants physically occupy the space both of Malebolge and of Cocito, while thematically they allow the juxtaposition of Biblical with classical stories of rebellion and retribution. Their position offers illustration of the division between the celestial and the terrestrial as physical and metaphorical opposites, and allows D. to reconcile the wisdom of his classical and his Christian *auctoritates* and acknowledge the double contribution of both Virgil and Beatrice to his spiritual regeneration. On *Inf.* xxxii: E. Pasquini, 'Lettura di *Inferno* xxxii', *L'Alighieri*, 49:29–37, emphasizes the meta-literary concerns and identity of D.'s narratorial persona in this 'linking' canto, outlining echoes of the language and imagery of the *Petrose* in descriptions of the icy topography of Caina, and also notes that a strongly Florentine, popular register of language draws attention to the physical and moral drop into the lowest level of Hell, by an equivalent lowering of rhetorical register. On canto xxxiii: G. Luti, 'Appunti sulla struttura del xxxiii dell'*Inferno*', *Mazzoni Vol.*, 189–97, outlines a careful, balanced architecture in the canto's seven-terzina 'prologue', the 23 terzine of Ugolino's story, and the 22 of the continuing journey. The article outlines a systematic pattern of repetition and reversal within the longer sequences, which ensures the mutual enhancement of the canto's rhetorical and thematic impact.

## PURGATORIO

Lino Pertile, *La puttana e il gigante: dal "Cantico dei Cantici" al Paradiso Terrestre di Dante*, Ravenna, Longo, 1998, 278 pp., takes the *sacra rappresentazione* of the final cantos of *Purg.* as its main point of departure. It addresses the question of D.'s intertextual references in the language and imagery of the pageant, tracing their relationship not only to the *Song of Songs* but also to a variety of receptions of the *Song*, ranging from learned Latin exegesis to vernacular parody, and placing them in a medieval context where the habit of syncretization makes intertextuality the norm rather than the individual and original exception. The study provides telling exposition of a variety of different concerns that D. brings together at the insistently autobiographical crisis-point of the meeting between the protagonist and Beatrice, in which political concerns, poetic reputation, personal experience, and universal history, coalesce. The *Song* was rendered acceptable, in the Middle Ages, by highly allegorical readings, often contextualized as part of a wider study of the Salomonic books, which made a narrative of psychological and spiritual maturation towards union with the Godhead: and P. shows that D.'s allusions to the *Song* form a continual subtext to the personal drama of the *personaggio* up to this point, allowing a similar reading of his own experience in relation to his knowledge of the spiritual via Beatrice. The thesis is supported by a plethora of citations from medieval texts on the *Song*, which provide an absorbing picture of contemporary approaches to reading, writing, and exegesis. An article that embraces much of the ante-Purgatory in its considerations is I. Baldelli, 'I morti di morte violenta: Dante e Sordello', *DaSt*, 115, 1997[1999]: 111–83, which presents an extremely thorough and detailed *lettura* of canti v to viii, with a wealth of reflections on theological, historical, and linguistic matters. A general consideration of the poetics of the *Purg.* as a whole is offered in R. L. Martinez, 'Lament and lamentations in *Purgatorio* and the case of Dante's Statius', *ib.*, 45–88. After a discussion of the stylistic analogues in Scripture for the registers of the three *cantiche*, the typical mode of *Purg.* is identified as lament: understood, on the basis of typological readings of *Lamentations* (*Threni*), as a penitential discipline leading to joy. While the Bible provides the main inspiration for D.'s purgatorial poetics of lament, other sources are identified in the Provençal *planh* and in S.'s *Thebaid*. Finally, D. and S., as protagonists of the *DC*, are carefully paired, each emblematically lamenting, first a city abandoning and abandoned by God, second the corrupting diffusion of cupidity in the world, and finally the insufficiency (from a Christian view) of their shared teacher and exemplar Virgil, culminating with the perfect classical/Biblical threnody for V. performed in *Purg.* xxx.

Single-canto studies include, on canto V, M. Picone, 'Il canto v del *Purgatorio* fra Orfeo e Palinuro', *L'Alighieri*, 49: 39–52, suggesting that D.-character suffers from an 'Orpheus complex', in his tendency to suffer distraction by music and by words from his progressive ascent towards Beatrice. Virgil must repeatedly remind him of the need for detachment from such retarding earthly concerns (literary, political, intellectual); an approach that is reinforced in this canto by the 'Palinurus complex' of the souls encountered, whose obsession with their places of burial or non-burial is being gradually purged towards a more appropriate focus on soul rather than body. On canto vi: G. Padoan, '*Purgatorio* vii 102: Arrigo VII o Federigo d'Asburgo?', *Mazzoni Vol.*, 225–31, presents a hypothesis relative to the Valley of the Princes episode (the misnumbering of the canto in the title is to be regretted). The article argues that the succession mentioned in the political pseudo-prophecy is not imperial and election-based, but rather dynastic, referring to the Habsburg territorial inheritance. On canto XIII: A. Kablitz, 'Videre–Invidere. Die Phänomenologie der Wahrnehmung und die Ontologie des Purgatoriums', *DDJ*, 74:137–87, is a dense and scholarly examination of the punishment accorded to the envious. It examines the 'etymological' explanation for their blinding offered in early commentary on the basis of the verbal pairing of *videre/invidere* (or *non-vedere*), in well-established theological tradition; and in a detailed, almost line-by-line *lectura* of the canto, unpicks its dense network of allusions to light-love-God vs blindness-envy. K. stresses the ontological aspect of the punishment: in a realm itself physically structured by the corporeal consequences of the Satanic and Adamic Falls, punishment demands a 'radical' connection between moral and material reality. On canto XIV: B. Guthmüller, ' "Che par che Circe li avesse in pastura" (*Purg*. XIV, 42). Mito di Circe e metamorfosi nella *Commedia*', Picone, *Dante*, 235–56, examines the use of myths of metamorphosis to describe political and dynastic degeneration in contemporary Romagna and, especially, Tuscany, and finds intertextual parallels with Boethius's discussion of vices that render humans bestial. The association of Tuscan cities with animals matches the examples used by B. in his categorizations of types of sin, which classification in turn corresponds to the scheme of *Inf.*, thereby making a direct analogy between the valley of the Arno and that of Hell. The transformative magic of C., like the temptations of Satan, 'dis-humanizes' its victims, and G. notes the numerous attributions of bestial qualities to the *Inf.*'s sinners; suggesting in conclusion that points of language and imagery reveal a connection between the dark myth of C. and the positive Ovidian myth of Glaucus in D.'s opposition between infernal *disumanar* and paradisal *trasumanar* (255). On canto XVI: M. Roddewig, '*Purgatorio* XVI — Zorn und Willensfreiheit', *DDJ*, 74:123–35. On canto XXIV, opposing conclusions are reached by two intriguing studies: C. Calenda, 'Ancora su Cino, la *Commedia*, e lo "stil novo" (*Purg*. XXIV e XXVI)', *Mazzoni Vol.*, 75–83, returns to the perennial problem of C.'s apparent absence from the *DC*. The article suggests however that there are implicit references to C. in the *Purg.*: in canto XXVI, 'li altri miei miglior' may include the poet hailed in the *DVE* as the Italian counterpart of Arnaut Daniel, supreme masters of the poetry of *venus*. This solution also bears on the issue of the 'dolce stil novo' of XXIV: it is suggested that while Bonagiunta refers to 'vostre penne', indicating a plural group of writers about *Amore-venus*, D.'s reply that 'i' mi son un' corrects this in his own case to identify his position as writer about *Amore-charitas*. R. Hollander, 'Dante's "dolce stil novo" and the *Comedy*', Picone, *Dante*, 263–81, addresses the same question, taking into consideration debates over terminology ('dolce' and 'novo'), possible schools ('vostre penne'), and the question of inspiration ('quando | Amor mi spira'). The first two points receive the joint conclusion that one other poet at least, Cino, may be understood as writing like D., and sharing his 'post-Franciscan' understanding of Beatrice as 'emanation of Christ among us in the world' (272). The question of inspiration is shown to be closely related to this overriding concern with theological issues, in love poetry and *poesia sacra* alike. An interesting additional suggestion appears in H.'s comments on the terminology of inspiration that D. applies to Justinian's codification of the law (*Par.* VI 10–12) at the inspiration of *amor*.

### PARADISO

A. M. Chiavacci Leonardi, 'Parole del *Paradiso*', *Mazzoni Vol.*, 95–103, is a brief but stimulating article on the language of the *Par.*, especially its copious Latinisms. C. L. suggests that these make deliberate use of the sacrality of the language of scripture and liturgy, but also of ·classical literature. As what the *DVE* calls a 'gramatica', a fixed and unchanging language, it provides access to a realm of metahistorical reality, allowing D.'s vernacular text to become transcendental, and to mimic the process whereby the Word of divine truth (eternal, unchanging and 'Latinate') becomes incarnate in the mutable (vernacular) world of human history, in order to remind its audience of history's eschatological orientation. M. Marietti, 'Au ciel du Soleil (*Paradis*, X–XIV)', *ChrI*, 57 : 28–48, examines a long sequence of cantos, focusing especially on two protagonists, St Francis and Solomon. The article investigates the use of inversion in the sequence's structure and, besides its rhetorical effects, explores its thematic implications with reference to the connections traced between F. and S., through their renunciations of worldly goods in exchange for access to divine Charity and Justice, which M. suggests both form part of D.'s conception of Wisdom. The same cantos are investigated in A. Meek-ins, 'Reflecting on the divine: notes on Dante's Heaven of the Sun', *The Italianist*, 18, 1998[1999] : 28–70, which investigates D.'s presenta-tion of contemporary approaches to salvation and argues that the cantos reveal a predilection for Neoplatonist and symbolic approaches to Scripture that at least in part runs counter to the traditional description of D. as a convinced Thomist and Christian Aristotelian and which reveals a strong response to the language and imagery of Bonaventuran and Salomonic mystical traditions.

I turn now to particular cantos. On *Par.* VI: V. Vianello, 'I segni della storia e i segni del testo: le maschere autobiografiche nel VI canto del *Paradiso*', *L'Alighieri*, 49:53–73. On *Par.* VIII: I. Baldelli, 'Dante e Catona', *Mazzoni Vol.*, 11–15, is devoted mainly to linguistic issues, investigating their political (and proto-'Italian') implications.

On *Par.* XIII: A. Cornish, 'I miti biblici. La sapienza di Salomone e le arti magiche', Picone, *Dante*, 391–403, shows how, whilst respecting the undisputable authenticity of the Bible, D. can manage to investigate and manipulate stories about Biblical figures derived from non-canonical sources, such as the legend of S. as magus. S.'s request for wisdom sufficient to govern, i.e. to perform his terrestrial duties, is read as a desire for knowledge not limited to the political or juristic spheres, but reflecting an engagement with the material world in general that suggests an elevated philosophical *forma mentis* which the reader in turn is invited to acquire. On *Par.* XIV: S. Gilson, '"Dal centro al cerchio": *Paradiso* XIV 1–9', *ISt*, 54:26–33, investigates evidence in these lines about D.'s understanding of the mechanics of human voice production, suggesting an emendation to Petrocchi's reading of line 3 in the process. G. suggests possible sources for D.'s physiological understanding, and for the images that he uses in illustration, in various classical and contemporary texts, which reveal that what initially appears to be a combination of empirical observation and poetic image can in fact be referred to a specific intellectual context. On *Par.* XVIII: F. Brunori Deigan and E. Liberatori Prati, '"L'emme del vocabol quinto": allegory of language, history and literature in Dante's *Paradiso* 18', *QI*, 19 (1998):7–26, explores the allegory in the transformation of graphic 'M' to iconic eagle, discussing a series of Christian and classical resonances produced by this metamorphosis and exploring its implications in a number of directions — spiritual, metalinguistic, historical. On *Par.* XX: L. Lazzerini, 'L'"allodetta" e il suo archetipo. La rielaborazione di temi mistici nella lirica trobadorica', *Mazzoni Vol.*, 165–88, takes as its starting-point the comparison of the Eagle in the heaven of Jupiter to a lark and traces the image's connections to Bernart de Ventadorn's *Can vei la lauzeta mover*, revealing intertextual allusions at a spiritual as well as literary level. Close reading of B. de V.'s lyric shows that beneath its ostensibly amorous subject-matter, the *lauzeta* functions as an allegory for the soul. The text's allusions to mirrors and reflections, bodies, and clothing, etc., draw on familiar Biblical imagery, and L. traces a tradition of such Scriptural borrowings from the troubadours through to the *stilnovisti*, stressing how such rhetorical repetitions enhance the impact of the mystical significance borne by particular images that D. employs in his own lyric verse, and in *Par.* XX's 'allodetta' allusion. On *Par.* XXIV: V. S. Benfell, 'Biblical truth in the examination cantos of Dante's *Paradiso*', *DaSt*, 115, 1997[1999]:89–109, while it surveys the examination cantos in general, takes as its start- and end-point the passage in *Par.* XXIV where D. apparently mis-cites or distorts the Biblical acount of Peter and John's visit to Christ's empty tomb, but to no obvious purpose.

The article suggests that the change forms part of the broader sequence's strategy of affirming the prophetic authority of the self-declared 'poema sacro'. The numerous references to text-production contained in these cantos draw together allusions to divine inspiration and to the physical copying of manuscript books; B. suggests that D.'s 'overwriting' of the Bible in *Par.* xxiv can be seen as analogous to the creation of a palimpsest, where new messages overwrite the old in an equally authoritative and Scriptural transmission of the divine Word. On *Par.* xxvi: P. Boyde, 'Essay on a line of Dante: "io ti farò vedere ogne valore" ', *Mazzoni Vol.*, 37–52, stresses how a single line (xxvi, 42) may be dense with philosophical and spiritual significance. B. works 'backwards' in the article: after opening with observations on the line's rhetorical and stylistic construction, he next takes us through a survey of the possible meanings of the single term 'valore' in D.'s culture, and then into a survey of the wider context of Aristotelian vs Christian moral schemes; finally, the closing pages provide a short *lettura* of the *Par.* xxvi passage itself. This 'backwards' organization of his argument allows B.'s final point, regarding the personal, 'I-thee' relationships that link D. and God, D.-character and V.-character, D.-poet and the reader, to convey a very full sense of what it means to make another individual 'vedere ogne valore'. On *Par.* xxxiii: R. Migliorini Fissi, ' "Come iri da iri" (*Par.* xxxiii 118)', *MR*, 12, 1998[1999]:49–79, examines the presentation in this canto of the Trinity in terms of light, colour, and geometrical form, alongside the rainbow simile. The science behind D.'s use of the rainbow image is explored, with possible sources cited, and considerable space given to the reception of the science and the theology in the early commentators. The article shows how the use of a rainbow image, in connection with the vision of a Godhead 'pinta della nostra effige', makes links with the story of Noah, and with the description of the Second Coming in *Revelations*, reminding us at the end of the *DC* of the salvific message that the poem carries.

# DUECENTO AND TRECENTO II
## (EXCLUDING DANTE)
### POSTPONED

# HUMANISM AND THE RENAISSANCE

By PAOLO. L. ROSSI, *Senior Lecturer in Italian Studies, Lancaster University* and GERALDINE MUIRHEAD, *Lecturer in Italian, Manchester Metropolitan University*

## 1. GENERAL

A number of studies further our understanding of the term Renaissance and explore important cultural issues of the period. Evelyn Welch, *Art and Society in Italy 1350–1500*, OUP, 1997, 351 pp., emphasizes the role played by mundane objects and images. Alison Brown, *The Renaissance*, London, Longman, 139 pp., is a radical revision of the 1992 edition with major changes to the sections and to the focus of individual chapters, and with an updated bibliography. Peter Burke, *The European Renaissance: Centres and Peripheries*, Oxford, Blackwell, 1998, x + 284 pp., sets out to present the Renaissance as a cultural movement centred on the 'enthusiasm for antiquity and the revival, reception, and transformation of the classical tradition' rather than an event or a period. His anthropological approach is applied to the whole of Europe and takes in neglected areas in the North and East. Id., *Varieties of Cultural History*, Oxford, Polity, 1997, x + 246 pp., contains 12 essays that explore the diversity of approaches to cultural history. Of particular significance are: 'The language of gesture in early modern Italy'; 'Frontiers of the comic in early modern Italy'. A. Tenenti, 'Aspetti del settentrione rinascimentale nel Quattrocento', *LItal*, 51:18–26. D. Burchell, 'Burckhardt redivivus: Renaissance pedagogy as self-formation', *RenS*, 13:283–302. Bette Talvacchia, *Taking Positions. On the Erotic in Renaissance Culture*, Princeton U.P., xiii + 302 pp., is a beautifully produced volume which argues that eroticism is an integral aspect of early modern culture of 'equal importance to the other historical documentation of the era'. It examines the genre of sexual representation, widespread throughout Europe, analyses the most famous (notorious) example, Giulio Romano's *I modi*, and investigates the motives that led Aretino to pen his sonnets linked to the images. It then explores the market-orientated strategies involved in the publishing of J. Carglio, *Gli amori degli dei*, and traces how Carglio's images were later transformed from mythologized art into medical illustrations in a textbook on anatomy. That political control can effect cultural change and a transformation in taste and style can be seen in: Giovanni Romano, *Gandolfino da Roreto e il Rinascimento nel Piemonte meridionale*, T, Fondazione Cassa di Risparmio di Torino, 1998, 359 pp. *Modelling the Individual. Biography and Portrait in the Renaissance. With a Critical Edition of Petrarch's 'Letter to Posterity'*, ed. Karl Enenkel, Betsy de Jong-Crane, and Peter Liebregts,

Amsterdam, Rodopi, 1998, 299 pp. + 43 pls, contains 12 articles covering Petrarch's adaptation of Boccaccio's biography of himself, the debate about philosophers versus soldiers in 'Portraits of Condottieri', and body and self-image in the autobiography of Gerolamo Cardano. *Educare il corpo educare la parola nella trattatistica del Rinascimento*, ed. Giorgio Patrizi and Amedeo Quondam, Ro, Bulzoni, 1998, 442 pp., consists of 17 essays on topics that include: S. Guazzo's *Civil conversazione*, and a re-assessment of N. Elias's 'civilising process'; the development of ideas, themes, and texts on courtliness and conduct before Della Casa; sources and themes in A. Piccolomini's *La instituzione di tutta la vita dell'homo nato nobile*; and Machiavelli as keeper of secrets in the *Principe*. Robert Williams, *Art, Theory and Culture in Sixteenth-Century Italy. From 'Techne' to 'Metatechne'*, CUP, 1997, 243 pp., uses the theoretical and literary writings of Vasari, Bocchi, Lomazzo, Zuccaro, and Tasso to propose that the 'Renaissance redefinition of art as a *metatechne* documents the awareness of its fundamental role in the constitution of reality, not just of the objects of knowledge and of the means of knowing them, but even of what it is we think does the knowing'. *Rabisch. Il grottesco nell'arte del Cinquecento*, ed. Giulio Bora, Manuela Kahn-Rossi, and Francesco Porzio, Mi, Skira, 1998, 358 pp., deals with the activities of the Accademia della Val di Blasio centred on Lomazzo. Reasons are put forward for the scatological side of Lomazzo that co-existed with his sober, public face, and the importance of carnival and the influence of a Northern European grotesque tradition are emphasized. The work includes a succint survey of Milanese literary academies, a study of the (*arabeschi*) dialect and the publishing history of *Rabisch*. Irene Fosi et al., *Dopo Sisto V. La transizione al Barocco (1590–1630)*, Ro, Istituto Nazionale di Studi Romani, 1997, 308 pp., comprises 13 essays highlighting the themes of continuity and experimentation in intellectual and cultural values and which examine poetry in Latin and the *volgare* to evaluate literary genres and intellectual positions. *Sasso Vol.* includes G. Inglese on the textual tradition in relation to his critical edition of the *Principe*, G. Cadoni on Florentine institutions to clarify Guicciardini's *Storie fiorentine and Discorso di Logrogno*, and C. de Frede on the favourable humanist reaction to the Turks and Islam. Trevor Dean and K. J. P. Lowe, *Marriage in Italy 1300–1650*, CUP, 1998, 304 pp., contains 14 essays. Of particular interest are: J. Musacchio on the humanist interest in classical literature and how theories were transformed into painted marriage panels; I. Fosi and M. A. Visceglia on the *Li nuptiali* of M. A. Altieri; and S. Kolsky on the circulation of discourses on women. The wedding ceremony features largely in Graham Hughes, *Renaissance Cassoni. Masterpieces of Early Italian Art. Painted Marriage Chests 1400–1550*, London, Art Books International, 1997, 256 pp., which covers the use of Christian and pagan images, the shift from feminine to masculine influence, and the adaptation of images from literature. D. Boccassini, 'Fifteenth-century "istoria": texts, images, contexts (Matteo Maria Boiardo and Jacopo Bellini)', *RenS*, 13 : 1–14. *Systems of Knowledge. Antiquity and Early Middle Ages, Middle Ages and Renaissance*, ed. Joseph Giordmaina, Malta U.P., 146 pp., is a useful student handbook that invites reflection on literature, art, politics, and the value of creativity. *Vatican Archives: an Inventory and Guide to Historical Documents of the Holy See*, ed. Francis X. Blouin Jr, OUP, 1998, xl + 588 pp., is a welcome addition to the existing material and lists the Agencies and Collections (College of Cardinals, Papal Court, Roman Curia, Apostolic Nunciatures, Papal States etc.) with all the attendant subdivisions. The conceptual framework for the guide is based, in fact, on the organizational structure of the Holy See and gives a valuable overview of the entire archive, an online database, the organization of specific collections, and bibliographical references and finding aids. Maria Grazia Vaccari, *La Guardaroba Medicea dell'Archivio di Stato di Firenze*, F, Regione Toscana, 1997, 375 pp., makes a welcome addition to existing catalogues with its clear descriptions of the various collections.

Recent scholarship has re-evaluated the importance of music and the uses to which it was put. Federico Ghisi, *Feste musicali della Firenze Medicea (1480–1580)*, Bo, Forni, xlviii + 89 pp., is a facsimile of the 1939 edition in two parts: *Canti carnascialeschi, Trionfi e Mascherate*; and *Intermedi fatti in occasione di feste e nozze alla corte Medicea*. The introduction gives references to the MS and printed sources, places the poems and music within a politico-cultural context, and points to the artists responsible for the visual aspect of the spectacles. James Haar, *The Science and Art of Renaissance Music*, ed. Paul Corneilson, Princeton U.P., 1998, xiv + 389 pp., includes an essay on Castiglione and the science and art of music and Cosimo Bartoli's ideas in the *Ragionamenti accademici*, and has a section on A. F. Doni which examines his library, the *Dialogo della musica*, and Doni as the possible compiler of the gift of madrigals to Cosimo I. Gianluca D'Agostino, 'Sul rapporto tra l'umanesimo e la musica. Proposte e annotazioni', *Annali dell'Istituto per gli Studi Storici*, 15, 1998 : 65–91, reviews recent studies, points to new approaches and sources for understanding the complexity of the humanist response to music, and assesses the problems inherent in using poetry to recreate the music. Jean Grundy Fanelli, *Musica e libri sulla musica nella Biblioteca Marucelliana di Firenze pubblicati fino al 1800*, Lucca, Libreria Musicale Italiana, xxviii + 161 pp., sets out a clear alphabetical listing with useful indexes of printers and publishers. Richard Sherr, *Music and Musicians in Renaissance Rome and other Courts*, Aldershot, Ashgate, xii + 338 pp., is a collection of already published essays. T. Carter, 'From the outside looking in: musicology and the Renaissance', *BSRS*, 17.2 : 1–7. A number of studies have concentrated on teaching and learning. Carlo Antinori and Maria Cristina Testa, *Università di Parma. Storia di un millennio*, Parma, Maccari, 109 pp., traces the origins of the university from the 8th c. and covers the periods of Visconti, Sforza, and Farnese rule, the teaching of theology, the organization of lessons, the provenance of students, the relationship between town and gown, the disciplines, the structure of the university and the development of Parma's 'collegio dei nobili, culla dell'aristocrazia'. Jonathan Davies, *Florence and its University during the Early Renaissance*, Leiden, Brill, 1998, 232 pp., examines the structure of the *Studio Fiorentino* and its relationship to social, economic, political, religious, and cultural forces. It then looks at its activities under Lorenzo de' Medici and the Republic. Donato Gallo, *Università e signoria a Padova dal XIV al XV secolo*, Trieste, Lint, 1998, viii + 149 pp., is a well-documented study of the complex relationship between public authority and university autonomy. Alberto Malfitano, *Alimentazione e studenti nella Bologna medievale e moderna*, Bo, CLUEB, 1998, 118 pp., is an entertaining study that adds another dimension to our knowledge of student life with analyses of contemporary descriptions, and texts of *novellieri* such as Sabbadino degli Arienti. *Educazione e istituzioni nell'Italia moderna*, ed. Roberto Sani, Mi, Università Cattolica, 822 pp., has important documentation relating to the thinking on, and development of, educational and teaching institutions. It gives the the texts of treatises by P. P. Vergerio, Maffeo Vegio da Lodi, Sadoleto, A. Piccolomini, S. Antoniano, O. Pescetti, B. Guarino and A. Possevino, together with decrees on education by the Council of Trent, and statutes and rules of religious institutions. P. F. Grendler, 'The university of Bologna, the city, and the papacy', *RenS*, 13 : 475–85.

BIBLIOGRAPHY, PRINTING AND PUBLISHING. *Catalogo dei manoscritti del Fondo Monreale della Biblioteca Centrale della Regione Siciliana*, Palermo, Regione Siciliana, 1998, xlvi + 248 pp., includes a history of the collection followed by a full description of 33 MSS which contain humanist studies. *Bibliotheca Encyclopaedica. Catalogo del fondo enciclopedico della biblioteca dell'Istituto dell'Enciclopedia fondata da Giovanni Treccani*, ed. Roberto Mauro and Massimo Menna, Ro, Istituto dell'Enciclopedia Italiana, 1997, xxii + 589 pp., has an introduction by Tullio Gregory on the methodology and rationale behind the early encyclopedias, and an essay by Madel Crasta on encyclopedia publishing, followed by a catalogue of 614 encyclopedias with full critical apparatus. *Per una bibliografia musicale: testi, trattati, spartiti. (Supplemento alle edizioni italiane del XVI secolo)*, ed. Isabella Ranieri and R. Maria Rosaria Boccadifuoco, Ro, Istituto Centrale per il Catalogo Unico, xiii + 248 pp., lists 3470 items with full critical apparatus. *Bibliografia delle edizioni palermitane antiche*, 1: *Edizioni del XVI secolo*, Palermo, Regione Siciliana, 1998, 253 pp., is the first volume of the project to catalogue all the works printed in Palermo from the 15th to the 18th c. It lists 437 works with full critical apparatus. Raffaele Tamalio, *La memoria dei Gonzaga. Repertorio bibliografico gonzaghesco (1473–1999)*, F, Olschki, xvii + 303 pp., lists 3860 studies starting with Pietro Adamo de' Micheli, *Della dichiaratione de l'horologio di Mantova*, 1473. This is however more than a list of titles. The section, 'La memoria dei Gonzaga', has a series of graphs that allow quantative analysis of authors, periods of scholarly activity, disciplines studied, distribution of articles with respect to books, and publishers. G. Rebecchini, 'The book collection and other possessions of Baldassare Castiglione', *JWCI*, 61, 1998[1999]:17–52. P. M. Galimberti, 'Il testamento e la biblioteca di Ambrogio Griffi, medico milanese, protonotario apostolico e consigliere sforzesco', *Aevum*, 71, 1998:447–83. C. Pulsoni, 'Per la ricostruzione della biblioteca bembiana: 1. I libri di Dante', *Critica del testo*, 2:735–49. S. Cecchetti, 'Una biblioteca erudita del Cinquecento: l'inventario dei libri letterari e storici di Pomponio Torelli (1359–1608)', *IMU*, 39, 1996[1999]:301–94. Dante Isella, *Bibliografia delle opere della letteratura in lingua milanese*, Mi, Biblioteca Nazionale Braidense, xxiv + 235 pp., lists 41 authors and groups, each with a brief biography and bibliography of works. The introduction investigates Lombard literary culture. Both *Catalogo dei manoscritti (nn. 2381–2600)* and *Catalogo dei manoscritti (nn. 2601–2900)*, ed. Emilio Lippi, Treviso, Biblioteca Comunale, 1997, 197 pp., and 1998, 205 pp., list MSS which contain a wealth of literary and historical material with indexes of names and subjects. Alison Adams, Stephen Rawles, and Alison Saunders, *A Bibliography of French Emblem Books*, Geneva, Droz, xxii + 670 pp., is not restricted to works by French authors but includes all texts printed within a certain area. The definition of emblem is carefully established as are the geographical parameters. There is a full critical apparatus with a facsimile of each frontespiece. This first volume lists 73 editions of Alciato, six of Cartari, two of Doni, and six of Giovio including five authored with G. Simeoni. A full set of indexes will appear in volume two. Marina Panetta and Paola Urbani, *In margine. Autografi e postille nelle raccolte casanatensi*, Ro, Aisthesis-Biblioteca Casanatense, 111 pp., discusses the importance of autograph works and annotations, and casts doubt on the relevance of graphology. There follow 37 examples of annotations relating to Poliziano, Egidio da Viterbo, F. Neri, and Stigliani. Alfredo Serrai, *Storia della bibliografia*, IX: *Manualistica, didattica e riforme*, Ro, Bulzoni, 886 pp., and Id., *Storia della bibliografia*, X: *Specializzazione e pragmatismo: i nuovi cardini della attività bibliografica*, 2 vols, Ro, Bulzoni, 551, 553–1123 pp., continue to contribute to our understanding of the organization of knowledge. Konstantinos Sp. Staikos, *Charta of Greek Printing. The Contribution of Greek Editors, Printers and Publishers to the Renaissance in Italy and the West*, I, *Fifteenth Century*, Cologne, Dinter, 1998, lxix + 557 pp., charts the movement of Greeks to Italy, their distribution in the peninsula, their impact on scholarship, the teaching of Greek, and the history of printing in Greek. There is a full analysis of Greek texts with a full list of Venetian editions of commentators and translators of Aristotle. Tables show Greek works printed by non-Greek scholars who had studied under Greek teachers. Two important chronological tables respectively list the Greeks involved in 15th-c. printing and 15th-c. texts in Greek. A chapter devoted to the major Greek scholars gives biographies and lists their contributions to printing. *Bibliografia testuale o filologia dei testi a stampa? Definizioni metodologiche e prospettive future*, ed. Neil Harris, Udine, Forum, 363 pp., is dedicated to Conor Fahy and opens with Harris's profile of the scholar. It includes essays by C. Fahy on textual bibliography, E. Barbieri on philology of printed texts, A. Cuna on 15th-c. printing in Greek, M. Villoresi on popular books of prose and poetry, N. Harris on the 1532 edition of the *Furioso*, R. Campioni on C. Fahy and the *Censimento*, D. Maltese on the problems of *bibliografia retrospettiva*, and C. M. Simonetti on the Compagnie dell'Aquila in 16th-c. Venice. Cristina Moro, *Gli incunaboli delle biblioteche ecclesiastiche di Udine*, Udine, Forum, 1998, xviii + 268 pp., has a scholarly introduction that traces the formation of the Biblioteca del Seminario, Biblioteca Vescovile, Biblioteca Bartoliniana, and Biblioteca Capitolare, followed by a catalogue of 190 volumes with full critical apparatus. *Prima edizione a stampa della Divina Commedia*, ed. Piero Lai and Anna Maria Menichelli, Foligno, Comune di Foligno, 107 pp., comprises five essays which cover: Gutenberg and the conditions which led to the first printed texts; the question of a literary language and the *edizioni folignate*; the first printed editions of Dante, Petrarch, and Boccaccio of 1470–72; the birth of the *libro volgare*; the publishing history of Johann Neumeister, his impact on Foligno, and the ramifications of the new technology. *Bibliotheca Franciscana. Gli incunaboli e le cinquecentine dei Frati Minori dell'Osservanza dell'Emilia–Romagna conservate presso il Convento dell'Osservanza di Bologna*, ed. Zita Zanardi, F, Olschki, xxxvi + 271 pp. + 17 pls, has an introductory essay on the development of the library collection, followed by a list of 121 incunables and 1,889 *cinquecentine* with full critical apparatus. Ermanno Segù, *Incunaboli e cinquecentine nella biblioteca del Seminario Vescovile di Pavia*, Pavia, Biblioteca del Seminario, 1998, 540 pp., has a useful list describing 1,941 volumes without full critical apparatus. *Il vino tra sacro e profano. Vite e vino nelle raccolte casanatensi*, ed. Angela Adriana Cavarra, Ro, Aisthesis-Biblioteca Casanatense, 294 pp., traces the theme of wine through MSS of Virgil, Apicius, and Pliny, through the writings of Piero de' Crescenzi, M. Savonarola, V. Polidoro, and others, and through edicts and music.

Andrea Capuccioni, *Cosimo detto Bianchino dal Leone: un tipografo a Perugia nel Cinquecento*, Perugia, Volumnia, 109 pp., traces his name and provenance, and charts his printing activity from 1513 to 1544, cataloguing 59 volumes together with 13 documents but no critical apparatus. Melissa Conway, *The Diario of the Printing Press of San Jacopo di Ripoli 1476–1484. Commentary and Transcription*, F, Olschki, viii + 366 pp., gives a detailed analysis of a unique document which reveals the origin of the printing press, and the entrepreneurial spirit of the Dominican, Fra Domenico, who ran it. In eight years of activity it produced more than 40 works including classical, humanistic, and literary texts, popular devotional works, as well as broad sheets, and prayer leaflets. It also printed the first edition of the Latin translation of Plato by Ficino, financed by Francesco Berlinghieri and Filippo Valori. Chapters cover the business of printing, managing a printing office, the Ripoli press and printing history. This is a most enjoyable study of the organization of a printing press during the incunable period. Jérome Delatour, *Une bibliothèque humaniste au temps des guerres de religion. Les livres de Claude Dupuy*, Villeurbanne, ENSSIB, 1998, xvii + 344 pp., lists a collection of some 2,000 works, comprising contemporary and classical texts and MSS, which reflect the world of intellectuals and antiquarians from 1545 to 1594. The volumes, 242 in Italian, give an insight into the study of Roman antiquity, Greek literature, and encyclopedism. G. Bertoli, 'Il giovane Borghini e la paternità del *De administratione nosocomii s. Mariae Novae* e di alcune marche tipografiche fiorentine', *LItal*, 51:85–93. E. Pierazzo, 'Le edizioni marcoliniane della *Zucca* del Doni (1551–52)', *Italianistica*, 28:49–72.

## 2. HUMANISM.

Gordon Griffiths, *The Justification of Florentine Foreign Policy offered by Leonardo Bruni in his Public Letters (1428–1444)*, Ro, Istituto Storico Italiano per il Medio Evo, 188 pp., based on archival research in Florence and Venice, takes as its starting point the theme of liberty in the *Laudatio* (1403–04) and questions whether Bruni took the same stance during his period as Chancellor responsible for Florentine foreign policy. It compares, from an historical perspective, the documents issuing from the chancery with Bruni's rhetorical works to show that, in the struggle against Milan, idealism had to wait on pragmatism. V. Schmidt, 'A humanist's life summarized. Leonardo Bruni's *Epitaph*', *HL*, 47, 1998: 1–14. G. Cambiano, 'L'Atene nascosta di Leonardo Bruni', *Rinascimento*, 38, 1998:3–26. J. Hankins, 'Unknown and little-known texts of Leonardo Bruni', *ib.*, 125–62. S. Rizzo, 'Omero, lingua volgare e lingua grammaticale: riflessioni in margine a luoghi di Pier Candido Decembrio, Angelo Decembrio, Annio da Viterbo', *ib.*, 337–44. Liliana Monti Sabia, *Un profilo moderno e due Vitae antiche di Giovanni Pontano*, Na, Accademia Pontaniana, 1998, 104 pp., has a scholarly biography followed by the Latin texts with translations of two little known sources: *Joannis Joviani Pontani vita brevis* by the Neapolitan humanist Tristano Caracciolo which, though written after 1512, is the first life of Pontano, covering the period from his childhood to 1475; and Calisto Fido's letter *De natali solo ac vita Johannis Joviani*, written after 1549. L. Monti Sabia, 'La mano di Giovanni Pontano in due Livii della Biblioteca Nazionale di Napoli', *IMU*, 39, 1996[1999]:171–208. Giovanni Pontano, *I libri delle virtù sociali*, ed. Francesco Tateo, Ro, Bulzoni, 278 pp., gives the Latin texts with translations of a series of interconnected philosophical works: *De liberalitate, De beneficentia, De magnificentia, De splendore*, and *De conviventia*, all written before 1493. The introduction sees them as a response to a social and political crisis and links them to his other writings on morality and ethics. Cecil Grayson, *Studi su Leon Battista Alberti*, ed. Paola Claut, F, Olschki, 1998, viii + 436 pp., has an introduction that reviews the publishing fortunes of Alberti's writings and the background to Grayson's own studies. There follow in chronological order 28 essays published between 1952 and 1994 and ranging from studies of Alberti's language to studies on humanism and humanists. Taken as a whole they represent a major contribution to Alberti scholarship. Leon Battista Alberti, *De statua*, ed. Mariarosa Spinetti, Na, Liguori, 52 pp., gives a translation with facing Latin text together with a short introduction that examines the innovative features of Alberti's methodology, and the history and structure of the work. Leon Battista Alberti, *Deifira. Analisi tematica e formale*, ed. Amalia Cecere, Na, Liguori, 120 pp., is an enlightening analysis of Alberti's theory of love in the *Ecatonfilea* and *Deifira*, and a detailed line-by-line stylistic and linguistic analysis of the *Deifira* which points to the close links between language and themes. Lucia Bertolini, *Grecus Sapor. Tramiti di presenze greche in Leon Battista Alberti*, Ro, Bulzoni, 1998, viii + 119 pp., studies the *Consolatoria* of C. Marsuppini and the *Homer* of Leonzio Pilato in order to assess Alberti's real knowledge of Greek and his debt to contemporary humanist scholars. It shows that the lines of transmission are obscure and that close comparisons of texts are required if one is to arrive at clear conclusions. A. Tenenti, 'Il Tempio. Riflessioni sul pensiero religioso di Leon Battista Alberti',

*Intersezioni*, 19:95–104. S. Simoncini, 'Le avventure di Momo nel Rinascimento. Il nume della critica tra Leon Battista Alberti e Giordano Bruno', *Rinascimento*, 38, 1998:405–54. A. Manfredi, 'Vicende umanistiche di codici Vaticani con opere di Sant'Ambrogio', *Aevum*, 72, 1998:559–89. D. Canfora, 'Il *De rege et tyranno* di Agostino Nifo e il *De infelicitate principum* di Poggio Bracciolini', *CLett*, 27:455–68. A. Carlini, 'Da Bisanzio a Firenze. Platone letto, trascritto, commentato e tradotto nei secoli XIV e XV', *AMAT*, 62, 1997[1998]:129–43. A. Rollo, 'La lettera consolatoria di Manuele Crisolora a Palla Strozzi', *Studi umanistici*, 4–5, 1993–94[1998]:7–86. *Malinconia ed allegrezza nel Rinascimento*, ed. Luisa Rotondi Secchi Tarugi, Mi, Nuovi Orizzonti, 575 pp., contains 41 essays including: J. Balsamo on melancholy in Guazzo; E. Bigi on *allegrezze umanistiche* in the letters of Bracciolini; P. G. Bietenholz on Valla's *De voluptate* and Erasmus's *Elogio della follia*; M. Lanfranchi on the themes of melancholy and joy in Valla; M. Davie on melancholy and laughter in Pulci; E. N. Girardi on melancholy and Saturnism in Michelangelo; S. Dall'Oco on E. S. Piccolomini's *De remedio amoris*; and L. Valcke on Pico della Mirandola. *Epistolae ad principes*, III, Sixtus V – Clemens VIII (1585–1605), ed. Luigi Nanni and Tomisalv Mrkonjic, Città del Vaticano, 1997, 784 pp., is a valuable resource for both literary scholars and historians. Anna Jolly, *Madonnas by Donatello and his Circle*, Bern, Lang, 1998, 360 pp. 146 pls, investigates the new interest in modelling in the early 15th c., which owed much to the writings of Pliny the Elder and was widely discussed in humanist circles. The genre is related to Alberti's *Della pittura* and P. Gaurico's treatise on sculpture. Francesco Barbaro, *La raccolta canonica delle epistole*, ed. Claudio Griggio, III, F, Olschki, liv + 807 pp., lists many addenda and corrigenda to the first volume (*La tradizione manoscritta e a stampa*, 1991) and gives a detailed account of the extant MS tradition and of the selection criteria, followed by the texts of 390 letters. The correspondents include Acciauoli, Beccadelli, Bracciolini, and Cosimo de' Medici. John M. McManamon, *Pier Paolo Vergerio the Elder and Saint Jerome. An Edition and Translation of Sermones pro sancto Hieronymo*, MRTS, xvii + 402 pp., is the first critical edition, with translation, of the ten panegyrics devoted to Saint Jerome. The introduction investigates what Jerome meant for the early humanists and why he became such an important, indeed inspirational, figure for Vergerio, who transformed him from 'an enemy of humanist learning to an advocate of its benefit for committed Christians'. The wealth of bibliographical information reflects the impeccable scholarship of this study. Paolo Cherchi, *Polimatia di riuso. Mezzo secolo di plagio (1539–1589)*, Ro, Bulzoni, 1998, 304 pp., sets out the subtle distinctions between *plagio* and *riscrittura*, and the methodologies and genres that gave rise to both phenomena. He points to a crisis in humanist culture around 1539 which led to false erudition. The works of both Doni and Guazzo are seen as the fruits of a new approach, and, though initially plagiarism and *riscrittura* may have been used within a polemical context, by the end of the century the very concept of erudition had been transformed. Nicholas Mann and Luke Syson, *The Image of the Individual. Portraits in the Renaissance*, London, British Museum, 1998, 240 pp., has 13 essays including a section, 'Classical precedents' with studies of: medallic portraits of the Este as products of courtly humanist culture; the classical debt of Medici glyptic portraits; humanist opinions, and the political function and sophisticated allusiveness of portrait likenesses. John Cunnally, *Images of the Illustrious. The Numismatic Presence in the Renaissance*, Princeton U.P., xi + 230 pp., shows how the many coin collections, linked to humanist scholarship and book illustrations, had a profound impact on the dissemination of knowledge of classical antiquity, and how they became a means of social intercourse. It presents a stimulating body of evidence which evokes the enthusiasm and excitement of the collectors.

That theorizing on architecture, the most socially engaged of the arts, represented a fundamental aspect of much humanist activity is only now being recognized. Alina A. Payne, *The Architectural Treatise in the Italian Renaissance. Architectural Invention, Ornament, and Literary Culture*, CUP, xv + 343 pp., places Renaissance architecture firmly within the world of literary and philosophical inquiry. It provides a close textual analysis of the works of Alberti, Francesco di Giorgio Martini, Serlio, and Scamozzi. It is about 'reading formats; about the humanist's and the architect's bookshelf, about what there was to provide a context for assimilating Vitruvius: it is [. . .] about the reader of Vitruvius who was also a reader of Aristotle, Cicero, Horace, and Ovid'. Mario Carpo, *L'architettura dell'età della stampa, oralità, scrittura, libro stampato e riproduzione meccanica dell'immagine della storia delle teorie architettoniche*, Mi, Jaca, 1997, 239 pp., charts the transformation of a 'mechanical' practice into a literary genre, then of a discourse based on words to one based on images. It proposes a convincing hypothesis for the lack of illustrations in classical and early Medieval texts. Annarita Angelini, *Sapienza, prudenza, eroica virtù, il mediomondo di Daniele Barbaro*, F, Olschki, xviii + 420 pp., analyses Barbaro's commentary to the Italian edition of Vitruvius and identifies a precise philosophical position as 'una struttura interpretativa della realtà conoscibile, che tende a identificarsi con un modello di enciclopedia come universitas del sapere umano'. Angelini rightly refuses to label Barbaro as either Aristotelian or Platonist; his cultural training, intellectual interests, and the circles in which he moved led him to develop a new language and new forms of rhetoric towards a reform and reorganization of knowledge where revelation was placed between the intelligible and the sensible universe. M. Vitruvio, *I dieci libri dell'architettura tradotti e commentati da Daniele Barbaro*, Ro, Bardi, xvii + 506 pp., is a facsimile of the 1567 Venetian edition, with an introductory essay by Tancredi Carunchio which identifies the importance of Vitruvius in Renaissance culture and the cultural and political aims of both Palladio and Barbaro to 'introdurre a Venezia la cultura classica romana, intesa a promuovere l'affrancamento della Serenissima dai legami della tradizione culturale tardo quattrocentesca'. Lionello Puppi, *Palladio*, ed. Donata Battilotti, Mi, Electa, 569 pp., a revision of the 1973 edition, traces divergent attitudes to classical studies and situates Palladio within the archeological and antiquarian tendency of Gian Giorgio Trissino, Alvise Cornaro, Giulio Camillo, Daniele Barbaro, and the Accademia Olimpica. Licia Asquini and Massimo Asquini, *Andrea Palladio e gli Antonini. Un palazzo 'Romano' nella Udine del Cinquecento*, Monfalcone, Laguna, 1997, xxiii + 167 pp., traces the links between the Antonini family and humanist circles and how their choice of palazzo design was a direct result of the links between them and patrician families in Venice and the Veneto. Vincenzo Scamozzi, *L'idea dell'architettura universale*, 2 vols, Vicenza, Centro Internazionale di Studi di Architettura Andrea Palladio, 1997, xxxviii + 352, 370 pp., provides a facsimile of the 1615 first edition with a scholarly introduction by F. Barbieri. This investigates why in the late 16th c. Scamozzi's works, along with those of Alberti, were regarded as *inutile erudizione*, a last attempt to present an exhaustive account of architecture on the model of Vitruvius. The text displays Scamozzi vast erudition and humanist training, particularly in history and philosophy, and his familiarity with the works of Plato, Aristotle, Galen, Vitruvius, and Alberti.

PHILOSOPHY AND HISTORY OF IDEAS. Cesare Vasoli, *Quasi sit deus. Studi su Marsilio Ficino*, Lecce, Conte, 357 pp., contains nine essays, two of them hitherto unpublished: 'Il mito dei prisci theologi come ideologia della renovatio' (11–50) examines the singular strain of Ficino's Christianity which aimed at a 'mediazione cosmica [..] del Cristo-verbo', whereas 'Marsilio Ficino e il suo rapporto con Agostino' (91–112) traces F.'s debt to Augustine for his ideas on art and beauty, and his role as a mediator of Platonic ideas. Marsilio Ficino, *Sopra lo amore ovvero convito di Platone*, ed. Giuseppe Rensi, Mi, SE, 1998, 166 pp., is a reprint, with corrections, of the Carabba 1914 edition without notes or critical apparatus. Michael J. B. Allen, *Synoptic Art. Marsilio Ficino on the History of Platonic Interpretation*, F, Olschki, 1998, xiv + 236 pp., consists of five studies which deal with:

Ficino's preoccupation with converting the intelligentsia to the truths of revelation; his concern with the *ingeniosus* and the attempt to establish Plotinus as inspired interpreter; the philosopher's tone of truth over and against the poet's love of the lie; Socrates as Christian philosopher and theologian who had become one with his daemon or guardian angel; the importance of Ficino's dialectic, its anti-Aristotelian character, and its function to apprehend the Good. *Friend to Mankind. Marsilio Ficino*, ed. Michael Shepherd, London, Shepheard-Walwyn, 215 pp., has 18 essays which celebrate 'his inspiration in his own times, his extending influence in subsequent centuries and [. . .] most of all, his continuing practical relevance today'. *The Letters of Marsilio Ficino*, vi: *Liber VII*, London, Shepheard-Walwyn, xxiv + 165 pp., comprises 44 letters written between 1481 and 1483 with a translation of 'On the star of the Magi' in the appendix. Some of the letters reflect the turbulent political events of the period, whilst others refer to his philosophical work, and to the themes of prophecy and astrology. This volume has a facsimile of the Venetian edition of 1495 and, as in the other volumes of this project, there is a full critical apparatus. *\*Marsilio Ficino e il ritorno di Ermete Trismegisto*, ed. Sebastiano Gentile and Carlos Gilly, F, Centro Di, 325 pp. V. Rees, 'Marsilio Ficino: philosopher and friend', *BSRS*, 16.1, 1998: 18–23. M. O'Rourke Boyle, 'Gracious laughter: Marsilio Ficino's anthropology', *RQ*, 52:712–41. C. S. Celenza, 'Pythagoras in the Renaissance: the case of Marsilio Ficino', *RQ*, 52:627–66. S. A. Farmer, *Syncretism in the West: Pico's 900 Theses (1486). The Evolution of Traditional Religious and Philosophical Systems*, MRTS, 1998, xv + 595 pp., is an excellent study which analyses Pico's 'new philosophy' and reconstructs his aims and debating strategies. It has chapters on syncretism, on deciphering the 900 theses, and on Pico and anti-Pico, and a scholarly review of the extant editions and MSS of the theses. The edition itself has full scholarly apparatus and gives both the Latin text and a translation. Clement Salaman et al., *The Way of Hermes*, London, Duckworth, 124 pp., presents the text of the *Corpus Hermeticum* with a short preface and that of *The Definitions of Hermes Trismegistus to Asclepius* with a scholarly introduction. Silvia Zoppi Garampi, *Tommaso Campanella: il progetto del sapere universale*, Na, Vivarium, 148 pp., investigates two treatises, the *Grammatica* and *Poetica*, of the *Philosophia rationales*. The *Grammatica* is shown to invest each particular language with specific scientific and cultural values, whereas the *Poetica* engages with the work of Horace. *Method and Order in Renaissance Philosophy of Nature: the Aristotle Commentary Tradition*, ed. Daniel A. Di Liscia, Eckhard Kessler, and Charlotte Methuen, Aldershot, Ashgate, 1997, xi + 416 pp., contains 17 essays which investigate the transformation of Aristotelian ideas with studies on:

Averroist commentaries on method; the philosophy of nature in Cardano and Telesio; Zabarella and F. Piccolomini on the differing views of academic and civil order and the place of the philosopher in that order; and Zabarella on the classification of the arts and sciences. Andrea Carlino, *Books of the Body. Anatomical Ritual and Renaissance Learning*, Chicago U.P., xiv + 266 pp., places dissection within a Roman ethical, legal, and medical framework, seeing it as an investigative tool, related more to the acquisition of knowledge than to medicine, and shows how professional interests hindered the revision of Galenic teaching that should have been promoted by new evidence. Maryanne Cline Horowitz, *Seeds of Virtue and Knowledge*, Princeton U.P., 1998, xviii + 373 pp., investigates the image and idea of the human mind as a garden and interprets the complex meanings in vegetative symbolism. Digging the foundations in Stoicism and moving to the flowering in Augustine and Aquinas the study branches out to encompass the writings of the Italian humanists.

BRUNO. Giordano Bruno, *Cause, Principle, and Unity and Essays on Magic*, trans. and ed. Richard J. Blackwell and Roberto de Lucca, CUP, 1998, xxxvi + 186 pp., gives a translation of *De la Causa, De Magia*, and *De vinculis in genere* with a scholarly introduction by A. Ingegno which discusses B. with respect to other philosophical positions and shows how his theory of the infinite universe impacts on the relationship between God, the world, and human beings. Michele Ciliberto, *Umbra Profunda. Studi su Giordano Bruno*, Ro, Storia e Letteratura, 330 pp., groups 11 essays in two sections. 'Filosofia e autobiografia' takes issue with Gentile's position by analysing B.'s reworking of autobiographical material, revisits the studies of F. Yates noting her lack of sensitivity to B. as a philosopher, points to the need to evaluate the different stages in B.'s use of Hermetic sources, and raises new questions about B.'s stay in England, with an analysis of the *Spaccio della bestia trionfante* and the *Cabala del cavallo pegaseo*. 'Bilanci e prospettive' reviews the state of B. studies. This is a stimulating collection that sheds new light on B. the philosopher and B. studies in general. Aniello Montano, *Giordano Bruno e Tommaso Campanella*, Na, Città del Sole, 62 pp., has two insightful short portraits. Giordano Bruno, *Opere italiane. Ristampa anastatica delle cinquecentine*, I: *Candelaio*; II: *La cena delle ceneri, De la causa principio et uno, De l'infinito, universo et mondi*; III: *Spaccio della bestia trionfante, Cabala del cavallo pegaseo*; IV: *De gl'heroici furori*, ed. Eugenio Canone, 4 vols, F, Olschki, xl + 324, 327–846, 849–1240, 1243–1592 pp., has an introduction pointing to the importance of referring to the original editions, commenting on the historiographical tradition and B.'s use of language, and giving a chronology of the Italian texts and their significance in the development of B.'s ideas. *Bruniana & Campanelliana*, 4, 1998, a collection of

19 essays, includes studies of B. on the themes of *ingegno*, atomism, religion, Machiavelli, cosmology, the English period, his trial, Christian Cabbala, and Ficino and Zoroaster. S. Nucciarelli, ' "Curiosus[. . .]in bonam et malam partem sumitur": la "curiositade" nei dialoghi italiani di Giordano Bruno', *NRLett*, 18.2, 1998:85–108. Guido de Rosa, *Il concetto di 'immaginazione' nel pensiero di Giordano Bruno*, Na, Città del Sole, 1997, 213 pp., uses the *De imaginum compositione* to assess the connotations of the terms *immaginazione* and *fantasia*. Giordano Bruno, *Il primo libro della Clavis magna ovvero il trattato sull'intelligenza artificiale*, trans. and introd. Claudio D'Antonio, Ro, Di Rienzo, 334 pp., identifies the *imaginum compositio* as the *clavis magna* followed by a translation and the Latin text without any critical apparatus.

RELIGIOUS THOUGHT AND THE CHURCH. Alberto Venturoli, *Il profeta della gioia. La mistica di San Filippo Neri*, Mi, Jaca, 108 pp., sets out a collection of prose, poetry, and maxims which reflect the quiet, pious, and devotional tone that had such a widespread impact in the late 16th century. *La Bibbia in Italiano tra Medioevo e Rinascimento*, ed. Lino Leonardi, F, Sismel, 1998, 442 pp., is an excellent collection of essays divided into five sections: 'La Bibbia e i volgarizzamenti', on production, circulation, and textual tradition; 'Verso un repertorio dei volgarizzamenti Italiani', with essays on the Apocalypse, glosses, the Gospels, and books of the Old Testament; 'La Bibbia nelle altre lingue romanze'; 'Libri e tradizioni particolari', covering humanism, Hebrew, biblical studies, and *lezionari*; 'La fine di un epoca', on Church reform and the return of Latin. Mario Zanchin, *Il primato del romano pontefice in un'opera inedita di Pietro del Monte del secolo XV*, Vigodarzere, Progetto Editoriale Mariano, 1997, 317 pp., is the first edition of a work dedicated to Pope Nicholas V by a Venetian Bishop, humanist, and diplomat. Diana Gisolfi and Staale Sinding-Larsen, *The Rule, the Bible and the Council. The Library of the Benedictine Abbey at Praglia*, Seattle, Washington U.P., 1998, xiii + 200 pp. + 77 pls, examines how the decoration of the library was used to comment on theological issues which stressed traditional dogma and 'right teaching', and the path to salvation via Divine wisdom. The study challenges some of the positions taken by H. Jedin on Trent and points out our lack of real understanding of the many issues involved. Antonio Samaritani, *Il Cinquecento religioso a Comacchio*, Ferrara, Corbo, 1997, 394 pp., while primarily concerned with tracing the gradual implementation of reformed practice, the study also has a great deal to offer on the links between the various Bishops and the worlds of humanism and literature. Franco Mormando, *The Preacher's Demons. Bernardino of Siena and the Social Underworld of Early Modern Italy*, Chicago U.P., xvi + 364 pp., concentrates on the preaching campaigns and the themes which most preoccupied his audience such as witchcraft, sodomy, and Judaism. It assesses the influences, and the social, intellectual, and religious climate that inspired his theology and programmes of reform. F. Mormando, 'Bernardino of Siena, "great defender" or "merciless betrayer" of women?', *Italica*, 75, 1998:22–40.

SAVONAROLA. *Savonarola rivisitato (1498–1998)*, ed. Massimiliano G. Rosito, F, Città di Vita, 229 pp., gathering a score of essays, includes: D. T. Verdan on painting, architecture, and S.'s ideas on morality; K. Eisenbichler on S.'s first published work (1491); L. Lunetta on the polemical exchange of letters between Angelo da Vallombrosa and the Dominicans of S. Marco; C. Vasoli on the defence of S. by the Franciscan Paolo da Fucecchio; A. Drigani on Gianfrancesco Pico Della Mirandola and S.'s innocence; and L. Sebregondi on the changing visual representations of Savonarola. *Quaderni del quarto centenario 1498–1998*, VII, Bo, Studio Domenicano, 1998, 127 pp., gathers three essays: T. S. Centi, 'I calunniati fanciulli di Fra Girolamo' (5–24), on the misrepresentation of Savonarola's ideas; E. Marino, 'Savonarola e la cultura poetico-artistica di Firenze' (58–78), on S.'s experience of humanist culture; E. Pucci, 'Savonarola, un maestro di vita' (79–108). It also includes the text of the *Predica prima sullo Spirito Santo*. G. Cadoni, 'Savonarola, Machiavelli, Guicciardini in una recente ipotesi interpretativa', *La Cultura*, 37:493–96. R. Catani, 'Girolamo Savonarola and astrology', *The Italianist*, 18:71–90.

INDIVIDUAL CENTRES. Ingrid D. Rowland, *The Culture of the High Renaissance. Ancient and Moderns in Sixteenth-Century Rome*, CUP, 1998, xiv + 384 pp., examines the Utopian aspirations in late 15th and early 16th-c. Rome to create a new order, by assimilating the best from the past, involving important cultural figures such as T. Inghirami, A. Chigi, and A. Colucci. Rowland delves into a vast array of sources from the world of literature, philosophy, mathematics, and polemics and succeeds in bringing to life the cultural ferment of a moment of hope, and charts its ultimate failure.

## 3. POETRY

Charles S. Ross, *The Custom of the Castle: from Malory to Macbeth*, Berkeley, California U.P., 1997, xvii + 205 pp., provides a fresh appraisal of certain customs found in chivalric narratives to introduce the reader to 'the challenging legal and cultural conceptions of custom in France, Italy and England'. In his section 'The Italian Transition' he examines how the stock episode (a knight arriving at a castle and being compelled to conform to an unjust custom) developed from the French model and in the works of Boiardo and Ariosto demonstrates new attitudes to tradition and the exercise of authority. C. Lastraioli, 'Le pasquinate italiane del MS N.A.F. 3107 della Biblioteca Nationale di Parigi', *FC*, 23, 1998:72–116, attributes the satirical epitaphs written upon the death of Pope Pius IV (9 December 1565) to Camillo della Croce. The brief overview of this figure's biography and his correspondence illustrate how diplomatic letters between the Papal and French courts (1530s and 1540s) frequently contained allusions to or had actual transcripts of *pasquinate* in Latin or the vernacular attached to them. L. shows how, following the anti-*pasquinata* campaign waged by the court of Pius V, the power of the *pasquinata* waned in Italy whereas in France it had become by the 1570s one of the most powerful weapons of the 'polemica anti-aulica e riformata'. In a detailed philological critique of the anonymous chivalric romance *Falconetto*, A. Canova, 'Problemi e proposte per l'edizione critica del *Falconetto* (1483)', *Aevum*, 72, 1998:647–69, attempts to undo the scathing review it received from Dionisotti. While admitting its metrical idiosyncrasies and repetition of character and plot from the Carolingian cycle, he nevertheless supports a reappraisal of the text especially in comparison to others of the same genre. D. Javitch, 'La nascita della teoria dei generi poetici del Cinquecento', *Italianistica*, 27, 1998:177–98, argues convincingly that the unprecedented Cinquecento explosion of treatises on poetic forms derived from what he calls 'progressive classicism'. Using Tasso, Vida, and especially Giraldi's *Discorso* on theatre as his reference point, he contends that the application of Aristotle's *Poetics* and the theories consequently produced represented a modernization of ancient genres. Giancarlo Mazzacurati, *Rinascimenti in transito*, Ro, Bulzoni, 1996, 225 pp., builds a picture of Renaissance Classicism by tracing the beginnings, evolutionary 'crisi', and European diffusion of the 'archetipi . . . transiti . . . trasformazioni' of Italian Cinquecento culture. Chapters include 'Le carte del Boiardo' (27–59); 'Il laboratorio ariostesco nella trasmissione dei "generi"' (59–79); and '1528–1532: Luigi Alamanni, tra la piazza e la Corte' (89–113). *Antologia della poesia italiana*, ed. Cesare Segre and Carlo Ossola, II, *Quattrocento e Cinquecento*, T, Einaudi, 1639 pp., has excellent philological and biographical essays. The Quattrocento is structured according to themes: 'Poesia dell'Umanesimo latino'; 'Poesia dell'Umanesimo volgare'; 'Lorenzo de' Medici'; 'Poliziano'; 'Poesia realistica e burlesca'; 'Matteo Maria Boiardo'; 'Poeti regionali e di corte'; 'Poesia per musica, laudi e composizioni religiose'. The Cinquecento deals with Sanazzaro, Ariosto, Folengo, Bembo, Castiglione, 'Petrarchisti e Manieristi', 'Rime spirituali', Tasso. Aretino is curiously excluded from the collection which provides an invaluable selection of poems and an incipit index. *Lepschy Vol.* contains two essays of particular interest to Renaissance scholars: L. Pertile, 'Plurilinguismo di Trifon Gabriele o Giason Denores' (177–95), with reference to *Regole Grammaticali* (1545), to writings on eminent poets (such as Dante) attributed to Gabriele, as well as to some minor Latin and unpublished texts, attempts to distinguish their author and show how Latin texts were read in the Veneto in the mid-16th c. The composite nature of these works is highlighted to reveal that, if Gabriele diminishes in stature, his school, with pupils such as Denores, does not and deserves greater critical attention; M. Davie, 'The connotations of *riso*, *ridere* in Pulci's *Morgante*' (165–76), through a detailed reading of the *Morgante*, shows the evolution of *ridere* in the poem from *riso* in the Dantesque sense of spiritual serenity to the destructive force of derision. These contrasting thematic layers ultimately point the way for 'chivalric poetry as the mixed genre par excellence in the Renaissance'. *La Raxone de la Pasca. Opus aureum et fructosum*, ed. R. Bagnasco, N. Boccalatte and F. Toso, Genoa, Le Mani, 1997, 63 pp., is the first modern edition with ample comment-ary of the 1473 text which is a description of Liguria in vernacular verse which besides linguistic interest provides an insight into the local and regional political and social issues of the time. R. Nigro, *Poeti e baroni nel Rinascimento lucano*, Venosa, Osanna, 1997, 87 pp., gathers a selection of 15th-c. verse from various noble authors centred around the noted jurist Roberto Maranta to portray the absorption of humanist and Petrarchan trends in the literary context of the region. *Miti del Cilento, cantati da Berardino Rota*, trans. G. Liuccio, Casalvelino Scalo, Galzerano, 1997, 68 pp., is a fluid and highly readable modern verse translation with explanatory notes and bibliography of the original Latin poem of the noted 16th-c. Neapolitan man of letters.

ARETINO. A. N. Mancini, 'Aretino italo e americano', *Italica*, 75, 1998:441–53, reviews two volumes of papers, *Pietro Aretino nel cinquecentenario della nascita*, produced as a result of the convention organized in 1992 by the Centro Pio Rajna in conjunction with the Comitato per l'Edizione Nazionale delle Opere. The volumes contain valuable contributions from many eminent A. scholars. For the poetry: M. Ciavolella looks at 'La produzione erotica di Pietro Aretino' (49–66), at its dating, P. Larivaille, 'Sulla datazione dei *Sonetti lussuriosi* di Pietro Aretino' (599–618); A. Romano, 'Come lavorava Aretino nelle poesie' (335–48); R. Bruscagli examines the narrative production in 'Aretino e la tradizione cavalleresca' (45–74). The one criticism to be levelled at these two essential volumes for Aretino scholars is that there is not enough coverage of the reception of A.'s texts in Italy and abroad.

ARIOSTO. M. A. Groesbeck, ' "Tra noi non resto più di differenza": men, transvestites and power in the *Orlando Furioso*' *AnI*, 16:65–84, explores the irony in A.'s veiled critique of Ferrara's ruling dynasty. The thematic extremes of power and impotence are illustrated in a radical way through the female warrior knights Marfisa and Bradamante. It is shown how although A. inevitably must conform to his task of glorifying the Este rulers, he undermines traditionally male attributes of power by this blurring of gender identities, which permits him to criticize subtly his masters. M. Praloran, \**Tempo e azione nell'*"*Orlando Furioso*', F, Olschki, pursues an analysis of how the events in the text are related which is 'narratologica', 'stilistica', and 'linguistica'. P. makes constant reference to literary precedents from classical to Arthurian romance but in particular highlights Boiardo as a key source.

ARLOTTO. F. Pignatti, 'I "motti e facezie del Piovano Arlotto" e la cultura del 400', *GSLI*, 176:54–86, while stating that Arlotto's text deserves to be considered on a par with the major works of 'letteratura faceta e giocosa', for example Poggio's *Liber facetiarum* and Poliziano's *Detti piacevoli* claims that the text can be linked to the *comicità* of Cinquecento texts like *Mandragola* and *La Cortegiana* as well as the plays of Gonnella and Barlacchi. Through a close reading of the text he furthermore argues convincingly that Quattrocento humanist biography is the source of Arlotto's peculiar trait of the pivotal role of a central character around which the *libro faceto* revolves.

BEMBO. A. Roncaccia, 'Un frammento critico sulle *Rime* del Bembo attribuibile a Lodovico Castelvetro', *Aevum*, 72, 1998:707–34, analyses a fragment ('Annotationi sopra i sonetti del Bembo') found in the Gamle Kongelige Samling of the Kongelige Bibliotek in Copenhagen, which he argues is a systematic commentary on Bembo's *Rime* carried out between 1535 and 1558. The fragment, which reached Copenhagen most probably through Castelvetro's nephew Giacomo, is analysed by Roncaccia who uncovers what he sees as characteristic features, not least C.'s style, the critical method applied to the *Rime*, the application of Aristotelian categories to verse. Particular attention is paid to his frequent controversial comments concerning Bembism: the alternation between admiration for the Petrarchan model and repudiation of Bembism.

BERNI. G. Giampieri, *Francesco Berni, I Toscani*, Fucecchio, Erba, 1997, 140 pp., attempts to overcome the scarcity of information about this well-known figure of the Renaissance by throwing new light on his poetic output which is 'originale e trasgressiva'.

BOIARDO. Matteo Maria Boiardo, *Amorum Libri Tres*, ed. T. Zanato, T, Einaudi, lx + 593 pp., has an introduction that illuminates the structure of the work with an excellent analysis of style, sources, textual tradition, and language complemented by exemplary notes. S. Carrai, 'La formazione di Boiardo. Modelli e letture di un giovane umanista', *Rinascimento*, 38, 1998:345–404, attempts to remedy the lack of information available about B.'s education and reading tastes by analysing the poetic output of the first 30 years of his life. From the fundamental influence of his uncle Tito Vespasiano Strozzi and the youthful works *Pastoralia* and the *Carmina de Laudibus Estensium*, the analysis culminates in the precedents for the *Amorum Libri* by suggesting that over and above the standard Ovidian and Petrarchan sources direct comparisons, especially in innovative use of metre, can be traced between the *Amorum* and Alberti's verse. M. Villoresi, 'Le donne e gli amori nel romanzo cavalleresco del '400', *FC*, 23, 1998:3–43, isolates certain patterns with regard to female figures and the process of falling in love in B.'s *Orlando innamorato*. He reviews minor works which precede B. to reveal the female stereotypes of the beautiful saracen, the witch seductress, and the amazon before launching into an in-depth study of the figure of B.'s Angelica, his concept of love, and the language he uses to depict it. Elio Monducci and Gino Badini, *Matteo Maria Boiardo: la vita nei documenti del suo tempo*, Modena, Aedes Muratoriana, 1997, lxi + 499 pp., sets Boiardo within a social and political framework and presents a series of documents relating to the lost first edition of the *Innamorato* of 1482–83. There is a brief chronology followed by archival references to all the letters together with sources of published material. This is followed by 744 documents, 370 of which are previously unpublished.

BRACCIOLINI. Like Boccaccio, Poggio Bracciolini as shown by G. Maglio, 'Poggio Bracciolini e il "Bugiale" come osservatore del suo tempo', *EL*, 23.2, 1998:43–62, casts a sardonic eye over the human behaviour of his time, particularly through the stock characters of the *Facetiae*. The comic nature of these cliches (e.g. *meretrix, vir indoctus*) does not prevent a more serious principle being expressed, i.e. that the virtues are not defined by status in society.

CAMMELLI. A. Mauriello, 'L'edizione dei sonetti faceti di Antonio Cammelli', *EL*, 24.3:51–68, looks again at E. Percopo's 1908 edition of Cammelli's work published in Naples. Percopo's text, the product of 20 years of research, attempted to refocus attention on this forgotten author who frequented the courts of Northern Italy between 1436 and 1502. Mauriello justly looks at Percopo's editorial choices in great detail and completes this essential source book of Cammelli's work by placing it in the general context of Tuscan mock poetry of the Quattrocento and Cinquecento.

CAPORALI. Cesare Caporali, *Gli orti di Mecenate*, ed. G. Lana, Ellera Umbra, Era Nuova, 71 pp., is a new edition, based on the 1898 edition, of the verse of a 16th-c. Umbrian man of letters, with ample bibliography and biographical notes.

CARMIGIANO. C. Mauro, *'Le cose vulgare* (1516) e *Le Operette* (1535) di Colantonio Carmigiano: un primo confronto', *CLett*, 27:225–46, attempts to undo Dionisotti's damning assessment of the noble Neapolitan poet known more by the pseudonym Partenopeo Suavio. Two texts are examined, *Le cose vulgare*, Venice, 1516, the principal object of D.'s ire and *Le Operette*, Bari, 1535. A thorough comparison of the two works, is intended to show the merits of the work of a poet who hitherto has only been mentioned in passing in bibliographies of 16th-c. southern writing.

CHIABRERA. Gabriello Chiabrera, *Maniere, scherzi e canzonette morali*, ed. Giulia Raboni, Parma, Guanda, xliv + 556 pp., is the first critical edition, based on the 1599 edition and with full philological apparatus and a useful *incipitario*. The scholarly introduction traces Chiabrera's sources.

CIGALA CASERO. Barnaba Cigala Casero, *Quarche gran maravegia, qualche gran meraviglia: liriche d'amore*, ed. F. Toso, Genoa, Le Mani, 61 pp., publishes the love verse of a 16th-c. Genoese Petrarchist renowned for encomiastic verse in Genoese.

COLONNA. The status enjoyed by Vittoria Colonna is revealed in C. Cinquini, 'Rinaldo Corso editore e commentatore delle *Rime* di Vittoria Colonna', *Aevum*, 73:669–96, which analyses two noted works regarding V. Colonna: the *Dichiaratione fatta sopra la seconda parte delle Rime della Divina Vittoria Colonna, Marchesana di Pescara, da Rinaldo Corso*, Bologna, Faelli, 1543, and *Tutte le rime della Illustrissima et Eccellentissima signora Vittoria Colonna Marchesana di Pescara, con l'esposi-tione del Signor Rinaldo Corso*, Venezia, Sessa, 1558, containing 120 examples of love poetry plus a new edition of the *Dichiaratione*. Normally only male poets of the highest calibre had their collections of poetry organized according to a precise logical narrative line as well as being pre-empted by an *espositione* in prose. There being no instructions from the author herself, Rinaldo Corso's (1525) organiza-tion of the text which also includes commentary on individual poems creates a true *canzoniere* which ratifies her status *post mortem*. M. Bianco, *\*'Le due redazioni del commento di Rinaldo Corso alle rime di Vittoria Colonna'*, *SFI*, 56, 1998[1999]:271–95. T. R. Toscano. *\*'La formazione "napoletana" di Vittoria Colonna e un nuovo manoscritto delle sue *Rime*', *SPCT*, 57, 1998:79–106.

DAL CARRETTO. S. Tomassini, 'Nel tribunale d'amore (a pro-posito di un'edizione recente del *Tempio d'Amore* di Galeotto dal Carretto)', *SPCT*, 58:89–102, argues that this hugely successful and monumental autobiographical work of some 7000 verses (four editions between 1518 and 1525) modelled on the *Roman de la Rose* deserves a special place in the history of allegorical and didactic verse and benefits greatly from the index and commentary on sources.

DELLA CASA. S. Carrai, *'Ancora sull'edizione delle *Rime* di Giovanni Della Casa', *SPCT*, 56, 1998:95–118.

FELICIANO. E. M. Duso, 'Un nuovo manoscritto esemplato da Felice Feliciano', *LItal*, 50, 1998:566–86, considers the interest to lie not so much in the verse of Marco Piacentini, the prolific Venetian Petrarchist as in the role of the noted copyist Felice Feliciano. The Veronese antiquarian added illustrations to P.'s text (probably from the 1460s - the Antichrist and Cupid) which synthesize the thematic poles of the *rime*. The changes illustrate the criteria which influenced F.'s choice of text, in this case predominantly political poetry, critical of the Curia. By the same author, *'Appunti per l'edizione critica di Marco Piacentini', *SFI*, 56, 1998[1999]:57–127.

FILELFO. Francesco Filelfo, *De Psychagogia* ed. G. Cortassa and E. V. Maltese, Alessandria, Orso, 1997, vii + 150 pp., is the first complete edition of the 15 Greek poems from MS Laurenziano 58, which illustrate F.'s great erudition and knowledge of rhetorical forms as well as introducing many contemporary figures.

FONTE. Although the two most famous pieces attributed to the 16th-c. feminist poet Moderata Fonte (*Tredici canti del Floridoro* and the dialogue *Il merito delle donne*) are the principal subject of S. D. Kolsky, 'Per la carriera poetica di Moderata Fonte: alcuni documenti poco consociuti', *EL*, 23.4, 1998:3–18, two other types of poetry she produced are analysed, i.e. sonnets used as an introduction/dedication to a larger work and occasional poetry with a political function, in order to illustrate the cultural context she worked within and also the way occasional poetry directed at Venetian society permitted her to pursue her career after marriage.

GIUSTINIAN. Orsatto Giustinian, *Rime*, ed. Ranieri Mercatanti, F, Olschki, 294 pp., provides a useful insight into the output of Petrarchists in Venice of the latter half of the Cinquecento through the publication of the first edition of G.'s *Rime* with author's corrections.

GRANDI. Ascanio Grandi, *Il Tancredi (e La vergine desponsata)*, ed. Antonio Mangione, Galatina, Congedo, 1997, 1154 pp., adds to the *Biblioteca di Scrittori Salentini's* reputation for uncovering and restoring the reputation of writers from the 'cultura periferica'. In this case, the 16th-c. Apulian scholar Ascanio Grandi (1567–1647) and his largest and most significant work, the heroic poem, *Tancredi*.

JACOPONE. G. Jori, '"Sentenze maravigliose e dolci affetti". Jacopone tra Cinque e Seicento', *LItal*, 50, 1998:506–27, traces the publishing history of the medieval text of the *Laudi*, and the essential role of St Philip Neri, to show how J. was viewed by humanists especially in his influence on late Cinquecento 'poesia sacra' and how later editions and especially commentaries on his text inspired the development of the oratorio.

ODASI.    The fourth Marquis of Mantua was reputed to have referred to the subject of R. Signorini, 'L'anno di morte di Michele "Tifi" Odasi (1492)', *GSLI,* 175, 1998:265–67, as 'padre della poesia macaronica'. This very brief biographical note casts light upon a neglected Paduan vernacular poet.

PIGNA.    Giovan Battista Pigna, *I Romanzi,* ed. S. Ritrovato, Bo, Forni, 1997, lxxiv + 258 pp., has a scholarly introduction examining the MSS in the Biblioteca Estense and Modena State Archive (1556–75), analysing the evolution of themes in the three books of the *Romanzi,* and tracing P.'s continuous dialogue with classical and Italian literature, especially Virgil and Ariosto.

PULCI, LUCA.    S. U. Baldassare, 'Lodi medicee in un dimenticato best seller del Quattrocento fiorentino. Il Driadeo di Luca Pulci', *FoI,* 32, 1998:375–402, attempts to show that critics have over-emphasized the laudatory nature of P.'s *ottava rima* love poem dedicated to *Lorenzo.* The eulogy is central to the text but must not be seen purely as an example of 'letteratura eziologica'. The work is not without its complexities, not least of which is its diversity of register.

PULCI, LUIGI.    Luigi Pulci, *Morgante e opere minori,* ed. A. Greco, T, UTET, 1997, 2 vols, 1477 pp., includes a range of P.'s work including letters, *frottole* and *ballate, La Giostra, La Beca, sonetti, La Confessione.* The informative introduction gives an account of the cultural background to the chivalric genre, the cultural milieu surrounding the Medici, the innovative linguistic and other features of P.'s other works.

SORANO.    M. Martini, *L'opera poetica di Domizio Palladio Sorano,* Sora, Centro di Studi Sorani Vincenzo Patriarca, 385 pp., includes a biographical essay on his activity as a teacher in Venice and gives the Latin text with facing translation of epigrams, elegies, orations, and his poem *Mariana.*

TASSO.    G. Rabitti, 'Discussioni tassiane ancora sulla canzone al Metauro', *FC,* 23, 1998:303–14, provides a systematic response to the criticism of her article by A. di Benedetto. Using analysis carried out by Leopardi, she maintains that the *canzone* is not merely a fragment but a valid piece of work which illuminates the problematic relationship between Torquato and Bernardo. E. Russo, 'Giotto e l'arte dell'infingere nel Tasso', *ib.,* 418–35, reveals the influence of Giotto on T.'s *Malpiglio overo de la corte* (1584) particularly regarding the theme of *infingere.* Conscious of the changes between his work and *Il Cortegiano,* T. controversially and poignantly puts forward his model of truth during the period of his imprisonment in Sant'Anna. M. Swensen Ruthernberg, 'Death of an epic, death of an epoch:

Ariosto and Tasso in Tomasi di Lampedusa's *Il Gattopardo*', *FoI, 32,* 1998:403–26, isolates a new 'temporal–literal' interpretation of Lampedusa's novel which derives from the echoes between the novel and the two Renaissance poems, the *Gerusalemme Liberata* and the *Furioso.* A. Villa, ' "Molto egli oprò col senno e con la mano". Esempi di ricontestualizzazione dantesche nella *Gerusalemme Liberata*', *LItal,* 51:27–51, clarifies the relationship between the imagery of the *Gerusalemme* and other texts like the *Aeneid* and the *Furioso* in order ultimately to underline her primary point, Tasso's indebtedness to Dante. M. T. Girardi, 'Scrittori greci nel *Giudizio* sulla *Conquistata* di Torquato Tasso', *Aevum,* 73:735–68, links T.'s justification of the Greek sources in his work and in particular his defence of Homer against charges of falsehood and the moral inacceptability of his work to the *Giudizio sovra la sua Gerusalemme da lui medesimo riformata,* which can be seen as a synthesis of T.'s poetic thought all the more significant as this was to be his last literary work, a defence of his own concept of false 'eccesso della verità' and truth in poetry. R. Loda, 'Il *Mondo Creato* di Torquato Tasso e la Bibbia glossata', *Aevum,* 72, 1998:733–57, analyses the classical sources that inspired T. in relation to how they would have been received in his time. By comparing the text of the *Mondo* with original sources and glosses, he underlines the breadth and diversity of T.'s sources and the way that often led to interpretations especially of the Bible that were considered inappropriate at the time. G. Da Pozzo, 'Ultimi assalti e vittoria differita nei canti finali della *Gerusalemme Liberata*', *ItStudien, 19,* 1998:83–108, uses an analysis of the language of the last three cantos of the poem before revision (XVIII, 45–XX, 108) as a focus around which to discuss the problematic issue of terminology in Cinquecento literature and to propose calling literary *manierismo* either *sincrezionismo* or *diacostruttismo.*

TEBALDEO. M. P. LaValva, 'Per un'assenza nelle *Rime* tebaldeane', *SPCT, 58*:45–81, opts to ignore the 791 well-known pieces of verse (which predominantly celebrate the Este family and in particular Eleonora d'Aragona) in favour of examining lesser known lyric such as the autobiographical *Stanze,* a small unnamed poem of 17 octaves, and his 'silloge epicedica'.

TRISSINO. C. Gigante, 'Azioni formidabili e misericordiose: l'esperimento epico del Trissino', *FC, 24*:44–71, compares and contrasts the use of allegory in Trissino's *Italia liberata dai Goti* and Ariosto's *Furioso.* Gigante points out what he sees as original aspects of the text, basing his views on an apparently self-conscious declaration of poetic intent on Trissino's part in Book V of his poem to modulate his ponderous style the product of the 'greve fama' associated with him.

ZANE. Giacomo Zane, *Rime*, ed. G. Rabitti, Padua, Antenore, 1997, 269 pp., a critical edition based on an investigation of the textual tradition, also offers a great deal of new biographical material.

## 4. THEATRE

Cynthia M. Pyle, *Milan and Lombardy in the Renaissance: Essays in Cultural History*, Ro, Fenice, 1997, xviii + 247 pp., attempts to overturn the negative critical attitude towards the *favole mitologiche* produced and performed at the Po Valley courts in the Quattrocento. A detailed reading of a number of works — *Poliscena* by L. della Serrata, *Parsithea* by G. Visconti, *Orbecche* by G. B. Giraldi — is provided, but it is the participation of Poliziano in this type of Renaissance *volgare* theatre with his *Fabula di Orfeo* that is intended by the author to restore its critical standing today. This broad overview may sometimes lack depth, but it provides a valuable insight into a neglected area of Renaissance theatre which, as Pyle contends, was a peculiarly Lombard phenomenon. Robert Henke, *Pastoral Transformations: Italian Tragicomedy and Shakespeare's Late Plays*, Cranberry, N.J., Univ. of Delaware Press, 1997, 239 pp., successfully argues for the international influences, cultural and theatrical, present in Shakespeare's late plays. Although his analysis of the development and theory of Italian tragicomedy and his application of Tasso's *Aminta* and Guarini's *Pastor Fido* are laudable, the argument would have further benefited from a review of the inspiration Shakespeare drew from pastoral romance (Sannazaro) and romantic epic (Ariosto, Tasso). L. J. Oldani and S.J. and V. R. Yanitelli, 'Jesuit theatre in Italy: its entrances and exit', *Italica*, 76:18–33, attempts to show how Italian Jesuit drama, deriving from the liturgical pageant (*sacra rappresentazione*) achieved its greatest success in the 16th c. with five-act plays such as Tuccio's *Golia* (1563). It is shown how the Jesuits viewed and used the theatre as a didactic tool. It is also maintained that the Jesuit drama pointed the way towards a national tragic drama. As the title suggests, *Il Teatro nelle Marche. Architettura, scenografia e spettacolo*, ed. F. Mariano, Fiesole, Nardini, 355 pp., is preoccupied with reconstructing the physical reality of theatrical production in the Marche especially in the 16th c. This useful illustrated book is the first synthesis of the history and enduring patrimony of theatres in the region. *Teatro del Quattrocento. Sacre rappresentazioni*, ed. Luigi Banfi, T, UTET, 1997, 856 pp., is a revised edition of a work first published in 1963 which covers a range of authors: Antonio Araldo, Castellano Castellani, Bernardo Pulci, Antonia Pulci, and Tommaso Benci. Antonio Stefani, *Edipo all'Olimpico, 1585–1997*, Vicenza, Accademia

Olimpica, 1997, 110 pp., looks at the staging and cultural background to the 1585 production followed by a survey of the tradition.

ARETINO. M. L. Doglio, 'P. Aretino e il teatro a Venezia' (753–61), isolates the figure of the pedant as essential in tracing the evolution of A.'s plays. C. Cairns, 'Teatro e festa la scenografia per *La Talanta* del 1542 e l'influenza del Vasari (231–44). Id., 'Pietro Aretino e la scena: testo, recita e stampa nella preistoria della commedia dell'arte' (959–80).

BRUNO. The concept of *mutatione* dominates Giordano Bruno's only play, explored in C. Pesca-Cupolo, 'Oltre la scena comica: la dimensione teatrale bruniana e l'ambientazione napoletana del *Candelaio*', *Italica*, 76:1–18. Written after Bruno's flight from Naples in 1576, the intertwined stories of three separate characters (the lover Bonifacio, the alchemist, Bartolomeo, the pedant Merfurio) explore peculiarly Neapolitan themes such as food and the sacred. A. B. Hodgart, *Giordano Bruno's The Candle Bearer: an enigmatic Renaissance play*, Lampeter, Mellen, 1997, xiii + 209 pp., is a stimulating, well-researched study establishing B.'s reasons for writing and the work's relationship with existing traditions and pointing to the originality of the play.

DELLA PORTA. B. Ferraro, 'L'estetica della fame e dell'eros nella *Sorella* di Giambattista Della Porta', *CLett*, 27:51–75, provides an in-depth analysis of the play's character and plot, which is seen firstly in the context of the author's work, as a bridge between his earlier and later production and then in the wider context as reflecting many characteristics of Cinquecento theatre, such as the predominant themes of hunger and love, exemplary character names, plurilingualism. However, it is the combination of classical, tragic, and popular influences present in one play which sets Della Porta's work apart and, above all, points to the important role his work played as a transition point between popular theatre in dialect and the Commedia dell'Arte.

DE' SOMMI. K. Hecker, 'Il concetto di regia di Leone de' Sommi nel contesto della trattistica del suo tempo', *Schede umanistiche*, 12, 1998:67–85, examines the theoretical views of De' S. (1525/7–1582) on the practicalities of theatre contained in his *Quattro dialoghi in materia di rappresentazioni sceniche* and sets them in the context of the time. Three principal elements of De' S.'s theory distinguish him as an essential transitional figure between the theatre of tragedy and comedy and, at the end of the century, the pastoral and commedia dell'arte: the requirement that the play should 'al general servir', the elevation of the actor to the status of creative poet, De' S.'s diffidence with regard to language.

GIRALDI. G. B. Giraldi, *Gli Eudemoni. An Italian Renaissance Comedy*, ed. Philip Horne, pref. Richard Andrews, Lampeter, Mellen, lxxxi + 140 pp., follows up H.'s editions of G.'s *Selene* and *Epizia* in the same series with G.'s only comedy, based on one of his own *novelle* and hitherto known in an unfortunate late-19th-c. edition. The text is judiciously annotated as well as meticulously edited. A three-part introduction explores the play's genesis and relates it to G.'s comic theory, concluding that 'it seems to be addressed to a circle of humanistically educated *literati* not much concerned, maybe, about its qualities as entertainment, but well equipped to appreciate its theoretical foundations and to assess it as a literary exercise in the tradition of classically inspired comedy'.

MACHIAVELLI. A. Russell Ascoli, 'Pyrrhus rules: playing with power from Boccaccio to Machiavelli', *MLN*, 114:14–54, examines the interplay of power and ethics in one story of Boccaccio's *Decameron* (the ninth of Day VII, a day he characterizes generally as 'pyrrhic'), comparing it with Machiavelli's *Clizia*. This in-depth review of the similarities between the two texts concludes satisfyingly by describing the play as being in a 'transformative relationship with Boccaccio's novella'. F. Masciandoro, *La conoscenza viva. Letture fenomenologiche da Dante a Machiavelli*, Ravenna, Longo, 195 pp., contains an essay (ch. 8) on M.'s *Mandragola* where Pirandello's criterion of 'il sentimento del contario' is applied through a close reading of plot and character, and their interaction, to unlock the meaning and especially the humour of the play.

MARTELLI. Ludovico Martelli, *Tullia (Tragedia)*, T, RES, 1998, xxx + 94 pp., gives the text of the play published by B. Varchi with biographical details and an assessment of its place and context in Cinquecento literary theory.

RICCHI. Agostino Ricchi, *I tre tiranni*, ed. Anna Maria Gallo, Mi, Il Polifilo, 232 pp., is the first publication of a little–known text (first performed at Bologna in 1530). Over and above the useful critical introduction and comparisons with the subversive tone of Aretino's theatre, the editor concludes convincingly that the historical moment, with the proliferation of Court theatre such as this, had a profound influence on the development of European theatre as a whole.

STEFONIO. Bernardino Stefonio, *Cristus Tragoedia*, ed. L. Strapponi, Ro, Bulzoni, xxvi + 146 pp., illustrates the culture of Jesuit theatre by reproducing the Latin text of the play first published in 1601 and performed at the Jesuit Collegio Romano in 1597. The introduction gives useful background information about the production and the literary context, and includes good biographical and bibliographical profiles.

TASSO. N. Borsellino, ' "S'ei piace, ei lice". Sull'utopia erotica dell'*Aminta*', *FC*, 23, 1998:144–54, shows how the eroticism of the myth of *Aminta* ensured the popularity and influence of the Italian model especially in French pastoral literature. T. in particular is seen as a continuer and renewer of the tradition. Maria Grazia Accorsi, '*Aminta*'. *Ritorno a Saturno*, Soveria Mannelli, Rubbettino, 1998, 146 pp., is an illuminating two-part essay examining T.'s pastoral from contrasting, but in some ways complementary, points of view: ch. 1 'Musicato. Per Musica. Musicale', reviewing critical opinion on the questiion of the work's relationship to music, and arguing that it was not set to music or written for the purpose, nor is it appropriate to define its style as 'musical'; ch. 2, 'Amore. Poesia. Sapienza', analysing it from a thematic and conceptual angle to conclude: 'in quel *collage* che è Aminta, scritta con il *furor* dell'amante, del poeta, del filosofo, dello studioso dei classici, c'è tutto, esplicito e mascherato: i simboli, le dichiarazioni di poetica, le posizioni ideologiche . . . l'Età del ferro con le sue passioni e il sogno di Saturno . . .'

TUCCIO. M. Saulini, 'Drammaturgia gesuitica: il *Christus nascens* e il *Christus patiens* del p. Stefano Tuccio S.J.', *CLett*, 26, 1998:627–52, analyses the first two plays in T.'s famed trilogy on the life of Christ dating from 1573 and 1569 respectively. Analysis of structure and plot reveals the vast difference between the two texts, the first largely a one-act play and eclogue preceded by a prologue, the second, on a far larger scale (five acts), weaving together the story told in the Gospels and containing features which were to become standard in Jesuit performances: the struggle between good and evil and the evident intent to *impressionare* the public, especially through crowd scenes.

## 5. PROSE

Among the various prose genres the novella is particularly well represented. I note: J. B. Jiménez, 'Filippo di Ser Brunellesco tra *Novella del grosso legniauolo* e le *Spicciolate fiorentine* del '400', *CLett*, 102:3–49; N. Marcelli, '*Favole, parabole, istorie*. Le forme della scrittura novellistica dal Medioevo al Rinascimento', *ASI*, 157:593–604; 'La novellistica volgare e latina fra Trecento e Cinquecento. Risultati e prospettive di una ricerca interuniversitaria', ed. R. Bessi, *MR*, 12, 1998[1999]:257–324, which includes: M. Martelli, 'Le linee generali del progetto' (259–62); G. Albanese, 'Per la storia della fondazione del genere novella tra volgare e latino. Edizioni di testi e problemi critici' (262–84); R. Bessi, 'La novella in volgare nel Quattrocento italiano: studi e testi' (285–307); M. Masoero, 'Fonti, plagi e "furti": la riscrittura della novella volgare fra Quattrocento e Cinquecento' (321–24).

For other prose genres: F. Pignatti, 'Il dialogo del Rinascimento. Rassegna della critica', *GSLI*, 176:408–43. '*Visibil parlare*'. *Le scritture esposte nei volgari italiani dal Medioevo al Rinascimento*, ed. Claudio Ciociola, Na, ESI, 1997, 484 pp., with 16 essays investigating texts and inscriptions on sculpture and plaques, and in paintings. It is divided into three sections: 'Paleologia'; 'Filologia e storia della lingua'; and 'Temi, generi, iconografie'. There is an analysis of the debate in the 15th and 16th c. about the didactic need and propriety of using such techniques. *Cento e dieci ricordi che formano il buon fattor di villa*, ed. Ulderico Bernardi and Enzo Dematté, Vicenza, Neri Pozza, 1998, 451 pp., gives an insight into the learning and experience displayed by a professional *fattore*. The text, though aimed primarily at imparting information on agriculture, encompasses scientific matters, precise technical data, social etiquette, and reference manuals. Biagio Buonaccorsi, *Diario dall'anno 1498 all'anno 1512 e altri scritti*, ed. Enrico Niccolini, Ro, Istituto Storico Italiano per il Medio Evo, xxxvi + 441 pp., has a scholarly introduction that gives a biography and points to Buonaccorsi's importance as a source for Guicciardini. Gherardo Sergiusti, *Sommaria de' successi della città di Lucca*, ed. Riccardo Ambrosini and Albarosa Belegni, Pisa, ETS, 1997, 163 pp., gives the text together with the *Vita di G. Sergiusti, Vita di Nicolao di Gherardo Sergiusti*, and *Chroniche della città di Lucca composte per Mess. Bastiano Puccini*, all from two MSS (98, 927) in the Biblioteca Statale di Lucca. The introduction investigates the MSS, gives an analysis of the texts, notes on the language and a useful glossary. Scipione Mazzella, *Descrittione del regno di Napoli*, Bologna, Forni, 1997, is a facsimile of the 1601 edition published by G. B. Cappello. It is a compendium which deals with geography, social history, anthropology, the lives of famous men, noble families and houses, and descriptions of coats of arms. Muzio Muzii, *Della storia di Teramo dalle origini all'anno 1559*, Bo, Forni, 1998, 356 p., is a facsimile of the 1893 edition which gives the variations between five different MSS of a work, set out as seven dialogues, that discuss the city of Teramo, the kingdom of Naples and finally the whole of Italy. An entertaining vision of Neapolitan life is to be found in Mario Forgione, *I Viceré 1503–1707. Cronache irriverenti di due secoli di dominazione spagnola a Napoli*, Na, Tempo Lungo, 1998, 510 pp. *Dispacci sforzeschi da Napoli, vol. 1, 1444–2 Luglio 1458*, ed. Francesco Senatore, Na, Istituto Italiano per gli Studi Filosofici, 1997, xx + 707 pp., is the first volume of the project 'Fonti per la storia di Napoli aragonese'. This first volume begins with a detailed description of the city, countryside and the nobility. Marco Bellabarba, *Racconti famigliari. Scritti di Tommaso Tabarelli de Fatis e altre storie di nobili cinquecenteschi*, Trent, Società di Studi Trentini di Scienze Storiche, 1997, 144 pp., is a scholarly reconstruction of the historical events which sparked off the literary response to the death of Paolo Tabarelli in 1524 by his son Tommaso.

The epitaphs, funeral orations, and poetry cover themes of violence, aristocratic honour, and the perennial problem of individual rights and justice. Giacomo Agostinetti, *Et io ge onsi le juncture*, ed. Giuseppe Palermo, Genoa, Le Mani, 1997, 63 pp., is the text of a MS written in Genoese dialect at the end of the 15th c., which fits into the 'Books of Secrets' genre.

ARETINO. Folke Gernert, *Francisco Delicados 'Retrato de la Lozana Andaluza' und Pietro Aretinos 'Sei Giornate'. Zum literarischen Diskurs über die käufliche Liebe im frühen Cinquecento*, Geneva, Droz, 302 pp., is a detailed study of an erotic literary genre that analyses, via a set of comparative tables, how framework, structure, dialogue, and characters, reflect social, philosophical, and religious trends.

BEMBO. S. D. Bowd, 'Pietro Bembo and the "monster" of Bologna (1514)', *RenS*, 13:40–54.

CARO. *Annibal Caro: lettere familiari e le traduzioni patristiche*, ed. Stanislao Tamburri, Comune di Civitanova Marche, 1997, vii + 115 pp., gathers four essays: T. Temperini concentrates on the *lettere burlesche*, classicism, and mannerist invention; T. Monaco, on language and style, examines the comic elements, letters on culture and art, and the polemical exchange with L. Castelvetro; S. Tamburri discusses Caro as a translator of patristic texts, and analyses Caro's first Latin epigram, which gives an insight into his methodology and ideas.

CASTIGLIONE. U. Motta, 'La *questione della lingua* nel primo libro del *Cortegiano*: dalla seconda alla terza redazione', *Aevum*, 73:707–34. D. A. Northrop, '"The ende therfore of a perfect courtier" in Baldassare Castiglione's *The Courtier*', *PQ*, 77, 1998:295–306.

COLONNA. Francesco Colonna, *Hypnerotomachia Poliphili. The Strife of Love in a Dream*, trans. Joscelyn Godwin, London, Thames and Hudson, 466 pp., is a handsome production that retains the size, format, font, woodcuts, and binding signatures of the original. It includes translations of the Greek and Latin inscriptions and has appendices which give the significance of allegorical names, a glossary of terms, and a diagram of the island of Cytherea. The introduction sets out the themes in each book, discusses the problems of translation, the question of authorship and the financial problems linked to the original printing. There is a useful schematic analysis that allows the structure of the entire work to be seen at a glance. A quibble would be to lament the lack of attention to bibliographical references.

GALATEO. S. Valerio, 'Le maschere dell'*Eremita* di Antonio Galateo', *CLett*, 27:419–54.

GUICCIARDINI. F. Manche, 'Per fas et nefas. Le concept de prudence chez Guicciardini', *ChrI*, 15.4:63–75. G. Tanturli,

*'Quante sono le edizioni dei *Ricordi* di Francesco Guicciardini', *SFI*, 56, 1998[1999]:271–95.

MACHIAVELLI.   Joseph V. Femia, *The Machiavellian Legacy. Essays in Italian Political Thought*, Houndmills, Macmillan, 1998, 169 pp., consists of five essays including a stimulating study which establishes links between Gramsci and Labriola, neo-Hegelian Marxists, and two advocates of elite theory, G. Mosca, and V. Pareto. The link lies in their adherence to M.'s 'hostility to essentialism, to the positing of *a priori* goals, imposed on men by God or nature'. It explores the implications of this stance, pointing to the importance of M.'s desire to study man via history rather than theology or philosophy, and highlights his rejection of abstract universals. Niccolò Machiavelli, *Opere*, ed. Rinaldo Rinaldi, 2 vols, T, UTET, 956, 945–1680 pp., are divided *De principatibus, Discorsi sopra la prima deca di Tito Livio (I-II)* and *Discorsi sopra la prima deca di Tito Livio (III), Dell'arte della guerra, Dalle legazioni.* A long scholarly introduction reviews critical positions, concentrates on placing the texts within an historical and literary framework, examines M.'s sources and sets out the relationship between the works. This is followed by a biographical sketch. The texts have excellent notes, and there is a full critical apparatus, though the bibliography is disappointing. Oreste Tommasini, *La vita e gli scritti di Niccolò Machiavelli nella loro relazione col Machiavellismo*, Na, Istituto Italiano per gli Studi Storici, xxvi + 964 pp., is a facsimile of part 1 of volume 2, originally published in 1911 (volume 1, 1883, was published in 1994), and covers the return of the Medici to Florence, M.'s misfortunes at the hand of fate, and the writing of the *Principe, Discorsi, Discorso per rassettare le cose di Firenze*, and *L'arte della guerra.* It examines M.'s letters, his activity as a dramatist, and an unpublished epigram. Tommasini's massive scholarly study, though now super-seded, still has valuable insights, and a wealth of archival material. Leo Paul de Alvarez, *The Machiavellian Enterprise. A Commentary on the Prince*, Dekalb, North Illinois U.P., 144 pp., gives a detailed textual commentary, then suggests that the illogical and haphazard manner in which M. sets out his chapters 'does not reflect the authentic argument of the work'. The study raises some interesting questions but suffers from lack of clarity and an excess of rhetoric. Rosanna Scavo, *Storia della storiografia: dalle cronache comunali all'Illuminismo*, Bari, Archivio di Stato, 1997, 273 pp., has assessments of humanist historiography in Venice and Rome, and history written for republics and princes, with particular reference to M. and Guicciardini. A. Fontana, G. Saro, X. Tabet, 'Trois chapitres des *Discours sur la première Décade de Tite-Live de Machiavel*', *ChrI*, 14.1, 1998:77–87. L. Gerbier, 'Temps historique et *virtù* politique chez Machiavel', *ib.*,

61–75. I. Cervelli, 'Machiavelli e la successione degli imperi universali', *Rinascimento*, 38, 1998:27–80. F. Verrier, '*L'arte della guerra*, trattato militare dialogato del Machiavelli: un felice ibrido retorico', *LItal*, 51:405–17. N. Rubinstein, 'An unknown version of Machiavelli's *Ritratto delle cose della Magna*', *Rinascimento*, 38, 1998:227–46.

## SEICENTO

POSTPONED

## SETTECENTO

By G. W. SLOWEY, *Senior Lecturer in Italian, University of Birmingham*

### 1. GENERAL

V. Romani, 'Tra giansenisti ed ex-gesuiti: note sulle origini della Biblioteca pubblica di Macerata', *NASSAB*, 13:91–101, traces the acquisition, for the establishment of a public library, of items which were taken from the Jesuits after their suppression. It illustrates some of the difficulties of Catholic reform and the inability of the Church to adapt to more radical pressures for cultural renewal. *L'abate in biblioteca: i libri di Tommaso Valperga di Caluso*, ed. Lucetta Levi Momigliano and Laura Tos, T, Allemandi, 57 pp. C. M. Grafinger, 'Die Erwerbung einer Sammlung von päpstlichen Briefen durch den Präfekten des vatikanischen Archives Giuseppe Garampi im Jahre 1754', *NASSAB*, 13:81–89, deals with the Vatican Archive's purchase of a manuscript containing several hundred letters from the papacy of Urban IV to that of Martin IV. A. Coco, 'Appunti per la storia del Parlamento Siciliano del 1714. Gli archivi e i documenti', *Siculorum Gymnasium*, 50, 1997[1999]:111–21, details documents referring to Sicily in the early 18th c. in archives in Palermo and Turin. *Editoria e cultura a Napoli nel 18. secolo. Atti del Convegno organizzato dall'Istituto Universitario Orientale, dalla Società Italiana di Studi sul secolo 18. e dall'Istituto Italiano per gli studi filosofici, Napoli 5–7 dicembre 1996*, ed. Anna Maria Rao, Na, Liguori, 1998, xi + 951 pp.

*Il Granducato di Toscana e i Lorena nel secolo XVIII. Incontro internazionale di studio, Firenze 22–24 settembre 1994*, ed. Alessandra Contini and Maria Grazia Parri, F, Olschki, 678 pp., is divided into four sections: *Tradizioni politiche della dinastia ed esperienze di governo in Toscana*, which contains a number of articles on the historical background, including S. Landi, 'Libri, norme, lettori. La formazione della legge sulle stampe in Toscana (1737–1743)' (143–86); *Funzionari e ministri lorenesi nel Granducato*; *Tradizioni culturali nella Toscana lorenese*, which contains J. Boutier, 'De l'Académie Royale de Lunéville à l'"Accademia dei Nobili" de Florence. Milieux intellectuels et transferts culturels au début de la Régence' (327–54); A. Courbet, 'Le bibliothécaire du Grand-Duc de Toscane, Valentin Jamerey-Duval (1695–1775) et sa correspondance de Florence' (355–84); M. Rosa, 'Il "Cuore del re": l'*Institution d'un prince* del giansenista Duguet' (385–416); J. Garms, 'Jean-Nicolas Jadot' (417–26); C. Cresti, 'Architettura e politica nell'età lorenese' (427–34); C. Sodini, 'Vincenzio Martinelli e la sua *Istoria della Famiglia Medici*' (435–54); M. A. Morelli Timpanaro, 'Francesco di Giovacchino Moücke stampatore a Firenze, tra Medici e Lorena, ed i suoi rapporti con il dottor Antonio Cocchi' (455–578); section four is entitled *Società ed economia*. F. Cristelli, 'Alle origini della massoneria fiorentina', *RST*, 45:187–207, traces the development of freemasonry in the period, examining its disagreements with the Church, as well as discussing masonic links with organizations such as the Accademia Etrusca di Cortona. G. Fiori, 'Gaetana Moruzzi, la "sfinge fiorenzuolana"', in un documento inedito', *BSPia*, 94, 1:121–50, looks at a work by Gian Domenico Rossi about Moruzzi, who gained enormous religious and political influence over Duke Ferdinand of Parma, and publishes the text of her *Memorie*. E. Frasson, 'Giuseppe Gennari: notizie giornaliere di quanto avvenne specialmente in Padova dal 1739 al 1800', *AMAP*, 110.3, 1997–98: 181–240, provides an index of names for Gennari's work, published in 1982–84, edited by Loredana Oliveto. N. Del Bianco, 'I "Pensieri diversi" di Francesco Melzi d'Eril', *NA*, 134, 2:330–49, edits various thoughts of Melzi on politics and other aspects of society from his journeys in Spain and England. C. Sodini, 'Vincenzio Martinelli, un cosmopolita toscano del '700 (parte prima)', *RST*, 45: 85–139, deals with Martinelli's journeys through Italy and the rest of Europe, including a long period spent in England where he met Casanova and Baretti and where his first work, *Istoria critica della vita civile*, was published in 1752. For Martinelli, see also the article by Sodini itemized above under *Il Granducato di Toscana e i Lorena nel secolo XVIII*. Christopher Storrs, *War, Diplomacy and the Rise of Savoy, 1690–1720*, CUP, xiv + 345 pp., contains much useful background information. P. Bianchi, 'Università e riforme: la "Relazione dell'università di Padova" di Francesco Filippo Picono (1712)', *QSUP*, 31, 1998: 165–203, discusses the influence of Picono's report to Vittorio Amedeo II on the establishment of the University of Turin, highlighting Picono's emphasis on the need to secularize university education.

K. Fabene, 'Vincenzo Ludovico Gotti e la *Via notarum* nell'apologetica cattolica del XVII-XVIII secolo', *Acme*, 52:249–60, looks at *La vera vita di Cristo* (1719) of Gotti, Inquisitor General in Milan, which refutes Calvinist arguments on the basis of the *via notarum*, a system of identifying and interpreting historical signs as infallible indicators of God's true Church. Gotti's arguments underline the Church's conviction as to the importance of miracles and prophecies. A. Batelli, 'Il cattolicesimo democratico nel triennio 1796–99 in Italia', *RiS*, 29:115–24, examines the Jansenist aspect of Catholicism with its tendency towards reform, drawing on the work of people such as Gaspare Morardo who spoke of a universal brotherhood united by religion. S. Ciccarelli, 'Notizie su un monaco giacobino di Siena', *RiS*, 29:89–113, considers the case of Egidio Holler, who challenged papal authority in articles for the *Monitore Bolognese*. Also on the influence of periodicals is *Il 'Monitore napoletano' (1799)*, ed. Mario Battaglini, Na, Guida, 918 pp., which is the first near-complete publication of an important Jacobin newspaper, lacking only a few supplements that do not seem to exist any longer. Connected with the same Neapolitan theme is V. Caianiello, 'Mario Pagano e la riforma delle istituzioni nella Repubblica Napoletana del 1799', *NA*, 134, 1:50–73, discussing Vincenzo Cuoco's influence on the interpretation of the achievement of the 1799 republic, which, according to the author, has led to an undervaluing of its importance. The article goes on to assess Pagano's contribution to the abolition of feudalism and the drafting of the constitution. *\*Napoli 1799*, ed. Roberto De Simone, Sorrento, Di Mauro, 390 pp. *\*Te Deum per un massacro: Napoli prima e dopo il 1799*, ed. Domenico Scafoglio, Cava de' Tirreni, Avagliano, 109 pp. Luciano Guerci, *\*Istruire nelle verità repubblicane. La letteratura politica per il popolo nell'Italia in rivoluzione (1796–1799)*, Bo, Il Mulino, 374 pp. Domenico Scafoglio, *\*Lazzari e giacobini. Cultura popolare e rivoluzione a Napoli nel 1799*, Mi, Ancora, 206 pp. *\*Folle controrivoluzionarie: le insorgenze popolari nell'Italia giacobina e napoleonica*, ed. Anna Maria Rao, Ro, Carocci, 388 pp.

*StSet*, 18, 1998[1999], devotes the second half of the issue to the topic *Dalla filosofia naturale alla fisica. Disciplina e didattica in Italia all'epoca di Volta*, which includes M. Ciardi, 'Medicina, tecnologia civile e militare, filosofia naturale. L'insegnamento della fisica nel Regno di Sardegna' (217–48); C. Farinella, 'I "luoghi" della fisica a Genova fra Settecento e Ottocento' (249–78); A. Ferraresi, 'La fisica sperimentale fra università e ginnasi nella Lombardia austriaca' (279–320); M. Cavazza, 'Fisica generale e fisica sperimentale nelle istituzioni scientifiche emiliane del Settecento' (321–42); S. Contardi, 'Visibilità e autoapprendimento. Aspetti della didattica della fisica nella Toscana di Pietro Leopoldo' (343–66); E. Schettino, 'L'insegnamento della fisica sperimentale a Napoli nella seconda metà del Settecento' (367–76); P. Nastasi, 'Domenico Scinà e la fisica palermitana fra Settecento e Ottocento' (377–406); L. Pepe, 'Matematica e fisica nei collegi del Settecento' (407–20). T. Alfieri Tonini, 'Iscrizioni greche della Lombardia nella cultura del '700', *Quaderni di Acme*, 39:99–111, examines how works such as Muratori's *Novus Thesaurus* treated these inscriptions, concluding that they were interested in them primarily as writings rather than as material to draw on in treating broader epigraphic questions.

## 2. Prose, Poetry, Drama

*Il Settecento*, Ro, Salerno, 1998, 1028 pp., is volume VI of the *Storia della letteratura italiana*, ed. Enrico Malato, containing important sections on the philosophical and political background as well as entries on major figures and themes. *Parigi / Venezia. Cultura, relazioni, influenze negli scambi intellettuali del Settecento*, ed. Carlo Ossola, F, Olschki, 1998, 495 pp., contains G. Benzoni, 'Dalla fitta conversazione al corrucciato silenzio' (1–38); M. Vovelle, 'Les échanges culturels aux XVIIIème siècle: un chantier ouvert' (39–54); F. Diaz, ' "Philosophie" e utopia da Rousseau agli idéologues' (55–84); L. Sozzi, 'Il paese delle chimere. L'idea di illusione nella stagione dei tardi lumi' (85–104); G. Ricuperati, 'Illuminismo e Settecento dal Dopoguerra ad oggi' (105–28); F. Jarauta, 'Viaje, "Bildung"', escritura' (129–36); J. Starobinski, 'Rousseau et l'espression musicale' (137–72); G. Gronda, 'Scelte poetiche italiane nelle "Consolations des misères de ma vie" ' (173–92); A. Wyss, 'La Venise intérieure. L'accent, le melodrame et les musiques de Venise' (193–210); R. Leydi, 'Rousseau, pioniere dell'antropologia e dell'etnomusicologia' (211–42); G. Morelli, 'La banalità conquistata (en travaillant Métastase)' (243–310); J. Rousset, 'Une confrontation idéale: le théâtre et l'acteur selon Rousseau et Goldoni' (311–23); M. Hobson, 'Diderot, Goldoni: les "espèces" et les caractères' (323–44); F. Fido, 'La ragione in ombra e le tentazioni della follia nelle commedie francesi' (345–64); G. Pizzamiglio, 'Carlo Goldoni, lettere da Parigi a Venezia' (365–82); P. Rosenberg, 'Fragonard et Venise' (383–88); L. Ritter Santini, 'Gli angeli del sonno' (389–410); B. Papasogli, 'Letture settecentesche di Pascal' (411–30); P. Del Negro, 'Tra Versailles, Rousseau e gli Inquisitori di Stato: il primo saggio politico veneziano sulla Rivoluzione francese' (431–56); C. Ossola, 'Piccoli improvvisi su "arie" e "affetti" ' (457–78). With a similar theme is D. Gallingani, 'Il libro del "sapere" tra Italia e Francia all'epoca dei lumi', *NA*, 134, 3 : 324–35, which examines the contribution made by Tiraboschi, Gravina, Denina, and Giovanni Andres and how far they were affected by Enlightenment culture. The article looks at the growth of cosmopolitan interest amongst Italians alongside the development of history of ideas and notions of progress in learning.

M. P. Donato, 'Accademie e accademismi in una capitale particolare: il caso di Roma, secoli XVIII-XIX', *MEFR*, 3. 1 : 415–30, traces the development of academies in Rome from the 17th c., pointing out the fact that although the city was an international centre for the formation of the clergy, it did not develop the role of a European cultural capital. The author asserts, however, that this situation changed in the second half of the 18th c., only to be reversed in the early years of the 19th c., where the academies were dependent for their existence on personal contacts rather than on any major public support from the Church. M. Verga, 'Per una storia delle accademie di Palermo nel XVIII secolo. Dal "lettorato" al professore universitario', *ASI*, 157:453–536, deals with the early founding of the Accademia del Buon Gusto and the Accademia dei Geniali, the first of which developed through the 18th c. into the major academy of Palermo. The article points out that the members were originally few in number and that the academy was lay in character and composition, interested in the public role of the *letterati*, challenging the scholastic culture of the ruling class, and initiating debate about the education of the nobility. The article continues with an examination of the academy's links particularly with Tuscan academies, and considers the short-lived Accademia degli Agricoltori Oretei in 1753, and the restructuring of much of the educational system after the expulsion of the Jesuits, with the establishment of new university chairs, especially in the sciences and law. The author, however, introduces a note of caution by referring to 'la fragilità culturale della realtà universitaria palermitana di fine Settecento'. A. Montanari, 'Due maestri riminesi al Seminario di Bertinoro. Lettere inedite (1745–51) a Giovanni Bianchi (Iano Planco)', *StRmgn*, 47, 1997[1999]:195–208, is concerned with the troubled academic careers of Mattia Giovenardi and Lucantonio Cenni, both pupils of Bianchi. M. Catto, *' "Se sia permessa agli ecclesiastici la lettura de' scrittori profani": una relazione dell'Accademia delle Scienze Esatte in Udine (1731–1747)', *Ce fastu?*, 75:141–58. A. Scotto Di Luzio, 'Il *Nuovo Giornale de' Letterati d'Italia*: riscrittura della tradizione zeniana ed impegno civile della cultura erudita', *Archivio di Storia della Cultura*, 11, 1998:5–106, demonstrates the links of the *Nuovo Giornale* (founded in 1772 by Gregorio Settari) with Zeno's early-18th-c. Venetian *Giornale de' Letterati*, which had flanked Muratori's reformism as outlined in the *Primi disegni* and the *Riflessioni sopra il buon gusto*. Among other things, the article discusses the debates sparked off by Catholic opposition to Enlightenment and hence to French ideas, illustrating the *Nuovo Giornale*'s criticism of the *Encyclopédie* and its emphasis on the status of Italian, which develops alongside the idea of nation. *Alle origini di una cultura riformatrice. Circolazione delle idee e modelli letterari nella Comacchio del Settecento*, ed. Andrea Cristiani, Bo, CLUEB, 360 pp. Emilia Mirmina, *Settecento in Friuli. Letteratura italiana e cultura nella patria del Friuli e nel Friuli imperiale. Disegno storico e profili di protagonisti*, Padua, CLEUP, 190 pp. Gian Paolo Romagnani, *Sotto la bandiera dell'istoria. Eruditi e uomini di lettere nell'Italia del Settecento: Maffei, Muratori, Tartarotti*, Sommacampagna, Cierre, xiv + 274 pp. Mario Rosa, *Settecento religioso. Politica della ragione e religione del cuore*, Venice, Marsilio, 312 pp. *Il misogallo romano*, ed. Marina Formica and Luca Lorenzetti, Ro, Bulzoni, 764 pp., is a collection of late-18th-c. verse in Italian and dialect attacking democracy and the French, with a 200 page introduction. *Tragedie del Settecento*, ed. Enrico Mattioda, 2 vols, Modena, Mucchi, 571, 604 pp., comprises (in vol. 1) Gianvincenzo Gravina, *Servio Tullio*; Scipione Maffei, *Merope*; Pier Jacopo Martello, *I Taimingi*; and Antonio Conti, *Druso*; and (in vol. 2): Alfonso Varano, *Giovanni di Giscala*; Saverio Bettinelli, *Serse re di Persia*; Alessandro Verri, *La congiura di Milano*; Alessandro Pepoli, *Adelinda*; and Giovanni Pindemonte, *Elena e Gerardo*. In addition, each volume has an extensive appendix of selections from 18th-c. writers dealing with such things as the theory of tragedy, acting style, happy endings, and the *melodramma*, as well as comments from contemporary travellers to Italy and debate on the *dramma borghese*. *Divina libertà. La rivoluzione della tragedia, la tragedia della rivoluzione: Pagano, Galdi, Salfi*, ed. Alberto Granese, 2 vols, Salerno, Edisud, xix + 238, 228 pp. B. Alfonzetti, 'Storiografia e teatro nel Settecento', *Siculorum Gymnasium*, 50, 1997[1999]:7–32, analyses French dramatic models, looking at themes such as history and conspiracy, with Italian examples such as Tiberio Carafa, Gravina, Saverio Pansuti. It draws on Vincenzo Cuoco's *Saggio storico sulla rivoluzione di Napoli del 1799*, emphasizing the rhetorical and dramatic structures which are present in that work too. Maria Grazia Accorsi, *Pastori e teatro: poesia e critica in Arcadia*, Modena, Mucchi, 308 pp., gathers together four previously published items. *Scenari*, ed. Marco Fioravanti, Lucca, Pacini Fazzi, 126 pp., contains two plays transcribed from the MS *Commedie diverse di Accademici Rozzi, 1775*. Folco Portinari, *Le regole del gioco: saggi sulla cultura letteraria del Settecento*, Lecce, Manni, 150 pp. *Italian autobiography from Vico to Alfieri (and beyond)*, ed. John Lindon, a *Supplement* to the *Italianist*, 17, 1997[1999], contains: A. Battistini, 'Genesi e sviluppo dell'autobiografia moderna' (7–21), which offers a solid historical survey of the genre, noting the broad differences between Vico early in the century and Alfieri at the end; B. Haddock, 'The philosophical significance of Vico's autobiography' (23–33), which points out the problems of treating Vico's *Vita* as a conventional autobiography, suggesting instead that the *Vita* applies to Vico's own life the critical principles established in the *Scienza nuova*; G. Gronda, 'Goldoni e i *Mémoires* teatrali' (34–41), which set the *Mémoires* in the context of a non-Italian genre of theatre memoirs; F. Baker, 'Lorenzo Da Ponte's witticisms: the implication of Jewish identity in the *Memorie*' (42–79), which takes issue with earlier suggestions that Da Ponte deliberately hid his Jewish origins and closely examines how Da Ponte presents his partially Jewish identity; J. Lindon, 'Design, distortion and ideology in Alfieri's *Vita*' (80–92), which looks at the *Vita* from the point of view of 'design', or the author's purpose and self-interpretation; F. D'Intino, 'Da Alfieri a Leopardi. La dissoluzione dell'autobiografia' (93–124), which shows how Leopardi, after an initial attempt in 1825 to imitate Alfieri, finds his true autobiographical voice in the poetry of *A Silvia* and *Le ricordanze*. Federica Martignago, \**La poesia delle stagioni: tempo e sensibilità nel Settecento*, Venice, IV, viii + 198 pp. V. Gallo, \*'La commedia dialettale napoletana del primo '700. Nicolò Maresca e Gennaro Antonio Federico', *EL*, 24.2:39–62. G. Gronda, 'Taglia e incolla: sulla tradizione testuale dei libretti d'opera', *Fahy Vol.*, 295–309, discusses the often brutal alterations made to opera libretti even in the course of printing, since the libretto is, up to a point, infinitely perfectible. As examples, the article draws on Rinuccini's *La Dafne* and Da Ponte's *Così fan tutte*. P. Howard, 'Guadagni in the dock: a crisis in the career of a castrato', *EMus*, 27:87–95, discusses the career of Gaetano Guadagni in England. On a similar subject is J. Grundy Fanelli, 'A sweet bird of youth: Caffarelli in Pistoia', *ib.*, 27:55–63, which looks at Gaetano Maiorano, known as Caffarelli, and his period spent in Pistoia between 1729 and 1731, with some useful information on the cultural background to the city. T. M. Gialdroni, ' " . . . questo giudizioso giro di parole": Niccolò Jomelli tra metrica e musica', *StMus*, 28:218–42, discusses J.'s approach to the poetic text and identifies his ability to retain a correct metrical structure even through repetitions of words and phrases. The article deals mainly with Metastasio's *Didone abbandonata*, comparing J.'s treatment of the words with that of other composers who set the same text. L. Cosi, 'Settecento musicale inedito tra Napoli e Terra d'Otranto: professioni e società di musica attraverso nuove fonti d'archivio', *Fonti musicali italiane*, 3, 1998:131–54, explores the world of music societies in addition to providing information on musical instrument makers. L. Pancino, 'Le opere di Vivaldi nel raffronto fra libretti e partiture, IV: *Dorilla in Tempe*; *Farnace*', *ISV*, 20:5–56, uses a comparison between libretti and musical scores to explore dramaturgical presentations of these works. Maria Aurelia Mastronardi, \**Gargano Trifone: feste a corte e commedie di principi. Teatro e musica in Puglia fra Sei e Settecento*, Fasano, Schena, 344 pp.

## 3. INDIVIDUAL AUTHORS

ALFIERI. Giuseppe Antonio Camerino, *Alfieri e il linguaggio della tragedia: verso, stile, topoi*, Na, Liguori, 296 pp., gathers ten articles, all but one of which have previously appeared. The unpublished article, 'Il modello tradito. La volontà di fuga e di morte nel linguaggio della *Mirra*' (227–44), points out that unhappiness and innocence go together in Mirra, in whom 'la infelicità sembra decretata da una natura avvertita come un nume terribile e irato' and Mirra's innocence is only preserved by her death. Lanfranco Caretti, *Studi sulle lettere alfieriane*, ed. Angelo Fabrizi and Clemente Mazzotta, Modena, Mucchi, 242 pp., collects 18 of Caretti's writings on Alfieri's letters which appeared between 1955 and 1994. Guido Santato, *Tra mito e palinodia: itinerari alfieriani*, Modena, Mucchi, 393 pp., comprises ten chapters all of which, except one, have previously appeared between 1978 and 1998. The new item is 'Tra "pensieri" e "ardentissimi desiderj". Mito politico e mito letterario nei trattati alfieriani' (55–85), which shows how in *Della tirannide* and *Del principe e delle lettere* A. addresses only those few who are capable of understanding his political and literary theory. The article suggests that the two tracts share a common perspective as 'il manifesto di una nuova "poetica della politica"'.

For the first time ever, two volumes of *AnAlf* have appeared in successive years. *AnAlf*, 6, 1998, carries: B. Alfonzetti, '"Mi piace il quint'atto". Tipologia dello scioglimento in Alfieri' (7–32); G. Santato, 'Saggio d'un commento alle *Satire*' (33–84); C. Forno, 'Cleopatra: "regina tragediabile" e occasione di incontro di innumerevoli autori' (85–128) and 'Sciolto un piccolo mistero: chi era "il prete Ivaldi"?' (147); P. Trivero, 'Una favola senza lieto fine: la *Rosmunda*' (129–46); M. Sterpos, '"Gli insorgenti aretini" a Firenze nel 1799: un "Alfieri codino"?' (149–80); S. Carrai, 'Schede sulla presenza alfieriana nei *Sepolcri*' (181–85); and P. Nason, 'Messinscene alfieriane (1953–1960)' (187–201). *AnAlf*, 7, contains the following items: D. Cutino, 'Le strategie dei personaggi nella *Mirra*' (1–21), which uses the image of Mirra at the bottom of a cone with all the other characters oscillating on the outer rim, each concerned to bring her back into their own sphere of belonging; A. Fabrizi, 'Alfieri e Tasso' (23–56), which traces the influence of Tasso in A.'s search for the ideal tragic style, from the various drafts of *Cleopatra* to a number of subsequent tragedies, such as *Saul* and *Filippo*; S. Jacomuzzi, 'Lettura della *Rosmunda*' (57–68), which examines the only one of A.'s plays to draw on medieval material, describing it as a play of hatred and love where the theme of regal power takes second place to the dominant passion; C. Barbolani, 'Utopia contro storia nella *Sofonisba* alfieriana' (69–86), which points out that even the heroism of the protagonist, as in other A. plays, has no impact on power relationships, while, as in *Mirra*, Sofonisba's suicide is an affirmation of individuality; E. Mattioda, '*Epponina* a Torino' (87–109), which considers the criticism of Giuseppe Bartoli's *Epponina* (1768) that appears in A.'s *I poeti*, and also looks at 18th-c. marginal comments on Bartoli in the copy in the Biblioteca Nazionale in Turin; V. Colombo, '"Chiamavasi Aillaud":

una ricerca sull'abate letterato amico di Vittorio Alfieri' (111–30), which attempts to identify in the person of Jean-Antoine Aillaud the figure mentioned by A. in the *Vita*; by the same author is 'Curiosità e inediti alfieriani' (131–60), which covers various matters, including a possible Nantes edition of the tragedies, a sonnet and other unpublished documents; S. Carrai, 'Una lettera inedita di Alfieri a Francesco Morelli' (161–65). F. Betti, 'Itinerari alfieriani: Saul e Mirra', *FoI*, 33:27–38, points out that Saul's interior torment is made human and becomes a metaphor for human weakness, as Mirra's isolation condemns her to be alienated from society because of her inconfessable passion. The author asserts that the two works are complementary in that they present 'in senso junghiano la proiezione di se stesso nell'eroico maschile e nella controparte femminile'. G. Bárberi Squarotti, 'Saul o la sfida a Dio', *RLettI*, 17:9–28, discusses A.'s presentation of Saul as a figure unable even to accept the authority of God, so that his suicide is seen as a titanic act of defiance: God has condemned and persecuted him, but cannot prevent his last act of liberty, death as a king. P.-E. Leuschner, 'La tragedia traviata: Alfieris *Mirra* zwischen *Phèdre* und den *melodramma romantico*', *ItStudien*, 20:73–107. C. Del Vento, 'L'edizione Kehl delle *Rime* di Alfieri (contributo alla storia e all'edizione critica delle opere di Alfieri)', *GSLI*, 176:503–27, considers the editorial vicissitudes of the *Rime* following A.'s decision not to issue the copies printed at Kehl (1789) and Giovanni Claudio Molini's unauthorized use of them for his own edition of the work. P. Bernaschina, *\*'Sugli autoritratti in versi di Alfieri e di Foscolo'*, *Versants*, 35:135–63. Massimo Manghi, *\*Il nano e il gigante e altri studi alfieriani*, Bo, Pendragon, 1998, 193 pp.

BARETTI.     M. Domenichelli, 'Scriblero in Arcadia: l'Inghilterra di Giuseppe Baretti', *RLMC*, 52:105–14, explores the influence of writers such as Pope on B., particularly in his savage attacks on petty writers.

BECCARIA.     *Atti di Governo (serie IV: 1787)* is the ninth volume in the *Edizione Nazionale delle Opere di Cesare Beccaria*, ed. Luigi Firpo and Gianni Francioni, Mi, Mediobanca, 1998, 947 pp.

BERTOLA.     A. Di Benedetto, 'Immagini dell'idillio nel secolo XVIII: Bertola e le poetiche della poesia pastorale', *GSLI*, 176:321–40, discusses 18th-c. theoretical concepts of the pastoral, particularly B.'s *Ragionamento sulla poesia pastorale*, which remained unpublished, and examines the complex analogies in B. between Arcadia and the modern day. G. A. Camerino, ' "… una maniera che la pittura mal sa ricopiare". Bertola e il gusto letterario dell'ultimo Settecento', *GSLI*, 176:341–54, analyses how B.'s 'Schema del gusto' is based on the notion of 'grazia' with its double structure of 'sensibilità' and 'sentimentalismo', asserting that the deep conflict between design and colour is what lies at the basis of late Settecento taste. M. F. Turchetti, 'Aurelio de' Giorgi Bertola e l'agricoltura', *Acme*, 52: 271–81, assesses B.'s contribution to the *Giornale letterario* of Siena, which he founded, noting that, in addition to his poetry, he also took part in the debate over agriculture in the Grand Duchy. Aurelio de' Giorgi Bertola, *Viaggio sul Reno e ne' suoi contorni*, Rimini, Luisè, 1998, xxxi + 191 pp., is a handy facsimile reprint of the original edition (1795), preceded by a new introduction.

CASANOVA.   Giorgio Ficara, *\*Casanova e la malinconia*, T, Einaudi, xii + 99 pp.

COMI.   M. C. Regali, 'Le *Ricerche storiche sull'Accademia degli Affidati* di Siro Comi. Edizione delle postille d'autore', *BSPSP*, 51:167–260, looks at the historical origins of this Pavia academy.

CUOCO.   Vincenzo Cuoco, *Saggio storico sulla rivoluzione di Napoli*, Mi, Rizzoli, 395 pp., reproduces Pasquale Villari's introduction alongside the definitive second edition of the 1806 text.

DA PONTE.   Lorenzo Da Ponte, *Libretti viennesi*, ed. Lorenzo della Chà, Parma, Guanda, 2 vols, xcvii + 1852 pp., as well as all the texts of Da P.'s 20 or more works for Vienna, contains nearly 300 pages of *notizie storiche* and an excellent, up-to-date bibliography. F. Ermini Polacci, 'Il *Mezenzio*, una tragedia dimenticata di Lorenzo Da Ponte', *ParL*, 19–20, 1998[1999]:58–90, outlines the genesis of this 1791 work, with its claimed stylistic derivation from Metastasio, and notes its connections with Ferdinando Casorri's libretto on the same subject for Cherubini. R. Mellace, 'Nel laboratorio di Da Ponte: *Così fan tutte, le nozze di Figaro* e la librettistica coeva', *RIM*, 33, 1998[1999]: 279–300, argues that even works such as *Così fan tutte*, long considered original, depend to a certain extent on Da P.'s long acquaintance with other writers' works, and by examining the libretti of figures such as Chiari and Galuppi shows that Da P. rewrote linguistic fragments and added his own poetic expression.

CALZABIGI.   G. Muresu, 'Ranieri de' Calzabigi e l'opera buffa', *CL*, 27, 104:469–87, examines C.'s *Lulliade* and its comments on Italian theatre and the *Dissertazione*, which is devoted to an analysis of Metastasio's work. The author contradicts those critics who would see C. as hostile to comic theatre, pointing out that it was the degradation of the genre, not the genre itself, that C. criticized. Id., 'Il Metastasio di Ranieri de' Calzabigi: le ragioni di un abiura', *RLI*, 103:379–405, deals with C.'s *Risposta* of 1790 which is full of the most savage attacks on M., especially on his style and *bellezze poetiche*, comparing it with C.'s earlier praise in the *Dissertazione* of 1755. The author suggests that this is due not only to differences of personality, but also of ideology, whereby C. rejects M.'s religious beliefs and takes pleasure in the bizarre and ridiculous.

FINETTI. S. Cavazza, 'Polemiche vichiane: Bonifazio Finetti, Carlantonio Pilati e lo "stato ferino" dell'umanità', *AASLAU*, 91, 1998[1999]:93–113, examines F.'s *De principiis juris naturae et gentium* (1765), which attacks various philosophical positions for their ambiguous attitude to the state of nature and devotes a final section to a critique of Vico's interpretation of the human state after the flood. The article also considers F.'s correspondence with Pilati in 1766.

GIANNONE. Lia Mannarino, *Le mille favole degli antichi. Ebraismo e cultura europea nel pensiero religioso di Pietro Giannone*, F, Le Lettere, 252 pp., considers G.'s *Triregno*, particularly the recently discovered *Prefazione*, in order to show how G. saw the Old Testament not as universal revelation but as the history of a single people, and how his comparison between sacred and profane history led him to believe in the inevitable decline of Christianity as of all religions.

GOLDONI. There are three new publications in the *Edizione Nazionale*: Carlo Goldoni, *L'amante militare*, ed. Piero Del Negro; *La guerra*, ed. Bianca Danna; *Il matrimonio per concorso*, ed. Andrea Fabiano, Venice, Marsilio, 291, 207, and 239 pp. respectively. Id., *Don Juan, Friends and Lovers, The Battlefield*, trans. Robert MacDonald, Oberon, 196 pp., contains three translations for the Citizens' Theatre in Glasgow. *Problemi di Critica Goldoniana*, 6, contains the following studies: L. Riccò, 'Goldoni, Chiari, Gozzi fra scritto e non scritto' (7–67), concerned with the particular difficulties of improvisation in the theatre and arguing that the three authors each produce different solutions to the transition from stage to written word: Chiari transfers the stage production as it is to the printed text, G.'s versions are always after the stage production, while Gozzi is interested in showing how the work develops from its beginnings into the stage performance; C. D'Angeli, 'La riforma messa in scena: il metateatro goldoniano' (69–96), which explores G.'s presentation of themes concerning the theatre, and also examines the element of autobiography; M. Pagan, 'Sulle forme dell'allocuzione in Goldoni, I: *La bottega del caffè*; II: *La figlia obbediente*' (97–141), which examines G.'s language in direct address and forms of respect, concluding that in *La bottega del caffè* variations in such forms emphasize the crucial points in the development of the relationship between characters with, in addition in *La figlia obbediente*, a certain consistency with the social use of the day, while in both cases the author stresses that G. was extremely attentive to what he was doing; A. Scannapieco, ' " . . .gli erarii vastissimi del Goldoniano repertorio". Per una storia della fortuna goldoniana tra Sette e Ottocento' (143–238), which examines in detail the theatre production of G. in the major centres of Italy, pointing out that it goes hand in hand with G.'s editorial success; M. Bordin, ' "Rimediare al disordine". Sintomatologia del lieto fine goldoniano dagli *Innamorati* al *Sior Todero brontolon'* (239–376), which is a substantial investigation into the period 1759–62, exploring parallels between G.'s work and the social system in Venice and concluding that G.'s writing moves from the ' "ritratti di famiglia" di gusto longhiano al nervosismo caricaturale che investe le ridicole e patetiche figurine . . . di Giandomenico Tiepolo'; N. Jonard, 'A propos du *Vero amico*. L'amitié dans le théâtre de Goldoni' (377–93), which discusses *Il vero amico* of 1751, looking at French models and claiming that G.'s celebration of friendship as a sovereign virtue has its roots in a well-established tradition.

GOZZI, G. Gasparo Gozzi, *Lettere*, ed. Fabio Saldini, Parma, Guanda, clxvi + 1299 pp., has an excellent bibliographical introduction.

LAVAGNOLI. F. L. Marcolungo, 'Antonio Lavagnoli (1718–1806): un metafisico dell'età dei Lumi, tra Vico e Rousseau', *AMAP*, 110.3, 1997–98:39–67, examines L.'s Latin writings between 1756 and 1764, emphasizing his insistence on a critical approach (and independence of thought within the Aristotelian system) and his stress on the primacy of rhetoric and the important social role of education.

LEANTI. Giuseppe Leanti, *Satira contro il Settecento galante in Sicilia*, ed. Maria Carmela Coco Davani, Palermo, Leopardi, 120 pp.

MAFFEI. *Scipione Maffei nell'Europa del Settecento*, ed. Gian Paolo Romagnani, Verona, Cierre, 1998, xxi + 745 pp., the proceedings of a conference held at Verona in 1996, covers the whole range of M.'s activities in the following sections: 'Scipione Maffei fra storiografia e politica'; 'Economia, governo e aristocrazia nella riflessione di Scipione Maffei'; 'Scipione Maffei nella "Repubblica delle lettere" '; 'Maffei, Muratori e l'Europa erudita'; 'Scipione Maffei fra lettere e arti'; 'Scipione Maffei epigrafista ed antiquario'.

MANZONI, F. F. Milani, 'Le poesie milanesi di Francesca Manzoni e un lettore di teologia a Pavia', *BSPSP*, 51:143–55, deals with eleven compositions by M. in dialect and her literary links with Carlo Maria Maggi and Marcantonio Zucchi.

METASTASIO. G. De Van, 'Les jeux de l'action. La construction de l'intrigue dans les drames de Métastase', *ParL*, 19–20, 1998[1999]:3–57, suggests that a study of M. should begin with the *argomenti* which preface each of his plays, and analyses M.'s preference for a happy ending and his use of chance, contrast and 'ornamenti episodici'. C. Pellegrino, 'Parole e silenzio delle eroine dei drammi di Metastasio', *ItStudien*, 20:58–72, talks of 'silenzio "chiuso" ' as an expression, willed or otherwise, of emotional disturbance, while soliloquy, or 'silenzio "aperto" ', effectively complements silence, since it is closed off from the outside world. The article also examines M.'s use of words and expressions of incommunicability. S. Olcese,

'Poesia e musica in Metastasio', *RLI*, 102:452–66, emphasizes the structural nature of music in M.'s *melodrammi*, pointing out that they were specifically written to be set to music and discussing the relative importance of recitative and aria. W. Spaggiari, 'Scheda per l'epistolario di Metastasio', *GSLI*, 176:99–109, discusses two unpublished letters to Giuseppe Rovatti. F. Lippmann and L. Tufano, 'Lettere edite e inedite di Pietro Metastasio nell'Archivio Caetani di Roma', *StMus*, 28:411–24, concerns, among other things, three unpublished letters to Andrea Ratti which are reproduced in an appendix.

PARINI.    Giuseppe Parini, *Odi: edizioni 1791 e 1802*, ed. Stefano Carrai, Trent, Università di Trento, xviii + 361, is a facsimile of the two editions with an introduction. C. Annoni, 'Parini, il "locus amoenus" e la città della giustizia', *RLI*, 103:406–28, analyses the Hegelian aspect of P.'s ideas, asserting that 'non c'è, infatti, il cielo sopra le opere del Parini', and examining his work as poet of the 'gente di picciolo affare'. Licia Badesi, *Rivisitando la vita di Giuseppe Parini*, Rimini, Luisè, 132 pp.

PIMENTEL.    Eleonora de Fonseca Pimentel, *Una donna tra le muse: la produzione poetica*, ed. Daniela De Liso, Na, Loffredo, 316 pp.

RIZZETTI.    F. Giudice, 'Giovanni Rizzetti, l'ottica newtoniana e la legge di rifrazione', *StSet*, 18, 1998[1999]:45–63, shows how R.'s opposition to Newton's theory of optics is based on a critique both of Newton's experimental procedures and of the accuracy of scientific instruments.

SERIO.    Raffaele Giglio, *Un letterato per la rivoluzione: Luigi Serio (1744–1799)*, Na, Loffredo, 279 pp.

VERRI, A.    B. Scalvini, 'L'*Iliade* tra compendio e dramma: Alessandro Verri traduttore di Omero', *StSet*, 18, 1998[1999]:159–78, asserts that V. was attracted by the 'estraneità' and the 'sapore esotico' of Homer, and that his decision in favour of a prose translation was partly due to his emphasis on the differences between the original idiomatic structures and the modern. Id., 'Notizie intorno alla *Storia d'Italia* di Alessandro Verri', *RSI*, 111:65–96.

VERRI, P.    *Pietro Verri e il suo tempo. Atti del convegno, Milano 9–11 ottobre 1997*, ed. Carlo Capra, Bo, Cisalpino, 2 vols, 540 and 600 pp., covers the whole range of V.'s activities. Vol. 1 has two sections, 'Pietro Verri e la memoria storica' and 'La felicità privata e pubblica', while Vol. 2 contains two main sections, 'Lo scrittore e il memorialista', 'L'economista e il riformatore', followed by a short section entitled 'La mostra *Pietro Verri e la Milano dei Lumi*.

VICO.    T. M. Costelloe, 'The concept of a "state of nature" in Vico's *New Science*', *History of Philosophy Quarterly*, 16:321–39, explores V.'s hypothetical use of the concept of a 'first time', discussing V.'s juxtaposition of poetic and philosophical modes of consciousness and stressing V.'s argument that the products of the mentality of the first men are inaccessible. F. Tessitore, 'Senso comune, teologia della storia e storicismo in Giambattista Vico', *Sasso Vol.*, 413–36, considering the problem of Vico in the transition between two centuries, examines his approach to history in the context of the awareness of the limits of reason as outlined in *De Antiquissima*, where he talks of 'sensus communis' as springing from 'similitudo morum'. The article explores the centrality of this idea in the *Scienza Nuova*, where in accordance with the limits of reason history too is recognized as not being an absolute reality.

# OTTOCENTO

By JOHN M. A. LINDON, *Professor of Italian Studies, University College London*
(This survey covers the years 1998 and 1999)

## 1. GENERAL

Publication of the imposing *Storia della letteratura italiano*, ed. Enrico
Malato, has reached the Ottocento with VII: *Il primo Ottocento*, Ro,
Salerno, 1998, xii + 1181 pp., and VIII: *Tra l'Otto e il Novecento*, Ro,
Salerno, xii + 1258 pp. Traditional in conception, the work sets high
scholarly, as well as typographical, standards. At the level of
popularization for an English-speaking readership, *The Cambridge
History of Italian Literature*, ed. Peter Brand and Lino Pertile, CUP,
xxi + 699 pp., revises in paperback what, when first brought out in
hard covers in 1996, was publicized as 'the first substantial history of
Italian literature to appear in the English language' and was generally
well received. Mistakes have been put right and omissions made
good; the index has been thoroughly revised. The chapters covering
our period — G. Carsaniga, 'The age of Romanticism (1800–1870)'
(397–456) and R. Dombroski, 'The literature of united Italy
(1870–1910)' (457–90) — are sound but, in the compass allowed,
inevitably skimpy: the *scapigliati*, for instance, merit a mere 14 lines.
In a series of surveys published by *Esperienze letterarie*, the Spanish,
British, and Irish contributions to Ottocento studies over the past
decade are examined in: F. Ardolino, 'Gli studi di italianistica in
Spagna negli ultimi dieci anni (Settecento e Ottocento)', *EL*, 23.3,
1998:111–22, and J. Lindon, 'Studi recenti d'italianistica in Gran
Bretagna e Irlanda: il Sette-Ottocento', *EL*, 24.3:103–14.

*La scrittura infinita: Bibbia e poesia in età romantica e contemporanea, con
antologia di testi dal 5. al 20. secolo. Atti del Convegno, Firenze 25–26 giugno
1997*, ed. Francesco Stella, F, Olschki, xiii + 216 pp. Paolo Giovannetti, *Nordiche superstizioni: la ballata romantica italiana*, Venice, Marsilio,
284 pp. Margherita Ganeri, *Il romanzo storico in Italia: il dibattito critico
dalle origini al postmoderno*, Lecce, Manni, 161 pp. Francesca Testa,
*Tristram Shandy in Italia*, Ro, Bulzoni, v + 286 pp., refers extensively
to pioneers such as G. Rabizzani (1920) and C. Varese (1948 and
1982) — and also to more recent predecessors such as L. Felici (1983),
or G. Mazzacurati (1991) and the other authors of the volume *Effetto
Sterne* (see *YWMLS*, 54:524) — in a new survey sensitive to essential
distinctions and marked by a sense of the historical moment.
Benedetta Montagni, *Angelo consolatore e ammazzapazienti: la figura del
medico nella letteratura italiana dell'Ottocento*, F, Le Lettere, 351 pp.,

articulates a fascinating spectrum of material in five chapters; 'Missione medico. Fede e idealismo di primo Ottocento'; 'Maschere e machiette: i nipoti di Balanzone'; 'Esculapio al bivio tra arte e scienza'; 'Un uomo nuovo per la nuova Italia: lo scienziato positivo'; and 'Professionisti alle soglie del Novecento'.

The corpus comprises mainly narrative and some verse, but also includes extracts from non-literary works such as *Nuovo galateo medico* or *Sui pregi e doveri del medico* to illustrate the idealization of the profession as a form of priesthood, but focuses on 19th-c. narrative (and occasionally verse) and indeed researches it with rigour and competence, to show how it reflects the developing image not only of the doctor in society but of illness itself, as for example in the transition from positivist optimism to the *fin-de-siècle* preoccupation with the occult and the paranormal, and the accompanying fashion, in literature, for hysteria and mental illness. B. Montagni, 'Dissezioni di cuore. Corpi di donna sul tavolo di anatomia dalla Scapigliatura a Pirandello', *ParL*, 13–14, 1997[1998]: 96–112. Laura Billi, and Manuela Bruni, *Le giardiniere del cuore: una lettura di scritti femminili della seconda metà dell'Ottocento*, Ferrara, Tufani, 136 pp., investigates the lives and writing (verse and prose) of women (often educators, hence the title) connected with Pistoia: mainly an anthology, it includes work by the 'poetessa pastora' Beatrice di Pian degli Ontani, Giannina Milli Cassone, Louisa Grace Bartolini, Erminia Fuà Fusinato, Anna Corsini, and Giulia Civinini Arrighi. C. Pestelli, 'L'arte della prosa tra Otto e Novecento. La crisi dell'*io* lirico e il romanzo impossibile negli studi di Tellini', *CLett*, 27:257–81. A. Santorsola, 'Gualdo critico e lettore, nella Francia della fine secolo', *Italianistica*, 27, 1998:37–56, following the rediscovery of G.'s novels (published between 1871 and 1892), looks at his criticism with particular reference to the French component: he is said to have shown 'una sempre vigile attenzione alla più avanzata ... produzione letteraria del tempo' and to have played a significant role in the evolution of literary taste. Gino Tellini, *Il romanzo italiano dell'Ottocento e Novecento*, Mi, B. Mondadori, 1998, x + 566 pp.

On 19th-c. theatre: F. Fido, ' "Fin de partie": the early romantics and comedy', *RLMC*, 51, 1998:379–90; G. Nicastro, 'Mogli e amanti nel teatro italiano dell'Ottocento', *CLett*, 27:721–42; Paolo Puppa, *Parola di scena: teatro italiano tra '800 e '900*, Ro, Bulzoni, 331 pp., for the Ottocento includes only 'Boito e le madri' (15–29), an engaging excursus on A. Boito's comedy *Le madri galanti*, written with Praga's collaboration and performed just once at the Teatro Carignano in 1863. V. Rea, 'Il teatro La Fenice di Napoli. 1813–1846', *ASPN*, 114, 1996[1998]:295–386, documents multiple aspects of the theatre's history, including its Romantic repertoire. Annamaria Sapienza, *La parodia dell'opera lirica a Napoli nell'Ottocento*, Na, Lettere italiane, 1998,

161 pp. *Seminario sulla drammaturgia*, ed. Luigi Rustichelli, Bordighera, West Lafayette, 1998, 87 pp., the proceedings of a seminar held at Reggio Emilia in 1991.

I note several collections of essays relating to more than one literary author. Marco Santagata, *Il Tramonto della Luna e altri studi su Foscolo e Leopardi*, Na, Liguori, 133 pp. Floriano Romboli, *La letteratura come valore: scritti su Carducci, D'Annunzio, Fogazzaro*, T, Tirrenia, 1998, 136 pp., gathers in revised form articles all but one (cf. *YWMLS*, 57:566) not noted in these pages: 'Contributo a una lettura critica delle *Rime di San Miniato* di Giosuè Carducci' (11–21); 'La prima stagione dell'arte dannunziana e la critica a lei contemporanea (da *Primo vere* alle *Laudi*) (23–41); 'Gabriele D'Annunzio e Angelo Conti. Il poeta e l'estetismo' (43–68); 'L'ebbrezza di *Alcyone* nella prosa notturna come "ricordo" e come "desiderio" (69–81); 'Da *Daniele Cortis* a *Il mistero del poeta*: alcune note sulla narrativa fogazzariana' (105–22); 'Evoluzione e letteratura nel tardo Ottocento italiano' (123–33). Niva Lorenzini, *Le maschere di Felicita: pratiche di riscrittura e travestimento da Leopardi a Gadda*, Lecce, Manni, 157 pp., revises and republishes '*Alla sua donna*: canzone amorosa' (11–30) together with pieces focusing on D'Annunzio in Gozzano, D'Annunzio in Cardarelli, and Pascoli in Caproni. Jone Gaillard Corsi, *\*Il libretto d'autore, 1860–1930: Boito, Verga, Capuana, Di Giacomo, D'Annunzio, Pascoli, Pirandello*, Bordighera, West Lafayette, 1997, 192 pp. I also note: Tommaso Scappaticci, *\*Dal mito alla storia: studi sulla letteratura italiana dell'800–'900*, Na, ESI, 274 pp., containing some new material; Rinaldo Rinaldi, *\*Dall'esempio al fantasma: percorsi di letteratura ottocentesca*, Soveria Mannelli, Rubbettino, 182 pp.

On minor literary episodes and figures: G. Brescia, 'La Repubblica Partenopea e le vicende dell'*Inno* del Cimarosa', *ArSP*, 51, 1998:233–40, highlighting the contradiction between Luigi Rossi's words for the 'Neapolitan Marseillaise', set to music by Cimarosa, and the anti-French text copied by the composer into his autograph of the piece after the Bourbon restoration; B. De Donà, 'Il Cadore tra francesi e austriaci nelle testimonianze letterarie', *Archivio storico di Belluno, Feltre e Cadore*, 69, 1998:138–47, covering writing (mainly occasional verse) published between 1809 and 1816 and reflecting the fluctuating local political situation; M. Perale, 'Belluno tra Venezia e Austria: una lirica di Carlo Vienna del 1816 dedicata a Francesco I', *ib.*, 148–56, discussing a blank-verse 'dream' (redolent of the *Somnium Scipionis, Aeneid* vi, and, of course, the *Divina Commedia*) where Austrian emperors keep company with the great ones of antiquity in the Elysean Fields.

For dialects and dialect literature: *La poesia in dialetto: storia e testi dalle origini al Novecento*, ed. Franco Brevini, 3 vols, Mi, Mondadori, c + 4509 pp., purports to be first systematic analysis of dialect poetry of all regions viewed as a whole from its 15th-c. origins to the present. *Croce e la letteratura dialettale. Atti della giornata di studi, Roma, Biblioteca Nazionale Centrale, 11 dicembre 1996*, ed. Laura Biancini, Leonardo Lattarulo, and Franco Onorati, Ro, BNCR, 196 pp. M. Piotti, 'Note sul *Vocabolario bresciano-italiano* di Giovan-Battista Melchiori', *Acme*, 52:83–103, analyses one of the earliest 19th-c. dialect dictionaries (1817), modelled on F. Cherubini's *Vocabolario milanese italiano*. G. Serrao, ' "Filologia" ed "antropologia culturale": motivi dell'antica poesia greca in un poeta dialettale calabrese dell'Ottocento', *RCCM*, 91:67–74, concerns a 'canzone' by Giuseppe Monaldo, not published until 1977, and its antecedents in Sappho and Theocritus.

Output of writing on travellers and travel literature has been particularly extensive during the past year. *Il viaggiatore meravigliato: Italiani in Italia (1714–1996)*, ed. Luca Clerici, Mi, Il Saggiatore, 372 pp. Id., *Viaggiatori italiani in Italia (1700–1996). Per una bibliografia*, Mi, Sylvestre Bonnard, 405 pp. *Il viaggio in Italia: modelli, stili, lingue. Atti del Convegno, Venezia 3–4 dicembre 1997*, ed. Ilaria Crotti, Na, ESI, 231 pp. Gianni Rosa, *La Sardegna vista da lontano: asterischi, storia, giornalismo, viaggiatori dell'Ottocento*, Oristano, S'Alvure, 255 pp., includes the writings of 19th-c. visitors to the island. *Italia e Italie: immagini tra Rivoluzione e Restaurazione. Atti del Convegno di studi, Roma, 7–9 novembre 1996*, ed. Maria Silvia Tatti, Ro, Bulzoni, 286 pp. Giorgio Maria Nicolai, *Il grande orso bianco: viaggiatori italiani in Russia*, Ro, Bulzoni, 577 pp., assembles some 30 Italian travellers who left accounts of Russia from Giovanni da Pian di Carpine and Marco Polo to the 20th c.: his accounts (chronologically arranged, with an introduction) of the accounts are followed by illustrations, a Russian glossary (385–445), notes to each of the travel accounts and the glossary (447–548) and an index of people, places, and Russian words.

Not concerned with travel as such, but with the Italian image of other cultures, are: A. Di Benedetto, ' "Le rovine d'Atene": letteratura filellenica in Italia tra Sette e Ottocento', *Italica*, 76:335–54, owns that the phenomenon only really begins in the 1820s and reviews in turn the role of its leading Italian representatives: 'Ugo Foscolo e i primi filelleni italiani', 'Giovanni Berchet, poeta filellenico', etc. F. Soldini, 'Svizzera e svizzeri: tracce in scrittori italiani degli ultimi due secoli', *Versants*, 34, 1998:49–65, includes many 19th-c. names, such as Foscolo, T. Dandolo, De Sanctis, Belli, and Fogazzaro, and highlights the role of deformation, generalization/ stereotyping, and subjectivism.

On aspects and moments of Ottocento intellectual history: Gian Paolo Romagnani, *'Fortemente moderati': intellettuali subalpini fra Sette e*

*Ottocento*, Alessandria, Orso, 240 pp., with a title that adapts Cesare Balbo's definition (1836) of a whole generation of late-18th-/early-19th-century Piedmontese intellectuals, presents a dozen individual portraits (of particular interest for literary culture are those of Galeani Napione, Diodata Saluzzo, and Ottavio and Tancredi Falletti di Barolo) which reveal considerable diversity among a group marked by common (conservative) traits: 'vario e non sempre lineare fu ad esempio il rapporto con la cultura settecentesca . . . Sono convinto, ad esempio, che l'estraneità o l'ostilità alle idee dei "philosophes" non escluda un'adesione convinta alla cultura delle riforme' (6). The reductive tendency of the traditional 'moderatist' interpretation of intellectual history (going back to Balbo's *Speranze d'Italia* of 1844) is exposed and corrected. R. Damiani, 'Carlo Vidua, riformatore della cultura italiana del primo Ottocento', *LItal*, 51:272–80, examines V.'s 'illuministic' programme for Italian education in *Dello stato delle cognizioni in Italia* (1816) and considers why it passed unnoticed at the time. A. Varni, 'L'"enciclopedismo" e la formazione della cultura risorgimentale', *NA*, 2210:321–29. Simone Casini, *Un'utopia nella storia: Carlo Botta e la 'Storia d'Italia dal 1789 al 1814'*, Ro, Bulzoni, 225 pp., approaches at various levels the prize-winning (over Leopardi's *Operette morali*) *Storia*: its extraordinary *fortuna* (1830–60) among the Risorgimento generation, its ideology (the drive to recover a political and linguistic Utopia situated in the Italy of city republics), its anachronistic, rhetorical prose, which is analysed at length. G. Talamo, 'Gli "antiromani" nel Risorgimento', *Sasso Vol.*, 603–15. N. Del Bianco, *\*'I "Pensieri diversi" di Francesco Melzi d'Eril'*, *NA*, 2210:330–49. A. Scirocco, *\*'Ruggiero Bonghi fra cultura e politica'*, *ib.*, 76–87. *\*Carteggio Lambruschini-Vieusseux*, F, Le Monnier–Fond. Spadolini Nuova Antologia, vol. 1, 1826–34, ed. Veronica Gabbrielli, pref. Giuseppe Galasso, 1998, vii + 356 pp.; vol. 2, 1835–37, ed. Aglaia Paoletti Langé, vii + 332 pp. F. Danelon, 'A lumi spenti. L'"Illuminismo" nella storiografia letteraria italiana primottocentesca', *CLett*, 26, 1998:653–70, examines Italian historicization of the (Italian) Enlightenment with particular reference to C. Ugoni, A. Lombardi, P. Emiliani Giudici, C. Cantù, L. Settembrini, and F. De Sanctis. M. Palumbo, 'Settembrini lettore di Machiavelli', *ib.*, 671–80, looks at S.'s positive interpretation of M. in the *Lezioni di letteratura italiana* (1866–72), bringing out the analogies with De Sanctis. M. Tarantino, 'Un capitolo (quasi) sconosciuto della fortuna ottocentesca di Machiavelli', *Sasso Vol.*, 573–602. Dante Della Terza, Matteo D'Ambrosio, and Giuseppina Scognamiglio, *\*Tradizione e innovazione: studi su De Sanctis, Croce e Pirandello*, Na, Liguori, 218 pp. M. T. Imbriani, 'Indici ragionati delle Carte Torraca', *CLett*, 26, 1998:741–85, gives alphabetical and chronological indexes of the correspondence (1875–1936) in the Torraca papers at Naples. M. Moretti, 'La dimensione ebraica di un maestro pisano', *ASNP*, n.s. 1, 1996[1998]: 209–48, analyses and richly documents the Jewish component of Alessandro D'Ancona's career and character as a scholar. A. Brambilla, 'Ancora su un opuscolo giovanile di G. I. Ascoli', *Ce fastu?*, 75: 267–77, discusses Ascoli's national and cultural identity in the wake of Dionisotti's *Appunti su Ascoli* and B.'s own 1996 volume on the great glottologist. V. Bagnoli, 'Scritture della persuasione: la nascita dell'*Idea Liberale* tra letteratura e propaganda (1891–1906)', *LItal*, 50, 1998: 19–47, illuminates the historical context that gave rise to this weekly, aimed at the bourgeois elite. *\*Adolfo Carolis e il suo mondo, 1892–1928: l'arte e la cultura attraverso i carteggi De Carolis, D'Annunzio, Maraini, Ojetti*, ed. Alessia Lenzi, Anghiari, ITEA, 190 pp. On the fringes of intellectual history I note: M. Canella, 'La creazione dei cimiteri nella Lombardia tra Settecento e Ottocento: tipologia per la gestione civile della morte o lusso per la celebrazione monumentale della memoria familiare?', *ChrI*, 14.2, 1998: 93–107, which invokes the views of Milanese *literati* such as L. Lambertenghi, A. and P. Verri, and U. Foscolo; and A. Candolini, 'Interpretazioni del "giardino moderno" nel Friuli ottocentesco', *Ce fastu?*, 74, 1998: 267–80, focusing on how the landscape garden fashion was introduced and adapted in 19th-c. Friuli, beginning with Quirico Viviani's 'Degli edifizj rustici e suburbani, e delle loro adjacenze', the first theoretical work on the English Garden to appear in Friuli.

The posthumous volume Carlo Dionisotti, *Ricordi della scuola italiana*, Ro, Storia e Letteratura, 1998, 620 pp., contains much of relevance, and of importance, for the history of Ottocento literary culture: 'Appunti su Giuseppe Taverna' (143–64); 'Petrarca, Rossetti e Hortis' (165–78); 'Panizzi esule' (179–208); 'Panizzi professore' (209–26); 'Torino, Milano e Genova' (227–40); 'Milano dal Regno Italico al Regno d'Italia' (241–50); 'Premessa a Sigismondo dei Conti' (251–62); 'Rinascimento e Risorgimento' (263–75); 'Appunti su Ascoli' (277–90); 'La lingua dell'unità' (291–319); 'Appunti sul carteggio D'Ancona' (321–68); 'Appunti sulla scuola padovana' (369–89); 'Letteratura e storia a Torino' (389–400); 'Giovanni Crocioni' (401–09); 'Ancora per Giovanni Crocioni' (411–20).

## 2. INDIVIDUAL AUTHORS

ABBA. A. Del Vecchio, 'Le *Noterelle* di Giuseppe Cesare Abba tra Romanticismo ed estetismo', *Testo*, 35, 1998: 103–22.

BELLI. B. Garvin, 'Oralità e poesia in Belli', *Lepschy Vol.*, 223–52, is an interesting analysis of the characteristic 'spoken' features (parataxis, syntactical reduction, interjections, etc.) used by Belli in

474     *Italian Studies*

his transposition of Roman into writing. With *Il Belli: quadrimestrale di poesia e di studi sui dialetti*, 1.1, Ro, Oleandro, 1999, the journal resumes publication under the auspices of the Centro Studi Gioachino Belli. Giuseppe Gioachino Belli, *Tutti i sonetti romaneschi*, ed. Marcello Teodonio, 2 vols, Ro, Newton Compton, 1998, iii + 1195, 1274 pp. CAPUANA. Luigi Capuana, *Novelle inverosimili*, ed. with an essay by Manuela La Feria, Cava de' Tirreni, Avagliano, 185 pp. M. L. Zito, 'Avventura di Luigi Capuana fra amore e morte. Un testo dimenticato', *RLettI*, 16, 1998:373–82, looks briefly at a text suffused with *fin-de-siècle* (Nordic) exoticism. By the same scholar, 'Psicologia e scienza in *Mostruosità* di Luigi Capuana', *CLett*, 27:767–74. M. Bocola, 'Capuana ritrovato: otto scritti critici sconosciuti', *ib.*, 323–40, discusses theatre and literary criticism, and articles on spiritualism, overlooked by G. Raya in his Capuana bibliography.

CARDUCCI. E. N. Girardi, 'Poesia e attualità. A proposito di Carducci', *Testo*, 36, 1998:3–26. A. Palermo, 'Su Carducci critico', *CLett*, 26, 1998:489–501, reviews C.'s 20th-c. fortunes as a critic and prose-writer, highlighting recognition of his strengths despite Croce's influential strictures (1914). M. Marti, 'La xxix delle *Barbare* e la modernità del Carducci', *GSLI*, 176:16–37, working outwards from 'Alla stazione in una mattina d'autunno', vindicates C.'s modernity, conceptual, linguistic, and metrical (even in his use of 'la metrica barbara'). G. Bianciardi, 'Gli autografi carducciani della collezione Finazzi', *ib.*, 174–95, examines a heterogeneous collection of Carducciana preserved among the Finazzi papers at the Novara State Archive: three opuscules sent (with autograph dedications) to Pietro Zambelli, two unpublished letters, and two copies of verse, one of which is the Alcaic ode *Ideale*, the other a fragment of C.'s projected translation of Hölderlin's *Griechenland*. B. Londero, 'A tavola con Carducci', *ItStudien*, 20:176–84, documents at length C.'s gourmet (and particularly bibulous) tendency from his letters. See also PELOSINI, below.

CASTELNUOVO. 'Enrico Castelnuovo o dell'infelicità', *Levia Gravia*, 1:31–51, examines the output (some ten novels and above 100 short stories, 1870–1908) of a minor but representative Jewish-Italian writer.

CIAMPOLI. Domenico Ciampoli, *Racconti abruzzesi*, Cerchio, Polla, 271 pp., is a facsimile of the 1880 edition.

COLLODI. Riccardo Campa, *La metafora dell'irrealtà: saggio su 'Le avventure di Pinocchio'*, Lucca, Pacini Fazzi — Pescia, Fondazione Nazionale Carlo Collodi, 1999, 85 pp., contains stimulating passages of commentary on the narrative but also much rather turgid abstraction. An absence of structure in reflected in the fact that the four chapters into which the essay is divided are without titles. *Sterne e*

*Collodi: Tavola rotonda, Collodi, 16 dicembre 1995*, Lucca, Pacini Fazzi — Pescia, Fondazione Nazionale Carlo Collodi, 59 pp., gathers R. Bertacchini, 'Digressioni d'autore sui nasi' (11–17); 'F. Tempesti, 'Sterne era davvero *sterniano?*' (19–22); and D. Marcheschi, 'Giornalismo umoristico e linea sterniana' (23–32) and the concluding discussion (33–44). While Tempesti reacts against the current tendency to categorize as 'Sternian' any manifestation of humour in Italian writing of the past two centuries, his colleagues document Collodi's familiarity with Sterne's novels. P. M. Toesca, 'La filosofia di Pinocchio ovvero l'Odissea di un ragazzo per bene con memoria di burattino', *FoI*, 31, 1997[1998]:459–86, concludes that the book was written, and can therefore be read, 'come la storia di un percorso di autoeducazione, di scoperta della propria identità'. Its meaning will vary according to the reader: 'l'effetto di questo ritrovamento [i.e. discovery of identity] sarà una conferma o una trasformazione'. Carlo Collodi, *Le avventure di Pinocchio. Storia di un burattino*, ann. Carlo Fruttero and Franco Lucentini, Mi, Mondadori, 254 pp., a reprint of the 1995 'Oscar Leggere i Classici' edition, usefully updates the bibliography of the 1981 'Oscar narrativa' edition.

COLOMBI. Clotilde Barbarulli and Luciana Brandi, *L'arma di cristallo: sui 'discorsi trionfanti', l'ironia della Marchesa Colombi*, Ferrara, Tufani, 1998, 93 pp., explores the irony that upsets the prescriptive power of the 'canone di femminilità codificato dai "discorsi trionfanti" del periodo'. As well as listing her publications in volume (1873–1900), the authors give a bibliography that evinces a surge of 'feminist' interest in Marchesa Colombi over the past two decades. E. Genevois, 'Une lettre inédite de la marchesa Colombi (1886)', *ChrI*, 14.1, 1998:123–29, publishes a letter of June 1886, addressed to the publisher Galli, concerning a second edition of *Prima morire* and her forthcoming children's book *I ragazzi d'una volta e i ragazzi di adesso*. E. Genevois, 'La marchesa Colombi (études et recherches)', *ib.*, 14.3–4, 1998:131–218, comprises an essay on C.'s best-seller 'Bon goût, bon sens: un traité de savoir-vivre du XIX$^e$ siècle: la *Gente per bene* de la Marchesa Colombi' and four of her short stories, two of them accompanied by essays.

D'ANNUNZIO. Pietro Nicolai, *Itinerario intellettuale di Gabriele D'Annunzio dalla 'Laus vitae' al 'Libro segreto'*, Ro, Città Nuova, 184 pp. Carmine Chiodo, *Di alcuni miti dannunziani delle 'Laudi'*, Ro, Vecchiarelli, 99 pp., glances at *Primo vere* and *Canto novo*, as well as the *Laudi*, *Maia* and *Alcyone* in particular, in a rapid and uncontroversial survey of Greek mythology in D.'s poetry which comes to predictable conclusions. More than a third of the slim volume usefully consists of notes containing copious bibliographical references, but regrettably there is no index. F. Ferrucci, 'Whitman e D'Annunzio', *StCrit*, 13,

1998:185–98, defines D'A.'s debt to Whitman in the *Laudi*. D. Dell'A-quilano, 'D'Annunzio e il leonardismo *fin de siècle*', *CLett*, 26, 1998:553–77, shows D'A. indulging in decadent *leonardismo* in, for instance, the Medusa-like women of his poetry (*Chimera*) and his novels. Marinella Cantelmi, *Il cerchio e la figura: miti e scenari nei romanzi di Gabriele D'Annunzio*, Lecce, Manni, 180 pp. L. Ricaldone, 'Dalla parodia dell'antico all'iperbole dell'immortalità: sulle tracce del suicidio in D'Annunzio', *ItStudien*, 19, 1998:161–70, elaborates a lucid and fascinating contrast between *Trionfo della morte* and *Libro segreto* with respect to suicide: in the former 'l'aspetto . . . parodistico risulterebbe proprio dal contrasto tra la maestosità degli apparati predisposti da D'Annunzio e la piccolezza del romanzo famigliare irrisolto del protagonista. Nel caso delle tentazioni di morte narrate nel *Libro segreto*, si tratta invece di suicidi non portati a termine, che permettono all'autore di narrarli trasformandoli in episodi epici, inseriti in una cornice cristiana . . . secondo un progetto di autoedi-ficazione agiografica modellata sul genere letterario dell'*ars moriendi* . . .' I. Crotti, 'La biblioteca a sé: appunti sull'autocitazione dannunzi-ana tra *Leda* e *Notturno*', *REI*, 45:115–32.

John Woodhouse, *Gabriele D'Annunzio: Defiant Archangel*, OUP, xi + 406 pp., researched with impressive thoroughness, seeks to provide the first fully documented critical biography of the author. Id., 'Per uno studio della rottura tra D'Annunzio e Santi Ceccherini. Con un carteggio inedito', *Rassegna dannunziana*, 34, 1998:1–10. Many of the other items to have appeared are of primarily biograph-ical interest. Gabriele D'Annunzio, *Lettere ai Treves*, ed. Gianni Oliva, Katia Berardi, and Barbara Di Serio, Mi, Garzanti, 837 pp., comprises (7–52) introductory material as well as the rich correspond-ence itself. *Benco-D'Annunzio: epistole d'irredentismo*, ed. Cristina Benussi and Giancarlo Lancellotti, Trieste, LINT, 1998, 125 pp., brings to light 34 unpublished letters between Silvio Benco (1894–1949) and D'Annunzio. *Il carteggio tra Gabriele D'Annunzio e Gian Francesco Malipiero, 1910–1938*, ed. Chiara Bianchi, Clusone, Ferrari, 1997, 195 pp. A. Pavetto, 'Affetti ed affari: le lettere di Ariel e di Mimì', *Levia Gravia*, 1:181–38. *Gabriele D'Annunzio e Arturo Toscanini: scritti*, ed. Carlo Santoli, Ro, Bulzoni, 107 pp. *Il piacere del corpo: D'Annunzio e lo sport*, ed. Mario Pancera e Guido Vergani, Mi, Electa, 143 pp. *Terre, città e paesi nella vita e nell'arte di Gabriele D'Annunzio*, II-III: *la Toscana, l'Emilia-Romagna, l'Umbria e la Francia. Atti del 24. Convegno internazionale, Firenze-Pisa, 7–10 maggio 1997*, ed. Silvia Capecchi, Pescara, Ediars, 573 pp. Milva Maria Cappellini, *D'Annunzio e Prato: documenti e lettere ritrovate*, F, Zella, 118 pp. Mark Choate, 'D'Annun-zio's political dramas and his idea-state of Fiume', *FoI*, 31,

1997[1998]:459–86, lucidly rehearses D'A.'s involvement in irre-
dentist politics and the Fiume episode, bringing out the relevance of
his imperialist dramas *La Nave* and *La Gloria*.

D'AZEGLIO. *Massimo d'Azeglio pittore*, Mi, Mazzotta, 1998, 171 pp.
DE AMICIS. L. Fournier, 'La fabrique de l'identité nationale en
Italie dans *Cuore* de De Amicis', *ChrI*, 15.2–3:63–78, analyses *Cuore*
as an exercise in patriotic indoctrination.

DE ROBERTO. M. Ganeri, 'La svolta dei *Viceré*', *Belfagor*,
54:539–48, argues against detractors that the work is indeed a
historical novel, situated at a turning point and the forerunner of
Pirandello's *I vecchi e i giovani* (1913) and Lampedusa's *Il Gattopardo*
(1957): it is 'il primo romanzo storico che nasce dal tramonto dello
storicismo romantico e dalla crisi del positivismo e si pone come
critica radicale del romanzo portatore delle ideologie risorgimentali'.
Yet 'nella trama dei *Viceré* la presenza dei modelli risorgimentali
[Manzoni and Nievo] resta sempre ben avvertibile'. A. Cavalli Pasini,
'Il punto su De Roberto. Inediti e nuovi studi', *CLett*, 26,
1998:695–708, bears witness to the ongoing revival of interest in De
Roberto since publication of her own monograph in 1996 with a
review article centring on the work of Antonio Di Grada, *\*La vita, le
carte, i turbamenti di Federico De Roberto, gentiluomo*, Catania, Fond. Verga,
1998, and of his pupil Rosario Castelli, who has edited the short-story
collection *\*L'albero della scienza*, Caltanissetta, Lussografica, 1997.
Particularly interesting among the *inediti* are the narratives contained
in Federico De Roberto, *\*Adriana, un racconto inedito, e altri 'studi di
donna'*, Catania, Aimone, 1998.

DE SANCTIS. A. Palermo, 'Il paradosso di De Sanctis', *EL*, 23.3,
1998:3–26, borrows G. Petronio's 1986 title for a reconsideration of
20th-c. Crocean and Marxist interpretations of De S.'s thought,
urging the need to accept its vital contradictions. C. Battista, 'La
funzione della *Storia:* De Sanctis e il presente', *LCrit*, 25–27,
1993–95[1997]:155–70.

DI GIACOMO. E. Soglia, 'Alla "fiamma della candela": le novelle
di Salvatore Di Giacomo', *Levia Gravia*, 1:1–30, is concerned not with
his seven collections of *novelle veriste* but with Di G.'s little-known
*racconti fantastici* (written for Neapolitan newspapers) with their
'sognatori di candela' (cf. G. Bachelard's study of *rêverie: La flamme
d'une chandelle*). Those (and they are the majority) dating from 1879–80
represent his earliest published work, reflecting the influence of
E. T. A. Hoffmann, E. A. Poe, and particularly the Alsatian writers
É. Erckmann and A. Chatrian.

DOSSI. M. Cassano, 'Testo e dintorni: per una geografia dossiana',
*LCrit*, 25–27, 1993[1997]:233–37. E. Cesaretti, '*Locus desacrationis* nel
"monastero" della *Desinenza in A*', *RStI*, 16.1, 1998:227–40, analyses

the scene 'In monastero' as typifying *scapigliato* writing. R. Cadonici, 'Gemiti dai torchi. Carlo Dossi e Dante Isella', *FC*, 23, 1998:436–43, suggests 'qualche dato . . . integrativo' in the wake of Carlo Dossi, *Opere*, ed. Dante Isella, Mi, Adelphi, 1995.

FERRETTI. *Jacopo Ferretti e la cultura del suo tempo. Atti del Convegno di studi, Roma 28–29 novembre 1996*, ed. A. Bini and F. Onorati, Mi, Skira, 352 pp.

FOGAZZARO. R. Cavalluzzi, 'Daniele Cortis', *LCrit*, 25–27, 1993–95[1997]:133–52, discusses F.'s bourgeois *contemporaneizzazione* of the novel, which eschews any polemical, 'veristic' representation of the poor and reveals F., despite all statements to the contrary, to be a conservative. Id., 'Piccolo mondo fogazzariano', *RLettI*, 16, 1998: 109–28, reconsiders *Piccolo mondo antico* with reference, among other things, to its 'charge' of symbolism, particularly in the climactic death-of-Ombretta sequence.

FOSCOLO U. Petry, 'Vitae parallele. Zur Poetik von Foscolos Roman *Ultime lettere di Jacopo Ortis* und seiner Bezugnahme auf *Die Leiden des jungen Werthers*', *ItStudien*, 20:108–37. A. Beniscelli, 'Wertherismo in scena: tra Sografi e Foscolo', *LItal*, 50, 1998:220–36, ranges from Sografi's comic stage adaptation *Verter* (1794) and Vordoni's *Jacopo Ortis* (1807) to Monti's *Aristodemo* (1786) via F.'s parallel between Werther and Ortis in the 1816 *Notizia bibliografica*. Ugo Foscolo and Angelo Sassoli, *Vera storia di due amanti infelici ossia Ultime lettere di Jacopo Ortis*, ed. Pino Fasano, Ro, Bulzoni, 166 pp., is a timely reproduction of the original *Ortis*, in the bicentenary of publication (Bologna, Marsigli, 1799), based on the second version of the Bologna text and on G. Gambarin's critical edition (1955) of the same. In the wake of C. Goffis (1942, 1958, and 1978), M. Martelli (1970), and G. Padoan (1993), and his own *Stratigrafie foscoliane* (1974), Fasano returns, in an important introduction (9–47), to the problematic authorship of the 'parte seconda' and demonstrates its attribution to Angelo Sassoli. G. Nuvoli, 'L'*Orazione a Bonaparte* di un "giovine e libero scrittore"', *GSLI*, 176:239–60, undertakes a useful running commentary, section by section, of the *Orazione*. R. Zucco, 'Note sui metri della *Caduta* e delle *Odi* foscoliane', *LS*, 34:109–32, reverting to the vexed question of the derivation of Parini's and Foscolo's rare metrical forms, suggests the importance of Italian translations of Horace's *Odes* by F. Venini, O. Dalla Riva, F. Cassoli, and L. Brami. P. Frare, 'Foscolo e Manzoni: rapporti biografici e polemiche testuali', *RLettI*, 17:29–50, critically re-examines the two writers' relations and revises Gavazzeni's arguments on the direct links between their poetry in the period 1801–03: notably the two self-portrait sonnets and the odes *All'amica risanata* and *Qual su le cinzie cime*. C. Del Vento, 'Sul *Diario italiano* di Ugo Foscolo. Note e precisazioni', *GSLI*,

176:222–38, concerns the newspaper run by F. in the last weeks of 1803 but suspended for lack of funds. Of three numbers published only one is extant (among the Mocenni-Magiotti papers at the Marucelliana). An appendix reproduces the two more substantial articles, the second being Luigi Bossi's review of *La Chioma di Berenice*. Laura Alcini, *Studio di varianti d'autore nella traduzione foscoliana di 'A sentimental journey through France and Italy'*, Perugia, Guerra, 1998, 120 pp., includes some useful collation of ch. 1–5 in the 1805–06 and 1812 autographs and the 1813 and 1817 editions; the discussion of variants lacks depth, but important generalities are confirmed, such as the literariness of the 1813 version as compared with that of 1805–06. A. Colombo, *'Princeps ingenii et operis. I restauri della Cena di Leonardo nell'Hypercalypsis foscoliana'*, *SPCT*, 56, 1998:31–62, offers a searching and subtle interpretation of F.'s censures against the painter Giuseppe Bossi in the *Hypercalypsis* and the *Clavis*. A. De Crescenzo, 'Il Foscolo critico: struttura e motivi degli *Essays on Petrarch*', *Italica*, 75, 1998:62–77. C. Pestelli, 'Giuseppe Chiarini e le edizioni dell'epistolario foscoliano', *Italianistica*, 27, 1998:235–49, develops broad considerations on C.'s work as a Foscolo scholar, defining him as 'il filologo del classicismo letterario secondottocentesco in Italia'. D. Isella, 'Su un ritratto inglese del Foscolo', *RLMC*, 52:251–65, identifies Mario Praz's copy of the famous Fabre portrait of the poet as the work of Henri-François Fradelle, probably executed for Foscolo in 1819. For the engraving of the Fradelle copy made by Elizabeth, daughter of Dawson Turner and wife of Foscolo's translator, Francis Palgrave, the article leans heavily on J. Lindon, who drew Isella's attention to his own work published in *Italianistica*, 17, 1988 (see *YWMLS*, 51:510).

FUCINI. T. Iermano, 'Umorismo e leggerezza nei racconti di Renato Fucini', *EL*, 24.4:19–52.

GIOBERTI. B. Haddock, 'Political union without social revolution: Gioberti's *Primato*', *The Historical Journal*, 41, 1998:23–33. M. Mustè, 'Gioberti e Cartesio', *Sasso Vol.*, 547–71, investigates the transition from G.'s *Teorica del sovranaturale* (1837) to his *Introduzione allo studio della filosofia* (1839–40) and defines the concomitant shift in his interpretation of Descartes: in the former G. draws support from D. for an ontological critique of sensationalism; in the latter Cartesianism is seen as a radical negation of ontology, and the subjectivism of the *cogito* as the source of corruption of modern philosophy.

GIORDANI. S. Timpanaro, 'Di una recente edizione del carteggio Giordani-Vieusseux', *BSPia*, 93, 1998:81–90, in Giordani's birth-place, draws attention to, and here and there corrects, Laura Melosi's excellent edition (see *YWMLS*, 59:579).

GIUSTI. G. Capovilla, 'Per un'analisi dell'esperienza metrica del Giusti', *SPCT*, 56, 1998:63–89, reviewing the metrical range of G.'s verse, also figures in *Giuseppe Giusti. Il tempo e i luoghi*, ed. Maurizio Bossi and Mirella Branca, F, Olschki, 454 pp., gathering 16 papers presented at studies days (Florence–Monsummano Terme, 1994–95) devoted to G. and Restoration Tuscany. The reappraisal aims to break out of the post-Risorgimento ideological cliché of G., based on his satire, and to set him in an altogether broader perspective. Thus, his *oeuvre* is represented in a balanced set of contributions that cover language as well as metre (Giovanni Nencioni, 'La lingua in Giuseppe Giusti', 277–98) and extend beyond poetry (Nicolò Mineo, 'La poesia di Giuseppe Giusti', 163–74) to include his autobiographical writings (G. Nicoletti, 'Le forme del racconto negli scritti autobiografici del Giusti', 259–75) and his letters, drastically censored by Gino Capponi and their first editors to exclude all that conflicted with the aforementioned cliché (E. Ghidetti, 'Preliminari all'*Epistolario* del Giusti', 235–58).

GROSSI. In complementary articles on the lexis of G.'s novel A. Zangrandi, 'Il lessico del *Marco Visconti* di Tommaso Grossi nella prima edizione milanese. La componente dialettale e popolare', *LS*, 33, 1998:267–300, looks in some detail at the dialectal component in relation to G.'s (and Manzoni's) *Sentir messa*, their reply to the anti-Lombard strictures of Michele Ponza, and finds substantial coherence: G.'s Lombardisms correspond to expressions also found in Tuscan as represented by the Crusca dictionary; while in 'Il lessico del *Marco Visconti* di Tommaso Grossi nella prima edizione milanese. La componente aulica', *ib.*, 34:227–51, she illustrates the presence of archaic literary lexis and 14-c. terms for objects (weapons, clothes, etc.) specific to that period, in which the novel is set.

LANCETTI. Vincenzo Lancetti, \*Memorie intorno alla mia vita, studi e impieghi: le vicende autobiografiche di un erudito cremonese ed intellettuale milanese tra antico regime e restaurazione, 1766–1851, ed. Emma Cristina Vantador, Cremona, Linograf, 1998, li + 209 pp., also contains an essay by Andrea Battistini.

LARA. A. Zoggia, 'Un'emblematica presenza nel giornalismo di fine '800: la Contessa Lara', *LItal*, 51:281–307, traces the career of the best known (and most notorious) professional woman writer of the late-19th c., the Florentine Evelina Cattermole Mancini, and then analyses the novel *La scalata alla fortuna* (1890) into which she projected that career.

LEOPARDI. The Leopardi bicentenary has predictably brought a proliferation of editions, critical volumes and articles, and conference papers (given the usual delays, these last can be expected to go on appearing well beyond 1999). Review of this vast output must needs be even more summary than usual. Giacomo Leopardi, *Tutte le opere*, ed. Lucio Felici, Ro, Lexis, 1998, the computerized version of Felici's hard-copy edition (Ro, Newton Compton), opens up interesting prospects for systematic study of Leopardi's *oeuvre*, especially of the *Zibaldone*. Editions of the *Canti* include: Giacomo Leopardi, *Canti*, ed. Franco Gavazzeni and Maria Maddalena Lombardi, Mi, Rizzoli, 1998; Giacomo Leopardi, *Canti*, ed. Emilio Peruzzi, 2 vols, Mi, Rizzoli, 1998, a revised and expanded version of the 1981 edition; and *Cantos*, trans. and ed. María de la Nieves Muñiz Muñiz, M, Cátedra, 1998, 954 pp., which must be one of the best non-Italian editions ever produced. It gives translation and original in parallel and with excellently documented notes and commentary. The translation sticks remarkably close to the letter of the original and to this end eschews rhyme. This would seem to be the one substantial loss. Giacomo Leopardi, *Canzoni*, ed. Marco Santagata, Mi, Mondadori, 1988, 182 pp., controversially 'translates' the ten *canzoni* into present-day prose. Giacomo Leopardi, *Della natura degli uomini e delle cose*. *Edizione tematica dello Zibaldone di pensieri stabilita sugli Indici leopardiani*, ed. Fabiana Cacciapuoti, pref. Antonio Prete, Ro, Donzelli, lxxxiv + 378 pp. M. Nieves Muñiz, 'Malefatte leopardiane di stato a Barcellona', *Belfagor*, 54:744–46, notes basic shortcomings in a Catalan translation of the *Zibaldone* (*El Zibaldone dels pensaments*, trans. and ed. Assumpta Camps, Barcelona, Columna-l'Albí, 1998, 612 pp.) published with public funding from Italy and a preface by Franco Foschi, Director of the Centro Nazionale di Studi Leopardiani.

Many minor works have received editorial attention: *Saggio sugli errori popolari degli antichi*, ed. G. B. Bronzini, Venosa, Osanna, 1997; *Storia dell'astronomia*, Mi, La Vita Felice, 1997, with an essay by A. Massarenti and an appendix by L. Zampieri; *Giulio Africano*, ed. C. Moreschini, Bo, Il Mulino, 1997; *Discorso di un italiano intorno alla poesia romantica*, ed. R. Copioli, Mi, Rizzoli, 1998; *Contro il romanticismo: il Discorso di un italiano di Giacomo Leopardi*, ed. Anna Clara Bova, Bari, Graphis, 1998, 156 pp.; *Manuale di Epitteto*, ed. F. Brioschi, Mi, Gallone, 1998; *La varietà delle lingue*, ed. Stefano Gensini, F, La Nuova Italia, 1998, an anthology of linguistic reflections from the *Zibaldone*; *Discorso sopra lo stato presente dei costumi degl'Italiani*, ed. Mario Andrea Rigoni, testo critico di Marco Dondero, commento di Roberto Melchiori, Mi, Rizzoli, 1998, 139 pp.; *I Paralipomeni*, ed. Fabio Russo, Mi, Angeli, 1997, 207 pp.; Giuseppe Savoca, *Concordanza dei 'Paralipomeni' di Giacomo Leopardi. Testo con commento, concordanza, lista di frequenza*, F, Olschki, 1998, xxiv + 330 pp.; Giacomo Leopardi, *Epistolario*, 2 vols, ed. Franco Brioschi and Patrizia Landi, T, Bollati Boringhieri, 1998, cxxvi + 1250–2540 pp., the first complete edition of Leopardi's correspondence (comprising all known letters from and to L.) since that of F. Moroncini (1934–41); *The Letters of Giacomo Leopardi*, ed. and trans. Prue Shaw, Leeds, Northern Universities Press, 1998, 296 pp., offering a judicious selection in English.

The bicentenary has been marked by the launch of a *Rivista internazionale di studi leopardiani*. The first issue (1999) comprises: Andrea Zanzotto, 'Sere del dì di festa' (5–6); S. Carrai, 'Lettura del *Sabato del villaggio*' (7–17); C. Galimberti, 'Sull'inferno dei *Paralipomeni*' (19–24); G. Panizza, 'Perché lo *Zibaldone* non s'intitolava *Zibaldone*'(25–35); L. Felici, 'La nuova edizione dell'*Epistolario*' (37–45); M. A. Rigoni, 'Sul nulla e sulla negazione del pensiero di Leopardi' (47–56); G. Serra, 'Leggere i Greci con Leopardi' (57–64); M. Castoldi, 'Il soffio che viene dall'isola lontana. *Odisseo*, Tristano e *La ginestra* nell'interpretazione di Giovanni Pascoli' (65–89); M. Orcel, 'Baudelaire avant la lettre' (91–99); M. Mandolini Pesaresi, 'Tragedia della memoria: Byron e Leopardi' (101–07); E. Giordani, 'Leopardi nell'ultimo ventennio: percorsi bibliografici' (109–29).

Several long-running journals have devoted whole issues to Leopardi for the bicentenary. *RLI*, 103, contains: L. Blasucci, 'I cinquant'anni della *Nuova poetica leopardiana*' (7–17); W. Binni, 'La ginestra e l'ultimo Leopardi' (18–29); S. Carrai, 'Leopardi lettore di Young' (30–45); I. Innamorati, 'Il *Pompeo in Egitto*: radiografie di personaggi tra libri e vita domestica' (46–60); E. Ghidetti, 'La "conversione" letteraria tra progetto e destino' (61–80); P. Girolami, 'L'"office du miroir": autobiografia, pensiero e poesia nel *Diario del primo amore*' (81–99); N. Bellucci, 'Il "gener frale": appunti sulle canzoni "rifiutate"' (100–11); F. D'Intino, 'Scene di caccia. Analisi di un topos leopardiano' (112–31); L. Felici, 'Paesaggio leopardiano: dalle Marche all'Umbria, dai *Canti* ai *Paralipomeni*' (132–46); M. Dondero, 'Appunti sul *Discorso sopra lo stato presente dei costumi degl'Italiani*' (147–61); O. Innocenti, 'L'altra faccia della luna. Una lezione di astronomia nelle *Operette morali*' (162–73); R. Bessi, 'Leopardi commenta Petrarca' (174–92); R. Carnero, ' "Eccelsa imago" e "cristallisation": le teorie amorose di Leopardi e Stendhal' (193–209); G. Tellini, '*Lo spettatore fiorentino*, giornale di "nessuna utilità" ' (210–22); J. Alcorn and D. Del Puppo, '*La ginestra*: un esempio di arte sociale' (223–51); P. Williams, 'La leopardiana filosofia della consolazione ne *La ginestra*' (252–61); G. Ferroni, 'I fiori di Leopardi o la forza della fragilità' (262–73); F. Mecatti, ' "Per isvagamento del lettore". Firenze e Napoli nei *Pensieri*' (274–301); L. Melosi, 'Ancora sul discorso di Pietro Giordani sulle *Operette morali* (la redazione fiorentina e le correzioni del 1846)' (302–21); E. Benucci, 'Alessandro Luzio e un articolo cestinato di Giacomo Leopardi' (322–30);

A. Marinotti, 'Luporini, Leopardi e la filosofia del '900' (331–65);
E. Giordano, 'Con Leopardi attraverso gli anni Novanta' (366–77).
*RStI*, 16.2, 1998, a tribute to L. edited by Anthony Verna,
comprises: J. M. Baker, 'Dialectics of mourning in *Sopra un bassorilievo
antico sepolcrale*' (1–18); C. Ball, ' "O famoso scopritor": rediscovering
*Ad Angelo Mai*' (19–40); D. Bini, '*Il tramonto della luna*' (41–57);
R. Bodei, 'Il "solido nulla". Male e sofferenza in Leopardi' (58–81);
A. Bonadeo: '*La ginestra*, il male, il piacere e la vitalità' (82–98);
A. Carrera, 'L'amore al telescopio. *Alla sua donna* e il platonismo
leopardiano' (99–123); G. Carsaniga, 'Ai margini della *Palinodia*.
Scienza, tecnologia e natura in Leopardi' (124–59); D. Castronuovo,
'Metamorphosis of the occasion in *Nelle nozze della sorella Paolina*'
(160–84); G. Cecchetti, 'Su *La sera del dì di festa*' (185–200); F. Di
Mieri, '*Il risorgimento*' (201–33); V. Esposito, 'Rilettura delle canzoni
patriottiche' (234–42); C. Federici, 'Leopardi's *Canto notturno*'
(243–57); L. Fontanella, '*Il sogno* di Giacomo Leopardi' (258–88);
P. Garofalo, 'Living in a material world: *Inno ai Patriarchi, o de' principi
del genere umano*' (289–311); E. Giordano, 'Autobiografia leopardiana:
*Le ricordanze*' (312–36); A. Illiano, 'Sul *Bruto minore*' (337–58); C. La
Porta, 'History and poetic vocation in *Sopra un monumento di Dante*'
(359–75); M. Lollini, 'La canzone *Alla primavera*. Leopardi e la lirica
moderna' (376–401); J. Marchegiani, '*Amore e morte*: ri-immaginare il
vero' (402–27); A. Musumeci, ' "Silvia ossia del ricordare" ' (428–37);
D. O'Connor, 'From Venus to Proserpine: *Sappho's last song*' (438–53);
P. Possiedi, '*Sopra il ritratto di una bella donna scolpita nel monumento
sepolcrale della medesima*' (454–68); G. Rimanelli, 'Giacomo Leopardi'
(469–85); T. C. Riviello, 'Dualities in *Il sabato del villaggio* by Giacomo
Leopardi' (486–96); A. Rossini, ' "Non è un'imitazione di Pindaro".
Alcune osservazioni sull'ode *A un vincitore nel pallone*' (497–509);
G. Singh, '*Aspasia*: an appreciation' (510–18); A. Urbancic,
'Reflecting on a moment of calm: Leopardi's *La quiete dopo la tempesta*'
(519–36).

*Antichi e moderni*, Bo, CLUEB, 1998, 121 pp., suppl. to *Schede
umanistiche*, includes: L. Avellini, 'Leopardi: per cominciare' (5–6),
F. Tateo, 'Su Leopardi e gli antichi' (7–19); R. Bonavita, 'Descrizione
di una battaglia. Leopardi e la *querelle* classico-romantica' (21–73);
A. Forlini, 'Stratone e l' "ospitale" dei viventi. Tradizioni filosofiche e
contesti scientifici per il Leopardi bolognese' (75–93); G. Benvenuti,
' "Non so se il riso o la pietà prevale". La saggezza degli antichi nelle
*Operette*' (95–121).

Bicentenary conference papers include: *Giacomo Leopardi, poeta e
filosofo. Atti del convegno dell'Istituto italiano di cultura, New York, 31 marzo-1
aprile 1998*, ed. Alessandro Carrera, pref. Gioacchino Lanza Tomasi,
Fiesole, Cadmo, xviii + 112 pp., comprising: E. Sanguineti, 'Invito a

Leopardi' (3–7); F. Ferrucci, 'Leopardi e Kafka' (9–13); C. Wright, 'To Giacomo Leopardi in the sky/A Giacomo Leopardi in cielo' (14–24); G. Ficara, 'Sistemi leopardiani: bellezza e felicità' (25–32); Sergio Givone, 'Severino e Baldacci interpreti di Leopardi' (33–38); P. Possiedi, 'Leopardi progressivo?' (39–50); T. J. Harrison, 'Leopardi, Unabomber' (51–57); M. Riva, 'Leopardi, l'inattuale. Tristano contro Zarathustra' (59–80); A. Carrera, 'La favola e il mondo vero. La questione della verità in Leopardi e Nietzsche' (81–108). *Il riso leopardiano: comica, satira, parodia. Atti del IX Convegno internazionale di studi leopardiani, Recanati, 18–22 settembre 1995,* 1998 + 670 pp. *L'ultimo orizzonte . . . Giacomo Leopardi: A Cosmic Poet and His Testament,* ed. Roberto Bertoni, T, Trauben — Dublin, Trinity College, 100 pp., comprises: N. Lorenzini, 'Leopardi e la poesia cosmica' (9–33); P. Williams, '*La ginestra*: the last will and testament of a poet and philosopher' (35–68): R. Bertoni, 'Note sul dialogo di Calvino con Leopardi' (69–100). *Ripensare Leopardi,* ed. Michele Dell'Aquila, Fasano, Schena, 192 pp., reproduces a series of bicentenary lectures organized by the Apulian Academy of Sciences with the financial support of the Fondazione Piazzolla: F. Tateo, 'Leopardi e gli antichi' (9–27, but cf. *Antichi e moderni,* above); S. Natoli, ' "Io nel pensier mi fingo". Leopardi e le illusioni' (29–45); A. Placanica, 'Leopardi. Il Mezzogiorno in idea e l'Italia' (47–91); M. Dell'Aquila, 'Leopardi. Le fondazioni del cuore' (93–117); M. Marti, "Leopardi: il "momento" di Arimane' (119–41), for which see also *GSLI* item below; G. Papuli, 'Leopardi. Filosofia e antisistema' (143–85); F. Foschi, 'Leopardi nel mondo' (187–92).

Other more or less occasional publications in volume form fall into several distinct categories. There are, for example, the various introductory volumes. Ugo Dotti, *Lo sguardo sul mondo. Introduzione a Leopardi,* Ro–Bari, Laterza, 175 pp., does not attempt to give a systematic account even of L.'s major works within such a narrow compass (120 small-format pages) but focuses, with reference to some, on his intellectual quest from 'the negation of spiritualism' to 'the last message'. Giuseppe Savoca, *Giacomo Leopardi,* Ro, Marzorati–Editalia, 1998, 206 pp., in the series LIME (Letteratura Italiana Carlo Marzorati–Editalia), is a clear, concise, reliable critical profile. Another work of a similar kind is Vincenzo Guarracino, *Guida alla lettura di Leopardi,* Mi, Mondadori, 1998, 519 pp. Other volumes are more biographical in character: Michele Ruggiano, *\*Leopardi: la pena di vivere,* Benevento, Edimedia, 1998, 202 pp.; Renato Minore, *Leopardi. L'infanzia, la città, gli amori,* Mi, Bompiani, 297 pp.

L. criticism by deceased writers has been republished: Giovanni Pascoli, *\*Saggi e lezioni leopardiane,* ed. Massimo Castoldi, La Spezia, Agorà, ccxiv + 253 pp., a critical edition preceded by the editor's lengthy introduction; Alfonso Gatto, \*Ritratto di Giacomo Leopardi, Bo, Boni, 93 pp.; Piero Bigongiari, La poesia pensa. Poesie e pensieri inediti, Leopardi, e la lezione del testo, ed. Enza Biagini, Paolo Fabrizio Iacuzzi, Adelia Noferi, F, Olschki, 302 pp., with a short section comprising texts already publ. in part: 'I Canti come voce desiderante dell'io (1987–1988– . . .)' (69–88); 'La poesia pensa (1989)' (89–93); 'Lo stupore del testo (luglio 1993–1996)' (95–97). Living scholars have themselves brought out new editions of earlier work. Bruno Biral, La posizione storica di Giacomo Leopardi, T, Einaudi, 1997, 429 pp., the sixth edition of a work first published in 1974, expands the previous version (1992), notably with chapters on Leopardi as philosopher (in particular on Amerio's Catholic philosopher thesis) and on Prete's conception of 'pensiero poetante' in Leopardi. Fabio Russo, Leopardi politico, o Della felicità impossibile, Ro, Bulzoni, 291 pp., first publ. 1979, is expanded by the addition of the three essays: 'Leopardi e il mondo politico greco antico' (203–33); 'Il quinto personaggio nel "Senofonte e Machiavello" di Leopardi' (235–44); and 'I popoli europei visti da Leopardi' (245–71). Domenico De Robertis, Leopardi. La poesia, Bo, CLUEB, 1998, xii + 360 pp., usefully gathers ten essays all already published except the lengthy 'Le canzoni o l'"inganno del desiderio"' (27–85).

Volumes of essentially new writing have been timed to coincide with the centenary. Cesare Luporini, Decifrare Leopardi, Na, Macchiaroli, 1998, xxi + 281 pp., posthumously assembles much of the material elaborated by Luporini for a projected comprehensive monograph left unfinished at his decease. It reflects his professional interests as a professor of moral philosopher, with chapters on 'Dall'Inno ai Patriarchi alla Storia del genere umano' (77–155); 'Poesia e filosofia' (157–224); 'Assiologia e ontologia nel nichilismo di Leopardi' (225–34); 'Nichilismo e virtù nel percorso leopardiano' (235–47); 'Leopardi e Bruto: il rinnegamento della virtù' (249–81). Two opening chapters deal with L.'s poetics and L'infinito. Luigi Baldacci, Il male nell'ordine. Scritti leopardiani, Mi, Rizzoli, 1998, 195 pp. Paolo Rota, Leopardi e la Bibbia: sulla soglia di 'alti Eldoradi', Bo, Il Mulino, 274 pp., systematically traces the intertextual links between L.'s writings and particular scriptural texts: Genesis, the Psalms, Ecclesiastes, Job, the Gospels.

Other volumes are more difficult to pigeon-hole in this fashion, especially where it has not been possible to examine them: Vittoriano Esposito, \*Religione e religiosità nel Leopardi. Questioni vecchie e nuove tra biografia, filosofia e poesia, Foggia, Bastogi, 112 pp.; Marco Manotta, \*Leopardi: la retorica e lo stile, F, Le Lettere, 339 pp.; \*Leopardi e l'età romantica, ed. Mario Andrea Rigoni, Venice, Marsilio, x + 450 pp., which includes two previously unpublished poems by Zanzotto;

Odoardo Spoglianti, *Leopardi lontano da Recanati*, pref. Renato Minore, Ro, Nuova Editrice Spada, 119 pp.; Carmen Cinzia Santoro, *E il suon di lei: la concezione estetico-musicale in Giacomo Leopardi*, Chieti, NoUbs, 1998 158 pp.; C. Ferrucci, *Un'estetica radicale: Leopardi*, Ro, Lithos, 126 pp. *Leopardi: altre tracce*, ed. Ugo Piscopo, Na, Guida, 142 pp.; Marco Santagata, *Il tramonto della luna e altri studi su Foscolo e Leopardi*, Na, Liguori, 133 pp.; Fanny Targioni Tozzetti, *Aspasia siete voi . . .; lettere di Fanny Targioni Tozzetti e Antonio Ranieri*, ed. Elisabetta Benucci, Venosa, Osanna, 246 pp.; Salvatore Natoli and Antonio Prete, *Dialogo su Leopardi: natura, poesia, filosofia*, Mi, B. Mondadori, 1998, 183 pp., comprising, as well as the dialogue, five separate essays by the two participants followed by P. Rota's, 'Percorsi di lettura sul pensiero leopardiano'; Augusto Placanica, *Leopardi e il mezzogiorno del mondo*, Cava de' Tirreni, Avagliano, 1998, 153 pp.; A. Prete, *Finitudine e infinito*, Mi, Feltrinelli, 1998, 174 pp.; G. A. Camerino, *L'invenzione poetica in Leopardi. Percorsi e forme*, Na, Liguori, 1998, 144 pp.; Giancarlo Bolognese, *Leopardi e l'armeno*, Mi, Vita e Pensiero, 144 pp.

Finally, miscellaneous articles are listed alphabetically by periodical. G. Ronconi, 'Soci dell'Accademia studiosi del Leopardi', *AMAP*, 110.3, 1998:69–86, reviews the Paduan academy's contribution to Leopardi studies through the work of members from G. Guerzoni and G. Zanella to G. Mazzoni, L. Lazzarini, M. Dazzi, G. Aliprandi and D. Valeri. V. Zaccaria, 'Due accademici traduttori e il Leopardi e il Foscolo (Preromanticismo nel Veneto)', *ib.*, 87–98, returns to the intermediary role played by Cesarotti and Costa with their translations of Gray's *Elegy* and expands the perspective to include Veneto editions and translations of other British pre-Romantic texts. M. Dell'Aquila, 'Memoria e scrittura nelle *Ricordanze* di G.Leopardi', *EL*, 24.3:3–17. G. Rando, 'Leopardi: la pedagogia negativa. Locke e la formazione del genio', *ib.*, 19–50, documents L.'s view that it is nurture, and not nature, which determines intelligence. M. Marti, ' "Leopardi": il 'momento' di Arimane, *GSLI*, 175, 1998:321–40, develops stimulating reflections on the principle of evil and the metaphysics of suffering in the late Leopardi, relating 'Ad Arimane' (spring 1833) to 'A se stesso' and the end of L.'s love for 'Aspasia'. E. Bigi, 'Materialismo e fantasia nel *Frammento apocrifo di Stratone di Lampsaco*', *ib.*, 176:1–15, in discussion with C. Galimberti's spiritualist interpretation of L.'s materialism, suggests that the second part of the *operetta*, on the infinity of worlds, is poetic fantasy on a par with the vision of total annihilation imagined in the *Cantico del gallo silvestre*. S. Verhulst, 'Il "coup d'oeil" dei Lumi e la teoria dell'immaginazione in Leopardi', *Intersezioni*, 19:61–71, traces the link between the cognitive *coup d'oeil* of Enlightenment epistemology and Leopardi's notion of ecstatic 'apprensione totale' via the imagination.

F. D'Intino, 'Da Alfieri a Leopardi. La dissoluzione dell'auto-biografia', pp. 93–124 of *Italian autobiography from Vico to Alfieri (and beyond)*, ed. John Lindon, Supplement to *The Italianist*, 17, 1977[1999]. A. Casadei, 'Schede leopardiane', *Italianistica*, 27, 1998:495–97, briefly signals some new editions and current critical tendencies. F. De Rosa, 'Sulla cronologia e la collocazione del *Passero solitario*', *ib.*, 23–46, reverting to a vexed question, rejects D. De Robertis's dating of the poem (1834–35) and (with L. Russo and others) assigns it, on the basis of language, style, and metre, to the period of the *grandi idilli* or, in any case, to the years between then and the composition of *Il pensiero dominante* (1832). G. Cecchetti, 'Un altro Leopardi in inglese', *Italica*, 75, 1998:242–52. G. Di Stefano, '*(. . .) ove per poco il cor non si spaura*. Le traduzioni tedesche de *L'infinito* di Giacomo Leopardi', *ItStudien*, 20:140–59, reviews 25 of the many German translations of the poem (he claims that they run to well over thirty) and finds that the majority misread the 'per poco'. L. Martellini, 'Giacomo Leopardi: la *Dissertazione sopra la felicità*', *ib.*, 160–75. M. Grilli, 'Giacomo Leopardi poeta della noia e del nulla', *LetP*, 102, 1998:25–37. A. Ferraris, 'L'enciclopedia infernale di Leopardi. Sul *Saggio sopra gli errori popolari degli antichi*', *LItal*, 50, 1998:176–85, points out the young scholar's marked taste for 'il teatro della crudeltà', i.e. the Underworld/Hell in the classical and Judeo-Christian traditions. C. Galimberti, 'Dal paesaggio marchigiano a quello campano', *ib.*, 374–80, opens up interesting perspectives on the presence and function of landscape in L.'s verse. P. Zellini, 'Leopardi, il pensiero matematico e il linguaggio dell'infinito', *ib.*, 606–15. A. M. Bazzocchi, 'Leopardi: intorno al bicentenario. Rassegna di studi 1993–1998', *ib.*, 51:112–41. G. Zaccaria, 'Le *Operette morali* come romanzo', *Levia Gravia*, 1:159–67. P. Williams, 'Leopardi's philosophy of consolation in *La ginestra*', *MLR*, 93, 1998:985–96. B. Nacci, 'Leopardi teorico della traduzione', *MLN*, 114:58–82, traces L.'s thinking through the *Zibaldone* and in published writings, claiming it to be 'una delle concezioni più originali e motivate dell'Ottocento'. M. Luzi, 'I *Canti* di Leopardi con l'interpretazione di De Robertis', *NA*, 2209:152–59. A. Di Preta and C. Delfino, 'Note lessicali ai *Canti* di Leopardi', *ib.*, 236–41. S. Timpanaro, 'L'edizione del *Giulio Africano* di Giacomo Leopardi', *ib.* 190–95. M. Fattori, 'Le poète et le philosophe: Leopardi et Descartes', *NRLett*, 18.1, 1998:61–72, stresses L.'s attribution of exemplary value to D.'s scepticism, his principle of methodological doubt. G. Magrini, '*Alla primavera*, o di Leopardi e Foscolo', *ParL*, 11–12, 1997[1998]:9–25. A. R. Romani, 'La teoria della lingua nel pensiero di Giacomo Leopardi', *RLettI*, 16, 1998:73–108, seeks to show how, in the *Zibaldone*, L. elaborates (albeit in fragmentary form) a complete linguistic theory and in conclusion stresses the importance of his meditation on language for his achievement as poet and thinker. M. Dell'Aquila, 'Leopardi: la canzone *Alla Primavera*', *ib.*, 17:155–67. M. Righini, 'Leopardi bolognese, Bologna leopardiana', *SUm*, 12.2, 1998:103–19. M. Dondero, 'La datazione del *Discorso* sui costumi degli italiani di Giacomo Leopardi', *SFI*, 56, 1998[1999]: 297–319. E. Capodaglio, 'Due impronte stilistiche nello *Zibaldone* di Giacomo Leopardi', *StCrit*, 88, 1998:321–62, lacks focus in addressing style in/the style of the *Zibaldone*. N. Jonard, 'Cristianesimo e pessimismo nella formazione intellettuale di Leopardi', *Testo*, 35, 1998:35–60. E. Landoni, 'Dall'infinito di Leopardi al Leopardi infinito. Un'interpretazione inesauribile', *ib.*, 61–88. G. Amoretti, 'Il dì natale. Il simbolismo della nascita in *Ad Angelo Mai* e *Canto notturno* di Giacomo Leopardi', *Versants*, 36:103–20, is based on the continuity and obvious contrast between *Ad Angelo Mai* (L.'s 'prima organica dichiarazione . . . della negatività del reale') and the *Canto notturno*, where that negativity has become inherent in Nature's cycle of production and destruction of life. C. Genetelli, 'Appunti sull'*Appressamento della morte* di Giacomo Leopardi', *ib.*, 33, 1998:83–104, situates the 'vision' in relation to L.'s other writings of the time (notably the *Discorso di un italiano*) and to models such as Dante, Petrarch, and Monti. G. Bonacchi Gazzarrini, 'Puccini e Leopardi', *Il Veltro*, 42, 1998:313–30.

MANZONI.     An important research tool to have recently appeared is *Bibliografia manzoniana 1980–1995*, ed. Mariella Goffredo De Robertis, Mi, Biblioteca Nazionale Braidense, 1998, xi + 480 pp. *Annali manzoniani* continues after a five-year interval with n.s. 3, a particularly rich volume comprising some two dozen items (and 430 pp.) divided between 'Studi', 'Testi', and 'Note e discussioni', plus a score of reviews (or a further 155 pp.). In G. Vigorelli, 'Premessa all'Edizione Nazionale delle Opere di Alessandro Manzoni' (7–18), the editor of the *Annali* and president of the Centro Nazionale di Studi Manzoniani describes the new 'Edizione Nazionale ed *Europea*' (thus dubbed in the three volumes just out) of Manzoni's *oeuvre*, which was cerimonially announced to the media and public in May 1998: a 35-volume critical edition (in two versions, de luxe and 'economica') promoted by the Ministero dei Beni Culturali, lavishly financed by the Fondazione Cariplo, and published by the Centro. The 'Studi' include: G. Cospito, 'Il giovane Manzoni, Vico e la Milano napoleonica' (21–50), which, taking the reality of Manzoni's 'vichismo' as now generally accepted, re-examines his brief but intense relations with the southern exiles Lomonaco and Cuoco by whom he was influenced; I. Botta 'Manzoni e Fauriel: un dialogo europeo' (53–94), anticipating (with only minor variants) her introduction, for volume 27 of the 'Edizione Nazionale ed *Europea*', to

Manzoni's longest epistolary dialogue, his correspondence with Claude Fauriel: ground often covered by M.'s biographers, though without ever having had so much documentation *a disposizione*; I. Becherucci, ' "Una storia così bella . . .": suggestioni per l'*Adelchi*' (95–114), arguing that M.'s reading of Angelo Maria Ricci's *Italiade* (Livorno 1819) in August 1820 played a decisive part in his choice of subject in *Adelchi*. Clara Leri, 'Le due scritture dell'*Apologia manzoniana* di Gadda' (129–95). Other essays concern, respectively, Carlo Porta and Tommaso Grossi (see PORTA, below) and Manzoni in Gadda. 'Testi' likewise contains items concerning not Manzoni himself but persons more or less connected with him: Henriette Blondel and Costanza Arconati, Giuseppe Gorani and Giovanni Verri, Stefano Stampa (his MS annotations in his copy of the fifth edition of Beccaria's *Dei delitte e delle pene*). For Manzoni himself they include: M. Vitale ' "Cette question éternelle . . .": sulla lettera di Manzoni al Delécluze' (199–207), republishing with commentary a letter mistakenly printed by G. P. Marchi as previously unknown (see below) and now owned by the Centro di Studi Manzoniani, which in May–June 1997 displayed it in an exhibition and transcribed it in the catalogue *Libri e manoscritti dalle nuove acquisizioni. Con quattro lettere inedite di Alessandro Manzoni*, Mi, Casa del Manzoni, 1997; E. Travi, 'L'edizione illustrata del romanzo manzoniano nelle lettere da Parigi di Sigismondo Trechi' (235–64), drawing at length on Trechi's copious missives at the Braidense; J. Riva, 'La dispensa di Casa Manzoni nelle lettere a Francesco Viani' (265–77), bringing to light three hitherto unpublished letters; G. Gaspari, 'Due lettere autografe ritrovate' (279–83), republishing from the originals letters to G. Bovara (1817) and F. Rossi (1842); L. A. Biglione di Viarigi, 'Trittico manzoniano. Documenti e inediti dagli Archivi privati di Brescia' (285–303), transcribing and discussing three sonnets (a version of the well-known self-portrait and two hitherto unknown), a satire against Gaetano Volpini, and references to Manzoni in the album of Countess Clara Maffei; N. Crespi and M. Santagiuliana, 'Dovera, 11 giugno 1605. Un "rapto di donna honesta" quasi manzoniano' (315–27), publishing, from originals in the Milan State Archive, two letters recounting an abduction with clear affinities to that of Lucia in *I Promessi Sposi*; S. Bertolucci and G. Meda, 'Documenti manzoniani. Inediti e curiosità dalle raccolte del Centro italo-tedesco Villa Vigoni' (365–74).

Looking at other work in the broad chronological perspective of M.'s *oeuvre* (minus the novel): the early verse is mentioned *passim* by Cospito (previous paragraph) and discussed by Frare (see FOSCOLO, above); on *Carmagnola* and *Adelchi*, M. Boaglio, 'La figura della *conversione* nelle tragedie manzoniane', *CLett*, 26, 1998:449–71, points

out that essential ingredients of the tragic genre are precluded by the
presence of Christian conversion ('l'eroe cristiano non può che
configurarsi come anti-eroe rispetto alla tradizione'): the result is 'uno
spettacolo più elegiaco che tragico, in cui l'espiazione prelude ormai
alla salvezza e alla redenzione'; for *Carmagnola* in particular: \**Una
storia, una tragedia. Maclodio 1427*, Maclodio, Comune di Maclodio —
Fond. Civiltà Bresciana, 1997, and for *Adelchi* the Becherucci item
mentioned above. The Ur-novel is represented by Valter Puccetti,
\**'Come biscie all'incanto'. Retoriche e simboli della visione nel Fermo e Lucia*,
Ro, Carocci, 127 pp. I note several recent editions of minor works:
\**Osservazioni sulla morale cattolica*, ed. Giorgio De Rienzo, Mi, Monda-
dori, 1997, 244 pp.; *Lettera al signor Chauvet sull'unità di tempo e di luogo
nella tragedia*, ed. Barbara Maj, F, Aletheia, 128 pp.; \**Storia della colonna
infame: tradizione critica, redazioni e varianti*, ed. Alma Maria Ioni, Ro,
Ediz. A. S., 1997, 223 pp.; \**Storia della colonna infame*, introd. Mino
Martinazzoli, Lecco, Periplo, 1997, 159 pp.; \**Storia della colonna infame*,
pref. Giancarlo Vigorelli, Locarno, Dadò, 163 pp., also containing
(151–62) an essay by Salvatore Veca. On the *Storia* I note a lengthy
chapter (67–123) of Ezio Raimondi, \**Letteratura e identità nazionale*, Mi,
Mondadori, 1998, 235 pp. E. Travi, ' "La giovane è bella": Manzoni
e la rivoluzione francese', *RLettI*, 16, 1998:439–71, traces the long
gestation of the late essay *La rivoluzione francese del 1789 e la rivoluzione
italiana del 1859*.

Vincenzo Di Benedetto, *Guida ai Promessi Sposi. I personaggi, la gente,
le idealità*, Mi, Rizzoli, 431 pp., rises above the level of interest
suggested by the title. L. Parisi, 'Il tema della provvidenza in
Manzoni', *MLN*, 114:83–105, views the Bossuet of the *Oraisons
funèbres*, the *Discours sur l'histoire universelle*, and the sermons *Sur la
Providence* as the source of M.'s theology of Providence in *Adelchi*,
which is then developed and deepened in *I promessi sposi*. A. M. Negri,
'Sulla struttura dei *Promessi sposi*', *GSLI*, 175, 1998:416–19, briefly
argues for an intentionally bipartite and symmetrical structure (ch.
1–19 and 20–38). Verina R. Jones, *Le 'dark ladies' manzoniane e altri
saggi sui 'Promessi sposi'*, Ro, Salerno, 1998, 167 pp., gathers together
her interesting Manzoni essays, focusing on intertextuality or text/
'extra-text' relations with reference to such phenomena as the silk
industry, illiteracy and literacy, or folk culture. The two dimensions
come together to good effect in the discussion of M.'s 'dark ladies',
Gertrude and Lucia, and the reasons for his infringement of the
stereotypical dark–blonde dichotomy of the literary tradition: Lucia's
black hair, in a girl endowed with the characteristics of the blonde
home-maker, reflects M.'s social realism and the model of 'la bella
Tetton' in Carlo Porta's *Lament del Marchionn di gamb avert*. \*Clareece
G. Godt, \**The Mobile Spectacle. Variable perspective in Manzoni's 'I Promessi*

*Sposi*', NY, Lang, 1998, xvi + 167 pp. Glenn Pierce, \**Manzoni and the Aesthetics of Lombard Seicento Art assimilated into the narrative of 'I Promessi Sposi*', London, Associated University Presses, 1998, 254 pp. F. Crescentini, 'Dall'arte figurativa lombarda: luci sui *Promessi Sposi*', *Intersezioni*, 19:39–59, following on from Mina Gregori's pioneering work (1950), extends discussion of the importance of Lombard art for M. further into the field of visual documentation (which alongside written documents enables him to 'penetrate' the historical period of *I promessi sposi*) and into that of M.'s research for the Gonin illustrations of the *quarantana*. A not entirely dissimilar connection, with music, emerges in A. Di Stefano, '*I promessi sposi* cantano', *RLI*, 102, 1998:484–99, examining operatic works of the 1830s inspired by the first edition of M.'s in some respects operatic novel: G. Ceccherini for L. Bordese (Naples 1830), A. Gusella for P. Bresciani (Padua 1833), and anon. for L. Gervasi (Rome 1834). In the same area I also note R. Candiani, 'Quegli eterni *Promessi sposi*. La fortuna musicale del romanzo manzoniano', *CLett*, 27:675–720.

Particular episodes or moments of the novel are discussed in: S. Ferlito, 'Fear of the mother's tongue: secrecy and gossip in Manzoni's *I Promessi Sposi*', *MLN*, 113, 1998:30–51, attempting a feminist reading of M.'s suppression of Lucia's desire (present in *Fermo e Lucia*) to tell her mother the secret only revealed to Fra Cristoforo in *I promessi sposi*; D. Isella, ' "In capo di tavola". Nota su un passo manzoniano', *StCrit*, 14:205–07, dismissing the problem (the position of Don Rodrigo at his own dinner table in ch. 5 of the novel) raised by G. Savelli, 'Intorno a una descrizione "sbagliata" di Manzoni', *ib.*, 13, 1998:105–27, and hinging around the meaning of the phrase 'in capo di tavola': the head of the table, in Italian, is wherever the master of the house chooses to sit; P. A. Perotti, 'Personaggi manzoniani: Tonio e Gervaso', *CLett*, 26, 1998:258–71, making interesting observations on Gervaso's half-wittedness in relation to the surprise wedding and Tonio's dementia after infection in the plague; R. Piazza, '*I promessi sposi*, VIII, 89–99, tra retorica e poesia', *Testo*, 89–102, analysing the concluding pages of ch. VIII in terms of classical figures and tropes, and of the frequent presence of metrical segments in the prose: this from the foremost representative of Italy's antirhetorical Romanticism; R. Luperini, 'Il silenzio dell'allegoria: la vigna di Renzo', *Belfagor*, 54:11–23, following up suggestions made by S. Agosti, A. Stella, and C. Repossi, and seeing in the famous passage not a piece of bravura description, or a mere display of botanical learning, but an allegory of nature in man and society which leaves the problem of evil unanswered.

Important for M.'s thought and intellectual biography are: \**Manzoni e Rosmini: 2 ottobre 1997*, Mi, Istituto Lombardo di Scienze e

Lettere–Centro Nazionale di Studi Manzoniani, 1998, 257 pp.; *Le Stresiane. Dialoghi tra Antonio Rosmini e Alessandro Manzoni raccolti a Stresa da Ruggero Bonghi*, ed. Pietro Prini, Piemme, Casale Monferrato, 1997, 253 pp. Other contributions of biographical relevance include: Giovanni Albertocchi, *Sull'epistolario di Alessandro Manzoni. Disagi e malesseri di un mittente*, pref. Cesare Segre, F, Cadmo, 1997, xi + 140 pp., incorporating articles already noted in *YWMLS*, 57:576; E. Travi, 'Alessandro Manzoni e la mancata collaborazione all'*Antologia*', *NA*, 2208, 1998:194–99; G. P. Marchi, 'Studi danteschi di Étienne-Claude Delécluze: appunti critici con una lettera inedita di Alessandro Manzoni', *LItal*, 50, 1998:237–47, publishing a letter (2 October 1841), formerly preserved inside D.'s complimentary copy of the *quarantana*, in which M. thanks him for the gift of his translation of the *Vita Nuova* (on this see the Vitale piece in *Annali manzoniani*, above); S. F. Ferlito, 'Mapping European philosophy: the coy politics of Manzoni's *Lettera a Victor Cousin*', *MLQ*, 59, 1998:195–229, reading the letter as politely voicing dissent from C.'s 'authoritarian and colonializing politics' through a critique of C.'s 'disembodied Cartesian subject always present to itself'; A. Bassi, 'Verdi e Manzoni: un'amicizia', *NA*, 2209:199–204; M. G. Bajoni, 'Un momento della biografia di Alessandro Manzoni: l'incontro con Giuseppe Verdi', *Aurea Parma*, 81, 1997:297–304; E. Travi, 'Alessandro Manzoni nella fantasia del giovane Giuseppe Giacosa', *Cenobio*, 47, 1998:36–39, transcribing from the Braidense MS Giacosa's 1872 letter to M. recounting his father's reminiscences of meeting M. at Azeglio castle as a boy; Giovanni Nardi, *Alessandro Manzoni e il dottor Azzeccagarbugli*, introd. Remo Ceserani, F, Le Lettere, 80 pp., concerning M.'s little-known activity as his own legal representative in asserting copyright in his own defence; Alessandra Dattero, *La famiglia Manzoni e la Valsassina. Politica, economia e società nello Stato di Milano durante l'antico regime*, Mi, Angeli, 1997, 223 pp. Also deserving of mention in this context is the elegant brochure *Immagini di casa Manzoni*, ed. Jone Riva, Mi, Centro Nazionale Studi Manzoniani, 1998, 126 pp., alternating colour photographs (interior views, portraits, title-pages, and other documents) with quotations (mainly from letters or memoirs) and also containing R.'s interesting annotations to the illustrations.

We are unable to specify the scope of Manzoni items contained in the following volumes, which have not been seen: M. Sansone, *Carte vecchie e nuove sul Manzoni*, ed. Michele Dell'Aquila, Fasano, Schena, 1998, 264 pp.; Angelo Stella, *Il piano di Lucia: Manzoni e altre voci lombarde*, F, Cesati, 323 pp., which gathers already publ. writings.

MONTI. A. Bruni 'Lettere montiane inedite', *StCrit*, 13, 1998:109–21, edits and annotates five letters (1796–1826) from

Monti to a brother, to an anonymous colleague, to T. Manza, V. Benzoni, and A. Calderara, and one to him from G. Cicognara. L. Tomasin, 'Carte montiane alla Biblioteca Querini Stampalia di Venezia', *SPCT*, 59:55–65.

NIEVO. M. Gallot, 'Cachotterie et indiscrétion dans *Le confessioni di un italiano*', *REI*, 45:109–14, explores 'les très nombreuses altérations dans les *Confessioni di un italiano* du code d'écriture de l'autobiographie'. With a similar attention to genre codes, P. Pellini, 'Il romanzo senza antagonista. Costanti strutturali della narrativa nieviana', *Italianistica*, 27, 1998:377–92, looks at the ideology underlying N.'s presentation of rural society in his works, but focuses mainly on divergences between the early *Angelo di bontà* and such antecedents as *Don Pasquale* (the comic libretto by Giovanni Ruffini) and *I promessi sposi*, seeing the resultant pattern as applicable also to later narratives, including the *Confessioni di un italiano*.

PANZINI. C. Marabini (ed.), ' "Scrivimi, Clotilde mia" '. Lettere inedite di Alfredo Panzini', *NA*, 2211:236–62.

PASCOLI. Renato Aymone, *\*Il Bruco e la Bella. Saggi pascoliani*, Cava de' Tirreni, Avagliano, 220 pp. Mario Pazzaglia, *Pascoli, la storia, la morte*, F, La Nuova Italia, vii + 168 pp. Rosamaria LaValva, *\*The Eternal Child: the Poetry and Poetics of Giovanni Pascoli*, Chapel Hill, Annali d'Italianistica, 226 pp. Vittorio Roda, *La folgore mansuefatta. Pascoli e la rivoluzione industriale*, Bo, CLUEB, 164 pp., brings together five articles — including Id., 'Un tema pascoliano: l'incontro fra cultura industriale e cultura pre-industriale', *SPCT*, 57, 1998:177–204 — which explore Pascoli's response to the technology of his time: electricity, the telegraph, the locomotive (central to his imagery and particularly charged with symbolic meanings). P. Gir, 'Il "ponte d'argento" (Dal mito alla lirica)', *Cenobio*, 47, 1998:131–36, reflects on symbolism with reference to P.'s 'silver bridge' in the madrigal 'Mare' (*Myricae*). G. Ponte, 'Giovanni Pascoli dal bozzettismo al sublime', *EL*, 24.2:3–16, traces P.'s growing symbolist tendency from *c.* 1890 onwards. M. Calella, 'Giovanni Pascoli e la poesia di Victor Hugo', *ib*, 73–90, finds reminiscences of (especially) 'un Hugo volto alle piccole cose e ad esseri umili, oltre che al nucleo famigliare'. D. Pisano, 'Il rapporto tra Giovanni Pascoli e Francesco d'Ovidio attraverso lettere inedite', *FC*, 23, 1998:411–17, brings to light three letters (one from P. to D'O., two the other way) documenting D'O.'s hardening opposition to P.'s Dante interpretations. P. M. Forni, 'L'aquilone, lo svagato e gli ireos gialli (tra Pascoli ed Erba)', *FC*, 23, 1998:459–72, taking much further a suggestion made by E. Gioanola, presents E.'s *Svagato* and *Gli ireos gialli* as 'riscrittura' of P.'s *Aquilone*. M. G. Bajoni, 'Pascoli e la musica. Una cartolina del Pascoli a Parmenio Bettoli', *RIL*, 131, 1998:165–72. E. Graziosi, 'Pascoli

edito e ignoto: sonetto per Sveno', *GSLI*, 175, 1998: 396–415, situates
'Già tempo un reo procurator romano' in the ideological context of
P.'s youth, where Christ figured as the first and greatest socialist.
E. Pappalardo, 'Semantica dei colori nei *Canti di Castelvecchio*', *RLI*,
102, 1998:500–20, explores colour references in the *Canti* with
regard to their frequency and connotations. M. Castoldi, 'Calypso e
la coscienza del nulla. Nota in margine a *Semantica pascoliana* di Laura
Bellucci', *SPCT*, 57, 1998: 159–75, is prompted by Bellucci's 'Chi è
Calypso? (Nota a *L'ultimo viaggio* di Giovanni Pascoli)' in her recent
volume (F, La Nuova Italia, 1996). Giovanni Pascoli, *La befana e altri
racconti*, ed. Giovanni Capecchi, Ro, Salerno, 125 pp., is the first
collected edition of P.'s known narrative output, consisting of six
stories published in local journals between 1882 and 1908, and
reflecting the poetic of the 'fanciullino' in their fantastic perception of
the ordinary.

PELOSINI. G. Tognoni, 'Spigolature pelosiniane III', *CLett*,
27:246–56, interprets the first part of Carducci's *Carnevale* (1863),
though dedicated to P., as documenting the break between the two
friends as their ideological convictions diverged (with P. moving back
towards Catholic, neo-Guelf positions): C. remained uncompre-
hending towards P.'s *Augusta* which expresses an attitude of abstention
and ataraxia.

PORTA. C. Carena 'Il vero "abaa Ovina" di Carlo Porta', *Annali
manzoniani*, 3:115–27, documents the exploits of the real priest on
whom the 'abate' (from *La guerra di pret*). D. Isella, 'Versi inediti di
Carlo Porta', *ib.*, 383–91, brings two poems to light: a sonnet
(1814–15) and a sixth poem for the servant Akmett which helps to
explain the other five.

RANIERI. F. Brancaleoni, 'La *Ginevra* di Antonio Ranieri ed il
*Twist* di Charles Dickens. Il romanzo sociale agli esordi', *CLett*,
27:163–88, conducts a lengthy parallel between Italy's first 'romanzo
sociale' *Ginevra o l'orfano della Nunziata* (partial ed. in instalments 1836,
complete ed. 1839) and *Oliver Twist* (1837–38). E. Benucci, 'Antonio
Ranieri all'amico Vincenzo Salvagnoli. Dal carteggio', *AMAT*, 62,
1997[1998]: 145–74, introduces and edits R.'s letters to S., almost all
dating from 1838–40 and relating to R.'s major historical work *Della
storia d'Italia . . . da Teodosio a Carlomagno*. G. Tessitore, 'Lettere inedite
di Maria Giuseppina Guacci Nobile', *CLett*, 26, 1998:89–138, edits
from the MSS 25 letters (1833–37) from the noted Neapolitan poetess
to Antonio Ranieri and one (1844) to Vincenzo Torelli.

RUFFINO. Martino Marazzi, *Il romanzo risorgimentale di Giovanni
Ruffini*, F, La Nuova Italia, viii + 205 pp., offers an illuminating
analysis of the *oeuvre* — seven English novels written in Paris — of the
noted Genoese exile and friend of Mazzini.

SALFI. *\*Salfi tra Napoli e Parigi: carteggio 1792–1832*, ed. Rocco Froio, Na, Macchiaroli, 1997, 503 pp., includes the essay: Fabiana Cacciapuoti, *Salfi: la Revue encyclopédique, Leopardi*.

SANTA ROSA. Santorre di Santa Rosa, *\*Ricordi, 1818–1824 (Torino, Svizzera, Parigi, Londra)*, ed. M. Montersino, F. Olshki, 1998, XX + 112 pp.

SERAO. P. Bianchi, 'La riscoperta di "Tuffolina": le prime prove narrative di Matilde Serao', *FC*, 23, 1998:444–58, for S.'s bibliography, records the first publication in the magazine *Novelliere* of stories republished with minor variants in *Dal vero* and other early texts. The variants of *Opale* are listed at length.

TOMMASEO. A. Paoletti Langè, 'Il primo soggiorno fiorentino di Niccolò Tommaseo (1827–1834)', *NA*, 2209:276–86. Niccolò Tommaseo, *Quaresimale*, ed. U. Carpi, Città Nuova, 1999, 112 pp.

VERGA. G. Longo, 'Vérisme et naturalisme: Verga et/ou', *ChrI*, 15.1:77–99, discusses the efforts (1880–1910) of Édouard Rod, C. Dejob, H. Muret, and others, to champion *verismo*, and Verga in particular, in France as an antidote to naturalism. *Verga e i verismi regionali*, ed. Gianni Oliva and V. Moretti, Ro, Studium, 410 pp., a rich compilation of material, contains more than might appear from the title. Thus, chapters on 'Naturalismo e verismo', 'Giovanni Verga', and 'Il realismo nelle regioni' are preceded by others outlining the political and cultural context and followed by a section of 'Documenti e testimonianze' and a region-by-region anthology of texts. G. P. Marchi, 'Giovanni Verga per le vie di Milano', *Quaderni di lingue e letterature* (University of Verona), 24, 1999:46–63, concludes that 'lo spazio poetico di Verga è uno spazio soprattutto mentale . . . si cimenta costantemente con studi di paesaggio, di ambientazione, è attento al dato sociale, è sensibile al colore locale; ma gli preme soprattutto l'interiorità morale dei personaggi, la loro parola-gesto'. V. Roda, 'La finestra della Capinera', *SPCT*, 58:103–34, takes a stimulating look at the function of the window in *Storia di una capinera*, 'amaro resoconto d'un vivere alla finestra, effettivo e metaforico al tempo stesso'. G. Longo, '*Cavalleria rusticana* au cinéma. Les séries d'art', *ChrI*, 15.1:101–09. F. De Cristofaro, 'Corporale di Gesualdo. Il bestiario selvaggio della malattia', *MLN*, 113, 1998:52–78, focuses on animals and animal imagery, particularly in the accounts of the deaths of Gesualdo and his father. Claiming to be tackling 'un tema mai esplorato sinora nella narrativa verghiana', but in fact anticipated by others (cf. *YWMLS*, 55:617, and 59:591), *Animali e metafore zoomorfe in Verga*, ed. Gianni Oliva, Ro, Bulzoni, 450 pp., gathers some dozen contributions arising out of seminars held at Chieti University and analysing V.'s use of animal imagery, with reference either to particular animals or to a particular work or works; the volume is rounded off (285–437) with a fascinating appendix 'Dizionario di etologia verghiana', ed. Mafalda Di Berardino, an alphabetical 270 *lemmi*, alphabetically arranged, and for each of them the list of occurrences (based on virtually the whole Verga corpus). The volume N. Vacante, 'Dal *Mastro don Gesualdo* alla *Duchessa di Leyra*. Sulla recente critica verghiana', *GSLI*, 176:261–85, attests to the growing sophistication of Verga criticism, which has produced its best recent results in the fields of textual philology and narratology. G. Verga, *Romanzi, ed. Marzio Pieri, T, UTET, 1998, 998 pp. Giovanni Verga, *Felis-mulier*, ed. Rita Verdirame, Palermo, Sellerio, 136 pp. Giorgio Cavallini, *Verga, Tozzi, Biamonti: tre trittici con una premessa comune*, Ro, Bulzoni.

## NOVECENTO

By ROBERTO BERTONI, *Senior Lecturer in Italian, Trinity College Dublin* and CATHERINE O'BRIEN, *Professor of Italian, National University of Ireland, Galway*

### 1. GENERAL

1999 has seen a number of publications on historical aspects of Italian literature in the 20th c. They are listed in this paragraph. A. Asor Rosa, 'Introduzione. Un altro Novecento', pp. vii-xiv of *Un altro Novecento*, F, La Nuova Italia, 410 pp., is the introduction to a collection of essays written between 1976 and 1993. A. R. argues, among other things, that contemporary 'literariness' comprises various language registers; and he sees Fortini, Pasolini, and Calvino as the interpreters of a contradictory literary world where what used to be considered classical has expired, while ontological uncertainty prevails. Piero Cudini, *Breve storia della letteratura italiana. Il Novecento*, Mi, Bompiani, 317 pp., focuses on literary values (especially on the combination of realism and experimentalism, and of visual and written languages) rather than on ideological debate; he stresses the importance of individual works, rather than the complete works of individual authors, and at the end of each chapter includes interesting passages called *corsivi* where literary phenomena, normally considered of minor importance (for instance, Pitigrilli and Liala), are highlighted. Giulio Ferroni, *Passioni del Novecento*, Ro, Donzelli, 248 pp., contains essays on a number of authors, including Pier Paolo Pasolini, Italo Calvino, Elsa Morante, Andrea Zanzotto, and Vincenzo Consolo. *Raccontare il Novecento. Histoire littéraire et littérature italienne du XX^e siècle. Actes de la Journée d'études de Caen (23–4–1998)*, ed. Paolo Grossi and Silvia Fabrizio-Costa (in association with the Italian Cultural Institute, Paris), Caen, LEIA, Presses Universitaires, 156 pp. Eugenia Ocello, *Spigolature letterarie. Il Novecento da Pirandello a Tomasi di Lampedusa, da Moravia a Rosso di San Secondo, da Eco a Lauretta*, F, L'Autore Libri, 128 pp. R. Scrivano, 'Svolgimenti di letteratura triestina', *RLettI*, 16:163–79, outlines some themes and authors in literature written by writers from Trieste in the 20th c. G. Turi, 'Le Accademie nell'Italia fascista', *Belfagor*, 54:403–24, argues that the foundation of the Accademia d'Italia constituted the turning point in the growing Fascist character of Italian cultural life.

Literary theory is represented by the following essays. Some are on the rhetoric of fiction. G. L. Beccaria, 'Variabili tensioni novecentesche', *LItal*, 51:70–84, explores some aspects of the concept of 'tension' (especially between low and high styles) in Italian 20th-c. prose and poetry, and devotes the last few pages to G. Caproni.

Andrea Berardinelli, *La narrazione*, Ro–Bari, Laterza, 136 pp., runs through some of the main definitions and procedures of fiction, examines some examples (such as *I promessi sposi*), and makes reference to semioticians and theorists of narratology (especially R. Barthes, G. Genette, and M. Bakhtin). Claudia Sebastiana Nobili, *Il lavoro della scrittura. Analisi e retorica del testo*, F, Sansoni, 293 pp., is a manual on various aspects of literary texts, including textual typologies, language registers and functions of the author's voice, and the reader's responses. Carla Benedetti, *L'ombra lunga dell'autore. Indagine su una figura cancellata*, Mi, Feltrinelli, 236 pp., defines Barthes's extinction of the author as a 'myth' created in late modernity and, though maintaining that the figure of the author is problematic in the 20th c., she defends its function as an important aspect of literary communication and of a historical interpretation of literature. Linda Pennings, *I generi letterari nella critica letteraria del primo Novecento*, F, Cesati, 406 pp.

Some essays are concerned with interpretation and value judgements in relation to literary criticism. G. Guglielmi, 'Lo spazio letterario', *il Verri*, 9:48–57, argues in favour of a critical approach to texts based upon constant variability of interpretation throughout history. Romano Luperini, *Il dialogo e il conflitto. Per un'ermeneutica materialistica*, Ro–Bari, Laterza, 186 pp., argues in favour of a historical and anthropological interpretation of literary texts, championing allegory as opposed to the symbol and analysing a number of works by authors such as Pirandello and Montale. Pier Vincenzo Mengaldo, *Giudizi di valore*, T, Einaudi, 215 pp., gathers miscellaneous essays written by M. over the years.

Some essays explore topics related to postmodernism and late modernity. F. Pellizzi, 'L'ipertesto critico: potenzialità e limiti', *Intersezioni*, 19:125–32, attempts a definition of the 'hypertext' through an analysis based on pragmatic linguistics. G. Petronio, 'Postmoderno?', *Problemi*, 112, 1998:210–22, examines some of the difficulties of defining the concept of postmodernism and explores its ambiguity in relation to the notions of modernism and modernity. Giuseppe O. Longo, *Il nuovo Golem*, Ro–Bari, Laterza, 1998. See also Muzzioli in the following paragraph.

A number of essays are about writers and politics. Vittorio Giacopini, *Scrittori contro la politica*, T, Bollati Boringhieri, 179 pp., discusses the work of a number of Italian and foreign writers who, though politically and socially engaged, are opposed to literature's exploitation by politicians. Included among these writers are Carlo Levi and Gerardo Chiaromonte. The last chapter ('Dopo la politica: il contrario dell'utopia', 161–79) sees renunciation of Utopian ideals as the premise to a realistic type of engagement in a democratic

society. F. Muzzioli, 'Una proposta di "avanguardia materialistica"',
*Karenina.IT* (Internet http://www.geocities.com/Paris/Lights/
7323/muzzioliɪ.html), detects a neo-traditionalist and a postmodern
trend in contemporary literary debate — the former is an escapist
journey into traditional literary values, while the latter adapts
modernism to the needs of the globalized market. According to M.,
both trends evade the issue of social and political commitment which
truly avant-garde literature ought to practice through a "demistifica-
zione materialistica' and a reformulation of its textual strategies in
the contemporary world. M. Paladini Musitelli, 'Osservazioni gram-
sciane di "politica culturale delle masse"', *Problemi*, 112, 1998:
123-33, shows how Gramsci paid attention to the artistic value of
literary works, to the political function of art, to the relationship
between writers and their readers, and to the need for transcendence
of national barriers as a 'vera e propria necessità della cultura
moderna'. Also on literature in Gramsci's thought: Bartolo Anglani,
*\*Egemonia e poesia. Gramsci: l'arte, la letteratura*, Lecce, Manni, 204 pp.
On intellectuals: Ugo Dotti, *\*Storia degli intellettuali in Italia*, ɪɪɪ: *Temi e
ideologia dagli illuministi a Gramsci*, Ro, Editori Riuniti, 330 pp.

On national identity: R. Luperini, 'Letteratura e identità nazionale:
la parabola novecentesca', *L'immaginazione*, 161:1-3, argues that,
even though modern Italian writers have exhibited a less pronounced
interest in national identity than their predecessors, such an interest
can still be found in politically and socially committed writers such as
Pasolini, Volponi, and Consolo; he also points out that those
contemporary writers who see national boundaries as 'annebbiati
all'interno del network universale' are nonetheless both global and
local; yet international globalized realities prevail, and perhaps the
end of an Italian national literature *strictu sensu* could be seen as taking
place in the 1970s.

Giorgio Bertone, *Lo sguardo escluso. L'idea di paesaggio nella letteratura
occidentale*, Novara, Interlinea, 272 pp., is a phenomenological reading
(based on M. Merleau-Ponty's theory and practice of perception) of
landscape in literature. It includes an introduction ('Introduzione in
dieci quadri') on the relationship between the reality and imagery of
landscape (11-83), and a chapter ('La Liguria e il paesaggio') on
E. Montale and Calvino (235-58).

On the relationship between science and literature: *\*La realtà e i
linguaggi. Ai confini tra scienza e letteratura*, ed. Mimma Bresciani Califano,
F, Le Lettere, 333 pp.

On comedy: Concetta D'Angelo and Guido Paduano, *Il comico*, Bo,
Il Mulino, 296 pp., sees comedy as subversion of social norms and
exorcism against death, and gives examples from a variety of authors.

On the literature of exile: A. Ciccarelli, 'La letteratura dell'emigrazione oggi in Italia: definizioni e correnti', *Intersezioni*, 19:105–24, builds on G. P. Biasin's, J.-J. Marchand's and A. Gnisci's definitions of the literature of emigration and exile in order to examine literary work written by Italians who live abroad, bicultural authors, and immigrants to Italy who have chosen to write in Italian.

Various topics of a general nature are as follows: \*Mappe dell'immaginario. Per una storia culturale del contemporaneo, ed. Mario Gervasani, Mi, Unicopli, 220 pp. 'La messinscena di scritto e figurato', *Autografo*, 38:9–73, contains essays by M. Corti, E. Tadini, A. Modena, P. Mazzucchelli, E. Vicini, and C. Carotenuto on the relation of drawing and painting to writing. Pino Fasano, *Letteratura e viaggio*, Ro–Bari, Laterza, 84 pp., is about travel literature but also about literature interpreted in terms of the metaphor of travel, and sees Italo Calvino's *Il cavaliere inesistente* as a quest for truth. Claudio Magris, *Utopia e disincanto*, Mi, Garzanti, 326 pp., is a selection of M.'s essays. Renato Nisticò, *La biblioteca*, Ro–Bari, Laterza, 100 pp., looks into the functions and contents of libraries and works quoted by authors in a number of texts, including Umberto Eco's *Il nome della rosa*. Giorgio Rimondi, *La scrittura sincopata. Jazz e letteratura nel Novecento italiano*, Mi, B. Mondadori, 264 pp., examines the influence of jazz on 20th-c. literature in general and, in particular, on the Futurists and other subsequent writers such as Massimo Bontempelli, Cesare Pavese, and Elio Vittorini. Giorgio Zanetti, *Il Novecento come visione*, Ro, Carocci, 255 pp., examines the relationship between music, the visual arts, and literature in a number of authors (amongst them Dino Campana and Gabriele D'Annunzio).

On comparative literature: *Introduzione alla letteratura comparata*, ed. Armando Gnisci, Mi, B. Mondadori, 362 pp., includes F. Sinopoli, 'La storia comparata della letteratura' (1–50), and 'Gli strumenti di lavoro del comparatista' (341–48); A. Trocchi, 'Temi e miti letterari' (51–90); E. Pantini, 'La letteratura e le altre arti' (91–114); D. Nucera, 'I viaggi e la letteratura' (115–59); M. Guglielmi, 'La traduzione letteraria' (160–210); N. Noll, 'Immagini dell'altro. Imagologia e studi interculturali' (211–49); F. Neri, 'Multiculturalismo, studi postcoloniali e decolonizzazione' (250–95); and E. Gajeri, 'Studi femminili e di genere' (296–340).

On the theory and practice of translation: *Autografo*, 36, 1997:7–110, is devoted to 'Il complesso e ambiguo mondo delle traduzioni' and includes essays on various aspects of translating. Specifically on the Italian field are: M. A. Terzoli, 'Le insidie della fedeltà. A proposito di una poesia di Montale tradotta' (9–26), and S. Corsi, '*Istruzioni*: Tonino Guerra traduttore di Ezra Pound' (71–85), where the translating is from English into Romagnol.

The following texts concern the history of criticism: D. De Martino, 'Manara Valgimigli–Luigi Russo: lettere e cartoline dal 1919', *Belfagor*, 54:453–88, reproduces a number of letters and postcards, and comments briefly upon the exchange. Luigi De Vendittis, *\*Luigi Russo e la sua metodologia critica*, Alessandria, Orso, 242 pp. The following essays focus on periodicals. 'Cinquant'anni di *Lettere italiane*', *LItal*, 51:3–17, includes short items by V. Branca (4–7) and E. Raimondi (7–9), and an essay by G. L. Beccaria (10–17), on the journal *Lettere italiane* from the 1950s to the 1970s. P. Ponti, '*Trifalco*, voce giovanile della pubblicistica milanese degli anni Venti', *RLettI*, 16, 1998:129–61, analyses the role played by *Trifalco* (a journal directed by Giovan Battista Angioletti) in promoting young writers, and examines its affinity with Futurism. F. Curi, 'Una "sapienza quotidiana"', *Poetiche*, n.s. 1:3–9, proposes a new series of *Poetiche* — following in the footsteps of Gobetti, Gramsci, and Anceschi — that will have the 'serietà di propositi e di comportamenti' and the 'novità e vivacità di iniziative meditate e durevoli' often missing in Italian contemporary journals, and be against the 'cannibali' in favour of a canon comprising writers such as Montale, Sereni, Caproni, Bertolucci, and Zanzotto. Piersandro Pallavicini, *Riviste anni '90. L'altro spazio della nuova narrativa*, Ravenna, Fernandel, 160 pp., examines journals such as *Versodove*, *Tratti*, *Fernandel*, and *La Bestia*, and highlights their role in publishing texts originating from Italian models (especially Tondelli) and foreign sources.

On publishing: *La mediazione editoriale*, ed. Alberto Cadioli, Enrico Decleva, and Vittorio Spinazzola, Mi, Il Saggiatore, 140 pp., contains several essays on publishing in Italy, among them G. Turi, 'L'intellettuale tra politica e mercato editoriale: il caso italiano' (63–80), and A. Cadioli, 'Pubblico e lettore nella storia dell'editoria italiana' (91–110). Luisa Mangoni, *Pensare i libri. La casa editrice Einaudi dagli anni trenta agli anni sessanta*, T, Bollati Boringhieri, 976 pp., reconstructs the cultural politics of the publishing firm Einaudi from archive material and through discussion of the role played by Vittorini, Pavese, and others. Dario Moretti, *Il lavoro editoriale*, Ro–Bari, Laterza, 98 pp., is about various aspects of editing. Giovanni Ragone, *\*Un secolo di libri. Storia dell'editoria in Italia dall'Unità al post-moderno*, T, Einaudi, 277 pp.

## 2. POETRY

Arnaldo Di Benedetto, *\*Poesia e critica del Novecento: studi e frammenti critici*, Na, Liguori, vi + 269 pp. Alberto Asor Rosa, 'Sulle antologie poetiche del Novecento', *Critica del testo*, 2, 1999:323–39, shows how the main anthologies published from 1903 to 1996 provide a reliable guide to developments in the literary field. *The Promised Land: Italian Poetry after 1975*, ed. Luigi Ballerini, Giuseppe Cavatorta, Elena Coda, and Paul Vangelisti, Los Angeles, Sun and Moon, 570 pp., offers a critical outline of poetry written between 1975 and 1995. S. Barsella, 'Bicicletta: il mito e la poesia', *Italica*, 76:70–97, examines how the bicycle is used in poetry to represent the epic or the social, as a symbol of the rejection of urban civilization or a vehicle that brings man closer to nature. It shows how these topics are used by Campana, Cucchi, Sereni, Penna, Erba, Gozzano, Saba, Montale, Caproni, Stecchetti, and Tessa. G. L. Beccaria, 'Variabili tensioni novecentesche', *LItal*, 51:70–84, outlines the tension created by words and language in 20th-c. prose and poetry. Walter Binni, *Poetica e poesia: letture novecentesche*, ed. Giulio Ferroni, F, Sansoni, 360 pp., brings together Binni's articles on 20th-c. Italian literature. *Come leggere la poesia italiana del Novecento. Saba, Ungaretti, Montale, Sereni, Caproni, Zanzotto*, ed. Stefano Carrai and Francesco Zambon, Vicenza, Neri Pozza, 1997, 137 pp., offers a lively analysis of a selected poem by each of these poets. *Le notti chiare erano tutte un'alba*, ed. Andrea Cortellessa, Mi, B. Mondadori, 1998, 514 pp., is a valuable anthology that outlines poetry written during or after the Second World War. It delineates the new perception of space and time brought about by the war and how this is voiced in the work of different poets. Fausto Curi, *La poesia italiana del Novecento*, Ro–Bari, Laterza, 1999, x + 445 pp., presents 21 essays on different aspects of 20th- c. poetry and poets. A useful number of articles also appeared on Futurism and the impact it had on the literature of its time. These include: M. Manotta, 'La scrittura futurista', *il Verri*, 10–11:115–29, who discusses the idea of the liberation of language. He makes a case for the need to give a vertical and linear meaning to language, looking at two forms of expression in the language of poetry and their graphic transposition, and also discussing the influence of Mallarmé on Futurist writing. K. L. Knauth, 'Il poliglottismo futurista', *Italienisch*, 41, 1999:16–34, shows how Futurism was the matrix for future 'poliglottismo' in Italy and Europe. Matteo D'Ambrosio, *\*Futurismo e altre avanguardie*, Na, Liguori, 205 pp., gathers seven essays, one published here for the first time. Giuseppe Farinella, *Vent'anni o poco più. Storia e poesia del movimento crepuscolare*, Mi, Ediz. Otto/Novecento, 1998, 645 pp. Marco Forti, *Tempi della poesia. Il secondo Novecento da Montale a Porta*, Mi, Mondadori, 368 pp. N. Lorenzini, 'Le nuove modalità della forma chiusa', *il Verri*, xxxx:124–34, analyses how different poets use new types of closed form in their work. By the same scholar, *La poesia italiana del Novecento*, Bo, Il Mulino, 206 pp., defines the major developments in 20th-c. poetry. Giorgio Luti, *La letteratura italiana del Novecento*, Ro, Editori Riuniti, 1998, 120 pp., sees the First World War as the great 20th-c.

watershed and discusses the changes apparent in the role of prose, poetry, and literary criticism in the post-war years. \**Nel caldo del mondo. Lettere sull'Italia. Dialoghi con Geno Pampaloni, Sandro Veronesi, Andrea Zanzotto*, ed. Alfonso Berardinelli, F, Liberal, 100 pp. S. Carrai, 'Leopardismi novecenteschi', *AnVi*, 13:53–60, briefly surveys Leopardi's influence on Montale, Cardarelli, Saba, and Solmi, and argues that in Italian literature in the 20th c., rather than imitation of Leopardi, we find a 'latente funzione Leopardi' consisting of an influence of some aspects of Leopardi's poetics on the ideologies and styles of subsequent authors. *La scrittura infinita: Bibbia e poesia in età romantica e contemporanea*, ed. Francesco Stella, F, Olschki, 216 pp., contains one article analysing the link between the Bible and the language of contemporary Italian poetry, and also 1997 interviews on this topic with Piero Bigongiari, Maura Del Serra, and Mario Luzi. *I poeti italiani della Voce*, ed. Paolo Febbraro, Mi, Marcos y Marcos, 1998, 345 pp., gives historical information on *La Voce*, while poets and their poetry are presented following the order of their appearance in that journal. *Nostos: poeti degli anni Novanta a Firenze*, ed. Franco Marescalchi, F, Polistampa, 1997, 283 pp., examines the Florentine dimension of poets in and about Florence from 1985 to 1997. Guglielmina Otter, *Ritratti della poesia. I visi comunicanti*, Faenza, Circolo degli Artisti, 1998, 336 pp., offers a huge overview of contemporary Italian poets, together with poetic and prose texts that discuss the objectives of contemporary Italian poetry and the place it occupies in Italy today. Chemello, *Parole scolpite* presents profiles of various women writing in Italy in the 1990s, including the poets Jolanda Insana and Lea Canducci. Grazia Maria Poddighe, *Oscura come l'ombra: la parola poetica nel '900*, Ro, Bulzoni, 99 pp., outlines the ability of various writers to empower poetic language. *Antologia della poesia italiana*, ed. Cesare Segre and Carlo Ossola, 3 vols, T, Einaudi, 1942 pp., provides a useful assessment of and full commentary on poetry from Monti to Sanguineti. Enrico Testa, *Per interposta persona. Lingua e poesia nel secondo Novecento*, Ro, Bulzoni, 161 pp. is a helpful lexical, syntactical, and textual analysis of a number of works by Sereni, Caproni, and Giudici. S. Verdino, 'Annali di poesia italiana 1994–98', *NC*, 123:161–213, details the most important collections of poetry published in those years. Giorgio Zanetti, *Il Novecento come visione: dal simbolismo a Campana*, Ro, Carocci, 1999, 256 pp., highlights the magical and ecstatic dimension of 20th-c. literature and examines the work of poetry where words, music, and pictorial images meet. \**Quando eravamo strutturalisti*, ed. Gian Luigi Beccaria, Alessandria, Orso, 134 pp. Paola Bianco, \**Tra ermetismo e realismo: la poesia siciliana da Quasimodo a Cattafi ad Aliberti*, Foggia, Bastogi, 117 pp. \**La poesia in dialetto: storia e testi dalle origini al Novecento*, ed. Franco Brevini, 3 vols,

Mi, Mondadori, c + 4509 pp., purports to be the first systematic analysis of dialect poetry from all regions of Italy, viewed as a whole from its 15th-c. origins to the present. Notable too are those publications that relate to the language of poetry. These include: Stefano Giovannuzzi, *\*Tempo di raccontare: tramonto del canone lirico e ricerca narrativa 1939–1956*, Alessandria, Orso, 214 pp. R. Luperini, 'Il canone, la scuola e l'insegnamento', *Allegoria*, 32:61–70, discusses the link between the canon and its presentation and interpretation in 20th-c. poetry. Romano Luperini, *\*Controtempo. Critica e letteratura fra moderno e postmoderno: proposte, polemiche e bilanci di fine secolo*, Na, Liguori, viii + 220 pp. *LS*, 34.2, has a number of articles that relate to metaphor. They include: C. Bazzanella, 'La metafora tra mente e discorso: alcuni cenni' (150–58), which considers metaphor as a cognitive process, delineates its functions, and provides a basis that allows for understanding or misinterpreting metaphor and its linguistic forms; C. Cacciani, 'La metafora: un ponte fra il linguaggio e l'esperienza percettiva' (159–66); F. Casadei, 'Alcuni pregi e limiti della teoria cognitivista della metafora' (167–80); C. Casadio, 'Aspetti logici e cognitivi della metafora' (181–90); N. R. Norrick, 'Paradox and metaphor: a discourse approach' (191–200); M. Prandi, 'La metafora come costruzione linguistica: le forme interne del conflitto concettuale' (201–10). A most useful addition to handbooks on metre is Giorgio Bertone, *Breve dizionario di metrica italiana*, T, Einaudi, 1999, 264 pp.

### 3. NARRATIVE, THEATRE

Vincenzo Arnone, *La figura del prete nella narrativa italiana del Novecento*, Cinisello Balsamo, San Paolo, 220 pp., is a selection of passages on priests from novels written both by priests and by lay authors (such as L. Sciascia and G. Parise) — each entry has a brief critical introduction.

Some essays examine the historical novel: Margherita Ganeri, *\*Il romanzo storico in Italia. Il dibattito critico dalle origini al postmoderno*, Lecce, Manni, 162 pp. M. Baker, 'Some thoughts on historical narrative in twentieth century Italian literature', *SpR*, 14:97–103, reviews the theories of A. Banti, G. Tomasi di Lampedusa, V. Spinazzola, and others, and concludes that 'the contemporary historical novel shows the adaptability of the genre to new conditions, and the readiness of writers to draw lessons from the past'. See also BANTI, below.

The following essays are about Italian narrative in the 1990s. Mario Barenghi, *Oltre il Novecento. Appunti su un decennio di narrativa (1988–1998)*, Mi, Marcos y Marcos, 320 pp., contains a number of short essays and reviews on various authors including Antonio

Tabucchi (121–23), Rosetta Loy (195–99), Paolo Maurensig (200–05) and Susanna Tamaro (210–15). *Stesso sangue. DNA di una generazione*, ed. Luca Beatrice, Ro, Minimum Fax, 187 pp., contains a number of interviews with Italian contemporary novelists such as N. Ammanniti, S. Ballestra, G. Caliceti, and T. Scarpa. Luminita Beiu-Paladi, *Generi del romanzo italiano contemporaneo* (AUSRS, 18), Stockholm, Almqwist & Wicksell International, 203 pp., discusses genre theory in the context of postmodernist changes due to which traditional literary genres have changed (14–53), and analyses a number of novels from the 1980s and 1990s under the following headings: the historical novel (47–77), the biographical novel (78–98), the autobiographical novel (99–128), the fantastic novel (129–62), and 'il romanzo dei professori: un genere editoriale erudito' (193–71). Filippo La Porta, *La nuova narrativa italiana. Travestimenti e stili di fine secolo*, T, Bollati Boringhieri, 256 pp., is a reprint of the 1995 edition with the addition of three new chapters. Filippo La Porta, *Manuale di scrittura creatina: per un antidoping della letteratura*, Ro, Minimum Fax, 76 pp. Fulvio Panzeri, *Senza rete. Conversazioni sulla nuova narrativa italiana*, Ancona, Pequod, 290 pp., contains a number of interviews with writers such as E. Palandri (35–54), C. Piersanti (55–77), and E. Fileno Carabba (189–94).

On theatre: Luciano Bottoni, *Storia del teatro italiano 1900–1945*, Bologna, Il Mulino, 212 pp., examines theatre criticism, in particular that of S. D'Amico and A. Gramsci, and outlines the history of texts and productions, with particular focus on G. D'Annunzio, R. Di San Secondo, M. Bontempelli, Futurist theatre, L. Pirandello, and the social and textual aspects of plays and companies in the Facist Italy of the 1930s and 1940s. Gunter Berghaus, *Italian Futurist Theatre, 1909–1944*, OUP, 1998, 604 pp., conducts a thorough analysis of the theory and practice of Futurist theatre, examines known and previously unpublished material, pays attention not only to theatre but also to the visual arts, poetry, and the Manifestoes, and concludes that Italian Futurism, from its beginnings to 1944, was 'discordant, contradictory, battling against the forces of tradition, but also compromised by its involvement with Fascist institutions and politics'. Paolo Puppa, *Parola di scena. Teatro italiano tra '800 e '900*, Ro, Bulzoni, 331 pp. Pippo Di Marca, *Tra memoria e presente. Breve storia del teatro di ricerca in Italia nel racconto dei protagonisti. Teatrografia (1959–1997)*, Ro, Artemide, 182 pp. Luca Ronconi, *Utopia senza Paradiso. Sogni disarmati al Laboratorio di Prato*, Venice, Marsilio, 132 pp. Luca Ronconi, *La ricerca di un metodo. L'opera di un maestro raccontata da lui stesso al VI Premio Europa per il Teatro a Taormina Arte*, Mi, Ubulibri, 189 pp.

4. INDIVIDUAL AUTHORS

ALVARO.    *Corrado Alvaro, *Il viaggio: Memoria a vita; poesie grigioverdi (1914–1916); Il viaggio (1941), con appendice di liriche e prose poetiche disperse*, ed. Anne Christine Faitrop Porta, Reggio Calabria, Falzea, 1999, 315 pp. Giovanni Carteri, *Il Dio nascosto. Viaggio nel cristianesimo di Corrado Alvaro*, Soveria Mannelli, Rubbettino, 132 pp., examines the letters exchanged by A. and the noted Catholic priest Don Giuseppe De Luca in the 1930s and 1940s, and shows how they are related to A.'s creative work.

ARBASINO.    *La scrittura infinita di Alberto Arbasino. Studio su 'Fratelli d'Italia'*, ed. Clelia Martignoni, Novara, Interlinea, 122 pp.

BANTI.    P. Carù, ' "Uno sguardo acuto dalla storia": Anna Banti's Historical Writings', pp. 87–101 of *Gendering Italian Fiction. Feminist Revisions of Italian History*, ed. Maria Ornella Marotti and Gabriella Brooke, Cranbury, NJ, Fairleigh Dickinson U. P., 253 pp., illustrates B.'s interest in Manzoni's early concept of the verisimilar as 'that which is invented but historically verifiable', and sees her protagonists' strategies of self-assertion against the 'invisibility of history' and the importance of 'female bonding' in her work as aspects of a 'gendered perspective' which anticipates modern feminist theory.

BARICCO.    I. Lanslots, 'Alessandro Baricco's infinite tales', *SpR*, 14:47–57, detects two fields of infinity (or pluralism and multiplicity) in B.'s fiction: the multiplicity of character and the sense of infinity in the space and time dimensions of the narrative. She links this to the relationship between cosmos and chaos, and concludes that, thanks to these aspects, B.'s narrative is 'quite extraordinary'. A. Longoni, 'Alessandro Baricco: *City*', *Autografo*, 39:165–69, examines narrative voices, 'romanzo labirinto', 'equivocità dei rudi e delle storie', and style in B.'s novel. F. Senardi, 'Alessandro Baricco, ovvero ... che storia mi racconti?', *Problemi*, 112, 1998:261–96, is about Baricco in general and especially his postmodern sense of perplexity *vis-à-vis* the false assumptions of his fictional characters.

BASSANI.    Guia Risani, *The Document within the Walls: The Romance of Bassani*, Market Harborough, Troubadour, 47 pp.

BENNI.    *Leggere, scrivere, disobbedire*, ed. Goffredo Fofi, Ro, Minimum Fax, 110 pp., is an interview granted to Fofi, in which B.'s political and literary ideas are expressed and tested.

BERTO.    Darop Biagi, *Vita scandalosa di Giuseppe Berto*, T, Bollati Boringhieri, 278 pp.

BERTOLUCCI.    F. Magro, 'La metrica del primo Bertolucci', *StN*, 26:109–56, outlines metrical characteristics and change in Bertolucci's early work. Carmelo Vero Saura, *La poesia di Attilio Bertolucci de 'Sirio' (1929) a 'La cabaña india' (1955)*, Seville U.P., 1997, 228 pp., offers a semantic analysis of B.'s early work from 1929 to the 1950s together with a thematic and linguistic analysis of *La capanna indiana*. E. Siciliano, 'Rossa alba baudelairiana per Attilio Bertolucci', *AnVi*, 13:131–38, examines B.'s translations from Baudelaire in relation to his own collection *Sirio* published in 1929.

BETOCCHI. E. Grandesso, 'Silenzio e verità nelle *Poesie del sabato* di Betocchi', *Atelier*, 15.4:29–31, looks at the way Betocchi deals with the themes of old age and death in these poems. G. Landolfi, 'Carlo Betocchi: tra realismo e classicismo', *ib.*, 5–18. S. Ramat, ' "Qualcosa che sa di leggenda". La madre (e il figlio) nella poesia di Betocchi', *ib.*, 19–28, analyses Betocchi's declared debt of gratitude to his mother in a number of selected poems.

BIAMONTI. Giorgio Cavallini, *Verga, Tozzi, Biamonti. Tre trittici con una premessa comune*, Ro, Bulzoni, 193 pp.

BIGONGIARI. T. O'Neill, 'Piero Bigongiari, 7 ottobre 1997', *Italica*, 76:175–92, written after B.'s death in 1997, outlines the way in which personal memories and encounters cast a particular light on selected poems. M. C. Papini, 'La poesia pensa: riflessione teorica e prassi poetica nell'ultimo Bigongiari', *RLI*, 103:449–53, shows how Bigongiari's writings and lyrics create and inform his philosophy as opposed to philosophy determining how he wrote. Piero Bigongiari, *L'azzurro e altri racconti*, ed. Paolo Fabrizio Iacuzzi, Pistoia, Via del Vento, 29 pp., adds to the 1991 first edition of the hitherto unpublished story 'Pistoia e la musica'. Piero Bigongiari, *E non vi è alcuna dimora (1990)*, ed. Paolo Fabrizio Iacuzzi, Porto Sant'Elpidio, L'Albatro, 76 pp., brings to light hitherto unpublished poems.

BILENCHI. Ferdinando Bianchini, *Bilenchi: analisi e cronistoria*, Mi, Laboratorio delle Arti, 454 pp., is a revised and enlarged edition of a work published in 1992. *Romano Bilenchi*, Fucecchio, Erba d'Arno, 97 pp., is a monographic issue (no. 78) of the quarterly *Erba d'Arno* published on the tenth anniversary of the writer's death and containing letters and other writings, in part published for the first time, as well as *interventi* by Mario Luzi and Gino Pampaloni. *I miei amici pittori: Romano Bilenchi e l'arte contemporanea*, ed. Marcello Ciccuto and Luca Lenzini, Fiesole, Cadmo, 118 pp., is the catalogue of an exhibition held in the Museo di San Pietro at Colle di Val d'Elsa.

BONAVIRI. Franco Musarra, *Scrittura della memoria. Memoria della scrittura. L'opera narrativa di Giuseppe Bonaviri*, F, Cesati, 130 pp., examines a number of B.'s works, and in particular explores the relationship between autobiography and storytelling, seriousness and irony, in his fiction.

BORGESE. G. Grifoni, 'Borgese antifascista: ancora nuovi inediti', *Intersezioni*, 19:283–301, examines published and unpublished material, and in particular *Goliah*, in an examination of B.'s complex situation in his self-imposed exile to the U.S.A. L. Parisi, 'La critica militante di Giuseppe Antonio Borgese', *ISt*, 54:102–17.

BUZZATI. A. Brambilla, 'Appunti sulle *Cronache terrestri* di Dino Buzzati', *Cenobio*, 47, 1998:1–11, points to shortcomings in D. Porzio's 1972 anthology republished (Mi, Mondadori, 1995) on the occasion of *Buzzati giornalista*, an international conference held at Feltre and Belluno.

CALVINO. Contributions of a biographical or general character include: Paola Castellucci, \**Un modo di stare al mondo: Italo Calvino e l'America*, Bari, Adriatica, 239 pp. \**Calvino da Sanremo a New York: dal fondo dell'opaco io scrivo / Calvino from Sanremo to New York: from the Depths of the Opaque I Write*, ed. Laura Guglielmi, Genoa, De Ferrari — Bordighera, Istituto Internazionale di Studi Liguri, 131 pp.; Manuela Dini, *Calvino critico. I percorsi letterari, gli scritti critici, le scelte di poetica*, Ancona, Transeuropa, 155 pp., reviewing C.'s work as an essayist. Enrica Ferrara, \**Calvino e il mare dell'altro*, Na, Magma, 236 pp.; Domenico Scarpa, *Italo Calvino*, Mi, B. Mondadori, 294 pp., examining a number of key concepts in alphabetical sequence (these include some innovative entries on 'implosione', 'identità', 'microstoria', and 'paesaggio'.)

Several contributions focus on individual works. Stefano Anselmi, *Il barone rampante: riassunto guidato, personaggi, critica*, Mi, Mursia, 87 pp. L. Cazzato, 'Italo Calvino: la via cosmicomica alla letteratura', *Allegoria*, 31:136–50, sees *Le cosmicomiche* as postmodernist by virtue of its combined low and high literary dimensions, and examines it in relation to science fiction but also within the framework of C.'s poetics. B. Ferraro, 'Dallo scudo di Agilulfo al tappeto di Eudossia: geometrie narrative in alcune opere di Italo Calvino', pp. 133–49 of *Italo Calvino: a Writer for the Next Millennium*, ed. Giorgio Bertone, Alessandria, Orso, 1998, 358 pp., highlights C.'s familiarity with the notion of *mise en abyme*, through reading Gide's correspondence, in the description of Agilulfo's shield in *Il cavaliere inesistente*, and detects reference to Escher's graphic design in *Lezioni americane*. L. Knapp, 'Ist Calvinos *Se una notte d'inverno un viaggiatore* ein postmodernes Werk?', *ItStudien*, 20:224–39. B. Ferraro, 'Figure e forme di conoscenza in alcuni testi di Italo Calvino', *CLett*, 26, 1998:313–22, through the imagery of crystal and fire in a number of his texts, illustrates C.'s concern with order, culminating in his preoccupation with communication in the *Lezioni americane*.

On intertextuality: R. Bertoni, 'Aspetti del dialogo di Calvino con Leopardi', pp. 69–100 of *L'ultimo orizzonte . . . Giacomo Leopardi: a Cosmic Poet and His Testament*, ed. Roberto Bertoni, T, Trauben and Dublin, Trinity College Italian Department, 103 pp., examines C.'s approach as a critic and a creative writer to Leopardi's *Operette morali*,

*Zibaldone*, and the *Canti*. L. Perlini, 'Strategie della vertigine: Calvino, Levi e i "black holes" ', *Il Ponte*, 55.4 : 119–33, analyses C.'s and Levi's ways of using the concept and image of 'black holes'. Silvio Perrella, *Calvino*, Ro–Bari, Laterza, 240 pp., an overview of C.'s work, combines biographical aspects and literary appreciation.

CAMILLERI.  M. Polacco, 'Andrea Camilleri: la re-invenzione del romanzo giallo', *ib.*, 55.3 : 138–50, shows how Montalbano, one of C.'s characters, is similar to Carvalho, the protagonist of a number of novels by the writer V. Montalban: it examines in particular Montalbano's 'istinto di fuga' from reality, and his 'riduzione (o semplificazione) del principio di realtà'. B. Porcelli, 'Due capitoli per Andrea Camilleri', *Italianistica*, 28: 207–20, examines intertextuality in C., and his slow yet fluent rhythm especially in stories like *Il corso delle cose* and *Il birraio di Preston*.

CAMPANA.  P. L. Ladron de Guevara Mellado, 'I *Canti orfici* del 1928', *RLI*, 102 : 537–45, recalling Campana's criticism of textual errors in the 1928 edn of his poems, indicates a further 65 variants from C.'s own 1914 edn in Falqui's (1973) despite the significant advances in printing technology of the intervening period. Christophe Mileschi, *Dino Campana, le mystique du chaos*, Lausanne–Paris, L'Age de l'Homme, 1998, 332 pp., is the first complete work on Campana in French by this Campana specialist. D. Campana, *Chants Orphiques / Canti Orfici*, Lausanne–Paris, L'Age de l'Homme, 1998, 183 pp., provides an introduction to and translation of Campana's *Canti Orfici* by Christophe Mileschi. Giuseppe Savoca, *\*Concordanza dei Canti orfici di Dino Campana: testo, concordanza, lista di frequenza, indici*, pref. Mario Petrucciani, F, Olschki, xx + 297 pp. P. Palmieri, 'Madonna Laldomine da Giosuè Carducci a Dino Campana', *StRmgn*, 47, 1996[1999] : 661–68. Carlo D'Alessio, *\*Il poema necessario. Poesia e orfismo in Dino Campana e Arturo Onofri*, Ro, Bulzoni, 244 pp.

CANDUCCI.  L. Canducci, 'Poesia e psiche', Chemello, *Parole scolpite*, 41–62.

CAPRIOLO.  G. Ania, 'At Capriolo's hotel: Heaven, Hell, and otherworlds in *Il doppio regno*', *ISt*, 54 : 132–56, sees C.'s narrative in a broad European context, deals with philosophical and metaphysical issues, and explores the blurred boundaries between reality and fantasy.

CAPRONI.  M. Billi, '*Anniversario 1, IX*. Per un'interpretazione dei sonetti caproniani', *Poetiche*, 2 : 299–315, compares parallel sound patterns in Leopardi's 'A Silvia' with selected Caproni sonnets. *Per Giorgio Caproni*, ed. Giorgio Devoto and Stefano Verdino, Genoa, Ediz. San Marco dei Giustiniani, 1997, 500 pp., has three sections that outline the context in which Caproni wrote, the texts themselves and memories associated with Caproni. G. Leonelli, *Giorgio Caproni*,

Mi, Garzanti, 1997, 153 pp., looks at Caproni's poetry, his use of language, and his work in prose. M. Modesti, 'La stagione di Sereni, Caproni, Luzi', *CV*, 54:607–16, identifies a stylistic and formal similarity in the work of these poets. A. Montani, 'Caproni, le bugie, Pascal', *The Italianist*, 18, 1998[1999]:155–69. G. Caproni, *Quaderni di traduzioni*, ed. Enrico Testa, T, Einaudi, 1998, 323 pp., is an anthology of C.'s translations (Apollinaire, Char, Frénaud, García Lorca, and Baudelaire) which Einaudi failed to bring out in the early 1980s. Roberto Orlando, *La via contraria. Sul Novecento di Giorgio Caproni*, Lecce, Pensa Multi-media, 1998, 235 pp., outlines C.'s religious outlook and then looks at the way C. incorporates unfamiliar and uncomfortable aspects of the *Novecento* into his poetry.

CARDARELLI. Charles F. Burdett, *\*Vincenzo Cardarelli and his Contemporaries. Fascist Politics and Literary Culture*, OUP, 236 pp. S. Jansen, 'Coesione e coerenza in una poesia di Cardarelli. Analisi letteraria e linguistica testuale', *Revue Romane*, 34:87–116, applies textual analysis to the poem 'Alla morte'.

CARIFI. M. Merlin, 'Il pathos del sublime. La poesia di Carifi', *Atelier*, 15.4:37–45, defines stylistic and thematic parameters in Carifi's poetry.

COMISSO. Giovanni Comisso, *Solstizio metafisico*, ed. Annalisa Colusso, pref. Ricciarda Ricorda, Padua, Il Poligrafo, 149 pp., is a posthumous first edition of these poems.

CONSOLO. R. Glynn, 'Metaphor and philosophy of history: motifs of representation in Consolo's *Sorriso dell'ignoto marinaio*', *ISt*, 54:118–31, is about C.'s 'philosophy of history' and 'anti-illusionist' poetics.

D'ARZO. R. Carnero, 'Il moderno disagio della diversità. Per *Essi pensano ad altro* di Silvio D'Arzo', *Il Ponte*, 55.7:148–71, re-appraises D.'s work in a modern critical context with reference to writers such as W. Benjamin, M. Blanchot, and A. Guglielmi.

DE CÉSPEDES. E. Gagliardi, 'Il rimorso di Alba de Céspedes: ipotesi sul romanzo epistolare del Novecento', *LetP*, 105:3–24, shows how De C. employs the epistolary novel as a specifically 20th-c. source of metafictional reflection.

DEL GIUDICE. M. Colummi Camerino, 'Daniele Del Giudice: narrazione del luogo, percezione dello spazio', *StCrit*, 14:61–81, examines spatial (and especially geographical) dimensions in Del G.'s fiction. R. Cepach, 'L'origine delle comete. Appunti sulla poetica dello stupore nell'opera di Daniele Del Giudice', *ItStudien*, 20:240–49.

DE LIBERO. G. Salvadori, 'Libero de Libero, memoria e scrittura', *CLett*, 27:283–321, considers the sentiments presented by this poet and examines poetic memory mechanisms in his work.

D'ERAMO. *Io sono un'aliena*, Ro, Lavoro, 120 pp., is a text generated by a number of conversations with Paola Gaglianone who reconstructs D'Eramo's intellectual and biographical itinerary.

DE SIGNORIBUS. P. Zublena, 'Lo sguardo duro e amoroso del "senzacasa"'. Su *Istini e chiuse* di Eugenio De Signoribus, *NC*, 123:117–60.

DESSÌ Giuseppe Dessì, *\*Diari*, II, *1931–1948*, ed. Franca Linari, Ro, Jouvence, xxxvi + 240 pp.

ECO. Michael Caesar, *Umberto Eco: Philosophy, Semiotics and the Work of Fiction*, Oxford, Polity, 198 pp., reconstructs E.'s theory from presemiotic to semiotic views and beyond, and to his recent philosophy of language. Ch. 6 and 7 (120–61) illustrate E.'s narrative theory in relation to his creative work and argue that the novels are in some respects independent of the essays.

FABBRI. E. De La Boetie, 'L'urgenza della scrittura: le "fragili chiusure" di Valerio Fabbri', *LetP*, 106:73–4, assesses the way Fabbri uses poetic language to express depth and urgency.

FALSETTI. G. Fozzer, 'Poesia neovolgare e religiosità in Giovanni Falsetti', *CV*, 54, 363–82, details the influence of Franco Scataglini's work on Falsetti's approach to poetry.

FENOGLIO. Luca Bufano, *Beppe Fenoglio e il racconto breve*, Ravenna, Longo, 184 pp., follows the itinerary of F.'s life, the story of his publications, and has a ch. (71–84) on the intertextual relation of F. to Maupassant. L. Bufano, 'L'esordio mancato di Fenoglio: I *Racconti della guerra civile* cinquant'anni dopo', *Il Ponte*, 55.3:121–37.

FO. J. Farrell, 'Dario Fo: Where's the Literature?', *Italia & Italy*, 1.1:16–29, advocates Fo's literariness, compares him with Ruzante and Molière, shows how F.'s writing and performance are interwoven, and defends his political theatre. Elena De Pasquale, *\*Il segreto del giullare: la dimensione testuale nel teatro di Dario Fo*, Na, Liguori, 93 pp.

FORTINI. Luca Lenzini, *\*Il poeta di nome Fortini: saggi e proposte di lettura*, Lecce, Manni, 231 pp.

GADDA. M. G. Bajoni, 'L'impronta di Fedro nell'opera di Carlo Emilio Gadda', *Testo*, 37:87–104, is about G.'s *Il primo libro delle favole* in relation to Phaedrus and Juvenal. D. Fairservice, '"Il peso di un paragone": Gadda and Joyce', *SpR*, 14:91–96, shows how Gadda was indebted to his reading of the French translation of some of Joyce's work. S. Giusti, 'Gadda verso Céline', *Levia Gravia*, 1:121–34. Rodica Diaconescu-Blumenfeld, *\*Born Illiterate: Gender and Representation in Gadda's Pasticciaccio*, Market Harborough, Troubadour, 87 pp.

GINZBURG. Giancarlo Borri, *\*Natalia Ginzburg*, Rimini, Luisè, 155 pp. Natalia Ginzburg, *\*È difficile parlare di sè. Conversazione a più voci condotta da Marino Sinibaldi*, ed. Cesare Garboli and Lisa Ginzburg, T, Einaudi, viii + 251 pp., is the text of conversations with various literary critics recorded in May 1990 during the four parts of a 'Radio Tre Antologia' programme.

GIOTTI. A. Benevento, 'Virgilio Giotti. L'edizione critica di *Colori*', *CLett*, 26, 1998:709–29, discusses the importance of the work of Rossana Esposito, Anna Modena, and Franco Brevini on Giotti, and suggests that G.'s originality stems from his use of the Triestine dialect and his presentation of a world imbued with memories of Trieste together with the memory of years spent in Tuscany.

GIOVENE DI GIRASOLE. V. Bonito, 'Andrea Giovene di Girasole: un problematico e inquieto letterato da riscoprire', *CLett*, 27:147–62, evaluates the prose and poetry of this Neapolitan writer.

GIUDICI. L. Surdich, 'Giovanni Giudici, la semplicità, il tempo', *NC*, 123:67–110, examines the idea of simplicity (taken from the poem 'Con tutta semplicità') together with the concept of time in G.'s work.

GOZZANO. L. Bossina, 'Circe, Cocotte e gli amori ancillari', *Levia Gravia*, 1:53–102.

GUIDACCI. D. Camiciotti, 'Margherita Guidacci: una vita di fedeltà all'amore', *CV*, 54:591–606, suggests that Guidacci's friendship with the American soldier Francisco Canepa provides a key to understanding much of her love poetry and wonders why this topic has not been pursued to date by Guidacci critics. *Margherita Guidacci: la parola e le immagini*, ed. Margherita Ghilardi, F, Polistampa, 77 pp., is the catalogue of an exhibition documenting her work as poet and translator. Margherita Guidacci, *Le Poesie*, ed. Maura Del Serra, F, Le Lettere, 1999, 567 pp., offers a valuable introduction to G.'s work and also publishes her collected work for the first time.

INSANA. J. Insana, 'Parole che trascinano senso', Chemello, *Parole scolpite*, 63–71, looks at Insana's dextrous manipulation of language in her poetry.

LAMARQUE. G. Petrucci, 'Il sonno di Alice: l'enunciazione del trasfert nella poesia di Vivian Lamarque', *Italianistica*, 27:89–98, evaluates the effectiveness of transfer therapy in L.'s poetry.

LEVI, C. *\*Il germoglio sotto la scorza. Carlo Levi cent'anni dopo*, ed. Franco Vitello, Cava de' Tirreni, Avagliano, 1998, 319 pp.

LEVI, P. P. D. Gambetta, 'Gli ultimi momenti di Primo Levi', *Belfagor*, 54:325–39, reflects upon the social, historical, and personal reasons behind L.'s death to maintain that it is more likely to have been due to an accident rather than suicide. Guglielmina Morelli, *Se questo è un uomo. Riassunto guidato, personaggi, critica*, Mi, Mursia, 56 pp.

LUCINI. S. U. Baldassarri, 'L'"anarcheggiare stoicamente" di Gian Pietro Lucini', *Italianistica*, 28:73–85, analyses L.'s interpretation of the concept of anarchy both politically and aesthetically. It also shows how his politics characterized his criticism of Italian

Futurism and outlines the way he viewed political consciousness as an essential element in the work of every writer.

LUZI. Marco Marchi, *Invito alla lettura di Mario Luzi*, Mi, Mursia, 1998, 158 pp., provides a useful analysis of Luzi's work and is a valuable addition to the Mursia series of 20th-c. poets and writers. Mario Luzi, *L'opera poetica*, ed. Stefano Verdino, Mi, Mondadori, 1998, liv + 1908 pp., an omnibus of Luzi's poetry, also contains a useful introductory essay to his poetry by Stefano Verdino. C. Viviani, 'La fine che si fa inizio', *Atelier*, 15.4:35–37, examines Luzi's method of presenting the continuity of life and the theme of resurrection in his poetry. *Fede e poesia: omaggio a Mario Luzi*, ed. Vitaliano Tiberia, Todi, Ediart, 1999, 78 pp., examines the link between Christian faith and belief in L.'s poetry. S. Givone, 'Per Luzi', *NC*, 124:279–82, details L's quest for truth in *Per il battesimo dei nostri frammenti* and *Viaggio terrestre e celeste di Simone Martini*. M. Cacciari, 'Insostenibile incarnazione', *ib.*, 273–77, looks at the emphasis placed on Luzi's use of language in his recent poetry. Interviews with Luzi were the subject of the following books: Mario Luzi, *Conversazione. Interviste 1953–1998*, ed. A. Murdocca, F, Cadmo, 289 pp., which covers topics that Luzi considered essential in those years. Mario Luzi, *Colloquio. Un dialogo con Mario Specchio*, Mi, Garzanti, 308 pp., outlines the thoughts, ideals, people and events that have had a lasting impact on Luzi the person and poet. A. Fongaro, 'Valeurs maternelles dans la poésie de Mario Luzi', *REI*, 43:87–96, makes reference to the importance given to the female figure in L.'s poetry. M. Modesti, 'La creaturalità in Mario Luzi', *CV*, 54:453–62, outlines various identities assigned to women in certain Luzi poems.

MAGRELLI. F. Sepe, 'A colloquio con Valerio Magrelli', *Italienisch*, 41:7–15, is an interview where Magrelli explains the genesis and meaning of *Ora serrata retinae* together with the importance given to Latin and medical science in this work.

MALERBA. F. Portinari, 'Scrittura di ricerca . . . e intrigo', *L'immaginazione*, 161:28–29, examines M.'s novel *La superficie di Eliane* (1999) as an intricate detective story as well as a political and experimental novel.

MARINETTI. *Le Commemorazioni in avanti di F. T. Marinetti: futurismo e critica letteraria*, ed. Matteo D'Ambrosio, Na, Liguori, viii + 184 pp. A. Frattini, 'F. T. Marinetti: l'industria e le macchine nella sua invenzione poetica', *LItal*, 51:434–48, outlines M.'s fascination with the development of science and technology and its application to poetic forms. M. Gragnolati, 'Marinetti e la lingua francese alle soglie del Futurismo: l'eclettismo ambiguo de *La ville charnelle*', *REI*, 45:115–32, looks at Marinetti's 1908 composition and evaluates the importance of French language and culture on this work.

MICHELSTAEDTER. Angela Michelis, *Carlo Michelstaedter. Il coraggio dell'impossibile*, Ro, Città Nuova, 1997, 240 pp., studies the middle-European cultural influences on and the Jewish dimension of M.'s writings. A. Perli, 'La metafora eroica. Sulla mitologia poetica di Michelstaedter', *CLett*, 27:77–108, stresses the importance for M. of the mountain as a symbol of freedom in *La leggenda di San Valentin*, the wind as symbol of heroic resistance in *Bora* and the sun as symbol of the vertical dimension of life in 'Amico — mi circonda il vasto mare'. Id., 'Eros e inerzia: la poetica dell'inquietudine in Michelstaedter', *Italianistica*, 28:235–45, is a lexical and thematic analysis of poems written by M. in 1907 highlighting the erotic inertia that creates the theme of restlessness in M.'s poetry. Id., 'Le "mal du siècle"': Michelstaedter et la *decadence*', *EL*, 24.1:79–97, relates M.'s denunciation of intellectual 'maladie' and 'Arcadia' to the polemic conducted by *La Voce* against D'Annunzio, links M.'s concept of persuasion to Leopardi, and examines various aspects of M.'s analysis of decadence in the context of contemporary cultural history.

MONTALE. Franco Contorbia, *Montale, Genova, il modernismo e altri saggi montaliani*, Bo, Pendragon, 175 pp., includes a ch. 8 of particular interest as dealing with M.'s formation, friendships, and literary career from the early 1920s to the post-war period. *Fondazione Mario Novaro: Il secolo di Montale. Genova 1896–1996*, Bo, Il Mulino, 714 pp. Giuseppe Mercenaro, *Eugenio Montale*, Mi, B. Mondadori, 213 pp., combines a biographical résumé, a bibliography, and a dictionary of terms, titles, and words associated with Montale. Giampaolo Borghello, *Il getto tremulo dei violini. Percorsi montaliani*, T, Paravia, 129 pp., suggests various ways of interpreting M.'s poetry and prose, looks at the diversity of critical opinion, and also considers the reception of M.'s work in Hungary. Laura Barile, *Montale, Londra e la luna*, F, Le Lettere, 1998, 199 pp., assesses the impact of London and English poetry on the young Montale and provides a critical assessment of the *Ossi*. Two other chapters deal with the *Bufera* while the final section looks at the impact of Leopardi on M.'s poetry. Ernesto Citra, *Trittico montaliano: In limine, Il balcone, Il tu*, Ro, Bulzoni, 91 pp. *Le muse di Montale*, ed. Giusi Baldissone, Novara, Interlinea, 1996, 100 pp., identifies the women muses — his mother and wife, Clizia, Maria Luisa Spaziani, Carla Fracci, and Annalisa Cima — in M.'s poetry. Eugenio Montale, *Mottetti*, ed. Dante Isella, Mi, Adelphi, 1998, 131 pp., provides a structured critical reading of the 21 'mottetti' dedicated to Clizia. It also gives a lexical, critical, thematic, and biographical guide to these poems. M. Gaetani, 'Opacità e motivazione nel mottetto XVIII di Montale', *LetP*, 105:47–61, links the 18th 'mottetto' thematically with the others and shows how its theme of time places everything in a negative perspective. L. Lomiento, 'I

*Fliaci* di Eugenio Montale: una metafora "cercidea"', *RLI*, 102:575–78, notes how Montale presents the ancient metaphor for farce (used by the poet Cercida di Megalopoli) as the satirical force in this poem. M. Villoresi, *Come leggere 'Ossi di seppia' di Eugenio Montale*, Mi, Mursia, 1997, 182 pp. Eugenio Montale, *Poesia travestita*, ed. Maria Corti and Maria Antonietta Terzoli, Novara, Interlinea, 1999, 66 pp., brings together the 'Nuove stanze' of *Le occasioni* and translations of the poem into Arabic and nine other languages. F. De Rosa, 'Profilo di *Satura*', *ChrI*, :111–28. G. Mazzoni, 'Il *Diario postumo* di Montale e la critica letteraria', *Allegoria*, 31:107–11. 'Su Eugenio Montale', *REI*, 44, 1998:163–298, includes essays by a number of authors. 'Montale postumo', *AnVi*, 13:85–112, includes essays by V. Scheiwiller, A. Cima, R. Bettarini, G. Savoca, P. Dyerval Angelini, and A. Parronchi on *Diario postumo*. Maria Cristina Santini, *\*Farfalla di Dinard e la memoria montaliana*, La Spezia, Agorà, 152 pp. F. Borio, 'Clizia e la Volpe: un capitolo della biografia poetica montaliana', *ON*, 23:179–99, suggests that while both figures were quite separate in M.'s mind one often recalls the other in certain poems. Angelo Fabrizi, *Montale e Proust*, F, Polistampa, 117 pp. Maria Antonietta Grignani, *Dislocazioni. Epifanie e metamorfosi in Montale*, Lecce, Marini, 1998, 144 pp. G. Lonardi, 'Montale, il fantasma dell'opera', *LItal*, 50:186–219, outlines the complicity of M. the musician and music critic with M. the poet and shows the important role it occupies at various levels in M.'s poetry. *Montale a teatro*, ed. R. T. Castria, Ro, Bulzoni, 189 pp., identifies the draw of the theatre and opera for Montale all his life. L. M. Marchetti, "Prima le parole, dopo la musica": Montale ed Euterpe', *LItal*, 51:649–56, analyses M.'s fondness for music, particularly opera. Claudio Scarpati, *Sulla cultura di Montale. Tre conversazioni*, Mi, VP, 1997, 104 pp., outlines in ch. 1 M.'s relationship with the philosopher Giuseppe Rensi (7–32), in ch. 2 has a complex series of references involving Montale, Eliot, Praz, Dante's *Vita Nuova*, and Contini's introduction to Dante's *Rime* (33–56), while ch. 3 discusses the relationship between Montale and Contini from 1945 to 1949 when both chronicled international meetings in Geneva (57–84). G. Genco, 'Il leopardismo di Montale', *Testo*, 37:105–33. A. Rondini, ' "Quando vado al cinematografo non comprendo quasi nulla di quanto avviene sullo schermo": Eugenio Montale sociologo della letteratura', *EL*, 24.1:59–78, a sociological reading of *Auto da fé*, highlights M.'s anticipation of current debate on literature in a mass society. M. Corti, 'Riflessioni su Montale ticinese', *Cenobio*, 47, 1998:263–66.

MORANTE. Marco Bardini, *Morante Elsa. Italiana. Di professione poeta*, Pisa, Nistri-Lischi, 778 pp., a full-scale study of M.'s work, focuses especially on *L'isola di Arturo* and *Menzogna e sortilegio*, examining M. from an existentialist angle and insisting on her sense of life rather than on autobiography. R. Donnarumma, '*Menzogna e sortilegio* oltre il bovarismo', *Allegoria*, 31 : 121–35, defines bovarism in *Menzogna e sortilegio* as a belief in illusory ideals, and sees M.'s novel as tending towards symbolism and therefore removed from the canon of Flaubert's realism. U. Pirotti, 'Intorno a *Menzogna e sortilegio*', *SPTC*, 57 : 205–23.

MORAVIA.    Silvana Palmieri, *Il mare dell'opacità. Una lettura di Moravia*, Ro, Oleandro, 138 pp.

MORETTI.    *Nelle più care dispute. Vito Moretti e i suoi trent'anni con la poesia*, ed. Toni Iermano, Ro, Bulzoni, 1998, 242 pp., brings together several critical essays that provide an updated outline of the work of this poet from the Abruzzi.

MORSELLI.    F. Pierangeli, ' "Nell'imminenza di un prodigio". Per un inedito di Guido Morselli', *RLettI*, 16: 383–97, examines some of the concepts in *Fede e critica*, especially the relationship between subjectivity, religion, and negativity.

MUCCI.    S. Luciani, 'Un romanzo dimenticato: *L'uomo di Torino* di Velso Mucci', *Il Ponte*, 55.9 : 162–70, reappraises M.'s novel with attention to its Joycian nature and its significance as an anti-Fascist story set in 1925.

NIGRO.    Marco Gaetani, *Il guardiano della luna. Commento alla narrativa di Raffaele Nigro*, Lecce, Milella, 500 pp.

NOVE.    V. Spinazzola, 'Gli integrati di Aldo Nove', *L'Indice*, 16.1 : 14, shows how N.'s young characters in *Woobinda* (1998) e *Plata market* (1997) are integrated in the value system propagated by the mass media; contrasts N.'s vision of superficial youth deviance with Pasolini's portrayal of authentic marginal youth; and sees N.'s language as derived both by slang and colloquial registers and by Testori's and Tessa's expressive literary language.

ONOFRI.    P. Pepe, 'L' "io" e l' "altro". Frammenti di un colloquio nella poesia lirica italiana fra Ottocento e Novecento', *CLett*, 27 : 109–23, explores the dynamics of the relationship between self and others in the poetry of Arturo Onofri, also showing how it parallels or contrasts with a similar mechanism employed in Ungaretti's poetry.

ORENGO.    F. Portinari, 'Il reale storico-lirico', *L'immaginazione*, 161 : 27–28, is about O.'s novel *L'ospite celeste* (1999), seen as an innovative piece of prose where traditional narrative structures are questioned and fantasy is combined with reference to real-life figures such as Kepler, Tycho Brahe, and J. L. Borges.

ORTESE.    G. Traina, 'Anna Maria Ortese. La denuncia sussurrata, tutte le metamorfosi', *Il Ponte*, 55.1 : 123–35, is a brief reappraisal of O.'s work following her decease.

OTTOLIA. Stefano Termanini, \**La roccia e l'uragano di Giovanni Ottolia: analisi di un romanzo contemporaneo*, introd. Roberto Trovato, Alessandria, Orso, 1999, 94 pp.

PALAZZESCHI. Lina Passione, *Il nulla e il suo doppio*, pref. Valentino Brosio, Catania, CUECM, 1998, 75 pp., deals with Palazzeschi's first novel :*riflessi*: (1908).

PAPINI. Carmine Di Biase, \**Giovanni Papini*. *L'anima intera*, Na, ESI, 520 pp.

PARISE. D. Scarpa, 'Goffredo Parise tra Darwin e Montale', *Belfagor*, 54:453–88, examines Montale's and Darwin's influence on P., but specifies that, even though P. did not read Darwin until the 1960s, his early work exhibits some interest in topics dealt with by Darwin, such as the relationship between life and death, the organic nature of reality, and disorder.

PARRONCHI. *Per Alessandro Parronchi*, ed. Isabella Bigazzi and Giovanni Falaschi, Ro, Bulzoni, 1998, 258 pp., is a collection of articles on P. presented at a 1998 conference in Florence. It includes: L. Baldacci, 'Parronchi poeta' (15–31); S. Ramat, 'Parronchi e *I giorni sensibili*' (33–48); L. Lenzini, 'Prosa e poesia in Alessandro Parronchi' (49–60); M. Fanfani, 'Sul linguaggio poetico di Parronchi' (61–101); O. Macrì, 'La vita rivissuta tra fede e forma (su *Replay*)' (181–88); V. Melani, 'Parronchi lettore e critico di Leopardi' (189–228); A. Mackie, 'La prospettiva nello spazio e nel tempo. La poesia e l'arte. Imitazione della *Tempesta* di Alessandro Parronchi' (229–44); S. Zamboni, 'Per un'immagine di Parronchi' (245–50).

PASOLINI. Marco Antonio Bazzocchi, *Pier Paolo Pasolini*, Mi, B. Mondadori, 1998, 253 pp., provides an updated bibliography on Pasolini, outlines his life and supplies a glossary of words associated with his poetry. Giordano Meacci, \**Improvviso il Novecento: Pasolini professore*, Ro, Minimum Fax, 408 pp. Andrea Miconi, *Pier Paolo Pasolini. La poesia, il corpo, il linguaggio*, Genoa, Costa e Nolan, 1998, 169 pp., reviews P.'s life and work and tries to find an answer for P.'s rejection of the canon of literary expression and language in favour of a personal one. Ilario Quirino, *Pasolini sulla strada di Tarso*, Lungro, Marco, 194 pp., sees P.'s death as the culmination of a literary and symbolic project discernible in his work. He also points to a strong parallel between the writer from Casarso and the Christian Paul from Tarsus. Giuseppe Zigaina, *Pasolini. 'Un'idea di stile: uno stilo'*, Venice, Marsilio, 138 pp., discusses the sense of death in P.'s work in relation to his own life. First rejected by P.'s family, the hypothesis of suicide now has greater credence and Zigaina furnishes added evidence to support the claim that P.'s violent death was 'in tutti i sensi un'opera d'autore'. Lino Miccichè, \**Pasolini nella città del cinema*, Venice, Marsilio, 217 pp. *Pasolini Old and New*, ed. Zygmunt G. Barański,

Dublin, Fourt Courts Press (published for The Foundation of Italian Studies, University College Dublin), 420 pp., runs counter to the mythicizing of Pasolini which has taken place after his death. The essays included in this volume are: R. Gordon, 'Pasolini's strategies of self-construction' (41–76), which highlights aspects of subjectivity that influenced P.'s creative expression; A. G. Meekins, 'Pier Paolo Pasolini: *Narcís tal Friúl*' (229–51), showing how autobiographical reference to the myth of Narcissus in P.'s early poetry was subsequently integrated with his political commitment; M. Caesar, 'Outside the palace: Pasolini's journalism (1973–1975)' (363–90), detecting P.'s 'physical immersion on the reality of things' beneath the political topics of P.'s newspaper articles; D. Ward, 'Pier Paolo Pasolini and the events of May 1968: the "Manifesto per un nuovo teatro"' (321–44) examining P.'s ideology combined with cultural analysis, and concluding that the 'Manifesto' offers 'genuinely disruptive modes of protest'; Z. Barański, 'The texts of *Il Vangelo secondo Matteo*' (281–320), highlighting P.'s politicization of the Gospel; J. Francese, 'The latent presence of Crocean aesthetics in Pasolini's "Critical Marxism"' (131–62), sees Croce's influence in some of P.'s concerns, such as the 'primacy of the writer-artist' and 'separation of theory from praxis'; T. De Mauro, 'Pasolini's linguistics' (77–90), arguing that P. owes to Gramsci his awareness of the fact that language is 'woven into the fabric of social relations and conflicts'; J. P. Welle, '*Pasolini traduttore*: translation, tradition and rewriting' (91–129), showing how P.'s activity as a translator of literary texts influenced his creative output; Z. Barański, 'Pasolini, Friuli, Rome (1950–1951): philological and historical notes' (253–80), observing that P. integrated *prosa d'arte* with realism; S. Rohdie, 'Neorealism and Pasolini: the desire for reality' (163–83), which asserts that P.'s film-making was removed from naturalism but shared themes and ideology with the neorealists; C. Wagstaff, 'Reality into poetry: Pasolini's film theory' (185–227), analysing his attempt to embrace two divergent visions of the world, realism and semiotics; P. Rumble, 'Contamination and excess: *I racconti di Canterbury* as a "struttura da farsi"' (345–61), examines P.'s film based on Chaucer's *Canterbury Tales*. M. A. Bazzocchi, 'Buona e mala mimesi (Pasolini, Dante e la poetica del romanzo)', *Poetiche*, n.s. 1:50–65, examines Dante's influence on the formation of P.'s poetics of realism, experimentalism, and cinema, particularly P.'s dissension from Contini's multilinguistic interpretation of D., and P.'s own use of D.'s *Commedia* in *Divina Mimesis*. S. De Matteis, 'Il Sud di Pasolini', *Lo Straniero*, 9:199–207, examines P.'s ethnological and linguistic attraction to the South of Italy. P. Bellocchio, *'Introduzione', pp. i-cxxii of Pier Paolo Pasolini, *Saggi sulla politica e sulla società*, ed. Walter Siti and Silvia De Laude, Mi, Mondadori, 1900 pp. C. Segre, *'Introduzione', pp. I-CXVIII of Pier Paolo Pasolini, *Saggi sulla letteratura e sull'arte*, ed. Walter Siti and Silvia De Laude, Mi, Mondadori, 3150 pp. Giuseppe Zigaina and Christa Steinle, *Organizzar nel trasumanar*, Venice, Marsilio, 228 pp.

PASTONCHI. *Pastonchi: ricordo di un poeta ligure, con antologia. Atti del Convegno di Riva Ligure e Sanremo, 5–6 dicembre 1997*, ed. Giorgio Bertone, Novara Interlinea, 142 pp.

PAVESE. C. Bonnetin, '*Paesi tuoi* et *Le facteur* de Cain', *Levia Gravia*, 1:103–19. E. Solera, ' "Un tema, per me ..." I componimenti scolastici di Cesare Pavese', *ib.*, 239–58. S. Savioli, "L'ALI di Pavese', *ib.*, 259–88.

PAVOLINI. Massimiliano Soldani, *L'ultimo poeta armato: Alessandro Pavolini, segretario del Partito fascista repubblicano*, Cusano Milanino, Barbarossa, 359 pp.

PENNA. L. Ferrara, 'Sandro Penna. Lo stile, l'illusione', *Atelier*, 16.4:16–20, examines Penna's use of illusion in his poetry. G. Landolfi, 'Sandro Penna: il mondo ad una dimensione', *ib.*, 7–15, suggests a psychological explanation for Penna's originality as a poet. S. Montalto, 'Sandro Penna. Nota bibliografica', *ib.*, 4–7, outlines areas of interest for literary critics in P.'s work. E. Pecora, 'Sandro Penna', *Belfagor*, 54:425–38, provides a personal interpretation of the poet and person as deduced from his papers and writings.

PIAZZOLLA. Antonella Calzolari, *Piazzolla. Mistero della parola*, Ro, Fermenti, 110 pp., provides a timely analysis of the work of Marino Piazzolla, poet, critic, painter, and French scholar whose generous financial bequest funds the Fondazione Piazzolla publications of non-Italian poetry in Italian translation.

PIERRO. Franco Trifuoggi, *Lettura della lirica tursitana di Albino Pierro*, Na, L'Istituto Italiano di Napoli, 1997, 336 pp., offers the most complete study to date of Pierro's work.

PIOTTI. G. Farinella, 'Pier Luigi Piotti poeta solitario', *ON*, 23:109–20, defines the feeling of isolation in Piotti's poetry.

PIOVENE. Guido Piovene, *Inferno e paradiso: racconti (1929–1931)*, ed. Monica Giachino, Treviso, Canova, xxviii + 207 pp., gathers P.'s short stories in volume for the first time. Sandro Gerbi, *Tempi di malafede. Una storia italiana tra fascismo e dopoguerra. Guido Piovene ed Eugenio Colorni*, T, Einaudi, 302 pp. A. Tommasi, '*Le stelle fredde* di Piovene in prospettiva psicanalitica', *ItStudien*, 20:200–23.

PIRANDELLO. Alfredo Barbina, *L'ombra e lo specchio. Pirandello e l'arte del tradurre*, Ro, Bulzoni, 290 pp. *Luigi Pirandello: Contemporary Perspectives*, ed. Gian Paolo Biasin and Manuela Gieri, Toronto U.P., 232 pp. W. Moretti, ' "Pena di vivere così" di Luigi Pirandello fra angoscia e prosa ritmata', *EL*, 24.1:3–18, by analysing the narrative sequences in P.'s story, detects some poetically rhythmic patterns in his style and highlights the *pathos* of Signora Leuca's existential experience. P. Pellini, ' "Effetti d'un sogno interrotto". Interpretazione di un racconto di Pirandello', *Il Ponte*, 55.4:134–42, examines the dream-like nature of P.'s short story and relates it to Gautier's, James's and Savinio's fiction, and more in general to the fantastic genre at the turn of the century. A. Perli, 'La vita e la forma: Michelstaedter e Pirandello', *LetP*, 105:25–37, compares M.'s *rettorica* and P.'s *umorismo*. E. Providenti, 'Pirandello impolitico nell' "era fascista" ', *Belfagor*, 54:15–45, sees P.'s consent to Fascism as motivated by essentially non- political reasons, by his expectations of social regeneration and by the fact that he did not foresee the rise of a dictatorial regime. W. Sahlfeld, 'La cultura tedesca e Pirandello negli anni '20', *ItStudien*, 20:185–99. C. Terribile, '*Questa sera si recita a soggetto* o il teatro sovvertito dalla narrazione', *Italianistica*, 28:193–205, detects narrative structures in P.'s plays and theatrical aspects in his fiction, and concludes that in his work we find 'forme estetiche mobili, ove teatro e narrazione si contaminano reciprocamente'.

PIZZUTO.    A. Pane, 'Pizzuto ai Parioli. Verifica di *Bilancio*', *Cenobio*, 48:24–40, links the intriguing piece with a Parioli cocktail party for creative writers attended by P. in February 1968.

POMILIO.    F. Parmeggiani, 'Pomilio scrittore del dissesto', *Italianistica*, 28:289–309, builds on P.'s self-definition as 'scrittore del dissesto' and concludes that he is an experimental and autobiographical writer bending towards a 'complesso esercizio delle orme ermeneutiche sul reale'.

PORTA.    V. Accame, 'Antonio Porta, *Poesie visive*', *Avanguardia*, 12:5–29, provides an analysis of Porta's collaboration with Achille Perilli and his momentary dalliance with visual poetry in the 1960s. C. Bello, 'Antonio Porta, l'ostinazione del conflitto originario', *ib.*, 30–49, highlights Porta's propensity towards a 'voluttà mortuaria' in his work. Antonio Porta, *Poesie 1956–1988*, Mi, Mondadori, 1998, viii + 200 pp., contains a useful introduction to P.'s work by Maurizio Cucchi.

PRATOLINI.    Francesco Paolo Memmo, *Vasco Pratolini. Bibliografia 1931–1997*, F, Giunti, 1998, 352 pp., includes works by and on the writer. D. Tomasello, 'Nota sulle redazioni di *Lo scialo* di Vasco Pratolini', *StN*, 25:273–89. M. Paoli, '*Cronaca familiare* di Vasco Pratolini, tra vita e politica', *Italianistica*, 28:267–88, conducts not only a biographical study of P., but also a thematic analysis of *Cronaca*.

QUASIMODO.    C. Del Popolo, 'Quasimodo, "Al padre" (v.1)', *Italianistica*, 37:73–85, noting that the words 'acque viola' are normally linked to the 1908 Messina earthquake, suggests a possible derivation from Quasimodo's translation of poem LXXXIV by Catullus, where the 'acque viole' of the Ionian sea become 'acque tempestose', thereby proposing a mythical transformation of the meaning of this line.

RAMONDINO. S. Lucamante, 'Le scelte dell'*antifiction*: il romanzo della memoria contro il potere della storia', *StN*, 25, 1998:367–68, is an analysis of *Althénopis* in the psychological light of the myths of childhood and of the building of an adult consciousness.

REBORA M. Dalla Torre, 'Questioni metriche dell'ultimo Rebora', *ON*, 23:129–78, shows a strong link between metrical forms in R.'s earlier and later poems and disproves the view that, following his conversion, R. rejected all links with his earlier poetry. *Le prose di Clemente Rebora*, ed. Gualtiero De Santi and Enrico Grandesso, Venice, Marsilio, xi + 151 pp., is a collection of essays on Rebora's prose writings and letters.

RÉPACI. *Leonida Répaci, *Poesie*, ed. Dante Maffia, Soveria Mannelli, Rubbettino, 220 pp.

RISI. W. Rupolo, 'Quando un poeta traduce un poeta', *NA*, 2206:211–18, records an interview with Nelo Risi on his translations into Italian of work by Apollinaire, Jouve, Queneau, Micheaux, Supervielle, and Kavafis.

ROCCATAGLIATA CECCARDI. F. Benozzo, 'Il puro paesaggio nelle poesie di Ceccardo Roccatagliata Ceccardi', *SPCT*, 58:153–71.

ROSSELLI. S. Giovanuzzi, '*La libellula*: Amelia Rosselli e il poemetto', *ParL*, 44:584–86, looks at the differences between the 1958 version of the poem and the one published in 1969 and 1985. It questions the different interpretation of Rosselli's use of the *poemetto* as a way of presenting the present in a prose- like poetic form while also suggesting that the past is characterized by forms no longer acceptable to her.

RUBINO. K. Pizzi, 'L'"intuizione del fantastico": Antonio Rubino', *MLR*, 94:394–408, argues that some aspects of R.'s cartoons and popular poetry could be seen as related to Futurist poetics.

RUFFATO. D. Maffia, 'Riflessioni su un poeta: *Scribendi licentia* di Cesare Ruffato', *LetP*, 105:110–12, points to Ruffato's changing moods and ideas in poems that he wrote from 1960 to 1998. Massimo Pamio, *Parola etica: la poesia di Cesare Ruffato*, Chieti, NoUbs, 165 pp., describes Ruffato's inventiveness with language and poetry, especially dialect poetry. A. Stussi, 'Tutta la "poesia in volgare padovano" di Cesare Ruffato', *Belfagor*, 54:439–52, outlines the way Ruffato focuses on the linguistic flexibility of the Paduan dialect.

SANGUINETI. Antonio Pietropaoli, *Unità e trinità di Edoardo Sanguineti*, Na, ESI, 205 pp. V. Hand, '*Laborintus II:* a neo-avant-garde celebration of Dante', *ISt*, 53, 1998:122–49, examines *Laborintus II*, a piece of musical theatre commissioned in 1963 from Edoardo Sanguineti and Luciano Berio. It looks at the question of 'connections' between the words and the music in specific parts of the libretto in particular.

SANVITALE.   Francesca Sanvitale, \*Camera ottica: pagine di letteratura e realtà, T, Einaudi, viii + 290 pp.

SATTA.   F. Petroni, 'A vent'anni dal *Giorno del giudizio*', *Allegoria*, 31 : 112–19, reappraises S.'s novel twenty years after its first edition, highlights its moral aspects and its experimental language, and concludes that, though realistic, this novel is mainly metaphysical.

SAVINIO.   Silvana Cirillo, \*Alberto Savinio. Le molte facce di un artista di genio, Mi, B. Mondadori, 1997, 367 pp. S. Lanuzza, 'Alberto Savinio in USA', *Il Ponte*, 56.1 : 147–52, details the work done on S. in U.S.A., particularly that of M. E. Gutiérrez. F. Secchieri, *Dove comincia la realtà e dove finisce. Studi su Alberto Savinio*, F, Le Lettere, 1998, 191 pp., examines real and oniric dimensions in S.'s poetry. Gerd Roos, \*Giorgio De Chirico e Alberto Savinio. Ricordi e documenti: Monaco, Milano, Firenze, 1906–1911, Bo, Bora, 447 pp. Alessandri Tinterri, \*Savinio e altro, Genoa, Il Melangolo, 126 pp. \*Un'amicizia senza corpo. La corrispondenza Parisot-Savinio, 1938–1952, ed. Giuditta Isotti Rosowski, Palermo, Sellerio, 1999, 250 pp.

SBARBARO.   Stefano Pavarini, \*Sbarbaro prosatore, Bo, Il Mulino, 1997, 193 pp.

SCATAGLINI.   Massimo Raffaeli, *El vive d'omo: scritti su Franco Scataglini*, Ancona, Transeuropea, 1998, 109 pp.

SCIASCIA.   Gaspare Giudice, *Leonardo Sciascia. Lo stemma di Racalmuto*, Na, L'Ancora, 160 pp., discusses the themes of *mafia* and political commitment, and intertextual questions, including and S.'s debt to Pirandello. T. O'Neill, 'Foscolo, Montale e Sciascia alle soglie del Duemila', pp. 9–34 of *Da un paese indicibile*, ed. Roberto Cincotta, Mi, La Vita Felice, identifies common intertextual ground between S. and a number of poets (more prominently Foscolo and Montale), and comments on other works read by Sciascia. Giuseppe Traina, *Leonardo Sciascia*, Mi, B. Mondadori, 271 pp., sets concepts and works in alphabetical order, like a short encyclopaedia or a hypertext.

SCOTELLARO.   P. Cisternino, 'Diagramma semantico dei lemmi: *casa, parola, silenzio* e *attesa* in "È fatto giorno" e "Margherite e rosolacci" di Rocco Scotellaro', *ON*, 23 : 233–39.

SERANTINI.   Graziella Malgaretti, *Francesco Serantini. La vita e l'opera letteraria*, Ravenna, Longo, 240 pp., reconstructs S.'s life and the chronology of his work, and argues in favour of religiosity in his fiction.

SERENI.   L. Barile, 'Una luce mai vista. Bocca di Magra e "Un posto di vacanza" di Vittorio Sereni', *LItal*, 51 : 383–404, shows how the physical Bocca di Magra — where Sereni spent his holidays — is metamorphosed in the emotional dimension of the poem "Un posto di vacanza" (*Stella variabile*). F. D'Alessandro, 'Sulla formazione intellettuale di Vittorio Sereni', *Aevum*, 63:891–912, evaluates the impact that Antonio Banfi, Luciano Anceschi, Enzo Paci, and their Milanese circle had on Sereni's work. It also marks the importance of Paul Valéry's poetry on Sereni who saw artistic creation as a constantly developing form of work in progress. F. D'Alessandro, 'Vittorio Sereni e gli anni di *Frontiera*', *ON*, 23:45–71, analyses the impact of the years 1935–40 on Sereni's earliest poetry when he had a palpable sense that an era was drawing to a close. Gian Carlo Ferretti, *Poeta e di poeti funzionario: il lavoro editoriale di Vittorio Sereni*, Mi, Il Saggiatore, 1999, 204 pp., examines a neglected aspect of Sereni's activity, viz. his work as literary editor (from 1958 onwards) and director of Mondadori. S. Ghidinelli, 'L'infaticabile "ma" di Sereni', *StN*, 26:157–84, examines Sereni's use of the word 'ma' in *Strumenti umani*, particularly its function in grammar and intonation. Renato Nisticò, *Nostalgia di presenze. La poesia di Sereni verso la prosa*, Lecce, Manni, 1998, 166 pp., delineates Sereni's effort to engage with the reader through poetry or prose. *Vittorio Sereni. La tentazione della prosa*, ed. Giovanni Raboni, Mi, Mondadori, 1998, 551 pp., presents published and unpublished prose by Sereni and suggests that the poet was also greatly tempted to devote his time to prose writing.

SILONE. F. De Core, 'Il caso Silone', *Lo Straniero*, 9:209–19, surveys a number of articles on S.'s suspected collaboration with Fascism. B. Falcetto, 'Introduzione', pp. ix–xxviii of Ignazio Silone, *Romanzi e saggi*, vol. 2 (1945–1978), ed. Bruno Falcetto, Mi, Mondadori, 1680 pp., detects biographical and imagined dimensions in S.'s fiction, and sees it as characterized by an interaction of the ordinary with the extraordinary. Diocleziano Giardini, *Ignazio Silone. Cronologia della vita e delle opere*, pref. Darina Silone, Cerchio, Polla, 183 pp.

SINIGAGLIA. G. Gorni, 'Il *Regesto* postumo di Sinigaglia', *Cenobio*, 47, 1998:47–51, a brief and personal appraisal of the poet prompted by the edition Sandro Sinigaglia, *Poesie*, introd. Silvia Longhi, ed. Paola Italia, Mi, 1997, xlviii + 440 pp., analyses 'Ti piace il piccolo' from *Il Regesto della Rosa e altre vanterie*. The same collection is further sampled in Id., 'Sinigaglia ultimo e penultimo', *Levia Gravia*, 1:169–78, where the author is defined as being 'di accusata, incontinente letterarietà'.

SINISGALLI. Marino Faggella, *Leonardo Sinisgalli. Un poeta nella civiltà delle macchine*, Potenza, Ermes, 1996, 225 pp., an analysis of the link that binds S. to Lucania, places him between the technological-mathematical and the literary Muses.

SOFFICI.　L. Tondelli, 'La poesia in tipografia. Lettura dei *Chimismi lirici* di Ardengo Soffici', *Poetiche*, 2: 229–65, is a critical analysis of this work. *\*Omaggio a Soffici: nel 35. anniversario dalla scomparsa*, ed. Mario Richter and Jean-François Rodriguez, Prato, Pentalinea, 131 pp. Jean-François Rodriguez, *\*Barbantini-Soffici: un'amicizia intellettuale fra Apollinaire ed Agnoletti. Parigi, Firenze, Venezia, 1913–1932*, Signa, Masso delle Fate, 86 pp.

SOLDATI.　Mario Soldati, *\*Un viaggio a Lourdes*, introd. Marziano Guglielminetti, Novara, Interlinea, 66 pp. I. Crotti, 'Le *24 ore* di Mario Soldati', *RLettI*, 16:193–214, compares S.'s cinematic and literary procedures as they are expressed in *24 ore in uno studio fotografico*, a text published in 1935.

SPALLICI.　M. A. Biondi and D. Pieri, 'Bertinoro tra mito e realtà negli scritti di Aldo Spallici', *StRmgn*, 47, 1996[1999]:247–58. A. Silvestri, 'Aldo Spallici poeta della Romagna agreste', *ib.*, 291–312.

SPAZIANI.　A. Napoli, 'L'Angelo nell'oasi', *Atelier*, 16.4:23–27, looks at the role of the sea and how it is linked to the key words *sogno*, *memoria* and *angelo* in Spaziani's latest work *La radice del mare*. S. Wright, 'Maria Luisa Spaziani: *principium individuationis* e progetto poetico nell'incontro con venti voci liriche femminili', *ItQ*, 137–138:35–47, gives details of Spaziani's para-psychological interviews and imaginary encounters with 20 women poets that give rise to lively dialogue. In 'Intervista a M. L. Spaziani', *ib.*, 49–81, S. Wright conducts an interview with the poet on her formation and relationship with poetry. This ranges from questions of metre and rhythm to such concerns as women's poetry, and the link between life and poetry, which Spaziani deals with in her work.

STUPARICH.　Bruno Vasari, *\*Giani Stuparich: ricordi di un allievo, con otto testimonianze sull'internamento alla risiera di San Sabba a Trieste*, ed. Giovanna Stuparich Criscione, introd. Elvio Guagnini, Trieste, LINT, 72 pp.

SVEVO.　S. Carrai, 'Come nacque *La coscienza di Zeno*', *StN*, 25, 1998:239–56, analyses the genesis of S.'s novel, and especially the structural aspect of its subdivision into chapters. Guido Baldi, *\*Le maschere dell'inetto. Lettura di 'Senilità'*, T, Paravia, 250 pp.

TABUCCHI.　B. Ferraro, 'Antonio Tabucchi e il fascino della pittura', pp. 829–48 of *I segni incrociati*, Viareggio, Baroni, 1998, starting out from T.'s study of Velasquez's *Las Meninas* in *Il gioco del rovescio*, traces his interest in both classical and contemporary painting — the latter being evidenced by his long-standing association with the artist Davide Benati. A. Guidotti, 'Aspetti del fantastico nella narrativa di Antonio Tabucchi', *StN*, 25, 1998:351–65, analyses some essential ingredients of T.'s narrative work, such as the journey, dreams, and time.

TESSA. Delio Tessa, *L'è el dì di mort, alegher!; De là dei mur; Altre liriche*, ed. Dante Isella, 2 vols, T, Einaudi, xxx + 585 pp., is a critical edition of Milanese dialect poems first published in 1985.

TONDELLI. Elena Buia, *Verso casa. Viaggio nella narrativa di Pier Vittorio Tondelli*, Ravenna, Fernandel, 128 pp., finds fragmentation of identity, the sense of separateness from and desire for integration in society, postmodernism, and multilayered language registers in T.'s fiction. S. Zappoli, 'Pier Vittorio Tondelli, solitario in fuga', *Il Ponte*, 55.9:146–61, examines the development of T.'s work from the rebel youth of *Altri libertini* to a more normalized approach to life.

TOZZI. F. Andorlino, 'Unità e dispersione. Alcune note su *Bestie* di Federigo Tozzi', *AnVi*, 13:61–75, examines, among other aspects, intertextual reference to James and Janet. M. Codebò, 'La rappresentazione del tempo in *Giovani* di Federigo Tozzi', *RStI*, 16.1, 1998:241–54. E. Baccarani, 'Psicologia e psicofisiologia: intorno alla cultura scientifica di Tozzi', *Poetiche*, 1:67–133, explores T.'s debt to the psychology of William James, Ribot, and Janet. In Federigo Tozzi, *Ricordi di un giovane impiegato. Edizione critico-genetica, introduzione e apparati*, ed. Riccardo Castellano, pref. Romano Luperini, Fiesole, Cadmo, xiii + 101 pp., elegant philological scholarship is applied to a text with a chequered, ten-year compositional history, not only to produce a meticulously corrected text but to reveal, line by line, its 'complessità stratigrafica'. In a short postface (89–99) Franco Petroni considers 'La figura della negazione nei *Ricordi di un giovane impiegato*'.

TRAVAINI. A. Rondini, 'L'anatomia del mondo: società e medicina nella narrative di Eugenio Travaini', *RLettI*, 16:217–78, analyses T.'s fiction, focusing especially on his criticism of malfunctions in Italian society.

TUROLDO. David Maria Turoldo, *Teatro*, introd. Giovanni Bianchi, Sotto il Monte, Servitium, 458 pp., presents six plays, one published for the first time.

UNGARETTI. Daniela Baroncini, *Ungaretti e il sentimento del classico*, Bo, Il Mulino, 288 pp., details the attraction and tension created in Ungaretti's poetry by his love of classical writers. R. Gennaro, 'La poetica di Ungaretti e il pensiero di Bergson. Continuità di un rapporto, *RLI*, 103:429–48, views the influence of Bergson on U.'s work as important but not all-pervasive because U. also acknowledged his debt to Plato and other Platonic philosophers in his poetry and writings. Gérard Genot, *La fiction poétique: Foscolo, Leopardi, Ungaretti*, Paris, Université Paris–Sorbonne, 1998, 160 pp., traces parallels and links between the work of these three poets. P. Cataldi, ' "I fiumi" di Ungaretti. La linea e il cerchio', *Allegoria*, 11:20–42, provides a structural, metrical and thematic analysis of Ungaretti's poem. M. Brose, 'Dido's turn: cultural syntax in Ungaretti's *La terra promessa*',

*AnI*, 16:121–43, examines the textual and psychological complexities of U.'s use of the figure of Dido in this work. Isabel Violante Picon, *Une oeuvre originale de poésie. Giuseppe Ungaretti traducteur*, Paris, Sorbonne, 1998, 348 pp. F. Musarra and R. Gennaro, 'La musique, la mémoire et les mots. Notes sur Ungaretti traducteur de Phèdre', *RLC*, 63:195–204.

VALERI. B. Rosada, 'Diego Valeri', pp. 82–109 of *Profili veneziani del Novecento*, Venice, Supernova, 110 pp., argues that V.'s work was never fully appreciated or understood by the critics.

VALASSINA. Luigi Picchi, *Valassina parroco scrittore e poeta*, Como, Dialogo, 1998, 60 pp., gives a broad outline of the poetry and prose of Valsassina, a friend of David Maria Turoldo.

VOLPONI. Paolo Volponi, *Del naturale e dell'artificiale*, ed. Emanuele Zinato, Ancona, Il Lavoro Editoriale, 195 pp., presents V.'s collected writings, some of them published for the first time.

ZANZOTTO. Andrea Zanzotto, *\*Le poesie e prose scelte*, ed. Stefano Dal Bianco and Gian Mario Villalta, Mi, Mondadori, cxxxvi + 1802 pp., includes essays by Stefano Agosti and Fernando Bandini together with some previously unpublished poems. Claudio Pezzin, *Zanzotto e Leopardi: il poeta come 'infans'*, Verona, Cierre, 153 pp., explores the relationship between L. and Z. and later with Hölderlin, Lacan, Bataille, Montale, Eliot, Husserl and Celan.

# ROMANIAN STUDIES*

## LANGUAGE

By MARTIN MAIDEN, *Professor of the Romance Languages, University of Oxford*
(This survey covers the years 1998 and 1999)

### 1. GENERAL

Cynthia Vakareliyska, *Romanian*, Munich, Lincom, 60 pp., is a brief sketch of the language, incl. an overview of its history, of phonological, morphological, and syntactic structures, and a comparison with non-Daco-Romanian dialects. Radu Daniliuc and Laura Daniliuc, *A Descriptive Grammar of Romanian*, Munich, Lincom, 240 pp. G. Ernst, 'Rumänisch und andere Sprachen', Holtus, *Lexikon*, 7, 757–78, is a useful contrastive structural study of Romanian.

Gabriela Bidu-Vrănceanu, Cristina Călăraşu, Liliana Ionescu-Ruxăndoiu, Mihaela Mancaş, and Gabriela Pană-Dindelegan, *Dicţionar de ştiinţe ale limbii*, Editura Ştiinţifică, 1997, 573 pp., provides the basis for G. Pană Dindelegan, 'Terminologia lingvistică actuală, între tradiţie şi inovaţie', *LiL*, 42.2, 1997:5–12, which considers the light thrown on the development of Romanian linguistic thought by the *Dicţionar*. P. Ţugui, 'Unele completări la "Precizări la precizări . . ." de Magdalena Vulpe', *LiL*, 43.1, 1998:26–30, marks yet another round in the debate about the circumstances attending the publication of vol. II of Puşcariu's *Limba română*. Id., 'Emil Petrovici şi unele probleme ale lingvisticii româneşti contemporane (I)', *LiL*, 43.3–4, 1998:80–87, details the life and scholarly activity of the Cluj linguist. B. Techtmeier, 'Sprachtheoretische Positionen, sprachkritische Aktivitäten und praktisches Sprachverhalten: das Beispiel Titu Maiorescu', Hassler, *Kontinuität*, 311–23, assesses this controversial figure's contribution to the modernization of the standard language, not only as a theorist and critic but also in his use of new orthographies, diffusion of neologisms, and in public and parliamentary activities. V. Arvinte, 'Denumiri pentru limbile României de sud-est', *LiL*, 43.1, 1998:5–20, examines the names for the Romance languages of south-eastern Europe (incl. Romanian and Dalmatian) in non-Romance varieties of that area.

---

* The place of publication of books is Bucharest unless otherwise stated.

## 2. History of the Language

Gheorghe Chivu, Mariana Costinescu, and Constantin Frâncu, *Istoria limbii române literare: epoca veche (1532–1780)*, Editura Academiei Române, 1997, 496 pp., focuses on the crystallization of the literary norm (or norms), and constitutes a useful synthesis of thinking on the emergence of literary Romanian (from both an external and a structural perspective); the lack of a subject index is regrettable. Marius Sala, *De la latină la română*, Univers Enciclopedic, 1998, 164 pp., approaches the task of narrating the history of Daco-Romanian from a comparative perspective, seeking to identify how much of the structure of Romanian is shared with other Romance languages. S. gives particular weight to the lexicon, observing among other things the interesting phenomenon of parallel patterns of borrowing (albeit from different languages) linking Romanian and other Romance varieties. V. Guţu Romalo, ' "Centralitatea" limbii române', *LiL*, 44.1, 5–11, argues for the linguistic 'centrality' of Romanian, given an interpretation of 'centre' as an interference point or crossroads of different linguistic influences from east and west. A succinct historical sketch of Romanian is offered by G. Price, 'Romanian', in Price, *Encyclopedia*, 355–61, which is particularly handy for its account of the history of the spelling system. The fascinating question of early grammaticography is discussed in W. Dahmen, 'Die Anfänge der rumänischen Grammatikschreibung', *Fest. Wunderli*, 57–68, which appraises particularly Eustatievici's *Gramatica rumânească* (with interesting remarks on E.'s sometimes cumbersome attempts to create native Romanian grammatical terminology — such as *de doao ori glăsuitoare* = 'diphthong'!).

Romanian has a prominent place in R. Windisch, 'Die historische Klassifikation der Romania, II: Balkanromanisch', Holtus, *Lexikon*, 7, 907–37. M. Trummer, 'Südosteuropäische Sprachen und Romanisch', Holtus, *Lexikon*, 7, 134–84, devotes a section (163–74) to Romanian (incl. the dialects) offering a fairly thorough survey of the effects of contact with Albanian, Slav, Turkish, and Hungarian. Contact phenomena are also the subject of D. Dumitrescu, 'Fenómenos paralelos de contacto con el inglés entre el español y el rumano hablados en los Estados Unidos', *Atti* (Palermo), V, 275–83. Peter Petrucci, *Slavic Features in the History of Rumanian*, Munich, Lincom, 200 pp., is a dissertation which methodically ascertains those features which are genuinely due to early contact with Slavic languages and shows that the Thomason and Kaufman model of language contact forms a useful framework for interpreting the effects of Slavic influence on Romanian.

L. Fassel, 'Der Begriff "Altrumänisch"' in den Überblickdarstellungen zur rumänischen Sprachgeschichte. Periodisierungsfragen', *Balkan-Archiv*, 22–23, 1997–98: 153–69, reviews different scholars' use of the term 'Old Romanian', singling out Ivănescu for having provided a valid periodization of the language and calling for support for a new, modified, edition of Ivănescu's history of the language. Victoria Vlad-Nedelcoviciu, *Limbă şi literatură medievală: Grigore Ureche, Miron Costin, Ion Neculce*, Arad, Multimedia, 1997, 250 pp., examines the language of these early chroniclers.

The recent history of the language of Moldova continues to attract lively scholarly interest. Donald Dyer, *The Romanian Dialect of Moldova: a study in language and politics*, Lampeter, Mellen, xii + 205 pp., is a collection of seven studies reflecting the author's research in this field. These are: an introduction giving the general historical background to the Moldovan 'language question', and studies on 'Politics', 'Dialects', 'Phonology', 'Morphosyntax', 'Sociolinguistics', and 'Language in Contact' (the last dealing with contact between Moldovan and both Gagauz and Bulgarian). There follow six appendices, four of which report interviews (conducted in 1996) with Moldovan politicians and academics. Because the seven central studies reproduce (with some new introductory comment) conference papers and other material produced by the author since the mid 1980s, there is a certain amount of redundant repetition, but this book is a valuable and informative assessment of the historical background and of the linguistic differences between standard Romanian, 'Moldovan', and the dialects of Moldova. The role played by Russian models in distinguishing Moldovan morphosyntax is made very clear in the chapters on morphosyntax and sociolinguistics. The question why the Soviets did not capitalize on the distinctive dialect features of Moldova in constructing the Moldovan language, although raised in the chapter on 'dialects', does not seem to get a satisfactory answer. C. King 'The ambivalence of authenticity, or How the Moldovan language was made', *Slavic Review*, 58: 117–42, deals with the process of 'language construction' in early Soviet cultural policy in the Moldovan Autonomous Soviet Socialist Republic (1924–40), where literary Romanian was considered 'bourgeois' and gallicized. K. examines the attitudes of the peasantry towards such innovations and the ambivalence of the cultural elite to adopting forms of speech and writing which they found uncultured. In fact, Moldova seems to have seen one of the more successful attempts by the Soviets to 'indigenize' the languages of the USSR, and it appears that in the interwar years there was a real attempt to build on the differences between Moldovan speech and literary Romanian, but by the mid 30s a new ideology emerged, based on promoting 'correct' and 'educated' speech (far more like literary Romanian) among Moldovan peasants. Changes in contemporary perceptions of the language question, against the background of changing political circumstances, are the subject of V. Dumbrava, 'Auf der Suche nach einer Identität. Veränderungen des Sprachbewusstseins in der Republik Moldova in den neunziger Jahren', *Grenzgänge*, 10, 1998:45–54, written from the perspective of somebody who himself participated in the demonstrations and debates which regularly took place from early 1989, and analysing the positions of partisans of the three major groups involved in the question — pro-Moldovan, pro-Romanian and pro-Russian. S. Berejan, 'La langue roumaine en République Moldova', *ib.*, 38–44, reviews some distinctive features of the speech of Moldova, but upholds its status as 'Romanian'. J. Erfurt, 'Sprachpolitik und Sprachpraxis in der Republik Moldova', *ib.*, 9, 1998:113–21, discusses among other things post-independence attitudes towards Moldovan/Romanian, as against the more prestigious Russian language, and calls for further detailed sociolinguistic investigation into the Moldovan situation. I. Robu, 'Moldova. Cultural Awareness', *Transitions*, 5.10, 1998:8–9, discusses the fate of the Romanian language in Moldova's radio-broadcasting in the face of pressure from Russian-language programming. D. Dyer, 'What price language contact: is there Russian influence on the syntax of Moldovan?', *Nationalities Papers*, 26, 1998:73–86, shows that Russian influence is essentially lexical, rather than syntactic. Price, *Encyclopedia*, 301, has a brief section on 'Moldavian'.

## 3. TEXTS

A. Avram, 'Trăsături fonetice arhaice în partea românească a "Lexiconului heptaglot de la Oxford"', *FD*, 16, 1997:5–22. V. Barbu, 'Prima traducere românească a cântării *stabat mater (I)*', *LiR* 46.1–3, 1997:29–41, deals with an 18th-c. Catholic 'Evangheliar', translated from Lat. into Romanian using the Roman alphabet. M. Teodorescu, 'În legătură cu grafia *vrădzimaţi* în Psaltirea Hurmuzaki', *ib.*, 205–06. G. Chivu, 'O versiune bănăţeană a *Visurilor lui Mamer*', *ib.*, 47–54, examines a rare example from the Banat of an 17th- or 18th-c. *carte populară*. G. Piccillo, 'Su un MS romeno-italiano della seconda metà del Settecento', *ib.*, 175–80, treats the linguistic significance of A. M. Mauro's 'Diverse materie in lingua moldava'. F. Vîrban, 'Un cronograf românesc de tip Danovici din secolul al XVIII-lea, păstrat în colecţia de manuscrise a Bibliotecii de Stat din Moscova', *ib.*, 209–17. E. Munteanu, 'Slavon ou latin? Une réexamination du problème de la langue-source des plus anciennes traductions roumaines du *Psautier*', *Atti* (Palermo), VI, 351–64. J. Kramer,

'Probleme der Edition älterer rumänischer Texte', *Balkan-Archiv*, 22–23, 1997–98:201–12, argues that reproductions of early texts should take the form of facsimiles or transliteration into cyrillic, but never roman, letters.

## 4. ORTHOGRAPHY AND PHONOLOGY

G. Mihăilă, 'Ecouri ale alfabetului chirilic în literatua română din secolul al XIX-lea și de la începutul secolului nostru'. *LiR*, 46.1–3, 1997:141–53. A. Avram, 'Alternanțe fonologice accentuale condiționate sintactic', *ib.*, 13–20, discusses the status of stress shifts such as *spúneți* vs *spunéți-mi*, and *zéro* vs *zeróuri*. Perceptual phonetics are treated in M. Mărdărescu-Teodorescu and A. Lăzăroiu 'Importanța benzilor de zgomot în percepția fricativelor din limba română', *FD*, 16, 1997:47–73.

Historical phonology is the subject of A. Avram, 'Remarques sur la nasalisation des voyelles et sur les consonnes nasales non étymologiques en portugais et en roumain', *Atti* (Palermo), 1, 51–56, which considers particularly the historical incidence in Romanian of nasalization produced by a *preceding* nasal consonant, showing that the phonological environments in which it occurs are more extensive than is usually claimed and drawing parallels with developments in Portuguese. D. Urițescu, 'Evolution des voyelles nasales en roumain et en roman: aspects formels et naturels', *ib.*, 409–19, also makes comparisons with Portuguese, and argues that although the nasalization process is partly 'natural', other aspects of it, such as the influence of labial and palatal consonants, and the differentiation of front and back vowels, are the result of a reinterpretation of natural processes at the level of the 'norm'. Id., 'Changement de conditionnement en phonologie: un exemple roumain', *La Linguistique*, 33, 1997:35–44, examines the partial resistance of pretonic [o] to raising peculiar to Daco-Romanian, dating it (and its morphologically constrained distribution) to a period before the intensive influx of Slav vocabulary, and suggesting that it provides evidence for a common Daco-Romanian stage.

## 5. MORPHOLOGY AND SYNTAX

Wim van Eeden, *\*Grammatica van het Roemeens. Syntaxis van de samgestelde zin*, Amsterdam, Grammar Publications, 1997, 311 pp., is the second volume of the projected five-volume descriptive grammar of Romanian, and deals with the syntax of simple sentences.

W. Zwanenburg, 'Homonymie systématique en morphologie: les dérivés de forme participiale du roumain', *RLFRU*, 18, 1999, 103–13, discusses the systematic formal identity between past participles, supines, and nominalized verbs in Romanian, and challenges Aronoff's analysis of phenomena of systematic homophony between functionally disjoint elements as belonging to a distinct 'morphomic' level. Z.'s analysis of the Romanian facts seems to me to prove nothing either way about their possible 'morphomic status', and the proposed alternative of deriving one form from the other by a 'morphophonological rule' overlooks some fundamental issues, such as the need arbitrarily to stipulate a direction of derivation, and loss of the insight that the systematically homonymous forms are mutually implicational.

Two studies dealing with historical morphology are M. Maiden, 'La tesi di Reichenkron e le origini delle desinenze -*i* e -*e* nel romanzo "orientale" ', *Atti* (Palermo), I, 177–86, which argues that these inflectional endings in Romanian (as well as Italian and Dalmatian) must be principally phonetic developments of desinences originally in -s; and Id., 'Il ruolo dell'"idoneità" in morfologia diacronica. I suffissi romeni -*ea*, -*ică* ed -*oi*', *RLiR*, 63, 321–45, demonstrating that the diachronic development of these suffixes (especially the frequent substitution of -*ea* by -*ică*) is explicable in terms of a kind of 'ideal shape' for derivational affixes — sign-like behaviour which contradicts recent claims that such affixes are not signs.

The theoretical significance of two facts about the morphology of the Romanian second person singular imperative (inflectional distinctions between transitive and intransitive forms, and the structure of the negative imperative) is touched on in M. Pîrvulescu and Y. Roberge, 'Objects and the structure of imperatives', *LSRL, 28*, 211–26. S. Reinheimer Rîpeanu, 'Le futur roumain et le futur roman', *Atti* (Palermo), I, 319–27, describes the sociolinguistic and semantic (especially modal) features which differentiate the various future forms available in Romanian. R. Iordache and G. Scurtu, 'Autour des structures périphrastiques verbales du français et de leur équivalence en roumain', *ib.*, II, 483–93, compares the various structures for expressing different types of 'imminence' in the two languages (among them *aller* + infinitive in Fr. and *a avea să* + subjunctive in Romanian). E. Pîrvu, 'Sulle cause della diversa distribuzione degli ausiliari temporali in italiano e in romeno', *ib.*, 673–78, considers semantic motivations for the different uses of 'have', 'be', and 'want' auxiliaries in the tense-systems of the two languages. The notion that Romanian uses 'have' in the present perfect because 'have' indicates an action 'whose concrete results are known', supposedly appropriate to this tense, whilst 'be' somehow indicates a 'possible state' (for instance, *să fi mers, aş fi vorbit*) is not convincingly argued, and P. seems surprisingly unaware of the literature in this subject in the wider Romance domain. Ilinca Crăiniceanu, *The Category of Aspect in English and Romanian with Special Reference to the Progressive Aspect*, Craiova U.P., 1997, 292 pp. M. Manoliu-Manea, 'Un revenant: le supin roumain', *Atti* (Palermo), II, 619–30, considers the conditions governing the choice of supine or subjunctive in Romanian, particularly in causative, impersonal, and final constructions. The supine is analysed as a mixed category representing a 'summary scanning' of the activity (whence its indifference to categories such as voice, tense, aspect, and mood), which is selected under circumstances of low 'prééminence discursive', where there is close coherence between the verb and its arguments, on the one hand, and between main and subordinate verb on the other. The highest degree of coherence occurs in modal constructions expressing necessity (for example, *am de*) followed by aspectual verbs such as *a termina de*, psychological verbs such as *a se plictisi de*, and the reflexive causative *a se apuca de*. The supine is also considered in T. Van Hecke, 'Aspects de la construction causative en roumain', *ib.*, 839–48, examining the choice of subjunctive or supine after causative *a pune* and *a da*, and the choice of the propositions *de* or *la* before the supine, *de* being agent-focused (*Mi-a dat de spălat niște ciorapi*) and *la* object-focused (*Mi-a dat la spălat niște ciorapi*).

A. Niculescu, 'Sur la position de l'article défini en roumain', *ib.*, VI, 247–58, claims that the Romanian definite article is not exclusively enclitic, although his over-emphatically asserted position seems to hold water only if the distinction between demonstratives and articles is not too rigidly maintained: what he really shows is that reflexes of Latin ILLE are not necessarily enclitic. S. Paliga, 'Romanian definite article revisited', *Linguistica*, 39, 71–82, argues, but falls considerably short of demonstrating, that some forms of the Romanian definite article (for example, popular *-u*, and, allegedly, the *-a* found in adverbial and demonstrative forms) go back to a Thracian substrate. E. Tănase, 'Y a-t-il en roumain un article génitival ou possessif?', *Atti* (Palermo), II, 807–14, deals with the status of the 'articles' *al ai a ale* (as in *o carte a studentului*) and proposes that they have pronominal status, marking a '(ré)actualisation (du nom déterminé)'.

P. Monachesi, 'Linearization properties of the Romanian verbal complex', *RLFRU*, 17, 1998:57–66, argues, within an HPSG framework, that the rigid ordering of Romanian verbal pronominal clitics, negators, and intensifiers (for example, *mai*, *prea*) need not be stipulated and is derivable from the different (syntactic vs lexical) status of these elements and the general architecture of the grammar. G. Cincilei, 'Les virtualités des pronoms réfléchis en français et en roumain', *La Linguistique*, 34, 1998:113–20, identifies differences between the two languages in respect of reciprocal reflexive and 'pronominal', reflexive verbs (for example, *a se ruga* vs *prier*). C. Dobrovie Sorin, 'Impersonal *se* constructions in Romance and the passivization of unergatives', *LI*, 29, 1998:399–437, uses the status of Romanian *se* as an accusative middle-passive to throw light on the Italian middle-passive *si* construction. D. Gierling, 'Clitic doubling, specificity and focus in Romanian', in Black, *Clitics*, 63–85, offers Romanian data showing that focus cannot project from a clitic doubled direct object DP (and also that specificity is not, in fact, the most important factor in determining clitic doubling). V. Motapanyane, 'Focus, checking theory and fronting strategies in Romanian, *SL*, 52, 1998: 227–43.

L.-S. Florea, 'Deux descendants de *in* face à face: le français *en* et le roumain *în*', *Atti* (Palermo), II, 309–23, makes a detailed and insightful comparison of the uses of these cognate prepositions and related forms in the two languages, pointing out that the lack of a Fr. equivalent to *din* (vs *de la*) means that Fr. signals a less nuanced set of spatial relations than Romanian. D. Crașoveanu, 'Despre folosirea unor prepoziţii în presa actuală vorbită', *LiL*, 44.1, 29–35, deals with aberrant uses of the prepositions in constructions such as *a se ocupa despre, a fi vorba de către, din elevi, cu ce preț* in the language of television and radio. A. Halvorsen, 'Le complément comparatif et le marqueur PE en roumain', *Atti* (Palermo), II, 393–403, is a revealing treatment of the near-constant use of the (apparent) object marker *pe* in comparative constructions (for example, *Le iubise pe toate* ca pe *niște prietene*), according to principles which violate the general rules for use of *pe* as object marker. Comparing this use with apparently different constructions with *pe* (for instance, *a face pe nebunul*), A. concludes that a fundamental property of *pe* is to mark a nominal syntagm as belonging to what he calls the 'zone objectale' and to indicate that the syntagm in question is considered 'salient', where 'salience' may be the non-conformity of the noun to reality. Different perspectives on the same preposition are offered by G. Pană Dindelegan, 'Din nou despre statutul prepoziziţiei. Cu referire specială la prepoziţia *pe*', *LiR*, 46.1–3, 1997:165–74, suggesting, among other things, that *pe* in constructions such as *a face pe prostul* should be analysed as constituting part of the verb. A historical perspective is taken in C. Ditvall, 'Sur l'expression du génitif de *tot* roumain en langue ancienne et moderne', *RevR*, 33, 1998:7–38, who argues from a study of the genitive formation of *tot* (old Romanian *a tot* vs modern *tuturor*) that the older *tot* had the status of a 'quantifier' whereas the modern word has the status of what she terms a 'caractérisant-quantifiant' (like *fiecare, ambii*); see also her 'Remarques sur la place du quantifiant *tot* en roumain ancien et moderne', *Actes*, Jyväskylä, 99–111.

D. Dumitrescu and M. Saltarelli, 'Two types of predicate modification. Evidence from the articulated adjectives of Romanian', *LSRL 26*, 175–92, deals with the semantic distinction between the type *săracul om* and *omul sărac*, taking a Fregean-inspired thematic approach and identifying various grammaticalized features of the language which attest to attributive vs predicative adjectival categories.

Ioana Ştefănescu, *The Syntax of Agreement in Romanian* (MIT Occasional Papers in Linguistics, 14), MIT, Cambridge Ma., 1997, xii + 307 pp., discusses the relationship between finite verb movement to the highest functional head in the clause architecture ('AGRo') and the licensing of number and person agreement with syntactically complex subject phrases such as partitives, possessives, and coordinate noun phrases. Ş argues that the highest functional head be split into two heads (Number and Person), based on the observation that Romanian has a number exponent different from the person exponents. There is also discussion of agreement patterns in relative clauses formed on personal pronouns and of the pattern with equative sentences containing *a fi*.

D. Nica, 'Le parole particelle nel romeno. Con riferimento ad altre lingue romanze', *Atti* (Palermo), v, 503–08, analyses the formal and semantic characteristics of 'adverbial' particles such as *chiar, mai, tot, prea, şi, doar, măcar*.

6. Lexicon, Phraseology, and Onomastics

Virtually all studies in these domains have a historical orientation, although modern usage is addressed in Anca Volceanov and George Volceanov, *Dicţionar de argou şi expresii familiare ale limbii române*, Livpress, 1998, 302 pp., presented by its authors as an expression of new, post-revolutionary, linguistic freedom from the formal, wooden constraints of the Ceauşescu era. The dictionary offers a fascinating overview of current slangs, jargons, and popular terms and phrases, and contains a brief history of earlier writings on Romanian argot, with bibliography. Included are communist-era terms such as *nechezol* 'coffee substitute', terms from Romany which have entered current slang usage, and new adjectives derived from verbs. Entries include information on register (for instance, ironic or old fashioned), domain (for example, thieves' slang, erotic, regionalisms), and there is a brief glossary of synonyms for standard forms.

H. Haarman, 'Language variation in a qualitative and quantitative perspective: assessing the influence of Lat. on south-eastern Europe', *Journal of Quantitative Linguistics*, 5, 1998:27–34, evaluates quantitative methods in establishing the 'Latinness' of Romanian, reaching the less than earth-shaking conclusion that it is the high frequency of Lat. elements in basic vocabulary, rather than the absolute number of Latin-based lexemes, which makes Romanian lexically Romance. W. Dahmen and J. Kramer, 'De la *Etymologicum Graeco-Slavo-Romanicum* à la *Etymologicum Graeco-Slavo-Romanicum*', *Atti* (Palermo), IV, 391–402, describes the reasons for their deciding to put aside, for the moment, their large-scale project to create an etymological dictionary of Greek and Slav elements in the Romance languages and concentrate on these elements in Romanian. This article contains discussion of their proposed methodology (particularly with regard to Greek elements — a subject which has not been well treated in Romanian historical lexicology). C. Moroianu, 'Dublete etimologice în sincronie şi diacronie', *LiL*, 42.2, 1997 : 20–27. Adrian Poruciuc, *Confluenţe şi etimologii*, Iaşi, Polirom, 1998, 131 pp., incl. discussions of the etymology of Romanian *codru* and its Balkan congeners (suggesting that the two meanings 'wood' and '(biggish) piece of something, etc.' reflect different, non-Lat., etyma), and of the probable Old Germanic origin of *teafăr*. T. Hristea, 'Corectări şi precizări etimologice', *LiR*, 46.1–3, 1997 : 109–17, covers 'ceasornic', 'a (se) turmenta' and 'zămos'. A. Mareş, 'Note filologice', *ib.*, 137–39, incl. discussion of 'pută (asserted to be 'non-existent'), 'robi' (whose status as a 'Romanian' word in Slavo-Romanian chancelry documents is challenged), a new 17th-c. attestation of the word 'socaci', the word 'şeşi', and '3 ştuchi din *bucoavna* tipărită la Bălgrad în 1699'. M. Mitu, ' "Cap" sau "pajură" şi unele consideraţii etimologice', *ib.*, 155–60, examines the etymology of 'pajură', the term used for 'tails' in children's coin-tossing games. A. Moraru, 'O expresie arhaică', *ib.*, 161–64, suggests that the expression 'a avea pe sine' found in the Bucharest Bible was a popular expression meaning 'menstruate' (which survives in some modern dialects). M. Popescu-Marin, 'Despre lat. *pavimentum* în română şi în alte limbi romanice', *ib.*, 181–84. M. Vulpe, 'Un argument în favoarea etimologii latine a rom. *mire*', *ib.*, 219–21. M. Purdela Sitaru, 'Compléments roumains au REW3 (éléments du Banat)', *Atti* (Palermo), III, 717–28, brings insights from the regional lexicon of the Banat to throw light on some etymologies in the third edition of *Romanisches Etymologisches Wörterbuch*.

M. Iliescu, 'Etymologie und Konnotation: Wörter griechischer Herkunft in der rumänischen Umgangssprache', Hassler, *Kontinuität*, 325–34, examines the reasons behind the often ironic or derogatory connotations of terms (such as *a se pricopsi, a sfeterisi*) that entered the language in the Phanariot period. F. Dimitrescu, 'Consideraţii asupra limbii române de la 1848. Lexicul social-politic în "Pruncul român" ', *LiL*, 43.3–4, 1998 : 5–24, observes how neologisms (especially lexical ones) contributed to the 'Westernization' of Romania. P. Zugun,

'Între atitudine antineologică şi realitatea lingvistică', *ib.*, 43.1, 1998:36–39, shows that English and Fr. loanwords considered 'useless' in 1990 in fact remain in use to this day. M. Avram, 'Noutăţi reale şi noutăţi aparente în vocabularul românesc actual', *ib.*, 31–35, assesses the status of apparent lexical innovations in Romanian and mentions the creation of a database for lexical innovations at the Institute of Linguistics in Bucharest. Id., 'Un formant terminologic devenit expresiv în limbajul publicistic: -*zaur*', *LiR*, 46.1–3, 1997:21–27, discusses neologisms formed on -*zaur* (from *dinozaur*, etc.). V. Guţu Romalo, 'Nou şi vechi în limba română actuală', *LiL*, 42.3–4, 1997:5–9, also studies the theme of modern innovations.

L. Onu, 'Priorités dans l'étude des néologismes grec-latins de l'ancien roumain', *Atti* (Palermo), III, 659–60, identifies some new neologisms, and provides earlier dates for some already known. M. Pavel, 'Les mots latins en ancien français et en ancien roumain', *ib.*, 673–83, draws interesting parallels concerning the shared Latin-based lexicon of the early history of both languages. G. Brâncuş, 'Ro. *ochi*, Alb. *sy* in expresii comune', *LiR*, 46.1–3, 1997:43–46, explores parallels between Romanian and Albanian in expressions involving 'eyes'. E. Toma, 'Etimologia multipla. Un problema di geolinguistica e di sociolinguistica: il caso romeno', *Atti* (Palermo), I, 393–402, looks at words of 18th-c. and 19th-c. medical-biological terminology each of which may have come from more than one language and have entered Romanian at different times and in different places (Transylvania, Moldavia, Wallachia). I. Oancea and L. Vasiluţă, 'Il super-strato culturale latino. Modello lessicale di integrazione romanza', *ib.*, III, 641–52, pays particular attention to Romanian participation in the absorption of Lat. words. T. Hristea, 'Tipuri de calc în limba română, *LiL*, 42.3–4, 1997:10–29, deals particularly with Fr. calques in Romanian. A. Nicolescu 'Prestiti russi di origine latino-romanza in romeno', *Atti* (Palermo), III, 621–27, asserts that most loans from Russian, are actually Russian words of Latin-Romance origin, and part of 'international' vocabulary. Mioara Avram, *Anglicismele în limba română actuală*, Editura Academiei Române, 1997, 31 pp., is the text of a lecture to the Romanian Academy. S. Stati, 'Gli italianismi nella lingua romena', *Italiano* 1997:307–11. C.-M. Tănase, 'Concordances lexicales franco-roumaines', *Atti* (Palermo), III, 877–82, examines lexical parallels between non-standard varieties of Fr. and Romanian, such as *cœur/inimă* in the sense 'stomach'; a number of these seem, however, to be purely accidental.

R. Sufleţel Moroianu, 'Mots d'origine latine dans la toponymie roumaine', *Atti* (Palermo), III, 865–75, is based on fieldwork in Banat, Oltenia, and southern Crişana. A. Rezeanu, 'Categoria numărului în toponimia urbană', *LiL*, 44.1:12–18, deals with singular and plural forms in toponyms. C. Mujdei, 'Structuration diachronique et système sémantique dans les langues romanes. Termes météorologiques', *Atti* (Palermo), III, 589–95, incl. discussion of Romanian terms. D. Tomescu, 'La recherche onomastique dans la République Moldave', *Onoma*, 34, 1998–99, 7–12, reports on the activities and methodology of the flourishing onomastic research being conducted in Moldova. E. Munteanu, 'La Bible comme source d'innovation lexicale pour le vieux roumain écrit', *Balkan-Archiv*, 22–23, 1997–98:213–22, deals with Romanian lexicalizations of the Biblical concepts of 'conscience', 'one's neighbour' and 'providence', whose uses go well beyond the purely ecclesiastical lexicon. The relative presence of Slav forms in religious and non-religious texts and religious vocabulary is the subject of A. Hetzer, 'Das Heilige und das Profane. Zur Funktion des slavichen Wortschatzes in rumänischen Texten des 17. Jahrhunderts', *ib.*, 171–99. M. Purdela Sitaru, 'Calcuri lexicale de structură în vechea română literară', *ib.*, 285–94, deals with the Old Romanian formation of structural calques such as *atotmâncătoriu* 'omnivorous', *atotvăzătoriu* 'all-seeing'.

7. DIALECTS

Brief external overviews of 'Aromanian', 'Istro-Romanian', and 'Megleno-Romanian' appear in Price, *Encyclopedia*, 16, 299, 231. N. Saramandu, 'Despre structura dialectală a dacoromânei', *LiR*, 46.1–3, 1997:185–89. A. Ulivi, 'Observaţii în legătură cu structura fonetică a opoziţiilor în graiurile dacoromâne', *FD*, 16, 1997:131–48. A welcome addition to *Noul atlas lingvistic român* is Ionel Stan and Dorin Uriţescu, *Crişana* (vol. I, *Corpul omenesc*), Editura Academiei Române, 1996, xlvi pp. + 201 maps (with 60 additional synoptic maps showing the distribution of phonological and other structural phenomena and nine introductory maps showing physical, demographic, and historical information). This is accompanied by Id., *Date despre localităţi şi informatori*, Editura Academiei Române, 1996, xxii + 172 pp. M. Marin and I. Mărgărit, 'Glosar dialectal Muntenia, p. iv: R-Z', *FD*, 16, 1997:167–291. I. Mărgărit and V. Neagoe, 'Cercetări asupra graiurilor româneşti vorbite în nord-estul Bulgariei (regiunea Loveci)', *ib.*, 75–96. N. Saramandu, 'Cercetări dialectale la un grup necunoscut de vorbitori ai Românei: Băiaşii din nordul Croaţiei', *ib.*, 97–130.

Id., 'Die Aromunen in der Dobrudscha und ihre Mundart', *Grenzgänge*, 10, 1998:28–37, draws on recent dialect surveys of those Aromanians (and their descendants) who came to settle in Dobrogea between 1925 and 1938. S. provides a list of the localities now inhabited by the Aromanians and some indications about the origins of the different groups of settlers. In a brief discussion of aspects of phonology, S. shows that some developments are peculiar to the Dobrogea varieties and cannot, despite appearances, be ascribed to the influence of Romanian. A. Androutsopoulou, 'Genitives in Aromanian dialects', *LSRL 26*, 1–21, argues that in Aromanian (and in Romanian) the prepositional genitive of the *a(l)* type occurs only if N-to-D raising takes place, but does not occur when a noun raising to D pied-pipes a larger projection containing the noun. E. Scarlătoiu, 'Remarques sur le vocabulaire actuel de l'istroroumain', *Atti* (Palermo), III, 789–92. T. Ferro, 'Etimi attestati ed etimi postulati nel lessico latino dell'aromeno: osservazioni in margine al DDA di Papahagi', *ib.*, 231–42, updates, using newly available materials, a number of Papahagi's etymologies.

8. PRAGMATICS AND STYLISTICS

The language of religion is the subject of the text of a lecture delivered to the Romanian Academy: Gheorghe Chivu, *Civilizaţie şi cultură, Consideraţii asupra limbajului bisericesc actual*, Editura Academiei Române, 1997, 17 pp. (with another seven pages of illustrative texts), and M. M. Deleanu, 'Stilul religios al limbii române literare', *LiL*, 42.2, 1997:28–39. A. Stoichiţiu Ichim, 'Strategii persuasive în discursul publicitar', *ib.*, 51–56, and *ib.*, 3–4, 45–54, provides some useful information on the under-researched area of Romanian advertising language. Developments in two domains of post-revolutionary Romanian usage, the language of the press and the speech of young people, are the respective subjects of B. Techtmeier, 'Sprachlich-kommunikative Entwicklungen in rumänischen Pressetexten nach 1989', *Grenzgänge*, 10, 1998:6–15, and W. Dahmen and S. Hecht, 'Jugendsprache vor und nach 1989 in Rumänien', *ib.*, 16–27. A. Borbély, 'Stiluri de vorbire în comunitatea românească din Chitigaz (Ungaria)', *FD*, 16, 1997:23–32. M. Ciolac, 'Observaţii privind comunicarea orală în context formal a unor categorii de intelectuali din mediul rural', *ib.*, 33–46. A. Şerbănescu, 'Les interrogatives en roumain, conséquences conversationnelles de la structure syntaxique', *Atti* (Palermo), II, 759–64, examines the structural and conversational characteristics of Fr. and Romanian interrogatives, observing that Romanian is more sensitive than Fr. to shared and non-shared information between interlocutors, and stressing the greater role played in Romanian by pragmatic context in determining leftward movement of interrogative pronouns. C. Ilie, 'The ideological remapping of semantic roles in totalitarian discourse, or, how to paint white roses red', *Discourse and Society*, 9, 1998:57–80, is a fascinating examination of how strategies of demotion of (human) agents to instrument or patient roles, and promotion of instruments and patients to agent roles, were employed in Ceauşescu's speeches as ideologically based techniques of reshaping social reality. J. Kramer, 'Sprachliche Eindrücke bei der Lektüre rumänischer Zeitungen vom Jahreswechsel 1995/6', *Balkan-Archiv*, 22–23, 1997–98:93–102, incl. reproductions of some of the newspaper articles considered, concludes that the time has come to move beyond the mere collection of neologisms (which, however, need to be separated from merely ephemeral phenomena), to look more systematically at syntax and pragmatics. K. also calls for investigation of the characteristic styles of individual newspapers and integration of Romanian into a general Romance 'media linguistics'. S. Sora, 'Neue Entlehnungen aus dem Französischen in der rumänischen Pressesprache nach der Wende', *ib.*, 135–49, lists various facets of Fr. lexical influence on the language of the press since the Revolution.

L. Schippel, 'Gesprochenes Rumänisch', *Grenzgänge*, 10, 1998:55–85, is a very detailed, and richly referenced, critical overview of the history of research into spoken Romanian.

## LITERATURE

By MIRCEA ANGHELESCU, *Professor of Romanian Literature in the University of Bucharest*

### 1. WORKS OF REFERENCE AND OF GENERAL INTEREST

Much continues to be published on Romanian literature, but in 1999 the quality has again remained uneven. *Dicţionarul analitic de opere literare româneşti*, ed. Ion Pop, vol. 2, Cluj-Napoca, Casa cărţii de ştiinţă, 422 pp., the continuation of a work (see *YWMLS*, 60:510) produced by a team of professors from the University of Cluj, comprises 178 entries describing literary works (famous poems, novels, short stories, plays or whole books) whose title begins with the letters E to L. It is a highly reliable work, systematically researched and verified. Each entry ends with bibliographies of editions of the work in question and of the critical literature on it. However, more than in the first volume, it seems to us that the selection of titles could have been improved upon. No doubt these options reflect a hierarchy of values and preferences peculiar to the authors, but as justified as any other. Yet it seems strange that the volume comprises five titles of a second-rate modernist such as Adrian Maniu, while no place is found for the major work of a great 19th-c. author (*Echilibru între antiteze*, 1869, by Heliade Rădulescu), or for two of the most important comedies by Alecsandri, *Iorgu de la Sadagura*, 1844, and *Iaşii în carnaval*, 1845, which exerted a rich influence on Caragiale's plays. Or, if mention is made of books by young contemporaries whose significance is as yet unclear (Mariana Bejan, Alex. Vlad or Vasile Vlad, for instance), why are there no entries for important books by famous contemporary authors: *Exil pe o boabă de piper* by Mircea Dinescu, the first openly anticommunist volume of the well-known poet, *Euridice şi umbra*, the last and probably best volume published by the late poet Cezar Baltag, or *Enciclopedia armenilor* by the important prose writer Bedros Horasangian? An important work of a lifetime was unfortunately issued a few weeks after the author's death: Valeriu Cristea, *Dicţionarul personajelor lui Creangă*, Fundaţiei Culturale Române, 373 pp., dealing with the 151 characters of *Amintiri din copilărie* and the 189 of all Creangă's other texts.

The only dictionary of writers to have been published in a foreign language, in English, is Ion Bogdan Lefter, *Romanian Writers of the '80s and '90s. A Concise Dictionary*, Piteşti, Paralela 45, 336 pp., comprising the names of 193 writers, including some from Bessarabia (the Republic of Moldavia), who published their first volume in any year since 1979. As the author confesses in his short *Introduction*, the idea on which the selection was based was suggested by Dumas's novel: that of seeing what had happened to these writers 'vingt ans après'. They do certainly include writers whose place in contemporary Romanian literature is very important: Mircea Cărtărescu, Mircea Nedelciu, Matei Vişniec, Magda Cârneci, Liviu Ioan Stoiciu, and others. The disadvantage of this criterion is that it allows wide differences in age although the initial intention was to present a single generation of writers: the oldest author registered in the dictionary was born in 1935, as compared with an average somewhere in the 1950s or 1960s. Several regional dictionaries of authors have also been published. The most substantial and useful is Victoria Ibolya Bitte, Tiberiu Chiş, and Nicolae Sîrbu, *Dicţionarul scriitorilor din Caraş-Severin*, Reşiţa, Timpul, 1998, 304 pp., which has a postface by Gh. Jurma. The volume is part of a larger project, which is to include in thematic volumes all the county's important names in research and culture, and it is printed under the auspices of the County Library. The volume contains 270 names of writers born in the county or who have settled there, whether permanently or on a temporary basis. It is one of the rare dictionaries of this kind, comprising authors who write in Croatian, French, German, Hungarian, and Serbian. The work has a clear, logical organization (not, however, maintained with perfect consistency); the entries are substantial and contribute valuable information. More arbitrary is Mihai Barbu, *Dicţionarul scriitorilor din Vale*, Petroşani, Matinal/Cameleonul, 392 pp., which refers to the Valea Jiului, the mining area from which the 1990 miners' march on Bucharest started out. It comprises data on only 71 writers, some of whom have only the slightest connection with the area. That is why we find, among those included, Frenchman Jules Verne (author of the novel *The Castle in the Carpathians* of 1892, whose action takes place in and around these places), prose writer Geo Bogza, author of a famous volume of reports, *Oameni şi cărbuni*, 1947, etc. The data, however, do not always have consistency, and the information is not wholly accurate, even when it could have been found in works already published (e.g. in *Dicţionarul scriitorilor români*). Victor Petrescu and Serghie Paraschiva, *Dicţionar de literatură al judeţului Dîmboviţa. 1508–1998*, Tîrgovişte, Bibliotheca, 311 pp., is a reference-book of the same kind for Dîmboviţa county, compiling entries on 204 writers, 76 literary or cultural journals, and 14 literary societies or circles, with some minor errors and misinformation. Slightly different is the volume Iulian Negrilă, *Presa literară arădeană (1864–1944)*, Arad, Multimedia International Publishing House, 388 pp., which comprises a number of studies on the Arad press, especially the literary journals and main political newspapers of the area ( *Tribuna poporului*,

1896–1912, and *Românul*, 1911–1938) and finally a *Catalog alfabetic al presei româneşti arădene* (1869–1944), containing a brief description of the 129 periodicals published during this period. The volume mentions material by famous writers as published at Arad without also mentioning the fact that it was merely reproduced from other periodicals.

No less important than the dictionaries are the bibliographies. *Bibliografia relaţiilor literaturii române cu literaturile străine în periodice (1919–1944)*, vol. 2, Saeculum I.O., 318 pp., produced by a team of researchers at the Institute for Literary History and Theory of the Romanian Academy, and organized according to the principles of decimal classification, contains 7,390 entries concerning English, Canadian, American, and Australian literature, i.e. translations of texts belonging to the literature of these countries, or articles, book reviews, and studies by Romanian authors relating to these literatures. It is the second volume of a second series of bibliographies of the articles published in Romanian literary periodicals (the first series, on worked published between 1858–1918, was printed in 1980–85 at the Publishing House of the Romanian Academy). Another biblio-graphy, Mircea Handoca, *Bibliografia Mircea Eliade: III, Receptarea critică*, Jurnalul literar, 429 pp., is completed (see *YWMLS*, 60:511) by presenting the critical response to Mircea Eliade's work in books, periodicals (both in Romania and abroad), and letters he received. There are also autographs signed by him or for him, and addenda to the first two volumes, making a grand total of 3,634 bibliographical entries, from 5,993 to 9,627. The volume also comprises three indexes: of names, of titles of Eliade's works, and of titles of the periodicals quoted in the three volumes. Nae Antonescu, *Revista 'Jurnalul literar'*, Iaşi, Timpul, 245 pp., combines a complete index of the two series of G. Călinescu's *Jurnalul literar* (in 1939 as a weekly magazine, then in 1947–1948 five issues published at irregular intervals) with a literary-historical introduction to the magazine and a small selection of representative texts. Another ambitious work in this field, coordinated by Mariana Iova and Dan Matei at the Institute of Cultural Memory, is Robertina Stoica, *Bibliografia de referinţă a cărţii vechi (manuscrisă şi tipărită)*, Ministry of Culture, 457 pp. The volume contains 1,990 references, published in keeping with the international bibliographical norms UNIMARC, which are meant to facilitate national and international publishing exchange. The book has author and subject indexes. It is unfortunate that disproportionately extens-ive entries are sometimes dedicated to minor articles or information.

Especially noteworthy among collections of literary documents is Helmut Frisch, *Sursele germane ale creaţiei eminesciene*, 2 vols, Saeculum I.O., 415 + 415 pp., which gathers the notes and reading excerpts made by Mihai Eminescu during his Berlin and Vienna years from such political and cultural journals of the period as *Magazin für die Literatur des Auslandes, Blätter für Theater, Musik und Kunst, Literatur Centralblatt für Deutschland.* Made without any indication of their source, and indeed sometimes taken for original texts, they had never been systematically identified. This is the service now performed by Dr Frisch (University of Bochum). His volume provides the original German texts with Romanian translations: very reliable and extremely valuable material for anyone who wishes to study the great poet's sources of inspiration.

*Mircea Eliade şi corespondenţii săi,* ann. M. Handoca with indexes, vol. 2, Minerva, 363 pp., comprises E.'s letters from correspondents F to J (among them Arturo Farinelli, Olga Froebe-Kapteyn, Miron Grindea, Alain Guillermou, Vintilă Horia, Eugen Ionesco, C. G. Jung, Ernst Jünger) which constitute an impressive set of documents. For E.'s own missives we have from the same editor: Mircea Eliade, *Europa, Asia, America . . . Corespondenţă,* ed. Mircea Handoca, vol. 1, Humanitas, 486 pp., gathers letters addressed to foreign researchers such as Carlo Bronne, Ananda Coomaraswamy, and Arturo Farinelli, or Romanians such as Sergiu Al-George, Lucian Blaga, Al. Busuioceanu, Ioan P. Culianu, and Vintilă Horia. A selection from the letters sent to the German-Romanian writer Oscar Walter Cisek (1897–1966) by Romanian writers and artists such as I. Minulescu, I. Pillat, Th. Pallady and others is published in: *Oscar Walter Cisek în scrisori,* ed. Constandina Brezu and Ioana Cisek, Eminescu, 246 pp. Again, a documentary volume of a special kind is Ana Selejan, *Literatura în totalitarism, 1957–1958,* Cartea românească, 530 pp., recalling as it does, by extensive quotation from the press of the period, the oppressive atmosphere, the ideological and factual censureship of writers and magazines. Writers' diaries and journals are also documentary texts: Radu Petrescu (1927–1982), *Catalogul mişcărilor mele zilnice. Jurnal, 1946–1951, 1954–1956,* Humanitas, 456 pp.; Marin Sorescu (1936–1996), *Jurnal. Romanul călătoriilor,* ed. Mihaela Constantinescu and Virginia Sorescu, Fundaţiei 'Marin Sorescu', 327 pp.; Alexandru Baciu, *Din amintirile unui secretar de redacţie. Pagini de jurnal, 1979–1989,* Cartea românească, 292 pp. One of the leading Romanian exiles in France, a poet and a prose writer herself, publishes also a book of recollections: Sanda Stolojan, *Au balcon de l'exil roumain. Avec Cioran, Eugène Ionesco, Mircea Eliade, Vintilă Horia,* Paris, L'Harmattan, 352 pp.

Among new editions of important writers, mention must first be made of editions of authors little, incompletely, or poorly published before 1989, primarily for political reasons. Max Blecher, *Întîmplări în irealitatea imediată, Inimi cicatrizate, Vizuină luminată, Corp transparent,*

*Corespondenţă*, ed. Const. Popa and Nicolae Tone, pref. Radu
G. Teposu, Craiova, Aius — Bucharest, Vinea, 421 pp., brings
together B.'s complete works in a single volume, which opens with
two recently rediscovered novels: little noticed on first publication,
they are profoundly marked by his Jewishness and his experience of
incurable disease (bone tuberculosis, from which he died in 1938 at
29). Also, we can mention the volume V. Voiculescu, *Integrala operei
poetice*, ed. Roxana Sorescu, Anastasia, 782 p.; Aron Cotruş, *Opere*, ed.
and introd. Al. Ruja, 1, Minerva, 320 pp.; Gala Galaction, *Opere*, vol.
5, ed. and ann. T. Vârgolici, Minerva, 341 pp., consisting of the novel
*La răspîntie de veacuri*. The third volume in a series entitled *Cărti populare*
and dedicated to the oldest chap-books in Romanian literature
includes two ancient stories: *Călătoria lui Zosim la Blajini*, ed. Maria
Stanciu-Istrate, and *Bertoldo*, ed. Magdalena Georgescu, Minerva,
248 pp.

2. LITERARY MONOGRAPHS AND CRITICISM

The book market was dominated this year by publications marking
the 150th anniversary of the death of Mihai Eminescu. The most
interesting was probably the anthology *Cazul Eminescu. Polemici,
atitudini, reacţii din presa anului 1998*, ed. Cezar Paul Bădescu, Piteşti,
Paralela 45, 253 pp., which assembles a series of interviews (with
N. Manolescu, M. Cărtărescu, Al. Paleologu, E. Simion, G. Munteanu, and others) initiated by B. in the weekly *Dilema* about what
Eminescu and his poetry might mean for present-day readers. An
important essay about the structure of the poetic universe in
Eminescu's work was Dan Mănucă, *Pelerinaj spre fiinţă. Eseu asupra
imaginarului poetic eminescian*, Iaşi, Polirom, 283 pp., studying some of
the symbolic characters in his poetry: the Disciple, the Wise Man
('Magul'), Hyperion, The Old Man, and so on. Cristian Tiberiu
Popescu, *Eminescu. Antiteză*, Libra, 308 pp., is an inquiry into antithesis
in Eminescu's poetry and journalism. There was also a collection of
essays by various authors: *Studii eminescologice*, ed. Ioan Constantinescu
and Cornelia Viziteu, Cluj-Napoca, Clusium, 190 pp. Last but not
least, mention must be made of the pocket edition of his complete
works in three volumes (*Poezii*; *Proză, Teatru, Literatură populară*;
*Publicistică, Corespondenţă, Fragmentarium*) with an appendix of essential
notes, brought out on India paper under the auspices of the Academy:
Mihai Eminescu, *Opere*, ed. D. Vatamaniuc, Univers enciclopedic,
1001, 1262, 1263 pp.
  Points of broad interest emerge from a number of books focusing
on a particular writer or problem. Postmodernism is viewed in a
European perspective in Mihaela Constantinescu, *Forme în mişcare*.

*Postmodernismul,* Univers enciclopedic, 232 pp., with, however, some references to the Romanian phenomenon. For postmodernism in Romanian literature we have Mircea Cărtărescu, *Postmodernismul românesc,* Humanitas, 558 pp., the Ph.D. thesis of the controversial novelist and academic much debated in the literary journals, and Mihaela Ursa, *Optzecismul şi promisiunile postmodernismului,* Piteşti, Paralela 45, 140 pp., debating the influence of the French and American models on the Romanian prose of the eighties. Lelia Nicolescu, *Ion D. Sîrbu despre sine si lume,* Craiova, Scrisul românesc, 262 pp., studies the celebrated dissident writer who died in 1989. For Benjamin Fondane, the French writer of Romanian origin, there has appeared a compilation of his Judaic contributions, as a young essayist, to the Romanian journals of the Jewish community before and shortly after the First World War: B. Fundoianu, *Iudaism şi elenism,* ed. Leon Volovici and R. Zăstroiu, Hasefer, 200 pp. *Fundoianu/ Fondane et l'avant-garde,* ed. Petre Răileanu and M. Carassou, Bucharest, Fondation Culturelle — Paris, Méditerranée, 171 pp., is a French translation of a selection of Fondane's letters and articles dealing with the Romanian and general avangarde. *Cahiers Benjamin Fondane,* 3, ed. Monique Jutrin and Leon Volovici (in Paris and Jerusalem), carries articles by Alain Virmaux, Louis Soler, and C. Safirman, on Fondane and film, and by O. Salazar-Ferrer on the writer as viewed by British and American criticism. A well-known critic's sixtieth birthday is marked with N. Manolescu, *Arhivele Paradisului: un dialog cu Mircea Mihaes,* Timişoara, Brumar, 67 pp. And so on.

A number of monographs, generally in the academic mould but well informed, are to be recorded. The most interesting is probably a book originally written as a Ph. D. thesis by a young academic at Cluj University: Ioana Bot, *D. Caracostea, teoretician şi critic literar,* Minerva, 241 pp. Others include: N. Mecu, *Iacob Negruzzi sau vocaţia comunicării,* Minerva, 241 pp.; Emil Manu, *Ion Caraion,* Universal Dalsi, 245 pp.; Ion Bălu, *Viaţa lui Lucian Blaga,* vol. 4, Libra, 438 pp., the last volume of a comprehensive reconstitution of the poet's life; Liviu Papadima, *Caragiale, fireşte,* Fundaţiei Culturale Române, 195 pp., and *Literatură şi comunicare,* Iaşi, Polirom, 284 pp., on the author-reader relationship in Romanian romantic prose; Mihai Botez, *În oglinzi paralele,* Fundaţiei Culturale Române, 155 pp., a study of Ion Barbu's poetry by the late dissident and Romanian ambassador to the U.S.A.; Mircea Tomuş, *Romanul romanului românesc,* vol. 1, ('în căutarea personajului'), Gramar, 485 pp.; Ruxandra Tudoreanu, *Personajul dilematic la Augustin Buzura,* Chişinău, Arc, 175 pp.; and Alex. Burlacu, *Proza basarabeană: fascinaţia modelelor,* Chişinău, 156 pp., on the influence of interwar Romanian writers on contemporary Bessarabian prose. A special kind of monograph is Gheorghe Carageani, *Invito alla lettura di Sorescu,*

Naples, Istituto Universitario Orientale, 289 pp., where about 40 poems by M. Sorescu, in the originals with an Italian translation, are discussed from philological, stylistic, and typological perspectives. Ion Munteanu, *Istoricul societăților scriitorilor români, 1899–1949*, Eminescu, 114 pp., is a documentary reconstitution of Romanian writers' attempts to organize themselves before the Communist era. Closely connected to the literary problems of the period between the World Wars is the monograph Z. Ornea, *The Romanian Extreme Right. The Nineteen Thirties*, NY, Boulder/Columbia U. P., 437 pp., dealing with 'totalitarian ideologies and literature', the 'Jewish problem' and contemporary literature, the 'autochthonist' trend in literature, and so on.

Essays or articles discussing Romanian writers, trends or problems as topics of literary history are to be found in individual books as well as the *acta* of colloquia and conferences. Sorin Alexandrescu, *La modernité à l'est. Treize aperçus sur la littérature roumaine*, Pitești, Paralela 45, 347 pp., contains studies focusing on, *inter alia*, the literary society 'Junimea' and its political discourse, the Romanian novel between the wars, and the literary work of Mircea Eliade. Corin Braga, *10 studii de arhetipologie*, Cluj-Napoca, Dacia, 231 pp., has a final chapter on Romanian postmodernism. Gheorghe Gheorghiu, *Destine literare*, Chișinău, Tipografiă Centrală, 179 pp., collects essays on Bessarabian writers between the two wars, when the province was part of Romania. Ioana Pârvulescu, *Alfabetul doamnelor*, Crater, 164 pp., deals with female characters in 19th-c. Romanian literature. Eugen Simion, *Fragmente critice*, vol. 3, Fundația Scrisul românesc/Univers enciclopedic, 391 pp., collects essays on 19th- and 20th-c. Romanian authors. A volume entirely devoted to Romanian literature written in exile (papers presented at a symposium held in Freiburg, Germany, in autumn 1998) is *Rumänische Exilliteratur 1945–1989 und ihre Integration heute*, ed. Eva Behring (Aus der Südosteuropa-Forschung, 11), Munich, Südosteuropa-Gesellschaft, 180 pp., with studies and testimonies by Paul Miron, D. Țepeneag, Walter Althammer, Mircea Anghelescu, Paul Cornea, Anke Pfeiffer, Ilina Gregori, Fl. Manolescu. Dissident Romanian literature between 1947 and 1989 was also the focus of the colloquium held at the Sorbonne in 1991. The papers, published as *La Littérature contre la dictature, en et hors de Roumanie*, ed. Alvaro Roquetti, D. Costineanu et Alain Vuillemin, Paris-Bucarest, Hestia-Certel-CIRER, 232 pp., comprise articles by Monica Lovinescu, Alain Vuillemin, Marco Cugno, R. Stanceva, I. Barthouil-Ionesco, Ileana Mălâncioiu, Mircea Anghelescu, G. Carageani, and others. The role of the open field in Romanian prose, from Odobescu to Bănulescu, is explored in Ramona Bordei Boca, 'L'éspace steppique dans la matrice spatiale roumaine', pp. 271–82 of *L'Homme et la steppe*, ed. Maryvonne Perrot and D.Pitavy, Dijon, Éditions Universitaires de Dijon. The Romanian myth of the lamb 'Miorita' and Mircea Eliade's theory is the subject of Eva Behring, *Die Mythentheorie des Schriftstellers und Religionsforschers Mircea Eliade — ihre Innovationskraft im Hinblick auf den rumänischen Nationalmythos 'Miorita'*, pp. 11–21 of *Geschichtliche Mythen in den Literaturen und Kulturen Ostmittel- und Südosteuropas*, ed. Eva Behring, Ludwig Richter, and Wolfgang Schwarz, Stuttgart, Steiner. Romanian literature and culture are involved in the collective volume *Kulturdialog und akzeptierte Vierfalt? Rumänien und rumänische Sprachgebiete nach 1918*, ed. Horst Förster and Horst Fassel, Stuttgart, Jan Thorbecke, 288 pp. Contributions include H. Fassel, 'Kultursymbiose oder etnische Isolierung? Das Theater im Temesvar'; Eduard Schneider, 'Banater deutsche literarische Übersetzungen aus dem Rumänischen, Ungarischen und Serbischen'; St. Dumistrăcel, 'Das Bild des Deutschen bei den Rumänen'. Aspects of Romanian-Italian literary relations (for example 'Ritratti rumeni nella storiografia italiana' or 'La cultura rumena sotto i principi fanarioti') are discussed in some of the essays contained in Luisa Valmarin, *Percorsi rumeni. Fra storia e letteratura*, Rome, Bagatto Libri, 173 pp.

There are also a number of interesting volumes gathering day-to-day criticism by writers old and young: Florin Faifer, *Faldurile Mnemosynei*, Iaşi, Junimea, 151 pp.; Em. Galaicu-Păun, *Poezia de după poezie*, Chişinău, Cartier, 278 pp., a book by 'the literary agent of Bessarabian poetry in Romania' (as Al. Cistelecan dubs him in a foreword) dealing with contemporary Bessarabian writers; Marius Ghica, *Paşii lui Hermes*, Craiova, Scrisul românesc, 290 pp.; Gh. Grigurcu, *Peisaj critic*, vol. 3, Cartea românească, 397 pp.; Aurel Rău, *Expo 99. De la Olahus la Emil Cioran*, Cartea românească, 308 pp.; Cassian Maria Spiridon, *Atitudini literare*, Cartea românească, 270 pp.; Z. Ornea, *Portrete*, Minerva, 442 pp., a volume consisting entirely of reviews of classical texts in new scientific editions.

An anthology that gathers theoretical texts about the literature of the eighties ('optzeciştii') is Gheorghe Crăciun, *Competiţia continuă. Generaţia '80 în texte teoretice*, Piteşti, Paralela 45, 551 pp., ending with a chapter of selections from the opinions of older critics (N. Manolescu, Adrian Marino, C. Regman, Ion Pop, and others).

# XI.  RHETO-ROMANCE STUDIES

By INGMAR SÖHRMAN, *Gothenburg University*

## 1.  BIBLIOGRAPHICAL AND GENERAL

G. Holtus and J. Kramer, 'Neue Forschungen zum Bündnerromanischen, Dolomitenladinischen und Friaulischen (1993–1995)', *Mondo Ladino*, 21, 1997:515–53, provides an excellent overview of linguistic work done in the Rheto-Romance field during the period indicated. H. Goebl, 'Vergleichende ethnolinguistische Betrachtungen zu den romanischen Minderheiten im Alpenraum', pp. 17–33 of *\*Mehrsprachigkeit im Alpenraum*, ed. Iwar Werlen, Aarau, Sauerländer, 1998, draws interesting ethnolinguistic comparisons between the different Romance dialects spoken in the Alpine region. G. B. Pellegrini, *\**'Popoli e documenti linguistici antichi dell'Italia alpina', *Mes Alpes à moi*, 131–42.

MORPHOSYNTAX.  Laura Vanelli, *I dialetti italiani settentrionali nel panorama romanzo. Studi di sintassi e morfologia*, Rome, Bulzoni, 279 pp., deals also with Friulan and Ladin, especially in the chapter on personal pronouns and the Friulan plural formation.

ONOMASTICS AND LEXIS.  J. Kramer, *\**'Latinus — ladino, nome di lingua parlata in Italia e nelle Alpi', *Mes Alpes à moi*, 165–74. A. Zamboni, *\**'I dialetti alto-veneti', *ib.*, 185–200, deals with several lexical parallells between the dialects of the northern Veneto, on the one hand, and Friulan and Ladin, on the other.

## 2.  FRIULAN

HISTORY OF THE LANGUAGE.  G. Frau, 'I tedeschismi nel friulano', *Ce fastu?*, 75:7–36, documents over 600 words of Germanic origin in Friulan lexis, toponyms, and surnames, mainly dating from the medieval period to the present day. P. Merkù, 'Aggiornamenti al lessico del dialetto tergestino', *ib.*, 75:309–15, adds from medieval documents to knowledge of the lexis of Trieste's now extinct Friulan dialect. L. Spangher, '*Il parlare di Gorizia* e la grammatica constrastiva di Carlo Vignoli del 1917', *ib.*, 297–304, situates V.'s work in the context of the linguistic situation in the former county of Gorizia at the turn of the 20th c., when Friulan was the chief medium of communication.

LEXIS AND ORTHOGRAPHY.  Gianni and Luca Nazzi, *Dizionario Friulano. Italiano-Friulano/Friulano-Italiano*, Milan, Vallardi, 1997, 500 pp., is modern but fairly limited in range, covering only 12,000 lexemes, but the general dearth of Friulan dictionaries makes even this an important contribution. Olivier Joy et al. (ed.), *Vocabolari inlustrât furlan*, ed. Olivier Joy *et al.*, Recanati, European Language Institute, 1997, 80 pp., is an illustrated basic dictionary. Marian Brecelj and Gianni Nazzi, *Lingue d'Europa — Dizionario pratico Italiano–Friulano–Sloveno–Tedesco–Inglese*, 2nd ed., S. Pietro al Natisone, Comunità montana delle Valli del Natisone, 1997, 622 pp., although only a small dictionary, is interesting by virtue of its regional perspective in combining the languages spoken in north-east Italy and its addition of English.

MORPHOSYNTAX. The long-felt lack of a reasonably complete Friulan grammar has finally come to an end with the publication of Giorgio Faggin, *Grammatica friulana*, Udine, Ribis, 1997, 338 pp. A thorough description of the so-called analytical verbs in Friulan is provided by the published thesis Federico Vicario, *I verbi analitici in friulano*, Milan, FrancoAngeli, 1997, 330 pp.

## 3. LADIN

GENERAL. The continuation theory and the controversial ethnogenesis of Ladin, as well as how it should be defined within the Romance family, especially in regard to Italian, is discussed in: M. Alinei, 'Il problema dell'etnogenesi ladina alla luce della "teoria della continuità" ', *Mondo Ladino*, 22, 1998:459–87; and H. Goebl, 'Il problema dell'entità ladina delle Dolomiti in vent'anni di studi e ricerche: linguistica, storiografia, antropologia', *ib.*, 43–68.

LEXIS AND ORTHOGRAPHY. In a long and illuminating article, Paola Barbierato, 'Il lessico retoromanzo secondo alcuni studiosi', pp. 3–54 of *Dialetti, cultura e società*, ed. M. Alberto Mioni *et al.*, Padua, Centro di Studi di Dialettologia Italiana, 1998, analyses how some renowned linguists have described Rheto-Romance vocabulary, confronting its uniqueness and lexical influences. An important, thoroughly researched project has continued with *\*Etymologisches Wörterbuch des Dolomitenladinischen (EWD)*, vol. 8, ed. Johannes Kramer and Birgitt Arendt, Hamburg, Buske, 1998, 147 pp.

Amalia Anderlan-Obletter, *\*La vedla massaría da lauré alalergia, te tubla y te cësa*, San Martin de Tor, Istitut Cultural Ladin 'Micurá de Rü', 1997, 251 pp., devotes a serious monograph to typical agricultural and household vocabulary.

MORPHOSYNTAX, SOCIOLINGUISTICS, AND LANGUAGES IN CONTACT. Linguistic policy and politics are controversial: the complexities of the current situation in the South Tyrol are described in Reiner Arntz, 'Sprachenrecht und Sprachenpolitik im dreisprachigen Südtirol', pp. 10–20 of *Neue Forschungsarbeiten zur Kontaktlinguistik*, ed. Wolfgang W. Moelleken and Peter J. Weber, Bonn, Dümmler,

1997. Giovanni Mischì, *'Sprachpolitische Aspekte zum Ausbau der Ladinischen', pp. 41–52 of *Incontri di linguistica*, ed. Daniela Veronesi, Bolzano, 1998, advances some considerations on the modernization of Ladin. From the architect of unified Romansh, Heinrich Schmid, *Wegleitungen für den Aufbau einer gemeinsamen Schriftsprache der Dolomitenladiner*, San Martin de Tor, Istitut Cultural Ladin 'Micurá de Rü', 1998, 152 pp., draws up the principles for a standardized written Ladin. The same problem is dealt with in P. Videsott, 'Der Mythos der "schlechten" Plansprache. Zur Ausarbeitung einer dolomitenladinischen Schriftsprache', pp. 317–28 of *Sprache und Mythos. Mythos der Sprache*, ed. Beate Burscher-Bechter *et al.*, Bonn, Romanistischer Verlag, 1998, and in Id., 'Ladin Dolomitan. Die dolomitenladinischen Idiome auf den Weg zu einer gemeinsamen Schriftsprache', *Der Schlern*, 72, 1998:169–87. The present sociolinguistic situation, and code switching, in the Badia Valley are presented in Carla Willeit, *'Aspetti della situazione linguistica e della commutazione di codice nella lingua parlata della Valle Badia', pp. 53–61 of *Incontri di linguistica*, ed. Daniela Veronesi, Bolzano, 1998.

## 4. Swiss Romansh

GENERAL.    Ricarda Liver, *Rätoromanisch. Eine Einführung in das Bündnerromanische*, Tübingen, Narr, 180 pp., is an extensive introduction that ranges well beyond the work's basic scope and gives a good overview of the structure of Rheto-Romance.

MORPHOSYNTAX AND PHONOLOGY.    B. Coray, *Grammatik sursilvan*, Ruschein, proRo, 35 pp., is a concise and handy Sursilvan grammar which, however, does not replace that of A. Spescha (1989). Philipp Walter, *Ortografia e grammatica putera*, Champfèr, Walther, 44 pp., is a concise grammar and orthography of the Puter dialect, useful for basic grammatical needs. D. Andry, 'Verbs particulars', *ASR*, 112:11–41. Wolfgang Eichenhofer, *Historische Lautlehre des Bündnerromanischen*, Tübingen, Francke, 575 pp.

LEXIS.    G. Darms and G. Dazzi, *Langenscheidt vocabulari rumantsch*, 6th ed., 1998, 635 pp., is a revised dictionary of standardized Rumantsch Grischun. T. Ebeneter, *Die romanisch-deutsche Sprachlandschaft am unteren Hinterrhein*, Frankfurt, Kommissionsverlag Sauerländer Aarau, 1998. Manfred Gross and Daniel Telli, *Romansch-English/English-Romansch. Dictionary and Phrasebook*, NY, Hippocrene, x + 193 pp, although of modest size, is well compiled and is the first modern, and only available, Romansh–English/English–Romansh dictionary, which in itself is an achievement. F. Signorelli, *Vocabulari / Wörterbuch. Surmiran–tudestg, deutsch–surmiran*, Chur, Chasa editura per meds d'instrucziun, xxix + 547 pp., is the first substantial modern dictionary of the central Romansh dialect. Detlef Thierling, *Taschen-wörterbuch Rätoromanisch Deutsch–Sursilvan / Vocabulari tascabel tudestg–sursilvan*, Wetzikon, Thierling, 1998, is a small dictionary that serves its purpose. W. Eichenhofer, 'Bündnerromanisches im Etymologischen Wörterbuch des Dolomitenladinischen (EWD.), Bände 1–7', *ASR*, 112:43–67. T. Ebneter, 'Bündnerromanische Entsprechungen deutscher Adjektive und Adverbien', *ib.*, 83–101. G. Hoyer, 'Les désignations des batraciens et du lézard en romanche', *ib.*, 103–46.

PHILOLOGY, SOCIOLINGUISTICS, AND LANGUAGES IN CONTACT   I. Söhrman, 'Från nationellt till officiellt språk. Om rätoromanskans nya status och dess ställning i Schweiz', pp. 49–66 of *Migration och mångfald. Essäer om kulturkontakt och minoritetsfrågor tillägnade Harald Runblom*, ed. Dag Blanck *et al.*, Uppsala, Centrum för multietnisk forskning, deals with whether the promotion of Romansh to partly official language affects its use and status. The conclusion is that it probably does, but the process is slow and may be too late. R. Cathomas and W. Carigiet, 'Princips da la didactica da linguatg', *ASR*, 112:69–81.

# 3

# CELTIC LANGUAGES

## I. WELSH STUDIES

### LANGUAGE

By David Thorne, *Reader in Welsh Language and Literature,*
*University of Wales, Lampeter*

### 1. General

D. Thorne, 'Y Gymraeg ym "Mhrifysgol Ruhleben"', *NLWJ*,
31:75–105, discusses the provision made for the teaching of Welsh
language, Welsh history and Welsh literature to civilian internees at
Ruhleben Camp, Berlin during the period 1914–18. Id., 'Celtic
Studies at the "University of Ruhleben" 1914–18', Heinz, *Keltologie*
59–70, describes the teaching of Celtic Studies at Ruhleben Intern-
ment Camp and includes some background material on the recordings of the Celtic languages made at the camp under the supervision
of Professor Kuno Meyer; these materials are at present conserved in
the *Lautarchiv der Humboldt-Universität zu Berlin.* D. E. Evans, 'Linguistics
and Celtic Ethnogenesis', *ICCS*, 10:1–18, is a thoughtful overview of
the study of linguistics in relation to the tracing of Celtic ethnogenesis;
J. Renales and V. M. Renera-Arribas 'Celtiberian Studies and
Spanish Celtic historiography in the nineteenth century' *ib.*, 108–25,
sketch the diversity of views of the Celtic world propounded by 19th-
c. Spanish historiographers. The study focuses on ethnogenesis, on
relationships between Celts and other peoples in Iberia, and on Celtic
society, religion and language.

### 2. Phonetics and Phonology

J. F. Eska, *Tau Gallicum*, *SC*, 32:115–27, explores the wide variety of
orthographies used to represent the Gaulish segment known as 'tau
Gallicum' and attempts to disentangle the complex nature of the
evidence.

### 3. Grammar

B. Morris Jones, 'Necessity and obligation: Part 2, children's Welsh',
*SC*, 32:231–69, extends the author's earlier study of *dylai, i fod, gorfod*

and *rhaid* in adult speech. The present discussion, based on corpus data, examines the lexemes in children's speech with the primary aim of attempting to establish whether contrasts of meaning are responsible for the different frequencies of these lexemes in the data. Phyl Brake, *Cymraeg Graenus*, Llandysul, Gomer, 168 pp., is a useful description of contemporary Welsh usage which includes valuable revisionary units and exercises. G. Price, 'A possible Celtic influence in Romance syntax', *ICCS*, 10: 126–32, explores the possible common origin for the discontinuous negative construction in Old French and Welsh, possibly carried over from Gaulish into the Romance speech of Gaul during a period of Celtic/Romance bilingualism.

### 4. ETYMOLOGY AND LEXICOGRAPHY

Parts 51 and 52 of *GPC* (ed. G. A. Bevan) cover s — SEISAF, SEISAF — SILICAT respectively. Gwynedd O. Pierce and Tomos Roberts, *Ar Draws Gwlad 2*, Llanrwst, Carreg Gwalch, 113 pp., is a discussion of place names across Wales. S. Zimmer, 'Vieux-Gallois gener et autres problèmes à propos de la Minute "Surexit"', *EC*, 33: 143–58, reviews the problems associated with the interpretation of the *Surexit Memorandum*, preserved in the Book of St Chad. P. Schrijver, 'Henbane and early European narcotics', *ZCP*, 51: 17–45, is a discussion of the plant name henbane and also includes references to W. *bele, bela*. A. Breeze, *ib.*, 170–72 has a note on W. *lloring*.

### 5. SOCIOLINGUISTICS

*Miliwn o Gymru Cymraeg! Yr Iaith Gymraeg a Chyfrifiad 1891*, Gwenfair Parry a Mari A. Williams, Cardiff, Univ. of Wales Press xii + 476 pp., presents a detailed picture of the socio-economic pattern of ability in Welsh and English and the pattern of language change in Wales at the end of the 19th c. The study concentrates on twenty communities and provides a detailed analysis of the linguistic evidence given in the enumerators' returns for the 1891 census when Welsh speakers were counted for the first time. Particular attention is given to migration streams thus shedding light on the penetration of English into traditional Welsh speaking areas. Edwards, *Ebwy*, has two contributions relevant to this section: S. Rh. Williams ' "Pentref mwyaf Cymreig Sir Fynwy": Rhymni a chyfrifiad iaith 1891' (137–61), explores the linguistic returns relating to Rhymni in Monmouthshire in the 1891 census and sees the signs of the decline of the Welsh language reflected in those returns; Mary Wiliam, 'Tafodiaith eithriadol o rymus' (162–76), is a popular description of the Gwentian sub-dialect of Tafarnau Bach in Monmouthshire. J. Aitchison and

H. Carter 'The Welsh language today', pp. 91–109 of *Wales Today*, ed. David Dunkerley and Andrew Thompson, Cardiff, Univ. of Wales Press, 326 pp., is a succinct analysis of the contemporary condition of the Welsh language. R. Merfyn Jones, *Cymru 2000*, Cardiff, Univ. of Wales Press, 224 pp., has a section 'Dau dafod y ddraig: ieithoedd Cymru' (176–192), which is a useful historical account of Welsh and English in Wales. Jenkins, *Gwnewch Bopeth*, analyses the status of Welsh in areas such as the rural and industrial economy, education, politics, the law, culture and religion in 19th-c. Wales. Attitudes towards the language are explored and also the attempts made to withstand its marginalization. R. O. Jones, 'The Welsh language: does it have a future?', *ICCS*, 10:425–56, discusses the changes, improvements and innovations in the sociology of Welsh which generally give hope and optimism for the future health of the language.

## EARLY AND MEDIEVAL LITERATURE

By JANE CARTWRIGHT, *Department of Welsh, University of Wales, Lampeter*

J. T. Koch, 'The place of *Y Gododdin* in the history of Scotland', *ICCS*, 10:199–210, draws upon his historical and linguistic study of the Book of Aneirin to discuss six interpretations of the relationship between the *Gododdin* and the socio-political history of Northern Britain in the 6th and 7th centuries. G. R. Isaac, 'Readings in the history and transmission of the *Gododdin*', *CMCS*, 37:55–78, criticizes Koch's theory of the *Gododdin*'s textual history and proposes that there was a greater mixing of lines of transmission with an increased number of copies and recensions being proposed for the 12th c. and 13th c. and earlier. Id., '*Trawsganu Kynan Garwyn mab Brochuael*: a tenth-century political poem', *ZCP*, 51:173–85, argues that *Trawsganu Kynan Garwyn* is not a 6th c. composition and provides a new edition and English translation of the poem. A. Breeze, '*Armes Prydein*, Hywel Dda, and the reign of Edmund of Wessex', *EC*, 33:209–22, maintains that *Armes Prydein* presents a political alternative to the policies of Hywel Dda and suggests 940 as the date of composition. R. M. Jones, 'Ffurf y cywydd a'r englyn', *YB*, 25:16–40, provides a useful summary of the history and development of Welsh metrics from the *Cynfeirdd* to the 14th c., focusing in detail on the *cywydd* and the *englyn*.

A. E. Lea, 'The nightingale in medieval Latin lyrics and the *Gorhoffedd* by Gwalchmai ap Meilyr', *ZCP*, 51:160–69, notes that there is a marked similarity between the presentation of the nightingale in medieval Latin love poetry and Gwalchmai ap Meilyr's *Gorhoffedd*. She suggests that Latin poetry may have influenced the work of the early *Gogynfeirdd*, rather than poetry from Provence. N. A. Jones, 'The Mynydd Carn "prophecy": a reassessment', *CMCS*, 38:73–92, provides a thorough review of previous interpretations of an *awdl gywydd* relating the Mynydd Carn prophecy which may have been erroneously attributed to Meilyr Brydydd. She suggests several fresh interpretations including the thesis that it contains a combination of *post eventum* prophecy and elegy. Id., 'Canu gofyn a diolch Beirdd y Tywysogion', *Dwned*, 5:23–33, discusses the few extant examples of poems thanking royal patrons for gifts. The majority are concise *englynion* offering thanks for gifts which do not appear to have been formally requested by the poets. Id., 'Y canu mawl i deulu brenhinol Powys yn y ddeuddegfed ganrif: arolwg', *LlC*, 22:25–41, surveys formal praise poetry composed for the royal house of Powys in the 12th c., most of which was produced during the reign of Madog ap Maredudd. Medieval Powys is also the subject of A. D. Carr, 'Powys: y cefndir hanesyddol yng nghyfnod Beirdd y Tywysogion',

*LlC*, 22 : 12–24, whose historical analysis of the period is relevant to an appreciation of the work of *Beirdd y Tywysogion*. N. A. Jones, 'Hela'r wyach', notes that references to a bird called 'gwyach' in the poetry of Cynddelw Brydydd Mawr refer to a vicious bird of prey and not the gentle grebe. A. Breeze, 'The battle of Brunanburgh and Welsh tradition', *Neophilogus*, 83 : 479–82, interprets references to 'kattybrydawt' in medieval poetry as the battle of Brunanburgh. Id., 'Sidney's *Apology For Poetry* and the Welsh bards', *NQ*: 244 : 198–99, refers to the tradition that Ysgolan burnt Welsh books. T. Hallam, 'Croesholi tystiolaeth y llyfrau cyfraith: pencerdd a bardd teulu', *LlC*, 22 : 1–11, discusses references to the *pencerdd* and *bardd teulu* in the different versions of the Welsh law texts.

Several editions of poetry associated with *Beirdd yr Uchelwyr* have appeared this year, including a further two volumes in the important UWCASWC series, *Cyfres Beirdd yr Uchelwyr. Gwaith Casnodyn*, ed. R. Iestyn Daniel, Aberystwyth, UWCASWC, xvii + 193 pp., provides new editions of twelve poems attributed to Casnodyn, a poet from Cilfái near Swansea who flourished in the first half of the 14th c. and wrote in the style of the *Gogynfeirdd*. Modern Welsh translations of the poems are provided. *Gwaith Siôn ap Hywel ap Llywelyn Fychan*, ed. A. Cynfael Lake, Aberystwyth, UWCASWC, xvii + 214 pp., edits the work of Siôn ap Hywel, an amateur poet from Holywell in Flintshire who flourished in the first half of the 16th c. His work includes formal praise poems, love poetry and religious verse, as well as *englynion* and couplets which form part of a bardic contention with Tudur Aled and other well-known poets. Both volumes include an introductory section on the poets' careers and brief notes. D. Johnston and A. Parry Owen, 'Tri darn o farddoniaeth yn Llawysgrif Peniarth 10', *Dwned*, 5 : 35–45, edit and discuss three sections of poetry found in Aberystwyth, National Library of Wales, MS Peniarth 10, including a particularly fine example of an early *cywydd serch* which they cautiously suggest could be the love poem to Lleucu Llwyd that Llywelyn Goch ap Meurig Hen refers to in his *awdl gyffes*. D. J. Bowen, 'Tri chywydd gan Hywel ap Dafydd ab Ieuan ap Rhys', *Dwned*, 5 : 71–88, edits three praise poems by Hywel Dafi (*fl.* 1450–80): two to Gwilym ap Hywel of Argoed and one to Morgan ap Rhys, the vicar of Merthyr Cynog. All three poems celebrate the erection of medieval halls and provide important historical evidence relating to medieval architecture in Wales. R. W. Evans, 'Englynion brud', *LlC*, 22 : 131–35, categorizes vaticinatory *englynion* and provides editions of a selection of poems from each category. C. A. Charnell-White, 'Alis, Catrin a Gwen: tair prydyddes o'r unfed ganrif ar bymtheg. Tair chwaer?', *Dwned*, 5 : 89–104, provides important new research on three 16th-c. female poets. Although Alis, Catrin and Gwen are listed as sisters in

Peter C. Bartrum, *Welsh Genealogies AD 1400–1500* (1983), Charnell-White demonstrates that ascertaining authorship of these rare *englynion* by Welsh women is rather more complex than it first appears. Editions of the *englynion* are appended.

H. M. Edwards, 'Murnio marwnadau: golwg ar y ffug-farwnad yng nghyfnod y cywydd', *Dwned*, 5:47–70, provides a thorough investigation into the composition of the pseudo-elegy, focusing primarily on 14th-c. *cywyddau marwnad* which can be interpreted as employing the artifice of a fellow poet's death and memorial for the purposes of satire. G. A. Williams, 'Cywydd Iolo Goch i Rosier Mortimer: cefndir a chyd-destun', *LlC*, 22:57–79, discusses the historical and political background to Iolo Goch's *cywydd* to Rhosier Mortimer, the fourth earl of the March of Wales (1374–98), suggesting that the poem was composed in the summer of 1394, that it was inspired by political events in England and Ireland, and that Iolo Goch may have received encouragement and information from Phylip ap Morgan, Rhosier Mortimer's steward, at Denbigh. G. Williams, 'Diwedd a dechrau: Margam a'r Mawnseliaid', *YB*, 25:41–60, briefly discusses poetry composed for the abbots of Margam. M. P. Bryant-Quinn, ' "Y Mab o Emlyn": golwg ar waith Syr Phylib, bardd-offeiriad', *Ceredigion*, 13.3:18–42, sheds light on the poetic career of the 15th-c. priest Phylib of Emlyn. Id., 'Marchog Mai', *LlC*, 22:128–30, points out that the month of May is frequently personified as a knight in medieval art, thus explaining why the two are associated in the poetic imagery of Dafydd ap Gwilym. B. O. Huws, 'Posau', *LlC*, 22:130–31, corrects the entry on riddles in *Y Cydymaith i Lenyddiaeth Cymru*, ed. Meic Stephens (1997), noting that the *cywydd* 'Y Niwl', which appears in *Cywyddau Dafydd ap Gwilym a'i Gyfoeswyr*, ed. Ifor Williams and Thomas Roberts (1935), is an example of *dyfalu* rather than a riddle.

A number of publications on religious themes have appeared this year. *Ystorya Gwlat Ieuan Vendigeit (Llythyr y Preutur Siôn) Cyfieithiadau Cymraeg Canol o Epistola Presbyteri Johannis*, ed. Gwilym Lloyd Edwards, Cardiff, Univ. of Wales Press, cxxvii + 97 pp., provides a critical edition of two Middle Welsh translations of *Epistola Presbyteri Johannis*, a 12th-c. letter which was assumed to have been written by Prester John and addressed primarily to Manuel Comnenus, Emperor of Constantinople. The volume includes an informative introduction to this much-neglected text, which comprises a discussion of the historical background, sources, dating, authorship and previous interpretations of the text, as well as an analysis of the relationship between the Welsh and Latin versions of the letter and a brief survey of references to Prester John in the poetry of the *Cywyddwyr*. Vocabulary and notes are provided. Jane Cartwright, *Y Forwyn Fair, Santesau a Lleianod: Agweddau ar Wyryfdod a Diweirdeb yng Nghymru'r*

*Oesoedd Canol*, Cardiff, Univ. of Wales Press, xi + 219 pp. + 20 pls, is an exploration of feminine sanctity in medieval Wales which highlights the importance of virginity and chastity in a wide-range of literary sources. The first chapter traces the cult of the Virgin Mary in medieval Wales and focuses on images of the virgin birth and Mary's virginity in the work of the *Cywyddwyr, Buched Meir*, and *Llyma Vabinogi Iessu Grist*. This is followed by a study of the female saints of Wales which synthesizes sources on native saints and Middle Welsh translations of the lives of internationally popular saints. The final section discusses the history of the Welsh nunneries and analyses attitudes towards the female religious in medieval Wales via a study of courtly love poetry to nuns and *cywyddau* to devout wives, as well as historical documentation. Throughout links are made between literary and visual representations of feminine sanctity and its related iconography. O. Davies, 'Der poet als Priester soteriologie des Gedichts im mittelalterlichen Wales', in *Fest. Haas*, 353–66, surveys the cultural and social situation of the poet as quasi-priest, and specifically the understanding of poetry as gift of the Holy Spirit, in medieval Wales. Id., 'Rhetoric of the gift: inspiration, pneumatology and poetic craft in medieval Wales', in *The Medieval Mystical Tradition England, Ireland, Wales*, ed. Marion Glasscoe, Cambridge, Brewer, 268 pp. (21–31), again discusses the development of the concept of the Holy Spirit as author of poetic inspiration focusing primarily on the work of Meilyr ap Gwalchmai, Cynddelw Brydydd Mawr and Siôn Cent. In the same volume R. I. Daniel 'Medieval mysticism: an example from Wales' (33–46), highlights the importance of *Ymborth yr Enaid* in the context of European medieval mysticism and spiritual literature. T. O'Loughlin, 'Rhygyfarch's *Vita Dauidis*: an *Apparatus biblicus*', *SC*, 32:179–88, elucidates references to scriptural images, notions and phrases in Rhygyfarch's *Vita Dauidis*. The apparatus is based on J. W. James's edition of the text (1967). *Celtic Spirituality*, trans. Oliver Davies with the collaboration of Thomas O'Loughlin, NY, Paulist Press, xxii + 550 pp., includes translations of a number of Middle Welsh and Latin hagiographical texts and religious poems.

Rhiannon Ifans, *Gwerthfawrogi'r Chwedlau*, Aberystwyth, CAA, 256 pp., provides a simple introduction to storytelling and legends in medieval Wales, suitable for use in secondary schools. The volume guides students through a selection of fragments of Middle Welsh tales and offers a list of vocabulary, notes on the language and style of the texts and a brief discussion of the main themes. I. Hughes, '*Math fab Mathonwy* a Gwydion fab Dôn, *Dwned*, 5:9–21, criticizes W. J. Gruffydd's hypothesis that *Math fab Mathonwy* is structured according to 'The King and his prophesized death' tale archetype and proposes that we view Gwydion fab Dôn, rather than Math fab Mathonwy, as the protagonist. A. Breeze, 'Politics and the *Four Branches of the Mabinogi*', *Memoria y Civilización* 2 : 243–60, reads *Pedeir Keinc y Mabinogi* as a reflection of 'the experience of government and politics we would expect a Welsh princess of the twelfth century to have', assuming from the outset that the reader agrees with his hypothesis that Gwenllïan ferch Gruffudd ap Cynan 'wrote' PKM. M. J. Aldhouse-Green, 'Pagan Celtic religion and early Celtic myth: connections or coincidence?', *ICCS*, 10 : 82–90, searches for resonances of pre-Christian beliefs in medieval Welsh and Irish literature focusing on PKM and *Culhwch ac Olwen*. J. F. Nagy, 'Esyllt observed' *ib.*, 222–32, interprets the name Esyllt as 'she who is gazed at' and emphasizes the importance of the visual register in Isolde's/Esyllt's story. Referring to *Culhwch ac Olwen* and the triad *Tri Gwrdueichyat Enys Prydein*, he suggests a connection between the theme of the Arthurian pig-hunt and the theme of impeded wooing. P. Russell, 'What did medieval Welsh scribes do? The scribe of the Dingestow Court Manuscript', *CMCS*, 37 : 79–96, sheds further light on medieval scribal activity via a detailed analysis of the orthographical features of the version of *Brut Dingestow* found in Aberystwyth, National Library of Wales, MS 5266B. He suggests that this text and a fragment of *Trioedd Ynys Prydein* found in Peniarth 16, both of which were copied by the same scribe, had similar exemplars. C. Sterckx, 'De Cassivellaunos à Caswallon', *SC*, 32 : 95–114, discusses references to Caesar's invasion of Britain in Geoffrey of Monmouth's *Historia Regum Britanniae* and associates Cassibellanus, son of Heli, with Caswallon ap Beli who is mentioned in PKM. He suggests further parallels between the narrative structure of *Breuddwyd Macsen* and the legendary material associated with Caswallon. H. Fulton, 'Cyd-destun gwleidyddol *Breuddwyt Ronabwy*', *LlC*, 22 : 42–56, suggests that *Breudwyt Ronabwy* is a political, rather than a literary, satire and demonstrates that an awareness of political changes in Powys at the turn of the 12th c. may considerably enhance our understanding of the text. K. L. Maund, 'Dynastic segmentation and Gwynedd *c.* 950–*c.* 1000', *SC*, 32 : 155–67, refers to a number of prose sources including *Annales Cambriae*, *Brut y Tywysogyon* and *Historia Grufud vab Kenan*, in his discussion of Welsh political life in the period *c.* 950–*c.* 1000. D. Wyatt, 'Gruffudd ap Cynan and the Hiberno-Norse world', *WHR*, 19 : 595–617, is also of interest to those studying *Historia Grufud vab Kenan*.

C. Lloyd-Morgan, 'Medieval manuscripts at the National Library of Wales', pp. 1–12 of *Sources, Exemplars and Copy-texts: Influence and Transmission*, ed. William Marx, Lampeter, *Trivium*, xvi + 176 pp., is a useful guide to the manuscript collection at the National Library of Wales, Aberystwyth. A brief history of the medieval acquisitions is given and the library's collecting policy is explained.

## LITERATURE SINCE 1500

By A. CYNFAEL LAKE, *Lecturer in Welsh, University of Wales Swansea*

D. Ifans, 'Dwy lawysgrif farddoniaeth o eglwys gadeiriol Llanelwy', *NLWJ*, 31:1–10, describes the contents of two 16th-c. MS collections of poems. Nia Powel, 'Robert ap Huw: A wanton minstrel of Anglesey', *Welsh Music History*, 3:5–29, outlines Robert's career and shows how closely-related the musicians and the poets were in late-medieval Wales. D. Klausner, 'Statud Gruffudd ap Cynan', *ib.*, 282–98, offers a new edition and translation of the statute based on BL Add MS 19711. Geraint Bowen, *Welsh Recusant Writings*, Cardiff, Univ. of Wales Press, 90 pp., surveys the religious and scholarly works undertaken by Gruffudd Robert, Siôn Dafydd Rhys and Morus Clynnog. G. W. Owen, 'Morgan Llwyd a'r Crynwyr', *Y Traethodydd*, 154:49–53, refers briefly to Llwyd's links with the Quaker movement. B. F. Roberts, 'Dialedd Taffy', *YB*, 25:61–78, explains how Edward Lhuyd induced Thomas Richards to compose his *Hoglandiae Descriptio* in response to Edward Holdsworth's *Muscipula sive Cambro-muo-maxia*.

A. R. Jones, examines some of the characteristics of Lewis Morris's letters in two articles, '"Ymrwbio yn ein gilydd mal ceffylau": llythyrau Lewis Morris', *LIC*, 22:80–92, and '"Talking upon paper": Lewis Morris's letters', *SC*, 32:211–30. Id., '"Vermin [who] creep into all corners through the least crevices": Lewis Morris and the Methodists', *THSC*, 5:24–35, compares English and Welsh versions of a sermon composed by Morris to rebuke the Methodists. Id., 'Apocryffa Lewis Morris', *NLWJ*, 31:41–44, considers two poems erroneously attributed to Morris. Dafydd Wyn Wiliam, *Cofiant Richard Morris (1702/3–79)*, Llangefni, p.p., 174 pp., deals in detail with the life and works of the second of the famous Morris brothers from Anglesey. Dafydd Glyn Jones, *Un o Wŷr y Medra: Bywyd a Gwaith William Williams Llandygái (1738–1817)*, Denbigh, Gee, 355 pp., is a comprehensive study of the life and family connections of Williams, and an invaluable introduction to his works, both poetry and prose, creative and descriptive. An adaptation of the first chapter can be seen in 'William Williams and "William Trotter"', *CHST*, 60:77–98. Id. also discusses one of Williams's works in '"Y Misoedd", gan William Williams, Llandygái', *LIC*, 22:93–107. Id., 'Bardd y Nant', *Canu Gwerin*, 22:11–42, sees the poetry of Twm o'r Nant falling into three clearly-defined categories. Huw Walters, 'Rhagor am ganu i'r ychen', *ib.*, 22:52–9, brings to light a reference by Dewi Haran to the custom of singing to the oxen. D. M. Lewis, 'Ai mawl yw hwyl alawon?', *Y Traethodydd*, 154:156–76, considers themes and imagery in 18th and 19th-c. hymns. An English rendering of Ann Griffiths's hymns and letters are made available in Kathryn Jenkins et al., *Hymns and Letters*, London, Stainer & Bell, 62 pp. Gwynn ap Gwilym ed., *Gogoneddus Arglwydd, Henffych Well*, Llandysul, Cytûn, xliv + 325 pp., is a balanced anthology of religious verse.

Robert Rhys, 'Llenyddiaeth Gymraeg y bedwaredd ganrif ar bymtheg', Jenkins, *Gwnewch bopeth*, 251–74, discusses poetry and prose in his enlightened introduction to Welsh literature in the nineteenth century. Dewi M. Lloyd, *Talhaiarn*, Cardiff, Univ. of Wales Press, 256 pp., sheds light on Talhaiarn's unusual career, and his desire to win recognition as a poet of the people. I. Jenkins and J. Jenkins, 'Tri chymwynaswr llên a chân', Edwards, *Ebwy*, 108–25, discuss Ossian Gwent and Dewi Carno who settled in the north-east but whose works were inspired by their upbringing in west Wales. D. Islwyn, 'Aneurin Fardd 1822–1904', *ib.*, 85–107, deals with Aneurin's career as poetic teacher, competitor and adjudicator. Huw Walters, 'David Rees Griffiths ('Amanwy'), 1882–1953', *CarA*, 35:89–103, depicts Amanwy who 'represented the cultured Welsh miner at his best'. Rhianydd Morgan, *Ioan Pedr (John Peter) 1833–1877*, Caernarfon, Pantycelyn, 115 pp., considers in detail Ioan's literary and linguistic pursuits, and also his scientific interests and social concerns. B. F. Roberts, 'Welsh scholarship at Merthyr Tydfil', *MerH*, 10:51–62, describes the conflict between fact and fiction, and sees at Merthyr 'a microcosm of the way in which Welsh scholarship faced its crisis in the mid-nineteenth century and [...] overcame it'. Ll. P. Roberts, 'Yr athro yn ei elfen', *Taliesin*, 105–06:117–44, amplifies on the mission of John Morris-Jones as poetic teacher and adjudicator.

Branwen Jarvis's collection of published papers, *Llinynnau: Detholiad o Ysgrifau Beirniadol*, Bodedern, Gwasg Taf, 238 pp., deals primarily with various literary figures of the 18th, 19th, and 20th centuries. Emyr Edwards, *Beirdd y Mynydd Bach*, Llandybïe, Barddas, 148 pp., in the series 'Bro a Bywyd', introduces four Cardiganshire poets, namely, T. Hughes Jones, J. M. Edwards, Prosser Rhys and B. T. Hopkins. Jon Meirion Jones, *Teulu'r Cilie*, Llandysul, Barddas, 294 pp., traces the remarkable history of Jeremiah Jones and his siblings, and quotes liberally from their compositions. Joseph P. Clancy, *Other Words*, Cardiff, Univ. of Wales Press, viii + 147 pp., comments on modern Welsh poetry and his own work as translator. M. Wynn Thomas, *Corresponding Cultures: The Two Literatures of Wales*, Cardiff, Univ. of Wales Press, 295 pp., is a pioneering cross-cultural study analysing the similarities and the actual links between the two cultures, especially in the 20th c. R. Gerallt Jones, *T. H. Parry-Williams*, Cardiff, Univ. of Wales Press, 277 pp., abounds with penetrating comments on Parry-Williams's poems and essays, and on the influence of a catalogue of events at critical junctures in his life. Alan Llwyd, 'Cerddi rhyfel eisteddfodol Cynan', *Barddas*, 251:4–12, 252:4–11, underlines the influence of World War I on the younger generation, and demonstrates how Cynan's early cynicism gradually gives room to hope and faith. Id. analyses Gwenallt's ode 'Y Sant' and considers its significance in *Barddas*, 253:4–10, 254:4–8, 255:4–8. R. G. Gruffydd, ' "Haf bach Mihangel 1941" gan Saunders Lewis', *YB*, 25:79–85, discusses the background and significance of the poem in question. Dewi Stephen Jones, *Bobi Jones: Y Canu Canol*, Caernarfon, Pantycelyn, 82 pp., comments on three volumes of verse by Bobi Jones published between 1965 and 1971. Bobi Jones continues his series 'Beirniadaeth ar feirniadaeth' in *Barddas* with references to Robert ap Gwilym Ddu, 250:12–15, Waldo, *ib.*, 252:45–47, and T. H. Parry-Williams, *ib.*, 254:12–14. B. G. Owens, 'Tato sir Benfro a'r bardd', *ib.*, 252:42–44, and 'Yr "ambell donc" olaf', *ib.*, 255:24–26, quotes some hitherto unknown verses in a light vein by Waldo. Alan Llwyd, 'Gilbert Ruddock ac R. Gerallt Jones', *ib.*, 250:30–34, draws attention to important themes in the poetry of Ruddock and Jones, as does Ll. Roberts, 'Nid llestri gweigion', *Barn*, 433:46–49 in a brief discussion on the poetry of Ifor ap Glyn.

*Rhyddid y Nofel*, ed. Gerwyn Williams, Cardiff, Univ. of Wales Press, xii + 322 pp., brings together comments on 15 contemporary novels and articles on the 20th-c. novel. U. Wiliam, 'Llenyddiaeth hanesyddol', *Taliesin*, 104:71–80, is a general survey of historical novels. J. G. Jones, 'Agweddau ar gydastudio hanes a llenyddiaeth yng Nghymru', *YB*, 25:144–67, contemplates the use by historians of literature as source material. N. M. Williams, 'Nofelau am gylch Cadwgan gan ddau aelod', *YB*, 25:86–104, compares the way two novels, by Pennar Davies and Rhydwen Williams, portray the Cadwgan Circle. Geraint H. Jenkins, *'Doc Tom' Thomas Richards*, Cardiff, Univ. of Wales Press, 224 pp., although primarily concerned with Doc Tom's historical writings, emphasises the merits of his two volumes of recollections of his childhood days in Cardiganshire, and also describes his dealings with that enigmatic bookworm, Bob Owen, Croesor. In her introduction to Caradog Prichard's *One Moonlit Night: Un Nos Ola Leuad*, London, Penguin, xix + 336 pp., Menna Baines sets the work and author in their context, and analyses the novel's framework and main themes. A. Price, 'Dim ond doe tan yfory, a heddiw o hynny 'mlaen', *Y Traethodydd*, 154:101–13, considers the rewriting of the myths of the past, with particular reference to Robin Llywelyn's *Seren Wen ar Gefndir Gwyn*, but also looks at works by Christoph Ransmayr, Salmon Rushdie and Italo Calvino. L. M. Roberts, 'Y normal a'r annormal yn ffuglen Mihangel Morgan',

*Taliesin*, 107:32–46, describes the juxtaposition of contrasting elements in Morgan's prose. Grahame Davies, *Sefyll yn y Bwlch*, Cardiff, Univ. of Wales Press, 201 pp., looks at the works and ideas of four antimodernist figures, T. S. Eliot, Saunders Lewis, Simone Weil and R. S. Thomas. He comments on Lewis's paradoxical modernist style, and suggests that his nationalism represented one aspect of his antimodernism. J. Owen, 'Llwyfan hanes', *CHCHMC*, 23:13–32, deals with two plays, by Islwyn Ffowc Elis and Cynan, which are based on the life of Howel Harris. W. R. Lewis, 'Areithiau hirion dramâu John Gwilym Jones (1): Y Brodyr', *LIC*, 22:108–24, identifies the problems faced by the author in his prose play, *Y Brodyr*, in his search for a befitting language. G. M. Roberts, 'Methu torri dros y tresi? Y ferch a theatr gyfoes Gymraeg', *Taliesin*, 105–06:58–75, compares the portrayal of women in plays by male and female dramatists.

Hywel Teifi Edwards, '*Y Gymraeg yn yr eisteddfod*', Jenkins, *Gwnewch bopeth*, 275–96, shows how the English became the dominant medium in the 19th-c. *eisteddfodau* in spite of the efforts of the pro-Welsh faction. Id. outlines the contrasting fortunes of one the protagonists in *Llew Llwyfo: Arwr Gwlad a'i Arwrgerdd*, Llanrwst, Llys yr Eisteddfod, 23 pp. Id., 'The Merthyr Tydfil National Eisteddfod, 1881', *MerH*, 10:81–100, explains the background of the 1881 event and comments on the promoters' intentions. Id., 'Eisteddfod Genedlaethol Caerffili, 7–12 Awst 1950', Edwards, *Ebwy*, 190–218, looks in particular at the implications of the Welsh Rule and the festival's literary encounters. F. Olding's survey, 'Traddodiad Cymraeg y Fenni a'r cylch', *ib.*, 60–84, covers the Abergavenny *eisteddfodau* and the response to the Treachery of the Blue Books.

H. M. Davies, 'Morgan John Rhys, *Y Cylchgrawn Cynmraeg* a'r Cymry uniaith', *Efrydiau Athronyddol*, 62:40–54, examines the 'first Welsh-language political journal' and its attempts to promote the ideals of the Enlightenment. P. H. Jones, 'Argraffu a chyhoeddi yn yr iaith Gymraeg 1800–1914', Jenkins, *Gwnewch bopeth*, 297–325, examines the forces which account for the decline of a most remarkable era in Welsh printing. Id., 'Thomas Gee: y dyn busnes', *Y Traethodydd*, 154:13–20, examines the entreprenerial qualities of Gee. Huw Walters, 'Y Gymraeg a'r wasg gylchgronol', Jenkins, *Gwnewch bopeth*, 327–52, surveys 19th-c. Welsh journals, and comments on the prominence of denominational publications, and efforts to publish material of a more popular nature. Id., 'Y "Prophwyd" a'r "Udgorn": dau gylchgrawn Mormonaidd', *Y Traethodydd*, 154:177–84, follows the course of two Mormon journals. Id., '*Llais Llyfrau* Pryse, Llanidloes', *Y Casglwr*, 65:11, draws attention to the only known issue of the *Cambrian Book Register* which listed current Welsh publications.

The one number of a journal which sought to aid the monoglot Welsh speaker to master English is also described by Walters in 'Lamp y Cymro', *ib.*, 67 : 3. Aled Jones, 'Yr iaith Gymraeg a newyddiaduraeth', Jenkins, *Gwnewch bopeth*, 353–74, analyses the language used by 19th-c. journalists and their attitudes towards the Welsh language. Bleddyn Owen Huws, *Hanes Cyhoeddi* Cerddi Eryri (*1927*) *Carneddog*, Llandybïe, Barddas, 24 pp., shows how Carneddog endeavored to publish the anthology which won him a prize at the Pwllheli National Eisteddfod of 1925.

## II.  BRETON AND CORNISH STUDIES
### POSTPONED

## III.  IRISH STUDIES

### EARLY IRISH
#### POSTPONED

### MODERN IRISH
#### POSTPONED

## IV.  SCOTTISH GAELIC STUDIES
### POSTPONED

# 4

# GERMANIC LANGUAGES

## I. GERMAN STUDIES

### LANGUAGE

By CHARLES V. J. RUSS, *Reader in the Department of Language and Linguistic Science, University of York*

### 1. GENERAL

SURVEYS, COLLECTIONS, BIBLIOGRAPHIES. A fascinating insight is given into the attitudes of speakers towards German in earlier times by W. J. Jones, *Images of Language. German Attitudes to European Languages from 1500 to 1800* (Studies in the History of Language Sciences, 89), Amsterdam–Philadelphia, Benjamins, x + 297 pp. which contains the following: ' "König Deutsch zu Abrahams Zeiten": perceptions of the place of German in the family of languages from Aventinus to Zedler' (1–24); ' "Mit rainem teutschen lispeln" ': attitudes to German among earlier German purists' (35–57); ' "Die Söhne wollen nicht der eignen Mutter schonen": lexis and metaphor in the formation of German puristic discourse' (59–83); ' "Mit den Feinden Teutsch reden": Abraham Kolbinger and the purity of German military language' (85–110); ' "Französisch kauder-walsch macht unsre sprache falsch": diagnoses of Gallomania' (111–69); and ' "Spuma linguarum": on the status of English in German-speaking countries before 1700' (171–213), which shows how speakers of other European languages regarded English with contempt as being a mixed language. How times have changed! These studies are all characterized by extremely detailed documentation and the discussion of the issues shows measured scholarly judgement. A general survey of modern German is presented by F. Debus, *Entwicklungen der deutschen Sprache in der Gegenwart — und in der Zukunft?* (Akademie der Wissenschaften und der Literatur — Mainz. Abhandlungen der Geistes- und sozialwissenschaftlichen Klasse, 2), Stuttgart, Steiner, 56 pp. A number of different topics which relate to the status and use of German are treated in '*Werkzeug Sprache.' Sprachpolitik, Sprachfähigkeit, Sprache und Macht*, ed. Union der deutschen Akademien der Wissenschaften: Sächsische Akademie der Wissenschaften zu Leipzig, Hildesheim, Olms, 198 pp., which contains the following contributions: U. Ammon, 'Deutsch oder Englisch als Wissenschaftssprache der Deutschen. Fakten, Probleme, Perspektiven' (13–33); P.H. Nelde, 'Perspektiven einer europäischen Sprachenpolitik' (35–56); M. Bier-wisch, 'Das Organ des Denkens und die Grenzen des Ausdrückbaren' (57–101); A. Neubert and M. Zeh-Glöckler, 'Neue Erfahrungen in der Lehre und im Gebrauch der englischen Sprache in Sachsen' (103–16); H.-M. Gauger, 'Gewalt in der Sprache?' (117–40); U. Fix, 'Was hindert die Bürger am freien Sprechen? Die Ordnung des Diskurses in der DDR' (141–63); E. Gülich, ' "Experten" und "Laien": der Umgang mit Kompetenzunterschieden am Beispiel medizinischer Kommunikation' (165–96). The topics treated are very disparate but stimulating in their approach. The most radical suggestion coming from these essays concerns the use of German in higher education. U. Ammon, 'Zur Frage der Teutonismen und zur nationalen Symmetrie in der wissenschaftlichen Behandlung der deutschen Gegenwartssprache', *Fest. Moser*, 385–94, concerns Ger-man as a pluricentric language, and the same volume contains several contributions on German in Austria: M. Clyne, 'Australische Sprach-gegenwart und österreichischen Sprachgeschichte. Gemeinsamkeiten und Unterschiede' (395–408); J. Ebner, 'Österreichischer Standard und westösterreichischer Wortschatz' (409–26); G. Retti, '*malta — Malter* — MALTER. Ein Beitrag zur Austriazismenforschung' (459–66). Also noted: G. Steinegger, *\*Sprachgebrauch und Sprachbeurtei-lung in Österreich und Südtirol. Ergebnisse einer Umfrage* (Schriften zur deutschen Sprache in Österreich, 26), Frankfurt, Lang, 1998, 395 pp.

GERMAN IN OTHER COUNTRIES. O. Putzer, 'Die deutsche Spache in Südtirol', *Fest. Moser*, 449–56. P. Gilles, *Dialektausgleich im Lëtzebuer-geschen. Zur phonetisch-phonologischen Fokussierung einer Nationalsprache* (Phonai 44), Tübingen, Niemeyer, viii + 279 pp., uses a sample of 23 young Luxembourg ladies to investigate the development of an interdialectal koine. He has kept all the linguistic variables constant except dialect provenance. He gathered material using a question-naire, and by recording conversations between informants from the same or from different areas, and the results of his survey indicated that one finds a spread of features that could be termed Central Luxembourgish, but that no koine of new or compromise forms is to be found. It also appears that standard German has played no role in the development of these dialects. The book is well-researched and repays careful study. *Essays on Politics and Society in Luxembourg*, ed. G. Newton, Lewiston–Queenston–Lampeter, Mellen, xv + 275 pp., is a spendidly produced volume which has a number of contributions highlighting different aspect of language use in Luxembourg: J. Kar-theiser, ' "Ech léiere Lëtzebuergesch, well ech . . .": learning Luxem-bourgish as a means of social and professional integration' (63–75); F. Fehlen, 'Die Sprachen in Luxemburg und die Sprachen der

Luxemburger' (77–90); J. Cajot, 'Die luxemburgische Sprachland-schaft zwischen Belgien und Deutschland. Ein lexikalischer Vergleich von vier Arealen' (91–112); S. Hughes, 'Germanic dialect spoken in Lorraine, with reference to the use of dialect by cross-border workers in Germany and Luxembourg' (113–34); G. Newton, 'The spelling of Luxembourgish. Systems and developments since 1824' (135–61); C. V. J. Russ, 'Word formation in Luxembourgish. Nominal and adjectival suffixes' (163–79); and H. Wickens, '*Hausnamen* in Waldbil-lig — an echo of traditional rural society in Luxembourg' (181–96). F. Krier, 'Idiomverwendung in der luxemburgischen Abgeordeten-kammer', *ZDL*, 66:280–95. German-speaking minorities in other countries feature in: P. Rosenberg, 'Deutsche Minderheiten in Lateinamerika', *Fest. Weydt*, 261–91; A. Burkhardt, ' "Mein geliebtes Deutsche" und seine "Schrecken" ', *Muttersprache*, 108, 1998:110–33; S. Gadeanu, *\*Sprache auf der Suche. Zur Identitätsfrage des Deutschen in Rumänien am Beispiel der Temeswarer Stadtsprache* (Theorie und For-schung, 574, Sprachwissenschaften, 8), Regensburg, Roderer, 1998, 436 pp.; *\*Sprachgebrauch — Sprachanpassung. Eine Untersuchung zum heutigen Gebrauch der deutschen Sprache in Westrumänien und zur sprachlichen Anpassung der Donauschwaben*, ed. H. Gehl, Tübingen, Institut für donauschwäbische Geschichte und Landeskunde, 1998, 214 pp.; N. Bradean-Ebinger, *\*Deutsch in Kontakt als Minderheits- und als Mehrheitssprache in Mitteleuropa. Eine soziolinguistische Untersuchung zum Sprachgebrauch bei den Ungarndeutschen, Donauschwaben und Kärtner Slo-wenen*, Vienna, Praesens, 1997, 118 pp.; I. Reiffenstein, *\*Sprachpflege und Sprachgeschichte. Rede Ingo Reiffensteins anlässlich der Ehrung mit dem Konrad Duden-Preis der Stadt Mannheim* (Duden Beiträge zu Fragen der Rechtschreibung, der Grammatik und des Stils, 54), Mannheim, Duden, 1998, 31 pp.; *\*Sprache — Sprachwissenschaft — Öffentlichkeit*, ed. G. Stickel, (Institut für deutsche Sprache, Jahrbuch 1998), Berlin, de Gruyter, viii + 348 pp.

INTERDISCIPLINES. Feminist approaches include M. Jonas, 'Sollen in Zukunft beim Bundesheer, wenn dereinst Damen zum Bundesheer dürfen, Angelobungen der "Jungmänner und Jungfrauen" vorge-nommen werden? Zwanzig Jahre feministische Sprachkritik. Der österreichische Weg', *Fest. Moser*, 285–96.

The acquisition of German as a foreign language appears in J. Dittmann and C. Schmidt, 'Verbales Arbeitsgedächtnis, Lernen und Fremdsprachenerwerb. Ein Forschungsüberblick', *DSp*, 27:304–36; D. Rösler, 'Die Form zum Sprechen bringen? Universi-täre Grammatikarbeit mit Übungsbüchern für Fortgeschrittene', *Fest. Weydt*, 251–60; Z. Wawrzyniak, 'Zu einigen Prinzipien des Fremdsprachenlernens', *Fest. Szulc*, 353–64; A. Debski, 'Wechselwir-kungen. Noch einmal zur interlingualen Interferenz in offenen und geschlossenen Subsystemen', *ib.*, 365–90; S. Katsikas, 'Zur Interferenz im Bereich der Wortbetonung. Vorschläge für eine Typologie von Interferenzerscheinungen im Fremdsprachenerwerb', *ib.*, 391–410; W. Abraham, 'DaF-Typologie. Die logische Struktur typologischer DaF-Grammatiken', *PapL*, 59, 1998:181–222. Translation features in G. Stieg, 'Der Übersetzungsfehler als kulturhistorische Fehlleistung. Eine "Causerie" zwischen Pfarrer-Symphonie und Löwenwurst', *Fest. Moser*, 275–84. Politics is the subject of S. Jäger, 'Sprache — Wissen — Macht. Victor Klemperers Beitrag zur Analyse von Sprache und Ideologie des Faschismus', *Muttersprache*, 109:1–18; R. Geier, 'Protest ohne Inhalt — zur Wahlwerbung der DVU', *ib.*, 19–23. Language and computing are discussed in T. Niehr, 'Halbautomatische Erforschung des öffentlichen Sprachgebrauchs oder vom Nutzen computerlesbarer Textkorpora', *ZGL*, 27:205–14; J. Runkehl et al., 'Sprache und Kommunikation im Internet', *Muttersprache*, 108, 1998:97–109. Also noted: E. W. B. Hess-Lüttich, 'Fachsprachen als Register', *Fest. Weydt*, 133–51; R. Hessky, 'Phraseologie in der Diskussion. Kritische Würdigung des Ansatzes von Czaba Földes', *ZDP*, 118:420–30; I. Behr and H. Quintin, 'Doppelt gemoppelt hält besser', *Fest. Faucher*, 85–100; J. Petit, 'Struktur und Chaos in natürlichen Sprachen. Konsequenzen für den Erwerb', *ib.*, 101–13; G. Lipold, ' "... denn deine Sprache verrät dich." Zur Autorenbestimmung in der forensischen Linguistik', *Fest. Szulc*, 241–58; Z. Berdychowska, 'Fachsprachliche Kollokationen und terminologisierte Ausdrücke in der Sprache der Rechtswissenschaft', *ib.*, 259–73; P. Braun, Annäherung an die Fussballsprache', *Muttersprache*, 108, 1998:134–45. Sociolinguistics features in: G. Siebert-Ott, 'Frühe Mehrsprachigkeit — Problem und Chance', *Fest. Vater*, 457–71; *\*Jugendliche und 'ihre' Sprache. Sprachregister, Jugendkulturen und Wertesysteme. Empirische Studien*, ed. P. Schlobinski et al., Opladen, Westdeutscher Vlg, 1998, 236 pp.; J. K. Androutsopoulos, *\*Deutsche Jugendsprache. Untersuchungen zu ihren Strukturen und Funktionen* (VarioLingua, 6), Frankfurt, Lang, 1998, 684 pp.

C. Bergmann, *Die Sprache der Stasi. Ein Beitrag zur Sprachkritik.* Göttingen, Vandenhoeck & Ruprecht, 133 pp., is an unusual work, based firmly on linguistic data, which examines how through the use of different meanings and abbreviations the *Stasi* created a secret language that was only brought to general notice after 1989. Among those in the upper echelons of the service a certain amount of unformity of usage prevailed, but the *Inoffizielle Mitarbeiter* showed a wide variety of usage in their language. The language was characterized by the use of euphemisms, nominalization, and long sentences.

B. sees his volume as a contribution to the culture of remembering, rather than suppressing.

GENERAL LINGUISTICS, PRAGMATICS AND TEXTLINGUISTICS. A. Gardt, *Geschichte der Sprachwissenschaft in Deutschland. Vom Mittelalter bis ins 20. Jahrhundert*, Berlin, de Gruyter, ix + 410 pp., examines the history of linguistics in German. H. Otto, 'Die Sprachursprungsfrage im 18. Jahrhundert: Schlaglichter auf die Konstituierung einer Leitlinie philologischer Wissenschaft', *Spillmann Vol.*, 171–91, analyses 18th-c. debate on the origins of language. Other items on language in general include: L. Seppänen, 'Über den modistischen Sprachbegriff', *Fest. Stellmacher*, 237–41; P. Plöger, 'Der Metawissenschaft auf der Spur — zu den Typologien sprachwissenschaftlicher Stile bei Jäger, Grewendorf und Schnelle', *LBer*, 178:230–36; K. Kucharczik, 'Organisch — "um den beliebten aber vildeutigen ausdruck zu gebrauchen". Zur Organismusmetaphorik in der Sprachwissenschaft des 19. Jahrhunderts', *Sprachwissenschaft*, 22, 1998:85–111; W. P. Lehmann, 'The structural approach of Jacob Grimm and his contemporaries', *JIES*, 27:1–13. The linguistic theories of Hans Glinz are disentangled in: H. Eto, 'Die Neuartigkeit der Grammatik von Hans Glinz. Historische Interpretation auf dem Hintergrund von zwei Haupttypen in der traditionellen Grammatikbeschreibung des Abendlandes. Mit der besonderen Berücksichtigung der Glinzschen "Fünf-Wortarten-Lehre"', *BGS*, 9:21–58; H. Glinz, 'Germanistik und Sprachtheorie in Aachen 1969–1975. Versuch einer Bilanz. Abschlussvorlesung gehalten am 16. Februar 1979', *ib.*, 59–88.

Text linguistic studies include H. Ortner, 'An den Grenzen der Sprachgeschichte: geschichtslose Textnormen. Normen "hinter" den Buchrezensionen', *Fest. Moser*, 297–324; H. Wellmann, 'Der offene Brief und seine Anfänge. Über Textart und Mediengeschichte', *ib.*, 361–84; R. Mayer, 'Textoptimierung aus mikroökonomischer Sicht', *LBer*, 177:3–51; S. Wichter, 'Texte, Diskurse, Querschnitte unter Berücksichtigung vertikaler Strukturen', *Fest. Stellmacher*, 253–62; H.-W. Eroms, ' "Auch ich war in Arkadien." Der Konnektor *auch* in Textzusammenhängen', *Sprachwissenschaft*, 22, 1998:185–216; M. Schecker, 'Textorganisationsprozesse beim kommunikativen Schreiben (anhand der Verbalisierung von 'Skript-Wissen' in alltäglichen Situationen)', *Fest. Faucher*, 115–36; S. Grosse, 'Sprechen und Schreiben', *Fest. Szulc*, 205–22; M. Pérennec, 'Von Zeitdeiktika zu Text- und Diskurskonnektoren: Überlegungen zur sprachlichen Temporalität', *ib.*, 299–314; H. Fuhrmann, 'Inhalts- und Beziehungsaspekt in fiktionaler Kommunikation C.F. Meyers Novelle *Der heilige*', *Spillmann Vol.*, 77–97; B. Hufeisen, 'Schnittstellen: interdisziplinäre

Ansätze fachsprächlicher Textwissenschaften. Diskussion verschiedener Ansätze und Anwendung auf einen authentischen Text im Hinblick auf curriculare Konsequenzen', *ib.*, 99–127; K.-H. Best, 'Zur Interaktion der Wortarten in Texten', *PapL*, 58, 1998:83–96; M. Schwarz, 'Anaphern und ihre diversen Antezedenten: Koreferenz und Konsorten', *Fest. Vater*, 445–55; U. Stephany, 'Endophorische Anapher und Textkohärenz in deutschen und griechischen Kindergeschichten', *ib.*, 473–94. Discourse studies include R. Wolf, 'Soziale Positionierung im Gespräch', *DSp*, 27:69–94; J. Meier, 'Prosodische Merkmale von Diskursrelationen', *LBer*, 177:65–86; B. Ahrenholz, 'Korrekturen in One-to-One Tutorien', *Fest. Weydt*, 9–30; W. Buddecke, 'Herrschaftsfreie Kommunikation? Der Fall Botho Strauss und das Elend unserer Streitkultur', *Spillmann Vol.*, 9–37; J. Förster, ' "Die Zeit der anderen Auslegung." Zur Renaissance philologischer Wissenschaftstradition im Diskurs der germanistischen Literaurwissenschaft', *ib.*, 55–76; J. Kopperschmidt, 'Vom Diana-Mythos zum Mythos Diana. Nachbemerkung zur Rhetorik eines bemerkenswerten Trauerdiskurses', *Muttersprache*, 108, 1998:167–73; N. Sauer, *\*Werbung — wenn Worte wirken. Ein Konzept der Perlokution, entwickelt an Werbeanzeigen* (Internationale Hochschulschriften, 274), Münster, Waxmann, 1998, 326 pp.

## 2. HISTORY OF LANGUAGE

The magnificent history of the German language by P. von Polenz is concluded with the third and final volume: *Deutsche Sprachgeschichte vom Spätmittelalter bis zur Gegenwart.* III. *19. und 20. Jahrhundert*, Berlin, de Gruyter, xiii + 757 pp. A second edition of the first volume of *\*Sprachgeschichte. Ein Handbuch zur Geschichte der deutschen Sprache und ihrer Erforschung*, ed. W. Besch et al., 1998, 1014 pp., has appeared (see *YWMLS* 46:632 on the first edition). *\*Sprachgeschichte als Kulturgeschichte*, ed. A. Gardt et al. (SLG, 54), viii + 418 pp. M. Selting. 'Kontinuität und Wandel der Verbstellung von ahd. *wanta* bis gwd. *weil*. Zur historischen und vergleichenden Syntax der *weil*-Konstruktionen', *ZGL* 27:167–204, examines the historical development of word order.

The study of Germanic continues to have its devoted followers: A. Bammesberger, 'The Germanic preterite-present *\*ann/unn-*', *NOWELE*, 34:15–21; T. K. Nilsson, 'Notationes Germanicae X-XIV', *ib.*, 35:49–65; K. G. Goblirsch, 'The correlation of voice in Germanic', *ib.*, 115–40; K.-H. Mottausch, 'Das Präteritum der 4. und 5. starken Verbklassen im Germanischen', *ib.*, 36:45–58; L. Benarczuk, 'Germanic and North Indo-European', *Fest. Szulc*,

37–50; J. Rusek, 'Über einige germanische Lehnwörter im Slawischen', *ib.*, 51–62; D. F. H. Boutkan, 'On the form of North European substratum words in Germanic', *HSp*, 111, 1998:102–33; K.-H. Mottausch, '"Gehen" und "stehen" im Germanischen', *ib.*, 134–62. Gothic studies feature in W. Binnig, \**Gotisches Elementarbuch*, 5th edn (based on the work by H. Hempel), Berlin, de Gruyter, 169 pp.; K. Dietz, 'Die gotischen Lehnwörter mit *au* im Altprovenzalischen und die Rekonstruktion des gotischen Lautsystems', *Sprachwissenschaft*, 25:127–56; C. van Bree, 'The strange simplicity of Gothic', *NOWELE*, 35:67–75; S. K. Sen, '\*Kw in Gothic', *ib.*, 36:67–68. Old Saxon is examined in J. Erickson, 'Some observations on word order in Old Saxon', *Fest. Vater*, 95–105.

OHG is the subject of J. Riecke, 'Pseudopartizipien im Althochdeutschen. Ein Beitrag zur Geschichte eines Wortbildungstyps', *Sprachwissenschaft*, 25:157–93; G. Neumann, 'Althochdeutsch *bergita* "eine Gebäcksorte" ', *HSp*, 111, 1998:163–68; \**Etymologisches Wörterbuch des Althochdeutschen*, ed. A. L. Lloyd et al., vol. 2, *bî — ezzo*, Göttingen, Vandenhoeck & Ruprecht, 1998, xv pp. + 1194 cols.

Medieval German is the subject of A. Mihm, 'Funktionen der Schriftlichkeit in der städtischen Gesetzgebung des Mittelalters', *ZGL*, 27:13–37; E. Meinecke, ' "Die ergiebigkeit des feldes ist noch von solcher art, dass es nie versagt." Überlegungen zur Erforschung des Mittelhochdeutschen', *ZDL*, 66: 147–83; S. Kaleta, 'Entlehnungen aus dem Polnischen in deutschsprachigen Urkunden der Krakauer Kanzlei des 14.–16. Jahrhunderts', *Fest. Szulc*, 63–86; F. Patocka, 'Zur Verbstellung in Nebensätzen mittelhochdeutscher Prosatexte', *ib.*, 131–44; K. Waligóra, 'Zur Graphematik einer Zunftsatzung der Krakauer Bäcker in Orginal und Abschrift', *ib.*, 145–58.

The linguistic history of Low German is illuminated by M. Durrell, 'Zum Ausgleich der Ablautalternanzen im Niederdeutschen', *Fest. Stellmacher*, 39–47; H. Kröger, 'Niederdeutsche Autographe in Walsroder Gebetbüchern von 1649', *ib.*, 51–56; M. Lehmberg, 'Zur Göttinger Schreibsprache bei Beginn des Sprachenwechsels', *ib.*, 57–65; A. Mihm, 'Gesprochenes Hochdeutsch in der norddeutschen Stadt. Zur Modalität des Sprachwechsels im 16. und 17. Jahrhundert', *ib.*, 67–88; C. Fischer, \**Die Stadtsprache von Soest im 16. und 17. Jahrhundert. Variationslinguistische Untersuchungen zum Schreibsprachenwechsel vom Niederdeutschen zum Hochdeutschen* (NdS, 43), 1998, x + 259 pp.; P. Hoheisel, \**Die Göttinger Stadtschreiber bis zur Reformation. Einfluss, Sozialprofil, Amtsaufgaben* (Studien zur Geschichte der Stadt Göttingen, 21), Göttingen, Vandenhoeck & Ruprecht, 21), x + 287 pp., and

M. Lehmberg, \**Der Amtssprachenwechsel im 16. Jahrhundert. Zur Sprachge-schichte der Stadt Göttingen* (Name und Wort, 15), Neumünster, Wach-holtz, xvii + 462 pp. J. Schwitalla, *Flugschrift* (Grundlagen der Medienkommunikation, 7), Tübingen, Niemeyer, vi + 106 pp., concentrates on the early NHG period. S. outlines in very succint and readable form the production, distribution, and reception of the *Flugschrift* as well as its linguistic form. He then gives a history of the medium and its use during the Reformation. Also noted: I. Warncke, \**Wege zur Kultursprache. Die Polyfunktionalisierung des Deutschen im juridischen Diskurs (1200–1800)* (SLG, 52), xv + 467 pp. An up-to-date survey of the role of Martin Luther in the history of German is ably presented in W. Besch, *Die Rolle Luthers in der deutschen Sprachgeschichte* (Schriften der Philosophisch-historischen Klasse der Heidelberger Akademie der Wissenschaften, 12), Heidelberg, Winter, 70 pp., who sees L.'s role as crucial in the development of a standard language and in breaking the shackles of linguistic regionalism. B.'s thesis is further supported by the immense popularity of the Luther Bible from the 17th to the 19th century. Other items on Martin Luther include: R. Grosse, 'Phonetische, phonologische und graphematische Strukturen bei der sprachräumlichen Umlagerung. Beobachtungen zur Entwicklung des Nordobersächsischen und zu Luthers Schriftlautung', *Fest. Szulc*, 159–69; H. Endermann, 'Zu einigen Texten Martin Luthers über Schule und Bildung', *RBS*, 7 : 151–64; S. Seyfarth, 'Zu lexikalisch-syntaktischen Veränderungen der frühneuhochdeutschen Biblespra-che in Martin Luthers Bibelübertragungen (1522–2545)', *ib.*, 269–88; and W. Besch, 'Martin Luther und "die Veldegge, die Eschilbache, die Reimare"', *Fest. Schupp*, 311–14. Early NHG in its wider sphere is considered by E. Koller, 'Bibeldeutsch zwischen Mentel und Luther. Neutestamentliche Schriftstellen in Predigten Geilers von Kaisersberg', *Fest. Moser*, 51–81. E. Müller-Bollhagen, 'Substantiv-komposita und kompositionsähnliche Strukturen in Schreiben der Kanzlei Kaiser Maximilians I', *ib.*, 83–100; H. Günther, 'Entwick-lungen in der deutschen Orthographie 1545–1797. Eine Etüde', *ib.*, 171–82; C. Lecointre, 'Ex (Germaniae) oriente lux', *Fest. Faucher*, 71–81, deals with the grammarian Clajus; E. Neuss, 'Satz oder "Nebensatz"? Beobachtungen zur Syntax komplexer Konstruktionen in einem Traktat von Martin Bucer', *Sprachwissenschaft*, 25 : 297–336; H. Boková, 'Beobachtungen zur Prager Druckersprache des 16. Jahrhunderts', *Fest. Pensel*, 11–20; D. Nübling, 'Wie die Alten sungen ... Zur Rolle von Frequenz und Allomorphie beim präteritalen Numerusausgleich im Frühneuhochdeutschen', *ZS*, 17, 1998 : 185–203; and S. Predota, 'Das älteste Fachwörterbuch mit einem deutschen, niederländischen und polnischen Teil', *Fest. Stellmacher*, 339–43. 18th-c. issues are dealt with by P. Wiesinger, 'Schwierigkeiten bei der Umsetzung der österreichischen Sprachreform im 18. Jahrhundert. Am Beispiel der "Christlichen Erinnerungen über die sonntäglichen Evangelien" von Franz Borgia Tausch von 1765', *Fest. Moser*, 207–24; Id., 'Die deutsche Orthographie im Rahmen der beginnenden Sprachpflege in Österreich im 18. Jahrhundert. Zu Johann Balthasar Antespergers "Kayserlicher deutscher Sprachtabelle" von 1734', *Fest. Szulz*, 183–204; K. Jakob, 'Die Sprachnormierungen Johann Christoph Gottscheds und ihre Durchsetzung in der zweiten Hälfte des 18. Jahrhunderts', *Sprachwissenschaft*, 24:1–46; M. Kauffer, 'Die Graphie der deutschen Nominalkomposita in elsässischen Handschriften seit dem 18. Jahrhundert', *ZDL*, 66:255–79; J.-L. Risse, 'Bemerkungen zu Adelungs Lexik und Sprache im Lehrgebäude und in der Stilistik', *Fest. Faucher*, 55–69; B. Djubo, 'Die grammatischen Anschaungen der Aufklärung bei Gottsched und Lomonosov', *DSp*, 26, 1998:369–77; D. Döring, 'Johann Georg Wachter in Leipzig und die Entstehung seines *Glossarium Etymologicum*', *Fest. Pensel*, 29–63; and S. Orgeldinger, *\*Standardisierung und Purismus bei Joachim Heinrich Campe* (SLG, 51), ix + 481 pp. The *Goethe Wörterbuch* concludes vol. 3 with fasc. 12, *Gemäldeausstellung — Gesäusel*, cols 1409–1535, Stuttgart, Kohlhammer, 1998.

Articles on more recent language history are *\*Sprache und bürgerliche Nation. Beiträge zur deutschen und europäischen Sprachgeschichte des 19. Jahrhunderts*, ed. D. Cherubum, Berlin, de Gruyter, 1998, ix + 456 pp.; K.-H. Jakob, 'Politische und religiöse Texte um 1900. Ein deutsch-englischer Vergleich', *Fest. Moser*, 225–36, and L. Ortner, 'Stellenanzeigen und Geschlecht: Sprachwandel in österreichischen Zeitungen des 20. Jahrhunderts', *ib.*, 325–59.

The history of German in GDR times is studied in N. Nail, 'In Vorbereitung des X. Parteitages. "Brigadetagebücher" als Quelle für die Sprachgeschichtsforschung', *Fest. Stellmacher*, 229–35. *\*Das 20. Jahrhundert. Sprachgeschichte — Zeitgeschichte*, ed. H. Kämper and H. Schmidt, 1998, Berlin, de Gruyter, vi + 446 pp.

## 3. ORTHOGRAPHY

T. A. Francis, 'Streitfrage Nummer eins', *NOWELE*, 36:121–34, compares the arguments for the reform of the use of capitals in German and Danish. W. Mentrup, 'Sprache — Schreibbrauch — Schreibnorm — Amtliche Norm. Diskussion der Neuregelung der Rechtschreibung: Beobachtungen und Überlegungunen', *Fest. Moser*,

183–205; H. Krieger, *Der Rechtschreib-Schwindel. Zwischenrufe zu einem absurden Reformtheater*, St. Goar, Leibniz Vlg Matthias Dräger, 1998, 152 pp.; R. Bergmann, 'Das morphologische Prinzip in der Rechtschreibreform und ihrer Diskussion. Synchronisches Prinzip und historischer Schreibgebrauch bei den Umlautgraphien <ä> und <äu>', *Sprachwissenschaft*, 22, 1998:217–61; K.-H. Ramers, 'Vokalquantität als orthographisches Problem: zur Funktion der Doppelkonsonanzschreibung im Deutschen', *LBer*, 177:52–64; P. Ewald and D. Nerius, 'Grossschreibung der Substantive und *das/dass*-Differenzierung. Zur Annahme eines "grammatischen Prinzips" in der deutschen Orthographie', *RBS*, 7:165–86; P. Ernst, 'Graphem-Phonem-Korrespondenzen in der deutschen Schriftsprache', *Fest. Szulc*, 223–40; H. Günther, 'Zur grammatischen Basis der Getrennt-/Zusammenschreibung im Deutschen', *Fest. Vater*, 3–16.

## 4. PHONOLOGY

K. H. Ramers, *Historische Veränderungen prosodischer Strukturen. Analysen im Licht der nichtlinearen Phonologie* (LA, 400), ix + 165 pp., seeks to examine three problems of historical phonology from a non-linear viewpoint. Two concern German: Verner's Law, which is seen as the spreading of a laryngeal feature [slack vocal cords] from a sonorant to a following obstruent, and the NHG vowel lengthening in open syllables, which is a process of syllable readjustment, although there are many exceptions. R. admits that he is presenting no new theory of sound change. There are plenty of examples in his discussion but it is hard not to feel that we are looking at the same old problems in fashionable new clothes which may, or may not, stand the test of time.

Some other historical studies from all stages of German are: G. W. Davis et al., 'Peripherality and markedness in the spread of the High German consonant shift', *BGDSL*, 121:177–200; G. K. Iverson and J. C. Salmons, 'Glottal spreading bias in Germanic', *LBer*, 178:135–51; W. König, 'Eine Ausnahme der neuhochdeutschen Monophthongierung. Zugleich ein Beitrag zur neuhochdeutschen Phonetik und Phonologie', *Fest. Moser*, 135–44; E. Koller, '200 Jahre Ach-Laut', *Fest. Weydt*, 187–94.

Synchronic phonetic and phonological studies feature in: W. Brockhaus, 'The syllable in German: exploring an alternative', Hulst, *Syllable*, 169–218; T. Becker, *Das Vokalsystem der deutschen Standardsprache* (Arbeiten zur Sprachanalyse, 32), Frankfurt, Lang, 1998, 200 pp.; W. H. Vieregge and P. M. Hettinga, 'Effiziente Zuverlässigkeitsbestimmung phonetisch-segmentaler Transkriptionen', *ZDL*, 66:31–47; B. Schönherr, 'So kann man das heute nicht mehr spielen! Über den Wandel der sprecherischen Stilideale auf der Bühne seit den 6oer Jahren', *LBer*, 177:145–70; M. Neef, 'Die Alternationsbedingung: ein deklarative Neubetrachtung', *Fest. Vater*, 17–31; B. J. Kröger, *\*Ein phonetisches Modell der Sprachproduktion* (LA, 387), xi + 308 pp.; F. Missaglia, *\*Phonetische Aspekte des Erwerbs von Deutsch als Fremdsprache durch italienische Muttersprachler* (Forum Phoneticum, 68), Frankfurt, Hector, 206 pp.

5. MORPHOLOGY

A comprehensive work on all aspects of morphology is F. Simmler, *Morphologie des Deutschen, Flexions- und Wortbildungsmorphologie* (GL, 4), Berlin, Weidler, 1998, 736 pp. A. Kühne, *Zur historischen Lexikostatistik der starken Verben im Deutschen* (Studien zur Geschichte der deutschen Sprache, 2), Heidelberg, Winter, 327 pp., is a complex and comprehensive investigation with a plethora of tables, abbreviations, and even a CD-ROM. Once the reader has made the effort to assimilate how the corpus has been put together and how it is presented, a detailed picture of the development of strong verbs can be traced. One of the strengths of this work is that it deals not only with simplexes but also with prefixed verbs, which, of course, are more numerous. The author presents a corpus of prefixed verbs whose development we can follow from OHG to NHG. K. points out difficulties such as that the Early NHG dictionary is only at the start of its publication. The main message is clear: that the number of strong verbs has become reduced since OHG, something that has been known but here we find it quantified and the use of prefixed verbs treated.

Lexical morphology features in the theoretical work of S. Siebert, *Wortbildung und Grammatik. Syntaktische Restriktionen in der Struktur komplexer Wörter* (LA, 408), vi + 167 pp. S. argues for morphology and syntax to be treated not as two separate components, but as one. She uses evidence from adjectives in -*bar* and noun compounds to substantiate her claim. Also noted: W. Motsch, *\*Deutsche Wortbildung in Grundzügen* (SIDS, 8), xi + 451 pp.; R. K. Bloomer, 'The obscured nominal compounds in German and English. Synchronic stations and processes of change', *STUF*, 52:52–63; A. Koskensalo, 'Die von deutschen Baiswörtern abgeleiteten Verben mit dem Suffix -*ieren* — eine verschwindende, weil schwach produktive Verbgruppe. Bemerkungen zur Karriere der deutschen -*ieren*-Verben im Wandel der Sprache und Zeit', *Fest. Stellmacher*, 215–28; W. Wilss, '*inter*-. Zur Wortbildung in der deutschen Gegenwartssprache', *Muttersprache*, 109:124–35; M. Nekula, 'Diminutive bei Franz Kafka', *Fest. Weydt*, 245–49; L. M. Eichinger, 'Wegweiser durch Textwelten. Wozu komplexe Substantive gut sind', *Fest. Faucher*, 169–82; M. Kauffer, 'Die feindlichen Brüder der Wortbildung', *ib.*, 197–215; K.-H. Ramers, 'Die Kunst der Fuge: zum morphologischen Status von Verbindungselementen in Nominalkomposita', *Fest. Vater*, 33–45.

## 6. Syntax

T. Buck, *A Concise German Grammar*, OUP, 185 pp., is a very useful, accessible account of German grammar which includes a good section on pronunciation. General items on theoretical syntax from various points of view include: E. Leiss, 'Aristotelische Linguistik. Der Neubeginn einer philosophischen Grammatik durch Jean-Marie Zemb', *Sprachwissenschaft*, 22, 1998:141–65.

Word classes are treated in: P. Baerentzen, 'Zur Definition der Wortarten des Deutschen', *Fest. Weydt*, 31–42; D. Busse, 'Wortarten und semantische Typen. Überlegungen zu den Grundlagen der lexikalisch-syntaktischen Wortarten-Klassifikation', *Fest. Vater*, 219–40.

Nouns and their morpho-syntactic features form the basis of the following articles: H. Weber, 'Substanz und Substantiv. Zur kategoriellen Bedeutung einer grammatischen Kategorie', *Fest. Weydt*, 349–61; W. Abraham, '*Ein Schatz von einem Kind*. Zur Prädikatsyntax binominaler Nominalkonstituenten', *DSp*, 27:337–47; J. David, 'Dauert ein dreistündiger Flug lange oder nicht lange: Überlegungen zur paradigmatischen Definition des Adverbialakkusativs', *Fest. Faucher*, 13–18; J.-F. Marillier, 'Koordination in Nominalgruppen', *ib.*, 259–74; J.-M. Zemb, 'Stete Tropfen. Zum Objektsprädikativ', *Sprachwissenschaft*, 22, 1998:1–31; C. Dürscheid, *\*Die verbalen Kasus des Deutschen. Untersuchungen zur Syntax, Semantik und Perspektive* (SLG, 53), xii + 305 pp.

There are several items on prepositions: M. Helmantel, 'Position und Distribution der PP', *NOWELE*, 34:23–42; W. Köller, 'Die Perspektivierungsfunktionen von Präpositionen', *Spillmann Vol.*, 129–49; M. van de Velde, 'Zum Stellungsverhalten von PG-DA-Verbindungen', *Fest. Faucher*, 39–52; C. Di Meola, 'Semantisch relevante und semantisch irrelevante Kasusalternation am Beispiel von *entlang*', *ZS*, 17, 1998:204–35; and R. Steinitz, 'Valenznotwendige Präpositionalphrasen weder Argument- noch Adjunktposition', *Fest. Vater*, 329–50.

Recent studies on the verb have concentrated on the passive: J. Sabel, 'Das Passiv im Deutschen. Derivationale Ökonomie vs. optionale Bewegung', *LBer*, 177:87–112; V. Agel, 'Reflexiv-Passiv, das (im Deutschen) keines ist. Überlegungen zu Reflexivität, Medialität, Passiv und Subject', *Fest. Vater*, 147–87; P. Bassola,

Language 579

'Erweiterungsverben mit passivischen Infinitivkonstruktionen im Deutschen', *Sprachwissenschaft*, 22, 1998:33–84. On the subjunctive: E. Morgenthaler, 'Zur Problematik des Konjunktivs in seiner Rolle bei der Redeerwähnung', *DSp*, 27:348–68; on tense: J.-P. Confais, 'Die Behandlung der Ambiguität in der Grammatik: das Beispiel des deutschen Perfekts', *Fest. Faucher*, 151–66; H. A. Welker, 'Das *futurum praeteriti* im Deutschen', *Fest. Weydt*, 363–77; J. Lenerz, '*Werden* und das deutsche Futur', *Fest. Vater*, 399–412. Compound verbs are treated by H. Härtl and J. Witt, 'Lokale Konzepte und Partikelverben in einem Modell der Sprachproduktion', *ZS*, 17, 1998:3–34. The auxiliaries feature in: M. L. Cotin, 'Die "Basisrelationen" des Deutschen und die Auxiliarisierung von Haben, Sein und Werden', *ZDP*, 118:391–419; W. Abraham, 'Modalverben als Sekundärprädikatoren', *Fest. Faucher*, 139–50; and T. Harden, 'Verpflichtung und Wissen. Unvollständige Überlegungen zur Funktion einiger Modalverben', *Fest. Weydt*, 111–18. Also noted: B. Lenz, 'Objektvariation bei Genitiv-Verben', *PapL*, 58, 1998:3–34; S. Olsen, Der Dativ bei Partikelverben', *Fest. Vater*, 307–28.

Word order and sentence structure are covered in: E. Faucher, 'Der zusammengesetzte Satz. Zu einem obligaten Kapitel jeder DaF-Gebrauchsgrammatik', *Fest. Weydt*, 85–97; P. Valentin, 'Subordination', *Fest. Faucher*, 29–37; M. Dalmas, 'Begleiterscheinungen bei Konditionalsätzen', *ib.*, 247–58; G. Webelhuth and F. Ackermann, 'A lexical-functional analysis of predicate topicalization', *AJGLL*, 11:1–61; A. Kiklewitsch, 'Zur funktionalen Modellierung der Aussage', *PapL*, 59, 1998:157–80; K. Farrar, 'Explanation for word order change in modern German', *ZDL*, 66:1–30; D. Clément, 'Syntaktische Mehrdeutigkeit bei Satzverknüpfungen', *ZS*, 17, 1998:236–68; B. Gerlach, 'Optimale Klitiksequenzen', *ib.*, 35–91; S. Uhmann, 'Verbstellungsvariation in *weil*-Sätzen: lexikalische Differenzierung mit grammatischen Folgen', *ib.*, 92–139; H. Wegener, 'Syntaxwandel und Degrammatikalisierung im heutigen Deutsch?', *DSp* 27:3–26; W. Abraham, 'Zur Basisstruktur des deutschen Satzes unter Berücksichtigung diskursfunktionaler Erwägungen', *Fest. Vater*, 59–67; H. Altmann, 'Verbstellungsprobleme bei subordinierten Sätzen in der deutschen Sprache', *ib.*, 69–84; T.N. Höhle, 'Vorangestellte Verben und Komplementierer sind eine natürliche Klasse', *ib.*, 107–20; M. Reis, 'Zum syntaktischen Status unselbständiger Verbzweit-Sätze', *ib.*, 121–44.

Contrastive studies include: K. Fischer, 'Englische und deutsche Satzstrukturen: ein valenztheoretischer Vergleich mit statistischen Anmerkungen', *Sprachwissenschaft*, 25:221–55; C. Scholz, 'Zur syntaktosemantischen Schnittstelle von Komparativkonstruktion im Deutschen und Ungarischen', *PapL*, 58, 1998:35–66; C. Küper,

'Thema und Rhema als ein zentrales linguistisches Konzept. Am Beispiel des Deutschen und Englischen', *Fest. Weydt*, 219–31; A. Ogawa, 'Reflexivierung im Deutschen und Verbsuffigierung im Japanischen', *Fest. Vater*, 291–305.

Some historical studies against a Germanic backdrop are: E. Ronneberger-Sibold, 'Typology and the diachronic evolution of German morphosystanx', Fisiak, *Reconstruction*, 313–35; W. Abraham, 'The interdependence of case, aspect and referentiality in the history of German: the case of the verbal genitive', Kemenade, *Parameters*, 29–61; J. Philippi, 'The rise of the article in the Germanic languages', *ib.*, 62–93.

*Fest. Weydt* contains a number of contributions on particles: W. Abraham, '*even-sogar*-Exerzitie' (1–8); A. Burkhhardt, 'Interjektionen: Begriff, Geschichte(n), Paraphrasen' (43–73); E. Hentschel, 'Die Emphase des Schreckens: *furchtbar nett* und *schrecklich freundlich*' (119–32); W. P. Klein, 'Über Schriftpartikel, oder: warum man manchmal aus einer Mücke einen Elefanten machen darf' (177–86); M. Krause, 'Überlegungen zu *hin-/her-* + Präposition' (195–217); M. Rost-Roth, 'Modalpartikeln in Argumentation und Handlungsvorschlägen' (293–324); B. Schlieben-Lange, 'Partikeln bei Bernhardi' (325–32); and W. Wolski, 'Partikeln im Werk Paul Celans' (379–402).

Also noted: K. Ezawa, 'Sekiguchis Sprachstudium und Grundkonzept der Grammatik', *Fest. Weydt*, 75–83; J. Trabant, 'Verspätete Bemerkungen über den unendlichen Gebrauch von endlichen Mitteln (UGVEM)', *ib.*, 333–47; P. Colliander, 'Partikelvalenz im Deutschen. Eine prototypenlinguistische Studie über die Valenzverhältnisse', *DSp* 27:2–51; J. M. Zemb, 'Den Gral hüten oder den Gral suchen?', *Fest. Faucher*, 19–27; D. Wunderlich, 'Der unterspezifizierte Artikel', *Fest. Vater*, 47–55; J. Ballweg, 'Die Männer sind alle Verbrecher. Zum Status gefloateter Quantoren', *ib.*, 189–203; C. Dürscheid, 'Perspektivierte Syntax', *ib.*, 241–57; V. Ehrich, 'Wertsteigerung und Wertverlust — die Veränderung der Valenz', *ib.*, 259–76; K. Pittner, *\*Adverbiale im Deutschen. Untersuchungen zu ihrer Stellung und Interpretation* (SDG, 60), Tübingen, Stauffenburg, ix + 390 pp.

## 8. Dialects

H. Niebaum and J. Macha, *Einführung in die Dialektologie des Deutschen* (GA, 37), xvi + 226 pp., is a general work suitable for beginners. It covers a wide range of material, sometimes perhaps too succinctly. There are exercises with questions to be answered, but most are only suitable for native German speakers. All in all this volume provides a detailed overview of German dialectology. A totally different kind of work is *Wilhelm Buschs Plisch und Plum in 40 deutschen Mundarten*, ed. M. Görlach, Heidelberg, Winter, 281 pp. The *deutsch* in the title refers to a wide variety of dialects, e.g. colonial dialects in Canada, and some in Romania. A single text is presented in 40 different dialects, allowing comparisons of dialectal features. Also noted: *\*Mundart in Deutschland. Vademekum zu Vereinen, Forschungseinrichtungen und anderen Institutionen* (Mitteilungen des Internationalen Mundartarchivs 'Ludwig Soumagne' des Kreises Neuss), Krefeld, Van Aken, 1998, 400 pp. *Fest. Stellmacher*, predictably has several articles dealing with Low German: I. Schröder, 'Niederdeutsche Zaubersprüche. Konstanz und Variation' (81–92); K. Stackmann, 'Die Borchlingschen 'Reiseberichte', ein Göttinger Beitrag zur Niederdeutschen Philologie' (93–99); H.-W. Appel, 'Zur Syntax des Verbs *doon* im Neuniederdeutschen' (101–10); U. Föllner, 'Zur Situation des Niederdeutschen zwischen Wittenberg und Salzwedel. Zwischenbilanz einer soziolinguistischen Untersuchung in Sachsen-Anhalt' (111–19); E. Isakson Biehl, 'Forschungsstand und Regionalsprachenförderung in Ostfriesland. Allgemeines zum Stand des Niederdeutschen in Norddeutschland' (121–35); D. Möhn, 'Norddeutsche Geräuschlexeme. Sprachschöpfungen für Comics' (137–46); E. Piirainen, '"Se lött nix te Potte braanen." Geschlechtsspezifische Idiome in der westmünsterländischen Mundart' (147–56); F. Schnibben, 'Wörterbuchbenutzer und Informationstheorie. Die Lexikographie als "Störquelle" im Übertragungskanal Sprache — Benutzer' (157–68); and J. Wirrer, 'New Melle, MO 63365: Sprecherin 21, Sprecher 34' (169–81). Dialect literature in Low German is treated in: J. Böger, 'Der ostfriesische Dichter Enno Hektor und der "Gesang eines finnischen Landmädchens"' (183–91); and U. Tinnemeyer, 'Eine niederdeutsche Welt. Bemerkungen zu Adolf Stuhlmann (1838–1924)' (193–202). Also noted on Low German: B. Scheuermann, *\*Zur Funktion des Niederdeutschen im Werk Uwe Johnsons. 'In all de annin Saokn büssu hie nich me- to Hus'* (Johnson-Studien, 2), Göttingen, Vandenhoeck & Ruprecht, 1998, 474 pp.; D. Stellmacher, *\*Das Saterland und das Saterländische* (Vorträge der Oldenburgischen Landschaft, 30), Oldenburg, Isensee, 1998, 43 pp.; Id., *\*Helmstedt und seine Sprachen. Ein sprachgeschichtlicher Überblick. Ergänzt um die Dokumentation einer Diskussionsveranstaltung zum Ostfälischen* (Veröffentlichungen des Ostfälischen Instituts der Deuregio Ostfalen, 3), 70 pp.

West Central German varieties feature in K.-P. Lange, 'Die fränkischen Lautverschiebungen im niederländisch-ripuarischen Gebiet', *NOWELE*, 34, 1998:43–74; P. Wagener, *'Auf Schalke! Auf* als lokative Präposition ohne Artikel im Ruhrdeutschen', *Fest. Stellmacher*, 243–51; W.V. Davies, ' "Geregeltes Miteinander oder ungeregeltes

Durcheinander?" Versuch einer Beschreibung der sogenannten "Umgangssprache" in Mannheim-Neckerau', *LBer*, 178:205–29; O. Kies, 'Weingärtnersprache in Lauffen am Neckar', *Muttersprache*, 109:75–80; K.-H. Mottausch, \*Geschichte der Mundart der Stadt Lorsch. *Mit Berücksichtigung des gesamten 'südhessischen' Mundartgebietes*, 2 vols, Giessen, W. Schmitz, xix + 394, xxix + 395–662 pp.; and C. Chapman, 'Diminutive plural infixation and the "West Franconian" problem', Fisiak, *Reconstruction*, 73–88.

East Central German is discussed by K. Spangenberg, \*Die Umgangssprache im Freistaat Thüringen und im Südwesten des Landes Sachsen-Anhalt, Rudolstadt, Hain, 1998, 198 pp.

G. Schunk, *Regionalisierung von Dialekten. Ein lautlicher Stadt-Land-Vergleich in Mainfranken* (Schriften zum Bayerischen Sprachatlas, 1), Heidelberg, Winter, 247 pp., is a detailed investigation of ten localities in the Würzburg dialect area, five towns and five villages near towns. Four field workers, using questionnaires, gathered the data which will also be used for the Franconian Sprachatlas. The informants were (as usual) elderly people who had lived in the locality most of their lives and were engaged in agricultural or craft activities. Three to five informants were used for each locality. S.'s emphasis is on phonology, and for the dialect of each locality there is a description of the phonemic oppositions among the short and long vowels, and diphthongs. Dialect development is largely due to the influence of other dialects rather than of standard German. There are less basic dialectal forms but they have spread throughout the region. The villages near towns and smaller towns have played a decisive role in the formation of regional characteristics, and larger cities such as Würzburg and Schweinfurt have played a lesser role. This study confirms changes at the phonetic-phonological level and these must be tested to see if they are reflected at other levels of language. Also on Franconian: N. R. Wolf, '*Die Kelter harrt des Weines*. Zu Mechanismen des Kultur- und Sprachkontextes anhand von Winzerwörtern an Rhein und Main', *Fest. Moser*, 115–22.

Alemannic features in H. Bickel, 'Dialektologie und Sprachgeschichte: Probleme der *p*-Verschiebung im Schweizerdeutschen', *Fest. Moser*, 123–34; \*Einleitung zum Südwestdeustchen Sprachatlas. ii, ed. H. Steger and V. Schupp, Marburg, Elwert, 1998, 274 pp.; W. König and R. Schrambke, \*Die Sprachatlanten des schwäbisch-alemannischen Raumes. Baden-Württemberg, Bayerisch-Schwaben, Elsass, Liechtenstein, Schweiz, Vorarlberg (Themen der Landeskunde, 8), Bühle, Konkordia, 156 pp.; and A. Ruoff and E. Gabriel, \*Die Mundarten Vorarlbergs. Ein Querschnitt durch die Dialektologie des Landes. Mit einem Katalog des Tonarchivs der Mundarten Vorarlbergs (Schriften der Vorarlberger Landesbibliothek, 3), Graz, Neugebauer, 1998, 183 pp.

On Bavarian: H. Hahn and I. Wörgötter, 'Sprachgeschichte erfahrbar machen. Das "Altern" von Dialektausdrücken als Unterrichtsthema', *Fest. Moser*, 427–48; P. Wiesinger, 'Zum Problem der phonetisch-phonologischen Beschreibung in Zeiten dialektalen Wandels', *Fest. Stellmacher*, 263–72; H. Weiss, *\*Syntax des Bairischen. Studien zur Grammatik einer natürlichen Sprache* (LA, 391), 1998, vii + 291 pp.; C. Ferstl, *\*Altbayerische Wörtersammlungen des 20. Jahrhunderts* (Jahrbuch der Johann-Andreas-Schmeller-Gesellschaft, 1998), Bayreuth, Rabenstein, 1998, xii + 119 pp.; P. Mauser, *\*Die Morphologie des Salzburger Lungaus* (Schriften der deutschen Sprache in Österreich, 27), Frankfurt, Lang, 440 pp.; *\*Sprachatlas von Oberösterreich. 1. Lautgeographie*, ed. S. Gaisbauer and H. Scheuringer, Linz, Adalbert-Stifter-Institut des Landes Oberösterreich, 1998, 20 maps.

Speech islands are the subject of P. Zürrer, *Sprachinseldialekte. Walserdeutsch im Aostatal (Italien)* (Sprachlandschaften, 23), Aarau, Sauerländer, 470 pp., produced by a dedicated enthusiast and linguist who has spent over 30 years researching these varieties. In this volume he homes in on Gressoney and Issime. Z. uses a wide range of material to illustrate the dialect, from his own dialect recordings to 19th-c. texts. He sketches the multilingual situation, then contrasts the phonological and grammatical systems of the two dialects, then in the main part of the book he treats the inflexion of the noun and pronoun, finishing with a documentary appendix. The inflexional system of nouns is becoming more analytic, i.e. the case endings are being replaced by prepositional and other constructions. The pronominal system is undergoing changes, with compound forms being formed, clitics being supported by Romance forms, reanalysis of pronouns as endings and complex phonological changes. This is a beautifully produced book in a series which unfortunately is not being continued.

H. Gehl, *Kommentierte Donauschwäbische Texte* (*ZDL*, Beihefte, 103), Stuttgart, Steiner, 226 pp., presents 16 transcribed texts of the dialects originally spoken near the Danube in eastern Europe from eight localities. The texts contain a large amount of crafts and technical vocabulary and were recorded mostly by speakers now living in Germany, but several have been recorded in the countries themselves. There are probably about 150,000 speakers of these dialects left today, although the number has been shrinking over the years. There are a number of maps with place-names both in German and Hungarian, Romanian, etc. to help the reader. There is a detailed index of topics and languages. This is not just a book of texts, which are given with word explanations, but also an account of a whole area and its history. The different dialects which the settlers originally spoke in the 18th c. have for the most part developed into

*Mischmundarten.* A unique situation has arisen in the case of one group of speakers who emigrated to Brazil and form a 1,500 strong settlement where they continue to use their dialect. This is a fascinating study of a world that is slipping away. Dialects in former East Prussia are discussed by J. Pinnow, *Tausend Worte Danzigerisch. Kurze Einführung in das Danziger Missingsch*, 2nd edn, Westerland, Pinnow, 215 pp. The following dialect dictionaries continue their publication: *Preussisches Worterbuch*, VI.2, *tollen — Ufer*, cols 129–256; VI.3, *ufern — verprahlen*, cols 257–384; VI.4, *verprassen — wahrsagen*, cols 389–512, Neumünster, Wachholtz; *Hamburgisches Wörterbuch*, fasc. 16, *Kaakappel — Kiep*, Neumünster, Wachholtz, 1998, cols 897–1024, fasc. 17, *Kiephoot — Knööpnadel*, cols 1025–1152; *Oberharzer Wörterbuch*, ed. K.-H. Weidemeier, Clausthal-Zellerfeld, Oberharzer Geschichts- und Museumsverein, 1998, I, *A-C*, 355 pp.; II, *D-F*, 334 pp.; *Wörterbuch der obersächsischen Mundarten*, ed. D. Helm et al., I, A-F, Berlin, Akademie, 1998, xii + 712 pp.; *Bayerisches Wörterbuch*, ed. A. Rowley et al., Munich, Oldenbourg, fasc. 3, [*Milch*]*almer — Appolonia*, cols 287–476, 1997; fasc. 4, *Apostel — Atmetzer*, cols 477–664, 1998; fasc. 5, *atmig — [an]packen*, cols 665–852; *Wörterbuch der bairischen Mundarten in Österreich*, vol. 4, fascs 9 and 10, *Temper — tetzig*, cols 1473–1814, Vienna, Österreichischen Akademie der Wissenschaften, 1998; *Schweizerisches Idiotikon*, vol. 16, fasc. 201, *Wald-wuld — Walt-wult*, cols 1537–1664, Frauenfeld, Huber, 1998; *Badisches Wörterbuch*, vol. 4, fasc. 57, *N-narri(ch)t*, Lahr, Moritzschauenburg, pp. 1–32.

9. ONOMASTICS

General items include: G. Koss, 'Rumpelstilzchens Gretchenfrage. Namengebung und Interpretationswissen', *Fest. Szulc*, 319–52; T. Vennemann, 'Volksetymologie und Ortsnamenforschung. Begriffsbestimmung und Anwendung auf ausgewählte, überwiegend bayerische Toponymie', *BNF*, 34:269–322; *Namenforschung und Namendidaktik. Gerhard Koss zum 65. Geburtstag*, ed. K. Franz and A. Greule, Baltmannsweiler, Schneider Vlg Hohengehren, 248 pp.; and *Die Welt der Namen, Sechs namenkundliche Beiträge*, ed. N. Nail (Schriften der Universitätsbibliothek Marburg, 87), Marburg, Universitätsbibliothek, 1998, vii + 135 pp. *Österreichische Namenforschung*, 27, contains a number of articles on different aspects of names in the German-Slav contact area: P. Jordan, 'Slowenische Ortsnamen in den amtlichen topographischen Karten Österreichs. Heutiger Zustand und Vorschläge zu seiner Verbesserung' (41–54); J. Malenínská, 'Orographische Termini in der Toponymie Böhmens' (69–74); J. Matúsova, 'Das deutsche Appellativum *Berg* in der

Oroymie Böhmens' (75–81); H. D. Pohl, 'Zum Namengut slowenischer Herkunft in Österreichs Süden und Südosten' (89–114). The same volume contains contributions treating other areas and general concerns: P. Anreiter, 'Isonymie, Tautonomie und semantische Entsprechungsrelationen' (137–49); Id., 'Der Stanzer Ortname *Grins*' (151–54); H. Bergmann, 'Hausnamen auf *-nig* im Gemeindegebiet von Ainet (Osttirol)' (155–74); M. Hintermayer Wellenberg, 'Zum Problem der Identifizierung von Ortsnamen' (175–80), and J. Kahn, 'Primäre und sekundäre Belebung am Beispiel von Graubündner und St. Gallener Flurnamen' (181–96). Also noted on contact studies: \*Romania Germania. Die Bedeutung von Ortsnamen für die Sprachgeschichte im Grenzgebiet zweier Sprachen, ed. F. Debus (*BNF*, Beihefte n.F., 52), Heidelberg, Winter, 61 pp. Studies on first and family names include: M. Siller, 'Von *Johannes* bis *Hans*. Die frühe Verbreitung und Entwicklung eines Rufnamens im südlichen romanisch-germanischen Grenzbereich', *Fest. Moser*, 32–49; M. Markefka, 'Ethnische Schimpfnamen — kollektive Symbole alltäglicher Diskriminierung. 1. Teil', *Muttersprache*, 109:97–123; R. Schumann, '*Aurinia* und *Veleda*: zwei germanische Seherinnen? Personennamen im Sprachkontakt', *BNF*, 34:131–43; and K. Kunze, \*dtv-Atlas Namenkunde. Vor- und Familiennamen im deutschen Sprachgebiet (dtv-Atlas, 3234), 2nd edn, Munich, dtv, 240 pp.

Several articles deal with names in the context of school: W. Kany, 'Einmal Grizzlybär? Persistenz und Veränderung von Schülerspitznamen', *Muttersprache*, 109:43–53; I. Kühn, 'Schulnamengebung im politisch-kulturellen Symbolkanon', *ib.*, 136–43; K.-E. Sommerfeldt, 'Von Stichling bis Schliemadonna. Schülerzeitungen in den neuen Bundesländern und deren Namen', *ib.*, 144–47; and D. Bering et al., 'Wegbeschreibungen. Entwurf eines Kategorienrasters zur Erforschung synchroner und diachroner Strassennamenkorpora', *Muttersprache*, 109:135–66.

On family names: P. Wagener, '*Stellmacher* und *Wagener*. Zur Frequenz und Geographie der aus der Berufsbezeichnung für den Wagenmacher abgeleiteten deutschen Familien Namen', *Fest. Stellmacher*, 349–56; B. Kewitz, \*Coesfelder Beinamen und Familiennamen vom 14. bis 16. Jahrhundert (*BNF*, Beihefte n.F., 51), Heidelberg, Winter, 588 pp.; W. Seibicke, \*Historisches deutsches Vornamenbuch, 2: F-K, Berlin, de Gruyter, 1998, xv + 724 pp. Plant names are treated in P. Seidensticker, \*Pflanzennamen. Überlieferung — Forschungsprobleme — Studien (*ZDL*, Beiheft, 120), Stuttgart, Steiner, 141 pp.

Studies on older names include: A. Bammesberger, 'MANNUM/MANNO bei Tacitus und der Name der *m*-Rune', *BNF*, 34:1–8; N. Wagner, 'SwabaharjaR', *ib.*, 9–16; Id., 'Lat.-wfrk. *Rauchingus*, ahd. *Roh-* sowie lat.-germ. *C(h)rocus*', *ib.*, 17–24; Id., '*Eobanus* und *Dadanus*', *ib.*, 145–50; Id., '*Ilbogo* und *Ilteri*', *ib.*, 151–57; Id., 'Zu einigen Germanennamen bei Papst Gregor dem Grossen', *ib.*, 255–67; Id., 'Die Namen von Lakringen, Sabalingen und Inkrionen', *HSp*, 111, 1998: 169–76, and Id., 'Freio et Frigatto und Hviteribus', *ib.*, 177–83. Place, river and field name studies include: R. Möller, \**Nasalsuffixe in niedersächsischen Siedlungsnamen und Flurnamen in Zeugnissen vor dem Jahre 1200* (BNF, Beihefte n.F., 50), Heidelberg, Winter, 1998, 146 pp.; L. Reichardt, \**Ortsnamenbuch des Ostelbkreises. Teil 1: A-L* (Veröffentlichungen der Kommission für Geschichtliche Landeskunde in Baden-Württemberg, Reihe B, 139, 140), Stuttgart, Kohlhammer, v + 402 pp.; \**Hydronymia Germaniae*, ed. W. P. Schmid, Reihe A, fasc. 17, *Das Flussgebiet der Havel (ohne die Spree)* (Kommission für vergleichende Sprachwissenschaften und der Literatur Mainz), Stuttgart, Steiner, v + 216 pp.; U. Ohainski and J. Udolph, \**Die Ortsnamen des Landkreises Hannover und der Stadt Hannover* (Veröffentlichungen des Instituts für Historische Landesforschung der Universität Göttingen, 37: Niedersächsisches Ortsnamenbuch, Teil 1), Bielefeld, Vlg für Regionalgeschichte, 1998, xxiv + 593 pp.; R. Richard et al., \**Die Ortsnamen des politischen Bezirkes Vöcklabruck (Südliches Hausruckviertel)*, (Ortsnamenbuch des Landes Oberösterreich, 4), Vienna, Österreichischen Akademie der Wissenschaften, 1997, xi + 186 pp.; Id. and P. Wiesinger, \**Die Ortsnamen des politischen Bezirkes Gmunden (Südwestliches Traunviertel)*, (Ortsnamenbuch des Landes Oberösterreich, 6), Vienna, Österreichischen Akademie der Wissenschaften, x + 186 pp.; \**Über Jena. Das Rätsel eines Ortsnamens. Alte und neue Beiträge*, ed. N. Nail and J. Göschel (*ZDL*, Beihefte, 194), Stuttgart, Steiner, 134 pp.; G. Plangg, 'Zu einigen Berg- und Passnamen in Tirol', *Tiroler Chronist*, 73, 1998: 14–16.

## MEDIEVAL LITERATURE

By DAVID A. WELLS, *Professor of German at Birkbeck College, University of London*

### 1. GENERAL

The *Lexikon des Mittelalters* is now completed with *Registerband*, ed. Charlotte Bretscher-Gisiger, Bettina Marquis, and Thomas Meier, Stuttgart–Weimar, Metzler, vii + 775 pp., of which the first of its three main parts is perhaps the most interesting. There are indexes of names and themes relating to relatively peripheral or non-Christian areas, e.g. Arabic and Islamic, Jewish, Byzantine, Russian, Irish, and Scandinavian cultures; of the major vernacular languages and literatures, including historiography and Classical reception; and of specialized areas, including architecture, medicine, numismatics, weapons, towns, and monastic foundations. There follows a list of the main cross-referenced headings in the work. The third and largest part lists the individual contributors and their articles. Meanwhile the work as a whole is made more accessible by its publication under a new imprint as a 'Studienausgabe' at greatly reduced price, *Lexikon des Mittelalters*, 9 vols, Stuttgart–Weimar, Metzler. The only changes are a lighter binding and slightly reduced page and font size, while the index volume is incorporated into the ninth, shorter volume. Among the outstanding features of the concluding volumes not previously mentioned in these pages is further welcome emphasis on vernacular literary works, including articles on *Straßburger Alexander* (N. H. Ott), *Streitgedicht* (U. Müller), *Stricker, Thüring von Ringoltingen, Volksbuch* (W. Röcke), *Steinmar, Tagelied, Thomasin von Zerklaere, Wirnt von Grafenberg* (H.-J. Schiewer), *Tierepos* (F. P. Knapp), *Trojadichtung* (E. Lienert), *Übersetzer / Übersetzungen* (N. Henkel), *Visionsliteratur* (P. Dinzelbacher), *Walther von der Vogelweide* (U. Schulze), *Tatian, Wiener Genesis und Exodus* (D. Kartschoke), *Wolfdietrich, Wolfram von Eschenbach* (J. Heinzle), besides many lesser authors, works, and topics. The effect is to complement entries in the *Verfasserlexikon* while often placing the German material in much wider contexts. Also of particularly impressive detail in the final volumes are the comprehensive treatments of *Stadt, Stand / Stände(-lehre), Universität, Vers- und Strophenbau*, and *Wasser*, besides 116 Williams and a sumptuous array of family trees. Carl Paschek, *Praxis der Literaturinformation Germanistik* (GL, 48), 2nd rev. edn, Berlin, Weidler, 314 pp., is completely revised since the first edition of 1986, taking the reader into the electronic age with an attempt at a systematic and comprehensive account of the application of bibliographical methods and techniques, and above all of the tasks relating to information search and retrieval operations.

While numerous theoretical questions, sometimes provocative, are asked in the opening sections, the emphasis falls on the illustration of problems through practical examples of different kinds of information known and required in literary and linguistic aspects of German studies and the means by which they can be found. There is also much practical information on the basic bibliographical tools in the discipline. H. Brunner, *Fest. Walliczek*, 217–30, comments in broad terms on the state of the discipline, with suggestions for further work. Volker Meid, *Sachwörterbuch zur deutschen Literatur*, Stuttgart, Reclam, 571 pp., seeks to give essential information in the form of encyclopaedia articles on current thought and knowledge relating to German literature, following established literary history and scholarship while remaining open to more recent approaches. There is a wealth of information on terminology, epochs, genres, literary themes and traditions, and the production and reception of literature. It is regrettable that the individual entries are not accompanied by bibliography; a very brief listing of major reference works does duty for the latter. Elisabeth Frenzel, *Motive der Weltliteratur. Ein Lexikon dichtungsgeschichtlicher Längsschnitte*, 5th rev. edn (KTA, 301), xvi + 935 pp., has been reset and revised, with some bibliographical updating. There is a wholly new and substantial article on *Zigeuner*. The work maintains its value as a comprehensive source of interdisciplinary material not brought together in this way elsewhere. Matias Martinez and Michael Scheffel, *Einführung in die Erzähltheorie*, Munich, Beck, 198 pp., is a systematically organized introduction, explicitly aiming at answering 'how' fictional narrative operates and not merely 'what' it does. There are chapters on fact and fiction, the relation of narration and narrative, time, mode, voice, narrative situations and elements, narrated worlds, deep structures, and the approaches implied by sociolinguistics, cognitive psychology, anthropology, and history. Besides moving easily among a host of modern theories the authors also range over a very wide spectrum of world literature, among which Hartmann von Aue, the *Nibelungenlied*, *Kudrun*, and *König Rother* yield exemplary insights. Rolf Bergmann, Peter Pauly, and Claudine Moulin-Fankhänel, *Alt- und Mittelhochdeutsch. Arbeitsbuch zur Grammatik der älteren deutschen Sprachstufen und zur deutschen Sprachgeschichte*, 5th rev. edn, Göttingen, Vandenhoeck & Ruprecht, 240 pp., is a welcome reissue of what is intended not as a grammar, but rather as a linguistic introduction to the period focusing above all on the text, and with wider cultural implications which emerge from the notes on the linguistic forms. Chapters on the morphology of OHG and MHG and on the historical linguistic background are followed by an introduction to the written culture of the period, with a representative selection of texts. The bibliography of standard works takes account of the latest editions. R. Panikkar, *Fest. Haas*, 585–604, understands medieval civilization as a link between the modern West and other cultures, and W. Röcke, *Fest. Brackert*, 265–84, considers alterity in medieval literature in terms of the foreign and exotic, and its transformation at the end of the period, while S. Fuchs, *ib.*, 365–84, discusses the impact of H. R. Jauss's thesis on alterity and modernity. H. Kleinschmidt, *NOWELE*, 35, 1999:77–114, supplies interesting examples from literature and art of forms of communication in medieval Europe, and S. Sonдеregger, *Fest. Haas*, 649–66, points to the significance of oral communication as expressed in a range of texts of different genres in the period, while G. Althoff, *FmSt*, 31, 1997:370–89, includes vernacular literary examples in a survey of the significance of symbolic communication. In Palmer, *Kloster*, J.-D. Müller (149–66) comments in broad theoretical terms on the problems currently attending the understanding of conceptions of authorship, text, and performance, and U. Peters (167–92) takes a broad-brush historico-anthropological approach to questions of literary activity in a courtly or religious milieu, while K. Grubmüller (193–210) elaborates the difficulties inherent in attempts at genre classification for medieval literature. *Das Mittelalter*, 4.1, includes a range of short contributions by F. Fürbeth, H. Hundsbichler, U. Ernst, H.-W. Goetz, W. Röcke, H. Keller, and others on interdisciplinarity in medieval studies. Hans-Werner Goetz, *Moderne Mediävistik. Stand und Perspektiven der Mittelalterforschung*, Darmstadt, Primus, 412 pp., is a bold attempt to take stock of the discipline as a whole (though with an inevitable emphasis on German and historical studies) in the light of the current state of the art. The theme of a relevant 'modernes Mittelalter' which has found a resonance in literary studies as advanced by J. Heinzle (*YWMLS*, 56:714–15; and see below) is revealed as one of many comparable trends. The first part of the book (pp. 7–149) is a major review of research classified into such themes as the legitimacy of medieval studies, the image of the period, the historical development of scholarship, the past generation, and the organization of the discipline. The second part is more specialized and addresses specific developments in research in areas such as sources, historical themes, social and economic history, the rise of historical anthropology, and topics concerned with transmission and communication. This is a most welcome study which is certain to both stimulate and provoke. *Modernes Mittelalter. Neue Bilder einer populären Epoche*, ed. Joachim Heinzle (IT, 2513), 495 pp., is a handy paperback reprint of a collection which first appeared in 1994 (see *YWMLS*, 56:714–15), doubtless partly elicited by the overtly populist approach to the

Middle Ages. This has, not surprisingly, fallen foul of critics such as Werner Schröder (see p. 591 below). Nevertheless, the underlying conception of a cultural and social continuity establishing a contemporary relevance is certainly a stimulus to work in our period.

Leander Petzoldt, *Einführung in die Sagenforschung*, Konstanz, UVK Universitätsverlag Konstanz, 238 pp., is a concise yet multi-faceted introduction which does justice to the historical development of the subject as well as to the range of current approaches. A first section on Herder, the Grimm Brothers, and other Romantics identifies the early collections; the problem of authenticity leads into treatments of definition, typology, and more recent anthropological and social approaches. The account of form, style, and structure includes mention of theories with a high degree of literary relevance. The longest section, a categorization of legendary motifs, contains numerous themes familiar from the literature of the period. *Legenden. Heiligengeschichten vom Altertum bis zur Gegenwart*, ed. Hans-Peter Ecker, Stuttgart, Reclam, 519 pp., includes a clear definition and discussion of the *Legende* as the conclusion to an anthology focused upon the very wide chronological and thematic range of the genre. The medieval texts, presented in modern German and as excerpts where space dictated, include, besides early Christian examples and apocryphal literature, *Georgslied*, Hrotsvitha, *Annolied*, Hartmann's *Gregorius*, and a selection from the *Legenda Aurea*; but as much space again is devoted to examples from German literature of the 16th-20th cs, besides a section of non-Catholic examples and one on polemic and parody on the genre from Luther onwards. F. J. Worstbrock, Haug, *Mittelalter*, 128–42, distinguishes renarration from translation in a review of common medieval narrative practice, and J. Heinzle, Lutz, *Literatur*, 79–93, comments critically on the value of the concept 'literarische Interessenbildung', seeing it as an essentially unsystematic attempt to evaluate literary history as human history. K. Grubmüller, Robertshaw, *Natur*, 3–17, interprets the use of *natûre* in OHG and MHG.

Klaus von See, *Europa und der Norden im Mittelalter*, Heidelberg, Winter, 452 pp., contains 12 essays on subjects originally published between 1972 and 1994. The reworking of the material, though varying considerably from one subject to another, is generally much more substantial than is usually the case with such collections. The overall impression is that the author has drawn the material together and presents a coherent vision of the early Middle Ages which, according to his expressed intentions, places greater emphasis on the Scandinavian tradition than is usual in German *Germanistik*, but at the same views a range of Old Norse texts clearly in the context of Continental and insular Christian culture. Even if the author often deals with topics more usually associated with an older generation of scholarship — e.g. the Germanic sacral theory — his approach aligns him firmly with current views, as in his corroboration of the pervasive influence on medieval literature of a well-known school text, the *Disticha Catonis*. Werner Schröder, *Frühe Schriften zur ältesten deutschen Literatur* (Schriften der Wiss. Gesellschaft an der Johann Wolfgang Goethe-Univ. Frankfurt am Main, Geisteswiss. Reihe, 13), Stuttgart, Steiner, 372 pp., complements the other volumes of S.'s collected essays with reprints of seven miscellaneous earlier works of the prolific author. The project is welcome, given that most of these items appeared in relatively obscure and today inaccessible publications in the first instance. The subject-matter ranges by way of early OHG and the *Hildebrandslied* to the detailed analyses supporting S.'s views on the structure of shorter EMHG religious poems and Wolfram's relationship to *Nibelungenlied* and *Klage*. Werner Schröder, *Critica Selecta. Zu neuen Ausgaben mittelhochdeutscher und frühneuhochdeutscher Texte*, ed. Wolfgang Maaz and Fritz Wagner (Spolia Berolinensia, 14), Hildesheim, Weidmann, vii + 311 pp., contains photographic reproductions of 21 contributions, helpfully including the paginations of the first places of publication. Most of the items are pungent reviews from the 1990s and cover a wide range of textual criticism from the MHG classical period to late-medieval romances and didactic literature and Meister Eckhart. S. is particularly devastating in his opinion of the 'new philology' and related approaches. A helpful index of names and works draws the subject-matter together. Alois Wolf, *Erzählkunst des Mittelalters. Komparatistische Arbeiten zur französischen und deutschen Literatur*, ed. Martina Backes, Francis G. Gentry, and Eckart Conrad Lutz, Tübingen, Niemeyer, vii + 404 pp., brings together 12 of W.'s essays which originally appeared between 1971 and 1993. The placing of German literature in a wider European context is everywhere apparent, from the broad-brush yet intimately sympathetic treatment of OHG and 11th-c. literature by way of the heroic epic to the classical courtly romance with which eight of the items are concerned. These include the convincing demolition of the chauvinistic *adaptation courtoise* dogma, where W. is generous enough to point to its one redeeming feature, the emphasis on the need to take account of the Old French models when interpreting the German: an approach which he perhaps more than any other current practitioner has made his own with a consistency of detail and of vision which abundantly justify these reprints. H. J. Heringer, *Fest. Eroms*, 235–43, studies Hermann Paul, and S. Müller, *Fest. Walliczek*, 231–57, writes on the satirical treatment of *Altgermanistik* by Moriz Haupt and Heinrich Hoffmann von Fallersleben.

Karin Schneider, *Paläographie und Handschriftenkunde für Germanisten. Eine Einführung* (Sammlung kurzer Grammatiken germanischer

Dialekte, B 8), Tübingen, Niemeyer, x + 237 pp., is a major addition to this series of standard handbooks which will certainly run into many future editions. A brief introduction concentrates on the most important German manuscript collections and is followed by a substantial treatment of palaeography, taking the reader chronologically through the scripts with practical illustrations and a focus on the problems specific to the vernacular. A longer chapter on codicology is equally clear in its subdivisions and in the detail of its examples. A final short chapter addresses provenances, patrons, private and monastic libraries, and the movement of manuscripts. There is a detailed index and list of manuscripts cited. A. Mentzel-Reuters, *DAEM*, 54, 1998:583–611, supplies a bibliography and review of recent manuscript catalogues, and E. Horváth, *ZDA*, 128:62–65, documents Hamburg manuscripts rediscovered since the Second World War. *Fest. Pensel* includes documentation of neglected manuscripts by B. C. Bushey (the Herzogin Anna Amalia Bibliothek, Weimar, 21–28); U.-D. Oppitz (manuscripts of the Princes Dietrichstein from Nikolsburg/Mikulov, 187–214); I. T. Piirainen (Sprottau/Szprotawa, 233–37); and R. D. Schiewer and H.-J. Schiewer (Amorbach manuscripts in Moscow, 239–61). C. Mackert, *BW*, 32:1–31, studies the library of Count Wolfgang zu Fürstenberg (1465–1509).

OTHER WORKS

H. Meyer, *FmSt*, 31, 1997:390–413, focuses on the conceptions of *intentio* and *utilitas* in a study of *accessus* prologues of the 11th-13th cs, while G. Björkvall and A. Haug, Schaefer, *Artes*, 309–23, survey medieval Latin versification and intonation, and D. Schaller, *DAEM*, 54, 1998:613–21, comments in broad terms on literature of the *prosimetrum* type. E. Feistner, Bennewitz, *Konstruktion*, 131–42, interprets clerical literature about women thought to be men, and B. Spreitzer, *ib.*, 249–63, interprets medieval legends which show a disruption of the natural order of the sexes. *Dämonen, Monster, Fabelwesen*, ed. Ulrich Müller and Werner Wunderlich (Mittelaltermythen, 2), St. Gallen, UVK, 696 pp., illustrates a movement towards both interdisciplinarity and an encyclopaedic approach in the treatment of a major nexus of themes. Following an introduction by W. Wunderlich there are 39 chapters by a range of specialists, not all of them mutually exclusive, on topics including the late-medieval world of demons (L. Petzoldt), bestiaries (L. A. J. R. Houwen), Arthurian demonology (R. Bräuer), *mappae mundi* (M. Hoogvliet), architectural monsters (P. Dinzelbacher, A. Classen), dragons (W. McConnell), witches (C. Habgier-Tuczay), Laurin (J. L. Flood),

the devil and Antichrist (W. Wunderlich, F. G. Gentry, G. Mahal,
B. Könneker), sirens (R. Krohn), wild men (E. R. Hintz), and wild
women, dwarfs, and giants (C. Habgier-Tuczay). The numerous
separate headings are listed alphabetically with definitions, and, while
most of the information is couched at a level of essential information,
there are numerous references to the literary sources where appropriate and abundant bibliography for further study.

Robert Luff, *Wissensvermittlung im europäischen Mittelalter. 'Imago
mundi'-Werke und ihre Prologe* (TTG, 47), xi + 586 pp., takes *imago mundi*
as a loose generic term for a body of literature of encyclopaedic
character — 'encyclopaedia' itself being unknown — and attaches
considerable importance to the fairly constant prologues of the works
as supplying insight into the author's perception of, and reflection on,
their function. The study seeks to trace authorial intention, intended
audience, type of knowledge conveyed, treatment of sources, and
world-view of such works from the 12th c. to the later Middle Ages.
The selection of eight paradigmatic authors and works is carefully
justified: the *Elucidarium* of Honorius Augustodunensis, the MHG
*Lucidarius* tradition, Herrad von Hohenburg, *Le Livre de Sidrac*, Alfonso
el Sabio, Brunetto Latini, Hiltgart von Hürnheim, and Christine de
Pizan. A wide-ranging appendix of texts from these works and related
passages for comparison from other authors fills over 100 pages. Not
all the conclusions are surprising: the frequent use of anonymity of
authorship, of teams of authors, the rise of the vernacular, the use of
dialogue and of vivid imagery, and the organization of knowledge
either according to *Heilsgeschichte* or an anthropocentric plan, but also
a significant focus on unsystematic works which prefer spontaneity of
presentation to any clear model. C. Meier, *FmSt*, 31, 1997 : 1–31 + 28
pls, reviews the function of illustration in medieval encyclopaedic
manuscripts, and *ib.*, 33 : 252–86, studies the images of learning in the
illustrations to the *Speculum maius* of Vincent of Beauvais in their
encyclopaedic context, while S. Schuler, Keller, *Schriftlichkeit*, 243–66,
examines the treatment of architectural science in Vincent's work.

*Lexikon der christlichen Antike*, ed. Johannes B. Bauer, Manfred
Hutter, and Anneliese Felber (KTA, 332), xxxi + 387 pp., focuses on
Western Christendom, with about 1,000 articles by a team of 24
authors, each accompanied by bibliographical leads for further study.
The period is understood as extending from the first to the eighth c.
and, while there is inevitably a degree of arbitrariness in the inclusion
or exclusion of some entries, the material as a whole provides a
comprehensive introduction to the major aspects of the history of the
Church, its institutions, concepts, beliefs, authors, and literature.
Erhard Gorys, *Lexikon der Heiligen* (dtv, 32507), DTV, 1997, has
essential information, including feast days, on about 600 saints,

focusing mainly but by no means exclusively on the Western Church and the early Middle Ages. There is a brief introduction to the subject-matter and lists of attributes, patrons, and a glossary of technical terms. Heinz Meyer and Rudolf Suntrup, *Lexikon der mittelalterlichen Zahlenbedeutungen* (MMS, 56), xlv pp. + 1016 cols, is a welcome paperback reissue of the monumental reference work from F. Ohly's Münster school which first appeared in 1987, without revision. The systematic clarity and care with which the biblical and exegetical documentation is set out and the indexes of numbered *res significantes* besides the allegorical *significata* — the latter in fact relatively few in number — make the work easy to use and indeed probably the first recourse for anyone working in this field for generations to come. Friedrich Ohly, *Zur Signaturenlehre der Frühen Neuzeit. Bemerkungen zur mittelalterlichen Vorgeschichte und zur Eigenart einer epochalen Denkform in Wissenschaft, Literatur und Kunst. Aus dem Nachlaß herausgegeben*, ed. Uwe Ruberg and Dietmar Peil, Stuttgart–Leipzig, Hirzel, x + 129 pp., contains, following an introduction by the editors, eight essays and a conclusion relating to a programme of research dating back to the 1970s. The introduction gives a clear definition of *Signaturenlehre* as analogous to the spiritual sense of Scripture, the immanent character implanted by God in all aspects of Creation, the meaning of which can be read in two possible directions: the hidden interior of the subject, or the analogy within the cosmos. Hence the doctrine of macrocosm and microcosm forms a significant expression of the medieval antecedents. Other studies relate to the formula *omnia in omnibus*, Paracelsus, Jacob Böhme, the role of language, Giuseppe Arcimboldo, and further examples from art, poetry, and music. F. Ohly, *FmSt*, 32, 1998 : 1–27, ed. B. Reudenbach, in a final posthumous study links the round towers of ecclesiastical architecture to the pillars of Solomon's temple, while G. Binding, *MJ*, 34.1 : 7–28, discusses the meaning of *architectus, wercmeistere*, and related terms. M. Schumacher, *Poetica*, 31 : 81–99, includes a survey of the exegetical treatment of the frog in a study of Rupert of Deutz, and N. Harris, Robertshaw, *Natur*, 65–75, considers the panther and its attributes. Also noted: *De generatione Christi. Ein typologisches Lehrgedicht des hohen Mittelalters (inc. Prima luce deum)*, ed. and comm. Martin Rödel (EH, xv, 79), 209 pp. *Fest. Haas* includes a study of illegitimacy in canon law by R. Schnell (117–38). Arvid Göttlicher, *Die Schiffe im Neuen Testament*, Berlin, Gebr. Mann, 379 pp. + 222 pls, is with a rich body of illustrations and copious documentation a worthy companion to G.'s treatment of the Old Testament aspects of the topic (*YWMLS*, 59 : 668). G. addresses in turn the seven major events associated with the Sea of Galilee; some commentary on the biblical background precedes, and serves to illuminate, the following iconographical studies, which are replete with examples. A discussion of the archaeological and metaphorical significance of the boat precedes comparable treatments of the sea voyages of the apostles and of the exegetical and artistic interpretation of the ships of the Apocalypse. Aspects of literary reception are addressed in a concluding chapter. Heinz Schreckenberg, *Die christlichen Adversus-Judaeos-Texte und ihr literarisches und historisches Umfeld. (1.–11. Jh.)*, 4th rev. edn, (EH, XXIII, 172), 795 pp., is a revised and updated edition of the standard handbook of which the third edition appeared only in 1995 (see *YWMLS*, 58 : 718). The inclusion of vernacular German literature is an important aspect of the subject-matter. The new edition follows the same pagination as its predecessor for the body of the text, but there is substantial expansion and updating of the addenda and corrigenda section, above all in the bibliographical area. Heinz Schreckenberg, *Christliche Adversus-Judaeos-Bilder. Das Alte und Neue Testament im Spiegel der christlichen Kunst* (EH, XXIII, 650), 469 pp., is an immensely valuable iconographic compendium to accompany the three textual handbooks on the subject, the material similarly arranged in chronological sequence from the 1st to the 20th c. About 400 illustrations appear, not always particularly well reproduced but with sufficient clarity for ordinary purposes of study. Where S. adds explanatory captions they are both concise and illuminating. Vernacular texts represented in manuscript illustration include *Kaiserchronik*, *Alexanderlied*, Der Wilde Mann, Eike von Repgow's *Sachsenspiegel*, Michel Beheim, and Hans Folz. Gilbert Dahan, *The Christian Polemic against the Jews in the Middle Ages*, trans. Jody Gladding, Notre Dame U.P., 1998, xii + 130 pp., is a lucid translation of a standard introduction to the subject which first appeared in French in 1991. The work is strong in its classification of the forms of polemic used, less so as regards comprehensiveness of coverage and the implications of a historical development. An index would have been welcome. Leonard B. Glick, *Abraham's Heirs. Jews and Christians in Medieval Europe*, Syracuse U.P., xv + 323 pp., is a readable basic history of the topic, the author describing his perspective as that of a 'social historian and anthropologist' focusing on the actual experience of Jews in the Franco-German Christian world of north-western Europe, but his narrative is all the better for avoiding the jargon too often associated with such approaches to socially marginal groups. The treatment is chronological, the 12th c. being seen as pivotal in the progression from protection to decline and persecution. There is some treatment of the intellectual evidence of interaction between Jews and Christians, notably the Victorine school, Gilbert Crispin, Peter Abelard, and the religious drama, although at too cursory a level to draw out the subtle nuances in the literature.

M. Curschmann, Haug, *Mittelalter*, 378–470, supplies a major survey of the relationship between vernacular literature and art from the 12th to the 16th c., and E. König, Palmer, *Kloster*, 141–48 + 9 pls, questions the extent to which book illumination should be seen as a narrative art, while J. Paul, Haug, *Mittelalter*, 471–98, takes a broadbrush view of change and continuity in late-medieval art, and U. Küsters, Müller, *Mittelalter*, 81–109, studies the semiotic role of wounds in late-medieval literature and art. C. Kaden, *ib.*, 333–67, characterizes the conflicting perception in the medieval aesthetic of music. Michael Hauskeller, *Geschichte der Ethik: Mittelalter* (dtv, 30727), DTV, 231 pp., is an excellent brief introduction to medieval ethics, not over-simplified merely because it focuses in three main chapters on Augustine, Abelard, and Aquinas respectively. Major topics are treated in precisely categorized sections (sin, love, Adam, freedom, etc.). There are full indications of sources for further reference, and a comprehensive index.

Wolfgang Trapp, *Kleines Handbuch der Münzkunde und des Geldwesens in Deutschland* (UB, 18026), 320 pp., has essential information on almost everything to do with the currency of Germany in different periods. For the Middle Ages the sections on coin production and metals, a brief history of the coinage from the Age of the Migrations onwards, and a concluding review of the state of prices and wages — in effect an introduction to economic history — are of particular interest. Hans-Werner Goetz, *Geschichtsschreibung und Geschichtsbewusstsein im hohen Mittelalter* (Orbis mediaevalis, 1), Berlin, Akademie, 501 pp., is a substantial contribution to medieval historiography as a whole, starting from the insight that, while much is now understood about the conception of history, relatively little work has been done on the consciousness of history in the period. Rather than focus on the better known and much studied major historiographical writers, G. sees the necessity of covering a wide range of less distinguished figures in order to identify the leading ideas. Chapters on central aspects of the world of the medieval imagination lead on to treatments of the narrative structure, content, and function of the works, and the institutional basis and bias of their approach. At intervals 16 exemplary cases are discussed in detail in order to illustrate the treatment of specific features such as universality, awareness of time, partisanship, polemic, and crisis. The threads are drawn together in a summary which is all the more convincing for the wealth of detail on which the arguments are based. A. Kablitz, Haug, *Mittelalter*, 499–549, considers changing attitudes to historiography between Dante and Petrarch, above all in the view of the *sacrum Imperium*. Alfred Heit and Ernst Voltmer, *Bibliographie zur Geschichte des Mittelalters* (dtv, 33008), DTV, 1997, 352 pp., is a well organized bibliographical guide well suited to the needs of literary scholars. The theoretical introduction itself has a practical application to scholarly needs, and the subdivisions of each section, used in conjunction with the comprehensive index and list of abbreviations, quickly identify sources on every conceivable subject. Electronic literature is also included. *The New Cambridge Medieval History*. III. *c. 900–c. 1024*, ed. Timothy Reuter, CUP, xxv + 863 pp., is introduced by R. who emphasizes the relative paucity of sources for the 'long 10th c.' and the differences of approach among historians of different nationalities. The political history of post-Carolingian Europe is divided up territorially, the German dimension being covered by E. Müller-Mertens (the Ottonians), G. Althoff (Saxony), H. Wolfram (Bavaria), and M. Parisse (Lotharingia). Non-Carolingian Europe receives almost at much attention, with chapters on Eastern Europe, Iberia, and substantial treatment of Byzantium and Bulgaria in several chapters by J. Shepard. As with the other published volumes the economic and cultural background is given due prominence, with chapters on the rural economy (R. Fossier), merchants and towns (P. Johanek), the Church (R. McKitterick), artists and patrons (H. Mayr-Harting), and intellectual life (C. Leonardi), which lucid surveys nevertheless scarcely conceal the relative lack of creative literary culture. There are admirable genealogical tables and documentation of sources. *The New Cambridge Medieval History*. V. *c. 1198–c. 1300*, ed. David Abulafia, CUP, xxiii + 1045 pp., continues the complete reworking of the standard work already heralded in the volume for the 8th and 9th cs (see *YWMLS*, 58:715). Instead of the theme of triumphalist 'completion' in the 13th c. characteristic of its 70-year-old predecessor, this work, by 35 contributors, emphasizes rather the expansion of the Latin West and its interaction with bordering civilizations and other cultures, exemplified in chapters on heresy and the Albigensians (B. Hamilton), the Church and the Jews (K. R. Stow), Byzantium (D. Jacoby and M. Angold), besides Islam, the Mongols, and Eastern Europe. A chapter is dedicated to a succinct survey of German political history and social change in the period (M. Toch). For economic history the reader is referred elsewhere, but developments of wider significance than narrowly political history are given prominence with opening chapters on social change and the orders of society, art and architecture (P. Binski), and the use of the vernacular (C. C. Smith; necessarily with a bias towards Romance). The universities and scholasticism (J. Verger) are prominent in the substantial treatment of the role of the Church. Genealogical tables, classified bibliographies, and full index aid the user of this work of first recourse for fundamental information on the period. Hans-Joachim Schmidt, *Kirche, Staat, Nation. Raumglie-derung der Kirche im mittelalterlichen Europa* (Forschungen zur mittelalter-lichen Geschichte, 37), Weimar, Böhlau, 580 pp., is a highly detailed work on the organizational and geographical structures of the medieval Church, including chapters on the historical position in the early Middle Ages, Innocent III and the effect of the Fourth Lateran Council, developments in diocesan organization, centralized papal power and the jurisdiction of legates, and the impact of later ecumenical councils. Of greatest interest for literary scholarship is the substantial section on monasteries and religious orders and the relationships between them. Brunner, *Krieg*, derives from a major Würzburg project on war in the period and includes work by G. Althoff (the limitations on the use of force and the rules governing its employment, 1–23); V. Schmidtchen (legal constraints on conduct in war, 25–56); K.-H. Ziegler (late-medieval legal literature on the conduct of war, 57–71); E. Walde (the use of the peace to make the feud illegal, 73–91); J. Fehn-Claus (analysis of the reasons for feuding in 15th-c. vernacular sources, 93–138); and R. Leng (musketeers' books on the justification of professional killing, 307–48, with texts). Richard van Dülmen, *Kultur und Alltag in der Frühen Neuzeit. 16.–18. Jahrhundert. I. Das Haus und seine Menschen. II. Dorf und Stadt. III. Religion, Magie, Aufklärung*, 3 vols, Munich, Beck, 316, 373, 343 pp., are a major contribution to social and cultural history, covering the three substantial areas of the private and domestic sphere, the hierarchy of public and social life, and, with the greatest development in the period covered, forms of religion, superstition, and education. In the surveys of *haus* and family, the stages of life, town, village, festival, social class and conflict, and popular Catholic piety the continuity with the late Middle Ages is undeniable, even though the evidence often derives from later periods. Though written in an accessible, semi-popular style, the work is fully documented with scholarly sources, and enhanced by a well-chosen corpus of illustrations. Paul Freedman, *Images of the Medieval Peasant*, Stanford U.P., xxi + 460 pp., takes a synchronic, thematic view of the image of the peasant from the Carolingian period to the war of 1525, on a European basis and including a German dimension so substantial that the book fills an important lacuna for our discipline, given its relatively neglected subject-matter. F. notes the significant inconsistencies in portrayal but sees these as secondary to the variety of ideas associated with the peasant. Great emphasis is placed on the social role, with five substantial sections on peasant labour as a support of society, the limits of mutual dependence, and its breakdown; equality, freedom, the biblical basis of the understanding of class origins, and related national myths; degrading images, and peasant bodies of both sexes;

peasants crossing class boundaries and clever and virtuous peasants; and the problem of servitude and rebellion against it late in the period. All the better-known German literary examples fit admirably into this framework.

## 2. GERMANIC AND OLD HIGH GERMAN

A. Bammesberger, *BNF*, 34:1–8, comments on *Manno* in Tacitus. Georg Scheibelreiter, *Die barbarische Gesellschaft. Mentalitätsgeschichte der europäischen Achsenzeit 5.–8. Jahrhundert*, Darmstadt, Primus, 661 pp., attempts, through a 'history of mentalities' approach to the period, to define its individual 'barbaric' character and rescue it from condemnation as either late-Classical decadence or mere prelude to the Middle Ages. Hence the initial treatment of the 'decline of antiquity' concludes with a section on the 'change of mentality'. Subsequent chapters deal with the idea of authority, characteristics of daily life, warfare and the individual's attitude to it, the sense of space and the afterlife, the exposure and vulnerability of the individual, and the dynamics of life. S. writes in the spirit of J. Huizinga and has too many concrete examples for the style to descend into *Geistesgeschichte*. For Germanists there are vivid and readable accounts of the historical background to the heroic epic. Id., Kooper, *Chronicle*, 251–59, studies Fredegar's 7th-c. chronicle. K. Hauck, *FmSt*, 32, 1998:28–56, continues his series of monographs on the gold bracteates. *Pforzen und Bergakker. Neue Untersuchungen zu Runeninschriften*, ed. Alfred Bammesberger and Gaby Waxenberger (*Historische Sprachforschung*, supp., 41), Göttingen, Vandenhoeck & Ruprecht, 304 pp., is a substantial collection of articles on recent runological scholarship. The first section is devoted to the inscription on the recently discovered buckle from Pforzen (Allgäu), with contributions on the context of the archaeological find (V. Babucke), meticulous transcription and description of the individual runes (P. Pieper), attempts at interpretation (K. Düwel, U. Schwab), and comments by other scholars on various details including the possible relevance to the heroic epic (R. Nedoma) and the name *Eigil* (N. Wagner). Description (V. Babucke) and interpretation (K. Düwel) of the ivory ring from the same find point to female domination of South Germanic runic culture. Six comparable articles are then devoted to the Bergakker (Gelderland) scabbard mount discovered in 1996, with opinions about the language(s) of the runes ranging over Gothic, Scandinavian, and Latin. There follow four contributions on miscellaneous topics, and discussion of the Brunswick whalebone casket (R. Marth, G. Waxenberger). U. Schwab, *Fest. Schupp*, 12–27, studies two runic inscriptions from Alemannic sites, characteristically drawing on literary monuments in their interpretation. *Runeninschriften als Quellen interdisziplinärer Forschung. Abhandlungen des Vierten Internationalen Symposiums über Runen und Runeninschriften in Göttingen vom 4.–9. August 1995*, ed. Klaus Düwel and Sean Nowak (Reallexikon der germanischen Altertumskunde: Ergänzungsbände, 15), Berlin, de Gruyter, 1998, xiv + 812 + 35 pp., includes work on numerous aspects of runology. Heinz Ritter-Schaumberg, *Der Schmied Weland. Forschungen zum historischen Kern der Sage von Wieland dem Schmied*, ed. Hans Martin Ritter (Historische Texte und Studien, 19), Hildesheim, Olms, 201 pp., concludes the unusual and highly individualistic series of the studies in which the now deceased author seeks to trace the origins of events recorded in heroic epic. Half of the book is occupied with a comparative presentation, in modern translation, of the accounts of Wieland in the two major versions of the *Thidrekssaga*. The author's radically historical and geographical approach places his work apart from the mainstream of literary scholarship, even of an older generation more inclined to speculative genetic theories, but his attempt to draw conclusions about 5th-c. historical figures on the basis of the texts and a range of archaeological artefacts will certainly continue to provoke controversy.

Matthias Becher, *Karl der Grosse* (Beck'sche Reihe, 2120), Munich, Beck, 128 pp., is a concise but highly readable introduction to Charlemagne's life, dynasty, and reign. The subject-matter is treated chronologically, and accompanied by time-chart and select bibliography. Treatment of the cultural significance of Charlemagne is inevitably restricted. B. Reudenbach, Schaefer, *Artes*, 283–308, comments on book illustration as an expression of Charlemagne's educational reform, and E. J. Goldberg, *Viator*, 30:41–78, includes literary references in a study of ritual and knighthood at the court of Louis the German. Dhuoda, *Handbook for William. A Carolingian Woman's Counsel for her Son*, trans. and introd. Carol Neel, Washington, DC, Catholic Univ. of America Press, xxviii + 163 pp., is a handy translation of a work which has come into prominence only recently, not least as a result of feminist approaches. The introduction reviews the historical background, the composition, sources, and structure of the work, its moral perspective, and view of Christian society. The translation is clearly set out and the notes include biblical references and brief explanations with reference to P. Riché's standard edition.

Birgit Kochskämper, *'Frau' und 'Mann' im Althochdeutschen* (GASK, 37), xxxix + 507 pp., is a Kiel dissertation with a feminist slant, combining the insights that modern German terminology for the two sexes is asymmetric and that feminist linguistics has paid scant attention to date to the historical aspects of the language. The conclusions suggest that the linguistic — and social — treatment of the man as the norm and the woman as the deviant have nothing to do with courtly culture but are present from the earliest OHG period and, indeed, of Indo-European antiquity. This for K. depressing conclusion is less interesting than the substance of the study, which analyses 22 words in great detail with a wealth of examples from the admirably documented sources. This makes it a valuable reference and source work for the student of this basic vocabulary. B. Kochskämper, Bennewitz, *Konstruktion*, 15–33, applies T. Laqueur's theoretical model of gender anthropology to an analysis of the OHG vocabulary for 'man' and 'woman'. H. D. Schlosser, *Fest. Brackert*, 162–73, reviews the worlds of life and experience in different OHG texts. Albrecht Greule, *Syntaktisches Verbwörterbuch zu den althochdeutschen Texten des 9. Jahrhunderts. Altalemannische Psalmenfragmente, Benediktinerregel, Hildebrandslied, Monseer Fragmente, Murbacher Hymnen, Otfrid, Tatian und kleinere Sprachdenkmäler* (RBDSL, B, 73), 309 pp., was conceived as part of a wider project for a structuralist grammar of OHG. The present dictionary is based on the insight that within limits the syntactical relations of OHG verbs can be described in terms of valency theory, their semantic and predicative function linking them to other parts of the sentence. Besides its obvious function of providing quick access to examples of verbal usage in the major monuments, the organization of the dictionary supplies under each headword a careful, syntactically based definition of meaning and usage; morphosyntactic analyses and relations to other components; and specific examples.

R. Bergmann and U. Götz, *Fest. Wiesinger*, 445–61, address the linguistic identity of the earliest glosses, and K. Gantert, *Fest. Schupp*, 28–42, interprets the *Wiener Hundesegen*. Michael Flöer, *Altêr uuîn in niuuen belgin. Studien zur Oxforder lateinisch-althochdeutschen Tatianabschrift* (SA, 36), 464 pp., readdresses the status of MS Junius 13 against the background of A. Masser's edition and related studies of Codex Sangallensis 56 (*YWMLS*, 54:663; 56:734) and the attempts of P. Ganz to demonstrate the independence of Junius 13. A comprehensive collation of the two versions seeks further insights into their relationship as well as into the work of Franciscus Junius. After an investigation of the structure of the MS the two most substantial chapters compare the material in vernacular and Latin respectively in meticulous detail. The evidence points to a close affiliation of the two MSS even in their bilingual character, with the establishment of a coherent, planned tradition and a high estimation of the efforts of Junius and his contemporaries. F. Simmler, *Fest. Eroms*, 299–335, analyses the macrostructures in the *Tatian*, and H. Löffler, *Fest. Schupp*, 255–68, illustrates the persistence of particular formulations in German prose Bible translations from the *Tatian* on.

B. Taeger, *NdW*, 39 : 157–77, applies semantic studies to the textual criticism of the *Heliand*, and in *Rauch Vol.*, J. E. Cathey (163–72) considers its Christian adaptation of Germanic concepts, while G. R. Murphy (183–88) interprets its vocabulary for alcoholic drinks, S. Suzuki (189–99) analyses its use of anacrusis, and D. R. Krooks (173–82) supplies specimens of an English translation. U. Winter, *Fest. Pensel*, 337–46, presents Old Saxon Psalm fragments. T. E. Hart, *Rauch Vol.*, 269–84, takes the structure of Otfrid's work to exemplify a project relating to the influence of early music theory on medieval literature, and E. E. Metzner, *Fest. Brackert*, 174–201, reviews the background to the *Ludwigslied* in the light of recent research. Notker der Deutsche von St. Gallen, *Die Hochzeit der Philologie und des Merkur. 'De nuptiis Philologiae et Mercurii' von Martianus Capella. Diplomatischer Textabdruck, Konkordanzen und Wortlisten nach dem Codex Sangallensis 872*, ed. Evelyn Scherabon Firchow, Richard Hotchkiss, and Rick Treece, 2 vols, Hildesheim, Olms, xxxi + 558, 559–1171 pp., is a major new aid to the study of Notker and a tribute both to F.'s persistence and to the sophistication of modern computer technology in the production of concordances. The basis of the work is a complete transcription, in which F.'s judgements necessarily do not always correspond to those of earlier editors, with assignation of a number to each line. The complex text in both German and Latin contains a wide array of special signs, but the abbreviations are kept to a manageable list to which the user quickly adapts. The first volume includes a concordance, reverse index, and word frequencies for the Latin text. The second volume, a typographic *tour de force*, is wholly occupied with the same aids for the German text. There is a clear implication that Notker's works as a whole deserve similar treatment, although on-line and CD-ROM developments might supersede such efforts. A. A. Grotans, *AJGLL*, 10, 1998 : 1–43, explains the pedagogical basis of Notker's treatment of Latin syntax, and E. Hellgardt, *Fest. Walliczek*, 131–66, studies his treatment of Psalm 95(96). *St. Gallen. Geschichte einer literarischen Kultur. Kloster — Stadt — Kanton — Region. 1. Darstellung.* II. *Quellen*, ed. Werner Wunderlich, 2 vols, St. Gallen, UVK, 1600 pp., is a monumental collection of studies and documentation on all aspects of the history and culture of St Gall. Among the major contributions are essays by W. Wunderlich (introduction), S. Sonderegger (linguistic background; OHG), W. Berschin (beginning of literary culture), P. Ochsenbein (role of the monastery school; monastic literature), K. Schmuki (chronicle and hagiography in the 11th-13th cs), and R. Schnell (secular lyric and epic). There is similar treatment of later epochs, and a section on literary institutions and media includes R. Kalkofen's survey of the context of literary life in general in which the medieval period receives concise but detailed treatment. B. K. Vollmann, Palmer, *Kloster*, 17–28, comments on the place of the court in early medieval monastic literature.

## 3. MIDDLE HIGH GERMAN

### GENERAL

C. März, Müller, *Mittelalter*, 317–32, considers a 'semantics' of metrical structures. M. Backes, *Fest. Schupp*, 1–11, reviews the literary interests of medieval Freiburg/Br., and H. Freytag, *NdJb*, 122:7–24, surveys literature in Lübeck during the period, while V. Bok, *Fest. Pensel*, 1–10, reviews German literature in Bohemia 1310–46, and H. Kästner, *Fest. Schupp*, 237–53, documents the evidence of the graves of some medieval poets and the rise of interest in visiting them. Lutz, *Literatur*, includes work by C. Meckseper (15–43) on the architecture of castle and town as the focus of social and literary activity, and P. Johanek (45–78) on the representation of the ruler at court, with a wealth of examples. H. Wenzel, *ZGer*, 9:549–56, comments on the imagery of visual perception, H. E. Keller, *ib.*, 598–615, treats other aspects, and H.-J. Bachorski and J. Klinger, *ib.*, 655–73, include the courtly festival in a theoretical study of changes in literary communication. L. Mirianashvili, F. Müller, and U. Müller, *Fest. Pensel*, 163–86, present a Georgian analogue to epic and romance themes. W. Haug, *ZDA*, 128:1–16, adopts a broad cultural approach to the isolation of the epic hero, with examples from MHG. H.-G. Roloff, Schwarz, *Text*, 219–29, comments on the tension between 'text' and 'context' from the later Middle Ages on. M. J. Schubert, *ABÄG*, 51:197–207, considers the pedagogical implications of translating Shakespeare and other texts into MHG.

L. Peter Johnson, *Die höfische Literatur der Blütezeit (1160/70–1220/30)* (Geschichte der deutschen Literatur von den Anfängen bis zum Beginn der Neuzeit, II, 1), Tübingen, Niemeyer, xi + 465 pp. + 16 pls, continues this literary history by a number of authors by emphasizing that, while the guiding principle of the work was the focus on literary production as a social and economic process, in the case of this of all periods aesthetic considerations are paramount and affect poets, audience, and patrons, the latter, following a discussion of the usual terminology applied to the period, being exemplified by Landgrave Hermann I of Thuringia. A particular feature of the book is the relative detail in which the lyric is treated (pp. 45–225), all the *Minnesangs Frühling* poets, Wolfram, and the *Tagelied* being subjected to a treatment which combines informative introduction with pungent and sometimes provocative critical insight. While the enthusiastic and vivid approach is maintained with the epic, there is relatively less thorough coverage here of authors and works other than Veldeke,

Hartmann, Gottfried, Wolfram, and the *Nibelungenlied*. Other forms of literary activity are treated cursorily, following the rather contentious assertion that 'literature' essentially means *belles-lettres*! Werner Paravicini, *Die ritterlich-höfische Kultur des Mittelalters* (Enzyklopädie deutscher Geschichte, 32), 2nd edn, Munich, Oldenbourg, viii + 137 pp., is a most welcome addition to this series of handbooks with basic information set out clearly and systematically. Although the orientation is primarily historical, the significance of the subject-matter for literary scholarship is an inevitable result which focuses closely on subjects such as the terminology associated with courtly culture, its relationship to other medieval classes and roles, and the place of women. The classified bibliography numbers 280 items. C. Stephen Jaeger, *Ennobling Love. In Search of a Lost Sensibility*, Philadelphia, Pennsylvania U.P., xiii + 311 pp., is a stimulating and provocative approach to the problems associated with 'courtly love', based on close reading of a range of mainly Latin but also vernacular texts from the mainstream European tradition. J. argues that the class-bound early medieval ideal of love and charismatic friendship, drawing on Classical Latin and biblical sources, was primarily a social rather than a personal condition, emerging in court, cathedral, and monastic environments as a form of behavioural self-representation rather than sexually based emotion. Hence, because of the restriction to relationships between men before the late 11th c., the association of 'ennobling love' with homosexuality is rejected. Faced with the inclusion of women in the social code, the aristocracy from the 12th c. made the ideal even more widespread, but the problem of sexuality results in an ultimately unresolvable 'romantic dilemma' already present in the inner contradictions of Andreas Capellanus and repeatedly addressed in romance literature where the ethical dimension of 'courtly love' proves unviable. A great merit of the study is its investing the earlier period with its own 'courtly behaviour' so often seen as a phenomenon of the 12th c. on. C. Haag, Bennewitz, *Konstruktion*, 228–48, identifies the figure of the *mulier fortis* in a number of MHG texts and seeks to trace its biblical origins. R. Schnell, *FmSt*, 32, 1998:307–64, detects competing images of masculinity in the period, and R. Weichselbaumer, Bennewitz, *Konstruktion*, 326–41, compares five texts in which men cross-dress as women. In *JOWG*, 11, love-letters are the subject of M. J. Schubert (oral and written, 35–47), F. Fürbeth (early humanism, 49–64), J. Schulz-Grobert (comic and ridiculous examples, 65–74), and M. Schiendorfer (a booklet of six letters from Zurich, *c.* 1300, 75–82). H. Brall, *ZDP*, 118:354–71, studies homosexuality in a range of texts.

A. Classen, *SM*, 39, 1998:833–63, includes MHG examples in a survey of *rois fainéants*, viewing them as criticism of contemporary rulers, and U. Friedrich, Müller, *Mittelalter*, 149–79, considers the discourse of violence in some 12th-c. works, while G. Althoff, Palmer, *Kloster*, 53–71, examines the communicative function of ritual submission (*deditio*) in *Herzog Ernst D*, Hartmann's *Iwein, Rolandslied, Nibelungenlied*, and elsewhere. W. Wegner, *Mediaevistik*, 11, 1998:113–34, discusses the communication of medical matters in MHG works, and D. Kimmich, *Fest. Schupp*, 125–33, includes MHG text in a commentary on the understanding of the diaphragm as the vital organ of life. Bettina Spoerri, *Der Tod als Text und Signum. Der literarische Todesdiskurs in geistlich-didaktischen Texten des Mittelalters* (DLA, 27), 345 pp., adopts a dual approach, based in the first part on rhetorical and philosophical considerations relating to the paradox of treating death through the medium of language, and on etymology and exegesis in the second part. The wide range of authors and texts applied to themes such as earthly vanity and transience, *ubi sunt?*, death as a thief, return journeys to the other world, and the personification of death, include Heinrich von Melk, Guibert of Nogent, Caesarius of Heisterbach, visionary literature, Hartmann's *Der Arme Heinrich*, Wirnt von Grafenberg's *Wigalois*, Konrad von Würzburg's *Der Welt Lohn* and *Elegie*, the *Ackermann aus Böhmen*, and a range of legendary and miracle literature besides iconographic examples. The second part includes a comprehensive overview of the interpretative history of the letter or symbol T and is relevant for Wolfram's *Willehalm*, Heinrich Hesler's *Evangelium Nicodemi*, and the *Legenda Aurea* among other works. Matthias Weimayr, *Der Stachel des Todes. Allmachtphantasien und Unsterblichkeitsstrategien im Mittelalter* (EH, XXXI, 390), 460 pp. T. R. Jackson, Robertshaw, *Natur*, 41–52, reviews the artifical depiction of nature in MHG works, and C. Fasbender, *ib.*, 53–64, considers other instances of artificial imitations of living beings and the problem of interpreting them. N. Largier, *ZGer*, 9:616–36, considers the 'speculative' function of the image of the mirror in a range of texts.

A. Wolf, *Fest. Schupp*, 160–76, points to the comments on their poetic activity by MHG poets themselves. Ruth Finckh, *Minor Mundus Homo. Studien zur Mikrokosmos-Idee in der mittelalterlichen Literatur* (Palaestra, 306), Göttingen, Vandenhoeck & Ruprecht, 475 pp., is primarily of value for the manner in which it draws together a wide range of medieval sources on the microcosm. An introductory chapter surveys the Oriental, Platonic and other Classical references, the early medieval authors and their 12th-century reception. There follow substantial treatments of the theme in Bernardus Silvestris, Alan of Lille, and Hildegard of Bingen among other Latin writers. A more interpretative dimension is then introduced with studies of Gottfried von Strassburg, focusing on the cave of lovers as a harmonious, paradisiacal utopia of the heart, of Albrecht's *Jüngerer Titurel*, leading to a reinterpretation of the prologue, and of Frauenlob, where various enigmatic texts underscore the centrality of his cosmological conception of love. The conclusions point, not surprisingly, to considerable diversity of treatment, but also to the recurrence of common themes. Ursula Peters, *Dynastengeschichte und Verwandtschaftsbilder. Die Adelsfamilie in der volkssprachigen Literatur des Mittelalters* (Hermaea, n.F., 85), Tübingen, Niemeyer, x + 376 pp., takes a 'history of mentalities' approach to the problem of the knowledge and awareness of the noble family in medieval literature which has no direct link to the genre of vernacular dynastic history. The introductory review of research has much literature on the family in the period as a whole, and points of contact with literary scholarship include, not surprisingly, the *chanson de geste*, the Percival romances, and romances dealing with mythical family origins. Treatment of the chronicle literature focuses on a wide range of German, French, and Dutch sources, while the place of the historical family in literature includes discussion of the Lohengrin and Melusine legends besides a chapter on literary references to patrons. The final section, on the noble family as a theme of courtly literature, includes chapters on the beast epic (fox and wolf!), the *Nibelungenlied*, Wolfram's *Parzival*, and the nexuses of brothers and nephews in the William epics, besides Wolfram's *Willehalm* in particular. The conclusions point to the diversity of the evidence, but nevertheless reveal convincing insights into the culture which informs the works. Andreas Daiber, *Bekannte Helden in neuen Gewändern? Intertextuelles Erzählen im 'Biterolf und Dietleib' sowie am Beispiel Keies und Gaweins im 'Lanzelet', 'Wigalois' und der 'Crone'* (Mikrokosmos, 53), Frankfurt, Lang, 288 pp., adds to the increasing number of studies of MHG works taking an intertextual approach, and by focusing on the theme of established heroes who feature in subsequent works contributes much to the re-evaluation of such texts in the light of the still often assumed judgement on their 'epigonality'. The success of this dissertation, however, lies less in any rigidly conceived theoretical framework for the approach — D. in any case insists that 'intertextuality' is to be broadly understood — than in the carefully worked-through analyses of the treatment of the main figures in the epics studied against the background of an excellent knowledge of the classical models. The conclusions point to a variety of potential and actual references to the 'original' texts, which certainly enrich our understanding of the later works. M. Bärmann, Lutz, *Literatur*, 147–90, investigates the name *Biterolf* and its significance for the *Wartburgkrieg* and for the Alexander tradition. N. H. Ott, *Fest. Walliczek*, 61–86, reconsiders the murals of epics and romances in

Rodenegg, Runkelstein, and Wildenstein, tracing a development in their relation to literature.

T. Klein, *Fest. Wiesinger*, 537–68, adopts a wide-ranging statistical approach to the relationship between verse and syntax in the EMHG corpus. K. Klein, *Fest. Pensel*, 95–100, presents hitherto disregarded fragments of the *Kaiserchronik* from Gnesen. Stephan Müller, *Vom Annolied zur Kaiserchronik. Zu Text- und Forschungsgeschichte einer verlorenen deutschen Reimchronik*, Heidelberg, Winter, ix + 340 pp., has as its concluding chapter (pp. 255–319) a substantial new comparative analysis of the *Annolied* in relation to the passages shared by the *Kaiserchronik*, in which M. favours a two-stage genesis, strophes 2–6 and 34–49 of the early 12th c. being followed by the prologue and the central world-historical portion under the influence of Rupert of Deutz. While this perhaps does less than justice to the force of early medieval historiographical tradition in general, M.'s necessarily partly speculative contribution to a time-honoured problem is justified by the rest of the Munich dissertation: a fascinating account of the literature on the subject from the early 19th c. on and in particular the hypothesis of an earlier lost rhyming chronicle, fiercely contested for a time but lost since the 1950s among the vested scholarly interests of debate surrounding new approaches, e.g. the numerological and typological. M.'s claim that the postulated chronicle still deserves serious consideration is countered by the history of scholarship on works such as the *Ezzolied* and the *Lob Salomons* and — in contrast to the alleged diversity of approaches — by a tendency to accept that the simplest solutions are often the most plausible and that Ockham's razor justly excises the many hypothetical *Vorlagen* beloved of earlier scholarship. Nevertheless, E. C. Lutz, Lutz, *Literatur*, 95–145, interprets the *Ezzolied* in its historical context, including the postulation of a 30-strophe version based not least on number symbolism, and at the same time casts an eye over *Annolied* and *Kaiserchronik*. Id., Palmer, *Kloster*, 29–52, places *Ezzolied* and *Rolandslied* at the centre of a reconsideration of the complex personal interactions, as distinct from the courts as institutions, which determine the nature of courtly cultural activity. H. Brall, *Das Mittelalter*, 3.2, 1998:45–61, focuses on *Ezzolied, Navigatio Brendani*, and *Herzog Ernst* in a study of the fascination of foreign travel, while C. Mackert, *Fest. Schupp*, 43–60, addresses the cultural background of Lamprecht's *Alexander* in relation to its sources, and B. Quast, Müller, *Mittelalter*, 197–216, examines the narrative technique of Der Wilde Mann's *Veronika*. In *FZPT*, 46, E. Tremp (52–66) surveys views of

Hildegard of Bingen expressed by her contemporaries, and U. Kühne (67–78) her understanding of her role as authoress, while R. Dabke, *Parergon*, 16.1, 1998:1–18, investigates the states of the souls in her *Ordo Virtutum*, and L. Gnädinger, *Fest. Haas*, 175–206, elucidates her theology of Adam's voice and the role of music.

MIDDLE HIGH GERMAN HEROIC LITERATURE

D. Gottschall, *ZDA*, 128:251–81, studies the semantic associations of *recke* from OHG to the *Nibelungenlied*. Bettina Geier, *Täuschungshandlungen im Nibelungenlied. Ein Beitrag zur Differenzierung von List und Betrug* (GAG, 659), 227 pp., is a very detailed and subtle treatment of the topic, based on the fundamental insight that the very wide range of semantic nuance associated with MHG *list* often excludes deceit, while the modern and medieval moral evaluations of deception often do not coincide. The highly differentiated analysis, which focuses on various aspects of language, silence, and gesture, identifies different usage in parts I and II of the *Nl.*, finds that — in contrast to the opinions of some earlier researchers — the poet's evaluation of deceitful behaviour is largely negative, and above all emphasizes that the whole subject is an inherent and carefully conceived component of the structure of the work. An excursus presents a comparative analysis of *Kudrun*. K. Kröhnke, *Fest. Brackert*, 148–61, studies the exchange of weapons in the *Nl.* and the *Iliad*. U. Störmer-Caysa, *Neophilologus*, 83:93–113, asks why Kriemhild betrays the secret of Siegfried's vulnerability, with various legal speculations, and M. Schausten, *ZDP*, 118:27–49, interprets *âventiure* 6 in terms of body and gender, while E. C. Tennant, *Müller, Mittelalter*, 273–316, studies the 'gender dynamics' of *âventiure* 11, and O. Ehrismann, *Fichtner, Doppelgänger*, 175–200, surveys the themes of the magic cloak and disguise from medieval heroic literature to its modern reception. C. Brinker-von der Heyde, *ABÄG*, 51:105–24, interprets the polyvalent figure of Hagen, emphasizing that the Hagen of *Kudrun* is not that of the *Nl. The Saga of the Volsungs. The Norse Epic of Sigurd the Dragon Slayer*, trans., introd., and comm. Jesse L. Byock, Harmondsworth, Penguin, ix + 145 pp., is a handy reprint of an excellent recent translation, which in this format will prove invaluable to those teaching and researching the *Nl.* The introduction focuses on the subject-matter in general, its representation in art, the mythical, heroic, legendary, and historical background, and Wagner. Notes and glossary are brief but informative. Walter Hansen, *Wo Siegfried starb und Kriemhild liebte. Die Schauplätze des Nibelungenliedes*, Vienna, Uebberreuter, 1997, 179 pp., vividly introduces the topography of the *Nl.* A major editorial project reaches fruition with *Die 'Nibelungenklage'*.

*Synoptische Ausgabe aller vier Fassungen*, ed. Joachim Bumke, Berlin, de Gruyter, 582 pp., and N. Henkel, Palmer, *Kloster*, 73–98, argues that the *Klage* was always a factor in the understanding of the events of the *Nl. c.* 1200, while T. Bein, *Editio*, 12, 1998:38–54, makes an intertextual correlation between the *Klage* and the obscure Walther von Grieven (*c.* 1300).

Joachim Heinzle, *Einführung in die mittelhochdeutsche Dietrichepik*, Berlin, de Gruyter, xi + 221 pp., is an informative introduction. *Die aventiurehafte Dietrichepik. Laurin und Walberan, der jüngere Sigenot, das Eckenlied, der Wanderer. Mittelhochdeutscher Text und neuhochdeutsche Übersetzung*, trans. Christa Tuczay (GAG, 599), 368 pp., is an attractive volume which aims to present the minor Dietrich epics to a student readership, but also the general reader. The texts follow the *Deutsches Heldenbuch* and other large inaccessible editions, and their collection in this format is itself of great benefit to the professional scholar. The translations in facing columns are unpretentious and seek accuracy above all. A pleasing range of illustrations from various early printed sources features on almost every page. E. Lienert, *BGDSL*, 121:23–46, confronts the Dietrich epic with the Nibelungen tradition, and B. Kellner, Müller, *Mittelalter*, 43–62, studies the role of genealogy in the *Buch von Bern*, while in *Dämonen, Monster, Fabelwesen* (see pp. 592–93 above) the relevant heroic literature is cited, together with other sources, in treatments of Laurin and the Wild Hunt (J. L. Flood), and of the demonic in the epic (H.-J. Behr). *Das Eckenlied. Sämtliche Fassungen. I. Einleitung. Die altbezeugten Versionen $E_1$, $E_2$ und Strophe 8–13 von $E_4$. Anhang: Die Ecca-Episode aus der Thidrekssaga. II. Dresdener Heldenbuch und Ansbacher Fragment $E_7$ und $E_3$. III. Die Druckversion und verwandte Textzeugen $e_1$, $E_4$, $E_5$, $E_6$*, ed. Francis B. Brévart (ATB, 111), 3 vols, xxxiv + 103, vi + 112, vi + 108 pp., is the culmination of many years' work, founded on the basic insights that the relatively recent edition of the L version by M. Wierschin (see *YWMLS*, 36:601) is defective — corrections appeared in B.'s handy Reclam edition of 1986 (see *YWMLS*, 48:689) — and that there is an overriding need in any case for a modern, text-critical edition of all manuscripts and the earliest printed version. The introductory material is — unusually for recent additions to the ATB series — concerned exclusively with codicology and transmission. There is minimal intervention in the texts apart from moderate graphemic normalization and correction of obvious errors. The problem of presentation of the inordinately complex textual relationships is admirably solved in a user-friendly manner: texts are organized synoptically in three volumes representing the three main versions, with full cross-referencing. C. Händl, *Fest. Walliczek*, 87–129, examines the role of text and illustration in the *Sigenot* transmission, and U. Störmer-Caysa, *ZDA*, 128:282–308, studies the role of Ortnit in various works, while S. Coxon, Robertshaw, *Natur*, 189–98, considers the hero as midwife in *Wolfdietrich*, and N. Voorwinden, *ZDA*, 128:47–61, returns to an old debate about the presence of *Wolfdietrich* in the Low Countries, arguing that there are no grounds for linking the Dutch *De Jager uyt Grieken* to the German epic. C. Gerhardt, *WW*, 49:27–45, studies a neglected *Rosengarten* manuscript, and B. Gotzkowsky, *ZDA*, 128:198–203, documents the sources of the illustrations of the 1560 edition of the *Heldenbuch*.

THE COURTLY ROMANCE

W. Haug, Palmer, *Kloster*, 211–28, sets up theoretical theses to explain the fictionality of the new courtly romance in the 12th c. U. Ernst, *FmSt*, 31, 1997:252–369, is a major monograph on literacy in the courtly romance, asserting the primarily literary environment in which they were produced and rejecting such received opinions as the largely oral reception of the works, the notion that private reading was performed aloud, and that the knights were illiterate and only ladies literate, etc. In Wolfzettel, *Erzählstrukturen*, F. P. Knapp (3–22) emphasizes the interplay of historiography and fiction in the greater part of 12th-c. romance, P. Ihring (47–65) studies the role of prophetic discourse as exemplified by the figure of Merlin, and E. Schmid (69–85) attacks the critical emphasis on structural reduplication as an oversimplified approach to the complexity of the classical Arthurian work, while F. Wolfzettel (119–41) also sees it as a relatively peripheral device, and M. Meyer (145–63) proposes a tripartite conception of literary character as an alternative. B. Haupt, *ZGer*, 9:557–85, studies pictorial description in the romance, and H. Wandhoff, *ib.*, 586–97, the poetics of the visual. Astrid Eitschberger, *Musikinstrumente in höfischen Romanen des deutschen Mittelalters* (Imagines medii aevi, 2), Wiesbaden, Reichert, ix + 357 pp. + 56 pls, is a Würzburg dissertation based on the analysis of the references to musical instruments in 30 works broadly defined as courtly romances from Lamprecht's *Alexander* to Johann von Würzburg's *Wilhelm von Österreich*, a period of somewhat over 150 years. Taking due note of possible exaggeration and idealization in the literary sources, E. addresses these in the context of the evidence from musical history and artistic representation. The terminology falls into four classes, the chordophonic, idiophonic, membranophonic, and aerophonic instruments. The discussions of individual and groups of instruments are fascinating reading, and comprise in essence an encyclopaedic treatment of the subject-matter which will form a permanent source for consultation. The brief conclusion summarizes the material and provides statistical analysis. H. Brall, Schaefer, *Artes*, 215–29, reviews magicians in the courtly romances, and H. Bleumer, Robertshaw, *Natur*, 77–89, addresses their complement of wild women, while A. Classen, *JOWG*, 11:153–71, surveys their presentation of Spain. Monika Schausten, *Erzählwelten der Tristangeschichte im hohen Mittelalter. Untersuchungen zu den deutschsprachigen Tristanfassungen des 12. und 13. Jahrhunderts* (FGÄDL, 24), 325 pp., a Cologne dissertation from the school of J. Bumke, devotes substantial separate chapters to Eilhart, Gottfried, Ulrich von Türheim, and Heinrich von Freiberg, and instead of dwelling on the common features and differences of the subject-matter in the manner of older genetic scholarship points rather to the quite different 'narrative worlds' created by each author, Gottfried's model in particular being seen as provoking the differing realizations and emphases of a fundamentally compelling story of love, deception, and betrayal. The study is of fundamental interest to the extent that it explores different forms of intertextuality inherent in different medieval treatments of a given narrative, and also questions the basis and substance of the idea of 'continuations' of existing narrative by later poets. H. Zutt, *Fest. Schupp*, 284–304, analyses the use of performative verbs of speaking to cause or persuade someone to do something, in *Iwein*, *Tristan*, and *Parzival*. J. Klinger, Müller, *Mittelalter*, 127–48, addresses the problem of identity and self-reflection in the heroes of Gottfried's *Tristan* and the *Prosa Lancelot*. K. Ridder, *Chloe*, 29:303–29, compares the treatment of death from love and suicide in Gottfried, in Rudolf von Ems's *Wilhelm von Orlens*, and in Konrad von Würzburg's *Partonopier und Meliur*. A. Krass, *LiLi*, 114:66–98, studies the friendship of Achilles and Patroclus in the Trojan romances of Herbort von Fritzlar and Konrad von Würzburg, and in Benoît de Sainte-Maure. R. G. Dunphy, *GRM*, 49:1–18, compares the story of the knight with the chemise in Jacques de Baisieux, Jans Enikel, and the *Weihenstephaner Chronik*, and S. G. Nichols, Müller, *Mittelalter*, 217–40, finds an allegorical complexity in the demonic image of the Melusine legend. M. Schausten, Bennewitz, *Konstruktion*, 143–58, examines the power and gender relations in Veldeke's treatment of Dido and Aeneas, and N. Halač, *JOWG*, 11:9–20, studies the descriptions of Dido in Veldeke and elsewhere.

### HARTMANN VON AUE

B. Schirok, *Fest. Schupp*, 184–211, interprets a range of passages in H.'s Arthurian romances as evidence of a concern with literary theory, and E. Feistner, *ASNS*, 236:241–64, writes on the identity of the hero in *Erec* and *Iwein*, while J. Margetts, *Fest. Brackert*, 11–23, comments on H.'s Enite in comparison with Chrétien, and R. Schipke, *Fest. Pensel*, 263–77, edits a newly-discovered fragment of *Gregorius* from Berlin. P. W. Tax, *ABÄG*, 51:125–46, returns to the problem of *Gregorius*, l. 108, discussing recent conjectures and favouring *âne geschôz* with an allusion to the prelapsarian nakedness of Adam; and L. Okken, *ib.*, 147–48, contributes further to the debate. C. Fasbender, *ZDA*, 128:394–408, investigates the understanding and treatment of *hôchvart* in *Der arme Heinrich* and other works by the scribe of Heidelberg Cpg 341, and D. Duckworth, *Mediaevistik*, 11, 1998:11–31, studies the theological background to Heinrich's *zwîvel*, while S. Grosse, *Fest. Schupp*, 329–45, studies the reception of *Der arme Heinrich* in various modern writers. W. Fritsch-Rössler, *GRM*, 49:241–47, finds both chiasmus and palindrome in the structural relationship of *Iwein* to *Erec*, and W. Haug, Wolfzettel, *Erzählstrukturen*, 99–118, interprets the *Yvain/Iwein* romances in terms of a misunderstanding by both the hero and the critics of Erec's fault, while M. Unzeitig-Herzog, *ib.*, 233–53, makes *Iwein* the focus of a study of the problems surrounding the conclusion of Arthurian narrative, with the change from hero to ruler, H. Wandhoff, Müller, *Mittelalter*, 111–26, takes a media-orientated approach to the question Iwein's identity and honour, and K. Freche, *Fest. Walliczek*, 201–15, includes reference to H. in a study of honour in the *Erex saga*.

### WOLFRAM VON ESCHENBACH

New versions of old editions include Wolfram von Eschenbach, *Parzival. Mittelhochdeutscher Text nach der 6. Ausgabe von Karl Lachmann*, trans. Peter Knecht, introd. Bernd Schirok, Berlin, de Gruyter, 1998, xcvi + 837 pp., and Wolfram von Eschenbach, *Parzival. Mittelhochdeutscher Text nach der 6. Ausgabe von Karl Lachmann. Einsprachige Studienausgabe*, introd. Bernd Schirok, Berlin, de Gruyter, xcvi + 420 pp. *A Companion to Wolfram's 'Parzival'*, ed. Will Hasty, Columbia, SC, Camden House, xxii + 295 pp., is a valuable collection of 12 essays which, if they cannot exhaustively cover the range of topics now associated with the greatest work of the period and occasionally show some uncertainty about their intended audience, do succeed in the more modest and perhaps more useful aim of conveying 'an impression of the current state of scholarship', and also demonstrate that a satisfactory single-author treatment is now a thing of the past. Following an introduction (W. Hasty, ix-xx) there are accounts of the Gahmuret books (F. G. Gentry, 3–11), the women characters (M. E. Gibbs, 12–36), Gawan (M. H. Jones, 37–76), the grail (S. Johnson, 77–95), sources (A. Stevens, 99–123), narrative presentation (N. Thomas, 124–39), theology (B. Murdoch, 143–58), tournaments and battles (W. H. Jackson, 159–88), literacy and learning (A. Classen, 189–202), symbols of transformation (W. McConnell, 203–22), P. in wider Arthurian perspective, 223–41), and modern reception (U. Müller, 245–58). There is a major advance in the prolonged process of supplying detailed commentaries on *Parzival*, earlier a surprisingly neglected activity, with three new consecutively arranged dissertations by Bochum pupils of E. Nellmann. Christa-Maria Kordt, *Parzival in Munsalvaesche. Kommentar zu Buch V/1 von Wolframs 'Parzival' (224,1–248,30)*, Herne, Vlg für Wissenschaft und Kunst, 1997, 309 pp., addresses the crucial episode of the first visit to the grail castle, prefacing each subdivided section with an analysis of subject-matter taken over from Chrétien or deviating from his version. The reader is obliged to move frequently between the densely informative main text and substantial additional material in footnotes. The brief introduction avoids theoretical and other problems posed by the commentary form and focuses on the substantial matters covered in the commentary: lexical and semantic problems, grammar and style, narrative technique, material culture, motifs, relation to the source and intertextual reference, and problems of interpretation. These in general receive an even balance of consideration in the body of the work. Three substantial excursuses, on the Abenberg/Wildenberg allusions, the grail procession, and interpretation of the failure to ask the question, are valuable surveys of research in their own right, leading to judicious conclusions. Susanna Backes, *Von Munsalvaesche zum Artushof. Stellenkommentar zum fünften Buch von Wolframs 'Parzival' (249,1–279,30)*, Herne, Vlg für Wissenschaft und Kunst, v + 222 pp., follows the same general format while keeping supplementary footnotes to a minimum. The introduction reflects briefly on the inevitably interpretative nature of any commentary and points to the same concerns as Kordt; it is noticeable that the chosen subject-matter, the Sigune and Jeschute episodes of Book V, is in itself relatively less rich than the grail-castle episode in material susceptible of very detailed comment. There are useful excursuses on Sigune in the linden tree and the grail sword. Gisela Garnerus, *Parzivals zweite Begegnung mit dem Artushof. Kommentar zu Buch VI/1 von Wolframs 'Parzival' (280,1–312,1)*, Herne, Vlg für Wissenschaft und Kunst, 310 pp., like the two previously mentioned works has its own individual stamp: how far this reflects the section of the work chosen for commentary or the personal interests of the author, is for consideration. G. sets out the same programme of areas for comment in her introduction, while also explicitly seeing her work as an aid for student use: an angle perhaps reflected in the relatively greater attention paid to matters of lexical comprehension, which results in information of a very general nature sitting together with arcane and very subject-specific explanations. Nevertheless, episodes as important as the blood drops in the snow and Parzival's relationship with Gawan at Arthur's court supply a wealth of material for which this commentary, like the others, will be a first recourse for those concerned with matters of textual detail. Randal Sivertson, *Loyalty and Riches in Wolfram's 'Parzival'* (EH, 1, 1720), 259 pp., is an uncomfortable but highly readable thesis which focuses on 'service for riches', confronting traditional interpretations based on chivalric, religious, courtly, or dynastic values with the bald fact that in many instances the pursuit of such high-flown ideals is often unequivocally subordinated to the attractions of worldly opulence. The argument is supported by numerous descriptive passages, but more cogently by detailed and convincing interpretations of such episodes as Parzival's initial idolization of riches before transferring his idolatry to richly clad knights and finally knighthood itself, his treatment of Jeschute, or the power of riches embodied by Feirefiz. In many cases the down-to-earth approach results in pungent polemic against some of the more fanciful and pretentious views of earlier critics. Also noted: Ulrike Grein Gamra, *Ein komplexer Ritter auf seiner dynamischen Queste. Wolframs Parzival und die Chaostheorie. Eine strukturelle Untersuchung* (DLA, 28), 275 pp. U. Ernst, Wolfzettel, *Erzählstrukturen*, 165–98, draws a parallel between *King Oedipus* and W.'s concealing and revealing technique, relating it to Bakhtin's theories, and W. Blank, *Fest. Schupp*, 212–32, reinterprets P.'s progress against the background of the tension betwen the Arthurian world and the grail world, while M. Swisher, *Neophilologus*, 83 : 253–65, interprets P.'s spiritual growth, C. J. Steppich, *JEGP*, 98 : 40–77, makes P.'s renunciation of joy (329,25–30) the focus of an interpretation of his quest, and K. Ridder, *LiLi*, 114 : 21–41, links P.'s grief to the themes of remembrance and forgetting. S. Heckel, Haas, *Frauen*, 35–52, studies the varying interpretations of Herzeloyde, and C. Young, Robertshaw, *Natur*, 243–52, considers childhood with reference to Obie and Obilot, while M. Baisch, Haas, *Frauen*, 15–33, discusses the figure and function of Orgeluse. M. Unzeitig-Herzog, *FmSt*, 32, 1998 : 196–217, considers the resolution of conflict in Book XIV, and W. Wunderlich, *JOWG*, 11 : 383–412, analyses the P. frescoes in Constance.

T. Tomasek, *FmSt*, 32, 1998 : 182–95, considers *Willehalm* as a *Legende*, and C. Brinker-von der Heyde, *Fest. Haas*, 337–51, interprets the various roles of Gyburg, both feminine and masculine, while M. Schnyder, *ib.*, 507–20, touches on similar themes in an account of her isolation. M. Kern, *DVLG*, 73 : 567–91, argues that the Amor of Noupatris's standard negates the allegory of Amor in Veldeke, and links into a traditional pattern, and W. G. Rohr, *LiLi*, 114 : 42–65, focuses on the theme of *klârheit* in a study of Willehalm's grief for Rennewart, while U. Gaebel, *JOWG*, 11:363–82, surveys cross-dressing in *chanson de geste* adaptations from Wolfram's *Willehalm* onwards. S. Christoph, *DVLG*, 73:211–27, interprets the 'Brackenseil' text of *Titurel* as offering Sigune authoritative knowledge, in conflict with her need to experience life, and E. Krotz, *Fest. Walliczek*, 167–200, compares W.'s treatment of the reader of *Titurel* to the hound and its leash.

GOTTFRIED VON STRASSBURG

A. Cowell, *Exemplaria*, 11:115–39, refers to G. in a study of the colours of rhetoric, and W. H. Jackson, Robertshaw, *Natur*, 175–87, interprets *natiure* in in Gottfried and related works, while T. Tomasek, *LiLi*, 114:9–20, interprets the conception of *truren* in *Tristan*, H. J. Scheuer, *BGDSL*, 121:406–39, studies the ritualistic aspects of T.'s baptism and of the dismemberment of the stag. In *Tristania*, 19, A. Deighton (1–12) contributes to the debate on G.'s biography, arguing that there is no basis for associating him personally with Augsburg; J. M. Jeep (13–43) analyses G.'s alliterating word-pairs; and A. Diem (45–95) sees the question of Marke's possible homosexuality as of secondary importance in the emotional context of the work as a whole. In *Chloe*, 29, H. Busch (203–18) returns to the question of suffering in *T.*, K. Usener (219–45) studies G.'s reception of Ovid, N. Werner (13–59) studies artistic representations of *T.*, and L. E. Saurma-Jeltsch (247–301) examines the illustrations of the Brussels manuscript. R. Günthart, *ASNS*, 236:94–101, shows G. introducing learned details into the orchard scene (*T.* 15087–105), and V. Mertens, Palmer, *Kloster*, 1–16, develops understanding of the allegory of the cave of love by demonstrating the monastic dimension of its significance, while E. Nellmann, *Fest. Schupp*, 305–10, returns to the latch on the door of the love-grotto, rejecting the erotic interpretations proposed by various critics. M. Titzmann, *Fest. Walliczek*, 295–322, considers Theodor Storm's reception of G.

OTHER ROMANCES

R. Chamberlin, *MGS*, 24, 1998:8–17, points to allegorical usage in Ulrich von Zatzikhoven's treatment of the marvellous. *Mauricius von Craûn. Mittelhochdeutsch/Neuhochdeutsch*, ed., trans., and comm. Dorothea Klein (UB, 8796), 244 pp., on the assumption that Hans Ried's unique copy followed a 13th-c. version close to the original, takes as its basis Edward Schröder's fairly cautious edition of 1929 rather than Ulrich Pretzel's more recent but highly conjectural and radical text of 1956. As with other works in the series, the translation aims to do no more than facilitate access to the original. The introduction also includes discussion of language, author, and subject-matter, with review of research. Besides an informative and fairly detailed commentary the French analogue, *Du chevalier qui recovra l'amour de sa dame*, is included with a line-by-line translation. R. Bauschke, Bennewitz, *Konstruktion*, 305–25, interprets *Moriz von Craûn* in terms of sex and gender theory. P. Kern, Wolfzettel, *Erzählstrukturen*, 199–218, identifies aspects of Heinrich von dem Türlin's *Diu Crône* which form a metadiscourse within the work, and D. Ganter, Haas, *Frauen*, 91–107, considers the implications for its structure of the figure of Gawein, while C. Schu, *ZDP*, 118:336–53, interprets the Gasozein episode, and J. Keller, *Fest.* Haas, 437–53, the place of death and the other world in the sequences of marvels. E. Schmid, *Fest.* Brackert, 42–57, interprets the Floris romances, while A. Schulz, *Fest.* Walliczek, 29–59, studies the narrative perspective of Rudolf von Ems's *Der Guote Gerhart*, and M. Schulz, *ib.*, 1–28, considers the idealization of its hero. Also noted: Erika Weigele-Ismael, *Rudolf von Ems, Wilhelm von Orlens. Studien zur Ausstattung und zur Ikonographie einer illustrierten deutschen Epenhandschrift des 13. Jahrhunderts am Beispiel des Cgm 63 der Bayerischen Staatsbibliothek München* (EH, XXVIII, 285), 1997, 365 pp.

Michael Waltenberger, *Das grosse Herz der Erzählung. Studien zu Narration und Interdiskursivität im 'Prosa-Lancelot'* (Mikrokosmos, 51), Frankfurt, Lang, 202 pp., is a highly original dissertation from the school of W. Harms which approaches the work in the light of the discourse theory of M. Foucault; the implications of the adaptation of this to a medieval romance, and especially the question of alterity, are addressed in a substantial theoretical introduction. The treatment of the text is necessarily highly selective and applicable to versions in all languages. But the real interest of the study in any case lies both in its detail and its broad-brush assessments of the narrative modes at different stages of the work. There is much on the description of the hero and other figures in terms of physiognomy and the humours, the narrative focus of the grail episodes against the background of T. Todorov's work, and the abandonment in the *Mort Artu* of a hierarchical narrative structure in favour of a series of multi-faceted changes in perspective, linked above all to the introduction of Fortuna. K. Ruh, *ZDA*, 128:194–97, studies references to the Round Table of the prose *Lancelot* cycle in a Franciscan work, and W. Haug, pp. 251–66 of *Das Ende. Figuren einer Denkform*, ed. Karlheinz Stierle and Rainer Warning (Poetik und Hermeneutik, 16), Munich, Fink, 1996, x + 680 pp., interprets the dénouement of the Arthurian tradition in the *Prosa Lancelot*, while E. Schmid, *Euphorion*, 49:373–89, includes the German text in a study of the theme of truth in the *Mort Artu*.

H. Fiedler, *Brüder Grimm Gedenken*, 13:78–94, studies Wilhelm Grimm's interest in, and transcription of, *Mai und Beaflor*. Ulrich von dem Türlin, *Arabel. Die ursprüngliche Fassung und ihre Bearbeitung*, ed. Werner Schröder, Stuttgart, Hirzel, xxi + 323 pp., is the culmination of many years' work, and effectively replaces S.'s six volumes of *Arabel-Studien* which appeared between 1982 and 1993. The text, which appeared there in varying and unsystematic order, now forms a coherent edition of enduring value. The introduction summarizes the essential facts and findings of the research underlying the work. R. Brandt, *ASNS*, 236:344–69, supplies a substantial critical bibliography of work on Konrad von Würzburg 1987–96, while W. G. Rohr, *Euphorion*, 93:305–48, interprets his *Engelhard*, and J. Eming, Haas, *Frauen*, 53–70, gives a psychological interpretation of Partonopier's mother in *Partonopier und Meliur*. K. Schmitt, Robertshaw, *Natur*, 151–62, examines gender roles in Ulrich von Etzenbach's *Alexander*, and W. Wunderlich, *JOWG*, 11:1–8, reviews its *ekphrasis* of the slaves of love. W. C. McDonald, *Tristania*, 19:97–113, interprets the masculinity of the hero of Heinrich von Freiberg's *Tristan*. K. Ridder, *Poetica*, 31:101–23, interprets the names of the protagonists in 14th-c. romances, and K. Ridder, Wolfzettel, *Erzählstrukturen*, 331–45, examines the narrative structure of *Reinfried von Braunschweig*, distinguishing medieval from modern forms of intertextuality, while S. Zöller, *Fest. Brackert*, 58–72, interprets the *triuwe* of *Die Rittertreue*. Cora Dietl, *Minnerede, Roman und historia. Der 'Wilhelm von Österreich' Johanns von Würzburg* (Hermaea, n.F., 87), Tübingen, Niemeyer, viii + 429 pp., for the first time places this early-14th-c. romance in its complete literary and historical context, building on a relatively limited number of recent studies which have finally disposed of the older dismissal of the work as *Epigonentum*. Detailed accounts of the content, transmission, author, and patronage of the work are followed by the three central chapters on the problem of *historia*, J.'s understanding of history and fiction and his treatment of his sources; the *Minnerede* as a genre and its adaptation by J. in the narrative structure; and the panegyric role of the *Minnerede* and its significance for the ending of the work in particular. The conclusions emphasize above all the complex generic mixture of the text, amplified with rerference to other comparable works of the period, and its treatment in reception. The documentation includes a print and translation of a hitherto unedited 'Liebesklage'.

*Chloe*, 29, is chiefly devoted to the late-medieval Tristan legend, and includes contributions by J. Küppers (magic potions in Classical literature, 61–102); A. Hartmann (the Persian analogue, 103–39);

X. von Ertzdorff (the narrative structures of various versions, 169–201); R. Voss (a comparison of different German versions, 331–54); B. Besamusca (Dutch reception, 413–28); besides work on the legend in various other languages, and its modern reception. J.-D. Müller, *Fest. Haas*, 455–70, interprets *Tristan als Mönch*. Id., Haug, *Mittelalter*, 143–63, supplies a critique of C. Lugowski's theory of the novel and its implications for the prose romance. H. E. Keller, *Fest. Haas*, 207–20, links ideas of Paracelsus to Thüring von Ringoltingen's *Melusine* among other works, and U. Störmer-Caysa, *BGDSL*, 121:239–61, writes on Melusine's children in Thüring's narrative.

LYRIC POETRY

B. Wachinger, Haug, *Mittelalter*, 1–29, takes a broad view of the love song from the 12th to the 16th c., focusing on the tension between oral and written traditions and on the conceptions of love implied. S. Obermaier, Cramer, *Lyrik*, 11–32, considers the thematization of 'poetry within poetry' as a tool for developing a poetic of the medieval lyric, and H. Haferland, *ib.*, 232–52, studies the assertions of integrity of a number of poets. F. Willaert, *ZDP*, 118:321–35, favours an intimate, esoteric milieu for the performance of the love-lyric, and M. Kern, *Neophilologus*, 83:577–99, studies references to Classical mythology and their function in a range of lyric texts, while R. Schnell, *ZDA*, 128:127–84, comments at length on gender roles and their interaction in the love-lyric. Also noted: Stefan Zeyen, *. . .daz tet der liebe dorn. Erotische Metaphorik in der deutschsprachigen Lyrik des 12.–14. Jahrhunderts* (Item mediävistische Studien, 5), Essen, Item, 1996, 255 pp. S. Fritsch-Staar, Bennewitz, *Konstruktion*, 182–203, considers the metaphorical treatment of the uterus in the lyric and elsewhere, and E. Wenzel, *ib.*, 264–83, identifies different types of images of women, while L. P. Johnson, Robertshaw, *Natur*, 31–40, interprets the conception of nature in the *Natureingang*. U. Ruberg, *Fest. Krummacher*, 15–29, seeks to identify the generic basic of the secular *Tagelied*, and A. Classen, *EG*, 54:173–96, studies its later variants.

*Romanisch beeinflußte Lieder des Minnesangs*, ed., trans., and comm. Olive Sayce (GAG, 664), x + 299 pp., builds on the work of I. Frank but applies a more rigorous test than Frank to the definition of influence, insisting on the presence of precise thematic and linguistic links between the German and the Romance texts and emphasizing that, while formal correspondences are usually also present, these do not in themselves prove prior knowledge of the Romance models. Twelve songs, two each by Hausen, Albrecht von Johansdorf, and Morungen, and one each by Veldeke, Bernger von Horheim, Ulrich von Gutenburg, Hartwig von Raute, Reinmar, and Walther, meet the criteria. Appropriate editions are selected, clear modern translations provided, together with very detailed commentary on the metre and on the German texts in relation to the originals. The question of Romance influence in each case is then helpfully summarized. A glossary is included in the supporting documentation. M. Chinca, pp. 199–213 of *Masculinity in Medieval Europe*, ed. D. M. Hadley, London, Routledge, x + 285 pp., studies the male and female voices in Kürenberger, considering them as relating either to the collective behaviour of noblemen, or to appreciation by both sexes. K. Hufeland, *Fest. Schupp*, 177–83, studies the Pseudo-Dietmar songs MF 37,4 and 37,18, while in Cramer, *Lyrik*, F. Willaert (33–56) considers the place of Veldeke among the early poets; J. Ashcroft (57–84) places Dido and Aeneas at the heart of an interpretation of the theme of *renovatio* in Hausen; M. Eikelmann (85–106) studies the development of the *Wechsel*; and J. Pfeiffer (122–38) interprets Morungen, MF 131,25. U. Wyss, *Fest. Brackert*, 24–41, writes on Morungen, MF 138,17, 'Ich waene, niemen lebe', and G. Callesen, *WW*, 49:17–26, reinterprets his 'Narcissus' song (MF 145,1), while M. Stock, *LiLi*, 114:156–66, interprets 'Ich wil eine reise' (MF 145,33) together with Burkhart von Hohenfels's 'Mich müet daz sô manger sprichet'. J.-D. Müller, *BGDSL*, 121:379–405, explains contradictions in the performative aspects of Reinmar's lyric, and I. Kasten, *Fest. Haas*, 419–35, notes the variations in the poetic role in Hartmann's songs, while A. Klare, Cramer, *Lyrik*, 139–68, finds at least three songs in a radical editorial approach to Hartmann, MF 207,11.

Manfred Günther Scholz, *Walther von der Vogelweide* (SM, 316), ix + 210 pp., is an entirely new treatment, focusing on the research of recent decades listed in a single concluding bibliography, and explicitly intended to complement, not replace, the serviceable series of volumes by Kurt Herbert Halbach (SM, 40) which concentrate on older research and its greater concern with biography and authenticity. S. possesses a magisterial knowledge of the literature, and the discussions of each work ably highlight the chief problems and place them in a perspective which repeatedly emphasizes the interpretative subtleties required for the understanding of a lyric poet who uses *ich* as much as any other. T. Nolte, *Poetica*, 30, 1998:351–76, considers theoretical discussions of irony in medieval literature and applies the concept to W.'s political poetry, and B. Plate, *Euphorion*, 93:293–304, examines the historical background to W.'s strophes L. 8,28, 18,19, and 19,5, while R. Luff, *ZDA*, 128:17–41, studies the background to the figure of the hermit in W. and elsewhere. Susanne Padberg, *'Ahî wie kristenlîche nû der bâbest lachet.' Walthers Kirchenkritik im Unmutston. (Edition, Kommentar, Untersuchungen)*, Herne, Vlg für Wissenschaft und

Kunst, 1997, 322 pp., is a Bochum dissertation which first places the *Unmutston* strophes in the context of W.'s political lyric as a whole, with introductory accounts of the communicative context and the relevant political and social developments of the period. Problems relating to the transmission, form, and chronology of the strophes are reviewed, with a survey of previous interpretations. The heart of the study is an extremely detailed treatment of each of the seven anticlerical strophes of the *Unmutston* considered very plausibly to be individual entities. A perceptive account of editorial principles indicates an approach based on a modified *Leithandschrift* accompanied, as in the case of P. Wapnewski's edition of W.'s lyric, by diplomatic print, detailed apparatus, exhaustive commentary, analysis, and interpretation. There are also brief excursuses on topics including W.'s national consciousness and his attitude to contemporary religious movements. Although the overall conclusions are not substantially new, this work with its wealth of detailed comment marks a fundamental updating of scholarship on the strophes. S. Ranawake, *ASNS*, 236:1–32, studies the cultural background to the crusading themes in W., finding them closer to troubadour lyric than to other possible sources, and J. Janota, Haug, *Mittelalter*, 78–99, focuses on the last transmission of W.'s love songs in the Weimar MS F, while H. Tervooren, *ZDP*, 118:431–32, comments on *hêre frowe* (39,24), and R.-H. Steinmetz, *ib.*, 69–86, interprets the four versions of W.'s 'Bin ich dir unmære'. Ricarda Bauschke, *Die 'Reinmar-Lieder' Walthers von der Vogelweide. Literarische Kommunikation als Form der Selbstinszenierung* (*GRM*-Beiheft, 15), Heidelberg, Winter, 343 pp., is a trenchantly written thesis of which the most enduringly valuable sections are perhaps the closely argued individual analyses of 12 songs which have a bearing on the alleged feud with Reinmar, each founded on detailed reviews of the text and transmission and adopting a primarily intertextual approach. The relatively brief concluding chapter is perhaps less original than it claims to be in emphasizing the primarily parodistic nature of W.'s comments, seeing these as marginal to his work as a whole, and rejecting the conception of a 'feud' as propounded in the older literature. More provocative is the concluding analysis of W.'s two memorial strophes on Reinmar, which reject the notion that W. was necessarily younger or Reinmar's 'pupil', and also dismiss the idea of a rivalry between them, finding in L. 83,5 *dich selben wolt ich lützel klagen* a hyperbolic eulogy of Reinmar's artistry through the negation of a known personal affection for the dead man. C. Edwards, *OGS*, 27, 1998:1–29, gives a wide-ranging interpretation of the fragmentary 'Ez sprach ein wîp bî Rîne', and T. Bein, Cramer, *Lyrik*, 169–96, studies the transmission of texts of W. and other poets in the *Rappoltsteiner Florilegium*.

*Die Lieder Neidharts. Mit einem Melodieanhang von Helmut Lomnitzer*, ed. Edmund Wiessner, Hanns Fischer, and Paul Sappler, 5th rev. edn (ATB, 44), xlii + 221 pp., is the first reissue of this text since 1984. There are notably revisions of text and apparatus, and the now substantial introduction and bibliography have been brought up to date. The font has been marginally reduced without loss of clarity. Reinhard Bleck, *Neidharts Kreuzzugs-, Bitt- und politische Lieder als Grundlage für seine Biographie* (GAG, 661), 1998, 310 pp. T. Tomasek, Wolfzettel, *Erzählstrukturen*, 347–61, points to Arthurian structures in Ulrich von Liechtenstein's *Frauendienst*, especially the Venus journey, and A. Moshövel, Bennewitz, *Konstruktion*, 342–69, considers the cross-dressing in the *Frauendienst* in the light of gender theory. P. Strohschneider, Cramer, *Lyrik*, 197–231, relates the *Leichs* of Ulrich von Winterstetten, Heinrich von Sax, and Tannhäuser to the question of the ritual significance of the lyric, and Id., Müller, *Mittelalter*, 19–41, places the *Wartburgkrieg* at the centre of a study of medieval textuality. J. Rettelbach, *ASNS*, 236:33–52, considers the medieval evidence of Heinrich von Ofterdingen, and Dietrich Gerhardt, *ZDP*, 118:103–10, comments on Süsskind von Trimberg's connection with Zurich, while K. Stackmann, *BGDSL*, 121:440–55, comments critically on Gerhardt's recent book on Süsskind (see *YWMLS*, 60:598). Patricia Harant, *Poeta Faber. Der Handwerks-Dichter bei Frauenlob. Texte, Übersetzungen, Textkritik, Kommentar und Metapherninterpretationen* (ES, 110), 1997, iv + 186 pp., takes as its theme the metaphor of the craftsman in Frauenlob but has significant wider implications, for by showing that most of the imagery reaches back to a pre-existing tradition a cautionary note is sounded about the adoption of an over-simplified understanding of S. Obermaier's recent study (see *YWMLS*, 57:686) as implying a fundamental dichotomy between Minnesang and later didactic poetry. After a preliminary chapter on problems of authenticity, the relevant texts are presented in turn with translations and interpretative commentary. A brief review of the theory of metaphor leads to a systematic survey of the metaphorical themes with parallels in earlier literature and a glance at the numinous implications of literary creativity in general. The added emphasis on Frauenlob's own new formulations rounds off this well-balanced and thoughtful study. T. A. Kemper, *BGDSL*, 121:201–13, studies a textual crux in Frauenlob's *Marienleich*, 'Der smit von oberlande'. Christoph März, *Die weltlichen Lieder des Mönchs von Salzburg. Texte und Melodien* (MTU, 114), x + 570 pp. + 17 pls + supp., is a monumental new edition of the secular songs which replaces the old standard edition of the 1890s and, given the current popularity of the author, may itself be in use at the end of the next century. As before, the 53 evidently authentic songs of MS D form the basis of the edition. An introductory survey of the different forms culminates in a tabulated concordance. The monumentally detailed codicological section takes account both of Spechtler's edition of the religious songs and seeks to do justice to peripheral and fragmentary aspects of the transmission. The texts are presented with great clarity, the apparatus distinguishing clearly between commentary on the *Leithandschrift*, which is followed fairly conservatively, and a history of text-critical conjecture. Modern notation is used for the music of the polyphonic songs, otherwise mensural notation. The commentary (pp. 365–505) also takes full account of the critical literature and serves as a detailed guide to understanding. A. Krass, *BGDSL*, 121:75–102, interprets the *Martinslied* of the Monk of Salzburg, and in particular its carnivalesque elements. K. Stackmann, *ZDA*, 128:377–93, takes a broad look at the literary and historical problems relating to the 500–strophe corpus of anonymous *Meisterlieder*, and A. Classen, *NMi*, 100:207–26, explores the focus on suicide in late dawn songs and ballads. The latter's *Deutsche Frauenlieder des fünfzehnten und sechzehnten Jahrhunderts. Authentische Stimmen in der deutschen Frauenliteratur der Frühneuzeit oder Vertreter einer poetischen Gattung (das 'Frauenlied')?*, introd., ed., and comm. Albrecht Classen (APSL, 136), xxxi + 228 pp., is a programmatic anthology, introduced by an essay which ranges widely over the question of the female contribution to medieval German literature and advances the view that the texts presented are indeed the work of women and not examples of male poets adopting a female persona. The impressive total of 120 texts are in many respects a revelation, showing that the term *Frauenlied* of medieval studies takes on a quite new dimension by the end of the period. The majority of the texts derive from the great song-book collections and are classified accordingly, with introductions and notes. Also noted: Gabriele Herchert, *'Acker mir mein bestes Feld.' Untersuchungen zu erotischen Liederbüchern des späten Mittelalters. Mit Wörterbuch und Textsammlung* (Internationale Hochschulschriften, 201), Münster, Waxmann, 1996, 325 pp. E. Glaser, *Fest. Wiesinger*, 479–94, has further work on Clara Hätzlerin's graphemic system.

### DIDACTIC, DEVOTIONAL AND RELIGIOUS LITERATURE

T. Broekmann, *FmSt*, 32, 1998:218–62, relates *Reinhart Fuchs* to medieval behavioural conventions, and E. Hesse, *Haas, Frauen*, 111–28, compares the Hersant episode in *Reinhart Fuchs* with other versions of the beast epic, while we also note Irmeli S. Kühnel, *Reinhart Fuchs. A Gendered Reading* (GAG, 634), 1997, 134 pp. J. Wolf, *ZDA*, 128:425–27, presents a new fragment of Stricker, and D. Rocher, *Palmer, Kloster*, 99–112, surveys the courtly and religious values running through Stricker's work; Id., *Fest. Schupp*, 233–36, points to elements in Stricker's works showing him appealing to a popular audience. R.-H. Steinmetz, *GRM*, 49:255–73, makes *Helmbrecht* the basis of a review of the problem of identifying the comic in medieval texts. *Karl und Galie. Karlmeinet, Teil 1. Eine rheinische Dichtung über Karl den Großen*, trans. Dagmar Helm (GAG, 666), 158 pp., builds on the 1986 edition (*YWMLS*, 48:701–02) which forms the basis of a lucid modern translation of the complete A text. The introduction and notes on fundamental concepts are directed at the student and general reader as much as the scholar, but the venture as a whole is worthwhile and deserves to stimulate interest in a seriously neglected epic. In Kooper, *Chronicle*, J. de Ruiter (96–102) comments on the uncertain genre of the Charlemagne epic, aligning it with chronicle literature. As a whole the collection Kooper, *Chronicle*, places the study of the medieval chronicle firmly within an interdisciplinary context, with work by G. M. Spiegel (the theoretical background to the reading of medieval chronicles, 1–12); A. Amberger (historiographical conceptions exemplified in murals, 56–68); A.-J. A. Bijsterveld (patronage and donations in chronicles of the 11th and 12th cs, 69–83); S. Evstatiev (the Islamic chronicle, 116–23); E. Freeman (Cistercian histories, 124–32); A. M. Piazzoni (Hugh of St Victor, 212–25); U. S. Olsen (Marie van Oss, 240–50); L. Veszprémy (Hungary, 260–68); J. Ward (dispute resolution in 12th-c. historiography, 269–84); and J. Wolf (changing attitudes to the present, especially in the *Sächsische Weltchronik* and Martin of Troppau, 285–99). There is a substantial body of textual studies on the most monumental of chronicles, *Studien zur 'Weltchronik' Heinrichs von München*, including *Überlieferung, Forschungsbericht, Untersuchungen, Texte*, ed. Horst Brunner (WM, 29), 1998, xii + 600 pp.; Johannes Rettelbach, *Von der 'Erweiterten Christ-herre-Chronik' zur Redaktion* α (WM, 30/1, 30/2), 2 vols, 1998, xvi + 636 pp. + 15 pls, vi + 426 pp.; and Dorothea Klein, *Text- und überlieferungsgeschichtliche Untersuchungen zur Redaktion* β (WM, 31/1, 31/2), 2 vols, 1998, x + 402, xvi + 648 pp. B. Studt, Keller, *Schriftlichkeit*, 203–18, addresses minor textual forms in the late-medieval historiographical tradition, and J. Schneider, *ib.*, 219–41, studies the documentation of social and political conflicts in Nuremberg in the period 1458–63. R. Bentzinger, *Besch Vol.*, 33–41, examines the language of the 15th-c. Erfurt *Historienbibeln*. In Brunner, *Krieg*, J. Schneider (139–82) studies the civic chronicles on the south German wars of the 1380s, and C. Hruschka (183–215) the Swiss and other chroniclers on Charles the Bold and war, while V. Honemann (217–27) analyses the sources on the Soest insurrection of 1444–49, and D. Mertens (279–306) assesses the value of the so-called 'Lake of

0

624 German Studies

Constance Map' for representing events of the Swabian War of 1499, Hans Lenz's rhyming chronicle on which forms the subject of R. Wetzel, Schwarz, *Text*, 319–32.

Stephanie Coué, *Hagiographie im Kontext. Schreibanlaß und Funktion von Bischofsviten aus dem 11. und vom Anfang des 12. Jahrhunderts* (Arbeiten zur Frühmittelalterforschung, 24), 1997, xi + 204 pp. G. Kornrumpf, *Fest. Pensel*, 101–12, presents a 13th-c. Marian lyric, possibly a contrafactura. Dominik Pietrzik, *Die Brandan-Legende. Ausgewählte Motive in der frühneuhochdeutschen sogenannten 'Reise'-Version* (BBLI, 26), 234 pp., is a Hamburg dissertation based on the text of the first Augsburg print of Anton Sorg (*c.* 1476). The preliminary material sets out with clarity much basic information on the definitions of terms such as *Motiv* and *Legende* and their subdivisions and affinities with related terms. The main body of the study focuses on the universal and archetypal nature of many of the motifs characteristic of the Brendan legend, although the general approach is anthropological rather than psychological. The documentation of motifs such as magic islands, the whale, the congealed sea, the magnet mountain, food from heaven, or sirens, in various periods and cultures is generally revealing, but the approach tends to be too reductive to be fruitful in the case of such basic conceptions as the ship or the sea voyage. M.-L. Rotsaert, *ABÄG*, 51:149–67, studies a version of the *Navigatio* of interest as a source of the Germanic versions of the Brendan legend, and C. Strijbosch, *ZDP*, 118:50–68, discusses the traditions of heaven and hell in the legend, two versions of which are compared by H. Neumann, Müller, *Mittelalter*, 181–96, in the light of M. Foucault's theory. Also of hagiographical interest, F. Roolfs, *NdW*, 39:411–28, considers the influence of the Low German St Anne legend on Scandinavian versions from the end of the period.

W. Haug, Haug, *Mittelalter*, 357–77, identifies significant changes in the history of mysticism. A three-volume study of female mysticism concludes with Wolfgang Beutin, *Anima. Untersuchungen zur Frauenmystik des Mittelalters. iii. Tiefenpsychologie — Mystikerinnen* (BBLI, 29), 261 pp., and we also note Marzena Górecka, *Das Bild Mariens in der Deutschen Mystik des Mittelalters* (DLA, 29), 647 pp. P. Schulze-Belli, *JOWG*, 11:211–32, analyses Mechthild von Magdeburg's imagery, and M. Hubrath, *ib.*, 233–44, understands the *Liber specialis gratiae* as a collective work, while H. Stadler, Haas, *Frauen*, 201–20, considers the view of Eve in Mechthild von Magdeburg. C. Rizek, *ib.*, 267–80, considers Eckhart in relation to his audience. Freimut Löser, *Meister Eckhart in Melk. Studien zum Redaktor Lienhart Peuger. Mit einer Edition des Traktats 'Von der sel wirdichait vnd aigenschafft'* (TTG, 48), ix + 604 pp., focuses on the reception of E.'s works in Melk in the first half of the 15th c. The opening chapters are concerned with knowledge of the scribe Lienhart Peuger in the context of the conditions of the monastery at the time, his own original works — printed in an appendix — with their naive Mariology being used to infer his approach to E., while his motivation and intended audience of lay brothers also receive attention. Detailed codicological documentation of the E. manuscripts, their texts, and Peuger's collection of E. sermons, occupies pp. 69–272, and there follows discussion of his editorial technique and role as compiler. The treatise *Von der sel wirdichait vnd aigenschafft* is revealed as an encyclopaedic compilation by Peuger, drawing together all statements by E. on the subject. A diplomatic edition of the unique Codex 1569, accompanied by a synoptic print of related texts on the right-hand pages, occupies pp. 330–497. There are detailed indexes. Katharina Ceming, *Mystik und Ethik bei Meister Eckhart und Johann Gottlieb Fichte* (EH, xx, 588), 270 pp. Y. Koda, Lutz, *Literatur*, 225–64, sees the mysticism of Eckhart's *Reden der Unterweisung* as rooted in his ambivalent attitude to the world outside the monastery, and K. Ruh, *ZDA*, 128:42–46, develops his thesis that none of Eckhart's sermons is of proven Cologne origin. P. Dinzelbacher, *ABÄG*, 51:195–96, draws attention to an Upper German translation of Seuse's *Horologium Sapientiae*, and N. Largier, Müller, *Mittelalter*, 241–71, examines the relationship between text and image in a 15th-c. Seuse manuscript. In *Fest. Haas*, W. Haug (79–96) writes on free will in the Neoplatonic concept of *ascensus* and its treatment by Bonaventura; B. McGinn (155–74) on suffering and annihilation in Hadewijch, Mechthild of Magdeburg, and Marguerite Porete; F. Löser (241–73) edits a variant text of Eckhart's sermon *Intravit Iesus in quoddam castellum* in which the role of Mary is enhanced; P. Michel (97–116) evaluates the encyclopaedic approach to exegesis of Petrus Berchorius; K.-E. Geith (59–77) studies a letter with mystical language from the milieu of the Colmar Dominicans; P. Ochsenbein (275–83) records elements of mysticism in the *Engelberger Gebetbuch*; B. Spoerri (299–315) interprets the imagery of the heart in Heinrich Seuse; and H. Stirnimann (317–21) interprets Seuse's prayer of greeting. The impressive volume includes work on other aspects of mysticism, among them studies by G. Bunge (Evagrios Pontikos, 27–41), G. Descœudres (visual media in late-Classical piety, 43–57), S. Ueda (philosophical commentary on the relation of faith and mysticism to experience, 323–34), S. Weigel (Jewish mysticism, 521–32), together with a range of philosophical topics. Kurt Ruh, *Geschichte der abendländischen Mystik. IV. Die niederländische Mystik des 14. bis 16. Jahrhunderts*, Munich, Beck, 340 pp., covers the area of perhaps the greatest affinity of Dutch and German literature, although R. points to the difficulties resulting from the limited bibliographical holdings outside the Low Countries. A substantial first chapter is devoted to Jan van Ruusbroec, including his contemporary reception, followed by lesser figures such as Willem Jordaens, Jan van Leeuwen, prominent as a critic of Eckhart, Jan van Schoonhoven, and Gheraert Appelmans. The Devotio Moderna is treated in relatively brief space, and includes sections on Geert Grote, Gerard Zerbolt van Zutphen, Hendrik Mande, and Thomas a Kempis. The third chapter addresses late-medieval Franciscan mysticism, seen as an area in which interest has all but dried up, although the clarity of R.'s presentation ought to serve as a stimulus to renewed interest. The final chapter deals with the later female mystics, among them Alijt Bake, Sister Bertken, and Maria van Hout, and sorority books. The work is introduced as R.'s final contribution to the series, but further volumes are promised from other hands. In *Fest. Haas*, 285–98, R. supplements the work with additional documentation of the Groenendaal mystics. Also noted: Kristina Freienhagen-Baumgardt, *Hendrik Herps 'Spieghel der Volcomenheit' in oberdeutscher Überlieferung. Ein Beitrag zur Rezeptionsgeschichte niederländischer Mystik im oberdeutschen Raum* (Miscellanea Neerlandica, 17), Leuven, Peeters, 1998, xi + 177 pp. S. de Tribolet-Aeschlimann, Lutz, *Literatur*, 343–57, supplies prolegomena to an edition of *Die hundert artickel von dem wirdigen liden unsers herren Jhesu Christi*, a mid-15th-c. Dominican mystical text on the Passion. M. Geisser, Haas, *Frauen*, 249–66, discusses the mystic Ursula Haider (1413–98).

H. Ulmschneider, *BW*, 32:112–32, adds to codicological knowledge of the *Schwarzwälder Predigten* and the *Lucidarius*, and R. Schnell, *FmSt*, 33:319–95, surveys the vernacular adaptation of Jacobus de Voragine's sermons on marriage, while H. Dworschak, Haas, *Frauen*, 177–99, emphasizes the unity of soul and body in the exemplum *Die Milch und die Fliegen* and other short religious texts, and K. Schneider, *Fest. Pensel*, 279–91, studies a German translation of the Dominican Guilelmus Peraldus's *Summa de vitiis*. K. Bertau, Palmer, *Kloster*, 113–40, includes elaborate geographical information in an attempt to link Konrad von Würzburg's *Goldene Schmiede* with the Teutonic Order and its religious Magdalen houses. Martina Probst, *Nu wache ûf, sünder træge. Geistliche Tagelieder des 13. bis 16. Jahrhunderts. Analysen und Begriffsbestimmung* (RBDSL, B 71), 186 pp., is a useful contribution to the relatively restricted and obscure transmission of the religious dawn song, in its origins inseparable from its better known secular counterpart. Building on the problems of definition highlighted by the two earlier substantial studies of T. Kochs and U. Ruberg, P. submits each of the six texts from the 13th c. to Hans Sachs, which are included in full, to detailed analysis and commentary in a chronological sequence. A development and refinement of earlier approaches to the texts is achieved, although at the occasional expense of generalizations about the cultural background in the different periods. K. Klein, *ZDA*, 128:66–72, reviews the manuscript transmission of Heinrich von Hesler's *Apokalypse*, the function of the preacher in which is studied by E. Tobler, *Fest. Haas*, 139–52. J. Thali, Lutz, *Literatur*, 265–315, examines the role of Mary in Friedrich Sunder's *vita*, and A. Vizkelety, *Fest. Pensel*, 325–36, studies a 14th-c. translation of the *Regula solitariorum* of Grimlaicus. G. Dunphy, Robertshaw, *Natur*, 91–102, discusses the understanding of the natural world in the Central German paraphrase of the Book of Job of 1338, and S. Flühler, Haas, *Frauen*, 221–48, studies the life of Berta von Herten from the St. Katharinental sorority book, while N. Staubach, Keller, *Schriftlichkeit*, 171–201, documents the literary reception and library activity among adherents of the Devotio Moderna, and F. Löser, *ZDP*, 118:1–26, writes on the late-14th-c. *Melker Evangelien*, linking the work with the Teutonic Order. V. Honemann and G. Diehl, *Fest. Pensel*, 79–93, edit and study Simon von Ruckersburg's translation of part of Robert Holcot's *Praelectiones*, and G. Roth, *ZDA*, 128:409–13, edits Meister Wilhelm's *Fünf Spiegel*, a brief catechetical tract, while K. Kunze, *Fest. Schupp*, 84–94, elucidates Margaretha Regula's adaptation of the *Legenda Aurea* for monastic use, and C. Rabenstein, Haas, *Frauen*, 305–23, reviews German examples of the legend of Pope Joan from the 1470s on. R.-H. Steinmetz, *ZDP*, 118:372–90, analyses the *Hystorij von Diocleciano*, an independent German version of the *Sieben weise Meister*.

Inés de la Cuadra, *Der 'Renner' Hugos von Trimberg: Allegorische Denkformen und literarische Traditionen* (GTS, 63), ix + 379 pp. + pls, claims with some justification to re-evaluate the monumental *Renner* by daring to address in its totality the complicated textual structure of a work too often limited to supplying isolated examples for thematic studies. The clearly argued thesis from the school of E. C. Lutz. The introductory study includes an analysis of Michael de Leone's index to the *Renner*, a contribution of value in its own right. The chapter on Hugo's allegorical technique emphasizes, in line with other recent work such as Anja Sommer's on the *Minneburg* (see p. 628 below), the mixing and juxtaposition of different forms of allegorical writing which are not susceptible of straightforward theoretical definition. There follow chapters on Hugo's poetics, including his reflection on the art of poetry, his use of literary models, and problems of generic definition, leading to a conclusion which emphasizes the work's productive reception of encyclopaedic literature of theological and moral content. I. de la Cuadra, Lutz, *Literatur*, 191–223, studies the historical references in the *Renner*, the treatment of *luxuria* in which is the subject of R. Schnell, *Fest. Schupp*, 71–83. C. Huber, Haug, *Mittelalter*, 187–212, compares continuity and innovation in the work of didactic authors including Thomasin von Zerclaere, Hugo von Trimberg, and Heinrich Wittenwiler. *Summa bonorum. Eine deutsche Exempelsammlung aus dem 15. Jahrhundert nach Stephan von Bourbon. Edition und Untersuchung*, ed. Susanne Baumgarte (TSM, 40), 335 pp., a Göttingen dissertation, is the first edition of a text consisting of translated excerpts from the mid-13th-c. collection of homiletic anecdotes *Tractatus de diversis materiis predicabilibus*, which B. places in the tradition of Konrad von Ammenhausen, the *Gesta Romanorum*, and Heinrich von Mügeln. The 250 brief *exempla* are understood as a source-book, not a text for reading. There is a full characterization of the treatment of the structure of the original and the dominant tendency of the German to simplify. The codicological and linguistic analysis of the two manuscripts leads to the selection of Munich, cgm 619, as *Leithandschrift*; the carefully prepared and legible edition is accompanied by an apparatus with the Vienna manuscript variants, a classified list of the *exempla* and their analogues, and index. P. Busch, *Fest. Schupp*, 95–113, reviews parliaments of fowls in late MHG literature, and F. P. Knapp, *Fest. Schupp*, 61–70, interprets the *Wiener Meerfahrt* as a satire on the Viennese patrician class, while K. Lerchner, *JOWG*, 11:333–49, studies Konrad von Ammenhausen's treatment of the *artes mechanicae* in the *Schachzabelbuch*. S. Kerth, Brunner, *Krieg*, 229–62, focuses specifically on the justification of war in the later lyric sources on the subject. Tilmann Walter, *Unkeuschheit und Werk der Liebe. Diskurse über Sexualität am Beginn der Neuzeit in Deutschland* (SLG, 48), 1998, viii + 597 pp., includes discussion of late-medieval didactic literature. Anja Sommer, *Die 'Minneburg'. Beiträge zu einer Funktionsgeschichte der Allegorie im späten Mittelalter. Mit der Erstedition der Prosafassung* (Mikrokosmos, 52), Frankfurt, Lang, 312 pp., by a pupil of W. Harms, transforms our understanding of the mid-14th-c. work and simultaneously brings new insight to the diversity of structures informing late-medieval allegory. On the basis of detailed analyses of the beast imagery, castle and pillar, battle and court of love, besides a more wide-ranging chapter on the strategies and perspectives of the allegorical discourse of the work, the thesis confirms that the definitions of allegory by scholars such as W. Blank and C. Meier fail to do justice to the complexity of secular and spiritual levels exemplified in the *Minneburg* which rather draws on a range of traditions and creates its own literary world. The edition of part of the short verse versions and of the prose version, which adapt the subject-matter in their own ways, is a welcome enhancement of the study. M. Bärmann and A. Bechtold, *Daphnis*, 28:61–91, document the life and family of Antonius von Pforr. T. Tomasek, *JOWG*, 11:259–67, surveys the tradition of medieval German riddles, and M. Eikelmann, *ib.*, 299–315, reviews gnomic and proverbial utterance, while S. Griese, Robertshaw, *Natur*, 215–29, illustrates the role of nature in various versions of the *Salomon und Markolf* tradition, included by U. Zitzlsperger, *ib.*, 253–65, in a study of the nature-culture dichotomy in the figure of the fool. Sabine Griese, *Salomon und Markolf. Ein literarischer Komplex im Mittelalter und in der frühen Neuzeit* (Hermaea, n.f., 81), Tübingen, Niemeyer, ix + 381 pp., is a comprehensive trteatment of the German tradition of a body of texts which, remarkably, show a 400-year interval between the first reference to the subject-matter and the date of the earliest surviving text, the *Dialogus Salomonis et Marcolfi* of 1410. G. deals in turn with the text, transmission, and essential features of the *Dialogus*, its 14th-c. verse adaptation *Markolfs buch*, Gregor Hayden's late-15th-c. version, various prose translations from the end of the period, *Fastnachtspiel* versions of Hans Folz, Hans Sachs, and Zacharias Bletz besides other works of Hans Sachs, and *Salman und Morolf*. The conclusions emphasize the diversity of forms and functions resulting from the committal to writing of an originally oral and fictional dialogue, and its raising to a topic of intellectual discourse at the end of the period covered. *Salman und Morolf. Mittelhochdeutsch/Neuhochdeutsch*, ed. and trans. Wolfgang Spiewok and Astrid Guillaume (Greifswalder Beiträge zum Mittelalter, 47; Texte des Mittelalters, 14), Greifswald, Reineke, 1996, xxiv + 214 pp. H. E. Keller, Schwarz, *Text*, 109–25, analyses the treatment of religious themes in *Des Teufels Netz*.

DRAMA. C. Dauven-van Knippenberg, Bennewitz, *Konstruktion*, 34–46, takes a feminist approach to the religious drama, and H. Linke, *ZDA*, 128:185–93, comments on the religious plays in the Codex Buranus, while U. Schulze, Haug, *Mittelalter*, 312–56, focuses on the themes of *repraesentatio* and its different forms of exemplification in the liturgical drama, and C. Gerhardt, *Euphorion*, 93:349–97, aligns *Von Luzifers und Adams Fall* with the tradition of the drama. K.-E. Geith, *Fest. Schupp*, 269–74, identifies the motif of the devil on a ladder of knives in the religious drama, and C. Kuné, *ZDA*, 128:414–24, edits the *Prague Last Supper Play*, while W. Frey, *Fest. Brackert*, 202–17, writes on the function of late-medieval civic Passion plays, and J. Janota, *Fest. Koopmann*, 65–80, places the *Alsfeld Passion Play* at the centre of a demonstration of the need for the text editor to follow a conception of extended authorship.

*Frühe Nürnberger Fastnachtspiele*, ed. Klaus Ridder, Hans-Hugo Steinhoff et al. (SME, 4), 1998, 202 pp., has seven plays, five from the Rosenplüt corpus (*Die verhinderten Ehemänner, Bauernprahlereien, Das Hofgericht vom Ehebruch, Ein Ehebrecher vor Gericht*, and *Eheliche Verdächtigungen*), the anonymous *Das Ungetüm*, and Hans Folz's *Der Juden Messias*. The texts have been deliberately selected to redress the relative absence from D. Wuttke's edition of the sexual, obscene, scatological, and anti-Semitic features which characterize the genre. The editions, which present a *Leithandschrift* in fairly conservative form with an apparatus of variants and editorial emendations, are very readable. Each play is accompanied by informative discussions of the text, authorship, structure, source of comedy, and relationship to analogous plays, and by textual commentary. K. Ridder, Schaefer, *Artes*, 391–409, surveys the mockery of learning and the learned in the *Fastnachtspiel*.

SCIENTIFIC AND SPECIALIZED LITERATURE

I. T. Piirainen, Schwarz, *Text*, 201–17, records specialized prose in Silesia and Slovakia, while *JOWG*, 11, includes work on legal texts and iconography by W. Schild (the nature of the relationship between text and illustration, 85–112), D. Hüpper (the illustrated *Sachsenspiegel*, 113–42), and G. Kocher (the use of illustration in presenting legal history, 143–51). R. Schmidt-Wiegand, *NdW*, 39: 393–409, interprets the illustrations of the author and title metaphors in Low German *Sachsenspiegel* manuscripts. On medical matters, we note Manfred Gröber, *Das wundärztliche Manual des Meisters Hans Seyff von Göppingen (ca. 1440–1518). Der Cod. med. et phys. 2⁰ 8 der Württembergischen Landesbibliothek Stuttgart* (GAG, 656), 1998, ix + 517 pp., while R. Wittern, Haug, *Mittelalter*, 550–71, characterizes continuity and change in late-medieval anatomy. Gynaecology features with Britta-Juliane Kruse, *'Die Arznei ist Goldes wert.' Mittelalterliche Frauenrezepte*, Berlin, de Gruyter, xiii + 414 pp., and M. Sherwood-Smith, Robertshaw, *Natur*, 163–74, interprets the misogynistic dimension of versions of the *Secreta Mulierum*. B. Fleith, Lutz, *Literatur*, 423–53, analyses a Geneva medical manuscript in the context of its history and likely users. F. Fürbeth, Robertshaw, *Natur*, 267–78, studies texts from 1416 and 1450 respectively on the benefits of bathing and visits to the waters. B. Schnell, *Fest. Pensel*, 293–312, prints herbal texts from Leipzig UB Ms. 1224, and N. Berend, *Besch Vol.*, 43–58, examines linguistic usage in the transmission of Konrad von Megenberg's *Buch der Natur*, while N. H. Ott, Robertshaw, *Natur*, 119–36, comments on the illustration of this and other works. Schaefer, *Artes*, contains an impressive range of contributions on medieval scientific and educational literature, including an introduction by U. Schaefer (1–10) and work by M. Haas (the function of music, 13–33), C. Brinker-von der Heyde (Thomasin von Zerclaere's view of the sciences, 34–52), B. Englisch (Roger Bacon, 53–67), J. Sarnowsky (the university curriculum, 68–82), B. R. Tammen and F. Hentschel (an interpretation of a Cologne wood-carving relating it to the theory and practice of music,

83–109), J. Pfeiffer (Heinrich von Mügeln and Konrad von Megenberg on the causes of the plague of 1348, 110–23), K. Kellermann (the rise of a scientific attitude to truth in the face of the old authorities at the end of the period, 124–40), F. Tinnefeld (encyclopaedic learning in Byzantium, 143–50), W. Knoch (the theological *summa*, 151–60), D. De Rentiis (the conception of *imitatio* in John of Salisbury, 161–73), W. Hirschmann (the transformation of music into a pragmatic science, 174–86), K. Herbers (Spain as a centre of the diffusion of learning, 230–48), F. Fürbeth (the magic arts, 249–62), T. Michalsky (aspects of the *artes mechanicae*, 324–43), A. Gross (the tarot, 344–57), K. Arnold (pictorial representation of the seven liberal arts, 361–75), and M. Schumacher (the understanding of *kunst* in Thomasin von Zerclaere and Heinrich der Teichner, 376–90).

Keller, *Schriftlichkeit*, is an important body of new research from the Münster centre for the pragmatic application of the written word. Following an introduction by C. Meier (1–7), A. Angenendt (9–23) classifies forms of association of written documents with the grave (miracles, indulgences, buried documents, donation lists); H. Keller surveys administrative documents in Italian communes (25–41); A. Mihm writes on written legal codes in German towns (43–67); J. Wild, on Bavarian enfeoffment registers (69–77); B. Tutsch, on Cluniac statutes (79–94); F. Cygler, on similar Carthusian documents (95–109); J. Van Engen, on the articles of government of the Brothers of the Common Life, with appendices of texts (111–69); and G. Keil examines a treatise on the distillation of brandy (267–78). D. Tophinke, *NdJb*, 122:25–43, places the Low German merchants' account books in the context of civic literacy. R. G. Pasler, *ZDA*, 128:428–33, edits a newly discovered fragment of the *Geometria Culmensis*. W. Kleiber and R. Steffens, *Fest. Wiesinger*, 516–37, analyse the Bavarian ducal land-register of 1231–34, and A. Greule, *Fest. Eroms*, 381–88, studies the language of the 15th-c. Gebenbach (Pfalz) parish register. R. M. Kully, *Fest. Schupp*, 134–51, classifies types of mnemonic and functional verse, and P. H. Weidmann, *Fest. Haas*, 395–417, comments on the place of the Queen of Sheba in Sibylline prophetic literature, while F. Fürbeth, *Fest. Brackert*, 218–32, explains the background to the gender-specific understanding of magic and witchcraft in the *Malleus Maleficarum*. N. Nagel, *NdW*, 39:179–227, documents 14th-c. vernacular wills from Lübeck and elsewhere in the North, and C. Fischer, *ib.*, 229–38, records 15th-c. High German — Low German correspondence, while S. Teuscher, Lutz, *Literatur*, 359–85, studies private letters from Berne of *c.* 1500. Doris Aichholzer, '*Wildu machen ayn guet essen . . .*' *Drei mittelhochdeutsche Kochbücher: Erstedition, Übersetzung, Kommentar* (WAGAPH, 35), 454 pp., is a first edition of the three cookery books in the Österreichische Nationalbibliothek, from Mondsee, the Vienna Dorotheenkloster, and Innsbruck; the first two show substantial correspondence. The background on medieval dietetics and its development from the pathology of the humours is of considerable interest, while the texts — A. identifies 46 German cookery books in all, of which only 11 have hitherto been edited — are presented on the left-hand pages in diplomatic form, accompanied on the facing pages by a straighforward modern translation which is indeed a significant aid to comprehension. The index, glossary, and bibliography are detailed, and the whole sufficiently appetizing to justify practical culinary experimentation. In *JOWG*, 11:351–62, A. pursues her work in this field.

OTHER LATER MEDIEVAL LITERATURE

I. Kasten, Haug, *Mittelalter*, 164–86, considers German fabliaux against the background of Boccaccio, and U. von Bloh, *BGDSL*, 121:214–38, interprets women's tournaments in various fabliaux, while R.-H. Steinmetz, *BGDSL*, 121:47–74, shows how Heinrich Kaufringer's moral values reflect a lay education. In Bennewitz, *Konstruktion*, fabliau literature is not surprisingly prominent in a collection of feminist and gender-orientated approaches. C. Brinker-von der Heyde (47–66) takes three fabliaux to exemplify the sexual and political connotations of the metaphor of horse and rider; C. Ortmann and H. Ragotzky (67–84) consider the gender aspects of Dietrich von der Glezze's *Der Gürtel*, which for U. Peters (284–304) features in a study of cross-dressing; R. Schlechtweg-Jahn (85–109) studies the *Nonnenturnier* and *Rosendorn*; and A. Schnyder (110–30) examines the presentation of the physical and sexual in three tales of adultery by Heinrich Kaufringer. M. Schiendorfer, *Fest. Haas*, 471–85, examines the narrative structure and strategy in *Die halbe Birne* and *Die Heidin*, and C. Tuczay, *Fabula*, 40:85–109, analyses the motif of three wishes in the fabliau and elsewhere, while O. Neudeck, Robertshaw, *Natur*, 201–13, interprets the sexual element in Hermann von Sachsenheim's *Grasmetze*, and J. Schulz-Grobert, *LiLi*, 114:99–112, considers late-medieval prototypes of the Eulenspiegel figure. Also noted: Paolo Marelli, *Gli 'Schwanklieder' nella tradizione Neidhartiana. Trascrizione dai manoscritti f/c/pr, traduzione, commento* (GAG, 658), 294 pp.

There is a Spanish translation of the *Ackermann aus Böhmen*, Johannes von Tepl, *El campesino de Bohemia y otros textos*, trans. Francisco M. Mariño (Clásicos medievales, 14), Madrid, Gredos, 161 pp. H. Kokott, *Fest. Brackert*, 73–84, analyses the structure of Heinrich

Wittenwiler's *Ring*, and K. Schmitt, Haas, *Frauen*, 129–52, studies sexuality in the work, while J. Keller, *ib.*, 153–74, focuses on the courtship of Bertschi and Mätzli, and W. Röcke, Brunner, *Krieg*, 263–77, analyses the mechanics of violence and the grotesque features of war in the *Ring*. H. Alex, *ZDA*, 128:337–41, revises the corpus of Eberhard von Cersne's songs. A. and U. M. Schwob, *Fest. Schupp*, 114–24, document Oswald von Wolkenstein's foundation of chapels in Brixen, and A. Robertshaw, *BGDSL*, 121:1–22, studies the distinction between *minne* and *liebe* in O. and other later poets, while W. von Kossak and S. Stockhorst, *Daphnis*, 28:1–33, survey the erotic and obscene dimensions of O. In *JOWG*, 11, J. Ogier (173–80) studies the background to Kl. 18 and 19; S. Hartmann (181–210) views O.'s pastorals in the context of comparable Spanish and French poetry; P. Voorn (413–36) finds him on the Ghent Altarpiece of Jan and Hubert van Eyck; and H. Melkert and M. J. Schubert (437–50) catalogue and review recent recordings of his songs. A. Schnyder, Schwarz, *Text*, 231–44, studies Kl. 2, while A. and U. M. Schwob, *Fest. Moser*, 101–14, interpret Kl. 26, in the *deditio* episode of which O. is ritually restored to the favour of Duke Frederick of Austria, and K. Helmkamp, Cramer, *Lyrik*, 107–21, focuses on Oswald, Kl. 76 and 83, in a study of the pastourelle. C. Edwards, *FMLS*, 35:70–80, interprets O.'s 'Frölich so wil ich' (Kl. 79).

W. Williams-Krapp, *Rottenburger Jb. für Kirchengeschichte*, 16, 1997:11–22, comments on the education of the laity in the 15th c. L. Schmitt, pp. 93–122 of *Autobiographie und Selbstportrait in der Renaissance*, ed. Gunter Schweikhart (Atlas: Bonner Beiträge zur Renaissanceforschung, 2), Cologne, König, 1998, 223 pp., characterizes art and artists in literature of the 15th and 16th cs. A. Mühlherr, Haug, *Mittelalter*, 213–36, compares views of learning and authority in Heinrich von Mügeln, Heinrich Wittenwiler, and Sebastian Brant, and N. H. Ott, *Fest. Pensel*, 215–32, seeks to identify the 'civic' aspects of late-medieval illustrated manuscripts, while F. Schanze, Keller, *Schriftlichkeit*, 299–331, reviews in detail the forms of transmission of political poetry in the 15th and 16th cs, and I. Simon, *NdW*, 39:429–52, comments on collections of proverbs. R. Damme and T. Hoffmann, *ib.*, 275–313, studies the fish names in the *Stralsunder Vokabular*. Peter Hoheisel, *Die Göttinger Stadtschreiber bis zur Reformation. Einfluß, Sozialprofil, Amtsaufgaben* (Studien zur Geschichte der Stadt Göttingen, 21), Göttingen, Vandenhoeck & Ruprecht, 1998, x + 287 pp. A. Näf and R. Wetzel, Lutz, *Literatur*, 317–42, assess the literary activity of Friedrich Kölner in St Gall in 1430–36 in its historical context. Christoph Roth, *Literatur und Klosterreform. Die Bibliothek der Benediktiner von St. Mang zu Füssen im 15. Jahrhundert* (Studia Augustana, 10), Tübingen, Niemeyer, viii + 438 pp., takes the 15th-c. reforming movements as the driving force behind the expansion of the St. Mang library as of others, and is able to draw on a wealth of historical documentation to trace the activity of the reforming abbots concerned. This forms the basis for a survey of the library holdings, while the donations and purchases during the office of Johannes Hess, and manuscripts produced in St. Mang before and during his abbacy, form the subject of a separate chapter with detailed analysis of the works concerned. Vernacular German texts receive special attention, and a concluding chapter identifies the chief themes and their relevance for the reforms. An appendix contains a short catalogue of the medieval holdings. K. Grubmüller, Haug, *Mittelalter*, 263–85, compares attitudes to the use of the German vernacular in the period 1484–1523.

Stephan Füssel, *Gutenberg und seine Wirkung*, Frankfurt, Insel, vii + 142 pp. + 62 pls, is a concise survey of G.'s life and activity and of the diffusion of early printing. The work remains at a scholarly level while presenting essential information in a concise and highly readable fashion. The reader is taken through the technical innovations, examples of the early work, the Bible, school texts, and pamphlets, and the subsequent activity of Fust and Schöffer. Rome, Venice, Paris, and London are taken to exemplify the spread of printing. Later chapters survey humanist printing, popular encyclopaedic works and fable collections, 16th-c. pamphlets, and the Reformation. A final chapter relates G. to the modern electronic revolution. The book is exquisitely produced in a manner befitting its subject: a timely reminder of the beauty of hot-metal typography, with admirable full-colour plates. F. Schanze, Haug, *Mittelalter*, 286–311, argues that the invention of printing resulted not in a 'revolution' but rather in the coexistence of different media and co-operation between them, and U. Rautenberg, *IASL*, 24.1:1–40, studies Hans Folz's press from the point of view of printing technology, while V. Honemann, S. Griese, and F. Eisermann, Keller, *Schriftlichkeit*, 333–48, make fundamental observations on the substance and significance of single-sheet pamphlets in the 15th and early 16th cs. S. Obermaier, *Reinardus*, 12:95–111, studies the fox fables in Anton von Pforr's *Buch der Beispiele*, and B. Weifenbach, *ABÄG*, 51:169–93, surveys versions of *Die vier Haimonskinder* and especially the Cologne printed text of 1493, while W. Röll, *BGDSL*, 121:103–08, documents further editions of the *Gesta Romanorum* from the end of the period.

*Das Mittelalter*, 3.2, 1998, is dedicated to travel literature, with documentation and bibliography by F. Reichert (5–17), and work by H. Hundsbichler (comments on the imaginative and intellectual context, 19–32); F. Wolfzettel (types of pilgrimage, 33–44);

M. Harbsmeier (Jewish literature, 63–80); K. Herbers (journeys to Spain, 81–106); A. Denke (Venice, 107–26); P. Schreiner (Constantinople, 127–39); D. Huschenbett (Jerusalem, 141–60); and I. Baumgärtner (cartography, 161–97). W. G. Rohr, *Bulletin Linguistique et Ethnologique*, 28, 1998:23–36, comments on the cultural significance of John Mandeville, and U. App, *Fest. Haas*, 13–26, cites the German translation of Marco Polo and later sources on Western knowledge of Zen Buddhism, while R. Birkmeyer, *JFL*, 59:109–27, characterizes the record of the journey to Jerusalem of Anselm von Eyb in 1468. P. Jorgensen, pp. 123–31 of *Beharrsamkeit und Wandel. Festschrift für Herbert Tatzreiter zum 60. Geburtstag*, ed. Werner Bauer and Hermann Scheuringer, Vienna, Praesens, 1998, 355 pp., studies a 15th-c. Ripuarian text of a pilgrimage narrative; Id., *Fest. Tatzreiter*, 123–31, distinguishes between factual and fictional narrative in Arnold von Harff's travelogue. Felix Fabri, *Die Sionpilger*, ed. Wieland Carls (TSM, 39), 596 pp., is an important first complete edition of the text of 1492 which will certainly stimulate still further research in an already popular field. The comprehensive introduction focuses not only on F.'s life and work but also on the genre as a whole and the question of what constitutes the contemplative, spiritual pilgrimage, given that F.'s work is itself a mixture of real experience and received topoi, and is primarily intended for nuns whose only visit to the Holy Land would be in the world of the imagination. The edition presents, with minor intervention, the Ulm text as *Leithandschrift*, with the variants of two other manuscripts. With use of bold and italic type the work, covering journeys to Jerusalem, Rome, and Santiago de Compostela, is clearly legible. Its value is enhanced by the addition of copious indexes of personal, saints', and place names, of Latin incipits and of headings. An appendix contains the prefaces and additional text from other manuscripts.

U. Wyss, Wolfzettel, *Erzählstrukturen*, 257–73, considers seminal structures in the prose romance, and D. Seitz, *Fest. Brackert*, 85–104, studies the dialogic features of the language of its early manifestations, while J. Eming, Bennewitz, *Konstruktion*, 159–81, shows how gender stereotypes begin to change in the genre. R. Schlechtweg-Jahn, Robertshaw, *Natur*, 231–41, interprets the place of culture and nature in Elisabeth von Nassau-Saarbrücken's *Huge Scheppel*, which is included in a treatment of the later development of the structural device of reduplication by G. Wild, Wolfzettel, *Erzählstrukturen*, 291–310. Also noted: Peter Bichsel, *Hug Schapler — Überlieferung und Stilwandel. Ein Beitrag zur frühneuhochdeutschen Prosaroman und zur lexikalischen Paarform* (ZGS, 53), 384 pp. G. S. Williams, Schwarz, *Text*, 333–43, discusses pacts with the devil in the chapbook, and A. Classen, *ib.*, 49–68, its treatment of the social position of women, while A. Simon, *Daphnis*, 28:35–59, focuses on the patterns of female behaviour exemplified in the *Ritter vom Turn*, H. E. Keller, Bennewitz, *Konstruktion*, 204–27, interprets the femininity of Frau Minne in late-medieval texts and illustrations with a dimension of bridal mysticism, and V. Hacker, Robertshaw, *Natur*, 139–49, considers feminine roles in Nicolosa Sanuda, Niklas von Wyle, and Albrecht von Eyb. C. Bertelsmeier-Kierst, *ZDA*, 128:73–83, discovers an unknown first edition of Niklas von Wyle's *Guiscard und Sigismunda*. Sebastian Brant, *Fabeln*. *Carminum et fabularum additiones Sebastiani Brant — Sebastian Brants Ergänzungen zur Aesop-Ausgabe von 1501. Mit den Holzschnitten der Ausgabe von 1501*, ed., trans., and comm. Bernd Schneider (Arbeiten und Editionen zur Mittleren Deutschen Literatur, n.F., 4), Stuttgart-Bad Cannstatt, Frommann-Holzboog, 454 pp., admirably complements the recent new edition of the shorter works (see *YWMLS*, 60:613). The edition consists of prefaces and 140 numbered short Latin texts of varied subject-matter which supplement the edition of Heinrich Steinhöwel's *Aesop* and in effect form an independent work. Each text is accompanied by a lucid German translation and the original woodcut. The introductory matter (pp. 409–47) is concise but informative, and complemented by an index of sources. Work on Brant also includes Vera Sack, *Sebastian Brant als politischer Publizist. Zwei Flugblatt-Satiren aus den Folgejahren des sogenannten Reformreichstags von 1495* (Veröffentlichungen aus dem Archiv der Stadt Freiburg im Breisgau, 30), Fribourg, Stadtarchiv, 1997, 211 pp., while D. Kartschoke, *Fest. Brackert*, 105–23, comments on the language of fools in the *Narrenschiff* and later works, T. Fritz, *Fest. Eroms*, 369–79, analyses Brant's epistolary syntax, and B. Lizinski, Schwarz, *Text*, 142–53, assesses the adaptation of Brant's *Von dem Fuchshatz* in a French moral satire. Work on *Reynke de Vos* includes Jan Goossens, *Reynke, Reynaert und das europäische Tierepos. Gesammelte Aufsätze* (Niederlande-Studien, 20), Münster, Waxmann, 1998, 220 pp., and *Reynke de Vos — Lübeck 1498. Zur Geschichte und Rezeption eines deutsch-niederländischen Bestsellers*, ed. Amand Berteloot (Niederlande-Studien: Kleinere Schriften, 5), Münster, Lit, 1998, 140 pp., includes essays by B., J. Goossens, and H. Menke.

## THE SIXTEENTH CENTURY

### By MARK TAPLIN

#### 1. GENERAL

*Das illustrierte Flugblatt in der Kultur der Frühen Neuzeit*, ed. Wolfgang Harms and Michael Schilling (Mikrokosmos, 50), Frankfurt, Lang, 1998, 290 pp., highlights the range of areas in which *Flugblätter* can contribute to our understanding of early modern European culture and seeks to modify the traditional perception of the *Flugblatt* as a purely 'popular' medium. The volume contains 11 essays covering the period 1500–1700. Items of interest include D. Peil, 'Das Sprichwort im illustrierten Flugblatt', which argues that proverbs serve both as a rich source of illustrations for *Flugblätter* and as a means of facilitating communication between author and reading public (11–34); F. Mauelshagen, on the changing interpretation of comets' significance in 16th.-c. and 17th.-c. *Flugblätter* (101–36); S. Homeyer, on the function of apocalypticism in 16th-c. *Flugblätter* (137–49); M. Knauer, 'Der erinnerte Tod: Überlegungen zu Form und Funktion retrospektiver Kunst am Beispiel der Vergänglichkeitsikonographie', which demonstrates continuity in the depiction of the figure of death throughout the early modern period (151–75); and B. A. Tlusty, on the ambiguous portrayal of drinkers and drinking in early modern *Flugschriften* (176–203). *Konversionen im Mittelalter und in der Frühneuzeit*, ed. Friedrich Niewöhner and Fidel Rädle (Hildesheimer Forschungen, 1), Hildesheim, Olms, vii + 216 pp., considers examples of religious conversion — between different Christian confessions, and between Christianity and Judaism — in Europe between the early 12th c. and late 17th c. Relevant items include J. Schilling, on the repudiation of monasticism in the early 1520s by Protestant reformers such as Martin Luther and Ambrosius Blarer (43–57); U. Mennecke-Haustein, on the conversion of the Königsberg theologian Friedrich Staphylus to Catholicism in the early 1550s (71–84); G. Frank, on the turbulent career of Simon Simonius of Lucca and his polemical exchange with the Tübingen philosopher Jakob Schegk (133–52); and H. Smolinsky, 'Konversion zur Konfession: Jüdische Konvertiten im 16. Jahrhundert', which examines confessional choices as a factor in Jewish conversions to Christianity during the course of the 16th c. and the function of Jewish conversion in Protestant-Catholic polemic (153–70). *Infinite Boundaries: Order, Disorder, and Reorder in Early Modern German Culture*, ed. Max Reinhart (SCES, 40), 1998, xiv + 408 pp. This volume, containing almost 20 essays by scholars from a variety of disciplines, highlights the defining role of boundaries — political, religious, social and intellectual — in the culture of early modern Germany. Of particular relevance are P. Casey, on the differing portrayals of Judas in plays by Thomas Naogeorgus, Paul Rebhun, and Wolfgang Schmeltzl (101–19); J. Chipps Smith, 'The Jesuit Church of St. Michael's in Munich: the story of an angel with a mission', which includes an analysis of the Jesuit play *Triumph unnd Frewdenfest Zu Ehren dem heiligen Erzengel Michael*, written to mark the dedication of St Michael's in 1597 (147–69); P. Cuneo, on the Reformation broadsheet *The Minter's Reply*, published in Augsburg by Wolfgang Roesch, as an example of the linking of religious and economic grievances in early Reformation propaganda (171–85); and S. Burnett, on the regulation of Hebrew printing in 16th-c. Germany (329–48). *Books have their own Destiny: Essays in Honor of Robert V. Schnucker*, ed. Robin B. Barnes, Robert A. Kolb, and Paula L. Presley (SCES, 50), 1998, viii + 168 pp., contains a number of short essays on aspects of print culture in early modern Europe, with the focus on German-speaking areas. Particularly relevant are R. Barnes, 'Astrology and popular print in Germany, c. 1470–1520' (17–26); R. Cole, 'Interpreting an early Reformation pamphlet by Urbanus Rhegius', which identifies a mixture of evangelical and traditionalist elements in R.'s *Predig der hailigenjunckfrawen Catharina* of 1521 (39–46); R. Kolb, on Johann Friedrich Coelestin's *Von Buchhendlern / Buchdruckern vnd Buchfurern* of 1569 (61–72); J. Mehl, on the use of the metaphor of light and dark by Reuchlin's defenders in the *Bücherstreit* and its subsequent adaptation by Reformation propagandists (83–92); and M. Wiesner-Hanks, on early modern defences of women's publishing by Katharina Zell, Elisabeth of Brandenburg, and others (143–52).

## 2. HUMANISM AND THE REFORMATION

*Renaissancekultur und antike Mythologie*, ed. Bodo Guthmüller and Wilhelm Kühlmann (FN, 50), xiii + 306 pp., explores aspects of the reception and function of Classical mythology in the art and literature of the European Renaissance. Although the volume is predominantly Italian in focus, it contains several contributions of interest to students of 16th-c. German literature and culture. They include W. Ludwig, on the use of mythological motifs in printer's marks and writers' coats of arms (113–48); W. Kühlmann, on pagan religious themes in Petrus Lotichius Secundus's elegy *Ad lunam* (149–66); and E. Klecker, on the mythological account of Habsburg origins presented in the *Europalia* of Johannes Baptista Fonteius Primo, written to mark the wedding of Charles II of Inner Austria in 1571. *In laudem Caroli: Renaissance and Reformation Studies for Charles G. Nauert*, ed. James V. Mehl (SCES, 49),

1998, x + 242 pp., includes E. Bernstein, on the development of a group identity among German humanists between 1450 and 1530 (45–64); J. Mehl, 'Hermann von dem Busche's poem in honor of Erasmus's arrival in Cologne in 1516' (65–74); and P. Casey, on Luther's use of song as a proselytizing tool in his first published hymn (75–94). W. Harms, 'Der Mensch als Mikrokosmos auf programmatischen Titelblättern der frühen Neuzeit', *Fest. Haas*, 553–65. S. Karant-Nunn, ' "Fragrant wedding roses": Lutheran wedding sermons and gender definition in Early Modern Germany', *German History*, 17:25–40, argues that wedding sermons were used by 16th-c. and 17th-c. preachers as an opportunity to reinforce patriarchal conceptions of gender and to encourage the belief in women's innate tendency to evil. R. Kolb, 'Altering the agenda, shifting the strategy: the *Grundfest* of 1571 as Philippist program for Lutheran concord', *SCJ*, 30:705–26, identifies in the *Grundfest* text a new willingness on the part of the Philippist theologians of Electoral Saxony to take the battle to their Gnesio-Lutheran opponents, which helped set the agenda, albeit negatively, for the Formula of Concord. C. Christensen, 'The reformation of Bible illustration: Genesis woodcuts in Wittenberg, 1523–1534', *AR*, 90:103–29, suggests that in early Reformation Bible editions illustration was used as a means of highlighting Old Testament scenes of particular significance for Luther's teaching on grace. J. Kittelson, 'The significance of Humanist educational methods for Reformation theology', *Lutherjb.*, 66:219–36.

## 3. Genres

### Drama and Dialogue

J. Kampe, 'Bildhafte Beschreibungen: die Darstellung von Freund und Feind in Dialogen der Reformationszeit', *JOWG*, 11:21–34, interprets early Reformation dialogues as a form of 'Super-Allegorie', in which the aim is to convince the common man of the need for reform of the church through the use of the rhetorical technique of *amplificatio*.

### Prose and Verse

J. Schulz-Grobert, *Das Strassburger Eulenspiegelbuch: Studien zu entstehungsgeschichtlichen Voraussetzungen der ältesten Drucküberlieferung* (Hermaea, Germanistische Forschungen, n.F., 83), Tübingen, Niemeyer, x + 424 pp., rejects the hypothesis of a Low German 'Ur-Ulnspegel', usually attributed to Hermann Bote, and seeks to refocus scholarly interest in *Till Eulenspiegel* on the first known printed edition of the work, published in Strasbourg by Johannes Grüninger in 1515. S.-G. argues that the collection derives in the main not from north German oral tradition as recorded by Bote, but from upper German literary sources for which Strasbourg — and, in particular, Grüninger's publishing house — was the production centre. He notes the paucity of Low German elements in *Till Eulenspiegel* and argues that those that can be identified are most likely to have been inserted by Grüninger and his collaborators as a means of adding local colour, sensitivity to dialect being a feature of Strasbourg printing. The suggestion that Bote might himself have written the work in High German is undermined, in S.-G.'s view, by the presence of specifically Alemannic elements in the language of *Till Eulenspiegel* and by the fact that it differs so profoundly from the 'Mischsprache' characteristic of Low German-speakers attempting to write High German in the early 16th century. Crucially, the author is able to demonstrate that approximately 50% of the narrative material in *Till Eulenspiegel* has identifiable parallels in earlier prose or verse works, none of which are of north or Low German origin (details are set out in an appendix). The key figure in the production of the finished text, he concludes, was not Bote, but Grüninger's corrector Johannes Adelphus Müling, who was involved in the publication of a number of works (such as Heinrich Bebel's *Facetiae*) that appear to have provided source material for the stories in the Eulenspiegel cycle. P. Bichsel, *Hug Schapler — Überlieferung und Stilwandel: Ein Beitrag zum frühneuhochdeutschen Prosaroman und zur lexikalischen Paarform* (ZGS, 53), 384 pp., tracks the stylistic evolution of this 15th-c. work by Elisabeth of Nassau-Saarbrücken through nine successive printed editions between 1500 and 1794. Of particular interest is the chapter on the 1537 edition of *Hug Schapler*, published in Strasbourg by Bartholomäus Grüninger, which was heavily reworked in an attempt to appeal to humanist-influenced readers of Latin and Italian Renaissance novellas. H. Rüther, 'Zur Druck- und Überlieferungsgeschichte des Strassburger Rätselbuches', *JOWG*, 11:269–98, distinguishes three groups of editions of this frequently published collection. I. Stahl, 'Nürnberger Handwerkerchroniken', *Fest. Pensel*, 313–24, compares the 16th.-c. chronicle of Sebastian Kopitz with a work by the 17th.-c. artisan Hans Leonhard Beck. K. Skow-Obenaus, 'Wives and mothers: a study of roles in *Herzog Herpin* and *Kaiser Octavian*', *GN*, 30:124–32. T. Althaus, 'Kleine Prosa der frühen Neuzeit: die *Adagia* des Erasmus von Rotterdam in ihrer Wirkung auf Johannes Agricola und Sebastian Franck', *JOWG*, 11:317–31.

### 4. OTHER WORK

C. Schnitzer, *Höfische Maskeraden: Funktion und Ausstattung von Verkleidungsdivertissements an deutschen Höfen der Frühen Neuzeit* (FN, 53), viii + 465 pp., draws on both written and pictorial sources to provide a comprehensive account of the role and significance of costumed entertainments at German courts between 1500 and 1800. S. argues against the tendency to dismiss such entertainments as a carnivalesque reaction to the rigidity and oppressiveness of court ceremonial. Instead, she views them as a form of 'verkleidetes Zeremoniell', conceived in response to the failure of traditional court ceremonial to prevent disputes over precedence, with the express purpose of uniting courtiers around the person of the ruler. The bulk of the work is given over to a typology of costumed entertainments in the early modern period, which illustrates how established forms such as mummeries and tournaments were gradually displaced by new ones such as costume banquets and masked balls, whose increasingly elaborate design reflected the power and aspirations of absolutist princes. It is supplemented by a helpful appendix containing a variety of written sources (clothing ordinances, occasional verse, contemporary descriptions of festivities etc.), along with more than 300 illustrations. U. Obhof, 'Aristoteles-Studium an der Universität Freiburg im Breisgau im 16. Jahrhundert: Studientexte aus der Offizin von Maternus Cholinus in Köln', *Gutenberg-Jb.*, 74:225–30. I. Bezzel, '*Ein nützlicher Tractat vom Pawmen peltzen*: die Erstedition des *Pelzbuchs* des Gottfried von Franken (Landshut: Johann Weissenburger, um 1530)', *Daphnis*, 28:205–26, examines the 16th-c. reworking of this 14th-c. text and assesses its influence on early modern horticultural literature more generally.

### 5. INDIVIDUAL AUTHORS AND WORKS

AGRIPPA VON NETTESHEIM, HEINRICH CORNELIUS. B. Spoerri, 'Ein ambivalentes Frauenlob: Agrippa von Nettesheim's *De nobilitate et praecellentia foeminei sexus*', Haas, *Frauen*, 283–303, detects the continued presence of misogynistic assumptions, along with Kabbalistic and other influences, in A.'s celebrated tract.

BOCER, JOHANNES. *Sämtliche Eklogen: Mit einer Einführung in Leben und Gesamtwerk des Verfassers*, ed. and trans. Lothar Mundt (FN, 46), lxxxiii + 200 pp., presents a critical edition and German prose translation of B.'s *Aeglogae septem* (1563), along with two other eclogues by the same author. In a helpful introduction, M. summarises B.'s career and places the eclogues within the context of his overall poetic output. Of particular interest is M.'s observation that pastoral subject-matter features far less prominently in B.'s verse than in the eclogues of his contemporary Simon Lemnius. That leads M. to postulate the existence in 16th-c. Neo-Latin poetry of a variant of the eclogue not restricted to pastoral themes and defined principally by form. Each poem included in the volume is accompanied by detailed notes that illustrate B's indebtedness both to the Classical bucolic poets and to contemporary writers, notably Petrus Lotichius Secundus.

BOTE, HERMANN. H. Blume, 'Eine bislang unbekannte mittelniederdeutsche Handschrift von Hermann Botes *Schichtbuch* und ihr Ort in der Überlieferung', *Fest. Stellmacher*, 27–37.

CORDUS, EURICIUS. G. Huber-Rebenich, 'Erfurter Humanisten und ihre Vorbilder — Euricius Cordus und Erasmus', *MJ*, 34: 101–16, examines C.'s creative use and adaptation of Erasmus's works in his verse.

CYSAT, RENWART. H. Greco-Kaufmann, 'Sinneslust und Eschatologie in Renward Cysats "Convivii Proces"', *Fest. Haas*, 367–79, notes the pronounced didacticism of C.'s play, which distinguishes it from the traditional *Fastnachtspiel* and reflects the strength of Jesuit influence in late 16th-c. Lucerne in its emphasis on repentance and moral reform.

DÜRER, ALBRECHT. J. Ashcroft, 'Zum Wort und Begriff "Kunst" in Dürers Schriften', Robertshaw, *Natur*, 19–28, identifies in some of D.'s unpublished writings an attempt to create an artistic discourse modelled on that of the Italian Renaissance.

EBERLIN VON GÜNZBURG, JOHANN. U. Petry, *Kommunikationsbezogene Syntax bei Johann Eberlin von Günzburg: Zur Funktion varianter Kompositionstypen in den 'Bundesgenossen'* (Documenta Linguistica, 3), Hildesheim, Olms, xiv + 421 pp., offers a systematic analysis of E.'s syntax in his *Bundesgenossen* and its significance for the reception of the work. The author concludes that E.'s style is tailored to the capacities of his main target audience — the illiterate 'common man' who features so prominently in early Reformation propaganda. The need for texts to be easily comprehensible when read aloud explains E.'s tendency to avoid Latinizing constructions; other techniques, such as repetition, are used to reinforce the evangelical message and to manipulate the emotions of the reader/hearer. However, E.'s syntax does not simply mirror the everyday speech of the 'common man'. More elaborate syntactical structures are used where necessary to put across complex ideas, in the expectation that the reader/hearer will gradually acquire the ability to assimilate them. E.'s pedagogical intent thus extends to language as well as doctrine. He also varies his style for different audiences, drawing heavily on the traditions of *Kanzleisprache* when addressing magistrates, for example. According to P., it is this that accounts for the 'Stilmischung' that scholars have identified in E.'s works.

FERNBERGER, GEORG CHRISTOPH. Georg Christoph Fernberger, *Reisetagebuch (1588–1593): Sinai, Babylon, Indien, Heiliges Land, Osteuropa*, ed. and trans. Ronald Burger and Robert Wallisch (Beiträge zur

Neueren Geschichte Österreichs, 12), Frankfurt, Lang, 358 pp., makes available for the first time F.'s lengthy and detailed account of his pilgrimage to Mount Sinai, subsequent travels in the Portuguese East Indies, and return to Austria via Persia, the Holy Land, and eastern Europe. The text published here is based on the earliest known manuscript of the diary, dating from shortly after F.'s death in battle against the Turks. Editorial corrections, marginal glosses, and variant readings are indicated in the footnotes, and the original Latin text is accompanied by an clear translation into modern German. A critical commentary on the work is to be published shortly.

FEYERABEND, SIGMUND. B. Gotzkowsky, 'Zur Herkunft der Illustrationen in der Frankfurter "Heldenbuch"-Ausgabe von 1560', *ZDA*, 128: 198–203.

GRATIUS, ORTWIN. W. Ludwig, 'Literatur und Geschichte: Ortwin Gratius, die "Dunkelmännerbriefe" und "Das Testament des Philipp Melanchthon" von Walter Jens', *MJ*, 34: 125–67, cautions against accepting at face value the characterization of G. in the *Epistolae obscurorum virorum* as a representative of unreconstructed scholasticism.

KLAUSER, KONRAD. E. Glaser, '*Qua uia itur Tigurum — Welches ist der recht wäg gen Zürich?* Lateinunterricht in der Schweiz des 16. Jahrhunderts als Quelle deutscher Sprachgeschichte', *Fest. Haas*, 629–48, examines K.'s *Sylvula formularum quotidiani sermonis*, a book of Latin phrases accompanied by translations into contemporary Alemannic German.

LUTHER, MARTIN. Martin Luther, *Werke. Kritische Gesamtausgabe*, continues with 68. *Lateinisches Sachregister zur Abteilung Schriften Band 1–60, s-zythum*, ed. Ulrich Köpf, Weimar, Böhlau, viii + 693 pp. *Eine glossierte Vulgata aus dem Umkreis Martin Luthers: Untersuchungen zu dem 1519 in Lyon gedruckten Exemplar in der Bibelsammlung der Württembergischen Landesbibliothek Stuttgart*, ed. Martin Brecht and Eberhard Zwink (*VB*, 21), 407 pp., contains papers presented at a 1997 colloquium on the annotated copy of the Vulgate recently rediscovered in Stuttgart by Manuel Santos Noya, which was at first suspected to be one of the bibles used by L. at the Wartburg. That proposition has now been ruled out on paleographical grounds, but scholars remain divided on what role (if any) the Stuttgart Vulgate played in L.'s work as a biblical translator — a division of opinion reflected in the articles published in this volume. They include H. Spilling, 'Paläographische Sichtung der anonymen Einträge und Glossen' (15–50), which indicates that although the glosses are not in L.'s hand, they show considerable familiarity with L.'s translation of the Bible, commentaries, and other works; S. Widmann, 'Von der Wartburgpostille bis zum

Septembertestament 1522: Luther als Übersetzer des Neuen Testaments' (61–93), which suggests that the glosses to the Stuttgart Vulgate may reflect detailed revisions to L.'s original translation of the New Testament undertaken by L. in collaboration with Melanchthon and others following his return to Wittenberg; M. Beyer, 'Luthers Übersetzerregel(n)' (95–116), which argues that the translations that appear in the glosses are inconsistent with Luther's approach to translation; M. Santos Noya, 'Die Notizen zu den paulinischen Briefen' (213–46), which seeks to demonstrate that the glosses form part of the preparatory work for the *Septembertestament* and contends that Erasmus's Latin Bible and the Vulgate, rather than the Greek New Testament, were the basis for L.'s translation; and S. Strohm, 'Eine protestantische Biblia cum Glosis und ein Plädoyer für Luthers Deutsche Bibel' (247–347), which argues, in opposition to Santos Noya, that the glosses are to be understood as the private biblical commentary of an anonymous writer heavily influenced by Luther's theology. The volume contains edited transcriptions of the glosses to Genesis and the shorter Pauline epistles, as well as reproductions of some annotated pages from the Stuttgart Vulgate. K. Hagen, 'Luther's so-called *Judenschriften*: a genre approach', *AR*, 90:130–58, disputes the existence of a specific category of writings by L. against the Jews, arguing that the works designated *Judenschriften* in modern editions are more convincingly understood as late representatives of several well established genres of medieval apologetic. T. Bell, 'Die Rezeption Bernhards von Clairvaux bei Luther', *AR*, 90:72–102, examines the different contexts in which Bernard features in L.'s works and notes L.'s generally positive image of this medieval theologian, whom later Protestant writers identified as a precursor of the Reformation. Although the precise extent of Bernard's influence on L.'s theology is as yet undetermined, there may be points of contact in their understandings of scripture and the role of faith. J. A. Steiger, 'Martin Luthers allegorisch-figürliche Auslegung der Heiligen Schrift', *Zeitschrift für Kirchengeschichte*, 110:331–51, notes that L.'s rejection of the traditional fourfold method of exegesis in favour of the *sensus literalis* was far from absolute and that his understanding of Christ as the ultimate referent of all scripture led him to continue to apply allegorical and typological interpretations to the Old Testament in particular. H.-J. Ziegeler, 'Wahrheiten, Lügen, Fiktionen: zu Martin Luthers "Lügend von S. Johanne Chrysostomo" und zum Status literarischer Gattungen im 15. und 16. Jahrhundert', Haug, *Mittelalter*, 237–62, argues that L. condemned traditional hagiography not because of its ahistoricity, but because of its use in support of religious practices and doctrines to which he was opposed. H. Otto, 'Die Herkunft der Vorlage zu

Luthers Edition der "Theologia Deutsch": ein Fund in London', *ZDA*, 128:434–43, presents evidence that L.'s 1516 edition of the *Theologia* was based on a manuscript borrowed from the Augustinian house in Cologne. K. Dienst, 'Martin Luther als Tischredner', *Luther*, 70:145–50.

MELANCHTHON, PHILIPP. *Melanchthon in Europe: His Work and Influence beyond Wittenberg*, ed. Karin Maag, Grand Rapids, Baker Books, 191 pp., aims to bring M. out from under Luther's shadow by highlighting two key aspects of his contribution to the Lutheran Reformation, his humanism and his international links. Of particular interest are B. Gordon, on the ambivalent relationship between M. and the Swiss churches (45–67); A. Nelson Burnett, on M.'s personal contacts with Basel and relationship with the city's printing industry (69–85); D. Buzogany, on M.'s application of dialectic to theology (87–101); J. Schneider, on M.'s conception of scripture as 'sacred oration' (141–59); and N. Kuropka, on M.'s humanist understanding of the relationship between rhetoric and effective political leadership (161–72). P. Walter, 'Melanchthon und die Tradition der "studia humanitatis"', *Zeitschrift für Kirchengeschichte*, 110:191–208, charts M.'s gradual abandonment of the medieval concept of the seven liberal arts in favour of a humanist educational programme based on the sound acquisition of the classical languages. T. Wengert, 'Melanchthon and Luther / Luther and Melanchthon', *Lutherjb.*, 66:55–88, attributes the differences in approach between the two reformers to their fundamentally different understandings of the origin of evil in the universe.

MOLLERUS, BERNARDUS. B. Czapla, 'Der Rhein, Europas Strom, nicht Deutschlands Grenze: Bernardus Mollerus' *Rhenus et eius discriptio elegans* und die Tradition lateinischer Flussdichtung in Europa', *JIG*, 30:8–31, argues that M.'s *Rhenus* should be read not as a patriotic poem but as an expression of the Latinate culture that bound together learned elites throughout Europe.

PELLIKAN, KONRAD. R. G. Hobbs, 'Conrad Pellican and the Psalms: the ambivalent legacy of a pioneer Hebraist', *Reformation and Renaissance Review*, 1:72–99, compares P.'s exegetical method with that of other biblical commentators from the 'Upper Rhineland School', notably Martin Bucer.

PISCATOR, HERMANNUS. U. Goerlitz, 'Wissen und Repräsentation: zur Auseinandersetzung des Hermannus Piscator mit Johannes Trithemius um die Rekonstruktion der Vergangenheit', Schaefer, *Artes*, 198–212, notes P.'s rejection in his *Chronicon urbis et ecclesiae Maguntinensis* of Trithemius's account of the early history of the diocese of Mainz. Id., 'The chronicle in the age of Humanism: chronological structures and the reckoning of time between tradition and innovation', Kooper, *Chronicle*, 133–43, argues that P.'s *Chronicon* is the first work of its kind to divide time into successively numbered centuries and points to its influence on Matthias Flacius Illyricus.

PLATTER, THOMAS. Thomas Platter, *Lebensbeschreibung*, ed. Alfred Hartmann, 2nd edn revised by Ueli Dill with an afterword by Holger Jacob-Friesen, Basle, Schwabe, 218 pp. In his afterword to this new edition of the *Lebensbeschreibung*, published to mark the 500th anniversary of P.'s birth, J.-F. traces the reception of the work from the first printed edition in the early 18th c. to the present, and summarizes the conclusions of recent scholarship. He argues that the *Lebensbeschreibung* is to be understood as a carefully drawn self-portrait, containing significant elements of literary stylization and organized around the theme of divine predestination.

REICHART, WOLFGANG. *Vater und Sohn im 16. Jahrhundert: Der Briefwechsel des Wolfgang Reichart genannt Rychardus mit seinem Sohn Zeno (1520–1543)*, ed. Walther Ludwig, Hildesheim, Weidmann, x + 446 pp., presents 235 letters and excerpts of letters written by, to, and about Zeno R., most of them previously unpublished. They include 98 letters from Wolfgang R., city doctor in Ulm from 1513 to 1547, to Zeno R., and 61 letters from Zeno to his father. The scholarly introduction provides an account of the history of the correspondence, a description of the manuscript volume from which it is drawn, and biographical information on the two Reicharts. The vast majority of the letters published here date from Zeno's time as a student in Freiburg, Tübingen, Heidelberg, and eventually Italy. They offer insights into the everyday difficulties (principally financial) encountered by early modern students, as well as 16th-c. pedagogical methods, medicine, and, as the title of the collection suggests, father-son relationships. Although the letters are personal in character, they contain some information on the early progress of the Reformation in Ingolstadt, Heidelberg, and Ulm, together with observations on contemporary political events such as the Peasants' War and the Turkish advance into central Europe. The Latin text of each letter is accompanied by a detailed summary of contents and explanatory notes.

REUCHLIN, JOHANNES. Johannes Reuchlin, *Sämtliche Werke*. IV. *Schriften zum Bücherstreit. 1. Reuchlins Schriften*, ed. Widu-Wolfgang Ehlers, Lothar Mundt, Hans-Gert Roloff, and Peter Schäfer, Stuttgart–Bad Cannstatt, Frommann-Holzboog, 480 pp., deals with the most celebrated episode in R.'s career: his dispute with the converted Jew Johannes Pfefferkorn and the Cologne theological faculty concerning whether Jewish books, above all the Talmud, should be tolerated in a Christian society. The volume contains the three works published by R. in the context of the dispute — the

*Augenspiegel, Ain clare verstentnis in Tütsch,* and the *Defensio,* addressed to the Emperor Maximilian I — along with an earlier work on the Jewish question, the *Tütsch missive, warumb die Juden solang in ellend sind.* Latin texts are accompanied by a translation into modern German. Although footnotes are kept to a minimum, all quotations and references are sourced, and there are several indexes covering, in particular, R.'s use of Jewish authorities and imperial law in support of his arguments. Editorial corrections are listed in an appendix. Two supplementary volumes of material relevant to the history of the *Bücherstreit,* along with an edition of the works of R.'s opponent Pfefferkorn, are planned. Johannes Reuchlin, *Briefwechsel.* I. *1477–1505,* ed. Matthias Dall'Asta and Gerald Dörner, Stuttgart–Bad Cannstatt, Frommann-Holzboog, lxv + 505 pp. This beautifully presented volume, the first of a projected four, contains 136 letters and poems from the critical formative phase of R.'s career, encompassing his student years, his Italian journeys, and his service at the courts of Tübingen and Heidelberg. The letters published here shed light on R.'s contacts with other Italian and German humanists — his correspondents during this period included Sebastian Brant, Rudolf Agricola, Heinrich Bebel, and Aldo Manuzio — and on his developing intellectual and, in particular, philological interests, which by 1505 were to see him emerge as Germany's foremost Christian Hebraist. However, as the editors note in their introduction, they also document R.'s less celebrated, but equally significant activities as a jurist and princely counsellor in Württemberg and the Palatinate. Each letter is accompanied by a detailed summary of contents and extensive notes. A selection of documents of particular biographical interest is published as an appendix.

ROT, LEONHARD. I. Bezzel, 'Eine "Bambergische Zeitung" von 1584 und ihr Drucker oder Verleger Leonhard Rot', *Gutenberg-Jb.,* 74:164–72.

SACHS, HANS. S. Wailes, 'Hans Sachs, John the Baptist, and the dark days of Nuremberg ca. 1548', *GLL,* 52:399–411, interprets S.'s *Enthauptung Johannis* as a commentary on the resistance of Andreas Osiander and Veit Dietrich to the implementation of the Interim in Nuremberg. J. Flood, 'Kultur auf einem dürren Ast: zu einem Einblattdruck des Hans Sachs', Robertshaw, *Natur,* 279–92, argues that S.'s *Clagred der Neün Muse oder Künst vber Teütschlandt* reflects contemporary humanists' dissatisfaction with their status in German society.

SACHS, MICHAEL. S. Wailes, 'Power and suffering in Michael Sachs' *Schoene Tragedia / von Stephano dem heiligen Marterer* (1565)', *Daphnis,* 28:93–115, argues that S.'s interpretation of his subject is informed by a peculiarly Lutheran understanding of martyrdom as confession in the face of magisterial opposition.

SCHÖFFERLIN, BERNHARD. C. Winter, *Humanistische Historiographie in der Volkssprache: Bernhard Schöfferlins 'Römische Historie'* (Arbeiten und Editionen zur Mittleren Deutschen Literatur, n.F. 6), Stuttgart–Bad Cannstatt, Fromann-Holzboog, ix + 284 pp., proceeds from the premise that S.'s work, first published in Mainz in 1505, was not merely a translation or reworking of Livy, but a substantially independent history, drawing on both classical and medieval traditions. As such, W. argues, it must be understood in the context of S.'s contacts with Italian humanism and of his lifelong connection with the ruling house of Württemberg. Through a close analysis of individual episodes treated in the work, the author shows how S.'s handling of his sources reflects his humanist understanding of history as a pedagogical tool for analysing human behaviour, especially in the political sphere, and his involvement in the tangled dynastic politics of late 15th-c. Württemberg and the Empire more generally. In his account of the early Roman kings, for example, S. selectively combines passages from Livy and the *Antiquitates Romanae* of Dionysus of Halicarnassus to present the institution of monarchy in a fundamentally positive light. In the same way, S.'s description of the struggle for power between patricians and plebeians in Rome during the period following the overthrow of the monarchy is informed by his experience of similar conflicts in the late medieval German cities. S.'s relatively free approach to his subject matter is also apparent in his treatment of religious and cultic themes and in his tendency to conflate or abbreviate material contained in his two main sources, Livy and Dionysus.

SPALATIN, GEORG. C. Meckelnborg and A.-B. Riecke, 'Die "Chronik von Sachsen und Thüringer" von Georg Spalatin', *Fest. Pensel*, 131–62, attempts to reconstruct the original conception of this unfinished work.

SPRENGER, BALTHASAR. B. Borowka-Clausberg, *Balthasar Sprenger und der frühneuzeitliche Reisebericht*, Munich, Iudicium, 220 pp., examines S.'s *Merfart*, the published account of his voyage in 1505–06 to Portuguese India as the agent of a consortium of Augsburg merchants, along with the woodcut illustrations to the text produced by Hans Burgkmair and Georg Glockendon. B.-C. contrasts S.'s restrained and 'factual' description of the places and peoples he encountered in the course of his travels with both the Classical and medieval tradition of writing about the Orient, as exemplified by Pliny, Isidore of Seville, and John Mandeville, and contemporary descriptions of the Americas, which tended to emphasize the fabulous and 'monstrous' aspects of life in the newly discovered lands. In her view, the absence of stylistic affectation in the work is to be understood as part of a narrative strategy aimed at convincing the reader of its 'Wahrhaftigkeit'. The 1509 edition of the *Merfart*, along with related documents, is included as an appendix.

STADEN, HANS. R. Schlechtweg-Jahn, 'Hans Stadens Brasilien-Reisebericht von 1557', Schaefer, *Artes*, 243–79, warns against an uncritical use of this text as an ethnographic source.

VADIAN, JOACHIM. F. Graf-Stuhlhofer, 'Vadian als Lehrer am Wiener Poetenkolleg', *Zwingliana*, 26:93–8.

## THE SEVENTEENTH CENTURY

By ANNA CARRDUS, *University of Bristol*

### 1. GENERAL

*Die Literatur des 17. Jahrhunderts*, ed. Albert Meier (Hansers Sozialgeschichte der deutschen Literatur vom 16. Jahrhundert bis zur Gegenwart, 2), Munich, dtv, 776 pp., is a most welcome collection of essays which outlines the social contexts of 17th-c. literary preoccupations. It is organized under four main headings: 'Historisch-politische' and 'Philosophisch-anthropologische Grundlagen', 'Literaturbezogene', and 'Literarische Institutionen'. The bibliography (679–746) is comprehensive, the index and list of contents so detailed that the collection is also useful as a reference work. Béhar, *Spectaculum*, is a unique and extremely substantial handbook presenting invaluable coverage of theatre and spectacle throughout Europe between 1580 and 1750. Conceived at a conference at the Centre d'Études Supérieures de la Renaissance at Tours in 1989, it aims above all to stimulate research into neglected topics. Chapters on Drama, Opera, Ballet, Entries, fireworks, and religious festivals are divided into sections on each European country which survey current knowledge, then pinpoint *lacunae* (the sections on neo-Latin drama, *commedia dell'arte*, and tournaments are Pan-European, but share this structural pattern). The European perspective is supported by a bilingual approach: sections on Romance-speaking countries are in French, all others in English. P. Béhar, 'Drama in the Empire', *ib.*, 257–87, illustrates that 'Of all European drama in this period that of the Empire is still one of the least examined'. The lavish attention already paid to Silesian tragedy is reflected in B.'s particularly coherent summary of it in relation to confessional conflict under Habsburg rule, Jesuit theatre, and rising interest in opera; and in his assessment of the part played in its development by Opitz, Gryphius, Lohenstein, Hallmann, and Haugwitz. Far briefer surveys cover comedy, 'historico-political' drama (a non-classical form which evolved with the rapid spread of wandering players after 1648 and influenced Weise's political school theatre), drama in Bohemia, and the spread of German theatre into Russia. B. insists that tracing primary souces is the most pressing research *desideratum*. W. Braun, 'Opera in the Empire', *ib.*, 437–64, indicates rich points of contact with drama, ballet, and tournaments, and is an informative and stimulating overview which claims to be 'a series of problems' rather than a 'linear history'. For example: while opera clearly thrived at Italianate courts in Vienna, Munich, and Dresden, at German-speaking courts in Wolfenbüttel and Weissenfels, and later in public opera houses in Braunschweig and Hamburg, little is known about smaller centres or travelling opera troupes. The urgent research *desideratum* of tracing documentation for productions is also problematic: texts may give only the arias from an opera, not the full libretto; scores date back to 1662 but are extant in representative quantity only from about 1680; series of illustrations exist for court but not for commercial productions. S. Smart, 'Ballet in the Empire', *ib.*, 547–70, surveys ballet as a spectacular type of 'Gesamtkunstwerk' with French, English, and Italian antecedents; it predated opera in Germany, yet was closely related to it, to tournaments, and — early in the 17th c. — to Jesuit theatre. S. traces the development of ballet after 1648 geographically, under the headings of courts whose dynastic interconnections and fundamental diversity encouraged both continuities and innovation; one constant feature was women's participation. Research has tended to neglect ballet in favour of opera; S. thus lists a number of pressing *desiderata*, all of which involve tracing source material. H. Watanabe-O'Kelly, 'Entries, fireworks and religious festivals in the Empire', *ib.*, 721–41, introduces new institutions as the organizers of later 17th-c. spectacle: not only courts but civic councils staged imperial or princely entries, while universities mounted elaborate ceremonies of their own. Towns and cities increasingly chose to mark festive occasions with illuminations, while courtly reliance on fireworks waned after culminating in unsurpassably grandiose firework operas (as at Munich in 1662). Religious festivals were predominantly Catholic, focusing on — for example — canonizations. With the exception of fireworks, these topics have hardly been researched. W.-O'K. urges studies of all important cities along the lines of K. Möseneder's 1986 volume on festivities in Regensburg. An important art-historical study with relevance to theatre, spectacle, and other aspects of 17th-c. culture is Schnitzer, *Maskeraden*, which surveys the role of 'fancy dress' in ceremonial at courts throughout Germany between 1500 and 1800. Initial discussion of day-to-day dress denoting court rank reveals the social and political function of 'fancy dress': just as 'incognito' lent certain freedoms to its wearers (when travelling, for example), so 'fancy dress' allowed rulers to relax routine ceremonial and modify court hierarchies. Current favourites or mistresses, visiting princes or diplomats could be honoured in the festive atmosphere of a masquerade without destabilising power relations at home or abroad; and (unlike 'incognito') masquerades enhanced rulers' prestige. In the 17th c., 'Ritterspiele' (various types of tournament) and 'Wirtschaften' (festive meals in fictional settings such as a rural inn) were favoured forms. The aesthetic potential of 'fancy dress' was augmented by the increasing flexibility of theme which S. traces through the era. In 'Ritterspiele' of the later 17th c., for instance, the colours of 'fancy dress' unified the lavish allegorical entertainments choreographed in large arenas. Discussion is supported by 318 illustrations from various court archives, and includes a section on how outfits and props were made and stored in Dresden. K. Conermann, 'Opitz auf der Dresdner Fürstenhochzeit von 1630. Drei satirische Sonette des Boberschwans', *Daphnis*, 29:587–630, describes the 1630 wedding festivities for Friedrich III of Schleswig-Holstein and Maria Elisabeth of Saxony, relating them to the weddings of M. E.'s sisters, Sophia Eleonora (to Georg II of Hessen-Darmstadt), and Magdalena Sybilla (to Christian IV of Denmark), and the part Opitz played in them, especially the latter (1634; examined in detail in Mara Wade's 1996 monograph, see *YWMLS*, 58:779). C. thus contextualizes three anonymous sonnets from the 1630 'Festbuch' which he compares with manuscript copies where Opitz's authorship is clear, and prints here for the first time. J. Bepler, B. Kümmel, and H. Meise, 'Weibliche Selbstdarstellung im 17. Jahrhundert. Das Funeralwerk der Landgräfin Sophia Eleonora von Hessen-Darmstadt', Wunder, *Geschlechterperspektiven*, 441–68, is an interdisciplinary examination of Sophia Eleonora's poems and graphic commissions in the *Mausolaeum* (1665), an opulent printed memorial to her husband, Georg II. Bepler defines the *Mausolaeum* in terms of book history, placing it beside the official 'Funeralwerk' organized by S. E.'s son Ludwig VI, in line with the representative memorial practices of other courts, but emphasizing its innovatory qualities: the realistic portraits of S. E. in 12 of the 82 engravings (reproductions in the article) mark the assertive entry of personal grief into the ritualized ceremonial of dynastic mourning. Meise examines S. E.'s poems in the *Mausolaeum* from a literary point of view, placing them within the range of various modes of self-presentation found in her manuscript ballets, prayer-book, and diaries. Kümmel elucidates the engravings in the *Mausolaeum* from an art historian's point of view, relating the portraits of S. E. to allegorical traditions which can accommodate personal grief in a dynastic setting. S. Smart, 'On the diverse duties of the servants of princes: Lorenz Beger (1653–1705), librarian, antiquarian, and court poet in Heidlberg', *MLR*, 94:1025–40, relates B.'s career to two princes of the Pfalz, Karl Ludwig (1617–80) and Karl II (1651–85); and two of Brandenburg, the Great Elector Friedrich Wilhelm (1620–88), and Friedrich III, first king of Prussia (1657–1713). As court librarian and antiquarian under Karl Ludwig, B. catalogued and published on Palatine collections which passed to Brandenburg on Karl's death, and thus became part of Prussia's great royal collections. As court poet under Karl, B. helped organize festivities which, S. argues, cannot help but reflect the diminished political status of the Palatinate in the wake of the 30 Years' War. M. Reinhart, 'Text and simultext: borrowing Claudian in seventeenth-century Germany (a case from the Fruchtbringende Gesellschaft)', *GLL*, 52:281–96, deals with the *Aulaea Romana* (1642), a Latin pamphlet by an anonymous member of the Fruchtbringende Gesellschaft which refutes Harsdörffer's translation into Latin of the francophile *Peristromata Turcica* (presented to the F. G. some months earlier), and concentrates on themes of peace and harmony. R. analyses the anonymous author's borrowings from Claudian in some detail, seeing them as complex instances of intertextuality which tactfully acknowledge political and confessional beliefs in Anhalt, the seat of Prince Ludwig, head of the F.G., and draw on recent contemporary recognition of Claudian as a non-pagan (Protestant) 'authority for an age in crisis'. J. J. Berns, 'Kriegs- und Friedensbilder. Mittel ihrer ästhetischen Reflexion im 17. Jahrhundert', *Morgenglantz*, 9:181–217, looks at the new military technologies of the 30 Years' War and at new media techniques which sought adequate aesthetic correlatives for them. B. analyses, for example, how visual images (Harsdörffer's 'Kriegsmonstrum' of 1647) and literary images (Grimmelshausen's account of the battle of Wittstock in *Simplicissimus*, II, 27) both arrive at an aesthetic of the grotesque, but by different means; and how onomatopoeia, conceived of by Schottelius and the 'Pegnitzschäfer' as an element of natural language, disturbingly provides acoustic images of mechanized weaponry. He finds images of peace less technically innovatory. Analysis is supported by eight illustrations. C. Woodford, 'Women as historians: the case of early-modern German convents', *GLL*, 52:271–80, discusses 17th-c. chronicles by two prioresses and one abbess who either established a historical tradition for their convents by recording internal events from the past, or recorded external events from the present when the 30 Years' War disrupted convent life. Few early modern women attempted historiography; these three, however, wrote in the knowledge that their records would be of value within their convents to future generations of nuns. B. Becker-Cantarino, '*Hexenküche* und *Walpurgisnacht*: Imagination der Dämonie in der Frühen Neuzeit und in *Faust I*', *Euphorion*, 93:193–225, sees witch-figures in *Faust* as standing for forces — imagination, physicality, desire, feeling — which enlightenment rationality treated as Other. B.-C. traces illuminating parallels between Goethe's demonization of the Other and early modern beliefs about witches, focusing in particular on notions of masculinity and sexuality. Bearing the predominantly male perspective in mind, she conducts detailed analysis of numerous (16th- and) 17th-c. representations — both visual and textual — of the 'Hexenküche' and 'Hexensabbat' motifs.

## 2. POETRY

### INDIVIDUAL AUTHORS

BIRKEN. H. Stauffer, 'Nachforschungen zur Chronologie der Werke Sigmund von Birkens', *Daphnis*, 28:137–86, gives a highly detailed account both of the problems attached to compiling a chronologically accurate bibliography of B.'s massive poetic output, and of means of solving them. Using B.'s (published) diaries, manuscript collections, and a contemporary genealogy of Nuremberg patrician families as sources, S. dates many occasional poems hitherto undated by modern bibliographies and editions of B.'s work. S. points out that occasional poetry, in particular, cannot be adequately understood until its context is restored by determining addressees and dates of composition, and throws new light on B.'s standing as 'Haus- und Hofpoet' to the Nuremberg patriciate.

DIESINGER. A. Haase, 'Die Freiung im Meistergesang. Bisher unveröffentlichte Lieder in Weimarer Handschriften', *Fest. Pensel*, 65–77, introduces and provides a scholarly edition of a cycle of three 'Lieder zur Freiung' — songs designed to gain admission to, or other privileges within a society of 'Meistersinger'. The songs were composed in Nuremberg in 1600/01 by Hans Diesinger (1572–1617) and are the oldest extant examples of this particular genre.

GRYPHIUS. *Andreas Gryphius: Herodes, Der Ölberg, Lateinische Epik*, ed. Ralf Georg Czapla (Bibliothek seltener Texte in Studienausgaben, 4), Berlin, Weidler, 349 pp., is a welcome, inexpensive and handsome edition of G.'s Latin epic poems *Herodis Furiae & Rahelis lachrymae* (1634), *Dei Vindicis Impetus et Herodis Interitus* (1635), and *Olivetum libri tres* (1646), made accessible to non-readers of Latin by lucid parallel translations into German. The generous critical apparatus includes commentary and a glossary of biblical and classical names. A similar edition of G.'s shorter Latin epic poems, epigrams and occasional poetry is forthcoming. D. Breuer, 'Andreas Gyphius als Bewunderer und Mittler römischer Barockkunst. Zu seinem Sonett *Als Er aus Rom geschidn*', *Morgenglantz*, 8, 1998:255–72, links aspects of G.'s poetic technique in his sonnets on Rome with contemporary attitudes towards appreciation of the arts which originated in Rome itself, in Jesuit circles. B. refers to this aesthetic of evocative amazement as the 'Argutia-Bewegung', emphasising that G.'s debt to it is literary, and so does not necessarily — as other critics have suggested — conflict with his religious beliefs as an orthodox Lutheran. S. Knöll, 'Gryphius' Erstes und Zweites Sonettbuch: neue Gedanken zu einer zahlensymbolischen Interpretation', *WBN*, 26:37–59, re-examines the numerical structuring of G.'s two books of sonnets as posited by Szyrocki and subsequent critics. K. then offers a new interpretation which takes account of the fact that the symbolic significance of numerical ordering systems was waning in the 17th c. and suggests G. displays an ironic awareness of this. Discussion is supported by a tabular diagram.

KNORR. I. M. Battafarano, 'Übersetzen und Vermitteln im Barock im Zeichen der kulturellen Angleichung und Irenik: Opitz, Harsdörffer, Hoffmannswaldau, Knorr von Rosenroth', *Morgenglantz*, 8, 1998:13–61, examines the 17th-c. concept of translating as mediation, a means of enriching German language and culture via intimate conversation with poets and scholars past or present, then sees K.'s monumental *Johannesapokalypse* (1670) and *Kabbala Denudata* (1677/84) as outstripping the aims of all three earlier translators. A. B. Kilcher, 'Hebräische Sprachmetaphysik und lateinische Kabbalistik. Knorr und das Metaphysische Problem der Übersetzung in der christlichen Kabbala', *ib.*, 63–108, deals with K.'s *Kabbala Denudata* in greater detail, while W. G. Marigold, 'Die englische Übersetzung von Knorrs Kommentar zur *Johannesapokalypse* und die Rezeption deutscher Erbauungsschriften in England im 17. Jahrhundert', *ib.*, 171–96, extends examination of the *Johannesapokalypse* to a German-English context. R. Zeller, 'Knorrs Übersetzung von Nicolas Fouquets *Le Chrestien desabusé du monde*', *ib.*, 109–24, is of interest because Fouquet's contemporary fate as a political prisoner was comparable with that of Boethius (d. 524), while K. is perhaps best known for his translation of B.'s *De consolatione philosophiae* (1677). G. van Gemert, 'Knorrs Nachdichtungen lateinischer Kirchenhymnen. Zu ihrem Stellenwert und zum Funktionszusammenhang im *Neuen Helicon*', *ib.*, 125–67, reprints the eight hymns in question (with parallel Latin texts) from *Neuer Helicon* (1684), K.'s collection of devotional songs. B. Bos, 'Knorrs *Helicon* und die Niederlande', *ib.*, 339–53, relates K.'s years in Holland (1663–64) to two poems from the collection: the first, which shows the influence of intellectual circles in Leiden; and no. LXX, translated from a poem by the mystic chiliast, Adam Boreel of Amsterdam. All three poems are reprinted in the article.

THOMAS. G. Riedl, 'Hochzeit in der literarischen Idylle. Ein exemplarischer Vergleich von Johann Thomas' *Lisille* (1663) mit Johann Heinrich Voss' *Luise* (1795)', *Daphnis*, 27, 1998:655–84, aims to resolve controversies over the literary quality and bourgeois nature of two somewhat neglected works which both treat pastoral as a retreat from public life (Thomas was a diplomat and 'Hofbeamter'). R. confirms *Lisille*'s exceptional status in 17th-c. literature as a forerunner of the bourgeois 'Privatroman' — it was inspired by T.'s own marriage and his portrayal of the wedded couple's everyday life is generically innovatory — but finds it typical of its time in its view of marital relationship as immune to transience and the vagaries of fortune.

OTHER WORK

H.-G. Kemper, 'Hölle und "Himmel auf der Erden"'. Liebes-,
Hochzeits- und Ehelyrik in der frühen Neuzeit', Haug, *Mittelalter*,
30–77, claims that Opitz's detachment of German love poetry from
the 'Minnesang' tradition in the *Poeterey* (1624) left it free to merge
with the Lutheran concept of marriage as an ideal earthly state. In
the light of this, K. traces reworkings of Petrarchan and Neoplatonic
elements in poetry by Opitz, Fleming, Hoffmannswaldau, and
Günther, and pays particular attention to H.'s treatment of eros as a
natural force and G.'s debt to the Song of Songs.

3. PROSE

INDIVIDUAL AUTHORS

CZEPKO. N. Largier, 'Die Mitte der Zeit. Apokatastasis als
Naturerfahrung in Daniel Czepko's "Consolatio ad Baronissam
Cziganeam"', *Fest. Haas*, 221–39, bases discussion of mystical
concepts of time and death on a substantial 'Trostschrift' (200 pp.)
written when Czepko was 27, suggesting that C. moves away from
the medieval traditions of mysticism which otherwise inform this
work towards a characteristically 17th-c. concept of nature as a site
of mystic experience.

GREIFFENBERG. L. Tatlock, M. Lindemann, and R. Scribner,
'Sinnliche Erfahrungen und spirituelle Autorität. Aspekte von Geschlecht in Catharina Regina von Greiffenbergs Meditationen über die
Empfängnis Christi und Marias Schwangerschaft', Wunder, *Geschlechterperspektiven*, 177–90, is an interdisciplinary approach to G.'s meditations on the Incarnation. Tatlock (a Germanist) argues that G.'s
descriptions of Christ's foetal growth derive from anatomical works
by male academics, while those of Mary's body derive from G.'s
experience of her own physical being as an authoritative source of
spiritual knowledge. Lindemann (a medical historian) counters this
sharp dichotomy by drawing attention to the overlap of medicine and
theology in 17th-c. discourse on conception in general, suggesting
points of contact between it and G.'s meditations. Scribner (a
theological historian) sees G. as synthesizing Catholic and Protestant
traditions, and suggests her personal religious experiences may be
characteristic of a type of piety which transcends confessional
differences. L. Tatlock, '*Scientia divinorum*: anatomy, transmutation,
and incorporation in Catharina von Greiffenberg's meditations on
the incarnation and the gestation of Christ', *German History*, 17:9–24,
is a valuably expanded version of T.'s contribution to the above-
mentioned article. T. develops her interest in 'representations of

bodies and bodiliness' in greater detail, discussing how G. links them with gender and what this reveals about a woman who wrote with authority on spiritual experience within cultural traditions dominated by men.

GRIMMELSHAUSEN. K. A. Zaenker, 'Grimmelshausen und die *Pícara Justina*', *Daphnis*, 27, 1998:631–53, claims that this early 17th-c. Spanish novel had a greater influence on G. than has so far been realized. Z. reveals the economy of G.'s narrative methods by comparing an episode from it with the 'Medicus-Novelle' in *Vogelnest, Zweiter Teil*, examines motifs in *Satyrischer Pilgram* and *Simplicissimus* which may reflect its influence, and argues that *Courasche* can be seen as a misogynistic counterpart to it.

MOSCHEROSCH. W. E. Schäfer, 'Der Dreissigjährige Krieg aus der Sicht Moscherochs und Grimmelshausens', *Morgenglantz*, 9:13–30, looks in particular at representations of social harmony in M.'s *Soldaten-Leben* (1644) and G.'s Simplician cycle, viewing them in the context of satire as generically appropriate counterweights to portrayal of 'die verkehrte Welt', and tracing their general relevance to differences between the authors' real-life experiences of war and peace.

SCHURMANN. *Anna Maria van Schurman: Whether a Christian Woman Should be Educated and other Writings from her Intellectual Circle*, ed. and trans. Joyce L. Irwin, Chicago U.P., xxvi + 148 pp., is a collection of otherwise not easily available writings by or to Schurman (1607–78), mostly translated from Latin. Schurman was Dutch, but her writings fed into late 17th-c. German debate on education for women and her name appears again and again in the catalogues of learned women that were such an important aspect of this debate — not least because they presented role models to women eager to learn or write.

SCHOTTELIUS. R. G. Czapla, ' "Wie man recht verteutschen soll." Der Traktat des Justus Georg Schottelius als Paradigma einer Übersetzungstheorie in der Frühen Neuzeit. Mit einem Exkurs zur Vergil-Übersetzung im 16. bis 19. Jahrhundert', *Morgenglantz*, 8, 1998:197–26, focuses on a treatise in dialogue form from S.'s *Ausführliche Arbeit der Teutschen HaubtSprache* (1663), examining the structure of his arguments and relating them to more modern theories of translation.

SPEE. I. M. Battafarano, 'Satanisierung des Alltags als verfehlte Sozialdisziplinierung in Spees *Cautio Criminalis* (1631)', *Morgenglantz*, 8, 1998:363–83, compares S.'s criticism of witch trials with Lipsius's concept of state discipline, showing, for example, that S. considers juristic follow-ups of popular rumour through torture and accusation to be a failure of public authority, which should seek control over the base ('satanic') emotions that start and spread rumours. I. M.

Battafarano, 'Absentia Dei in Spees *Cautio Criminalis*? Wesen und Wirkung einer epochemachenden Schrift', *ib.*, 385–400, discusses a statement from S.'s *Cautio Criminalis* which suggests God did not heed the cries of women burned as witches. ZESEN. *Philipp von Zesen: Sämtliche Werke*, vols 17.1, 17.2, ed. Ferdinand van Ingen, Ulrich Maché, and Volker Meid (Ausgaben Deutscher Dichter des XV. bis XVIII. Jahrhunderts), Berlin–NY, de Gruyter, 1998, 697, 333 pp., is the most recent volume of this splendid edition. The first part contains Z.'s mythological handbook *Der erdichteten Heidnischen Gottheiten wie auch Als= und Halb-Gottheiten Herkunft und Begäbnisse* (1688), the second his own very extensive index-glossary ('Blatweiser') to this work with the editors' critical apparatus.

## 4. DRAMA

### INDIVIDUAL AUTHORS

GRYPHIUS. D. Bourger, 'Schwert und Zunge: über die zweifache Prahlerei in Andreas Gryphius' *Horribilicribrifax*', *Daphnis*, 28 : 117–36, offers a text-immanent reading. Focusing on the central figures of two braggart soldiers, B. follows their comic replacement of deed by speech, 'Schwert' by 'Zunge', through the play and back to the mock prefatory letter, suggesting that G. deflates this final instance of linguistic boasting by departing from his practice in relation to the earlier *Peter Squentz* and claiming authorship on the title page.

### OTHER WORK

Sarah Colvin, *The Rhetorical Feminine. Gender and the Orient on the German Stage, 1647–1742*, Oxford, Clarendon, x + 332 pp., analyses dramatic and operatic representations of the early modern Other ('woman, the oriental, and the "infidel"'), seeing them as aimed at persuading audiences to accept normative notions of social order. C. shows these representations to be rhetorical constructs which combine and re-combine stereotypes of gender and exoticism: in *Catharina von Georgien*, for example, Gryphius adds the 'feminine' weaknesses of deceit, vacillation and ungoverned sensuality to exoticism in his portrayal of the Persian infidel Chach Abas, thus clinching condemnation of his tyranny. As would be expected, the Other is often embodied in Turkish characters, but C. reveals various permutations of stereotypes across a wide range of texts, including comedies, by both the well-known (Gryphius, Lohenstein, Haugwitz, Hallmann, Bostel) and the lesser-known. She devotes one chapter to close analysis of how music supports rhetorical constructs.

# THE CLASSICAL ERA

By JEFFREY MORRISON, *Lecturer in German, National University of Ireland, Maynooth*

## I. GENERAL

GENERAL STUDIES AND ESSAY COLLECTIONS. Ingrid Strohschneider-Kohrs, *Poesie und Reflexion: Aufsätze zur Literatur*, Tübingen, Niemeyer, 482 pp., contains a wide range of essays on a variety of topics, most of which have appeared elsewhere. Two are however new and relevant to our period: ' "Doppelreflexion" und "sokratische Ironie" in Lessings Spätschriften' (159–96); 'Bilder und Gegenbilder goethezeitlicher Antike-Rezeption' (249–76).

PERIODS: AUFKLÄRUNG. *Wanderzwang — Wanderlust: Formen der Raum- und Sozialerfahrung zwischen Aufklärung und Frühindustrialisierung*, ed. Wolfgang Albrecht and Hans-Joachim Kertscher (Hallesche Beiträge zur Europäischen Aufklärung, 11), Tübingen, Niemeyer, 314 pp., is the product of a 1995 conference in Halle and focuses on a fascinating sub-category of travel experience. Contributions focusing on our period include: W. Albrecht, 'Kultur und Physiologie des Wanderns: Einleitende Vorüberlegungen eines Germanisten zur interdisziplinären Erforschung der deutschsprachigen Wanderliteratur' (1–12); A. Opitz, 'Ein Schuhmacher auf dem "Schriftstellertheater": die Wanderschaften und Schicksale von Johann Caspar Steube im Kontext der spätaufklärerischen Reiseliteratur' (13–24); H.-J. Althaus, 'Bürgerliche Wanderlust: Anmerkungen zur Entstehung eines Kultur- und Bewegungsmusters' (25–43); I. Kuczynski, 'Die Lust zum Wandern — ein Hintergehen der bürgerlichen Moderne?' (44–60); T. Sadowsky, 'Gehen Sta(d)t Fahren: Anmerkungen zur urbanen Praxis des Füssgängers in der Reiseliteratur um 1800' (61–90); H. Ritter, 'Über Gehen, Spazieren und Wandern von Frauen in der zweiten Hälfte des 18. Jahrhunderts' (91–104); U. Meyer, ' "Fahren zeigt Ohnmacht, Gehen Kraft": Sozial- und stilgeschichtlicher Vergleich ausgewählter Wanderberichte der Spätaufklärung' (105–22); U. Hentschel, 'Zur politisch-aufklärerischen und gegenaufklärerischen Wanderliteratur' (122–34); H. Bosse, 'Zur Sozialgeschichte des Wanderliedes' (135–58); H.-J. Kertscher, 'Lektüre im "Buch der Natur": Johann Georg Sulzers Alpenwanderungen' (158–76); R. Baasner, 'Literarische Relexionen des Wanderns: Goethes frühe Gedichte und die Tradition' (177–91); C. Siegrist, 'Ausbruch aus der Enge: Ulrich Bräkers Wanderungen' (192–99); J. Drews, 'Ein Mann verwirklicht seine "Lieblingsträumerei": Beobachtungen zu Details von Seumes

"Spaziergang" nach Syrakus' (200–14). The publisher Frommann-Holzboog continues to provide an outstanding service to scholars of the period by publishing a series of texts which would otherwise be hard to locate, and yet which cast an interesting light upon patterns of Enlightenment thinking. As the title of the series suggests, the aim is to bring to our attention figures who were not necessarily part of the mainstream but whose activity clearly related to it. George Schade, *Die unwandelbare und ewige Religion*, ed. and intro. Martin Mulsow (Freidenker der europäischen Aufklärung, 1.4), Stuttgart–Bad Cannstatt, Frommann-Holzboog, 501 pp., consists, as do the other texts in the series, of a reprint of an early edition along with a critical introduction and bibliography. This text is valuable as an unconventional example of contemporary deism. *Aufklärungsforschung in Deutschland*, ed. Holger Dainat and Wilhelm Vosskamp (Beihefte zum Euphorion, 32), Heidelberg, Winter, 128 pp., includes seven analyses of the historical positions taken by scholars of German with respect to the Enlightenment. As the introduction suggests, the study of the Enlightenment has always had a paradigmatic character; it is seen as a test of prevalent methodologies but also, more importantly, forces the critic into self-reflection. The volume investigates various treatments of the Enlightenment from the 19th and 20th cs: W. Vosskamp, 'Aufklärungsforschung in Deutschland: Einleitung' (1–6); R. Rosenberg, ' "Aufklärung" in der deutschen Literaturgeschichtsschreibung des 19. Jahrhunderts' (7–20); H. Dainat, 'Die wichtigste aller Epochen: Geistesgeschichtliche Aufklärungsforschung' (21–38); J. Schönert, 'Konstellationen und Entwicklungen der germanistischen Forschung zur Aufklärung seit 1960' (39–48); F. Vollhardt, 'Aspekte der germanistischen Wissenschaftsentwicklung am Beispiel der neueren Forschung zur "Empfindsamkeit" ' (49–78); M. Schlott, ' "Politische Aufklärung" durch wissenschaftliche "Kopplungmanöver": germanistische Literaturwissenschaft und geschichtswissenschaftliche Jakobinerforschung zwischen 1965 und 1990' (79–98); W. Erhart, 'Nach der Aufklärungsforschung?' (99–128). Roger Paulin, *Der Fall Wilhelm Jerusalem: Zum Selbstmordproblem zwischen Aufklärung und Empfindsamkeit* (Kleine Schriften zur Aufklärung, 6), Göttingen, Wallstein, 167 pp., provides a concise treatment of the debate provoked by the life, death and works of J. It further provides 70 contemporary documents or extracts from documents pertaining to the particular suicide and the issue in general during this period with a natural focus on Werther. Holger Zaunstöck, *Sozietätslandschaft und Mitgliederstrukturen: Die mitteldeutschen Aufklärungsgesellschaften im 18. Jahrhundert* (Hallesche Beiträge zur Europäischen Aufklärung, 9), Tübingen, Niemeyer, 352 pp., is a slightly amended version of a doctoral thesis. It attempts to put flesh on the bones of our knowledge of the complex network of learned or 'enlightened' societies which flourished during the 18th c. It does so by examining how many of them existed in the given area, the nature of the membership and the nature of any co-operation or networking. In doing so, Z. illustrates a fundamental aspect of the dynamics of Enlightenment. Similarly exhaustive, and not unrelated in theme, is the work by Detlef Gaus, *Geselligkeit und Gesellige: Bildung, Bürgertum und bildungsbürgerliche Kultur um 1800*, Stuttgart–Weimar, Metzler, 1998, 502 pp. He details the dynamic developments in the Berlin salons of this period; their precise make-up is revealed in the extraordinarily detailed *Anhänge*. The historical changes in the social composition and intellectual focus of these groups are captured in great detail, particularly the shift towards more inclusive (women, Jews, young intellectuals) groupings at the end of the 18th c. Emanuel Peter, *Geselligkeiten: Literatur, Gruppenbildung und kultureller Wandel im 18. Jahrhundert* (SDL, 153), 359 pp., takes the study of *Geselligkeit* into broader territory. More than dealing with particular intellectual forums, it deals primarily with the theory of *Geselligkeit*, the political implications of different forms of social interaction and grouping and some 18th-c. experiments in this area. It also explores how *Geselligkeit* could (or indeed could not) be accommodated within feudal social structures and, later, how it coped with the demands of modern individuality. The international nature of the Enlightenment is explored in *Gelehrsamkeit in Deutschland und Italien im 18. Jahrhundert: Letterati, erudizione e società scientifiche negli spazi italiani e tedeschi del '700*, ed. Giorgio Cusatelli et al. (Hallesche Beiträge zur Europäischen Aufklärung, 8), Tübingen, Niemeyer, xv + 312 pp., which brings together 18 very varied articles on aspects of 18th-c. Italo-German intellectual relations, originally produced for a 1996 conference. Harro Zimmermann, *Aufklärung und Erfahrungswandel: Studien zur deutschen Literaturgeschichte des späten 18. Jahrhunderts*, Göttingen, Wallstein, 384 pp., is the author's *Habilitationsschrift* and brings together in revised form a great deal of work previously published and also three original pieces: 'Aufklärung — Epochendiskurs und Projekt der Moderne: Aspekte einer ausgebliebenen Debatte' (9–64); 'Despotie der Aufklärung: die anti-jesuitische Verschwörungstheorie in der *Berliner Monatsschrift*' (65–112); 'Erleuchtete Vernunft: Jung-Stillings Roman *Das Heimweh* und die Französische Revolution' (113–46). *Das achtzehnte Jahrhundert*, 23.2 is a special number on 'Haskala. Die jüdische Aufklärung in Deutschland 1769–1812'. Articles published on the period in general include: U. Zeuch, 'Kraft als Inbegriff menschlicher Seelentätigkeit in der Anthropologie der Spätaufklärung', *JDSG*, 43:99–122.

PERIODS: CLASSICISM. Articles published in the general area include: P. Bishop and R. H. Stephenson, 'Nietzsche and Weimar aesthetics', *GLL*, 52:412–29; P. Bishop, 'The birth of analytical psychology from the spirit of Weimar Classicism', *JES*, 29:417–40.

GENRES. Sibylle Schönborn, *Das Buch der Seele: Tagebuchliteratur zwischen Aufklärung und Kunstperiode*, Tübingen, Niemeyer, 303 pp., makes a forceful attempt to revise critical assumptions about the expansion in diary-literature during the 18th c. This expansion has been routinely, and perhaps plausibly, associated with the influence of pietism with its emphasis upon personal religious experience. S. indicates that the motivation behind such literature may be more complex in tracing the development of multi-faceted individuality and/or of a literary persona. The authors are often involved in a complex *Selbstdialog*, even if the diary may be ostensibly addressed to another (a friend, a relative, a god); the process is often given urgency by an awareness of the reality of death. This fascinating study covers works by: P. M. Hahn, A. von Haller, C. F. Gellert, J. C. Lavater, A. Pfranger, S. La Roche, J. W. Goethe, E. von der Recke, J. A. von Leisewitz, G. C. Lichtenberg. Aspects of a very specific genre are covered by: C. Zschirnt, 'Fainting and latency in the eighteenth century's romantic novel of courtship', *GR*, 74:48–66.

THEMES. Schnitzer, *Maskeraden*, ranges far beyond the literary confines, and indeed the period, of this section. It is, however, a text which could be extremely useful for those who find themselves dealing with literary manifestations of courtly rituals and entertainments since it deals in great detail with the nature and symbolic function of masquerades from the 15th to the 18th c. *Von der Geometrie zur Naturalisierung: Utopisches Denken im 18. Jahrhundert zwischen literarischer Fiktion und frühneuzeitlicher Gartenkunst*, ed. Richard Saage and Eva-Maria Seng (Hallesche Beiträge zur Europäischen Aufklärung, 10), Tübingen, Niemeyer, xi + 296 pp., covers an international and interdisciplinary field of study but contains some articles which have a specifically German slant and concern, above all, German aesthetics. To isolate these from the whole is rather artificial given the wide-ranging, international nature of utopian thinking and aesthetics of the period, but they include: H. Günther, 'Kult der Primitivität im Klassizismus' (62–108); U. Küster, 'Natur ordnen: Landschaftserfahrung im 18. Jahrhundert' (109–16); E.-M. Seng, 'Die Wörlitzer Anlagen zwischen englischem Landschaftsgarten und *Bon-Sauvage*-Utopie?' (117–50); E. Hirsch, 'Utopia realisata: Utopie und Umsetzung — aufgeklärt-humanistische Gartengestaltung in Anhalt-Dessau' (151–79); M. Niedermeier, 'Wörlitz als höfische Veranstaltung? Eros zwischen höfischer Selbstreflexion, pädagogischer Kontrolle und naturalisierter Utopie'

(180–208); J. Garber, 'Antagonismus und Utopie: Georg Forsters Städtebilder im Spannungsfeld von *Wirklichkeit und Idee*' (209–36). The apparently non-literary focus of the volume is deceptive since the debates on architecture and garden design echo contemporary debates in literary aesthetics, and indeed many of the locations discussed are powerfully associated with literary figures. Hans von Trotha, *Angenehme Empfindungen: Medien einer populären Wirkungsästhetik im 18. Jahrhundert vom Landschaftsgarten bis zum Schauerroman*, Munich, Fink, 384 pp., will prove a highly interesting text for anyone working in the area of 18th-c. aesthetics. The author takes an approach which embraces theology, theoretical aesthetics, literature, and garden design in order to investigate a variety of manifestations of the sublime, from the pleasant experience typical of the 18th c. to the more radical formulations of the 19th. The treatment of the apparent 'domestication' of a problematic aesthetic into pleasant literary or horticultural experience is most illuminating, as is the underlying discussion of the problematic aesthetic principles of *Aufklärung* and *Empfindsamkeit*. Michael Wetzel, *Mignon: Die Kindsbraut als Phantasma der Goethezeit*, Munich, Fink, 503 pp., is an important text. It addresses the issue of the near constant presence of young female characters in the male literature and intellectual debate of the *Goethezeit*. It examines the various, often contradictory, functions which they serve, not least as outlets for male fantasy. The analyses of the individual figures and of the contemporary discussions of the theme are exhaustive and allow multiple perspectives — literary-historical, psychoanalytical, socio-historical, aesthetic, pedagogical, medical. The conflation of these perspectives is one of the most interesting aspects of the text since we enter territory where the boundaries between the aesthetic and the sexual are blurred. The last part of the text is concerned with the Romantic period. Fritz Landsberger, *Die Kunst der Goethezeit: Kunst- und Kunstanschauung von 1750–1830*, ed. Werner Hofmann (Edition Logos), Berlin, Gebrüder Mann, 328 pp., is a welcome republication with a new *Nachwort* of a famous text. Its value for the literary scholar is in the powerful and compact illustrated survey of theory and practice in the visual arts of the period which cannot and should not be separated from the parallel literary theory and praxis. In this connection it is an extremely useful first port of call. Susanne M. Zantop, *Kolonialphantasien im vorkolonialen Deutschland (1770–1870)* (PSQ, 158), 314 pp., is substantially concerned with texts from our period. The text is an updated German version of a 1997 English-language original. It explores the fascinating fact that German writers, who were not, at that time, representatives of a colonizing nation, nonetheless harboured colonial fantasies. It was to be many years before reality could attempt to catch up with these. The fantasies took a variety of forms. They were, for historical reasons, focused on South America (as a separate bibliography indicates) and featured some disturbing if understandable traits. Zantop examines the way in which German writers styled themselves as representatives of the Enlightenment and so in a superior position and able to judge outsiders; and yet the discourse contains highly gendered, patronising, and racist language which would not seem to confirm this position. Given its unreal nature, the function of colonial discourse in the 18th and 19th c. would appear to be to reinforce a sense of (national) identity at home, albeit a white, male, middle-class version of the same. *GLL*, 52.2 is a special number on 'The body in German literature around 1800' and contains the following articles on our period: N. Saul, 'Introduction — from "Ideendichtung" to the *commercium mentis et corporis*: the body in German literature around 1800' (115–22); J. Morrison, 'The discreet charm of the Belvedere: submerged homosexuality in eighteenth-century writing on art' (123–35); S. Richter, 'Wieland and the phallic breast' (136–50); A. Košenina, 'Gläserne Brust, lesbares Herz: ein psychopathographischer Topos im Zeichen physiognomischer Tyrannei bei C. H. Spiess und anderen' (151–65); S. M. Schneider, 'Kunstautonomie als Semiotik des Todes? Digressionen im klassizistischen Diskurs der schönen Menschengestalt bei Karl Phillip Moritz' (166–83); L. Sharpe, 'Female illness and male heroism: the works of Caroline von Wolzogen' (184–96); M. Bell, 'The revenge of the "untere Seelenvermögen" in Schiller's plays' (197–210); C. Begemann, 'Poiesis des Körpers: künstlerische Produktivität und Konstruktion des Leibes in der erotischen Dichtung des klassischen Goethe' (211–37). Thematic articles on the period include: B. Jessing, 'Das Rom-Bild in der deutschen Literatur des 18. und 19. Jahrhunderts', *DUS*, 99.2:16–27; U. Spörl, 'Berge, Meer und Sterne als Erhabenes in der Natur? Eine Untersuchung zur Poetik der Frühaufklärung und der "poetischen" Malerei Brockes', *DVLG*, 73:228–66; A. Corkhill, 'Female language theory in the age of Goethe: three case studies', *MLR*, 94:1041–53; M. Gamper, ' "Die Verfassung sei republikanisch" — Verhandlungen über Ordnung und Unordnung in den Kunstdebatten des 18. Janrhunderts', *ZDP*, 118:189–215; W. Hettche, 'Im Hain, im Tunnel und im Teich. Autorschaft und Autorisation in literarischen Vereinen', *Editio*, 13:98–107; R. Baasner, 'Geschichte der deutschen Literatur des 18. Jahrhunderts als Computeranwendung. Ein Werkstattbericht', *Das achtzehnte Jahrhundert*, 22, 1998:165–71.

## 2. GOETHE

EDITIONS. *Fairy Tales, Short Stories, and Poems by Johann Wolfgang von Goethe*, ed. and trans. J. W. Thomas (Germanic Languages and Literature, 109), NY, Lang, 1998, 137 pp., contains good translations of the texts though without critical apparatus and with only a brief introduction. The translations of poetry have appeared previously, the prose translations appear to be new and include (to use the English titles): 'The Fairy Tale' (9–36); 'The New Paris' (37–48); 'The New Melusina' (49–68); 'The Ghost' (69–78); 'The Lawyer' (79–94); 'The Singular Children of Neighbours' (95–102); 'Novella' (103–22). *Goethe — The Flight to Italy: Diary and Selected Letters*, ed. and trans. T. J. Reed (Oxford World's Classics), OUP, xxxiv + 159 pp., provides a fine translation of the early version of G.'s Italian travels along with an at once succinct and engaging introduction. The text will clearly attract a new audience to this area of study. Johann Wolfgang von Goethe, *Poems of the West and East: West-Eastern Divan; Bi-Lingual Edition of the Complete Poems*, trans. John Whaley and introd. Katharina Mommsen (GSA, 68), 1998, xxx + 490 pp., is an extraordinary undertaking, here in a revised third edition. The fine verse translations of this inherently difficult collection will continue to make it accessible to a wider audience. Johann Wolfgang von Goethe, *Leiden des jungen Werthers: Edition der Handschrift von 1786*, ed. Matthias Luserke, Weimar, Böhlau, 141 pp., makes public the manuscript which formed the basis of the 1787 second edition of *Werther*. The manuscript is, however, not identical with the published version and so this publication serves a useful purpose in making an alternative version more visible. The republication of Goethe's *Schriften zur Naturwissenschaft* continues with the appearance of vol. 1/7 *Zur Farbenlehre: Anzeige und Übersicht, statt des supplementaren Teils und Erklärung der Tafeln*, ed. Ruprecht Matthaei, Weimar, Böhlau, 114 pp. This is an exact republication of a 1957 edition and so serves only to make the work more accessible than had previously been the case. Another digital version of Goethe's work has appeared in the form of *Goethe: Zeit — Leben — Werk*, ed. Jürgen von Esenwein and Harald Gerlach, Berlin, Aufbau–Hanover, Schroedel Lernverlag–Stuttgart, Metzler, CD-ROM, which contains the texts according to the 22-vol. Berlin edition, a presentation on 'Goethe und seine Zeit', a selection of letters and conversations and a selection from the *Goethe-Handbuch*. On that basis it is a highly useful disk, particularly for the newcomer to the field of study, with the presentational and search advantages which the medium offers.

GENERAL STUDIES AND ESSAY COLLECTIONS. The anniversary year 1999 clearly provided a great opportunity for the reworking or republication of established volumes and the commissioning of collective volumes. Dorothea Hölscher-Lohmeyer, *Johann Wolfgang Goethe* (BsR, 2127), 144 pp., is a revised second edition of an original 1991 publication which provides a useful and compact introduction to G. The further republication of Peter Boerner, *Johann Wolfgang von Goethe*, Reinbek, Rowohlt, 158 pp., fulfils a very similar purpose. Erich Trunz, *Ein Tag aus Goethes Leben: Acht Studien zu Leben und Werk* (BsR, 1303), 217 pp., brings together for the first time a number of papers previously published elsewhere (sometimes in a more exhaustive form). The individual papers include: 'Ein Tag aus Goethes Leben' (7–42); 'Das Haus am Frauenplan in Goethes Alter' (42–71); 'Goethe als Sammler' (72–100); 'Goethes lyrische Kurzgedichte' (101–38); 'Goethes Altersstil' (139–46); 'Goethes späte Lyrik' (147–66); 'Das Vergängliche als Gleichnis in Goethes Dichtung' (167–87); 'Vom Handwerk des Herausgebers: Aus der Werkstatt der Hamburger Goethe-Ausgabe' (188–214). *Goethes Rückblick auf die Antike: Beiträge des deutsch-italienischen Kolloquiums Rom 1998*, ed. Bernd Witte and Mauro Ponzi, Berlin, Schmidt, 219 pp., contains a powerful selection of papers including: V. Borsò, 'Der Rückblick auf die Antike: Formen der Vermittlung zwischen Kunst und Natur' (9–20); B. Witte, 'Goethe und Homer: ein Paradigmenwechsel' (21–38); M. Ponzi, ' "Eines Schattens Traum": Goethe und Pindar' (38–59); H.-J. Schrader, 'Götter, Helden, Waldteufel: zu Goethes Sturm-und-Drang-Antike' (59–82); S. Schönborn, 'Vom Geschlechterkampf zum symbolischen Geschlechtertausch: Goethes Arbeit am antiken Mythos am Beispiel der *Iphigenie auf Tauris*' (83–100); B. Zimmermann, 'Goethes Novelle und der Hirtenroman des Longus' (101–12); W. Vosskamp, 'Goethes Klassizismus im Zeichen der Diskussion des Verhältnisses von Poesie und bildender Kunst um 1800' (113–21); P. Chiarini, 'Verfälschung des klassischen Kanons oder moderne Rezeption der Antike? Antonio Canova zwischen August Wilhelm Schlegel und Goethe' (122–31); M. Cometa, 'Die Tragödie des Laokoon: Drama und Skulptur bei Goethe' (132–60); J. Schmidt, 'Helena im *Faust II*: die geschichtliche Vermittlung antiker Kultur in die Neuzeit und die Konzeption das Klassisch-Schönen' (161–75); G. Mattenklott, '*Faust II*: das Schöne als "Zwischenspiel" ' (176–90); H. Anton, 'Goethes eleusinische Hermeneutik' (191–205). Sebastian Donat (and Hendrik Birus), *Goethe — ein letztes Universalgenie*, Göttingen, Wallstein, 144 pp., is a text designed to accompany an exhibition of the same name organized by the Goethe-Institut and is correspondingly introductory in nature, although richly illustrated. *GJb*, 115, 1998[1999], provides the usual wide range of articles on aspects of G.'s work, the most substantial of which are: H. D. Irmscher, 'Prophet und Dichter: über Goethes Versuche, Hamann zu verstehen' (13–28); B. Nemeyr, 'Navigation mit "virtus" und "fortuna"': Goethes Gedicht *Seefahrt* und seine stoische Grundkonzeption' (29–44); S. Martus, 'Sinn und Form in Goethes *Egmont*' (45–62); A. Kornbacher, 'August Wilhelm Schlegels Einfluß auf den Aufsatz *Über epische und dramatische Dichtung von Goethe und Schiller* (1797)' (63–69); S. Matuschek, 'Was ist ein "Troubador der Erlebnislyrik"? Epochenblick durch ein Goethe-Sonett' (69–76); G. Ehrhardt, ' "Wahl-Anziehung" — Herders Spinoza-Schrift und Goethes *Wahlverwandtschaften*' (77–96); H.-J. Schings, 'Fausts Verzweiflung' (97–124); R. C. Zimmermann, 'Goethes Humanität und Fausts Apotheose: zur Problematik der religiösen Dimension von Goethes *Faust*' (125–46); A. V. Michajlov, 'Die Natur in Goethes schöpferischem Denken' (147–54); U. Enke and M. Wenzel, 'Wissbegierde contra Menschlichkeit — Goethes ambivalentes Verhältnis zur Anatomie in seiner Dichtung und Biographie' (155–70); E. Pielmann, 'Goethes Treppenhäuser' (171–82); G. Brude-Firnau, '*Die Wahlverwandtschaften* als Referenztext in Martin Walsers Erzählwerk' (183–98); Y. Wuneng, 'Goethe in China: Das Goethe-Jahr 1932 und die neuerliche Goethe-Verehrung' (199–210). Matthias Luserke, *Der junge Goethe: "Ich weis nicht warum ich Narr soviel schreibe"* (Sammlung Vandenhoeck), Göttingen, Vandenhoeck & Ruprecht, 181 pp., is not the introductory/biographical work that the title might suggest. The text makes a valiant attempt to lift the 'Goethe-Blockade', the vast body of inherited knowledge, scholarship, and plain prejudice about G., which inhibits access to the texts and biography. To do this L. focuses upon the emergent individuality of G. and upon the literary processing of his life and society in general, i.e. upon the G.'s contribution to the 'Medialisierung' of his own life and work. The outcome of this analysis of modern individuality is highly interesting, especially given the use of many less obvious textual examples. Momme Mommsen, *Lebendige Überlieferung: George — Hölderlin — Goethe*, ed. Katharina Mommsen (GSA, 69), 406 pp., brings together a number of articles on G. from a variety of sources which might otherwise be less accessible. They include: 'Spinoza und die Deutsche Klassik' (217–74); 'Goethes Verhältnis zu Christus und Spinoza: Blick auf die Werther-Zeit' (275–306); 'Goethe als Selbstdarsteller' (307–42); ' "Schwänchen" und "Schwan" im *Schenkenbuch des West-Östlichen Divan*' (343–52); 'Goethe und Zelter' (353–62); 'Goethe und Eckermann' (363–68). *Metzler Goethe-Lexikon*, ed. Benedikt Jessing, Bernd Lutz and Inge Wild, Stuttgart–Weimar, Metzler, 592 pp., provides much of the useful information that potential readers might expect about G.'s life and work and is a highly useful tool. It is also subject to the necessary limitations of such a project given the space available. This volume expands its horizons, however, through its treatment of topics which might not be expected. The reader is surprised by some of the subject headings, which range, to take a snapshot, from 'Gotthard-Pass', through 'Kirche und Staat' to 'Zähne'. The slightly unusual angle taken on known material means that this volume is more readable than many parallel texts and will not be used for reference only. *Goethe-Spuren: Ein Lesebuch zum Konzertprojekt — Konzerthaus Berlin 1998/99*, ed. Heike Hoffmann, Göttingen, Wallstein, 1998, 293 pp., delivers more than the title might suggest, and also ranges more widely than the connection with the *Konzerthaus* might suggest. The text enjoys very high production values and the individual contributions, which understandably do not include the usual academic apparatus, include: E. Budde, 'Goethe und die Musik' (15–35); D. Kimpel, 'Goethes gestaltästhetische Betrachtung der Natur' (39–55); H. Traber, 'Nichts ist musikalischer als ein Sonnenuntergang — wie Goethes Naturanschauung musikalische Wirkung zeigte' (57–75); W. Stellmacher, 'Goethe und die Volkspoesie' (79–95); V. Mertens, 'Neue bedeutende Melodien — Kunstmusik, Volkslied und Goethe' (97–107); D. Borchmeyer, 'Goethe — Universalist das Theaters' (113–26); G. Müller, 'Goethe und das musikalische Theater' (129–51); H.-K. Metzger, 'Metamorphose und Nomos — über den Sinn von Weberns Goethe-Anrufung' (155–67); V. Riedel, 'Goethe und die Antike' (171–87); P. Andraschke, 'Von Helden und Mythen' (191–210); H. Birus, '*Westöstlicher Divan* oder Versammlung deutscher Gedichte in stetem Bezug auf den Orient' (215–31); H. Danuser, 'Heimische Fremde: musikalische Orientalistikfragen im Anschluß an Goethes *West-östlichen Divan*' (233–46); C. Hamlin, ' "Nur nicht lesen! immer singen!" — Goethe im Lied' (249–67); W. Dinglinger, ' "Goethes Verlust ist eine Nachricht, die Einen wieder so arm macht!" — Begegnungen zwischen Goethe und Mendelssohn' (269–79); W. Markgraf, 'Musikstadt Weimar' (281–87). *Nru*, 110.1 styles itself as a *Goethe-Parcours* and correspondingly contains a number of very short (typically 4–8 pages) contributions. *RGI*, 12, is a special number devoted to Goethe and includes: J. Mondot, 'Goethe du nord au sud. *Le Voyage en Italie* et le paradigme du Sud' (7–18); D. Borchmeyer, 'La *vis comica* chez Goethe. *Faust* et la comédie' (19–34); G. Mattenklott, 'Les premières scènes de *Faust II*' (35–46); R. Krebs, '*Les souffrances du jeune Werther* lues par Goethe' (47–59); G. Stieg, 'Goethe et Spinoza' (63–75); J. Lacoste, 'Goethe et la science anglaise' (77–88); J. Golz, 'Existence et représentation dans le journal intime de Goethe et de Thomas Mann' (89–99); E. Zehm, 'La correspondance Goethe–Zelter: de l'écriture privée à l'écrit public' (101–109); G. Oesterle, 'Mascarade et mystification dans le *Journal de Tiefurt*' (111–23); G. Sauder, 'L'esthétique goethéene de l'autonomie entre la fin des

Lumières et le XIXe siècle' (125–35); E. Osterkamp, 'Goethe et l'art français' (137–52); C. Asman, ' "Le trésor de Goethe": Le collectionneur et ses dons' (153–60); E. Décultot, 'Le cosmopolitisme en question. Goethe face aux saisies françaises d'œuvres d'art sous la Révolution et sous l'Empire' (161–75); C. Helmreich, 'La traduction des *Souffrances du jeune Werther* en France (1776–1850). Contribution à une histoire de transferts franco-allemands' (179–93); M. Espagne, 'Humboldt à Paris, lecteur de Goethe' (195–209); J. Le Rider, 'Campagne de France en 1792. Parallèle entre Chateaubriand et Goethe' (211–27); P. Pénisson, 'Goethe traducteur du *Neveu de Rameau*' (229–39); M. Schneider, 'Freud, lecteur et interprète de Goethe' (243–56); W. Vosskamp, ' "Extinction". A propos de l'auto-réflexion du roman d'éducation au XXe s. chez Thomas Bernhard' (257–69); W. Bolle, 'Lever du soleil sur le fleuve Amazone' (271–85) (the latter concerns colour theory and 19th-c. German and Brazilian literature).

POETRY. Reiner Wild, *Goethes klassische Lyrik*, Stuttgart–Weimar, Metzler, x + 317 pp., seeks to correct a common perception of Weimar Classicism as something monumental. In G.'s case it is best seen as a dynamic series of processes and interactions. G.'s classical period is understood to cover broadly the period of his friendship with Schiller, but during this period his processing of the classical involves not only their intellectual interaction but also the processing of the experience of Italy, the exposure to classical verse forms and ancient history. What emerges is a productive tension between ancient and modern affecting literary production and personal development. Interestingly, W.'s text includes treatments of apparently more modern verses which he sees as part of the process of establishing a position with respect to the classical through opposition. Meredith Lee, *Displacing Authority: Goethe's Poetic Reception of Klopstock* (Neue Bremer Beiträge, 10), Heidelberg, Winter, 242 pp., is a highly interesting volume because it does not (only) understand Klopstock's influence upon G. in terms of forms and themes borrowed and adapted. Importantly, L. questions how the presence and influence of the poet figure K. helped to shape G.'s sense of his own standing as poet — the battle for authority mentioned in the title. In doing so L. helps to undermine G.'s monumental status as poet, revealing his natural dependence upon his forebears and showing the poem as the crucial site for interaction with them. Articles published on G.'s poetry include: G. Peters, 'Prometheus oder Epimetheus? Der Titanenmythos in Goethes Dichtung', *DUS*, 99.1:6–19; B. Leistner, ' "Reisezehrung": zu einem Goethesonett über die Liebe', *ib.*, 75–84; R. Otto, 'Meinungen und Redeweisen in Goethes Spruchdichtung', ib., 85–95; M. Mayer, 'Goethes vampirische Poetik: Zwei Thesen zur

*Braut von Corinth*', JDSG, 43:148–58; H. Lange, 'Goethe's strategy of self-censorship: the case of the *Venezianische Epigramme*', *MDU*, 91:224–240; J. Simpson, 'Freud and the Erl King', *OGS*, 27, 1998:30–63; R. Paulin, 'Art and immortality: Goethe's elegy *Euphrosyne*', *PEGS(NS)*, 68, 1998[1999]:61–69; Y. A. Elsaghe, 'Säbel und Schere: Goethes Revolutionierung des Epos und die Rezeptionskarriere von *Hermann und Dorothea*', *Seminar*, 34, 1998:121–36; T. Althaus, 'Ursprung in später Zeit: Goethes *Heidenröslein* und der Volksliedentwurf', *ZDP*, 118:161–88; J. Golz, '"Alle Ordnung ist vorläufig": über den Zusammenhang von Textgenese und Entstehungskontext in Goethes *Venezianischen Epigrammen*', *Editio*, 12, 1998:69–78; A. Leistner, '"Doch tückisch harrt das Lebewohl zuletzt"', *NDL*, 48.4:11–19 (on Goethes poem *An Werther*).

DRAMA. Recent articles on G.'s drama include: T. Buck, 'Goethes *Iphigenie* als dramaturgisches Modell des Bewusstseinstheaters', *DUS*, 99.1:30–39; I. Strohschneider-Kohrs, 'Proserpina im *Triumph der Empfindsamkeit*: Goethes Selbstmaskierung', *Euphorion*, 93:139–68; A. van Dijk, 'Das Dämonische als moderne Rezeptionskategorie: dargestellt an Goethes *Egmont* und *Torquato Tasso*', *Neophilologus*, 83:427–43.

FAUST. Bernd Mahl, *Goethes 'Faust' auf der Bühne (1806–1998)*, Stuttgart–Weimar, Metzler, xii + 284 pp., provides a very useful examination of the reception of this play in the form of theatrical productions. It provides in the case of each production a treatment of the motivation, the use of text, the detail of staging and cast, along with a brief examination of the critical reception of the individual production. 250 pls are incorporated into the body of the text and are an extremely useful feature. Whilst the treatment of individual productions is inevitably brief, patterns do emerge. Particularly interesting is the discussion of the ideological battles acted out in contrasting 20th-c. productions. Helmut Schanze, *Faust-Konstellationen: Mythos und Medien*, Munich, Fink, 144 pp., offers an 'archaeological' investigation of Faust in its own right and in its reception in a variety of media (including film and digital). The idea is to work down from the surface of the text or received text towards the deep structures, without prejudiced assumption about what will be found. The critic must not repeat Schliemann's archaelogical error in seeking a particular vision of Troy and almost destroying the real Troy in the process. The removal of assumptions, even of reverence towards the text, is productive since S. is able to highlight the complexities of individual scenes and broader units in the play revealing the unstable structure of the *Faust* project which cannot

necessarily be overcome by technical wizardry in modern productions. Jochen Schmidt, *Goethes 'Faust', Erster und Zweiter Teil: Grundlagen — Werk — Wirkung* (Arbeitsbücher zur Literaturgeschichte),
Munich, Beck, 383 pp., covers a great deal of the territory suggested
by its subtitle and reveals a meticulous understanding of the historical
determinants of literary production and reception. However, the
historical thread in the presentation is supplemented by textual
analysis of individual scenes in the *Faust* project. S. deals in detail with
the pre-history of the subject matter and form of the plays, G.'s
processing of those materials and subsequent reprocessings through
the medium of G. This latter section of the text is particularly
interesting in its analysis of the emergence of Faust as a 'nationale
Identifikationsfigur' in the 19th and 20th c. The supplememnts to this
volume are also worthy of note, so useful are they. We are offered a
bibliography of *Faust* in other media, a compact treatment of
versification, a useful *Faust* bibliography on a scene-by-scene basis
and graphic representations of the structure of the play. These
supplementary features along with the substance make this a very
useful critical volume and teaching tool. *Fest. Schupp,* contains a
fascinating short article by J. Schmidt, 'Die antike Helene und der
mittelalterliche Faust im drittem Akt des *Faust II*' (315–28). The title
is deceptive in suggesting a narrow focus since S. investigates, on the
basis of a limited portion of text, G.'s processing of the complex
relationships between antiquity, the medieval world, the Renaissance
and the modern age. Articles recently published on *Faust* include:
J. M. van der Laan, 'The virtual and the real in Goethe's Faust', *Acta
Germanica: German Studies in Africa,* 25:7–20; H.-D. Dahnke, '*Faust* am
Ende des 20. Jahrhunderts: Ergebnisse und Tendenzen der wissenschaftlichen Arbeit zur Goethe'schen Dichtung', *DUS,* 99.1:52–62;
M. Staiger, '*Faust* verfilmt', *ib.,* 120–27; B. Greiner, 'Margarete in
Weimar: die Begründung des *Faust* als Tragödie', *Euphorion,*
93:169–93; B. Becker-Cantarino, 'Hexenküche und Walpurgisnacht:
Imaginationen der Dämonie in der Frühen Neuzeit und in *Faust I*',
*ib.,* 193–226; C. König, 'Wissensvorstellungen in Goethes *Faust II*',
*ib.,* 227–50; F. J. Lamport, 'Goethes *Faust*: a cautionary tale?', *FMLS,*
35:193–206; F. Meier, 'Goethes Faust als Schiffbrüchiger und
Zuschauer: einige Überlegungen anknüpfend an Hans Blumenbergs
Studie zur Daseinsmetapher des Schiffbruchs mit Zuschauer', *GRM,*
49:55–78; F. Breithaupt, 'Dies-und Jenseits des Endes der Geschichte, Helena', *MLN,* 114:528–50; P. Delvaux, 'Hexenglaube und
Verantwortung. Zur Walpurgisnacht in Goethes *Faust I*', *Neophilologus,*
83:601–16; J. Nelles, 'Bedeutungsdimensionen zwischen dem Ge-
sagten und dem Ungesagten: intertextuelle Korrespondenz in Fontanes *Effi Briest* und Goethes *Faust*', *WW,* 48, 1998:192–214;

H. Rölleke, ' "Ein guten magen haben" ': zu einigen populären Versen in Goethes *Faust I'*, *ib.*, 317–18.

NARRATIVE. Gesa Dane, *"Die heilsame Toilette": Kosmetik und Bildung in Goethes 'Der Mann von fünfzig Jahren'*, Göttingen, Wallstein, 216 pp., offers a refreshing perspective on this text and by extension other fictional and theoretical/scientific works by G. Contemporary 'cosmetic' theory and treatises on external physical appearance and its implications are introduced and then shown in their manifestations in the literary text. In a particularly illuminating chapter (95–134), D. reveals how the discourse of cosmetics (broadly understood) is interwoven in G.'s work with his more general treatment of *Bildung*, self-development, and self-image. Not unrelated in theme is Italo Michele Battafarano, *Die im Chaos blühenden Zitronen: Identität und Alterität in Goethes 'Italienischer Reise'* (IRIS: FEK, 12), 262 pp. B., contrary to the current trend, takes G.'s mature reflections on the *Italian Journey* rather then the more spontaneous early diary/letters as his starting-point. He is concerned with the mature G.'s analysis of the formation of his self in Italy. Italy confronted him with the limitations of his self and so made him aware of the productive value of the experience of alterity. Particularly interesting is the substantial fourth part of the text ('Anthropologie' (109–244)) and its final section on 'mask' and 'carnival'. B. argues that the process of self-development is particularly well illustrated in this later version of the journey since it is presented in a concentrated literary form rather than in the rather more dilute form of the diary or letter. Ehrhard Bahr, *The Novel as Archive: The Genesis, Reception, and Criticism of Goethe's 'Wilhelm Meisters Wanderjahre'* (SGLLC), 1998, 121 pp., is an expansion of an article which appeared in the *Goethe-Handbuch* and makes the case for the modernity of the text in question, particularly in the matter of narration. B. argues that the use of an 'editor', and the introduction of novellas into the stream of the narrative have a consciously disruptive effect on the reading process and create an ironic distance between author and text. These modern features were not, B. shows, well received by contemporary critics and even created some difficulty for 20th-c. critics. Articles on narrative texts include: B. Meier, 'Goethes *Werther* — Prologomena für eine didaktische Rezeptionsgeschichte, *DUS*, 99.1 : 20–29; J. Golz, 'Der Tagebuchautor Goethe', *ib.*, 63–74; A. Koschorke, 'Die Textur der Neigungen: Attraktion, Verwandtschaftscode und novellistische Kombinatorik in Goethes *Mann von fünfzig Jahren*', *DVLG*, 73 : 592–610; G.-L. Fink, 'Die Pädagogik und die Forderung des Tages in *Wilhelm Meisters Wanderjahren*, *Euphorion*, 93 : 251–91; H.-J. Schings, 'Wilhelm Meister und das Erbe der Illuminaten', *JDSG*, 43 : 123–47; B. J. Dotzler, 'Werthers Leser', *MLN*, 114 : 445–70; J. Vogl, 'Nomos der Ökonomie:

# The Classical Era 673

Steuerungen in Goethes *Wahlverwandtschaften*', *ib.*, 503–27; J. S. Walker, 'Sex, suicide and the sublime: a reading of Goethe's *Werther*', *MDU*, 91 : 2, 208–23; ; J. Twardella, 'Experimente im Treibhaus der Moderne: Versuch einer kommunikationstheorischen Analyse von Goethes *Wahlverwandtschaften*', *Neophilologus*, 83 : 445–60; A. Dorschel, 'Utopie und Resignation: Schuberts Deutungen des Sehnsuchtliedes aus Goethes *Wilhelm Meister* von 1826', *OGS*, 26, 1997[1998] : 132–64; M. Koch, '*Memoria mobilis*: französische Revolution und kulturelle Gedächtnisbildung in Goethes Erzählwerk', *ColH*, 27, 1998 : 105–27 (on *Unterhaltungen deutscher Ausgewanderten*); G. Bersier, ' "Buchstäblich genommen"': zur parodistischen Machart von Goethes *Wahlverwandtschaften*', *JFDH*, 1998 : 15–35; S. Dickson, 'Two sides of an anorexic coin in *Die Wahlverwandtschaften* and *Die Verwandlung*: Ottilie as "Heilige", Gregor als "Mistkäfer"' ', *OL*, 54 : 174–84; C. Leimbach, 'Die Gegenbilder von Ehe und Leidenschaften in Goethes *Wahlverwandtschaften*', *WB*, 45 : 35–52; R. G. Renner, 'Text, Bild und Gedächtnis: Goethes Erzählen im *Mann von fünfzig Jahren* und in den *Wanderjahren*', *Poetica*, 31 : 149–74; M. Mandelartz, 'Bauen, erhalten, zerstören, versiegeln. Architektur als Kunst in Goethes *Wahverwandtschaften*', *ZDP*, 118 : 500–17.

THEMES. W. Daniel Wilson, *Unterirdische Gänge: Goethe, Freimaurerei und Politik*, Göttingen, Wallstein, 275 pp., constitutes a revisitation on the basis of new research of territory already examined by the same author in a controversial 1991 publication. The focus is on the problematic nature of G.'s relationship with secret societies. A search in the relatively limited pertinent historical material on freemasonry and on the order of the *Illuminaten* attempts to establish whether G.'s memberships were a matter of inclination, pragmatism or surveillance (particularly during the period 1780–82). The suggestion is that they were largely a matter of keeping an eye on movements with increasing influence in Weimar. The assessment of the detail of W.'s argument is a matter for a more initiated critic. It is, however, clear that the text has a valuable function in shifting freemasonry into the foreground of considerations of the political G. Recent thematic articles on G. include: E. Krippendorf, 'Goethe — Politik gegen den Zeitgeist', *DUS*, 99.1 : 40–51; G. Neumann, 'Naturwissenschaft und Geschichte als Literatur: zu Goethes kulturpoetischem Projekt', *MLN*, 114 : 471–502; D. Constantine, 'Goethe and the Hamiltons', *OGS*, 26, 1997[1998] : 101–31; K. H. Bohrer, 'Einsame Klassizität: Goethes Stil als Vorschein einer anderen Moderne', *Merkur*, 53 : 493–507.

INFLUENCE. RECEPTION. Thomas Wolf, *Pustkuchen und Goethe: Die Streitschrift als produktives Verwirrspiel* (UDL, 101), x + 447 pp., is a text with a manifold purpose. It introduces the — for many — obscure figure of Pustkuchen, his life, work and anti-G. stance. In this respect the various *Anhänge* to the main text are most valuable since they direct the reader to relatively unknown primary material in a very organized manner through the bibliography, and present some important letters and a short text (*Maria oder die Frömmigkeit des Weibes*, 377–94) in facsimile. The central treatment of P.'s literary response to G.'s writing, especially *Wilhelm Meisters Wanderjahre*, and P.'s production of a fake, parodistic text of the same name is highly interesting, particularly in the matter of the politics of *Bildung*. W. also provides an analysis of contemporary responses to P.'s undertaking and this can be usefully read in connection with the several other texts produced this year on the subject of the creation of the public persona of G. P. clearly hoped to contribute to the instability of the increasingly monumental image of G. Carl Paschek, *Das Goethe-Bild der Postmoderne 1975–1999 in Büchern und elektronischen Medien* (Frankfurter Bibliotheksschriften, 7), Frankfurt, Klostermann, 142 pp., surveys the material suggested in the title and was designed to accompany an exhibition of the same name in the *Stadt- und Universitätsbibliothek*, which has massive holdings in this area of study. In consequence it provides a useful and compact means of orientation in the area of postmodern Goethe-reception and the deconstruction of the Goethe myth. Wilfried Barner, *Von Rahel Varnhagen bis Friedrich Gundolf: Juden als deutsche Goethe-Verehrer* (Kleine Schriften zur Aufklärung, 3), Göttingen, Wallstein, 56 pp., explores the use made of the 'identifikatorische Vielfalt' available in G.'s life and work, and the desire to identify him with positive, humane aspects of German life. Recent articles on G. reception include: M. Jaeger, 'Goethe schmähen — Goethe loben: Martin Walsers Weg nach Weimar', *DUS*, 99.1 : 96–105; G. Tihanov, 'The ideology of "Bildung": Lukács and Bakhtin as readers of Goethe', *OGS*, 27, 1998 : 102–40; G. J. A. Burgess, 'A pale imitation of its forebear: Christa Schmidt's *Die Wahlverwandtschaften*', *ib.*, 169–89; J. Seng, ' "Ich kann von Goethe nicht anders sprechen als mit Liebe": Thomas Manns Briefwechsel mit Ernst Beutler', *JFDH*, 1998 : 242–76; I. Amodeo, 'Rolf Dieter Brinkmanns Versuch, ohne Goethe über Italien zu schreiben', *Arcadia*, 34 : 2–19.

BIOGRAPHY. Dieter Kühn, *Goethe zieht in den Krieg: Eine biographische Skizze*, Frankfurt, Fischer, 283 pp., employs a method used elsewhere by the same author: the combination of fact-based biographical and imaginative writing in the same volume, in this case to cover G.'s campaign in France from a lively perspective. Georg Schwedt, *Goethe in Göttingen und zur Kur in Pyrmont*, Göttingen, Vandenhoeck & Ruprecht, 166 pp., covers a Goethean summer in some detail but with a conscious focus upon places and personalities rather than upon work undertaken. It deals with the general significance of the location for G. rather than the specific achievements it enabled. Roberto

Zapperi, *Das Inkognito: Goethes ganz andere Existenz in Rom*, Munich, Beck, 299 pp., offers a lively version of this phase of Goethe's life and of life in Rome during the period. It also provides new suggestions as to the direction of G.'s love-life at this time on the basis of new archive research — although this appears a little less extensive and conclusive than we are led to expect. The focus is on the human, sexual individual rather than on the poet, aesthete, and statesman. H. Folkers, 'Ein Tag im Leben Goethes und sein Wort zur neueren Philosophie', *JFDH*, 1998:36–67. E Zehm, *Fest. Walliczek*, 259–69, studies G.'s correspondence with Carl Friedrich Zelter.

### 3. SCHILLER

LITERARY WORKS. Articles recently published in this area include: W. Müller-Seidel, 'Der Zweck und die Mittel: zum Bild des handelnden Menschen in Schillers *Don Carlos*', *JDSG*, 43:188–221; M. Hofmann, 'Die unaufhebbare Ambivalenz historischer Praxis und die Poetik des Erhabenen in Friedrich Schillers *Wallenstein*-Trilogie', *ib.*, 241–65; J. Guthrie, 'Schiller's early styles: language and gesture in *Die Räuber*', *MLR*, 94:438–59; D. Guth, 'George Eliot and Schiller: narrative ambivalence in *Middlemarch* and *Felix Holt*', *ib.*, 913–24; G. K. Hart, 'The stage and the state: the execution of Schiller's *Maria Stuart*', *Seminar*, 35:95–106; C. Steingiesser, 'Neues zu einem Brief an Schiller: aus der Arbeit an Band 39 II der Schiller-Nationalausgabe', *Editio*, 12, 1998:110–29 (letter from painter Johann Christian Reinhart); G. K. Hart, 'Re-dressing history: Mother Nature, mother Isabeau, the Virgin Mary and Schiller's Jungfrau', *WGY*, 14, 1998[1999]:91–107.

THEMES. Recent articles on aspects of S.'s life and work include: S. Grimm, 'Von der sentimentalischen Dichtung zur "Universalpoesie": Schiller, Friedrich Schlegel und die "Wechselwirkung" Fichtes', *JDSG*, 43, 159–87; D. Müller Niebala, 'Die "Gewalt" der "Vergleichung": zur Freiheit in Schillers Kant-Lektüre', *ib.*, 222–40; L. Sharpe, ' "Wahrheit allein sollte mich leiten": Caroline von Wolzogen's Schiller biography', *PEGS(NS)*, 68, 1998[1999]:70–81; F. Nies, 'Schiller, Werle et les autres: Racine en allemand', *MLR*, 73:185–93; A. Duncan, 'Remembering Schiller: the centenary of 1859', *Seminar*, 35:1–22.

### 4. INDIVIDUAL AUTHORS

#### (EXCLUDING GOETHE AND SCHILLER)

BRÄKER. A. Messerli, 'Vermittler, Herausgeber, Kritiker und Leser von Ulrich Bräkers Schriften: zum 200. Todestag des armen Mannes aus dem Tokenburg', *Das achtzehnte Jahrhundert*, 22, 1998:184–93.

FALK.  Johannes Demandt, *Johannes Daniel Falk: Sein Weg von Danzig über Halle nach Weimar (1768–1799)* (Arbeiten zur Geschichte des Pietismus, 36), Göttingen, Vandenhoeck & Ruprecht, 397 pp., provides a welcome insight into the life and work of this marginal figure, known largely by association with more central literary figures such as Goethe and Wieland. This work, which was originally a doctoral thesis, is especially useful in offering access to a wide range of archival material and unpublished work which would otherwise be less accessible. In this respect the Anhang is vital in presenting new material and providing bibliographical direction towards known texts.

FORSTER.  L. Uhlig, *'Die Humanität des Künstlers: Georg Forsters Genieästhetik im zeitgenössischen Kontext', ZDP*, 118:481–99.

GESSNER.  U. Hentschel, 'Salomon Gessners Idyllen und ihre deutsche Rezeption im 18. und beginnenden 19. Jahrhundert', *OL*, 54:332–49.

HAGEDORN.  Ulrike Bardt, *Literarische Wahlverwandtschaften und poetische Metamorphosen: Die Fabel- und Erzähldichtung Friedrich von Hagedorns*, Stuttgart–Weimar, Metzler, 343 pp., may help to revise H.'s position in literary history. In this publication of her doctoral thesis, B. goes to great lengths to contextualize H.'s literary enterprises, comparing them with contemporary and ancient models as well as locating them within his own oeuvre. She argues that these short works gain particularly from being read in the context of the collections in which they appeared, i.e. they depend on a kind of internal intertextuality along with demanding from the reader an awareness of the broader literary historical context. B. is particularly compelling in dealing with the self-conscious literary properties of the collections and with the tension between oral tradition and written form.

HALLER.  U. Hentschel, 'Albrecht von Hallers Alpen-Dichtung und ihre zeitgenössische Rezeption', *WW*, 48, 1998:183–91.

HAMANN.  W. Schmidt-Biggemann, 'Bemerkungen an Hamanns *Aesthetica in nuce*', *Fest. Haas*, 487–506, contains a dense treatment of the relationship beteen the experience of God, feeling, language, and aesthetics.

KLOPSTOCK.  M. Nenon, 'The psychology of the sublime: On the function of poetry in Klopstock's aesthetic essays', *Seminar*, 34, 1998:110–20.

KNIGGE.  *Zwischen Weltklugheit und Moral: der Aufklärer Adolph Freiherr Knigge*, ed. Martin Rector (Das Knigge-Archiv, 2), Göttingen, Wallstein, 232 pp., brings together contributions from a 1996 Hanover conference and includes: M. Rector, 'Knigge oder die Grenzen der Aufklärung' (9–20); P. Raabe, 'Knigges Nachlass — von der "alten Kiste" zur neuen Ausgabe: eine persönliche Rechenschaft'

(21–32); A. Bethmann and Gerhard Dongowski, 'Zum Verhältnis von Moral und Politik bei Knigge' (33–44); F. Vollhardt, '*Ueber Eigennutz und Undank*: Knigges Beitrag zur moralphilosophischen Diskussion der Spätaufklärung' (45–67); E.-O. Fehn, 'Zu Knigges *Predigten*' (68–82); W. Fenner, 'Knigge, Bode und Weishaupt: zu Knigges Mitgliedschaft im Illuminatenorden' (85–91); M. Grätz, 'Knigge als Erzieher in Theorie und Praxis' (92–102); B. Nübel, ' "jede Zeile von ihm mit dem wärmsten Interesse": Aspekte der Rousseau-Rezeption bei Knigge' (103–20); P.-A. Bois, 'Zwischen Revolution und aufgeklärtem Absolutismus: Knigges Vorstellung der Politik' (121–32); W. Daniel Wilson, 'Vom internalisierten "Despotismus" zur Mündigkeit: Knigge und die Selbstorganisation der aufgeklärten Intelligenz' (133–45); I. Fetscher, 'Hatte Knigge eine politische Philosophie?' (146–57); K.-H. Göttert, 'Agathon und seine Brüder: zu Knigges Romanen' (158–168); M. Rüppel, 'Instrument der Aufklärung oder "nothwendiges Uebel"? Knigge und das Theater' (169–85); H. Peitsch, 'Hans Georg Brenner *alias* Reinhold Th. Grabe: ein Knigge wider den Faschismus?' (186–206); M. Schlott, 'Zur Wirkungsgeschichte Knigges' (207–230).

LA ROCHE. Sophie von La Roche, *Herbsttage*, ed. Barbara Becker-Cantarino, Karben, Petra Wald, 1997[1999], 53 + 323 pp. (original pagination) + 3 sheets of music, is a welcome reprint of the 1805 edition of the text with a brief introduction to the text's genesis and, usefully, a 'Kommentiertes Werkverzeichnis' of the author which helps with orientation in her oeuvre. Recent articles in this area include: R. Umbach, 'The role of anglophilia in Sophie von La Roche's *Geschichte des Fräuleins von Sternheim* (1771)', *GLL*, 52:1–13; M. Archangeli, 'Charlotte von Hezel and *Das Wochenblatt fürs schöne Geschlecht*: an eighteenth-century challenge to gender and genre', *WGY*, 14, 1998[1999]:71–89 (built around a comparison with S. de la Roche's journal publications).

LENZ. *'Lenzens Verrückung': Chronik und Dokumente zu J. M. R. Lenz von Herbst 1777 bis Frühjahr 1778*, ed. Burghard Dedner, Hubert Gersch, and Ariane Martin (Büchner-Studien, 8), Tübingen, Niemeyer, 280 pp., is an extraordinary volume produced in the wake of research for the new critical edition of Büchner's work. It brings together 150 documents relating to Lenz's illness many of which would, according to the bibliography, be otherwise rather difficult to find, as well as 27 pictures and maps. These documents enable a much more rounded view of events that has been the case so far; the text will prove a vital asset to Lenz and Büchner scholars alike. Alan C. Leidner and Karin A. Wurst, *Unpopular Virtues: The Critical Reception of J. M. R. Lenz*, Columbia, Camden House, xvi + 167 pp., provides a critical survey of Lenz reception from the 1770s to the mid-1990s and details the consistent difficulty that critics have had in coping with the political implications of L.'s work. Often this has led to extensive periods of critical silence. Likewise critics have consistently struggled with the formal innovation in his texts and the refusal to offer closure in the traditional manner. The indication is that postmodern criticism is most likely to do justice to L.'s works since they contain 'the potential for their own destruction and reconstruction' and an 'unstable beauty'. M. Mayer, 'Erlösen durch Erzählen: Lenz' Ballade *Die Geschichte auf der Aar*', *JFDH*, 1998: 1–14.

LESSING. D. Müller-Nielaba, 'Schlafes Bruder, zu Wort gekommen: wie Lessing enden lässt', *DVLG*, 73: 266–89, deals with Lessing's denial of the use of terror for aesthetic effect; death is meant to be used only as commentary upon violence. Other recent articles on L. include: J. Golawski-Braunhart, 'Furcht oder Schrecken: Lessing, Corneille und Aristoteles', *Euphorion*, 93: 401–32; E. J. Engel, 'Relativ wahr? Jacobis Spinoza-Gespräch mit Lessing', *ib.*, 433–52; E. M. Batley, 'Lessing's templars and the reform of German freemasonry', *GLL*, 52: 297–313; A. Oesman, '*Nathan der Weise*: suffering Lessing's "Erziehung"', *GR*, 74: 131–45; E. Batley, 'Mysteries and mastery: English freemasonry in Lessing and Goethe', *PEGS(NS)*, 68, 1998[1999]: 1–19; D. Blakert, 'Grenzbereiche der Edition: die Paralipolemena zu Lessings Laokoon', *Editio*, 13: 78–97.

LICHTENBERG. *Georg Christoph Lichtenberg: Eine Hommage — Gewitzte Aufklärung*, ed. Jörg-Dieter Kogel and Harro Zimmermann, Göttingen, Wallstein (with Radio Bremen), Audio CD-ROM, presents a selection of aphorisms, letters and other writing, plus selected compact responses to L.'s work by critics and creative writers. Smail Rapic, *Erkenntnis und Sprachgebrauch: Lichtenberg und der englische Empirismus* (Lichtenberg-Studien, 8), Göttingen, Wallstein, 326 pp., is a reworked version of a doctoral thesis in philosophy and develops arguments which this reviewer is not competent to judge.

MENDELSSOHN. *Musik und Ästhetik im Berlin Moses Mendelssohns*, ed. Anselm Gerhard (WSA, 25), 263 pp., presents a wide range of contributions on the general theme indicated by the title in a declared attempt to shift the emphasis in M.- and related-studies away from his Jewishness and his relationship with the Enlightenment, although these issues necessarily re-emerge. Contributions include: A. Gerhard, 'Einleitung: die Bedeutung der jüdischen Minderheit für die Musikkultur der Berliner Aufklärung' (1–26); M. Maurer, 'Verbürgerlichung oder Akkulturation? Zur Situation deutscher Juden zwischen Moses Mendelssohn und David Friedländer' (27–57); J. Strauss, 'Aaron Halle-Wolfssohn: ein Leben in drei Sprachen' (57–76); G. Och, ' "Ess- und Theetisch": die Polemik gegen das akkulturierte Berliner Judentum im ausgehenden 18. und frühen 19.

Jahrhundert' (77–96); C. Zelle, 'Verwöhnter Geschmack, schauervolles Ergötzen und theatralische Sittlichkeit: zum Verhältnis von Ethik und Ästhetik in Moses Mendelssohns ästhetischen Schriften' (97–116); S. Gesse, 'Moses Mendelssohns Theorie der Empfindungen und die Poetik der Mischform' (117–34); L. Lütteken, 'Zwischen Ohr und Verstand: Moses Mendelssohn, Johann Philipp Kirnberger und die Begründung des "reinen Satzes" in der Musik' (135–64); H. Grimm, 'Moses Mendelssohns Beitrag zur Musikästhetik und Carl Philipp Emanuel Bachs Fantasie-Prinzip' (165–86); U. Leisinger, 'Die Ode in der poetischen Theorie und in der musikalischen Praxis' (187–216); P. Wollny, ' "Ein förmlicher Sebastian und Philipp Emanuel Bach-Kultus": Sara Levy, geb. Itzig, und ihr literarisch-musikalischer Salon' (217–56). *Mendelssohn-Studien*, 11, ed. Rudolf Elvers and Hans-Günther Klein, Berlin, Duncker & Humblot, 231 pp., contains two contributions relevant for our period: E. J. Engel, '1750: Moses Mendelssohns erste Veröffentlichung' (9–20); D. Krochmalnik, 'Das Andachtshaus der Vernunft: zur sakralen Poesie und Musik bei Moses Mendelssohn' (21–48). Recent articles on M. include: D. Sorkin, 'The Mendelssohn myth and its method', *NGC*, 77:7–28; A. Arkush, 'The questionable Judaism of Moses Mendelssohn', *ib.*, 29–44.

MEYERN. J. Kunisch, 'Die Denunzierung des ewigen Friedens: der Krieg als moralische Anstalt in der Literatur und Publizistik der Spätaufklärung', Brunner, *Krieg*, 427–39, analyses the work of the obscure figure J. W. F. von Meyern, as he preferred to be known, and suggests that beneath the rather unpromising surface of his fiction there lies an important figure who marks an important shift in attitudes towards patriotism and war. He envisaged an engaged *Bürger* willing to make sacrifices for the fatherland.

MÜLLER. P. Micha, '*L'Aufklärung* et le rire: Johann Gottwerth Müller ou le difficile "roman comique"', *RG*, 28, 1998:1–32.

RAUSEYSEN. R. Hillebrand, ' "Soldat und noch dazu gelehrt": Rettung des Poeten Philipp Ernst Rauseysen', *Euphorion*, 93:453–84.

WEZEL. D. Hill, 'Johann Karl Wezel and the art of illusion', *PEGS(NS)*, 68, 1998[1999]:45–60.

WINCKELMANN. E. Décultot, 'Winckelmann naturaliste. L'histoire naturelle et la naissance de l'histoire d'art', *DhS*, 31:179–94.

## THE ROMANTIC ERA

By LAURA MARTIN, *Lecturer in German, University of Glasgow*

### 1. GENERAL STUDIES

THEMES. In deceptively simple language, Bruno Hillebrand, *Aesthetik des Augenblicks: der Dichter als Überwinder der Zeit — von Goethe bis heute*, Göttingen, Vandenhoeck & Ruprecht, 156 pp., takes us through the post-Renaissance developments in western thought by focusing on the 'Augenblick', both in the sense of an instant of time and the meeting of eyes in human-to-human contact. The German Romantics were the first to experience the panic of meaninglessness brought on by the loss of belief in eternity; they sought solace in the 'erfüllter Augenblick' by means of their art. W. H. Wackenroder and L. Tieck are mentioned, and there are two chapters featuring Kleist. The discussion ranges from Bruno to Goethe, Nietzsche, Benn, Eco, and the deconstructionists. Susanne M. Zantop's *Kolonialphantasien im vorkolonialen Deutschland (1770–1870)*, Berlin, Schmidt, 314 pp., adds a bibliography of 18th-c. and 19th-c. German texts on South America to the original English version, first published in 1997. The study focuses on fantasies of colonialism in a variety of texts, including tractates, stories, and plays, from the time before Germany had any real colonies in which to put the theories into practice. Germany's privileged position outside the contingencies of colonial administration allowed it to imagine for itself a national identity in contrast not only to the countries to be dominated but also to countries which actually were dominating their own colonies. Unlike most post-colonial studies, Zantop's does not focus on the Anglo-Saxon world, and it does include an investigation of the role of ideas of the feminine in a concrete, not merely metaphorical way. Ethel Matala de Mazza, *Der verfasste Körper: zum Projekt einer organischen Gemeinschaft in der politischen Romantik*, Freiburg, Rombach Litterae, 476 pp., is a wide-ranging study which likewise finds that Germany's special status gave it a privileged position from which to theorize, this time about the body politic. Mazza's work carries on that of Foucault, but unlike his does not look at technical aspects of disciplining the body but rather at the discursive/symbolic speculations about it. This interdisciplinary study brings insights from literary anthropology, the history of medicine, discourse history, and gender studies to bear on the investigation of the 'phantasm' of the organic body and body politic in the poetic and theoretical works of Novalis, Schlegel, Adam Müller, Brentano, A. von Arnim, including the latter's institution of the *Christlich-deutsche Tischgesellschaft*. Wynfrid Kriegleder, *Vorwärts in die Vergangenheit: Das Bild der USA im deutschsprachigen Roman von 1776–1855,* Tübingen, Stauffenburg, 494 pp., takes a different aspect of colonial mentality as its subject. A very wide range of novels is investigated, with 'case studies' devoted to novels by D. C. Seybold, H. Frölich, C. Sealsfield, and F. Kürnberger. The material is divided chronologically according to mostly European historical developments. It traces the development of the Enlightenment adventure novel (1770–1805) into novels which depicted the USA as a land of asylum for Europe-weary emigrants (1805–30, following the Napoleonic Wars), culminating in the post-July Revolutionary era, which saw a return of the Enlightenment adventure novel but also a dystopic strand of writing as well as the sheer adventure novel with no social message. C. Sealsfield stands in a class of his own in this schema, and the inward-looking tendencies of programmatic Realism after 1848 puts an end to this longer era of German depictions of the USA.

R. Littlejohns, 'Crossing a threshold: the example of German Romanticism', Saul, *Schwellen,* 152–63, superimposes the idea of an historical epoch on the literary idea of movement in order to bring out similarities between contemporaries otherwise ignored. Early and Late Romantics have in some ways less in common with each other than with the Classical writers and the *Biedermeier* generation, respectively, because they lived through shared historical experiences. J. Daiber, 'Selbsexperimentation: zu einer romantischen Versuchspraxis', *Aurora,* 58, 1998:49–68, traces the development of a Romantic experimentation which focused on one's own body and soul, out of the Enlightenment tradition of experimentation on external, physical nature. L. Tieck, A. von Arnim, and J. W. Ritter are all discussed, as is the fascination with 'animal magnetism'. Two articles included in Fichtner, *Doppelgänger,* are broad general studies with mentions of German Romanticism. The first, H.-H. Hildebrandt, 'Das geschriebene Ich oder: wer ist wer im Spiegel?' (219–43), sweeps through the whole history of the Western tradition, from Homer, Hesiod and the Bible to Montaigne and Rousseau, from there through K. P. Moritz and Jean Paul (*Siebenkäs*) to S. Beckett in a truly impressive account of the formation of an I (and not-I) through language and representation. Not quite so interesting was O. Panagl, ' "Drei Frauen in ein und derselben Frau! Drei Seelen in einer einzigen Seele!" Zum Doppelgänger-Motiv in der Kunstgattung Oper' (157–74), which mentions many operas which have *Doppelgänger* or which have had them added in modern productions. One section of the three included is devoted to Offenbach's *Les Contes d'Hoffmann.*

Also noted: *Volk — Nation — Europa. Zur Romantisierung und Entromantisierung politischer Begriffe,* ed. Alexander von Bormann,

Würzburg, Königshausen & Neumann, 1998, 301 pp.; Rolf Toman, *Klassizismus und Romantik,* Cologne, Könemann, 464 pp.; Heiner Ullrich, *Das Kind als schöpferischer Ursprung: Studien zur Genese des romantischen Kindbildes und zu seiner Wirkung auf das pädagogische Denken,* Bad Heilbrunn, Klinkhardt, 387 pp.; Bettina Gruber, *Die Seherin von Prevorst: Romantischer Okkultismius in Religion, Wissenschaft und Literatur,* Paderborn, Schöningh, 260 pp.; Eckhard Lobsien, *Kunst der Assoziation: Phänomenologie eines ästhetischen Grundbegriffs vor und nach der Romantik,* Munich, Fink, 264 pp. *Romantik und Ästhetizismus: Festschrift für Paul Gerhard Klussmann,* ed. Bettine Gruber et al., Würzburg, Königshausen & Neumann, 343 pp.; Juliane Forssmann, *Intimations of Ambiguity: The Narrative Treatment of the Uncanny in Selected Texts of Romantic English and German Prose Fiction* (SAG, 362), 150 pp.; *Der Streit um die Grundlagen der Ästhetik (1795–1805): Mit Texten von Schlegel, Schelling, Humboldt, Jacobi, Novalis u.a.,* ed. Walter Jaeschke, Hamburg, Meiner, 748 pp.; H. I. Sullivan, 'Collecting the rocks of time: Goethe, the Romantics and early geology', *ERR,* 10:341–70.

GENRES. Two volumes of stories have appeared this year, *Erzählungen der deutschen Romantik,* ed. and comm. Albert Meier et al., Munich, DTV, 463 pp., which contains 11 stories plus approximately 10 pages per author and story consisting of a brief biography, material on the text, commentary, and further readings; and the less academic *Deutsche Erzähler des 19. Jahrhunderts von Heinrich von Kleist bis Adalbert Stifter,* ed. Rainer Hillebrand, Zurich, Manesse, 776 pp., which actually starts with C. M. Wieland and has 13 stories, even shorter biographies and commentary, and no further readings suggested. *Reclams Romanlexikon II: Von der Romantik bis zum Naturalismus,* ed. Frank Rainer Max and Christine Ruhrberg, Stuttgart, Reclam, 558 pp., has entries not only for novels but also novellas, stories, and other narratives, for example Grimms' *Kinder- und Hausmärchen.* The order of the entries for individual authors follows no apparent logic, but there is an index to assist the reader. Entries are brief, rarely exceeding 2–3 pages.

Cordula Braun, *Divergentes Bewusstsein: Romanprosa an der Wende zum 19. Jahrhundert,* Berne, Lang, 456 pp., traces the development of a Romantic concept of prose. Unlike Descartes's forward-looking, goal-orientated, rational discourse, and unlike J. G. Lindner's concept of the utility of prose (as opposed to the entertainment value of poetry), the Romantic prose of Schlegel (*Lucinde*), Brentano (*Godwi*), and Jean Paul (*Leben Fibels*) is complex, self-reflexive, interdisciplinary (mixing theory with poetry), and experimental. The three novels studied do not seek to reinstate order and unity (as does Goethe's *Wahlverwandtschaften*) yet nor do they disintegrate into Lichtenbergian aphorisms or fall into the nihilism of Tieck's *William Lovell* and the *Nachtwachen von Bonaventura.*

The Romantic poet as priest is the subject of Nicholas Saul, *'Prediger aus der neuen romantischen Clique': Zur Interaktion von Romantik und Homiletik um 1800*, Würzburg, Königshausen & Neumann, 219 pp. Literary texts are analysed side by side with the much neglected homiletic of the Romantic era, namely that of J. M. Sailer and F. Schleiermacher. Finally, various theories of discourse analysis are utilized to show that poets and preachers were contesting for authority in the changing times around the turn of the 18th century. Authors discussed include Novalis, Brentano, E. T. A. Hoffmann, Z. Werner, Kleist, and W. Hauff.

Helga Neumann, *Zwischen Emanzipation und Anpassung; Protagonistinnen des deutschen Zeitschriftenwesens im ausgehenden 18. Jahrhundert (1779–1795)*, Würzburg, Königshausen & Neumann, 194 pp., covers a little-known area in women's writing, concentrating on Sophie von la Roche and Marianne Ehrmann, but also including lesser-known writers and publications which we know of only through contemporary reviews. Elke Ramm, *Autobiographische Schriften deutschsprachiger Autorinnen um 1800*, Hildesheim, Olms, 1998, 214 pp., is another investigation of women's writing. The authors covered range from the last third of the 18th c. to the latter half of the 19th century. Many of them published anonymous autobiographies, and thus fall out of the range of most studies of autobiography, which posit the discovery of a self through the writing. Thus, a well-known problem in women's studies rears its ugly head again here.

Uwe Japp, *Die Komödie der Romantik: Typologie und Überblick*, Tübingen, Niemeyer, xiv + 138 pp., takes as its subject the much-ignored genre of Romantic comedy, which he divides into three categories, 'parabatisch', which steps out of character, so to speak, and mocks itself and others; 'illudierend', which is a less self-conscious comedy of intrigue; and lastly a third, catch-all category which he subdivides into four further categories. The authors studied include Brentano, A. von Arnim, Eichendorff and A. von Platen, but not Kleist. Michael Boehringer, *The Telling Tactics of Narrative Strategies in Tieck, Kleist, Stifter and Storm* (NASNCGL, 24), x + 204 pp., uses the narrative theory of structuralism to study the four texts, yet adds to the purely intratextual structuralist tradition extra- and intertextual elements. The relation between the narrator and the characters is taken as a focal point, and an attempt is made to trace a development from the earlier to the later works, though no claims are made for universal applicability of the tendencies. The exact nature of these changes remained, unfortunately, unclear to this reader.

*The Oxford Companion to Fairy Tales*, ed. Jack Zipes, OUP, 601 pp., will be a standard reference for those working on German or other fairy tales. It is mentioned here because of the importance of the German Romantic Era for the subject and hence its presence in Zipes's volume. Similarly, Maria Tatar, *The Classic Fairy Tales*, NY, Norton Critical Edition, xviii + 394 pp., provides a very handy overview of various versions of some of the best-known tales (almost all of which have a Grimm version) as well as extracts from criticism on fairy tales, and will prove a useful teaching text for the genre. Also noted: Jack David Zipes, *When Dreams Came True: Classical Fairy Tales and Their Tradition*, NY, Routledge, x + 238 pp.

## 2. Individual Authors

ARNIM, BETTINE VON.    Hildegard Baumgart, *Bettine Brentano und Achim von Arnim. Lehrjahre einer Liebe*, Berlin Vlg, 493 pp., is written by a Romance-language scholar with an interest in the idea of romantic love. The couple was chosen from other alternatives due to their suitability in time and because they exemplified Romantic love for the author. The double biography follows the protagonists from their first meeting up to their marriage. Bettina Brentano, . . . *Wer ein schön Gesicht hat . . . Originale und erdichtete Breife ausgewählt und kommentiert von Hannelore Schlaffer*, Munich, Hanser, 157 pp., is an interesting selection of B. v. A.'s real and fictional letters. The commentary is interspersed throughout the text in italics, making for easy reading, and the text itself is given as narrative, with little interruption by the formalities (headings and signatures) of real letter-writing. Ingeborg Drewitz, *'darum muss man nichts als Leben.' Bettine von Arnim*, Munich, Econ & List, 384 pp., is a posthumous reprint of the 1969 work, and it is still fascinating. T. Richter, 'Zwei Gestaltungen von "Schleiermachers Tod". Prinzipien der Literarisierung bei Bettina von Arnim im Vergleich mit dem Bericht Henriette Schleiermachers', *IJBAG*, 10, 1998:73–95, furthers our insight into the writer's method of mixing fact and fiction, for in this case, unlike much of what we have in *Goethes Briefwechsel mit einem Kinde*, we have another account with which to compare hers, and we have her own immediate response to the incident in her letters to Prinz Pückler. B. von A. is shown in *Ilius Pamphilius und die Ambrosia* to romanticize aspects of the account but not to make statements in outright contradicition to known fact. H. Pompe, 'Die Wiederholung der Gabe. Überlegungen zu Bettine von Arnims Briefbuch *Ilius Pamphilius und die Ambrosia*', *ib.*, 97–113, studies the same work in terms of M. Mauss's idea of the gift. The journal's reprint this year is M. Carriere, 'Bettina von Arnim', *ib.* 129–60, which was originally published by K. Gutzkow in 1844. Also noted: R. Moering, 'Bettine Brentanos Vertonung von Goethes "Ach neige, du Schmerzenreiche . . .". Ein unbekanntes Autograph im Goethe- und Schiller-Archiv,' *ib.*, 11–21; A. W. Lemke, 'Briefe einer Bettina-Verehrerin. Ein Beitrag zur frühen Rezeption von *Goethes Briefwechsel mit einem Kinde*', *ib.*, 23–46; B. Krehl, 'Bettina von Arnim in Milan Kunderas Roman *Die Unsterblichkeit*', *ib.*, 115–26; Hedwig Pompe, \**Der Wille zum Glück: Bettina von Arnims Poetik der Naivität im Briefroman 'Die Günderode*', Bielefeld, Aisthesis, 252 pp.; Bettina von Arnim, \**The Life of High Countess Gritta von Ratsinourhouse* (*Das Leben der Hochgräfin Rattenzuhausbeiuns*), trans. and introd. Lisa Ohm, Lincoln, Nebraska U.P., xxxv + 152 pp.; A. Corkhill, 'Female language in the age of Goethe: three case studies', *MLR*, 94: 1041–53.

BONAVENTURA. Linde Katritzky, *A Guide to Bonaventura's Nightwatches* (Ars Interpretandi, 9), NY, Lang, x + 291 pp., seeks not to determine the mysterious author of the text (though a strong case is made for G. C. Lichtenberg on the basis of similarity of preoccupations and style), but rather to 'understand and classify' the text and 'to recognize [its] conceptual originality'. The text with its vast array of allusions is 'decoded' for the reader; literary, scientific, artistic, and philosophical influences are convincingly spelled out and a case is made for viewing the work as Menippean satire. See also L. Katritzky, 'Defining the genre of Bonaventura's *Nachtwachen*', *GLL*, 52: 13–27.

BRENTANO, CLEMENS. An unual contribution to scholarship is presented by Hans Magnus Enzensberger, *Requiem für eine romantische Frau: Die Geschichte von Auguste Bussmann und Clemens Brentano*, Frankfurt, Insel, 356 pp. It includes letters and documents pertaining to the relationship of A. Bussmann and B., including material not published elsewhere; yet the edition is not really a scholarly one but seeks instead to tell a story, thus letters are edited according to different principles. This edition contains material not available in the 1996 edition as well as rather racy photos from a film version. More standard is Hartwig Schultz's *Clemens Brentano*, Stuttgart, Reclam, 223 pp., with biography and interpretations of the works.

Martina Vordermayer, *Antisemitismus und Judentum bei Clemens Brentano* (Forschungen zum Junghegelianismus, 4), Frankfurt, Lang, 300 pp. is an extremely thorough and differentiated study of the attitudes towards Jewishness in Brentano. V. sets the context with a reception history in which B. is supposed anti-Semitic by those who were like-minded and, paradoxically, assumed by others to be Jewish himself. She attempts to distinguish between religious '*Judenfeindlichkeit*' and the historically more recent racial anti-Semitism. B. is guilty of the former only, and even this, prevalent as it is in his work, must be seen in a context where B. also identified himself with the Wandering Jew and considered the Jews to be God's chosen people.

N. Saul, 'Leiche und Humor. Clemens Brentanos Schauspielfragment "Zigeunerin" und der Patriotismus um 1813', *JFDH*, 1998: 111–66, wishes to rehabilitate Romantic drama, which work he begins here by publishing for the first time a fragment comprising 21 pages. A commentary is also provided. B's anti-Semitism is not denied, but it is set beside his paradoxically positive portrayal of the other group of outsiders, the gypsies.

C. MacLeod, 'Sculpture and the wounds of language in Clemens B.'s *Godwi*', *GR*, 74:178–94, sets the 18th-c. context of ideas concerning aesthetics and the relationship between the arts (Winckelmann, Lessing, Goethe, Moritz), then proceeds to a psychoanalytically-influenced reading of *Godwi*, where a tension between the plastic and narrative modes is found. As allegory, the statues actually enact death, or the vegetative decay they would stop, in this *'verwilderten Roman'*, which is also falling apart at the seams.

Also noted: Kristina Hasenpflug, *\*Clemens Brentanos Lyrik an Luise Hensel: mit historisch-kritischen Edition einiger Gedichte und Erläuterungen* (EH, I, 1707), 350 pp.; Clemens Brentano, *\*Historisch-kritische Ausgabe sämtlicher Werke und Briefe: Frankfurter Brentano-Ausgabe*, III.1: *Gedichte 1816–1817;* III.2: *Gedichte 1818–1819*, ed. Michael Grus et al., Stuttgart, Kohlhammer, 648, 500 pp.; H. U. Treichel, 'Clemens Brentano's poetics', *Merkur*, 53:367–73.

CHAMISSO. A. Lorenczuk, 'Die *Geschichte von den drei Liebschaften*', *Aurora*, 59, 1998:125–32, discovers a source in C.'s poem 'Die drei Sonnen' for the character Mai-Sachme's story of falling in love with a woman, later with her daughter, and even later with her granddaughter in T. Mann's *Joseph der Ernährer*. Also noted: D. V. Chamisso, 'Ein wiederentdecktes Kinderbild Adalbert von Chamissos, *Studia Theodisca*, 6:171–77.

DE LA MOTTE FOUQUÉ, FRIEDRICH. *Der Doppelroman der Berliner Romantik*, ed. and comm. Helmuth Rogge, 2 vols, Hildesheim, Olms, 406, 359 pp., is a facsimile reprint of the 1926 edition. It will be of interest to scholars not only of M.F., but also of K. A. Varnhagen, W. Neumann, A. F. Bernhardi, K. W. S. Contessa, A. von Chamisso, and E. T. A. Hoffmann, all of whom collaborated on the ironic parody of contemporary writers. The first part (*Die Versuche und Hindernisse Karls*) was published in 1808 and the second (*Der Roman des Freiherrn von Vieren*) only in 1926 in Rogge's edition. Katja Diegmann-Hornig, *'Sich in die Poesie zu flüchten, wie in unantastbare Eilande der Seeligen': Analysen zu ausgewählten Romanen von Friedrich Baron de la Motte Fouqué*, Hildesheim, Olms, 211 pp., is a well-conceived effort to rehabilitate M.F., who has been unfairly accused of writing mere *Trivialromane*. Brief sections about his biography (a total of some 20 pages) are interspersed with discussions of seven novels (not including

*Undine*) where an attempt is made to give the reader enough of a sense of the language of these unfamiliar novels to be able to judge the quality for himself. Summaries are given of all the novels in an appendix, and there is a chapter on the history of the concept of *Trivialliteratur*. EICHENDORFF, JOSEPH VON. A. Riemen, 'Adelsleben und Zeitgeschehen. Beobachtungen Eichendorffs zur napoleonischen Zeit, *Aurora*, 58, 1998:69–88, studies *Pro Memoria*, a journal-like collection of sketches, together with *Ahnung und Gegenwart*, in order to extract a picture of the Silesian nobility in the Napoleonic era. Also noted: H. Korte, 'Taugenichts-Lektüren: Eichendorff im literarischen Kanon', *IASL* 24.2:17–70. FICHTE. Johann Gottlieb Fichte, *Gesamtausgabe der Bayrischen Akademie der Wissenschaften*, series II, vol. XII: *Nachgelassene Schriften 1810–1812*, ed. Reinhard Lauth et al., Stuttgart–Bad Canstatt, Frommann-Holzboog, xii + 464 pp., contains posthumous material from 1811, including 'Die Thatsachen des Bewusstseins', the 'Wissenschaftslehre' of 1811, and several other lectures, and it continues the editing and documenting of F.'s work. Georg Römpp, *Ethik des Selbsbewusstseins: Der Andere in der idealistischen Grundlegung der Philosophie. Kant, Fichte, Schelling, Hegel*, Berlin, Duncker & Humblot, 308 pp., shows how the philosophy of self-consciousness is based on the identity and difference with the other, which makes itself apparent in ethics. Katharine Ceming, *Mystik und Ethik bei Meister Eckhart und J. G. Fichte* (Philosophie, 588), Frankfurt, Lang, 270 pp., returns to Eckhart for a definition of mysticism in order to prove that even F.'s late work is not in a true sense mystical, because whereas F. believed ethical behaviour led to discovery of the divine in man, the true mystic Eckhart thought that it was the union of God and man that led to ethical behaviour. Bernd Kleinhans, *Der 'Philosoph' in der neueren Geschichte der Philosophie: 'Eigentlicher Philosoph' und 'vollendeter Gelehrter'. Konkretionen des praktischen Philosophen bei Kant und Fichte*, Würzburg, Königshausen & Neumann, 321 pp., sees in Kant's 'eigenticher Philosoph' and F.'s 'vollendeter Gelehrter' two attempts to bridge the divide between systematic and practical philosophy.

Also noted: Klaus Unterburger, *Determinismuswiderlegung in der kritischen Philosophie Immanuel Kants und bei J. G. Fichte in der Phase bis 1796*, Neuried, Ars Una, 194 pp.; Klaus Schaller, *Zur Grundlegung der Einzelwissenschaft bei Comenius und Fichte: Eine Studie zum Problem des Studiums Generale*, introd. Käte Meyer-Drawe, St Augustin, Academia Richarz, 256 pp.; Werner Volker Csech, *Die Raumlehre J. G. Fichtes: Mit Berücksichtigung philosophiegeschichtlicher Konstellationen* (EH, xx, 583), 463 pp.; Helmut Girndt et al., *Zur Einheit der Lehre Fichtes: Die Zeit der*

*Wissenschaftslehre nova methodo: Tagung der Internationalen J. G. Fichte-Gesellschaft*, Amsterdam–Atlanta, Rodopi, xiv + 452 pp.; Wolfgang Janke, *'Wissenschaftslehre 1805': Methodisch-systematischer und philosophischer Kommentar*, WBG, xiv + 214 pp.; Christoph Asmuth, *Das Begreifen des Unbegreiflichen: Philosophie und Religion bei J. G. Fichte 1800–1806*, Stuttgart–Bad Canstatt, Frommann-Holzboog, 411 pp.; Armin G. Wildfeuer, *Praktische Vernunft und System: Entwicklungsgeschichtliche Untersuchungen zur unsprünglichen Kant-Rezeption J. G. Fichtes*, Stuttgart–Bad Canstatt, Frommann-Holzboog, 596 pp.

GOETHE, CHRISTIANE. A rather unusual contribution to scholarship is provided by *Christiane Goethe Tagebuch 1816 und Briefe*, ed. Sigrid Damm, Frankfurt, Insel, 479 pp. The diary entries are short and trivial, mere lists of people seen and things done, and are not of any literary interest, as the hopeful reader in these days of the revival of women's writing might be led to expect. A much longer commentary is presented on the facing page, which may be of use for those curious about life in the Goethe household. The material by G. seems hardly able to support the speculative nature of Damm's introduction.

GRIMM, JACOB AND WILHELM. The following editions are noted: J.G. and W.G., *Sämtliche Werke*, 1: *Die Werke Jacob Grimms*. XV: *Geschichte der deutschen Sprache*, ed. Maria Herrlich, Hildesheim, Olms; *Die ursprünglichen Märchen der Brüder Grimm: Handschriften, Urfassung und Texte zur Kulturgeschichte*, ed. Kurt Derungs, Stuttgart, Amalia, 320 pp.; *Wiege und Kinderlieder gesammelt durch die Brüder Grimm*, ed. Heinz Rölleke, Weimar, Böhlau, 168 pp.; Lutz Röhrich, *Wage es, den Frosch zu küssen! Das Grimmsche Märchen Nummer Eins in seinen Wandlungen*, Bad Orb, Orbensien, 168 pp.; J.G. and W.G., *Grimms Märchen und Deutsche Sagen*, ed. Heinz Rölleke, Frankfurt, DKV, 2392 pp; and lastly a reprint with a new publisher is Arnold Bittlinger, *Es war einmal ... Grimms Märchen im Licht von Tiefenpsychologie und Bibel*, 3 vols, Kindhausen, Metanoia, 158, 150, 159 pp.

Wilhelm Solms, *Die Moral von Grimms Märchen*, Darmstadt, Primus, vi + 249 pp., shows that the moralizing of the psychoanalytic studies as well as the amoral stance of folklore and literary studies both miss the point somewhat. Grimms' tales do have a 'moral' in the sense that the hero/heroine is always rewarded, regardless of behaviour and against all odds; yet it is not because the hero/heroine is virtuous, but because he/she is selflessly open to experience. Not only the *Zaubermärchen*, but also the *Schwankmärchen* and the moralizing stories of the collection are discussed, with constant reference to previous scholarship. Susanne Meier, *Liebe, Traum und Tod: Die Rezeption der Grimmschen Kinder- und Hausmärchen auf der Opernbühne*, Trier, Wissenschaftlicher Vlg Trier, 331 pp., covers 41 librettos from over 200 years of opera, so it includes some of the precursors to the Gs' work.

Meier works out a type, if not exactly a genre, of fairy tale opera, which turns the original *Volksmärchen* into something resembling a *Kunstmärchen* because the stage productions add psychological depth, dramatize the magic (which is taken for granted in the *Volkmärchen*), and make the difference between dream and reality (also ignored in the *Volksmärchen*) an issue, where the dreamworld is an escape from harsh reality for the heroine or hero. Elisabeth Görner, *Konfliktreiche Mutter-Tochter-Beziehungen in der Urfassung der Grimmschen Märchen*, Erzabtei St. Ottilien, EOS Vlg, 150 pp., is somewhat disappointing, being directed to a general audience rather than a scholarly one. Although the interpretations of the tales are of some interest, they remain superficial, as there is no attempt to deal with modern scholarship which questions the pedagogical aspect of the tales or, for that matter, with feminist interpretations. Although Görner does take into account the differences in the various editions by the Grimms, their *Urfassung* is naively taken as a true representative of the *Volksmärchen* as it supposedly really existed, and so Görner makes unsubstantiated claims for universally valid interpretations of the tales. The interpretations may appeal, but an admission of their limitations would be welcome. Esther Gallwitz, *Schneewittchens Apfel. Pflanzen in Grimms Märchen. Mit farbigen Aquarellen von Maria-Therese Tietmeyer*, Frankfurt, Insel, 208 pp., is a very unusual contribution, mixing as it does real research into etymologies and the symbolic value of plants and herbs with a highly discursive style.

Maria Herrlich, *Organismuskonzept und Sprachgeschichtsschreibung. Die 'Geschichte der deutschen Sprache' von Jacob Grimm* (Schriftenreihe Werke der Brüder J. G. und W. G., 1), Hildesheim, Olms-Weidmann, 1998, 222 pp., rehabilitates the much-spurned 'Geschichte der deutschen Sprache' by showing how it represents J.G.'s concept of the organism. Arguments that J.G. was an inevitable precursor of National Socialist thinking are refuted, as the *Geschichte* is proved to show that 'organic' developments of language, and thus of culture, were open not just to the Germans, but to any nation. S. Heyer, 'Zum Ossian-Wagnis des alten Jacob Grimms', *Brüder Grimm Gedenken*, 13 : 1–58, traces J.G.'s later interest in the 1807 publication of the poems by 'Ossian'. From first intending merely to document motifs in the works, J.G. later wanted to prove their authenticity, which he never doubted. He was hindered in completing this task only by the overwhelming amount of work necessary to complete the dictionary. M. Halub, ' "Meine wege gehen auf Ihre strasse." Über die Wechselbeziehungen der Brüder Grimm mit den schwäbischen Romantikern', *ib.*, 59–77, documents the much neglected mutual influence of the brothers and L. Uhland, J. Kerner, G. Schwab, and other Swabian Romantics, proving that these writers were in more contact with the rest of

Germany than previously thought. P. Breukker, 'Der frühe Einfluss von Jacob Grimm in Friesland, insbesondere seine Einwirkung auf die Entstehung des Werkes von Paulus Scheltema', *ib.*, 150–62, shows that J.G.'s interest in old Frisian documents probably influenced the work of the Frisian scholar. Also noted in this volume: 'Abschrift des Romans von "Mai und Beaflor" durch Wilhelm Grimm', *ib.*, 78–94; M. Janssen, 'Jacob und Wilhelm Grimms Göttinger Vorlesungen. Hörerlisten aus den Jahren 1831–1837', *ib.*, 95–104; U. Schröter, ' "Sie wissen, wie schätzbar mir Ihre theilnahme an dem wörterbuch ist." Zum Briefwechsel Wilhelm Grimm—Gabriel Riedel', *ib.*, 121–34; D. Wagner, 'Christian Friedrich Wurm (1801–1861). Der von Jacob Grimm verschmähte DWB-Mitarbeiter und seine Wortsammlung', *ib.*, 135–43; E. Hexelschneider, 'Walther Friedrich Clossius und Jacob Grimm', *ib.*, 144–49; E. Ebel, 'Zu den Beziehungen der Brüder Grimm zu skandinavischen Wissenschaftlern', *ib.*, 163–70; I. T. Erdlélyi, 'Beziehungen Jacob Grimms zur volkstümlichen Literatur Ungarns', *ib.*, 171–83; M. Sutton, 'Ein neu bearbeitetes Inhaltsverzeichnis der ersten englischen Übersetzungen der KHM von Edgar Taylor', *ib.*, 184–89; and M. M. Cardoza and H. W. Rauth, 'Bibliographie der Übersetzungen Grimmscher Märchen in Brasilien und Portugal', *ib.*, 190–200. Also noted: W. P. Lehmann, 'The structural approach of Jacob Grimm and his contemporaries, *JIES*, 27 : 1–13.

GÜNDERRODE, KAROLINE. *Karoline von Günderrode: Gedichte, Prosa, Briefe*, ed. Hannelore Schlaffer, Stuttgart, Reclam, 1998, 148 pp., makes a selection of poetry and letters available and has an interesting epilogue. Wiebke Amthor, 'Der Tod als Zitat. Eine motivische Betrachtung zum Selbstmord Karoline von Günderrodes', *IJBAG*, 10, 1998:49–72, teases out the motif of suicide by dagger and drowning in G.'s writing. The suicide is neither an act of desperation in the face of unrequited (Romantic) love nor simply the expression of a (Romantic) death wish. Rather, at the same moment that G. expresses herself fully in this 'manly' act, she also fulfils her own ideals of 'womanly' self-abnegation. Also noted: Markus Hille, *\*Karoline von Günderrode*, Reinbek, Rowohlt, 153 pp.

HEBEL, JOHANN PETER. Johann Peter Hebel, *Die Kalender Geschichten*, ed. Hannelore Schlaffer and Harald Zils, Munich, Hanser, 847 pp., includes a commentary on and documentation supporting the stories of the *Rheinländischer Hausfreund*, which are published all together here. H. Fricke, ' "Ein-Bild-hielt-uns-gefangen": on Wittgenstein's notion of *Witz* as a therapy against intellectual rigidity', *LiLi*, 29:90–112, discusses H.'s *Kannitverstan* in terms of Wittgenstein's notion of the *Witz*. Also noted: Y.-G. Mix, 'Das Mass der Dinge und die kosmische Ordnung: Ereignisgeschichte, Zeit- und Raumsemantik in Johann Peter Hebel's "Rheinländischem Hausfreund"', *ZDP*, 118:518–29.

HOFFMANN, E. T. A.   R. Schmidt, 'Der Dichter als Fledermaus bei der Schau des Wunderbaren. Die Poetologie des rechten dichterischen Sehens in Hoffmanns *Der Sandmann* und *Das öde Haus*', *Mutual Exchanges. Sheffield-Münster Colloquium*, Frankfurt, Lang, 334 pp., illustrates the way H. ironizes, but does not reject outright, the Romantic hero in his depiction of Nathanael in *Der Sandmann*. Whereas the less well-known story portrays an acceptable attitude towards the uncanny, and thus becomes almost didactic, *Der Sandmann* hovers between final decisions about the truth value of what N. sees. Thus, N. goes too far, but H. himself still supports the Romantic commitment to poeticizing the world. A. Würker, 'Worüber uns E.T.A. Hoffmanns *Sandmann* die Augen öffnet', pp. 59–77 of *Grenzgänge: Literatur und Unbewusstes. Zu Heinrich von Kleist., E.T.A. Hoffmann, Alfred Andersch, Ingeborg Bachmann und Max Frisch*, ed. Achim Würker et al., Würzburg, Königshausen & Neumann, 147 pp., is an interesting development of Freud's interpretation of *Der Sandmann*. The text is read as literature, not as a case study of pathogenesis in the main character and not as the biography of the author; further, symbolic meanings gain force by sheer association, not by any concretized correspondences. Thus, the method, and not the theory, of Freudian psychoanalysis is the tool used to help explain the reader's experience of reality in a clearly fictional text. In Lutz Hagestedt, *Das Genieproblem bei E.T.A. Hoffmann: eine Interpretation seiner späten Erzählungen 'Des Vetters Eckfenster'*, Munich, Belleville, 170 pp., the two unnamed *Vetter* of the story each represent an opposing concept of the genius which was current in the *Goethezeit*. The *Vetter* of the title is selfish, egocentric, and conceited; he exaggerates his own abilities and is a failure as a writer. The narrating figure, on the other hand, quietly and without any vain posturing achieves what his cousin fails to do: to observe life and write about it. H.'s narrative strategy of having the narrating cousin both take part in the dialogue and report about it is unique; the splitting of a character into two 'doubles' is, of course, common practice in the literature of the period.

Several studies have variously tried to determine H.'s thought, as similar to or different from that of our postmodern age. Sabine Hillebrand, *Stratagien der Verwirrung. Zur Erzählkunst von E.T.A. Hoffmann, Thomas Bernhard und Giorgio Manganelli* (SDLNZ, 39), 190 pp., sees in H. the beginnings of a modern 'aesthetics of ambiguity', where an author intentionally obfuscates the meaning and makes the reader take part in a futile effort of detection. H. is known to have influenced

writers such as Baudelaire, Rimbaud, Mallarmé, Poe, and Dostoevsky, and in a sense he is the first writer to confront modern
psychological terror. Roughly one third of the book is dedicated to
each of the authors named in the title, the chapter on H. includes
sections on *Der Sandmann* and *Die Elixiere des Teufels*. Kenneth
B. Woodgate, *Das Phantastische bei E. T. A. Hoffmann* (BDL, 25),
273 pp., broadens the investigation of the fantastic in H. beyond the
two much-studied texts, *Der goldene Topf* and *Der Sandmann*. The history
of the fantastic and its cognates is laid out in order to show how
H. diverged from his contemporaries' use of the term. H. is a
mannered writer who drives the fantastic to extremes in his work but
also mockingly questions the efficacy of a fantastic attitude. Thus he
is neither Romantic nor yet Biedermeier, but tries to balance the
opposing claims of realism and fantasy in his work. R. Schmidt, 'The
narrative structures of Romantic subjectivity in E. T. A. Hoffmann's
*Die Elixiere des Teufels* and *Der Sandmann*, GRM, 49:143–60, rescues
H. from postmodern decentering by showing how the centrifugal
forces threatening the self in *Elixiere* and *Der Sandmann* are offset by
centripetal ones. Thus H. remains a Romanticist, despite the claims
of many modern, ahistorical critics. See also R. Schmidt, 'Ahnung
des Göttlichen und affizierte Ganglien. Die kontrapunktische Er-
zähltechnik des *Kater Murr* auf der Schwelle von Romantik zu
Moderne', Saul, *Schwellen*, 138–51.
    J. Daiber, 'Die Autofaszination des Blickes. Zu einem Motivkom-
plex in Erzählwerk E. T. A. Hoffmanns', *Euphorion*, 93:485–96,
distinguishes two aspects of the eye for H., the physiological and the
creative. In a series of examples, failed artist figures in the works are
shown to exaggerate the solipsistic inner eye over the reality of the
outer world. The true artist would instead follow the Serapion
principle by balancing the perception of the outer world with the
inner changing of what is perceived, which is then projected back out
on the world. The philistine, on the other hand, fails to do more than
register outer reality, having none of the inner working that the failed
artist has too much of.
    Also noted: P. Liedke Konow, 'Staging Serapion art works: E. T. A.
Hoffmann's frame story "Doge und Dogaresse" as part of the
anthology *Die Serapionsbruder*', GN, 30.2:134–42; Detlev Kremer, *E.
T. A. Hoffmann: Erzählungen und Romane*, Berlin, Schmidt, 241 pp.;
Heinz Schmitz, *Gegenwelten: Mythologische Strukturen in E. T. A.
Hoffmanns Traumwelten*, Essen, Die blaue Eule, 98 pp.; Klaus Detering,
*Magie des poetischen Raums: E. T. A. Hoffmanns Dichtung und Weltbild*,
Heidelberg, Winter, 359 pp.; Katrin Bomhoff, *Bildende Kunst und
Dichtung: Die Selbstinterpretation E.T.A. Hoffmanns in der Kunst Jacques
Callots und Salvator Rosas* (Rombach Wissenschaften, Reihe Cultura,

6), Freiburg, Rombach, 280 pp.; B. Dohm, 'Improbable probabilities — making possible the miraculous in E. T. A. Hoffmann's *Das Fräulein von Scuderi*', *DVLG*, 73:289–318; S. E. Gustafson, 'The cadaverous bodies of vampiric mothers and the genealogy of pathology in E. T. A. Hoffmann's *Tales*', *GLL*, 52:238–54; S. Kleine, 'E. T. A. Hoffmann, oder: die Fälschung der romantischen Welt', *Prospero*, 6:73–86; K. B. Woodgate, 'Revisiting Serapion: E. T. A. Hoffmann's principles of literary production and the limits of literary discourse', *AUMLA*, 92:33–50; L. Bryson, 'Romantic science: Hoffmann's use of natural sciences in *Der goldene Topf*', *MDLK*, 91:241–55; S. Kleine, '*Elixiere des Teufels*. Notes on E. T. A. Hoffmann's "Black Romanticism" and the idealist critical response', *AUMLA*, 91:27–44.

HÖLDERLIN. Friedrich Hölderlin, *Sämtliche Gedichte und Hyperion*, ed. Jochen Schmidt, Frankfurt, Insel, 665 pp. organizes the poetry chronologically and includes some sketches and fragments as well as post-1806 poetry. Emery E. George, *Hölderlin's Hymn 'Der Einzige': Sources — Language — Context — Form*, Bonn, Bouvier, 554 pp., will prove to be an invaluable source for the student of H.'s hymns. Facsimiles of the extant MS pages are provided, as well as chapters on the sources, on the linguistic difficulties presented by the poem, on its biographical context, and on the problems of poetic form which the poem itself makes apparent. An argument is made for the relevance of this poem and it is related to particularly English-language poems of Modernism. Fridolin Ganter, *Versus Heroicus: Eine sprech-, sprach- und textanalytische ästhetische Konstruktion von Hölderlins 'Archipelagus'* (EH, 1, 1708), Frankfurt, Lang, xii + 172 pp., also takes one poem only as its subject. This language-based approach uses phonetics, phonology, the rules of versification, and even chaos theory in order to analyse the text. Charles de Roche, *Friedrich Hölderlin: Patmos. Das scheidende Erscheinen des Gedichts*, Munich, Fink, 239 pp., discusses the hymn in relation to W. Benjamin's analysis of 'Dichtermut-Blödigkeit'.

Momme Mommsen, *Lebendige Uberlieferung: George — Hölderlin — Goethe* (GSA, 69), x + 406 pp., was published as a surprise for the author by Katharina Mommsen. It comprises essays written over four decades, including four on H. originally published in the 1960s. The first half of Gregor Wittkop, *Hölderlins Nürtingen: Lebenswelt und literarischer Entwurf*, Tübingen, Niemeyer, vii + 152 pp., uses letters and other documents to describe H.'s relationship to the town he grew up in, whereas the second half seeks to use this information to clarify H.'s concept of *Heimat* in his work. Robert Charlier, *Heros und Messias: Hölderlins messianische Mythogenese und das jüdische Denken*,

Würzburg, Königshausen & Neumann, 267 pp., traces Greek, Christian, and Jewish elements in H.'s vision of the function of poetry and the poet/priest. The reinscription of the Jewish concept of an external and politicized messianic belief in place of the inward Christian tradition is not to be seen as mere syncretism, but as a real return to a tradition that had been lost to Christianity.

Violetta L. Waibel, *Hölderlin und Fichte 1794–1800*, Paderborn, Schöningh, 384 pp., is the first full-length study to examine the developing influence of Fichte on H.'s philosophy, as evidenced in a variety of the latter's writings, both poetic and theoretical. The possible influence of H. on the *Wissenschaftslehre* is also described. H.'s coming to terms with Fichte culminates in his manuscript, *Die Verfahrungsweise des poetischen Geistes.* Jürgen Link, *Hölderlin — Rousseau: Inventive Rückkehr*, Opladen, Westdeutscher Vlg, 280 pp., shows that H. was much influenced by Rousseau, yet looked to the future, not simply to the past. In an unexpected move, Link speculates that H.'s alleged insanity was in some sense simulated, whether consciously or not, as there are no signs of schizophrenia in his behaviour or writings. It was instead possibly a case of severe depression and certainly a case of a 'return to nature' in the giving up of worldly ambitions, both political and poetic.

*The Solid Letter: Readings of Friedrich Hölderlin*, ed. Aris Fioretos, Stanford U.P., vii + 512 pp., provides modern interpretations to an English-speaking readership, and is a must for anyone interested in H. The basis of humanistic study and the political and historiographical implications of reading form the foundation of these readings by leading scholars in the field of Romanticism, who save H. from earlier nationalist interpretations as well as from the response to nationalism in *textimmanent* interpretations which ignored all political and social ramifications of the poetry. Included in the volume are the following: Peter Fenves, 'Measure for Measure: Hölderlin and the place of philosophy' (25–43), which turns to metre as central to H.'s ideas because it is what distinguishes Classical from modern poetry, and poetry itself from philosophy; Jean-Luc Nancy, 'The calculation of the poet' (44–73), which also distinguishes between poetry and philosophy in H. The poet measures and calculates time, unlike the philosopher, who uses time in which to unfold his arguments; the poet also seeks to give a synopsis, not a synthesis; Philippe Lacoue-Labarthe, 'Poetry's courage' (74–93), which follows Benjamin's interpetation of 'Dichtermut' (later called 'Blödigkeit') which sees the destination as a return to *das Gedichtete*, not, as Heidegger had read the poem, as some sort of return to *Volk* or nation; Hent de Vries, ' "Winke": Divine Topoi in Hölderlin, Heidegger, Nancy' (94–120), which traces the topos of the divine in

H. and Heidegger as well as in the interpretations by Derrida, de Man, and Nancy; Jean-François Courtine, 'Hölderlin's Christ' (121–41), which dicusses the Christology of three late poems, 'Der Einzige', 'Freidensfeier', and 'Patmos', where divine presence is real, not representational. Thus, H. does not nostalgically long for a return to the past in his poetry, but is very much caught up with present concerns; Edgar Pankow, 'Epistolary writing, fate, language: Hölderlin's "Hyperion"' (142–72), which looks at 'Hyperion' to investigate H.'s unusual concept of the epistolary not as something between stable subjects but rather as a mutual exploration of otherness, where thinking originates in the communicative act; Arnaud Villani, 'Figures of duality: Hölderlin and Greek tragedy' (175–200), which finds a doubleness or duplicity in the ancient texts 'Oedipus' and 'Antigone' taken up and re-doubled by H. in his translations and theoretical notes to the translations; Andrzej Warminski, 'Heidegger reading Hölderlin' (201–14), focusing on H.'s translation of Sophocles's *deinon* as *ungeheuer* and Heidegger's mistranslation of the same as *nicht heuer* or *unheimlich*, thus missing out on the monstrosity which, for H., accounts for the difference between Hesperians and the Orient; Stanley Corngold, 'Disowning contingencies in Hölderlin's "Empedocles"' (215–36), which argues that the *Verläugnung* is what makes it impossible for H. to complete his tragedy; Christopher Fynsk, 'Reading the "Poetics" after the "Remarks"' (237–46), which reads Aristotle's *Poetics* in terms of H.'s interpretation, where rhythmic structure is involved in catharsis; Rainer Nägele, 'Ancient sport and modern transport: Hölderlin's tragic bodies' (247–67), which discusses word-play as not accidental but integral to H.'s thinking; Aris Fioretos, 'Color read: Hölderlin and translation' (268–87), which relates the failure of meaning for the characters in Sophocles's *Antigone* to H.'s failure to carry the ancient into the modern; Cyrus Hamlin, 'The philosophy of poetic form: Hölderlin's theory of poetry and the Classical German elegy' (291–320), which attempts to focus attention away from the late hymns to the pre-1800 elegies, where, despite philosophical content, H. is proved once again to be primarily a poet, not a philosopher; Bernhard Böschenstein, ' "Brod und Wein': from the 'Classical' final version to the later revision' (321–39), which argues against any 'equalizing systematization' of various renditions of the text and instead wants the text to be considered as heterogeneous; Arne Melberg, 'Turns and echoes: two examples of Hölderlin's poetics' (340–54), which also sees rhythm as primary to H.'s meaning, and poetry and poetics to take precedence over philosophy, here illustrated in 'Brod und Wein' and 'Mnemosyne'; Hans-Jost Frey, 'Hölderlin's marginalization of language' (356–74), which takes seriously the implications of manuscript marginalia where H. theorizes on the nature of language, as this writerly practice has been much ignored in scholarship; and Thomas Schestag, 'The Highest' (375–411), which studies the fifth Pindar fragment to show the impossibility of translation of language or culture, an impossibility which H. enacts in his renditions of the Greek into German. H. D. Rauh, 'Die Schrift der Einsamkeit. Versuch über Hölderlin', *Aurora*, 58, 1998:89–114, finds H.'s 'Andenken', 'Menons Klage über Diotima', and other poems to be examples not of Romantic solipsism, but of a transcendental mourning which allows no return from the solitary autonomy of the subject. The context of late 18th-c. and early 19th-c. discourse on solitude and melancholy is set out. A. Thomasberger, 'Erinnerungsbilder. Das Konzept Hölderlins und eine Applikation auf Storm', Peil, *Erkennen*, 527–41, discusses the idea of an *erinnerndes Erkennen* in H.'s *Fragment philosophischer Briefe* and *Das untergehende Vaterland*, then moves on to a discussion of Storm's novella *Hans und Heinz Kunz*.

Also noted: Andreas Graeser, *\*Studien zu Spinoza, Herder, Hölderlin und Hegel*, St Augustin, Academia Richarz, 140 pp.; L. Michaelis, 'The deadly goddess: Friedrich Hölderlin on politics and fate', *HPT*, 20:225–49.

HUMBOLDT, WILHELM VON. Noted: Michael Losonsky, *\*Wilhelm von Humboldt. On Language: On Diversity of Human Language Construction and Its Influence on the Mental Development of the Human Species*, NY, CUP, xli + 296 pp.; Stefan Fröhling et al., *\*Die Humboldts: Lebenslinie einer gelehrten Familie*, Berlin, Nicolai, 144 pp.; J. E. Joseph, 'A matter of consequence: H., race and the genius of the Chinese language', *HistL*, 26:89–148.

KLEIST. This year (and last) has seen the publication of several important works on Kleist. Hilda Meldrum Brown, *Heinrich von Kleist: The Ambiguity of Art and the Necessity of Form*, Oxford, Clarendon, 1998, x + 409 pp., is an integrated approach to the life and writings of K. Starting with the letters, K.'s ideas about the visual and, more importantly, about the uses of illusion in art, are shown to develop at the same time as he is supposedly suffering his *Kant-Krise*. The occasional writings, stories, and plays are each individually discussed. This is a book not to be missed. Another very important work is Anthony Stephens, *Kleist. Sprache und Gewalt*, Freiburg, Rombach, 489 pp. Here articles written since 1981 are republished along with one new one, 'Wege der Sprache und der Macht' (13–48), which covers the full range of K.'s works in a discussion of the necessity of dialogue despite its inevitable violence. This work will be a welcome addition to many a scholar's shelf. Dirk Grathoff, *Kleist. Geschichte, Politik, Sprache*, Opladen, Westdeutscher Vlg, 250 pp., is a collection of essays, most already published though many are now virtually inaccessible. Topics range from particular works to K.'s relationship with contemporaries; these are framed by an essay on the 'beginnings' with the *Würzburger Reise* and ending with the theatrical suicide. Heinrich von Kleist, *Sämtliche Briefe*, ed. Dieter Heimböckel, Stuttgart, Reclam, 765 pp., has 233 letters from K. and just 22 to him. It is based on Georg Minde-Poet's 1936–38 work, though it returns to MSS or facsimiles in questionable cases where possible. There is a commentary and an index of people named. *Kleist im Speigel der Presse: Zeitungsausschnittsammlung 1998*, ed. Anton Philipp Knittel, Stadtbücherei Heilbronn, gives bibliographic information for any reference to K. in 1998. R. Wartusch, 'Neue Dokumente zum Nachruhm Ks auf dem Theater', *JFDH*, 1998:167–92, publishes a long 1819 passage by K. A. Böttiger about K.'s *Kätchen von Heilbronn* which shows that he was not so inimical to K. after all, but an understanding supporter. Tieck, K. von Brühl, de la Motte Fouqué and L. Robert all did their best to bring K. to the stage in the decades following the writer's death. S. Scheifele, 'Heinrich von Kleists *Penthesilea* oder: die Lust der Gewalt,' pp. 37–57 of *Grenzgänge: Literatur und Unbewusstes. Zu Heinrich von Kleist, E.T.A. Hoffmann, Alfred Andersch, Ingeborg Bachmann und Max Frisch*, Achim Würker et al., Würzburg, Königshausen & Neumann, 147 pp., discusses the problem of desire and violence in the play, moves to a discussion of M. Horkheimer and T. Adorno's *Dialektik der Aufklärung*, where Odysseus stands for the bourgeois male ego asserting itself against feminine desire, and ends with a biographical sketch to set the context of K.'s unique contribution to literature. In K. Jeziorkowski, 'Traum-Raum und Text-Höhle. Beobachtungen an dramatischen Szenen Heinrich von Kleists,' *Fest. Geith*, 215–24, K.'s language creates spaces, holes, places of contradiction and of speaking which yet remains silent. *Der zerbrochene Krug* and *Das Kätchen von Heilbronn* are discussed in terms of motifs as well as the way in which language is used to contain an emptiness, in this short but pithy essay. In a similar vein, and similary pithy, is N. Saul's 'Body, language and body language: thresholds in Heinrich von Kleist', Saul, *Schwellen*, 316–31, which takes the threshold instead as the defining metaphor and follows it through to ascertain a commitment to surface in Kleist. B. Greiner, *Grazie des unendlichen Bewusstsein. Prinz Friedrich von Homburg. Initiation in den Vernichtungskrieg*, Stadtbücherei Heilbronn, 27 pp., takes K.'s unique idea of *Grazie* as described in *Über das Marionettentheater* as a model for Prinz Freidrich. The prince is a *Gliedermann* in the hands of the *Kurfürst*, and must find his way to grace (which does not equal *Gnade*, or mercy) in the face of death. L. Martin, '*Die Marquise von O . . .* and *The Scarlet Letter*: a study in vicarious gender-jumping', Saul, *Schwellen*,

251–64, discovers a way to read the two authors that neither ignores their misogynist tendencies nor exaggerates their feminist ones, but rather uses an aesthetics of both/and rather than either/or to understand them. The topic of this year's *KlJb* was '*Kleists Duelle*', though K.'s preoccupation with the *Finte*, ruse or deception, also ran through the essays. G. Blamberger, 'Agonalität und Theatralität. Kleists Gedankenfigur des Duells im Kontext der europäischen Moralistik' (25–40), traces K.'s growing scepticism regarding truth in his essays. Underlying all his thought is the idea of an *agon*; one defines onself only through chance encounters with others, and these contests are won by whoever best dissimulates. Thus K. is shown to work in a tradition of the likes of Machiavelli, Montaigne, and La Rochefoucauld: he is an old-fashioned aristocrat, no precursor of the modern. Similarly, G. von Essen, 'Römer und Germanen im Spiel der Masken. Heinrich von Kleists *Hermannsschlacht*' (41–52), shows how K.'s Hermann is no typical upright, honest Germanic hero, but rather a clever tactician well-schooled in the political ploys of a Machiavelli or Gracián who uses simulation and dissimulation against friend and foe alike to achieve his political ambitions for the Cheruskers. M. Dönike, ' " . . . durch List und den ganzen Inbegriff jener Künste, die die Notwehr dem Schwachen in die Hände gibt." Zur Gedankenfigur der Notwehr bei Kleist' (53–66), takes the 'Notwehr Distichon' from the *Berliner Abendblättern* as an indication of how to read K.'s deceptive writing about the French occupiers. The political ploy seems more optimistic than the repeatedly failed attempts at simulation and dissimulation in K.'s fiction, but in the end, these fail too: K. is censored and, like Gustav in *Die Verlobung in St Domingo*, he takes his own life in an act of 'self-defence from the unbearable'. In S. Peters, 'Wie Geschichte geschehen lassen? Theatralität und Anekdotizität in den *Berliner Abendblättern*' (67–86), the replacement of swords by pistols in duels coincides with the change in the conception of history around 1800: in the pistol duel, structured, formal acting culminates in an unpredictable outcome. In his *Berliner Abandblättern*, K. uses a series of feints to act out history in advance in the hopes of causing a particular outcome. Simulation and dissimulation collapse into unity, as one simulates that which already exists. B. Theisen, 'Der Bewunderer des Shakespeare. Kleists Skeptizismus' (87–108), claims that unlike contemporary German admirers of Shakepeare, K. was not interested in poetological devices nor in the mixture of 'naive' and 'sentimental', but rather in the underlying scepticism. S. allowed his characters only partial glimpses of truth; K. drives the impossibility of complete knowledge even further in his depictions. In G. Brandstetter, 'Duell im Spiegel. Zum Rahmenspiel in Kleists *Amphitryon* (109–27), the

*Spiegelgefecht*, or a fencer's practice in front of a mirror, is taken as a paradigm for K.'s preoccupation in *Amphitryon* (and elsewhere) with the double nature of the mirror, which both reflects back the self and splits an identity into observer and observed. Amphitryon finds himself duelling to restore his honour — his identity — in a play where no one's identity is certain. M. Ott, ' "... ich will keine andre Ehre mehr, als deine Schande..." Zu Ehre, Duell und Geschlechterdifferenz in Kleists Erzählungen' (144–65), appeals to recent writings on the idea of honour (U. Frevert, J. Butler, P. Bourdieu) to discuss *Die Marquise von O*... and *Der Zweikampf* in terms of the 'casuist' arguments about honour. K. radically undermines discourse on the supposed norms of morality, law, and honour at a time when these ideas were in any case undergoing a radical shift. P. Dettmering, 'Die Sprachduelle in den Dramen Kleists' (166–73), uses psychoanalytic theory to show how *Sprachduellen* in the dialogue sequences where two or more characters talk at cross-purposes come about when one character concretizes a word in an attempt to deny (*verleugnen*) something unpleasant. Examples are taken from *Der zerbrochene Krug*, *Amphitryon*, and *Prinz Friedrich von Homburg*. E. Bronfen, 'Liebeszerstükkelung: *Penthesilea* mit Shakespeare gelesen' (174–93), boldly reads *Penthesilea* together with Tim Burton's 1990s film *Batman Returns* and Shakespeare's *A Midsummer Night's Dream* in order to 'cross-map' the fear of losing one's self in love. M. Schuller, 'Pfeil und Asche. Zu Kleists Erzählung *Der Zweikampf*' (194–202), seeks out linguistic associations between the names of the two enemy protagonists to show that they are one of a series of pairings in this story. The mediaeval setting reveals itself as a parody, as the battle between '*Bedeutungsfülle und Sinnesverlust*' remains unresolved. U. Frevert, 'Die Sprache der Ehre. Heinrich von Kleist und die Duellpraxis seiner Zeit' (215–21), studies K.'s challenging of F. von Raumer to a duel in the light of contemporary ideas about duelling. The duel is not an act of private revenge, but a public show of honour. Once a challenge is accepted, the original insult is forgotten, and the two duellists are on an entirely equal basis in terms of honour and risk, regardless of the outcome. Also in this volume: U. Fülleborn, 'Die Geburt der Tragödie aus dem Scheitern aller Berechnungen. Die frühen Briefe Heinrichs von Kleists und *Die Familie Schroffenstein*' (225–47); H. F. Weiss, 'Eine neuentdeckte Fassung von Heinrich von Kleists "Das letzte Lied" ' (251–65); C. Benthien, 'Gesichtsverlust und Gewaltsamkeit. Zur Psychodynamik von Scham und Schuld in Kleists *Familie Schroffenstein*' (128–43); W. Struck, 'Schwarz — Weiss — Rot, oder "Lernt des Verräthers Mitleid in Domingo." *Die Verlobung in St Domingo* zwischen Befreiungskrieg und Kolonialismus' (203–13).

C. Müller-Tragin, 'Hans Kolhase und Michael Kohlhaas. Unwahrscheinliche Wahrhaftigkeiten', *Heilbronner Kleist-Blätter*, 7:9–40, sets the context of the historical feud, the documents for which were only rediscovered a few years ago, and then investigates K.'s fictional working of the material. Also included in this volume is a report of a colloquium: B. Gribnitz, 'Erotik, Sexualität und Kleist. Das International Kolloquium des Kleist-Archivs Sembdner' (41–49), as well as a bibliography (64–86), information on the teaching of K. in German universities (87–90), the performance of his works on stage (91–92), and other matters relating to the archives. Also noted: László Földényi, *Heinrich von Kleist im Netz der Wörter*, Munich, Matthes und Seitz, 400 pp.; Bernd Hamacher, *Heinrich von Kleist. Prinz Friedrich von Homburg, Erläuterung und Dokumente*, Stuttgart, Reclam, 203 pp.; Nancy Nobile, *The School of Days: Heinrich von Kleist and the Traumas of Education*, Detroit, Wayne State U.P., 267 pp.; B. Franco, 'From popular genre to aesthetic model. The marionette theater according to Kleist', *EG*, 54:391–413; L. Van Eynde, 'Kleist's journey to Wurzburg and the epistolary birth of a "dramatic" work', *ib.*, 217–240; A. Esterhammer, ' "The Duel": Kleist's scandal of the speaking body', *ERR*, 19:1–22; F. Pan, 'Defending the premodern household against the bourgeois family: anti-Enlightenment anticolonialism in Heinrich von Kleist's *Die Verlobung in St Domingo*', *ColGer*, 32:165–99; J. Hibberd, 'Paris fashions in Kleist's *Berliner Abendblätter*', *MLR*, 94:122–31; W. Hulk, ' "Zerscherbtes Paktum" — "La tête sur un plat": über einige Bruchstücke bei Kleist und Flaubert', pp. 38–55 of *Über das fragment/Du fragment*, ed. Arlette Camion et al., Heidelberg, Winter, viii + 320 pp.

NOVALIS. Herbert Uerlings, *Novalis*, Stuttgart, Reclam, 1998, 248 pp., is a handy biography and interpretation of the poet. Irene Bark, *'Steine in Potenzen.' Konstruktive Rezeption der Minerologie bei Novalis* (Hermaea, n. F., 88), Tübingen, Niemeyer, xi + 509 pp., seeks to bring the poetological and scientific ideas of N. together within the context of contemporary scientific discoveries. The language seems unnecessarily difficult and thus the book presents a disappointingly rough read, though the interdisciplinary nature of the topic itself is quite exciting.

J. Endres, 'Novalis und das Lustspiel. Ein vergessener Beitrag zur Geschichte der Gattung', *Aurora*, 58, 1998:19–33, explains that although N. never produced any comedy, the comic figures strongly in his theoretical writings. The relief it could provide from the serious business of 'romanticizing' the world remained regettably out of N.'s own reach. L. Pikulik, ' "Sehnsucht nach dem Tode." Novalis' sechste *Hymne an die Nacht* im kontextuellen Zusammenhang', *ib.*, 35–47, reads the poem not as pathological nor as Christian, but as a thoroughly Modern(ist) preoccupation with death.

Also noted: Verena Anna Lukas, \**Der Dialog im Dialog: Das Inzitament bei Friedrich von Hardenberg* (ZGS, 55), 202 pp.; A. Kuzniar, 'The crystal revenge': the hypertrophy of the visual in Novalis and Tieck', *GR*, 74:214–28; L. Margantin, 'The figures of Orpheus and Jesus in the works of Novalis', *Romantisme*, 29:5–17; H. Schanze, 'Das romantische Fragment zwischen Chamfort und Nietzsche: über einige historische Widersprüche im Fragmentbegriff bei Friedrich Schlegel und Novalis', pp. 30–37 of *Über das fragment/Du fragment*, ed. Arlette Camion et al., Heidelberg, Winter, viii + 320 pp.

RICHTER, JEAN PAUL. This year saw a revival of interest in J.P., with three monographs solely or largely dedicated to him. Gustav Lohmann, *Jean Paul: Entwicklung zum Dichter*, Würzburg, Königshausen & Neumann, 668 pp., presents an inner, rather than outwardly directed biography, defining the man through his works. It is relatively hard-going for the reader, perhaps because the obscurity of the subject, J.P. himself, makes clear writing well-nigh impossible. The rather theory-laden Beatrice Mall-Grob, *Fiktion des Angfangs: Literarische und Kindheitsmodelle bei Jean Paul und Adalbert Stifter*, Stuttgart–Weimar, Metzler, 414 pp., justifies a comparison of the two authors because they stand in a close intertextual relationship to one another and they both wrote in times of great social change. As in several of the general studies of Romanticism this year, literary texts are taken as fruitful objects of study for extra-literary purposes — here the conception of childhood — because the fictional form allows for innovation, play, and a combination of opposing ideas in its alogical presentation. The opposing ideas studied here are conceptions of childhood that are separative (that the child is completely other, lost in time, irretrievable, *à la* Rousseau) versus those which are integrative (that the child remains instead an ineradicable part of the adult's psyche, in the manner of the much later Freud). Lastly Eckart Goebel, *Am Ufer der zweiten Welt: Jean Pauls 'poetische Landschaftsmalerei'*, Tübingen, Stauffenberg, 163 pp., uses the discussion of landscape painting in the novels to develop J.P.'s aesthetic theory, rather than looking at the overtly theoretical *Vorschule*. Three novels, *Hesperus*, *Titan*, and *Der Komet* are thus shown to hang together in a way previously not noted by scholars, as each novel expands upon and replaces the earlier one in terms of its aesthetic theory. J.P. does not create a theodicy in response to the Kantian critique of rationalism, but rather leads the reader to the 'bank' only, without carrying across into another world.

SCHELLING. Noted: Markus Hoffmann, \**Über den Staat hinaus: Eine historisch-systematische Untersuchung zu F. W. J. Schellings Rechts- und*

*Staatsphilosophie* (Zürcher Studien zur Rechtsgeschichte, 37), Zurich, Schulthess, 239 pp.; Jörg Ewertowski, *\*Die Freiheit des Anfangs und das Gesetz des Werdens: Zur Metaphorik von Mangel und Fülle in F. W. J. Schellings Prinzip des Schöpferischen*, Stuttgart–Bad Canstatt, Frommann-Holzboog, 444 pp.; Lothar Knatz, *\*Geschichte — Kunst — Mythos: Schellings Philosophie und die Perspektive einer philosophischen Mythostheorie*, Würzburg, Königshausen & Neumann, 351 pp.; F. Steinkamp, 'Schelling's concept of the will', *Idealistic Studies*, 29:103–19.

SCHLEGEL, FRIEDRICH. Berbeli Wanning, *Friedrich Schlegel: zur Einführung*, Hamburg, Junius, 172 pp., is a useful and concise introduction the the varied output of the writer, scholar, and philosopher. An argument pointing out S.'s innovativeness and his articulation of a feminine voice occurs in Peter Schnyder, *Die Magie der Rhetorik. Poesie, Philosophie und Politik in Friedrich Schlegels Frühwerk*, Paderborn, Schöningh, 248 pp. A forgotten chapter in Romanticism Studies is S.'s interest in rhetoric at a time when it had fallen out of favour in a reaction to the stilted, mechanical verse of the 18th century. Kant feared rhetoric as dangerously misleading for the masses, but S. appreciated its democratic potential, exemplified in the right to freedom of speech. Furthermore, as made evident in the much quoted Fragment 116 ('die Poesie mit der Philosophie und Rhetorik in Berührung zu setzen'), S. also saw its poetic potential and stressed language's function as a means of creating, not merely carrying, knowledge.

Also noted: Edith Höltenschmidt, *\*Die Mittelalterrezeption der Brüder Schlegel*, Paderborn, Schöningh, 900 pp.; P. D. Krause, 'Zu Errata in der Biographie des jungen Friedrich Schlegels', *ZDP*, 118:592–600; L.C. Roetzel, 'Positionality and the male philosopher: Friedrich Schlegel's "Über die Philosophie: An Dorothea"', *MDLK*, 91:188–207.

SCHLEGEL-SCHELLING, CAROLINE. Franziska Meyer, *Avantgarde im Hinterland: Caroline Schlegel-Schelling in der DDR-Literatur* (GLC, 25), xiii + 258 pp., is a reception history which stresses the author less than her function in a particular time and place. S.-S.'s existence as a woman between the social utopianism of the Mainzer Republic and the individualism of the Romantic Jena allowed her to function as a catalyst for pre-*Wende* thinking on the function of society, the relation of public to private spheres, and the role of the feminine in society. Despite its modern focus, the book will be of great interest to S.-S. scholars as well as those interested in the *Erbe-Debatte* in the DDR.

SCHOPENHAUER, JOHANNA. Noted: A. Gilleir, 'Discourse between empirical experience and aesthetic hermeneutics — sociocultural observations on Johanna Schopenhauer's travel books', *EG*, 54:196–215.

SPIESS, C. H.. A. Kosenina, 'Gläserne Brust, lesbares Herz: ein psychopathographischer Topos im Zeichen physiognomischer Tyrannei bei C. H. Spiess und anderen', *GLL*, 52:151–65, focuses on Spiess's *Biographien der Wahnsinnigen*, especially the story of 'Jakob W**r', to trace the growing fear of being 'read' by the sciences of physiognomy and 'pathognomy'. Other examples from classical and romantic authors include F. M. Klinger, Goethe, Jean Paul, E.T.A. Hoffmann, and the author of the *Nachtwachen*.

STEFFENS, HENRIK. *Henrik Steffens: Vermittler zwischen Natur und Geist*, ed. Otto Lorenz and Bernd Henningsen, Berlin Vlg, 163 pp., is the third volume in a series on Germany and its northern neighbours, and is thus of somewhat marginal interest to the student of German Romanticism. Yet the Norwegian-born philosopher taught at various German universities and was acquainted with leading figures of the Romantic and Classical movements, and so national boundaries prove inadequate for defining the field. Of particular interest to the Germanist will be the following articles: Jan-Erik Ebbestad Hansen, 'Böhme — Schelling — Steffens. Eine deutsche Filationslinie', *ib.*, 27–41; Bengt Algot Sørensen, 'Schellings Natur- und Kunstphilosophie im Kontext seiner Zeit', *ib.*, 43–65; and Dietrich von Engelhardt, 'Henrik Steffens im Spektrum der Naturwissenschaft und Naturphilosophie in der Epoche der Romantik', *ib.*, 89–112.

TIECK, LUDWIG. Noted: B. Prager, 'The contours of the visual arts in Tieck's 'Franz Sternbalds Wanderungen': text/image/phantasm', *Seminar*, 35:89–206; R. Hillenbrand, 'Tieck's Novella "Der Gelehrte" ', *ib.*, 283–94.

VARNHAGEN, RAHEL LEVIN. Noted: A. Elon, 'Rahel Varnhagen: the life of a Jewess', *The New York Review of Books*, 46.3:19–22.

WERNER, ZACHARIAS. Noted: *Helenik und Romantik: Ausgewählte Gedichte*, ed. Brigit Schmidt-Rösemann, Hanover, Revonnah, 48 pp.; N. Saul, 'The body, death, mutilation and decay in Zacharias Werner', *GLL*, 52:255–70.

WOLZOGEN, CAROLINE VON. Noted: L. Sharpe, 'Female illness and male heroism: the works of Caroline von Wolzogen', *GLL*, 52:84–96.

## LITERATURE, 1830–1880

By BOYD MULLAN, *Senior Lecturer in German in the University of St Andrews*

### 1. GENERAL

REFERENCE WORKS AND GENERAL STUDIES. The third, revised and enlarged edition of the *Quellenlexikon zur deutschen Literaturgeschichte: Personal- und Einzelwerkbibliographien der internationalen Sekundärliteratur 1945–1990 zur deutschen Literatur von den Anfängen bis zur Gegenwart*, ed. Heiner Schmidt et al., has reached the letter M with the appearance of vols 18–21, Duisburg, Vlg für pädagogische Dokumentation, 512 pp. per vol. A major new reference work is the *Encyclopedia of the Novel*, ed. Paul Schellinger et al., 2 vols, Chicago–London, Fitzroy Dearborn, 1998, xxv + 1613 pp. This is a collaborative effort by over 350 scholars from around the world and contains a total of some 650 articles on novelists, individual works, and various technical, theoretical, and historical aspects of the novel form. The 19th-c. German novel does not fare well in the inevitable process of selection. Only Fontane, Keller, and Stifter merit separate entries as novelists, and *Effi Briest* is the only work to merit an entry by title. There are however four 'thematic' entries by Germanists: Michael Minden on the *Bildungsroman*, Malcolm Humble on the 'German Novel', Peter Hutchinson on the 'Novella', and Andreas Solbach on the German-language 'Swiss Novel'. The full index in vol. 2 reveals references to a number of writers who do not merit their own headword (Raabe, Storm, Meyer, Sacher-Masoch). *Von der Romantik bis zum Naturalismus*, ed. Frank Rainer Max et al. (UB, 18002) 558 pp., is the second volume of *Reclams Romanlexikon* and a welcome addition to this useful set. It provides reliable new plot summaries, contributed by leading modern specialists, of novels and Novellen by almost 100 (mainly canonical) 19th-c. authors. The set is to comprise five volumes in all. *Metzler-Lexikon Literatur- und Kulturtheorie: Ansätze — Personen — Grundbegriffe*, ed. Ansgar Nünning, Stuttgart–Weimar, Metzler, 1998, 593 pp., covers a wide range of names and terms from ancient times to the most modern. Volker Meid, *Sachwörterbuch zur deutschen Literatur*, Stuttgart, Reclam, 571 pp., provides useful factual information on a large number of terms and topics. *Metzler Autorinnen Lexikon*, ed. Ute Hechtfischer et al., Stuttgart, Metzler, 1998, vi + 617 pp., contains over 400 articles, usually one or one and a half pages long, on women writers of many countries and languages. Where possible, the entries are accompanied by a picture or photograph of the subject and by short bibliogaphical references. Most, but not all, of the writers are from the 19th or 20th cs. Coverage of 19th-c. German literature is reasonably good. Most of the big names such as Droste-Hülshoff, Lewald, and Ebner-Eschenbach are included. Among the omissions are Louise Aston, Clara Mundt, and Eugenie Marlitt. *The Feminist Encyclopedia of German Literature*, ed. Friederike Eigler et al., Westport, Conn.–London, Greenwood, 1997, xiii + 676 pp., is not yet another guide to women's writing but a guide to German literature in general seen from a feminist perspective. Numerous entries pertain to the 19th century. The excellent *Companion to German Literature*, ed. Eda Sagarra and Peter Skrine, Blackwell, 1997 (see *YWMLS*, 59:783–84) has been reissued at a very affordable price in paperback. *The Cambridge Companion to Modern German Culture*, ed. Eva Kolinsky et al., CUP, 1998, xxiv + 365 pp., is marginally relevant to our period since most of the chapters take as their starting point either 1848 or 1871. Two especially useful chapters are those by J. Breuilly, 'German national identity' (44–66), and H.-G. Betz, 'Elites and class structure' (67–85). *Das unbekannte Erbe: Literarische Nachlässe und Literaturarchive in Österreich*, ed. Hildemar Holl et al. (Salzburger Beiträge, 33; SAG, 353), 1997, 137 pp.

THEMES. Hildegard Kernmayer, *Judentum im Wiener Feuilleton (1848–1903): Exemplarische Untersuchungen zum literarästhetischen und politischen Diskurs der Moderne* (CJ, 24), 1998, ix + 326 pp., is a 1997 Graz dissertation which examines literary and political aspects of a wide range of Jewish contributors to the Viennese *Feuilleton*, including among others Saphir, Kürnberger, and Schlögl. Also on the theme of Jewish literature is *Ghetto Writing: Traditional and Eastern Jewry in German-Jewish Prose Literature from Heine to Hilsenrath*, ed. Anne Fuchs et al. (SGLLC), 231 pp. Women's writing is another theme that continues to attract much attention. Ruth-Ellen Boetcher Joeres, *Respectability and Deviance: Nineteenth-Century German Women Writers and the Ambiguity of Representation* (Women in Culture and Society), Chicago U.P., xxxiv + 349 pp., writes from a strongly feminist perspective and portrays the careers, and the struggle for acceptance, of a wide range of 19th-c. women writers. Those discussed range from Droste-Hülshoff in the early part of the century through Louise Aston, Otto-Peters, Lewald, François, and Marlitt to Hedwig Dohm at the end. Some less well known names are also included, though there are surprising omissions too, such as the names of Johanna Schopenhauer or Gabriele Reuter. The emphasis is very much on the biographies of the selected writers, the place of women in society, and the interesting question of canon formation (which is discussed intelligently). There is much analysis of the women's letters and autobiographical writings, but almost no comment at all on their creative work. Karin Tebben, *Deutschsprachige Schriftstellerinnen des Fin de siècle*, WBG, viii + 350 pp., has an introductory chapter by the editor followed by 15 further chapters each portraying a leading female writer of the period. Among those treated are Ebner-Eschenbach and Gabriele Reuter. *Gender and Germanness: Cultural Productions of a Nation*, ed. Patricia Herminghouse et al. (Modern German Studies, 4), Providence, RI, Berghahn, 1997, vii + 344 pp., contains two contributions on the 19th c.: R. A. Berman, 'How to think about Germany: nationality, gender, and obsession in Heine's "Night thoughts"' (66–81); and P. Herminghouse, 'The lady's auxiliary of German literature: nineteenth-century women writers and the quest for a national literary identity' (141–58). *Gendering German Studies: New Perspectives on German Literature and Culture*, ed. Margaret Littler, Oxford, Blackwell, 1997, 216 pp., is an interdisciplinary collection of essays, ranging from the Middle Ages to the present day, that explore the impact of institutional and linguistic structures on women's lives. Christa Gürtler and Sigrid Schmid-Bortenschlager, *\*Eigensinn und Widerstand: Schriftstellerinnen der Habsburgermonarchie*, Vienna, Überreuter, 1998, 269 pp. Christoph E. Schweitzer, *\*Men Viewing Women as Art Objects: Studies in German Literature* (SGLLC), 1998, xiv + 103 pp., has material on Stifter's *Nachsommer*, Mörike's *Maler Nolten*, and Storm's *Immensee*. Irmgard Scheitler, *Gattung und Geschlecht: Reisebeschreibungen deutscher Frauen 1780–1850* (STSL, 67), ix + 312 pp. *Geschlecht—Literatur—Geschichte I*, ed. Gudrun Loster-Schneider et al. (Mannheimer Studien zur Literatur- und Kulturwissenschaft, 15), St Ingbert, Röhrig, 272 pp., has articles on Ebner-Eschenbach, Lewald, Stifter, and Raabe.

*Ottocento tedesco: Da Goethe a Nietzsche. Per Luciano Zagari*, ed. G. Catalano et al. (Il pensiero e la storia, 49), Naples, Città del sole, 1998, 388 pp., contains: S. Corrado, 'Platen, Kavafis: malincolia e ripetizione' (187–218); F. Brogelli, 'Sui sonetti di Heine: proposizione e dissoluzione della forma rigida nel *Buch der Lieder*' (219–36); A. Schininà, 'La crisi del narratore in *Der arme Spielmann* di Grillparzer' (237–54); P. Gheri, 'Franz Grillparzer: mito e critica della cultura in *Das goldene Vlies*' (255–78); E. Fiandra, 'Il sigillo dell'"eros": *Das alte Siegel* di A. S.' (279–309); G. Catalano, 'Reperti di un passato minore: Il "museo" del "Signore di Stechlin"' (311–26). *L'Allemagne, des lumières à la modernité: Mélanges offerts à Jean-Louis Bandet*, ed. Pierre Labaye, Rennes U.P., 1997, 422 pp., contains: J. Charue, 'L'espace et le temps dans la *Sappho* de Grillparzer' (121–31); J. Charue-Ferrucci, 'La notion de barbarie dans la trilogie de Grillparzer *La Toison d'or*' (133–43); L. Hay, 'Heinrich Heine, plume à la main' (145–56); R. Anglade, ' "Versifizirtes Lebensblut": Heines Gedicht "Der Asra"' (157–70); V. Croz, 'Expérience et représentation de l'histoire: quelques remarques sur la recherche de la forme dans *Witiko* d'Adalbert Stifter' (171–82); A. Cosic, 'Un autre "village" sur une autre "lande": la nouvelle de Theodor Storm *Draussen im Heidedorf.* Réécriture d'un fait divers et exploration du réel' (183–95); M. Haslé, 'Le pasteur de la Redoute Rouge: *Stopfkuchen* de Wilhelm Raabe et la religion' (197–210); D. Iehl, 'Büchner et Beckett' (405–13). Aude Locatelli, *La Lyre, la plume et le temps: Figures de musiciens dans le 'Bildungsroman'* (Communicatio, 19), Tübingen, Niemeyer, 1998, vii + 336 pp., compares ten French and German texts from the mid-19th c. to the present, including Grillparzer's *Der arme Spielmann*, Hesse's *Gertrud*, Mann's *Dr Faustus*, Bernhard's *Der Untergeher*, and Jelinek's *Die Klavierspielerin. Images modernes et contemporaines de l'homme baroque*, ed. Jean-Marie Paul (Bibliothèque le texte et l'idée, 8), Nancy, Centre de Recherches Germaniques de l'Université de Nancy, 1997, 310 pp., has two articles on the 19th c.: M.-O. Blum, ' "Les Albigeois" de Lenau: l'étrange et l'excessif' (133–42); and J. Charue-Ferrucci, 'Un avatar de l'homme baroque à l'époque Biedermeier' (167–76). *From Classical Shades to Vickers Victorious: Shifting Perspectives in British German Studies. Papers delivered at the Conference of University Teachers of German, University of Leicester, 6–8 April 1998*, ed. Steve Giles et al. (Conference of University Teachers of German, Proceedings, 1), Berne, Lang, 257 pp., has: A. Goodbody, 'From Raabe to Amery: German literature in ecocritical perspective' (77–99); R. Atkins, 'Versions of reality: Hochhuth's *Effis Nacht*, Fontane and Spielhagen' (97–110). P. Böckmann, *Dichterische Wege der Subjektivierung: Studien zur deutschen Literatur im 19. und 20. Jahrhundert*, ed. C. König et al., Tübingen, Niemeyer, viii + 484 pp., reprints 16 essays by Böckmann on a range of authors including Grillparzer, Stifter, Storm, Fontane, and Nietzsche.

Harald Steiner, *Das Autorenhonorar: Seine Entwicklungsgeschichte vom 17. bis 19. Jahrhundert* (Buchwissenschaftliche Beiträge aus dem Deutschen Bucharchiv München, 59), Wiesbaden, Harrassowitz, 1998, vii + 392 pp., documents the policy on authors' royalties of such major publishers as Cotta and Vandenhoeck & Ruprecht, albeit paying more attention to the 18th c. than to the 19th. This is nevertheless an important and interesting book. Peter Sprengel, *Von Luther zu Bismarck: Kulturkampf und nationale Identität bei Theodor Fontane, Conrad Ferdinand Meyer und Gerhart Hauptmann*, Bielefeld, Aisthesis, 120 pp. Gesa von Essen, *Hermannsschlachten: Germanen- und Römerbilder in der Literatur des 18. und 19. Jahrhunderts*, Göttingen, Wallstein, 1998, 288 pp., is a 1997 Göttingen dissertation that examines the use made of the Arminius myth in the process of cultural 'decolonization' by which Germany shook off foreign (French) influence and established its own national consciousness and cultural identity. The author selects four major treatments of the subject, those of J. E. Schlegel, Klopstock, Kleist, and Grabbe, and brings out well the different accents that they each placed on it. At the heart of the myth is the sharp contrast drawn by Tacitus between the freedom-loving, natural, morally upright 'Germanen' and the tyrannical, artificial, and decadent Romans. In the late 18th and early 19th cs the Germanic-Roman conflict was used as a paradigm for the cultural and political opposition of Germany and France, and the supposed virtues of the ancient 'Germanen' came to be identified as typical of the modern German. Reception of the Roman past was quite different in France, where the defeat of Vercingetorix could be welcomed because it meant the eclipse of barbarian Gaul and led ultimately to the creation of modern French civilization. Another treatment of the Arminius theme is that of H. Fröhlich, 'Arminius und die Deutschen: ein politischer Mythos des 19. Jahrhunderts', *Aurora*, 59 : 173–88. F. Apel, *Deutscher Geist und deutsche Landschaft: Eine Topographie*, Munich, Albrecht Knaus, 1998, 251 pp., examines the use of landscape in the writing of nearly 30 authors from Jakob Böhme in the 17th to Herta Müller in the late 20th century. Among the 19th-c. writers discussed are Droste-Hülshoff, Heine, and Fontane. Apel's main point is that there is a unique attitude over a long period of time on the part of German writers (and their readership) to the German landscape that they describe and the cultural and political weight that they place upon it. The imaginative experience of landscape, he argues, can be used to represent symbolically both the possibility of escape into individual freedom and the possibility of achieving a protective sense of belonging, of membership of a wider national and political community. Josef Nadler's *Literaturgeschichte des deutschen Volkes* attracts much negative comment. Apel's topic is an interesting one, but his short and rather woolly chapters — typically five to ten pages long — do not always do justice to the material and leave the impression that further research is needed. Swantje Christow, *Der Lilith-Mythos in der Literatur: Der Wandel des Frauenbildes im Schaffen des 19. und 20. Jahrhunderts*, Aachen, Shaker, 1998, 112 pp., gives prominence to the work of Isolde Kurz and Paul Heyse. *Der Streit um die Metapher: Poetologische Texte von Nietzsche bis Handke. Mit kommentierenden Studien*, ed. Klaus Müller-Richter et al., WBG, 1998, ix + 400 pp., prints the reflections of leading authors, beginning with Nietzsche, on the nature of metaphorical language. Susanne Zantop, *Kolonialphantasien im vorkolonialen Deutschland 1770–1870* (PSQ, 158), 314 pp., considers the persistent preoccupation of German writers, even before the first colonies were gained in the 1880s, with the portrayal in innumerable novels, *Singspiele*, dramas, and epics of an ideal German society located abroad. B. Jebing, 'Das Rom-Bild in der deutschen Literatur des 18. und 19. Jahrhunderts', *DUS*, 51 : 16–27, has brief comment on Platen and Heine. Stefan Andriopoulis, 'Besessene Körper:

"criminelle Suggestion" und "Körperschaftsverbrechen" in Literatur, Medizin und Rechtswissenschaft des späten 19. Jahrhunderts', *Scientia Poetica*, 2, 1998:129–50. C. Haug, ' "Das halbe Geschäft beruht auf Eisenbahnstationen . . .": zur Entstehungsgeschichte der Eisenbahnbibliotheken im 19. Jahrhundert', *IASL*, 23, 1998:70–117. H. Eggert, 'Roman und Wissenschaft im 19. Jahrhundert: ein Essay', *Fest. Lämmert*, 97–106. C. Begemann, 'Der steinerne Leib der Frau: ein Phantasma in der europäischen Literatur des 18. und 19. Jahrhunderts', *Aurora*, 59:135–59, has some comment on Keller, Stifter, Heine, and Sacher-Masoch among others. E. Joseph, 'Himmelhohe Zacken: über ein Motiv bei Ernst Ludwig Kirchner, Ludwig Richter, Friedrich Nietzsche und im *Zauberberg* von Thomas Mann', *LWU*, 32:225–35, is concerned with the treatment of the Tinzenhorn near Davos as a literary motif. U. J. Beil, 'Die "verspätete Nation" und ihre "Weltliteratur": deutsche Kanonbildung im 19. und frühen 20. Jahrhundert', Heydebrand, *Kanonbildung*, 323–40 and 443–45. V. Žmegač, 'Komparatistische Überlegungen zur Literatur des 19. Jahrhunderts', *ZGB*, 7, 1998:1–17.

LYRIC. Bernhard Sorg, *Lyrik interpretieren: Eine Einführung*, Bielefeld, Schmidt, 211 pp., offers definitions of critical terms and illustrative interpretations of poems from the 1600s to 1990. *Naturlyrik: Über Zyklen und Sequenzen im Werk von Annette von Droste-Hülshoff, Uhland, Lenau und Heine*, ed. G. Vonhoff (HKADL, 23), 1998, 283 pp., is a collective volume which publishes the results of a research project, conducted in 1996–97 in the university of Münster, into the process by which the tightly-structured lyric cycles such as Wilhelm Müller's *Winterreise* that were favoured by poets in the late 18th and early 19th cs gave way to more open, 'modern' groupings of poems such as Heine's *Buch der Lieder* or Baudelaire's *Les Fleurs du mal*. The nature poetry of Droste-Hülshoff, notably the *Haidebilder*, is seen by the Münster team as pivotal in this change. Most of the articles are by *Hauptseminar* students and it has to be said that their lack of experience sometimes shows, not least in the excessively heavy footnoting. The most substantial contribution is that of D. Jürgens, 'Der Schiffbruch des Ichs: Heines *Nordsee-Cyklen* als Teil des *Buchs der Lieder*' (119–60). The other articles in the volume are: D. Jürgens, ' "Im unbefriedeten Ganzen": Zyklen und Sequenzen in der Restaurationszeit' (9–17); G. Vonhoff, 'Aus Zyklus wird Sequenz: von Uhlands *Wanderliedern* zu Püttmanns *Wanderbildern*' (18–38); M. Binek, 'Eine Ordnung "zusammengebaut": "Die Elemente" von A. v. D.-H. im Vergleich mit Härsdorffers Tageszeiten-Zyklus' (39–55); T. Gombert, 'Kurzzyklen als Ausdruck der Krise: Lenaus "Winternacht" und A. v. D.-Hs "Am Weiher" ' (56–66); G. Bruch, ' "Mein Auge zündet sich — wo bin ich? — wo?": "Ein Sommernachtstraum" von A. v. D.-H." (67–79);

K. Ludwig, 'Gegen das Genrebild angeschrieben'': "Die Weiher" von A. v. D.-H.' (80–94); S. Pomp and T. Zumloh, 'Die Konkretion im Abstrakten: A. v. D.-Hs *Haidebilder*' (95–118); B. Bremer, ' "Wer heut draussen wandelt, braucht keine Gespenster'': A. v. D.-Hs "Volksglauben in den Pyrenäen" ' (161–76); S. Scho, 'Ihr Platz ist dazwischen: Heine und Courbet. Künstler in einer kunstlosen Zeit?' (177–206). *Frauen dichten anders: 181 Gedichte mit Interpretationen*, ed. M. Reich-Ranicki, Frankfurt–Leipzig, Insel, 1998, 859 pp., has interpretations of poems by 54 female writers. *Frankfurter Anthologie: Gedichte und Interpretationen*, 22, ed. Marcel Reich-Ranicki, Frankfurt, Insel, 300 pp., has interpretations of poems by Hoffmann von Fallersleben, Mörike, Storm, Fontane, and C. F. Meyer, all previously published in the *FAZ*. *Ein Fischer sass im Kahne: Die schönsten deutschen Balladen des 19. Jahrhunderts*, ed. Herbert Greiner-Mai et al. (ATV, 6026), 1998, 236 pp., contains a wide and varied selection of texts by authors ranging from Brentano to Liliencron. The obvious big names in the canon are well represented, but there are some intriguing novelties too. *Fundbuch der Gedichtinterpretation*, ed. Wulf Segebrecht, Paderborn–Munich, Schöningh, x + 530 pp. Rolf Selbmann, *\*Die simulierte Wirklichkeit: Zur Lyrik des Realismus*, Bielefeld, Aisthesis, 159 pp.

NARRATIVE. Todd Kontje, *Women, the Novel, and the German Nation 1771–1871: Domestic Fiction in the Fatherland*, CUP, 1998, xvi + 242 pp., gives an impressive survey of the historical development of 'domestic fiction' written by German women in the century from the beginnings of a national literature in Lessing's time to the foundation of the nation-state. Although 'domestic fiction' concentrates on the traditional feminine concerns of love, marriage, and family, these themes are inextricably bound up with wider issues of class, money, and politics so that the novels give a vivid picture of both private and public life in the Germany of the time. Kontje's method is traditional and empirical, avoiding all jargon and the modern obsession with methodology and arcane discourse theory. What he gives us instead is a series of beautifully clear and informative accounts of the main works of selected leading or representative writers, beginning with Sophie von La Roche and ending with Eugenie Marlitt. Other writers studied include Therese Huber, Johanna Schopenhauer, Droste-Hülshoff (*Ledwina*), Ida Hahn-Hahn, Fanny Lewald, and Louise Aston. We are at all times kept aware of the changing social and political background against which the texts were written. A particularly interesting aspect of the study is its focus on changing attitudes to sexuality. This excellent book is probably the best so far written in any language on 19th-c. German women's fiction. Wynfrid Kriegleder, *Vorwärts in die Vergangenheit: Das Bild der*

*USA im deutschsprachigen Roman von 1776 bis 1855* (Edition Orpheus, 13), Tübingen, Stauffenburg, 494 pp., is a 1997 Vienna *Habilitationsschrift*. Kriegleder has certainly uncovered a most interesting field of study, and he has done it justice, for the book is thoroughly researched with over 80 novels analysed and it is well and clearly written. The work is divided into three main chapters, the first covering the period 1776 to 1805 (the early years of American independence and the French Revolution in Europe), the second covering the period 1805 to 1830 (the time of consolidation of the American republic and of the Napoleonic era in Europe), and the third dealing with the years 1830 to 1855 (the age of American expansion and of renewed European interest in America following the revolutions of 1830). The *Amerikaroman* is seen as a genre rooted in the critical tradition of the *Aufklärung*. America is portrayed as a transatlantic Utopia which functions as a vehicle for implied criticism of conditions in Europe, though ironically what these novels often advocate as Utopia is a return to an idealized European past that in reality can never be restored. The genre declines rapidly in the 1850s because of the failure of the 1848 revolution and the tendency of the Realist writers to look inward to life in Germany. The *Amerikaroman* loses its critical function and descends into the novel of adventure (Karl May) intended only to entertain and devoid of serious political and social content. The work of Sealsfield is seen as the high point of the genre; other 19th-c. authors studied include Laube, Gerstäcker, Lewald, and Kürnberger. Marina Zitterer, *Der Frauenroman bei Fontane, Lewald und Marlitt: Eine Analyse des feministischen Ganzheitskonzepts im humanistischen Sinn* (Veröffentlichungen aus dem Forschungsprojekt 'Literatur und Soziologie', 18), Klagenfurt, Inst. für Interdisziplinäre Forschung und Fortbildung der Universitäten Innsbruck, Klagenfurt, Wien, 1997, 234 pp., is a 1996 Klagenfurt dissertation. John Pizer, *Ego — alter ego: Double and/as Other in the Age of German Poetic Realism*, North Carolina U.P., 1998, xi + 157 pp. Frauke Berndt, *Anamnesis: Studien zur Topik der Erinnerung in der erzählenden Literatur zwischen 1800 und 1900. Moritz — Keller — Raabe* (Hermaea, 89), Tübingen, Niemeyer, vi + 528 pp., is a 1999 Frankfurt dissertation which discusses *Anton Reiser, Der grüne Heinrich*, and *Die Akten des Vogelsangs*. R. Bürner-Kotzam, 'Der Parasit als Gast in Erzählungen des bürgerlichen Realismus', pp. 131–55 of *Figures der/des Dritten: Erkundung interkultureller Zwischenräume*, ed. Claudia Breger et al. (Internationale Forschungen zur Allgemeinen und Vergleichenden Literaturwissenschaft, 30), Amsterdam, Rodopi, 1998, 269 pp.

DRAMA.   Manfred Brauneck's massive enterprise, *Die Welt als Bühne: Geschichte des europäischen Theaters*, Stuttgart, Metzler, has added vol. 3, *19. Jahrhundert und Jahrhundertwende*, xviii + 965 pp. Sascha

Kiefer, *Dramatik der Gründerzeit: Deutsches Drama und Theater 1870–1890*
(SBL, 53), 1997, 256 pp., fills a significant gap in German theatre
history with his informative and lucid account of a period that has
been surprisingly little researched. He rightly observes that most
scholars concern themselves with either the period 1820–1850, the
age of Grillparzer, Grabbe, and Büchner, or the period after 1889
when Hauptmann's *Vor Sonnenaufgang* appeared, while the years
1870–1890 are largely ignored. He begins with a chapter on the
(unhappy) state of the theatre in the years after the foundation of the
Empire, outlining the effect of the 'Gewerbefreiheit' of 1869, the
expansion of commercial theatres, the impact of the Meininger in
Berlin, the opening of the Deutsches Theater, and the role of
censorship. The main part of the book however consists of two long
chapters that deal in turn with the writers of popular dramas on
contemporary social themes, among them Paul Lindau, Richard
Voss, and Adolph L'Arronge, and the 'academic' playwrights such as
Albert Lindner and Adolf von Wilbrandt who wrote historical and
classicizing dramas of the kind still encouraged by the conservatively
minded committees that award distinctions like the Schiller prize. A
particularly valuable feature of the work is the prominence it gives to
the ideas and influence of leading critics of the time such as Karl
Frenzel and Rudolf von Gottschall. Despite its modest origins as a
1996 Saarbrücken dissertation this is an excellent book. One regrets
only the lack of an index that would have made its first-rate contents
more easily accessible. Wolfgang Struck, *\*Konfigurationen der Vergangenheit: Deutsche Geschichtsdramen im Zeitalter der Restauration* (SDL, 143),
1997, vi + 355 pp., is a 1995 Tübingen dissertation. *Die dramatische
Konfiguration*, ed. K. K. Polheim (Uni-Taschenbücher, 1996), Paderborn, Schöningh, 1997, 377 pp., contains: A.-K. Schatz, 'Die Konfiguration in C. D. Grabbes *Scherz, Satire, Ironie und tiefere Bedeutung*'
(101–24); A. Hagedorn, 'Von der Zerrissenheit zur Harmonie: die
dramatische Konfiguration in Ferdinand Raimunds Zauberspiel *Der
Alpenkönig und der Menschenfeind*' (125–46); M. Deufert, 'Lustspiel der
verkehrten Welt: Bemerkungen zur Konfiguration von G. Büchners
*Leonce und Lena*' (147–65); C. Kretschmann, ' ". . . bis zu den untersten
Abstufungen herab"': zur Konfiguration von Friedrich Hebbels
*Herodes und Mariamne*' (167–210). *Dramen des 19. Jahrhunderts*, ed. Theo
Elm (UB, 9631), 1997, 352 pp., contains: R. Drux, 'Christian Dietrich
Grabbe, *Scherz, Satire, Ironie und tiefere Bedeutung*' (71–95); P. Haida,
'Johann Nestroy, *Der böse Geist Lumpazivagabundus*: "Die Welt steht auf
kein' Fall mehr lang" ' (96–119); J. Schröder, 'Ferdinand Raimund,
*Der Verschwender*: eine Trilogie des Abschiednehmens' (120–40);
T. Elm, 'Georg Büchner, *Woyzeck*: zum Erlebnishorizont der Vor-
märzzeit' (141–71); H. Höller, 'Franz Grillparzer, *Weh dem, der lügt!*'

(172–202); J. Hein, 'Johann Nestroy, *Der Talisman*' (203–33); G. Häntzschel, 'Christian Friedrich Hebbel, *Maria Magdalena*' (234–52); M. Ritzer, 'Christian Friedrich Hebbel, *Agnes Bernauer*' (253–85); K. Wagner, 'Ludwig Anzengruber, *Der Meineidbauer*' (286–305). *Der Milde Knabe oder Die Natur eines Berufenen: Ein wissenschaftlicher Ausblick, Oskar Pausch zum Eintritt in den Ruhestand gewidmet*, ed. Georg Geldner (Mimundus, 9), Vienna, Böhlau, 1997, 333 pp., contains: W. E. Yates, ' "Was ich abschreibe, das bleibt abgeschrieben" ': zur Überlieferung von Nestroys Possen' (68–76); Paul S. Ulrich, 'The role of souffleur journals in the 19th century as exemplified by those of the Meiningen theatre' (77–112). *Der literarische Einfall: Über das Entstehen von Texten*, ed. Bernhard Fetz et al., Vienna, Zsolnay, 1998, 208 pp., contains: W. Obermaier, 'Johann Nepomuk Nestroy (1801–1862): *Karrikaturen-Charivari mit Heurathszweck*' (27–35); Id., 'Franz Grillparzer (1791–1872): *Libussa*' (197–203). Jerzy Got, *Das österreichische Theater in Lemberg im 18. und 19. Jahrhundert: Aus dem Theaterleben der Vielvölkermonarchie*, 2 vols (Theatergeschichte Österreichs, 10, Donaumonarchie, 4), VÖAW, 1997, xxi + 490, x + 491–875 pp. Jean Dewitz, *De Franz Prüller à Ludwig Thoma: Le 'Volkstheater' à Munich (1850–1914)* (Contacts: Série I, Theatrica, 20), Berne, Lang, xix + 537 pp., traces the evolution of the Munich variant of the *Volksstück* and considers the impact on it of changing political and cultural pressures, among them the cultural aspirations of Maximilian II in the 1850s. K. Kratzsch, 'Zur Puppenspielhandschrift F 5136 aus der Faust-Sammlung der Herzogin Anna Amalia Bibliothek zu Weimar', *Fest. Pensel*, 113–30, describes a *Puppenspiel* version of the Faust legend written by one Johannes Lick in Munich in 1865, and compares it with other 19th-c. versions such as that of Karl Simrock. Petra Hartmann, \**Faust und Don Juan: Ein Verschmelzungsprozess, dargestellt anhand der Autoren Wolfgang Amadeus Mozart, Johann Wolfgang von Goethe, Nikolaus Lenau, Christian Dietrich Grabbe, Gustav Kühne und Theodor Mundt*, Stuttgart, Ibidem, 1998, 144 pp.

MOVEMENTS AND PERIODS. A valuable publication which testifies to the strength of *Biedermeier* studies in British and Irish universities is *The Biedermeier and Beyond: Selected Papers from the Symposium held at St Peter's College, Oxford from 19–21 September 1997*, ed. I. F. Roe et al. (British and Irish Studies in German Language and Literature, 17), Berne, Lang, 253 pp. The volume contains: E. Bruckmüller, 'Biedermeier und österreichische Identität' (21–44); S. P. Scheichl, 'Die vaterländischen Balladen des österreichischen Biedermeier: Bausteine des Habsburgischen Mythos. Zu Ludwig August Frankls *Habsburglied*' (45–61); E. Sagarra, 'Benign authority and its cultivation in the *Biedermeier*' (63–73); P. Kampits, 'Das Biedermeier und die

Ursprünge der österreichischen Philosophie' (75–85); P. Branscombe, 'Attitudes towards nature in Biedermeier Vienna' (87–97);
A. Barker, ' "Often sublime and always pathetic": settings of Scottish
texts in Biedermeier Vienna and beyond' (99–106); I. F.
Roe, *Die Jüdin von Toledo* and changing views on women in the Biedermeier
and beyond' (107–26); J. Warren, 'Eduard von Bauernfeld and the
beginnings of Austrian social drama' (127–45); D. Zumbusch-
Beisteiner, '. . . unter charakteristischer Musik fällt der Vorhang'
(147–68, on Nestroy's *Lumpazivagabundus*); H. Ragg-Kirkby, '*Witiko*
and the absurd' (169–81); M. Rogers, 'Wiener Wohnkultur' (183–91);
K. Rossbacher, 'Friedrich Schlögl: Beamter im "Biedermeier" und
Feuilletonist im "Beyond" ' (193–214); Colin Walker, 'Ludwig August
Frankl and the reflection of the *Biedermeier*' (215–24); Alexander
Stillmark, ' "Es war alles gut und erfüllt": Rudolf Hans Bartsch's
*Schwammerl* and the making of the Schubert myth' (225–34); W. E.
Yates, 'The image of the *Biedermeier* age in early-twentieth-century
Vienna' (235–47). Laudably, though unusually for volumes of
conference proceedings, the book is provided with a helpful index of
names. *Literatur und Politik in der Heinezeit: Die 48er Revolution in Texten
zwischen Vormärz und Nachmärz*, ed. H. Kircher et al., Cologne, Böhlau,
1998, xvi + 260 pp., is a collaborative effort by 17 scholars from the
universities of Cologne and Cracow who view the 1848 Revolution
from a distance of 150 years and from a variety of perspectives. Their
aim is to examine both the social and political climate of Germany as
it is portrayed in the literature of the *Vormärz* leading up to the
explosive events of 1848, and the echo of this failed attempt at radical
democratic change in the literature of the *Nachmärz*. Heine is seen as
the most important and influential writer of the period. The individual
articles are: N. Mecklenburg, 'Durch politische Brille und Butzen-
scheibe: literarische Lutherbilder in der Heine-Zeit' (1–15, on the
attempts of both conservatives and liberals to claim Luther for their
cause); K. Jastal, ' "Eine tadelhafte Unziemlichkeit": über eine
politische Episode E. T. A. Hoffmanns' (17–25, on Heine's criticism
of *Meister Floh*); K. Lipinski, 'Politik in Goethes *Faust II*' (27–39);
S. Frydel, 'Der deutsche Nationalismus und die europäische Einheit'
(41–47, on the growth of German nationalism in the period of
Romanticism and the *Befreiungskriege*); R. Drux, 'Mit romantischen
Traumfrauen gegen die Pest der Zeit: Heinrich Heines *Florentinische
Nächte* im "dritten Teil ses Salons" ' (49–64, on Heine's criticism of
*Restaurationszeit* society); A. Simonis, ' "Profezeien Sie uns die Zukunft
. . .": Allianz und (verborgene) Kontroverse zwischen Bettine von
Arnim und den "Jungdeutschen" ' (65–81, on Arnim's *Dies Buch gehört
dem König*); S. Grimm, 'Das Allgemeine im Subjektiven: Revolution
des Bewusstseins im Theater des Vormärz' (83–97, on Grillparzer,

Grabbe, Büchner, and Hebbel); D. Fulda, ' "Letzter Dichter in einer prosaischen Zeit": Grillparzers Kritik am Historismus und die dualistische Struktur seiner Habsburgerdramen' (99–121); A. Kuhlmann, 'Die Amazone im Salon: Frauenbilder und Revolutionsdarstellung bei Louise Aston' (123–36); J. Buszko, 'Ein weniger bekannter polnischer Aufstand: der Krakauer Aufstand des Jahres 1846' (137–48); H. Kircher, ' "Arznei auf Honigkuchen": zur sozialkritischen Dorfgeschichte im Vormärz am Beispiel Carl Arnold Schloenbachs' (149–67); M. Klanska, 'Wenzel Messenhauser: ein Dichter und Opfer der Revolution von 1848' (169–83); E. Kleinschmidt, 'Revolutionäre Spiegelungen: zu Moritz Hartmanns *Reimchronik des Pfaffen Maurizius* (1849)' (185–203); E. M. Siegel, 'Nach dem Vormärz oder von der *Emancipation des Fleisches* zur *Ästhetik des Hässlichen*' (205–18). *Vormärz und Klassik*, ed. L. Ehrlich et al. (*Vormärz-Studien*, 1), Bielefeld, Aisthesis, 300 pp., has: H. Bock, 'Deutscher Vormärz: immer noch Fragen nach Definitionen und Zäsuren einer Epoche' (9–32); J. A. Kruse, 'Zwischen Weltschmerz und Engagement: Heine. Über historische Grenzen und deren Bestimmbarkeit, fliessende Übergänge und die Nähe von Klassik und Romantik zur deutschen Literatur des Vormärz' (33–47); P. Stein, ' "Kunstperiode" und "Vormärz": zum veränderten Verhältnis von Ästhetizität und Operativität am Beispiel Heinrich Heines' (49–62); J. Fohrmann, 'Heines Marmor' (63–80); L. Ehrlich, 'Immermanns Verhältnis zur Weimarer Klassik' (81–97); H. G. Werner, 'Büchner und Goethe' (99–119); R. Schnell, 'Heine und der Junghegelianismus' (141–53); R. Rosenberg, 'Eine "neue Literatur" am "Ende der Kunst"?' (155–61); H. Steinecke, ' "Reisende waren wir beide": Pückler-Muskau und Heine, London, Frühjahr 1827. Aspekte der Reiseliteratur vor der Julirevolution' (163–80); B. Füllner, ' "Nur Unruhe! Unruhe! sonst bin ich verloren": Georg Weerth und die "Göttin der Langeweile" ' (181–97); W. Wülfing, '*Gleichzeitigkeit* als "Unendlichkeit": zur Darstellung von Raum- und Zeiterfahrungen in Texten des Vormärz' (199–219); N. O. Eke, ' "Ja, ja, wir leben schnell, schneller als die Menschen lebten": Beiläufige Anmerkungen zum Verhältnis von Revolution und Beschleunigung in Revolutionsdramen des Vor- und Nachmärz' (221–33); H. Müller, 'Idealismus und Realismus im historischen Drama: Schiller, Grabbe, Büchner' (235–47); P. U. Hohendahl, 'Fiktion und Kritik: Heines *Romantische Schule* im Kontext der zeitgenössischen Literaturgeschichte' (249–63); I. Pepperle, 'Georg Herweghs unbekannte Korrespondenzen aus Paris 1848 in Arnold Ruges Berliner Zeitung *Die Reform*' (265–75); F. Wahrenburg, 'Stadterfahrung im Genrewechsel: Glassbrenners Berlin-Schilderungen' (277–300). *Forum Vormärz Forschung*, 4, 1998[1999], *Juden und jüdische Kultur im Vormärz*, has: H. T. Tewarson, 'Die

Aufklärung im jüdischen Denken des 19. Jahrhunderts: Rahel Levin Varnhagen, Ludwig Robert, Ludwig Börne, Eduard Gans, Berthold Auerbach, Fanny Lewald' (17–61); A. Herzig, 'Jüdische Akkulturationsvorstellungen im Vormärz' (63–70); W. Beutin, '"In diesem Hause immer fremd"': Carl Spindlers historischer Roman *Der Jude*' (91–109); B. Budde, 'Verwahrungen aufklärerischer Vernunft: literarisch-publizistische Strategien in Börnes Schutzschriften für die Juden' (111–40); U. Zemke, 'Georg Weerths Juden-Bild' (141–63); S. P. Scheichl, 'Zur Freundschaftskultur von Prager und Wiener Juden im Vormärz' (165–80); G. Och, '"Judenwitz"': zur Semantik eines Stereotyps in der Literaturkritik des Vormärz' (181–99); M. Betz, '"Meine Lieder werden leben"': zum 150. Todestag der Annette von Droste-Hülshoff' (251–63); U. Walter, 'Franz Freiherr von Gaudy: *Mein Römerzug*. Eine vergessene italienische Reise' (281–304); T. Coppola, '"... meine Kunst/Reisst dir die Fern in den Gesichtskreis ..."': die göttliche Macht der Allschau. Zum Motiv der Entgrenzung des visuellen Raums in Grabbes *Don Juan und Faust*' (305–12); M. B. Füllner, '"... wie ein Lilienstiefel"': Anmerkungen zur illustrierten Ausgabe von Georg Weerths *Leben und Thaten des berühmten Ritters Schnapphahnski*' (313–27). *Die Achtundvierziger: Lebensbilder aus der deutschen Revolution 1848–49*, ed. Sabine Freitag, Munich, Beck, 1998, 354 pp., contains among other articles: I. Fellrath, 'G. H. — Emma Herwegh: Vive la république' (33–44, 305–06); S. Klabunde, 'Malwide von Meysenbug: mit den Waffen der Freiheit und der Zukunft' (225–36, 329–31). *1848 — Literatur, Kunst und Freiheit im europäischen Rahmen*, ed. Hartmut Melenk et al. (Ludwigsburger Hochschulschriften, 19), Freiburg, Fillibach, 1998, 220 pp., contains: K. Fingerhut, '"Die ganze Welt wird frei und bankrott"': Heinrich Heine, Georg Herwegh, Ludwig Pfau, Justinus Kerner und die unglücklichen poetischen Kommentierungen der verunglückten Revolution von 1848' (39–62); F. Genton, 'Lyoner Canuts und "Schlesische Weber"': noch einmal Heine und die Folgen' (119–35); M. Siguan, 'Heine und Spanien' (137–56). *1848 — Revolution in Österreich*, ed. Ernst Bruckmüller et al. (Schriften des Instituts für Österreichkunde, 62), Vienna, ÖBV, 173 pp., is mainly concerned with the political events of 1848, but there is an article on the literature of the period by H. Lengauer, '"Hab Achtung vor dem Menschenbild!"': zur Literatur der österreichischen Revolution im Jahre 1848' (70–88), which includes references to Stifter, Moritz Hartmann, Grillparzer, Nestroy (*Freiheit in Krähwinkel, Judith und Holofernes*), and Hebbel among others. Friedrich Sengle, *Biedermeierzeit: Deutsche Literatur im Spannungsfeld zwischen Restauration und Revolution 1815–1848*, 3 vols, Stuttgart, Metzler, 3039 pp., is a paperback reprint of the monumental work first published in the 1970s and

1980s. Its affordable price will now make it an attractive possibility for many Germanists to buy their own personal copies. A.-K. Henkel, 'Bibliotheken und Lektüreangebot in der Residenzstadt Hannover: Aspekte der Literaturversorgung im Vormärz', *AGB*, 49, 1998:221–65. S. Höhne, 'Böhmische Dörfer: zu sozialen und ethischen Kategorisierungen in der deutschböhmischen Vormärzliteratur', *Brücken*, 5, 1997:5–28. R. Weninger, 'Zur Dialektik des Dialekts im deutschen Realismus: zugleich Überlegungen zu Michail Bachtins Konzeption der Redevielfalt', *GQ*, 72:115–32, examines Berthold Auerbach's *Die Frau Professorin* in the light of Bakhtin's notion of *heteroglossia*. U. Landfester, ' "Heute soll hier die Revolution losgehen . . .": Anna von Baumbachs Briefe aus Berlin an ihren Mann Freimund vom Sommer 1848', *Fest. Steinsdorff*, 257–88.

LITERARY LIFE, JOURNALS, AND SOCIETIES. *Joseph Freiherr von Lassberg (1770–1855): Imaginierte Lebensformen des Mittelalters. Sonderheft zu dem Symposion Joseph Freiherr von Lassberg in Meersburg im Oktober 1988*, ed. Ulrich Gaier et al. (*MaM*, 82, Sonderheft), Marbach, Dt. Schillergesellschaft, 1998, 136 pp., is concerned with the career of this early Germanist who was married to Droste-Hülshoff's elder sister. A merit of the volume is that it gives an impression of literary life in the circle of Droste, Uhland and Gustav Schwab. G. Butzer, M. Günter, and R. von Heydebrand, 'Strategien zur Kanonisierung des "Realismus" am Beispiel der *Deutschen Rundschau*: zum Ausschluß österreichischer und schweizer Schriftsteller aus der deutschen Nationalliteratur', *IASL*, 24:55–81. Jutta Kleedorfer, 'Kinder- und Jugendzeitschriften in der zweiten Hälfte des 19. Jahrhunderts', pp. 68–73 of *Geschichte der österreichischen Kinder- und Jugendliteratur vom 18. Jahrhundert bis zur Gegenwart*, ed. Hans-Heino Ewers et al., Vienna, Buchkultur, 1997, 207 pp. B. Dölling, 'Der literarische Sonntagsverein ' "Tunnel über der Spree" ', *Lose Blätter*, 1, 1997:32–35. W. Hettche, 'Im Hain, im Tunnel und im Teich: Autorschaft und Autorisation in literarischen Vereinen', *Editio*, 13:98–107, discusses problems encountered in the editing of collective publications of members of the *Göttinger Hain*, the *Tunnel über der Spree*, and the Munich *Krokodil* circle.

REGIONAL LITERATURE. *Literatur und Regionalität*, ed. Anselm Maler (Studien zur neueren Literatur, 4), Frankfurt, Lang, 1997, 228 pp., publishes the papers given at a conference on the topic of regionalism in literature held in Kassel in 1994. Of the 13 articles in the volume the following four fall within our period: M. K. Wallach, 'Konstruktion und Dekonstruktion des Bildes einer Region: Talvj und Heine über Polen (101–15, on Talvj's Novelle *Verfehlte Bestimmung* and Heine's essay *Über Polen*); F. Schüppen, 'Region und Tradition im Werk Friedrich Wilhelm Webers: zum mentalitätsgeschichtlichen Ort

des westfälischen Dichters' (141–56, on the epic poem *Dreizehnlinden*);
E. Frederiksen, 'Der literarische Text im späten 19. Jahrhundert als
Schnittpunkt von regionalen, überregionalen und Geschlechts-
aspekten: Gabriele Reuters Roman *Aus guter Familie* zum Beispiel'
(157–66); J. L. Sammons, 'Ein Fall von fehlender Interregionalität:
die Abwesenheit des Amerikaschriftstellers Karl May in Amerika'
(167–79). *\*Habsburger Aporien? Geisteshaltung und Lebenskonzepte in der
multinationalen Literatur der Habsburger Monarchie*, ed. E. Reichmann
(Bielefelder Schriften zu Linguistik und Literaturwissenschaft, 10),
Bielefeld, Aisthesis, 1998, 194 pp. *Österreichische Literatur und Psychoana-
lyse: Literaturpsychologische Essays über Nestroy, Ebner-Eschenbach, Schnitzler,
Kraus, Rilke, Musil, Zweig, Kafka, Horvath, Canetti*, ed. Josef Rattner et
al., Würzburg, Königshausen & Neumann, 1998, 325 pp., has:
J. Rattner, 'Nestroys Komödien' (9–35); and G. Danzer, '"Es
schreibt keiner wie ein Gott, der nicht gelitten hat wie ein Hund"':
das Leben der Marie von Ebner-Eschenbach' (37–69). Werner
Michler, *Darwinismus und Literatur: Naturwissenschaftliche und literarische
Intelligenz in Österreich 1859–1914* (Literaturgeschichte in Studien und
Quellen, 2), Vienna, Böhlau, 560 pp., discusses the impact of
Darwinian ideas on a range of texts of the late 19th c., including
Sacher-Masoch's *Venus im Pelz*. Young-Kyun Ra, *\*Probleme der Litera-
turgeschichtsschreibung: Überlegungen zur österreichischen Literatur in deutschen
Literaturgeschichten, am Beispiel von Johann Nestroy, Adalbert Stifter und Karl
Kraus dargestellt* (EH, 1, 1710), 252 pp. A. Mádl, 'Das Ungarnbild in
der österreichischen Literatur im 19. Jahrhundert', pp. 83–96 of
*Österreichische Germanistik im Ausland: Ideal und Wirklichkeit. Beiträge der
Tagung der Österreichschen Gesellschaft für Germanistik in Pécs 1997*, ed.
Kurt Bartsch et al., Vienna, Praesens, 1997, 152 pp. M. Rózsa, 'Auf
Ungarn bezügliche Berichte des Wiener *Wanderer* 1851–1861', *Jb. der
ungarischen Germanistik*, 1997:173–89. S. Boronkai, 'Bedeutungsverlust
und Identitätskrise der ungarndeutschen Literatur des 19. Jahrhun-
derts. Am Beispiel der deutschsprachigen Literatur und Kultur in
Ödenburg 1790–1890', *ib.*, 1996[1997]:131–48. Rémy Charbon, '*O
Schweizerland, du schöne Braut': Politische Schweizer Literatur 1798–1848*,
Zurich, Limmat, 1998, 660 pp., reprints and comments on over 200
examples of political literature, including texts by some well-known
names like Freiligrath, Gotthelf, Herwegh, and Keller, who were
Swiss or were resident for some time in Switzerland. Regine
Schindler, *\*Johanna Spyri: Spurensuche*, Zurich, Pendo, 1997, 354 pp.
Karin Mahler, *Eduard Schmelzkopf und die Zensur: Niederdeutsche Lyrik und
politische Ausrichtung eines Braunschweiger Vormärzdichters*, Bielefeld, Vlg
für Regionalgeschichte, 1997, 171 pp. W. Freund, 'Der Hexenautor
von Usedom: Wilhelm Meinhold und die Bernsteinhexe', *Die Horen*,
43, 1998:97–109, on Meinhold's best-known novel *Maria Schweidler*,

*die Bernsteinhexe* of 1843. H.-J. Schrader, 'Klosterraub südwestlich, nördlich, südöstlich: vom Eigen-Sinn der humoristischen Erzählform in C. F. Meyers *Plautus im Nonnenkloster*, W. Raabes *Kloster Lugau* und A. Brandstetters *Die Abtei*', pp. 16–41 of *Humor und Regionalität*, ed. Heinrich Kröger (Soltauer Schriften, 5), Soltau, Freudenthal-Gesellschaft, 1997, 148 pp.

## 2. INDIVIDUAL AUTHORS

ALEXIS. The photomechanical reprint edition of A.'s *Romane und Erzählungen. Gesamtausgabe in 23 Bänden*, ed. Markus Bernauer et al., Hildesheim, Olms, has added Abt. II. 5, *Das Haus Düsterweg*, xvi + 734 pp. R. Stangenberger, 'W. A. Als Bühnendichter: ein Recherchebericht', *Palmbaum*, 6.2, 1998:76–91.

BACHERACHT, THERESE. Hugh Powell, who published a critical biography of B. in 1995, has now translated her novel *Heinrich Burkhart* (SGLLC), 1997, 126 pp. He claims in his introduction that this is the most interesting and topical of her novels because of its portrayal of the social and political unrest of the 1840s.

BECHSTEIN, LUDWIG. L. B., *Deutsches Märchenbuch*, ed. H.-J. Uther, Munich, Diedrichs, 1997, 394 pp., is a new edition of B.'s best known work, first published in 1845. Uther has revised the text of the 1857 'Ausgabe letzter Hand' and added an index.

BÜCHNER. The major DKV edition of B.'s *Sämtliche Werke, Briefe, Dokumente*, ed. Henri Poschmann, has been completed by the addition of vol. 2, *Schriften, Briefe, Dokumente*, 1283 pp. G. B., *Woyzeck: Studienausgabe*, ed. Burghard Dedner (UB, 18007), 211 pp. Jürgen Seidel, *Georg Büchner* (DTV, 31001), 1998, 154 pp., is a popularizing and academically unambitious biography. Karlheinz Hasselbach, *Georg Büchner* (UB, 15212), 1997, 107 pp. Peter Ludwig, '*Es gibt eine Revolution in der Wissenschaft': Naturwissenschaft und Dichtung bei Georg Büchner* (SBL, 63), 1998, 373 pp., in a 1997 Saarbrücken dissertation underlines the importance of B.'s medical training for his writing and argues that he brings an objective, scientific approach to the portrayal of his characters. *Lenzens Verrückung: Chronik und Dokumentation zu J. M. R. Lenz von Herbst 1777 bis Frühjahr 1778*, ed. B. Dedner et al. (Büchner-Studien, 8), Tübingen, Niemeyer, v + 280 pp., publishes 150 documents relating to the progress of Lenz's illness. Hubert Gersch, *Der (produktive) Unverstand des Abschreibers und die Literaturgeschichte: Johann Friedrich Oberlins Bericht 'Herr L . . .' und die Textüberlieferung bis zu Georg Büchners 'Lenz'-Entwurf* (Büchner-Studien, 7), Tübingen, Niemeyer, x + 198 pp. G. Stiening, 'Schönheit und Ökonomie-Prinzip: zum Verhältnis von Naturwissenschaft und Philosophiegeschichte bei G. B.', *Scientia Poetica*, 3:95–121. R. Taylor, 'Saint-Just's theodicy of history in *Dantons Tod*, *MGS*, 23, 1997[1998]: 24–38, argues that St Just's historical optimism shows similarities not just with Hegelian ideas but also with the thought of Fichte. L. Ginters, 'Before and after the Wall: G. B.'s *Dantons Tod* as social thermometer', pp. 87–99 of *Literature in Times of Crisis Conference: A Selection of Postgraduate Papers*, ed. Stephan Atzert, Melbourne U.P., 1997, 111 pp. O. Hildebrand, ' "Der göttliche Epicur und die Venus mit dem schönen Hintern": zur Kritik hedonistischer Utopien in Bs *Dantons Tod*', *ZDP*, 118:530–54, examines sexual motifs in B.'s play with special reference to the 'Marion' scene. G. Meisel, 'Eigenschaftslosigkeit: B., Musil, Cyberspace', *Fidibus*, 26, 1998:17–27, is concerned with *Dantons Tod* and Musil's *Der Mann ohne Eigenschaften*. R. Campe, 'Johann Franz Woyzeck: der Fall im Drama', pp. 209–36 of *Unzurechnungsfähigkeiten: Diskursivierungen unfreier Bewusstseinszustände seit dem 18. Jahrhundert*, ed. Michael Niehaus et al. (BBL, 20), 1998, 292 pp. C. Jakobi, 'Kritischer Zweischritt: G. Bs ästhetische Entmächtigung moralischer Sinnsysteme im *Woyzeck*', *ZDP*, 118:216–33, discusses B.'s use of the grotesque to invalidate contemporary concepts of meaning. T. Teraoka, 'Religiöser Fanatismus in Bs Brief an Gutzkow', *Forschungsberichte zur Germanistik* (Osaka), 39, 1997:1–16. F. Iurlani, 'Robert Musil e G. B.: Aspetti di un affinità intellettuale', *ConLet*, 14:1997:301–09.

BURCKHARDT. N. Meier, *Emilie Linder und Jacob Burckhardt: Stifter und Sammler für die Öffentliche Kunstsammlung Basel*, Basle, Schwabe, 1997, 140 pp., provides among other things an analysis of B.'s understanding of aesthetics and his approach to the study of art. Peter Ganz, 'J. B. und die Kulturgeschichte', *Fest. Brackert*, 334–47.

BUSCH. W. B., *Gedichte*, ed. T. Schlee (IT, 2531), 200 pp. *Plisch und Plum in 40 deutschen Mundarten*, ed. Manfred Görlach, Heidelberg, Winter, 281 pp. *Wilhelm Busch: Malerei, Zeichnungen, Bildergeschichten* ed. Carl Aigner et al., Vienna–Munich, Brandstätter, 208 pp., is a catalogue produced to accompany an exhibition held in Krems and Schloss Oberhausen in 1998–99. Daniel Ruby, *Schema und Variation: Untersuchungen zum Bildergeschichtenwerk Wilhelm Buschs* (EH, 1, 1638), 1998, 115 pp., is concerned mainly with *Max und Moritz* and *Die fromme Helene*. H. Ries, 'Der böse Hundsfänger und das arme Hündlein: Bilderstreifen bei W. B.', *Satire*, 1998:36–45.

DROSTE-HÜLSHOFF. A. v. D.-H., *Historisch-kritische Ausgabe. Werke, Briefwechsel*, ed. Winfried Woesler, Tübingen, Niemeyer, has added vol. VIII.2: *Briefe 1805–1838. Kommentar*, ed. Walter Gödden, xi + pp. 349–1306. A. v. D.-H., *Die Judenbuche*, ed. Christian Begemann (Suhrkamp BasisBibliothek), 128 pp. Walter Gödden and Jochen Grywatsch, *Annette von Droste-Hülshoff am Bodensee: Ein Reiseführer zu den Droste-Stätten in Meersburg und Umgebung*, Meersburg, Turm, 1998,

167 pp. Gertrud B. Pickar, *Ambivalence Transcended: A Study of the Writings of Annette von Droste-Hülshoff* (SGLLC), 1997, xiv + 381 pp., traces the development in D.-H.'s life and work from her diffident beginnings through the struggle for self-expression to the mature self-confidence that enabled her to find her creative voice and satisfy her ambition to get her work into print and see its value critically acclaimed. The book is divided into four fairly loosely connected chapters dealing with her portrayal of women (with special reference to the one-act comedy *Perdu*); the important role of fantasy in her personal life as well as her writing; the narrative modes she deployed in her poetry and her prose (with perceptive comment on *Ledwina, Die Judenbuche, Westphälische Schilderungen aus einer westphälischen Feder, Bei uns zu Lande auf dem Lande,* and *Joseph*); and her path to self-affirmation as an author. A strength of the book is that it pays close attention to texts like *Perdu* that are not often studied. Well written and cogently argued, it represents a valuable contribution to D. scholarship. Barbara Beuys, *Blamieren mag ich mich nicht: Das Leben der Annette von Droste-Hülshoff,* Munich, Hanser, 408 pp., is aimed at a general readership but is nevertheless a work of sound enough scholarship. *Annette von Droste-Hülshoff: Zwischen Fügsamkeit und Selbstverwirklichung,* ed. H. Galen, Münster, Stadtmuseum, 1997, 165 pp., is an exhibition catalogue which contains: R. Kauder-Steiniger, 'Zwischen Fügsamkeit und Selbstverwirklichung' (119–31); F. Schwarzbauer, ' "Das Städtchen ist so angenehm": A. v. D.-H. in Meersburg' (133–40); H. Kraft, 'Literarische Bilder aus Münster' (143–50); W. Woesler, 'A. v. D.-H., "Der Knabe im Moor": eine Interpretation' (152–62). B. Plachta, 'Editorischer Pragmatismus: zum Verfahren der genetischen Variantendarstellung in der historisch-kritischen Droste-Ausgabe', pp. 233–49 of *Textgenetische Edition,* ed. H. Zeller et al. (Beihefte zu *Editio,* 10), 1998, vi + 345 pp. H. Heselhaus, 'Memory, natural history and A. v. D.-H.'s *Heidebilder*', pp. 81–89 of *The Poetics of Memory,* ed. Thomas Wägenbaur (Stauffenburg Colloquium, 45), Tübingen, Stauffenburg, 1998, viii + 411 pp. E. Lenk, 'Die fremde Frau: A. v. D.-H. zum zweihundertsten Geburtstag', *Welfengarten,* 7, 1997:167–80. W. Gödden, 'Vom Schreiben: A. v. D.-Hs Umgang mit Feder, Tinte und Papier', *Jb. der Ernst-Meister-Gesellschaft,* 1998[1999]:39–53. M. Helfer, ' "Wer wagt es, eitlen Blutes Drang zu messen": reading blood in A. v. D.-Hs *Die Judenbuche*', *GQ,* 71, 1998:228–53. W. C. Donahue, ' "Ist er kein Jude, so verdiente er einer zu sein" ': D.-H.'s *Die Judenbuche* and religious anti-Semitism', *GQ,* 72:44–73. A. B. Kilcher, 'Das magische Gesetz der hebräischen Sprache: Ds *Judenbuche* und der spätromantische Diskurs über die jüdische Magie', *ZDP,* 118:235–65, is concerned with the status and function of the Hebrew inscription carved in the tree. S. Hilzinger,

'Ambivalenzstruktur und Geschlechterdifferenz in A. v. D.-Hs Prosafragment *Ledwina* (1820–1825)', *IASL*, 24 : 1–16. C. Tully, 'Placing D.'s *Ledwina*: 'Jugendwerk' or 'gescheiterte Frauenliteratur?', *GLL*, 52 : 314–24. S. Kirkbright, 'Sorrow, intrigue and circumstances: on A. v. D.-H.'s poetry of self-assertion', *LWU*, 32 : 323–37. See also the collective volume edited by G. Vonhoff, p. 709 above.

DULK, ALBERT. Astrid Schweimler, *Albert Friedrich Benno Dulk (1919–1884): Ein Dramatiker als Wegbereiter der gesellschaftlichen Emanzipation*, Giessen, Focus, 1998, 225 pp., is a 1997 Stuttgart dissertation.

EBNER-ESCHENBACH. M. v. E.-E., *Sämtliche Werke*, 12 vols, Freiburg, Echo, 1998, 4468 pp., is a photographic reprint of the plaintext edition published by Paetel of Berlin in 1920. M. v. E.-E., *Kritische Texte und Deutungen*, ed. K. K. Polheim et al., Tübingen, Niemeyer, has added *Ergänzungsband* 1, *Marie von Ebner-Eschenbach: Eine Bibliographie*, ed. Carsten Kretschmann, 226 pp., which contains over 1,200 main headings listing both primary and secondary literature up to the year 1998. M. v. E.-E., *Lotti, die Uhrmacherin*, ed. Marianne Henn (UB, 7463), 166 pp. Gudrun Gorla, *Marie von Ebner-Eschenbach: 100 Jahre später. Eine Analyse aus der Sicht des ausgehenden 20. Jahrhunderts mit Berücksichtigung der Mutterfigur, der Ideologie des Matriarchats und formaler Aspekte*, Berne, Lang, 222 pp., is a 1997 Rutgers Univ. dissertation concerned principally with E.-E.'s portrayal of the mother figure in *Bozena*. G. Langer, 'Kulturelle Verortung und literarische Topologie in M. v. E.-Es *Bozena* und Bozena Nemcovás *Babicka*', *Bohemia*, 39, 1998 : 17–32. S. Colvin, 'Disturbing bodies: Mary Stuart and Marilyn Monroe in plays by Liz Lochhead, M. v. E.-E. and Gerlind Reinshagen', *FMLS*, 35 : 251–60.

FEUCHTERSLEBEN. Karl Pisa, *Ernst Freiherr von Feuchtersleben: Pionier der Psychosomatik* (Literatur und Leben, 52), Cologne, Böhlau, 1998, 184 pp., is a biographical account of F.'s career.

FONTANE. T. F., *Grosse Brandenburger Ausgabe*, ed. Gotthard Erler, Berlin, Aufbau, is proceeding apace with *Das erzählerische Werk* and has added vol. 3, *Grete Minde*, ed. C. Schmitz, 1997, 220 pp.; vol. 4, *L'Adultera*, ed. G. Radecke, 1998, 278 pp.; vol. 6, *Schach von Wuthenow*, ed. K. Seebacher, 1997, 250 pp.; vol. 7, *Graf Petöfy*, ed. P. Kabus, 324 pp.; vol. 8, *Unterm Birnbaum*, ed. C. Hehle, 1997, 185 pp.; vol. 10, *Irrungen, Wirrungen*, ed. K. Bauer, 1997, 287 pp.; vol 12, *Quitt*, ed. Christina Brieger, 426 pp.; vol. 15, *Effi Briest*, ed. C. Hehle, 1998, 534 pp. In the same edition there has also appeared Emilie Fontane and T. F., *Der Ehebriefwechsel*, ed. G. Erler et al., 3 vols, 1998, xxxiv + 698, 821, 838 pp. In paperback there have appeared T. F., *Kriegsgefangen: Erlebtes 1870* (ATV, 5277), 199 pp.; *Jenseits des Tweed: Bilder und Briefe aus Schottland*, ed. G. and T. Erler (ATV, 5286), 313 pp.; *Ein Sommer in London*, ed. R. Muhs (ATV, 5276), 1998,

210 pp.; and *Jenseits von Havel und Spree: Reisebriefe*, ed. G. Erler (ATV, 5268), 1998, 417 pp. T. F., *Aus meinem bunten Leben: Ein biographisches Lesebuch*, ed. Gabriele Radecke et al., Munich–Vienna, Hanser, 1998, 326 pp., is a compilation of F.'s letters. T. F., *'Eine Zeitungsnummer lebt nur zwölf Stunden': Londoner Korrespondenzen aus Berlin*, ed. H. Streiter-Buscher, Berlin, de Gruyter, 1998, xvi + 222 pp., presents a short selection of the highlights from T. F., *Unechte Korrespondenzen: Ein Jahrzehnt Redakteur der Kreuzzeitung* (reviewed in *YWMLS*, 59:794).

Helga Bemmann, *Fontane: Ein preussischer Dichter*, Berlin, Ullstein, 1998, 440 pp., gives a strictly chronological account of F.'s life, paying relatively little attention to the novels. Norbert Mecklenburg, *\*Theodor Fontane: Romankunst der Vielstimmigkeit*, Frankfurt, Suhrkamp, 1998, 327 pp. The very title of Rolf Zuberbühler's *Fontane und Hölderlin: Romantik-Auffassung und Hölderlin-Bild in 'Vor dem Sturm'* (UDL, 91), 1997, vii + 125 pp., is likely to raise more than a few eyebrows. The author himself anticipates the predictable objections, for he opens his first chapter with a full and frank acknowledgement of the great differences between the poet of German Idealism and the representative of *bürgerlicher* or Poetic Realism. His main thesis is that *Vor dem Sturm* is, in Gutzkow's phrase, a *Roman des Nebeneinander* which gives a picture of Prussian society in the winter of 1812–13, engaged in a momentous national struggle and on the threshold of major change. He argues that the novel is not least a piece of intellectual and literary history — conversations about art and literature take up much space in it — and that the examination of Hölderlin is seamlessly integrated into the larger view of Prussian life. His ode 'An die Parzen' even runs as a leitmotif through the novel. What links Hölderlin firmly to the great national struggle of 1812–13 is his patriotism and his emphasis on the need for the most intense concentration of energy (as seen in 'An die Parzen') as a condition of success in the service of any 'great idea', whether it be political or artistic. The book is well and clearly written, and Zuberbühler supports his thesis convincingly. Sybil Gräfin Schönfeldt, *Bei Fontane zu Tisch: Wanderungen durch des Dichters Esslandschaften*, Zurich–Hamburg, Arche, 1997, 188 pp. Michael Fleischer, *\*'Kommen Sie Cohn': Fontane und die 'Judenfrage'*, Berlin, Fleischer, 1998, 391 pp. John Osborne, *Theodor Fontane: Vor den Romanen. Krieg und Kunst*, Göttingen, Vandenhoeck & Ruprecht, 218 pp. Christine Renz, *Geglückte Rede: Zu Erzählstrukturen in Theodor Fontanes 'Effi Briest', 'Jenny Treibel' und 'Der Stechlin'*, Munich, Fink, 228 pp., applies the ideas of Roland Barthes to Fontane. Hugo Aust, *Theodor Fontane: Ein Studienbuch* (UTB, 1988), Tübingen, Francke, 1998, 250 pp. Hans Schumann, *Der Schwefelgelbe: Fontane und Bismarck*, Zurich, Manesse, 1998, 78 pp.

*Fontane und sein Jahrhundert*, ed. Anne Franzkowiak et al., Berlin, Henschel, 1998, 279 pp., is a catalogue accompanying the exhibition held in the Stadtmuseum in Berlin from 11 September 1998 to 17 January 1999, and has: L. Schirmer, 'Stationen eines Jahrhunderts' (11–15); A. Franzkowiak, 'Schicksal als Chance?: Rückblicke auf die Kindheit' (23–30); B. Machner, 'Auf der Suche: vom Apotheker zum Staatsdiener, vom Tunnelianer zum freien Schriftsteller' (43–53); M. Weinland, 'Vormärz und Berliner Revolution' (70–76); Id., 'Im Dienste Preussens' (86–90); H. Schirmer, ' "Der Herr hat heut Kritik" ': T. F. und das Theater seiner Zeit' (101–14); T. Trunk, ' "Weiber weiblich, Männer männlich" ': Frauen in der Welt Fs' (137–54); T. Friedrich, 'Menschen des Übergangs, unfertige Stadt 1833–1898: Berlin als Fontanopolis' (178–86); B. Reissmann and H. Zettler, 'Reisebilder' (199–204); A. Teltow, 'Lehret uns Erinnerung, damit wir lernen, schlummernden Reichtum zu erschließen: Fs Blick auf die Mark — Variationen eines Themas' (211–18); B. Machner, 'Potsdamer Straße 134c: Der Dichternachlass' (251–60). *Theodor Fontane: Un promeneur dans le siècle*, ed. Marc Thuret (Publications de l'Institut d'Allemand, 26), Asnières, 323 pp., publishes the papers given at a conference held in Paris in October 1998 to mark the F. centenary, and contains: M. Thuret, 'Un promeneur dans le siècle: chronologie' (9–42); G. Krebs, 'F. et la révolution de 1848' (45–70); J. Ritte, 'Le voyage en France' (71–90); H. Streiter-Buscher, 'Présence de Bismarck dans l'œuvre romanesque de F.: politique et esthétique' (91–114); P. Wruck, ' "Monde nouveau" et "dieux anciens" ': T. F., chroniqueur provincial et romancier moderne' (115–30); E. Kaufholz-Messmer, 'L'art du roman chez F.' (133–48); M. Thuret, 'L'humour chez F.' (149–68); G. Guillard, '*F., Effi Briest* de R. W. Fassbinder: un vaste contrechamp' (169–82); E. Carstanjen, 'F. et ses filles' (183–98); M. Dubar, 'Portrait d'Effi Briest en Cendrillon, Nora, et ... Froufrou' (199–218); Y. Chevrel, 'T. F. critique du théâtre français' (221–234); J. Legrand, 'F. et Stendhal dans le droit fil d'une tradition d'élégance intellectuelle' (235–50); M. Thuret, 'F. en France et en français' (251–72); R. Stephan, 'L'œuvre de T. F. en France: un témoignage' (273–76); D. Modigliani, 'Lire-écrire F.: réflexions sur une pratique théorique du traduire' (277–99); J. Legrand, 'Les loches d'Altenbrak: un traducteur essaie de jouer sur les jeux de mots de F.' (301–10); E. Tophoven, ' "What's in a name ..." ': Beckett lecteur de F.' (311–18). *Fontane und die bildende Kunst*, ed. Claude Keisch et al., Berlin, Henschel, 1998, 335 pp., is a catalogue accompanying the exhibition held in the Nationalgalerie in Berlin from 4 September to 29 November 1998, and has: P.-K. Schuster, 'Die Kunst bei F.' (9–10); M. Wullen, 'Englische Malerei: "Kosmopolitismus in der Kunst". F. in England' (42–120); C. Keisch,

'Das klassische Berlin: Suche nach einer verlorenen Zeit. Berlin in der Mark Brandenburg' (121–68); M. Wullen, 'Deutsche Zeitgenossen: das Kunstwerk im Zeitalter seiner technischen Reproduzierbarkeit' (169–230); I. Wagner-Douglas, 'Alte Meister: von der Bildsprache zum Sprachbild' (231–51); M. Wullen, 'Über das Sehen bei F.' (257–61); H. Frank, 'Im Kunstschein des Konkreten: einige Grundbestimmungen des Kunsturteils bei F.' (262–65); H. Karge, 'Poesie und Wissenschaft: F. und die Kunstgeschichte' (267–78); C. Keisch, 'Aus der Werkstatt des Kunstkritikers: Fs Notizen aus Berliner Kunstausstellungen' (279–91); U. Finke, ' ". . . ein Musterschauplatz für die gesamte moderne Kunst": die Art Treasures Exhibition in Manchester' (292–302); W. Lottes, 'Englische Malerei zur Zeit Fs' (303–08); F. Forster-Hahn, ' "Die Ehe als Beruf " ' oder der Fall von der Schaukel: über die Moral in präraffaelitischen Bildgeschichten und in Fs *Effi Briest*' (309–17); A. Wesenberg, ' "Dass Sie mich mit F. vergleichen, ist mir sehr schmeichelhaft": vom Kritiker zum Künstlerkollegen. Der Romancier und der Maler' (318–24). *Berliner Hefte zur Geschichte des literarischen Lebens*, 2, 1998, has: R. Muhs, ' "Die Lilie der Legende": ein unbekanntes Huldigungsgedicht T. Fs an Königin Elisabeth von Preussen' (65–74); R. Berbig, 'Das Ganze als Ganzes oder: Pastor Schmutz und Geheimrat Stiehl. Zur Rezeptionssteuerung der *Wanderungen* durch F.' (75–94); P. Wruck, 'Stichproben die Editionen und den Status der Fontaneschen *Wanderungen durch die Mark Brandenburg* betreffend' (95–101); M. Kikawa, 'Prinz Heinrich in Rheinsberg: ein Beitrag zur Auseinandersetzung Fs mit der friderizianischen Zeit' (102–08).

*Fontane-Blätter*, 67, has: H. Karge, 'T. F. und Karl Schnaase: ein neugefundenes Gutachten beleuchtet die Anfänge der *Wanderungen durch die Mark Brandenburg*' (10–34); H. Fischer, 'Gordon oder die Liebe zur Telegraphie' (36–58); B. Losch, 'Widerstandsrecht bei F.: *Grete Minde* gegen Unterdrückung und Rechtsverweigerung' (59–74); H. Schlaffer, 'Die gesprächige Ehe: eine Utopie des späten F.' (75–90); E. Miller, 'Die roten Fäden des roten Hahns: zu einem Motivkomplex im *Stechlin*' (91–105); T. Küpper, ' ". . . leuchtet's wieder weit und breit": zur Popularität der Ribbeck-Ballade' (106–21); P. Schaefer and D. Strauch, 'F. in Film und Fernsehen: zwischen "Werktreue" und Neuinterpretation. Mit einer Filmographie' (172–200); E. Krauss, ' "Aus dem Hirschberger Tal kommen immer die romantischsten Geschichten . . ." ' (201–10); P. Schaefer, 'Auswahlbibliographie: Neuerscheinungen und -erwerbungen des F.-Archivs bis 31.1.1999' (224–64). *Fontane-Blätter*, 68, has: H. D. von Wolzogen et al., ' "Und auch zu viel Lob ist von Uebel": unbekannte Briefe T. Fs an Salo Schottländer' (10–17); M. Brosig, ' "Es sei dies die Geschichte eines Feldpredigers, der in gewissem Sinne [. . .] die

Schlacht bei Kesseldorf gewonnen . . ."': zwei unbekannte F.-Briefe aus der "Wanderungs"-Zeit' (18–28); K.-P. Möller, 'Die Verlagsverträge im T.-F.-Archiv (1. Teil)' (29–72); C. Klug, 'Die Poesie der Zeitung: Fs poetische Rezeption der Tagespresse und die Entdeckung der neuen Wirklichkeiten' (74–117); B. Plett, 'Frauenbilder, Männerperspektiven und die fragwürdige Moral: Applikation und Demontage von Rollenbildern und Wertzuschreibungen in Fs Romanen' (118–29); R. Dieterle, 'Die sieben Waisen und die Mädchenbildung: zur pädagogischen Diskussion in Fs *Frau Jenny Treibel*' (130–43); L. Zylinski, 'T. Fs Rezeption in Polen' (144–56); K.-P. Möller, 'Der vorgetäuschte Erfolg: zum Problem der Erstausgaben, Neuauflagen, Neudrucke bei T. F.' (192–216); H. Müller-Michaels, ' "F. in der Schule": ein Bericht über das internationale Symposium in Neuruppin vom 29.–31. Oktober 1998' (216–19); K.-P. Möller and P. Schaefer, 'Auswahlbibliographie: Neuerscheinungen und -erwerbungen des F.-Archivs bis 30. Juni 1999' (224–36).

R. Helmstetter, 'Literarische induzierte Liebe und "salonmäßig abgedämpfte Liebe"': T. Fs *Effi Briest*, pp. 229–51 of *Leidenschaft Literarisch*, ed. Reinhard M. Nischik (Texte zur Weltliteratur, 1), Konstanz U.P., 1998, 302 pp. H. Rohse, ' "Arme Effi"': Widersprüche geschlechtlicher Identität in Fs *Effi Briest*, pp. 203–16 of *Widersprüche geschlechtlicher Identität: Bibliographie. Literaturpsychologie 1992–1996*, ed. Johannes Cremerius (*FLG*, 17), 1998, 375 pp. I. von der Lühe, 'Fremdheit und Moderne: T. Fs Novellenfragment *Oceane von Parceval*', pp. 123–34 of *'Die andere Stimme': Das Fremde in der Kultur der Moderne. Festschrift für Klaus R. Scherpe zum 60. Geburtstag*, ed. Alexander Honhold et al. (Literatur — Kultur — Geschlecht. Grosse Reihe, 13), Cologne, Böhlau, 375 pp. V. Drehsen, 'Pfarrersfiguren als Gesinnungsfigurationen: zur Bedeutung des Pfarrers in T. Fs Romanen', pp. 37–55 of *Der "ganze Mensch": Perspektiven lebensgeschichtlicher Individualität. Fest. für Dietrich Rössler zum siebzigsten Geburtstag*, ed. Volker Drehsen, Berlin–NY, de Gruyter, 1997, xi + 477 pp. W. Siebers, 'Die romantische Hälfte Schottlands: T. Fs Reisebuch *Jenseit des Tweed*', pp. 59–66 of *Deutsche Schottlandbilder: Beiträge zur Kulturgeschichte*, ed. Winfried Siebers et al., Osnabrück, Rasch, 1998, 230 pp. G. Loster-Schneider, 'T. Fs *Wanderungen durch die Mark Brandenburg*: interkulturelle Identitätsentwürfe eines "in der Wolle gefärbten Preussen', *Fest. Storck*, 233–55. Jürgens, *Exchanges*, contains: L. Köhn, ' "Bei dem Fritzen-Denkmal stehen sie wieder"': Fs Preussen-Balladen als Schlüssel zu seinem Werk' (342–59); and D. Schilling, 'T. F.: *L'Adultera*' (360–69).

G. Radecke and W. Hettche, 'F. und sein Jahrhundert: eine Ausstellung des Stadtmuseums Berlin', *Aus dem Antiquariat*, 1998, Heft

12, A:845–49. I. Stolzenberg, 'Die Fontanehandschriften der Staatsbibliothek Preussischer Kulturbesitz: Altbestand und Neuerwerbungen bis 1991', *Staatsbibliothek (Berlin): Mitteilungen*, 6 (1997), Heft
2:211–19. E. Ziegler, 'Schriftsteller-Vater und Verleger-Sohn: T. F.
und der Verlag Fontane & Co', *Buchhandelsgeschichte*, 1997, Heft 3,
B:134–137. U. Diederichs, 'Der Dichter T. F. und der Verlagslehr-
ling Eugen Diederichs', *Aus dem Antiquariat*, 1998, Heft 4, A:271–73.
W. Hettche, 'Raffiniert und ledern: zwei Briefe Fs über norwegische
Erzähler', *ib.*, 273–74. G. Knoll, 'Johannes Schultze, Paul Wallich
und T. F.', *ib.*, Heft 12, A:838–45. E. H. Krause and S. V. Hicks,
'"O Himmel, jetzt kommt Hegel an die Reihe": F. and Hegel on
social substance', *Seminar*, 35:38–54. Konrad Ehlich, 'Die Fremde als
Spuk: Fontane', *DaF*, 24, 1998:83–96. F. Gordon, 'Legitimation and
irony in Tolstoy and Fontane', pp. 85–97 of *Scarlet Letters: Fictions of
Adultery from Antiquity to the 1990s*, ed. Nicholas White et al.,
Basingstoke, Macmillan, 1997, xi + 232 pp., has some comment on
*Effi Briest*. W. Hüffmeier, '"Alles ist Gnade": Beobachtungen zu
Kirche und Theologie bei T. F.', *Zeitschrift für Theologie und Kirche*, 95,
1998:250–76. E. Fiandra, 'La serra del desiderio: maniere del tragico
e tragico di maniera nell'*Adultera* di F.', *Cultura Tedesca*, 11:72–86.
T. Küpper, '"Herr von Ribbeck auf Ribbeck" — im Havelland und
in anderen Kontexten', *SPIEL*, 17, 1998[1999]:111–33, is based on
Niklas Luhmann's sociological systems theory and shows how F.'s
poem has been exploited in a variety of sometimes unexpected
contexts and non-literary media such as the world of advertising. H.-
J. Müllenbrock, 'T. Fs historischer Roman *Vor dem Sturm* und die
Scottsche Gattungstradition', *GRM*, 48, 1998:365–73. M. Schmidt,
'"Wie ein roter Faden": Fs Antisemitismus und die Literaturwissen-
schaft', *Jb. für Antisemitismusforschung*, 8:350–69. H. Schumann, 'T.
F. und die Juden', *Geschichte in Wissenschaft und Unterricht*, 49,
1998:530–43. J. Desel, 'T. F.: seine Familie und seine französische
Abstammung', *Genealogie*, 11–12, 1998:338–55. K. Goebel,
'"Offensichtlich eine Respektsperson": Heinrich Wolfgang Seidels
lebenslanger Umgang mit T. F.', *WW*, 48, 1998:355–66.
M. Schmidt, '"Geheimnisse [. . .] und Anspielungen" oder Caroline
und Effi von Briest: "Namenanspielung" und Protoemanzipation in
T. Fs Roman', *Nordlit* (Tromsø), 3, 1998:143–80. H. Steinmetz, 'Fs
Bildreihen', *ABNG*, 45:161–73, focuses on *Irrungen Wirrungen* and
discusses F.'s technique of dividing his novels into numerous short
sections by means of very precise indications of time. E. H. Krause,
'Desire and denial: F.'s *Effi Briest*', *GR*, 74:117–29. E. Miller, 'Der
Stechlinsee: Symbol und Struktur in Fs Altersroman', *JEGP*,
97:352–70, argues that *Der Stechlin* is not the tired work of an ageing
man and lacking in action, but 'ein durchkomponiertes Werk' resting

on quite new structural principles. B. Overton, 'Children and childlessness in the novel of female adultery', *MLR*, 94:314–27, includes some comment on F.'s *L'Adultera* (including the intriguing claim that its happy ending makes it unique in the canon of 19th-c. adultery fiction), *Unwiederbringlich*, and *Effi Briest*. M. Schlette, 'Fs Adelstypologie im *Stechlin*: eine Untersuchung ihres sozialgeschichtlichen Gehalts', *LitL*, 22:127–43.

FRANZOS.     *Karl Emil Franzos (1848–1904): Der Dichter Galiziens. Zum 150. Geburtstag*, ed. Herwig Pürtz, Vienna, Wiener Stadt- und Landesbibliothek, 1998, 72 pp., was published to accompany an exhibition held in the Vienna *Stadtbibliothek* from October 1998 to January 1999.

FREYTAG.     Martin Gubser, *Literarischer Antisemitismus: Untersuchungen zu Gustav Freytag und anderen bürgerlichen Schriftstellern des 19. Jahrhunderts*, Göttingen, Wallstein, 1998, 328 pp., is a 1995 Fribourg dissertation. The book is divided into two main parts, the first of which discusses the situation of Jews in the 19th c. with special reference to Prussia and defines various kinds of anti-Semitism (religious, economic, political, racial). This material will already be familiar to most interested readers, though it is competently enough presented. The most useful chapter in this first part of the work is the one which examines the stylistic devices characteristic of anti-Semitic writing (travesty, parody, the stereotypes of, for example, 'die schöne Jüdin' and 'die edlen Juden'). The second part of the book consists of a series of exhaustive analyses of F.'s works in an attempt to determine whether or not he should be labelled anti-Semitic. His progression from an anti-Semitic to a philo-Semitic position is traced in detail. Like the first part of the book it is well enough done, though nothing surprising or fundamentally new emerges. Walter Boehlich, 'Das "deutsche" Volk bei "seiner" Arbeit: ein befremdeter Blick auf G. Fs *Soll und Haben*', *Fest. Brackert*, 311–19.

GERSTÄCKER.     Anton Zangerl, *Friedrich Gerstäcker (1816–1872): Romane und Erzählungen. Struktur und Gehalt* (Narratio, 15), Berne, Lang, 301 pp., in a 1998 Zurich dissertation makes a plea for G. to be recognized as a serious literary figure rather than a purveyor of popular tales of travel and adventure.

GLASSBRENNER.     Patricia Calkins, *\*Wo das Pulver liegt: Biedermeier Berlin as Reflected in Adolf Glassbrenner's 'Berliner Don Quixote'* (STML, 23), 1998, x + 219 pp.

GOTTHELF.     *Gotthelf-Augenblicke: Beiträge zu Leben und Werk*, ed. Ulrich Knellwolf et al., Münsingen, Fischer-Media-Vlg, 1997, 144 pp., is a slight and popular publication which has: U. Knellwolf, ' "Zu Gs Zeiten": über die beklemmende Gegenwärtigkeit eines Altväterlichen' (18–25); S. Bosch, 'G. lebt' (26–33); E. Y. Meyer,

'Die Zeitgemässheit eines "Unzeitgemässen"' (46–50); R. Straumann, 'Der Revolutionär, der ein Konservativer wurde' (51–55); S. Bieri, 'Pfarrer, Prediger und Prophet: J. G. als Theologe' (58–65); O. A. Kambly, 'Motive und Botschaft' (80–82); P. von Matt, 'Der Diagnostiker unserer vernetzten Bosheit: Hinweis auf einen unbeschönigten G.' (84–89); B. Giger, 'Das schwarz-weiße Emmental: die sechs G.-Filme von Franz Schnyder' (98–103); W. Muschg, 'J. G.: eine Ansprache in der Kirche Lützelflüh' (124–29); E. O. Bohnenblust and G. Schütz, 'Synoptische Biographie' (135–39). *Erzählkunst und Volkserziehung: Das literarische Werk des Jeremias Gotthelf. Mit einer Gotthelf-Bibliographie*, ed. Walter Pape et al., Tübingen, Niemeyer, vii + 401 pp., is one of the most valuable collective volumes to appear on G. in recent years and goes some way towards making up for the comparative neglect of the bi-centenary of his birth in 1997. It embraces a wide range of topics, with articles not only on his prose fiction but also on his politics, his theology, and his place in the broader European literary and cultural context. The individual contributions are: W. Pape, ' "Gotthelf, suchet euch ein Wirtshaus aus": der *Bauern-Spiegel* — Bildungsroman, Schweizer Art' (3–25); W. Braungart, 'Hiobs Bruder: zur ästhetischen Theodizee der *Uli*-Romane' (27–41); P. Rusterholz, 'Gs *Wie Anne Bäbi Jowäger haushaltet und wie es ihm mit dem Doktern geht*: historischer Anlass und aktuelle Bedeutung' (43–54); S. A. Jørgensen, 'Humor, Komik und Satire in der *Käserei in der Vehfreude*' (55–65); R. Charbon, 'Tradition und Innovation: Gs Bedeutung für das Dorfgeschichte' (69–82); D. Fulda, 'Geburt der Geschichte aus dem Gedächtnis der Familie: Gs historische Erzählungen im Kontext vormärzlicher Geschichtsdarstellung' (83–110); S. S. Tschopp, ' "Predigen, gefasst in Lebenssprache": zur narrativen Strategie von Gs *Neuem Berner-Kalender*' (111–27); W. Pape, ' "Ein Wort, das sich in seine Seele hakte": Bild und Metapher bei J. G.' (131–50); R. Böschenstein, 'Mythos und Allegorie: zur Eigenart von Gs Schreiben' (151–70); P. Utz, 'Redeströme, Bilderbrücken, Schriftschwellen: Gs *Wassernot im Emmental* in literarischer Sicht' (171–83); K. Blaser, 'Todesfluten, Glaubensbrücken, Liebesströme: theologische Anmerkungen zu Gs *Wassernot im Emmental*' (185–98); R. Paulin, 'Der Kindertod in Predigt und Roman bei G.' (199–207); M. Andermatt, ' "Keinem wurde ein einziges Gericht geschenkt": Leiblichkeit bei G.' (209–23); H. Thomke, 'Gs "Konservatismus" im europäischen Kontext' (227–41); W. Hahl, 'Gs Liberalismus-Kritik im europäischen Kontext: ein Blick auf Benjamin Disraelis Roman *Sybil: Or the Two Nations* . . .' (243–63); R. Godwin-Jones, 'Soziale und politische Modelle in George Sands *Le Compagnon du Tour de France* und Gs *Jakobs des Handwerksgesellen Wanderungen durch die Schweiz*' (267–88); P. Skrine,

'Die Brautschauerzählung bei J. G. und Hannah More' (289–303);
H. Lauf hütte, 'Gs Bedeutung für die Selbstvergewisserung Gottfried
Kellers' (307–20); D. Müller, 'Illustration als Interpretation: Gs
*Schwarze Spinne als Bildvorlage*' (321–44); 'Bibliographie' (345–88).
H. Schmidt-Westman, 'Zwei Leben — ein Erinnerungsjahr: J. G.
und Jakob Burckhardt', *Aus dem Antiquariat*, 1997, Heft 12, A: 668–74.
*Dimensionen des Phantastischen: Studien zu E. T. A. Hoffmann*, ed. Jean-
Marie Paul (SBL, 61), 1998, 225 pp., has an article by the editor, 'Der
Teufel und das Diabolische in E. T. A. Hoffmanns *Ignaz Denner* und
in J. Gs *Die schwarze Spinne*', pp. 133–52.

GREGOROVIUS.    Gustav Seibt, *Das Komma in der Erdnussbutter: Essays
zur Literatur und literarischen Kritik* (FT, 13874), 1997, ·191 pp., has a
short essay 'Wider die Weltwoge der Moderne: die *Römische Tagebücher*
des F. G.', pp. 175–79.

GRILLPARZER.    William C. Reeve, *Grillparzer's 'Libussa': The Tragedy
of Separation*, McGill–Queens' U.P., 292 pp., is divided into five main
chapters and a conclusion. Each of the chapters is devoted to an act
of the play and gives an exhaustive textual analysis of it. An attempt
is made to situate the play in the development of the history of ideas
in the 19th century. The author argues that G. anticipates ideas of
Bachofen, Nietzsche, Freud, and Lacan among others. Use is made
of Freudian psychoanalysis in the interpretations. *Stile, Stilprägungen,
Stilgeschichte: Über Epochen-, Gattungs- und Autorenstile; sprachliche Analysen
und didaktische Aspekte*, ed. Ulla Fix et al. (Sprache — Literatur und
Geschichte, 15), Heidelberg, Winter, 1997, 416 pp., includes C. Leitgeb, 'Grillparzers *Jugenderinnerungen im Grünen*' (331–44), and R. Reichensperger, 'Dramentheorie und Stilanalyse: Franz Grillparzers *Die
Jüdin von Toledo*' (345–59). A. Reininger, '*Das goldene Vlies*', pp. 33–55
of *Studia Austriaca*, ed. Fausto Cercignani, vol. 6, Milan, Ed. dell'Arco,
1998, 271 pp. E. Reichmann, ' "Altwiener Amazonen": Gs
Frauenfiguren', pp. 171–85 of *Studien zu Forschungsproblemen der
deutschen Literatur in Mittel- und Osteuropa*, ed. Carola Gottzmann et al.
(Deutsche Literatur in Mittel- und Osteuropa. Mittelalter und
Neuzeit, 1), Frankfurt–Berlin, Lang, 1998, 278 pp. K. Feilchenfeldt,
'Die "Nobilitierung" der Prosa in Grillparzers *Der arme Spielmann*',
*Fest. Steinsdorff*, 223–35. U. H. Gerlach, 'Helferin oder Hindernis?: die
Frau in Gs *König Ottokars Glück und Ende*', *ZGB*, 6, 1997:13–28.
A. Focher, 'F. G. epigrammista musicale', *ConLet*, 14, 1997:63–92.
G. Stocker, 'Die zerstörerische Kraft des Eros bei G.', *Cultura Tedesca*,
11:45–63.

GROTH.    *Jahresgabe der K.-G.-Gesellschaft*, 41, contains: U. Bichel,
'K. G., "Int Fährhus" (Ein unvollendetes Vertellen)' (9–63, prints the
text of G.'s fragment for the first time, with a commentary and
annotations); F. Schüppen, 'Noch einmal: Liebe und Ökonomie:

Hauptthema der Erzählungen von K. G. VII. Von Möglichkeiten und
Gefahren einer neuen Welt im Manuskript "Int Fährhus"' (65–88);
U. Bichel and I. Bichel, 'Vor hundert Jahren: K. G. im Jahre 1899'
(89–120); R. Goltz, 'Vor fünfzig Jahren: die Gründung der K.-G.-
Gesellschaft' (121–26). J. Hartig, 'K. Gs *Heisterkrog*: Entstehung und
Wirkung', *Nordfriesisches Jahrbuch*, 34, 1998: 111–27.
GUTZKOW. K. G., *Schriften*, ed. Adrian Hummel (Haidnische
Althertümer), 2 vols, Frankfurt, Zweitausendeins, 1998, presents two
volumes of G.'s selected critical and autobiographical writings, vol. 1,
*Politisch-Zeitkritisches. Philosophisch-Weltanschauliches*, and vol. 2,
*Literaturkritisch-Publizistisches. Autobiographisch-Itinerarisches*, 859,
863–1942 pp. For most Germanists the more interesting material will
be found in the second volume which includes reviews of, and essays
on, works by Heine, Büchner, Grabbe, and Hebbel; essays on
contemporary literary debates (chiefly aspects of the novel) first
published in the *Unterhaltungen am häuslichen Herd* between 1853 and
1857; and the autobiographical writings *Eine Reise nach Wien* (1845)
and the *Jugenderinnerungen* of 1852. There is also a third volume of
*Materialien*, 556 pp., giving a full and informative commentary on the
contents of volumes 1 and 2 and a useful index of names. All three
volumes are attractively bound in covers of a 19th-c. style. The
publication, especially the commentary, will be of great value to
anyone interested in research on Gutzkow. In the same series is a
reprint of K. G., *Die Ritter vom Geiste: Roman in neun Büchern*, ed.
Thomas Neumann (Haidnische Althertümer), 3 vols, Frankfurt,
Zweitausendeins, 1998, 3609 pp. This contains the full texts of the
nine books of the novel, again bound in stylish covers characteristic
of the 19th c. There is also an accompanying *Materialband* by Adrian
Hummel and Neumann, 510 pp., with nearly 250 pages of commentary on the text of the novel; a summary of the action; a list of the
characters in it; and numerous documents pertaining to its reception
history. K. G., *Die Selbsttaufe: Erzählungen und Novellen*, ed. Stephan
Landshuter, Passau, Stuta, 1998, 414 pp.
HACKLÄNDER. Hans Peter Siebel, *F. W. Hackländer: Eine Bibliographie. Klassifikation, Beschreibung, Textvergleiche*, Heidelberg, Mattes,
1997, 581 pp. H. Herbst, 'Der Erfolgsschriftsteller F. W. H.
(1816–1877)', *Aus dem Antiquariat*, 1998, Heft 5: A 354–59.
HAHN-HAHN. J. Osinski, 'Von der Nachfolgerin George Sands zur
Grande Dame des katholischen Milieus', Heydebrand, *Kanonbildung*,
524–39.
HEBBEL. This year has seen the appearance of a major new
edition of the correspondence. F. H., *Briefwechsel 1829–1863*.
*Historisch-Kritische Ausgabe*, ed. Otfrid Ehrismann et al., 5 vols, Munich,
Iudicium, contains almost 2,900 letters of which 320 — 50 written by

H. and 270 addressed to him — are here published for the first time. The individual volumes of the 'Wesselburener Ausgabe' are: I: *1829–1848: Briefe Nr 1–648*, ed. U. Henry Gerlach, xx + 1085 pp.; II: *1849–1853: Briefe Nr 649–1342*, ed. Hermann Knebel, xxi + 730 pp.; III: *1854–59: Briefe Nr 1343–2089*, ed. Otfrid Ehrismann, xxii + 845 pp.; IV: *1860–1863: Briefe Nr 2090–2880*, ed. Hargen Thomsen, xxiii + 783 pp.; V: *Register und Nachträge*, ed. Günter Häntzschel et al., vii + 384 pp. Each volume has a full and clear critical apparatus and the *Registerband* provides excellent indexes arranged by the dates of the letters, the names of H.'s correspondents, names of people mentioned, and by topic. The set is in every way an outstanding achievement and a welcome replacement for the outdated edition of Felix Bamberg. Future research on H. will be unthinkable without it.

*Hebbel-Jb.*, 54, has: H. Knebel, 'Aspekte des "Briefschreibens"' im Briefwechsel F. Hs' (59–82); U. H. Gerlach, 'Hs Briefe der Lehr- und Wanderjahre: Hinweise für Benutzer' (83–94); O. Ehrismann, ' "Der Jude ist gerade so schlecht, wie der Mensch!": zu Hs Judenbild' (95–112); H. Thomsen, 'Philologische Späne, oder: wozu dient eine historisch-kritische Ausgabe? Mit Anhang: Zu Erinnerung an den Geh. Hofrath Dr James Marshall, † 28 Dezember 1881' (113–43); G. Häntzschel, 'Künftige Aufgaben der H.-Forschung' (145–51); S. Kiefer, 'Kritische Destruktion und literarische Produktion: über einen Grundzug von F. Hs Arbeitsweise, mit besonderer Berücksichtigung seiner *Genoveva*' (153–66); V. Nölle, ' "Politisierter Totenkult" in der *Antigone* und in *Agnes Bernauer*' (167–76); A. Tischel, ' "... ein Jeder, der hieher kommt, erst sehen lernen muss...": F. H. in Italien' (177–96); S. Schwabach-Albrecht, 'H. und die Deutsche Schillerstiftung' (197–210); H. Thomsen, 'Theaterbericht' (211–20).

*Hebbel — Mensch und Dichter im Werk: Problemdrama und Postmoderne*, ed. Ida Koller-Andorf et al. (Schriftenreihe der F.-H.-Gesellschaft Wien, 6), Hamburg, LIT, 1998, ii + 226 pp., has: M. M. Langner, 'Auf Spurensuche — Richard Maria Werner: "Alles regt sich, nur Wien bleibt stumm!" ' (5–18); A. Rudolph, 'Ferdinand Raimunds Edelsteinallegorie in F. Hs Komödie *Der Rubin* (1849): ein Beitrag zur Wirkung der Wiener Bühne auf H.' (19–46); G. Scheidt, 'Tragödie des Judentums — Komödie des Antisemitismus?: das Verhältnis zum Judentum in Hs *Judith* und Nestroys Parodie *Judith und Holofernes*' (47–59); A. T. Alt, 'Zu Hs partiellem Realismus und dem Ursprung seines Humanismus' (65–77); M. Ritzer, 'Skepsis und Vision: zur Konzeption von Tragik in Hs Spätwerk am Beispiel des *Demetrius*-Fragments' (79–96); H. Grundmann, 'F. H. — in seinen Helden gebar sich der moderne Mensch: oder was die Postmoderne von ihnen lernen kann' (97–113); G. Benesch-Tschanett, '*Genoveva* und

Mariamne: Menschenwürde und Gewalt im "Ehedrama" ' (115–30); H. Thomsen, ' "Nein, die Sache selbst interessirte mich . . .": H. als Briefschreiber' (131–41); G. Häntzschel, ' "Epigramme in einem höheren Sinn: F. H. und die deutsche Epigrammdichtung' (143–56); G. Scheibelreiter, 'Drei Untertanen des dänischen Königs in Rom: H., Mommsen, Andersen' (157–82); Y. M. Kim, 'F. H. in Korea' (183–90); I. Koller-Andorf, 'H. in Marienbad — und ein Versäumnis' (191–201). *Gefühl und Reflexion: Studien zu Friedrich Hebbels Lyrik*, ed. Günter Häntzschel, Neuried, Ars una, 1998, 268 pp., publishes the proceedings of a conference held by the H.-Gesellschaft in Wesselburen in 1997 and contains 14 articles of generally high quality: R. Baasner, 'F. H. als Lyriker: Die Entscheidung, Gedichte zu verfassen' (17–30); M. Ritzer, ' "Lebens-Resultate": zur Position der Lyrik in F. Hs Werk' (31–54); B. Sorg, ' "Alles Dichten aber ist Offenbarung": zu F. Hs Poetik des Lyrischen' (55–64); G. Häntzschel, 'F. H.: Tagebuch und Lyrik. Zur epigrammatischen Struktur seiner Lyrik' (65–75); L. L. Albertsen, 'Wozu und wie Sonette schreiben?: allgemeine Gesetzmäßigkeit auf Material bei F. H. appliziert' (77–87); H. Kaiser, ' "Hier gilt's den Pöbelfürst zu bezwingen: F. Hs ästhetisches Weltbild in seinen Sonetten' (89–102); W. Häusler, ' "Mein Päan": zum politischen Aspekt von F. Hs Sonetten' (103–46); F. Schüppen, 'Heimatliche Geographie und globale Historie in F. Hs realistischen Balladen' (147–60); W. Schwan, 'Blitze, Hexenspuk und Liebesgeständnisse: F. Hs Ballade "Liebeszauber" und die Gewitterepisode in Goethes *Werther*' (161–72); R. Selbmann, 'Schmetterlinge: F. H. und Gottfried Keller, die Intertextualität und die Lyrik des Realismus' (173–86); A. Tischel, 'Geschlechterverhältnisse in F. Hs Lyrik' (187–205); R.-R. Wuthenow, 'Produktivität und Kritik: F. H. und die Lyrik seiner Zeit' (207–19); M. Vogt, 'Versuch, F. Hs Lyrik mit Benn zu lesen' (221–36); J. Bark, 'F. Hs Anthologiegedichte. Mit einem Anhang von A. Reck, "Gedichte von F. H. in Anthologien des 19. Jahrhunderts" ' (237–68).

Claudia Pilling, *Hebbels Dramen* (HKADL, 26), 1998, 221 pp., is a 1994 Münster dissertation. Friedrich Kittler, *\*Hebbels Einbildungskraft — Die dunkle Natur* (FLK, 65), 154 pp. Christian Rochow, *Das bürgerliche Trauerspiel* (UB, 17617), 245 pp., treats the theory, history and examples of the genre from the 18th and 19th cs, including H.'s *Maria Magdalena* (206–14). A. Rudolph, 'Zur Kultursemantik der drei Kronen in F. Hs Tragödie *Gyges und sein Ring*', pp. 559–84 of *Texte über Texte: Interdisziplinäre Zugänge*, ed. I. Pohl et al. (Sprache — System und Tätigkeit, 24), Frankfurt–Berlin, Lang, 1998, 628 pp. Id., '(Schauer)romantische Sinnkonstitution, Dramaästhetik und soziale Frage in kritischer Perspektive: F. H. auf dem Weg zur Tragödie', pp. 471–99 of *Kritische Fragen an die Tradition: Festschrift für Claus Träger zum*

*70. Geburtstag*, ed. Marion Marquardt et al. (SAG, 340), 1997, 618 pp. P. von Matt, 'Canetti und Hebbel', pp. 252–63 of *'Ein Dichter braucht Ahnen': Elias Canetti und die europäische Tradition. Akten des Pariser Symposiums 16.–18. 11. 1995*, ed. Gerald Stieg, et al. (*JIG*, Reihe A, Kongressberichte, 44), Berne, Lang, 1997, 314 pp. E. Goebel, '*Die Kuh*: zur Kompositionskunst F. Hs', *Fest. Lämmert*, 63–73.

HEINE. B. Kortländer, 'H. in wechselnder Gestalt: die beiden historisch-kritischen H.-Ausgaben', *Jb. der Ernst-Meister-Gesellschaft*, 1998[1999]:21–38, compares the Düsseldorf edition with the *Säkularausgabe*. H. H., *Florentinische Nächte: Prosa*, ed. Tilman Spreckelsen, ATV, 191 pp., is a popular edition of texts by H. on the theme of travel and includes *Der Rabbi von Bacherach, Aus den Memoiren des Herren von Schnabelowopski*, and selections from the *Florentinische Nächte*. H. H., *Prinzessin Sabbat: Über Juden und Judentum*, ed. Paul Peters, Bodenheim, Philo, 1997, 697 pp., performs a useful function by collating in one thick volume all H. texts on the subject of Jews and Jewishness. The book replaces Hugo Bieber's *Heinrich Heine: Confessio Judaica* of 1925. *Die Von Geldern Haggadah und Heinrich Heines 'Der Rabbi von Bacherach'*, ed. Emile G. L. Schrijver et al., Vienna, Brandstätter, 1997, 80 pp. \**Heinrich Heines Höllenfahrt: Nachrufe auf einen streitbaren Schriftsteller. Dokumente 1846–1858*, ed. Ralf G. Bogner, Heidelberg, Palatina, 1997, 207 pp., prints a selection of texts by H. with an introduction by the editor.

The great tide of *Sammelbände* published to mark the bicentenary of H.'s birth continues almost undiminished. The most important and most voluminous of these to appear this year is *Aufklärung und Skepsis: Internationaler Heinrich Heine-Kongress 1997 zum 200. Geburtstag*, ed. Joseph A. Kruse et al., Stuttgart–Weimar, Metzler, xx + 950 pp., containing some 60 papers given in May 1997 in Düsseldorf by luminaries in H. research from all over the world. The articles are too numerous to list individually, but their general quality is high and the volume should certainly find its way into the library of any institution where H. is studied seriously. For ease of access the articles are grouped in nine main sections dealing with H. and the Enlightenment; his Europeanism; his Jewishness; his use of various myths (eg. Barbarossa); his support for *littérature engagée*; his attitude to revolution; his stance in philosophy and religion; the history of H. reception (with special reference to exile reception 1933–1945); and linguistic and stylistic features of his writing.

This year *GR*, 74, has one number devoted entirely to Heine's Jewish identity, and contains: W. Goetschel and N. Roemer, 'H.'s Judaism and its reception' (267–69); W. Goetschel, 'Rhyming history: a note on the "Hebrew melodies"' (271–82); R. C. Holub, 'H.'s conversion: reflections from the "Matratzengruft" ' (283–92); K. Weimar, 'A third meaning of the word *Jewish*: H. in German literary histories of the nineteenth century' (293–98); N. Roemer, 'Jew or German? H. H.'s German-Jewish reception in the nineteenth century' (301–12); S. J. Sasson, 'The dying poet: scenarios of a christianized H.' (314–26); P. Reitter, 'H. in the Bronx' (327–36); J. L. Sammons, 'The restoration of the H. monument in the Bronx' (337–39). *Romantisme*, 28, 1998, also has one number devoted entirely to H. with the title *Heine le médiateur*, and contains: G.-A. Goldschmidt, 'Un poète allemand en France' (7–16); M.-C. Hoock-Demarle, 'La médiation selon H.' (17–27); B. Kortländer, 'Le poète inconnu de la 'Loreley': le médiateur supprimé' (29–40); M. Perraudin, 'H. et l'Angleterre ou le médiateur en défaut' (41–49); L. Calvié, 'H., médiateur de l'idée de révolution' (51–61); B. Kortländer, 'Tribulations posthumes d'une figure de poète: images commentées par B. Kortländer' (63–71); I. Oesterle, 'Les *Lettres de Paris*: un genre heinéen' (73–83); G. Schlocker, 'H. journaliste, notes sur le langage d'un contrabandier' (85–88); I. Kalinowski, 'H. en français: brève histoire d'une réception difficile' (89–96); G. Schlocker, ' "Les yeux rivés sur l'avenir": une lecture d'Albrecht Betz' (105–08); I. Brendel, 'H. H. en 1997: bibliographie choisie et commentée' (109–12).

*Differenz und Identität: Heinrich Heine (1797–1856). Europäische Perspektiven im 19. Jahrhundert. Tagungsakten des internationalen Kolloquiuums zum Heine-Gedenkjahr. Lissabon 4.–5. Dezember 1997*, ed. Alfred Opitz (Schriftenreihe Literaturwissenschaft, 41), Trier, Wissenschaftlicher Vlg, 1998, 279 pp., includes among other articles too numerous to list: M. M. G. Delille, 'Die H.-Rezeption in Portugal: von der Romantik bis zur Gegenwart' (27–55); M. Dias, 'H. H. als utopischer Dichter Deutschlands' (135–41); H. Bergmeier, 'Die Eröffnung von Hs Salon' (169–80); F. M. Alves, 'Zwischen Miranda und Cleopatra gibt es Verschiedene: Hs weibliche Figuren' (225–35). *Heinrich Heine zum 200. Geburtstag: Kolloquium vom 14. März 1997 in Zusammenarbeit mit der Université Libre de Bruxelles*, ed. Bernhard Beutler et al., Brussels, Goethe-Institut, 1998, 94 pp., contains: J. Kruse, '200 Jahre H. H.: Wirkung, Ruhm und Kontroversen' (11–21); B. Witte, 'Hieroglyphenschrift: Poetologie und Anthropologie der Moderne in H. Hs *Lutezia*' (22–36); M. Hofmann, 'H. H. — ein Aufklärer?' (37–47); A. M. Jäger, 'H. Hs *Rabbi von Bacherach*: literarisches Projekt der jüdischen Aufklärung?' (48–67); H. Gehle, 'Heines *Denkschrift* über Ludwig Börne' (68–81); F. Höllerer, 'H. H. und das Ballett: *Der Doktor Faustus* im H.-Bild Gérard de Nervals' (82–92). *\*Heinrich Heine und die Religion, ein kritischer Rückblick: Ein Symposium der Evgl. Kirche im Rheinland vom 27.–30. Oktober 1997*, ed. Ferdinand Schlingensiepen et al., Düsseldorf, Archiv der Evang. Kirche im Rheinland, 1998, 244 pp.

\*_Dichter unbekannt, Heine lesen heute: Internationales Heine-Symposium Bonn, Mai 1997_, ed. Dolf Oehler et al., Bonn, Bouvier, 1998, 178 pp. _H.-Jb._, 38, contains: S. Ledanff, ' "Berlin ist gar keine große Stadt": der Ursprung eines Topos. Hs _Briefe aus Berlin_' (1–28); K. H. Götze, 'Die unmögliche und die mögliche Liebe: Hs Liebeslyrik in der Geschichte der Gefühle' (29–45); R. Anglade, 'H. H.: von der französischen "Spezialrevoluzion" zur deutschen "Universalrevoluzion"' (45–73); M. Glückert, ' "Rothe Pantoffeln"' (74–90, on the poem of that title); R. Francke, ' "Damit sie die Geister entzünde und die Herzen treffe, rede die Philosophie in verständlichen Tönen!": eine unbekannte Quelle für Hs philosophische Studien' (91–104); C. auf der Horst and A. Labisch, 'H. H., der Verdacht einer Bleivergiftung und Hs Opium-Abusus' (105–31); M. Folkerts, 'Wer war Hs "Mouche"? Dichtung und Wahrheit' (133–51); G. Hoffmeister, 'H. in der Romania: Vorstudie zu einer Rezeptionsgeschichte' (152–74); M. Maher, 'Die arabische Welt in Hs Werk und Hs Werk in der arabischen Welt' (175–96); R. Olwitz, 'Offenbarungen des Bildes: H. H. über Roberts Gemälde _Die Schnitter_' (197–204); S. Bierwirth, 'H.-Rezeption in Griechenland' (205–14); E. Wulf, 'Das Berliner H.-Denkmal von Waldemar Grzimek' (215–24); W. Zöller, 'H. H. im Spiegel der Philatelie' (225–30); M. Tilch, 'Bestandsverzeichnis der Düsseldorfer H.-Autographen. Neuerwerbungen 1993–1998' (231–41); T.-R. Feuerhake, 'H.-Literatur 1997–98 mit Nachträgen' (299–32).

Dietrich Gronau, \*_Heinrich Heine: "Nichts als ein Dichter"_, Munich, Heyne, 1997, 237 pp. _Die Jahre kommen und vergehen! 10 Jahre Heinrich-Heine-Universität Düsseldorf_, ed. Holger Ehlert et al., Düsseldorf, Grupello, 1998, 299 pp. Geertje Suhr, \*_Venus und Loreley: Die Wandlungen des Frauenbildes in der Lyrik Heinrich Heines_, Düsseldorf, Grupello, 1998, 208 pp., is a dissertation accepted in 1980 by the University of Illinois at Urbana. _Großer Mann im seidenen Rock: Heines Verhältnis zu Goethe_, ed. U. Roth et al. (Heinrich-Heine-Institut Düsseldorf–Archiv, Bibliothek, Museum, 8), Stuttgart–Weimar, Metzler, 195 pp., is an exhibition catalogue which attempts to illuminate the problematic relationship between H. and Goethe through texts by both of them and by others, and through numerous illustrations. Arnold Pistiak, '_Ich will das rote Sefchen küssen': Nachdenken über Heines letzten Gedichtzyklus_ (Heine-Studien), Stuttgart–Weimar, Metzler, 411 pp., offers a detailed study of H.'s _Gedichte. 1853 und 1854_. Hubert Wolf and Wolfgang Schopf, \*_Die Macht der Zensur: Heinrich Heine auf dem Index_, Düsseldorf, Patmos, 1998, 272 pp. George Peters, _The Poet as Provocateur: Heinrich Heine and His Critics_ (Literary Criticism in Perspective), Columbia, SC, Camden House, 256 pp., traces the history of critical debate on H. from his own lifetime to the present day. _Zwei Zeitmaler_ *in Paris: Honoré Daumier und Heinrich Heine*, ed. Werner Büsen et al. (Veröffentlichungen des H.-H.-Instituts, Düsseldorf) Düsseldorf, Droste, 1998, 159 pp. Martin van Amerongen, *\*Heine en Holland*, Amsterdam, Ambo, 1997, 92 pp. Roger E. Cook, *By the Rivers of Babylon: Heinrich Heine's Late Songs and Reflections* (German Literary Theory and Cultural Studies), Wayne State U.P., 1998, 399 pp. M.-C. Boerner, '*Die ganze Janitscharenmusik der Weltqual': Heines Auseinandersetzung mit der romantischen Theorie*, Stuttgart–Weimar, Metzler, 1998, 396 pp., is a 1996 Berlin dissertation. Anne Maximiliane Jäger,'*Besaß auch in Spanien manch' luftiges Schloss': Spanien in Heinrich Heines Werk*, Stuttgart, Metzler, 340 pp., is a 1998 Marburg dissertation which traces the influence of Spanish history and culture on H.'s writings and his sense of his Jewish identity. *\*Mit Heine im Exil: Heinrich Heine in der deutschsprachigen Exilpresse 1933 bis 1945*, ed. Wolfgang Schopf, Frankfurt, Neue Kritik, 1997, 167 pp.

G. Höhn, 'H. H., une figure européenne', pp. 313–22 of *Maison Heinrich Heine Paris 1956–1996: Quarante ans de présence culturelle*, ed. Martin Raether, Paris, Maison Heinrich Heine — Bonn, DAAD, 1998, 399 pp. A. Phelan, 'H.'s Metropolen: Berlin — London — Paris', pp. 169–90 of *Der fremde Blick: Perspektiven interkultureller Kommunikation und Hermeneutik. Ergebnisse der DAAD-Tagung in London, 17–19 Juni 1996*, ed. Ingo Breuer et al., Bolzano, Sturzflüge, 1997, 302 pp. L. Zagari, 'Säkularisation und Privatreligion: Novalis — H. — Benn — Brecht', pp. 474–508 of *Ästhetische Moderne in Europa: Gründzüge und Problemzusammenhänge seit der Romantik*, ed. Silvio Vietta et al., Munich, Fink, 1998, vii + 572 pp.

J. L. Sammons, 'Review essay: the bicentennial of H. H. 1997. An overview', *Goethe Yearbook*, 9 : 346–83, provides a penetrating and well-judged assessment of the flood of publications that marked the celebration. D. P. Meier-Lenz, 'Hs Modernität: Aspekte zu seinem politischen und philosophischen Denken', *Die Horen*, 43, 1998 : 161–75. M. Thiam, ' "Autonomie der Kunst" als Begegnungsebene: zu H. Hs und Leopold Sedor Senghers Ästhetik', *AGJSG*, 25, 1997[1999] : 21–33, compares H. with a modern Senegalese poet. C. Gellner, 'Schriftsteller als Bibelleser: H. H., Bertolt Brecht und Erich Fried', *Stimmen der Zeit*, 123, 1998 : 550–62. H. Wolf, 'H. H. auf dem Index der verbotenen Bücher: Häretiker, Religionskritiker, Revolutionär', *Forschung Frankfurt*, 16.2, 1998 : 4–11. B. Morawe, 'Hs "gefährliche Vielleichts" und die Anfänge des politischen Radikalismus in Deutschland', *Euphorion*, 93 : 1–59. G. F. Peters, 'Review Essay: H. at 200', *GQ*, 71, 1998 : 284–98. H. Wehrmann, 'Hs Musikanschauung', *Acta Musicologica*, 70, 1998 : 79–107. P. O'Doherty, 'The reception of H.'s Jewishness in the Soviet Zone/GDR, 1945–1961', *GLL*, 52 : 85–96. E. Petzoldt, 'Karl Kraus über

H. H.: ein politisches Missverständnis', *Welfengarten*, 7, 1997 : 133–48.
C. Sonino, 'Der Jude Gundolf und der "Fall" H.', *Menora*, 8,
1997 : 231–54. A. Meier, ' "vom Schwindel erfasst": Hs *Harzreise* als
Symptom eines kulturgeschichtlichen Paradigmenwechsels', *WW*,
49 : 329–54. O. Hildebrand, 'Sinnliche Seligkeit: Goethes heidnischer
Sensualismus und seine Beziehung zu H.', *Goethe-Jb.*, 114,
1997[1998] : 231–51.
    HERWEGH.    Michail Krausnick, *Nicht Magd mit den Knechten: Emma
Herwegh. Eine biographische Skizze* (*MaM*, 83, Sonderheft), 1998, 127 pp.
Id., 'Zeitlos zeitbezogen "Achtzehnter März": vor rund hundertfünf-
undzwanzig Jahren schrieb der Dichter G. H. eines seiner wichtigsten
Gedichte, die Erinnerung an ein Ereignis, das mittlerweile 25 Jahre
zurücklag', *Passagen*, 11.2, 1998 : 26–27.
    HEYSE.    The large Hildesheim reprint edition of P. H., *Gesammelte
Werke (Gesamtausgabe)*, ed. M. Bernauer et al., has added *Reihe* 5,
*Italienische Dichter in Übersetzungen*, ed. M. Bernauer et al., 5 vols,
Hildesheim, Olms. A sixth and final *Reihe* will reprint the dramatic
works. R. Hillenbrand, 'Paul Heyse als Ghostwriter für Franz
Lenbach', *Zeitschrift für Kunstgeschichte*, 60, 1997 : 549–55.
    HOFFMANN VON FALLERSLEBEN.    W. Freund, ' "Abend wird es
wieder": eine Erinnerung an den Dichter August Heinrich H. v. F.'
*Die Horen*, 43, 1998 : 111–24. F. Schüppen, 'Doppeljubiläum: August
Heinrich H. v. Fs (1789–1874) niederdeutsche Arbeiten und seine
Ausgabe des "Reineke Vos von 1498" ', *Quickborn*, 88, 1998, 37–50.
U. Müller, ' "Deutschland, Deutschland, Über Alles?": Walther von
der Vogelweide, H. v. F. and the "Song of the Germans". Medieval-
ism, nationalism and/or racism', *Workman Vol.*, 117–30.
    HOLTEI.    Georg Potempa, *Karl von Holtei: Eine Erinnerung an den
Dichter und Schauspieler aus Breslau*, Nettetal, Matussek, 1998, 35 pp.
    IMMERMANN.    Markus Fauser, *Intertextualität als Poetik des Epigonalen:
Immermann-Studien*, Munich, Fink, 443 pp.
    KAISER, FRIEDRICH.    R. Reutner, 'Ein kleines Dialektwörterbuch:
zusammengestellt aus Belegen in den gedruckten Volksstücken F. Ks',
*Fest. Tatzreiter*, 179–204.
    KELLER.    Martina Wagner-Egelhaaf, *Die Melancholie der Literatur:
Diskursgeschichte und Textfiguration*, Stuttgart, Metzler, 1997,
vi + 570 pp., is a Bochum *Habilitationsschrift* that discusses the interpretation of melancholy in a wide range of texts from various periods,
including K.'s *Der grüne Heinrich*. Annette Coen, *Literatur-Kartei zur
Novelle von Gottfried Keller 'Kleider machen Leute'*, Mühlheim, an der Ruhr,
1997, 84 pp. Helmut Naumann, *Aufsätze zur deutschen Literatur* (Deutsche und vergleichende Literaturwissenschaft, 31), Rheinfelden–Berlin, Schäuble, 1997, 170 pp., has two essays on *Der grüne Heinrich*: 'Das
Tell-Fest im Zürcher Unterland: ein Beispiel für G. Ks epische

Landschaftsmalerei' (2–27); and 'Die Heidenstube bei Glattfelden' (28–65). G. Marci-Boehncke, 'Imaging a hero: the fantastic rise of the tailor in K.'s and Käutner's *Kleider machen Leute*', pp. 45–52 of *Special Issues Devoted to the Fantastic and Related Genres and Revising the Canon: Culture and Pop Culture*, ed. Marilyn Bendena et al., Morgantown, West Virginia U.P., 1998, v + 156 pp. A. Azzone Zweifel, '"Trotz Goethe, Natur und gutem Lehrer . . .": pittura e letteratura in G. K., *Der grüne Heinrich* (erste Fassung)', pp. 113–55 of *Il gesto, il bello, il sublime: Arte e letteratura in Germania tra '700 e '800*, ed. Emilio Bonfatti (Proteo, 3), Rome, Artemide, 1997, 174 pp. P. Villwock, 'Was stand in G. Ks Bibliothek?', *Text*, 4, 1998: 99–118. W. Albrecht, 'Die Utopie der Liebe: über den rahmenstiftenden Sinnzusammenhang in Ks Novellenzyklus *Das Sinngedicht*', *MGS*, 23, 1997[1998]: 39–56. G. Brandstetter, 'Fremde Zeichen: Zu G. Ks Novelle *Die Berlocken*. Literaturwissenschaft als Kulturpoetik', *JDSG*, 43: 305–24.

KINKEL, GOTTFRIED. K. Schmidt, '"Was wir friedlich gewünscht hätten, wird in Sturm und Wetter erscheinen": G. K. und die rheinischen Demokraten', pp. 91–108 of *Das war 'ne heisse Märzenzeit: Revolution im Rheinland 1848–49*, ed. Frita Bilz et al., Cologne, PapyRossa, 1998, 196 pp.

LENAU. N. L., *Gedichte*, ed. Hansgeorg Schmidt-Bergmann (IT, 1986), 1998, 328 pp. N. Oellers, 'Der zerstörte Traum: N. Ls Amerika-Abenteuer', pp. 139–53 of *Literatur und Geschichte: Fest. für Wulf Koepke zum 70. Geburtstag*, ed. K. Menges (APSL, 133), 364 pp. A. Mádl, 'Ls Aktualität heute', *Jb. der ungarischen Germanistik*, 1997: 23–32.

LUDWIG. *Otto Ludwig: Das literarische und musikalische Werk, mit einer vollständigen Otto-Ludwig-Bibliographie*, ed. Claudia Pilling et al. (HKADL, 25), 567 pp.

MEYER. C. F. M., *Briefwechsel: Historische-kritische Ausgabe*, ed. Hans Zeller, I. *Conrad Ferdinand Meyer — Gottfried Keller: Briefe 1871 bis 1889*, Berne, Benteli, 1998, 383 pp., is a bibliophile edition with photographic facsimiles of each one of the 58 extant letters, postcards, etc. C. F. M., *Gedichte*, ed. Rüdiger Görner (IT, 2233), 1998, 153 pp. J. Schuster, '"Der Burg zerstörtes Wappen": Historismus und Modernität in C. F. Meyers Lyrik', *Hofmannsthal-Jb.*, 7: 289–306. K. S. Guthke, 'Lebenskunst, Sterbenskunst: C. F. Meyer und die Kultur des letzten Worts', *WW*, 49: 207–34, discusses M.'s treatment of the moment of death in his verse and Novellen.

MÖRIKE. *Mörike im Spiegel seiner Briefe von Velegern, Herausgebern und Redakteuren: 'Ihr Interesse und das Unsrige . . .'*, ed. Hans-Ulrich Simon (Veröffentlichungen der Deutschen Schiller-Gesellschaft, 48), Stuttgart, Cotta, 1997, 341 pp. S. Guarda, 'Hegel's "Schein": eine ästhetische Konsekration (unter Berücksichtigung von Ms Gedicht "Auf eine Lampe"', *MDU*, 91:305–22. F. Lösel, 'E. M., "Einer Reisenden": das Problem der Umkehr im Gedichtwerk', Kavanagh, *Exchanges*, 152–66.

MÜHLBACH, LUISE (MUNDT, CLARA). Cornelia Tönnesen, *Die Vormärz-Autorin Luise Mühlbach: Vom sozialkritischen Frühwerk zum historischen Roman*, Neuss, Ahasvera, 1997, ix + 269 pp., is a 1995 Düsseldorf dissertation.

NESTROY. The HKA of N.'s *Sämtliche Werke*, ed. Jürgen Hein et al., Vienna, Deuticke (formerly Jugend und Volk), has added *Stücke*, 8.2: *Weder Lorbeerbaum noch Bettelstab*, ed. Friedrich Walla, 1998, 462 pp.; *Stücke*, 11: *Die beiden Nachtwandler oder Das Notwendige und das Überflüssige. Der Affe und der Bräutigam*, ed. Jürgen Hein, 1998, xvi + 447 pp.; *Stücke*, 16.1: *Der Färber und sein Zwillingsbruder*, ed. Louise A. Huish, xiv + 306 pp.; and *Stücke*, 29: *Alles will den Prophet'n sehen. Verwickelte Geschichte!*, ed. Walter Obermaier, xxi + 426 pp.

*Nestroyana*, 19, has: G. Schlögl, W. Schlögl, and K. Schuster, 'Nestroy als Liedtexter: *Die Ballnacht* von Waldon und von Nestroy' (5–18); R. Theobald, J. Hein, and S. P. Scheichl, 'Hieronymus Lorm über Nestroy (2)' (19, supplements the note by Scheichl in *Nestroyana*, 18:39); G. Schlögl and W. Schlögl, 'Nestroy im Ausweichquartier' (20–26); U. Helmensdorfer, '*Himmelangst*: Nachtrag zu *Der alte Mann mit der jungen Frau* (*Stücke*, 27/1) und *Höllenangst* (*Stücke*, 27/2)' (27–47); S. P. Scheichl, 'Nestroy-Brief Nr 110 an Bauernfeld (1856)' (48, publishes a newly discovered letter by N.); B. Pargner, 'Theaterdirektor J. N.: "Der betrogene Betrüger"' (49–64); J. Hein and W. E. Yates, 'Zwei N.-Epiloge' (65–69); R. Reutner, 'Karl Meisls Nachruf auf Anton Linhart' (85–87); Id., 'Nachträgliches zu Adolf Bäuerles *Die Fremden in Wien* (1814) und Karl Meisls *Moisasuras's Hexenspruch* (1827)' (88–91); O. Pausch, 'Unbekannte Nestroyana im Österreichischen Theatermuseum: 3. Bericht' (92–97); R. Theobald, 'Der "confuse" N.: Beobachtungen an einem frühen Aufführungsdokument' (98–101); L. A. Huish, E. E. Smith, and W. E. Yates, 'Zu Ns *Werther*-Fragment' (101–06); L. A. Huish, 'Der experimentierende N.' (107–15); J. Hein, 'Wiener Volkstheater-Eindrücke eines finnischen Reisenden im Jahre 1841' (116–19); J. Hein and W. E. Yates, 'Ein Bericht aus dem Jahr 1843 über das Ensemble des Theaters an der Wien. Nebst Nachträgen zu den Bänden *Stücke*, 19 und *Stücke*, 20 der HKA' (119–37); S. In, 'Ns Theater als Abbild und Sinnbild der Welt: *Der Zerrissene* im Vergleich zu *L'homme blasé*' (138–49).

Herbert Hunger, *Das Denken am Leitseil der Sprache: Johann Nestroys geniale wie auch banale Verfremdung durch Neologismen* (Sitzungsberichte der phil.-hist. Klasse, 664), VÖAW, 201 pp. *Die Welt ist die wahre Schule . . .: Beiträge und Materialien zu Nestroy im Deutschunterricht*, ed.

Ulrike Tanzer (Publikationen der Internationalen Nestroy-Gesellschaft, 1), Vienna, Lehner, 1998, 70 pp. R. Reutner, 'Dialekt und Sprachspiel bei Ns Vorgängern und Zeitgenossen: am Beispiel von Franz Xaver Gewey (1764–1819) und Friedrich Kaiser (1814–1874)', pp. 105–24 of *Deutsche Sprache in Raum und Zeit: Festschrift für Peter Wiesinger zum 60. Geburtstag*, ed. Peter Ernst et al., Vienna, Praesens, 1998, 714 pp. W. Neuber, 'Erstarrte Welt? Zum Verhältnis von Bild und Wort in Ns Schlusstableaux', *ABNG*, 45 : 135–46.

NIETZSCHE. The Berlin HKA of N.'s *Werke*, ed. Giorgio Colli et al., Berlin, de Gruyter, has produced vol. III, 5, *Nachbericht zur dritten Abteilung*, ed. Wolfram Groddeck et al., 2 vols, 1997, vii + 916, 919–1704 pp. The first of the two *Halbbände* is of particular interest to Germanists because it contains the long-awaited commentary to *Die Geburt der Tragödie* and the *Unzeitgemäße Betrachtungen*. F. N., *Sämtliche Gedichte*, ed. Ralph-Rainer Wuthenow (Bibliothek der Weltliteratur), Zurich, Manesse, 258 pp. F. N., *The Birth of Tragedy and Other Writings*, ed. Raymond Geuss and Ronald Speirs (Cambridge Texts in the History of Philosophy), CUP, xxxvii + 163 pp., provides a fluent new translation by Speirs and an introduction by Geuss. The 'other writings' are two short pieces on 'The Dionysiac world view' and 'On truth and lying in a non-moral sense' that were never published in N.'s lifetime but are related in theme to *The Birth of Tragedy*. The book contains a useful index and a glossary of significant German terms (*Schein, Rechtfertigung*) occurring in the text.

Carol Diethe, *Historical Dictionary of Nietzscheanism* (Historical Dictionaries of Religions, Philosophies and Movements, 21), Lanham, Maryland–London, Scarecrow, xvi + 265 pp., has an introduction of 40 pages, followed by the dictionary itself which runs to nearly 200 pages and consists of brief notes (typically half a page or a page) on a variety of names (Apollo, Bakhtin, Barthes) and terms (Art, Dance, Transvaluation of Values). The result is frankly a thin hotch-potch of information that can for the most part be found easily and more reliably elsewhere. Curtis Cate, *Friedrich Nietzsche*, London, Hutchinson, 480 pp., is a biographical study. Peter D. Murray, *Nietzsche's Affirmative Morality: A Revaluation Based in the Dionysian World-View* (MTNF, 42), xvi + 320 pp., is a Sydney dissertation. *Nietzsche und die jüdische Kultur*, ed. Jacob Golomb, Vienna U.P., 1998, 284 pp., is a translation by Helmut Dahmer of *Nietzsche and Jewish Culture*, London, Routledge, 1997, xii + 282 pp, and includes: S. Aschheim, 'N., der Antisemitismus und der Holocaust' (13–30); W. Santaniello, 'N. und die Juden im Hinblick auf Christentum und Nazismus — nach dem Holocaust' (31–66); H. Cancik, '"Mongolen, Semiten, Rassengriechen": Ns Umgang mit den Rassenlehren seiner Zeit' (67–86); S. L. Gilman, 'Heine, N. and the idea of the Jew' (87–112); J. Simon,

'Das Judentum und Europa bei N.' (113–25); Y. Yovel, 'N. und die Juden: die Struktur einer Ambivalenz' (126–44); S. Corngold, 'Nietzsche, Kafka und die literarische Vaterschaft' (145–64); J. Golomb, 'N. und die "Grenzjuden"' (165–84); P. Heller, 'Freud in seinem Verhältnis zu Nietzsche' (185–209); W. J. McGrath, 'Mahler und der Wiener Nietzsche-Verein' (210–24); P. Mendes-Flohr, 'Zarathustras Apostel: Martin Buber und die "Jüdische Renaissance"' (225–35). Günter Figal, *Nietzsche: Eine philosophische Einführung* (UB, 9752), 293 pp. Barbara Smitmans-Vajda, *Melancholie, Eros, Muße: Das Frauenbild in Nietzsches Philosophie* (Nietzsche in der Diskussion), Würzburg, Königshausen & Neumann, 190 pp. Hubert Cancik and Hildegard Cancik-Lindemaier, *Philolog und Kultfigur: Friedrich Nietzsche und seine Antike in Deutschland*, Stuttgart–Weimar, Metzler, xi + 291 pp., examines among other things N.'s status as a cult figure in Weimar and elsewhere, before and after his death. Martina Hoffmann, *Von Venedig nach Weimar: Eine Entwicklungsgeschichte paradigmatischen Künstlertums* (BSDL, 51), 309 pp., is a 1997 Bochum dissertation which discusses N. and Schopenhauer as well as Goethe and Thomas Mann. Manfred Riedel, *Freilichtgedanken: Nietzsches dichterische Welterfahrung*, Stuttgart, Klett-Cotta, 1998, 375 pp. Erwin Schlimgen, *Nietzsches Theorie des Bewusstseins* (MTNF, 41), xiii + 253 pp., is a 1997 Jena dissertation. Katrin Meyer, *Ästhetik der Historie: Friedrich Nietzsches 'Vom Nutzen und Nachteil der Historie für das Leben'* (Ep, 238), 1998, vi + 215 pp., is a 1997 Basle dissertation. Douglas Thomas, *Reading Nietzsche Rhetorically*, NY–London, Guilford Press, x + 198 pp. Christian Lipperheide, *Die Ästhetik des Erhabenen bei Friedrich Nietzsche: Die Verwindung der Metaphysik der Erhabenheit*, Würzburg, Königshausen & Neumann, 103 pp. Massimo Ferrari Zumbini, *Untergänge und Morgenröten: Nietzsche — Spengler — Antisemitismus* (Studien zur Literatur- und Kulturgeschichte, 14), Würzburg, Königshausen & Neumann, 217 pp. Michael Thalken, *'Ein bewegliches Heer von Metaphern . . .': Sprachkritisches Sprechen bei Friedrich Nietzsche, Gustav Gerber, Fritz Mauthner und Karl Kraus* (Literatur als Sprache, 12), Frankfurt–Berlin, Lang, 393 pp., is a 1998 Münster dissertation concerned with the attitude of the four writers to the phenomenon of language and the way in which their ideas about it were influenced by journalism and the press.

*Nietzsche-Studien*, 28, 1998, includes: H. J. Pérez López, 'Shakespeare jenseits des Dramas: zur frühen Shakespeare-Rezeption Ns (1869–1872)' (238–67); M. Riedel, 'Ns Gedicht "Sils-Maria": Entstehungsgeschichte und Deutung' (268–82). *Nietzscheforschung*, 4, 1998, contains: H. J. Pérez López, 'Gesellschaftspolitische Argumente einer Artistenmetaphysik im Vorfeld der *Geburt der Tragödie aus dem Geiste der*

*Musik'* (101–17); I. Schulze, 'N. und Claude Lorrain' (217–25); D. Schubert, 'Ns Blick auf Delacroix als Künstlertypus' (227–42); S. Brömsel, 'Zur Nietzscherezeption der Jahrhundertwende: ein Gedicht von Stefan George' (243–57); J. Nolte, 'Die Rückkehr des Verdrängten: Savonarola im Urteil von Goethe, Jacob Burckhardt und N.' (259–70). *RGI*, 11, is a special volume devoted to N. and has: V. Gerhardt, 'Les temps modernes commencent avec Socrate' (2–25); A. Nehamas, 'Le visage de Socrate a ses raisons . . .: N. sur "le problème de Socrate"' (27–57); P. Choulet, 'Une anthropologie impossible?' (61–75); M. Crépon, 'Figures du "nous": note sur l'interprétation nietzschéen du judaïsme' (77–88); J. Lacoste, 'Goethe éducateur?' (89–107); M. de Launay, '"Ars vitae, Ars tacendi"' (109–21); W. Lauter-Müller, 'De l'économie et de la culture chez N.' (123–35); A. Münster, 'Le moi, l'unique et le néant: N. et Stirner' (137–55); J. I. Porter, 'N. et les charmes de la métaphysique: "La logique du sentiment"' (157–72); J. Salaquarda, 'L'enseignant de l'humanité' (173–89); A. Venturelli, 'Généalogie et évolution: N. et le darwinisme' (191–203); J. Le Rider, 'Oubli, mémoire, histoire, dans la *Deuxième Considération inactuelle*' (207–25); P. Pénisson, 'N. missionaire: le protestantisme et la question de l'auteur à la fin de la *Seconde considération intempestive*' (227–35).

L. Pinto, 'De la canonisation en philosophie: N. en France', Heydebrand, *Kanonbildung*, 467–82. A. del Caro, '"A N. in your corner or to each a N."', *MDU*, 91 : 132–41, is a review article which discusses five monographs of the 1990s on Nietzsche. U. Klingmann, 'Ein Dämon, welcher lacht: Lachen und Legitimation im Werk Ns', *AGJSG*, 25, 1997[1999] : 35–54. M. Milli, 'F. N.: un caso di antisemitismo', *Cultura Tedesco*, 10, 1998 : 125–45. P. Bishop and R. H. Stephenson, 'N. and Weimar aesthetics', *GLL*, 52 : 412–29, examines the presence of Goethe and Schiller in *Die Geburt der Tragödie*. C. Zittel, 'Ästhetik des Nihilismus: über Wahrheit und Lüge in Ns *Also sprach Zarathustra*', *OL*, 54 : 239–61. P. Bishop, 'Estrangement from the deed and the memory thereof: Freud and Jung on the Pale Criminal in N.'s *Zarathustra*', *ib.*, 424–38. E. Joseph, '"Dass es sich ebensogut anders hätte entscheiden können": Modernität in Thomas Manns *Zauberberg*, bei F. N., Walter Benjamin und Zygmunt Baumann', *LJb*, 39, 1998 : 165–86. F. Kenk, 'Comment Freud peut cacher N.: quelques réflexions sur la place dans l'histoire intellectuelle d'un auteur énigmatique: Elias Canetti', *Austriaca*, 47 : 147–67, investigates the impact of N. on Canetti. S. Kimoto, 'Die siebente Einsamkeit: vom Ursprung des "Willens zur Wahrheit" bei N.', *DB*, 102 : 106–15 (Japanese with German summary). K. Bauer, 'Strategies of identity construction in N.'s critique of Wagner', *Seminar*, 35 : 295–307.

PAOLI, BETTY. Karin S. Wozonig, *Die Literatin Betty Paoli: Weibliche Mobilität im 19. Jahrhundert* (Sonderpublikation der Grillparzer-Gesellschaft, 4), Vienna, Löcker, 221 pp., gives a feminist's account of the life and work of this lyricist, translator and journalist who was a friend of Grillparzer and Ebner-Eschenbach. Prominence is given to P.'s interest in the 'Frauenfrage' and her energetic involvement in the movement for women's emancipation.

PFEIFFER, IDA. P. Howe, ' "Die Wirklichkeit ist anders": I. P.'s visit to China 1847', *GLL*, 52 : 325–42.

PLATEN. *August Graf von Platen: Leben, Werk, Wirkung*, ed. Hartmut Bobzin et al., Paderborn, Schöningh, 1998, xi + 189 pp., has: H. Flachenecker, 'Die ungeliebte Pflicht: P. als bayerischer Offizier' (1–20); M. Riedel, ' "Das geheimnisvolle Wie der Dinge": Schelling und P.' (21–44); J. Link, 'Sprünge im Spiegel, Zäsuren: ein Faszinationskomplex und Ps lyrischer Stil' (45–62); H. Thomé, 'P. und das Epos' (63–83); J. C. Bürgel, 'P. und Hafis' (85–102); H. Bobzin, 'P. und Rückert im Gespräch über Hafis' (103–21); J. Heymann, 'Tristans Irrungen im Land seiner Träume: A. v. P. und Italien' (123–48); G. Och, ' "Lass tief in dir mich lesen": Platen-Spuren im Werk Thomas Manns' (149–68); W. Popp, 'Der Dichter und seine Gemeinde: P. in literarischen Texten seiner Verehrer. Hans von Hülsen, Albert H. Rausch, Hubert Fichte' (169–89). K. Wölfel, 'Über Johann Peter Uz — und A. v. P.: zur 200. Wiederkehr ihres Todes- und Geburtstages', pp. 249–63 of *Dichter und Bürger in der Provinz: Johann Peter Uz und die Aufklärung in Ansbach*, ed. Ernst Rohmer et al. (FN, 42), 1998, xxiv + 307 pp.

PRUTZ, ROBERT. Edda Bergmann, *Ich darf das beste, das ich kann, nicht tun: Robert Eduard Prutz (1816–1872) zwischen Literatur und Politik*, Würzburg, Ergon, 1997, 346 pp., is a 1997 Augsburg dissertation.

PÜCKLER-MUSKAU. S. Neuhaus, 'Das fehlerhafte Vorbild: zur Darstellung Großbritanniens in H. Fürst von P.-Ms Bestseller *Briefe eines Verstorbenen*', *Neophilologus*, 83 : 267–81.

RAABE. *Raabe und Braunschweig 1870–1910: Lebenszeugnisse und Werke des Schriftstellers und Zeichners aus den Beständen der Stadt Braunschweig. Katalog zur Ausstellung der Stadtbibliothek in Verbindung mit dem Städtischen Museum, 5. Juli bis 13. September 1998*, ed. Gabriele Henkel, Braunschweig, Stadt, 1998, 190 pp. Christoph Zeller, *Allegorien des Erzählens: Wilhelm Raabes Jean-Paul-Lektüre*, Stuttgart, M & P, 378 pp., is a 1998 Stuttgart dissertation. Son-Hyoung Kwon, *Das Groteske in Wilhelm Raabes Spätwerk 'Die Akten des Vogelsangs'* (EH, 1, 1706), x + 182 pp., is a 1998 Tübingen dissertation. *Raabe-Jb.*, 40, has: M. Wünsch, ' "Tod" in der Erzählliteratur des deutschen Realismus' (1–14); B. Kristiansen, 'W. R. und Arthur Schopenhauer: Überlegungen zu den Romanen *Das Odfeld* und *Hastenbeck*' (15–32);

R. G. Czapla, ' "Gedenk der Holunderblüte!" ' oder Schreiben wider das Vergessen. Erinnerte Geschichte bei W. R. und Johannes Bobrowski' (33–59); W. Struck, 'See- und Mordgeschichten: zur Konstruktion exotischer Räume in realistischen Erzähltexten' (60–70); S.-H. Kwon, 'W. R. als Schriftsteller des Grotesken: zum Hochzeitsfest in *Christoph Pechlin* und dem Plünderungsfest in *Die Akten des Vogelsangs*' (71–94); S. Meyer, 'Narreteien ins Nichts: Intertextualität und Rollenmuster in W. Rs *Die Akten des Vogelsangs*' (95–111); C. Zeller, 'Zeichen des Bösen: Rs *Die Akten des Vogelsangs* und Jean Pauls *Titan*' (112–43); W. Hettche, 'Nach alter Melodie: die Gedichte von Julius Rodenberg, Wilhelm Jensen und Paul Heyse zum 70. Geburtstag W. Rs' (144–56); W. Dittrich, 'R.-Bibliographie 1999 (208–13). *Mitteilungen der R.-Gesellschaft*, 85, 1998, has: G. Henkel, 'Ein Nachtrag zum Thema "R. und Grabbe" ' (41–42); H. Streuber, 'Einige Anmerkungen zum Thema "W. R. und Heinrich Heine" ' (43–45); U. Peschke, 'W. Rs *Kinder von Finkenrode* : gelesen durch die Brille einer Tierfreundin' (50–52); M. Thienel, 'Symbole für das Unbewusste: unter dem Holunderstrauch. Wege von Kleist zu R. und Fontane' (53–66).

REUTER, FRITZ.  Gudrun Osmann and Manfred Günther, ' *. . . dass ich immer Farbe gehalten habe . . .': Zeugnisse aus Fritz Reuters Eisenacher Zeit*, ed. Karlheinz Büttner, Eisenach, Antiquariat & Buchhandlung St Georg, 1997, 120 pp., was published to mark the centenary of the Reuter museum in Eisenach. *. . . damit ich nicht noch mehr als Idylliker abgestempelt werde: Ehm Welk im literarischen Leben Mecklenburg-Vorpommerns nach 1945*, ed. Reinhard Rösler et al., Rostock, Reich, 173 pp., has three items on Reuter: J. Grabow, 'Beim Wiederlesen der Reuter-Festschrift von 1960' (100–07); M. Schürmann, 'Ehm Welk und die *Kein Hüsing*-Verfilmung der DEFA von 1954' (108–26); and C. Schmitt, 'F. Rs *Kein Hüsing* als filmischer Text: zur DEFA-Verfilmung des niederdeutschen Versepos nach dem Drehbuch Ehm Welks' (143–69). *Fritz Reuter und die Literatur des 20. Jahrhunderts*, ed. Christian Bunners et al. (Beiträge der Fritz-Reuter-Gesellschaft, 7), Hamburg, von Bockel, 1997, 98 pp., includes: H. Matter, 'Thomas Mann und F. R.' (11–20); J. Borchert and H. Brun, 'Johannes Gillhoff und Fritz Reuter: die Sprache von "Jürnjakob Swehn" und die Sprache von "Unkel Bräsig" ' (21–32, on *Jürnjakob Swehn, der Amerikafahrer*); H. Suhrbier, 'Der "vagelbunte" Wortspieler: was Arno Schmidt an F. R. fand' (33–50); J. Grambow, 'Papenbrock heißt Johnsons Pomuchelskopp' (51–64).

REUTER, GABRIELE.  R.'s best-known work *Aus guter Familie* (1895) has been translated for the first time into English by Lynne Tatlock under the title *From a Good Family* (SGLLC), 220 pp. Ludmila Kaloyanova-Slavova, *Übergangsgeschöpfe: Gabriele Reuter, Hedwig Dohm,*

*Helene Böhlau und Franziska von Reventlow* (Women in German Literature, 2), Frankfurt, Lang, 1998, 188 pp. K. Tebben, ' "Man hat das Prinzip zur Geltung zu bringen, das man darstellt": Standortbestimmung Thomas Manns im Jahre 1904: *Gabriele Reuter'*, *TMJb*, 12:77–99, revisits Mann's essay of 1904 on Reuter. H. Detering, ' "Das Ewig-Weibliche": Thomas Mann über Toni Schwabe, Gabriele Reuter, Ricarda Huch', *ib.*, 149–69.

RÜCKERT. The HKA of R.'s works, ed. Hans Wollschläger et al., Göttingen, Wallstein, has added vol. 1: *Die Weisheit des Brahmanen: Ein Lehrgedicht in Bruchstücken*, ed. Rudolf Kreutner et al., 2 vols, Göttingen, Wallstein, 1998, 1112 pp. Ingeborg Forssmann, *Luise Rückert, geb. Wiethaus-Fischer. 'Mein guter Geist, mein besseres Ich!': Ein Lebensbild der Frau des gelehrten Dichters Friedrich Rückert* (Rückert zu Ehren, 10), Würzburg, Ergon, 139 pp. Ali Radjaie, *\*Das profan-mystische Ghasel des Hafis in Rückerts Übersetzungen und in Goethes Divan*, Würzburg, Ergon, 1998, 361 pp., is a 1997 Heidelberg dissertation. B. Frischmut, 'Verrückt wie Rückert', *NDL*, 45, 1997:195–200, is concerned with problems of translation. M. al Ali, 'Der dichtende Philologe: eine Untersuchung zu Rs Sprachanschauungen anhand seiner Gedichte', *Nouveaux cahiers d'allemand*, 16, 1998:21–32.

RUGE. W. Bunzel, ' "Die vollkommenste Einigung der Wissenschaft mit dem Leben": Briefe von Eduard Meyen and Arnold Ruge (1838–1841)', *Fest. Steinsdorff*, 143–203.

SAAR. The HKA of F. v. S., *Kritische Texte und Deutungen*, ed. K. K. Polheim et al., Tübingen, Niemeyer, has added vol. IX: *Dissonanzen: Die Familie Worel*, ed. Günther Karrasch, ix + 229 pp.

SACHER-MASOCH. I. Massey, 'S.-M. Talmudist', *Aschkenas*, 7, 1997:341–88. K. Wagner, 'S.-M. — ein "Naturdichter" auf Irrwegen', *Cultura Tedesca*, 11:64–71. Russell A. Berman, *Enlightenment or Empire: Colonial Discourse in German Culture*, Nebraska U.P., 1998, 270 pp., has some discussion of S.-M. in his concluding chapter.

SAPHIR, MORITZ GOTTLIEB. *Sprichwörter und Redensarten im Biedermeier: Prosatexte von Moritz Gottlieb Saphir (1795–1858)*, ed. Wolfgang Mieder, Vienna, Praesens, 1998, 298 pp. W. Wunderlich, 'Medieval images: J. V. v. S. 's *Ekkehard* and St Gall', *Workman Vol.*, 193–27.

SCHOPENHAUER, JOHANNA. A. Gilleir, 'Diskurs zwischen Empirie und ästhetischer Hermeneutik: kultursoziologische Betrachtungen über J. Ss Reisebeschreibungen', *EG*, 54:197–215.

SCHWAB, GUSTAV. D. Blamires, 'The later texts in G. S.'s *Volksbücher*: origins and character', *MLR*, 94:110–21. M.-V. Leistner, 'Wilhelm Müller und G. S.: zur Geschichte einer Dichterfreundschaft', *JDSG*, 43:9–32.

SEALSFIELD. Lars-Peter Linke, *Reise, Abenteuer und Geheimnis: Zu den Romanen Charles Sealsfields*, Bielefeld, Aisthesis, 237 pp., is a 1997 Freiburg dissertation. Prominence is given to S.'s treatment of social themes in the novels, and a competent account is given of his view of both antebellum America and Josephinian Austria. F. Schüppen, ' "Deutsche, die das Glück haben, Amerikaner zu sein!" ': das Bild der Deutschamerikaner bei C. S. und Theodor Fontane', *Yearbook of German American Studies*, 32, 1997:99–115. A. Ritter, 'C. S. (eigentl. Karl Postl): Bibliographie 1945–1998. Texteditionen und Forschungsliteratur (Stand: November 1998)', *ZGB*, 7, 1998:153–67.

STIFTER. The HKA of S.'s *Werke und Briefe*, ed. A. Doppler et al., Stuttgart, Kohlhammer, has added vol VI.1: *Die Mappe meines Urgroßvaters, dritte Fassung. Lesetext*, ed. H. Gottwald et al., 1998, 343 pp.; and vol. VI.3: *Die Mappe meines Urgrossvaters, dritte und vierte Fassung. Integraler Apparat*, ed. H. Gottwald et al., 207 pp. Cornelia Blasberg, *Erschriebene Tradition: Adalbert Stifter oder das Erzählen im Zeichen verlorener Geschichten* (Rombach Wissenschaft Reihe Litterae, 48), Freiburg, Rombach, 1998, 397 pp., is a Tübingen *Habilitionsschrift* which adopts an approach based on modern literary theory. Beatrice Mall-Grob, *\*Fiktion des Anfangs: Literarische Kindheitsmodelle bei Jean Paul und Adalbert Stifter*, Stuttgart, M & P, 414 pp., is a 1998 Basle dissertation. D. Naumann, 'Semantisches Rauschen: Wiederholungen in A. Ss Roman *Witiko*', pp. 82–108 of *Dasselbe noch einmal: Die Ästhetik der Wiederholung*, ed. Carola Hilmes et al. (Kulturwissenschaftliche Studien zur deutschen Literatur), Opladen, Westdeutscher Vlg, 1998, 266 pp.

*Austriaca*, 48, is devoted almost entirely to S. and has: J. Benay, 'S. épistolier: entre confidences esthétiques et chronique domestique' (7–32); J. Chambon, 'Le bel agir' (45–48, on the moral stance of S.'s characters in the face of hostile nature and death); P. Cimaz, 'Le jardin dans le paysage stiftérien' (49–61, mainly on *Zwei Schwestern, Der Nachsommer,* and *Die Mappe meines Urgrossvaters*); J. Le Rider, 'Les couleurs et le dessin chez A. S.' (63–75); I. Ruiz, 'Le rôle d'A. S. dans l'œuvre de Johannes Urdizil' (77–91); G. Stieg, 'Von der Hommage zum Verriss: der Austriophobe Arno Schmidt über A. S.' (93–106); J. Le Rider, 'Bibliographie chronologique des traductions françaises d'A. S.' (107–08); V. Croz, 'Bibliographie des études en français sur A. S.' (109–10).

E. Stehlíková, 'Ss Ideal der Vollkommenheit', *Listy filologické*, 120, 1997:79–89. U. Zeuch, 'Der Zugang zu den Phänomenen — für immer geschlossen? Zum Wissenschaftsbegriff in Ss *Nachsommer*', *Scientia Poetica*, 3:72–94. G. H. Hertling, 'A. Ss "Forewords" to *Bunte Steine* in English: his poetics, aesthetics, and *Weltanschauung*', *MAL*, 32:1–21, translates and comments on the unabridged texts of both the forewords that S. wrote in the autumn of 1852. H. Ester, 'Sprachbildlichkeit in A. Ss Roman *Der Nachsommer*', *ABNG*, 45:147–59. H. Ragg-Kirkby, ' "Die Kinder liebten ihre Eltern nicht mehr und die Eltern die Kinder nicht" ': A. S. and the happy family', *OGS*, 27, 1998:64–101, discusses a wide range of S.'s texts, arguing persuasively that he paints a far less rosy picture of family life than critics generally assume. Also by Ragg-Kirkby is ' "So ward die Wüste immer größer": zones of otherness in the stories of A. S.', *FMLS*, 35:207–22. E. Downing, 'A. S. and the scope of realism', *GR*, 74:229–41, is concerned principally with *Der Hochwald*. H. D. Irmscher, 'Die Verkündigung auf dem Berge: zur Theodizee in A. Ss Erzählung *Bergkristall*', *Sprachkunst*, 30:1–9.

STORM. A warm welcome will be extended to T. S., '*Hans and Heinz Kirch*', *with 'Immensee' and 'Journey to a Hallig*', trans. Denis Jackson et al., London, Angel, 189 pp. *Hans und Heinz Kirch* and *Eine Halligfahrt* are here translated into English for the first time. In an age when universities are increasingly obliged to provide literature courses in translation it has become urgently necessary to augment the number of good translations of 19th-c. German texts, and Jackson and his German collaborator have done an outstanding job. The translations of both the prose of Storm's stories, and of the inset poems in *Immensee*, are uniformly excellent. They remain admirably close to the surface meaning of Storm's German, yet they also capture very accurately the characteristic rhythms of his language and manage at the same time to read like natural English. A more eloquent refutation of the old charge 'traduttore traditore' would be hard to find. T. S., *Immensee*, ed. Joseph Kiermeier-Debre (Bibliothek der Erstausgaben; DTV, 2654), 85 pp., follows the text of Biernatzki's *Volksbuch auf das Jahr 1850*. This version is about 10% longer than that published by Duncker in 1852 in S.'s *Sommer-Geschichten und Liedern* and all subsequent printings in S.'s lifetime. There are a few pages of notes and a short *Nachwort*.

*Theodor Storm und die Medien: Zur Mediengeschichte eines poetischen Realisten* (Husumer Beiträge zur Storm-Forschung, 1), ed. Harro Segeberg et al., Berlin, Schmidt, 461 pp., publishes the majority of the papers given at a conference on Storm and the media held in Husum in 1996 (financial pressures forced the editors to publish the other papers in *STSG*, 48, and its *Beiheft*, noted below). The volume opens with two preliminary essays by J. Schönert on the sometimes prickly relationship between *Germanistik* and the new discipline of media studies, and H. Segeberg on some general problems and trends that can be discerned in the filming of Storm texts. The main body of the book is then divided into two sections, the first of which deals with S.'s own role and the treatment his texts received in the media that

were available in the 19th c., and the second with the history of 20th-
c. attempts to transfer his work to the medium of film. The first
section contains: G. Eversberg, 'Mündlichkeit/Schriftlichkeit/
Drucktext: literarische Produktion als Medienwechsel (am Beispiel
von Sagen und Spukgeschichten)' (49–66, on S.'s transformation of
real or fictitious oral and manuscript sources, particularly in *Am Kamin*
and *Der Schimmelreiter*); G. Plumpe, 'Gedächtnis und Erzählung: zur
Ästhetisierung des Erinnerns im Zeitalter der Information' (67–79,
on the narrator's entirely non-naturalistic reliance on memory — 'in
halbvisionären Zustande' — in the telling of a story that in other ways
has a good deal in common with Naturalism); G. Reichelt, 'T. Ss
Bildgebrauch im Kontext des Zeitschriftenmediums' (81–102, on the
use of paintings in for example *Aquis submersus*); E. Pastor, 'Transfor-
mationen in eigener und fremder Regie. Oder: zum Text-Prozess
Stormscher Novellen in den zeitgenössischen Medien' (103–27, on
the changes in the texts that may be traced in the progression from
the manuscript stage to the proofs, first publication in journals and
then in book form, and finally in the collected editions). The second
section of the book contains articles on film or television versions of
Storm Novellen and has: M. Schaudig (139–74), on *Ein Fest auf
Haderslevhuus*; U. von Keitz (175–207), on *Zur Chronik von Grieshuus*;
B. Wegner (209–45), on *Der Schimmelreiter*; N. Grob (247–68), on Veit
Harlan's *Immensee*; H. Krah (269–97), on Harlan's *Viola tricolor/Ich
werde dich auf Händen tragen*; H. H. Hiebel (321–49), and E. Viehoff-
Kamper (351–780), both on *Pole Poppenspäler*; and K. Kickethier
(321–49), on S. and television. To round off the volume G. Eversberg
(425–45), provides a comprehensive filmography which indicates
that since 1917 some 20 of S.'s Novellen have been filmed, some of
them several times. The book is not always easy to read — some of
the articles are more jargon-laden than is to the present reviewer's
taste — but it is undoubtedly one of the most innovative contributions
to research on S. to appear in recent years. Three of the papers
originally intended for the volume are published in *STSG*, 48. These
are: K. M. Schmidt, 'Novellentheorie und filmisches Erzählen vor
dem Hintergrund moderner Stormverfilmungen' (95–125, with
comment on film adaptations of no less than ten Novellen); B. Zimmermann, ' "Am grauen Strand, am grauen Meer": Annäherungen
ans literarische Erbe am Beispiel einer Storm-Adaption des
Fernsehens der DDR' (127–39, mainly concerned with *Hans und
Heinz Kirch*); F. R. Sammern-Frankenegg, 'Prolegomena zu einer
Neuverfilmung von Ss *Immensee*' (141–53). The other articles in this
volume of the *STSG* are : P. Wapnewski, 'T. S.: nach fünfzig und
hundertfünfzig Jahren' (13–42); D. Jackson, 'Frauenopfer und
Frauenverrat: T. Ss Novelle *Carsten Curator*' (43–56); M. Lowsky,

'Fritz Basch oder die Sensibilität für die Sprache: über T. Ss Novelle *Bötjer Basch*' (57–64); B. Kratz, 'Das "Wiedersehen an der Bahre"': ein Balladenmotiv in T. Ss Novelle *In St. Jürgen*' (65–72); L. M. Wang, 'Literarische Übersetzung: zur Rezeptionsgeschichte von Ss *Immensee* in Taiwan' (73–83); W. Hettche, 'T. S.: Brief an Hans Speckter vom 18. Dezember 1878. Ein Nachtrag zum Briefwechsel Storm — Speckter' (85–86); K.-L. Barkhausen, 'Der Schriftsteller Hans Bethge zu Besuch in Husum (1896)' (87–92); E. Jacobsen, 'S.-Bibliographie' (154–64); G. Eversberg, 'S.-Forschung und S.-Gesellschaft' (165–74). *Dichter und ihre Photographien: Frühe Photos aus der Storm-Familie und aus dem Freundeskreis*, ed. Gerd Eversberg (Beiheft zu den Schriften des T.-S.-Gesellschaft, 48), Heide, Boyens, 96 pp., publishes two more of the articles that could not be accommodated in Segeberg's *Theodor Storm und die Medien*. These are: F.-J. Albersmeier, 'Europäische Literatur und Photographie/Film' (9–21); and D. L. Dysart, 'T. S. und die Photographie' (23–31). Other articles in the book are: M. Davidis, 'Freunde und Zeitgenossen T. Ss in der Photographischen Sammlung des Schiller-Nationalmuseums in Marbach' (33–42); R. Articus, ' "und typen lassen will ich mich auch"': die Daguerreotypien von T. Ss Braut und Ehefrau Constanze Esmarch' (43–65); U. Steen, 'Portraitphotographien T. Ss und seiner Familie (1843–1864): Bemerkungen über die Anfänge der Lichtbildnerei in Schleswig-Holstein' (67–87); G. Eversberg, 'T. S. und die Entwicklung photographischer Reproduktionstechniken' (89–94). The quality of the 50 black-and-white plates reproduced in the book, and the historical and human interest attaching to them, support Eversberg's argument in his foreword that a new approach to S. based on extra-philological media research has much to teach us.

K. E. Laage, *Storm-Haus-Geschicht(en): Das Theodor-Storm-Museum gestern und heute*, Heide, Boyens, 1997, 88 pp. H. G. Peters, '*Der Schimmelreiter* als überlesene Ethnographie', Jürgens, *Exchanges*, 136–47. Jennifer D. Askey, 'Authority and community in T. S.'s *Draußen im Heidedorf*', *Seminar*, 35 : 23–37. K.-E. Laage, 'Thomas Manns Storm-Essay und sein neues Storm-Bild', *TMJb*, 12 : 191–203.

WAGNER. R. W., *Sämtliche Briefe*, ed. Werner Breig, Wiesbaden–Leipzig–Paris, Breitkopf & Härtel, has added vol. XI: *1. April bis 31. Dezember 1859*, ed. Martin Dürrer, 608 pp. *Im Schatten Wagners: Thomas Mann über Richard Wagner. Texte und Zeugnisse 1895–1955*, ed. Hans Rudolf Vaget (FT, 13835), 359 pp., is fuller and better than Erika Mann's *Wagner und unsere Zeit* of 1963. Maike Oergel, *The Return of King Arthur and the Nibelungen: National Myth in Nineteenth-century English and German Literature* (European Cultures, 10), Berlin, de Gruyter, 1998, viii + 325 pp., is principally concerned with the *Ring* and Tennyson's *Idylls of the King*. David J. Levin, *Richard Wagner, Fritz Lang and the*

*Nibelungen: The Dramaturgy of Disavowal*, Princeton U.P., 1998, xi + 207 pp., compares the *Ring* with Lang's film *Die Nibelungen*. B. Gruber, 'Parsifal als esoterischer Generator: Aspekte von Kommentar und Selbstkommentar zu Ws letzter Oper', pp. 120–34 of *Erfahrung und System: Mystik und Esoterik in der Literatur der Moderne*, ed. Bettina Gruber, Opladen, Westdeutscher Vlg, 1997, 254 pp. V. Stegemann, 'Brecht contra Wagner: the evolution of the epic music theatre', pp. 238–60 of *A Bertolt Brecht Reference Companion*, ed. Siegried Mews, Westport, Conn., Greenwood, 1997, xviii + 430 pp. H. R. Vaget, ' "Ein Traum von Liebe": Musik, Homosexualität und W. in Thomas Manns *Der Zauberberg*', pp. 111–41 of *Auf dem Weg zum 'Zauberberg': Die Davoser Literaturtage 1996*, ed. Thomas Sprecher (TMS, 16), 1997, 361 pp. A. Ebenbauer, 'R. Ws *Ring des Nibelungen*: Gold und Macht', *Fest. Brackert*, 298–310. I. Baxmann, 'Verbindung der Künste und Verknüpfung der Sinne: zur W.-Rezeption der Avantgarde in Frankreich', *Fest. Lämmert*, 179–87. W. Breig, 'Zur Überlieferung des Briefwechsels zwischen R. W. und Mathilde Wesendonk', *Die Musikforschung*, 51, 1998:57–63. P. Russell, 'Sexuality, self-division and guilt: W.'s *Tannhäuser* 150 years on', *AUMLA*, 88, 1997:21–36. E. Roch, 'Das Undine-Motiv in R. Ws Dramenkonzeption', *Die Musikforschung*, 51, 1998:302–15. M. Meier, 'Das Gericht der *Eumeniden* und der *Götterdämmerung*: ein weiterer Aspekt aischyleischen Einflusses auf das Werk R. Ws', *ib.*, 404–19. J.-F. Candoni, 'R. W.: texte, musique et drame', *EG*, 54:415–39.

WEERTH. *Georg Weerth und das Feuilleton der 'Neuen Rheinischen Zeitung': Kolloquium zum 175. Geburtstag am 14.–15. Febr. 1997 in Detmold*, ed. M. Vogt (Vormärz-Studien, 2), Bielefeld, Aisthesis, 198 pp. G. Vonhoff, ' "Eine frische Literatur": G. Ws Skizzen aus dem sozialen und politischen Leben der Briten', Kavanagh, *Exchanges*, 80–95.

ZSCHOKKE. D. Assmann, 'H. Z. — ein Preuße für die Schweiz', *Ginkgo-Baum*, 16, 1998:267–71.

# LITERATURE, 1880–1945
## POSTPONED

## LITERATURE FROM 1945
## TO THE PRESENT DAY

By OWEN EVANS, *Lecturer in German, University of Wales, Bangor*

### 1. GENERAL

*\*Literatur und Holocaust*, ed. Heinz Ludwig Arnold (TK, 144), 97 pp. A. Assmann, 'Ein deutsches Trauma? Die Kollektivschuldthese zwischen Erinnern und Vergessen', *Merkur*, 53:1142–54. Stephen Brockmann, *Literature and German Unification* (CSG, 4), 245 pp., is a thought-provoking and delightfully engaging contribution to recent works which have examined German culture and national identity since 1989. In the course of his thorough survey, B. uncovers a myriad, often conflicting, strands of thought that have surrounded debates pertaining to events in 1989–90. He reveals the complexity of those debates and how the process of political and economic union did not carry all in its wake, and least of all in the cultural and intellectual sphere. In his consideration of various themes, B. is able to explain how Kohl failed to achieve the 'normalization' he sought merely by locking the two Germanies together politically. The main problem, B. asserts, lies in the problem of locating the German Nation, which is explored at length in the introduction and is returned to time and again throughout the study. B. repeatedly rejects the view that literature has lost its political significance and asserts that, on the contrary, it is central to the debates on national identity. To reinforce his view, he cites in his introduction the row between Grass and Reich-Ranicki over *Ein weites Feld,* and the controversial *Spiegel* cover of 1995. B. goes on to explore the major concerns in discrete chapters, which makes for a very accessible division of the material covered. Some of the issues are not unfamiliar, such as his coverage of the divergence/convergence of West and East German literature, or the unease of some intellectuals about reunification, but it is no weakness to revisit these ideas. His chapter exploring the feasibility of the 'third way' expounded by the likes of Wolf and Heym is lucid, and his synopsis of the row surrounding *Was bleibt* is exceedingly good. Although not the first to identify parallels between the *Literaturstreit* of the early 1990s and the *Historikerstreit* of the 1980s, a point B. himself concedes, he does examine the similarity of the central issues of both more thoroughly than hitherto, concluding that both rested upon a desire to normalize the relationship with the past. At the core of the later debate was the wish for a 'normalization of literary and aesthetic standards and an escape from the burden of coming to terms with the difficult German past in literature'. Unsurprisingly, B. turns his

attention to the impact of the *Stasi* on GDR literature, listing some of what might be termed '*Stasi* works' and devoting some time to Wolfgang Hilbig's '*Ich*', in particular. The linguistic strategies employed by the Prenzlauer Berg poets, in a bid to create a self-reflexive, non-communicative anti-language, form an important part of B.'s survey here. He does not ignore the irony that the *Stasi* involvement of Sascha Anderson and Rainer Schedlinski severely tarnished what Uwe Kolbe defined as this group's attempt to place literature in a 'land beyond meaning', beyond politics. B. points out in the subsequent chapter that it was not only the demise of the GDR that was mourned; in some corners, indeed, on the so-called 'New Right', represented by writers such as Botho Strauss, a sense of foreboding abounded as the old Federal Republic was to disappear as well. A revision of identity and attitudes would inevitably follow reunification, yet conservatives were as divided on the question of nationhood as those on the left in the GDR had been about the possibility of the 'third way'. In his final chapter, he reiterates his belief that 'literature very much retains a political and identificatory power, at least for certain segments of the population'; in truth it is 'the commonality implied by the word"nation" that is in question', rather than literature itself. B. elucidates the various ideas advanced by intellectuals since 1989 in pursuit of how best to define Germanness, whilst himself stressing that the role of culture as a unifying force was built into the unification treaty. The one proposal to be rejected vehemently is Grass's notion that Auschwitz offers the key to German identity: 'It is unclear how any positive political identity can emerge solely on the basis of Auschwitz'. B. is sensible enough not to propose his own definitive answer to the problem, but neatly suggests instead that 'it is the existence of the problem itself that will be characteristic of German intellectual and cultural life'. Although it is still too soon for the great German Reunification novel, B. argues convincingly that it is literature's ongoing consideration of this particular problem which will be crucial. Thus concludes a most engaging analysis of the contemporary literary scene in Germany, which will doubtless stimulate and enrage in equal measure. \**Germany and Eastern Europe: Cultural Identities and Cultural Differences*, ed. Keith Bullivant, Geoffrey Giles, and Walter Pape, Amsterdam–Atlanta, Rodopi, vi + 366 pp. Jörg Drews, \**Eichendorffs Untergänge: Rezensionen deutschsprachiger Gegenwartsliteratur von 1967 bis 1999*, Frankfurt, Suhrkamp, 250 pp. Amir Eshel, \**Zeit der Zäsur: Jüdische Dichter im Angesicht der Shoah* (BNL, 169), 320 pp. D. Gutzen, 'Vom Fremdwerden des Vertrauten. Die Vereinigung im Spiegel der Literatur oder: "Ein weites Feld"', *EG*, 53, 1998:619–34. R. Kellermann, 'Was man schon immer über den Tod lesen wollte? Neuere Publikationen über das Erzählen vom Tod in der Moderne', *LWU*, 5:271–90. Sven Kramer, *Auschwitz im Widerstreit. Zur Darstellung der Shoah im Film, Philosophie und Literatur*, Leverkusen, Deutscher Universitätsverlag, vi + 143 pp. H. Krauss, 'Literatur — Wende — Literatur', *DUS*, 51.4:37–45. M. Kublitz-Kramer, 'Literatur von Frauen der neunziger Jahre', *DUS*, 51.4:46–58. Sigrid Lange, *Authentisches Medium. Faschismus und Holocaust in ästhetischen Darstellungen der Gegenwart*, Bielefeld, Aisthesis, 256 pp. G. Lauer, 'Erinnerungsverhandlungen. Kollektives Gedächtnis und Literatur fünfzig Jahre nach der Vernichtung der europäischen Juden', *DVLG*, 73:215–45. Birgit Schütter, *Weibliche Perspektiven in der Gegenwartsliteratur* (BSDL, 50), 234 pp. W. G. Sebald, *Luftkrieg und Literatur, mit einem Essay über Alfred Andersch*, Hamburg, Hanser, 184 pp.

WEST GERMANY, AUSTRIA, SWITZERLAND. *Bestandsaufnahme: Studien zur Gruppe 47*, ed. Stephan Braese (PSQ, 157), 300 pp. *Towards the Millenium: Interpreting the Austrian Novel, 1971–1996*, ed. Gerald Chapple, Tübingen, Stauffenburg, x + 300 pp. *Centre Stage: Contemporary Drama in Austria*, ed. Frank Finlay and Ralf Jeutter (APSL, 137), vii + 240 pp. *Berliner Beiträge zur Prosa der Nachkriegsjahre (1945–1960)*, ed. Ursula Heukenkamp, Berlin, Schmidt, 420 pp. Jürgen Lieskounig, *Das Kreuz mit dem Körper. Untersuchungen zur Darstellung von Körperlichkeit in ausgewählten westdeutschen Romanen aus den fünfziger, sechziger und siebziger Jahren* (EH, I, 1722), 249 pp. Beatrice von Matt, *Frauen schreiben die Schweiz. Aus der Literaturgeschichte der Gegenwart*, Frauenfeld, Huber, 1998, 248 pp. *The 'Gruppe 47' Fifty Years on. A Re-appraisal of its Literary and Political Significance*, ed. Stuart Parkes and John J. White, Amsterdam–Atlanta, Rodopi, 296 pp. C. Ruthner, ' "Habsburger Mythos" versus k.(u.)k. (Post-)Kolonialismus. Neuere Publikationen zum österreichischen Heimat-Bild', *GM*, 49:95–103. Ernestine Schlant, *The Language of Silence: West German Literature and the Holocaust*, London–NY, Routledge, 288 pp. Klaus Zeyringer, *Österreichische Literatur 1945–1998: Überblicke, Einschnitte, Wegmarken*, Innsbruck, Haymon, 640 pp.

EAST GERMANY. Gerrit-Jan Berendse, *Grenz-Fallstudien: Zur DDR-Literatur der 80er Jahre* (PSQ, 156), 160 pp. W. Emmerich, 'Versungen und vertan? Rückblicke auf 40 Jahre DDR-Literatur und Geschichtsschreibung der DDR-Literatur', *OGS*, 27, 1998:141–68. Daniel J. Farrelley, *Goethe in East Germany, 1949–1989. Toward a History of Goethe Reception in the GDR*, Columbia, Camden House, 1998, 178 pp. Antje Janssen-Zimmermann and Elke Kasper, *Grenzenlos. Literatur zwischen Ost und West von 1949 bis 1989. Eine Bibliographie* (LU, 32), 736 pp. B. Leistner, ' "Gross meine Mühe, würdevoll zu fliehn." Ostdeutsche Literatur nach der "Wende" ', *NDL*, 47.2:16–32. Franziska Meyer, *Avantgarde im Hinterland. Caroline Schlegel-Schelling in der*

*DDR-Literatur* (GLC, 25), xiii + 258 pp. P. O'Doherty, 'The reception of Heine's Jewishness in the Soviet Zone/GDR, 1945–1961', *GLL*, 52:85–96. R. J. Owen, 'The ex-GDR poet and the people', *ib.*, 490–505. *Wendezeichen? Neue Sichtweisen auf die Literatur der DDR*, ed. Roswitha Skare and Rainer B. Hoppe (ABNG, 46), 243 pp., is a collection of papers from an interdisciplinary conference held in Tromsö in 1997, which contributes to the ongoing debate about the study of GDR literature in the post-unification period. As the title indicates, the papers here are designed to promote new ways of perceiving work produced in the GDR. As the preface remarks, for all the diversity in evidence in the volume, three common issues can be isolated in most of the articles pertaining to the treatment of East German writing: attention is paid to aesthetic elements rather than merely the political aspects; the question of the relationship between literature and society is examined and to what extent there has been a shift; and the issue of how best to define GDR literature, as a discrete element, as part of post-1945 German writing as a whole, or as the work not of a Nation, but of a European region? The contributions fall into two categories; those focusing on particular aspects and themes of GDR society and culture, and those concentrating on individual authors. There are interesting articles on Brecht, Bobrowski, Reimann, Hein, Braun, and Soviet author Vladimir Dudinzew, most of which take as their theme the re-assessment of the past in the works selected. In this regard, the most apposite of these articles to the overall thrust of the collection as a whole is V. Kirchner's essay on Volker Braun. Kirchner looks at Braun's *Das Nichtgelebte*, and explores the inner crisis of the protagonist, a critical but loyal intellectual, after the collapse of the GDR. Braun, like his protagonist, retained a belief in a socialist utopia, despite the stagnation of the GDR which he had explored in texts such as *Unvollendete Geschichte*. Kirchner is not the first to underline the importance of Ernst Bloch's *Das Prinzip Hoffnung* for many GDR intellectuals, but it is interesting that the text in question, published in 1995, should still draw on the philosopher's concept of utopia. The thematic essays are, in some ways, the most provocative here, since they tackle the broader nature of the discussion. T. Jung explores the writing of Jewish authors in the GDR which was long repressed or marginalized, whilst M. Scholz considers the way in which GDR history has been studied. In common with a number of former East German authors, he proposes research into the mentality of the GDR as a meaningful approach to understanding the country's evolution. It is the articles by the two editors, however, which reflect the issues most cogently. R. Skare underlines the problem of how best to define GDR literature by analysing recent literary histories of the GDR and finding flaws in each of them. As well as the problem of isolating the key characteristics of GDR writing, a necessarily reductive, and unsatisfactory, process, Skare demonstrates the problem of selection facing the aspirant literary historian. Should one include the likes of Erich Loest, Sarah Kirsch, Monika Maron, and Jurek Becker in any study of GDR literature, since all published widely once they left the GDR? Are such works by 'exile' writers truly GDR texts? Skare sensibly offers no solution to the problem, but suggests it is one all academics specializing in the GDR should address. By contrast, R. Hoppe calls on literary critics in the new Germany not merely to consign GDR literature to the history books, but to engage in a new reading of such work, employing contemporary interpretative methods. The continuing popularity of GDR writers in German department syllabuses not only lends substantial weight to Hoppe's appeal, but also underlines the importance of this provocative volume and the questions it raises.

## 2. LYRIC POETRY

Andreas Böhn, *Das zeitgenössische deutschsprachige Sonett: Vielfalt und Aktualität einer literarischen Form*, Stuttgart, Metzler, 200 pp. H. Korte, 'Ein neues Jahrzehnt des Gedichts? Deutschsprachige Lyrik der neunziger Jahre', *DUS*, 51.4:21–36. P. B. Kory, 'Lyrik im Zeichen der Diktatur. Subversität als Phänomen der Interkulturalität', *Temeswarer Beiträge zur Germanistik*, 2:92–112.

## 3. DRAMA

M. Hofmann, 'Rosa Riese, guter König. Dramatische Texte der neunziger Jahre', *DUS*, 51.4:9–20. Jeanette R. Malkin, *Memorytheater and Postmodern Drama*, Michigan U.P., 276 pp.

## 4. PROSE

Ursula Bredel, *Erzählen im Umbruch, Studie zur narrativen Verarbeitung der 'Wende' 1989*, Tübingen, Stauffenburg, 208 pp. Eva-Maria Fahmüller, *Postmoderne Veränderungen. Zur deutschen Erzählkunst um 1990*, Munich, Iudicium, 215 pp. Nikolaus Förster, *Die Wiederkehr des Erzählens: Deutschsprachige Prosa der 80er und 90er Jahre*, WBG, 272 pp. Lars Jacob, *Bildschrift–Schriftbild: Zu einer eidetischen Fundierung von Erkenntnistheorie im modernen Roman* (Ep, 266), 350 pp. Mirjam Sprenger, *Modernes Erzählen: Metafiktion im deutschsprachigen Roman der Gegenwart*, Stuttgart, Metzler, 300 pp.

## 5. INDIVIDUAL AUTHORS

AICHINGER, ILSE.   D. L. Colclasure, 'Erzählkunst und Gesellschaftskritik in I. As *Spiegelgeschichte*: eine Neuinterpretation', *MAL*, 32.1 : 67–89. B. Desbrière-Nicolas, '*Engel in der Nacht*: l'ange dans la prose de jeunesse d'I. A.', *Germanica*, 24 : 117–35. Tanja Hetzer, *\*Kinderblick auf die Shoah: Formen der Erinnerung bei I. A., Hubert Fichte and Danilo Kiš* (Ep, 271), 130 pp. \**Verschwiegenes Wortspiel. Kommentare zu den Werken I. As*, ed. Heidy Margrit Müller, Bielefeld, Aisthesis, 198 pp. ANDERSCH, ALFRED.   U. Kinzel, 'Das Ende der Reise. Orientierung und Erfahrung in A. As *Hohe Breitengrade*', *JDSG*, 63 : 403–30. Reiner Poppe, *\*A. A.*, Stuttgart, Reclam, 100 pp. Anne Raabe, *\*Das Wort stammt von Kierkegaard. A. A. und Søren Kierkegaard* (BLL, 18), 236 pp. ANDRES, STEFAN.   *\*S. A. Zeitzeuge des 20. Jahrhunderts*, ed. Michael Braun, Georg Guntermann, and Birgit Lermen (TSL, 32), 270 pp. AUSLÄNDER, ROSE.   Helmut Braun, *\*R. A.: Zu ihrer Biographie*, Stuttgart, Radius, 220 pp. Annette Jael Lehmann, *\*Im Zeichen der Shoah. Aspekte der Dichtungs- und Sprachkrise bei R. A und Nelly Sachs*, Tübingen, Stauffenburg, xxvi + 248 pp. BACHMANN, INGEBORG.   *\*Poetische Korrespondenzen. Vierzehn Beiträge. I. B. und Paul Celan*, ed. Bernhard Böschenstein and Sigrid Weigel, Frankfurt, Suhrkamp, 1997, 268 pp. Jens Brachmann, *\*Enteignetes Material: Zitathaftigkeit und narrative Umsetzung in I. Bs 'Malina'*, Wiesbaden, Deutscher Universitätsverlag, 277 pp. E. Brüns, 'Portrait of the artist as a young woman. Die Schauspielerin in Lilly Stepaneks *Malina* und in I. Bs Werk', *ZDP*, 118 : 266–78. Ariane Huml, *\*Silben im Oleander, Wort im Akaziengrün: Zum literarischen Italienbild I. Bs*, Göttingen, Wallstein, 304 pp. Christine Kranz, *\*Angst und Geschlechterdifferenz: I. Bs 'Todesarten'-Projekt in Kontexten der Gegenwartsliteratur* (EFF, 52), 270 pp. *\*In die Mulde meiner Stummheit leg ein Wort': Interpretationen zur Lyrik I. Bs*, ed. Primus-Heinz Kucher, Vienna, Böhlau, 272 pp. Leslie Morris, *\*'Ich suche ein unschuldiges Land': Reading History in the Poetry of I. B.*, Tübingen, Stauffenburg, 136 pp. M. Schmitz-Emans, 'Stein und Wasser — Dauer und Wandel — Gründe und Grundlosigkeit. Poetische Rom-Bilder bei Giuseppe Ungaretti und I. B.', *DUS*, 51.2 : 68–87. Jost Schneider, *\*Die Kompositionsmethode I. Bs. Erzählstil und Engagement in 'Das dreissigste Jahr', 'Malina', und 'Simultan'*, Bielefeld, Aisthesis, 512 pp. M. Tzaneva, 'Das "neue Aufreissen einer Vertikale": dreidimensionale Sprache in I. Bs *Malina*', *MAL*, 31.3–4, 1998 : 188–211. See also JOHNSON, UWE.

BECKER, JÜRGEN.   T. Geiger, 'Als käme ich aus den Ferien zurück. Gespräch mit J. Bs neuen Roman', *StZ*, 152 : 506–22.

BERNHARD, THOMAS. Claudia Albes, *Der Spaziergang als Erzählmo-dell: Studien zu Jean-Jacques Rousseau, Adalbert Stifter, Robert Walser und T. B.*, Tübingen, Francke, 290 pp. V. C. Dörr, 'Leben und Wahrheit. Zu den autobiographischen Büchern T. Bs', *MAL*, 32.2:39–57. Hermann Helms-Defert, *Die Last der Geschichte. Interpretationen zur Prosa von T. B.* (KGS, 39), 1997, 266 pp. Gregor Hens, *T. B.'s 'Trilogie der Künste': 'Der Untergeher', 'Holzfällen', 'Alte Meister'*, SGLLC, 300 pp. Sabine Hillebrand, *Strategien der Verwirrung. Zur Erzählkunst von E. T. A. Hoffmann, T. B. und Giorgio Manganelli* (Studien zur deutschen und europäischen Literatur des 19. und 20. Jahrhunderts, 39), Frankfurt, Lang, 190 pp. *T. B.: Traditionen und Trabanten*, ed. Joachim Hoell and Kai Luehrs-Kaiser, Würzburg, Königshausen & Neumann, 240 pp. *T. B.: Die Zurichtung des Menschen*, ed. Alexander Honold and Markus Joch, Würzburg, Königshausen & Neumann, 240 pp. Dirk Jürgens, *Das Theater T. Bs* (HKADL, 28), 321 pp. Alexandra Ludewig, *Grossvaterland. T. Bs Schriftstellergenese dargestellt anhand seiner (Auto-) Biographie* (EH, I, 1718), 366 pp. Barbara Mariacher, *'Umspringbilder'. Erzählen — Beobachten — Erinnern. Überlegungen zur späten Prosa T. Bs* (EH, I, 1709), 195 pp. A. Milanowski, 'Immanuel Kant auf dem Weg nach Amerika. T. B., Krystian Lupa, Gerhard Hauptmann, Tadeusz Rittner: Der Untergang der Titanic oder die Beschreibung des Paradigmenwechsels in der Kultur', *MAL*, 31.3–4, 1998:49–64. Suitbert Oberreiter, *Lebensinszenierung und kalkulierte Kompromißlosigkeit: Zur Relevanz der Lebenswelt im Werk T. Bs*, Vienna, Böhlau, 436 pp. Alfred Pfabigan, *T. B. Ein österreichisches Weltexperiment*, Vienna, Zsolnay, 438 pp. W. Vosskamp, ' "Extinction." A propos de l'autoré-flexion du roman d'éducation au XXe siècle chez T. B. traduit de l'allemand par Olivier Mannoni', *RGI*, 12:257–69. Walter Wagner, *'Franzose wäre ich gern gewesen'. Zur Rezeption französischer Literatur bei T. B.* (EH, XVIII, 92), 148 pp.

BEYER, MARCEL. P. Bekes, ' "Ab diesem Punkt spricht niemand mehr." Aspekte der Interpretation von M. Bs Roman *Flughunde* im Unterricht', *DUS*, 51.4:59–69.

BIERMANN, WOLF. E.-U. Pinkert, *'Die deutsche Misere* und *Das Himmelreich auf Erden.* Anmerkungen zu W. Bs Auseinandersetzung mit Heinrich Heine', *ChrA*, 7:125–38.

BIONDI, FRANCO. I. Amodeo, 'Die Ästhetik der Differenz im Werk F. Bs', *Cultura tedesca*, 10, 1998:43–56. M. E. Brunner, ' "Weder einen Platz noch eine Feuerstelle haben": traurige Helden in der Migra-tionsliteratur von F. B.', *LiLi*, 29:113–23.

BOBROWSKI, JOHANNES. Holger Gehle, *J.B. Erläuterungen der Romane, der Erzählungen, vermischten Prosa und Selbstzeugnisse*, Stuttgart, DVA, 380 pp. B. Leistner, 'Bs Gedichtsprache der Erinnerung',

*Convivium*, 1998:157–77. John P. Wieczorek, *Between Sarmatia and Socialism: The Life and Works of J. B.* (APSL, 139), xii + 269 pp.

BÖLL, HEINRICH. B. Balzer, 'Bs erste Publikation: ein Schlüssel zu seinem Werk?', *Orbis Linguarum*, 11:5–19. Werner Bellmann and Christine Hummel, *Erläuterungen und Dokumente zu H. B.: Die verlorene Ehre der Katharina Blum*, Stuttgart, Reclam, 220 pp. Lawrence F. Glatz, *H. B. als Moralist: Die Funktion von Verbrechen und Gewalt in seinen Prosawerken* (STML, 42), 344 pp. Beate Schnepp, *Vogelflug — Vertreibungen — Fürsorgliche Belagerung. Studien zu H. Bs Roman 'Fürsorgliche Belagerung'*, Trier, Wissenschaftlicher Vlg, 1997, 288 pp. M. Stebler, 'Die Todesmotivik in H. Bs *Der Zug war pünktlich*', *Orbis Linguarum*, 12:81–88.

BRASCH, THOMAS. Jens Ponath, *Spiel und Dramaturgie in T. Bs Werk* (Ep), 250 pp.

BRAUN, VOLKER. D. Haffad, 'In den Bahnen literarischer Tradition gegenwärtiger Geschichte auf der Spur. V. Bs Erzählung *Die vier Werkzeugmacher*', *CEtGer*, 36.1:119–36. J. Krätzer, 'Eine Wendezeit wird besichtigt. V. B., Uwe Kolbe, Klaus Schlesinger: Versuche, die eigene Erfahrung zu behaupten', *NDL*, 47.3:148–62. T. Rosenlöcher, 'Der Engel der 11. Feuerbachthese. Laudatio für V. B.', *ib.*, 47.1:143–53.

BREDEL, WILLI. Brigitte Nester, *Bibliographie W. B.* (HBG, 27), 709 pp.

BŘEZAN, JURIJ. D. Scholze, 'Postmoderne Tendenzen in der sorbischen Literatur? J. Bs *Krabat*-Romane (1976; 1994/95)', *WB*, 45:423–31.

BRINKMANN, ROLF DIETER. Karsten Herrmann, *Bewusstseinserkundungen im 'Angst- und Todesuniversum'. R. D. Bs Collagebücher*, Bielefeld, Aisthesis, 325 pp. See also KOEPPEN, WOLFGANG.

DE BRUYN, GÜNTER. W. Schemme, 'Diesseits der Kanondebatte: das Thema "Vereinigung"'. G. d. B, *Vierzig Jahre. Ein Lebensbericht*, *DUB*, 50, 1997:585–97. *G. d. B. in Perspective*, ed. Dennis Tate, Amsterdam–Atlanta, Rodopi, 234 pp., is the latest monograph in Rodopi's German Monitor series which publishes new work on authors from the former GDR. The subject here is arguably the only prominent eastern German writer to have survived the *Wende* unscathed. T.'s introduction attributes the enthusiastic reception accorded this noticeably reticent author in the new Germany to an attempt by western German critics to adjust a previously rather dismissive view of his work. T.'s volume contributes to this ongoing reassessment by including articles from an array of academics which range over de B.'s entire career. Key works are examined in detail, and in particular the recent autobiographies, but room is also made for exploration of the author's essays, lesser-known works, and comparisons with other authors. The two contributions devoted to *Vierzig Jahre* mirror the mixed reception of the second volume of the autobiography on its publication in 1996. For O. Evans it builds on the success of the initial instalment, *Zwischenbilanz*, in its tone and the interweaving of personal and public experience, whereas K. Hirdina, whilst not doubting the author's integrity, feels the work lacks sufficient rigour to be anything other than an oversimplified self-justificatory view of GDR life. The ironic tone of de B.'s fiction is missing, and the autobiography suffers as a result. M. Kane uses the autobiographies as a springboard for re-examining *Der Hohlweg*, de B.'s debut novel, and defends it persuasively, despite its inherent weaknesses, from criticisms levelled at it by the author himself. J. White underlines the greater sophistication of de B.'s second novel, *Buridans Esel*, teasing out Freudian strategies employed by the author to expose the central figure's hypocrisy and mendacity, as well as to undercut GDR Socialist Realism. D. Gwosc considers *Neue Herrlichkeit* a prophetic statement of the demise of the GDR and documents the elements which comprise its social critique, in particular its unremitting bitterness. Alongside these assessments of the major works in de B.'s canon, the volume casts light on some of the minor publications. For instance, the short story *Freiheitsberaubung* is the subject of two contributions. A. Hollis provides an accessible and informative account of the complicated genesis of the text, which was originally conceived as part of an anthology of Berlin tales obstructed by the *Stasi*, and juxtaposes it with an analysis of Plenzdorf's theatrical adaptations of the story. Y.-G. Mix similarly looks at the story, along with *Märkische Forschungen* and aspects of de B.'s Jean Paul biography, as examples of the author's *Versteckspiel* with censorship. Both articles thereby reveal the hoops through which a typical GDR author had to jump. A pleasing inclusion is N. Harris's examination of de B.'s reworking of *Tristan and Isolde*, a text too often excluded from work on the author, as Harris himself observes. Despite certain conscious omissions for the sake of producing an accessible new version for a contemporary young audience, de B.'s craftsmanship and the joy he evidently derived from the project are praised by Harris, who stoutly defends the author from those experts who might bemoan his choice of sources or the concision of the finished product. L. Kube's contribution is also welcome, interpreting the essay collection *Mein Brandenburg* as both addition and corrective to Fontane's *Wanderungen*, and finding in the essays a mixture of identification with and critical distance from the region. Comparisons between de B. and other authors, such as Walser, are drawn elsewhere in the volume, but two articles adopt a more directly comparative approach. J. H. Reid takes disparaging comments made on 'Literarisches Quartett' about de

B. and Heinrich Böll as a starting point for the defence of their work and an examination of the ways in which Böll served as a role model during the early phase of the GDR writer's career, before *Buridans Esel* finally established his own literary voice. R. Rechtien sets de B. alongside Christa Wolf, detailing their relationship as friends and colleagues, before turning her attention to a comparison of *Zwischenbilanz* and *Kindheitsmuster*. Rechtien underlines the importance of subjectivity in their work, but concludes that Wolf's text calls into question the traditional autobiographical narrative of de B.'s text. Whilst praising the latter's integrity, Rechtien emphasizes the challenge presented by *Kindheitsmuster* with its problematization of the 'ich'. The difference in approach, between the more conventional and the more experimental, it is argued, is one similarly found in the fictional work of both authors. The volume concludes with an interview with de B. conducted by C. Lewis which neatly highlights many of the aspects and themes elucidated in the earlier chapters. Lewis ponders on the extent to which de B.'s earlier work is truly autobiographical and detects a continuing tendency in the author towards self-censorship in the *post-Wende* period. In conclusion, T.'s volume is certain to sustain interest in one of Germany's finest contemporary authors and stimulate further exploration of his canon. Whilst acknowledging de B.'s importance as an author and praising his craftsmanship, the combined effect of the contributions here does suggest a more realistic appraisal of his role is appropriate, which de B. himself would doubtless welcome.

BURMEISTER, BRIGITTE. M. Gebauer, 'Erzählen als Sujet. Ein Interview mit der Berliner Schriftstellerin B. B.', *TeK*, 21.1, 1998:94–111.

CANETTI, ELIAS. F. Kenk, 'Comment Freud peut cacher Nietzsche. Quelques réflexions sur la place dans l'histoire intellectuelle d'un auteur énigmatique: E. C.', *Austriaca*, 23, 1998:47–48. K. Jastal, '*Die gerettete Zunge* von E. C. Eine Autobiographie am Rande der Habsburger Monarchie? Einige Bemerkungen zur erzählerischen Perspektivierung des kulturgeschichtlichen Kontextes', *Convivium*, 1998:143–56. David Scott, *Metaphor as Thought in E. C.'s 'Masse und Macht'* (ANZSGLL, 18), xiv + 206 pp. Z. Światlowski, 'E. C. oder die Ehrenrettung der Literatur', *Orbis Linguarum*, 11:41–51.

CELAN, PAUL. *Arcadia*, 32.1, 1997, includes: M. Broda, 'Présence de P. C. dans la poésie contemporaine' (274–82); Id., 'Traduit du silence: les langues de P. C.' (269–73); R. Ertel, 'La résonance des cendres' (263–68); H. Fricke, 'Sentimentalität, Plagiat und übergrosse Schönheit? Über das Missverständnis "Todesfuge"' (195–209); C. Ivanović, '"Auch du hättest ein Recht auf Paris". Die Stadt und der Ort des Gedichts bei P. C.' (65–96); L. Koelle, 'Pneumatisches

Judentum, oder: Die gestaltete Polarität. Die Jerusalem-Koordinate als innere Disposition Cs' (38–64); J. P. Lefebvre, ' "P. C. — unser Deutschlehrer" ' (97–108); H. Mayer, 'Interview zu P. C. Gespräch von Jürgen Wertheimer mit Hans Mayer über P. C. am 11.03.1997' (298–300); M. Pajević, 'Erfahrungen, Orte, Aufenthalte und die Sorge um das Selbst' (148–61); M. Pfeiffer, 'P. C. aus spanischer Sicht' (254–62); H. Schmull, 'Übersetzen als Sprung. Textgenetische und poetologische Beobachtungen an Cs Übersetzungen von Shakespeares Sonetten' (119–47); P. Solomon, 'L'adolescence d'un adieu' (162–68); Y. Tawada, 'Rabbi Löw und 27 Punkte. Physiognomie der Interpunktion bei P. C.' (283–86); L. Terreni, 'Forschungsprojekt zu den Neologismen von P. C.' (230–53); U. Vogt, 'P. C. in Italien' (210–29); A. Werberger, 'P. C. und Osip Mandel'štam oder "Pavel Tselan" und "Joseph Mandelstamm" — Wiederbegegnung in der Begegnung' (6–27); B. Wiedemann, ' "Im Osten weilt mein Herz." Gedichte von Jehuda Halevi in der Übersetzung P. Cs' (28–37); and A. Zanzotto, 'Aufzeichnungen zu C.' (287–90). *Poetik der Transformation: P. C. — Übersetzer und übersetzt*, ed. Alfred Bodenheimer and Shimon Sandbank (CJ, 28), 190 pp. T. Böning, ' "Fahlstimmig" — P. Cs"Einspruch" gegen"Das Wort" Stefan Georges und Martin Heideggers. Ein Versuch', *DVLG*, 73:529–61. Anne Carson, *Economy of the Unlost*, Princeton U.P., 160 pp. E. Dalmaso, 'Cs Begegnung und Gespräch mit Ungaretti durch die Übersetzung', *ÖGL*, 43:250–64. Wolfgang Emmerich, *P. C.* (RoM, 50397), 190 pp. F. Helzel, 'Nibelungische Echos. Ost-westliche Bilder in Gedichten P. Cs von 1944 bis 1968', *ZDA*, 128:309–36. B. Malinkowski, ' "...den Himmel als Abgrund unter sich": zu einer Poetik des Endes bei P. C.', *Germanica*, 24:177–203. Sabine Markis, *"mit lesendem Aug': Prinzipien der Textorganisation in P. Cs 'Niemandsrose'*, Bielefeld, Aisthesis, 128 pp. L. Naiditsch, 'P. Cs Gedicht"Eine Gauner- und Ganovenweise" im Blick auf die Frage "Celan — Mandelstam" ', *EG*, 53, 1998:687–700. Werner Wolski, *Gedeutetes verstehen — Sprachliches wissen. Grundfragen der Philologie zum Werk P. Cs aus sprachwissenschaftlicher Sicht* (Studien zur Germanistik und Anglistik, 14), Frankfurt, Lang, 482 pp. See also BACHMANN, INGEBORG.

CZURDA, ELFRIEDE.   G. C. Howes, 'Therapeutic murder in E.C. and Lilian Faschinger', *MAL*, 32.2:79–93. K. Thorpe, 'Aggression and self-realization in E. C.'s novel *Die Giftmörderinnen*', *ib.*, 31.3–4, 1998:175–87.

DAHL, EDWIN WOLFRAM.   E. J. Krzywon, 'Gedichte gegen den Tod in der Welt. Zum lyrischen Gesamtwerk von E. W. D. anlässlich seines 70. Geburtstages', *Orbis Linguarum*, 12:105–24.

DÖBLIN, ALFRED.  Friedrich Wambsganz, *Das Leid im Werk A. Ds. Eine Analyse der späten Romane in Beziehung zum Gesamtwerk* (EH, 1, 1728), 289 pp.

DODERER, HEIMITO VON.  Slawomir Piontek, *Der Mythos von der österreichischen Identität. Überlegungen zu Aspekten der Wirklichkeitsmythisierung in Romanen von Albert Paris Gütersloh, H. v. D. und Herbert Eisenreich* (EH, 1, 1713), 250 pp.

DRAWERT, KURT.  C. Cosentino, '"Ich komme nirgendwo her .../Wie es weitergeht, weiss ich nicht": Ortswechsel und Nirgendwo in K. Ds Lyrikband *Wo es war*', *Neophilologus*, 83:121–31.

DÜRRENMATT, FRIEDRICH.  Liliana Mitrache, *Intertextualität und Phraseologie in den drei Versionen der 'Panne' von F. D.: Aspekte von Groteske und Ironie* (SGU, 38), 154 pp. See also HEIN, CHRISTOPH.

EICH, GÜNTER.  J. Fetscher, 'Das Empire bläst zum Angriff Saxophon. Text und Kontext von G. Es "Rebellion in der Goldstadt"', *WB*, 45:584–97.

ENZENSBERGER, HANS MAGNUS.  Jörg Lau, *H. M. E.: Ein öffentliches Leben*, Berlin, Alexander Fest, 288 pp.

FALKNER, GERHARD.  Neil H. Donahue, *Voice and Void. The Poetry of G. F.* (BNL, 157), 1998, 234 pp., is a useful introduction to a challenging poet and is sure to provide fertile ground for further analysis. After publishing his first volume, *so beginnen am körper die tage*, in 1981, F. was to remain on the fringes of cultural life representing 'a poetic idiom that was not commonly favoured in West Germany'. Ironically, on the brink of recognition with his third volume of poetry, *wemut*, in 1989, F. decided to end his career, disillusioned with the prospects for poetry in a climate where contemporary culture was infected by modern media. D. reveals that the poet has, nevertheless, published individual poems since 1989, but maintains that this is not a retreat from his earlier renunciation. The picture emerges in this study of a poet totally committed to his art, and D. dissects F.'s work in very great detail with extensive chapters devoted to each of F.'s volumes in turn. It is hermetic work, linguistically playful but not without a critical perspective', albeit not overtly political. D. argues passionately that F.'s 'poetry encompasses a range of sensation that is singular in contemporary German verse'. The monograph is certainly at its best when setting F. alongside others. In some respects, D. observes that the mood of the first volume of poetry is reminiscent of Trakl, whereas his later poetry is more akin to work produced by the poets of the Prenzlauer Berg, with whom F. felt some affinity prior to 1989. In particular, it is the exploration of language as a means to subvert ideology and 'create a free space' or 'a "no-place" in language' which brings F. close to the work of Bert Papenfuss-Gorek, for example. In contrast, D. juxtaposes F.'s poetry with that of Wolf Biermann, whose work is driven much more by its overtly polemical tone. Although both are described as moralists and sharing a tenacity in their aims, D. concludes that the epistemological element of F.'s poetry sets it apart. A little oddly, perhaps, D. then proceeds to insert a short excursus focusing explicitly on the work of Durs Grünbein, the successful Dresden poet. D. argues that Grünbein's career is a useful counterpoint to F.; whereas the latter is original, D. finds much of the former's poetry to be derivative. Indeed, he describes Grünbein somewhat disparagingly as an 'interesting and clever epigone', and quotes others who share this view. Although D.'s admiration of F.'s work is axiomatic, this excursus rests uneasily in what is an otherwise objective academic study. One feels that D. resents the acclaim Grünbein has enjoyed, compared to F.'s relative lack of success. In the process, though, D. seems to ignore at the same time how F. is described as being happy in what is termed a self-imposed 'exile'. Whereas the contrastive approach adopted elsewhere in the monograph is enlightening, the section on Grünbein appears rather partial and ill-judged. In conclusion, D. lays before us an exhaustive study of G. F. which is both perceptive and provocative. It remains to be seen whether others will share D.'s conviction about F.'s primacy amongst contemporary lyric poets, but there is sufficient material here to promote further discussion.

FLEISSER, MARIELUISE. Gérard Thiériot, *M. F. (1901–1974) et le théâtre populaire critique en Allemagne* (Contacts, 1, 19), Berne, Lang, xii + 387 pp.

FORTE, DIETER. M. Durzak, 'Die drei Leben des D. F. Zum Abschluß seiner Romantrilogie', *NRu*, 110.2 : 145–52.

FRIED, ERICH. *Gedichte von E. F.*, ed. Volker Kaukoreit, Stuttgart, Reclam, 160 pp.

FRISCH, MAX. Régine Battiston-Zuliani, *M. F. romancier. Son évolution de 'Mein Name sei Gantenbein' à 'Der Mensch erscheint im Holozän'* (EH, 1, 1732), xii + 300 pp. Sonja Rüegg, *'Ich hasse nicht die Schweiz, sondern die Verlogenheit'. Das Schweiz-Bild in M. Fs Werken 'Graf Öderland', 'Stiller' und 'Achtung: die Schweiz' und ihre zeitgenössische Kritik*, Zurich, Chronos, 1998, 475 pp.

FRISCHMUTH, BARBARA. P. Fachinger, 'Orientalism Reconsidered. Turkey in B. F.'s *Das Verschwinden des Schattens in der Sonne* and Hanne Mede-Flock's *Im Schatten des Mondsichel*', *STCL*, 23 : 239–54.

FUCHS, ANTON. M. L. Caputo-Mayr, 'A. F. Eine Würdigung', *MAL*, 32.2 : 125–35.

FÜHMANN, FRANZ. J. Krätzen, '"Das mythische Element in der Literatur" F. Fs', *DUS*, 51.6 : 51–61.

FUSSENEGGER, GERTRUD. *Grenzüberschreitungen. Festschrift für G. F.*, ed. Frank-Lothar Kroll, Munich, Langen Müller, 1998, 494 pp.

GRANZOW, KLAUS. W. Knütel, 'Erinnerungen an die Heimat in K. Gs Pommernbüchern', *SSG*, 6, 1998:111–20.

GRASS, GÜNTER Stephan Füssel, *Erläuterungen und Dokumente zu G.G.: Das Treffen in Telgte*, Stuttgart, Reclam, 160 pp. R. Geier, 'Grenzüberschreitungen — Vom Ritual zum Fanal. Die Lobrede des G. G. zur Verleihung des Friedenpreises des deutschen Buchhandels 1997 als Philippika', *CEtGer*, 36.2:99–109. R. Geissler, 'Ein Ende des"weiten Feldes"?', *WB*, 45:65–81. A. M. Haslach, 'Die Stadt Danzig-Gdańsk und ihre Geschichte im Werk von G. G.', *SGGed*, 6, 1998:93–110. S. Mohr-Elfadl, 'Jeu de tambour: la phraséologie dans l'oeuvre de G. G. et sa traduction', *NCA*, 17:401–11. Theodor Pelster, *G. G.*, Stuttgart, Reclam, 110 pp. L. Quinkenstein, 'Entsiegelte Geschichte. Zur Bildfunktion der Stadt Danzig in der polnischen Gegenwartsliteratur unter Berücksichtigung der Wirkungsgeschichte von G. G.', *Convivium*, 1998:209–21. T. Rahner, *G. G.: 'Die Blechtrommel'. Inhalt, Hintergrund, Interpretation*, Munich, Mentor, 64 pp. Dieter Stolz, *G. G. zur Einführung*, Hamburg, Junius, 200 pp. S. Taberner, ' "sowas läuft nur im Dritten Programm": winning over the audience for political engagement in G. G's *Kopfgeburten oder Die Deutschen sterben aus*', *MDU*, 91:84–100.

GRÜNBEIN, DURS. W. Riedel, 'Poetik der Präsenz. Idee der Dichtung bei D. G.', *IASL*, 24.1:82–105.

HANDKE, PETER. Johanna Bossinade, *Moderne Textpoetik: Entfaltung eines verfahrens, mit dem Beispiel P. Hs*, Würzburg, Könighausen & Neumann, 250 pp. C. E. Paver, ' "Die verkörperte Scham": the body in P. H.'s *Wunschloses Unglück*', *MLR*, 94:460–75. See also STRAUSS, BOTHO.

HÄRTLING, PETER. M. Zielińska, 'P. H. — Erinnerung als literarischer Stoff', *Orbis Linguarum*, 11:221–30.

HARIG, LUDWIG. *Sprache fürs Leben, Wörter gegen Tod. Ein Buch über L. H.*, ed. Benno Rech, Blieskastel, Gollenstein, 1997, 381 pp.

HAUSHOFER, MARLEN. *'Eine geheime Schrift aus diesem Splitterwerk enträtseln . . .': M. Hs Werk im Kontext*, ed. Anke Bosse and Clemens Ruthner, Tübingen, Francke, 350 pp.

HEIN, CHRISTOPH. G. Jackman, ' "Nur wo er spielt, ganz Mensch"? C.H.'s *Das Napoleon-Spiel*, *GQ*, 72:17–32. David W. Robinson, *Deconstructing East Germany: C. H.'s Literature of Dissent*, SGLLC, 240 pp. A. Schalk, 'Geschlossene Kreisläufe. Mythische Bilder im modernen Drama. Überlegungen zu C. H., Tankred Dorst, Heiner Müller, Friedrich Dürrenmatt und Botho Strauß', *DUS*, 51.6:19–28.

HERMLIN, STEPHAN. A. Solbach, 'Antifaschismus und Schuld. Zur Diskussion um S. H.', *WB*, 45:325–47.

HEYM, STEFAN. L. Hyunseon, 'Im Schatten der stalinistischen Prozesse: zur Dialektik des Geständnisses in S. Hs Roman *Collin*', *LiLi*, 29:143–55. Herbert Krämer, *Ein dreissigjähriger Krieg gegen ein Buch: Zur Publikations- und Rezeptionsgeschichte von S. Hs Roman über den 17. Juni 1953*, Tübingen, Stauffenburg, 210 pp.

HILDESHEIMER, WOLFGANG. J. Long, 'Time and narrative: W. H.'s *Tynset* and *Masante*', *GLL*, 52:457–74.

HOCHGATTERER, PAULUS. R. G. Weigel, 'Zerfetztheit und Ganzheit: zu P. Hs Roman *Über die Chirurgie*', *MAL*, 31.3–4, 1998:161–74.

HOFFER, KLAUS. J. E. Michaels, 'Interview mit K. H.', *MAL*, 32.2:105–12.

HOFMANN, GERT. D. Pinfold, ' "Das war schon einmal da, wie langweilig!" ? : "Hörspiel" and narrative in the work of G. H. (1931–1993)', *GLL*, 52:475–85. Hans-Georg Schede, *G. H.: Werkmonographie* (Ep, 289), 400 pp.

HOHL, LUDWIG. Sabine Haupt, *Schwer wie ein weisser Stein.' L. Hs ambivalente Bewältigung der Melancholie* (ZGS, 48), 1997, 326 pp.

HONIGMANN, BARBARA. L. Harig, 'Aufbruch in ein neues Leben. Der Weg der Schriftstellerin B. H.', *NDL*, 47.1:154–60.

HUCHEL, PETER. Thomas Götz, *Die brüchige Idylle. P. Hs Lyrik zwischen Magie und Entzauberung* (EH, 1, 1702), 236 pp. Wolfgang Heidenreich, *'...eine Notheberge für meine letzten Jahre'. P. H. in Staufen im Breisgau 1972–1981*, Marbach, Deutsche Schillergesellschaft, 16 pp. M. Jacob, 'Le temps des rêves et l'évocation du passé dans l'oeuvre lyrique de P. H.', *CEtGer*, 36.1:83–99. S. Kiefer, 'Zwischen Brecht, Mao und Ulbricht. P. Hs Fragment "Bericht aus Malaga"', *WB*, 45:368–86. *Die Ordnung der Gewitter. Positionen und Perspektiven in der internationalen Rezeption P. Hs. Akten der P.-H.-Konferenz, Potsdam 1996*, ed. Knut Kiesant, Berne, Lang, 202 pp.

JAHNN, HANS HENNY. H. L. Arnold, ' "Die Menschen sind Sklaven geworden ..." H. H. J. war ein "Alleingänger", der Wahrheiten meist zu persönlichen Schaden aussprach. Der umstrittene Autor starb vor vierzig Jahren', *SchwM*, 79.12:8–16.

JELINEK, ELFRIEDE. Eva Glenk, *Die Funktion von Sprichwörtern im Text. Eine linguistische Untersuchung anhand von Texten aus E. Js Werken*, Vienna, Praesens, 196 pp. R. S. Thomas, 'Subjectivity in E. J.'s *Clara S.*: resisting the vanishing point', *MAL*, 32.1:141–58.

JOHNSON, UWE. *Johnson-Jb.*, 6, includes: ' "Andere über mich." Schriftsteller (und Politiker) über U. J. Zweiter Teil: Von Berlin über New York nach Sheerness. Nach Belieben zusammengestellt von Uwe Neumann' (277–304); R. Berbig, ' "dieser Junge muss diesen Preis haben." U. J. als Preisträger und Juror des Fontane-Preises' (105–45); I. Gerlach, 'Ein Ring für D. E. Zum Tageseintrag des 1. Juli 1968' (305–10); M. Göritz, 'Die Ethik des Geschichtenerzählens in U. Js *Mutmassungen über Jakob*' (38–56); J. Grambow, 'Westkrankheit à la Weyrauch. U. J. in der DDR: eine Episode' (25–37); H. Helbig, 'Über die ästhetische Erziehung der Staatssicherheit in einer Reihe von Thesen. J. liest Schiller' (57–84); D. L. Horzen, 'Fitting the news to the novel. U. J.'s use of *The New York Times* in *Jahrestage*' (183–207); N. Jückstock, 'Unter Realisten. U. Js *Rede zur Verleihung des Raabepreises*' (146–62); K. Leuchtenberger, ' "Nachrichten über die Lage." Argumente für eine Lesart der *Zwei Ansichten*' (85–104); R. Paasch-Beeck, 'Eine Rede über Kirche und Tod. U. Js *Rede zum Bußtag*' (163–82); T. Schmidt, 'U. Js Jahrestage. Ein synoptisches Kalendarium' (208–76); and G. F. Seelig, 'Weil er hinhören, zusehen, auf Leute aufpassen konnte. Ein Gespräch' (9–24). G. Bond, ' "Der Brunnen der Vergangenheit": historical narration in U. J.'s *Heute Neunzig Jahre* and Thomas Mann's *Joseph und seine Brüder*', *GLL*, 52:68–84. K. Fickert, 'The identity of "Der Genosse Schriftsteller" in J.'s *Jahrestage*', *MDU*, 91:256–67. \**Js 'Jahrestage': Der Kommentar*, ed. Holger Helbig, Göttingen, Vandenhoeck & Ruprecht, 1100 pp. Annekatrin Klaus, \**'Sie haben ein Gedächtnis wie ein Mann, Mrs Cresspahl!' Weibliche Hauptfiguren im Werk U. Js*, Göttingen, Vandenhoeck & Ruprecht, 410 pp. Nicolai Riedel, \**U. J-Bibliographie 1959–1998*, Stuttgart, Metzler, 480 pp. M. Schweda, 'U. Js *Jahrestage* und Ingeborg Bachmanns *Todesarten* — Eine Zusammenschau', *LiLi*, 29:146–55.

JONKE, GERT. \**Die Aufhebung der Schwerkraft. Zu G. Js Poesie*, ed. Klaus Amann, Vienna, Sonderzahl, 1998, 208 pp. W. Hemecker, 'G. Js "Geblendeter Augenblick": eine Annäherung', *MAL*, 31.3–4, 1998:301–07.

JÜNGER, ERNST. \**Jung und Jünger: Gemeinsamkeiten und Gegensätzliches in den Werken von Carl Gustav Jung und E. J.*, ed. Thomas Arzt, Würzburg, Königshausen & Neumann, 284 pp. Elliott Y. Neaman, \**A Dubious Past: E. J. and the Politics of Literature after Nazism*, Berkeley, California U.P., 320 pp. Horst Seferens, \**'Leute von übermorgen und von vorgestern.' E. Js Ikonographie der Gegenaufklärung und die deutsche Rechte nach 1945*, Bodenheim, Philo, 1998, 399 pp. T. Weitin, 'Auflösung und Ganzheit. Zur Maschine bei E. J. und Heiner Müller', *WB*, 45:387–407. Tobias Wimbauer, \**Personenregister der Tagebücher E. J.*, Freiburg, Rombach, 296 pp.

KASCHNITZ, MARIE-LUISE. M. Kublitz-Kramer, ' "Es war einmal eine Zeit, da hatten die Götter in der Stadt gewohnt." Rom-Gänge mit K. und Koeppen', *DUS*, 51.2:55–67. Nikola Rossbach, \**'Jedes Kind ein Christkind, jedes Kind ein Mörder': Kind- und Kindheitsmotivik im Werk von M.-L. K.*, Tübingen, Francke, viii + 347 pp.

KEUN, IRMGARD. Ingrid Marchlewitz, \**I. K.: Leben und Werk* (Ep, 261), 195 pp.

KIPPHARDT, HEINAR.   Tilmann Fischer, *\**Gesund ist, wer andere zermalmt.'* H. Ks 'März' im Kontext der Antipsychiatrie-Debatte*, Bielefeld, Aisthesis, 208 pp.

KLUGE, ALEXANDER.   Herbert Holl, *\*La fuite du temps. 'Zeitenzug' chez A. K. Récit. Image. Concept* (Contacts, 3, 46), Berne, Lang, xx + 455 pp. Peter C. Lutze, *\*A. K. The Last Modernist*, Detroit, Wayne State U.P., 1998, 296 pp. Rainer Stollmann, *\*A. K. zur Einführung*, Hamburg, Junius, 1998, 163 pp.

KOEPPEN, WOLFGANG.   T. Fiedler, ' "eine sehr komplizierte Rechtslage wegen der Urheberrechte." Zu Jakob Littner und W. K.', *ColGer*, 32:103–04. B. Künzig, 'Die Schrift der Architektur. Der Städtebau Roms als geistiges Modell bei W. K., Paul Nizon und Rolf Dieter Brinkmann', *DUS*, 51.2:43–54. R. Ulrich, 'Vom Report zum Roman. Zur Textwelt von W. Ks Roman *Jakob Littners Aufzeichnungen aus einem Erdloch*', *ColGer*, 32:135–50. S. Ward, 'W. K. and the bridge of memory', *GLL*, 52:97–111. R. Zachau, 'Das Originalmanuskript zu W. Ks *Jakob Littners Aufzeichnungen aus einem Erdloch*', *ColGer*, 32:115–33. See also KASCHNITZ, MARIE-LUISE.

KÖHLMEIER, MICHAEL.   R. L. Burt, 'Heimweh im Paradies: the role of narrative in M. K's *Kalypso*', *MAL*, 31.3–4, 1998:240–51. B. Laman, 'Ein Gespräch mit M. K. am 9. April 1998 in Dickinson, North Dakota', *MAL*, 32.2:94–104.

KOLBE, UWE.   H. Krauss, 'Rom, Worte. Gespräch mit U. K.', *DUS*, 51.2:99–103.

KONSALIK, HEINZ G.   Matthias Harder, *\*Erfahrung Krieg. Zur Darstellung des Zweiten Weltkrieges in den Romanen von H. G. K. Mit einer Bibliographie der deutschsprachigen Veröffentlichungen des Autors von 1943–1996* (Ep, 232), 310 pp.

KRACAUER, SIEGFRIED.   Dirk Oschmann, *\*Auszug aus der Innerlichkeit: Das literarische Werk S. Ks*, Heidelberg, Winter, 336 pp.

KUNZE, REINER.   P. W. Lorkowski, 'Egzystencjalizm Reinera Kunzego i jego filozoficzno-poetyckie powinowactwa', *SGGed*, 6, 1998:121–35 (in Polish).

LAEDERACH, JÜRG.   D. Komorowski, 'Der Flaneur auf dem Boulevard der Imagination — zu Ls *Emanuel*', *Orbis Linguarum*, 11:231–38.

LÄNGLE, ULRIKE.   A. Daigger, ' "Schöne Aussichten" . . . U. Ls neuer Roman *Vermutungen über die Liebe in einem fremden Haus*', *MAL*, 31.3–4, 1998:278–87.

LANDER, JEANNETTE.   M. E. Goozé, 'The interlocution of geographical displacement, cultural identity, and cuisine in works by J. L.', *MDU*, 91:101–20.

LANGGÄSSER, ELISABETH.   *\*E. L. 1899–1950*, ed. Ulrich Ott (*MaM*, 85), 119 pp.

LANGNER, ILSE. F. Edmonds, 'Contested memories: *Heimat* and *Vaterland* in I. L.'s *Frau Emma kämpft im Hinterland*', *WGY*, 14:163–82. C. C. Marshall, 'I. L.'s Klytämnestra: a feminist response to the rhetoric of war', *ib.*, 183–99.

LENZ, HERMANN. *\*H.L.*, ed H. L. Arnold (TK, 114), 104 pp.

LUBOMIRSKI, KARL. R. Weigel, 'Mächtiger als die Strömeme des Leids, sind die Brücken — Zur Lyrik K. Ls', *MAL*, 32.2:58–78.

MAYRÖCKER, FRIEDERIKE. H. Kasper, 'Polyphone Aussagestruktur im Werk F. Ms', *CEtGer*, 36.2:163–72. Klaus Kastberger, *\*Reinschrift des Lebens: F. Ms 'Reise durch die Nacht'*. Edition und Analyse, Vienna, Böhlau, 496 pp.

MEIER, GERHARD. Dorota Sośnicka, *\*Wie handgewobene Teppiche. Die Prosawerke G. Ms*, Berne, Lang, 402 pp.

MEISTER, ERNST. Hans-Günther Huch, *\*Sage vom Ganzen den Satz: Philosophie und Zeichensprache in der Lyrik E. Ms* (Ep), 250 pp. Id., 'Das Spiel im Nirgendblau. Vom Sein und Raum in der Lyrik E. Ms', *Akzente*, 46:514–25. R. Keifer, 'Zum Stand der E. M. Forschung (II)', *Ernst-Meister-Jb.*, 1998[1999]:131–45.

MERKEL, INGE. G. K. Schneider, 'Zur Themenpalette I. Ms: eine österreichische Dichterin europäischer Prägung', *MAL*, 31.3–4, 1998:148–60.

MICKEL, KARL. J. Drews, 'Sein Nachbild auf meiner Netzhaut. Laudatio auf K. M.', *NDL*, 47.2:143–51.

MITTERER, FELIX. E. Bourke, 'F. Ms Volksstück *Kein Platz für Idioten*', *ZGB*, 7, 1998:39–50. A. Strasser, 'Biblische Motive in F. Ms Stück *Abraham*', *Germanica*, 24:69–78.

MOOG, CHRISTA. H. Mundt, 'Katherine Mansfield revisited: constructions of the self in C. M.'s *Aus tausend grünen Spiegeln*', *WGY*, 14:225–43.

MORGNER, IRMTRAUD. M. E. Eidecker, 'An den Grenzübergängen zum dominanten Diskurs. Entdeckungsreisen der Kinderfigur Wesselin in den Salman-Romanen I. Ms', *WB*, 45:53–64. Id., 'I. Ms *Das heroische Testament*. Zeugnis fehlender Spiegelung und fortgesetzter Suche nach der "Utopie Mensch"', *WB*, 45:444–48. C. Teissier, 'Aspects du rire dans le roman d'I. M. *Leben und Abenteuer der Trobadora Beatriz*: la mise en oeuvre du grotesque dans le livre neuf', *CEtGer*, 36.1:101–17.

MÜLLER, HEINER. Norbert Otto Eke, *\*H. M.*, Stuttgart, Reclam, 300 pp. M. Fröhlich, 'The void of utopian potentials: H. M.'s production of *Tristan und Isolde*', *GQ*, 72:153–66. Helmut Fuhrmann, *\*Warten auf "Geschichte". Der Dramatiker H. M.*, Würzburg, Königshausen & Neumann, 1997, 182 pp. C. Klein, 'M. et le misère allemande', *ChrA*, 7:139–50. M. Krajenbrink, '"Der Fall H. M.:

Probleme und Perspektiven.'' Impressionen einer Konferenz', *DeutB*, 28, 1998:237–41. See also JÜNGER, ERNST, and HEIN, CHRISTOPH.

NOLL, INGRID.   K. Drebes, 'Mordende Frauen — auch in der Schule? I. N. in Unterricht', *DUS*, 51.4:91–98.

NOSSACK, HANS ERICH.   G. Ociepa, 'Re-Konstruktion des Ich. H. E. Ns *Nekyia*. *Bericht eines Überlebenden* (1. Teil)', *Orbis Linguarum*, 12:95–104.

ÖZDAMAR, EMINE SEVGI.   M. E. Brunner, 'Die Türkei, ein Mutterland — Deutschland, ein Bitterland? E. S. Ös *Das Leben ist eine Karawanserei, IDF*, 26:556–65. S. Ghaussy, 'Das Vaterland verlassen: nomadic language and "feminine writing" in E. S. O.'s *Das Leben ist eine Karawanserei*', *GQ*, 72:1–16.

RABINOVICI, DORAN.   L. Silverman, ' "Der richtige Riecher"': the reconfiguration of Jewish and Austrian identities in the work of D. R.', *GQ*, 72:252–64.

RANSMAYR, CHRISTOPH.   L. Cook, 'The novels of C. R.: towards a final myth', *MAL*, 31.3–4, 1998:225–39. I. Foster, 'Alternative history and C. R.'s *Morbus Kitahara*', *ib.*, 32.1:111–25. E. Pascu, 'Interkulturelle Aspekte der Literatur: C. Rs Roman *Die letzte Welt*', *Temeswarer Beiträge zur Germanistik*, 2:128–42.

RATHENOW, LUTZ.   U. Struve, 'Gespräch mit L. R.', *DeutB*, 28, 1998:162–86.

REIMANN, BRIGITTE.   Margret Gottlieb, *' ...als wäre jeder Tag der letzte'* — B. R., Munich, Econ & List, 240 pp.

REZZORI, GREGOR VON.   *G. v. R. Essays, Anmerkungen und Erinnerungen*, ed. Gerhard Köpf, Oberhausen, Laufen, 316 pp.

ROTH, GERHARD.   P. S. Saur, 'G. R.'s *Die Archive des Schweigens*: a new genre', *MAL*, 31.3–4, 1998:89–102.

RÜHMKOPF, PETER.   E. Jarosz-Sienkiewicz, 'P. Rs Parodiebegriff', *Orbis Linguarum*, 12:129–38.

SACHS, NELLY.   A. Lerousseau, 'Le personnage d'Abraham dans l'oeuvre poétique et dramatique de N. S.', *Germanica*, 24:55–68.

SAIKO, GEORGE.   W. Klier, 'Unter den Grossen der Unbekannteste. Über den österreichischen Romancier G. S.', *Merkur*, 53:742–48.

SCHINDEL, ROBERT.   H. Nabbe, 'Die Enkelkinder des Doppeladlers. Einblendung von politischer Vergangenheit in den Alltag der Gegenwart in R. Ss Roman *Gebürtig*', *MAL*, 32.2:113–24.

SCHLINK, BERNHARD.   J. Köster, 'B. S.: *Der Vorleser* (1995) — Eine Interpretation für die Schule', *DUS*, 51.4:70–81.

SCHMIDT, ARNO.   W. Albrecht, 'Bewährungsprobe eines Editionsverfahrens. Zum Druck der Typoskriptbücher A. Ss innerhalb der Bargfelder Ausgabe', *Editio*, 12, 1998:130–37. G. Graf, 'Selbstgespräch mit Schüler. A. S und Hans Wollschläger', *Merkur*, 53:521–29. Frank Schäfer, *Lichtenberg — S. — Rühmkorf. Eine kleine Analogie- und

*Ableitungskunde*, Hanover, Wehrhahn, 77 pp. Julia Schmidt, *\*Karneval der Überlebenden*. *Intertextualität in A. Ss Novellen-Comödie 'Die Schule der Atheisten'* (APSL, 131), 1998, 187 pp. Stefan Voigt, *\*In der Auflösung begriffen*. *Erkenntnismodelle in A. Ss*, Bielefeld, Aisthesis, 325 pp.

SCHNEIDER, ROBERT. Rainer Moritz, *\*Erläuterungen und Dokumente zu R. S.: 'Schlafes Bruder'*, Stuttgart, Reclam, 101 pp. A. Steets, 'R. Ss *Schlafes Bruder*. Anregungen für eine Unterrichtssequenz', *DUS*, 51.4:82–90. N. Vazsonyi, 'Of genius and epiphany. *Schlafes Bruder, Das Parfum*, and *Babette's Feast*', *STCL*, 23:331–51.

SCHNURRE, WOLFDIETRICH. Daniela Schwardt, *\*'Fabelnd denken.' Zur Schreib- und Wirkungsabsicht von W. S.*, Oldenburg, Igel, 294 pp.

SCHUMANN, GERHARD. K.-H. Schoeps, 'Zur Kontinuität der völkisch-nationalkonservativen Literatur vor, während und nach 1945: der Fall G. S', *MDU*, 91:45–63.

SCHWAB, WERNER. G. U. Sanford, 'Zu W. Ss *Faust: Mein Brustkord: Mein Helm*', *MAL*, 31.3–4, 1998:332–55.

SEGHERS, ANNA. F. Albert, 'Das letzte Buch. Zu A. Ss Zyklus *Drei Frauen aus Haiti*', *WB*, 45:348–67. M. Bircken, 'Verhängtes oder verlorenes Schicksal? Über A. Ss *Das Argonautenschiff* (1949)', *DUS*, 51.6:29–40. Ursula Elsner, *\*A. S., Das siebte Kreuz. Interpretation von Ursula Elsner*, Munich, Oldenbourg, 184 pp.

SIMMEL, JOHANNES MARIO. *\*J. M. S. lächelt*, ed. Friedbert Aspetsberger, Innsbruck–Vienna, Studien Vlg, 280 pp.

STRAUSS, BOTHO. D. Byrnes, C. Schobess and F. Schröder, '"...Übersetzung von Lektüre im Schauspiel." B. Ss *Ithaka* am Deutschen Theater', *DUS*, 51.6:101–04. Jan Eckhoff, *\*Der junge B. S.: Literarische Sprache im Zeitalter der Medien*, Tübingen, Niemeyer, 300 pp. J. J. Rosellini, ' "Balkanische Bocksgesänge"? Neuartige Meldungen von B. S. und Peter Handke', *TeK*, 21.1, 1998:112–32. See also HEIN, CHRISTOPH.

STREERUWITZ, MARLENE. A. Schininà, 'M. S' Stücke: vom Wiener Volksstück zum Theater der Grausamkeit', *MAL*, 31.3–4, 1998:118–34. H. Schreckenberger, 'Die"Poetik des Banalen" in M. S' Romanen *Verführungen* und *Lisa's Liebe*', *ib.*, 135–47.

TABORI, GEORGE. *\*Verkörperte Geschichtsentwürfe. G. Ts Theaterarbeit*, ed. Peter Höyng, Tübingen, Francke, 1998, 220 pp. T. B. Malchow, 'G. T.'s *Jubiläum*: jokes and their relation to the representation of the Holocaust', *GQ*, 72:167–84.

TESCHKE, HOLGER. A. Kuhlmann, ' "Und an den starrenden Mauern ein Traum." H. Ts *Berliner November*', *WB*, 45:408–22.

TIMM, UWE. *U. T.*, ed. David Basker, Cardiff, Univ. of Wales Press, xi + 148 pp., continues the stimulating series of monographs on contemporary writers with a look at a writer whose early career was moulded by his involvement in the student movement in the late

1960s, and whose work as a whole incorporates exploration of the exotic and the everyday. The volume adheres to the now familiar pattern including an original essay from T. which deals with his love of distant lands, a theme revisited in several of the articles here. In a slight departure, Basker presents an overview of T.'s career not as an outline biography, but as a short essay which functions as a useful primer for the topics to follow. T. proves an eloquent and forthcoming subject in C. Riordan's interview, in which he stresses his positive view of the student movement. Above all, he is at pains to underscore the 'gesellschaftliche Relevanz der Literatur' and its need to provoke the reader, but does not see it as possessing a moralizing duty. Harking back to T.'s opening essay, K. Bullivant presents T. as an anthropologist and argues that even the novels set in the Federal Republic have an essentially ethnographic dimension with their fascination with the trappings of everyday life. R. Williams explores T.'s early work and finds elements of the *Bildungsroman* in their composition. Most striking, in Williams's survey, are the echoes he reveals between T. and the work of Peter Handke. Although critical of the Austrian's non-political stance, T. nevertheless 'shares Handke's fascination with the manifestations of popular culture which obtrude upon our consciousness'. The 'Innerlichkeit' Williams identifies in T.'s writing of the 1970s differs from the norm inasmuch as the central figures must actively strive for a solution, rather than come across one. C. Riordan examines the ecological aspects of T.'s novels *Morenga* and *Der Schlangenbaum*, and includes a brief, but illuminating, survey of Peter Kropotkin's work, which plays a role in the former text. Riordan argues that T.'s stance in these novels is complex and not without ambivalence, so that the abiding message is one of pessimism concerning the ability of the individual and the collective to avert ecological disaster. In perhaps the most engaging article here, D. Basker concentrates on T.'s preoccupation with 'die Ästhetik des Alltags', offering a fascinating insight into rhetorical devices employed in the author's later works supported by detailed reference to T.'s theoretical writings in *Erzählen und kein Ende*. Objects such as a toothpick or a potato are used to deflect the narrative of these later works into different, often fantastic, directions. Such digressions serve to relativize the omniscience of the narrator by offering further possible or probable sequences of events. What we have in texts such as *Der Mann auf dem Hochrad* or *Die Entdeckung der Currywurst* then is a narrative approach which goes beyond a simple collation of facts; it embraces an imaginative recreation of what might have occurred which is reminiscent of devices employed by Uwe Johnson in *Mutmassungen über Jakob* or Max Frisch in *Mein Name sei Gantenbein*, for example. In T.'s eyes the storyteller is not merely a chronicler of the past. The same technique is applied in *Johannisnacht*, where objects and stories trigger other stories, in which 'personal experience is repeatedly seen to intersect with wider cultural, political and historical factors'. Thus, Basker concludes, the texts in question lend credence to T.'s contention that narration is a means of interpreting the outside world. Therein lies literature's social relevance, even in the observation of mundane, everyday objects. As ever, the volume concludes with a highly detailed and accessible bibliography. It is to be hoped that this fine addition to Swansea's series will serve as a useful research tool for the expert, stimulate further academic interest, and bring the author to the attention of a wider audience.

TREICHEL, HANS-ULRICH. C. Kammler and M. Krallmann, ' "Ich wollte niemandem ähnlich sein . . .". H.-U. Ts Erzählung "Der Verlorene" als Beitrag zur inneren Geschichtsschreibung der Nachkriegsgeneration', *DUS*, 51.4:99–102.

WAGNER, RICHARD. G. L. Predoiu, 'Die Kategorie des Fremden bei R. W.', *Temeswarer Beiträge zur Germanistik*, 2:81–91.

WALSER, MARTIN. J. L. Plews, 'M. W.'s *Ein fliehendes Pferd*: good food, health, and immortality', *MGS*, 23.2, 1997:158–171. *Die Debatte: Der Streit um M. Ws Friedenspreisrede*, ed. Frank Schirrmacher, Frankfurt, Suhrkamp, 500 pp. S. Taberner, ' "Wie schön wäre Deutschland, wenn man sich noch als Deutscher fühlen und mit Stolz als Deutscher fühlen könnte." M. W.'s reception of Victor Klemperer's *Tagebücher 1933–1945* in *Das Prinzip Genauigkeit* and *Die Verteidigung der Kindheit*', *DVLG*, 73:710–32.

WECKMANN, ANDRÉ. B. Bach, 'W. et l'écologie: exemple d'une approche possible de la littérature régionale', *NCA*, 17:207–221.

WEISS, PETER. *'Marat/Sade', 'The Investigation' and 'The Shadow of the Body of the Coachman'*, ed. Robert Cohen (The German Library, 92), NY, Continuum, xxvii + 303 pp., compiles existing translations of three of W.'s better known publications. The result is a fine and engaging addition to the German Library series. C.'s introduction is insightful and thorough, placing the works translated here into the wider context of W.'s career as a whole and illuminating the author's key aesthetic and thematic concerns, as well as casting light on one of the post-war period's most innovative authors in a manner accessible for students at all levels, the volume could prove a useful stimulus for those working on more advanced planes. A full chronology of W.'s life and career is included, and the volume is supplemented by a very useful select bibliography. The introduction begins with a detailed description of the author's family background, and C. provides evidence of W.'s early preoccupation with the nature of suffering and pain both in his painting and writing. Attention is then turned to each text in chronological order, beginning with *Der Schatten des Körpers des Kutschers* (1952), perceived as both linguistic experiment and satire of the mores of the bourgeoisie. With regard to the former, C. concludes that the text 'often seems closer to Kafka than to the *nouveau roman*'. Parallels with *Waiting for Godot* are remarked upon, although the hopelessness of Beckett's work is absent in W.'s text. A more telling comparison might be with Buñuel's French films of the same period; C. refers at an earlier juncture to the influence surrealists such as the Spanish director had on W.'s early artwork. In contrast to the hermeticism of the prose piece, the many-layered *Marat/Sade* (1963) offers a different challenge. With its 'complex and disorientating structure' a hindrance to easy interpretation, C. sees the play on one level as a 'precursor of a postmodern drama of playful arbitrariness and undecidability'. On another level, the motif of the body is interpreted as a sign of W.'s incipient attraction to Marxism. W. revised the text many times, and the translation here is enriched by C.'s addition of new portions. The editor underlines that the final text here, *Die Ermittlung* (1965), is striking for its minimalism and marks the 'collapsing of boundaries between document and fiction'. Constructed from actual transcripts from the Auschwitz trials, the drama does not seek to recreate the Holocaust on stage: in fact, reference to nationalities, ethnic background and place are expunged in a bid for universality. C. observes that W.'s approach was not without its critics in the USA and it might appear that W., a member of the Swedish Communist Party, was advocating an interpretation of German history dangerously close to the conservative view espoused later during the *Historikerstreit* in the 1980s. However, reference in the play to several of the companies who exploited slave labour during the Third Reich and to the treatment of Soviet prisoners underscores that W.'s critical gaze is directed principally at the restitution of old forces and attitudes in capitalist postwar West Germany; his aim is not to relativize the Holocaust, but to ensure it does not fade as a distant memory. C. duly concludes by stressing the play's significant, and enduring, contribution to *Vergangenheitsbewälti- gung* by virtue of its 'power to disturb, to provoke, to anger'. The introduction is rounded off with an ample analysis of W.'s later work, with particular mention made of his mammoth *Die Ästhetik des Widerstands*, 'a work without precedent, a vast and heroic undertak- ing'. It is a measure of C.'s achievement that he has been able in a mere 17 pages to pinpoint the crucial coordinates of W.'s life and work sufficiently to both facilitate meaningful interaction with the texts collated here and whet the appetite for further study of this remarkable author. Stefan Schwöbel, \**Autonomie und Auftrag. Studien zur Kunsttheorie im Werk von P. W.* (Studien zur deutschen und europäischen Literatur des 19. und 20. Jahrhunderts, 41), Frankfurt, Lang, 349 pp.

WELLERSHOFF, DIETER. W. Jung, 'Bloss eine Anleitung für Mitläufer? Ws Arbeiten über Benn', *WB*, 45:240–55.

WERNER, MARKUS. G. Schiavoni, 'Julia sulle orme di Lou. Percorsi dell'Eros in *Terraferma* di M. W.', *Cultura tedesca*, 11:149–56.

WIMMER, HERBERT J. B. Schmidt, 'Über den Realismus des Formalen. Rede zur Inauguration des Ambivalenzromans *das offene schloss* von H. J. W.', *Wespennest*, 116:24–29.

WOHMANN, GABRIELE. Sigrid Mayer and Martha Hanscom, *The Critical Reception of the Short Fiction by Joyce Carol Oates and G. W.*, Columbia, Camden House, 1998, 249 pp.

WOLF, CHRISTA. J. Engler, 'Normalität und Argwohn. C. Ws *Kindheitsmuster* — wiedergelesen', *NDL*, 47.2:7–14. Suzanne Legg, *Zwischen Echos leben. C. Ws Prosa im Licht weiblicher Ästhetikdebatten*, Essen, Die Blaue Eule, 1998, 207 pp. Matti Luukkainen, *These, Antithese, Synthese. Zu Wandel und Beständigkeit des Sprachstils im Werk von C. W. 1961–1996* (BGS, 13), 1997, ix + 301 pp. E. Prak-Derrington, '"Wer spricht?" Über Tempora, Pronomina und Grenzverwischungen in C. Ws *Kein Ort. Nirgends*', *CEtGer*, 36.2:173–84. Tanja Walenski, *C. W. und Sowjetrussland 1945–1991* (Deutsch-russische Literaturbeziehungen, 9), Frankfurt, Lang, 150 pp.

ZAUNER, FRIEDRICH C. J. Thunecke, 'Weder Idylle noch Hölle; F. C. Zs Heimatroman Zyklus: *Das Ende der Ewigkeit*', *MAL*, 31.3–4, 1998:252–77.

## II. DUTCH STUDIES

### LANGUAGE

POSTPONED

### LITERATURE

By WIM HÜSKEN, *Senior Lecturer in Dutch, University of Auckland*

1. GENERAL

Modern-day technology is gradually infiltrating the humanities. In June 1992, the first electronic journal on Dutch language and literature was established: *Neder-L: Elektronisch tijdschrift voor de neerlandistiek.* This periodical mainly contains announcements of conferences, literary events, and academic vacancies but it also publishes reviews of recent books. *Neder-L*, an initiative of Ben Salemans, is free of charge and it is also accessible through the Internet: <http://baserv.uci.kun.nl/ ~ salemans/ >, or on email. Electronic editions of Dutch classic texts written between the Middle Ages and the mid-20th c. are available at the *Laurens Jansz Coster* webpages: <http://www.dds.nl/ ~ ljcoster/ >, a project initiated by Marc van Oostendorp. Together with another website, *De Nederlandse letteren* <http://www.letteren.nl/ >, the *Laurens Jansz Coster* webpages give access to an increasing number of computerized versions of Dutch literary texts. An impressive collection of 150 texts composed between the Middle Ages and the beginning of the 20th c. have been united on CD-ROM, *\*Klassieke literatuur: Nederlandse letterkunde van de Middeleeuwen tot en met de Tachtigers*, Utrecht, Arjen de Boer. Some of the texts come with sound; songs on this CD-ROM are performed by *Camerata Trajectina*, while Letty Kosterman and Gerrit Komrij lend their voices to recite texts. In addition to the texts edited on this CD-ROM, it also contains interviews with literary historians such as W. Kuiper, H. Pleij, M. A. Schenkeveld-van der Dussen, and J. Fontijn.

The *Nieuwe encyclopedie van de Vlaamse beweging*, ed. Reginald de Schryver et al., Tielt, Lannoo, 1998, 3 vols, 3799 pp., is a thoroughly revised and greatly enlarged edition of the *Encyclopedie van de Vlaamse beweging*, previously published between 1973 and 1975. The Board of Editors admit that it is not easy to give a definition of the 'Flemish Movement'. Over the centuries the concept appears to have been dominated by three elements: the language conflict ('taalstrijd') between speakers of Dutch and French, the cultivation of a national consciousness, and the spiritual and material development of Flanders as a nation. Apart from hundreds of entries the three volumes also include some 80 articles meant to be read as miniature monographs. Annette Portegies and Ron Rijghard, *Nederlandse literatuur in een notendop*, Amsterdam, Prometheus, 132 pp., present one of the shortest histories of Dutch literature ever written. Portegies and Rijghard limit themselves to the canon of Dutch literature to satisfy the appetite of those members of the wider public who want to obtain a quick insight into major movements and authors of Dutch literature between the Middle Ages and the present. A rich and voluminous history of Dutch literature for the French market has been edited by Hanna Stouten and Jeanne Verbij-Schillings, *Histoire de la littérature néerlandaise (Pays-Bas et Flandre)*, Paris, Fayard, 915 pp., with chapters written by leading literary historians such as F. van Oostrom, H. Pleij, E. K. Grootes, and J. Goedegebuure. *Een wandeling door het vak: Opstellen voor Marijke Spies*, ed. Henk Duits and Ton van Strien (Stichting Neerlandistiek VU, 29), Amsterdam, Stichting Neerlandistiek VU–Münster, Nodus, 134 pp., has been written in honour of Marijke Spies, formerly professor of Dutch Literature at the Free University of Amsterdam. The authors of the essays focus on rhetorical and argumentative aspects of Dutch literary texts.

In 1642, Prince Henry of Orange and the English Queen, Henrietta Maria, visited the Portuguese Synagogue in Amsterdam. One of the rabbis, Menasseh ben Israël, delivered a Latin eulogy in their honour which he subsequently had translated into Dutch. This eulogy represents the first non-religious text in Dutch published by a Jew. An anthology of prose texts, written in Dutch between 1642 and the present, in which Jewish authors reflect on living in a Dutch society, at times hostile to them but at others protecting them against external threats, has been edited by Daphne Meijer in *Levi in de Lage Landen: 350 jaar joodse schrijvers in de Nederlandse literatuur*, Amsterdam–Antwerp, Contact, 592 pp. The book contains work by some 48 authors. *Oost-Indische inkt: 400 jaar Indië in de Nederlandse letteren*, ed. Alfred Birney, Amsterdam–Antwerp, Contact, 1998, 559 pp., is an anthology of literary texts and fragments on 400 years of Dutch and Indonesian involvement with the Dutch East Indies. The book not only contains texts by authors travelling eastward but also includes observations written by first and second generation Indonesians who decided to live in the Netherlands once their country had become a Republic. A. M. Hagen, *O schone moedertaal: Lofzangen op het Nederlands 1500–2000*, Amsterdam, Contact, 123 pp., is an edition of laudatory poems on the Dutch language, written over the last five centuries.

## 2. The Middle Ages

Between 1280 and 1308, two different authors worked on a rhymed chronicle of the provinces of Holland and Zeeland, the first document in this genre in the Low Countries. The name of the second author is known: Melis Stoke, town clerk of Dordrecht who was employed, at a later stage in his career, in the chancellery of the dukes of Holland at The Hague. J. W. J. Burgers, *De Rijmkroniek van Holland en zijn auteurs: Historiografie in Holland door de Anonymus (1280–1282) en de grafelijke klerk Melis Stoke (begin veertiende eeuw)* (Hollandse studiën, 35), Haarlem, Historische Vereniging Holland–Hilversum, Verloren, 492 pp., describes the way the two authors composed this work, their aims, their sources, and their respective political and cultural contexts. Ever since it was published for the first time, in 1591, the *Rijmkroniek* has enjoyed a large popularity amongst historians and men of letters, but scholars have only recently embarked on a study of the six manuscripts left behind by Claes Heynensoon, herald to Willem VI, second duke of the House of Bavaria and Hainault. 'Heraut Beyeren' was one of the highest officials at court, responsible, among other things, for the accurate historiography of his master's duchy and related areas of interest. *Het Haagse handschrift van heraut Beyeren, Hs. Den Haag, Koninklijke Bibliotheek, 131 G 37*, ed. Jeanne Verbij-Schillings (Middeleeuwse verzamelhandschriften uit de Nederlanden, 6), Hilversum, Verloren, 273 pp., is an edition of one of these codices. The manuscript is characterized by the generous attention it pays to the history of the duchy of Brabant in an adaptation of one of Jan van Boendale's works. The book not only offers a complete transcription of the text but it also includes an integral facsimile of the original MS with its 55 colourful coats of arms.

Corrie de Haan, *Dichten in stijl: Duitse kleuring in Middelnederlandse teksten*, Amsterdam, Prometheus, 235 pp., studies the impact German literature had on texts in the Low Countries. Nico Lettinck, *Praten als Brugman: De wereld van een Nederlandse volksprediker aan het einde van de Middeleeuwen* (Verloren verleden, 5), Hilversum, Verloren, 80 pp., reviews the life and the works of Jan Brugman, a 15th-c. Franciscan preacher whose rhetorical qualities were, and still are, proverbial in the Dutch language.

*Pade crom ende menichfoude: Het Reynaert-onderzoek in de tweede helft van de twintigste eeuw*, ed. Hans van Dijk and Paul Wackers (Middeleeuwse studies en bronnen, 67), Hilversum, Verloren, 283 pp., is a reprint of 14 articles published between 1956 and 1996 by leading scholars of the Dutch version of Renart the Fox, *Reynaert de vos*. The book includes essays by, among others, W. Hellinga, K. Heeroma, L. Peeters, F. van Oostrom, and F. Lulofs. History and reception of the Dutch and

Low-German renditions of the story are studied in *Reynke de Vos —
Lübeck 1498: Zur Geschichte und Rezeption eines deutsch-niederländischen
Bestsellers*, ed. Amand Berteloot, Loek Geeraedts, and Hubertus
Menke (Niederlande-Studien, Kleinere Schriften, 5), Münster–Ham-
burg, Lit, 1998, 140 pp. Berteloot concentrates on the history of the
story prior to the publication of the Low German edition of 1498 in
' "Were al dat laken pergement dat dar wert ghemaket tho Gent, men
scholdet dar nicht in konen schryuen . . .": zur Vorgeschichte des
*Reynke de Vos*' (11–44). Details about the author of the Low German
text are given by Goossens in 'Der Verfasser des *Reynke de Vos*: ein
Dichterprofil' (45–79). Some people view the fox as a rascal, others
as a hero. Menke discusses the fox's character in 'Schurke, Schelm
und rebellischer Held: die Wandlungen der Reineke-Fuchs-
Auffassung' (81–101). The concluding essay is by W. Günther Rohr
who studies the reception of the Low German chapbook edition in
'Zur Rezeption des *Reynke de Vos*' (103–25). *Reinaert de vos*, ed. Hubert
Slings (Tekst in context, 3), Amsterdam U.P., 104 pp., is a translation
into modern Dutch of this famous beast epic with explanations of the
text.

Meant for a wider audience, *Jacob van Maerlant*, ed. Ingrid
Biesheuvel and Frits van Oostrom (Tekst in context, 2), Amsterdam
U.P., 103 pp., presents a selection of noteworthy fragments from Van
Maerlant's works with explanatory essays about the context of the
four fragments selected. *Poetry of Hadewijch*, ed. Marieke van Baest
(Studies in Spirituality, Supp., 3), Leuven, Peeters, 330 pp., is a new
edition of English translations of one of the best-known female mystic
authors.

One of the richest manuscripts ever compiled in the Low Countries,
named after its first owner, Charles Van Hulthem, has been edited
for the first time as one book: *Het handschrift-Van Hulthem, hs. Brussel,
Koninklijke Bibliotheek van België, 15.589–623*, ed. Herman Brinkman
and Janny Schenkel (Middeleeuwse verzamelhandschriften uit de
Nederlanden, 7), Hilversum, Verloren, 2 vols, 1295 pp. Many of the
texts in this collection, such as the *abele spelen* (serious secular plays
mostly on chivalric topics) and *sotternieën* (farces), have seen numerous
editions after the manuscript became available in the 1830s, but for a
substantial number of texts this edition is their first. A detailed
description of the Van Hulthem manuscript is published by M. E. M.
Jungman and J. B. Voorbij, *Repertorium van teksten in het handschrift-Van
Hulthem (hs. Brussel, Koninklijke Bibliotheek van België, 15.589–15.623)*,
Hilversum, Verloren, 96 pp. + CD-ROM. The authors give a complete inventory of the texts in the manuscript, including *incipit* and
*explicit* formulae, aspects identifying the codicological characteristics
of the items in the volume, information about the authors of the texts,

references to about 250 MSS containing parallel versions, and a bibliography of some 1,300 titles of books and articles on the manuscript and its 212 constituting texts. *'s Levens felheid in één band: Handschrift-Van Hulthem*, ed. Ria Jansen-Sieben, Brussels, Centrum voor de Bibliografie van de Neerlandistiek, 147 pp., is a catalogue of an exhibition dedicated to the famous manuscript held in the Royal Library in Brussels from 9 April to 22 May 1999. *\*Jeesten van rouwen ende van feesten, een bloemlezing uit de Lancelotcompilatie*, ed. Bart Besamusca (Middelnederlandse tekstedities, 6), Hilversum, Verloren, 240 pp., presents editions of a number of fragments of Dutch Arthurian novels. Each fragment is followed by an essay shedding light on the text's background. *Lanceloet: De Middelnederlandse vertaling van de Lancelot en prose overgeleverd in de Lancelotcompilatie*, vol. 4, ll. 16264–26636, ed. Ada Postma (Middelnederlandse Lancelotromans, 7), Hilversum, Verloren, 1998, vii + 518 pp., is another slice of the complete edition of the bulky Middle-Dutch compilation (*c.* 90,000 lines) of adaptations and translations of French Arthurian novels. *De kikker die zichzelf opblies en andere Middelnederlandse fabels*, ed. Anda Schippers (Griffioen), Amsterdam, Querido, 109 pp., offers modernized versions of some 50 fables, mostly from the 1498 and 1548 editions of Aesop's stories. Schippers defines a fable as any short story with a moral lesson in which animals or inanimate objects such as pots and pans think and talk like people. Frequently recurring themes are gluttony, lack of a sense of honour, and club-law.

## 3. THE RHETORICIANS' PERIOD

*Uilenspiegel: De wereld op zijn kop*, ed. Jozef Janssens, Leuven, Davidsfonds, 271 pp., concentrates on the early 16th-c. story of Till Eulenspiegel, relating aspects of his life, his jokes, and his pranks. In 'De wereld op zijn kop omstreeks 1500: De merkwaardige lotgevallen van een Nederduitse schalk' (15–58), Janssens reviews the motif of a topsy-turvy world as it was presented in the Dutch and Low German versions of the story. E. de Bruyn explores owl symbolism in late medieval iconography in 'De uil als spiegelbeeld: over uilsymboliek in de laatmiddeleeuwse iconografie' (59–86). Two 16th-c. editions of the chapbook are studied by V. Uyttersprot in 'Uilenspiegel in de drukken van Straatsburg (1515) en Antwerpen (1525/1546)' (87–109). The popularity of the story between the 16th and 20th cs is dealt with by P. Visscher in 'Uilenspiegel in volksboek en prent: van de 16de tot de 20ste eeuw' (111–145), while J. Hutsebaut researches the importance of a Flemish town for the history of Uilenspiegel in 'Damme: een Uilenspiegelstad?' (146–159). The two concluding contributions take us to modern adaptations of the chapbook.

V. Nachtergaele, 'De *Légende d'Ulenspiegel*, haar mythe en literaire navolgers in Vlaanderen' (160–211) studies the reception of Charles de Coster's version in Hugo Claus, Jan Eekhout, and Herman Teirlinck. Finally G. Segers writes about the reception of the story in 20th-c. children's literature in 'Een middeleeuwse schalk met vele gezichten: aspecten van de Uilenspiegelreceptie in de 20ste eeuw' (212–251).

T. C. J. van der Heijden and F. C. van Boheemen, *Met minnen versaemt: De Hollandse rederijkers vanaf de middeleeuwen tot het begin van de achttiende eeuw: Bronnen en bronnenstudies*, Delft, Eburon, 415 pp., study the archives of the province of Holland in search of traces of Chambers of Rhetoric and activities of rhetoricians from their first appearance in the 15th c. until the beginning of the 18th c. In the first part of the book, Van der Heijden discusses the relationship between rhetoricians and civic authorities, followed in part two by Van Boheemen's observations regarding poetry and drama competitions between various Chambers of Rhetoric. The third part, also by Van Boheemen, deals with financial aspects of the staging of rhetoricians' drama, related to the costs involved as well as to the proceeds of performances used for charitable purposes. The records unearthed in the many archives studied by Van Boheemen and Van der Heijden are published in *Retoricaal memoriaal: Bronnen voor de geschiedenis van de Hollandse rederijkerskamers van de middeleeuwen tot het begin van de achttiende eeuw*, Delft, Eburon, 842 pp. This material has also been made available on a CD-ROM.

*Het album J. Rotarii: Tekstuitgave van het werk van Johan Radermacher de Oude (1538–1617) in het 'Album Rotarii', Handschrift 2465 van de Centrale Bibliotheek van de Rijksuniversiteit te Gent*, ed. K. Bostoen et al., Hilversum, Verloren, 118 pp., is a facsimile edition with transcriptions on facing pages of texts written by Johan Radermacher, a merchant and humanist who spent a number of years in London as local agent of the influential puritan Antwerp merchant Gillis Hooftman. Raderma-cher's poetry includes epitaphs for family members, mottos and epigrams suitable to be engraved on knives and other presents. In 1607 he wrote a refrain in which he criticized a hymnal written by a doctoral student of theology. Prior to this edition K. Bostoen and C. Binnerts-Kluyver published a biography of Radermacher: *\*Bonis in bonum: Johan Radermacher de Oude (1538–1617), humanist en koopman* (Zeven Provinciën-reeks, 15), Hilversum, Verloren, 1998, 80 pp.

### 4. THE SEVENTEENTH CENTURY

Johan Verberckmoes, *Laughter, Jestbooks and Society in the Spanish Netherlands* (Early Modern History: Society and Culture), Houndsmill,

# 782 *Dutch Studies*

Macmillan–NY, St. Martin's Press, x + 214 pp., presents a throughly revised and amended English translation of his Dutch dissertation, *Schertsen, schimpen en schateren* (see *YWMLS*, 60:783). Jeroen Salman, *\*Populair drukwerk in de Gouden Eeuw: De almanak als lectuur en handelswaar* (Bijdragen tot de geschiedenis van de Nederlandse boekhandel, n.s., 3), Zutphen, Walburg, 495 pp., concentrates on the popular genre of the almanac viewing these booklets from a dual perspective, as material for easy reading and as a commercial product. *De spreek-woorden van Jacob Cats*, ed. M. A. van den Broek, Antwerp–Rotterdam, De Vries-Brouwers, 1998, 179 pp., provides an alphabetically arranged list with commentary of proverbs in the works of Jacob Cats, one of the most widely read authors of the century.

Marijke Spies, *Rhetoric, Rhetoricians and Poets: Studies in Renaissance Poetry and Poetics*, ed. Henk Duits and Ton van Strien, Amsterdam U.P., 169 pp., is a reprint of 12 essays by a former professor of Dutch Literature at the Free University of Amsterdam, previously published between 1982 and 1999. The first three chapters in the book focus on Neo-Latin and French literature: 'The rhetoric of Ronsard's "Hymne de l'Or"' (5–11), 'From disputation to argumentation: the French morality play in the sixteenth century' (13–19), 'Between epic and lyric: the genres in J. C. Scaliger's *Poetices Libri Septem*' (21–27).

A relatively large number of text editions have appeared in print. *Het hart naar boven: Religieuze poëzie uit de zeventiende eeuw*, ed. Ton van Strien and Els Stronks (Delta), Amsterdam, Ambo–Amsterdam U.P., 447 pp., is an anthology of religious poetry by 46 authors some of whom, such as Bernardus Busschoff and Geertruyd Gordon, have until now barely received any attention. Preceding each chapter the author and his or her works are introduced, enabling the reader to reconstruct the context from which he or she worked. The editors limit their choice to texts explicitly dealing with religious topics excluding the many poems showing religious inspiration in a general sense. The collection therefore contains poems in which biblical stories are related or in which an individual's relationship with God is described. In a concluding essay the editors concentrate on the personal implications of belief in the 17th c., on the clerical landscape of the Dutch Republic, and on the various ways poets expressed religious feelings in their poetry.

Between 1643 and 1649 the Haarlem printer Claes Albertsz Haen published four volumes of poems and songs in a series of 'Haerlemsche Bloempjes'. A selection from these, supplemented with poems from four other Haarlem songbooks is *De Haarlemse bloempjes: Bloemlezing uit een zeventiende-eeuwse liedboekenreeks*, ed. Natascha Veldhorst (Haarlemse Doelenreeks, 4), Haarlem, Stadsbibliotheek–Arcadia, 96 pp.

Erycius Puteanus, born in Venlo in 1574, was trained as a humanist scholar. At the tender age of 25 he became professor of rhetoric at the University of Milan. Appointed as successor of the famous scholar Justus Lipsius, P. returned to the Spanish Netherlands in 1606 where he lectured in the Collegium Trilingue of the University of Leuven (Louvain). In 1638 he published, under the pseudonym Honorius Vanden Born, a first collection of epigrammic poetry entitled *Sedigh leven*, announcing an enlarged edition for the next year. *Sedigh leven, daghelycks broodt (1639)*, ed. Hugo Dehennin (Literaire tekstedities en bibliografieën, 1), Ghent, KANTL, 278 pp., is the first reprint of this collection of poems, which has never received any attention in literary history despite Constantijn Huygens's appreciation of the work. In his introduction to the edition Dehennin discusses various aspects of *Sedigh leven*, including P.'s poetics and style, metre and rhyme, the way the collection was arranged, moral issues, influences and parallels, and the position of the book in Dutch literature.

Two of Bredero's most popular comic plays have been reprinted in a new edition: *G. A. Bredero's Moortje en Spaanschen Brabander*, ed. E. K. Grootes (Delta), Amsterdam, Athenaeum–Polak & Van Gennep, 421 pp. In an essay following the texts of these plays Grootes elaborates on the position they occupy in the dramatic tradition between the Rhetoricians' farces and the fully-fledged genre of Renaissance comedy, the sources and the way Bredero adapted them in accordance with the taste of his Amsterdam audience, the time frame in which these plays are assumed to take place (*c.* 1580 for *Moortje* and the mid-1570s for *Spaanschen Brabander*), and the tenor of the two plays. W. D. Hooft, *Door-trapte Meelis* & J. Noozeman, *Lichte Klaartje*, ed. Arjan van Leuvensteijn and Jeanine Stuart (Stichting Neerlandistiek VU, 28), Amsterdam, Stichting Neerlandistiek VU–Münster, Nodus, 169 pp., presents an edition of farces by two minor poets.

*In een web van vriendschap: Brieven van Nederlandse vrouwen uit de zeventiende eeuw*, ed. Mieke B. Smits-Veldt and Martha S. Bakker (Griffioen), Amsterdam, Querido, 143 pp., has editions in modern Dutch of letters by women, some known as writers themselves, others relatives or acquaintances of well-known men. The collection includes letters by two of Constantijn Huygens's sisters, Constance and Geertruyd, by his mother Susanna Hoefnagel, and by one of his first girlfriends, Dorothea van Dorp; it also publishes letters by Maria van Reigersberch, the wife of Hugo de Groot, and by the women poets Maria Tesselschade and Anna Roemersdochter Visscher. A selection from the poems written by the last-mentioned is *Gedichten van Anna Roemersdochter Visscher: een bloemlezing*, ed. Riet Schenkeveld-van der Dussen and Annelies de Jeu (De Amazone-reeks), Amsterdam U.P.,

143 pp. *D'openhertige juffrouw, of d'ontdekte geveinsdheid (1680)*, ed. Joost Kloek, Inger Leemans, and Wijnand Mijnhardt (Duivelshoekreeks, 10), Leiden, Astraea, 1998, 194 pp., is an edition of a prostitute's life story narrated by herself. In 1683, an English translation of the book appeared in print as *The London Jilt, or The Politick Whore*.

## 5. The Eighteenth Century

The first part of W. R. D. van Oostrum, *Juliana Cornelia de Lannoy (1738–1782): Ambitieus, vrijmoedig en gevat*, Hilversum, Verloren, 376 pp., discusses the ways in which De Lannoy dealt with the gender straitjacket enforced upon her, an intelligent woman living in the second half of the 18th century. Annoyed with her social limitations, De Lannoy managed to use literature to express her thoughts about the position of women in the world, criticizing those, men and women alike, who wanted to maintain the status quo. In her poems, published in two volumes between 1780 and 1783, the author frequently repeated the idea that women are not inferior to men and that they are, compared to their male competitors, equally well capable of reaching the top of Mount Parnassus. Key to achieving this, as well as to success in other areas of public life, is, according to De Lannoy, good education. These matters were already central to her first publication, the long poem *Aan myn geest* (1766), comprising a dialogue between the author herself and her spirit. Unlike similar works, notably those by Boileau and Frederic II of Prussia (*Le Philosophe de Sans-Souci*), De Lannoy's poem shows a distinct difference between the two speaking personages, the spirit representing the ideal poet the I-character would like to be. However, the author's preferred poetic genre was not the didactic poem but the satirical *sonnet du coude*, in which a topsy-turvy world is shown. Acknowledging the fact that De Lannoy saw herself in the first place as a playwright, Van Oostrum gives special attention to her three tragedies, *Leo de Grote* (1767), *De belegering van Haerlem* (1770), and *Cleopatra, koningin van Syriën* (1776). The main character in the second play is Kenau Hasselaer, leader of the belligerent women involved in the defence of Haarlem when it was besieged and eventually captured by the Spaniards in 1572–73. Kenau — the name has become a saying in the Dutch language for a strong bossy woman — refuses to surrender and when at the end of the play, despite her efforts to prevent it, Haarlem yields to the enemy, she forces the Spanish army captain to have a good look at the blood-soaked result of the last stages of the siege during which many citizens were killed. In this play De Lannoy tried to depict Kenau as a warm, feeling mother as well as a brave hero, in no

respect whatsoever different from her male combatants. The third
part of this rich book consists of a biographical sketch of De Lannoy's
life and works.

José de Kruif, *Liefhebbers en gewoontelezers: Leescultuur in Den Haag in
de achttiende eeuw* (Bijdragen tot de geschiedenis van de Nederlandse
boekhandel, 4), Zutphen, Walburg, 360 pp., analyses the culture of
reading in literary societies at The Hague and the way these societies
influenced the dissemination of literature.

On 20 August 1731, a new weekly appeared in print named *De
Hollandsche Spectator*. By the time the last (360th) issue came out, on 8
April 1735, its readers knew the name of the author, Justus van Effen.
Moulded upon the example of Steele and Addison's *Spectator*, *De
Hollandsche Spectator* discussed topics related to dozens of areas
appertaining to 18th-c. social life. In 1985, the first 30 issues were
reprinted in a facsimile edition. Recently the continuation of this
project was taken up by a group of scholars, and so far four further
sections have been made available. Nos 31–195, covering the period
between 8 February 1732 and 7 September 1733, ed. Elly Groenenboom-Draai, W. R. D. van Oostrum, Susanne Gabriëls, and Marco
de Niet (Duivelshoekreeks, 8, 9, 12, and 13), Leiden, Astraea, 4 vols,
262, 356, 352, 376 pp.

Before the end of 1778, Hieronymus van Alphen published an
adaptation of Riedel's *Theorie der schönen Künste und Wissenschaften*
(1767), preceded by a lengthy introduction. In it Van Alphen proposes
to approach poetry from a philosophical point of view. Compared to
the literatures of surrounding countries, Dutch poetry is of a much
lower quality and future poets are therefore advised to study foreign
examples. Central to any attempt to improve standards is the study
of aesthetics. This, according to Van Alphen, leads to better taste;
*ingenium* (poetic genius) does not suffice to achieve this aim. Four years
later Van Alphen published two further treatises, one on the ways
Dutch poetry could be improved and one on the innate in poetry. A
unique criterion introduced in the first of the two works is the author's
demand that poetic language be 'sensual': through sounds and images
it has to be able to evoke sensual feelings. Jacqueline de Man presents
new editions of these treatises in Hieronymus van Alphen, *Literair-
theoretische geschriften* (Monumenta literaria neerlandica, 10.1, 10.2),
The Hague, Constantijn Huygens Instituut, 2 vols, 277, 319 pp.

Gerrit Paape and Maria van Schie, *Kinderpligten, gebeden en
samenspraaken, geschikt naar de vatbaarheid der jeugd: Negentien gedichten uit
een verdwenen boekje*, ed. Anne de Vries (Stichting Neerlandistiek VU,
30), Amsterdam, Stichting Neerlandistiek VU–Münster, Nodus,
57 pp., is an edition of 19 poems from a lost collection of nursery

rhymes. Since no copies of the original work have survived, De Vries had to rely on a later anthology of nursery rhymes, *Verzameling van gedichtjens ten dienste der schoolen* (1782). Gerrit Paape, *Vrolijke Caracterschetsen & De Knorrepot en de Menschenvriend*, ed. Peter Altena, Nijmegen, Vantilt, 256 pp., is an edition of two satirical stories, written in August and December 1797, shortly after Paape had been dismissed as judge. Not a lawyer by training, Paape had by way of experiment been appointed in that profession in 1796 to allow lay people to have a greater influence on the legal system in the recently established Batavian Republic.

## 6. THE NINETEENTH CENTURY

*Hoofdstukken uit de geschiedenis van de Vlaamse letterkunde in de negentiende eeuw, I,* ed. Ada Deprez, Walter Gobbers, and Karel Wauters (Studies op het gebied van de moderne Nederlandse literatuur, 1), Ghent, KANTL, xiii + 319 pp., has been conceived to compensate for the lacking (8th) vol. on 19th-c. Flemish literature in the authoritative *Geschiedenis van de Letterkunde der Nederlanden* (published between 1939 and 1988). This volume includes two chapters: W. Gobbers, 'Inleiding tot de Vlaamse literatuur van de negentiende eeuw: de socio-culturele achtergrond en het geestelijk en artistiek tijdsklimaat' (1–147), depicts the spiritual, artistic, and socio-cultural background of 19th-c. Flemish literature from a comparative point of view. In the period under scrutiny Flanders saw only one novelist and one poet of international standing, Hendrik Conscience and Guido Gezelle. In keeping with the national character, the far greater majority of Flemish authors were more interested in literature in which moral and didactic lessons prevail. Consequently, literary European movements appear here, as well as in the north where the situation was very similar, in mitigated forms. Hence, Romanticism was recast in a realist way and Realism appeared in a moderated, idealistic version. In the second chapter, K. Wauters, 'Het Vlaamse fictionele proza van Conscience tot Loveling' (147–310), reviews Flemish fictional prose written between 1830 and 1890. The author holds the opinion that negative value judgments related to 19th-c. Flemish prose overlook the fact that without it both the Flemish movement and the rich 20th-c. narrative literature would be unimaginable. Major authors in this period are H. Conscience, D. Sleeckx, A. Bergmann (Tony), and V. Loveling.

J. R. van der Wiel, *\*De geschiedenis in balkostuum: De historische roman in de Nederlandse literaire kritiek (1808–1874)* (Literatuur in veelvoud, 12), Leuven, Garant, 770 pp., studies the reception in literary criticism of historical novels by, among others, A. Bosboom-Toussaint, A. Drost, A. Loosjes, J. Oltmans, and H. Schimmel. Nop Maas has edited a collection of reactions by 19th-c. humorist authors and designers in one of the oldest Dutch periodicals: *De Opregte Haarlemsche Courant in negentiende-eeuwse literatuur en karikatuur* (Haarlemse Doelenreeks, 2), Haarlem, Arcadia, 1998, 96 pp. Together with Wim Vogel he has also edited a selection of poems on the town of Haarlem: *\*Een steen in goud gevat: Twee eeuwen gedichten over Haarlem*, Haarlem, Arcadia, 1998, 96 pp.

J. C. Streng, *Het is thans zeer briljant: Aspecten van het Zwolse culturele leven tijdens de overgang van ancien régime naar moderne tijd*, Hilversum, Verloren, 238 pp., reviews cultural life in the north-eastern town of Zwolle between 1780 and 1840, a provincial city with some 12,000 inhabitants and, since 1802, the capital of the province of Overijssel. S. highlights seven aspects of culture ranging from sociability and public life to Enlightenment, tradition, nature, and monuments to famous Zwolle citizens cast in paper, marble, or iron. The most prominent of all Zwolle's citizens was Rhijnvis Feith but Streng does not forget to include a number of minor poets, such as Pieter Leon de Beer and Hendrik Doyer. In a final chapter he reviews the reputation of Zwolle's cultural life in the rest of the Netherlands and the perception of Dutch culture by its inhabitants. The only poet, next to Feith, who, on a modest scale, received national fame was the notary public L. Rietberg. Painters and musicians living in Zwolle were less favoured. The town was too small to entertain a substantial cultural life, until in 1839 an Odeon was established where music and theatre performances could be held, and only then did cultural life become truly brilliant.

*\*De as van de Romantiek: Opstellen aangeboden aan prof. dr. W. van den Berg bij zijn afscheid als hoogleraar Moderne Nederlandse Letterkunde aan de Universiteit van Amsterdam*, ed. K. D. Beekman, M. T. C. Mathijsen-Verkooijen, and G. F. H. Raat, Amsterdam, Vossiuspers AUP, 320 pp., is a collection of essays presented to Wim van den Berg on his retirement as professor of modern Dutch literature at the University of Amsterdam. The authors attempt answers to questions as to the conditions in which the term Romanticism can be used and they study the many occasions when it has been incorrectly applied to authors and literary developments. Willem van den Berg, *Een bedachtzame beeldenstorm: Beschouwingen over de letterkunde van de achttiende en negentiende eeuw*, ed. Klaus Beekman, Marita Mathijsen, and George Vis, Amsterdam U.P., 351 pp., is a reprint of 14 of his essays, published on the occasion of the previously mentioned retirement, concentrating among other things on Romanticism, 19th-c. sociability, epistolarity as a literary concept, and literary intellectual relations.

Jacob Israël de Haan, *Mijn belijdend lied: 31 gedichten*, ed. Louis Putman, Amsterdam, Putman, 128 pp., is an edition with an introductory essay (11–39) by the poet and former professor of Dutch Literature at Leiden University, P. N. van Eyck. *Huiselijke poëzie*, ed. Ellen Krol (Griffioen), Amsterdam, Querido, 195 pp. is an anthology of comely poetry in the *Biedermeier* style which many 19th-c. Dutch poets felt attracted to over the decades following the turbulent times of the French occupation of the Netherlands between 1795 and 1815. The commemoration of the centenary of Guido Gezelle's death, on 27 November 1899, led to an overwhelming number of publications. In *Gezelle humorist*, Leuven, Davidsfonds–Clauwaert, 261 pp., Johan van Iseghem highlights the humorous aspects of the poetry written by the Flemish priest who is otherwise known for a tone of melancholy and piety in his works. Further publications include Karel M. C. Platteau, *Guido Gezelles vertaling van 'The song of Hiawatha' van Longfellow en de doorwerking daarvan in zijn poëzie*, n.p., Van der Borght, 381 pp.; Piet Couttenier, *Het Guido Gezellemuseum te Brugge*, Bruges, Stad Brugge, 127 pp. *'Reizen in den geest': De boekenwereld van Guido Gezelle*, ed. Els Depuydt and Ludo Vandamme, Bruges, Stad Brugge, 208 pp., is the catalogue of a exhibition on Gezelle, held in Bruges between 30 April and 10 July 1999. The author's complete poetry, previously published in eight volumes, has been reprinted in one volume: Guido Gezelle, *Volledig Dichtwerk: Jubileumuitgave 1899–1999*, ed. Jozef Boets, Tielt, Lannoo–Kapellen, Pelckmans, 1998, 1963 pp. *Als de ziele luistert: De mooiste religieuze gedichten van Guido Gezelle*, ed. Piet Thomas, Tielt, Lannoo, 212 pp., is an anthology of Gezelle's religious poetry. *De allermooiste gedichten van Guido Gezelle over vriendschap en geluk*, and *De honderd mooiste gedichten Guido Gezelle*, ed. Katrien Bruyland, Aartselaar, Deltas, 46 pp., 100 pp., are two further selections of his best poems on friendship and happiness.

## 7.  1880 TO 1945

On 1 November 1881, the poet Jacques Perk died, a mere 22 years old. Only 23 of his poems had been published before his death but they had attracted the attention of a young generation of poets consisting of urban professionals who wanted to abolish the old-fashioned style of their predecessors, scornfully referred to as 'domineedichters', poetic parsons. Like Dante and Petrarch, Perk was inspired by a distant beloved, named Mathilde. Dominated by a long cycle of sonnets dedicated to this girl, his collected poems were for the first time edited in 1882 by Willem Kloos, with introductions by the editor and the famous critic Carel Vosmaer. Jacques Perk,

*Gedichten*, pref. C. Vosmaer, introd. Willem Kloos, ed. Fabian R. W. Stolk (Delta), Amsterdam, Bert Bakker, 278 pp., is an amended reprint of this first edition. In his afterword, Stolk presents Perk's poetry as located halfway between a more traditional kind of writing and the new 'l'art pour l'art' style embraced by the 'Tachtiger' (Eighties) movement. J. D. F. van Halsema, *Dit eene brein: Opstellen over werk en dichterschap van J. H. Leopold*, Groningen, Historische Uitgeverij, 332 pp., is a reprint of six essays on the poet Leopold, supplemented with two hitherto unpublished articles. Two of the essays deal with the sources of his best-known poem, *Cheops* (1915). In the other chapters Van Halsema discusses, among other things, the relationship between religion and philosophy in Leopold's works, the philosophical background of his poems, 'Oinou' (1910) and 'Kinderpartij' (1906) in particular, intertextuality in the poetic cycle 'Morgen' (1897), and the motif of the deceased beloved in his early poetry.

An analytical bibliographical description of the first ten years, 1885–95, of the important literary periodical *De Nieuwe Gids* was published on CD-ROM, *Literaire Tijdschriften in Nederland*, 7, ed. Ramona Land, Leiden, Masters Software. Josette de Groot, *\*De verleidingstechnieken van Couperus: Over 'De boeken der kleine zielen'*, Leiden, Stichting Neerlandistiek te Leiden, 95 pp., argues that Couperus deliberately made extensive use of the technique of changing the narrative point of view in telling his story. By doing so, De Groot thinks, Couperus manages to show us what the true moral values are that emerge, once the sundry layers of social convention and the many shells of vain exterior pomp have been removed from the individual. The impressionist author and painter, Jacobus van Looy, had, apart from writing and painting, one other passion: travelling. On his many trips through Europe and Africa he used both means of expression for his viewpoints and ideas. *Looy met den noorderzon, weg!! De reizen van Jacobus van Looy*, ed. Esther Scheepers and Chris Will, Zutphen, Walburg, 1998, 128 pp., published in connection with an exhibition on the same topic held in Haarlem's 'Teylers Museum', reviews ten of Van Looy's voyages, from nearby Utrecht as a 20-year old to Spain and Morocco in the late 1880s and early 1900s.

Thomas Vaessens, *Circus Dubio & Schroom: Nijhoff, Van Ostaijen en de mentaliteit van het modernisme*, Amsterdam–Antwerp, De Arbeiderspers, 1998, 267 pp., reiterates the importance of the year 1916 in the history of modern Dutch literature. In 1916, Martinus Nijhoff published his first collection of poems, *De Wandelaar*, and in Flanders Paul van Ostaijen's firstling, *Music-Hall*, came out. Traditionally, the first mentioned author is seen as an intellectual modernist, the second as an avant-garde agitator and a revolutionary. Vaessens, however, attempts to prove that at the deeper level of their mentality and world picture, the two poets had much more in common than one would, at first glance, expect. Nijhoff and Van Ostaijen reacted in similar ways to the changing world surrounding them by functioning as intermediaries between the artistic and intellectual circles in Flanders and the Netherlands. *Paul van Ostaijen, die Avantgarde und Berlin*, ed. Lut Missinne and Loek Geeraedts (Niederlande-Studien, Kleinere Schriften, 4), Münster, Lit, 1998, 132 + [16] pp., publishes five essays on topics such as avantgarde and radicalism in Van Ostaijen's poetry.

Esther Blom, *De vlam van het menselijk denken: Nico van Suchtelen (1878–1949)*, Amsterdam, Wereldbibliotheek, 239 + [12] pp., is a biography of the almost forgotten poet, novelist, and playwright Van Suchtelen, who was thoroughly influenced by the works of the philosopher Spinoza. His pacifist novel *De stille lach* (1916) was among the best-read books of the 1920s. Gé Vaartjes, *Herman de Man: Een biografie*, Soesterberg, Aspekt, 716 + [16] pp., describes the life and the works of the author of regional novels, Herman de Man (pseudonym of S. H. Hamburger), who became famous for his novel *Het wassende water* (1925). Jaap Goedegebuure, *Zee, berg, rivier: Het leven van H. Marsman* (Open Domein, 35), Amsterdam, De Arbeiderspers, 343 + [32] pp., has written a new biography of the poet and critic Hendrik Marsman, which relates many events in Marsman's early life back to his semi-autobiographical novel, *Zelfportret van J.F.* (1932–37).

*Tussen twee generaties, briefwisseling A. Roland Holst en H. Marsman (1922–1940)*, ed. H. T. M. van Vliet (Achter het boek, 34), The Hague, Letterkundig Museum, xiii + 425 pp., is an edition of the correspondence between two of the most important poets of the Interbellum period. In June 1935, Roland Holst destroyed most of the letters he had received over the years, and thus the proportion of Marsman's correspondence in this edition is relatively small.

Wilfred Jonckheere, *Van Mafeking tot Robbeneiland: Zuid-Afrika in de Nederlandse letterkunde, 1896–1996*, Nijmegen, Vantilt, 224 + [16] pp., studies the image of South Africa created by Dutch and Flemish authors in their works. Central to the first part of the book is the aura of heroism bestowed upon the boers in Dutch literature after the Boer War, 1899–1902. Until the 1950s visiting young poets and novelists saw South-Africa as an ideal country. The second part of the book is dedicated to that period in literature, followed by observations in part three on the way writers reacted to Apartheid.

When he was 29 years old, the painter Harm Kamerlingh Onnes made a journey to East Asia. He was accompanied by his uncle, director of a trust office in Medan on the island of Sumatra, who was making this trip for the 30th time. Harm kept a diary of this journey which brought him to various plantations in the Dutch East Indies and to places such as Singapore, Shanghai, Beijing, Kyoto, and Tokyo. Complete with their drawings his impressions have been published as *De reis van Harm Kamerlingh Onnes: Brieven uit de Oost, 1922–1923*, ed. Dirk A. Buiskool, Hilversum, Verloren, 282 pp. Although the literary value of Kamerlingh Onnes's observations is limited, the edition deserves special attention as being of interest for those researching early 20th-c. involvement of Europeans, the Dutch in particular, with East Asian society, politics, and culture. *In het klad: Tekstgenetische studies*, ed. Dirk Van Hulle and Edward Vanhoutte, Antwerp, Archief en Museum voor het Vlaams Cultuurleven, 176 pp., tries to draw our attention to the many literary manuscripts waiting in the archives for a thorough scrutiny by devoted scholars. The book includes essays by M. De Smedt and Van Hulle on Willem Elsschot, by P. De Bruijn on Gerrit Achterberg, by A. De Vos on Guido Gezelle, by Y. T. Sjoen on Richard Minne, and by Y. van der Fraenen on Maurice Gilliams. One of those hitherto unpublished manuscripts has now been edited by Ludo Stynen and Sylvia Van Peteghem, *In Oorlogsnood: Virginie Lovelings dagboek 1914–1918*, Ghent, KANTL, 791 pp. It contains the diary of one of Flanders' most successful late 19th-c. and early 20th-c. female novelists, Virginie Loveling. Compared to other diaries by literary authors of the time Loveling's stands out in that it covers the entire period between 29 July 1914 when Belgium started mobilization and 2 December 1918 when the nation was slowly getting back on its feet again. As one of the most famous Flemish authors of her time she was frequently asked whether she did not keep a diary but she always denied it, because it could have endangered her safety. Unfortunately, the complete diary has not survived. Stynen discovered a few years ago that the first stack of unbound pages had disappeared. Even though Loveling had been suspected by the Germans of being a spy and despite the severity of the way they behaved towards Belgians, she bore deep feelings of sympathy for certain Germans, acknowledging in her diary that not all Germans could be equated with the system they represented.

José Buschman, *Den Haag, stad, boordevol Bordewijk: Een literaire wandeling door het Den Haag van F. Bordewijk*, Amsterdam, Lubberhuizen, 111 pp., takes readers and walkers on four tours through The Hague, the town in which the novelist Bordewijk lived for most of his lifetime and in which a number of his novels are set. F. Bordewijk, *Huis te huur: Elf surrealistische verhalen*, ed. Hans Anten and J. A. Dautzenberg, Amsterdam, Nijgh & Van Ditmar, 384 pp., presents editions of eleven surrealist stories by the same author.

## 8. 1945 TO THE PRESENT DAY

Piet Calis, *De vrienden van weleer: Schrijvers en tijdschriften tussen 1945 en 1948*, Amsterdam, Meulenhoff, 417 pp., is a sequel to two previously written books by Calis, one on illegal and clandestine periodicals during the Second World War, another on the history of three literary journals published between 1945 and 1948. In this volume the author concentrates on the histories of three further periodicals: *Het Woord*, *Criterium*, and *Libertinage*.

Redbad Fokkema, *Aan de mond van al die rivieren: Een geschiedenis van de Nederlandse poëzie sinds 1945*, Amsterdam, De Arbeiderspers, 318 pp., sketches a history of Dutch poetry after 1945. In the first three chapters the author gives a chronological outline of modern Dutch poetry. In 'Dromen aan de dijk' (13–47) he discusses the preceding period, roughly between 1880 and 1945, followed by 'De proefondervindelijke zee' (48–81) in which he deals with the Experimentalists of the 1950s. In 'Een landschap van rivieren' (82–121) the period between 1960 and the present is covered. The following four chapters have a thematic approach. Problems such as the extent to which post-War Dutch poetry can be termed post-modern, the relationship between realism and idealism, the question of whether language itself speaks in poetry, and the role of emotions in writing and reading poetry are tackled. Jan Oegema, *\*Lucebert, mysticus*, Nijmegen, Vantilt, 352 pp., deals with the 'Emperor' of the Experimentalist poets, Lucebert.

*In droomcadans bedwongen: over Hendrik de Vries*, ed. Bart Slijper (Over . . ., 7), [Groningen], Historische Uitgeverij, 183 pp., unites six essays on Hendrik de Vries, a poet commonly regarded as one of the *dii minores* in Dutch literature. A. L. Sötemann reviews the author's poetic conceptions in 'Harken in een tovertuin' (14–30). P. H. Dubois publishes excerpts from his correspondence with De Vries and comments on his letters in 'Het zal de maan wel zijn' (31–50). Aspects of horror and humour in his fairy-tales are discussed by W. Wilmink in 'Eigenaardige vrouwen' (51–60), and H. Hillenaar offers a psychological analysis of the poems written shortly after De Vries married: 'De "Levensroman" van Hendrik de Vries' (72–101). J. van der Vegt studies the origin of *De Tovertuin*, a collection of poems regarded as his best, written between 1938 and 1945, in 'Een tuin vol demonie' (102–51). Finally, H. Hermans returns to the sources of De Vries's many translations of Spanish *coplas* in 'Rood-geel-rood! Zijn eigen noot!' (152–82). Anneke Reitsma, *\*'Een naam en ster als boegbeeld': De poëzie van Ida Gerhardt in symbolistisch perspectief*, Assen, Van Gorcum, 1998, ix + 226 pp., studies Ida Gerhardt's poetry from a symbolist point of view.

P. Kralt, '*Paradoxaal is het gehele leven*': *Het œuvre van Vestdijk*, Amsterdam U.P., 200 pp., reviews the work of Simon Vestdijk, one of the most prolific modern Dutch novelists. Kralt discusses themes such as love, death, treason, power, and guilt, and a number of Vestdijk's novels are analysed. In addition, the author shows that Vestdijk was largely inspired by paintings. Albert Helman (pseudonym of Lou Lichtveld) was the first important author from Surinam, until 1975 part of the Kingdom of the Netherlands. Michiel van Kempen gives a personal account of the life and the works of Helman, whom he interviewed on many occasions, in *Kijk vreesloos in de spiegel: Albert Helman 1903–1996, notities, nota's, noteringen*, Haarlem, In de Knipscheer, 1998, 125 pp. Hans van Straten, *Hermans: Zijn tijd, zijn werk, zijn leven*, Soesterberg, Aspekt, 606 + [12] pp., presents the first fully-fledged biography of the famous critic and novelist, Willem Frederik Hermans, who died five years ago. See also René Marres, \**Willem Frederik Hermans, de geschiedkunde en het fenomeen Friedrich Weinreb* (Leidse opstellen, 33), Leiden, Stichting Internationaal Forum voor Afrikaanse en Nederlandse Taal en Letteren, 123 pp.

Harry Mulisch has received wide acclaim, both in the Netherlands and abroad, for his novels but he also published collections of essays and documentaries on political, social, and historical topics. Jos Buurlage, *Onveranderlijk veranderlijk: Harry Mulisch tussen literatuur, journalistiek, wetenschap en politiek in de jaren zestig en zeventig*, Amsterdam, De Bezige Bij, 285 pp., reviews Mulisch's social and politic stance in the 1960s and 1970s expressed in pamphlets such as *Bericht aan de rattenkoning* (1966), which shows the author's open support of the revolutionary 'Provo' movement, and *De zaak 40/61: Een reportage* (1962) on the trial of Adolf Eichmann. Even though Mulisch made himself heard as a critic of society in these documentaries, Buurlage thinks that his essays prove that the author basically remained a novelist.

Bart Vervaeck, *Het postmodernisme in de Nederlandse en Vlaamse roman* (Tekst en tijd, 1), Brussels, VUB–Nijmegen, Vantilt, 222 pp., studies Postmodernism in Dutch and Flemish novels by some 25 authors published between the 1970s and the present, reviewing their world picture, view of mankind, concept of language, and aspects of time, narration, meta-fiction, and intertextuality. Tijn Boon, *Het koppige hoofd dat niet wilde scheuren: Over Frans Kellendonk*, Amsterdam, Meulenhoff, 1998, 167 pp., concentrates on the conflicts Kellendonk fought with himself, regarding these as the key to his writings. B. discusses Kellendonk's ambiguous relationship with realism and his urge to look for some kind of social engagement while at the same time being much more interested in a life of seclusion. His works show a delicate balance between irony and moral behaviour, expressed for example in his fascination with Roman Catholicism while at the same time in essence being an atheist.

*Een zondagmiddag met J. J. Voskuil: 27 meest academische reacties op 'Het bureau'*, ed. Joris Bekkers et al., Nijmegen, Boekhandel Roelants, 1998, 143 pp., presents 27 essays in which various critics and literary scholars reflect on the success of J. J. Voskuil's cycle of novels currently being published as *Het bureau*.

*Hun kleine oorlog: De invloed van de Tweede Wereldoorlog op het literaire leven in België*, ed. Dirk de Geest, Paul Aron and Dirk Martin, Leuven, Peeters–Soma, 1998, vi + 339 pp., reviews the impact of the German occupation on literary life in Flanders during World War II and shortly after. The authors of the essays in this book concentrate on topics such as the world of publishers, literary criticism, and the position of literary journals. A French version of the same book was published in 1997 as *Leurs occupation: L'impact de la Seconde Guerre Mondiale sur la littérature en Belgique*, ed. P. Aron, D. de Geest & A. vanden Braembussche, Brussels, Textyles.

Marcel Janssens, *De L van lezen: Essays over hedendaagse literatuur*, Leuven, Davidsfonds–Literair, 295 pp., publishes a collection of 16 essays on modern Flemish literature ranging from Guido Gezelle to Herman Brusselmans and Kristien Hemmerechts. J. questions the usefulness of the term Postmodernism in 'De postmoderne mixing van hoog-en laagcultureel' (27–57). In 'Gezelles positie en betekenis in de Europese literatuur' (59–76), he places the Flemish poet Guido Gezelle in a European context. Next Janssens discusses poems written by the Expressionist poet Paul van Ostaijen: ' "Februarie", een boodschap vol wind' (77–87), and 'Een "Fatalisties liedje" van angst en pijn' (89–100). Special attention is given to William Faulkner's influence on two Flemish novelists: 'Louis Paul Boon en William Faulkner' (111–25), deals with Boon's tale *Menuet* (1955); 'Hugo Claus en William Faulkner: Een beknopte receptiegeschiedenis' (145–57), 'Hugo Claus en William Faulkner: Textuele confrontaties' (159–73), deal with Claus's novel *De Metsiers* (1950). Both stories show a remarkable resemblance to Faulkner's *The sound and the fury* (1929) and *As I Lay Dying* (1930). In 'Plagiaat, "plagiaat" of (plagiaat)?' (175–95), the author discusses the concept of plagiarism and the extent to which modern and postmodern authors can be accused of it. With an allusion to the poet's real name, Cyriel Coupé, Janssens reviews Anton van Wilderode's poetry in 'Beelden in Cyrielisch schrift' (197–205). The four concluding essays deal with Christian concepts, God and Christ in particular, in literature and art, including the applied art of advertising.

P. Hadermann, *Tijd en ruimte bij Herman Teirlinck* (Mededelingen van de Afdeling Letterkunde, 61.10), Amsterdam, Koninklijke Nederlandse Akademie van Wetenschappen, 1998, 17 pp., discusses aspects of space and time in the novels of Herman Teirlinck. Elke Brems, *\*Alles is leugen: De vroege romans van Gerard Walschap*, Antwerp, Manteau, 308 pp., concentrates on the early novels of Gerard Walschap. Commemorating the 20th anniversary of his death, Jos Muyres, *Louis Paul Boon, het vergeefse van de droom* (De school van de literatuur), Nijmegen, SUN–[Antwerp], Kritak, 157 pp., presents a concise biography of the Flemish author who died the day before he was to be told, in the Swedish embassy at Brussels, that he had been awarded the Nobel Prize for Literature. Kris Humbeeck, *Onder de giftige rook van Chipka: Louis Paul Boon en de fabrieksstad Aalst*, Ghent, Ludion–Amsterdam, Querido, 311 pp., is an impressive account of the life and the works of the same Flemish novelist, in which the author focuses on Boon's love-hate relationship with his native town of Aalst. The social environment in which he grew up had an enormous influence on his work. Special attention is paid to Boon's graphic works with splendid full-colour reproductions of 28 of his oil paintings. The book also includes an edition of the diary Boon kept during the last 18 months of his life, *Het dagboek van meneerke Boin, behandelende het jaar 1978–1979*. Boon's special relationship with Aalst is studied in more detail by Kris Humbeeck, *\*Louis Paul Boon en de fabrieksstad Aalst* (Boon-studies, 10), Antwerp, L. P. Boon-Documentatiecentrum–Antwerp U.P., 150 pp. Louis Paul Boon, *Het boek Jezebel*, ed. Johan Dierinck and Britt Kennis (Boon-studies, 11), Ghent, KANTL, xxvi + 236 pp., is an edition of an allegorical novel Boon wrote on the occasion of one of the most infamous sex scandals of the 1960s. Preceded by an edition of the texts of a number of semi-documentary accounts on the affair, *De nieuwe lady's Hamilton*, Boon comments on the Profumo Affair. The edition is supplemented by appendices including detailed annotations and a comprehensive list of textual variations.

*Hugo Claus, 'Wat bekommert zich de leeuw om de vlooien in zijn vacht': Vijftig jaar beschouwing in citaten, tekeningen en overzichten*, ed. Georges Wildemeersch and Gwennie Debergh, Leuven, Peeters, viii + 158 pp., reviews 50 years of criticism on the poems, novels, and plays of Hugo Claus. Within each of these genres Claus displayed great diversity (he feared being pinpointed as the mouthpiece of a particular literary movement), as a result of which he greatly confused his critics.

Sylvia Witteman and Thomas van den Bergh, *S. Carmiggelt: Een levensverhaal*, Amsterdam, De Arbeiderspers, 1998, 151 pp., present the life history of one of the best representatives of the genre of the humorous short story in modern Dutch literature, the highly popular

author Simon Carmiggelt. Between the lines of his witty stories
Carmiggelt betrayed a passionate character, showing himself a man
full of doubts and obsessions, by no means without weaknesses.
Together with Godfried Bomans, Kees van Kooten, and Kees Stip,
poets and authors of stories of the 'lighter' genre, Carmiggelt also
figures in *Vier lichte letterheren*, ed. Aad Meinders and Dick Welsink
(Schrijversprentenboek, 44), The Hague, Letterkundig Museum–
Amsterdam, Thomas Rap, 121 pp., published on the occasion of an
exhibition in The Hague, from 16 April to 12 September 1999.
    Between 1938 and 1954 Ed. Hoornik had most of his poetry and
critical studies published by Alexander Stols. *'Geld verdienen zal ik er
nooit aan': Briefwisseling Ed. Hoornik en A. A. M. Stols, 1938–1954*, ed.
Anky Hilgersom (Achter het boek, 33), The Hague, Letterkundig
Museum, 562 pp., is an integral edition of their correspondence
comprising a total of 375 documents with a certain emphasis on the
years 1939–42 when Hoornik was the main editor of *Helikon*, a
periodical also published by Stols. Hoornik's correspondence shows
few gaps owing to the fact that Stols saw to it that his archives were
well kept.
    Well-known poets such as P. C. Boutens, H. Marsman, and
A. Roland Holst have not made it to *De selectie van de eeuw: De 200 beste
gedichten van Nederland en Vlaanderen*, ed. Hugo Brems, Rob Schouten,
and Rogi Wieg, Amsterdam, De Arbeiderspers, 255 pp., an anthology
of 200 of the best 20th-c. Dutch poems. The editors decided to
include only those poets who still appeal to modern readers, for the
selection of which they followed their own personal tastes. *\*Het geheim
dat ik draag: 500 gedichten over de vrouw uit de Nederlandstalige letterkunde*, ed.
Christine D'haen, Tielt, Lannoo–Amsterdam, Atlas, [1998], 664 pp.,
is an anthology of 500 poems in which women take central stage. In
*Dames gaan voor: Nieuwe Nederlandse schrijfsters van Hella Haasse tot Connie
Palmen*, Amsterdam, De Bijenkorf, 191 pp., Elsbeth Etty presents her
selection of 100 of the best novels or collections of short stories written
by women in the second half of the 20th c. In an introductory essay
Etty quotes from a recently published report on reading in which
women are found to spend between two and three hours per week on
reading as opposed to men who read less than 90 minutes. Women
also buy more books than men. Explanations for these differences are
not given. Dutch female authors have become very successful over
the last 25 years and have been accepted as equal to their male
colleagues. Etty observes that feminism and the urge in women to
write about topics close to their own hearts are two of the most
important reasons for this remarkable success.
    *\*Een leven lang: Auteursportretten in woord en beeld*, The Hague, Biblion
Uitgeverij–Hilversum, NPS Radio, is a series of CD-ROMs on

modern Dutch authors. The four CD-ROMs available so far are geared towards a relatively young audience. They introduce Th. Beckman, M. Berk, R. van Dantzig, and H. Heeresma by way of interviews and reviews of their work, supplemented with their individual bio- and bibliographies.

## III. DANISH STUDIES*

### LANGUAGE

By T O M L U N D S K Æ R - N I E L S E N, *Queen Alexandra Lecturer in Danish, Department of Scandinavian Studies, University College London*

1. G E N E R A L

It seems fitting to begin this last survey of publications in the 20th c. with the discussion of language problems associated with the millennium and related issues that appears in H. Galberg Jacobsen, 'År 2000–problemer', *Nyt fra Sprognævnet*, no. 1 : 1–6. The current use of Danish in radio and TV, compared with the previous decades, is debated in three articles by present or former members of staff in *Sprog & Samfund*, 17.1: O. E. Riisager, 'Sproget på Radioavisen — eller: En afskedssalut' (4–7); M. Bähncke, 'Sproget i DR — set indefra' (7–10); and L. Trudsø, ' "Sproget" i DR-TV' (10–12). The 'comma debate' shows no sign of abating, as may be seen in N. Davidsen-Nielsen, 'Komma i engelsk og dansk', *Nyt fra Sprognævnet*, no. 1 : 7–15, and his follow-up comment 'Komma i engelsk og dansk nok en gang', *ib.*, no. 2 : 7–8, and in B. Pedersbæk, 'Ingen ro om kommaet', *Sprog & Samfund*, 17.1 : 3. A concise introduction to the 'new comma' is Susanne Nonboe Jacobsen and Ellen Bak Åndahl, *Færre kommaer*, Frederikshavn, Dafolo, 24 pp. *World Knowledge and Natural Language Analysis*, ed. Steffen Leo Hansen (Copenhagen Studies in Language, 23), Samfundslitteratur, Handelshøjskolen i København, 139 pp., contains six articles: B. Nistrup Madsen, H. Erdman Thomsen, and C. Vikner, 'The project "Computer-Aided Ontology Structuring" (CAOS)' (9–38); H. Erdman Thomsen, 'Typed feature specifications for establishing terminological equivalence relations' (39–55); S. W. Jørgensen, 'Can you be more specific? World knowledge and the analysis of specificity' (57–81); M. Nelson, 'What are proper names and how do we identify them?' (83–103); C. Philp, 'Properties of motion verbs' (105–18); and F. Sørensen, 'Locations. On the meaning of phrases like *i Paris* (in Paris) and *i fængsel* (in prison)' (119–39). H. J. Ladegaard, 'Dansk rigsmål i et socialpsykologisk perspektiv: En diskussion og empirisk analyse af rigsmålsbegrebet', *Rask*, 11, Odense U.P., 3–43. *Digte om sproget*, ed. Erik Skyum-Nielsen, Modersmål-Selskabets Årbog, C. A. Reitzel, 143 pp., reprints a large number of poems about the Danish language,

---

* The place of publication of books is Copenhagen unless otherwise indicated.

after an introduction by the editor (9–16). Some popular 'old wives' tales' about specific areas of language use are dealt with in E. Hansen, 'De hemmelige regler', *Mål & Mæle*, no. 4:17–20, and related issues in the field of oral communication in J. Rischel, 'Talesprogets sære strategier', *ib.*, no. 2:22–27. The perceived richness of Danish is emphasized in J. Bendix, 'Sprogets rigdom', *ib.*, no. 4:25–31, while more general political aspects of language are discussed in J. Rosendal, 'Sproget som politisk våben — om George Orwells sprogprojekt *nysprog*', *ib.*, no. 2:5–9. There are also strong political overtones in U. Ammon, 'On the language situation in the European Union (EU)', *Rask*, 9–10, Odense U.P, 135–56, and a comparison between language politics in Denmark and France is examined in B. Bakmand, 'Hvad kan vi lære af Frankrig — eller jagten på en dansk sprogpolitik', *NyS*, 25:85–103. Jørn Lund, *Tidens Sprog pejlet af Professor Higgins*, Spektrum, 95 pp., is a collection of earlier newspaper articles by the author. Some general and philosophical aspects of language are presented in Finn Collin and Finn Guldmann, *Sprogfilosofi — En introduktion*, Gyldendal, 311 pp.

2. HISTORY OF THE LANGUAGE, PHONOLOGY, MORPHOLOGY, LEXIS, SYNTAX, SEMANTICS, AND PRAGMATICS

E. Hansen, 'Volapyk', *Mål & Mæle*, no. 2:28–31. A. Karker, 'Udtrykket *i alt fald* — et grammatisk levn fra vikingetiden?' *Sprint*, no. 1–2:38–42. M. Akhøj Nielsen, 'Kønsskifte på gammeldansk — om genus af garth', *DSt*, 180–85. M. Lerche Nielsen, 'Runeindskrifterne fra Starigard/Oldenburg. Og andre runer fra det vestslaviske område', *ib.*, 16–36. J. Kousgård Sørensen, 'Etymologi — teori og praksis', *ib.*, 5–15. H. Basbøll, 'Prosodic issues in Danish compounding: a cognitive view', *Rask*, 9–10, Odense U.P., 349–68. H. Juul, 'Er der *r* i ordblind?' *Mål & Mæle*, no. 1:16–20. B. R. Pallesen, 'Om distinkthed', *ib.*, no. 2:17–21. Eugeniusz Rajnik, *Gramatyka Jezyka Dunskiego — Morfologia*, Poznan, Wydawnictwo Naukowe Uniwersytetu im. Adama Mickiewicza w Poznaniu (Adam Mickiewicz U.P.), 338 pp. V. Sandersen, 'Grammatisk eller naturligt køn', *Nyt fra Sprognævnet*, no. 4:1–5. B. Ørsnæs, 'Complex event compounds in Danish — an HPSG approach', *Acta Linguistica Hafniensia*, 31:59–90. A major work on lexis is Pia Jarvad, *Nye Ord — Ordbog over nye ord i dansk 1955–1998*, Gyldendal, 1084 pp., which is an updated expansion of the same author's previous recording of new words in Danish 1955–75 (under the name of Riber Petersen, 1984). Short presentations of this book are found in Id., 'Nye ord 1955–1998', *Mål & Mæle*, no. 3:5–8, and, incorporating Norwegian and Swedish aspects too, in the same author's article 'Årtusindparat?' *Sprog i Norden*, Novus, 51–66. She also makes some interesting comments about her approach to the task and the editorial work on the book in 'Hvordan finder man de nye ord?', *Sprog & Samfund*, 17.2:10–13. Blends or telescope words are discussed in J. Schack, 'Blandt sprogets kimærer', *DSt*, 37–52. Particles (in a very wide sense) is the theme of the double issue of *NyS*, 26–27, *Artikler om partikler*, Dansklærerforeningen, 245 pp. It contains nine articles: U. Hvilshøj, 'Om *sig* og *sig* selv. Medium og refleksiv i dansk' (11–34); L. Brink, 'Kongen af Danmark s bolsjer. Om tilhørspræpositionen s' (35–42); S. Nimb and P. Juel Henrichsen, 'Supersymmetrier i den danske *der*-konstruktion' (43–72); T. Juel Jensen, 'Kan man *ligge* i et mentalt rum? Om Lakoff, Fauconnier og den danske *der*-konstruktion' (73–99); M. Thestrup, 'Min kusine har haft hest — hun har også kommet af med den igen! Om hjælpeverbet "at have" som aspektuel mulighed i mundtlig diskurs' (101–29); P. Durst-Andersen, 'En kognitiv analyse af perfektum og imperfektum i dansk' (131–64); D. Bleses, 'Transparens og produktivitet i danske børns tilegnelse af verbers præteritum' (165–96); A. Gudiksen, 'Er orddannelse forudsigelig?' (197–223); and P. Juel Henrichsen, 'Tyrannocorpus Rex. Nogle indledende korpuslingvistiske undersøgelser af den danske del af www' (225–45). Kirsten Rask, *Sproglig tjekliste — for redaktører, grafikere og skribenter*, Grafisk Litteratur, 47 pp. Søren Brandt, *Modal Verbs in Danish* (Travaux du Cercle Linguistique de Copenhague, 30), C. A. Reitzel, 206 pp., is a major contribution to the study of Danish modal verbs. E. Hansen, 'Kriterier for inddeling af ledsætninger', *Ny forskning i grammatik*, ed. Peter Colliander and Iørn Korzen (Sophienbergsymposiet 1997: Fællespublikation, 5), Odense U.P., 1998, pp. 7–22. S. Hedegård Nielsen, 'Subjektakkusativ', *Mål & Mæle*, no. 1:26–31. C. Elbro, 'Stærke ordpar', *ib.*, no. 2:14–16. A discussion of the desirability of reducing the number of alternative spellings of words that appear in the official Danish work on spelling, *Retskrivningsordbogen*, is found in H. Galberg Jacobsen, 'Ud med dobbeltformerne?', *ib.*, no. 1:4–10. An analysis of reader responses to this article appears in H. Galberg Jacobsen, 'Fra dobbelt til enkelt?', *ib.*, no. 3:16–29. S. Foersom, 'Fuldtræffer eller ram forbi?', *ib.*, no. 1:11–15. P. Jarvad, 'Påkørsel af en fure i en mark?' *Nyt fra Sprognævnet*, no. 2:8–10. A. M. Ågerup, 'Den bare skjorte', *ib.*, no. 3:9–13. Jan Engberg, *Introduktion til Fagsprogslingvistikken*, Århus, Systime, 1998, 110 pp. Lis Holm, *Grundbog i tekstlingvistik*, Århus, Systime, 1998, 155 pp. Bodil Nistrup Madsen, *Terminologi 1–2*, 2 vols, Gad, 230, 91 pp.; vol. 1 deals with principles and methods, whereas vol. 2 is an exercise book. *Leksikalske datasamlinger. Indholds- og strukturbeskrivelse. 1: Taksonomi til klassifikation af oplysningstyper*, Dansk Standard, 1998, 74 pp.

3. DIALECTOLOGY, CONTRASTIVE LINGUISTICS,
BILINGUALISM, AND APPLIED LINGUISTICS

*Danske Folkemål*, 41, C. A. Reitzel, 197 pp., contains the following
contributions: M. Bjerrum, 'Fjolde-etymologier.' Supplement til Fjol-
deordbogen' (5–15); I. Ejskjær, '*strippe* og andre ord for malkespand i
danske dialekter' (17–33); I. Bévort, 'En ærøsk kilde fra 1869' (35–46);
B. Jul Nielsen, 'Hjælpeverberne *have* og *være* i danske dialekter. En
kommenteret gennemgang af nogle dialekttekster' (47–77); K. M.
Pedersen, 'Genusforenklingen i københavnsk' (79–105); F. Gregersen, 'Sociolingvistikkens forandringer. Indledende knæbøjninger
før Projekt Bysociolingvistik eventuelt genoptages' (107–38); T. Kristiansen, 'Unge sprogholdninger i Næstved 89 og 98' (139–62); and
J. Scheuer, 'Maskuliniteter, rekruttering og dialogiske idealer'
(163–84). Two articles by I. L. Pedersen, \*'Danskernes indstilling til
dialekter og de danske dialekters stilling blandt danskerne', *Dansknoter*
2:29–31, and \*'Regionalitet og sprogforandring i Danmark', *Stedet
som kulturell konstruksjon*, ed. B. Mæhlum, D. Slettan, and O. S. Stugu,
Trondheim, Historisk Institutt, NTNU, pp. 33–52. The debate about
the impact on Danish of the influx of foreign loan-words (especially
from English) continues to engage people's minds. Two important
books have appeared on the subject: Bent Preisler, *Danskerne og det
engelske sprog*, Roskilde U.P., 272 pp., and *Engelsk eller ikke engelsk? That
is the question*, ed. Niels Davidsen-Nielsen, Erik Hansen, and Pia
Jarvad (*Dansk Sprognævns skrifter*, 28), Gyldendal, 152 pp., which
includes the following articles: N. Davidsen-Nielsen and M. Herslund,
'Dansk han med sin tjener talte' (11–18); M. Herslund, 'Dansk som
"det andet sprog" ' (19–25); F. Larsen, 'Stands, eller jeg siger bang!'
(27–37); B. Preisler, 'Engelsk overfra og nedenfra: sprogforandring
og kulturel identitet' (39–64); E. Hansen, 'Det gode afløsningsord'
(91–102); and P. Jarvad, 'Den engelske påvirknings art og mængde'
(103–18). Among shorter contributions on the same topic are:
C. Elbro, 'Sproglig tolerance på engelsk', *Mål & Mæle*, no. 4:21–24;
B. Preisler, 'Hvorfor bruger de unge *engelsk* når de taler *dansk?' ib.*,
11–16; A. Szubert, 'Falske lån', *ib.*, no. 2:10–13; \*'Engelsk i
globaliseringens tidsalder', *Sprogforum*, 5.13:45–51; and, with reference to computer language, B. Pedersbæk, 'Computeren og sproget',
*Sprog & Samfund*, 17.3:6. The debate has even resulted in a proposal
(with an allusion to the new wave of Danish films) for 10 'dogmas' for
the use of Danish in O. Togeby, 'Dogmedansk', *Mål & Mæle*, no.
4:3–10. In continuation of her similarly entitled article last year,
H. Korzen, 'Se storken på cykel. Noget om frie prædikativer o.l. på
dansk og fransk', Parts 2 and 3, *Sprint*, no. 1–2:43–76, 77–120,
further explores the position of free adjunct constructions in Danish

and French. *Tekststrukturering på italiensk og dansk / Strutturazione testuale in italiano e in danese*, ed. Gunver Skytte, Iørn Korzen, Paola Polito, and Erling Strudsholm, 3 vols + 3 CDs, Museum Tusculanum, 689 pp. *Ny forskning i grammatik*, ed. Peter Colliander and Iørn Korzen (Sophienbergsymposiet 1997: Fællespublikation, 5), Odense U.P., 1998, contains two articles that compare Danish and Italian: B. L. Jensen, 'Om brugen af modalverber på italiensk og dansk; *dovere* sammenlignet med *måtte* og *skulle*' (109–28), and I. Korzen, 'Ellipsen i tekstgrammatisk perspektiv' (129–58). Jens Cramer and Erik Vive Larsen, *Dansk som nabosprog*. *Dansk grammatik for svensktalende*, Aarhus U.P., 96 pp. Elin Fredsted, *Analyser af dansk og tysk talesprog*, Oslo, Novus, 1998, 358 pp. An important contribution to the study of Danish as a second language is Anne Holmen and Karen Lund, *Studier i dansk som andetsprog*, Akademisk Forlag, 433 pp. Among its 13 articles are: K. Lund, 'Sprog, tilegnelse og kommunikativ undervisning' (11–69); B. Henriksen, 'Ordforråd og ordforrådsindlæring' (71–106); J. Normann Jørgensen, 'Om tilegnelse af dansk udtale hos voksne indlærere' (107–36); H. Vedel and G. Østergård, 'Alfabetisering i dansk som andetsprog' (237–305); L. Holm, 'Lytteforståelse' (323–52); and P. Frederiksen and S. Knudsen, 'Skriftlig dansk som andetsprog' (353–70). *Foredrag fra den fjerde konference om de nordiske sprog som andetsprog*, ed. A. Holmen, N. Jørgensen, P. Quist, and J. Møller (Københavnerstudier i tosprogethed). A. Horsbøl, 'Kommunikationsanalyse af dialoger til undervisning i dansk som andetsprog', *NyS*, 25:57–83. K. Lomholt, *\*'Skandināvu valoda politika attiecībā pret svešvārdiem un valodas ietekmes sfēru zudums'*, pp. 64–103 of *Sastatāmā un lietišķā valodniecība: Kontrastīvie pētījumi*, VII, Latvijas Universitātes Zinātniskie raksti (Acta Universitatis Latviensis), Riga, 1998. K. Lomholt, 'I got five pyramids off my chest: alphabetisation of idioms in dictionaries', pp. 184–202 of *Proceedings, The 2nd Riga Symposium on Pragmatic Aspects of Translation*, ed. Andrejs Veisbergs and Ieva Zauberga, Riga, University of Latvia–University of Mainz. J. C. Nielsen, 'Hvordan læser Azime og Ismet?' *Mål & Mæle*, no. 3:9–15. *\*'*The transformation of the culture and language of intimacy', *Psyke & Logos*, 2:435–55. B. Perregaard, 'Forskning i børns tidlige skriftsproglige udvikling: en oversigt og en kritik', *DSt*, 53–85. *NyS*, 28, *Muligheder og perspektiver i danskundervisningen i gymnasiet og på HF*, Dansklærerforeningen, 112 pp., is devoted to the teaching of Danish in upper-secondary educational institutions in Denmark. *Probing the Process in Translation: Methods and Results*, ed. Gyde Hansen (Copenhagen Studies in Language, 24), Samfundslitteratur, Handelshøjskolen i København, 187 pp., contains a number of articles about the methodology and practical results involved in the use of the computer programme 'Translog'. B. Norlyk, 'Translation and communication:

the influence of culture and context in Danish and British sales brochures', *Hermes*, 23 : 77–92, Det Erhvervssproglige Fakultet, Handelshøjskolen i Århus.

## 4. LEXICOGRAPHY, GRAMMARS, STYLISTICS, AND RHETORIC

A number of very useful dictionaries have been published: *Politikens Dansk Visuel Ordbog*, Politiken, 1998, 672 pp.; a new one-volume edition of *Politikens Nudansk Ordbog*, 17th ed., Politiken, 1287 pp.; *Politikens Nudansk Ordbog med etymologi*, 2 vols, Politiken, 1611 pp.; *Politikens Engelsk-Dansk med betydningsforklaringer*, ed. Arne Zettersten and Hanne Lauridsen, 2 vols, Politiken, 2279 pp.; *DanskOrdbogen*, Århus, Systime, 1175 pp. P. Bæk and I. Munk, 'Av min arm — en ordbog om kroppens sprog', *Mål & Mæle*, no. 1 : 21–25. E. Hjorth, 'Den Danske Ordbog — en kommende kollega til Retskrivningsordbogen', *Nyt fra Sprognævnet*, no. 3 : 1–9. B. B. Thomasen, 'Om ord og ordformer som glider ud af Retskrivningsordbogen', *ib.*, no. 4 : 6–8. Anne Marie Heltoft, Jørgen Wildt Hansen, and Helle Thoregaard, *Perleporten. Et introduktionsmateriale til grammatik*, Gad, 80 pp. Anne Hilt, Birgit Rehder, and Lilly Christensen, *Dansk gruppegrammatik — fokus på syntaks*, Akademisk Forlag, 95 pp. S. Kaas Andersen, 'Leif og lokalkoloritten', *Sprint*, no. 1–2 : 5–11. Poul Carlsbæk and Bent Møller, *Modern Public Sprog-Management*, Frederikshavn, Dafolo, 1998, 63 pp., warns against the invasion of management language into public sector publications. C. Grevy, 'Informationsmotorvejen og andre metaforer i computerfagsprog', *Hermes*, 23 : 173–201, Det Erhvervssproglige Fakultet, Handelshøjskolen i Århus. E. Hansen, 'Litteraturen og sproget', *Mål & Mæle*, no. 3 : 30–31. I. Livbjerg, 'Recipient roles in translation', *Hermes*, 23 : 203–20, Det Erhvervssproglige Fakultet, Handelshøjskolen i Århus.

'Sprogholdninger og sproglig variation', *Dansk*, 2 : 27–37. *NyS*, 25, has two articles of relevance here: M. Femø Nielsen, 'Grundbegreber i nyere samtaleanalyse' (9–55), and P. Steensbech Lemée and A. K. Lund, 'Et spørgsmål om retorik' (105–14).

## 5. ONOMASTICS

Bent Jørgensen, *Storbyens Stednavne*, Gyldendal, 348 pp. 'Stednavne i Thy med udgangspunkt i sognenavnet', *Historisk årbog for Thy*, 139–61.

## LITERATURE
POSTPONED

## IV. NORWEGIAN STUDIES*

### LANGUAGE

POSTPONED

### LITERATURE SINCE THE REFORMATION

By ØYSTEIN ROTTEM, *Cand. phil., Copenhagen*

1. GENERAL

Harald Gaski, *Skriftbilder. Samisk litteraturhistorie*, Karasjok, Davvi girji, 1998, 69 pp. Id., ' "The secretive text": Yoik lyrics as literature and tradition', *Nordlit*, Tromsø, 5: 3–28. Kaisa Lindbach, 'Skjønnlitteratur — et etnisk speil?', *ib.*, 55–72. Riita Kontio, ' "Midtimellomfenomen" i Nordkalottens litteratur: Forfatteren både inne i og utenfor sentrum og marginal', *ib.*, 73–94. The contributions in *Naturhistorier. Naturoppfatning, menneskesyn og poetikk i skandinavisk litteratur*, ed. I. Lærkesen, H. Bache-Wiig, and A. Lombnæs, LNU–Cappelen Akademiske, 384 pp., track the view on and function of nature in Scandinavian literature from early folk tales up to the poems of Olav H. Hauge. The role of nature in the national mythography is very well examined by Gudleiv Bø, and in an article on the poetry of Romanticism, Alvhild Dvergsdal shows how inanimate nature is transformed into spiritual poetry. Included are also articles on Maurits Hansen, Bjørnson, and Skram (by Per Bache), Jonas Lie (by H. Bache-Wiig), Hamsun (by H. H. Wærp), and Olav Aukrust and Tarjei Vesaas (by Ole M. Høystad).

2. THE SIXTEENTH TO NINETEENTH CENTURIES

GENERAL

Liv Bliksrud, *Den smilende makten. Norske Selskab i København og Johan Herman Wessel*, Aschehoug, 292 pp., is a popular, but nevertheless penetrating study of the ideology and aesthetics of the Norske Selskab in which B. takes a stand against an earlier understanding of the association as a predecessor of the patriotism of the 19th century. Of special interest is her examination of the relationship between love for the mother country and erotic motives in the writings of the society's members.

---

* The place of publication of books is Oslo unless otherwise indicated.

## 3. THE NINETEENTH CENTURY

### GENERAL

Jorunn Hareide, *Skrivefryd og penneskrekk*, LNU–Cappelen Akademiske, 213 pp., sheds light on autobiography as genre, focusing on five female writers, Camilla Collett, Hanna Winsnes, Gustava Kielland, Magdalene Thoresen, and Marie Wexelsen, and the psychological barriers they have to overcome to be able to express and understand themselves as writers.

### INDIVIDUAL AUTHORS

BJØRNSON. Aldo Keel, *Bjørnstjerne Bjørnson. En biografi. 1880–1910*, Gyldendal, 653 pp., is an excellent portrayal of the national hero par excellence of Norwegian literature. His private life, his public activities, the literary works, and not at least his political commitment are thoroughly examined and presented in a very readable way. The work provides much new information about the author and will be of great interest both to an academic audience and to a wider public, and must be considered as the standard work of Bjørnson scholarship. COLLETT. *Skrift, kropp og selv. Nytt lys på Camilla Collett*, ed. J. Hareide, Emilia, 1998, 240 pp. HAMSUN. In Martin Humpál, *The Roots of Modernist Narrative: Knut Hamsun's Novels 'Hunger', 'Mysteries' and 'Pan'*, Solum, 1998, H.'s first great novels are analysed from a narratological point of view. The main point is that H. must be considered as an early forerunner of Modernism. Harald Næss, *Knut Hamsuns brev 1925–1933*, Gyldendal, 560 pp. The collection of articles in *'Alles nur Kunst?' Knut Hamsun zwischen Ästhetik und Politik*, ed. R. Wolfert, Berlin, Arno Spitz, 149 pp., stems from a symposium in Berlin in 1997. The most interesting contributions deal with the well-known issue concerning the relationship between the ideology and the aesthetics of H., and are written by such Hamsun experts as W. Baumgartner, H. Detering, G. Gumbert, and H. Uecker. *Agora*, 17 : 1–2, is a special issue dedicated to the work of H. It presents new and valuable readings of individual works as well as overall views on H.'s literary method and ideological points of view and contains: A. Linneberg, 'Avantgardens andre ansikt: Hamsuns poetikk' (4–20); H. H. Wærp, 'Knut Hamsun som lyriker' (21–38); B. Jager, 'Melankoliska krypteringar i *Sult*' (39–66); E. B. Hansen, 'Frihet, spatialitet og tekstualitet i Hamsun. Noen spekulasjoner om "Dronningen av Saba" ', *Børn av Tiden* og *Ringen sluttet*' (67–95); O. Synnes, 'Mottakinga av *Mysterier* i samtida i Danmark og Noreg' (96–124); A. Skaftun, 'Nabobyen som diskursivt topos. Omkring Hamsuns sosialt situerte fortellerposisjon' (125–50); L. H. Nesby, 'Ironi og metafiksjonalitet i *Siste Kapitel*' (151–78); S. Dingstad,

'Innledning til *Landstrykere*' (179–212); T. Selboe, 'Ringen sluttet?'
Om Knut Hamsun, *På gjengrodde stier*' (213–31). Of special interest is
J. Langdal's polemic article 'Hvordan trylle bort det ubehagelige?
Et blikk inn i den magiske forskning' (232–59), in which he accuses
Norwegian scholars of having tried to explain away the traces of
Nazism in H.'s work. The papers presented at the international
Hamsun conference at the University of Tromsø, 1999, demonstrate
the diversity of interests and topics studied today: *Hamsun i Tromsø II.
Rapport fra den 2. internasjonale Hamsun-konferanse 1999*, ed. E. Arntzen,
N. M. Knutsen, and H. H. Wærp, Tromsø, Hamsun-Selskapet,
319 pp. Articles include Ø. Rottem, 'Har vi ham nå? Refleksjoner i
forkant av en eventuell ny Hamsunbiografi' (9–22); Id., '*Markens
grøde* — lovsang til jorddyrkingens pris eller landstrykerens ugjen-
nomførbare drøm' (269–86); E. Arntzen, 'Knut Hamsun som litterær
figur' (23–46); K. Brynhildsvoll, 'Knut Hamsuns *Siste kapittel*. Fin de
partie avant Fin de partie' (47–74); Å. Hennig, 'På turné' (75–87);
S. Dingstad, '*Ringen sluttet*: om Hamsun og kynismen' (89–108);
A. Skaftun, ' "Jeg bygger på mit personlige indtryk": om *På gjengrodde
stier*, en fortellerposisjon og litt til' (109–31); T. Selboe, 'Byens
betydning i *Sult*' (133–53); P. Graves, 'Gamla och nya horisonter:
något om mottagandet av Knut Hamsun och Selma Lagerlöf i
Storbritannien 1890–1940' (155–69); M. Žagar, ' "Nu var hun
fanget." Kvinner, barn, og fruktbarhet i *Markens grøde*' (171–93); F. C.
Brøgger, ' "Gud vet, hvad jeg i dag er vidne til": Naturen som "Det
andre" i *Pan*' (195–216); E. Egeberg, 'Tilbake til jorden — Hamsun
og Tolstoj' (217–38); H. H. Wærp, 'Knut Hamsun som reiseskildrer:
*I Æventyrland*' (239–61); N. M. Knutsen, 'Makt og maktmisbruk i
*Benoni* og *Rosa* (1908)' (287–97); B. Hemmer, 'Løytnant Thomas
Glahn og Hamsuns *Pan*' (299–319). L. B. Sønderby, 'Blodets hvisken
og benpibernes bøn. Kroppen som tematisk konstans: et fænomenolo-
gisk spor i Hamsuns forfatterskab', *Edda*: 222–31. Kari Wessely,
'Knut Hamsuns *Pan*, erotiken och det Onda', *ib.*, 233–44. M. Stecher-
Hansen, 'Whose Hamsun? Author and artifice: Knut Hamsun,
Thorkild Hansen and Per Olov Enquist', *ib.*, 245–51. M. Žagar, 'The
rhetoric of defense in Hamsun's *Paa gjengrodde Stier* (*On Overgrown
Paths*)', *ib.*, 252–61. S. Dingstad, 'Hamsun nå igjen — om seks nye
bidrag til forskningen', *ib.*, 262–71. S. König, ' "Deutschlands
bescheidener Freund." Die deutsche NS-Propaganda und Knut
Hamsun', *Skandinavistik*, 29:20–35. M. Sandberg, 'Writing on the
wall. The language of advertising in Knut Hamsun's *Sult*', *ScSt*,
71:265–96. Gunvald Hermundstad, *Psykiatriens historie*, Ad Notam
Gyldendal, 367 pp., includes an article on the proceedings against
Hamsun and the general condemnation of him, in which he takes a
stand against the psychiatrists' superficial understanding of H.'s

Literature since the Reformation 807

character, and explains the Nazi sympathies of H. as a late result of early childhood experiences.

HEIBERG. L. B. Haaland, 'Gunnar Heibergs etterliv som dramatiker', *NLÅ*, 68–89.

IBSEN, H. *Ibsen im europäischen Spannungsfeld zwischen Naturalismus und Symbolismus. Kongressakten der 8. Internationalen Ibsen-Konferenz. Gossensass 23.–28.6 1997*, ed. Maria Deppermann et al., Frankfurt, Lang, 1998, 489 pp. Asbjørn Aarseth, *Ibsens samtidsskuespill. En studie i glasskapets dramaturgi*, Oslo U.P., 376 pp. Egil Törnqvist, *Ibsen, Strindberg and the Intimate Theatre. Studies in TV Presentation*, Amsterdam U.P., 240 pp. Ellen Ugland, *Søkelys på Gengangere av Henrik Ibsen*, NKS, 113 pp. Egil A. Wyller, *Et enhetssyn på Ibsen fra 'Brand' til 'Når vi døde vågner'*, Spartacus–Andreas & Butenschøn, 217 pp. Odd B. Grønli, *I skyggen av Nora*, Steinkjer, Foreningen Gamle Steinkjer, 136 pp. 'Disputas. Frode Helland: *Melankoliens spill. En studie i Henrik Ibsens siste skuespill*. Universitetet i Oslo 28. januar 1998. Førsteopponent professor emeritus Inga-Stina Ewbank. Andreopponent professor, dr. philos. Atle Kittang, Universitetet i Bergen. Svar fra doktoranden', *Edda*, 170–94. B. Steene, 'Can this bird fly? The wild duck on the screen', *ib.*, 31–39. H. K. Sødal, 'Henrik Ibsens *Brand* — illustrasjon på en teleologisk suspensjon av det etiske?', *ib.*, 63–70. M. K. Norseng, 'Suicide and Ibsen's Hedda Gabler. The seen and unseen, sight and site, in the theater of mind', *ScSt*, 71:1–40.

IBSEN, S. T. Leiren, 'Catalysts of disunion. Sigurd Ibsen and *Ringeren*, 1898–1899', *ScSt*, 71:297–310.

JØLSEN. A. Skaftun, 'Diskursive omvegar til dyret bak dyden. Om Ragnhild Jølsens novelle "Hanna Valmoen"', *Nordlit*, Tromsø, 5:131–60.

KIELLAND. T. Rem, 'Posisjon og penger: Dickens og Kiellands forfattervirksomhet', *Norsk Litteraturvitenskapelig Tidsskrift*, 2:111–24. O. I. Apeland, 'Alexander Kiellands forhold til Bibel og kristendom', *Edda*, 40–49. H. Bache-Wiig, 'Kiellands roman *Jacob*: Fra krambod til supermarked — et kort oppgjør over dikterens fallitbo', *ib.*, 154–62.

LIE. O. Alfarnes, 'Eros i fugleham. Transcendens-motivet i Jonas Lies "Andværs-skarven"', *Edda*, 50–62.

WINSNES. *Hanna Winsnes og hennes tid*, ed. K. G. Svensøy and T. Alsvik, Drammen, Drammen museum, 191 pp.

## 4. THE TWENTIETH CENTURY

### GENERAL

Tom E. Hverven, *Å lese etter familien*, Tiden, 160 pp., concerns the revival of religion and family as focal points of interest in contemporary Norwegian fiction. Works by e.g. J. Kjærstad, J. Fosse,

T. Renberg, and H. Ørstavik are taken into account in order to illustrate the main points. G. Vestad, 'Minimalismens tiår', *NLÅ*, 150–68. Henning Hagerup, *Vinternotater*, Tiden, 344 pp., includes articles on e.g. Claes Gill, Gunvor Hofmo, Sigmund Mjelve, Dag Solstad, and Tor-Åge Bringsværd. U. Langås, 'Perspektiver på norsk 60-tallspoesi', pp. 52–90 of *Historier om nyere nordisk litteratur og kunst*, ed. A.-M. Mai and A. Borup, Copenhagen, Gads, 375 pp.

INDIVIDUAL AUTHORS

AMBJØRNSEN.   K. Imerslund, 'Outsidernes retorikk. Om språket i Ingvar Ambjørnsens roman *Hvite niggere*', *NLÅ*, 120–33.

ASKILDSEN.    *Festskrift til Kjell Askildsen på 70-årsdagen 30. september 1999*, Oktober, 190 pp.

BJØRNEBOE.    M. Mussari, 'Color: the material of immateriality in Jens Bjørneboe's *Blåmann*', *Edda*, 340–49.

BRYNILDSEN.   *Aasmund Brynildsen — en europeer fra Tjøme*. *Tønsberg 8.–9. oktober 1993*, Tønsberg, Tønsberg bibliotek, 1998, 144 pp.

DUUN.    Reidar Astås, B*arndommens eventyrland? Duun: I eventyre som kilde*, Tano Aschehoug, 1998, 266 pp.

FANGEN.    Jan Inge Sørbø, *Over dype svelg. Eit essay om Ronald Fangens aktualitet*, Gyldendal, 181 pp.

GRIEG.    Jan Tveita, *Om Vår ære og vår makt av Nordahl Grieg*, Ad Notam Gyldendal, 105 pp.

HERBJØRNSRUD.    F. Helland, 'Hans Herbjørnsruds novellesamling *Blinddøra*. En lesning', *NLÅ*, 134–49.

HOFMO.    F. Helland, ' "En tretthet som planter bilder" — om Gunvor Hofmos lyrikk', *Norsk Litteraturvitenskapelig Tidsskrift*, 2 : 56–70.

JONSSON.    Ingar S. Kolloen, *Berre kjærleik og død. Ein biografi om Tor Jonsson*, Samlaget, 441 pp., presents the life and work of J. in a congenial way. The book is well-written and well-documented. The impact of J.'s poor background on his writing and not least on his final suicide is convincingly clarified.

KØLTZOW.    Unni Langås, *Forandringens former. En studie i Liv Køltzows forfaterskap 1970–1988*, Aschehoug, 376 pp., is an exhaustive study of one of the leading feminist writers of contemporary fiction in which L. takes account of the main themes as well as the delicate and original style of K.'s prose fiction.

LUND.    F. Lønstad, 'Innsauset — om Thure Erik Lund', *Vagant*, no. 1 : 59–66.

LUNDEN.    A. Fosvold, 'De spinkle toner — sider af Eldrid Lundens forfatterskab', pp. 138–58 of *Historier om nyere nordisk litteratur og kunst*, ed. A.-M. Mai and A. Borup, Copenhagen, Gads, 374 pp.

MEHREN.  B. Aamotsbakken, 'Oxymoriske trekk i dikt fra Stein Mehrens *Evighet, vårt flyktigste stoff*', *Edda*, 91–101.

MJELVE.  K. Madsen, 'Sigmund Mjelve og det paradisiske', *Edda*, 365–69.

MYKLE.  Anders Heger, *Agnar Mykle. Et diktet liv*, Gyldendal, 552 pp., is biographical writing at its best. H. does not hide his fascination for the writer, but is at the same time very much concerned with the writer's use of models from real life. The fate of M., who suddenly stopped publishing books and went mad, has interested Norwegians for many years. In his very personal book Heger shows how and why it happened.

NEDREAAS.  Laila Aase, *Om Musikk fra en blå brønn av Torborg Nedreaas* (Veier til verket), Ad Notam Gyldendal, 151 pp.

ORVIL.  E. Stueland, 'Om spørsmål og svar og noe midt imellom (Om Ernst Orvil, vennskap og omdømme)', *Vagant*, no. 2:17–28.

SANDE.  *Jakob Sande 1998*, Dale i Sunnfjord, Jakob Sande-selskapet, 1998, 128 pp.

SANDEMOSE.  Anna F. Malm, *Kollisioner. Aksel Sandemose som outcast och monument*, Stockholm–Stehag, Brutus Östling, 1998, 389 pp. Jorunn Hareide, *Diktning som skjebne. Aksel Sandemose*, Aschehoug, 191 pp. J. Hareide, 'Mord og kjærlighet. Aksel Sandemose som kriminalforfatter', *Edda*, 297–306. S. K. Povlsen, 'Det utydelige. Om Aksel Sandemoses *Det svundne er en drøm*', *ib.*, 307–18. S. Andersen, 'Palimpsest eller genbrug? Forarbejder og eftertanker i Aksel Sandemoses forfatterskab', *ib.*, 317–32. J. Hareide, 'Aksel Sandemose i forskningtradisjonen', *ib.*, 333–39.

SCOTT.  Truls Erik Dahl, *Gabriel Scott. Et levnetsforløp*, Fjellhammer, Juni, 1998, 378 pp.

SOLSTAD.  F. Tveito, 'Ljoset frå det tragiske i *Professor Andersens natt*', *Agora*, 16, 1998:467–79. S. Ødegaard, 'Eksistensiell eskapisme. Antihelter i Dag Solstadss nittitallsprosa', *Edda*, 1998:318–30. K. A. Hoem, 'Om historia og realismen — og ikkje minst om tidsånden i Dag Solstads krigstrilogi og i romanen om skipsverftet Aker', *Vagant*, no. 3:41–50.

VESTLY.  O. Alfarnes, 'Anne-Cath. Vestly og realismens problem', *NLÅ*, 90–119.

VESAAS.  R. Greenwald, 'Tarjei Vesaas' lyrikk. Ei utfordring for natur- og modernismeomgrep', *NLÅ*, 22–57.

ULVEN.  T. Borge and H. Hagerup, 'Parantesen av lys. Om Tor Ulvens forfatterskap — noen nedslag', *Vinduet*, no. 1:8–14.

UNDSET.  O. Reiner, 'Unfashionable *Kristin Lavransdatter*', *ScSt*, 71:67–79.

## V. SWEDISH STUDIES*

### LANGUAGE

By GUNILLA HALSIUS, *Lektor in Swedish, University of Edinburgh*

### 1. GENERAL

*Språk i Norden 1999*, ed. Birgitta Lindgren et al., 174 pp., the yearly issue published by the Nordic Language Council, contains articles on language usage and different aspects of language and technology. Another publication from the Nordic Language Council is *\*Nordiskt klarspråkseminarium: rapport från ett seminarium den 14–16 maj 1998 i Stockholm*, ed. Birgitta Lindgren, Oslo, Nordiska språkrådet, 65 pp. Viveka Adelswärd, *Kvinnospråk och fruntimmersprat: forskning och fördomar under 100 år*, Bromberg, 229 pp., is a stimulating volume on 'female language' research and prejudices during the past 100 years. Sture Allén, *Modersmålet i fäderneslandet: ett urval uppsatser under fyrtio år* (Meijerbergs arkiv för svensk ordforskning, 25), Göteborg Univ., 731 pp., illus., reflects the diversity of Allén's work. Robert Zola Christensen, *Dansk grammatik for svenskere — med øvelser og facitliste*, Lund, Studentlitteratur, 111 pp., is a short introduction to the structure and function of Danish. *Svenskans beskrivning 23. Förhandlingar vid Tjugotredje sammankomsten för svenskans beskrivning. Göteborg den 15–16 maj 1998*, ed. Lars-Gunnar Andersson et al., Lund U.P., 461 pp., with English summaries, is a collection of papers from regularly held symposia on the structure and use of Swedish. This year the theme was language and the media and the volume includes: E. Reimers, 'Från olycksplats till gravplats — bärgningsdebatten som offentligt samtal i dagspressen' (355–64); U. Börenstam Uhlman, 'Om jag då helt enkelt spör ... Interskandinaviska intervjuer i etermedia' (38–47); and G. Tingbjörn 'Engelska inslag i tidningarnas sportspråk' (408–19). It also contains papers on other aspects of Swedish. Other collective volumes on Swedish language are: *Ordets makt och tankens frihet: om språket som maktfaktor*, ed. Rut Boström-Andersson, Uppsala Univ., 377 pp. *Språk och Stil NF 8 (1998)*, ed. Lennart Elmevik, Bengt Nordberg, and Mats Thelander, Uppsala, Institutionen för nordiska språk, 232 pp.; *\*Kultur och samhälle i språkets spegel. En essäsamling från språkvetenskapliga fakulteten*, ed. Gunilla Gren-Eklund, Uppsala Univ., 208 pp., illus., and *Nordiska vindar*, ed. Antti J. Pitkänen (Nordistica Tamperensia, A2), Tampere, Institutionen för filologi 11, 326 pp. *Alla*

---

* The place of publication of books is Stockholm unless otherwise indicated.

*tiders språk*, ed. Inger Haskå and Carin Sandqvist (LSNS, ser. A, 55), 245 pp., is a *Festschrift* in honour of Gertrud Pettersson on her retirement. Among the articles, showing the variety and range of the contributions in the volume, are: C. Falk, 'Om interna och externa förklaringar till språkförändringar' (88–95); L. Santesson, ' "förlåten mig kära Fruntimmer." ' Några 1700-tals röster om kvinnor och språk' (217–23); J. Svensson, 'Statsministertal — en jämförelse mellan Per Albin Hanssons och Göran Perssons talarstilar' (224–31); and U. Teleman, 'Orden, bilderna och världen. Om konstruktionen av hybrida budskap' (232–36). *Från dataskärm och forskarpärm* (Meddelanden från institutionen för svenska språket vid Göteborgs universitet, 25), 249 pp., is a *Festschrift* in honour of Birgitta Ernby on her 65th birthday containing 30 articles, the majority of which are on dialectology and lexicology.

## 2. PHONETICS AND METRICS

*Proceedings of Fonetik 99*, ed. Robert Andersson et al., Gothenburg Univ., 153 pp., is a collection of 35 papers given at the 12th Swedish Phonetics Conference at Gothenburg University, June 2–4, 1999, covering the following areas: prominence, prosody, speech perception, speech technology, speech and hearing disorders, and speech segments in dialects/languages. Robert Bannert and Peter E. Czigler, *Variations within Consonant Clusters in Standard Swedish* (Phonum, 7), Umeå, Department of Phonetics, 197 pp. M. Horne et al., 'Discourse markers and the segmentation of spontaneous speech. The case of Swedish *men* "but/and/so" ', pp. 123–39 of *Working Papers 47*, ed. Jan-Olof Svantesson, Lund, Department of Linguistics and Phonetics, 225 pp. As part of the research project 'Theory and description of Swedish poetry from an international viewpoint', three studies have been published: Eva Lilja and Marianne Nordman, *Bidrag till en nordisk metrik. Vol I* (Skrifter utgivna av Centrum för metriska studier, 9), 253 pp., contains Lilja's study 'The sound-structure of poetry. About the meaning of verse' (25–156), in which metrics is treated in a semiotic framework and models for understanding the relationship between form and meaning are presented; and Nordman's study 'Rhythm in prose' (157–246), which discusses prose rhythms at different levels of the text and how these are interlinked. *Bidrag till en nordisk metrik. Vol II*. Studier i äldre metrik: valda problem 1300–1650, efterlämnade skrifter av Krister Wåhlin, ed. Eva Lilja and Mats Malm (Skrifter utgivna av Centrum för metriska studier, 11), 169 pp., focuses on the old Nordic four-beat line. Jörgen Larsson, *Poesi som rörelse i tiden: om vers som källa till kognitiv rytmisk respons: exemplet Elmer*

*Diktonius* (Skrifter utgivna av Centrum för metrisk studier, 10), 403 pp. (with a summary in English).

### 3. MORPHOLOGY, SYNTAX, SEMANTICS

The long awaited standard grammar of Swedish, *Svenska Akademiens grammatik (SAG)*, ed. Ulf Teleman, Staffan Hellberg, and Erik Andersson, Norstedts Ordbok, 4 vols, 2744 pp., is an extensive description of contemporary written and also spoken Swedish. A positive feature is the emphasis on semantics, i.e. the relationship between linguistic utterances and the reality they mirror. Fredrik Harstad, *Prepositioner och prepositionsbruk. En analys av svenskans prepositioner och prepositionsbrukets förändring under perioden 1965–1997* (Meddelanden från Institutionen för svenska språket vid Göteborgs universitet, 29), 44 pp. Susanna Karlsson, *Svaga och starka verb — vilken styrka har de?* (Meddelanden från Institutionen för svenska språket vid Göteborgs universitet, 28), 32 pp., describes the development of strong and weak verbs with alternative declension patterns during the 20th century. Anna Lindström, *Language as Social Action. Grammar, Prosody and Interaction in Swedish Conversation* (SINSU, 46), 198 pp., diss., is a contribution to a larger research programme that links grammar and prosody with talk-in-interaction, assuming that language is key to the organization of social action. Using conversation analysis she describes and analyses the interactants' orientations as diplayed through the way they take turns in talking, and three phenomena are introduced that can be identified by and are constituted through aspects of grammar and prosody. *Working Papers in Scandinavian Syntax, 63*, Lund, Institutionen för nordiska språk, 147 pp., includes: E. Engdahl, 'Versatile parasitic gaps' (45–74); B. Lyngfelt, 'Optimal control. An OT perspective on the interpretation of PRO in Swedish' (75–104); and G. Josefsson, 'Non-finite root clauses in Swedish child language' (105–50). *Working Papers in Scandinavian Syntax, 64*, Lund, Institutionen för nordiska språk, 115 pp., includes: I. Rosengren, 'Rethinking the adjunct' (1–36); and M. Mörnsjö, 'Theories on the assignment of focal accent as applied to Swedish' (37–78), in which the assignment of focal accent in Swedish utterances is examined in the light of nuclear stress rule and focus theory. Jan Lindström, *Vackert, vackert! Syntaktisk reduplikation i svenskan* (SSLF, 617), 265 pp., diss., investigates formal, semantic, pragmatic, and stylistic properties of syntactic reduplication in modern Swedish. Mats Dahllöf, *Språklig betydelse. En introduktion till semantik och pragmatik*, Lund, Studentlitteratur, 189 pp. Harry Näslund, *Pengar som vetenskaplig term — en syntagmisk studie* (TeFa, text- och fackspråksforskning, 27), Institutionen för nordiska språk vid Stockholms universitet, 45 pp., investigates lexical, syntactic, and semantic aspects of the word 'money' as an economic term in Swedish scientific economic texts from six periods over the last 200 years.

4. RHETORIC AND STYLISTICS

The interface of rhetoric and politics is the subject of four works: Nicklas Håkansson, *Valretorik: om politiskt språk i partipropagandan* (Göteborg studies in politics, 65), 255 pp., diss., with a summary in English; Anders Sigrell, *Att övertyga mellan raderna*. *En retorisk studie om underförstådda inslag i modern politisk argumentation* (Meddelanden från Institutionen för nordiska språk vid Umeå univ., 28), 326 pp., diss., with a summary in English; A. Öhrberg, ' "Kommen nu I Swea inbyggare!"': kvinnliga författare och politisk retorik under frihetstiden', *Kvinnovetenskaplig tidskrift*, 20.2 : 17–30; and S.-G. Malmgren, 'Valspråk 98 — om språket i den politiska debatten, *Språkvård*, 1 : 7–18. Helena Jarl Kerzar's dissertation *Gammalt och nytt i predikospråket. Språklig-stilistisk analys av predikan i svenska kyrkans radio- och Tv-sända högmässor 1938–1984* (SINSU, 47), 259 pp., is a broad description of the linguistic and stylistic changes in the language of the church of Sweden's Sunday service sermons on radio and television between 1938 and 1984. Ingrid Zachrisson, *Med Reine i centrum* (Meddelanden från Institutionen för svenska språket vid Göteborgs universitet, 26), is a descriptive study of narrative techniques in P. C. Jersild's novel *Barnens Ö* and includes a stylistic analysis of the use of 'erlebte rede'. Per Lagerholm, *Talspråk i skrift. Om muntlighetens utveckling i svensk sakprosa 1800–1987* (LSNL, ser. A, 54), 196 pp., diss., with an English summary, is an interesting study of the concept of orality. The study is mainly descriptive and focuses on three questions: (i) what is orality? (ii) how has orality developed during the last 200 years in Swedish non-fiction? and (iii) what is the cause of this development?

5. DISCOURSE ANALYSIS, TEXT LINGUISTICS, GENRE HISTORY

Margareta Bredman, *Att göra det ovanliga normalt: Kommunikativ varsamhet med medicinska uppgifter i barnmorskors samtal med gravida kvinnor*, Linköping, Tema Institute, 343 pp., diss., with a summary in English, is a detailed analysis of how midwives manage sensitive topics and how they present medical technology in interaction with expectant mothers. Marie Andersson, *Språkattityder i Sverige* (TeFa, Text- och fackspråksforskning, 28), Institutionen för nordiska språk vid Stockholms universitet, 41 pp., investigates language attitudes in Sweden.

Anna-Malin Karlsson, *Svenska chattares hemsidor* (TeFa, Text- och fackspråksforskning, 29), Institutionen för nordiska språk vid Stockholms universitet, 76 pp., takes a socio-semiotic look at Swedish e-chatters' homepages. Åsa Kroon, *När folkhemmet blev folkhemskt — en näranalys av steriliseringsdebatten i svenska massmedier*, Linköping, Tema Kommunikation, 66 pp. Håkan Landqvist, *Det låter som de e hallå hallå här — om ansiktsrelaterade åtgärder i samtal till Giftinformationcentralen* (SoLiD, sociolingvistiska dokument, 11), Uppsala Univ., 36 pp. Bengt Nordberg and Eva Sundgren, *On observing real time language change: a Swedish case study* (SoLiD, 10), Uppsala, Enheten för sociolingvistik, 29 pp., deals with language change in the present-day spoken language of central Sweden. C. Norrby and J. Winter, 'Set-marking tags "and stuff"', in *Proceedings of the 1999 Conference of the Australian Linguistic Society*, ed. J. Henderson et al., <www.arts.uwa.edu.au/lingWWW/als99/proceedings.html> is a comparison between Australian and Swedish youth language and the use of set marking tags. *Samtal och språkanvändning i professionerna*, ed. Per Linell, Lars Ahrenberg, and Linda Jönsson, Uppsala, ASLA Svenska föreningen för tillämpad språkvetenskap, is a collection of 19 papers from the annual meeting of ASLA (Association Suédoise de Linguistique Appliquée) in Linköping 6–7 November 1997, on different aspects of discourse and the professions. Four reports have been published from the project 'Svensk sakprosa': Gudrun Alinder, *Ord och bild i samverkan* (Svensk sakprosa, 28), Lund, Institutionen för nordiska språk, 75 pp., examines different methods for analysing lexivisions and suggests new ones; Per Ledin, *Texter och textslag — en teoretisk diskussion* (Svensk sakprosa, 27), Lund, Institutionen för nordiska språk, 43 pp., is an illuminating theoretical discussion on what constitutes a text and how 'texts' have been approached by linguists; Lena Lötmarker, *Språkriktighet, affärsbrev — och retorik* (Svensk sakprosa, 25), Lund, Institutionen för nordiska språk, 151 pp., aims to identify the goals to which education has aspired, and the textual and pedagogical ideals that have characterized the teaching of writing in Swedish secondary schools 1860–1960, the emphasis being on the period 1900–40; and Björn Melander, *Vetenskap och underhållning* (Svensk sakprosa, 26), Lund, Institutionen för nordiska språk, 87 pp., who looks at the development over time of the prognosticon essays of the Swedish almanac with regard to both content and form.

6. First and Second Language Acquisition, Bilingualism, Languages in Contact

*Svenska på prov: arton artiklar om språk, litteratur, didaktik och prov*, ed. Catharina Nyström and Maria Ohlsson (Svenska i utveckling, 13;

FUMS rapport, 196), Uppsala Univ., 150 pp., is a *Festschrift* in honour of Birgitta Garme on her 60th birthday focusing on the subject of Swedish as a mother tongue taught in school. A couple of articles discuss specific aspects of language, but a great number deal with the relation between tests and the development of language skills. Anne Palmér, *Tankar om tal — lärares och elevers syn på muntlig framställning i undervisning och bedömning* (Svenska i utveckling, 10; FUMS rapport, 193), Uppsala Univ., 57 pp., is a pilot study of the role of speech in language development. Annika Persson, *Texten och inspirationskällan. En studie av förlagans betydelse för elevers fria textproduktion i skolår 5* (Svenska i utveckling, 9; FUMS rapport, 191), Uppsala Univ., 42 pp., investigates to what extent pupils integrate test materials in the texts that they produce in test situations. Eva Östlund-Stjärnegårdh, *Principen och praktiken: en enkätundersökning av lärares syn på bedömning av gymnasieelevers texter* (Svenska i utveckling, 13; FUMS rapport, 195), Uppsala Univ., 40 pp. N. Abrahamsson, 'Vowel epenthesis of / sC(C)/ onsets in Spanish/Swedish interphonology: a longitudinal case study', *Language Learning*, 49.3:473–508, studies the variables conditioning vowel epenthesis of initial /sC(C)/ clusters in the L2 production of L1 Spanish speakers using a longitudinal corpus of spontaneous/natural speech. *Facksprak och översättningsteori. VAKKI-symposium XVIII. Vasa 14–15.2.1998*, ed. Detlef Wilske (Publikationer av forskargruppen för översättningsteori och fackspråk vid Vasa universitet, 24), Vasa Univ., 325 pp., includes: M. Buss 'Språk-badsflickors och -pojkars bruk av ordförrådet i andraspråket' (58–69); and B. Haagensen, 'Främmande element i vuxna språkbadsstuder-andes svenska' (82–93). Margareta Holmgaard, *\*Språkmedvetenhet och ordinlärning. Lärare och inlärare reflekterar kring en betydelsefältsövning i svenska som andraspråk* (Göteborg Studies in Educational Sciences, 135), viii + 292 pp., diss., with an English summary. Christer Laurén, *\*Språkbad. Forskning och praktik. Proceedings of the University of Vaasa. Research Papers 226*, Vasa Univ., 205 pp. I. Lindberg, 'Interaktion med fokus på form', pp. 1–21 of *Foredrag fra den fjerde konference om de nordiske sprog som andetsprog*, ed. A. I. Holmen et al., Copenhagen, Københav-nerstudier i tosprogethed. *Sveriges sju inhemska språk — ett minoritets-språksperspektiv*, ed. Kenneth Hyltenstam, Lund, Studentlitteratur, 366 pp., is a highly informative book describing, from a socio-linguistic and language policy point of view, the situation of minority languages in Sweden. Swedish is also considered from a minority-language point of view. Two contributions on Swedish in Finland have appeared: A.-M. Ivars, 'Har svenskan i Finland en framtid? Föredrag vid Svenska litteratursällskapets i Finland årshögtid den 5 februari 1999', pp. 7–17 of *Historiska och litteraturhistoriska studier, 74*,

Helsingfors, Sällskapet, 260 pp.; and M. Saari, 'Schwedisch in Finnland in soziokulturellem Licht', pp. 125–35 of *Sprachen in Finnland und Estland*, ed. Pekka Lehtimäki, Wiesbaden, Harrassowitz, 147 pp. An interesting comparison between Swedish and Dutch as pluristic languages looking in particular at the similarities between Finnish-Swedish and Flemish is E. Bijvoet and G. Laurey, 'Svenska och nederländska som pluricentriska språk — en jämförelse', *Språkbruk*, 4: 10–15.

7.  ONOMASTICS AND RUNOLOGY

Bertel Fortelius, *\*Ortnamnen i Korpo*, Åbo, Åbo akademis förlag, 485 pp. *I hast hälsar*, ed. Stig Isaksson (Dialekt- och ortnamnsarkivet, 9), Lund, 286 pp., is a collection of 56 articles in honour of Gösta Hallberg on his 60th birthday. *Namn och bygd, 87* (Tidskrift för nordisk ortnamnsforskning), Uppsala, Gustav Adolfs Akademien, 199 pp., contains: T. Andersson, 'Hundare och det germanska hundratalet' (5–12); L.-O. Berg, 'Var låg Gestilren?' (81–86); L. Elmevik, '*Bäsna* och *Bäsinge*' (57–64); S. Fridell, '\*Lø' (65–70); S. Göransson, 'Öländska by- och godsnamn i ett senmedeltida jordeskiftesbrev. Ortidentifieringar' (87–103); G. Holm, 'Ortnamnselementet fornnordiskt *-staðir* — innebörd och ursprung' (43–46); K. I. Sandred, 'Det engelska *stead* och det nordiska *stad* "kant, rand"' (47–55); G. Widmark, '*Normlösa, rättlösa* och den lösa jorden. Till tolkningen av ortnamnselementet *-lösa*' (25–42); and P. Vikstrand, 'Ortnamn, centralplatser och det meningsfulla landskapet' (13–24). All the articles have short summaries in English. *Ortnamnssällskapets i Uppsala årsskrift, 1999*, ed. Karl Inge Sandred, Lund, Ortnamnssällskapet i Uppsala, 56 pp., includes six articles with summaries in English: J. Agertz, 'On the identification of the name in *a: tiura: biærh: e* from a Runic inscription in Småland' (5–9); S. Brink, 'Controlled naming: the case of Canberra' (9–22); F. Jönsson, 'Mysterious Påskallavik' (23–30); M. Kalske, 'What the horse is not called' (31–35); L. Moberg, 'Alsike — *Als-ēke* or *Al-sēke*?' (36–41); and E. Salberger, 'The name in *atruakn* on Sö 45' (43–56). *Sydsvenska ortnamnssällskapets årsskrift*, 1999[2000], Lund, Sydsvenska ortnamnssällskapets förlag, 96 pp., contains two articles concerning Swedish place names: B. Ejder (15–32) argues that some names ending in '-bukt' are of Dutch origin and that the difference between 'vik' and 'bukt' has a communicational rather than a topographical basis; and E. Salberger (35–54) gives an interpretation of the inscription on the runestone of Rörbro. *Folkliga växtnamn i Västerbotten samlade av Gustav Fridner*, ed. Sigurd Fries, Jan Nilsson, and Margit Wennstedt (SDOFU, ser. E, Växtnamn, 2), 217 pp. In *SASc, 17*, J. Owe suggests an interpretation of two uninterpreted runic names, *alah* and *uhi* (21–26), and L. Pettersson introduces a new research project on a dictionary of personal names used in runic inscriptions (99–102). *Från Adam till MY: ett färggrannt knippe namn*, ed. Marianne Blomqvist (Meddelanden från Institutionen för nordiska språk och nordisk litteratur vid Helsingfors universitet, B: 20), 273 pp., consists of 12 essays, mainly on personal names among Swedish-speaking Finns, divided into two parts: one deals with the Finland-Swedish almanac and name-day celebrations, and the other with different aspects of forenames, surnames, and animal names. In *Den nordiska namnforskningen: I går, i dag, i morgon. Handlingar från NORNAs 25e symposium i Uppsala 7–9 februari 1997*, ed. Mats Wahlberg (NORNA-rapporter, 67), Uppsala, 270 pp., L. Hellberg (9–22), and M. Wahlberg (23–34), present the history and the present activities of NORNA; G. Harling-Kranck (63–76), discusses the classification of place-names; S. Strandberg (119–32), gives an account of the main features of Swedish name-research in the 20th c. and points out some areas that remain to be investigated; M. Blomqvist (175–88), presents a study of names of blocks of houses in Finland; and L.-E. Edlund (189–203), discusses the relationship between linguistic geography and place-name geography. *Runor och namn. Hyllningsskrift till Lena Petersson den 27 januari 1999*, ed. Lennart Elmevik (Namn och samhälle, 10), Uppsala Univ., xx + 167 pp., comprises 17 articles, seven of which deal with place-names (including S. Strandberg, 'Sörmländska ortnamn som vittnar om finnars närvaro och verksamhet' (95–103), investigating place-names from Söder-manland containing *Finn-* as their first element, two articles concen-trate on personal names, and one on canine names, while the last seven focus partly on personal names but primarily on runic inscriptions and runology. Lars Magnar Enoksen, *\*Skånska runstenar*, Lund, Historiska media, 124 pp. David N. Parsons, *Recasting the Runes: The Reform of the Anglo-Saxon Futhorc* (Runrön, 14), 148 pp., argues that there was a conscious reform of the *futhorc* which established the characteristic appearance of Anglo-Saxon runes in the Christian period; in order to make his case he draws runic evidence from, among other things, the Scandinavian and Continental inscriptions that use the original 'older *futhark*'. Per Stille, *Runstenar, runristare i det vikingatida Fjädrundaland. En studie i attribuering* (Runrön, 13), 245 pp., diss., with a summary in German, aims to attribute all rune-carvings from the late Viking Age in Fjädrundaland using criteria from four areas: ornamentation, rune forms, orthography, and formulation; the relative importance of the various criteria in attributing stones is also dicussed.

8. DIALECTOLOGY, HISTORY OF LANGUAGE, TEXTUAL
STUDIES

Lennart Brodin, *Ord som vandrat: En studie över lågtyska lånord i svenska
dialekter* (Meijerbergs arkiv för svensk ordforskning, 26), Gothenburg,
296 pp., diss., with a summary in German, is a study of Low German
loanwords found in regional Swedish but not in Standard Swedish. A
corpus of 350 words has been studied from two aspects: the semantic
range of the dialectal loanwords compared with that of the standard
language, and a search for individual loanwords in dictionaries of
early Swedish written language. Reinert Kvillerud, *Bohuslänska —
språkprov med kommentarer*, Gothenburg, Språk och folkminnesinstitutet,
130 pp. + CD, is a popular description of the dialects of the province
of Bohuslän and contains 12 samples of written dialect as well as 22
taped samples of spoken dialect. In *Svenska landsmål och svenskt folkliv
1999*, ed. Maj Reinhammar, Uppsala, Kungliga Gustav Adolfs
Akademien, 205 pp., S. Björsten et al. (7–23), exemplify how
experimental phonetics today can help to set Swedish dialects in a
universal context, explain historical sound change processes, and
provide technical tools to achieve these aims in an effective manner;
S. Fridell (25–28), examines the noun 'stol' and the verb 'stola' which
occur in two dialects in two different parts of Sweden; an etymological
study centred on the Jämtland dialect word 'sjäken', 'sjecken', is
presented by V. Reinhammar (29–52); and G. Söderberg (53–75),
comments on the words 'gästabud' and 'bröllop'. The fourth part of
Gösta Sjöstedt's *Ordbok över folkmålen i Västra Göinge härad snabel —
övning* (Skrifter utgivna genom Dialekt- och ortnamnsarkivet i Lund,
1), Lund, Gleerup, pp. 563–782, has appeared. Asbjørg Westum, *Ris,
Skäver och Skärva. Folklig kategorisering av några barnsjukdomar ur ett kognitivt
semantiskt perspektiv* (SDOFU, ser. A, Dialekter, 13), 235 pp., diss., with
a summary in English, aims to demonstrate how people experiencing
an illness will assign their illness to a certain category, and it
investigates also how popular names for illnesses have originated in
folk conceptions. In *ANF*, 114, two articles deal with Swedish: L.-O.
Delsing (151–232), discusses the transition of Swedish from being a
language with mainly an OV word order to a language with VO
word order, and concludes that there is some support for the so-called
'principle of economy' at work in this language change; and B.-A.
Wendt (129–42), discusses how medieval manuscripts can be dated.
*Nordiska språk — synkront och diakront*, ed. Jurij Kusmenko and Sven
Lange, Berlin, Nordeuropa Institut, 114 pp. A useful overview of the
development of Finnish-Swedish over the past 1,000 years is M. Tandefelt 'Finlandssvenskan i tusen år', *Språkbruk*, 3:3–9, and *ib.*, 4:3–9.
Sven Lange, *Till frågan om ortografisk norm på 1600-talet* (MINS, 47),

63 pp., is a comparison between 19 clerical reports from the 17th c. and contemporary Swedish in order to quantify the concept of linguistic distance. *Greger Mattssons kostbok för Stegeborg 1487–1492*, ed. Zeth Alvered, with comments and registers, Uppsala, Svenska fornskriftssällskapet, 314 pp. *Petrus Lagerlöfs collegium 1691 angående wårt Swenska språks cultiverande*, ed. Hans H. Ronge, Börje Tjäder, and Gun Widmark (Nordiska texter och undersökningar, 27), Uppsala, Institutionen för nordiska språk, 256 pp., illus., is the first publication of the manuscripts of a series of lectures on Swedish language given by Petrus Lagerlöf in 1691.

9. LEXICOGRAPHY AND TRANSLATION STUDIES

The Swedish Academy's *Ordbok över svenska språket*, Lund, Gleerupska, continues with fascs 339–43, cols 14505–15382: Sull-Sväpa. *Norstedts svenska ordbok + uppslagsbok*, Norstedts Ordbok AB, 1370 pp., is a combination of dictionary and encyclopaedia. It contains 70,000 words and phrases and 14,000 encyclopaedic entries. *Dictionary of Anglicisms in Swedish*, ed. Rudolf Filipović, Zagreb, Faculty of Philosophy, Institute of Linguistics, Croatian Academy of Arts and Sciences, Institute of Linguistic, 254 pp., is the first volume in the second series of publications written for the research project 'The English element in European languages' under the title 'Dictionaries of Anglicisms in European Languages' compiled by Goranka Antunović. Knut Söderwall, *Ordbok öfver svenska medeltids-språket H. 6–7*, Svenska fornskriftssällskapet, 353–504. Hans Andersson, *Vokabler på vandring. Ordimport till Sverige under tusen år*, Lund, Studentlitteratur, 156 pp., deals with borrowings into Swedish during the past 1,000 years, mainly from Greek and English. Anna Hallström and Urban Östberg, *Fasta fraser*, Lund, Studentlitteratur, 105 pp., is a practical workbook on verb and noun phrases. Jerker Järborg *Lexikon i konfrontation*, Språkdata, Institutionen för svenska språket, Gothenburg Univ., 31 pp. Margaretha Svahn, *Den liderliga kvinnan och den omanlige mannen: skällsord, stereotyper och könskonstruktioner*, Carlsson, 219 pp., with a summary in English. Maria Ålander, *Nyord i svenskan sedan 1985. Hur väl förstås de och hur mycket används de?* (Meddelanden från Institutionen för svenska vid Göteborgs universitet, 27), 41 pp., is a study of the extent to which a number of new words in Swedish are used and understood. *Terminologi och språkvård*, ed. Birgitta Lindgren, Oslo, Nordisk Språkråd, 75 pp., is a report from a conference held at Gentofte, Denmark, 24–26 April 1999. *Word, Text, Translation: Liber Amicorum for Peter Newmark*, ed. Gunilla Anderman and Margaret Rogers, Clevedon–Buffalo–Toronto–Sydney, Multilingual Matters Ltd, 240 pp., is a collection of essays from scholars in the field of translation studies and of particular interest to Swedish are G. Anderman's discussion (35–46), on the perils of particle translation; and H. Lindquist's contribution (179–89), on electronic corpora as tools for translation.

## 10. BIBLIOGRAPHY

Two very useful bibliographies on sociolinguistic research published in Sweden and Finland or by Swedish/Finnish researchers in 1998 can be found in *Sociolinguistica* 13. The section on Swedish (368–72), has been compiled by B. Nordberg and the Finnish section (340–41), by M. Tandefelt.

# LITERATURE

By BIRGITTA THOMPSON, *Lecturer in Swedish, University of Wales, Lampeter*

## I. GENERAL

*Finlands svenska litteraturhistoria. Första delen: åren 1400–1900*, ed. Johan Wrede, Helsinki, Svenska litteratursällskapet i Finland–Atlantis, 480 pp., is the first Swedish literary history of Finland-Swedish literature for three decades; the first volume deals with the 500-year period from the Middle Ages to about 1900, while the second volume will cover the 20th c. and include a reference section and indexes. It is an impressive quarto-sized richly illustrated book which gives surveys of literary periods, individual writers, and not least insight into the political and cultural history of Finland. What sets it apart from its predecessor is the focus on history and the common elements of the cultural development of both Finland and Sweden. The diverse aims of this literary history, such as reinforcing national cultural identity on the one hand and the transgressional functions of literature on the other, are reflected in the scholarly breadth of the contributors. This is an immensely readable standard reference work of authority for decades to come. *Den svenska litteraturen*, ed. Lars Lönnroth and Sven Delblanc, 3 vols, Bonniers, xi + 659, x + 681, xi + 792 pp., is an updated and revised new edition (see *YWMLS*, 49:879, 50:965, 51:901, 52:896). C.-G. Holmberg, 'Konsten att berätta en (litteratur)historia', *Fest. Thavenius*, 141–50, compares the literary histories of Schück-Warburg and Lönnroth-Delblanc. Louise Vinge, *Skånska läsningar*, Malmö, Corona, 204 pp., is an anthology of essays on the literature of Skåne. Following on from the major project *Skånes litteraturhistoria* (1996–97), it discusses various reasons why a regional literary history is necessary, gives glimpses of readers and writers in the 1760s, refers to dialect writings and to problems in general that became obvious in the course of working on the regional literary history of Skåne. *Författare i Småland*, ed. Ingrid Nettervik, Karl Lindqvist, and Claes Evenäs, Carlssons, 1998, 336 pp., introduces Småland writers from Linnaeus to the present day. Carl Fehrman, *Litteraturhistorien i Europaperspektiv. Från komparatism till kanon* (Absalon, 15), SLILU, 140 pp., discusses European aspects of comparative literature and literary histories, a context in which Sweden receives only marginal attention. *Aspects of Modern Swedish Literature*, ed. Irene Scobbie, 2nd rev. and augmented edn, Norwich, Norvik Press, 474 pp., has been updated from the 1988 edition. As the title indicates, it does not constitute an encyclopaedic literary history; it deals with 'aspects' of literary trends and important works from

Strindberg onwards. The updating concerns mainly the chapters on poetry of the 20th c. and on the novel, 'Twelve modern novelists' (325–406), which gives an account of a number of writers who have 'won general approval'. Like the earlier edition, the target readership is students of Swedish and the more general reader. Å. Arping and A. Nordenstam, 'Inne eller inte? Åsa Arping och Anna Nordenstam om litteratur och genus i svensk offentlighet', *TidLit*, 28.2:85–89. P. Sheppard, 'Modern drama studies. An annual bibliography', *ModD*, 42:59–170, includes a Scandinavian section (151–54). *TidLit*, 28.3–4, is a special issue on literature and new technology, and includes: J. Svedjedal, 'Bortom bokkedjan. Bokmarknadens funktioner — en ny modell och några exempel' (3–18); E. Peurell, ' "…bakom kundens blekhet." Textuell kvalitet på webben' (64–86), examines a number of web sites, such as those of Almqvist's collected works by Svenska Vitterhetssamfundet, and versions of Selma Lagerlöf's and Karin Boye's works, and provides information on relevant WWW addresses. S. Brantly, 'Att söka Sverige i Karl XII:s porträtt', *Horisont*, 46.1–2:14–22, discusses literary portraits of Karl XII. Henrik Schück, *Anteckningar till Svenska Akademiens historia 1883–1912*, ed. Bo Svensén, Svenska Akademien — Norstedts, 228 + 279 + 138 + 214 + 247 pp., brings together in one single volume the five parts of Schück's notes which have been published previously in five consecutive volumes of *Svenska Akademiens Handlingar*, 19–24 (1994–98).

## 2. THE MIDDLE AGES

Gisela Vilhelmsdotter, *Riddare, bonde och biskop. Studier kring tre fornsvenska dikter jämte två nyeditioner* (AUSt, Stockholm Studies in History of Literature, 42), Almqvist & Wiksell International, 276 pp., diss. with a summary in German, discusses the parallel historical contents — the right to dethrone an unrighteous king — in three Old Swedish epics, namely *Erikskrönikan* (1320–21), *Dikten om kung Albrekt* (1388–89), and *Engelbrektsdikten* (1439); the differences between them are due, it is argued, not to time factors, but to the fact that the three authors have adopted different social perspectives, namely that of the nobleman, the peasant, and the bishop. Sven-Bertil Jansson, *Den levande balladen. Medeltida ballad i svensk tradition*, Prisma, 271 pp., examines the ballad, the popular epic song that appeared in Scandinavia some 700 years ago. It was transmitted orally, and written documentation of only a few of these songs dates back to the 16th c., since when they have been and still are being gradually transcribed; in addition there have been sound recordings since the 1950s. The emphasis in this book is the living ballad tradition in our own age, and tracing those who passed on these songs to later generations; the evidence is scant from earlier cs, but from the 19th c. onwards it is possible to give some information about names and social class. K. Nykvist, 'Mimetiska mönster i medeltida landskapslag', *Edda*, 272–79.

BIRGITTA. Bridget Morris, *St Birgitta of Sweden* (Studies in Medieval Mysticism, 1), Woodbridge, Boydell, 202 pp., is the result of many years of research and provides an account of the life and achievements of 'this towering Swedish saint', based mainly on the primary sources but also on research over the past 30 years. The study places B. in the context of the society from which she emerges and assesses the way in which her public voice and reforming zeal are underpinned by a deep private spirituality at all stages of her life. The major primary sources are the revelations themselves and the *Vita*, written shortly after B.'s death in 1373 by her two Swedish confessors. This impressive narrative biography presents B. in the light of several varying perspectives in order to demonstrate the breadth of her achievement that culminated in the founding of a monastic order primarily for women.

3. FROM THE RENAISSANCE TO THE GUSTAVIAN AGE

*Om barocken i Norden*, ed. Kristina Malmio (Meddelanden från avdelningen för nordisk litteratur, Nordica), Helsinki U.P., 146 pp., includes papers presented at a symposium in April 1999, among them: M. Malm, 'Barocken och textens auktoritet' (28–61), on early novels by Jacob Mörk, and on the pioneer authority of Georg Stiernhielm; H. K. Riikonen, 'Till frågan om barocken i finsk litteratur' (63–79), on a study by George C. Schoolfield. B. Olsson, 'Skillnaden mellan poesi och prosa', *Fest. Thavenius*, 74–86, discusses quantitative style research into the period 1641–1760. Hans Östman, *Gustavian Non-Academic Criticism 1772–1809* (AUSt, Stockholm Studies in History of Literature, 40), Almqvist & Wiksell International, 196 pp., highlights the complexity of the Gustavian literary scene. It analyses the uniforming and normative effect on literature that was achieved outside the universities by various academies under royal protection, by articles and reviews in the press, and last but not least by prefaces to literary works at a time when literature was regarded as an integrated part of the social fabric. The most influential of the Gustavian theorists based their ideals mainly on the central critical concepts of late neoclassicism, but the analysis of this extensive material also identifies opponents to the accepted rules; the exchange of views between the two parties helped to widen the intellectual horizon to make this period a golden age of Swedish letters.

BELLMAN, CARL MICHAEL. *Bellman 1998 — och sedan? Symposium om Bellman och framtidens Bellmansforskning i Växjö 24–25 april 1998*, ed. Anders Ringblom (Acta Wexionensia, Humaniora, 3), Växjö U.P., 152 pp., includes papers and a panel discussion from the symposium: G. Hillbom, on B.'s collected works; T. Stålmarck, on B. as a prose writer; A. Ankarcrona, on the B. pastoral; J. Stenström, on the B. tradition in the 19th c.; S. Sørensen, on Danish research; J. Huldén, on Fredman's epistle no. 19. S. Ekman, ' "ditt Minne jag bereder." Om retorisk tradition och poetisk egenart i Bellmans gravdiktning', *Samlaren*, 119, 1998[1999]:29–39. T. Stålmarck, 'Kellgren vs Bellman — en utdragen process', *ib.*, 96–99. B. Lewan, ' "Herdar utan lamb och får" ', *Fest. Thavenius*, 21–32. A. Palm, 'Kontextens betydelse(r)', *ib.*, 97–115. K. Nykvist, 'Bellman och mimesis. Mimetiska perspektiv på Fredmans epistel No: 9', *TidLit*, 28.2:21–30.

DALIN, OLOF VON. A. Swanson, 'The epigraphs of *Then Swänska Argus*', *Scandinavica*, 38:147–70.

HORN, AGNETA. M. von Platen, 'Agneta Horn än en gång. Reflexioner och presentationer', *Samlaren*, 119, 1998[1999]:100–11.

LINNAEUS, CARL. Ove Torgny, *Linnés skånska resa. Berättad 250 år senare*, Wahlström & Widstrand, 224 pp., relates selected parts of L.'s journey with explanatory comments and brief articles from today's perspective. *Carl Linnaei Skånska resa förrättad år 1749*, ed. Carl-Otto von Sydow, Wahlström & Widstrand, 563 pp., a reprint from 1959, is a complete version with notes and an afterword.

SPEGEL, HAQUIN. Nils Ekedahl, *Det svenska Israel. Myt och retorik i Haquin Spegels predikokonst* (Studia Rhetorica Upsaliensia, 2), Hedemora, Gidlunds, 270 pp., diss. with a summary in English, analyses rhetorical qualities in S.'s sermons and their political impact. Although known to posterity as one of the most important writers of the Carolingian era, S., a leading cleric and finally archbishop, was better known to his contemporaries as a brilliant preacher. His close contacts with the court and its political élite made his sermons an important political propaganda tool for the absolute monarchy, not least in the confessionally shaped national myth of Sweden as the new Israel. Id., '*Dygdz och Dödz åminnelse* — om tillkomsten av en nyupptäckt dikt av Haquin Spegel', *Samlaren*, 119, 1998[1999]:112–22.

SWEDENBORG, EMANUEL. Lars Bergquist, *Swedenborgs hemlighet. Om ordets betydelse, änglarnas liv och tjänsten hos Gud. En biografi*, Natur och Kultur, 560 pp., declares modestly that this is just a biography, not a scholarly work giving comprehensive accounts of S.'s religious system; that type of book would have needed quite a different kind of scope. It is nevertheless an admirable effort, the result of research over the past two decades into the thought of S. who continues to influence artists and writers through the ages. The secret of S., according to this book, is 'evighetens nu', the present of eternity.

THORILD, THOMAS. K. Frostenson, 'Thomas Thorild', pp. 29–37 of *Svenska Akademiens Handlingar*, 25, 1998[1999], Svenska Akademien — Norstedts, 109 pp.

WALLENBERG, JACOB. Jacob Wallenberg, *Samlade skrifter*. II. *Min son på galejan. Susanna*, ed. and comm. Torkel Stålmarck (Svenska författare. Ny serie), Svenska Vitterhetssamfundet, 327 pp., is the second volume of the new text-critical edition of W.'s works in three volumes (see *YWMLS*, 60:835). It includes W.'s masterpiece, his travel book *Min son på galejan*, and the lyrical play *Susanna*.

## 4. ROMANTICISM AND LIBERALISM

P. Söderlund, 'De svenska romantikernas läsare. Om sång som läsarpraktik', *TidLit*, 28.2:71–84.

ALMQVIST, CARL JONAS LOVE. L. Burman, 'Inledning', pp. vii-xx of C. J. L. Almqvist, *Syster och bror. En af Stockholms hemligheter*, ed. and comm. Lars Burman (Samlade Verk, 29), Svenska Vitterhetssamfundet — Almqvistsamfundet, xx + 246 pp., refers to A.'s writing as his only source of income and his precarious financial situation; it discusses contemporary reception, A.'s comments on the novel, and later scant recognition. B. Glienke, 'Almqvist in Paris und den USA', Glienke, *Metropolis*, 45–66, discusses A.'s writings following his four-month stay in Paris in the autumn of 1840 and during his later exile in the USA, as part of the major project on the city theme in Scandinavian literature from 1830 onwards.

BLANCHE, AUGUST. G. Syréhn, 'Johan Ludvig Heiberg och den svenska vådevillen', *NT*, 75:149–160.

BREMER, FREDRIKA. Laurel Ann Lofsvold, *Fredrika Bremer and the Writing of America* (Litteratur Teater Film, Nya serien, 22), Lund U.P., 256 pp., diss., discussses *Hemmen i den nya verlden* from the American perspective; it is 'not only an account of her own adventures, but also a unique, impressionistic portrait of the United States, and of a national literature in the process of defining itself'. The three main sections illustrate the use B. made of a number of American writers, and how their books and ideas helped to form her impressions, not least of the most sensitive domestic political question of the day, the slavery issue.

FALKMAN, CHARLOTTA. P. Forssell, 'Charlotta Falkmans förbisedda författarskap. En berättelse om dygd, bildning och försörjning', *HLS*, 74:61–84 (SSLF, 618).

FLYGARE-CARLÉN, EMILIE. Ida Ivarsson, *Pål och Nora. En feministisk läsning av Emilie Flygare-Carléns 'Pål Värning'* (Emilie Flygare-Carlén

Sällskapet, 2), Gothenburg, 96 pp., is a stimulating undergraduate dissertation that discusses one of F.'s less familiar novels. The declared feminist perspective cannot hide the fact that F.'s main concern was to depict men and women equally as human beings, an aspect that is brought to the fore in a convincing and refreshing way. G. D. Hansson, 'Hur bilden av Bohuslän förändrades. "Jesus Christ! there's a man left on board!" ', Hansson, *Ärans hospital*, 286–313, discusses the literary depiction of the province Bohuslän, and stresses that F.'s novels had a pioneering impact. There are references to later contributions by Hilma Angered-Strandberg, Selma Lagerlöf, and Evert Taube.

GEIJER, ERIK GUSTAF. Anders Ehnmark, *Minnets hemlighet. En bok om Erik Gustaf Geijer*, Norstedts, 206 pp., reintroduces the national poet as a modern democrat and European intellectual, well aware of the wind of political change and its possibilities. The present is linked with the past: 'the secret of memory is that the past does not desert us'.

KNORRING, SOPHIE VON. Å. Arping, 'Bakom manlighetens mask. Sophie von Knorring, *Cousinerna* och spelet med författarrollen', *TidLit*, 28.2 : 50–70.

RUNEBERG, JOHAN LUDVIG. B. Pettersson, 'Om Runeberg och mytbildning. Bonden Paavo i går och i dag', *FT*: 14–21.

RYDBERG, VIKTOR. G. D. Hansson, 'Hur död är Viktor Rydberg? Om ett hundraårsminne', Hansson, *Ärans hospital*, 179–82, laments the non-commemoration of the centenary of R.'s death. B. Sjöberg, 'Varför arkebuseras Gustaf Drake? Sjöröveri och statskuppsförsök i Viktor Rydbergs *Fribytaren på Östersjön*', *Fest. Thavenius*, 153–66.

SJÖBERG, ERIK (VITALIS). G. D. Hansson, 'Vitalis och ärans omäteliga hospital', Hansson, *Ärans hospital*, 144–50, discusses this largely forgotten Romantic writer.

STAGNELIUS, ERIK JOHAN. P. S. Larsen, 'Modernistiske rødder. Skønhed og forrådnelse. Stagnelius' digtning mellem nordisk romantik og europaeisk modernisme', pp. 23–38 of Peter Stein Larsen, *Modernistiske outsidere. Underbelyste hjørner af dansk lyriktradition fra 1800 til i dag* (OUSSLL, 39), 1998, 192 pp., argues in a close textual reading of his poems 'Endymion' and 'Till förruttnelsen' that Stagnelius's poetry differs from traditional Scandinavian Romanticism. The chapter is part of an attempt to reinstate into the Danish modernist lyrical canon some forgotten names through close readings of sample texts and to advocate a more varied understanding of literary tradition. It is argued that established romantic writers, such as Oehlenschläger and Stagnelius, show striking similarities with symbolist and modernist poetry.

TEGNÉR, ESAIAS. G. D. Hansson, 'Solens portar i Riddarhuset —
om Tegnér och helgdagsbetänkandet', Hansson, *Ärans hospital*,
153–55. Lennart Sjögren, *När hararna vitna och rönndruvan glöder*, Lund,
Tegnérsamfundet, 27 pp., on T.'s poetry.

## 5. THE LATER NINETEENTH CENTURY

Inga-Lisa Petersson, *Statens läsebok* (Litteratur Teater Film, Nya serien,
18b), Lund U.P., 215 pp, diss. with a summary in German, discusses
the origin and publication of the national project *Läsebok för folkskolan*
in 1868, in the wake of the introduction of general education for all in
the 1840s. This interdisciplinary study is based on the assumption
that contributions by individual people were of decisive importance,
not least C. J. L. Almqvist, as was the Scandinavian political situation
in general. *Nordic Letters 1870–1910*, ed. Michael Robinson and Janet
Garton, Norwich, Norvik Press, 422 pp., has a wide range of relevant
essays that were originally presented as papers at a symposium in
September, 1997; it includes: M. Robinson, an introductory survey
of letters written at the time of the Modern Breakthrough (11–32);
K. Dahlbäck, on the vocabulary of Strindberg's letters (108–22);
B. Lide, on Strindberg's epistolary wit (123–45); M. Robinson, on
Strindberg's correspondence with actors and directors (146–71);
R. Holmström, on the correspondence between Mikael Lybeck and
his publisher Werner Söderström (335–51). *Parnass*, no. 4, is a special
issue on the 1890s.

BENEDICTSSON, VICTORIA. I. Hammar, 'Med dunkla brev på
djupa vatten. Victoria Benedictsson och offerrollen', *Samlaren*, 119,
1998[1999]:40–53. S. Death, 'Translator's afterword', pp. 179–86
of Victoria Benedictsson, *Money*, trans. Sarah Death, Norwich,
Norvik Press, 186 pp., introduces B. to an English-speaking audience
in this welcome translation of her first novel.

ENGSTRÖM, ALBERT. *Årsbok 1999*, ed. Esse Jansson (Albert Engström Sällskapet, 18), Grisslehamn, 157 pp., includes among its
varied articles: R. S. Samuelsson, 'Tre Strix — Strindberg, Engström
och tidskriften' (11–18); H. Lång, on E. and songs (55–62);
H. Lönegren, on E. and the Swedish Academy (63–88).

FRÖDING, GUSTAF. Staffan Bergsten, *Gustaf Fröding* (Litterära
profiler), Natur och Kultur, 248 pp., is a life-and-letters monograph
on F. In line with the policy of this particular series it addresses the
general reader rather than the scholar, hence footnotes are banned
and any references to previous research restricted to some final pages
under the heading 'Källor och litteratur'. Even though it is said to be
of current interest, the book is largely based on this previous research.
Not surprisingly then, it presents a traditional picture of the author: it

examines chronologically the close relationship between life and work
without dwelling on new methods and theses. What might have been
given more emphasis in the light of recent research is where F.
stands in relation to Modernism. Knut Warmland, *Gustaf Fröding — mannen
från månen*, Bilda, 189 pp., is a similar but shorter life-and-letters
monograph, also based largely on previous research; the title stresses
F.'s feelings of always being an outsider. It refers briefly to the
question of Modernism and recent research, and concludes that
through F. Modernism arrived unusually early in Sweden. G. D.
Hansson, 'Vid myren med Böök', Hansson, *Ärans hospital*, 213–18.

HANSSON, OLA.    Inger Månesköld-Öberg, *Ola Hanssons livsdikt. Om
mottagandet i Sverige och det sena författarskapet*, Carlssons, 1998, 403 pp.,
re-evaluates the traditional picture of H. in the literary canon; it
examines firstly, reception in Sweden from 1890 to 1925, secondly,
his later works. It reveals various tensions in the 'literary field'
between literary factions and the political views of radical and
bourgeois critics which were crucial in shaping the established view.
U. Linde, 'Mullens outsider. Om Ola Hansson', Linde, *Svar*, 72–82,
regards his poetry as firmly rooted in his native soil, in contrast to his
later nomadic continental life.

HEIDENSTAM, VERNER VON.    *Verner von Heidenstam och August Strindberg. Brev 1884–1890*, ed. Magnus von Platen and Gudmund Fröberg,
Wahlström & Widstrand, 261 pp., is a welcome source of reference;
this is the first time that the whole of this correspondence has been
published. It includes an informative survey by M. von Platen (5–15),
and comments by G. Fröberg (for Strindberg's letters they are based
on the notes by T. Eklund in parts IV-VII of the Collected Letters).
While scholars have devoted themselves to Strindberg's letters, those
by H. are largely unknown; out of some eighty letters only half a
dozen or so had been published before. U. Linde, 'Den sentimentale
satyren. Om Heidenstams Hans Alienus', Linde, *Svar*, 38–71, analyses
links to possible sources, above all Nietzsche's *Die Geburt der Tragödie*.

KARLFELDT, ERIK AXEL.    Carin von Sydow, *Jag ville ha sagt dig det
ömmaste ord. Kärleken mellan Gerda och Erik Axel Karlfeldt* (Karlfeldtsam-
fundets skriftserie, 31), Wahlström & Widstrand, 267 pp., is an
important first detailed account of K.'s love and marriage, based on
the couple's letters and Gerda's diaries, and the biographer's intimate
personal knowledge. Written by K.'s well-informed and well-qualified
great-niece, it helps to further a deeper understanding of K., his
writing, and his private life together with the woman who became his
wife fifteen years and three children after they first met. G. D.
Hansson, 'Det moderna genombrottets himmelsfärd', Hansson, *Ärans
hospital*, 183–88, compares K. with Erik Lindegren and the Hungarian
poet Endre Ady.

LAGERLÖF, SELMA. K. E. Lagerlöf, 'Auktoritär tolkning', *BLM*, 68.1:30–42, is a polemic on P. O. Enguist's interpretation of the novel *Kejsaren av Portugallien*; the discussion is continued in subsequent issues of *BLM*: B. Holm, 'Selma Lagerlöf och syskonrivaliteten', *ib.*, 2:52–56; K. E. Lagerlöf, 'Läsa Selma Selma där det står Klara Gulla Klara Gulla', *ib.*, 2:57; H. Wivel. 'Om Selmas suveränitet', *ib.*, 3:68. LEFFLER, ANNE CHARLOTTE. Mona Lagerström, *Dramatisk teknik och könsideologi. Anne Charlotte Lefflers tidiga kärleks- och äktenskapsdramatik* (SLIGU, 36), 262 pp., diss. with a summary in English, refutes from a gender perspective the standard claim that L. was an unoriginal imitator; a comparison with Bjørnson as an innovative dramatist in his early plays is much to the latter's disadvantage. It argues instead that the efforts of L. and those of Carl Rupert Nyblom and Anders Flodman were decisive for Swedish drama in the period between August Blanche and August Strindberg. STRINDBERG, AUGUST. *August Strindberg. Diktare och mångfrestare* (Kungl. bibliotekets utställningskatalog, 127), ed. Margareta Brundin, Kungl. biblioteket, 160 pp., is not at all the usual exhibition catalogue. As befits a National Library publication to celebrate the 150th anniversary of the birth of S., who was also a former Library colleague, the editor has made full use of the Library archive holdings of S. manuscripts, beautifully reproduced in colour. Apart from unsigned informative chapters by M. Brundin, the contributions are written by editors of various volumes of S.'s Collected Works, focusing on S.'s multiple roles, and include: B. Bennich-Björkman, on the historian of culture; L. Dahlbäck, on the collected unwritten works, and the documentary reports from France in 1886 and Sweden in 1890–91; H.-G. Ekman, on the dramatist; B. Meidal, on the letter-writer, and the social critic; A. Lalander, on the painter, and, together with E. Höök, on the photographer; E. Höök, on music; G. Ollén, on scientific speculations; K. Petherick, on *Ockulta Dagboken*; A.-C. Gavel Adams, on the gold-maker and occultist. *Expressionism and Modernism. New Approaches to August Strindberg*, ed. Michael Robinson and Sven Hakon Rossel (WSS, 1), Vienna, Praesens, 264 pp., includes most of the papers given at the October 1997 Linz symposium on S., under the title 'S. and Expressionism', among them: L. Gavel Adams, '*The Dance of Death*. 1. The hells of August Strindberg and Lars Norén — from Swedenborgian vastation to bourgeois waste land' (17–23); P. Bukowski, 'August Strindberg and the expressionist aesthetics of Pär Lagerkvist' (47–52); H. G. Carlson, 'Theme, image and style in August Strindberg's Expressionism' (53–61); B. Jacobs, 'Expressionist elements in August Strindberg's *Charles the Twelfth*' (63–77); H. Rodlauer, 'Franz Kafka reads August Strindberg' (161–74). Elena Balzamo, *August Strindberg. Visages et destin. Essai biographique*, Paris,

Hamy, 320 pp., provides not a chronological, but a thematic survey of S.'s life and work for the benefit of the French reader who might know him at best only from his plays and a couple of biographies in French translation. With numerous quotations from the letters, it places his writings in their literary, historical, and cultural context to show S. as a European intellectual; the chapters cover aspects such as S. and history, geography, society, women, and literature. *August Strindberg: 'Ich dichte nie.' Ein Werk-Porträt in einem Band*, ed. Renate Bleibtreu and Wolfgang Butt, Hamburg, Rogner & Bernhard, 790 pp., includes introductory and concluding essays by Peter Weiss (15–23), and Erland Josephson (747–50); it provides a commentated version in a new or revised German translation of a generous selection of S.'s short prose in chronological order. Together with extracts from his letters it gives good insight into S., not the dramatist but the narrator in a number of different genres, a side of him that surprisingly enough seems to have been overlooked and forgotten in Germany, as also in Britain. Björn Meidal and Carl Olof Johansson, *Vänligen August Strindberg. Ett år — ett liv i brev*, Prisma, 342 pp., presents one commented S. letter per day over a full year; the dates of the letters are in chronological order, but the years are all taken at random from the whole of S.'s life, thus providing an overall picture of the letter-writer S. Originally compiled for the Swedish Radio programme series 'Dagens Strindbergsbrev' (broadcast 22 January, 1999–21 January, 2000) with a commentary by Björn Meidal, the letters were selected by Carl Olof Johansson. *Köra och vända. Strindbergs efterlämnade papper*, ed. Magnus Florin and Ulf Olsson, Bonniers, 149 pp., is an unashamedly subjective selection on aesthetic grounds of the miscellaneous material that S. left behind as his 'Gröna säcken': notes, unfinished manuscripts, drafts, currently kept in the archives of the Swedish National Library. Most of the material is as yet unpublished and therefore little known, something which this book seeks to remedy. *Strindbergs förvandlingar*, ed. Ulf Olsson, Eslöv, Symposion, 233 pp., is an anthology of ten inspiring essays by Swedish and foreign scholars that bring S. to the fore in new readings that explore his very modernity, hence the title. *Strindbergiana*, ed. Birgitta Steene (Strindbergssällskapet, 14), Atlantis, 192 pp., stresses the international perspective, and includes essays on the dramatist and his reception abroad by international scholars from Australia, Britain, Italy, and the Netherlands, as well as Swedish contributions on relations with S. Egil Törnqvist, *Ibsen, Strindberg and the Intimate Theatre. Studies in TV Presentation*, Amsterdam U.P., 240 pp., challenges the view that 'there is as yet hardly any serious criticism of drama on television' by comparing various Scandinavian and British TV versions of six of Ibsen's and seven of S.'s best known plays; this is the first book to deal with the adaptation of stage drama to the small screen — although television drama is now, in terms of audience participation, the dominant form of theatre. A substantial part of the book has appeared earlier in various publications. Björn Meidal, *August Strindberg. Ursvensk och europé* (Svenska porträtt), Svenska Institutet, 32 pp., a Swedish version of the series booklet. B. Glienke, ' "Ich glaube an die Aufhebung der Städte." ' August Strindberg: *Röda rummet* (1879)', Glienke, *Metropolis* (93–121), unmasks the relevance of the Stockholm scene in the novel *Röda rummet*. B. Sundberg, 'Sonen blir patriark — om Strindbergs *Riksföreståndaren*', *Samlaren*, 119, 1998[1999]:54–76. M. J. Blackwell, 'Strindberg's early dramas and Lacan's "law of the father" ', *ScSt*, 71:311–24. *TsSk*, 20.1, is devoted to S. and the film directors Alf Sjöberg and Ingmar Bergman; the issue includes eleven of the papers given at a Stockholm symposium in August 1998 on the theme of the artist and cultural identity, edited by Birgitta Steene and Egil Törnqvist: I.-S. Ewbank, 'Strindberg and British culture' (7–28); M. Robinson, 'Maid in England. Anglicizing *Miss Julie*' (29–33); P. Livingston, 'Self-reflexivity in Strindberg and Bergman' (35–43); V. Hockenjos, 'Strindberg through Bergman. A case of mutation' (45–60); E. Törnqvist, 'Strindberg, Bergman and the silent character' (61–72); M. Wirmark, 'Strindberg versus Bergman. The end of *Spöksonaten*' (73–83). *Scandinavica*, 38.1, is devoted to S, and includes: M. Robinson, 'Sesquicentennial Strindberg. An Anglo-Swedish editorial note' (5–12); U. Olsson, 'The blue void. Dialogicity, narration and the future in Strindberg's *Röda rummet*' (13–33); P. Stounbjerg, 'A modernist hell. On August Strindberg's *Inferno*' (35–59); E. Törnqvist, 'Unreliable narration in Strindbergian drama' (61–79). *Parnass*, no. 1, is devoted to S. *Modernism in European Drama: Ibsen, Strindberg, Pirandello, Beckett. Essays from Modern Drama*, ed. Frederick J. Marker and Christopher Innes, Toronto U.P., 1998, xv + 293 pp., includes: B. K. Bennett, 'Strindberg and Ibsen. Toward a cubism of time in drama' (69–91); D. F. Gillespie, 'Strindberg's *To Damascus*. Archetypal autobiography' (110–26); B. Parker, 'Strindberg's *Miss Julie* and the legend of Salome' (92–109). Erik Østerud, 'August Strindberg's *Svarta handsken* as a modern morality play', pp. 83–100 of Id., *Theatrical and Narrative Space. Studies in Strindberg, Ibsen and J. P. Jacobsen*, Aarhus U.P., 1998, 152 pp., is one of five essays on the experience of modernity, and deals with one of S.'s last plays in which 'echoes of the mysteries and moralities of the Midle Ages are more abundant than elsewhere in S.' The basis is Harry G. Carlson's suggested contrast between the Greek Ibsen and the post-Inferno medieval S., as well as theories about 'modernity

on stage' advanced by Peter Szondi and Rainer Nägele. J. Westerström, 'Från Lill-Jan till Rosenbad. Om Stockholmsbohemens inpla-
cering', *Fest.* *Thavenius*, 167–77, discusses the Stockholm bohemian
on the basis of S.'s *Röda rummet* and later in the 20th century.

### 6. THE TWENTIETH CENTURY

*Svenska Akademiens Handlingar*, 24, 1997[1998], Svenska Akademien–
Norstedts, 138 + 247 pp.; the first section includes two inaugural
addresses: P. Wästberg, on Werner Aspenström (15–53); H. Engdahl,
on Johannes Edfelt (57–85); the second section is devoted to the final
part of Henrik Schück's notes on the history of the Swedish Academy:
'V. Svenska Akademien och litteraturen 1901–1912', ed. Bo Svensén
(1–247); it deals with the new concern of the Academy to award the
Nobel Prize for literature from 1901. Ingemar Haag, *Det groteska.*
*Kroppens språk och språkets kropp i svensk lyrisk modernism*, Aiolos, 392 pp.,
diss. with a summary in English, gives valuable insight into Swedish
Modernism; it traces the historical and conceptual development of
the grotesque and then discusses representatives of lyrical Modernism
on the theoretical basis of Michail Bakhtin and Wolfgang Kayser,
including Pär Lagerkvist, his 'ars poetica' *Ordkonst och bildkonst* (1913),
and his early poetry, the Finland-Swedish modernists Edith Södergran, Elmer Diktonius, and Gunnar Björling. Swedish writers of the
1920s neither absorbed nor developed Lagerkvist's initial approach
to Modernism: 'with a few exceptions they indulged in an idyllic and
restrained ideal'. The opposition to this ideal came with Artur
Lundkvist and other young writers, in particular the two who
indisputably contributed to the breakthrough of Modernism, Gunnar
Ekelöf and Harry Martinson. Bengt Landgren, *Dödsteman. Läsningar*
*av Rilke Edfelt Lindegren* (AUU, Historia litterarum, 21), Uppsala U.P.,
155 pp., with a summary in English, examines selected poems by
Rilke and his Swedish translators Johannes Edfelt and Erik Lindegren; it argues that Edfelt's three collections of poetry from 1947,
1956, and 1983 develop Rilkean themes of memory and death in 'a
highly suggestive, elaborated, euphonic poetical language'. An analysis of two poems by Lindegren in *mannen utan väg* (1942) and *Sviter*
(1947) concludes that 'the modernist word-music accompanies Rilkean themes of death and rebirth, the secret hidden unity of life and
death'. Magnus Jansson, *Genom tidsspegeln. Diktanalysen som texttyp*
(SLIGU, 37), 296 pp., diss. with a summary in English, discusses
analysis of poetry as a specific form of text on the basis of theories
expounded by Michel Charles re 'explication de texte', and by
examining how this metatextual text form has been used in the period
1900–60. Attention is focused on the anthology *Lyrisk tidsspegel* (1947)

by Gunnar Tideström et al.; its analyses of individual poems are compared with both earlier texts and later similar books. It concludes that the material proves to be more than merely 'interpretations of poems'; it has a rhetorical effect that changes the object, the poem that is studied. Leif Dahlberg, *Tre romantiska berättelser. Studier i Eyvind Johnsons Romantisk berättelse och Tidens gång, Lars Gustafssons Poeten Brumbergs sista dagar och död och Sven Delblancs Kastrater*, Eslöv, Symposion, 608 pp., diss. with a summary in English, is a comparative study of three novels by three 20th-c. writers — Johnson's novel is in two parts; what these novels have in common is the title or sub-title 'romantic story'. One of the aims of the study is to reveal the meaning of this concept, whether or not it differs in the three novels, and what allusions there are to Romanticism in general in this late return to the roots of Modernism. Lars Wendelius, *Rationalitet och kaos. Nedslag i svensk kriminalfiktion efter 1965* (Avdelningen för litteratursociologi, 40, SLIUU), Hedemora, Gidlunds, 276 pp., with a summary in English, discusses recent criminal fiction on the basis of three books, each of which is one in a series of novels: Maj Sjöwall and Per Wahlöö, *Det slutna rummet* (1972), Jan Guillou, *Den hedervärde mördaren* (1990), and Henning Mankell, *Den vita lejoninnan* (1993). The aim is to describe, explain, and analyse the changes in the genre that followed in the wake of the decreasing status of the cosy, classical British detective story. It is argued that, together with their escapist functions, the three novels reflect in various ways social and moral chaos in the rational society of the welfare state.

L. Furuland, 'Arbetardiktningen i Sverige och syndikalismen. Översikt av ett försummat forskningsfält', Furuland, *Syndikalismen*, 9–31, is the introductory essay in an anthology that includes papers given in March 1998 at a symposium on the Syndicalist movement. Furuland gives a summarizing survey, and fills in some gaps regarding writers who are not dealt with in other papers. He argues that several working-class writers contributed to the Syndicalist publications *Brand* and *Arbetaren* and stresses the important link between proletarian writers and the Syndicalist movement which has largely been overlooked by scholars. Ulf I. Eriksson, *Exempel. Anteckningar i levnadskonst*, Eslöv, Symposion, 287 pp., is an anthology of previously published essays in various journals over the past three decades; it is labelled 'unfashionable notes on attempted escapes from social dictatorship', i.e. homogeneous, bourgeois reality. The essays deal largely with modern writers who have risen in revolt, Swedish as well as foreign; among them are Vilhelm Ekelund, Maria Gripe, Artur Lundkvist, Emilia Fogelklou — and not surprisingly Almqvist. I. Schöier, 'Berättandets återkomst? Svensk litteratur 1998', *NT*, 75:275–84. G. Widén, 'Ett eldorado för poeter. Finlandssvensk litteratur 1998', *ib.*, 241–248. *SBR*, Supplement, is devoted to new writers. U. Lindberg, 'Högt, lågt och lyrisk modernism. Lagerkvist, Södergran, Ekelöf', *Edda*: 107–28. B. Wallén, 'Poesins logos, kritikens ethos. Poesiöversikt 1998', *FT*: 394–408. N. Olsson, 'Estetik och kritik — vad det ena är och det andra bör', *OB*, no.2: 14–17, includes critical comments on contemporary novels and literary criticism. The discussion is followed up in the next issue: J. H. Swahn, 'Om den atrofierade litteraturen', *ib.*, no.3: 8–9; J. Thente, ' "Nils Olsson letar på fel ställe" ', *ib.*, 9–10; N. Olsson, ' "Förena perspektiven" ', *ib.*, 10. K. Fjelkestam, 'Beramade bilder. Sexualitetens mimesis i mellankrigs-tidens kvinnliga samtidsromaner', *TidLit*, 28.3–4: 94–108. B. Hedén, 'Pingis — puts väck', *Fest. Thavenius*, 33–39, discusses sports in literature. Merete Mazzarella, *Där man aldrig är ensam. Om läsandets konst*, Forum, 235 pp., deals with the rewards of reading, and reading widely. Being a writer, on the other hand, 'is to live in a world without frontiers', in the words of Christer Kihlman. An index would have been helpful to find references to Edith Södergran, Sonja Åkesson, Bo Carpelan, Carina Rydberg et al. *Sidor av samma sak? Sex uppsatser om översättning*, ed. Björn Meidal (MLIÅA, 26), 105 pp., includes papers presented at a symposium on translation in November 1998: A.-C. Gavel Adams, on translating Strindberg's *Legender* into Swedish from the original French (69–80); F. Hertzberg, on Björling in English (81–92). D. Bölöni, 'Vid horisonten. Finlandssvenska berättare i ungersk översättning', *Horisont*, 46.3: 66–67. O. Larsmo et al., '*BLM*, Blemman, Bonniers Litterära Metro', *OB*, no.6: 7–11: 67 years after its launch it is time for Bonniers to say goodbye to *BLM*; reactions come from four latter-day *BLM* editors, namely O. Larsmo, M. Schot-tenius, S. Farran-Lee, and J. H. Swahn, and also D. Karlsson, the publisher. T. Forser, 'BLM in memoriam. Sju decenniers litterära magasin — ett bokslut', *ib.*, 12–20. See also J. H. Swahn, 'Farväl', *BLM*, 68.4: 2.

Karin Helander, *Från sagospel till barntragedi. Pedagogik, förströelse och konst i 1900–talets svenska barnteater* (SSBI, 65), Carlssons, 304 pp., discusses the development and dominant trends of children's theatre in the 20th c., and how it reflects the contemporary view of children and childhood; there is a lack of good plays and a constant battle to improve the status of this type of theatre. Lena Kåreland, *Modernismen i barnkammaren. Barnlitteraturens 40–tal* (SSBI, 66), Rabén & Sjögren, 400 pp., examines the influence of Modernism on children's literature in the forties. Unlike previous studies it presents the interaction of children's and adult literature, and the possible impact this might have on both, and is based on Pierre Bourdieu's field theory. Books by writers such as Lennart Hellsing and Astrid Lindgren are discussed against the background of primitivism, dadaism, and surrealism; this is a refreshingly new approach. Lena Kjersén Edman, *Författare som stör — och berör. Nio författarporträtt för dig som är ung*, Lund, Bibliotekstjänst, 1998, 116 pp., includes presentations of Swedish and foreign writers for young people: Inger Edelfeldt, Anita Eklund Lykull, Maria Gripe, Per Nilsson, and Peter Pohl. Ulla Forsén, *Äventyr, spänning, saga och fantasi. Nio författare för dig som är bokslukare*, Lund, Bibliotekstjänst, 142 pp., is a similar book on a selection of writers for young people. Lennart Hellsing, *Tankar om barnlitteraturen* (SSBI, 67), Rabén & Sjögren, 156 pp., with an afterword (139–52) by Sonja Svensson on Svenska barnboksinstitutet, is a new edition of Hellsing's discussion document of 1963 about the state of children's literature and his vision for the future. A lot has happened since then: Svenska barnboksinstitutet, 'the National Library of children's literature', was founded in 1965 at his instigation; children's literature has finally attained academic respectability on entering departments of literature and attracting scholarly research. Lars Wolf, *Snabbare, högre, starkare. Idrottsmotivet i svensk ungdomslitteratur 1940–1990* (SSBI, 68), Bonnier Carlsen, 336 pp., examines sports in literature for young people 1940–90. In spite of the ever-increasing popularity of sport, the somewhat surprising result is that very few authors choose to depict sports; according to Wolf the total number of such books is no more than 80, bearing in mind that the total number of books for young people in the same period is several thousand. Over the decades there are noticeable differences: the 1940s' series 'Idrottsböckerna' is mainly didactic; in the 1950s Stig Malmberg's books stress comradeship as an attitude to life; Max Lundgren and Stig Ericson are the main authors of the 1960s and 1970s; in the 1980s no one single author stands out, while the number of sports books almost doubled compared to the two previous decades. Ewa Teodorowicz-Hellman, *Svensk-polska litterära möten. Tema: barnlitteratur* (SSBI, 69), Svenska Institutet, 175 pp., includes seven studies of children's literature and literary and cultural relations between Sweden and Poland, e.g. reception, and also a bibliography of Swedish children's books translated into Polish 1890–1998; summaries of each study are in both English and Polish. After the very first translation of a Swedish folk-tale into Polish in 1890, interest in Swedish literature for children and young people grew steadily in Poland; at the beginning of the 20th c. books by Selma Lagerlöf, such as *Nils Holgersson*, were popular, as were the picture-books by Elsa Beskow. Her illustrations were even used with a newly written and adapted Polish text. After 1945 the most translated writers were not surprisingly Selma Lagerlöf, Astrid Lindgren, Gösta Knutsson, Hans Peterson, Maria Gripe, Frans G. Bengtsson, and Gunnel Linde. M. Österlund, 'Från flätor till flickmakt. Flickskildringar i ungdomslitteraturen', *FT*: 546–55, discusses writers such as Maria Gripe, Astrid Lindgren, Peter Pohl, and Ulf Stark. A. Rombach, 'Medeas barn — ein schwedisches Kindertheaterstück und seine Karriere auf deutschen Bühnen', *Skandinavistik*, 28, 1998: 24–29, on the play by Suzanne Osten and Per Lysander. AHLIN, LARS. G. D. Hansson, 'Ögonblicket för diktarens födelse', Hansson, *Årans hospital*, 353–57; 'Den enkle Lars Ahlin', *ib.*, 358–69. C. Ekholm, 'Lars Ahlins presterade tystnad', *BLM*, 68.3 : 60–63. ARONSON, STINA. Petra Broomans, '*Jag vill vara mig själv.*' *Stina Aronson (1892–1956), ett litteraturhistoriskt öde. Kvinnliga författare i svensk litteraturhistorieskrivning — en metalitteraturhistorisk studie*, Groningen U.P., 290 pp., diss. with a summary in Dutch, is a meta-literary monograph. A. is the central figure as portrayed in seven Swedish literary histories in the period 1965–89 and in the third volume of *Nordisk kvinnolitteraturhistoria* (1996). In addition, the treatment of three other contemporary women writers is brought in as a comparison, namely Karin Boye, Agnes von Krusenstjerna, and Moa Martinson. The discussion concerns Swedish literary research in general and the literary history of women writers in particular, treating the history of literature as a genre, in many ways akin to reception studies, and applying terms borrowed from recent research in history writing. The main benefit of this balanced study is that we are made aware of the pitfalls in writing a supposedly objective literary history and thereby creating an accepted canon. ASPENSTRÖM, WERNER. N. Åkesson, 'Den envisa besvärjelsen. Om besvärjelsen i Werner Aspenströms *Litania*', *TidLit*, 28.2 : 31–49. G. D. Hansson, 'Hellre eldflugor än fyrtorn', Hansson, *Årans hospital*, 370–72. AURELL, TAGE. L. Andersson, 'Efterord', pp. 265–71 of Tage Aurell, *Grindstolpe. Berättelser*, Bonniers, 274 pp., a representative selection of A.'s late short prose fiction, gives good insight into the main features of his narrative technique. BECKMAN, ERIK *OB*, no.6: 52–88, 114–26, is devoted to B., and includes a CD with texts by the author. A. Johansson, 'Det finns inga hjältar. En intervju med Erik Beckman', *BLM*, 68.1: 46–49. G. D. Hansson, 'Döden och sällskapet. 3 x Erik Beckman', Hansson, *Årans hospital*, 373–79. BERGMAN, HJALMAR. Sten Wistrand, *Att slås till insikt. Hjalmar Bergmans roman Clownen Jac* (Hjalmar Bergman Samfundet, 12 — Örebro studies, 16), Örebro U.P., 255 pp., diss. with an English summary, sheds some new light on B.'s last novel from 1930. It has generally been looked upon as a biographical legacy of the author trying to come to terms with his own writing and artistic creativity. On the basis of modern theories of narrative structure, Wistrand argues convincingly that the novel should not be regarded exclusively as a depiction of the author's own conflict between art and life; his analysis of the narrative structure reveals a tragedy of the same kind as *King Oedipus*, a modern story about Oedipus in Hollywood. In the end, the clown is 'struck by insight', forced to accept his destiny and remain a clown, whether he likes it or not. Ö. Lindberger, 'Hur tolka Clownen Jac?', *NT*, 75 : 329–34. *En sann europé — Hjalmar Bergman i ett internationellt perspektiv* (Hjalmar Bergman Samfundet, 11 — Högskolan i Örebro Skriftserie, 65), Örebro U.P., 1998, 255 pp., includes papers given at an Örebro colloquium in 1996. Although B. depicts the provincial Swedish town, he is still at home in a general European setting and familiar with the trends of the international modern novel. K. Dahlbäck's introductory paper examines the question whether B. was a true European or not; L. Gustafsson and S. Wistrand both refer to Thomas Mann's *Tonio Kröger* and Hermann Hesse's *Steppenwolf* in their contradictory analyses of the novel *Clownen Jac*; K. Petherick reflects on 'forbidden relations'; S. R. Ek discusses B.'s fairy-tales and their debt to a European influence; M. C. Lombardi discusses the short story *Damen i svart*, about a lady who travels through Europe in search of a suitable grave for her dead daughter; J. Balbierz reflects on B.'s links with the cultures of Italy and Central Europe; M. Wirmark examines the one-act play *Herr Sleeman kommer*, commedia dell'arte, and film; U.-L. Karahka discusses theatrical aspects of the novel *En döds memoarer* in a European context; L.-Å. Skalin considers B.'s modern novel technique from *Blå blommor* onwards.

BERGMAN, INGMAR. Margareta Wirmark, *Smultronstället och dödens ekipage*, Carlssons, 1998, 194 pp., is a study of B.'s film *Wild Strawberries* of 1957; it provides wide-ranging comparisons with works by Strindberg, Lagerlöf, and Hjalmar Bergman.

BOYE, KARIN. Barbro Gustafsson Rosenqvist, '*Att skapa en ny värld.*' *Samhällssyn, kvinnosyn och djuppsykologi hos Karin Boye*, Carlssons, 314 pp., diss. with a summary in English, focuses on the final words of the novel *Kallocain*, 'att skapa en ny värld', 'creating a new world', in its attempt to present three essential themes in B. that have so far not been given enough emphasis, according to Gustafsson. These converge at their most mature in *Kallocain*, where B. defines her views on society, women and depth psychology; these themes are, however, also relevant to earlier works. What is new here is the stress on the continuity of these themes throughout B.'s writings, and the central importance of *Kallocain*. *Karin Boyes liv och diktning IX. Minnesskrift*, ed. Bengt Davidsson, Huddinge, Karin Boye Sällskapet, 86 pp., includes: Ö. Svedberg, on B. and *Clarté*; P. Helgeson, on B. as a letter writer; C. Chevallier, on religion in B.'s poetry; K. and C. Björk, on B. and

China; S. Didon, on B. as a translator; P. E. Sandén, on a review of B.'s last public appearance; M. and H. Mehlin, B. on the Internet. DAGERMAN, STIG. T. Karlsson, 'Stig Dagerman — författaren som anarkist', Furuland, *Syndikalism*, 133–63. *Parnass*, no. 3, is devoted to D.

DAHLSTRÖM, MAGNUS. M. McEachrane, 'Att låta läsaren ta ansvar', *BLM*, 68.3:65–67.

DELBLANC, SVEN. Helene Blomqvist, *Vanmaktens makt. Sekulariseringen i Sven Delblancs Samuelsvit och Änkan* (SLIGU, 35), 323 pp., diss. with a summary in English, examines secularization as the central theme in first the Samuel tetralogy and secondly the novel *Änkan*. The four earlier works deal with the process itself, while *Änkan* takes this further by dealing with the consequences of a secularized society; the analyses lead to the unravelling of two vital questions, one concerning ontology, or how to understand the nature of existence, the other ethics, or how to get to grips with living in this world, once the paradigm of obedience has been rejected together with the idea of an authoritarian almighty God. It is suggested that the solution lies, not in the rejection, but in the revision of faith, and the acceptance of the alternative of dualism.

DIKTONIUS, ELMER. A. Nilsson, ' "Så är vi två, min dikt och jag." Språk och poetik hos Diktonius', *Horisont*, 46.3:21–29. Jörgen Larsson, *\*Poesi som rörelse i tiden. Om vers som källa till kognitiv, rytmisk respons. Exemplet Elmer Diktonius* (Centrum för metriska studier, 10), Gothenburg, U.P., 405 pp., diss. with a summary in English.

EKELUND, VILHELM. *Den största lyckan. En bok till Vilhelm Ekelund*, ed. Per Erik Ljung and Helena Nilsson, Lund, Vilhelm Ekelundsamfundet — Ellerströms, 268 pp., is an anthology by members of the E. Society to commemorate the 50th anniversary of E.'s death and the 60th birthday of the Society; in spite of the miscellaneous nature of the contributions it has still been possible to achieve a thematic order central to E.'s writings.

EKLUND, RAGNAR RUDOLF. R. Åsbacka, 'Ekonomisk brist, litterär nödvändighet. R. R. Eklund och arvet', *Horisont*, 46.4:3–17.

EKMAN, KERSTIN. L. Wendelius, 'En mångtydig kriminalhistoria. En läsning av Kerstin Ekmans *Händelser vid vatten*', *TidLit*, 28.1:21–51.

ENQUIST, PER OLOV. M. Stecher-Hansen, 'Whose Hamsun? Author and artifice: Knut Hamsun, Thorkild Hansen and Per Olov Enquist', *Edda*:245–51. U. Lindberg, ' "Mannen i båten." Om P. O. Enquists förskjutningar', *TidLit*, 28.1:3–20.

FAGERBERG, SVEN. Carl Johan Ljungberg, *Fagerberg. Sven Fagerberg som romanförfattare och polemiker*, Timbro, 205 pp., provides valuable insight into F.'s novels and other books on individual freedom and self-fulfilment by stressing their cultural and long-term social criticism, a humanistic message that was only too often ignored in the ideological climate of the 1970s and early 1980s. The pictures of life in literature, art and myth have a lot to say about human nature and man's hidden creative forces, according to F.

FAHLSTRÖM, ÖYVIND. Teddy Hultberg, *Öyvind Fahlström i etern — Manipulera världen; Öyvind Fahlström on the Air — Manipulating the World*, Sveriges Radios förlag — Fylkingen, 337 pp., with a parallel text in English and two CDs (from Fylkingen), is the most comprehensive study so far of F.'s bewildering genre-transcending art, his concrete poetry and its significance for the second half of the 20th c. The study focuses on two 'acoustic compositions' for radio from the early 1960s, *Fåglar i Sverige* and *Den helige Torsten Nilsson*, 'among the most remarkable works ever produced by Swedish Radio', according to Hultberg; both texts are reproduced in the book and on CD.

FERLIN, NILS. *Parnass*, no. 2, is a special issue on F.

FRIDEGÅRD, JAN. E. Peurell, 'Den solidariska individualismen. Jan Fridegårds sociala patos och samhällskritik', Furuland, *Syndikalismen*, 82–104.

FRIDELL, FOLKE. B. Sund, 'Folke Fridell — taylorismen och den "moderne fursten"', Furuland, *Syndikalismen*, 105–32.

GRANQVIST, WILLY. *BLM*, 68.3:2–34, is devoted to G.

GULLBERG, HJALMAR. U. Linde, 'Tal', pp. 7–15 of *Svenska Akademiens Handlingar*, 25, 1998[1999], Svenska Akademien — Norstedts, 109 pp.

GYLLENSTEN, LARS. C. Brudin Borg, 'Lust och lärdom. Gyllenstens *Sju vise mästare om kärlek* och erotiska motiv hos Kierkegaard', *TidLit*, 28.1:86–104.

HEDBERG, OLLE. R. Aho, 'Olle Hedberg och den felande länken', *Horisont*, 46.1–2:50–55.

HEDMAN, KAJ. C. Braw, 'En stege mot tystnadens mur. Kaj Hedmans poesi', *Horisont*, 46.1–2:40–49.

HOLMBERG, ÅKE. Karl G. and Lilian Fredriksson, *'Använd bara pitolerna i nödfall!' — en bok om Ture Sventon*, Jury, 88 pp., is a captivating and very informative introduction to the books for young people about Ture Sventon, possibly the best liked and most popular fictional detective ever in Sweden. This brief study manages to pinpoint a number of details that contribute to the alluring aspects of the books in the series, obviously well worth a more comprehensive analysis.

ISAKSSON, FOLKE. Håkan Sandgren, *Landskap på jorden och i drömmen. Studier i Folke Isakssons lyrik* (Litteratur Teater Film, Nya serien, 19), Lund U.P., 269 pp., diss. with a summary in English, focuses on the analyses of individual poems as paradigms of I.'s writings, based on an assumed thematic unity in his poetry. This unity, it is argued, stems from the poet's constant preoccupation with the relations between the I of the poem and the external landscape. The study reveals the complexity of I.'s poetry and identifies its most important thematic elements.

JOHNSON, EYVIND.  Örjan Lindberger, *Berättaren Eyvind Johnson. En kort vägledning*, Eyvind Johnson-sällskapet, 38 pp., published by the J. Society as a centenary celebration of his birth, is a brief but nevertheless informative introduction to his life and work. U. Linde, 'Syn och sak hos Eyvind Johnson', Linde, *Svar*, 243–61, discusses J.'s eidetic ability as an essential aspect of his writing. P.-O. Mattsson, 'Eyvind Johnson och syndikalismen', Furuland, *Syndikalismen*, 32–48. O. Widhe, 'Det levande förflutna. En essä om att minnas', *Horisont*, 46.1–2:5–10, deals with J. and Willy Kyrklund.

KANDRE, MARE.  S. Broomé, 'Möte med Mare Kandre', *BLM*, 68.4:37–40.

KOCH, MARTIN.  G. D. Hansson, 'Att hopsummera livets siffror — om Martin Koch', Hansson, *Ärans hospital*, 192–209; 'Barnet i det stängda rummet', *ib.*, 210–12.

LAGERKVIST, PÄR.  Jöran Mjöberg, *Ångest var hans arvedel. Om Pär Lagerkvist som lyriker* (Pär Lagerkvist-Samfundet, 9), Växjö U.P., 136 pp., is an important book, despite its slimness, that discusses L.'s ten collections of poetry from the point of view of his existential *angst*. The main aim is a survey of the individual collections; selected poems are discussed and compared together with generous excerpts from contemporary sources illustrating their reception, and scholarly comments. Although Mjöberg admits that some of L.'s poetry is weak and inferior, his final collection *Aftonland* (1953) deserves the highest praise and is also his most lauded book of poetry. Anders Ringblom, *Småland i världen. Om Lagerkvist och Moberg* (Pär Lagerkvist-Samfundet, 8), Växjö U.P., 1998, 35 pp., originally presented as a paper at the symposium 'Småland berättar' in September, 1998, is a comparative study of two fundamentally different writers, in spite of their similar Småland background.

LARSMO, OLA.  L. Schenck, 'Ola Larsmo's *Maroon mountain*', *SBR*, no.1 : 2–3.

LECKIUS, INGEMAR.  J. Stenström, 'Kolonialism och poesi. Ingemar Leckius' dikt "I öknen går de vilda fåren"', *Fest. Thavenius*, 178–89.

LINDGREN, ASTRID.  Margareta Strömstedt, *Astrid Lindgren. En levnadsteckning*, Rabén & Sjögren, 411 pp., is a welcome revised and extended edition of the classical original biography, published in 1977. After more than 20 years, perspectives have changed; since her 70th birthday in 1977, L. has published one of her most remarkable books, *Ronja rövardotter*. Her international reputation is continuously

Literature 841

growing, and she has also devoted time and energy to influencing public opinion on issues such as the environment and animal welfare. Lena Törnqvist, *Astrid från Vimmerby*, Eriksson & Lindgren, 1998, 68 pp., is a brief, but informative presentation of L., lavishly illustrated with unique family photographs. It provides valuable insight into her childhood environment, and recurring themes and incidents in her work.

LINDORM, ERIK. G. D. Hansson, 'Lyckans minuter', Hansson, *Ärans hospital*, 349–57.

LYBECK, MIKAEL. A. Hållner, *'Breven till Cecilia* — en roman för 1990-talet', *Horisont*, 46.1–2:95–105.

MARTINSON, HARRY. I. Holm, 'Havet som drömspel och verklighet', pp. 295–322 of Harry Martinson, *Resor utan mål, Kap Farväl!*, ed. Stefan Sandelin, Harry Martinson-sällskapet — Bonniers, 333 pp., presents M.'s two books of 1932 and 1933 in this 10-vol. edition of M.'s collected works; it stresses the parallels between them which are reflected in the two poems that introduce *Resor utan mål* — life at sea, world nomadic travelling, and the creation of dynamic literary compositions, associated with M.'s travels. M. Sjöström and R.-E. Sjöström, 'Varför sjunger Harry Martinson en Sång om Karelen?', *Horisont*, 46.5:55–56.

MARTINSON, MOA. E. Witt Brattström, 'Stor padda i liten pöl — Moa Martinson och syndikalismen', Furuland, *Syndikalismen*, 49–81.

MOBERG, VILHELM. Bengt Forslund, *Vilhelm Moberg, filmen och televisionen. Fakta och kommentarer. Brevväxlingar och debattinlägg* (Vilhelm Moberg-sällskapets skrifter, 9), Carlssons, 1998, 179 pp., examines the numerous films based on M.'s works, and his attitude to film production.

NORÉN, LARS. Patrik Mehrens, *Mellan ordet och döden. Rum, tid och representation i Lars Noréns 70-talslyrik* (AUU, SLIUU, 37), 330 pp., diss. with a summary in German, is the first to deal exclusively with N. and his poetry. The study focuses on the text in a close reading of the relevant collections of poetry to explore their metapoetical features. It explores important aspects of N.'s artistic technique and the complexity of the texts; instead of leading to an overall view, this complexity forces the reader to re-examine the text. B. Lundberg, 'Konstruktiv konflikt och livsförnyelse. Lars Noréns pjäs *Höst och vinter* tolkad utifrån Rolo May', *Samlaren*, 119, 1998[1999]:77–95. M. Wirmark, 'Framtidens teater', *Fest. Thavenius*, 56–62.

OLSSON, HAGAR. R. Holmström, 'Innerlighetens färdvägar. Hagar Olsson och det bysantinska', *HLS*, 71:85–103 (SSLF, 618). E. Rees, 'Hagar Olsson's *Chitambo* and the ambiguities of female modernism', *ScSt*, 71:191–206.

RANELID, BJÖRN.  A.-S. Ljung Svensson, ' "Sången mellan själ och materia." Om platsen för människoblivandet i Björn Ranelids textvärld', *TidLit*, 28.1:52–75.

RIBICH, EVA.  M. McEachrane, 'Eva Ribichs poetiska realism', *BLM*, 68.4:33–36.

RINGNÉR-LUNDGREN, ESTER.  C. Ödman, 'Kära Lotta. En studie i Ester Ringnér-Lundgrens Lottaböcker, Wahlströms mest lästa flickboksserie', *Horisont*, 46.4:58–69.

SCHILDT, RUNAR.  J. Mattlar, 'De röda och upproret i Runar Schildts *Hemkomsten och andra noveller*', *Horisont*, 46.1–2:106–10. A.-L. and M. Murrell, 'Runar Schildt's "The weaker one"', *SBR*, no.2:2–5.

SCHOULTZ, SOLVEIG VON.  Solveig von Schoultz, *Det som har varit, det som är. En brevbiografi*, ed. and comm. Inga-Britt Wik, Esbo, Schildts, 316 pp., supplements the picture of S., who died in 1996, with this compilation of letters which are kept in the archives of the Svenska litteratursällskapet in Finland. These letters from her childhood to her final years partly make up for the fact that she never wrote her memoirs, although she published a few autobiographical books. They cover her correspondence with Tito Colliander in the early 1920s, with the writer Helen af Enehjelm from the war years onwards, and with the Norwegian writers Halldis Moren Vesaas and Tarjei Vesaas. S. von Schoultz, 'Ur författarens verkstad med en inledning av Inga-Britt Wik', *HLS*, 74:105–31 (SSLF, 618).

SJÖBERG, BIRGER.  Johan Svedjedal, *Skrivaredans. Birger Sjöbergs liv och diktning*, Wahlström & Widstrand, 768 pp., looks upon S. as a modern type of writer, a professional as both a journalist and an author; the first and hitherto only biography was published over 50 years ago. His life, characterized here by the significant title of the introductory poem in *Kriser och kransar*, provides a key-hole perspective of Swedish society during the first three decades of the 20th c. Svedjedal can, however, draw on subsequent comprehensive research for this welcome and eminently readable book, not least the year-book of the S. Society from 1962 onwards. He characterizes his biography as a 'litteratursociologiskt präglad livsstudie', in which the focus is on how private and social life is transposed into literature, and on the function of literature in society — surely a book that will serve both scholars and general readers for a long time to come.

SONNEVI, GÖRAN.  P. Henrikson, 'Ansikte mot ansikte. Apokalyps och utopi i Göran Sonnevis *Små klanger; en röst*', *TidLit*, 28.2:3–20.

STIERNSTEDT, MARIKA.  Margaretha Fahlgren, *Spegling i en skärva. Kring Marika Stiernstedts författarliv*, Carlssons, 1998, 320 pp., is part of the Uppsala literary project 'Kvinnorna på det litterära fältet. Kön,

värderingar och makt från det moderna genombrottet till post-
modernismen (c:a 1880–1990)'. Without attempting to provide a
complete and definitive picture of S.'s writings, all but forgotten
today, it nevertheless gives an informative depiction of her life as a
celebrated and controversial woman writer and her marriage to the
author Ludvig Nordström.

STRÖM, CARL-ERIK.   H. Boij, 'Hermelinen bland tallkottarna. Ett
samtal med Carl-Erik Ström', *Horisont*, 46.1–2:28–39.

SUNDMAN, PER OLOF.   *OB*, no.1:8–15, continues the discussion on
S. and Nazism initiated in *OB*, 1998, no. 6 (see *YWMLS*, 60:857),
and includes: L. Bäckström, 'Sundman är inte pessimist'; L. Jakobsson, 'Helgledig vänskap och försök att läsa oskriven text'; M. Löfgren,
'Den pessimistiske logistikern. Om nazism som modernitetskritik i en
berättelse av Per Olof Sundman', an analysis of the short story
*Vadaren*.

SUNDSTRÖM, MIKAELA.   M. Holmström, 'Att hitta sig själv och att
hitta tillbaka. Möte med debutanten Mikaela Sundström', *Horisont*,
46.5:26–29.

SÖDERBERG, HJALMAR.   Jaana Tarakkamäki, *Manligt och kvinnligt
språk. En studie i Hjalmar Söderbergs Den allvarsamma leken och Gun-Britt
Sundströms För Lydia* (Scripta minora, 38), Växjö U.P., 1997, 34 pp.,
examines the language in the two novels of 1912 and 1973, and
concludes that S. has managed to give his male and female characters
realistic linguistic features that correspond to those of men and
women writing at the time. Although Sundström is particularly
successful with the language of her female characters, she is less so
with that of her male counterparts.

SÖDERGRAN, EDITH.   J. Hedberg, 'Naturbeskrivningens funktion i
Edith Södergrans "Dikter"', *FT*:453–465. K. Mikkonen, 'The
metamorphic resolutions of Edith Södergran', *Scandinavica*,
38:193–216.

TRANSTRÖMER, TOMAS.   Niklas Schiöler, *Koncentrationens konst.
Tomas Tranströmers senare poesi*, Bonniers, 335 pp., diss. with a summary
in English, is the first doctoral dissertation on this important writer
who has been widely translated into various languages, and has
gained an international reputation. It focuses on T.'s three latest
collections of poetry, *Det vilda torget* (1983), *För levande och döda* (1989),
and *Sorgegondolen* (1996). Its strength lies in the analyses of individual
poems; it is a welcome publication as the first major work on T. after
Kjell Espmark's book *Resans formler* (1983).

WEISS, PETER.   Magnus Bergh, *Mörkrets litteratur. Peter Weiss i
Motståndets estetik* (Bonnier Essä), Bonniers, 106 pp., analyses W.'s
novel trilogy (1975–81) as an autobiographical account on the basis
of his published diaries, *Notisböckerna*.

WESTÖ, KJELL. M. Mazzarella, 'Idyllens kronotorp. Kjell Westös novell "Moster Elsie"', *HLS*, 74:135–40 (SSLF, 618). R.-E. Sjöström, 'Kjell Westös Helsingforssymfoni *Drakarna över Helsingfors*', *Horisont*, 46.3:14–20.

WÄGNER, ELIN. H. Forsås-Scott, 'Inledning', pp. 13–60 of Elin Wägner, *Vad tänker du, mänsklighet? Texter om feminism, fred och miljö*, ed. Helena Forsås-Scott, Norstedts, 302 pp., claims that the foresight and radicalism in W.'s texts on feminism, peace, and the environment make them relevant today, even half a century or more after they were written. A large number of her articles and essays have never been reprinted or appeared in book form, a gap that this book tries to fill on the 50th anniversary of W.'s death. Together with the selected texts, the informative and robustly academic introduction is no mean attempt to reintroduce W. Åsa Nilsson, *Föränderlighet och oföränderlighet. En studie av Elin Wägners Vinden vände bladen* (Scripta minora, 39), Växjö U.P., 1998, 55 pp., is a study of W.'s last novel in the light of modern narratological theories; it concludes that the message of the text is similar to W.'s earlier books, but that the sophisticated composition is entirely new and unique. *Att berätta historia. Tusen år i Småland sextio år efteråt* (Elin Wägner-sällskapet, 10), Växjö U.P., 56 pp., brings together papers given at an interdisciplinary symposium in September, 1998 on *Tusen år i Småland*, among them H. Forsås-Scott, 'Modernitet, ekofeminism, text. En narratologisk studie av *Tusen år i Småland*' (7–26). B. Cain and Ulla Sweedler, 'Elin Wägner', *SBR*, no.1:19–20.

# 5
# SLAVONIC LANGUAGES

## I. CZECH STUDIES

### LANGUAGE

POSTPONED

### LITERATURE

POSTPONED

## II. SLOVAK STUDIES

### LANGUAGE

POSTPONED

### LITERATURE

POSTPONED

## III. POLISH STUDIES

### LANGUAGE

By Nigel Gotteri, *University of Sheffield*

### 1. Appreciations and Surveys

F. Sławski, 'Aleksander Brückner jako badacz słownictwa polskiego', *JPol*, 79:250–58. A. Kadyjewska and K. Waszakowa, 'Bibliografia prac Prof. Jadwigi Puzyniny', *PFil*, 43, 1998:27–44. M. Jurkowski, 'Wybrane publikacje B. Strumińskiego', *SFPS*, 35:12–18. H. Popowska-Taborska, 'O profesorze Januszu Siatkowskim — (oficjalnie i mniej oficjalnie)', *PFil*, 44:9–12, precedes 'Bibliografia prac Janusza Siatkowskiego za lata 1951–1998', *ib.*, 13–34. The third issue of *JPol*, 79:161–240, is devoted to Stanisław Urbańczyk; in addition to Z. Wójcikowa, 'Bibliografia prac Profesora Stanisława Urbańczyka za lata 1979–1999', *JPol*, 79:227–40, containing 862 items, there are extracts from and reprints of a number of Urbańczyk's writings: 'Wyjątki ze wspomnień' (162–76); 'Rola języka w historii narodu polskiego' (177–84); 'Nazwy staropolskich centrów organizacyjnych a typologia i chronologia słowiańskich nazw miejscowych'

(184–86); 'Sytuacja językowa w Polsce XVII wieku' (187–98); 'Sytuacja języka polskiego w Polsce niepodległej' (199–209); 'Polski kresowy dialekt literacki?' (209–16); 'Uwagi o polszczyźnie Melecjusza Smotryckiego' (216–22); 'Polska i czeska praktyka w nazywaniu ulic. Szkic porównawczy' (223–26). J. Gierała et al., 'Przegląd polskich prac językoznawczych ogłoszonych drukiem w roku 1997. (Uzupełnienia)', *PJ*, 1998, no.6:42–58, (cf. *YWMLS*, 60:870). M. Kornacka, 'Bibliografia autorów piszących o języku słowackim i o wpływach słowackich na pograniczu polsko-słowackim (lata 1981–1995)', *SFPS*, 34, 1998:387–415. Z. Wąsik, 'The development of general linguistics within the history of the language sciences in Poland, 1868–1968', *HistL*, 26:149–98, follows an issue (*HistL*, 25, 1998) devoted entirely to the history of linguistics in Poland; I. Bobrowski, *\*Zaproszenie do językoznawstwa*, Kw, Instytut Języka Polskiego PAN, 134 pp., is an introduction by a current practitioner.

## 2. PHONETICS, PHONOLOGY, ORTHOGRAPHY

In *Handbook of the International Phonetic Association. A Guide to the Use of the International Phonetic Alphabet*, CUP, x + 204 pp., Bulgarian, Czech, and Slovene are among the languages used to illustrate the IPA, while Polish is not. For phonetic transcription of Polish using IPA conventions, curly-tail < c > and < z > remain to represent alveolopalatal fricatives (pp. ix, 22, 112); there is still no curly-tail < n > to represent an alveolopalatal nasal, for which underbarred < n > followed by superscript < j > (p. 112) can be used. Superscript < j > has for over a decade now been the normal IPA symbol representing palatalization, and the underbar represents retraction. Important differences between Slavistic and IPA usage remain, e.g. the use of the tailed < z > (ezh or yogh) symbol in IPA to represent a voiced postalveolar fricative (in Slavistic usage represented by a < z > wedge); in Slavistic usage a tailed < z > represents a voiced dental affricate ( < dz > in IPA). Christina Y. Bethin, *Slavic Prosody. Language Change and Phonological Theory* (Cambridge Studies in Linguistics, 86), CUP, 1998, xvi + 349 pp., argues that sound change and accentual change are systematically related in Late Common Slavonic by means of syllable structure, best represented in a non-linear manner. Evidence drawn from the full range of Slavonic languages includes, for example, Polish penultimate stress (176–78) and the ongoing importance to Polish of the realizations of underlying jers (206–10). Continuing the theme of penultimate stress is N. Ukiah, 'The stress of Polish phrases of the type *'na dół'*, *'na wsi'*, *ZSl*, 44, 268–85, who finds that there does indeed remain much to be said about Polish stress, a claim which should also be seen in the context of Id., 'Stress retraction in phrases of the type на день, зá сорок, не был in Modern Russian', *RLing*, 22 (1998):287–319. On orthography: J. Bugajski, 'O stanie i potrzebach polskiej ortografii', *PJ*, no.7:2–7; A. Dąbrowska, 'Poprawność ortograficzna a zrozumiałośc tekstu', *ib.*, 16–29; P. Zbróg, 'Naruszanie normy ortograficznej i interpunkcyjnej w ogłoszeniach prasowych a pragmatyka', *ib.*, 51–59; S. Drewniak, 'Wydruk komputerowy i co dalej', *ib.*, 74–79; I. Kosek, 'O kłopotach z pisownią cząstki *by* (na przykładzie połączeń ze spójnikami i zaimkami)', *PJ*, nos.2–3:34–38, finds hierarchies of perceived rules and intuitions; J. Miodek, 'Nie ma zgody na tę regułę interpunkcyjną', *PJ*, no.1:65–67, is concerned with the use of the dash (*myślnik*).

## 3. Morphology, Word-Formation

S. Bąba, '*Bogu* czy *bogowi*? O formie celownika lp. rzeczownika *bóg*', *JPol*, 79:156–57, inclines towards *Bogu* with a capital letter and *bogowi* without, depending on the meaning of the word; M. Białoskórska, 'Wstępna analiza polskich gniazd słowotwórczych z centrum czasownikowym (cz. I)', *PJ*, nos.5–6:1–27. Dana Bielec, *Polish: An Essential Grammar*, London, Routledge, 1998, xiv + 294 pp., is pedagogical in orientation. J. Chludzińska-Świątecka, 'Korona Kazimierzów', *PFil*, 41, 1996:7–12. M. Danielewiczowa, 'O szczególnych właściwościach 1. os. l. poj. czasu teraźniejszego pewnych czasowników mentalnych', *PFil*, 43, 1998:119–30. K. Długosz-Kurczabowa and S. Dubisz, *\*Gramatyka historyczna języka polskiego. Podręcznik dla studentów polonistyki*, Warsaw UP, 1998, 334 pp., adopts a scholarly approach, and gives priority to issues rather than to comprehensive coverage of details (see also *YWMLS*, 57:968); Bogdan Walczak, *Zarys dziejów języka polskiego*, WUW, 305 pp., is but a second edition with new publisher, format and pagination (see *YWMLS*, 57:968). A. Dyszak, 'Rzeczowniki defektywne', *JPol*, 79:79–92, distinguishes between *singularia tantum*, *pluralia tantum*, and countable nouns like *spodnie* which do not show number in their declension. M. Honowska, 'Ślady imiennych modeli typologicznych w polskiej gramatyce historycznej', *PFil*, 44:233–37; H. Jadacka, 'Opis gniazdowy jako podstawa badania łączliwości formantów', *PFil*, 43, 1998:205–12; A. Kępińska, 'Wyrównania międzydeklinacyjne oraz negacja a problem genezy rodzaju męsko- i niemęskoosobowego', *PFil*, 42, 1997:91–120; A. Kiklewicz, 'Czy w języku polskim istnieją zaimki dzierżawcze?', *ib.*, 121–34; K. Kleszczowa, 'Rzeczownikowe derywaty mutacyjne w polszczyźnie', *PFil*, 44:297–305; B. Kreja, 'Formacje na -*ownictwo* i -*alnictwo* we współczesnym języku polskim', *PFil*, 43, 1998:273–80; Id., 'Deminutiva (itd.) na -*iczka* i augmentativa (itp.) na -*ica* w perspektywie historycznej', *PFil*, 44:319–32; Id., 'Drobiazgi słowotwórcze. 45. Formacje typu *nadworze, nawsie* — problem ich natury i genezy', *JPol*, 79:259–65. M. Majewska, 'O potrzebie rejestrowania haseł morfemowych w słownikach języka polskiego', *PJ*, 1998, nos.8–9:8–21, puts a case not only for entries for the like of *auto-* or *homeo-* but also for *-logia* or *-nauta*. W. Mańczak, 'Pochodzenie gwarowych form *rękamy, my, mę, między*', *PFil*, 41, 1996:267–74; T. Menzel, 'Zur formalen und kategoriensemantischen Entwicklung des Duals im Alt- und Mittelpolnischen', *ŽSl*, 44:22–45. A. Nagórko, 'Słowotwórstwo w polskich pracach językoznawczych XIX i początków XX wieku', *PFil*, 41, 1996:43–74; and her 'Słowotwórstwo poza słowotwórstwem', *PFil*, 44:397–404. M. Olejniczak, 'Odbicie bliskoznaczności wyrazów w strukturze gniazd słowotwórczych od podstaw czasownikowych', *PJ*, nos.2–3:1–15. R[oxanna] S[inielnikoff], 'Kilka słów o przyrostku *-ówka*', *PJ*, no.4, 52–56, notes the continued productivity of shorthand forms in *-ówka*. J. Wierzchowski, 'W sprawie tzw. słowników gniazdowych', *PFil*, 42, 1997:53–62; M. Załęska, 'Grammaticalizzazione della categoria del congiuntivo in polacco', *RicSl*, 44, 1997[1999]:18–207.

## 4. Syntax

K. Dziwirek, 'Reduced constructions in UG: evidence from Polish object control constructions', *NLLT*, 16, 1998:53–99, presents a richly exemplified Relational Grammar analysis of double-function constructions like *Jan kazał Ewie kupić chleb*; Polish provides some evidence in W. Petrovitz, 'The syntactic representation of understood subjects', *Word*, 50:47–56. M. Gawełko, 'O głównej funkcji inwersji podmiotu w polszczyźnie', *PFil*, 41, 1996:127–46. K. Kallas, 'Zaimki przeczące w polskim zdaniu', *PFil*, 43, 1998:229–36. J. Miodek, 'ABC — jakie?, czego?, o czym?', *PJ*, 1998, no.6:59–60, accepts *ABC o Internecie* on at least two grounds: *ABC* is like *informator*, and there is a trend towards prepositional constructions such as even *dobry wieczór dla państwa*. D. Pawlak, 'Użycie form analitycznych czasu przyszłego we współczesnej polszczyźnie', *PFil*, 42, 1997:135–46. H[alina] S[atkiewicz], 'Czy z używaniem zaimków nie mamy żadnych kłopotów?', *PJ*, 1998, no.7:60–61 opines that the use of *mi* and *ci* in *Mi się to nie podobało, a ci?*, if not jocular, remains erroneous; forms like *twe, swych* and *mego* are stylistically marked, would be comical outside poetry, and are dying out altogether. R[oxanna] S[inielnikoff], 'Jeszcze o czasownikach', *PJ*, 1998, nos.8–9:52–57, notes a move from genitive to accusative objects with *oszczędzać*, examines similar tendencies with *spróbować, dotknąć, dostarczać*, and *przestrzegać*, and discusses a number of common contaminations. Polish receives most of the attention in *Slavic in Head-Driven Phrase Structure Grammar*, ed. Robert D. Borsley and Adam Przepiórkowski, Stanford, Center for the Study of Language and Information Publications, xiv + 345 pp.: T. Avgustinova et al., 'Typological similarities in HPSG: a case study on Slavic verb diathesis' (1–28); R. D. Borsley, 'Auxiliaries, verbs and complementizers in Polish' (29–60); T. H. Höhle, 'An architecture for phonology' (61–90); A. Kupść, 'Haplology of the Polish reflexive marker' (91–124); M. Marciniak, 'Towards a binding theory for Polish' (125–47); A. Przepiórkowski, 'On complements and adjuncts in Polish' (183–210); A. Przepiórkowski and A. Kupść, 'Eventuality negation and negative concord in Polish and Italian' (211–46); F. Richter and M. Sailer, 'LF conditions on expressions of Ty2: an HPSG analysis of negative concord in Polish' (247–82). D. Szumska, 'Nadmiar czy umiar? Refleksje nad redundancją pleonastyczną', *PFil*, 43, 1998:445–54; M. Szupryczyńska, 'Tzw. "beneficjent" a przeznaczenie i cel w zdaniach typu *X kupuje Y Z-owi // dla Z-a*', *ib.*, 455–62; M. Świdziński, 'Negacja w polszczyźnie: uwikłania składniowe imiesłowów, gerundiów i quasi-gerundiów', *ib.*, 463–72; H. Świeczkowska, 'O zdaniach jednostkowych w języku polskim (uwagi na marginesie ontologii Leśniewskiego)', *PFil*, 41, 1996:147–58; B. Taras, 'Staropolskie partykuły wprowadzające zdania pytajne', *PFil*, 42, 1997:153–70; E. Walusiak, 'Syntagmatic contextual units', *RicSl*, 44, 1997[1999]:169–88. finds problems in the division between contextuality and valency; often the distinctions seem to depend on arbitrary, or at least not essentially syntactic, decisions about intonation or punctuation on the part of a speaker or writer. P. Żmigrodzki, 'Oddziaływanie analitycznych konstrukcji werbo-nominalnych na inne składniki zdania', *PJ*, 1998, no.7:1–16.

## 5. LEXICOLOGY AND PHRASEOLOGY

J. Basara, 'Siewca słowa rozsiewa', *PFil*, 43, 1998:67–70; S. Bąba, '*Gwóźdź do trumny — wbić gwóźdź do trumny*', *JPol*, 79:316–18; M. Borejszo, 'Nazwy roślin pokojowych we współczesnej polszczyźnie, *PJ*, 1998, nos.8–9:22–34, and her 'Nazwy roślin pokojowych w współczesnej polszczyźnie (dokończenie)', *PJ*, 1998, no.10:6–14. K. Cyra, 'Struktura semantyczna leksemu *nigdy*', *PJ*, 1998, nos.8–9:1–7; W. Decyk, 'O nazwach początkowego i końcowego odcinka rzeki w wybranych XVIII-wiecznych podręcznikach do geografii', *PFil*, 43, 1998:131–39; R. Dźwigoł, 'Słowiańskie demony domowe zarejestrowane w Słowniku wileńskim', *JPol*, 79:270–75. J. Gardzińska, '*Przestukaj na komórkę* . . ., czyli o językowych zachowaniach Polaków w sytuacji rozmowy telefonicznej', *PJ*, no.4:30–38, examines a wide range of current alternatives to *dzwonić*.

M. Grochowski, 'Ekwiwalencja funkcjonalna i semantyczna wykładników następstwa w wypowiedzeniu prostym i złożonym', *SFPS*, 34, 1998:43–53; K. Handke, '*Tło* czy *dno?*', *PFil*, 44:221–25; G. Hentschel, 'Zu Status und Funktion von polnisch *to (jest)* — II: Kopula — Pronomen — Konjunktion — Partikel', *PFil*, 43, 1998:191–204. I. Kamińska-Szmaj, 'Słownictwo charakterystyczne dla tekstów reklamowych', *PJ*, 1998, no.6:5–11; K. Kleszczowa, 'Staropolskie nazwy czynności', *PFil*, 43, 1998:243–50; Z. Leszczyński, 'Światłocień pozostaje', *ib.*, 307–12. J. Liberek, 'Skrzydlate słowa w perspektywie frazeologicznej', *PJ*, no.4 (563), 41–51, pleads for clarification of the relationship between phraseology and *skrzydlatologia* 'quotationology'. M. Majewska, 'Polskie słowniki homonimów', *PJ*, 1998, no.6:27–41, compares four dictionaries published between 1984 and 1993; and her 'Analiza historyczna przymiotnikowych homonimów całkowitych', *PFil*, 42, 1997:271–76. N. Mikołajczak-Matyja, 'Podstawowe reguły definiowania a praktyka leksykograficzna', *SFPS*, 35:67–107; T. Minikowska, 'Z rozważań o *błogosławieństwie*', *PFil*, 43, 1998:319–27; E. Młynarczyk, 'Gdzie targowano dawniej w Polsce, czyli o staropolskich wyrazach nazywających place, stoiska i pomieszczenia handlowe', *JPol*, 79:54–67; L. Moszyński, 'Wybrane zagadnienia staropolskiej i starosłowieńskiej leksykografii (Jan Mączyński 1564 — Matija Kastelec 1680)', *SFPS*, 35:193–213; A. Nagórko, 'Synonimia kontekstowa i sytuacyjna. Implikacje leksykograficzne', *PFil*, 43, 1998:327–41; A. Nagórko, 'Die Synonyme und ein polnisches Synonymwörterbuch für Deutsche', *ŽSl*, 44, 46–60; M. Preyzner, 'Czy można skserować kasetę?', *JPol*, 79:314; R. Roszko, 'Tendencje rozwoju terminologii popularnej związanej z techniką wideo', *Slavia*, 68:45–52. H[alina] S[atkiewicz], 'Nowy filar', *PJ*, nos.2–3:561–62, notes *filar* being used in constructions appropriate to words like *bank* and *kasa*. T. Smółkowa, 'Słownictwo — zmienność i stabilność', *PFil*, 43, 1998:425–32; A. Tworek, ' "Nigdy mi, kto majętny, nie był obojętny . . ." ', *JPol*, 79:363–70, in fact examines the word *szlachetny*. E. Walusiak, 'Metatekstowa funkcja hierarchizująca ciągu *przy*', *SFPS*, 34, 1998:117–27; Z. Wanicowa, 'Na marginesie prac nad Słownikiem staropolskim. Trzy zagadkowe wyrazy: *zamisać, ziele* i *zielony*', *JPol*, 79:68–69; A. Zajda, 'Staropolska terminologia prawnicza odznacza się wybitną rodzimością', *ib.*, 47–53. P. Żmigrodzki, '*Derby* nadal kłopotliwe', *ib.*, 312–13, is concerned with whether the word, when used in the sense of '(local) Derby', is declinable.

## 6. SEMANTICS, PRAGMATICS

J. Bartmiński, 'Dynamika polskiego pojęcia ojczyzny', *PFil*, 43, 1998:53–60; L. Bednarczuk, 'Transcendencja i transkomunikacja', *ib.*, 71–82; A. Bogusławski, 'O "pożytkach karmienia człowieka piersią"', *ib.*, 83–91; J. Bralczyk, 'Wspólny język?' (uwagi o reklamie)', *ib.*, 91–94. K. Cyra, 'Warunki ekwiwalencji wybranych wykładników regularnego współwystępowania faktów', *PJ*, 1998, no.10:15–25, deals with *co noc, każdej nocy, w każdą noc* and the like. A. Gałczyńska, 'Honoryfikatywne zróżnicowanie aktów odmowy w języku polskim', *PJ*, nos.2–3:16–24, is a gem of socio-pragmatic description. M. Gębka-Wolak, 'O możliwości interpretowania grup apozycyjnych z członem wyodrębnionym interpunkcyjnie jako konstrukcji współrzędnych', *PJ*, no.1:21–29. M. Grochowski, 'Antonimy *na szczęście — niestety*. Próba analizy semantycznej', *PFil*, 43, 1998:163–68; A. Grybosiowa, 'Człowiek współczesny — jednostka precyzyjnie oznakowana', *ib.*, 169–75; R. Grzegorczykowa, 'Obraz "sumienia" w języku polskim na tle porównawczym', *ib.*, 175–84; and her 'Opozycja 'wierzch' — 'spód' jako składnik językowej konceptualizacji przestrzeni', *PFil*, 44:185–92; G. Habrajska, 'O pewnym sposobie językowego wyrażania centralności wybranych cech prototypowych', *ib.*, 213–19. K. Handke, 'Doraźny prestiż słowa', *PFil*, 43, 1998:185–90. A. Karaś and E. Nowak, 'Znaczenie predykatu a wybór werbalizatora w konstrukcjach analitycznych (na przykładzie konstrukcji z predykatami *chęć, ochota, pragnienie, żądza*)', *PJ*, no.1:11–20. M. Karpluk, 'Do zagadnień polskiego światopoglądu językowego: próba nazwania człowieka oszczędzającego', *PFil*, 43, 1998:237–42. T. Malec and M. Kucała, '*Popełnić książkę*', *JPol*, 79:157–58, leave open the question of whether such current jocular expressions imply an echo of earlier, wider usage of *popełnić*; similarly, D. Piekarczyk, 'Językowy obraz świata w metaforze *świat to teatr*', *JPol*, 79:96–104, precedes W. J. Darasz, '*Cały świat to scena*', *ib.*, 308–09, who points out that popular and fashionable imagery may have a long and distinguished history. K. Pisarkowa, '*Układała swe włosy* — erotyk intersemiotyczny w przekładzie', *PFil*, 43, 1998:363–70. J. Puzynina, 'Słownictwo wartościujące w porównawczych badaniach slawistycznych', *PFil*, 44:435–39. J. Sambor, 'Rangi znaczeń wyrazów polisemicznych w ocenach licealistów a studentów (Próba rekonesansowa)', *PFil*, 43, 1998:385–94. D. Sarzyńska, 'Leksykalne sposoby akceptowania wypowiedzi odbiorcy w dialogowych kazaniach dla dzieci', *PJ*, 1998, nos.8–9:35–41. H. Satkiewicz, 'Kreowanie rzeczywistości w wiadomościach prasowych z roku 1952', *PFil*, 43, 1998:395–400; G. Sawicka, '*Konwencja — kontekst — znaczenie*', *ib.*, 401–08. K. Sobstyl, ' "Porzuć samotność" — illokucyjne aspekty w polskich ogłoszeniach towarzysko-matrymonialnych', *PJ*, 1998, no.6:19–26. G. Szpila, 'Przysłowie —

semantyka tekstu jednozdaniowego', *JPol*, 79:371–78. M. Suszczyńska, 'Apologizing in English, Polish and Hungarian: different languages, different strategies', *JP*, 31:1053–65. K. Waszakowa, 'Jakiego
koloru jest człowiek?', *PFil*, 44:545–56. B. Witosz, 'Pojęcia *wyboru* we
współczesnej refleksji tekstologicznej', *PJ*, nos.5–6:28–38. T. W.
Wiernikowskaja, 'O zaimkowym wyrażaniu aktantu adresatywnego
w języku polskim', *JPol*, 79:266–69. Z. Zaron, 'Czy zwierzę to ktoś?
Językowe dowody podmiotowości zwierząt', *PFil*, 43, 1998:507–14.

7. Sociolinguistics and Dialectology

*II Forum Kultury Słowa. Edukacja językowa Polaków*, ed. Władysław
Miodunka, Kw, Upowszechnianie Nauki — Oświata 'UN-O', 1998,
148 pp., includes: W. Miodunka, 'Edukacja językowa Polaków.
Koncepcja II Forum Kultury Słowa' (7–12); I. Białecki, 'Alfabetyzm
funkcjonalny. Kultura tworzenia i wykorzystywania informacji'
(13–35); A. Szumowski, 'Kwestie językowe integracji europejskiej'
(36–39); W. Pisarek, 'Edukacja językowa Polaków w programie prac
Rady Języka Polskiego' (40–45); J. Puzynina, 'Język — edukacja —
wartości' (46–52); M. Sawicki, 'Istota reformy proponowanej w
oświacie' (53–54); B. Chrząstowska and T. Patrzałek, 'Jakiej reformy
kształcenia językowego potrzebuje szkoła?' (55–70); M. Małachowska, 'Program nauczania języka polskiego w szkole podstawowej. Dla
kogo i po co?' (71–76); H. Mrazek, 'Rozwijanie języka dziecka w
klasach IV-VIII szkoły podstawowej — umiejętności i wiedza'
(77–82); J. Podracki and J. Porayski-Pomsta, 'Przygotowanie nauc-
zycieli do edukacji jezykowej' (83–89); W. Przyczyna and G. Siwek,
'Edukacja językowa księży' (90–97); T. Gizbert-Studnicki, 'Edukacja
językowa prawników' (98–102); M. Zieliński, 'O potrzebie nauczania
języka prawa' (103–11); H. Jadacka, 'Edukacja językowa prawników'
(112–16); W. Miodunka, 'Język polski w edukacji społeczeństw
zachodnich' (117–29); J. Mazur, 'Specyfika nauczania języka polskiego na Wschodzie' (130–38); M. Gumkowska, 'Promocja kultury
polskiej w kontekście zadań Ministerstwa Kultury i Sztuki' (139–44);
W. Pisarek, 'Podsumowanie II Forum Kultury Słowa' (146–48).
I. Bajerowa, 'Dwa spojrzenia na ewolucję języka ogólnopolskiego',
*PFil*, 43, 1998:45–52; her '*Nie* z imiesłowami (w zasadzie) zawsze
razem', *JPol*, 79:318–20; her 'Przestroga przed natrętstwem *jakby*',
*ib.*, 320; her 'Wstyd nie odmieniać nazwisk', *ib.*, 320, particularly
deplores failures to decline surnames whose declension is in no way
troublesome. J. Basara, 'Id *siewiatki* do *siewnika*', *PFil*, 43, 1998:51–58;
T. I. Bendina, 'Польские диалекты в западнославянском языко-
вом континууме: к вопросу о каталогизации зон архаики и

Language 853

инноваций (по материалам Общеславянского лингвистического атласа)', *PFil*, 44:557–66. M. Dawlewicz, 'Neologizmy w socjolekcie młodzieży polskiego pochodzenia w Wilnie', *PJ*, nos.5–6:45–53. M. Gabrych-Owsianko, 'O wyrazach obcych i tłumaczeniach', *JPol*, 79:314–15, expresses some reasonable concerns of a Pole living abroad about the standard of some Polish published in Poland. S. Gajda, 'Program polskiej polityki jezykowej', *PJ*, nos.5–6:1–10, describes the programme drawn up with support from PAN and four ministries. K. Geben, 'Cytaty i przełączanie kodów w zachowaniach językowych przedstawicieli wielojęzycznej grupy lokalnej (na podstawie badań wileńskich rodzin heterogenicznych językowo)', *PJ*, 1998, no.10:26–32. Z. Greń and B. Kubok, 'Komunikacja językowa w handlu przygranicznym na Śląsku Cieszyńskim', *SFPS*, 35:31–40. H. Grochoło-Szczepanek, 'O sposobie przejmowania złożeń niemieckich przez gwary polskie', *JPol*, 79:73–78, examines German influence on compound nouns in Polish dialects. H. Karaś, 'Wahania i zmiany rodzaju rzeczowników w języku studentów polonistyki wileńskiej', *PFil*, 44:257–68. M. Kucała, 'O polonijnych normach językowych', *PFil*, 43, 1998:287–94. *Język polski w kraju i za granicą. Materiały Międzynarodowej Konferencji Naukowej Polonistów Warszawa 14–16 września 1995 r.*, ed. Barbara Janowska and Józef Porayski-Pomsta, Wa, Elipsa, 1997, 2 vols, 260, 270 pp., deals with language contacts (1:29–162), translation studies (1:163–246), Polish language teaching methodology (2:11–146) and Polish as a foreign language in Poland and abroad (2:147–270). J. Kobylińska, 'Z Mszany Górnej, powiat limanowski', *JPol*, 79:283–87, presents dialect texts. B. Kubok, 'Z badań nad zmianami w słownictwie gwary zachodniocieszyńskiej', *SFPS*, 34, 1998:55–68. E. Malinowska, 'Wypowiedzi administracyjne i ich poprawność', *PFil*, 44:363–72. W. Mańczak, 'W sprawie gwarowego *ino*', *JPol*, 79:307–08. I. Maryniakowa, 'Nazwy kłamcy w gwarach na polsko-białoruskim pograniczu językowym', *PFil*, 44:373–79. M. Michalik, 'Interteksty w organizacji dyskursu na temat *cierpienia*', *PJ*, nos.5–6:39–44. J. Miodek, 'Gust w języku', *Polonistyka*, 333–35, notes a pathological vulgarisation of everyday Polish. M. Ostrowska and A. Zielińska, 'Polacy z Kresów północno-wschodnich o swojej polszczyźnie (na podstawie badań terenowych w latach 1992–1995)', *SFPS*, 34, 1998:69–83. Language education surfaces repeatedly in *Polonistyka*, 87–446; a section of *PJ*, 1998, no.10:41–60, is devoted to *kultura języka*, including discussion of the future of Polish in Europe (42–44), the official and popular names of Caucasian and Central Asian states (*Republika Uzbecka*, popularly *Uzbekistan*) (44–49), and an appeal for vulgarisms to be rigorously excluded from all dictionaries aimed at young people (49). A. Pospiszylowa, 'Zadwerbializowane formy przypadkowe rzeczowników z gwarze wsi Istebna', *PFil*, 41, 1996:85–86. B. Walczak, 'Kto nie rozumie i czego nie rozumie?' O (nie)znajomości słownictwa społeczno-politycznego i ekonomicznego w różnych środowiskach użytkowników współczesnej polszczyzny', *PFil*, 43, 1998:489–501. Published under the aegis of the Language Council of PAN, *Polszczyzna 2000. Orędzie o stanie języka na przełomie tysiącleci*, ed. Walery Pisarek, Kw, Ośrodek Badań Prasoznawczych, 326 pp., includes: W. Pisarek, 'Wprowadzenie' (5–11); S. Gajda, 'Język nauk humanistycznych' (12–32); J. Doroszewski, 'Polski język medyczny' (33–49); M. Zieliński, 'Języki prawne i prawnicze' (50–74); E. Malinowska, 'Język w urzędach' (75–96); A. Cieślikowa, 'Nazwy własne we współczesnym języku polskim' (97–115); W. Przyczyna and G. Siwek, 'Język w Kościele' (130–48); H. Synowiec, 'Język polski w szkole' (115–29); B. Zeler, 'Język innych kościołów chrześcijańskich (na przykładzie Kościoła Ewangelickoaugsburskiego)' (149–65); J. Kornhauser, 'Język we współczesnej literaturze polskiej' (166–80); G. Majkowska and H. Satkiewicz, 'Język w mediach', (181–96); J. Bralczyk, 'O używaniu języka w polskiej polityce w latach dziewięćdziesiatych' (197–218); Id., 'O językowych zwyczajach polskiej reklamy', (218–226); B. Dunaj et al., 'Język na co dzień' (227–51); H. Zgółkowa, 'Język subkultur młodzieżowych' (252–61); J. Reichan, 'Gwary polskie w końcu XX w.' (262–78); W. Kajtoch, 'Języki mniejszości narodowych w Polsce' (279–306); W. T. Miodunka, 'Język polski poza Polską' (306–25). A. Rejter, 'Wtórny gatunek mowy jako obiekt badań lingwistycznych', *PJ*, no.1:35–43; J. Rieger, 'Kilka uwag o gwarze polskiej wsi Gwozdawa (Hwozdawa) w rejonie berdyczowskim', *PFil*, 44:447–56. D. Rytel-Kuc et al., 'Miejsce kobiet i mężczyzn w ogłoszeniach o pracę', *ib.*, 471–78. D. Sarzyńska, 'Perswazyjność dialogów kaznodziejskich (na przykładzie kazań dla dzieci)', *PJ*, 1998, no.7:43–51, analyses 60 dialogic sermons recorded in Lublin between 1994 and 1998. M. Skarżyński, 'Między tradycją i zdrowym rozsądkiem. Uwagi o naszym piśmiennictwie poprawnościowym', *JPol*, 79:112–21, written while the Polish language law was still being discussed, and concluding with a moderating comment by Marian Kucała (120–21), encapsulates useful information on current usage. B. Strumiński, 'Bugaj. Z poszukiwań substratu przedpolskiego', *SFPS*, 34, 1998:103–15; I. Szczepankowska, 'Perspektywy badań lingwistycznych nad językiem prawnym', *PJ*, nos.5–6:11–17; R. Tokarski, 'Wspólnota kulturowa — kultura języka', *PFil*, 43, 1998:473–80. P. Żmigrodzki, 'Kogo i jak gramatyki uczyć? (w związku z dyskusją nad Składnią polską … Jerzego Podrackiego)', *JPol*, 79:141–44, argues for including linguistic theory in all kinds of teaching about grammar;

I. Bobrowski, 'O kulturowej wartości gramatyki tradycyjnej i poradnictwa językowego (na marginesie artykułów P. Żmigrodzkiego i M. Skarżyńskiego)', *ib.*, 397–400. T. Ulewicz, 'Ludowość i barbaryzmy, czyli w praktyce *wio, basta, łajza* itd.', *ib.*, 310–11, and F. Sławski, 'Do artykułu Tadeusza Ulewicza', *ib.*, 312. Grzegorz Walczak, 'Funkcje spójnika *bo* w gwarach warmińsko-mazursko-ostródzkich', *PFil*, 41, 1996:159–74. K. Wojtczuk, 'Wariantywne nazwy dziecka o ekspresji pozytywnej i/lub negatywnej w języku familijnym siedlczan', *ib.*, 111–26. E. Wolańska, 'Renarracja jako gatunek potocznego języka mówionego', *PJ*, no.4:11–17. H. and T. Zgółko, 'Polonistyczna dydaktyka uniwersytecka a *Podstawa programowa języka polskiego*', *Polonistyka*, 335–41, discusses a document signed by Minister Handke in 1998.

8. INDIVIDUALS, INDIVIDUAL WORKS

ABRAMOW-NEWERLY. W. Kupiszewski, 'Socjolingwistyczna charakterystyka bohaterów sztuki Jarosława Abramowa-Newerlego *Gęsi za wodą*', *PFil*, 43, 1998:295–306.

ANTON. H. Popowska-Taborska, 'Oryginalna wersja "Kaszubskiego słowniczka" Karla-Gottloba Antona', *SFPS*, 34, 1998:145–56, is first introduced by A. D. Dulichenko, *ib.*, 129–44.

BACZYŃSKI. P. Paziak, 'Funkcja semantyczna przymiotników na -*awy* w poezji Krzysztofa Kamila Baczyńskiego', *PJ*, 1998, no.7:52–59.

BAR POETRY. S. Dubisz, 'Lamentacyjne incipity utworów wierszowanych okresu konfederacji barskiej', *PFil*, 43, 1998:139–42.

BARTHOLOMEW OF BYDGOSZCZ. E. Kędelska, 'Nowa edycja Słownika Bartłomieja z Bydgoszczy', *SFPS*, 35:41–53.

BAUDOUIN DE COURTENAY. Z. Leszczyński, 'Deklaracja polskości Baudouina', *PFil*, 44:345–47.

BIBLE. L. Moszyński, 'Udział Biblii w kształtowaniu się polskiego nazewnictwa kamieni szlachetnych', *PFil*, 44:387–96.

CARROLL IN TRANSLATION. J. Szerszunowicz, 'Polskie odpowiedniki translatoryczne czasowników angielskich (na podstawie *Alicji w Krainie Czarów*)', *PFil*, 42, 1997:277–92.

CHATA RODZINNA. T. Graczykowska, 'Nazwy zawodów i funkcji w kowieńskim tygodniku "Chata rodzinna"', *PJ*, 1998, no.7:34–42, illustrates archaisms, Russianisms, Lithuanianisms, local innovations, and a dialect word.

CONFESSION. W. R. Rzepka and W. Wydra, 'Mazowiecka wersja spowiedzi powszechnej z końca XV wieku', *PFil*, 44:479–89.

DRUŻBACKA. Teodozja Rittel, 'Style funckjonalne w jezyku Elżbiety Drużbackiej. Warianty kontaktowe — wyraz poetycki', *SFPS*, 34, 1998:85–101.
FRYC. E. Siatkowska, 'Fonetyka J.B. Fryca na przykładzie jego tłumaczenia "Księgi Genesis" (1796) w porównaniu ze współczesną normą literacką', *PFil*, 41, 1996:181–92.
GOSZCZYŃSKI. A. Kępińska, 'Rzeczowniki podzielne słowotwórczo w *Dzienniku Sprawy Bożej*. S. Goszczyńskiego (z wyjątkiem nazw czynności)', *PFil*, 41, 1996:13–42.
GÓRNICKI. F. Pepłowski, 'Dwa wydania *Dworzanina polskiego* Łukasza Górnickiego', *PFil*, 43, 1998:357–62.
HERBERT. K. Pisarkowa, '*To jest ów owoc*. O Brewiarzu Zbigniewa Herberta', *JPol*, 79:1–14.
KAMIEŃSKA. A. Pajdzińska, 'Semantyka *ciemności* w poezji Anny Kamieńskiej', *PFil*, 43, 1998:347–56.
KOCHANOWSKI. M. Kucała, 'Nazwy ludów słowiańskich w pismach Jana Kochanowskiego', *PFil*, 44:333–38.
KONOPNICKA. M. Jurkowski, 'Rutenizmy i orientalizmy w baśni *O krasnoludkach i sierotce* Marii Konopnickiej (w setną rocznicę wydania dzieła)', *PFil*, 41, 1996:315–26.
LINDE. A. Nowakowska, 'Nazwy drzew w *Słowniku języka polskiego* S. B. Lindego', *PJ*, 1998, no.6:12–18.
MICKIEWICZ. J. Damborský, 'O dwujęzyczności *Dziadów*', *PFil*, 44:85–95. W. J. Darasz, '*I zliczyć każdy dźwięk* — spojrzenie strukturalisty', *JPol*, 79:400, deals with the poem *Wsłuchać się w szum wód głuchy*; also Id., 'Amfibrach', *ib.*, 105–11, and 'Jamb', *ib.*, 288–96. B. Kreja, 'Ze słownictwa Pana Tadeusza', *ib.*, 158–60, discusses *obora* and *ogrójec*. A. Krupianka, 'Nazwy doktryn z formantem *-izm // -yzm* w tekstach Mickiewiczowskich', *PFil*, 43, 1998:281–86; L. Mariak, 'Funkcje parafraz przysłów w tekstach A. Mickiewicza', *PFil*, 42, 1997:233–52; A. Merdas, 'Jezus Mickiewicza', *PFil*, 43, 1998:313–18; D. Kozaryn, 'Parafrazy biblijne w *Listach Adama Mickiewicza*', *PFil*, 42, 1997:221–32; M. J. Mikoś, 'Words, words, words: on translating Mickiewicz's *Crimean Sonnets*', *PolR*, 43:387–95, opines, 'there is no need whatsoever to depart wilfully from the original'. E. Smółkowa, ' "Lubia" — "To lubię" ', *PFil*, 44:509–12; E. Stachurski, 'Wyrazy-klucze Mickiewiczowskiej epopei', *JPol*, 79:15–29; M. Szpiczakowska, 'Formy i funkcje imiesłowów w *Panu Tadeuszu* A. Mickiewicza na tle normy językowej XIX w.', *ib.*, 79:30–34. M. Zarębina, 'Wartościowanie związane z *małżeństwem* w "Panu Tadeuszu" A. Mickiewicza', *PFil*, 43, 1998:501–06.
MONIUSZKO. M. Czardybon, 'Słownictwo muzyczne w korespondencji Stanisława Moniuszki', *PFil*, 41, 1996:223–46.

NESTOR. W. Decyk, 'Transpozycja wschodniosłowiańskich nazw geograficznych na język polski (na przykładzie materiału z kroniki Nestora)', *PFil*, 41, 1996:247–66.

NORWID. K. Chodorowska-Zdebiak, 'Metaforyka przestrzenna w wierszach Cyprian Norwida z lat 1842–1851', *PFil*, 43, 1998:101–10. J. Chojak, 'Święte, istotne, szczere czy fałszywe i okrutne? (uwagi o Norwidowskim serio)', *ib.*, 111–18. A. Dunajski, 'Norwidowe piękno jako "kształt miłości"', *ib.*, 143–46. K. Konecka, 'Norwidowskie Kwiaty w asocjacjach sakralnych', *PFil*, 42, 1997:189–202; T. Korpysz, '*Swoboda* i jej derywaty w idiolekcie Cypriana Norwida na tle dziewiętnastowiecznej polszczyzny ogólnej i języka Adama Mickiewicza', *ib.*, 203–20; Id., 'Kilka uwag na temat norwidowego rozumienia zwrotu *szczęść Boże*', *PFil*, 43, 1998:257–64; T. Skubalanka, 'Uwagi o kształcie językowym *Pierścienia Wielkiej-Damy* Norwida', *ib.*, 417–24.

PILOT. W. Kupiszewski, 'Gwara w wybranych utworach M. Pilota', *PFil*, 44:339–43.

POLICARP. S. Dubisz, 'Czy w *Rozmowie mistrza Polikarpa ze Śmiercią* występuje mazurzenie?', *PFil*, 44:113–17.

PSALTER. S. Kaziara, '*Miłować* i jego synonimy w polskich przekładach Psałterza', *PFil*, 43, 1998:265–72.

RÓŻEWICZ. J. Jankowska, 'Elementy stylu religijnego w poezji Tadeusza Różewicza', *PJ*, no.4:1–10.

ROZMYŚLANIE PRZEMYSKIE. W. R. Rzepka and W. B. Twardzik, 'Archaizmy fleksyjne w Rozmyślaniu przemyskim. 6. Archaiczne formy part. praet. act. I typu *przyszed, kupiw, lizw* "przyszedłszy, kupiwszy, liznąwszy"', *JPol*, 79:35–46; B. Taras, 'Średniowieczne słownictwo domowe i rodzinne. Cz. I. Wyrazy, wyrażenia i zwroty związane z narodzinami, pielęgnacją i wychowaniem małego dziecka znajdujące się w tekście *Rozmyślania przemyskiego*', *PFil*, 41, 1996:275–82.

RZEWUSKI. B. Bartnicka, 'Przymiotnikowe archaizmy leksykalne i semantyczne w języku powieści Henryka Rzewuskiego', *PFil*, 41, 1996:299–314; her 'Archaizmy gramatyczne w tekstach Henryka Rzewuskiego', *PFil*, 42, 1997:171–88; and her 'Dziewiętnastowieczne funkcje składniowe bezokolicznika (na materiale powieści Henryka Rzewuskiego)', *PFil*, 43, 1998:61–66.

SŁOWACKI. T. Skubalanka, 'Juliusz Słowacki — artysta słowa', *JPol*, 79:339–51, concentrates chiefly on linguistic creativity in *Bieniowski*. F. Sławski, 'Słownictwo Juliusza Słowackiego', *ib.*, 322–38. M. Wojtak, 'Juliusza Słowackiego kunszt stylizatorski — wybrane aspekty stylu Fantazego', *ib.*, 351–62.

ŚCIBOR-RYLSKI. M. Sadecka, 'Konstrukcje potoczne (składnia, frazeologia) w dialogach *Człowieka z marmuru* według scenariusza

Aleksandra Ścibor-Rylskiego', *PJ*, no.1 : 44–54; and her 'Konstrukcje potoczne w *Człowieku z marmuru* (dokończenie)', *PJ*, nos.2–3 : 25–33. TAMUTIS. M. Marszałek, 'Odzwierciedlenie północnokresowych cech fonetycznych w Słowniku litewsko-polskim K. Tamutisa (r. 1940)', *JPol*, 79 : 276–82. TARANOWSKI. W. Decyk, 'Zmiany w języku a praktyka wydawnicza (na przykładzie wydań relacji J. Taranowskiego: 1597, 1611, 1860)', *PFil*, 44 : 97–105. TWARDOWSKI. A. Mazan, 'Z tajników warsztatu artystycznego Jana Twardowskiego', *PP*, 53 : 244–68, looks at phraseological innovations and metamorphoses of Christian religious language. WENKER. E. Rzetelska-Feleszko, 'Rozważania o kaszubskiej *warzączhwi* i *białce* (w związku z materiału Georga Wenkera)', *PFil*, 44 : 491–98.

## 9. POLISH AND OTHER LANGUAGES

I. M. Doliński, 'Bułgarskie nazwy środków czynności (w porównaniu z polskimi)', *PFil*, 44 : 107–12. M. Korytkowska, 'Uprzedniość, rezultatywność a zdania czasowe w języku bułgarskim i polskim', *SFPS*, 34, 1998 : 205–24; her 'Tekst w tekście a procesy desemantyzacji wykładników imperceptywności (na materiale języka bułgarskiego i polskiego)', *Slavia*, 68 : 99–106; and her 'Z problematyki opisu styku diatezy oraz kategorii czasu i aspektu (na materiale bułgarskim i polskim)', *SFPS*, 35 : 173–92. V. Koseska-Toszewa, 'O wieloznaczności wyrażeń kwantyfikujących w językach bułgarskim i polskim', *PFil*, 44 : 313–18. B. Bartnicka, 'Przymiotniki dzierżawcze w języku polskim i czeskim', *ib.*, 41–50; M. Godlewski, 'Adnominalny genetivus jakościowy w językach: czeskim, słowackim i słoweńskim na tle polszczyzny', *PFil*, 42, 1997 : 147–52; Z. Greń, ' "Swój" i "obcy" na Śląsku Cieszyńskim — wyznaczenie zakresu na podstawie wyboru kodu w warunkach diglosji', *SFPS*, 34, 1998 : 27–41; M. Karpluk, 'Do wpływu czeskiego na epistolografię staropolską', *PFil*, 44 : 269–74. C. Koch, 'Weiterung des relativen Attributivkonnexes. Die westslavischen Adverbialadjektiva auf *-ějьš-*, *ZSl*, 44 : 455–75; E. Lotko, 'Ke konfrontaci příbuzných jazyků (na materiálu češtiny a polštiny)', *Slavia*, 68 : 75–82; N. Nübler, 'Anmerkungen zu den infiniten Verbformen im Tschechischen und Polnischen', *ASP*, 36, 1998 : 75–86. K. Oliva, 'Czy polskie *owszem* to czeskie *ovšem*? Owszem, lecz nie zawsze', *PFil*, 44 : 405–07. E. Mańczak-Wohlfeld, 'Anglicyzmy w terminologii marynistycznej', *PJ*, no.1 : 30–34. K. Feleszko, 'Charakterystyka punktów prudnickich w archiwum Deutscher Sprachatlas', *PFil*, 44 : 173–78; K. Pisarkowa, 'Glose polonaise sur la symbolique de l'Union européenne', *RSl*, 78 : 793–814, discusses translations of Schiller's *An die Freude*; J. Reichan, 'Interpretowanie fonetycznych form zapożyczeń niemieckich w *Słowniku gwar polskich* PAN', *PFil*, 44:441–46; S. Schmidt, 'Kultura języka w Polsce i w Niemczech. O kształtowaniu się postaw wobec języka', *PJ*, no.1:1–10. J. Bańczerowski, 'Grupy fonemów spółgłoskowych w śródgłosie wyrazowym języka polskiego i węgierskiego II', *SSH*, 43, 1998:1–22. H. Popowska-Taborska, 'Specyfika kaszubskich innowacji leksykalnych w *Słowniku polsko-kaszubskim* Jana Trepczyka', *Slavia*, 68:69–74. J. Borzęcki, 'Issues of language and national identity in the population censuses of the Polish-Russian borderlands: reexamination and comments', *PolR*, 43:29–46; J. Chludzińska-Świątecka, 'Przyjaciele Moskale', *PFil*, 43, 1998:95–100; M. Moser, 'Die einfachen verba loci stativa und ihr idiomatischer Gebrauch im Russischen und Polnischen', *WSlA*, 42, 1998:251–80; B. Wiemer, 'Aktuelles Präsens bei russ. *приходить* und poln. *przychodzić*?', *ZSP*, 58:85–105; E. A. Zemskaja, O. P. Ermakova and Z. Rudnik-Karwatowa, 'Tendencje rozwojowe w słowotwórstwie języka polskiego i rosyjskiego końca XX stulecia', *Slavia*, 68:9–18. H. Popowska-Taborska, 'O polskim *wrzeciądzu* i jego północnosłowiańskich odpowiednikach', *PFil*, 44:429–33. B. Falińska, 'Słowiańskie przywoływania kur i kurcząt (na materiale materiałów OLA)', *ib.*, 155–62. F. Buffa, 'O formálnych zhodách v oblasti poľskej a slovenskej lexiky', *SlSl*, 34:124–36; J. Dudášová-Kriššáková, 'Fonologický system spisovnej slovenčiny a poľštiny z typologického hľadiska', *ib.*, 16–24, also in *PFil*, 44:119–27. H. Mieczkowska, 'Ujęcie typologiczne deklinacji rzeczowników słowackich w konfrontacji z polskimi', *ib.*, 381–86; M. Papierz, 'Zaimek zwrotny w językach słowackim i polskim', *ib.*, 415–19. E. Siatkowska, 'Czasowniki typu *katować* // *katowaś* w języku polskim i dolnołużyckim', *ib.*, 503–07. A. Dąbrowska-Kamińska, 'Kategoria rodzaju rzeczowników zakończonych na spółgłoskę miękką i historycznie miękką w języku polskim i ukraińskim', *PFil*, 42, 1997:63–80; M. Jurkowski, 'Rodzaj gramatyczny rzeczowników obcego pochodzenia w języku polskim i ukraińskim', *ib.*, 81–90.

## 10. Onomastics

E. Breza, 'Nazwa jeziora Mausz i wsi Mojusz w Kartuskiem', *SFPS*, 35:23–29; Id., 'Nazwiska *Czapa, Czap(p), Czapeli* i podobne', *PFil*, 44:65–73; Id., 'Staropolskie imię *Bog(o)dal*, nazwisko *Bugdoll* i jego warianty', *JPol*, 79:70–73. W. Decyk, 'Motywacja nazw własnych krów', *PFil*, 42, 1997:253–60; her 'Toponimy w języku zbiorowości polonijnych w sferze oddziaływania języka angielskiego', *PJ*, 1998, no.7:17–33; and her 'Nazwy organizacji i instytucji europejskich w polszczyźnie', *PJ*, no.4:18–29. H. Duda, 'Nazwiska typu *Janów*,

*Józków, Pańków* są odmienne!', *JPol*, 79:93–95. J. Duma, 'Niektóre aspekty zmian leksykalnych, morfologicznych i fonetycznych w nazwach rzek środkowej Polski', *SFPS*, 34, 1998:17–25. Id., 'Rozmieszczenie na Pomorzu Zachodnim nazw terenowych zawierających rdzeń *běl-* 'biały, biel'' *PFil*, 44:129–38. Z. Gałecki, '*Płosodrza*', *PFil*, 42, 1997:261–70. Id., 'Nazwa miejscowa *Harachwosty* i jej podstawa imienna', *PFil*, 44:179–83. A. Kępińska, 'Wyrównania międzydeklinacyjne w M. lm. a geneza dzisiejszych końcówek miejscowych nazw patronimicznych, służebnych, etnicznych i rodowych typu *Biskupice* (zamiast pierwotnego *Biskupicy*), *Kuchary* (zamiast *Kucharze*), czy *Zabłocice* (zamiast *Zabłocicy*)', *ib.*, 281–89. W. Mańczak, 'W sprawie nazwiska *Mudlaf*', *JPol*, 79:140–41. A. Pisowicz, 'Czy regres polskiej transkrypcji? Uwagi sprowokowane pisownią obcych nazw geograficznych w nowym "Atlasie encyklopedycznym PWN"', *ib.*, 379–82, examines the confusions and inconsistencies caused by taking over English, French or other foreign spellings and transliterations of names into Polish. E. Rzetelska-Feleszko, 'Procesy globalizacji a niektóre rodzaje nazw własnych', *Slavia*, 68:53–59. S. Sochacka, 'Elementy czeskie w nazwach miejscowych ziemi kłodzkiej', *PFil*, 44:513–19. J. Strzelecka, 'O nazwach osobowych w "Księdze ławniczej miasta Nowej Warszawy" z lat 1416–1485', *SFPS*, 35:109–21.

## LITERATURE

By JOHN BATES, *University of Glasgow*

### 1. GENERAL

Brigitte Schultze, *Perspektywy polonistyczne i komparatystyczne*, Kw, Universitas, 500 pp., mainly examines selected aspects of 19th- and 20th-c. Polish drama and reflects on translations thereof in what is largely a collection of previously published essays. Henryk Machalski, *Przestrzeń przedstawiona*, IBL, 146 pp., contains sketches on the poetics of mimesis in 18th- and 19th-c. Polish literature with reference to writers like J. I. Kraszewski and I. Krasicki. *Literatura i komunikacja. Od listu do powieści autobiograficznej*, ed. Artur Blaim and Zbigniew Maciejewski, UMCS, 1998, 434 pp., includes contributions on L. Tyrmand's *Dziennik 1954*, as well as on A. Tolstoi, I. Bashevis Singer, D. Defoe, V. Woolf. *W kręgu etyki, poetyki i dydaktyki słowa*, ed. Tadeusz Patrzałek, WUW, 1998, 179 pp., includes M. Inglot on C. K. Norwid's concretization of the Romantics' vision of word and deed with particular reference to the poem *Słowotwór*, and essays on A. Mickiewicz, S. Brzozowski, and the poetic ethos of language in Z. Herbert's work. *Oniryczne tematy i konwencje w literaturze polskiej w XX wieku*, ed. Ilona Glatzel, Jerzy Smulski, and Anna Sobolewska, Toruń, Wyd. Uniwersytetu Mikołaja Kopernika, 393 pp., is immensely wideranging, with contributions from leading Polish specialists on poetry, prose and drama. *Lustra historii. Rozprawy i eseje ofiarowane Profesor Marii Żmigrodzkiej z okazji pięćdziesięciolecia pracy naukowej*, ed. Maria Kalinowska and Elżbieta Kiślak, Wa., Wyd. IBL, 1998, 278 pp., includes articles by leading Polish scholars such as R. Przybylski and M. Janion on works and authors such as *Dziady* and *Kordian*, E. Orzeszkowa, and W. Szymborska. *Od oświecenia do romantyzmu. Prace ofiarowane Piotrowi Żbikowskiemu*, ed. Gustaw Ostasz and Stanisław Uliasz, Rzeszów, WSP, 1997, 283 pp., contains essays on the occasional poetry produced during the Four Year Sejm, on K. Ujejski, K. Koźmian and F. Wężyk, C. K. Norwid, J. Lechoń's poem *Kniaźnin i żołnierz*, as well as a bibliography of works written by Żbikowski between 1958 and 1996.

Włodzimierz Bolecki, *Polowanie na postmodernistów (w Polsce) i inne szkice*, WL, 427 pp., reprints an eclectic series of essays written since the 1970s, grouped under three headings: History, Theory and Post-Theory. Stefan Szymutko, *Rzeczywistość jako zwątpienie w literaturze i literaturoznawstwie*, Katowice, Wyd. Uniwersytetu Śląskiego, 1998, 195 pp., contains essays on W. Gombrowicz, T. Parnicki, J. Lechoń, and W. Broniewski, as well as W. Wharton and J. Joyce.

Maria Delaperrière, *Dialog z dystansu*, Kw, Universitas, 1998, 277 pp., contains essays on J. Przyboś, A. Kuśniewicz, S. Grochowiak, Gombrowicz, J. Brzękowski and others. W. Bolecki, ' "Emigracyjność" — "polityczność" historia literatury', *TD*, no.3:151–60. H. C. Trepte, 'Switching languages in emigre literature', *CanSS*, nos.2–4:215–22, a general treatment, focuses ultimately on J. Kosiński. R. Nycz, ' "Każdy z nas jest przybyszem". Wzory tożsamości w literaturze polskiej XX wieku', *TD*, no.5:41–51, argues that there are two main strands, represented by C. Miłosz, whose credo was one of 'being at home' everywhere, and Gombrowicz, whose dictum was always to 'be other'. Dorota Sapa, *Między polską wyspą a ukraińskim morzem*, Kw, Universitas, 1998, 249 pp., examines, on the basis of texts written between 1918 and 1988, the reconstruction of a vision of the world of the *kresy*, as exemplified in the works of M. Pankowski, W. Odojewski, J. Wittlin, S. Vincenz, and others.

Henryk Dubowik, *Fantastyka w literaturze polskiej. Dzieje motywów fantastycznych w zarysie*, Bydgoszcz, Towarzystwo Miłośników Wilna i Ziemi Wileńskiej Oddział w Bydgoszcy, 324 pp., is a very wideranging study that examines fantastic motifs from the Middle Ages, through J. Słowacki and Mickiewicz, to the postwar period. Jolanta Ługowska, *Folklor — tradycje i inscenizacje. Szkice literacko-folklorystyczne*, WUW, 208 pp., devotes its third part to the application of folklore in folk and fairy tales, with specific reference to works by J. Korczak, B. Ostrowska, and C. S. Lewis's *Narnia* stories, among others. *Natura Naturata. Gegenständliche Welt und Kultureme in der polnischen Literatur von der zweiten Hälfte des 19. Jahrhunderts bis zur Gegenwart*, ed. Dagmar Burkhart and Waldemar Klemm, Amsterdam, Rodopi, 1997, 361 pp., contains contributions by H. Gosk, A. Z. Makowiecki, and B. Schultze on gastronomic customs as depicted in works by Gombrowicz, W. Berent, Konwicki, and W. Reymont, and writers who made their prose debuts in the period 1956–64. Bogdan Burdziej, *Super Flumina Babylonis. Psalm 136 (137) w literaturze polskiej XIX–XX w.*, Toruń, Wyd. Uniwersytet Mikołaja Kopernika, 364 pp., is an exhaustive examination of the roles, references, and uses to which the famous psalm has been put. *Idee i obrazy religijne w literaturze XIX i XX wieku*, ed. Grzegorz Igliński, Olsztyń, WSP, 1998, 426 pp., is a wide-ranging collection which examines religious imagery and ideas in the works of the Romantic poets, Young Poland writers (T. Miciński, J. Kasprowicz), and contemporary writers (e.g. G. Herling-Grudziński), as well as lesser-known writers such as Z. Ułaszynówna and J. S. Wierzbicki. *Z Bogiem przez wieki. Inspiracje i motywy religijne w literaturze polskiej i literaturach zachodnioeuropejskich XIX i XX wieku*, ed. Piotr Żbikowski, Rzeszów, WSP, 1998, 440 pp. *TD*, nos.1–2, contains two essays on gender-related themes: I. Iwasiów,

'Osoba w dyskursie feministycznym' (49–63) is exemplified on the basis of K. Kofta's novel *Złodziejka pamięci*, while G. Ritz's 'Seks, gender i tekst albo granice autonomii literackiej' (165–74) examines more extensive material, including Mickiewicz's *Wielka Improwizacja*, M. Komornicka's late lyrics, and E. Łuskina's *Żelazna maska* cycle. M. A. Packalen, 'Uwarunkowania kulturowe literackiego obrazu kobiet w polskiej i szwedzkiej prozie o tematyce wiejskiej z pierwszej połowy XX wieku', *PL(W)*, 90.3:59–70. U. Phillips, 'The upbringing and education of women as represented in novels by nineteenth-century Polish women writers', *SEER*, 77:201–22, examines the issues in relation to lesser-known novels and novellists, such as E. Jaraczewska, K. Tańska-Hoffmanowa, and N. Zmichowska's *Biała Róża*.

*Pierwsza wojna światowa w literaturze polskiej i obcej. Wybrane zagadnienia*, ed. Eugenia Loch and Krzysztof Stępnik, UMCS, 332 pp., has a second part devoted to essays on Z. Nałkowska, J. Wittlin, J. Stryjkowski, and E. Zegadłowicz, and contains a comparative study of B. Ostrowska's *Bohaterski miś* and H. Zakrzewska's *Dzieci Lwowa*. M. G. Levine, 'Bezdomność w literaturze wojennej — typologia obrazowania', *TD*, no.4:7–17, a wide-ranging article, examines works largely set in Warsaw by J. Andrzejewski, B. Wojdowski, I. Fink, M. Białoszewski, and W. Szlengel. K. Pisarkowa, 'Glose polonaise sur la symbolique de l'Union européene', *RSl*, 70:793–814.

## 2. FROM THE MIDDLE AGES UP TO ROMANTICISM

Janusz Andrzej Drob, *Trzy zegary. Obraz czasu w polskich kazaniach barokowych*, Towarzystwo Naukowe KUL, 1998, 225 pp. Jadwiga Koterska, *\*Theatrum Mundi. Ze studiów nad poezją staropolską*, Gdańsk U.P., 1998, 266 pp., discusses primarily emblems by such diverse writers as M. Sęp Szarzyński, H. and Z. Morsztyn, W. Potocki, and J. Baka. Jacek Sokolski, *Bogini, pojęcie, demon. Fortuna w dziełach autorów staropolskich*, WUW, 1996, 148 pp., considers the changing guises of the figure of Fortune in the work of M. Rej, H. Morsztyn, J. Kochanowski and others in terms of Fortune's relationship with destiny, virtue, and wisdom, and finally Fortune as demonic power. He concludes that by the 17th c., Fortune was no longer merely a personification, and that in Baroque works there are medieval elements that are non-classical in origin. *Zmierzch kultury staropolskiej. Ciągłość i kryzysy (wieki XVII-XIX)*, ed. Urszula Augustyniak and Adam Karpiński, Wa, Semper, 1997, 135 pp., includes M. Prejs's 'Ciągłość i kryzys epoki staropolskiej w literaturze późnego baroku' (78–91). *Lektury polonistyczne. Średniowiecze — Renesans — Barok. Tom III*, ed. Janusz S. Gruchała, Kw, Universitas, 301 pp., starts from *Kazania*

*Świętokrzyskie* and goes on to discuss Władysław z Gielniowa's *Żołtarz Jezusow, literatura sowizdrzalska,* M. K. Sarbiewski, J. Kochanowski, J. A. Morsztyn, S. Twardowski, and S. H. Lubomirski. *The Annals of Jan Długosz,* ed. Maurice Michael, Chichester, IM Publications, 1997, xxviii + 673 pp., is an abridged translation of the Latin original with a critical commentary by P. Smith (603–12). *Polish Enlightenment and Baroque Literature: An Anthology,* ed. Michael J. Mikoš, Columbus, Slavica, 1996, 382 pp., is principally an anthology of translations of key works with a brief introduction (38–58), continuing the series of such works.

K. Croxen, 'Thematic and generic medievalism in the Polish neo-Latin drama of the Renaissance and Baroque', *SEEJ,* 43:265–98, considers works by S. Szymonowic, as well as lesser-known writers such as Gregorius Cnapius and J. Joncre. M. Cybulski, 'O dwóch XVII-wiecznych polskich przekładach Psałterza. *Psałterz Dawidow* Mikołaja Reja i *Psałterz Dawida* Jakuba Lubelczyka', *RKJŁ,* 44:13–29, is principally linguistic. R. Grzesik, 'Legitimierungs-funktion der ungarisch-polnischen Chronik', Kooper, *Chronicle,* 144–54. R. Krzywy, 'Konwencja i autopsja w opisie dzieła sztuki. Na przykładzie ekfraz kościoła Mądrości Bożejw poezji barokowej', *PrLit,* 36, 1998:25–47, examines descriptions of the Hagia Sophia in Polish Baroque poetry.

Przemysława Matuszewska, *Gry z adresatem. Studia o poezji i epistemologii wieku oświecenia,* WUW, 219 pp., considers the role of Voltaire's works in Krasicki's oeuvre, the poetic epistle and the role of the addressee in A. Naruszewicz, *inter alia.* Jerzy Snopek, *Oświecenie. Szkic do portretu epoki* (Mała Historia Literatury Polskiej), PWN, 288 pp., comprises two parts: (i) devoted to the general intellectual and social background, (ii) literary matters *per se.* Piotr Żbikowski, *Klasycyzm postanisławowski. Zarys problematyki,* PWN, 354 pp. + 16 pls, is a changed and expanded version of the 1984 edition. *Wśród pisarzy oświecenia. Studia i portrety,* ed. Antoni Czyż and Stanisław Szczęsny, Bydgoszcz, WSP, 1997, 369 pp., includes T. Kostkiewiczowa on Naruszewicz, and other contributions on Krasicki, L. Węgierski, J. Jasiński, and J. P. Woronowicz.

INDIVIDUAL WRITERS

GÓRNICKI. Jakub Zdzisław Lichański, *Łukasz Górnicki — Sarmacki Castiglione,* Wa, DiG, 1998, 158 pp.

KOCHANOWSKI. Joanna Senderska, *\*Zależności między schematami zdań a strukturą wiersza Jana Kochanowskiego,* Kielce, WSP im. Jana Kochanowskiego, 250 pp. J. Sokolski, '"Sybilla prorokuje ..." o fraszce *Do Stanisława* Jana Kochanowskiego', *PL(W),* 90.3:149–52.

KRASICKI. E. Aleksandrowska, 'Problemy *Monitorowego* autorstwa Krasickiego. Z warsztatu bibliografa *Monitora*', *PL(W)*, 90.1 : 153–66.
LUBOMIRSKI. E. Lasocińska, 'O *Eklezjastesie* Stanisława Herakliusza Lubomirskiego — słowo i Słowo', *PL(W)*, 90.2 : 133–52.
H. MORSZTYN. A. Kochan, 'Niektóre problemy stylu *Światowej Rozkoszy* Hieronima Morsztyna. Próba charakterystyki', *PrLit* , 36, 1998 : 11–24.
NIEMCEWICZ. Izabela Kusinowa, *Pana Juliana przypadki życia. Julian Ursyn Niemcewicz 1797–1841*, Wa, TRIO, 404 pp., is a biographical account.
SĘP SZARZYŃSKI. A. Komaromi, 'The aporia of temporal existence in Sęp Szarzyński's poetry', *SEEJ*, 43 : 122–36.

## 3. ROMANTICISM

Bogusław Dopart, *Romantyzm polski. Pluralizm prądów i synkretyzm dzieła*, Kw, Wyd. Naukowe — Księgarnia Akademicka, 215 pp., a major new study, examines its theme in relation to *Maria, Dziady, Pan Tadeusz*, A. Fredro's plays, *Lalka*, and the Gothic novel. Włodzimierz Szturc, *O obrotach sfer romantycznych. Studia o ideach i wyobraźni*, Bydgoszcz, Homini, 1997, 197 pp., examines various aspects of Słowacki's writing, such as his millenarianism and the language of the late dramatic works, foundation myths in Norwid's *Wanda*, Mickiewicz, A. Malczewski, as well as Novalis and F. H. Hölderlin. Marian Śliwiński, *Motywy romantyczne*, Piotrków Trybunalski, WSP w Kielcach, 237 pp., addresses such key motifs as 'North-South' and 'sailor'. Jan Tuczyński, *Herder i herderyzm w Polsce*, Gd, Marpress, 179 pp., analyses Herder's influence on Polish culture from the late 18th to the mid-19th century.

Maria Cieśla-Korytowska, *O Mickiewiczu i Słowackim*, Kw, Universitas, 227 pp., is principally on S.'s messianism and mystical writings. Mieczysław Inglot, *Postać Żyda w literaturze polskiej lat 1822–1864*, WUW, 296 pp., is part-analysis, part-anthology, focusing on the Jewish image in the works of the Romantics and Realists.

S. Makowski, 'Kazimierz Pułaski — bohater romantycznej legendy literackiej', *PrzH*, 43.2–3 : 73–92, considers the portrayal of Pułaski in works by Słowacki and lesser-known Romantics. M. Siwiec, 'Między piekłem a niebem. Paryż romantyczny', *TD*, no.4 : 111–36, considers the responses of Mickiewicz and Słowacki as well as those of G. de Nerval and V. Hugo.

### INDIVIDUAL WRITERS

FREDRO. H. Markiewicz, 'Lekcje *Pana Jowialskiego*', *PL(W)*, 90.3 : 153–66.

GODEBSKI. A. Timofiejew, '*Powieści* Cypriana Godebskiego wobec konwencji powiastki oświeceniowej', *PL(W)*, 90.3: 133–48.

KRASIŃSKI. T. Łuczkowski, 'Melancholijny obraz średniowiecza w genewskiej korespondencji Zygmunta Krasińskiego', *PP*, 1998, 53: 104–18.

LENARTOWICZ. M. Laskowska, 'Lirnik mazowiecki jako poeta kultury. O *Album włoskim* Teofila Lenartowicza', *PP*, 1998, 53: 84–103.

MICKIEWICZ. Jan Ciechanowicz, *Droga geniusza (O Adamie Mickiewiczu)*, Ww, Wyd. Nortom, 1998, 131 pp. Mieczysław Inglot, *Wieszcz i pomniki. W kręgu XIX- i XX-wiecznej recepcji dzieł Adama Mickiewicza*, WUW, 307 pp., collects previously published pieces written over the past thirty years on various aspects of M.'s reception. Bolesław T. Łaszewski, *Poglądy i działalność społeczno-polityczna Adama Mickiewicza po roku 1830*, Radom, Wyd. i Zakład Poligrafii Instytutu Technologii Eksploatacji, 111 pp. Dariusz Seweryn, '. . . *jak tam zaszedłeś*'. *Mickiewiecz w szkole klasycznym*, KUL, 1997, 144 pp., considers the Hellenic spirit as exhibited mainly in M.'s early work. His *O wyobraźni lirycznej Adama Mickiewicza* (Rozprawy literackie, 74), IBL, 1996, 135 pp., focuses on the *Crimean Sonnets* as well as the later verse, the poems immediately prior to, as well as, the Lausanne poetry. *Mickiewicz i kresy*, ed. Zofia Kurzowa and Zofia Cygal-Krupowa, Kw, Universitas, 324 pp., is a selection of papers from a conference held in Cracow on 4–6 December 1997, with *Pan Tadeusz* as the principal focus of contributors' essays, which are concerned with linguistic elements (forms of address), the *styl kresowy*, and elements of English culture.

*RSl*, 70, contains four essays devoted to M.: Z. Mitosek, 'Mickiewicz, Napoleon et les Francais' (739–50); P. Karagyozov, 'Курс Адама Мицкевича по славяним литературам в Коллеж де франс в контексте сравнитьного славянского литературоведения' (751–69); S. Makowski, 'Le romantisme polonais dans *Les Slaves* d'Adam Mickiewicz (771–81); and M. Delaperrière, 'Mickiewicz, un moderne' (783–91). *PrzH*, 43.4, contains four essays on M.-related matters: O. Cybienko, 'Włodzimierz Sołowjowi Adam Mickiewicz' (31–44); T. Kizwalter, who answers the question posed in his title 'Czy Mickiewicz stworzył naród polski?' (45–60) with a qualified 'yes', in view of M.'s reinterpretation of Sarmatian culture; and the complementary M. Michajłowa, 'Obchody stulecia urodzin Adama Mickiewicza w Rosji' (73–81) and Z. Przybyła, 'Obchody setnej rocznicy urodzin Adama Mickiewicza na ziemiach polskich' (61–71). R. Fieguth, 'Zur Frage der zyklischen Komposition von Mickiewiczs Sonettbuch (1826)', *WSl*, 43.2, 1998:201–28. H. Filipowicz, 'Performing bodies, performing Mickiewicz. Drama as problem in Performance Studies', *SEEJ*, 43:1–18. E. Kasperski,

'Zabójczy jad poezji. Iwan Franko i Adam Mickiewicz na rozstajnych szlakach historii', *PrzH*, 43.5:57–75, analyses the fall-out from Franko's highly critical article about M., 'Ein Dichter des Verrathes', published in the Vienna daily *Die Zeit* on 8 May 1897. NORWID. Grażyna Halkiewicz-Sojak, *Wobec tajemnicy i prawdy o Norwidowskich obrazach całości*, Toruń, Wyd. Uniwersytet Mikołaja Kopernika, 1998, 226 pp. M. Piasecka, ' "[. . .] w wilię chrześciańskiej prawdy objawienia". Obraz upadającego Rzymu w *Quidamie* Cypriana Kamila Norwida', *PP*, 1998, 53:68–83. PODCZASZYŃSKI. Michał Strzyżewski, *Michał Podczaszyński, zapomniany romantyk*, Toruń, Wyd. Adam Marszałek, 238 pp. examines the work and influence of a little-known figure of Polish Romanticism. SŁOWACKI. Marta Piwińska, *Juliusz Słowacki od duchów*, Wa, OPEN, 502 pp., considers S.'s *Genesis* poems and *Król-Duch*. Ryszard Przybylski, *Rozhukany koń. Esej o myśleniu Juliusza Słowackiego*, Wa, Sic, 215 pp., examines such issues as the archaic and eschatological dimensions of S.'s thinking. *Juliusz Słowacki. Wielkokulturowe źródła twórczości*, ed. Adam Bajcar, Wa, Ogólnopolskie Klub Miłośników Litwy, 256 pp. + 1 map, contains contributions by scholars from the Ukraine, Lithuania, and Poland. *Słowacki współczesny*, ed. Marek Troszyński, IBL, 276 pp., contains contributions by leading Polish scholars on S.'s continuing relevance. B. Mucha, 'Pisarze rosyjscy w opinii Juliusza Slowackiego', *PrzH*, 43.4:23–30. STARZYŃSKI. D. Kowalewska, 'Proza Stanisława Doliwy Starzyńskiego jako wyraz jego światopoglądu', *PP*, 1998, 53:30–67.

## 4. FROM REALISM TO NEO-REALISM

Wojciech Gutowski, *Mit — Eros — Sacrum. Sytuacje młodopolskie*, Bydgoszcz, Homini, 262 pp. His *Nagie dusze i maski. O młodopolskich mitach miłości*, Kw, Wyd. Literackie, 1997, 399 pp., examines certain common decadent themes in the work of Young Poland writers, such as the *femme fatale*, religion of love, and erotic myths, on the basis of their representation in the work of Leśmian and others. Magdalena Popiel, *Oblicza wzniosłości. Estetyka powieści młodopolskiej*, Kw, Universitas, 288 pp. Jerzy Tyniecki, *Światopogląd Pozytywizmu. Wybór pism*, Łódź U.P., 1996, 285 pp., contains essays on *Fachowiec*, *Rodzina Połanieckich*, *Nad Niemnem* and lesser-known works such as J. Narzymski's *Ojczym. Inspiracje i motywy biblijne w literaturze pozytywizmu i Młodej Polski*, ed. H. Filipkowska and S. Fita, KUL, 293 pp., considers biblical motifs in the work of such writers as S. Żeromski, M. Konopnicka and others. *Piotr Chmielowski i Antoni Gustaw Bem*, ed. Zbigniew Przybyła, Częstochowa, WSP, 349 pp., marks the anniversary of the two publicists' births. A. Kępa, 'Adam Chmielowski jako postać historyczna w świetle faktów i opinii', *PP*, 1998, 53 : 158–79. Krystyna Ratajska, *Neomesjanistyczni spadkobiercy Mickiewicza*, Łódź U.P., 1998, 217 pp., examines the impact of Mickiewicz's mystical and messianic works on the work and activities of the Galician Neomessianists, focusing on the Lwów periodical *Odrodzenie* and Warsaw's *Legion*, A. Górski's *Monsalwat*, and S. Pigoń's early activity. Andrzej Romanowski, *Młoda Polska wileńska*, Kw, Universitas, 406 pp. + 94 pls, explores a hitherto under-researched dimension of the Young Poland movement. Marta Wyka, *Światopoglądy młodopolskie*, Kw, Universitas, 1996, 241 pp., deals with, *inter alia*, S. Brzozowski's *Sam wśród ludzi*, S. Przybyszewski's novels, L. Staff, and J. Ruffer's lyrics. A. Nasiłowska's 'Liryzm I podmiot modernistyczny', *TD*, nos. 1–2 : 7–30, goes back to Classicism in her overview of developments. M. Podraza-Kwiatkowska, 'Wzniosłość, Słowacki i młodopolski ekspresjonizm', *TD*, 3 : 33–43.

INDIVIDUAL WRITERS

KASPROWICZ.　Grzegorz Igliński, *Pieśni wieczystej tęsknoty. Lyrika Jana Kasprowicza w latach 1906–1926*, Olsztyn, WSP, 576 pp.

LICIŃSKI.　J. Raźny, 'Bohater opowiadań Ludwika Stanisława Licińskiego — *Z pamiętnika włóczęgi*', *PP*, 1998, 53 : 119–57.

T. MICIŃSKI.　Jolanta Wróbel, *Misteria Czasu. Problematyka temporalna Tadeusza Micińskiego*, Kw, 138 pp., concludes that M.'s conception of time is closer to the Bergsonian notion of duration, rather than mechanical time.

PRZYBYSZEWSKI.　P. Dybel, 'Choroba jako postęp, czyli dekadencka historiografia Przybyszewskiego', *PL(W)*, 90.2 : 27–46.

SIENKIEWICZ.　Tadeusz Bujnicki, *Światopogląd i poetyka. Szkice o powieściach historycznych Henryka Sienkiewicza*, Rzeszów, WSP, 173 pp. *Motywy religijne w twórczości Henryka Sienkiewicza*, ed. Lech Ludorowski, Kielce, Kielickie Towarzystwo Wydawnicze, 1998, 185 pp. A. Kuniczak-Trzcinowicz, 'Rozważania o melodramatyzmie w *Na marne* Henryka Sienkiewicza', *Literatura i kultura popularna*, 8 : 33–59.

WITKIEWICZ.　Jan Majda, *Góralszczyzna i Tatry w twórczości Stanisława Witkiewicza*, Kw, Universitas, 1998, 154 pp., examines the role of Highlander culture in, among other works by W., the novel *Na przełęczy*.

WYSPIAŃSKI.　Ewa Miodońska-Brookes, '*Mam ten dar bowiem: patrzę się inaczej.' Szkice o twórczości Stanisława Wyspiańskiego*, Kw, Universitas, 1997, 241 pp., examines the chorus as one of the dramatis personae, the religious aspects of the dramas, and W.'s vision of *Dziady*, among other issues. M. Freise, 'Historismus und Symbolismus in Wyspiańskis Dramen', *WSl*, 44.2 : 255–70.

Literature 869

ZAPOLSKA. K. Kłosińska, 'Fortepian. Muzyka w *Przedpiekle* Gabrieli Zapolskiej', *PL(W)*, 90.2:113–32.

## 5. FROM 1918 TO 1945

Ewa Kraskowska, *Piórem niewieścim: z problemów prozy kobiecej dwudziestolecia międzywojennego*, Wyd. Naukowe UAM, 224 pp., containing chapters on Nałkowska, H. Boguszewska, A. Gruszecka, and E. Szemplińska, also examines the depiction of motherhood in female interwar prose as well as women's journalism. Jerzy Święch, *Literatura polska w latach II wojny światowej*, PWN, 1997, 584 pp., is a major volume on this period and is divided, as with other tomes in the series, into general generic overviews and chapters devoted to specific authors. Ewa Tenzer, *Nation Kunst Zensur. Nationalstaatsbildung und Kunstzensur in Polen (1918–1939)*, Frankfurt–NY, Campus Vlg, 1998, 342 pp., provides material on the censorship of works by Zegadłowicz and Wat. E. Kraskowska, 'Nałkowska i Schulz, Schulz i Nałkowska', *TD*, nos.1–2:211–27. M. Skwara, 'Schulz i Witkacy — głos drugi', ibid., no.6:121–37, while allowing that there is little textual evidence, considers Witkacy to have exerted an influence on Schulz.

### INDIVIDUAL WRITERS

BACZYŃSKI. Wiesław Budzyński, *Testament Krzysztofa Kamila*, Wa, Twój Styl, 1998, 323 pp.

GOMBROWICZ. M. Inglot, 'Romantyczne konteksty *Operetki* Witolda Gombrowicza', *PL(W)*, 90.3:47–58. Z. Majchrowski, 'Mickiewicz in Gombrowicz's Theater', *Periphery*, 1998–99:113–21, discusses Mickiewicz's influence in relation to *The Marriage, Operetta* and *History*. M. Masłowski, ' "Kościół międzyludzkiej" w *Ślubie* Witolda Gombrowicza', *TD*, nos.1–2:175–87. L. Neuger, '*Kosmos* Witolda Gombrowicza. Genologiczne podstawy hipotez sensowności', ibid., no.6:57–70. J. Orska, 'Logos i Bigos — o dyskusjach nad *Opętanymi*', *Literatura i kultura popularna*, 7, 1998:43–54. K. Szczuka, 'Gombrowicz subwersywny', *TD*, no.5:171–80. S. Tynecka-Makowska, 'Między jawem i snem — u źródeł literackiej konwencji (*Ferdydurke* Witolda Gombrowicza a *Metamorfozy albo złoty osioł* Apulejusza z Madaury), *PP*, 1998, 53:7–29.

IWASZKIEWICZ. Zbigniew Chojnowski, *Poetycka wiara Jarosława Iwaszkiewicza*, Olsztyn, WSP, 397 pp., also includes an appendix of poems considered for, but not included in, the collection *Ciemne ścieżki*. Tomasz Wójcik, *Pociecha mieszka w pięknie. Studia o twórczości*

*Jarosława Iwaszkiewicza*, Wa, ELIPSA, 1998, 216 pp. *Powroty Iwaszkiewicza*, (Poznańskie studia polonistyczne, 18), ed. Agnieszka Czyżak, Jan Galant and Katarzyna Kuczyńska-Koschana, Pń, Abedik, 203 pp., includes essays on I.'s poetry and prose. A. Dziadek, 'Rytm i podmiot w *Oktostychach* i *muzyce wieczorem* Jarosława Iwaszkiewicza', *PL(W)*, 90.2: 27–66.

JASIEŃSKI. J. Holý, 'Der tschechische utopische Roman der Zwischenkriegzeit und *Palę Paryż* von Bruno Jasieński', *ŻRL*, 42:61–71.

KORCZAK. Aleksander Lewin, *Korczak znany i nieznany*, Wa, WSP Związku Nauczycielstwa Polskiego, 547 pp.

LECHOŃ. B. Dorosz, 'Archiwum Jana Lechonia w Polskim Instytucie Naukowym w Nowym Jorku. Relacja z Badań', *PL(W)*, 90.3:167–93, also contains an annex (185–93) of fragments and works published for the first time.

LEŚMIAN. E. Zarych, 'Postacie kalek w utworach Bolesława Leśmiana — zwycięstwo ciała czy ducha?', *TD*, no.6:149–60, is inconclusive.

NAŁKOWSKA. I. Kaluta, 'Pisać Nałkowską', *TD*, nos.1–2:189–210.

SCHULZ. Jerzy Jarzębski, *Schulz*, Ww, Wyd. Dolnośląskie, 243 pp. R. Lachmann, 'Demiurg i jego fantazmaty. Spekulacje wokół mitologii stworzenia w dziele Bruno [*sic*] Schulza', *TD*, 103–19.

WAT. Krystyna Pietrych, *O wierszach śródziemnomorskich Aleksandra Wata* (Rozprawy literackie, 77), IBL, 183 pp. Józef Olejniczak, *\*Wtajemniczanie — Aleksander Wat (PNUS*, 1,797), 289 pp.

WITKACY. J. Błoński, 'Estetyka Witkacego. Kilka uwag', *TD*, 3:45–53. K. Obremski, 'Witkacy Arystotelesem "podszyty" *Mimesis* i Czysta Forma', ibid., no.6:139–47. A. Pastuszek, 'Witkacy: ucieczka od absurdu jako pogoń za nim', *Filozofia*, 33, 1998:65–73. P. Rudzki, '*W małym dworku* Stanisława Ignacego Witkiewicza a *W małym domku* Tadeusza Rittera — analiza porównawcza', *PrLit*, 36, 1998:105–21.

WYSZOMIRSKI. T. Śmigielski, 'Między Wilnem i Łodzią. O życiu i twórczości Jerzego Wyszomirskiego (1897–1955)', *PP*, 1998, 53:180–209.

## 6. 1945 TO THE PRESENT DAY

*Literatura polska XX wieku: przewodnik encyklopedyczny, T. 1: A-O*, ed. Artur Hutnikiewicz and Andrzej Lam, PWN, 496 pp. *\*Współcześni polscy pisarze i badacze literatury: słownikencyklopedyczny. Tom 6: N-P*, ed. Jadwiga Czachowska and Alicja Szałagan, WSiP, 555 pp. Agnieszka Czyżak, *Życiorysy polskie. 1944–1989*, Pń, Abedik, 1997, 174 pp., is an interesting investigation of the relations between writers' biographies and their work, which concludes with chapters on I. Newerley,

K. Brandys and W. Myśliwski. Andrzej Fabianowski, *Konwicki, Odojewski i romantycy. Projekt interpretacji intertekstualnych*, Kw, Universitas, 284 pp., commences from an analysis of the field, before examining K. and O.'s views of the Romantics, and then examines their work under the categories of Man, Love, Knowledge, God, and Nations and History. Zygmunt Ziątek, *Wiek dokumentu*, IBL, 224 pp., explores the relationship between documentary work and fiction in chapters devoted to Myśliwski, T. Borowski, H. Krall and R. Kapuściński, Newerley, and Z. Kruszyński and O. Tokarczuk.

Anna Legeżyńska, *Gest pożegnania* (Poznańskie studia polonistyczne, 17), Pń, Abedik, 192 pp., considers valedictory poems by Iwaszkiewicz, Białoszewski, Herbert, Różewicz, E. Lipska, and S. Barańczak. Arendt van Nieukerken, *Ironiczny konceptyzm. Nowoczesna polska poezja metafizyczna*, Kw, Universitas, 1998, 422 pp., examines Polish writers such as Szymborska, Barańczak, Herbert and Miłosz in relation to the Anglo-American context of metaphysical poetry. Dariusz Pawelec, *Debiuty i powroty. Czytanie w czasie przełomu*, Katowice, Agencja Artystyczna PARA, 1998, 206 pp., examines the poetry of Miłosz, Barańczak, the poetry of Martial Law and the latter half of the 1980s. A different *przełom* is marked in E. Balcerzan's 'W stronę genologii multimedialnej', *TD*, no.6:7–24, which examines the impact of multimedia on form, with particular reference to the work of Szymborska and Barańczak.

*O dialogu kultur wspólnot kresowych*, ed. Stanisław Uliasz, Rzeszów, WSP, 1998, 366 pp., has essays on Vincenz, T. Konwicki, S. Piasecki, Odojewski, A. Rudnicki, Kuśniewicz, and W. Mach, by G. Ritz, J. Arlt, and others. Ewa Wiegandt, *Austria Felix, czyli o micie Galicji w polskiej prozie współczesnej*, Pń, Bene Nati, 1997, 253 pp., contains an account of the functioning of the myth of Galicia in works by Kuśniewicz, Stryjkowski, Odojewski, A. Stojowski, and L. Buczkowski in the third chapter devoted to private mythologies, while other chapters consider the myth as Arcadian, as cultural metatext, and in relation to war.

A number of works have appeared concerning the relations between politics and literature. The most general and novel of these is Carl Tighe, *The Politics of Literature*, Cardiff, University of Wales Press, 412 pp., a sociological approach, which deals with seven writers united by their criticism of the Communist regime: Andrzejewski, J. Kott, S. Lem, K. Brandys, T. Konwicki, R. Kapuściński, and A. Michnik. As ever, more attention has been paid to Socialist Realism. Zbigniew Jarosiński, *Nadwiślański socrealizm*, IBL, 328 pp., consists of two parts: accounts of major features of the period in Part I, while Part II, containing some previously published essays, details individual cases, such as corrected versions of Socialist Realist

works and children's literature. Wojciech Tomasik, *Inżynieria dusz.*
*Literatura realizmu socjalistycznego w planie 'propagandy monumentalnej'*, Ww,
Leopoldinum, 219 pp + 20 pls, an intriguing collection of six essays,
mainly considers the interconnections between architecture and
literature. Mariusz Zawodniak, *Literatura w stanie oskarżenia. Rola krytyki*
*w życiu literackim socrealizmu*, Wa, Upowszechnianie Nauki — Oświata
'UN-O', 1998, 136 pp., is a thorough analysis of the forms of criticism
practised in the early 1950s, from the mechanism of self-criticism,
through 'corrected' second editions, to denunciations of such figures
as Miłosz and K. I. Gałczyński. Grzegorz Wołowiec, *Nowocześni w*
*PRL. Przyboś i Sandauer*, Ww, Leopoldinum, 291 pp., an important
new study, examines the paths of the outstanding poet and critic from
their interwar avantgardism to the Socialist Realist project. *Październik*
*56. Odwilż i przełom w życiu literackim i kulturalnym Polski*, ed. Adam
Kulawik, Kw, Antykwa, 1996, 301 pp., contains contributions to a
session held on 23–25 September 1996 by leading scholars from
within and outwith Poland, on individual writers such as Andrzejewski and Stryjkowski.

CanSS, nos. 2–4, contains two essays on the reception of postwar
émigré literature in Poland: M. Czermińska, 'The reception of Polish
émigré writing in Poland' (179–89) and J. Bates, 'Making approaches:
Official attitudes and practice in People's Poland towards Polish
émigré literature after 1956' (191–213). A. Mirosław, 'The achievements and perspectives of Polish émigré bibliography after 1939 (an
overview of issues)', *Solanus*, 13:44–59. E. Chuchro, 'Czasopisma
drugiego obiegu lat 1981–1989 — pytanie o tożsamośćkultury', *PP*,
1998, 53:221–43.

Karol Maliszewski, *Nasi klasycyści, nasi barbarzyńscy. Szkice o nowej*
*poezji*, Bydgoszcz, Instytut Wydawniczy Świadectwo, 174 pp. P. Czapliński, 'Wznoszenie autobiografii — proza polska lat dziewięćdziesiątych w poszukiwaniu utraconego czasu', *TD*, no.3:55–76.
M. Hamkało, 'Prywatny romantyzm. O tradycji w wierszach debiut-
antów początku lat dziewięćdziesiątych', *PrLit*, 36, 1998:171–90,
examines this theme in relation to A. Sosnowski and M. Swietlicki's
work. J. Orska's 'Polska i świat. Nowojorskie historie i nowa poezja
polska', *TD*, no.5:53–70, examines the influence of O'Hara and
Ashbery on contemporary poets, such as M. Stala and B. Zadura.

## INDIVIDUAL WRITERS

BARAŃCZAK.  Joanna Dembińska-Pawelec, *Światy możliwe w poezji*
*Stanisława Barańczaka*, Katowice, Wyd. Uniwersytetu Śląskiego,
165 pp. *Barańczak — poeta lector* (Poznańskie studia polonistyczne.
Seria literacka), ed. Barbara Judkowiak, Anna Legeżyńska and

Barbara Sienkiewicz, Pń, Abedik, 319 pp., contains essays on B.'s own poetry as well as translations done by him. A. Hejmej, 'Słuchać i czytać: dwa źródła jednej strategii interpretacyjnej. *Podróż zimowa* Stanisława Barańczaka', *PL(W)*, 90.2:67–94, an intriguing intersemiotic and intertextual play of the cycle, compares it with F. Schubert and W. Müller's texts.

BIAŁOSZEWSKI. Jarosław Fazan, *'Ale Ja nie Bóg.' Kontemplacja i teatr w dziele Mirona Białoszewskiego*, Kw, Universitas, 1998, 197 pp. Romuald Cudak, *Czytając Białoszewskiego*, Katowice, Śląsk, 316 pp., consists of a general academic introduction followed by interpretations of specific poems. Anna Sobolewska, *Maksymalnie udana egzystencja. Szkice o życiu i twórczości Mirona Białoszewskiego*, IBL, 1997, 127 pp. W. Jajdejski, 'Symbolika czystości i brudu w twórczości szpitalnej Mirona Białoszewskiego', *PL(W)*, 90.3:95–106.

K. BRANDYS. M. Wołk, 'Autotekstualność i pierwsza osoba. Przypadek *Nierzeczywistości* i *Ronda* Kazimierza Brandysa', *PL(W)*, 90.3:107–31.

BUCZKOWSKI. S. Buryła, 'Poza konwencją. Poszukiwania artystyczne w prozie Leopolda Buczkowskiego', *PL(W)*, 90.3:71–93.

CHCIUK. Bogumiła Żongołłowicz, *Andrzej Chciuk: Pisarz z antypodów*, WL, 222 pp. + 20 pls.

GROCHOWIAK. *Lektury Grochowiaka* (Poznańskie studia polonistyczne. Seria literacka), ed. Tomasz Mizerkiewicz and Agata Stankowska, Pń, Abedik, 208 pp., comprises new readings by S. Makowski, J. Grądziel, P. Czapliński, and others.

HERBERT. E. Węgłowska, 'Zbigniew Herbert i krytyka', *PrzH*, 43.5:103–19, is a highly useful overview of H.'s critical reception with a bibliography.

HERLING-GRUDZINSKI. A. Morawiec, 'Opowiadania Gustawa Herlinga-Grudzińskiego (Podstawowe zagadnienia genologiczne)', *ŻRL*, 42:125–39.

HUELLE. S. Gromadzki, *'Weiser Dawidek* jako powieść-poszukiwanie czyli o paradoksie książki nie napisanej', *PrzH*, 43.1:103–20.

KONWICKI. E. Możejko, 'Models of represented reality in the prose of Tadeusz Konwicki', *CanSP*, 39:487–94.

LUBKIEWICZ-URBANOWICZ. M. Sugiera, 'Leworęczna i wilkołak: "inny" w dramatach Lubkiewicz-Urbanowicz', *TD*, no.5:145–55, would appear to be the first scholarly article on the popular female radio dramatist from the first half of the 1970s.

MIŁOSZ. Jan Błoński, *Miłosz jak świat*, Kw, Znak, 1998, 239 pp., comprises mostly previously published pieces on the poet dating from the late 1950s onwards, and a new sketch, the title essay, which deals with M.'s work in the 1990s. *Periphery*, 1998–99, contains four substantial essays on M.: A. Fiut, 'Facing the river' (88–91), mostly on the recent work; J. Illg, ' "An invisible rope." ' Czesław Miłosz in the literary underground in Poland' (92–98); J. Błoński, 'Who is Miłosz?'; and Lillian Vallee, 'The exile in California' (102–04). B. Karnowska, 'Czesław Miłosz's self-presentation in English-speaking countries', *CanSP*, 40:273–95. E. Kiślak, 'Dialog w maskach', *TD*, no.3:131–49, considers M.'s *Trzy zimy*. D. Kozińska, 'Inspiracje filozoficzne poezji Czesława Miłosza. Czas i światopogląd', *PrLit*, 36, 1998:151–70.

MROZEK. *Mrożek w Gdańsku*, ed. J. Ciechowicz, Gdańsk U.P., 1998, 69 pp., includes essays on M. as parodist, philosopher and artist.

MYŚLIWSKI. A. Lubaszenka's ' "W daguerotyp raczej pióro zamieniam" ', *TD*, no.4:165–83, on the relations between literature and photography, deals largely with M.'s novel *Widnokrąg*.

RÓŻEWICZ. *PL(W)*, 90.1, has six essays devoted to aspects of R.'s work, generally placing him in his European context: K. Klosiński, 'Imię Róży' (5–20); J. Ward, 'Thomas Stearns Eliot w twórczości poetyckiej Tadeusza Różewicza' (21–46); R. Cieślak, 'Próba nowej całości. *Opowiadania dydaktyczne* Tadeusza Różewicza wobec sztuk wizualnych' (47–64); A. Ubertowska, 'Przygodność wiersza i istotność poezji. O motywach goetheańskich w twórczości Różewicza' (65–74); L. Wiśniewska, 'W centrum *Białego małżeństwa* Tadeusza Różewicza' (75–116); T. Zukowski, 'Skatalogiczny Chrystus. Wokół Różewiczowskiej epifanii' (117–31).

RYMKIEWICZ. Adam Poprawa, *Kultura i egzystencja w poezji Jarosława Marka Rymkiewicza*, WUW, 140 pp.; and his 'Anioł i nicpoń. Kreacja poety w wierszach Jarosława Marka Rymkiewicza', *PrLit*, 36, 1998:131–49.

SŁUCKI. Sławomir Jacek Żurek, ' . . . *lotny trud półistnienia.*' *O motywach judaistycznych w poezji Arnolda Słuckiego*, Kw, Księgarnia Akademicka, 204 pp., appears to be the first substantial monograph on the author.

SZYMBORSKA. J. Brodal, 'Wisława Szymborska — poet in evolution', *ScSl*, 45:35–48, is an overview of the poet's development.

TWARDOWSKI. A. Mazan, 'Z tajników warsztatu artystycznego Jana Twardowskiego', *PP*, 1998, 53:244–68.

TYRMAND. Ryszard K. Przybylski, *O tym jak Leopold Tyrmand wałęsał się w świecie kultury popularnej* (Poznańskie studia polonistyczne, 14), Pń, Abedik, 1998, 181 pp.

VINCENZ. P. Nowaczyński, 'Vincenz — filozof dziejów', *TD*, no.3:103–19; J. Wolski, 'Adalbert Stifter — Stanisław Vincenz', ibid.:121–29.

WAŃKOWICZ. Aleksandra Ziółkowska-Boehm, *Na tropach Wańkowicza*, Wa, Prószyński i S-ka, 364 pp.

ZAGAJEWSKI.  Z. Ziątek, 'Trzecie miasto Adama Zagajewskiego',
*TD*, no.4 : 155–64, examines Z.'s views of Cracow.

# IV.  RUSSIAN STUDIES

## LANGUAGE
POSTPONED

## LITERATURE TO 1700
POSTPONED

## LITERATURE 1700–1820
POSTPONED

## LITERATURE 1820–1800
POSTPONED

## LITERATURE 1880–1917
POSTPONED

## LITERATURE 1917 TO THE PRESENT DAY
POSTPONED

# V.  UKRAINIAN STUDIES
POSTPONED

# VI.  BELARUSIAN STUDIES
POSTPONED

# VII.  SERBO-CROAT STUDIES

## LANGUAGE
POSTPONED

## LITERATURE
POSTPONED

# VIII.  BULGARIAN STUDIES
POSTPONED

# ABBREVIATIONS

## I. ACTA, FESTSCHRIFTEN AND OTHER COLLECTIVE AND GENERAL WORKS

*Actas* (APL 1996): *Actas do XIIé Encontro Nacional da Associação Portuguesa de Linguística (Braga-Guimarães, 30 de Setembro a 2 de Outubro de 1996)*, I. *Linguística*, II. *Linguística Histórica e História da Linguística*, ed. Ivo Castro, 2 vols, Lisbon, Associação Portuguesa de Linguística, 1997, 355, 625 pp.

*Actas* (Birmingham), I: *Actas del XII Congreso Internacional de Hispanistas (Birmingham, 21–26 de agosto de 1995)*. I. *Medieval y lingüística*, ed. Aengus Ward, Birmingham, Department of Hispanic Studies, xiii + 359 pp.

*Actas* (Birmingham), IV: *Actas del XII Congreso Internacional de Hispanistas (Birmingham, 21–26 de agosto de 1995)*. IV. *Del romanticismo a la guerra civil*, ed. Derek Flitter, Birmingham, Department of Hispanic Studies, xiii + 301 pp.

*Actas* (Corunna): *Edición y anotación de textos. Actas del I Congreso de Jóvenes Filólogos (A Coruña, 25–28 de septiembre de 1996)*, ed. C. Parrilla et al., 2 vols, Corunna U.P., 350, 381 pp.

*Actes* (Barcelona): *Actes del Congrés Europeu sobre Planificació Lingüística, Barcelona, 9 i 10 de novembre de 1995*, Barcelona, Institut de Sociolingüística Catalana–Generalitat de Catalunya, Departament de Cultura, 1997, 430 pp.

*Actes* (Jyväskylä): *Actes du XIIIe Congrès des Romanistes scandinaves I*, ed. Outi Merisalo and Teija Natri, 2 vols, Jyväskylä, University of Jyväskylä, 1998, 415, 416–845 pp.

*Actes* (Spa): *Les niveaux de vie au Moyen Âge. Actes du colloque international de Spa 21–25 octobre 1998*, ed. Jean-Pierre Sosson et al., Louvain-la-Neuve, Academia–Bruylant, 462 pp.

*AHLM 7: Actes del VII Congrés de l'Associació Hispànica de Literatura Medieval (Castelló de la Plana, 1997)*, ed. S. Ortuño and T. Martínez, 3 vols, Castelló de la Plana, Univ. Jaume I, 446, 480, 502 pp.

*Alarcos Vol.: Homenaje al profesor Emilio Alarcos García en el centenario de su nacimiento, 1895–1995*, ed. Cesar Hernández Alonso, Valladolid, 1998.

*Aleza, Estudios: Estudios de historia de la lengua española en América y España*, ed. Milagros Aleza Izquierdo, Valencia, Departamento de filología española, Univ. de València, 288 pp.

*ALFAL 11: Actas del XI congreso internacional de la Asociación de Lingüística y Filología de la América Latina, Las Palmas de Gran Canaria, del 22 al 27 de julio de 1996*, ed. José Antonio Samper Padilla and Magnolia Troya Déniz, 3 vols, Las Palmas, Servicio de Publicaciones de la Universidad de Gran Canaria, vol. I, 844 pp.

*Alonso Montero Vol.: Cinguidos por unha arela común. Homenaxe a Xesús Alonso Montero*, ed. R. Álvarez and Dolores Vilavedra, 2 vols, Santiago de Compostela U.P., 1377, 1649 pp.

*APL 14: Actas do XIV Encontro Nacional da Associação Portuguesa de Linguística (Aveiro, 28–30 de Setembro de 1998)*, ed. A. C. M. Lopes and Cristina Martins, 2 vols, Braga, APL, 614, 634 pp.

*Atti* (Milan): *Sogno e scrittura nelle culture iberiche. Atti del XVII Convegno, Associazione Ispanisti Italiani, Milano 1996*, vol. I, Rome, Bulzoni, 1998, 456 pp.

*Atti* (Palermo): *Atti del XXI Congresso Internazionale di Linguistica e Filologia Romanza (Palermo, 18–24 settembre 1995)*, ed. Giovanni Ruffino, 6 vols, I. *Grammatica storica delle lingue romanze;* II. *Morfologia e sintassi delle lingue romanze;* III. *Lessicologia e semantica delle lingue romanze;* IV. *Le strutture del parlato - Storia linguistica e culturale del Mediterraneo;* V. *Dialettologia, geolinguistica, sociolinguistica;* VI. *Edizione e analisi linguistica dei testi letterari e documentari del Medioevo — Paradigmi interpretativi della cultura medievale*, Tübingen, Niemeyer, xviii + 494, xii + 940, xii + 1032, xi + 627, xi + 813, xi + 825 pp.

*Axeitos, Exilio: 'Sesenta años después. Actas I'. Os escritores do exilio republicano*, ed. X. L. Axeitos and C. Portela,

*Baum Vol.: Kunst und Kommunikation. Betrachtungen zum Medium Sprache in der Romania. Festschrift zum 60. Geburtstag von Richard Baum,* ed. Maria Lieber and Willi Hirdt, Tübingen, Stauffenburg, 1997, xvi + 554 pp.

Béhar, *Spectaculum: Spectaculum Europeae. Theatre and Spectacle in Europe / Histoire du spectacle en Europe (1580–1750),* ed. Pierre Béhar and Helen Watanabe-O'Kelly (Wolfenbuetteler Arbeiten zur Barockforschung, 31), Wiesbaden, Harrassowitz, x + 818 pp.

Bennewitz, *Konstruktion: Manlîchiu wîp, wîplîch man. Zur Konstruktion der Kategorien 'Körper' und 'Geschlecht' in der deutschen Literatur des Mittelalters. (Internationales Kolloquium der Oswald von Wolkenstein-Gesellschaft und der Gerhard-Mercator-Universität Duisburg, Xanten 1997),* ed. Ingrid Bennewitz and Helmut Tervooren (*Zeitschrift für deutsche Philologie,* Beihefte, 9), Berlin, Schmidt, 375 pp.

*Besch Vol.: Das Frühneuhochdeutsche als sprachgeschichtliche Epoche. Werner Besch zum 70. Geburtstag,* ed. Walter Hoffmann, Jürgen Macha, Klaus J. Mattheier, Hans-Joachim Solms, and Klaus-Peter Wegera, Frankfurt am Main, Lang, 294 pp.

Billy, *Onomastique: Onomastique et histoire / Onomastique litteraire. Actes du VIIIe Colloque de la Société Française d'Onomastique (Aix-en-Provence le 26–29 octobre 1994),* ed. Pierre-Henri Billy and Jacques Chaurand, Aix-en-Provence U.P., 1998, iii + 386 pp.

Black, *Clitics: Clitics, Pronouns and Movement,* ed. James Black and Virginia Motapanyane, Amsterdam–Philadelphia, Benjamins, 1997, 375 pp.

Blackmore, *Queer Iberia: Queer Iberia. Sexualities, Cultures, and Crossings from the Middle Ages to the Renaissance,* ed. J. Blackmore and G. S. Hutchenson, Duke U.P., 478 pp.

Blecua, *Grafemática: Estudios de grafemática en el dominio hispánico,* ed. José Manuel Blecua, Juan Gutiérrez, and Lidia Sala, Salamanca U.P.–Bogotá, Instituto Caro y Cuervo, 1998.

Boitani, *Produzione: Lo spazio letterario del Medioevo, 2: Il Medioevo volgare, 1: La produzione del testo,* ed. Piero Boitani, Mario Mancini, and Alberto Varvaro, vol. I, Rome, Salerno, 745 pp.

Botta, *Inês: Inês de Castro. Studi. Estudos. Estudios,* ed. P. Botta, Ravenna, Longo–Rome, Facoltà di Lettere dell'Università di Roma 'La Sapienza'–Lisbon, Instituto Camões, 389 pp.

Brunner, *Krieg: Der Krieg im Mittelalter und in der Frühen Neuzeit: Gründe, Begründungen, Bilder, Bräuche, Recht,* ed. Horst Brunner (Imagines medii aevi, 3), Wiesbaden, Reichert, xix + 454 pp.

Canavaggio, *Novela: La invención de la novela,* ed. Jean Canavaggio, Madrid, ·Casa de Velázquez, 211 pp.

Cardinale, *Insegnare italiano: Insegnare italiano nella scuola del 2000. Atti del convegno internazionale, Trieste, 7–9 novembre 1996,* ed. Ugo Cardinale, Padua, Unipress, 367 pp.

*Chant et Enchantement: Chant et Enchantement au Moyen Age. Travaux du Groupe de Recherches 'Lectures Médiévales', Université de Toulouse II* (Collection Moyen Age), Toulouse, Editions Universitaires du Sud, 1997, 235 pp.

Chemello, *Parole scolpite: Parole scolpite: profili di scrittrici degli anni Novanta,* ed. Adriana Chemello, Padua, Il Poligrafo, 134 pp.

*CHLE 4: Actas del IV Congreso Internacional de Historia de la Lengua Española,* ed. Claudio García Turza, Faian González Bachiller, and Javier Mangado Martínez, 2 vols, Logroño, Asociación de Historia de la Lengua Española, 1998, 910, 973 pp.

*CIEG 4, 1: Proceedings of the 4th International Conference on Galician Studies (Univ. of Oxford, 1994). Actas do IV Congreso Internacional de Estudios Galegos (Univ. de Oxford, 1994). 1. Language. Lingua,* ed. B. Fernández Salgado, Oxford, Centre for Galician Studies, 1997, 000 pp.

*CIEG 5: Actas do V Congreso Internacional de Estudios Galegos. Akten des 5. Internationalen Kongresses für Galicische Studien,* ed. D. Kremer, 2 vols, Trier, Galicien Zentrum der Universität Trier — O Castro, 557, 1181 pp.

*Colón Vol.: Estudios de lingüística y filología españolas. Homenaje a Germán Colón,* Madrid, Gredos, 1998, 468 pp.

Cox, *Virgil:* Fiona Cox, *Aeneas Takes the Metro: The Presence of Virgil in Twentieth-Century French Literature,* Oxford, Legenda, 228 pp.

Cramer, *Lyrik: Mittelalterliche Lyrik: Probleme der Poetik*, ed. Thomas Cramer and Ingrid Kasten (Philologische Studien und Quellen, 154), Berlin, Schmidt, 252 pp.

*CRISIMA 4: Le Sang au Moyen Âge: actes du quatrième colloque international de Montpellier Université Paul-Valéry (27–29 novembre 1997)*, ed. Marcel Faure (Cahiers du CRISIMA, 4), 476 pp.

Crosta, *Récits: Récits de vie de l'Afrique et des Antilles. Exil, errance, enracinement*, ed. Suzanne Crosta (GRELCA, collection 'essais'), Laval U.P., 1998, 238 pp.

Dagen, *Épicure: Entre Épicure et Vauvenargues: principes et formes de la pensée morale*, ed. Jean Dagen (Moralia, 1), Paris, Champion, 442 pp.

Dagen, *Morale: La Morale des moralistes*, ed. Jean Dagen (Moralia, 2), Paris, Champion, 244 pp.

Debaisieux, *Violence: Violence et fiction jusqu'à la Révolution*, ed. Martine Debaisieux and Gabrielle Verdier (ELF, 660), Tübingen, Narr, 1998, 480 pp.

Díez de Revenga, *Tres poetas: Tres poetas, tres amigos. Estudios sobre Vicente Aleixandre, Federico García Lorca y Dámaso Alonso*, ed. Francisco Javier Díez de Revenga and Mariano de Paco, Murcia, CajaMurcia, Obra Cultural, 348 pp.

Dionisotti, *Ricordi:* Carlo Dionisotti, *Ricordi della scuola italiana*, Rome, Edizioni di Storia e Letteratura, 1998, 620 pp.

Edwards, *Ebwy: Ebwy, Rhymni a Sirhywi*, ed. Hywel Teifi Edwards, Llandysul, Gomer, 240 pp.

*Eustis Vol.: Le Labyrinthe de Versailles: parcours critiques de Molière à La Fontaine, à la mémoire d'Alvin Eustis*, ed. Martine Debaisieux (Faux Titre, 147), Amsterdam–Atlanta, GA, Rodopi, 1998, 215 pp.

Fernández, *Estudios: Estudios de sociolingüística románica. Linguas e variedades minorizadas*, ed. F. Fernández Rei and A. Santamarina Fernández, Santiago de Compostela U.P., 512 pp.

*Fest. Brackert: Der fremdgewordene Text. Festschrift für Helmut Brackert zum 65. Geburtstag*, ed. Silvia Bovenschen, Winfried Frey, Stephan Fuchs, Walter Raitz, and Dieter Seitz, Berlin, de Gruyter, 1997, x + 476 pp.

*Fest. Eroms: Deutsche Grammatik — Thema in Variationen. Festschrift für Hans-Werner Eroms zum 60. Geburtstag*, ed. Karin Donhauser and Ludwig M. Eichinger, Heidelberg, Winter, 1998, 427 pp.

*Fest. Faucher: Rand und Band. Abgrenzung und Verknüpfung als Grundtendenzen des Deutschen. Festschrift für Eugène Faucher zum 60. Geburtstag*, ed. René Métrich and Marcel Vuillaume (Eurogermanistik, 7), Tübingen, Narr, 339 pp.

*Fest. Haas: Homo Medietas. Aufsätze zu Religiosität, Literatur und Denkformen des Menschen vom Mittelalter bis in die Neuzeit. Festschrift für Alois Maria Haas zum 65. Geburtstag*, ed. Claudia Brinker-von der Heyde and Niklaus Largier, Berne, Lang, 703 pp.

*Fest. Koepke: Literatur und Geschichte. Festschrift für Wulf Koepke zum 70. Geburtstag*, ed. Karl Menges (Amsterdamer Publikationen zur Sprache und Literatur, 133), Amsterdam, Rodopi, 1998, 364 pp.

*Fest. Koopmann: 'In Spuren gehen . . .'. Festschrift für Helmut Koopmann*, ed. Andrea Bartl, Jürgen Eder, Harry Fröhlich, Klaus Dieter Post, and Ursula Regener, Tübingen, Niemeyer, 1998, xi + 515 pp.

*Fest. Krummacher: Traditionen der Lyrik. Festschrift für Hans-Henrik Krummacher*, ed. Wolfgang Düsing, Hans-Jürgen Schings, Stefan Trappen, and Gottfried Willems, Tübingen, Niemeyer, 1997, vi + 286 pp.

*Fest. Lämmert: Literaturwissenschaft und politische Kultur. Für Eberhard Lämmert zum 75. Geburtstag*, ed. Winfried Menninghaus and Klaus R. Scherpe, Stuttgart, Metzler, ix + 320 pp.

*Fest. Moser: Sprache — Kultur — Geschichte. Sprachhistorische Studien zum Deutschen. Hans Moser zum 60. Geburtstag*, ed. Maria Pümpel-Mader, Beatrix Schönherr, and Astrid Obernosterer (Innsbrucker Beiträge zur Kulturwissenschaft. Germanistische Reihe, 59), Innsbruck, Institut für Germanistik an der Universität Innsbruck, 474 pp.

*Fest. Pensel: Fata libellorum: Festschrift für Franzjosef Pensel zum 70. Geburtstag*, ed. Rudolf Bentzinger and Ulrich-Dieter Oppitz (Göppinger Arbeiten zur Germanistik, 648), Göppingen, Kümmerle, 348 pp.

*Fest. Rischbieter: Theater als Ort der Geschichte. Festschrift für Henning Rischbieter*, ed. Theo Girshausen and Henry Thorau, Velber, Friedrich, 1998, 400 pp.

*Fest. Schupp: 'Ze hove und an der strâzen.' Die deutsche Literatur des Mittelalters und ihr 'Sitz im Leben'. Festschrift für Volker Schupp zum 65. Geburtstag*, ed. Anna Keck and Theodor Nolte, Stuttgart–Leipzig, Hirzel, xiv + 351 pp.

*Fest. Steinsdorff: Schnittpunkt Romantik. Text- und Quellenstudien zur Literatur des 19. Jahrhunderts. Festschrift für Sibylle von Steinsdorff*, ed. Wolfgang Bunzel, Konrad Feilchenfeldt, and Walter Schmitz, Tübingen, Niemeyer, 1997, viii + 354 pp.

*Fest. Stellmacher: Sprachformen. Deutsch und Niederdeutsch in europäischen Bezügen. Festschrift für Dieter Stellmacher zum 60. Geburtstag*, ed. Peter Wagener (*Zeitschrift für Dialektologie und Linguistik*, Beihefte, 105), Stuttgart, Steiner, 374 pp.

*Fest. Storck: Korrespondenzen. Festschrift für Joachim W. Storck aus Anlaß seines 75. Geburtstages*, ed. Rudi Schweikert and Sabine Schmidt (Mannheimer Studien zur Literatur- und Kulturwissenschaft, 20), St. Ingbert, Röhrig, 719 pp.

*Fest. Szulc: Vielfalt der Sprachen. Festschrift für Aleksander Szulc zum 75. Geburtstag*, ed. Maria Kłańska and Peter Wiesinger, Vienna, Praesens, 529 pp.

*Fest. Tatzreiter: Beharrsamkeit und Wandel. Festschrift für Herbert Tatzreiter zum 60. Geburtstag*, ed. Werner Bauer and Hermann Scheuringer, Vienna, Praesens, 1998, 355 pp.

*Fest. Thavenius: Skeptiska betraktelser* [Festskrift till Jan Thavenius], ed. Lars Gustaf Andersson et al. (Absalon, 17), SLILU, 219 pp.

*Fest. Walliczek: 'helle döne schöne.' Versammelte Arbeiten zur älteren und neueren deutschen Literatur. Festschrift für Wolfgang Walliczek*, ed. Horst Brunner, Claudia Händl, Ernst Hellgardt, and Monika Schulz (Göppinger Arbeiten zur Germanistik, 668), Göppingen, Kümmerle, v + 453 pp.

*Fest. Weydt: Particulae particularum. Festschrift zum 60. Geburtstag von Harald Weydt*, ed. Theo Harden and Elke Hentschel (Stauffenburg-Festschriften, 5), Tübingen, Stauffenburg, 1998, viii + 402 pp.

*Fest. Wiesinger: Deutsche Sprache in Raum und Zeit. Festschrift für Peter Wiesinger zum 60. Geburtstag*, ed. Peter Ernst and Franz Patocka, Vienna, Praesens, 1998, 714 pp.

*Fest. Wunderli: Et multum et multa. Festschrift für Peter Wunderli*, ed. Edeltraud Werner, Ricarda Liver, Yvonne Stork, and Martina Nicklaus, Tübingen, Narr, 1998, xii + 447 pp.

*Fest. Ziolkowski: Themes and Structures. Studies in German Literature from Goethe to the Present.* [A Festschrift for Theodore Ziolkowski], ed. Alexander Stephan, Columbia, SC, Camden House, 1997, 331 pp.

Fichtner, *Doppelgänger: Doppelgänger. Von endlosen Spielarten eines Phänomens*, ed. Ingrid Fichtner (Facetten der Literatur, 7), Berne, Haupt, ix + 269 pp.

Fisiak, *Reconstruction: Linguistic Reconstruction and Typology*, ed. Jacek Fisiak (Trends in Linguistics, Studies and Monographs, 96), Berlin–New York, Mouton de Gruyter, 1997, x + 368 pp.

*Flores Vol.: Homenaxe ó profesor Camilo Flores*, ed. X. L. Couceiro et al., 2 vols, Santiago de Compostela U.P., 479, 746 pp.

*Fourquet Vol.: Littérature épique au Moyen Age: hommage à Jean Fourquet pour son 100ème anniversaire*, ed. Danielle Buschinger, Griefswald, Reineke, 409 pp.

Fumaroli, *Rhétorique: Histoire de la Rhétorique dans l'Europe moderne 1450–1950*, ed. Marc Fumaroli, Paris, PUF, 1359 pp.

Furuland, *Syndikalismen:* Lars Furuland et al., *Arbetarförfattarna och syndikalismen*, Stockholm, Federativs, 167 pp.

*Gallagher Vol.: A Lifetime's Reading. Hispanic Essays for Patrick Gallagher*, ed. Don W. Cruickshank, Dublin, University College Dublin Press, 229 pp.

Goebl, *Kontaktlinguistik: Kontaktlinguistik/Contact Linguistics/Linguistique de contact, Kontaktlinguistik/Contact Linguistics/Linguistique de contact*, ed. Hans Goebl, Peter H. Nelde, Zdeněk Starý, and Wolfgang Wölck, Vol. 1, Berlin–New York, de Gruyter, 1996, xxxix + 936 pp.

Glienke, *Metropolis:* Bernhard Glienke, *Metropolis un nordische Moderne. Großstadtthematik als Herausforderung literarischer Innovationen in Skandinavien seit 1830*, ed. Annika Krummacher et al. (Beiträge zur Skandinavistik, 15), Frankfurt, Lang, 190 pp.

*Guenée Vol.: Saint-Denis et la Royauté. Études offertes à Bernard Guenée, Membre de l'Institut*, ed. Françoise Autrand, Claude Gauvard, and Jean-Marie Moeglin (Histoire ancienne et médiévale, 59), Paris, Publications de la Sorbonne, 814 pp.

Guijarro, *Humanismo: Humanismo y literatura en tiempos de Juan del Encina*, ed. J. Guijarro, prol. P. M. Cátedra, Salamanca U.P., 446 pp.

Gutiérrez-Rexach, *Advances: Advances in Hispanic Linguistics. Papers from the 2nd Hispanic Linguistics Symposium*, ed. Javier Gutiérrez-Rexach and Fernando Martínez-Gil, 2 vols, Sommerville NJ, Cascadilla Press, xiv + 1–300, 303–578 pp.

Haas, *Frauen: Schwierige Frauen — schwierige Männer in der Literatur des Mittelalters*, ed. Alois M. Haas and Ingrid Kasten, Berne, Lang, 326 pp.

Haigh, *Caribbean Francophone Writing: An Introduction to Caribbean Francophone Writing. Guadeloupe and Martinique*, ed. Sam Haigh, Oxford, Berg, vii + 230 pp.

Hansson, *Årans hospital:* Gunnar D. Hansson, *Årans hospital. Valfrändskpaper, tolkningar, essäer, småstycken, anmälningar*, Stockholm, Bonniers, 404 pp.

Hassler, *Kontinuität: Kontinuität und Innovation. Studien zur Geschichte der romanischen Sprachforschung vom 17. bis zum 19. Jahrhundert*, ed. Gerda Hassler and Jürgen Storost, Münster, Nodus, 334 pp.

Haug, *Mittelalter: Mittelalter und frühe Neuzeit. Übergänge, Umbrüche und Neuansätze*, ed. Walter Haug (Fortuna Vitrea, 16), Tübingen, Niemeyer, ix + 585 pp.

Heinz, *Keltologie: Die Deutsche Keltologie und ihre Berliner Gelehrten bis 1945. Beiträge zur internationalen Fachtagung 'Keltologie an der Friedrich-Wilhelms-Universität vor und während des Nationalsozialismus' vom 27.–28.03.1998 an der Humboldt-Universität zu Berlin*, ed. Sabine Heinz, Frankfurt am Main, Lang, 292 pp.

Heydebrand, *Kanonbildung: Kanon-Macht-Kultur: Theoretische, historische und soziale Aspekte ästhetischer Kanonbildung*, ed. Renate von Heydebrand (Germanistische Symposien, 9), Stuttgart, Metzler, 1998, xvi + 648 pp.

Heyndels, *L'Autre: L'Autre au XVIIème siècle. Actes du 4e colloque du Centre International de rencontres sur le XVIIe siècle, Université de Miami 23 au 25 avril 1998*, ed. Ralph Heyndels and Barbara Woshinsky (Biblio 17, 117), Tübingen, Narr, 451 pp.

*Hipp Vol.: Grandeur et servitude au siècle de Louis XIV: journée d'étude à la mémoire de Marie-Thérèse Hipp, 27 novembre 1997*, ed. Roger Marchal (Collection Publications du Centre d'Étude des Milieux Littéraires, 1), Nancy U.P., 106 pp.

Holtus, *Lexikon*, VII: *Lexikon der Romanistischen Linguistik*, VII. *Kontakt, Migration und Kunstsprachen. Kontrastivität, Klassifikation und Typologie. Langues en contact, langues des migrants et langues artificielles. Analyses contrastives, classification et typologie des langues romanes*, ed. Gunter Holtus, Michael Metzeltin, and Christian Schmitt, Tübingen, Niemeyer, 1998, xliii + 1085 pp.

Hulst, *Prosodic Systems: Word Prosodic Systems in the Languages of Europe*, ed. Harry van der Hulst (Empirical Approaches to Language Typology; Eurotyp, 20–4), Berlin–New York, Mouton de Gruyter, xxx + 1050 pp.

Hulst, *Syllable: The Syllable. Views and Facts*, ed. Harry van der Hulst and Nancy A. Ritter (Studies in Generative Grammar, 45), Berlin–New York, Mouton de Gruyter, xvii + 777 pp.

*ICCS 10*, I: *Celtic Connections. Proceedings of the 10th International Congress of Celtic Studies*, ed. Ronald Black, William Gillies, and Roibeard Ó Maolalaigh, vol. 1. *Language, Literature, History, Culture*, Edinburgh, Tuckwell Press, xxiv + 568 pp.

*ICOS 18: Onomastik. Akten des 18. Internationalen Kongresses für Namenforschung (Trier 12.–17. April 1993)*, ed. D. Kremer, vols III–IV, Tübingen, Niemeyer, vii + 299, vii + 330 pp.

*ICOS 19: Proceedings of the XIXth International Congress of Onomastic Sciences, Aberdeen, August 4–11, 1996*, ed. W. F. H. Nicolaisen, 3 vols, Department of English, University of Aberdeen, 1998, xviii + 356, vi + 402, vi + 405 pp.

*Jaeggli Vol.: Beyond Principles and Parameters. Essays in Memory of Osvaldo Jaeggli*, ed. Kyle Johnson and Ian Roberts (Studies in Natural Language and Linguistic Theory, 45), Dordrecht, Kluwer, vi + 648 pp.

Jenkins, *Gwnewch bopeth: 'Gwnewch bopeth yn Gymraeg': Yr Iaith Gymraeg a'i Pheuoedd 1801–1911*, ed. Geraint H. Jenkins, Cardiff, University of Wales Press, 598 pp.

Jürgens, *Exchanges: Mutual Exchanges: Sheffield-Münster Colloquium II*, ed. Dirk Jürgens, Frankfurt–Berlin, Lang, 418 pp.

Kavanagh, *Exchanges: Mutual Exchanges: Sheffield-Münster Colloquium I*, ed. R. J. Kavanagh, Frankfurt–Berlin, Lang, 334 pp.

Keller, *Schriftlichkeit: Schriftlichkeit und Lebenspraxis im Mittelalter. Erfassen, Bewahren, Verändern. (Akten des Internationalen Kolloquiums 8.–10. Juni 1995)*, ed. Hagen Keller, Christel Meier, and Thomas Scharff (Münstersche Mittelalter-Schriften, 76), Munich, Fink, ix + 361 pp. + 21 pls.

Kemenade, *Parameters: Parameters of Morphosyntactic Change*, ed. Ans van Kemenade and Nigel Vincent, Cambridge University Press, 1997, viii + 544 pp.

*Koerner Vol.*, II: *The Emergence of the Modern Language Sciences. Studies on the Transition from Historical-Comparative to Structural Linguistics in Honour of E. F. K. Koerner*. Vol. II. *Methodological Perspectives and Applications*, ed. Sheila Embleton, John E. Joseph, and Hans-Josef Niederehe, Amsterdam, Benjamins, lv + 335 pp.

Kooper, *Chronicle: The Medieval Chronicle. Proceedings of the 1st International Conference on the Medieval Chronicle Driebergen/Utrecht 13–16 July 1996*, ed. Erik Kooper (Costerus, n.s., 120), Amsterdam–Atlanta, vi + 299 pp.

Krause, *Verleiblichungen: Verleiblichungen. Literatur- und kulturgeschichtliche Studien über Strategien, Formen und Funktionen der Verleiblichung in Texten von der Frühzeit bis zum Cyberspace*, ed. Burkhardt Krause and Ulrich Scheck (Mannheimer Studien zur Literatur- und Kulturwissenschaft, 7), St. Ingbert, Röhrig, 1996, 273 pp.

Kronegger, *Esthétique: Esthétique baroque et imagination créatrice. Colloque de Cérisy–la Salle (June 1991)*, ed. Marlies Kronegger (Biblio 17, 110), Tübingen, Narr, 1998, ix + 296 pp.

*Latin vulgaire V: Latin vulgaire — latin tardif V. Actes du Ve Colloque international sur le latin vulgaire et tardif, Heidelberg, 5–8 septembre 1997*, ed. Hubert Petersmann and Rudolf Kettemann, Heidelberg, Winter, xviii + 567 pp.

*Lepschy Vol: In amicizia. Essays in honour of Giulio Lepschy*, ed. Zygmunt Barański et al. (*The Italianist*, 17, special supp.), 1997, 536 pp.

Linde, *Svar:* Ulf Linde, *Svar*, ed. Lars Nygren, Stockholm, Bonniers, 285 pp.

*Lloyd Vol.: Essays in Hispanic Linguistics Dedicated to Paul Lloyd*, ed. Robert J. Blake, Diana L. Ranson, and Roger Wright (Juan de la Cuesta Hispanic Monographs; *Homenajes*, 14 / *Estudios lingüísticos*, 6), Newark, DE, Juan de la Cuesta, x + 258 pp.

Lorenzo, *Dinamización: Dinamización e normalización lingüística*, ed. A. M. Lorenzo Suárez, Vigo, U. P., 1997, 255 pp.

*Lorenzo Vol.: Homenaxe a Ramón Lorenzo*, ed. Dieter Kremer, Vigo, Galaxia, 2 vols, xxxvi + 547, 555–1138 pp.

*LSRL 28: Formal Perspectives on Romance Linguistics. Selected Papers from the 28th Linguistic Symposium on Romance Languages (LSRL, XXVIII), University Park, 16–19 April 1998*, ed. J.-Marc Authier, Barbara Bullock, and Lisa A. Reed (Current Issues in Linguistic Theory, 185), Amsterdam, Benjamins, xii + 333 pp.

Lutz, *Literatur: Mittelalterliche Literatur im Lebenszusammenhang. Ergebnisse des Troisième Cycle Romand 1994*, ed. Eckart Conrad Lutz (Scrinium Friburgense, 8), Fribourg U.P., 1997, 480 pp. + 19 pls.

Maninchedda, *Sardegna: La Sardegna e la presenza catalana nel Mediterraneo. Atti del VI congresso (III Internazionale) dell'Associazione Italiana di Studi Catalani*, ed. P. Maninchedda, 2 vols, Cagliari, Cooperativa Universitaria Editrice Cagliaritana, 1998, 581, 462 pp.

Martínez-Gil, *Issues: Issues in the Phonology and Morphology of the Major Iberian Languages*, ed. Fernando Martínez-Gil and Alfonso Morales-Front, Washington D.C., Georgetown University Press, 1997, xiv + 694 pp.

Marzys, *Variation:* Zygmunt Marzys, *La Variation et la Norme. Essais de dialectologie galloromane et d'histoire de la langue française*, Univ. of Neuchatel–Geneva, Droz, 1998, 296 pp.

*Mazzoni Vol.: Sotto il segno di Dante. Scritti in onore di Francesco Mazzoni*, ed. Leonella Coglievina and Domenico De Robertis, Florence, Le Lettere, 1998, xlviii + 367 pp.

*Mes Alpes à moi: Mes Alpes à moi. Civiltà storiche e comunità culturali delle Alpi. Atti del Convegno (dal 6 all'8 giugno 1996)*, ed. E. Cason Angelini, Belluno, Fondazione Angelini, 1998, 438 pp.

Müller, *Mittelalter: Mittelalter. Neue Wege durch einen alten Kontinent*, ed. Jan-Dirk Müller and Horst Wenzel, Stuttgart–Leipzig, 379 pp.

*NML 2: New Medieval Literatures, 2*, ed. Rita Copeland, David Lawton, and Wendy Scase, Oxford, Clarendon Press, 1998, viii + 282 pp.

*NML 3: New Medieval Literatures, 3*, ed. Rita Copeland, David Lawton, and Wendy Scase, Oxford, Clarendon Press, vi + 334 pp.

*Nykrog Vol.: The World and its Rival: Essays on Literary Imagination in Honor of Per Nykrog*, ed. Kathryn Karczewska and Tom Conley, Amsterdam, Rodopi, xxviii + 301 pp.

*Ouimette Vol.: Luz vital. Estudios de cultura hispánica en memoria de Victor Ouimette*, ed. Ramón F. Llorens and Jesús Pérez Magallón, McGill University, Dept of Hispanic Studies — Alicante, Caja de Ahorros del Mediterráneo, 227 pp.

*OWPLPP 4: Oxford Working Papers in Linguistics, Philology and Phonetics, no. 4*, ed. Rafaella Folli and Roberta Middleton, Oxford, Centre for Linguistics and Philology, 128 pp.

Palmer, *Kloster: Mittelalterliche Literatur und Kunst im Spannungsfeld von Hof und Kloster. Ergebnisse der Berliner Tagung, 9.–11. Oktober 1997*, ed. Nigel F. Palmer and Hans-Jochen Schiewer, Tübingen, Niemeyer, x + 239 pp.

Parrilla, *Estudios: Estudios sobre poesía de cancionero*, ed. C. Parrilla and J. I. Pérez Pascual, Noia, Toxosoutos, 135 pp.

Peil, *Erkennen: Erkennen und Erinnern in Kunst und Literatur. Kolloquium Reisensburg, 4.–7. Januar 1996*, ed. Dietmar Peil, Michael Schilling, Peter Strohschneider, and Wolfgang Frühwald, Tübingen, Niemeyer, 1998, ix + 675 pp.

Pfersmann, *Fondements: Fondements, évolutions et persistance des théories du roman*, ed. Andréas Pfersmann and Bernard Alazet (Études romanesques, 5), Paris–Caen, Lettres Modernes Minard, 1998, 322 pp.

Picone, *Dante: Dante, mito e poesia. Atti del II Seminario dantesco internazionale, Monte Vertià, Ascona, 23–27 giugno 1997*, ed. Michelangelo Picone and Tiziana Crivelli, Florence, Cesati, 460 pp.

Price, *Encyclopedia: Encyclopedia of the Languages of Europe*, ed. Glanville Price, Oxford, Blackwell, 1998, xviii + 499 pp.

Rafanell, *Estudis: Estudis de Filologia Catalana. Dotze anys de l'Institut de Llengua i Cultura Catalanes. Secció Francesc Eiximenis*, ed. A. Rafanell and P. Valsalobre, Montserrat, PAM, 358 pp.

*Rauch Vol.: Interdigitations. Essays for Irmengard Rauch*, ed. Gerald F. Carr, Wayne Harbert, and Lihua Zhang, New York. Lang, xxii + 762 pp.

Riemsdijk, *Clitics: Clitics in the Languages of Europe*, ed. Henk van Riemsdijk (Empirical Approaches to Language Typology; Eurotyp, 20–5), Berlin–New York, Mouton de Gruyter, xxii + 1026 pp.

Robertshaw, *Natur: Natur und Kultur in der deutschen Literatur des Mittelalters. Colloquium Exeter 1997*, ed. Alan Robertshaw, Gerhard Wolf, Frank Fürbeth, and Ulrike Zitzlsperger, Tübingen, Niemeyer, viii + 297 pp.

Rolfe, *Quebec: Focus on Quebec. Five Essays on Québécois Society and Culture*, ed. Christopher D. Rolfe, Edinburgh, GRECF, 63 pp.

*Rölleke Vol.: Romantik und Volksliteratur: Beiträge des Wuppertaler Kolloquiums zu Ehren von Heinz Rölleke*, ed. Lothar Bluhm and Achim Hölter (Beihefte zum Euphorion, 33), Heidelberg, Winter, viii + 214, pp.

Rovira, *Ciudad: Escrituras de la ciudad*, ed. José Carlos Rovira, Madrid, Palas Atenea, 282 pp.

Sala Di Felice, *Sardegna sabauda: Lingua e letteratura per la Sardegna sabauda. Tra ancien régime e restaurazione*, ed. Elena Sala Di Felice and Ines Loi Corvetto, Rome, Carocci, 144 pp.

*Saltarelli Vol.: Grammatical Analyses in Basque and Romance Linguistics. Papers in Honor of Mario Saltarelli*, ed. Jon Franco, Alazne Landa, and Juan Martín (Current Issues in Linguistic Theory, 187), Amsterdam, Benjamins, viii + 307 pp.

*Santiago-Otero Vol.: Pensamiento medieval hispano. Homenaje a Horacio Santiago-Otero*, ed. J. M. Soto, 2 vols, Madrid, CSIC–Junta de Castilla y León–Diputación de Zamora, 915, 1689 pp.

*Sarmiento: O Padre Sarmiento e o seu tempo. Actas do Congreso Internacional do Tricentenario de Fr.*
   *Martín Sarmiento (1695–1995)*, Santiago de Compostela, Consello da Cultura Galega–
   Universidade de Santiago de Compostela, 2 vols, 1997, 485, 464 pp.
*Sasso Vol.: Storia, filosofia e letteratura. Studi in onore di Gennaro Sasso*, ed. Marta Herling and
   Mario Reale, Naples, Bibliopolis, 1999, 919 pp.
Saul, *Schwellen: Schwellen Germanistiche Erkundungen einer Metapher*, ed. Nicholas Saul et al.,
   Würzburg, Königshausen & Neumann, 382 pp.
Schaefer, *Artes: 'Artes' im Mittelalter*, ed. Ursula Schaefer, Berlin, Akademie, x + 409 pp.
Schnitzer, *Maskeraden:* Claudia Schnitzer, *Höfische Maskeraden. Funktion und Ausstattung von
   Verkleidungsdivertissements an deutschen Höfen der Frühen Neuzeit* (Frühe Neuzeit, 53),
   Tübingen, Niemeyer, viii + 465 pp. + 318 pls.
Schwarz, *Text: Text im Kontext. Anleitung zur Lektüre deutscher Texte der frühen Neuzeit*, ed.
   Alexander Schwarz and Laure Abplanalp (Tausch, 9), Berne, Lang, 1997, 343 pp.
*SFLP 1: I Seminário de Filologia e Língua Portuguesa*, ed. Angela Cecília de Souza Rodrigues,
   Ieda Maria Alves, and Norma Selzer Goldstein , Rio de Janeiro, Humanitas, 183 pp.
*SLI 31: Fonologia e morfologia dell'italiano e dei dialetti d'Italia. Atti del XXXI Congresso della
   Società di linguistica italiana*, ed. Paola Benincà, Alberto Mioni and Laura Vanelli, Rome,
   Bulzoni, iii + 637 pp.
*Spillmann Vol.: Usus linguae. Der Text im Fokus sprach- und literaturwissenschaftlicher Perspektiven.
   Hans Otto Spillmann zum 60. Geburtstag*, ed. Ingo Warnke and Britta Hufeisen
   (Germanistische Texte und Studien, 62), Hildesheim, Olms-Weidmann, 270 pp.
*Studia Hispanica Medievalia IV: Studia Hispanica Medievalia IV. Actas de las V Jornadas
   Internacionales de Literatura Española Medieval*, ed. A. A. Fraboschi, C. Stramiello, and
   A. Rosarossa, Buenos Aires, Universidad Católica Argentina, 350 pp.
*Suard Vol.: Plaist vos oir bone cançon vaillant? Mélanges de Langue et de Littérature Médiévales offerts
   à François Suard*, ed. Dominique Boutet, Marie-Madeleine Castellani, Françoise
   Ferrand, and Aimé Petit, 2 vols, Lille, Université Charles-de-Gaulle–Lille 3, 1–554,
   555–1049 pp.
Taylor, *Gender Transgressions: Gender Transgressions: Crossing the Normative Barrier in Old French
   Literature*, ed. Karen J. Taylor, New York, Garland, 1998, xv + 203 pp.
Touriñán, *Interculturalidad: Interculturalidad y educación para el desarrollo. Estrategias sociales para
   la comprensión internacional*, ed. J. M. Touriñán López and M. A. Santos Rego, Santiago
   de Compostela, Xunta de Galicia, 335 pp.
Treviño, *Semantic Issues: Semantic Issues in Romance Syntax*, ed. Esthela Treviño and José
   Lema (Current Issues in Linguistic Theory, 173), Amsterdam, Benjamins,
   viii + 309 pp.
Vogeleer, *Modalité: La Modalité sous tous ses aspects*, ed. Svetlana Vogeleer et al. (Cahiers
   Chronos, 4), Amsterdam–Atlanta, GA, Rodopi, 353 pp.
Vogeleer, *Temps: Temps et discours*, ed. Svetlana Vogeleer et al., Louvain-la-Neuve, Peeters,
   1998, 297 pp.
*Wilmet Vol.: La Ligne claire de la linguistique à la grammaire. Mélanges offerts à Marc Wilmet à
   l'óccasion de sa 60e anniversaire*, ed. Annick Engelbert et al., Paris–Brussels, Duculot,
   1998, 398 pp.
Wolfzettel, *Erzählstrukturen: Erzählstrukturen der Artusliteratur. Forschungsgeschichte und neue
   Ansätze*, ed. Friedrich Wolfzettel and Peter Ihring, Tübingen, Niemeyer, xi + 366 pp.
*Workman Vol.: Medievalism in the Modern World: Essays in Honour of Leslie J. Workman*, ed.
   Richard Utz et al. (Making the Middle Ages, 1), Turnhout, Brepols, 1998,
   xiv + 452 pp.
*Wunberg Vol.: Von der Natur zur Kunst zurück. Neue Beiträge zur Goethe-Forschung. Gotthart Wunberg
   zum 65. Geburtstag*, ed. Moritz Bassler, Christoph Brecht, and Dirk Niefanger,
   Tübingen, Niemeyer, 1997, vi + 265 pp.
Wunder, *Geschlechterperspektiven: Geschlechterperspektiven. Forschungen zur Frühen Neuzeit*, ed.
   Heide Wunder and Gisela Engel, Koenogstein /Ts., Helmer, 1998, 489 pp.

## II.  GENERAL

| | |
|---|---|
| abbrev. | abbreviation, abbreviated to |
| Acad., Akad. | Academy, Academia, etc. |
| acc. | accusative |
| ann. | annotated (by) |
| anon. | anonymous |
| appx | appendix |
| Arg. | Argentinian (and foreign equivalents) |
| Assoc. | Association (and foreign equivalents) |
| Auv. | Auvergnat |
| Bel. | Belarusian |
| BL | British Library |
| BM | British Museum |
| BN | Bibliothèque Nationale, Biblioteka Narodowa, etc. |
| BPtg. | Brazilian Portuguese |
| bull. | bulletin |
| c. | century |
| *c.* | circa |
| Cat. | Catalan |
| ch. | chapter |
| col. | column |
| comm. | commentary (by) |
| comp. | compiler, compiled (by) |
| Cz. | Czech |
| diss. | dissertation |
| ed. | edited (by), editor (and foreign equivalents) |
| edn | edition |
| EPtg. | European Portuguese |
| fac. | facsimile |
| fasc. | fascicle |
| *Fest.* | Festschrift, Festskrift |
| Fin. | Finnish |
| Fr. | France, French, Français |
| Gal.-Ptg. | Galician-Portuguese (and equivalents) |
| Gasc. | Gascon |
| Ger. | German(y) |
| Gk | Greek |
| Gmc | Germanic |
| IE | Indo-European |
| illus. | illustrated, illustration(s) |
| impr. | impression |
| incl. | including, include(s) |
| Inst. | Institute (and foreign equivalents) |
| introd. | introduction, introduced by, introductory |
| It. | Italian |
| izd. | издание |
| izd-vo | издательство |
| *Jb.* | Jahrbuch |
| Jg | Jahrgang |
| Jh. | Jahrhundert |
| Lang. | Languedocien |
| Lat. | Latin |
| Lim. | Limousin |

| | |
|---|---|
| lit. | literature |
| med. | medieval |
| MHG | Middle High German |
| Mid. Ir. | Middle Irish |
| Mil. | Milanese |
| MS | manuscript |
| n.d. | no date |
| n.f. | neue Folge |
| no. | number (and foreign equivalents) |
| nom. | nominative |
| n.p. | no place |
| n.s. | new series |
| O Auv. | Old Auvergnat |
| O Cat. | Old Catalan |
| Occ. | Occitan |
| OE | Old English |
| OF | Old French |
| O Gasc. | Old Gascon |
| OHG | Old High German |
| O Ir. | Old Irish |
| O Lim. | Old Limousin |
| O Occ. | Old Occitan |
| O Pr. | Old Provençal |
| O Ptg. | Old Portuguese |
| OS | Old Saxon |
| OW | Old Welsh |
| part. | participle |
| ped. | педагогический, etc. |
| PIE | Proto-Indo-European |
| Pied. | Piedmontese |
| PGmc | Primitive Germanic |
| pl. | plate |
| plur. | plural |
| Pol. | Polish |
| p.p. | privately published |
| Pr. | Provençal |
| pref. | preface (by) |
| *Procs* | Proceedings |
| Ptg. | Portuguese |
| publ. | publication, published (by) |
| Ren. | Renaissance |
| repr. | reprint(ed) |
| Rev. | Review, Revista, Revue |
| rev. | revised (by) |
| Russ. | Russian |
| s. | siècle |
| ser. | series |
| sg. | singular |
| Slg | Sammlung |
| Soc. | Society (and foreign equivalents) |
| Sp. | Spanish |
| supp. | supplement |
| Sw. | Swedish |
| *Trans.* | Transactions |

| | |
|---|---|
| trans. | translated (by), translation |
| Ukr. | Ukrainian |
| Univ. | University (and foreign equivalents) |
| unpubl. | unpublished |
| U.P. | University Press (and foreign equivalents) |
| Vlg | Verlag |
| vol. | volume |
| vs | versus |
| W. | Welsh |
| wyd. | wydawnictwo |

\* before a publication signifies that it has not been seen by the contributor.

## III. PLACE NAMES

| | | | |
|---|---|---|---|
| B | Barcelona | NY | New York |
| BA | Buenos Aires | O | Oporto |
| Be | Belgrade | Pń | Poznań |
| Bo | Bologna | R | Rio de Janeiro |
| C | Coimbra | Ro | Rome |
| F | Florence | SC | Santiago de Compostela |
| Gd | Gdańsk | SPo | São Paulo |
| Kw | Kraków, Cracow | StP | St Petersburg |
| L | Lisbon | T | Turin |
| Ld | Leningrad | V | Valencia |
| M | Madrid | Wa | Warsaw |
| Mi | Milan | Ww | Wrocław |
| Mw | Moscow | Z | Zagreb |
| Na | Naples | | |

## IV. PERIODICALS, INSTITUTIONS, PUBLISHERS

*AA*, Antike und Abendland

AAA, Ardis Publishers, Ann Arbor, Michigan

*AAA*, Archivio per l'Alto Adige

AAASS, American Association for the Advancement of Slavic Studies

*AABC*, Anuari de l'Agrupació Borrianenca de Cultura

*AAC*, Atti dell'Accademia Clementina

*AAL*, Atti dell'Accademia dei Lincei

*AALP*, L'Arvista dl'Academia dla Lenga Piemontèisa

AAM, Association des Amis de Maynard

*AAPH*, Anais da Academia Portuguesa da História

*AAPN*, Atti dell'Accademia Pontaniana di Napoli

*AAPP*, Atti Accademia Peloritana dei Pericolanti. Classe di Lettere Filosofia e Belle Arti

*AARA*, Atti della Accademia Roveretana degli Agiati

*AASB*, Atti dell'Accademia delle Scienze dell'Istituto di Bologna

*AASF*, Annales Academiae Scientiarum Fennicae

*AASLAP*, Atti dell'Accademia di Scienze, Lettere ed Arti di Palermo

*AASLAU*, Atti dell'Accademia di
Scienze, Lettere e Arti di Udine
*AASN*, Atti dell'Accademia di
Scienze Morali e Politiche di
Napoli
*AAST*, Atti dell'Accademia delle
Scienze di Torino
*AAVM*, Atti e Memorie
dell'Accademia Virgiliana di
Mantova
AAWG, Abhandlungen der
Akademie der Wissenschaften in
Göttingen, phil.-hist. Kl., 3rd
ser., Göttingen, Vandenhoeck &
Ruprecht
*AB*, Analecta Bollandiana
*ABa*, L'Année Balzacienne
*ABÄG*, Amsterdamer Beiträge zur
älteren Germanistik
*ABB*, Archives et Bibliothèques de
Belgique — Archief– en
Bibliotheekswezen in België
*ABDB*, Aus dem Antiquariat.
Beiträge zum Börsenblatt für den
deutschen Buchhandel
*ABDO*, Association Bourguignonne
de Dialectologie et
d'Onomastique, Fontaine lès
Dijon
*ABHL*, Annual Bulletin of Historical
Literature
*ABI*, Accademie e Biblioteche
d'Italia
*ABN*, Anais da Biblioteca Nacional,
Rio de Janeiro
ABNG, Amsterdamer Beiträge zur
neueren Germanistik,
Amsterdam, Rodopi
*ABNG*, Amsterdamer Beiträge zur
neueren Germanistik
*ABor*, Acta Borussica
*ABP*, Arquivo de Bibliografia
Portuguesa
*ABR*, American Benedictine Review
*ABr*, Annales de Bretagne et des
Pays de l'Ouest
*ABS*, Acta Baltico-Slavica
*ABSJ*, Annual Bulletin of the Société
Jersiaise
*AC*, Analecta Cisterciensa, Rome
ACCT, Agence de Coopération
Culturelle et Technique
*ACer*, Anales Cervantinos, Madrid

ACIS, Association for
Contemporary Iberian Studies
*ACo*, Acta Comeniana, Prague
*AColl*, Actes et Colloques
*Acme*, Annali della Facoltà di
Filosofia e Lettere dell'Università
Statale di Milano
*ACP*, L'Amitié Charles Péguy
*ACUA*, Anales del Colegio
Universitario de Almería
AD, Analysen und Dokumente.
Beiträge zur Neueren Literatur,
Berne, Lang
ADEVA, Akademische Druck- und
Verlagsanstalt, Graz
AE, Artemis Einführungen,
Munich, Artemis
*AE*, L'Autre Europe
*AEA*, Anuario de Estudios
Atlánticos, Las Palmas
AECI, Agencia Española de
Cooperación Internacional
AEd, Arbeiten zur
Editionswissenschaft, Frankfurt,
Lang
*AEF*, Anuario de Estudios
Filológicos, Cáceres
*AEL*, Anuario de la Escuela de
Letras, Mérida, Venezuela
*AELG*, Anuario de Literarios
Galegos
*AEM*, Anuario de Estudios
Medievales
*AF*, Anuario de Filología, Barcelona
*AFA*, Archivo de Filología
Aragonesa
*AfAf*, African Affairs
*AfC*, Afrique Contemporaine
*AFe*, L'Armana di Felibre
*AFF*, Anali Filološkog fakulteta,
Belgrade
*AFH*, Archivum Franciscanum
Historicum
*AFHis*, Anales de Filología
Hispánica
*AfHR*, Afro-Hispanic Review
*AfL*, L'Afrique Littéraire
*AFLE*, Annali della Fondazione
Luigi Einaudi
*AFLFUB*, Annali della Facoltà di
Lettere e Filosofia dell'Università
di Bari

*AFLFUC*, Annali della Facoltà di Lettere e Filosofia dell'Università di Cagliari

*AFLFUG*, Annali della Facoltà di Lettere e Filosofia dell'Università degli Studi di Genova

*AFLFUM*, Annali della Facoltà di Lettere e Filosofia dell'Università di Macerata

*AFLFUN*, Annali della Facoltà di Lettere e Filosofia dell'Università di Napoli

*AFLFUP(SF)*, Annali della Facoltà di Lettere e Filosofia dell'Università di Perugia. 1. Studi Filosofici

*AFLFUP(SLL)*, Annali della Facoltà di Lettere e Filosofia dell'Università di Perugia. 3. Studi Linguistici-Letterari

*AFLFUS*, Annali della Facoltà di Lettere e Filosofia dell'Università di Siena

*AFLLS*, Annali della Facoltà di Lingua e Letterature Straniere di Ca' Foscari, Venice

*AFLN*, Annales de la Faculté des Lettres et Sciences Humaines de Nice

AFLS, Association for French Language Studies

*AFP*, Archivum Fratrum Praedicatorum

AFrP, Athlone French Poets, London, The Athlone Press

*AG*, Anales Galdosianos

*AGB*, Archiv für Geschichte des Buchwesens

*AGF*, Anuario Galego de Filoloxia

*AGI*, Archivio Glottologico Italiano

*AGJSG*, Acta Germanica. Jahrbuch des Südafrikanischen Germanistenverbandes

*AGP*, Archiv für Geschichte der Philosophie

*AH*, Archivo Hispalense

AHAW, Abhandlungen der Heidelberger Akademie der Wissenschaften, phil-hist. Kl

AHCP, Arquivos de História de Cultura Portuguesa

*AHDLMA*, Archives d'Histoire Doctrinale et Littéraire du Moyen Âge

*AHF*, Archiwum Historii Filozofii i Myśli Społecznej

*AHP*, Archivum Historiae Pontificae

*AHPr*, Annales de Haute-Provence, Digne-les-Bains

*AHR*, American Historical Review

*AHRF*, Annales Historiques de la Révolution Française

*AHRou*, Archives historiques du Rouergue

*AHSJ*, Archivum Historicum Societatis Jesu

*AHSS*, Annales: Histoire — Science Sociales

*AI*, Almanacco Italiano

*AIB*, Annali dell'Istituto Banfi

*AIBL*, Académie des Inscriptions et Belles-Lettres, Comptes Rendus

*AIEM*, Anales del Instituto de Estudios Madrileños

AIEO, Association Internationale d'Études Occitanes

*AIFMUR*, Annali dell'Istituto di Filologia Moderna dell'Università di Roma

*AIFUF*, Annali dell'Istituto di Filosofia dell'Università di Firenze

AIHI, Archives Internationales d'Histoire des Idées, The Hague, Nijhoff

*AIHS*, Archives Internationales d'Histoire des Sciences

AIL, Associação Internacional de Lusitanistas

AILLC, Associació Internacional de Llengua i Literatura Catalanes

*AISIGT*, Annali dell'Istituto Storico Italo-Germanico di Trento

*AION(FG)*, Annali dell'Istituto Universitario Orientale, Naples: Sezione Germanica. Filologia Germanica

*AION(SF)*, Annali dell'Istituto Universitario Orientale, Naples: Studi Filosofici

*AION(SL)*, Annali dell'Istituto Universitario Orientale, Naples: Sezione Linguistica

*AION(SR)*, Annali dell'Istituto Universitario Orientale, Naples: Sezione Romanza

890     *Abbreviations*

*AION(SS)*, Annali dell'Istituto Universitario Orientale, Naples: Sezione Slava
*AION(ST)*, Annali dell'Istituto Universitario Orientale, Naples: Sezione Germanica. Studi Tedeschi
*AIPHS*, Annuaire de l'Institut de Philologie et de l'Histoire Orientales et Slaves
*AIPS*, Annales Instituti Philologiae Slavica Universitatis Debreceniensis de Ludovico Kossuth Nominatae — Slavica
*AITCA*, Arxiu informatizat de textos catalans antics
*AIV*, Atti dell'Istituto Veneto
*AJ*, Alemannisches Jahrbuch
*AJCAI*, Actas de las Jornadas de Cultura Arabe e Islámica
*AJFS*, Australian Journal of French Studies
*AJGLL*, American Journal of Germanic Linguistics and Literatures
*AJL*, Australian Journal of Linguistics
*AJP*, American Journal of Philology
*AKG*, Archiv für Kulturgeschichte
AKML, Abhandlungen zur Kunst-, Musik- und Literaturwissenschaft, Bonn, Bouvier
*AL*, Anuario de Letras, Mexico
*AlAm*, Alba de América
ALB, Annales de la Faculté des Lettres de Besançon
*ALC*, African Languages and Cultures
*ALE*, Anales de Literatura Española, Alicante
*ALEC*, Anales de Literatura Española Contemporánea
*ALet*, Armas y Letras, Universidad de Nuevo León
*ALEUA*, Anales de Literatura Española de la Universidad de Alicante
*ALFL*, Actes de Langue Française et de Linguistique
*ALH*, Acta Linguistica Hungaricae
*ALHA*, Anales de la Literatura Hispanoamericana
*ALHa*, Acta Linguistica Hafniensia

*ALHisp*, Anuario de Lingüística Hispánica
*ALHist*, Annales: Littérature et Histoire
*ALit*, Acta Literaria, Chile
*ALitH*, Acta Litteraria Hungarica
*ALLI*, Atlante Linguistico dei Laghi Italiani
*ALM*, Archives des Lettres Modernes
*ALMA*, Archivum Latinitatis Medii Aevi (Bulletin du Cange)
*ALo*, Armanac de Louzero
*ALP*, Atlas linguistique et ethnographique de Provence, CNRS, 1975–86
*AlS*, Almanac Setòri
*ALT*, African Literature Today
*ALUB*, Annales Littéraires de l'Université de Besançon
*AM*, Analecta Musicologica
*AMAA*, Atti e Memorie dell'Accademia d'Arcadia
*AMAASLV*, Atti e Memorie dell'Accademia di Agricultura, Scienze e Lettere di Verona
*AMal*, Analecta Malacitana
*AMAP*, Atti e Memorie dell'Accademia Patavina di Scienze, Lettere ed Arti
*AMAPet*, Atti e Memorie dell'Accademia Petrarca di Lettere, Arti e Scienze, Arezzo
*AMAT*, Atti e Memorie dell'Accademia Toscana di Scienze e Lettere, La Colombaria
AMDLS, Arbeiten zur Mittleren Deutschen Literatur und Sprache, Berne, Lang
*AMDSPAPM*, Atti e Memorie della Deputazione di Storia Patria per le Antiche Province Modenesi
AMGG, Abhandlungen der Marburger Gelehrten Gesellschaft, Munich, Fink
*AmH*, American Hispanist
*AMid*, Annales du Midi
AML, Main Monographien Literaturwissenschaft, Frankfurt, Main
*AmIn*, América Indígena, Mexico
*AMSSSP*, Atti e Memorie della Società Savonese di Storia Patria
АН, Академия наук

*AN*, Americana Norvegica

ANABA, Asociación Nacional de Bibliotecarios, Arquiveros y Arqueólogos

*AnAlf*, Annali Alfieriani

*AnEA*, Anaquel de Estudios Arabes

*ANeo*, Acta Neophilologica, Ljubljana

*ANF*, Arkiv för nordisk filologi

*AnI*, Annali d'Italianistica

*AnL*, Anthropological Linguistics

*AnM*, Anuario Medieval

*AnN*, Annales de Normandie

*AnnM*, Annuale Medievale

ANPOLL, Associação Nacional de Pós-graduação e Pesquisa em Letras e Lingüística, São Paulo

*ANQ*, American Notes and Queries

*ANS*, Anglo-Norman Studies

ANTS, Anglo-Norman Text Society

*AnVi*, Antologia Vieusseux

ANZSGLL, Australian and New Zealand Studies in German Language and Literature, Berne, Lang

*AO*, Almanac occitan, Foix

*AÖAW*, Anzeiger der Österreichischen Akademie der Wissenschaften

*AOn*, Acta Onomastica

*AP*, Aurea Parma

*APIFN*, Актуальные проблемы истории философии народов СССР.

*APK*, Aufsätze zur portugiesischen Kulturgeschichte, Görres-Gesellschaft, Münster

*ApL*, Applied Linguistics

APL, Associação Portuguesa de Linguística

APPP, Abhandlungen zur Philosophie, Psychologie und Pädagogik, Bonn, Bouvier

*APr*, Analecta Praemonstratensia

*AProu*, Armana Prouvençau, Marseilles

*APS*, Acta Philologica Scandinavica

APSL, Amsterdamer Publikationen zur Sprache und Literatur, Amsterdam, Rodopi

APUCF, Association des Publications de la Faculté des Lettres et Sciences Humaines de l'Université de Clermont-Ferrand II, Nouvelle Série

*AQ*, Arizona Quarterly

*AqAq*, Aquò d'aquí, Gap

*AR*, Archiv für Reformationsgeschichte

*ARAJ*, American Romanian Academy Journal

*ARAL*, Australian Review of Applied Linguistics

ARCA, ARCA: Papers of the Liverpool Latin Seminar

*ArCCP*, Arquivos do Centro Cultural Português, Paris

*ArEM*, Aragón en la Edad Media

*ArFil*, Archivio di Filosofia

*ArI*, Arthurian Interpretations

*ARI*, Архив русской истории

ARL, Athlone Renaissance Library

*ArL*, Archivum Linguisticum

*ArLit*, Arthurian Literature

*ArP*, Археографски прилози

*ArSP*, Archivio Storico Pugliese

*ArSPr*, Archivio Storico Pratese

*ArSt*, Archivi per la Storia

ART, Atelier Reproduction des Thèses, Univ. de Lille III, Paris, Champion

*AS*, The American Scholar

*ASAHM*, Annales de la Société d'Art et d'Histoire du Mentonnais, Menton

*ASAvS*, Annuaire de la Société des Amis du vieux-Strasbourg

*ASB*, Archivio Storico Bergamasco

ASCALF, Association for the Study of Caribbean and African Literature in French

*ASCALFB*, ASCALF Bulletin

*ASCALFY*, ASCALF Yearbook

*ASE*, Annali di Storia dell'Esegesi

*ASEES*, Australian Slavonic and East European Studies

*ASELGC*, 1616. Anuario de la Sociedad Española de Literatura General y Comparada

*ASGM*, Atti del Sodalizio Glottologico Milanese

*ASI*, Archivio Storico Italiano

*ASJ*, Acta Slavonica Japonica

*ASL*, Archivio Storico Lombardo

*ASLSP*, Atti della Società Ligure di Storia Patria

*ASMC*, Annali di Storia Moderna e
Contemporanea
*ASNP*, Annali della Scuola Normale
Superiore di Pisa
*ASNS*, Archiv für das Studium der
Neueren Sprachen und
Literaturen
*ASocRous*, Annales de la Société J.-J.
Rousseau
*ASolP*, A Sol Post, Editorial Marfil,
Alcoi
*ASP*, Anzeiger für slavische
Philologie
*AsP*, L'Astrado prouvençalo. Revisto
Bilengo de Prouvenco/Revue
Bilingue de Provence, Berre
L'Etang.
*ASPN*, Archivio Storico per le
Province Napoletane
*ASPP*, Archivio Storico per le
Province Parmensi
*ASR*, Annalas da la Societad
Retorumantscha
*ASRSP*, Archivio della Società
Romana di Storia Patria
*ASSO*, Archivio Storico per la Sicilia
Orientale
*ASSUL*, Annali del Dipartimento di
Scienze Storiche e Sociali
dell'Università di Lecce
*AST*, Analecta Sacra Tarraconensia
*ASt*, Austrian Studies
*ASTic*, Archivio Storico Ticinese
*AŞUI*, (e), (f), Analele Ştiinţifice ale
Universităţii 'Al. I. Cuza' din Iaşi,
secţ. e, Lingvistică, secţ. f,
Literatură
*AT*, Athenäums Taschenbücher,
Frankfurt, Athenäum
*ATB*, Altdeutsche Textbibliothek,
Tübingen, Niemeyer
*ATCA*, Arxiu de Textos Catalans
Antics, IEC, Barcelona
*Ate*, Nueva Atenea, Universidad de
Concepción, Chile
*ATO*, A Trabe de Ouro
*ATS*, Arbeiten und Texte zur
Slavistik, Munich, Sagner
*ATV*, Aufbau Taschenbuch Verlag,
Berlin, Aufbau
*AtV*, Ateneo Veneto
*AUBLLR*, Analele Universităţii
Bucureşti, Limba şi literatura
română

*AUBLLS*, Analele Universităţii
Bucureşti, Limbi şi literaturi
străine
*AUC*, Anales de la Universidad de
Cuenca
*AUCP*, Acta Universitatis
Carolinae Pragensis
*AuE*, Arbeiten und Editionen zur
Mittleren Deutschen Literatur,
Stuttgart–Bad Cannstatt,
Frommann-Holzboog
*AUL*, Acta Universitatis Lodziensis
*AUL*, Annali della Facoltà di Lettere
e Filosofia dell'Università di
Lecce
*AUMCS*, Annales Uniwersytetu
Marii Curie-Skłodowskiej, Lublin
*AUML*, Anales de la Universidad de
Murcia: Letras
*AUMLA*, Journal of the Australasian
Universities Modern Language
Association
*AUN*, Annali della Facoltà di Lettere
e Filosofia dell'Università di
Napoli
*AUNCFP*, Acta Universitatis Nicolai
Copernici. Filologia Polska,
Toruń
*AUPO*, Acta Universitatis
Palackianae Olomucensis
*AUS*, American University Studies,
Berne — New York, Lang
*AUSP*, Annali dell'Università per
Stranieri di Perugia
*AUSt*, Acta Universitatis
Stockholmiensis
*AUTŞF*, Analele Universităţii din
Timişoara, Ştiinţe Filologice
*AUU*, Acta Universitatis Upsaliensis
*AUW*, Acta Universitatis
Wratislaviensis
*AVen*, Archivio Veneto
*AVEP*, Assouciacien vareso pèr
l'ensignamen dòu prouvençou,
La Farlède
*AVEPB*, Bulletin AVEP, La Farlède
*AvT*, L'Avant-Scène Théâtre
*AWR*, Anglo-Welsh Review

*BA*, Bollettino d'Arte
*BAAA*, Bulletin de l'Association des
Amis d'Alain

*BAAG*, Bulletin des Amis d'André Gide

*BAAJG*, Bulletin de l'Association des Amis de Jean Giono

*BAAL*, Boletín de la Academia Argentina de Letras

*BaB*, Bargfelder Bote

BAC, Biblioteca de Autores Cristianos

*BACol*, Boletín de la Academia Colombiana

BÄDL, Beiträge zur Älteren Deutschen Literaturgeschichte, Berne, Lang

BADLit, Bonner Arbeiten zur deutschen Literatur, Bonn, Bouvier

BAE, Biblioteca de Autores Españoles

*BAEO*, Boletín de la Asociación Española de Orientalistas

*BAFJ*, Bulletin de l'Association Francis Jammes

*BAG*, Boletín de la Academia Gallega

*BAIEO*, Bulletins de l'Association Internationale d'Études Occitanes

*BAJR*, Bulletin des Amis de Jules Romains

*BAJRAF*, Bulletin des Amis de Jacques Rivière et d'Alain-Fournier

*BALI*, Bollettino dell'Atlante Linguistico Italiano

*BALM*, Bollettino dell'Atlante Linguistico Mediterraneo

*BalS*, Balkan Studies, Institute for Balkan Studies, Thessaloniki

BAN, Българска Академия на Науките, София

BAO, Biblioteca Abat Oliva, Publicacions de l'Abadia de Montserrat, Barcelona

*BAPC*, Bulletin de l'Association Paul Claudel

*BAPRLE*, Boletín de la Academia Puertorrigueña de la Lengua Española

BAR, Biblioteca dell'Archivum Romanicum

*BARLLF*, Bulletin de l'Académie Royale de Langues et de Littératures Françaises de Bruxelles

BAWA, Bayerische Akademie der Wissenschaften. Phil.-hist. Kl. Abhandlungen, n.F.

BB, Biblioteca Breve, Lisbon

*BB*, Bulletin of Bibliography

*BBAHLM*, Boletín Bibliografico de la Asociación Hispánica de Literatura Medieval

BBB, Berner Beiträge zur Barockgermanistik, Berne, Lang

*BBGN*, Brünner Beiträge zur Germanistik und Nordistik

*BBib*, Bulletin du Bibliophile

BBL, Bayreuther Beiträge zur Literaturwissenschaft, Frankfurt, Lang

BBLI, Bremer Beiträge zur Literatur- und Ideengeschichte, Frankfurt, Lang

*BBMP*, Boletín de la Biblioteca de Menéndez Pelayo

BBN, Bibliotheca Bibliographica Neerlandica, Nieuwkoop, De Graaf

BBNDL, Berliner Beiträge zur neueren deutschen Literaturgeschichte, Berne, Lang

*BBSANZ*, Bulletin of the Bibliographical Society of Australia and New Zealand

*BBSIA*, Bulletin Bibliographique de la Société Internationale Arthurienne

*BBSMES*, Bulletin of the British Society for Middle Eastern Studies

*BBUC*, Boletim da Biblioteca da Universidade de Coimbra

*BC*, Bulletin of the 'Comediantes', University of Wisconsin

BCB, Boletín Cultural y Bibliográfico, Bogatá

*BCEC*, Bwletin Cymdeithas Emynwyr Cymru

*BCél*, Bulletin Célinien

*BCh*, Болдинские чтения

*BCLSMP*, Académie Royale de Belgique: Bulletin de la Classe des Lettres et des Sciences Morales et Politiques

*BCMV*, Bollettino Civici Musei Veneziani

*BCRLT*, Bulletin du Centre de
Romanistique et de Latinité
Tardive
*BCS*, Bulletin of Canadian Studies
*BCSM*, Bulletin of the Cantigueiros
de Santa Maria
*BCSS*, Bollettino del Centro di Studi
Filologici e Linguistici Siciliani
*BCSV*, Bollettino del Centro di Studi
Vichiani
*BCZG*, Blätter der Carl Zuckmayer
Gesellschaft
*BD*, Беларуская думка
*BDADA*, Bulletin de documentation
des Archives départementales de
l'Aveyron, Rodez
*BDB*, Börsenblatt für den deutschen
Buchhandel
*BDBA*, Bien Dire et Bien Aprandre
*BDL*, Beiträge zur Deutschen
Literatur, Frankfurt, Lang
BDP, Beiträge zur Deutschen
Philologie, Giessen, Schmitz
*BEA*, Bulletin des Études Africaines
*BEC*, Bibliothèque de l'École des
Chartes
BelE, Беларуская энцыклапедыя
*BelL*, Беларуская лінгвістыка
*BelS*, Беларускі сьвет
*BEP*, Bulletin des Études
Portugaises
*BEPar*, Bulletin des Études
Parnassiennes et Symbolistes
*BEzLit*, Български език и
литература
*BF*, Boletim de Filologia
*BFA*, Bulletin of Francophone Africa
*BFC*, Boletín de Filología, Univ. de
Chile
*BFE*, Boletín de Filología Española
*BFF*, Bulletin Francophone de
Finlande
*BFFGL*, Boletín de la Fundación
Federico García Lorca
*BFï*, Bollettino Filosofico
*BFLS*, Bulletin de la Faculté des
Lettres de Strasbourg
*BFo*, Biuletyn Fonograficzny
BFPLUL, Bibliothèque de la Faculté
de Philosophie et Lettres de
l'Université de Liège
BFR, Bibliothèque Française et
Romane, Paris, Klincksieck

*BFR*, Bulletin of the Fondation C.F.
Ramuz
*BFr*, Börsenblatt Frankfurt
BG, Bibliotheca Germanica,
Tübingen, Francke
*BGB*, Bulletin de l'Association
Guillaume Budé
*BGDSL*, Beiträge zur Geschichte der
deutschen Sprache und Literatur,
Tübingen
BGKT, Беларускае грамадска-
культуральнае тавырства
*BGL*, Boletín Galego de Literatura
BGLKAJ, Beiträge zur Geschichte
der Literatur und Kunst des 18.
Jahrhunderts, Heidelberg, Winter
BGP, Bristol German Publications,
Bristol U.P
*BGREC*, Bulletin du Groupe de
Recherches et d'Études du
Clermontais, Clermont-l'Hérault
*BGS*, Beiträge zur Geschichte der
Sprachwissenschaft
BGS, Beiträge zur germanistischen
Sprachwissenschaft, Hamburg,
Buske
BGT, Blackwell German Texts,
Oxford, Blackwell
*BH*, Bulletin Hispanique
*BHR*, Bibliothèque d'Humanisme et
Renaissance
*BHS(G)*, Bulletin of Hispanic
Studies, Glasgow
*BHS(L)*, Bulletin of Hispanic
Studies, Liverpool
BI, Bibliographisches Institut,
Leipzig
BibAN, Библиотека Академии
наук СССР
*BIDS*, Bulletin of the International
Dostoevsky Society, Klagenfurt
*BIEA*, Boletín del Instituto de
Estudios Asturianos
*BIHBR*, Bulletin de l'Institut
Historique Belge de Rome
*BIHR*, Bulletin of the Institute of
Historical Research
*BIO*, Bulletin de l'Institut Occitan,
Pau
*BJA*, British Journal of Aesthetics
*BJCS*, British Journal for Canadian
Studies
*BJECS*, The British Journal for
Eighteenth-Century Studies

*BJHP*, British Journal of the History of Philosophy

*BJHS*, British Journal of the History of Science

*BJL*, Belgian Journal of Linguistics

*BJR*, Bulletin of the John Rylands University Library of Manchester

*BKF*, Beiträge zur Kleist-Forschung

*BL*, Brain and Language

*BLAR*, Bulletin of Latin American Research

*BLBI*, Bulletin des Leo Baeck Instituts

*BLe*, Börsenblatt Leipzig

BLFCUP, Bibliothèque de Littérature Française Contemporaine de l'Université Paris 7

*BLI*, Beiträge zur Linguistik und Informationsverarbeitung

*BLi*, Беларуская літаратура. Міжвузаўскі зборнік.

*BLJ*, British Library Journal

BLL, Beiträge zur Literatur und Literaturwissenschaft des 20. Jahrhunderts, Berne, Lang

*BLM*, Bonniers Litterära Magasin

BLR, Bibliothèque Littéraire de la Renaissance, Geneva, Slatkine–Paris, Champion

*BLR*, Bodleian Library Record

BLVS, Bibliothek des Literarischen Vereins, Stuttgart, Hiersemann

BM, Bibliothek Metzier, Stuttgart

*BMBP*, Bollettino del Museo Bodoniano di Parma

*BMCP*, Bollettino del Museo Civico di Padova

*BML*, Беларуская мова і літаратура ў школе

*BMo*, Беларуская мова. Міжвузаўскі зборнік

BNE, Beiträge zur neueren Epochenforschung, Berne, Lang

*BNF*, Beiträge zur Namenforschung

BNL, Beiträge zur neueren Literaturgeschichte, 3rd ser., Heidelberg, Winter

BNP, Beiträge zur nordischen Philologie, Basel, Helbing & Lichtenhahn

*BO*, Biblioteca Orientalis

*BOCES*, Boletín del Centro de Estudios del Siglo XVIII, Oviedo

*BOP*, Bradford Occasional Papers

ВР, Български писател

*BP*, Lo Bornat dau Perigòrd

*BPTJ*, Biuletyn Polskiego Towarzystwa Językoznawczego

*BR*, Болгарская русистика.

BRA, Bonner Romanistische Arbeiten, Berne, Lang

*BRABLB*, Boletín de la Real Academia de Buenas Letras de Barcelona

*BRAC*, Boletín de la Real Academia de Córdoba de Ciencias, Bellas Letras, y Nobles Artes

*BRAE*, Boletín de la Real Academia Española

*BRAH*, Boletín de la Real Academia de la Historia

*BrC*, Bruniana & Campanelliana

BRIES, Bibliothèque Russe de l'Institut d'Études Slaves, Paris, Institut d'Études Slaves

*BRJL*, Bulletin ruského jazyka a literatury

*BrL*, La Bretagne Linguistique

*BRP*, Beiträge zur romanischen Philologie

*BS*, Biuletyn slawistyczny, Łódź

*BSAHH*, Bulletin de la Société archéologique et historique des hauts cantons de l'Hérault, Bédarieux

*BSAHL*, Bulletin de la Société archéologique et historique du Limousin, Limoges

*BSAHLSG*, Bulletin de la Société Archéologique, Historique, Littéraire et Scientifique du Gers

*BSAM*, Bulletin de la Société des Amis de Montaigne

*BSAMPAC*, Bulletin de la Société des Amis de Marcel Proust et des Amis de Combray

*BSASLB*, Bulletin de la Société Archéologique, Scientifique et Littéraire de Béziers

*BSATG*, Bulletin de la Société Archéologique de Tarn-et-Garonne

*BSBS*, Bollettino Storico–Bibliografico Subalpino

*BSCC*, Boletín de la Sociedad Castellonense de Cultura

BSD, Bithell Series of Dissertations — MHRA Texts and Dissertations, London, Modern Humanities Research Association

*BSD*, Bulletin de la Société de Borda, Dax

BSDL, Bochumer Schriften zur deutschen Literatur, Berne, Lang

BSDSL, Basler Studien zur deutschen Sprache und Literatur, Tübingen, Francke

BSE, Галоўная рэдакцыя Беларускай савеюкай энцыклапедыі

*BSEHA*, Bulletin de la Société d'Études des Hautes-Alpes, Gap

*BSEHTD*, Bulletin de la Société d'Études Historiques du texte dialectal

*BSELSAL*, Bulletin de la Société des Études Littéraires, Scientifiques et Artistiques du Lot

*BSF*, Bollettino di Storia della Filosofia

BSG, Berliner Studien zur Germanistik, Frankfurt, Lang

*BSHAP*, Bulletin de la Société Historique et Archéologique du Périgord, Périgueux

*BSHPF*, Bulletin de la Société de l'Histoire du Protestantisme Français

BSIH, Brill's Studies in Intellectual History, Leiden, Brill

*BSIS*, Bulletin of the Society for Italian Studies

*BSLLW*, Bulletin de la Société de Langue et Littérature Wallonnes

*BSLP*, Bulletin de la Société de Linguistique de Paris

*BSLV*, Bollettino della Società Letteraria di Verona

BSM, Birmingham Slavonic Monographs, University of Birmingham

*BSOAS*, Bulletin of the School of Oriental and African Studies

*BSP*, Bollettino Storico Pisano

*BSPC*, Bulletin de la Société Paul Claudel

*BSPia*, Bollettino Storico Piacentino

*BSPN*, Bollettino Storico per le Province di Novara

*BSPSP*, Bollettino della Società Pavese di Storia Patria

BsR, Beck'sche Reihe, Munich, Beck

*BSR*, Bulletin de la Société Ramond. Bagneres-de-Bigorre

*BSRS*, Bulletin of the Society for Renaissance Studies

*BSSAAPC*, Bollettino della Società per gli Studi Storici, Archeologici ed Artistici della Provincia di Cuneo

*BSSCLE*, Bulletin of the Society for the Study of the Crusades and the Latin East

*BSSP*, Bullettino Senese di Storia Patria

*BSSPin*, Bollettino della Società Storica Pinerolese, Pinerolo, Piemonte, Italy.

*BSSPHS*, Bulletin of the Society for Spanish and Portuguese Historical Studies

*BSSV*, Bollettino della Società Storica Valtellinese

*BSZJPS*, Bałtosłowiańskie związki językowe. Prace Slawistyczne

*BT*, Богословские труды, Moscow

*BTe*, Biblioteca Teatrale

*BTH*, Boletim de Trabalhos Historicos

*BulEz*, Български език

*BW*, Bibliothek und Wissenschaft

*BySt*, Byzantine Studies

*CA*, Cuadernos Americanos

*CAAM*, Cahiers de l'Association Les Amis de Milosz

*CAB*, Commentari dell'Ateneo di Brescia

*CAC*, Les Cahiers de l'Abbaye de Créteil

*CadL*, Cadernos da Lingua

*CAG*, Cahiers André Gide

*CAIEF*, Cahiers de l'Association Internationale des Études Françaises

*CalLet*, Calabria Letteraria

CAm, Casa de las Américas, Havana

*CAm*, Casa de las Américas, Havana

*CanJL*, Canadian Journal of Linguistics

*CanJP*, Canadian Journal of Philosophy

*CanL*, Canadian Literature

*CanSP*, Canadian Slavonic Papers

*CanSS*, Canadian–American Slavic Studies

*CarA*, Carmarthenshire Antiquary

*CARB*, Cahiers des Amis de Robert Brasillach

*CarQ*, Caribbean Quarterly

*CAT*, Cahiers d'Analyse Textuelle, Liège, Les Belles Lettres

*CatR*, Catalan Review

*CAVL*, Cahiers des Amis de Valery Larbaud

*CB*, Cuadernos Bibliográficos

*CC*, Comparative Criticism

*CCe*, Cahiers du Cerf XX

*CCend*, Continent Cendrars

*CCF*, Cuadernos de la Cátedra Feijoo

*CCMe*, Cahiers de Civilisation Médiévale

*CCol*, Cahiers Colette

*CCU*, Cuadernos de la Cátedra M. de Unamuno

*CD*, Cuadernos para el Diálogo

*CdA*, Camp de l'Arpa

CDA, Christliche deutsche Autoren des 20. Jahrhunderts, Berne, Lang

CDB, Coleção Documentos Brasileiros

*CDr*, Comparative Drama

*ČDS*, Čeština doma a ve světě

*CDs*, Cahiers du Dix-septième, Athens, Georgia

CDU, Centre de Documentation Universitaire

*CduC*, Cahiers de CERES. Série littéraire, Tunis

*CE*, Cahiers Élisabéthains

*CEA*, Cahiers d'Études Africaines

CEAL, Centro Editor de América Latina

*CEC*, Cahiers d'Études Cathares, Narbonne

CEC, Conselho Estadual de Cultura, Comissão de Literatura, São Paulo

CECAES, Centre d'Études des Cultures d'Aquitaine et d'Europe du Sud, Université de Bordeaux III

*CEcr*, Corps Écrit

CEDAM, Casa Editrice Dott. A. Milani

*CEG*, Cuadernos de Estudios Gallegos

CEL, Cadernos de Estudos Lingüísticos, Campinas, Brazil

CELO, Centre d'Etude de la Littérature Occitane, Bordes.

*CEM*, Cahiers d'Études Médiévales, Univ. of Montreal

*CEMa*, Cahiers d'Études Maghrebines, Cologne

*CEMed*, Cuadernos de Estudios Medievales

CEPL, Centre d'Étude et de Promotion de la Lecture, Paris

CEPON, Centre per l'estudi e la promocion de l'Occitan normat.

*CEPONB*, CEPON Bulletin d'échange.

*CER*, Cahiers d'Études Romanes

*CERCLiD*, Cahiers d'Études Romanes, Centre de Linguistique et de Dialectologie, Toulouse

CEROC, Centre d'Enseignement et de Recherche d'Oc, Paris

*CERoum*, Cahiers d'Études Roumaines

*CeS*, Cultura e Scuola

CESCM, Centre d'Études Supérieures de Civilisation Médiévale, Poitiers

CET, Centro Editoriale Toscano

*CEtGer*, Cahiers d'Études Germaniques

*CF*, Les Cahiers de Fontenay

*CFC*, Contemporary French Civilization

*CFI*, Cuadernos de Filologia Italiana

*CFLA*, Cuadernos de Filología. Literaturas: Análisis, Valencia

*CFM*, Cahiers François Mauriac

CFMA, Collection des Classiques Français du Moyen Âge

*CFol*, Classical Folia

*CFS*, Cahiers Ferdinand de Saussure

*CFSLH*, Cuadernos de Filología: Studia Linguistica Hispanica

CFTM, Classiques Français des Temps Modernes, Paris, Champion

*CG*, Cahiers de Grammaire

*CGD*, Cahiers Georges Duhamel

CGFT, Critical Guides to French Texts, London, Grant & Cutler

CGGT, Critical Guides to German Texts, London, Grant & Cutler

*CGP*, Carleton Germanic Papers

*CGS*, Colloquia Germanica Stetinensia

CGST, Critical Guides to Spanish Texts, London, Támesis, Grant & Cutler

*CH*, Crítica Hispánica

*CHA*, Cuadernos Hispano-Americanos

*CHAC*, Cuadernos Hispano-Americanos. Los complementarios

*CHB*, Cahiers Henri Bosco

*ChC*, Chemins Critiques

*CHCHMC*, Cylchgrawn Hanes Cymdeithas Hanes y Methodistiaid Calfinaidd

*CHLR*, Cahiers d'Histoire des Littératures Romanes

*CHP*, Cahiers Henri Pourrat

*ChR*, The Chesterton Review

*ChRev*, Chaucer Review

*ChrA*, Chroniques Allemandes

*ChrI*, Chroniques Italiennes

*ChrL*, Christianity and Literature

*ChrN*, Chronica Nova

*ChS*, Champs du Signe

*CHST*, Caernarvonshire Historical Society Transactions

*CHum*, Computers and the Humanities

*CI*, Critical Inquiry

*CiD*, La Ciudad de Dios

CIDO, Centre International de Documentation Occitane, Béziers

CIEL, Centre International de l'Écrit en Langue d'Òc, Berre

CIEM, Comité International d'Études Morisques

*CIF*, Cuadernos de Investigación Filológica

*CIH*, Cuadernos de Investigación Historica

CILF, Conseil International de la Langue Française

*CILH*, Cuadernos para Investigación de la Literatura Hispanica

*CILL*, Cahiers de l'Institut de Linguistique de l'Université de Louvain

*CIMAGL*, Cahiers de l'Institut du Moyen Âge Grec et Latin, Copenhagen

*CIn*, Cahiers Intersignes

CIRDOC, Centre Inter-Régional de Développement de l'Occitan, Béziers

CIRVI, Centro Interuniversitario di Ricerche sul 'Viaggio in Italia', Moncalieri

CISAM, Centro Italiano di Studi sull'Alto Medioevo

*CIt*, Carte Italiane

CIUS, Canadian Institute of Ukrainian Studies Edmonton

*CivC*, Civiltà Cattolica

CJ, Conditio Judaica, Tübingen, Niemeyer

*CJb*, Celan-Jahrbuch

*CJC*, Cahiers Jacques Chardonne

*CJG*, Cahiers Jean Giraudoux

*CJIS*, Canadian Journal of Italian Studies

*ČJL*, Český jazyk a literatura

*CJNS*, Canadian Journal of Netherlandic Studies

*CJP*, Cahiers Jean Paulhan

*CJR*, Cahiers Jules Romains

CL, Cuadernos de Leiden

*CL*, Comparative Literature

*ČL*, Česká literatura

*CLA*, Cahiers du LACITO

*CLAJ*, College Language Association Journal

*CLCC*, Cahiers de Littérature Canadienne Comparée

*CLCWeb*, Comparative Literature and Culture, A WWWeb Journal, <http://www.arts.ualberta.ca/clcwebjournal/>

*CLE*, Comunicaciones de Literatura Española, Buenos Aires

*CLe*, Cahiers de Lexicologie

CLEAM, Colección de Literatura Española Aljamiado–Morisca, Madrid, Gredos

CLESP, Cooperativa Libraria Editrice degli Studenti dell'Università di Padova, Padua

*CLett*, Critica Letteraria

CLEUP, Cooperativa Libraria Editrice, Università di Padova

*CLF*, Cahiers de Linguistique Française

*CLHM*, Cahiers de Linguistique Hispanique Médiévale

*CLin*, Cercetări de Lingvistica

*CLit*, Cadernos de Literatura, Coimbra

*ClL*, La Clau lemosina

*CLO*, Cahiers Linguistiques d'Ottawa

*ClP*, Classical Philology

*CLS*, Comparative Literature Studies

*CLSl*, Cahiers de Linguistique Slave

*CLTA*, Cahiers de Linguistique Théorique et Appliquée

*CLTL*, Cadernos de Lingüística e Teoria da Literatura

CLUEB, Cooperativa Libraria Universitaria Editrice Bologna

*CLus*, Convergência Lusíada, Rio de Janeiro

*CM*, Classica et Mediaevalia

*CMA*, Cahier Marcel Aymé

*CMar*, Cuadernos de Marcha

CMCS, Cambrian Medieval Celtic Studies

*CMERSA*, Center for Medieval and Early Renaissance Studies, State University of New York at Binghamton. Acta

*ČMF (PhP)*, Časopis pro moderni filologii: Philologica Pragensia

*CMHLB*, Cahiers du Monde Hispanique et Luso-Brésilien

*CMi*, Cultura Milano

*CML*, Classical and Modern Literature

*ČMM*, Časopis Matice Moravské

*CMon*, Communication Monographs

*CMP*, Cahiers Marcel Proust

*CMRS*, Cahiers du Monde Russe et Soviétique

*CN*, Cultura Neolatina

*CNat*, Les Cahiers Naturalistes

CNCDP, Comissão Nacional para a Comemoração dos Descobrimentos Portugueses, Lisbon

*CNor*, Los Cuadernos del Norte

CNR, Consiglio Nazionale delle Ricerche

CNRS, Centre National de la Recherche Scientifique

*CO*, Camera Obscura

*CoF*, Collectanea Franciscana

*COJ*, Cambridge Opera Journal

COK, Centralny Ośrodek Kultury, Warsaw

*CoL*, Compás de Letras

*ColA*, Colóquio Artes

*ColGer*, Colloquia Germanica

*ColH*, Colloquium Helveticum

*ColL*, Colóquio Letras

*ComB*, Communications of the International Brecht Society

*ComGer*, Comunicaciones Germánicas

*CompL*, Computational Linguistics

*ConL*, Contrastive Linguistics

*ConLet*, Il Confronto Letterario

*ConLit*, Contemporary Literature

*ConS*, Condorcet Studies

CORDAE, Centre Occitan de Recèrca, de Documentacion e d'Animacion Etnografica, Cordes

*CP*, Castrum Peregrini

*CPE*, Cahiers Prévost d'Exiles, Grenoble

*CPL*, Cahiers Paul Léautand

*CPr*, Cahiers de Praxématique

*CPR*, Chroniques de Port-Royal

*CPUC*, Cadernos PUC, São Paulo

*CQ*, Critical Quarterly

*CR*, Contemporary Review

*CRAC*, Cahiers Roucher — André Chénier

*CRCL*, Canadian Review of Comparative Literature

*CREL*, Cahiers Roumains d'Études Littéraires

CREO, Centre régional d'études occitanes

*CRev*, Centennial Review

*CRI*, Cuadernos de Ruedo Ibérico

*CRIAR*, Cahiers du Centre de Recherches Ibériques et Ibéro-Américains de l'Université de Rouen

*CRIN*, Cahiers de Recherches des Instituts Néerlandais de Langue et Littérature Françaises

*CRLN*, Comparative Romance Linguistics Newsletter

*CRM*, Cahiers de Recherches Médiévales (XIIIe–XVe siècles), Paris, Champion

*CRQ*, Cahiers Raymond Queneau

*CRR*, Cincinnati Romance Review

*CRRI*, Centre de Recherche sur la Renaissance Italienne, Paris

*CRRR*, Centre de Recherches Révolutionnaires et Romantiques, Université Blaise-Pascal, Clermont-Ferrand.

*CS*, Cornish Studies

*CSAM*, Centro di Studi sull'Alto Medioevo, Spoleto

*ČSAV*, Československá akademie věd

*CSDI*, Centro di Studio per la Dialettologia Italiana

*CSem*, Caiete de Semiotică

*CSFLS*, Centro di Studi Filologici e Linguistici Siciliani, Palermo

*CSG*, Cambridge Studies in German, Cambridge U.P.

*CSGLL*, Canadian Studies in German Language and Literature, Berne — New York — Frankfurt, Lang

*CSH*, Cahiers des Sciences Humaines

*CSIC*, Consejo Superior de Investigaciones Científicas, Madrid

*CSJP*, Cahiers Saint-John Perse

*CSl*, Critica Slovia, Florence

*CSLI*, Center for the Study of Language and Information, Stanford University

*CSM*, Les Cahiers de Saint-Martin

*ČSp*, Československý spisovatel

*CSS*, California Slavic Studies

*CSSH*, Comparative Studies in Society and History

*CST*, Cahiers de Sémiotique Textuelle

*CSt*, Critica Storica

*CT*, Christianity Today

*CTC*, Cuadernos de Teatro Clásico

*CTE*, Cuadernos de Traducción e Interpretación

*CTe*, Cuadernos de Teología

*CTex*, Cahiers Textuels

*CTH*, Cahiers Tristan l'Hermite

*CTh*, Ciencia Tomista

*CTL*, Current Trends in Linguistics

*CTLin*, Commissione per i Testi di Lingua, Bologna

*CUECM*, Cooperativa Universitaria Editrice Catanese Magistero

*CUER MA*, Centre Universitaire d'Études et de Recherches Médiévales d'Aix, Université de Provence, Aix-en-Provence

*CUP*, Cambridge University Press

*CUUCV*, Cultura Universitaria de la Universidad Central de Venezuela

*CV*, Città di Vita

*CWPL*, Catalan Working Papers in Linguistics

*CWPWL*, Cardiff Working Papers in Welsh Linguistics

*DAEM*, Deutsches Archiv für Erforschung des Mittelalters

*DaF*, Deutsch als Fremdsprache

*DAG*, Dictionnaire onomasiologique de l'ancien gascon, Tübingen, Niemeyer

*DalR*, Dalhousie Review

*DanU*, Dansk Udsyn

*DAO*, Dictionnaire onomasiologique de l'ancien occitan, Tübingen, Niemeyer

*DaSt*, Dante Studies

DB, Дзяржаўная бібліятэка БССР

*DB*, Doitsu Bungaku

*DBl*, Driemaandelijkse Bladen

DBO, Deutsche Bibliothek des Ostens, Berlin, Nicolai

*DBR*, Les Dialectes Belgo-Romans

*DBr*, Doitsu Bungakoranko

*DCFH*, Dicenda. Cuadernos de Filología Hispánica

*DD*, Diskussion Deutsch

DDG, Deutsche Dialektgeographie, Marburg, Elwert

*DDJ*, Deutsches Dante-Jahrbuch

*DegSec*, Degré Second

*DELTA*, Revista de Documentação de Estudos em Lingüística Teórica e Aplicada, São Paulo

*DESB*, Delta Epsilon Sigma Bulletin, Dubuque, Iowa

*DeutB*, Deutsche Bücher

*DeutUB*, Deutschungarische Beiträge
*DFC*, Durham French Colloquies
*DFS*, Dalhousie French Studies
DGF, Dokumentation germanistischer Forschung, Frankfurt, Lang
*DgF*, Danmarks gamle Folkeviser
DHA, Diálogos Hispánicos de Amsterdam, Rodopi
*DHR*, Duquesne Hispanic Review
*DhS*, Dix-huitième Siècle
DI, Deutscher Idealismus, Stuttgart, Klett-Cotta Verlag
*DI*, Декоративное искусство
DIAS, Dublin Institute for Advanced Studies
*DiL*, Dictionnairique et Lexicographie
*DiS*, Dickinson Studies
*DisA*, Dissertation Abstracts
*DisSlSHL*, Dissertationes Slavicae: Sectio Historiae Litterarum
*DisSlSL*, Dissertationes Slavicae: Sectio Linguistica
*DK*, Duitse Kroniek
*DkJb*, Deutschkanadisches Jahrbuch
DKV, Deutscher Klassiker Verlag, Frankfurt
*DL*, Детская литература
DLA, Deutsche Literatur von den Anfängen bis 1700, Berne — Frankfurt — Paris — New York, Lang
*DLit*, Discurso Literario
*DLM*, Deutsche Literatur des Mittelalters (Wissenschaftliche Beiträge der Ernst-Moritz-Arndt-Universität Greifswald)
DLR, Deutsche Literatur in Reprints, Munich, Fink
*DLRECL*, Diálogo de la Lengua. Revista de Estudio y Creación Literaria, Cuenca
*DM*, Dirassat Masrahiyyat
DMRPH, De Montfort Research Papers in the Humanities, De Montfort University, Leicester
DMTS, Davis Medieval Texts and Studies, Leiden, Brill
*DN*, Дружба народов
*DNT*, De Nieuwe Taalgids

DOLMA, Documenta Onomastica Litteralia Medii Aevi, Hildesheim, Olms
*DOM*, Dictionnaire de l'occitan médiéval, Tübingen, Niemeyer, 1996–
*DosS*, Dostoevsky Studies
*DoV*, Дошкольное воспитание
*DPA*, Documents pour servir à l'histoire du département des Pyrénées-Atlantiques, Pau
DPL, De Proprietatibus Litterarum, The Hague, Mouton
*DpL*, День поэзии, Leningrad
*DpM*, День поэзии, Moscow
*DR*, Drama Review
*DRev*, Downside Review
*DRLAV*, DRLAV, Revue de Linguistique
*DS*, Diderot Studies
DSEÜ, Deutsche Sprache in Europa und Übersee, Stuttgart, Steiner
DSL, Det danske Sprog- og Litteraturselskab
*DSp*, Deutsche Sprache
DSRPD, Documenta et Scripta. Rubrica Paleographica et Diplomatica, Barcelona
*DSS*, XVIIe Siècle
DSt, Deutsche Studien, Meisenheim, Hain
*DSt*, Danske Studier
DT, Deutsche Texte, Tübingen, Niemeyer
*DteolT*, Dansk teologisk Tidsskrift
*DtL*, Die deutsche Literatur
DTM, Deutsche Texte des Mittelalters, Berlin, Akademie
DTV, Deutscher Taschenbuch Verlag, Munich
*DUB*, Deutschunterricht, East Berlin
*DUJ*, Durham University Journal (New Series)
*DUS*, Der Deutschunterricht, Stuttgart
*DUSA*, Deutschunterricht in Südafrika
*DV*, Дальний Восток
DVA, Deutsche Verlags-Anstalt, Stuttgart

*DVLG*, Deutsche Vierteljahresschrift für Literaturwissenschaft und Geistesgeschichte

E, Verlag Enzyklopädie, Leipzig
*EAL*, Early American Literature
EALS, Europäische Aufklärung in Literatur und Sprache, Frankfurt, Lang
*EAS*, Europe-Asia Studies
*EB*, Estudos Brasileiros
*EBal*, Etudes Balkaniques
*EBM*, Era Bouts dera mountanho, Aurignac
*EBTch*, Études Balkaniques Tchécoslovaques
EC, El Escritor y la Crítica, Colección Persiles, Madrid, Taurus
*EC*, Études Celtiques
*ECan*, Études Canadiennes
*ECar*, Espace Caraïbe
*ECent*, The Eighteenth Century, Lubbock, Texas
*ECentF*, Eighteenth-Century Fiction
*ECF*, Écrits du Canada Français
*ECI*, Eighteenth-Century Ireland
ECIG, Edizioni Culturali Internazionali Genova
*ECla*, Les Études Classiques
*ECon*, España Contemporánea
*EconH*, Économie et Humanisme
*EcR*, Echo de Rabastens. Les Veillées Rabastinoises, Rabastens (Tarn)
*ECr*, Essays in Criticism
*ECS*, Eighteenth Century Studies
EdCat, Ediciones Cátedra, Madrid
EDESA, Ediciones Españolas S.A.
*EDHS*, Études sur le XVIIIe Siècle
*EDL*, Études de Lettres
EDT, Edizioni di Torino
*EE*, Erasmus in English
EEM, East European Monographs
*EEQ*, East European Quarterly
EF, Erträge der Forschung, Darmstadt, Wissenschaftliche Buchgesellschaft
*EF*, Études Françaises
*EFAA*, Échanges Franco-Allemands sur l'Afrique
*EFE*, Estudios de Fonética Experimental

EFF, Ergebnisse der Frauenforschung, Stuttgart, Metzler
*EFil*, Estudios Filológicos, Valdivia, Chile
*EFL*, Essays in French Literature, Univ. of Western Australia
EFR, Éditeurs Français Réunis
*EG*, Études Germaniques
EH, Europäische Hochschulschriften, Berne–Frankfurt, Lang
*EH*, Estudios Humanísticos
*EHF*, Estudios Humanísticos. Filología
*EHN*, Estudios de Historia Novohispana
*EHQ*, European History Quarterly
*EHR*, English Historical Review
EHRC, European Humanities Research Centre, University of Oxford
*EHS*, Estudios de Historia Social
EHT, Exeter Hispanic Texts, Exeter
*EIA*, Estudos Ibero-Americanos
*EIP*, Estudos Italianos em Portugal
*EJWS*, European Journal of Women's Studies
*EL*, Esperienze Letterarie
El, Elementa, Würzburg, Königshausen & Neumann –Amsterdam, Rodopi
*ELA*, Études de Linguistique Appliquée
*ELF*, Études Littéraires Françaises, Paris, J.-M. Place — Tübingen, Narr
*ELH*, English Literary History
*El'H*, Études sur l'Hérault, Pézenas
*ELin*, Estudos Lingüísticos, São Paulo
*ELit*, Essays in Literature
*ELL*, Estudos Lingüísticos e Literários, Bahia
*ELLC*, Estudis de Llengua i Literatura Catalanes
*ELLF*, Études de Langue et Littérature Françaises, Tokyo
*ELM*, Études littéraires maghrebines
*ELR*, English Literary Renaissance
*EMarg*, Els Marges
*EMH*, Early Music History

EMus, Early Music
ENC, Els Nostres Clàssics,
  Barcelona, Barcino
ENSJF, École Nationale Supérieure
  de Jeunes Filles
EO, Édition Orpheus, Tübingen,
  Francke
EO, Europa Orientalis
EOc, Estudis Occitans
EP, Études Philosophiques
Ep, Epistemata, Würzburg,
  Königshausen & Neumann
EPESA, Ediciones y Publicaciones
  Españolas S.A.
EPoet, Essays in Poetics
ER, Estudis Romànics
ERab, Études Rabelaisiennes
ERB, Études Romanes de Brno
ER(BSRLR), Études Romanes
  (Bulletin de la Société Roumaine
  de Linguistique Romane)
ERL, Études Romanes de Lund
ErlF, Erlanger Forschungen
ERLIMA, Équipe de recherche sur
  la littérature d'imagination du
  moyen âge, Centre d'Études
  Supérieures de Civilisation
  Médiévale/Faculté des Lettres et
  des Langues, Université de
  Poitiers.
EROPD, Ежегодник рукописного
  отдела Пушкинского дома
ERR, European Romantic Review
ES, Erlanger Studien, Erlangen,
  Palm & Enke
ES, Estudios Segovianos
EsC, L'Esprit Créateur
ESGP, Early Studies in Germanic
  Philology, Amsterdam, Rodopi
ESI, Edizioni Scientifiche Italiane
ESk, Edition Suhrkamp, Frankfurt,
  Suhrkamp
ESor, Études sorguaises
EspA, Español Actual
ESt, English Studies
EstE, Estudios Escénicos
EstG, Estudi General
EstH, Estudios Hispánicos
EstL, Estudios de Lingüística,
  Alicante
EstR, Estudios Románticos
EStud, Essays and Studies
ET, L'Écrit du Temps
EtCan, Études Canadiennes

ETF, Espacio, Tiempo y Forma,
  Revista de la Facultad de
  Geografía e Historia, UNED
EtF, Etudes francophones
EtH, Études sur l'Hérault, Pézenas
EthS, Ethnologia Slavica
ETJ, Educational Theatre Journal
ETL, Explicación de Textos
  Literarios
EtLitt, Études Littéraires, Quebec
EUDEBA, Editorial Universitaria
  de Buenos Aires
EUNSA, Ediciones Universidad de
  Navarra, Pamplona
EUS, European University Studies,
  Berne, Lang
ExP, Excerpta Philologica
EzLit, Език и литература

FAL, Forum Academicum
  Literaturwissenschaft,
  Königstein, Hain
FAM, Filologia Antica e Moderna
FAPESP, Fundação de Amparo à
  Pesquisa do Estado de São Paulo
FAR, French-American Review
FAS, Frankfurter Abhandlungen zur
  Slavistik, Giessen, Schmitz
FBAN, Фундаментальная
  бібліятэка Акадэміі навук
  БССР
FBG, Frankfurter Beiträge zur
  Germanistik, Heidelberg, Winter
FBS, Franco-British Studies
FC, Filologia e Critica
FCE, Fondo de Cultura Económica,
  Mexico
FCG — CCP, Fondation Calouste
  Gulbenkian — Centre Culturel
  Portugais, Paris
FCS, Fifteenth Century Studies
FD, Fonetică şi Dialectologie
FDL, Facetten deutscher Literatur,
  Berne, Haupt
FEI, Faites entrer l'infini. Journal de
  la Société des Amis de Louis
  Aragon et Elsa Triolet
FEK, Forschungen zur
  europäischen Kultur, Berne,
  Lang
FemSt, Feministische Studien
FF, Forma y Función

FF, Forum für Fachsprachenforschung, Tübingen, Narr

FFM, French Forum Monographs, Lexington, Kentucky

FGÄDL, Forschungen zur Geschichte der älteren deutschen Literatur, Munich, Fink

FH, Fundamenta Historica, Stuttgart-Bad Cannstatt, Frommann-Holzboog

*FH*, Frankfurter Hefte

*FHL*, Forum Homosexualität und Literatur

*FHS*, French Historical Studies

FIDS, Forschungsberichte des Instituts für Deutsche Sprache, Tübingen, Narr

*FHSJ*, Flintshire Historical Society Journal

*FilM*, Filologia Mediolatina

*FilMod*, Filologia Moderna, Udine –Pisa

*FilN*, Филологические науки

*FilR*, Filologia Romanza

*FilS*, Filologické studie

*FilZ*, Filologija, Zagreb

*FiM*, Filologia Moderna, Facultad de Filosofía y Letras, Madrid

*FinS*, Fin de Siglo

*FIRL*, Forum at Iowa on Russian Literature

*FL*, La France Latine

*FLa*, Faits de Langues

*FLG*, Freiburger literaturpsychologische Gespräche

*FLin*, Folia Linguistica

*FLinHist*, Folia Linguistica Historica

FLK, Forschungen zur Literatur- und Kulturgeschichte. Beiträge zur Sprach- und Literaturwissenschaft, Berne, Lang

*FLP*, Filologia e linguística portuguesa

*FLS*, French Literature Series

*FLV*, Fontes Linguae Vasconum

*FM*, Le Français Moderne

*FMADIUR*, FM: Annali del Dipartimento di Italianistica, Università di Roma 'La Sapienza'

FMDA, Forschungen und Materialien zur deutschen

Aufklärung, Stuttgart — Bad Cannstatt, Frommann-Holzboog

*FMLS*, Forum for Modern Language Studies

*FMon*, Le Français dans le Monde

*FmSt*, Frühmittelalterliche Studien

*FMT*, Forum Modernes Theater

FN, Frühe Neuzeit, Tübingen, Niemeyer

FNDIR, Fédération nationale des déportés et internés résistants

FNS, Frühneuzeit-Studien, Frankfurt, Lang

*FoH*, Foro Hispánico, Amsterdam

FNT, Foilseacháin Náisiúnta Tta

*FoI*, Forum Italicum

*FoS*, Le Forme e la Storia

*FP*, Folia Phonetica

*FPub*, First Publications

*FR*, French Review

*FrA*, Le Français Aujourd'hui

*FranS*, Franciscan Studies

*FrCS*, French Cultural Studies

*FrF*, French Forum

*FrH*, Französisch Heute

*FrP* Le Français Préclassique

*FrSoc*, Français et Société

FS, Forum Slavicum, Munich, Fink

*FS*, French Studies

*FSB*, French Studies Bulletin

*FSlav*, Folia Slavica

*FSSA*, French Studies in Southern Africa

FT, Fischer Taschenbuch, Frankfurt, Fischer

*FT*, Finsk Tidskrift

*FTCG*, 'La Talanquere': Folklore, Tradition, Culture Gasconne, Nogano

FUE, Fundación Universitaria Española

FV, Fortuna Vitrea, Tübingen, Niemeyer

*FZPT*, Freiburger Zeitschrift für Philosophie und Theologie

GA, Germanistische Arbeitshefte, Tübingen, Niemeyer

GAB, Göppinger Akademische Beiträge, Lauterburg, Kümmerle

GAG, Göppinger Arbeiten zur Germanistik, Lauterburg, Kümmerle

*GAKS*, Gesammelte Aufsätze zur Kulturgeschichte Spaniens

*GalR*, Galician Review, Birmingham

GANDLL, Giessener Arbeiten zur neueren deutschen Literatur und Literaturwissenschaft, Berne, Lang

GAS, German-Australian Studies, Berne, Lang

GASK, Germanistische Arbeiten zu Sprache und Kulturgeschichte, Frankfurt, Lang

GB, Germanistische Bibliothek, Heidelberg, Winter

*GBA*, Gazette des Beaux-Arts

*GBE*, Germanistik in der Blauen Eule

GC, Generalitat de Catalunya

*GCFI*, Giornale Critico della Filosofia Italiana

GEMP, Groupement d'Ethnomusicologie en Midi-Pyrénées, La Talvèra

GerAb, Germanistische Abhandlungen, Stuttgart, Metzler

*GerLux*, Germanistik Luxembourg

*GermL*, Germanistische Linguistik

*GeW*, Germanica Wratislaviensia

*GF*, Giornale di Fisica

*GFFNS*, Godišnjak Filozofskog fakulteta u Novom Sadu

*GG*, Geschichte und Gesellschaft

GGF, Göteborger Germanistische Forschungen, University of Gothenburg

GGVD, Grundlagen und Gedanken zum Verständnis des Dramas, Frankfurt, Diesterweg

*GGF*, Greifswalder Germanistische Forschungen

GGVEL, Grundlagen und Gedanken zum Verständnis erzählender Literatur, Frankfurt, Diesterweg

GIDILOc, Grop d'Iniciativa per un Diccionari Informatizat de la Lenga Occitana, Montpellier

*GIF*, Giornale Italiano di Filologia

GIGFL, Glasgow Introductory Guides to French Literature

GIGGL, Glasgow Introductory Guides to German Literature

*GJ*, Gutenberg-Jahrbuch

*GJb*, Goethe Jahrbuch

*GJLL*, The Georgetown Journal of Language and Linguistics

GK, Goldmann Klassiker, Munich, Goldmann

GL, Germanistische Lehrbuchsammlung, Berlin, Weidler

*GL*, General Linguistics

GLC, German Life and Civilisation, Berne, Lang

*GLL*, German Life and Letters

GLML, The Garland Library of Medieval Literature, New York –London, Garland

*GLR*, García Lorca Review

*GLS*, Grazer Linguistische Studien

*Glyph*, Glyph: Johns Hopkins Textual Studies, Baltimore

*GM*, Germanistische Mitteilungen

GML, Gothenburg Monographs in Linguistics

*GMon*, German Monitor

*GN*, Germanic Notes and Reviews

GPB, Гос. публичная библиотека им. М. Е. Салтыкова-Щедрина

GPI, Государственный педагогический институт

GPSR, Glossaire des Patois de la Suisse Romande

*GQ*, German Quarterly

*GR*, Germanic Review

GREC, Groupe de Recherches et d'Études du Clermontais, Clermont-l'Hérault

GREHAM, Groupe de REcherche d'Histoire de l'Anthroponymie Médiévale, Tours, Université François-Rabelais

GRELCA, Groupe de Recherche sur les Littératures de la Caraïbe, Université Laval

GRLH, Garland Reference Library of the Humanities, New York — London, Garland

GRLM, Grundriss der romanischen Literaturen des Mittelalters

*GRM*, Germanisch-Romanische Monatsschrift

*GrSt*, Grundtvig Studier

*GS*, Lo Gai Saber, Toulouse

GSA, Germanic Studies in America, Berne–Frankfurt, Lang

GSC, German Studies in Canada, Frankfurt, Lang

*GSI*, German Studies in India

*GSl*, Germano-Slavica, Ontario

*GSLI*, Giornale Storico della Letteratura Italiana

*GSR*, German Studies Review

GSSL, Göttinger Schriften zur Sprach– und Literaturwissenschaft, Göttingen, Herodot

GTN, Gdańskie Towarzystwo Naukowe

GTS, Germanistische Texte und Studien, Hildesheim, Olms

GV, Generalitat Valenciana

*GY*, Goethe Yearbook


H, Hochschulschriften, Cologne, Pahl-Rugenstein

*HAHR*, Hispanic American Historical Review

*HB*, Horváth Blätter

*HBA*, Historiografía y Bibliografía Americanistas, Seville

HBG, Hamburger Beiträge zur Germanistik, Frankfurt, Lang

HDG, Huis aan de Drie Grachten, Amsterdam

*HEI*, History of European Ideas

*HEL*, Histoire, Epistémologie, Language

*Her(A)*, Hermes, Århus

*HES*, Histoire, Économie et Société

*HeyJ*, Heythrop Journal

HF, Heidelberger Forschungen, Heidelberg, Winter

*HHS*, History of the Human Sciences

*HI*, Historica Ibérica

*HIAR*, Hamburger Ibero-Amerikanische Reihe

HICL, Histoire des Idées et Critique Littéraire, Geneva, Droz

HIGL, Holland Institute for Generative Linguistics, Leiden

*HisJ*, Hispanic Journal, Indiana–Pennsylvania

*HisL*, Hispanic Linguistics

*HistL*, Historiographia Linguistica

*HistS*, History of Science

*His(US)*, Hispania, Los Angeles

*HJ*, Historical Journal

*HJb*, Heidelberger Jahrbücher

*HJBS*, Hispanic Journal of Behavioural Sciences

HKADL, Historisch-kritische Arbeiten zur deutschen Literatur, Frankfurt, Lang

*HKZMTLG*, Handelingen van de Koninklijke Zuidnederlandse Maatschappij voor Taalen, Letterkunde en Geschiedenis

HL, Hochschulschriften Literaturwissenschaft, Königstein, Hain

*HL*, Humanistica Lovaniensia

*HLB*, Harvard Library Bulletin

*HLQ*, Huntington Library Quarterly

*HLS*, Historiska och litteraturhistoriska studier

HM, Hommes et Migrations

*HMJb*, Heinrich Mann Jahrbuch

*HP*, History of Psychiatry

*HPh*, Historical Philology

*HPos*, Hispanica Posnaniensia

HPS, Hamburger Philologische Studien, Hamburg, Buske

HPSl, Heidelberger Publikationen zur Slavistik, Frankfurt, Lang

*HPT*, History of Political Thought

*HR*, Hispanic Review

*HRef*, Historical reflections / Reflexions historiques

*HRel*, History of Religions

*HRev*, Hrvatska revija

*HRSHM*, Heresis, revue semestrielle d'hérésiologie médiévale

HS, Helfant Studien, Stuttgart, Helfant

*HS*, Hispania Sacra

*HSLA*, Hebrew University Studies in Literature and the Arts

*HSlav*, Hungaro-Slavica

HSMS, Hispanic Seminary of Medieval Studies, Madison

*HSp*, Historische Sprachforschung (Historical Linguistics)

*HSSL*, Harvard Studies in Slavic Linguistics

*HSt*, Hispanische Studien

*HSWSL*, Hallesche Studien zur Wirkung von Sprache und Literatur

HT, Helfant Texte, Stuttgart, Helfant

*HT*, History Today
*HTh*, History and Theory
*HTR*, Harvard Theological Review
*HUS*, Harvard Ukrainian Studies
*HY*, Herder Yearbook
*HZ*, Historische Zeitschrift

*IÅ*, Ibsen-Årbok, Oslo
*IAP*, Ibero-Americana Pragensia
*IAr*, Iberoamerikanisches Archiv
*IARB*, Inter-American Review of
 Bibliography
*IASL*, Internationales Archiv für
 Sozialgeschichte der deutschen
 Literatur
*IASLS*, Internationales Archiv für
 Sozialgeschichte der deutschen
 Literatur: Sonderheft
IB, Insel-Bücherei, Frankfurt, Insel
IBKG, Innsbrucker Beiträge zur
 Kulturwissenschaft.
 Germanistische Reihe
IBL, Instytut Badań Literackich
 PAN, Warsaw
IBLA, Institut des Belles Lettres
 Arabes
IBLe, Insel-Bücherei, Leipzig, Insel
IBS, Innsbrücker Beiträge zur
 Sprachwissenschaft
*IC*, Index on Censorship
ICALP, Instituto de Cultura e
 Língua Portuguesa, Lisbon
*ICALPR*, Instituto de Cultura e
 Língua Portuguesa. Revista
ICC, Instituto Caro y Cuervo,
 Bogotà
ICMA, Instituto de Cooperación
 con el Mundo Árabe
*ID*, Italia Dialettale
*IDF*, Informationen Deutsch als
 Fremdsprache
IDL, Indices zur deutschen
 Literatur, Tübingen, Niemeyer
*IdLit*, Ideologies and Literature
IEC, Institut d'Estudis Catalans
IEI, Istituto dell'Enciclopedia
 Italiana
IEO, Institut d'Estudis Occitans
IES, Institut d'Études Slaves, Paris
IF, Impulse der Forschung,
 Darmstadt, Wissenschaftliche
 Buchgesellschaft
*IF*, Indogermanische Forschungen

IFC, Institutión Fernando el
 Católico
*IFEE*, Investigación Franco-
 Española. Estudios
IFiS, Instytut Filozofii i Socjologii
 PAN, Warsaw
IFOTT, Institut voor Functioneel
 Onderzoek naar Taal en
 Taalgebruik, Amsterdam
*IFR*, International Fiction Review
*IG*, Information Grammaticale
*IHC*, Italian History and Culture
*IHE*, Índice Histórico Español
*IHS*, Irish Historical Studies
II, Information und Interpretation,
 Frankfurt, Lang
IIa, Институт языкознания
III, Институт истории искусств
*IIFV*, Institut Interuniversitari de
 Filologia Valenciana, Valencia
*IJ*, Italian Journal
*IJAL*, International Journal of
 American Linguistics
*IJBAG*, Internationales Jahrbuch
 der Bettina-von-Arnim
 Gesellschaft
*IJCS*, International Journal of
 Canadian Studies
*IJFS*, International Journal of
 Francophone Studies, Leeds
*IJHL*, Indiana Journal of Hispanic
 Literatures
*IJL*, International Journal of
 Lexicography
*IJP*, International Journal of
 Psycholinguistics
*IJSL*, International Journal for the
 Sociology of Language
*IJSLP*, International Journal of
 Slavic Linguistics and Poetics
*IK*, Искусство кино
IKU, Institut za književnost i
 umetnost, Belgrade
*IL*, L'Information Littéraire
*ILASLR*, Istituto Lombardo.
 Accademia di Scienze e Lettere.
 Rendiconti
*ILen*, Искусство Ленинграда
ILG, Instituto da Lingua Galega
*ILing*, Incontri Linguistici
ILTEC, Instituto de Linguistica
 Teórica e Computacional, Lisbon
*IMN*, Irisleabhar Mhá Nuad

*IMR*, International Migration Review
*IMU*, Italia Medioevale e Umanistica
INCM, Imprensa Nacional, Casa da Moeda, Lisbon
*InfD*, Informationen und Didaktik
INLF, Institut National de la Langue Française
INIC, Instituto Nacional de Investigação Científica
*InL*, Иностранная литература
INLE, Instituto Nacional del Libro Español
InstEB, Inst. de Estudos Brasileiros
InstNL, Inst. Nacional do Livro, Brasilia
*IO*, Italiano e Oltre
IPL, Istituto di Propaganda Libraria
IPZS, Istituto Poligrafico e Zecca dello Stato, Rome
*IR*, L'Immagine Riflessa
*IRAL*, International Review of Applied Linguistics
IRIa, Институт русского языка Российской Академии Наук
*IrR*, The Irish Review
*IRSH*, International Review of Social History
*IRSL*, International Review of Slavic Linguistics
ISC, Institut de Sociolingüística Catalana
ISI, Institute for Scientific Information, U.S.A.
ISIEMC, Istituto Storico Italiano per l'Età Moderna e Contemporanea, Rome
*ISLIa*, Известия Академии наук СССР. Серия литературы и языка
*ISOAN*, Известия сибирского отделения АН СССР, Novosibirsk
*ISP*, International Studies in Philosophy
*ISPS*, International Studies in the Philosophy of Science
*ISS*, Irish Slavonic Studies
*IsS*, Islamic Studies, Islamabad
*ISSA*, Studi d'Italianistica nell'Africa Australe: Italian Studies in Southern Africa
*ISt*, Italian Studies

*ISV*, Informazioni e Studi Vivaldiani
IT, Insel Taschenbuch, Frankfurt, Insel
*ItC*, Italian Culture
*ITL*, ITL. Review of Applied Linguistics, Instituut voor Toegepaste Linguistiek, Leuven
*ItQ*, Italian Quarterly
*ItStudien*, Italienische Studien
*IUJF*, Internationales Uwe-Johnson-Forum
IULA, Institut Universitari de Lingüística Aplicada, Universitat Pompeu Fabra, Barcelona
IUP, Irish University Press
*IUR*, Irish University Review
IV, Istituto Veneto di Scienze, Lettere ed Arti
IVAS, Indices Verborum zum altdeutschen Schrifttum, Amsterdam, Rodopi
IVN, Internationale Vereniging voor Nederlandistiek

*JAAC*, Journal of Aesthetics and Art Criticism
*JACIS*, Journal of the Association for Contemporary Iberian Studies
*JAE*, Journal of Aesthetic Education
*JAIS*, Journal of Anglo-Italian Studies, Malta
*JAMS*, Journal of the American Musicological Society
*JAOS*, Journal of the American Oriental Society
JanL, Janua Linguarum, The Hague, Mouton
*JAPLA*, Journal of the Atlantic Provinces Linguistic Association
*JARA*, Journal of the American Romanian Academy of Arts and Sciences
*JAS*, The Journal of Algerian Studies
*JASI*, Jahrbuch des Adalbert-Stifter-Instituts
*JATI*, Association of Teachers of Italian Journal
*JazA*, Jazykovědné aktuality
*JazŠ*, Jazykovedné štúdie

JAZU, Jugoslavenska akademija znanosti i umjetnosti

*JBSP*, Journal of the British Society for Phenomenology

*JČ*, Jazykovedný časopis, Bratislava

*JCanS*, Journal of Canadian Studies

*JCHAS*, Journal of the Cork Historical and Archaeological Society

*JCL*, Journal of Child Language

*JCLin*, Journal of Celtic Linguistics

*JCS*, Journal of Celtic Studies

*JDASD*, Deutsche Akademie für Sprache und Dichtung: Jahrbuch

*JDF*, Jahrbuch Deutsch als Fremdsprache

*JDSG*, Jahrbuch der Deutschen Schiller-Gesellschaft

*JEA*, Lou Journalet de l'Escandihado Aubagnenco

*JEGP*, Journal of English and Germanic Philology

*JEH*, Journal of Ecclesiastical History

*JEL*, Journal of English Linguistics

*JES*, Journal of European Studies

*JF*, Južnoslovenski filolog

*JFDH*, Jahrbuch des Freien Deutschen Hochstifts

*JFG*, Jahrbuch der Fouqué Gesellschaft

*JFinL*, Jahrbuch für finnisch-deutsche Literaturbeziehungen

*JFL*, Jahrbuch für fränkische Landesforschung

*JFLS*, Journal of French Language Studies

*JFR*, Journal of Folklore Research

*JG*, Jahrbuch für Geschichte, Berlin, Akademie

*JGO*, Jahrbücher für die Geschichte Osteuropas

*JHA*, Journal for the History of Astronomy

*JHI*, Journal of the History of Ideas

*JHispP*, Journal of Hispanic Philology

*JHP*, Journal of the History of Philosophy

*JHR*, Journal of Hispanic Research

*JHS*, Journal of the History of Sexuality

*JIAS*, Journal of Inter-American Studies

*JIES*, Journal of Indo-European Studies

*JIG*, Jahrbuch für Internationale Germanistik

*JIL*, Journal of Italian Linguistics

*JILAS*, Journal of Iberian and Latin American Studies (formerly *Tesserae*)

*JILS*, Journal of Interdisciplinary Literary Studies

*JIPA*, Journal of the International Phonetic Association

*JIRS*, Journal of the Institute of Romance Studies

*JJQ*, James Joyce Quarterly

*JJS*, Journal of Jewish Studies

*JL*, Journal of Linguistics

*JLACS*, Journal of Latin American Cultural Studies

*JLAL*, Journal of Latin American Lore

*JLAS*, Journal of Latin American Studies

*JLH*, Journal of Library History

*JLS*, Journal of Literary Semantics

*JLSP*, Journal of Language and Social Psychology

*JMemL*, Journal of Memory and Language

*JMEMS*, Journal of Medieval and Early Modern Studies

*JMH*, Journal of Medieval History

*JMHRS*, Journal of the Merioneth Historical and Record Society

*JML*, Journal of Modern Literature

*JMLat*, Journal of Medieval Latin

*JMMD*, Journal of Multilingual and Multicultural Development

*JMMLA*, Journal of the Midwest Modern Language Association

*JModH*, Journal of Modern History

*JMP*, Journal of Medicine and Philosophy

*JMRS*, Journal of Medieval and Renaissance Studies

*JMS*, Journal of Maghrebi Studies

*JNT*, Journal of Narrative Technique

*JONVL*, Een Jaarboek: Overzicht van de Nederlandse en Vlaamse Literatuur

*JOWG*, Jahrbuch der Oswald von Wolkenstein Gesellschaft

*JP*, Journal of Pragmatics

*JPC*, Journal of Popular Culture
*JPCL*, Journal of Pidgin and Creole
  Languages
*JPh*, Journal of Phonetics
*JPHS*, The Journal of the
  Pembrokeshire Historical Society
*JPol*, Język Polski
*JPR*, Journal of Psycholinguistic
  Research
*JQ*, Jacques e i suoi Quaderni
*JRA*, Journal of Religion in Africa
*JRG*, Jahrbücher der Reineke-
  Gesellschaft
*JRH*, Journal of Religious History
*JRIC*, Journal of the Royal
  Institution of Cornwall
*JŘJR*, Jazyk a řeč jihočeského
  regionu. České Budějovice,
  Pedagogická fakulta Jihočeské
  univerzity
*JRMA*, Journal of the Royal Musical
  Association
*JRMMRA*, Journal of the Rocky
  Mountain Medieval and
  Renaissance Association
*JRS*, Journal of Romance Studies
*JRUL*, Journal of the Rutgers
  University Libraries
*JS*, Journal des Savants
*JSEES*, Japanese Slavic and East
  European Studies
*JSem*, Journal of Semantics
*JSFWUB*, Jahrbuch der
  Schlesischen Friedrich-Wilhelms-
  Universität zu Breslau
*JSH*, Jihočeský sborník historický
*JSHR*, Journal of Speech and
  Hearing Research
*JSL*, Journal of Slavic Linguistics
*JSS*, Journal of Spanish Studies:
  Twentieth Century
*JTS*, Journal of Theological Studies
JU, Judentum und Umwelt, Berne,
  Lang.
*JUS*, Journal of Ukrainian Studies
*JV*, Jahrbuch für Volkskunde
*JVF*, Jahrbuch für
  Volksliedforschung
*JVLVB*, Journal of Verbal Learning
  and Verbal Behavior
*JWCI*, Journal of the Warburg and
  Courtauld Institutes
*JWGV*, Jahrbuch des Wiener
  Goethe-Vereins, Neue Folge

*JWH*, Journal of World History
*JWIL*, Journal of West Indian
  Literature
*JZ*, Jazykovedný zborník


KANTL, Koninklijke Akademie
  voor Nederlandse Taal- en
  Letterkunde
KASL, Kasseler Arbeiten zur
  Sprache und Literatur, Frankfurt,
  Lang
KAW, Krajowa Agencja
  Wydawnicza
KAWLSK, Koninklijke Academie
  voor Wetenschappen, Letteren en
  Schone Kunsten van België,
  Brussels
*KB*, Književni barok
*KBGL*, Kopenhagener Beiträge zur
  germanistischen Linguistik
*Kbl*, Korrespondenzblatt des
  Vereins für niederdeutsche
  Sprachforschung
KDPM, Kleine deutsche
  Prosadenkmäler des Mittelalters,
  Munich, Fink
KGOS, Kultur- und
  geistesgeschichtliche
  Ostmitteleuropa-Studien,
  Marburg, Elwert
KGS, Kölner germanistische
  Studien, Cologne, Böhlau
*KGS*, Kairoer germanistische
  Studien
*KH*, Komparatistische Hefte
KhL, Художественная
  литература
*KI*, Književna istorija
KiW, Książka i Wiedza
*KJ*, Književnost i jezik
*KK*, Kirke og Kultur
*KlJb*, Kleist-Jahrbuch
*KLWL*, Krieg und Literatur: War
  and Literature
Klage, Klage: Kölner linguistische
  Arbeiten. Germanistik, Hürth-
  Efferen, Gabel
*KN*, Kwartalnik Neofilologiczny
*KnK*, Kniževna kritika
КО, Университетско
  издателство
  'Климент Охридски'
*KO*, Книжное обозрение

KP, Книжная палата
KRA, Kölner Romanistische Arbeiten, Geneva, Droz
*KS*, Kúltura slova
KSDL, Kieler Studien zur deutschen Literaturgeschichte, Neumünster, Wachholtz
KSL, Kölner Studien zur Literaturwissenschaft, Frankfurt, Lang
*KSt*, Kant Studien
KTA, Kröners Taschenausgabe, Stuttgart, Kröner
KTRM, Klassische Texte des romanischen Mittelalters, Munich, Fink
KU, Konstanzer Universitäts-reden
KUL, Katolicki Uniwersytet Lubelski, Lublin
KuSDL, Kulturwissenschaftliche Studien zur deutschen Literatur, Opladen, Westdeutscher Verlag
*KZG*, Koreanische Zeitschrift für Germanistik
KZMTLG, Koninklijke Zuidnederlandse Maatschappij voor Taal- en Letterkunde en Geschiedenis, Brussels
*KZMTLGH*, Koninklijke Zuidnederlandse Maatschaapij voor Taal- en Letterkunde en Geschiedenis. Handelingen

LA, Linguistische Arbeiten, Tübingen, Niemeyer
*LA*, Linguistic Analysis
*LaA*, Language Acquisition
*LAbs*, Linguistics Abstracts
*LaF*, Langue Française
*LAILJ*, Latin American Indian Literatures Journal
*LaLi*, Langues et Linguistique
*LALIES*, LALIES. Actes des sessions de linguistique et de littérature. Institut d'Etudes linguistiques et phonétiques. Sessions de linguistique. Ecole Normale Supérieure Paris, Sorbonne nouvelle
*LALR*, Latin-American Literary Review
*LaM*, Les Langues Modernes

*LangH*, Le Langage et l'Homme
*LArb*, Linguistische Arbeitsberichte
*LARR*, Latin-American Research Review
*LaS*, Langage et Société
*LATR*, Latin-American Theatre Review
*LatT*, Latin Teaching, Shrewsbury
*LB*, Leuvense Bijdragen
*LBer*, Linguistische Berichte
*LBIYB*, Leo Baeck Institute Year Book
*LBR*, Luso-Brazilian Review
*LC*, Letture Classensi
*LCC*, Léachtaí Cholm Cille
*LCh*, Literatura Chilena
*LCP*, Language and Cognitive Processes
*LCrit*, Lavoro Critico
*LCUTA*, Library Chronicle of the University of Texas at Austin
*LD*, Libri e Documenti
*LdA*, Linha d'Agua
*LDan*, Lectura Dantis
*LDanN*, Lectura Dantis Newberryana
*LDGM*, Ligam-DiGaM. Quadèrn de lingüística e lexicografía gasconas, Fontenay aux Roses
*LE*, Language and Education
*LEA*, Lingüística Española Actual
*LebS*, Lebende Sprachen
*LEMIR*, Literatura Española Medieval y del Renacimiento, Valencia U.P.; http://www.uv.es/~lemir/Revista.html
*Leng(M)*, Lengas, Montpellier
*Leng(T)*, Lengas, Toulouse
*LenP*, Ленинградская панорама
*LetA*, Letterature d'America
*LetD*, Letras de Deusto
LETHB, Laboratoires d'Études Théâtrales de l'Université de Haute-Bretagne. Études et Documents, Rennes
*LetL*, Letras e Letras, Departamento de Línguas Estrangeiras Modernas, Universidade Federal de Uberlândia, Brazil
*LetMS*, Letopis Matice srpske, Novi Sad
*LetP*, Il Lettore di Provincia
*LetS*, Letras Soltas
*LevT*, Levende Talen

*Lex(L)*, Lexique, Lille
*LF*, Letras Femeninas
*LFil*, Listy filologické
*LFQ*, Literature and Film Quarterly
LGF, Lunder Germanistische Forschungen, Stockholm, Almqvist & Wiksell
LGGL, Literatur in der Geschichte, Geschichte in der Literatur, Cologne–Vienna, Böhlau
LGL, Langs Germanistische Lehrbuchsammlung, Berne, Lang
LGP, Leicester German Poets, Leicester U.P.
LGW, Literaturwissenschaft — Gesellschaftswissenschaft, Stuttgart, Klett
*LH*, Lingüística Hispánica
*LHum*, Litteraria Humanitas, Brno
*LI*, Linguistic Inquiry
LIÅA, Litteraturvetenskapliga institutionen vid Åbo Akademi, Åbo Akademi U.P.
*LiB*, Literatur in Bayern
*LIC*, Letteratura Italiana Contemporanea
*LiCC*, Lien des chercheurs cévenols
LIE, Lessico Intellettuale Europeo, Rome, Ateneo
*LiL*, Limbă şi Literatură
*LiLi*, Zeitschrift für Literaturwissenschaft und Linguistik
LingAk, Linguistik Aktuell, Amsterdam, Benjamins
*LingBal*, Балканско езикознание – Linguistique Balkanique
*LingCon*, Lingua e Contesto
*LingFil*, Linguistica e Filologia, Dipartimento di Linguistica e Letterature Comparate, Bergamo
*LingLett*, Linguistica e Letteratura
*LíngLit*, Língua e Literatura, São Paulo
*LinLit*, Lingüística y Literatura
*LINQ*, Linq [Literature in North Queensland]
*LInv*, Linguisticae Investigationes
*LiR*, Limba Română
*LIT*, Literature Interpretation Theory
*LIt*, Lettera dall'Italia
*LitAP*, Literární archív Památníku národního pisemnictví

*LItal*, Lettere Italiane
*LitB*, Literatura, Budapest
*LitC*, Littératures Classiques
*LitG*, Литературная газета, Moscow
*LitH*, Literature and History
LItL, Letteratura Italiana Laterza, Bari, Laterza
*LitL*, Literatur für Leser
*LitLing*, Literatura y Lingüística
*LitM*, Literární měsíčník
*LitMis*, Литературна мисъл
*LitP*, Literature and Psychology
*LitR*, The Literary Review
LittB, Litteraria, Bratislava
LittK, Litterae, Lauterburg, Kümmerle
*LittS*, Litteratur og Samfund
*LittW*, Litteraria, Wrocław
*LiU*, Література Україна
*LJb*, Literaturwissenschaftliches Jahrbuch der Görres–Gesellschaft
LK, Literatur-Kommentare, Munich, Hanser
*LK*, Literatur und Kritik
LKol, Loccumer Kolloquium
*LL*, Langues et Littératures, Rabat
*LlA*, Lletres Asturianes
LLC, Literary and Linguistic Computing
*LlC*, Llên Cymru
*LlLi*, Llengua i Literatura
LLS, Lenguas, Literaturas, Sociedades. Cuadernos Hispánicos
LLSEE, Linguistic and Literary Studies in Eastern Europe, Amsterdam, Benjamins
*LM*, Le Lingue del Mondo
*LN*, Lingua Nostra
*LNB*, Leipziger namenkundliche Beiträge
*LNL*, Les Langues Néo-Latines
*LNouv*, Les Lettres Nouvelles
LoP, Loccumer Protokolle
*LOS*, Literary Onomastic Studies
LP, Le Livre de Poche, Librairie Générale Française
*LP*, Lingua Posnaniensis
*LPen*, Letras Peninsulares
*LPh*, Linguistics and Philosophy
*LPLP*, Language Problems and Language Planning

*LPO*, Lenga e Païs d'Oc, Montpellier
*LPr*, Linguistica Pragensia
*LQ*, Language Quarterly, University of S. Florida
*LQu*, Lettres québécoises
LR, Linguistische Reihe, Munich, Hueber
*LR*, Les Lettres Romanes
*LRev*, Linguistic Review
*LRI*, Libri e Riviste d'Italia
LS, Literatur als Sprache, Münster, Aschendorff
*LS*, Lingua e Stile
*LSa*, Lusitania Sacra
*LSc*, Language Sciences
*LSil*, Linguistica Silesiana
LSNS, Lundastudier i Nordisk Språkvetenskap
*LSo*, Language in Society
*LSp*, Language and Speech
*LSPS*, Lou Sourgentin/La Petite Source. Revue culturelle bilingue nissart-français, Nice
*LSty*, Language and Style
LSW, Ludowa Spółdzielnia Wydawnicza
LTG, Literaturwissenschaft, Theorie und Geschichte, Frankfurt, Lang
ŁTN, Łódzkie Towarzystwo Naukowe
*LTP*, Laval Théologique et Philosophique
LU, Literarhistorische Untersuchungen, Berne, Lang
*LVC*, Language Variation and Change
LW, Literatur und Wirklichkeit, Bonn, Bouvier
*LWU*, Literatur in Wissenschaft und Unterricht
*LY*, Lessing Yearbook

*MA*, Moyen Âge
*MAASC*, Mémoires de l'Académie des Arts et des Sciences de Carcassonne
*MACL*, Memórias da Academia de Ciências de Lisboa, Classe de Letras
*MAe*, Medium Aevum

*MAKDDR*, Mitteilungen der Akademie der Künste der DDR
*MAL*, Modern Austrian Literature
*MaL*, Le Maghreb Littéraire – Revue Canadienne des Littératures Maghrébines, Toronto
*MaM*, Marbacher Magazin
MAPS, Medium Aevum. Philologische Studien, Munich, Fink
MARPOC, Maison d'animation et de recherche populaire occitane, Nimes
*MAST*, Memorie dell'Accademia delle Scienze di Torino
MatSl, Matica Slovenská
*MBA*, Mitteilungen aus dem Brenner-Archiv
*MBAV*, Miscellanea Bibliothecae Apostolicae Vaticanae
MBMRF, Münchener Beiträge zur Mediävistik und Renaissance-Forschung, Bachenhausen, Arbeo
MBRP, Münstersche Beiträge zur romanischen Philologie, Münster, Kleinheinrich
MBSL, Mannheimer Beiträge zur Sprach- und Literaturwissenschaft, Tübingen, Narr
*MC*, Misure Critiche
*MCV*, Mélanges de la Casa de Velázquez
*MD*, Musica Disciplina
*MDan*, Meddelser fra Dansklærerforeningen
MDG, Mitteilungen des deutschen Germanistenverbandes
MDL, Mittlere Deutsche Literatur in Neu- und Nachdrucken, Berne, Lang
*MDr*, Momentum Dramaticum
MDU, Monatshefte für deutschen Unterricht, deutsche Sprache und Literatur
MEC, Ministerio de Educação e Cultura, Rio de Janeiro
*MedC*, La Méditerranée et ses Cultures
*MedH*, Medioevo e Umanesimo
*MedLR*, Mediterranean Language Review
*MedP*, Medieval Perspectives

*MedRom*, Medioevo Romanzo
*MedS*, Medieval Studies
*MEFR*, Mélanges de l'École Française de Rome, Moyen Age
*MerH*, Merthyr Historian
*MerP*, Mercurio Peruano
*MF*, Mercure de France
MFDT, Mainzer Forschungen zu Drama und Theater, Tübingen, Francke
*MFS*, Modern Fiction Studies
MG, Молодая гвардия
*MG*, Молодая гвардия
MGB, Münchner Germanistische Beiträge, Munich, Fink
MGG, Mystik in Geschichte und Gegenwart, Stuttgart-Bad Cannstatt, Frommann-Holzboog
MGS, Marburger Germanistische Studien, Frankfurt, Lang
*MGS*, Michigan Germanic Studies
*MGSL*, Minas Gerais, Suplemento Literário
*MH*, Medievalia et Humanistica
*MHJ*, Medieval History Journal
*MHLS*, Mid-Hudson Language Studies
MHRA, Modern Humanities Research Association
*MichRS*, Michigan Romance Studies
MILUS, Meddelanden från Institutionen i Lingvistik vid Universitetet i Stockholm
MINS, Meddelanden från institutionen för nordiska språk vid Stockholms universiteit, Stockholm U.P.
*MiscBarc*, Miscellanea Barcinonensia
*MiscEB*, Miscel·lània d'Estudis Bagencs
*MiscP*, Miscel·lània Penedesenca
*MJ*, Mittellateinisches Jahrbuch
*MK*, Maske und Kothurn
MKH, Deutsche Forschungsgemeinschaft: Mitteilung der Kommission für Humanismusforschung, Weinheim, Acta Humaniora
*MKNAWL*, Mededelingen der Koninklijke Nederlandse Akademie van Wetenschappen, Afd. Letterkunde, Amsterdam

ML, Mediaevalia Lovaniensia, Leuven U.P.
*ML*, Modern Languages
*MLAIntBibl*, Modern Language Association International Bibliography
MLIÅA, Meddelanden utgivna av Litteraturvetenskapliga institutionen vid Åbo Akademi, Åbo Akademi U.P.
MLIGU, Meddelanden utgivna av Litteraturvetenskapliga institutionen vid Göteborgs universitet, Gothenburg U.P.
MLit, Мастацкая літаратура
*MLit*, Miesięcznik Literacki
MLIUU, Meddelanden utgivna av Litteraturvetenskapliga institutionen vid Uppsala universitet, Uppsala U.P.
*MLJ*, Modern Language Journal
*MLN*, Modern Language Notes
*MLQ*, Modern Language Quarterly
*MLR*, Modern Language Review
*MLS*, Modern Language Studies
*MM*, Maal og Minne
MMS, Münstersche Mittelalter-Schriften, Munich, Fink
*MN*, Man and Nature. L'Homme et la Nature
MNGT, Manchester New German Texts, Manchester U.P.
*ModD*, Modern Drama
*ModS*, Modern Schoolman
MoL, Modellanalysen: Literatur, Paderborn, Schöningh–Munich, Fink
MON, Ministerstwo Obrony Narodowej, Warsaw
MosR, Московский рабочий
*MoyFr*, Le Moyen Français
*MP*, Modern Philology
*MQ*, Mississippi Quarterly
*MQR*, Michigan Quarterly Review
MR, Die Mainzer Reihe, Mainz, Hase & Koehler
*MR*, Medioevo e Rinascimento
*MRev*, Maghreb Review
*MRo*, Marche Romane
*MRS*, Medieval and Renaissance Studies
MRTS, Medieval and Renaissance Texts and Studies, Tempe,

Arizona, Arizona State University
MS, Marbacher Schriften, Stuttgart, Cotta
*MS*, Moderna Språk
MSC, Medjunarodni slavistički centar, Belgrade
MSG, Marburger Studien zur Germanistik, Marburg, Hitzeroth
MSHA, Maison des sciences de l'homme d'Aquitaine
*MSISS*, Materiali della Socièta Italiana di Studi sul Secolo XVIII
MSL, Marburger Studien zur Literatur, Marburg, Hitzeroth
MSLKD, Münchener Studien zur literarischen Kultur in Deutschland, Frankfurt, Lang
*MSMS*, Middeleeuse Studies — Medieval Studies, Johannesburg
MSNH, Mémoires de la Société Néophilologique de Helsinki
*MSp*, Moderne Sprachen (Zeitschrift des Verbandes der österreichischen Neuphilologen)
*MSSp*, Münchener Studien zur Sprachwissenschaft, Munich
MTCGT, Methuen's Twentieth-Century German Texts, London, Methuen
MTG, Mitteilungen zur Theatergeschichte der Goethezeit, Bonn, Bouvier
MTNF, Monographien und Texte zur Nietzsche-Forschung, Berlin — New York, de Gruyter
MTU, Münchener Texte und Untersuchungen zur deutschen Literatur des Mittelalters, Tübingen, Niemeyer
*MTUB*, Mitteilungen der T. U. Braunschweig
MUP, Manchester University Press
*MusL*, Music and Letters
*MusP*, Museum Patavinum
*MyQ*, Mystics Quarterly

*NA*, Nuova Antologia
*NAFMUM*, Nuovi Annali della Facoltà di Magistero dell'Università di Messina
*NArg*, Nuovi Argomenti

*NAS*, Nouveaux Actes Sémiotiques, PULIM, Université de Limoges
NASNCGL, North American Studies in Nineteenth-Century German Literature, Berne, Lang
*NASSAB*, Nuovi Annali della Scuola Speciale per Archivisti e Bibliotecari
NAWG, Nachrichten der Akademie der Wissenschaften zu Göttingen, phil.-hist. Kl., Göttingen, Vandenhoeck & Ruprecht
*NBGF*, Neue Beiträge zur George-Forschung
*NC*, New Criterion
*NCA*, Nouveaux Cahiers d'Allemand
*NCEFRW*, Nouvelles du Centre d'études francoprovençales 'René Willien'
*NCF*, Nineteenth-Century Fiction
*NCFS*, Nineteenth-Century French Studies
*NCo*, New Comparison
NCSRLL, North Carolina Studies in the Romance Languages and Literatures, Chapel Hill
ND, Наукова думка
*NDH*, Neue deutsche Hefte
*NdJb*, Niederdeutsches Jahrbuch
NDL, Nachdrucke deutscher Literatur des 17. Jahrhunderts, Berne, Lang
*NDL*, Neue deutsche Literatur
NdS, Niederdeutsche Studien, Cologne, Böhlau
*NDSK*, Nydanske Studier og almen kommunikationsteori
*NdW*, Niederdeutsches Wort
*NE*, Nueva Estafeta
NEL, Nouvelles Éditions Latines, Paris
*NFF*, Novel: A Forum in Fiction
*NFS*, Nottingham French Studies
*NFT*, Német Filológiai Tanulmányok. Arbeiten zur deutschen Philologie
NG, Nordistica Gothoburgensia
*NGC*, New German Critique
*NGFH*, Die Neue Gesellschaft/ Frankfurter Hefte
*NGR*, New German Review
*NGS*, New German Studies, Hull
*NH*, Nuevo Hispanismo

*NHi*, Nice Historique
NHLS, North Holland Linguistic Series, Amsterdam
*NHVKSG*, Neujahrsblatt des Historischen Vereins des Kantons St Gallen
NI, Наука и изкуство
*NIMLA*, NIMLA. Journal of the Modern Language Association of Northern Ireland
*NJ*, Naš jezik
*NJL*, Nordic Journal of Linguistics
NKT, Norske klassiker-tekster, Bergen, Eide
*NL*, Nouvelles Littéraires
*NLÅ*, Norsk Litterær Årbok
*NLD*, Nuove Letture Dantesche
*NLe*, Nuove Lettere
*NLH*, New Literary History
*NLi*, Notre Librairie
*NLLT*, Natural Language and Linguistic Theory
*NLN*, Neo-Latin News
*NLT*, Norsk Lingvistisk Tidsskrift
*NLWJ*, National Library of Wales Journal
NM, Народна младеж
*NMi*, Neuphilologische Mitteilungen
*NMS*, Nottingham Medieval Studies
*NN*, Наше наследие
*NNH*, Nueva Narrativa Hispano-americana
*NNR*, New Novel Review
*NOR*, New Orleans Review
NORNA, Nordiska samarbetskommittén för namnforskning, Uppsala
*NovE*, Novos Estudos (CEBRAP)
*NovM*, Новый мир
*NovR*, Nova Renascenza
*NOWELE*, North-Western European Language Evolution. Nowele
NP, Народна просвета
*NP*, Nouvello de Prouvènço (Li), Avignon, Parlaren Païs d'Avignoun
*NQ*, Notes and Queries
*NR*, New Review
*NŘ*, Naše řeč
*NRe*, New Readings, School of European Studies, University of Wales, College of Cardiff

*NRE*, Nuova Rivista Europea
*NRF*, Nouvelle Revue Française
*NRFH*, Nueva Revista de Filología Hispánica
*NRL*, Neue russische Literatur. Almanach, Salzburg
*NRLett*, Nouvelles de la République des Lettres
*NRLI*, Nuova Rivista di Letteratura Italiana
*NRMI*, Nuova Rivista Musicale Italiana
*NRO*, Nouvelle Revue d'Onomastique
*NRP*, Nouvelle Revue de Psychanalyse
*NRS*, Nuova Rivista Storica
*NRSS*, Nouvelle Revue du Seizième Siècle
*NRu*, Die Neue Rundschau
*NS*, Die Neueren Sprachen
*NSc*, New Scholar
*NSh*, Начальная школа
NSL, Det Norske Språk- og Litteraturselskap
*NSlg*, Neue Sammlung
*NSo*, Наш современник . . . Альманах
*NSP*, Nuovi Studi Politici
*NSS*, Nysvenska Studier
*NSt*, Naše stvaranje
NT, Навука і тэхніка
*NT*, Nordisk Tidskrift
*NTBB*, Nordisk Tidskrift för Bok- och Biblioteksväsen
*NTC*, Nuevo Texto Crítico
*NTE*, Народна творчість та етнографія
*NTg*, Nieuwe Taalgids
*NTQ*, New Theatre Quarterly
NTSh, Наукове товариство ім. Шевченка
*NTW*, News from the Top of the World: Norwegian Literature Today
*NU*, Narodna umjetnost
*NV*, Новое время
*NVS*, New Vico Studies
*NWIG*, Niewe West-Indische Gids
*NyS*, Nydanske Studier / Almen Kommunikationsteori
NYSNDL, New Yorker Studien zur neueren deutschen

Literaturgeschichte, Berne, Lang
NYUOS, New York University Ottendorfer Series, Berne, Lang
*NZh*, Новый журнал
*NZh* (StP), Новый журнал, St Petersburg
*NZJFS*, New Zealand Journal of French Studies
*NZSJ*, New Zealand Slavonic Journal


*OA*, Отечественные архивы
*OB*, Ord och Bild
OBS, Osnabrücker Beiträge zur Sprachtheorie, Oldenbourg, OBST
OBTUP, Universitetsforlaget Oslo–Bergen–Tromsø
*ÖBV*, Österreichischer Bundesverlag, Vienna
*OC*, Œuvres et Critiques
*OcL*, Oceanic Linguistics
*Oc(N)*, Oc, Nice
*OCP*, Orientalia Christiana Periodica, Rome
*OCS*, Occitan/Catalan Studies
*ÖGL*, Österreich in Geschichte und Literatur
OGS, Oxford German Studies
*OH*, Ottawa Hispánica
OIU, Oldenbourg Interpretationen mit Unterrichtshilfen, Munich, Oldenbourg
*OL*, Orbis Litterarum
*OLR*, Oxford Literary Review
OLSI, Osservatorio Linguistico della Svizzera italiana
*OM*, L'Oc Médiéval
*ON*, Otto/Novecento
*OPBS*, Occasional Papers in Belarusian Studies
OPEN, Oficyna Polska Encyklopedia Nezależna
OPI, Overseas Publications Interchange, London
*OPL*, Osservatore Politico Letterario
*OPM*, 'Ou Païs Mentounasc': Bulletin de la Société d'Art et d'Histoire du Mentonnais, Menton

OPRPNZ, Общество по распространению политических и научных знаний
*OPSLL*, Occasional Papers in Slavic Languages and Literatures
*OR*, Odrodzenie i Reformacja w Polsce
ORP, Oriental Research Partners, Cambridge
*OS*, 'Oc Sulpic': Bulletin de l'Association Occitane du Québec, Montreal
*OSP*, Oxford Slavonic Papers
*OT*, Oral Tradition
OTS, Onderzoeksinstituut voor Taal en Spraak, Utrecht
OUP, Oxford University Press
OUSL, Odense University Studies in Literature
OUSSLL, Odense University Studies in Scandinavian Languages and Literatures, Odense U.P.
OWPLC, Odense Working Papers in Language and Communication


*PA*, Présence Africaine
*PAf*, Politique Africaine
*PAGS*, Proceedings of the Australian Goethe Society
*Pal*, Palaeobulgarica — Старобългаристика
PAM, Publicacions de l'Abadia de Montserrat, Barcelona
PAN, Polska Akademia Nauk, Warsaw
*PaP*, Past and Present
*PapBSA*, Papers of the Bibliographical Society of America
*PAPhS*, Proceedings of the American Philosophical Society
*PapL*, Papiere zur Linguistik
*ParL*, Paragone Letteratura
*PartR*, Partisan Review
*PaS*, Pamiętnik Słowiański
*PASJ*, Pictish Arts Society Journal
PAX, Instytut Wydawniczy PAX, Warsaw
PB, Д-р Петър Берон
*PBA*, Proceedings of the British Academy

PBib, Philosophische Bibliothek, Hamburg, Meiner

*PBLS*, Proceedings of the Annual Meeting of the Berkeley Linguistic Society

*PBML*, Prague Bulletin of Mathematical Linguistics

*PBSA*, Publications of the Bibliographical Society of America

*PC*, Problems of Communism

*PCLS*, Proceedings of the Chicago Linguistic Society

*PCP*, Pacific Coast Philology

PD, Probleme der Dichtung, Heidelberg, Winter

*PDA*, Pagine della Dante

*PdO*, Paraula d'oc, Centre International de Recerca i Documentació d'Oc, Valencia

*PE*, Poesía Española

*PEGS(NS)*, Publications of the English Goethe Society (New Series)

*PenP*, Il Pensiero Politico

*PerM*, Perspectives Médiévales

*PEs*, Lou Prouvençau à l'Escolo

*PF*, Présences Francophones

*PFil*, Prace Filologiczne

*PFPS*, Z problemów frazeologii polskiej i słowiańskiej, ZNiO

*PFSCL*, Papers on French Seventeenth Century Literature

*PG*, Païs gascons

*PGA*, Lo pais gascon/Lou pais gascoun, Anglet

PGIG, Publikationen der Gesellschaft für interkulturelle Germanistik, Munich, Iudicium

*PH*, La Palabra y El Hombre

*PhilosQ*, Philosophical Quarterly

*PhilP*, Philological Papers, West Virginia University

*PhilR*, Philosophy and Rhetoric

*PhilRev*, Philosophical Review

*PhLC*, Phréatique, Langage et Création

*PHol*, Le Pauvre Holterling

*PhonPr*, Phonetica Pragensia

*PhP*, Philologica Pragensia

*PhR*, Phoenix Review

*PHSL*, Proceedings of the Huguenot Society of London

PI, педагогический институт

*PId*, Le Parole e le Idee

PIGS, Publications of the Institute of Germanic Studies, University of London

*PiH*, Il Piccolo Hans

*PIMA*, Proceedings of the Illinois Medieval Association

PIMS, Publications of the Institute for Medieval Studies, Toronto

PIW, Państwowy Instytut Wydawniczy, Warsaw

*PJ*, Poradnik Językowy

*PLing*, Papers in Linguistics

*PLit*, Philosophy and Literature

*PLL*, Papers on Language and Literature

*PL(L)*, Pamiętnik Literacki, London

*PLRL*, Patio de Letras/La Rosa als Llavis

*PLS*, Přednášky z běhu Letní školy slovanských studií

*PL(W)*, Pamiętnik Literacki, Warsaw

*PM*, Pleine Marge

*PMH*, Portugaliae Monumenta Historica

PMHRS, Papers of the Medieval Hispanic Research Seminar, London, Department of Hispanic Studies, Queen Mary and Westfield College

*PMLA*, Publications of the Modern Language Association of America

*PMPA*, Publications of the Missouri Philological Association

*PN*, Paraulas de novelum, Périgueux

*PNCIP*, Plurilinguismo. Notizario del Centro Internazionale sul Plurilinguismo

*PNR*, Poetry and Nation Review

*PNUS*, Prace Naukowe Uniwersytetu Śląskiego, Katowice

*PoetT*, Poetics Today

*PolR*, Polish Review

*PortSt*, Portuguese Studies

*PP*, Prace Polonistyczne

*PPNCFL*, Proceedings of the Pacific Northwest Conference on Foreign Languages

*PPr*, Papers in Pragmatics

PPU, Promociones y Publicaciones Universitarias, S.A., Barcelona

*PQ*, The Philological Quarterly

*PR*, Podravska Revija
*PrA*, Prouvenço aro, Marseilles
*PraRu*, Prace Rusycystyczne
*PRev*, Poetry Review
PRF, Publications Romanes et Françaises, Geneva, Droz
PRH, Pahl-Rugenstein Hochschulschriften, Cologne, Pahl–Rugenstein
*PrH*, Provence Historique
*PrHlit*, Prace Historycznoliterackie
*PrHum*, Prace Humanistyczne
*PRIA*, Proceedings of the Royal Irish Academy
*PrIJP*, Prace Instytutu Języka Polskiego
*Prilozi*, Prilozi za književnost, jezik, istoriju i folklor, Belgrade
*PrilPJ*, Prilozi proučavanju jezika
PRIS-MA, Bulletin de liaison de l'ERLIMA, Université de Poitiers
*PrLit*, Prace Literackie
*PRom*, Papers in Romance
*PrRu*, Przegląd Rusycystyczny
*PrzH*, Przegląd Humanistyczny
*PrzW*, Przegląd Wschodni
*PS*, Проблеми слов'янознавства
*PSCL*, Papers and Studies in Contrastive Linguistics
*PSE*, Prague Studies in English
*PSGAS*, Politics and Society in Germany, Austria and Switzerland
*PSLu*, Pagine Storiche Luganesi
*PSML*, Prague Studies in Mathematical Linguistics
PSQ, Philologische Studien und Quellen, Berlin, Schmidt
*PSR*, Portuguese Studies Review
*PSRL*, Полное собрание русских летописей
PSS, Z polskich studiów slawistycznych, Warsaw, PWN
*PSSLSAA*, Procès-verbaux des séances de la Société des Lettres, Sciences et Arts de l'Aveyron
*PSV*, Polono-Slavica Varsoviensia
*PT*, Pamiętnik Teatralny
PUC, Pontifícia Universidade Católica, São Paulo
PUE, Publications Universitaires, Européennes, NY–Berne–Frankfurt, Lang

PUF, Presses Universitaires de France, Paris
PUG Pontificia Università Gregoriana
PUMRL, Purdue University Monographs in Romance Languages, Amsterdam — Philadelphia, Benjamins
PUStE, Publications de l'Université de St Étienne
*PW*, Poetry Wales
PWN, Państwowe Wydawnictwo Naukowe, Warsaw, etc

*QA*, Quaderni de Archivio
*QALT*, Quaderni dell'Atlante Lessicale Toscano
*QASIS*, Quaderni di lavoro dell'ASIS (Atlante Sintattico dell'Italia Settentrionale), Centro di Studio per la Dialettologia Italiana 'O. Parlangèli', Università degli Studi di Padova
*QCFLP*, Quaderni del Circolo Filologico Linguistico Padovano
*QDLC*, Quaderni del Dipartimento di Linguistica, Università della Calabria
*QDLF*, Quaderni del Dipartimento di Linguistica, Università degli Studi, Firenze
*QDLLSMG*, Quaderni del Dipartimento di Lingue e Letterature Straniere Moderne, Università di Genova
QDSL, Quellen zur deutschen Sprach- und Literaturgeschichte, Heidelberg, Winter
QFCC, Quaderni della Fondazione Camillo Caetani, Rome
QFESM, Quellen und Forschungen zur Erbauungsliteratur des späten Mittelalters und der frühen Neuzeit, Amsterdam, Rodopi
*QFGB*, Quaderni di Filologia Germanica della Facoltà di Lettere e Filosofia dell'Università di Bologna
*QFIAB*, Quellen und Forschungen aus italienischen Archiven und Bibliotheken
QFLK, Quellen und Forschungen zur Literatur- und

Kulturgeschichte, Berlin, de Gruyter

*QFLR*, Quaderni di Filologia e Lingua Romanze, Università di Macerata

*QFSK*, Quellen und Forschungen zur Sprach- und Kulturgeschichte der germanischen Völker, Berlin, de Gruyter

*QI*, Quaderni d'Italianistica

*QIA*, Quaderni Ibero-Americani

*QIGC*, Quaderni dell'Istituto di Glottologia, Università degli Studi 'G. D'Annunzio' di Chieti, Facoltà di Lettere e Filosofia

*QIICM*, Quaderni dell'Istituto Italiano de Cultura, Melbourne

*QILLSB*, Quaderni dell'Istituto di Lingue e Letterature Straniere della Facoltà di Magistero dell'Università degli Studi di Bari

*QILUU*, Quaderni dell'Istituto di Linguistica dell'Università di Urbino

*QINSRM*, Quaderni dell'Istituto Nazionale di Studi sul Rinascimento Meridionale

*QJMFL*, A Quarterly Journal in Modern Foreign Literatures

*QJS*, Quarterly Journal of Speech, Speech Association of America

*QLII*, Quaderni di Letterature Iberiche e Iberoamericane

*QLL*, Quaderni di Lingue e Letterature, Verona

*QLLP*, Quaderni del Laboratorio di Linguistica, Scuola Normale Superiore, Pisa

*QLLSP*, Quaderni di Lingua e Letteratura Straniere, Facoltà di Magistero, Università degli Studi di Palermo

*QLO*, Quasèrns de Lingüistica Occitana

*QM*, Quaderni Milanesi

*QMed*, Quaderni Medievali

*QP*, Quaderns de Ponent

*QPet*, Quaderni Petrarcheschi

*QPL*, Quaderni Patavini di Linguistica

*QQ*, Queen's Quarterly, Kingston, Ontario

*QR*, Quercy Recherche, Cahors

*QRCDLIM*, Quaderni di Ricerca, Centro di Dialettologia e Linguistica Italiana di Manchester

*QRP*, Quaderni di Retorica e Poetica

*QS*, Quaderni di Semantica

*QSF*, Quaderni del Seicento Francese

*QSGLL*, Queensland Studies in German Language and Literature, Berne, Francke

*QSt*, Quaderni Storici

*QStef*, Quaderni Stefaniani

*QSUP*, Quaderni per la Storia dell'Università di Padova

*QT*, Quaderni di Teatro

*QuF*, Québec français

*QuS*, Quebec Studies

*QV*, Quaderni del Vittoriale

*QVen*, Quaderni Veneti

*QVer*, Quaderni Veronesi di Filologia, Lingua e Letteratura Italiana

*QVR*, Quo vadis Romania?, Vienna


RA, Romanistische Arbeitshefte, Tübingen, Niemeyer

*RA*, Revista Agustiniana

*RAA*, Rendiconti dell'Accademia di Archeologia, Lettere e Belle Arti

*RABM*, Revista de Archivos, Bibliotecas y Museos

*RAct*, Regards sur l'Actualité

*Rad*, Rad Jugoslavenske akademije znanosti i umjetnosti

RAE, Real Academia Española

*RAfL*, Research in African Literatures

RAG, Real Academia Galega

*RAL*, Revista Argentina de Lingüística

*RAN*, Regards sur l'Afrique du Nord

*RANL*, Rendiconti dell'Accademia Nazionale dei Lincei, Classe di scienze morali, storiche e filologiche, serie IX

*RANPOLL*, Revista ANPOLL, Faculdade de Filosofia, Letras e Ciências Humanas, Univ. de São Paulo.

*RAPL*, Revista da Academia Paulista de Letras, São Paulo

*RAR*, Renaissance and Reformation

*RAS*, Rassegna degli Archivi di Stato

*RASoc*, Revista de Antropología Social

*RB*, Revue Bénédictine

RBC, Research Bibliographies and Checklists, London, Grant & Cutler

RBDSL, Regensburger Beiträge zur deutschen Sprach- und Literaturwissenschaft, Frankfurt–Berne, Lang

*RBG*, Reclams de Bearn et Gasconha

*RBGd*, Rocznik Biblioteki Gdańskiej PAN (Libri Gedanenses)

*RBKr*, Rocznik Biblioteki PAN w Krakowie

*RBL*, Revista Brasileira de Lingüística

*RBLL*, Revista Brasileira de Lingua e Literatura

*RBN*, Revista da Biblioteca Nacional

*RBPH*, Revue Belge de Philologie et d'Histoire

*RBS*, Rostocker Beiträge zur Sprachwissenschaft

*RC*, Le Ragioni Critiche

*RCat*, Revista de Catalunya

*RČAV*, Rozpravy Československé akademie věd, Prague, ČSAV

*RCB*, Revista de Cultura Brasileña

*RCCM*, Rivista di Cultura Classica e Medioevale

*RCEH*, Revista Canadiense de Estudios Hispánicos

*RCEN*, Revue Canadienne d'Études Néerlandaises

*RCF*, Review of Contemporary Fiction

*RCL*, Revista Chilena de Literatura

*RCLL*, Revista de Crítica Literaria Latino-Americana

*RCo*, Revue de Comminges

*RCSF*, Rivista Critica di Storia della Filosofia

*RCVS*, Rassegna di Cultura e Vita Scolastica

*RD*, Revue drômoise: archéologie, histoire, géographie

*RDE*, Recherches sur Diderot et sur l'‘Encyclopédie'

*RDM*, Revue des Deux Mondes

*RDsS*, Recherches sur le XVIIe Siècle

*RDTP*, Revista de Dialectología y Tradiciones Populares

*RE*, Revista de Espiritualidad

*REC*, Revista de Estudios del Caribe

*RECat*, Revue d'Études Catalanes

*RedLet*, Red Letters

*REE*, Revista de Estudios Extremeños

*REEI*, Revista del Instituto Egipcio de Estudios Islámicos, Madrid

*REH*, Revista de Estudios Hispánicos, Washington University, St Louis

*REHisp*, Revista de Estudios Hispánicos, Puerto Rico

*REI*, Revue des Études Italiennes

*REJ*, Revista de Estudios de Juventud

*REJui*, Revue des Études Juives, Paris

*REL*, Revue des Études Latines

*RELA*, Revista Española de Lingüística Aplicada

*RelCL*, Religion in Communist Lands

*RELI*, Rassegna Europea di Letteratura Italiana

*RELing*, Revista Española de Lingüística, Madrid

*RelLit*, Religious Literature

*ReMS*, Renaissance and Modern Studies

*RenD*, Renaissance Drama

*RenP*, Renaissance Papers

*RenR*, Renaissance and Reformation

*RenS*, Renaissance Studies

*RES*, Review of English Studies

*RESEE*, Revue des Études Sud-Est Européennes

*RESS*, Revue Européenne des Sciences Sociales et Cahiers Vilfredo Pareto

*RevA*, Revue d'Allemagne

*RevAl*, Revista de l'Alguer

*RevAR*, Revue des Amis de Ronsard

*RevAuv*, Revue d'Auvergne, Clermont-Ferrand

*RevEL*, Revista de Estudos da Linguagem, Faculdade de Letras, Universidade Federal de Minas Gerais

*RevF*, Revista de Filología
*RevHA*, Revue de la Haute-Auvergne
*RevG*, Revista de Girona
*RevIb*, Revista Iberoamericana
*RevL*, Revista Lusitana
*RevLM*, Revista de Literatura Medieval
*RevLR*, Revista do Livro
*RevO*, La Revista occitana, Montpellier
*RevP*, Revue Parole, Université de Mons-Hainault
*RevPF*, Revista Portuguesa de Filosofia
*RevR*, Revue Romane
*RF*, Romanische Forschungen
*RFe*, Razón y Fe
*RFE*, Revista de Filología Española
*RFHL*, Revue Française d'Histoire du Livre
*RFLSJ*, Revista de Filosofía y Lingüística de San José, Costa Rica
*RFLUL*, Revista da Faculdade de Letras da Universidade de Lisboa
*RFLUP*, Revista da Faculdade de Letras da Universidade do Porto
*RFN*, Rivisti di Filosofia Neoscolastica
*RFo*, Ricerca Folklorica
*RFP*, Recherches sur le Français Parlé
*RFR*, Revista de Filología Románica
*RFr*, Revue Frontenac
*RG*, Recherches Germaniques
*RGand*, Romanica Gandensia
*RGCC*, Revue du Gévaudan, des Causses et des Cévennes
*RGG*, Rivista di Grammatica Generativa
*RGI*, Revue Germanique Internationale
RGL, Reihe Germanistische Linguistik, Tübingen, Niemeyer
*RGo*, Romanica Gothoburgensia
*RGT*, Revista Galega de Teatro
RH, Reihe Hanser, Munich, Hanser
*RH*, Revue Hebdomadaire
*RHA*, Revista de Historia de America
*RHAM*, Revue Historique et Archéologique du Maine

*RHCS*, Rocznik Historii Czasopiśmiennictwa Polskiego
*RHDFE*, Revue Historique de Droit Français et Étranger
*RHE*, Revue d'Histoire Ecclésiastique
*RHEF*, Revue d'Histoire de l'Église de France
RHel, Romanica Helvetica, Tübingen and Basle, Francke
*RHFB*, Rapports — Het Franse Boek
*RHI*, Revista da Historia das Ideias
*RHis*, Revue Historique
RHL, Reihe Hanser Literaturkommentare, Munich, Hanser
*RHLF*, Revue d'Histoire Littéraire de la France
*RHLP*, Revista de História Literária de Portugal
*RHM*, Revista Hispánica Moderna
*RHMag*, Revue d'Histoire Maghrébine
*RHMC*, Revue d'Histoire Moderne et Contemporaine
*RHPR*, Revue d'Histoire et de Philosophie Religieuses
*RHR*, Réforme, Humanisme, Renaissance
*RHRel*, Revue de l'Histoire des Religions
*RHS*, Revue Historique de la Spiritualité
*RHSc*, Revue d'Histoire des Sciences
*RHSt*, Ricarda Huch. Studien zu ihrem Leben und Werk
*RHT*, Revue d'Histoire du Théâtre
*RHTe*, Revue d'Histoire des Textes
*RI*, Rassegna Iberistica
*RIA*, Rivista Italiana di Acustica
RIa, Русский язык
*RIAB*, Revista Interamericana de Bibliografía
*RIaR*, Русский язык за рубежом
*RICC*, Revue Itinéraires et Contacts de Culture
*RICP*, Revista del Instituto de Cultura Puertorriqueña
*RicSl*, Ricerche Slavistiche
*RID*, Rivista Italiana di Dialettologia
*RIE*, Revista de Ideas Estéticas

*RIEB*, Revista do Instituto de
Estudos Brasileiros
*RIL*, Rendiconti dell'Istituto
Lombardo
*RILA*, Rassegna Italiana di
Linguistica Applicata
*RILCE*, Revista del Instituto de
Lengua y Cultura Españoles
*RILP*, Revista Internacional da
Língua Portuguesa
*RIM*, Rivista Italiana di Musicologia
*RIndM*, Revista de Indias
*RInv*, Revista de Investigación
*RIO*, Revue Internationale
d'Onomastique
*RIOn*, Rivista Italiana di
Onomastica
*RIP*, Revue Internationale de
Philosophie
*RIS*, Revue de l'Institute de
Sociologie, Université Libre,
Brussels
*RiS*, Ricerche Storiche
*RITL*, Revista de Istorie și Teorie
Literară, Bucharest
*RivF*, Rivista di Filosofia
*RivL*, Rivista di Linguistica
*RJ*, Romanistisches Jahrbuch
*RKHlit*, Rocznik Komisji
Historycznoliterackiej PAN
*RKJŁ*, Rozprawy Komisji Językowej
Łódzkiego Towarzystwa
Naukowego
*RKJW*, Rozprawy Komisji
Językowej Wrocławskiego
Towarzystwa Naukowego
*RLA*, Romance Languages Annual
*RLaR*, Revue des Langues Romanes
*RLB*, Recueil Linguistique de
Bratislava
*RLC*, Revue de Littérature
Comparée
*RLD*, Revista de Llengua i Dret
*RLet*, Revista de Letras
*RLettI*, Rivista di Letteratura
Italiana
*RLex*, Revista de Lexicologia
*RLF*, Revista de Literatura
Fantástica
*RLFRU*, Recherches de Linguistique
Française et Romane d'Utrecht
*RLH*, Revista de Literatura
Hispanoamericana

*RLI*, Rassegna della Letteratura
Italiana
*RLib*, Rivista dei Libri
*RLing*, Russian Linguistics
*RLiR*, Revue de Linguistique
Romane
*RLit*, Revista de Literatura
*RLJ*, Russian Language Journal
*RLLCGV*, Revista de Lengua y
Literatura Catalana, Gallega y
Vasca, Madrid
*RLLR*, Romance Literature and
Linguistics Review
*RLM*, Revista de Literaturas
Modernas, Cuyo
*RLMC*, Rivista di Letterature
Moderne e Comparate
*RLMed*, Revista de Literatura
Medieval
*RLMexC*, Revista de Literatura
Mexicana Contemporánea
*RLMod*, Revue des Lettres
Modernes
*RLModCB*, Revue des Lettres
Modernes. Carnets
Bibliographiques
*RLSer*, Revista de Literatura Ser,
Puerto Rico
*RLSL*, Revista de Lingvistică și
Știință Literară
*RLT*, Russian Literature
Triquarterly
*RLTA*, Revista de Lingüística
Teórica y Aplicada
*RLV*, Revue des Langues Vivantes
*RLVin*, Recherches Linguistiques de
Vincennes
RM, Romance Monograph Series,
University, Mississippi
*RM*, Remate de Males
*RMAL*, Revue du Moyen Âge Latin
*RMar*, Revue Marivaux
*RMC*, Roma Moderna e
Contemporanea
*RMEH*, Revista Marroquí de
Estudios Hispánicos
*RMH*, Recherches sur le Monde
Hispanique au XIXe Siècle
*RMM*, Revue de Métaphysique et
de Morale
*RMon*, Revue Montesquieu
*RMRLL*, Rocky Mountain Review
of Language and Literature
*RMS*, Reading Medieval Studies

*RNC*, Revista Nacional de Cultura,
Carácas
*RNDWSPK*, Rocznik Naukowo-
Dydaktyczny WSP w Krakowie
*RO*, Revista de Occidente
*RoczH*, Roczniki Humanistyczne
Katolickiego Uniw. Lubelskiego
*RoczSl*, Rocznik Slawistyczny
*ROl*, Rossica Olomucensia
RoM, Rowohlts Monographien,
Reinbek, Rowohlt
*RomGG*, Romanistik in Geschichte
und Gegenwart
*ROMM*, Revue de L'Occident
Musulman et de la Méditerranée
*RoN*, Romance Notes
*RoQ*, Romance Quarterly
*RORD*, Research Opportunities in
Renaissance Drama
*RoS*, Romance Studies
*RoSl*, Роднае слова
РР, Радянський письменник
*RP*, Revista de Portugal
*RPA*, Revue de Phonétique
Appliquée
*RPac*, Revue du Pacifique
*RPC*, Revue Pédagogique et
Culturelle de l'AVEP
*RPF*, Revista Portuguesa de
Filologia
*RPFE*, Revue Philosophique de la
France et de l'Étranger
*RPh*, Romance Philology
*RPL*, Revue Philosophique de
Louvain
*RPl*, Río de la Plata
*RPLit*, Res Publica Litterarum
*RPN*, Res Publica nowa, Warsaw
*RPP*, Romanticism Past and Present
*RPr*, Raison Présente
*RPS*, Revista Paraguaya de
Sociologia
*RPyr*, Recherches pyrénéennes,
Toulouse
*RQ*, Renaissance Quarterly
*RQL*, Revue Québécoise de
Linguistique
*RR*, Romanic Review
*RRe*, Русская речь
*RRL*, Revue Roumaine de
Linguistique
*RRou*, Revue du Rouergue
RS, Reihe Siegen, Heidelberg,
Winter

*RS*, Revue de Synthèse
*RSC*, Rivista di Studi Canadesi
*RSCI*, Rivista di Storia della Chiesa
in Italia
*RSEAV*, Revue de la Société des
enfants et amis de Villeneuve-de-
Berg
*RSF*, Rivista di Storia della Filosofia
*RSH*, Revue des Sciences Humaines
RSh, Радянська школа
*RSI*, Rivista Storica Italiana
*RSJb*, Reinhold Schneider Jahrbuch
*RSL*, Rusycystyczne Studia
Literaturoznawcze
*RSl*, Revue des Études Slaves
*RSLR*, Rivista di Storia e
Letteratura Religiose
*RSPT*, Revue des Sciences
Philosophiques et Théologiques
*RSR*, Rassegna Storica del
Risorgimento
*RSSR*, Rivista di Storia Sociale e
Religiosa
*RST*, Rassegna Storica Toscana
*RSt*, Research Studies
*RStI*, Rivista di Studi Italiani
*RT*, Revue du Tarn
*RTAM*, Recherches de Théologie
Ancienne et Médiévale
*RTLiM*, Rocznik Towarzystwa
Literackiego im. Adama
Mickiewicza
*RTr*, Recherches et Travaux,
Université de Grenoble
*RTUG*, Recherches et Travaux de
l'Université de Grenoble III
*RUB*, Revue de l'Université de
Bruxelles
*RUC*, Revista de la Universidad
Complutense
*RuLit*, Ruch Literacki
*RUM*, Revista de la Universidad de
Madrid
*RUMex*, Revista de la Universidad
de México
*RUOt*, Revue de l'Université
d'Ottawa
*RUS*, Rice University Studies
*RusH*, Russian History
*RusL*, Русская литература, ПД,
Leningrad
*RusM*, Русская мысль
*RusMed*, Russia Medievalis
*RusR*, Russian Review

RUW, Rozprawy Uniwersytetu
Warsawskiego, Warsaw
*RVB*, Rheinische Vierteljahrsblätter
*RVF*, Revista Valenciana de
Filología
*RVi*, Revue du Vivarais
*RVQ*, Romanica Vulgaria Quaderni
RVV, Romanische Versuche und
Vorarbeiten, Bonn U.P.
RVVig, Reihe der Villa Vigoni,
Tübingen, Niemeyer
*RZLG*, Romanistische Zeitschrift für
Literaturgeschichte
*RZSF*, Radovi Zavoda za slavensku
filologiju

SA, Studien zum Althochdeutschen,
Göttingen, Vandenhoeck &
Ruprecht
*SAB*, South Atlantic Bulletin
*Sac*, Sacris Erudiri
SAG, Stuttgarter Arbeiten zur
Germanistik, Stuttgart, Heinz
*SAH*, Studies in American Humour
SANU, Srpska akademija nauka i
umetnosti
SAOB, Svenska Akademiens
Ordbok
*SAQ*, South Atlantic Quarterly
*SAR*, South Atlantic Review
*SAS*, Studia Academica Slovaca
*SaS*, Slovo a slovesnost
*SASc*, Studia Anthroponymica
Scandinavica
SATF, Société des Anciens Textes
Français
SAV, Slovenská akadémia vied
SAVL, Studien zur allgemeinen und
vergleichenden
Literaturwissenschaft, Stuttgart,
Metzler
SB, Slavistische Beiträge, Munich,
Sagner
*SB*, Studies in Bibliography
SBAW, Sitzungsberichte der
Bayerischen Akad. der
Wissenschaften, phil-hist. Kl.,
Munich, Beck
SBL, Saarbrücker Beiträge zur
Literaturwissenschaft, St. Ingbert,
Röhrig
*SBL*, Старобългарска литература
*SBR*, Swedish Book Review

*SBVS*, Saga-Book of the Viking
Society
*SC*, Studia Celtica, The Bulletin of
the Board of Celtic Studies
SCB, Skrifter utgivna av Centrum
för barnkulturforskning,
Stockholm U.P.
*SCC*, Studies in Comparative
Communism
*SCen*, The Seventeenth Century
SCES, Sixteenth Century Essays
and Studies, Kirksville, Missouri,
Sixteenth Century Journal
*SCFS*, Seventeenth-Century French
Studies
SchG, Schriftsteller der Gegenwart,
Berlin, Volk & Wissen
SchSch, Schlern-Schriften,
Innsbruck, Wagner
*SchwM*, Schweizer Monatshefte
*SCJ*, Sixteenth Century Journal
*SCL*, Studii şi Cercetări Lingvistice
*SCl*, Stendhal Club
*ScL*, Scottish Language
*ScM*, Scripta Mediterranea
*SCN*, Seventeenth Century News
SCO, Studii şi Cercetäri de
Onomasticä
*ScO*, Scriptoralia, Tübingen, Narr
SCR, Studies in Comparative
Religion
*ScRev*, Scandinavian Review
*ScSl*, Scando-Slavica
*ScSt*, Scandinavian Studies
SD, Sprache und Dichtung, n.F.,
Berne, Haupt
*SD*, Современная драматургия.
*SdA*, Storia dell'Arte
SDFU, Skrifter utgivna genom
Dialekt- och folkminnesarkivet i
Uppsala
SDG, Studien zur deutschen
Grammatik, Tübingen,
Stauffenburg
SDL, Studien zur deutschen
Literatur, Tübingen, Niemeyer
SDLNZ, Studien zur deutschen
Literatur des 19. und 20.
Jahrhunderts, Berne, Lang
*SdO*, Serra d'Or
SDOFU, Skrifter utgivna av
Dialekt-, ortnamns- och
folkminnesarkivet i Umeå

SDS, Studien zur Dialektologie in Südwestdeutschland, Marburg, Elwert

SDSp, Studien zur deutschen Sprache, Tübingen, Narr

*SDv*, Sprache und Datenverarbeitung

*SE*, Série Esludos Uberaba

*SeC*, Scrittura e Civiltà

*SECC*, Studies in Eighteenth-Century Culture

SEDES, Société d'Éditions d'Enseignement Supérieur

*SEEA*, Slavic and East European Arts

*SEEJ*, The Slavic and East European Journal

*SEER*, Slavonic and East European Review

*SEES*, Slavic and East European Studies

SEI, Società Editrice Internazionale, Turin

*SELA*, South Eastern Latin Americanist

*SemL*, Seminarios de Linguística, Universidade do Algarve, Faro

SEN, Società Editrice Napoletana, Naples

SEP, Secretaría de Educación Pública, Mexico

*SeS*, Serbian Studies

*SEz*, Съпоставително езикознание

SF, Slavistische Forschungen, Cologne — Vienna, Böhlau

SFAIEO, Section Française de l'Association Internationale d'Études Occitanes, Montpellier

*SFI*, Studi di Filologia Italiana

SFIS, Stanford French and Italian Studies

SFKG, Schriftenreihe der Franz–Kafka–Gesellschaft, Vienna, Braumüller

SFL, Studies in French Literature, London, Arnold

*SFL*, Studi di Filologia e Letteratura

*SFPS*, Studia z Filologii Polskiej i Słowiańskiej PAN

*SFR*, Stanford French Review

*SFr*, Studi Francesi

*SFRS*, Studia z Filologii Rosyjskiej i Słowiańskiej, Warsaw

*SFS*, Swiss-French Studies

*SFUŠ*, Sborník Filozofickej Fakulty Univerzity P. J. Šafárika, Prešov

SG, Sprache der Gegenwart, Düsseldorf, Schwann

SGAK, Studien zu Germanistik, Anglistik und Komparatistik, Bonn, Bouvier

*SGECRN*, Study Group on Eighteenth-Century Russia Newsletter

SGEL, Sociedad General Española de Librería

*SGesch*, Sprache und Geschichte, Stuttgart, Klett-Cotta

SGF, Stockholmer Germanistische Forschungen, Stockholm, Almqvist & Wiksell

*SGG*, Studia Germanica Gandensia

*SGGed*, Studia Germanica Gedanensia

*SGI*, Studi di Grammatica Italiana

SGLL, Studies in German Language and Literature, Lewiston-Queenston-Lampeter

SGLLC, Studies in German Literature, Linguistics, and Culture, Columbia, S.C., Camden House, Woodbridge, Boydell & Brewer

*SGP*, Studia Germanica Posnaniensia

SGS, Stanford German Studies, Berne, Lang

*SGS*, Scottish Gaelic Studies

SGU, Studia Germanistica Upsaliensia, Stockholm, Almqvist & Wiksell

SH, Slavica Helvetica, Berne, Lang

*SH*, Studia Hibernica

*ShAn*, Sharq al-Andalus

SHAW, Sitzungsberichte der Heidelberger Akademie der Wissenschaften, phil.-hist. Klasse, Heidelberg, Winter

SHCT, Studies in the History of Christian Thought, Leiden, Brill

SHPF, Société de l'Histoire du Protestantisme Français

*SHPS*, Studies in History and Philosophy of Science

*SHR*, The Scottish Historical Review

SI, Sprache und Information,
Tübingen, Niemeyer
*SIAA*, Studi di Italianistica
nell'Africa Australe
*SiCh*, Слово i час
SIDES, Société Internationale de
Diffusion et d'Édition
Scientifiques, Antony
SIDS, Schriften des Instituts für
deutsche Sprache, Berlin, de
Gruyter
*Siglo XX*, Siglo XX/20th Century
*SILTA*, Studi Italiani di Linguistica
Teorica ed Applicata
*SiN*, Sin Nombre
SINSU, Skrifter utgivna av
institutionen för nordiska språk
vid Uppsala universitet, Uppsala
U.P.
*SIR*, Stanford Italian Review
SISMEL, Società Internazionale
per lo Studio del Medioevo
Latino, Edizioni del Galluzzo,
Florence
*SIsp*, Studi Ispanici
SISSD, Società Italiana di Studi sul
Secolo XVIII
*SJLŠ*, Slovenský jazyk a literatúra v
škole
*SkSt*, Skandinavistische Studien
SKZ, Srpska Književna Zadruga,
Belgrade
SL, Sammlung Luchterhand,
Darmstadt, Luchterhand
*SL*, Studia Linguistica
*SLÅ*, Svensk Lärarföreningens
Årsskrift
*SlaG*, Slavica Gandensia
*SlaH*, Slavica Helsingensia
*SlaL*, Slavica Lundensia
*SlavFil*, Славянска филология,
Sofia
*SlavH*, Slavica Hierosolymitana
*SlavLit*, Славянските литератури
в България
*SlavRev*, Slavistična revija
*SlaW*, Slavica Wratislaviensia
*SLeg*, Studium Legionense
*SLeI*, Studi di Lessicografia Italiana
SLESPO, Suplemento Literário do
Estado de São Paulo
*SLF*, Studi di Letteratura Francese
SLG, Studia Linguistica
Germanica, Berlin, de Gruyter

SLI, Società di Linguistica Italiana
*SLI*, Studi Linguistici Italiani
SLIGU, Skrifter utgivna av
Litteraturvetenskapliga
institutionen vid Göteborgs
universitet, Gothenburg U.P.
SLILU, Skrifter utgivna av
Litteraturvetenskapliga
institutionen vid Lunds
universitet, Lund U.P.
SLit, Schriften zur
Literaturwissenschaft, Berlin,
Dunckler & Humblot
*SLit*, Slovenská literatúra
*SLitR*, Stanford Literature Review
SLIUU, Skrifter utgivna av
Litteraturvetenskapliga
institutionen vid Uppsala
universitet, Uppsala U.P.
SLK, Schwerpunkte Linguistik und
Kommunikationswissenschaft
SLL, Skrifter utg. genom
Landsmålsarkivet i Lund
SLM, Studien zur Literatur der
Moderne, Bonn, Bouvier
*SLN*, Slovenský národopis
*SLO*, Slavica Lublinensia et
Olomucensia
*SlO*, Slavia Orientalis
*SlOc*, Slavia Occidentalis
*SlOth*, Slavica Othinensia
SlPN, Slovenské pedagogické
nakladateľstvo
*SlPoh*, Slovenské pohľady
*SlPr*, Slavica Pragensia
*SLPS*, Studia Linguistica Polono-
Slovaca
*SLR*, Second Language Research
*SLS*, Studies in the Linguistic
Sciences
*SlSb*, Slezský sborník
*SlSl*, Slavica Slovaca
SlSp, Slovenský spisovateľ
*SLRev*, Southern Literary Review
*SLu*, Studia Lulliana
*SLWU*, Sprach und Literatur in
Wissenschaft und Unterricht
SM, Sammlung Metzler, Stuttgart,
Metzler
*SM*, Studi Medievali
*SMC*, Studies in Medieval Culture
SME, Schöninghs mediävistische
Editionen, Paderborn, Schöningh
*SMer*, Студенческий меридиан

SMGL, Studies in Modern German Literature, Berne – Frankfurt – New York, Lang

*SMLS*, Strathclyde Modern Language Studies

SMRT, Studies in Medieval and Reformation Thought, Leiden, Brill

*SMS*, Sewanee Medieval Studies

*SMu*, Советский музей

*SMV*, Studi Mediolatini e Volgari

*SN*, Studia Neophilologica

SNL, Sveučilišna naklada Liber, Zagreb

*SNM*, Sborník Národního muzea

*SNov*, Seara Nova

SNTL, Státní nakladatelství technické literatury

SÖAW, Sitzungsberichte der Österreichischen Akademie der Wissenschaften, phil.-hist. Klasse

*SOBI*, Societat d'Onomastica, Butlleti Interior, Barcelona

*SoCR*, South Central Review

SOH, Studia Onomastica Helvetica, Arbon, Eurotext: Historisch-Archäologischer Verlag

*SoK*, Sprog og Kultur

*SopL*, Sophia Linguistica, Tokyo

*SoRA*, Southern Review, Adelaide

*SoRL*, Southern Review, Louisiana

SOU, Skrifter utgivna genom Ortnamnsarkivet i Uppsala

SP, Sammlung Profile, Bonn, Bouvier

*SP*, Studies in Philology

*SPat*, Studi Patavini

*SpC*, Speech Communication

SPCT, Studi e Problemi di Critica Testuale

SPES, Studio per Edizioni Scelte, Florence

*SPFB*, Sborník Pedagogické fakulty v Brně

*SPFFBU*, Sborník prací Filosofické fakulty Brněnské Univerzity

*SPFHK*, Sborník Pedagogické fakulty, Hradec Králové

*SPFO*, Sborník Pedagogické fakulty, Ostrava

*SPFOl*, Sborník Pedagogické fakulty, Olomouc

*SPFUK*, Sborník Pedagogické fakulty Univerzity Karlovy, Prague

SPGS, Scottish Papers in Germanic Studies, Glasgow

*SPh*, Studia philologica, Olomouc

SPi, Serie Piper, Munich, Piper

*SPIEL*, Siegener Periodicum zur Internationalen Empirischen Literaturwissenschaft

*SPK*, Studia nad polszczyzną kresową, Wrocław

*SpLit*, Sprache und Literatur

*SpMod*, Spicilegio Moderno, Pisa

SPN, Státní pedagogické nakladatelství

*SPol*, Studia Polonistyczne

SPR, Slavistic Printings and Reprintings, The Hague, Mouton

*SpR*, Spunti e Ricerche

SPRF, Société de Publications Romanes et Françaises, Geneva, Droz

SPS, Specimina Philologiae Slavicae, Munich, Otto Sagner

*SPS*, Studia Philologica Salmanticensia

*SPSO*, Studia Polono–Slavica–Orientalia. Acta Litteraria

*SpSt*, Spanish Studies

*SPUAM*, Studia Polonistyczna Uniwersytetu Adama Mickiewicza, Poznań

*SR*, Slovenská reč

*SRAZ*, Studia Romanica et Anglica Zagrabiensia

*SRev*, Slavic Review

*SRF*, Studi e Ricerche Francescane

SRL, Studia Romanica et Linguistica, Frankfurt, Lang

*SRLF*, Saggi e Ricerche di Letteratura Francese

*SRo*, Studi Romanzi

*SRom*, Studi Romeni

*SRoP*, Studia Romanica Posnaniensia

*SRP*, Studia Rossica Posnaniensia

SRU, Studia Romanica Upsaliensia

SS, Symbolae Slavicae, Frankfurt–Berne–Cirencester, Lang

*SS*, Syn og Segn

SSBI, Skrifter utgivna av Svenska barnboksinstitutet

SSB, Strenna Storica Bolognese

SSCJ, Southern Speech Communication Journal

SSDSP, Società Savonese di Storia Patria

SSE, Studi di Storia dell'Educazione

SSF, Studies in Short Fiction

SSFin, Studia Slavica Finlandensia

SSGL, Studies in Slavic and General Linguistics, Amsterdam, Rodopi

SSH, Studia Slavica Academiae Scientiarum Hungaricae

SSL, Studi e Saggi Linguistici

SSLF, Skrifter utgivna av Svenska Litteratursällskapet i Finland

SSLP, Studies in Slavic Literature and Poetics, Amsterdam, Rodopi

SSLS, Studi Storici Luigi Simeoni

SSMP, Stockholm Studies in Modern Philology

SSPHS, Society for Spanish and Portuguese Historical Studies, Millersville

SSS, Stanford Slavic Studies

SSSAS, Society of Spanish and Spanish-American Studies, Boulder, Colorado

SSSlg, Sagners Slavistische Sammlung, Munich, Sagner

SSSN, Skrifter utgivna av Svenska språknämnden

SSSP, Stockholm Studies in Scandinavian Philology

SST, Sprache — System und Tätigkeit, Frankfurt, Lang

SSt, Slavic Studies, Hokkaido

ST, Suhrkamp Taschenbuch, Frankfurt, Suhrkamp

ST, Studi Testuali, Alessandria, Edizioni dell'Orso

StB, Studi sul Boccaccio

STC, Studies in the Twentieth Century

StCJ, Studia Celtica Japonica

STCL, Studies in Twentieth Century Literature

StCL, Studies in Canadian Literature

StCrit, Strumenti Critici

StD, Studi Danteschi

StF, Studie Francescani

StFil, Studia Filozoficzne

STFM, Société des Textes Français Modernes

StG, Studi Germanici

StGol, Studi Goldoniani

StH, Studies in the Humanities

StI, Studi Italici, Kyoto

StIt, Studi Italiani

StL, Studium Linguistik

StLa, Studies in Language, Amsterdam

StLi, Stauffenburg Linguistik, Tübingen, Stauffenburg

StLI, Studi di Letteratura Ispano-Americana

StLIt, Studi Latini e Italiani

StLM, Studies in the Literary Imagination

StLo, Studia Logica

StM, Studies in Medievalism

STM, Suhrkamp Taschenbuch Materialien, Frankfurt, Suhrkamp

STML, Studies on Themes and Motifs in Literature, New York, Lang

StMon, Studia Monastica

StMus, Studi Musicali

StMy, Studia Mystica

StN, Studi Novecenteschi

StNF, Studier i Nordisk Filologi

StO, Studium Ovetense

StP, Studi Piemontesi

StPet, Studi Petrarcheschi

StR, Studie o rukopisech

StRLLF, Studi e Ricerche di Letteratura e Linguistica Francese

StRmgn, Studi Romagnoli

StRo, Studi Romani

StRom, Studies in Romanticism

StRu, Studia Russica, Budapest

StS, Studi Storici

StSec, Studi Secenteschi

StSk, Studia Skandinavica

StSet, Studi Settecenteschi

STSL, Studien und Texte zur Sozialgeschichte der Literatur, Tübingen, Niemeyer

StT, Studi Tassiani

STUF, Sprachtypologie und Universalienforschung

StV, Studies on Voltaire and the 18th Century

STW, Suhrkamp Taschenbücher Wissenschaft, Frankfurt, Suhrkamp

*StZ*, Sprache im technischen Zeitalter

*SU*, Studi Urbinati

*SUBBP*, Studia Universitatis Babeş-Bolyai, Philologia, Cluj

SUDAM, Editorial Sudamericana, Buenos Aires

*SuF*, Sinn und Form

*SUm*, Schede Umanistiche

SUP, Spisy University J. E. Purkyně, Brno

*SupEz*, Съпоставително езикознание, Sofia

*SV*, Studi Veneziani

*SZ*, Studia Zamorensia


*TAL*, Travaux d'Archéologie Limousine, Limoges

*TAm*, The Americas, Bethesda

TAPS, Transactions of the American Philosophical Society

*TB*, Tempo Brasileiro

TBL, Tübinger Beiträge zur Linguistik, Tübingen, Narr

*TC*, Texto Critico

*TCBS*, Transactions of the Cambridge Bibliographical Society

*TCERFM*, Travaux du Centre d'Études et de Recherches sur François Mauriac, Bordeaux

*TCL*, Twentieth-Century Literature

*TCLN*, Travaux du Cercle Linguistique de Nice

*TCWAAS*, Transactions of the Cumberland and Westmorland Antiquarian and Archaeological Society

*TD*, Teksty Drugie

*TDC*, Textes et Documents pour la Classe

*TEC*, Teresiunum Ephemerides Carmeliticae

TECC, Textos i Estudis de Cultura Catalana, Curial — Publicacions de l'Abadia de Montserrat, Barcelona

*TeK*, Text und Kontext

TELK, Trouvaillen — Editionen zur Literatur- und Kulturgeschichte, Berne, Lang

*TeN*, Terminologies Nouvelles

*TeSt*, Teatro e Storia

TE(XVIII), Textos y Estudios del Siglo XVIII

TF, Texte zur Forschung, Darmstadt, Wissenschaftliche Buchgesellschaft

TFN, Texte der Frühen Neuzeit, Frankfurt am Main, Keip

TGLSK, Theorie und Geschichte der Literatur und der Schönen Künste, Munich, Fink

*TGSI*, Transactions of the Gaelic Society of Inverness

THESOC, Thesaurus Occitan

THL, Theory and History of Literature, Manchester U.P.

THM, Textos Hispánicos Modernos, Barcelona, Labor

THR, Travaux d'Humanisme et Renaissance, Geneva, Droz

*THSC*, Transactions of the Honourable Society of Cymmrodorion

*TI*, Le Texte et l'Idée

*TidLit*, Tidskrift för Litteraturvetenskap

*TILAS*, Travaux de l'Institut d'Études Latino-Américaines de l'Université de Strasbourg

TILL, Travaux de l'Institut de Linguistique de Lund

*TJ*, Theatre Journal

TK, Text und Kritik, Munich

*TKS*, Търновска книжевна школа, Sofia

*TL*, Theoretical Linguistics

TLF, Textes Littéraires Français, Geneva, Droz

*TLit*, Travaux de Littérature

*TLP*, Travaux de Linguistique et de Philologie

*TLQ*, Travaux de Linguistique Québécoise

TLTL, Teaching Language Through Literature

*TM*, Les Temps Modernes

*TMJb*, Thomas Mann-Jahrbuch

*TMo*, O Tempo e o Modo

TMS, Thomas-Mann Studien, Frankfurt, Klostermann

*TN*, Theatre Notebook

*TNA*, Tijdschrift voor Nederlands en Afrikaans

TNT, Towarzystwo Naukowe w Toruniu

*TOc*, Tèxtes Occitans, Bordeaux

*TODL*, Труды Отдела древнерусской литературы Института русской литературы АН СССР

*TP*, Textual Practice

*TPa*, Torre de Papel

*TPS*, Transactions of the Philological Society

*TQ*, Theatre Quarterly

*TR*, Телевидение и радиовещание

*TravL*, Travaux de Linguistique, Luxembourg

*TRCTL*, Texte-Revue de Critique et de Théorie Littéraire

*TRI*, Theatre Research International

TRISMM, Tradition — Reform — Innovation. Studien zur Modernität des Mittelalters, Frankfurt, Lang

*TrK*, Трезвость и культура

*TrL*, Travaux de Linguistique

*TrLit*, Translation and Literature

*TRS*, The Transactions of the Radnorshire Society

*TS*, Theatre Survey

*TSC*, Treballs de Sociolingüística Catalana

TSDL, Tübinger Studien zur deutschen Literatur, Frankfurt, Lang

*TSJ*, Tolstoy Studies Journal

TSL, Trierer Studien zur Literatur, Frankfurt, Lang

*TSLL*, Texas Studies in Literature and Language

TSM, Texte des späten Mittelalters und der frühen Neuzeit, Berlin, Schmidt

*TsNTL*, Tijdschrift voor Nederlandse Taal- en Letterkunde

TSRLL, Tulane Studies in Romance Languages and Literature

*TsSk*, Tijdschrift voor Skandinavistiek

*TsSV*, Tijdschrift voor de Studie van de Verlichting

*TSWL*, Tulsa Studies in Women's Literature

TT, Tekst en Tijd, Nijmegen, Alfa

*TT*, Travail Théâtral

TTAS, Twayne Theatrical Arts Series, Boston–New York

TTG, Texte und Textgeschichte, Tübingen, Niemeyer

*TTr*, Terminologie et Traduction

TUGS, Texte und Untersuchungen zur Germanistik und Skandinavistik, Frankfurt, Lang

TVS, Theorie und Vermittlung der Sprache, Frankfurt, Lang

TWAS, Twayne's World Authors Series, Boston–New York

*TWQ*, Third World Quarterly

UAB, Universitat Autònoma de Barcelona

UAC, Universidad de Antioquia, Colombia

UAM, Uniwersytet Adama Mickiewicza, Poznań

UB, Universal-Bibliothek, Stuttgart, Reclam

UBL, Universal-Bibliothek, Leipzig, Reclam

*UCLWPL*, UCL Working Papers in Linguistics

UCPL, University of California Publications in Linguistics

UCPMP, University of California Publications in Modern Philology

UDL, Untersuchungen zur deutschen Literaturgeschichte, Tübingen, Niemeyer

*UDR*, University of Dayton Review

UFPB, Universidade Federal da Paraíba

UFRGS, Univ. Federal do Rio Grande do Sul (Brazil)

UFRJ, Universidade Federal do Rio de Janeiro

UFSC, Universidade Federal de Santa Catarina

UGE, Union Générale d'Éditions

UGFGP, University of Glasgow French and German Publications

*UL*, Українське літературознавство, Lvov U.P.

*UM*, Українська мова і література
в школі
UMCS, Uniwersytet Marii Curie-
Skłodowskiej, Lublin
*UMov*, Українське мовазнавство
UNAM, Universidad Nacional
Autónoma de Mexico
UNC, Univ. of North Carolina
UNCSGL, University of North
Carolina Studies in Germanic
Languages and Literatures,
Chapel Hill
UNED, Universidad Nacional de
Enseñanza a Distancia
UNESP, Universidade Estadual de
São Paulo
UNMH, University of Nottingham
Monographs in the Humanities
UPP, University of Pennsylvania
Press, Philadelphia
*UQ*, Ukrainian Quarterly
*UR*, Umjetnost riječi
*USCFLS*, University of South
Carolina French Literature Series
*USFLQ*, University of South Florida
Language Quarterly
USH, Umeå Studies in the
Humanities, Stockholm, Almqvist
& Wiksell International
USLL, Utah Studies in Literature
and Linguistics, Berne, Lang
USP, Universidade de São Paulo
UTB, Uni-Taschenbücher
UTET, Unione Tipografico-
Editrice Torinese
UTPLF, Università di Torino,
Pubblicazioni della Facoltà di
Lettere e Filosofia
*UTQ*, University of Toronto
Quarterly
UVAN, Українська Вільна
Академія Наук, Winnipeg
UVK, Universitätsverlag Konstanz
*UVWPL*, University of Venice
Working Papers in Linguistics
UWCASWC, The University of
Wales Centre for Advanced
Studies in Welsh and Celtic
*UZLU*, Ученые записки
Ленинградского университета

VAM, Vergessene Autoren der
Moderne, Siegen U.P.

VAS, Vorträge und Abhandlungen
zur Slavistik, Giessen, Schmitz
VASSLOI, Veröffentlichungen der
Abteilung für Slavische Sprachen
und Literaturen des Osteuropa-
Instituts (Slavistiches Seminar) an
der Freien Universität Berlin
*VB*, Vestigia Bibliae
*VBDU*, Веснік Беларускага
дзяржаўнага ўніверсітэта імя
У. I. Леніна. Серыя IV
*VCT*, Les Voies de la Création
Théâtrale
VDASD, Veröffentlichungen der
Deutschen Akademie für Sprache
und Dichtung, Darmstadt,
Luchterhand
*VF*, Вопросы философии
VGBIL, Всесоюзная
государственная библиотека
иностранной литературы
*VH*, Vida Hispánica,
Wolverhampton
*VHis*, Verba Hispanica
VI, Военно издателство
*VI*, Voix et Images
*VIa*, Вопросы языкознания
VIN, Veröffentlichungen des
Instituts für niederländische
Philologie, Erftstadt, Lukassen
ViSH, Вища школа
*VIst*, Вопросы истории
*Vit*, Вітчизна
VKP, Всесоюзная книжная
палата
*VL*, Вопросы литературы
*VLet*, Voz y Letras
*VM*, Время и мы, New York —
Paris — Jerusalem
*VMKA*, Verslagen en Mededelingen,
Koninklijke Academie voor
Nederlandse Taal- en
Letterkunde
*VMUF*, Вестник Московского
университета. Серия IX,
филология
*VMUFil*, Вестник Московского
университета. Серия VII,
философия
VÖAW, Verlag der
Österreichischen Akademie der
Wissenschaften, Vienna
*Voz*, Возрождение
*VP*, Встречи с прошлым, Moscow

*VPen*, Vita e Pensiero
*VR*, Vox Romanica
*VRKhD*, Вестник Русского
   христианского движения
*VRL*, Вопросы русской
   литературы
*VRM*, Volkskultur am Rhein und
   Maas
*VS*, Вопросы семантики
VSAV, Vydavateľstvo Slovenskej
   akadémie vied
VSh, Вышэйшая школа
*VSh*, Визвольний шлях
*VSPU*, Вестник Санкт-
   Петербургского университета
*VSSH*, Вечерняя средняя школа
*VV*, Византийский временник
*VVM*, Vlastivědný věstník moravský
*VVSh*, Вестник высшей школы
VWGÖ, Verband der
   wissenschaftlichen Gesellschaften
   Österreichs
VySh, Вища школа
VysSh, Высшая школа
*VyV*, Verdad y Vida
VZ, Vukova zadužbina, Belgrade


WAB, Wolfenbütteler Arbeiten zur
   Barockforschung, Wiesbaden,
   Harrassowitz
WADL, Wiener Arbeiten zur
   deutschen Literatur, Vienna,
   Braumüller
WAGAPH, Wiener Arbeiten zur
   germanischen Altertumskunde
   und Philologie, Berne, Lang
WAiF, Wydawnictwa Artystyczne i
   Filmowe, Warsaw
WaT, Wagenbachs
   Taschenbücherei, Berlin,
   Wagenbach
*WB*, Weimarer Beiträge
WBDP, Würzburger Beiträge zur
   deutschen Philologie, Würzburg,
   Königshausen & Neumann
WBG, Wissenschaftliche
   Buchgesellschaft, Darmstadt
*WBN*, Wolfenbütteler Barock-
   Nachrichten
WF, Wege der Forschung,
   Darmstadt, Wissenschaftliche
   Buchgesellschaft

*WGCR*, West Georgia College
   Review
*WGY*, Women in German Yearbook
WHNDL, Würzburger
   Hochschulschriften zur neueren
   Deutschen Literaturgeschichte,
   Frankfurt, Lang
*WHR*, The Welsh History Review
*WIFS*, Women in French Studies
*WKJb*, Wissenschaftskolleg.
   Institute for Advanced Study,
   Berlin. Jahrbuch
WL, Wydawnictwo Literackie,
   Cracow
WŁ, Wydawnictwo Łódzkie
WLub, Wydawnictwo Lubelskie
*WLT*, World Literature Today
WM, Wissensliteratur im
   Mittelalter, Wiesbaden, Reichert
*WNB*, Wolfenbütteler Notizen zur
   Buchgeschichte
WNT, Wydawnictwa Naukowo-
   Techniczne
*WoB*, Wolfenbütteler Beiträge
WoF, Wolfenbütteler Forschungen,
   Wiesbaden, Harrassowitz
WP, Wiedza Powszechna, Warsaw
*WPEL*, Working Papers in
   Educational Linguistics
WPFG, Working Papers in
   Functional Grammar,
   Amsterdam U.P.
*WRM*, Wolfenbütteler Renaissance
   Mitteilungen
*WS*, Wort und Sinn
WSA, Wolfenbütteler Studien zur
   Aufklärung, Tübingen, Niemeyer
WSiP, Wydawnictwa Szkolne i
   Pedagogiczne, Warsaw
*WSJ*, Wiener Slavistisches Jahrbuch
*WSl*, Die Welt der Slaven
*WSlA*, Wiener Slawistischer
   Almanach
WSP, Wyższa Szkoła Pedagogiczna
*WSp*, Word and Spirit
*WSPRRNDFP*, Wyższa Szkoła
   Pedagogiczna w Rzeszowie.
   Rocznik Naukowo-Dydaktyczny.
   Filologia Polska
WSS, Wiener Studien zur
   Skandinavistik
*WuW*, Welt und Wort
WUW, Wydawnictwo Uniwersytetu
   Wrocławskiego

*WW*, Wirkendes Wort
*WWAG*, Woman Writers in the Age of Goethe
*WWE*, Welsh Writing in English. A Yearbook of Critical Essays
*WZHUB*, Wissenschaftliche Zeitschrift der Humboldt-Universität, Berlin: gesellschafts- und sprachwissenschaftliche Reihe
*WZPHP*, Wissenschaftliche Zeitschrift der pädagogischen Hochschule Potsdam. Gesellschafts- und sprachwissenschaftliche Reihe
*WZUG*, Wissenschaftliche Zeitschrift der Ernst-Moritz-Arndt- Universität Greifswald
*WZUH*, Wissenschaftliche Zeitschrift der Martin-Luther-Universität Halle-Wittenberg: gesellschafts- und sprachwissenschaftliche Reihe
*WZUJ*, Wissenschaftliche Zeitschrift der Friedrich-Schiller-Universität Jena/Thüringen: gesellschafts-und sprachwissenschaftliche Reihe
*WZUL*, Wissenschaftliche Zeitschrift der Karl Marx Universität Leipzig: gesellschafts- und sprachwissenschaftliche Reihe
*WZUR*, Wissenschaftliche Zeitschrift der Universität Rostock: gesellschafts- und sprachwissenschaftliche Reihe

*YaIS*, Yale Italian Studies
*YB*, Ysgrifau Beirniadol
*YCC*, Yearbook of Comparative Criticism
*YCGL*, Yearbook of Comparative and General Literature
*YDAMEIS*, Yearbook of the Dutch Association for Middle Eastern and Islamic Studies
YEEP, Yale Russian and East European Publications, New Haven, Yale Center for International and Area Studies
*YES*, Yearbook of English Studies

*YFS*, Yale French Studies
*YIP*, Yale Italian Poetry
*YIS*, Yearbook of Italian Studies
*YJC*, Yale Journal of Criticism
*YM*, Yearbook of Morphology
*YPL*, York Papers in Linguistics
*YR*, Yale Review
*YSGP*, Yearbook. Seminar for Germanic Philology
*YSPS*, The Yearbook of the Society of Pirandello Studies
*YWMLS*, The Year's Work in Modern Language Studies

*ZÄAK*, Zeitschrift für Ästhetik und allgemeine Kunstwissenschaft
*ZB*, Zeitschrift für Balkanologie
*ZBL*, Zeitschrift für bayerische Landesgeschichte
*ZbS*, Zbornik za slavistiku
*ZCP*, Zeitschrift für celtische Philologie
*ZD*, Zielsprache Deutsch
*ZDA*, Zeitschrift für deutsches Altertum und deutsche Literatur
*ZDL*, Zeitschrift für Dialektologie und Linguistik
*ZDNÖL*, Zirkular. Dokumentationsstelle für neuere österreichische Literatur
*ZDP*, Zeitschrift für deutsche Philologie
*ZFKPhil*, Zborník Filozofickej fakulty Univerzity Komenského. Philologica
*ZFL*, Zbornik za filologiju i lingvistiku
*ZFSL*, Zeitschrift für französische Sprache und Literatur
*ZGB*, Zagreber germanistische Beiträge
*ZGer*, Zeitschrift für Germanistik
*ZGKS*, Zeitschrift der Gesellschaft für Kanada-Studien
*ZGL*, Zeitschrift für germanistische Linguistik
ZGS, Zürcher germanistische Studien, Berne, Lang
*ZK*, Zeitschrift für Katalanistik
*ZL*, Zeszyty Literackie, Paris
*ZMS(FL)*, Zbornik Matice srpske za filologiju i lingvistiku

*ZMS(KJ)*, Zbornik Matice srpske za književnost i jezik
*ZMS(Sl)*, Zbornik Matice srpske za slavistiku
ZNiO, Zakład Narodowy im. Ossolińskich, Wrocław
*ZnS*, Знание — сила
*ZNTSh*, Записки Наукового товариства iм. Шевченка
*ZNUG*, Zeszyty Naukowe Uniw. Gdańskiego, Gdańsk
*ZNUJ*, Zeszyty Naukowe Uniw. Jagiellońskiego, Cracow
*ZNWHFR*, Zeszyty Naukowe Wydziału Humanistycznego. Filologia Rosyjska
*ZNWSPO*, Zeszyty Naukowe Wyższej Szkoly Pedagogicznej w Opolu
*ZO*, Zeitschrift für Ostforschung
*ZPŠSlav*, Zborník Pedagogickej fakulty v Prešove Univerzity Pavla Jozefa Šafárika v Košiciach-Slavistika, Bratislava
*ZR*, Zadarska revija
*ZRAG*, Записки русской академической группы в США

*ZRBI*, Зборник радова византолошког института, Belgrade
*ZRL*, Zagadnienia Rodzajów Literackich
*ZRP*, Zeitschrift für romanische Philologie
*ZS*, Zeitschrift für Sprachwissenschaft
*ZSJ*, Zápisnik slovenského jazykovedca
*ZSK*, Ze Skarbca Kultury
*ZSL*, Zeitschrift für siebenbürgische Landeskunde
*ZSl*, Zeitschrift für Slawistik
*ZSP*, Zeitschrift für slavische Philologie
*ZSVS*, Zborník Spolku vojvodinských slovakistov, Novi Sad
*ZT*, Здесь и теперь
*ZV*, Zeitschrift für Volkskunde
*ZvV*, Звезда востока
*ZWL*, Zeitschrift für württembergische Landesgeschichte

# NAME INDEX

Aamotsbakken, B., 809
Aarseth, A., 807
Aase, L., 809
Abad, Mercedes, 284
Abad Merino, M., 230
Abaurre, M. B. M., 313
Abba, Giuseppe Cesare, 473
Abdeljelil Temimi, E., 250
Abé, A., 35
Abelard, J., 114
Abelard, Peter, 5, 6, 595, 596
Abouda, L., 30
Abplanalp, L., 884
Abraham de Béziers, 215
Abraham, C., 127
Abraham, W., 19, 570, 578, 579, 580
Abrahamsson, N., 815
Abramow-Newerly, J., 855
Abreu, Caio Fernando, 371
Abreu, R., 371
Abuín, A., 334
Abulafia, Abraham, 301
Abulafia, D., 301, 597
Accame, V., 520
Accarie, M., 50
Acciauoli, A., 431
Accorsi, M. G., 449, 459
Achard-Bayle, G., 39
Achas, Francisco Xavier de, 343
Achterberg, Gerrit, 791
Ackermann, F., 579
Acquaviva, P., 379
Acuña, A., 338
Acuña, Father Cristobal de, 367
Adam de la Halle, 68, 79
Adams, A., 427
Adams, A., 96
Adams, H., 217
Adams, T., 60
Adelswärd, V., 810
Adelung, J. C., 575
Adenet le Roi, 69
Ader, Guilhem, 116
Aderaldo Castello, J., 366
Adler, H., 346, 357
Adorno, F., 414
Adorno, Theodor, 697
Adoum, Jorge Enrique, 349
Ady, Endre, 828

Aegidius of Corbeil, 7
Aelfric, 2
Aeschbach, M., 85
Aeschylus, 334, 405
Aethelwold, 2
Agawu-Kakraba, Y., 287
Agel, V., 578
Ageno, F., 402
Agertz, J., 816
Agerup, A. M., 800
Agnoletti, F., 524
Agosín, M., 370
Agosín, Marjorie, 347
Agosti, S., 491, 526
Agostinetti, Giacomo, 451
Agostini, Giacomo, 451
Agricola, Johannes, 640
Agricola, Rudolf, 647
Agrippa von Nettesheim, Heinrich Cornelius, 641
Aguado, Jesús, 289
Aguiar, C., 368
Aguilar, Rosario, 349, 361
Aguilar Piñal, F., 253, 255
Aguilera Sarramuño, Marco Tulio, 345
Aguirre, A. M., 263, 334
Agustín, José, 345, 360
Agustini, Delmira, 346, 347, 364
Ahlin, Lars, 836
Aho, R., 839
Ahokas, J. A., 43
Ahrenberg, L., 814
Ahrenholz, B., 572
Aichholzer, D., 631
Aichinger, Ilse, 757
Aigner, C., 720
Aigrot, E., 124
Ailes, M. J., 53
Aillaud, Jean-Antoine, 461, 462
Aimeric de Belenoi, 216
Ainaud Escudero, J., 303
Ainsworth, P. F., 83
Aitchison, J., 554
Åkesson, N., 836
Åkesson, Sonja, 834
Alabau, Magaly, 356
Alain de Lille, 605
Alamanni, L., 438
Ålander, M., 819
Alarcón Sierra, R., 259

Alarcos García, E., 877
Alazet, B., 883
Alba, N., 264, 282
Alba-Koch, B. de, 342
Albada, J. E., 353
Albanese, G., 449
Albano, E. C., 312
Albano Leoni, F., 377
Albanowski, A., 348
Albersmeier, F.-J., 750
Albert, F., 771
Albert, M., 262
Alberti, Leon Battista, 430, 431, 432, 433, 441
Alberti, Rafael, 260, 261, 262, 263, 265–67, 278, 281, 294
Albertocchi, G., 492
Albertsen, L. L., 733
Albertus Magnus, 9, 76
Albes, C., 758
Albornoz, Aurora de, 291
Albrecht, 606, 615
Albrecht von Eyb, 636
Albrecht von Johansdorf, 618
Albrecht, J., 17
Albrecht, W., 659, 739, 770
Alcalá, A., 234, 242
Alciato, A., 427
Alciato, Andrea, 96
Alcini, L., 479
Alcorn, J., 482
Alcover, M., 120
Aldhelm, 2, 3
Aldhouse-Green, M. J., 560
Alecsandri, Vasile, 541
Alegre, Francesc, 308
Aleixandre, Vicente, 260, 261, 262, 265, 267, 879
Aleksandrowska, E., 865
Alemany, R., 302, 307
Alemany Bay, C., 364
Alén Garabato, M. C., 210, 217
Alencar, José de, 366, 368
Alesch, J. S., 182
Alessio, G. C., 402
Alex, H., 633
Alexander Neckam, 9
Alexander, Frida, 370
Alexandrescu, S., 547
Alexandrescu, V., 150

Alèxis, L., 208
Alexis, Willibald, 719
Aleza Izquierdo, M., 15, 877
Alfarnes, O., 807, 809
Alfieri Tonini, T., 456
Alfieri, Vittorio, 459, 460–62, 487
Alfonso V (*King of Aragon*), 246
Alfonso X (*el Sabio, King of Castile and León*), 220, 235, 236, 237, 238, 242, 250, 332, 593
Alfonso Vegas, M., 222
Alfonzetti, B., 459, 461
Alfonzetti, G., 384
Algazi, L. G., 164
Al-George, S., 544
Ali, M. al, 746
Alibert, L., 204, 205, 209
Aliberti, C., 503
Alinder, G., 814
Alinei, M., 550
Aliprandi, G. 486
Allard, J., 186
Allegretti, P., 216
Allen, M. J. B., 433
Allen, R., 57
Allén, S., 810
Allende, Isabel, 353
Allmand, C., 85
Almeida, T. V. de, 369
Almeida Conrado, R. F. de, 370
Almqvist, Carl Jonas Love, 822, 823, 825, 827, 833
Almuzara, Javier, 289
Alonso, A., 250
Alonso, C. J., 346
Alonso, Dámaso, 261, 267–68, 879
Alonso Millán, Juan José, 293
Alonso Montero, Xesús, 332, 877
Alonso Nogueira, A., 333
Alonso Núñez, A. S., 321, 336
Alonso de Santos, José Luis, 292, 293
Alós, Concha, 282, 284
Alsvik, T., 807
Alt, A. T., 732
Altamira, R., 260
Altamiranda, D., 352
Altena, P., 786
Althammer, W., 547
Althaus, H.-J., 659
Althaus, T., 640, 670
Althoff, G., 589, 597, 598, 605
Altieri, M. A., 424
Altman, C., 309
Altmann, H., 579
Altolaguirre, M., 264
Alturo i Perucho, J., 215

Alvar, C., 233, 243, 246, 251
Alvar, M., 225, 226, 228
Alvarez, C., 56, 353
Alvarez, Julia, 357
Alvarez, L. P. de, 452
Álvarez, R., 877
Álvarez, V., 333
Álvarez, Valentin Andrés, 262
Álvarez Barrientos, J., 254, 255, 258
Álvarez Blanco, R., 322
Álvarez de Castro, Camilo, 333
Álvarez de la Granja, M., 323
Álvarez Junco, J., 264
Álvarez de Miranda, P., 256, 257
Álvarez Pellitero, A. M., 251, 252
Álvarez Saenz, Félix, 363
Álvarez-Ude, C., 259
Alvaro, Corrado, 506
Alvered, Z., 819
Alves, C., 368
Alves, F. M., 735
Alves, I. M., 310, 311, 884
Alves de Aguiar, J., 372
Alvilares, X., 336
Alzate, C., 356
Alzate Cadavid, C., 342
Amado, Jorge, 370, 372
Amado, M. T., 338
Amado Rodríguez, M. T., 337
Amanieu de la Broquiera, 215
Amanieu de Sescas, 215
Amann, E., 276
Amann, K., 767
Amanwy (David Rees Griffiths), 562
Amasuno, M., 250
Amat, Nuria, 284
Âmbar, M., 19, 314
Amberger, A., 623
Ambjørnsen, Ingvar, 808
Ambrière, M., 153, 158
Ambroise, 67
Ambrose (*Saint*), 431
Ambrosi, P., 271
Ambrosini, R., 450
Amerio, R., 485
Amerongen, M. von, 737
Amery, C., 707
Amícola, J., 350
Amis, Kingsley, 114
Amis, Martin, 114
Ammanniti, N., 505
Ammon, U., 567, 568, 799
Amodeo, I., 674, 758
Amor y Vásquez, J., 280
Amoretti, G., 488
Amorós, A., 251, 255, 269
Amorós, Amparo, 282

Amory, F., 371
Amthor, W., 690
Anceschi, L., 501, 523
Anchieta, José de, 367
Ancos García, P., 251
Åndahl, E. Bak, 798
Anderlan-Obletter, A., 550
Anderman, G., 819, 820
Andermatt, M., 729
Andersch, Alfred, 691, 697, 75
757
Andersen, Hans Christian, 270
287, 733
Andersen, H. L., 40
Andersen, Henning, 19
Andersen, S. Kaas, 803
Andersen, S., 809
Anderson, A. A., 269, 270
Anderson, C., 181
Anderson, Sascha, 753
Andersson, E., 812
Andersson, H., 819
Andersson, L. G., 810, 880
Andersson, L., 836
Andersson, M., 813
Andersson, R., 811
Andersson, T., 27
Andersson, T., 816
Andorlino, F., 525
Andrade, Jorge, 369
Andrade, M. L., 310
Andrade, Mário de, 366, 370
Andrade, Oswald de, 369
Andraschke, P., 668
Andreas Capellanus, 90, 604, 606
Andréoli, M., 160, 163
Andres, Giovanni, 457
Andres, Stefan, 757
Andrés-Suárez, I., 223
Andrews, R., 447
Andreyev, Leonid, 266
Andrieux-Reix, N., 54
Andriopoulis, S., 708
Androutsopoulos, J. K., 570
Androutsopoulou, A., 539
Andry, D., 551
Andrzejewski, J., 863, 871, 87
Andueza, M., 260
Aneau, Barthélemy, 96
Aneirin, 556
Anelli, L., 383
Aneurin Fardd (Aneurin Jone
562
Angel, Albalucía, 355
Angelini, A., 432
Angelo da Vallombrosa, 437
Angelomus of Luxeuil, 3, 4
Angenendt, A., 631

Angered-Strandberg, Hilma, 826
Anghelescu, M., 541, 547
Angioletti, Giovan Battista, 501
Anglade, R., 706, 736
Anglani, B., 499
Angold, M., 597
Angueira, A., 336
Angvik, B., 362
Ania, G., 509
Anis, P., 120
Ankarcrona, A., 824
Anne de Bretagne, 73, 89, 114
Annichiarico, A., 307
Annio da Viterbo, 430
Annoni, C., 466
Anouilh, Jean, 173
Anreiter, P., 585
Anselm von Eyb, 635
Anselmi, S., 508
Antelmi, D., 385
Anten, H., 791
Antesperger, Johann Balthasar, 575
Antinori, C., 426
Anton, H., 666
Anton, K.-G., 855
Antonaya, M. L., 249
Antonescu, N., 543
Antoniano, S., 426
Antonius von Pforr, 628, 634
Antunović, G., 819
Anzengruber, Ludwig, 713
Apel, F., 708
Apeland, O. I., 807
Apicius, 429
Apollinaire, Guillaume, 510, 521, 524
App, U., 635
Appel, H.-W., 581
Appelmans, Gheraert, 626
Aprile, M., 9, 16
Apter, R., 214
Apter-Cragnolino, A., 348
Apuleius, 133, 869
Aquin, Hubert, 184, 187
Aquinas v. Thomas
Aquino, Carlo d', 403
Araldo, Antonio, 446
Aranda, Count of, 254
Araújo, H., 362
Araújo, N., 342, 356
Arbaleste, Charlotte, 97
Arbasino, Alberto, 506
Arbor Aldea, M., 331
Archangeli, M., 677
Arcimboldo, 180
Arcimboldo, G., 594
Arcipreste de Hita v. Ruiz, Juan
Arconati, Costanza, 489

Arden, H., 86
Arderiu, Clementina, 290
Ardila, J. G., 276
Ardolino, F., 468
Arenas, F., 371
Arenas, M. A., 362
Arenas, M. I., 362
Arenas, Reinaldo, 346, 356, 357
Arends, J., 318
Arendt, B., 550
Aretino, Pietro, 423, 438, 439, 447, 448, 451
Arguedas, José María, 352, 362
Argueta, Manlio, 358
Arias, J., 372
Arias, S., 356
Arias-Alvarez, B., 224
Arias Cabal, A., 224
Arias Santos, F. J., 276
Ariosto, Ludovico, 1, 104, 438, 440, 444, 445, 446
Aristotle, 6, 120, 121, 126, 137, 396, 400, 420, 422, 428, 432, 433, 434, 438, 440, 578, 641, 678, 695
Ariza, M., 220, 228
Arizaleta, A., 236
Arkinstall, C., 364
Arkush, A., 679
Arlotto Mainardi (*Piovano*), 440
Arlt, J., 871
Arlt, Roberto, 346, 347, 348
Armangué, J., 299
Armijo Canto, C. E., 239
Arminius (or: Hermann, *Germanic warrior*), 707, 708
Armistead, S. G., 235, 228
Armour, P., 399
Armstrong, A., 79, 80
Armstrong, G. M., 57
Armstrong, N., 33
Armstrong, P., 370
Arn, M., 77
Arnal Purroy, M. L., 227
Arnau de Vilanova, 303-04
Arnau, Y. E., 193
Arnauld, Antoine, 144, 147, 148
Arnauld-d'Andilly, J.-A.-M. de S.-M. (Mère Angélique de Saint-Jean), 148
Arnaut Daniel, 419
Arnaut Guilhem de Marsan, 215
Arnaut Peire, 202
Arneodo, S., 212
Arnim, A. von, 680, 681, 683, 684
Arnim, Bettina von, 684-85, 714
Arnold von Harff, 635
Arnold, H. L., 766, 769
Arnold, K., 631

Arnone, V., 504
Arntz, R., 550
Arntzen, E., 806
Aron, P., 794
Aronna, M., 344
Aronoff, M., 378
Aronson, Stina, 836
Arozarena, Marcelino, 356
Arping, Å., 822, 826
Arreola, Juan José, 347, 359
Arrigoni, A., 142
Arrivé, M., 32
Arriví, F., 357
Arrufat, Antón, 357
Arteaga, E. de, 256
Artel, Jorge, 355
Articus, R., 750
Arveiller, R., 25
Arvidsson, K.-A., 32
Arvinte, V., 527
Arzt, T., 767
Åsbacka, R., 838
Aschheim, S., 741
Asclepius, 434
Ascoli, A. R., 448
Ascoli, G. I., 473
Ascunce, J. A., 272
Ashbery, John, 872
Ashcroft, J., 619, 642
Ashley, K., 64
Askey, J. D., 750
Askildsen, Kjell, 808
Asman, C., 669
Asmuth, C., 688
Asor Rosa, A., 497, 501
Aspenström, Werner, 832, 836
Asperti, S., 301
Asperto, S., 233
Aspetsberger, F., 771
Asquini, L., 433
Asquini, M., 433
Assaf, F., 134, 140
Assmann, A., 752
Assmann, D., 751
Astås, R., 808
Astell, A. W., 1
Aston, Louise, 705, 710, 715
Asturias, Miguel Angel, 335, 346, 358
Atencia, María Victoria, 290, 291
Athayde, F. de, 368
Atkins, R., 707
Ato, Cardinal Bishop of Ostia, 5
Atxaga, Bernardo, 283
Atzert, S., 720
Aub, Max, 273, 278, 282, 284
Aubanèl, T., 211
Aubigné, Agrippa d', 92, 94, 100, 111-12, 117, 118

Auden, W. H., 415
Auerbach, Berthold, 716, 717
Auger, J., 47
Augier, M.-L., 82
Augustine (*Saint*), 9, 75, 148, 244, 395, 431, 433, 435, 596
Augusto, C., 316
Augustyniak, U., 863
Aukrust, Olav, 804
Aulnoy, Marie Catherine, comtesse d', 134, 135
Aureau, B., 154
Aurell, Tage, 836
Ausländer, Rose, 757
Aust, H., 723
Authier, J.-M., 37, 882
Authier-Revuz, J., 34
Autrand, F., 881
Avelar, I., 344, 354
Avellini, L., 483
Avenoza, G., 248, 301, 332
Aventinus, Johannes, 567
Averroes, 435
Avgustinova, T., 849
Ávila, F. J., 290
Avolio, F., 389, 391
Avram, A., 530, 531
Avram, M., 537
Axeitos, X. L., 329, 877
Ayestarán Uriz, I., 282
Aymard, R., 207
Aymone, R., 493
Azara, J.-N. de, 257
Azara y Perera, José Nicolás de, 330
Azevedo, Aluísio, 368
Azevedo, Álvares de, 368
Aznar Soler, M., 264, 266, 282
Azorín (J. Martínez Ruiz), 260, 274–75, 278
Azzam, W., 54
Azzone Zweifel, A., 739


Baardewijk, J. van, 40
Baasner, R., 659, 664, 733
Bąba, S., 847, 849
Babucke, V., 599
Bacarisse, Mauricio, 259
Baccar, A., 122
Baccarani, E., 525
Bach, B., 773
Bach, Carl Philipp Emanuel, 679
Bach, Philipp Emmanuel, 679
Bache, P., 804
Bachelard, G., 477
Bacheracht, Therese, 719
Bache-Wiig, H., 804, 807
Bachmann, Ingeborg, 691, 697, 757, 767

Bachofen, Johann Jakob, 730
Bachorski, H.-J., 603
Baciu, A., 544
Backes, M., 591, 603
Backes, S., 613
Bäckström, L., 843
Bäckvall, H., 24
Bacon, Roger, 630
Baczyński, Krzysztof Kamil, 855, 869
Baddeley, S., 96
Badel, P.-Y., 70
Baden, N. T., 370
Bădescu, C. P., 546
Badesi, L., 466
Badia, L., 301, 303, 305, 307
Badia Margarit, A. M., 308
Badini, G., 441
Baehr, R., 411
Bæk, P., 803
Baena, Juan Alfonso de, 246
Baerentzen, P., 578
Baetens, J., 130
Báez de Aguilar González, F., 231
Baez Montero, C., 222
Bagnasco, R., 439
Bagnoli, V., 473
Bagués, A., 260
Bähncke, M., 798
Bahr, E., 672
Baïf, Jean-Antoine de, 92, 99, 114, 115
Bailbé, J.-M., 158, 168
Bailey, M., 233
Bailleul, Thomas de, 70
Baillie, R., 190
Baines, M., 563
Baisch, M., 614
Baixeras, X. R., 337
Bajarlía, J. J., 348
Bajcar, A., 867
Bajerowa, I., 852
Bajoni, M. G., 492, 493, 511
Baka, J., 863
Bake, Alijt, 626
Baker, F., 459
Baker, J. M., 483
Baker, M., 504
Bakhtin, Mikhail, 331, 370, 498, 614, 674, 832, 717, 741
Bakker, M. S., 783, 789
Bakmand, B., 799
Balbierz, J., 837
Balbo, Cesare, 472
Balcells, J. M., 265
Balcerzan, E., 871
Balconi, M., 383
Baldacci, L., 484, 485, 517
Baldassare, U., 444

Baldassarri, S. U., 512
Baldelli, I., 414, 418, 420
Balderston, D., 346, 349
Baldi, G., 524
Baldi, P., 14
Baldinger, K., 42, 201
Baldissone, G., 514
Baldit, J.-P., 211
Balès, I., 211
Ball, C., 483
Ballanche, Pierre Simon, 170
Ballerini, L., 502
Ballesteros, I., 284
Ballestra, S., 505
Ballweg, J., 580
Balme, C., 295
Balsamo, J., 95, 100, 431
Baltag, Cezar, 541
Baltanás, E., 235
Bălu, I., 547
Balzac, Honoré de, 153, 159–64, 270
Balzac, Jean-Louis Guez de, 120, 134, 135, 144
Balzamo, E., 829
Balzer, B., 759
Bambaglioli, Graziolo, 402
Bamberg, Felix, 732
Bammesberger, A., 572, 585, 599
Bańczerowski, J., 859
Bandeira, Manuel, 309, 368, 369
Banderier, G., 110, 111
Bandet, J.-L., 706
Bandini, F., 526
Banfi, Antonio, 523
Banfi, L., 446
Bannert, R., 811
Banniard, M., 14
Baños Vallejo, F., 236
Banti, Anna, 504, 506
Bănulescu, Ştefan, 547
Banville, Théodore de, 156
Barańczak, Stanisław, 871, 872, 873
Barański, Z. G., 398, 400, 409, 410, 517, 518, 882
Barbance, M., 192
Barbantini, 524
Barbaro, Daniele, 432, 433
Barbaro, F., 431
Barbarossa v. Frederick
Barbarulli, C., 475
Bárberi Squarotti, G., 462
Barbéris, P., 163, 164
Barbès, A., 168
Barbi, M., 406
Barbierato, P., 550
Barbieri, E., 428
Barbieri, F., 433

Barbina, A., 519
Barbolani, C., 461
Barbosa, P. A., 312
Barbry, F.-R., 195
Barbu, Ion, 546
Barbu, M., 542
Barbu, V., 530
Barca, D., 217
Barceló, Elia, 280
Barcelo, François, 186
Barchilon, J., 134
Bardini, M., 515
Bardout, J.-C., 149
Bardt, U., 676
Barei, S. N., 348
Barenghi, M., 504
Baretti, Giuseppe, 455, 462
Baricco, Alessandro, 506
Barile, L., 514, 522
Bark, E., 259
Bark, I., 700
Bark, J., 733
Barker, A., 714
Barkhausen, K.-L., 750
Barlacchi, D., 440
Barletta, V., 240
Bärmann, M., 606, 628
Barner, W., 674
Barnes, R. B., 638
Barnet, M.-C., 176
Barnett, R.-L., 129, 130
Barnwell, H. T., 130
Baroja, Pío, 259, 260, 264, 274
Barolini, T., 410
Baron, A.-M., 162, 163
Barón, E., 264
Baroncini, D., 525
Barquet, J.J., 357
Barra-Jover, M., 30
Barral, Carlos, 291
Barraqué, J.-P.,202
Barreca, R., 175
Barrera, T., 347
Barrès, M., 159
Barri, M., 298
Barros, D. L. P., 309, 310
Barros, João de, 309
Barros, Pía, 354
Barsella, S., 502
Barsotti, C., 210
Barthes, Roland, 112, 175, 283, 286, 287, 289, 498, 723, 741
Bartholomeus Anglicanus, 91
Bartholomew of Bydgoszcz, 855
Bartholomaeus of Capua, 7
Barthouil-Ionesco, I., 547
Bartl, A., 879
Bartmiński, J., 850
Bartnicka, B., 857, 858
Bartoli, Cosimo, 425

Bartoli, Giuseppe, 461
Bartolini, Louisa Grace, 469
Bartra, Agustí, 281
Bartrum, P. C., 558
Bartsch, K., 718
Bartsch, R. H., 714
Bas, E.-J., 148
Basara, J., 849, 852
Basbøll, H., 799
Bascoy, M., 332
Bashevis Singer, Isaac, 861
Basker, D., 771, 772, 773
Basnage de Beauval, Henri, 121
Bassani, Giorgio, 506
Bassetto, B. F., 206
Bassi, A., 492
Bassler, M., 884
Bassola, P., 578
Basterra, G. S., 271
Basterra, Ramón, 259
Bastos, H., 370
Bataille, Georges, 173, 177, 180, 263, 526
Batany, J., 75
Batelli, A., 455
Bates, E., 385
Bates, J., 861, 872
Batley, E. M., 678
Batlle, M., 305
Battafarano, I. M., 655, 657, 658, 672
Battaglini, M., 456
Battesti, J.-P., 129
Battilotti, D., 433
Battista, C., 477
Battistini, A., 459, 480
Battiston-Zuliani, R., 764
Baudelaire, Charles, 39, 153, 156, 159, 168, 259, 482, 507, 510, 692, 709
Baudelle-Michels, S., 54
Baudouin de Courtenay, J., 855
Bauer, J. B., 593
Bauer, K., 722, 743
Bauer, R., 387
Bauer, W., 635, 880
Bäuerle, Adolf, 740
Bauernfeld, Eduard von, 714, 740
Baum, R., 28, 878
Baumann, Z., 743
Baumbach, Anna von, 717
Baumbach, Freimund von, 717
Baumgart, H., 684
Baumgarte, S., 628
Baumgartner, E., 58
Baumgärtner, I., 635
Baumgartner, W., 805
Bauschke, R., 616, 620
Bautista, Amalia, 289

Bavent, M., 122
Baxmann, I., 751
Bayle, Pierre, 147
Bayley, P., 119
Bazalgues, G., 200
Bazzanella, C., 381, 382, 383, 504
Bazzocchi, A. M., 487
Bazzocchi, M. A., 517, 518
Beasley, F. E., 138
Beatrice, L., 505
Beauchemin, Yves, 185, 187, 189
Beaudet, M.-A., 185, 194
Beaudin, J.-D., 117
Beaudry, J., 183
Beaugrand, H., 187
Beaulieu, J.-P., 97
Beaulieu, Victor-Lévy, 184, 187
Beaumarchais, Pierre-Augustin Caron de, 117
Beaupied, A., 356
Beausoleil, Claude, 187, 193
Beauvais-Nangis, Nicolas de Brichanteau, marquis de, 120
Beauvoir, Simone de, 173–74, 178
Bebel, Heinrich, 640, 647
Bec, P., 216
Beccadelli, A., 431
Beccaria, Cesare, 462, 489
Beccaria, G. L., 497, 501, 502, 503
Becchi, Guglielmo, 6
Becher, M., 600
Becherelle, L.-N., 42
Becherucci, I., 489, 490
Bechstein, Ludwig, 719
Bechtold, A., 628
Beck, Hans Leonhard, 640
Becker, Jurek, 756
Becker, Jürgen, 757
Becker, K., 74
Becker, T., 576
Becker-Cantarino, B., 653, 671, 677
Beckett, S., 34
Beckett, Samuel, 174, 405, 681, 707, 724, 774, 831
Beckman, Erik, 836
Beckman, Thea, 797
Becq, A., 152
Becquer, A., 43
Bécquer, G., 264
Becquet, J., 203
Bede, 2, 3. 4, 6
Bedingfield, M. B., 2
Bednarczuk, L., 850
Beekman, K., 787
Beer, Pieter Leon de, 787
Begemann, C., 664, 709, 720

Beger, Lorenz, 652
Béguelin, M.-J., 43
Béhar, P., 650, 878
Beheim, Michel, 595
Behr, H.-J., 609
Behr, I., 570
Behring, E., 547, 548
Beigbeder, F., 204
Beil, U. J., 709
Bein, T., 609, 620
Beiu-Paladi, L., 505
Bejan, Mariana, 541
Bekes, P., 758
Bekkers, J., 794
Bel Gaya, A., 299
Béland, André, 187
Belegni, A., 450
Bell, D. F., 162
Bell, M., 664
Bell, T., 644
Bellabarba, M., 450
Belleau, Remy, 94, 115
Belleforest, François de, 93, 133
Bellenger, Y., 94, 95, 99, 104
Belletti, A., 20, 23
Belletti, G. C., 214
Belli, Gioconda, 347
Belli, Giuseppe Gioachino, 471, 473–74
Bellini, Jacopo, 425
Bellman, Carl Michael, 824
Bellmann, W., 759
Bello, C., 520
Bellocchio, P., 518
Bellomo, S., 396
Bellon, R., 66
Bellour, R., 178
Bellucci, Laura, 494
Bellucci, N., 482
Belmonte-Serrano, J., 284
Belon, Pierre, 92, 110
Beltran, E., 11
Beltrán, R., 305, 306
Beltrán, Rosa, 360
Beltrán, V., 243, 303
Bem, Antoni Gustaw, 867
Bembo, Pietro, 375, 427, 438, 440, 451
Bemmann, H., 723
Benarczuk, L., 572
Benati, Davide, 524
Benavente, J., 278
Benay, J., 747
Benci, Tommaso, 446
Bencivenni, Zucchero, 374
Benco, Silvio, 476
Bencze, Á., 384
Bendena, M., 739
Bendina, T. I., 852
Bendix, J., 799

Benedetti, C., 498
Benedetti, Mario, 346, 364
Benedetti, M., 387
Benedictsson, Victoria, 827
Benesch-Tschanett, G., 732
Benet i Jornet, Josep M., 294
Benet, Juan, 282
Benevento, A., 512
Beneyto, María, 291
Beneyto, M., 358, 359
Benfell, V. S., 421
Bengtsson, A., 89
Bengtsson, Frans G., 835
Bénichou, P., 158
Benincà, P., 884
Beniscelli, A., 478
Benítez Ariza, José Manuel, 289
Benítez Reyes, Felipe, 289
Benjamin, Walter, 156, 510, 693, 694, 743
Benn, Gottfried, 680, 733, 737
Bennett, B. K., 831
Bennett, P. E., 53, 54
Bennewitz, I., 878
Benni, Stefano, 506
Bennich-Björkman, B., 829
Benoît de Sainte-Maure, 50, 60, 67, 611
Benozzo, F., 521
Benrekassa, G., 152
Bensoussan, D., 141
Benthien, C., 699
Bentley, D., 391
Bentzinger, R., 623, 879
Benucci, E., 482, 486, 494
Benussi, C., 476
Benvenuti, G., 483
Benvenuto da Imola, 402
Benzoni, G., 457
Benzoni, V., 493
Beolco, A. v. Ruzante
Bepler, J., 652
Berardi, K., 476
Berardinelli, A., 498, 503
Berbig, R., 725, 766
Bercé, F., 165
Bercegol, F., 154
Berceo, Gonzalo de, 220, 223, 236–37
Berchet, Giovanni, 471
Berdychowska, Z., 570
Bereau, J., 106
Berejan, S., 530
Berend, N., 630
Berendse, G.-J., 754
Berent, W., 862
Beresford, A., 245
Berg, L.-O., 816
Berg, W. van den, 787
Bergamín, José, 264, 266

Bergenthal, K., 353
Bergh, M., 843
Bergh, T. van den, 795
Berghaus, G., 505
Bergman, Hjalmar, 836–37
Bergman, Ingmar, 831, 837
Bergmann, A., 786
Bergmann, C., 570
Bergmann, E., 744
Bergmann, H., 585
Bergmann, R., 576, 588, 601
Bergmeier, H., 735
Bergquist, L., 824
Bergson, Henri, 173, 525
Bergsten, S., 827
Bering, D., 585
Berio, Luciano, 522
Berk, Marjan, 797
Berlinghieri, Francesco, 429
Berlioz, Hector, 158
Berman, A., 747
Berman, R. A., 706
Berman, Sabina, 361
Bernabé, J., 47
Bernal Muñoz, J. L., 274
Bernal Salgado, J. L., 267
Bernard of Clairvaux (*Saint*), 6, 148, 410, 644
Bernard, L. A., 235
Bernard-Griffiths, S., 171, 172
Bernardi, N., 391
Bernardi, U., 450
Bernardino da Siena (*Saint*), 436, 437, 448
Bernardus Silvestris, 6, 7, 605
Bernart de Ventadorn, 214, 216, 421
Bernaschina, P., 462
Bernauer, M., 719, 738
Bernazzoli, C., 123
Berndt, F., 711
Bernger von Horheim, 618
Bernhard, G., 26
Bernhard, Thomas, 669, 691, 707, 757, 758
Bernhardi, A. F., 686
Berni, Francesco, 440
Berns, J. J., 653
Bernstein, E., 639
Bernstein, S., 230
Béroul, 56
Berrada, M., 149
Berregard, S., 143
Berretta, M., 382
Berrini, B., 368, 369
Berriot-Salvadore, E., 95, 113
Berschin, W., 602
Bersier, G., 673
Bersuire, Pierre (Petrus Berchorius), 9, 625

Berta von Herten, 627
Bertacchini, R., 475
Bertau, K., 626
Bertaud, M., 137, 140
Berteloot, A., 636, 779
Bertelsmeier-Kierst, C., 636
Berthelot, A., 59, 72, 78
Berthiaume, P., 192
Berthier, P., 155, 161, 163
Berthonneau, A.-M., 39
Berthoud, Samuel-Henri, 153
Bertken (*Sister*), 626
Berto, Giuseppe, 506
Bertola, Aurelio de' Giorgi, 462–63
Bertoli, G., 429
Bertolini, L., 430
Bertolucci, Attilio, 501, 506–07
Bertolucci, S., 489
Bertolucci, V., 233
Bertone, G., 499, 504, 508, 519
Bertoni, R., 484, 497, 508
Bertot, L. D., 356
Bertrand, Aloysius, 153, 154
Bertrand-Jennings, C., 167
Beruete, A. de, 274
Besamusca, B., 618, 780
Besch, W., 572, 574, 878
Beskow, Elsa, 835
Besse, M., 18
Bessette, Gérard, 184, 185, 188
Bessi, R., 449, 482
Bessler, P., 36
Besson-Morel, A., 161
Best, K.-H., 572
Betensky, C., 167
Bethge, Hans, 750
Bethin, C. Y., 846
Bethmann, A., 677
Betocchi, Carlo, 507
Bettarini, R., 515
Betti, F., 462
Bettinelli, Saverio, 459
Bettoli, Parmenio, 493
Bettoni, A., 115
Bettoni, C., 393
Betz, A., 735
Betz, H.-G., 705
Betz, M., 716
Beugnot, B., 119, 146, 179
Beuter, Pere Antoni, 305
Beutin, W., 624, 716
Beutler, B., 735
Beutler, Ernst, 674
Beuys, B., 721
Bevan, G. A., 554
Beverido, F., 361
Beverley, J., 344
Bévort, I., 801
Beyer, M., 644

Beyer, Marcel, 758
Beyle, Henri v. Stendhal
Bèze, Théodore de, 96
Bezzel, I., 641, 647
Bhabha, Homi, 198
Białecki, I., 852
Białoskórska, M., 847
Białoszewski, Miron, 863, 871, 873
Biagi, D., 506
Biagini, E., 485
Biamonti, F., 496, 507
Bianchi, C., 476
Bianchi, G., 525
Bianchi, Giovanni, 458
Bianchi, N., 402
Bianchi, P., 455, 495
Bianchini, F., 507
Bianciardi, G., 474
Biancini, L., 471
Bianco, M., 442
Bianco, P., 503
Biasin, G. P., 500, 519
Bichel, U., 730, 731
Bichsel, P., 635, 640
Bickel, H., 582
Bidu-Vrânceanu, G., 527
Bieber, H., 734
Biedermann-Pasques, L., 33
Bielec, D., 847
Bieri, S., 729
Biermann, K., 167
Biermann, Wolf, 758, 764
Biernatzki, Karl, 748
Bierwirth, S., 736
Bierwisch, M., 568
Biesheuvel, I., 779
Biet, C., 129
Bietenholz, P. G., 431
Biffi, I., 410
Bigazzi, I., 517
Bigi, E., 431, 486
Biglione di Viarigi, L. A., 489
Bigongiari, Piero, 485, 503, 507
Bijsterveld, A.-J. A., 623
Bijvoet, E., 816
Bilbao, Francisco, 341
Bilenchi, Romano, 507
Bilharinho, G., 366
Billi, L., 469
Billi, M., 509
Billy, P.-H., 200, 202, 204, 207, 208, 209, 212, 878
Bilz, F., 739
Binding, G., 2, 594
Binek, M., 709
Binet, Etienne, 121
Bini, A., 478
Bini, D., 483
Binnerts-Kluyver, C., 781

Binni, W., 482, 502
Binnig, W., 573
Binoche, B., 151
Binski, P., 597
Biondi, Franco, 758
Biondi, M. A., 524
Bioy Casares, Adolfo, 348, 350
Biral, B., 485
Birberick, A. L., 135
Bircken, M., 771
Birgitta of Sweden (*Saint*), 821, 823, 830, 831
Birken, Sigmund von, 654
Birkmeyer, R., 635
Birney, A., 777
Biron, M., 184, 191
Birus, H., 666, 668
Bisanti, A., 4
Bishop, P., 662, 743
Bismarck, Otto von, 707, 723, 724
Bisset, J., 361
Bisson, C., 211
Bissonnette, Lise, 185
Bittlinger, A., 688
Bitzius v. Gotthelf
Bizer, M., 107
Bizzarri, H. O., 239, 249
Bjerrum, M., 801
Björk, C., 837
Björk, K., 837
Björkvall, G., 592
Björling, Gunnar, 832, 834
Bjørneboe, Jens, 808
Bjørnson, Bjørnstjerne, 804, 805, 829
Björsten, S., 818
Black, I., 76
Black, J., 878
Black, R., 881
Blackmore, J., 305, 878
Blackwell, M. J., 831
Blackwell. R. J., 423, 435
Blaeschke, A., 155
Blaga, Lucian, 544, 546
Blaim, A., 861
Blais, Marie-Claire, 185, 188, 193, 195
Blake, R. J., 882
Blake, William, 403
Blakert, D., 678
Blamberger, G., 698
Blamires, D., 746
Blampain, D., 34
Blanc, A., 95
Blanchard, J., 85, 87
Blanche, August, 825, 829
Blanchet, P., 46, 211
Blanchot, M., 510
Blanck, D., 552

Blanco, C., 337
Blanco, D., 329
Blanco, M. E., 346, 356
Blanco, X., 26
Blanco Soler, L., 262
Blanco Torres, Roberto, 332–33
Blanco White, José, 256, 258
Blank, W., 614, 628
Blanquaert, H., 45
Blanquaert, M., 45
Blarer, Ambrosius, 637
Blas Arroyo, J. L., 28, 230
Blasberg, C., 747
Blasco-Dulbecco, M., 41
Blasco Ferrer, E., 14
Blasco Ibáñez, Vicente, 259,
    273, 275
Blaser, K., 729
Blasucci, L., 482
Blay, V., 246
Blecher, Max, 544
Bleck, R., 621
Blecua, A., 237, 240
Blecua, J. M., 878
Bleibtreu, R., 830
Bleses, D., 800
Bletz, Zacharias, 629
Bleumer, H., 611
Bliese, J. R. E. , 52
Bliggenstorfer, S., 75, 76
Bliksrud, L., 804
Bloch, Ernst, 755
Bloch, R. H., 50, 63
Block de Béjar, L., 349
Blocker, D., 136
Bloh, U. von, 632
Blois, J. de, 44
Blom, E., 790
Blomqvist, H., 838
Blomqvist, M., 817
Blondel, H., 489
Błoński, J., 870, 873, 874
Bloom, H., 397
Bloomer, R. K., 577
Blot-Labarrère, C., 176
Blouin, F. X., 425
Bluhm, L., 883
Blum, M.-O., 707
Blum, P., 95
Blume, H., 642
Blumenberg, Hans, 671
Blumenfeld-Kosinski, R., 84
Blunt, Anthony, 103
Bø, G., 804
Boadella, Albert, 293
Boaglio, M., 489
Boal, Augusto, 370
Bobrowski, I., 846, 855
Bobrowski, Johannes, 745, 755,
    758–59

Bobzin, H., 744
Boccaccio, Giovanni, 403, 404,
    408, 424, 428, 441, 448, 632
Boccadifuoco, R. M. R., 426
Boccalatte, N., 439
Boccassini, D., 425
Bocchi, F 424
Bocer, Johannes, 641–42
Boch, F., 34
Bock, H., 715
Böckmann, P., 707
Bocola, M., 474
Bode, Johann Joachim, 677
Bodei, R., 483
Bodenheimer, A., 762
Bodin, Jean, 146
Bodtorf, C., 354
Boehlich, W., 728
Boehringer, M., 683
Boendale, Jan van, 778
Boerner, M.-C., 737
Boerner, P., 666
Boetcher Joeres, R.-E., 705
Boethius, 5, 87, 419, 655
Boets, J., 788
Böger, J., 581
Bogner, R. G., 734
Bogusławski, A., 851
Boguszewska, H., 869
Bogza, Geo, 542
Boheemen, F. C. van, 781
Böhlau, Helene, 746
Böhme, Jakob, 594, 703, 708
Böhmer, H., 32
Böhn, A., 756
Bohnenblust, E. O., 729
Bohrer, K. H., 673
Boiardo, Matteo Maria, 425,
    438, 440–41
Boij, H., 843
Boileau, Etienne, 784
Bois, P.-A., 677
Boisclair, I., 186, 192
Boitani, P., 232, 234, 240, 398,
    410, 878
Boito, Arrigo, 469, 470
Boivin, A., 193
Boix, E., 231
Bok, V., 603
Bolecki, W., 861, 862
Bolívar, Simón, 341
Böll, Heinrich, 759, 761
Bolle, W., 669
Bologna, C., 396, 403
Bologne, J.-C., 42
Bolognese, G., 486
Bölöni, D., 834
Bolovan, M. M., 119
Bomans, Godfried, 796
Bombal, María Luisa, 353

Bombart, M., 93, 135
Bomhoff, K., 692
Bonacchi Gazzarrini, G., 488
Bonadeo, A., 483
Bonafin, M., 66
Bonagiunta Orbicciani, 419
Bonaparte, Louis Lucien, 320
Bonaparte, Louis-Napoleon, 167
Bonaventura (*Saint*), 412, 420,
    625
Bonaventura (*pseudonym*), 683,
    685
Bonaviri, Giuseppe, 507
Bonavita, R., 483
Bond, G., 767
Bonenfant, J., 187
Bonfatti, E., 739
Bonghi, Ruggiero, 472, 492
Bongie, C., 196
Bongiovanni-Bertini, M., 161
Bonhomme, M., 43
Böning, T., 762
Bonito, V., 512
Bonnard, H., 36
Bonnaud, P., 211
Bonnefoy, Yves, 174
Bonnemaison, J., 207
Bonnet, C., 200
Bonnet, M. R., 203
Bonnetin, C., 519
Bontempelli, Massimo, 500, 505
Boon, Louis Paul, 794, 795
Boon, R., 352
Boon, T., 793
Boone, A., 41
Boons, J. P., 39
Bora, G., 424
Borbély, A., 539
Borchert, J., 745
Borchling, C. B., 581
Borchmeyer, D., 668
Bordas, É., 161, 163
Bordei Boca, R., 547
Bordeleau, F., 186, 193
Bordese, L., 491
Bordewijk, Ferdinand, 791
Bordier, J.-P., 82, 117
Bordin, M., 464
Bordo, S., 148
Boreel, Adam, 655
Borejszo, M., 849
Börenstam Uhlman, U., 810
Boretz, E., 235
Borge, T., 809
Borges, Jorge Luis, 106, 346,
    348–50, 367, 516
Borges de Torre, Norah, 262
Borgese, Giuseppe Antonio,
    507–08
Borghello, G., 514

Borghi-Cedrini, L., 216
Borghini, Vincenzo, 429
Borillo, A., 38
Borio, F., 515
Bormann, Ludwig, von, 681
Börne, Ludwig, 716, 735
Boronkai, S., 718
Borowka-Clausberg, B., 648
Borowski, T., 871
Borrás, L., 352
Borrás, T., 278
Borràs Castanyer, L., 73
Borri, G., 511
Borriero, G., 7, 215
Borsellino, N., 448
Borsley, R. D., 849
Borsò, V., 666
Borup, A., 808
Borzęcki, J., 859
Bos, B., 655
Bosboom-Toussaint, A., 787
Bòsc, Zefir, 209
Bosch, S., 728
Böschenstein, B., 695, 757
Böschenstein, R., 729
Boschetto-Sandoval, S. M., 362
Bosquet, J., 34
Bosse, A., 765
Bosse, H., 659
Bossi, Giuseppe, 479, 480
Bossi, L., 479, 480
Bossi, M., 480
Bossina, L., 512
Bossinade, J., 765
Bossuet, Jacques-Bénigne, 119, 141, 154, 490
Bostel, L. von, 658
Bostoen, K., 781
Boström-Andersson, R., 810
Bot, I., 546
Bote, Hermann, 639, 640, 642
Botez, M., 546
Botta, Carlo, 472
Botta, I., 488
Botta, P., 241, 243, 250, 878
Böttiger, K. A., 697
Bottoni, L., 505
Bou, E., 268, 282
Boubat, E., 34
Bouchard, M., 184
Bouchard, P., 43
Bouchardeau, F., 349
Bouchart, A., 82
Bouchet, F., 73, 105
Bouchet, Jean, 113
Bouchette, Errol, 188
Boucicaut: Jehan le Maingre, 83–84
Boucoiran, L., 205
Boudet, J.-P., 75

Boudin, T., 164
Bouhours, Dominique, 122
Bouillaguet, A., 181
Bouillot, C., 63
Boulanger, J.-C., 41, 44
Boullón Agrelo, A. I., 27, 325
Boullosa, Carmen, 347, 360
Boulton, M., 89
Bouquet, S., 32
Bourciez, É., 14
Bourdieu, Pierre, 230, 280, 699, 834
Bourdin, P., 38
Bourgeois-Courtois, M., 145
Bourger, D., 658
Bourignon, Anne, 150
Bourke, E., 769
Bournardel, S., 346
Bourque, D., 184, 188
Bourqui, C., 126
Bousoño, Carlos, 291
Boutens, P. C., 796
Boutet, D., 55, 64, 884
Boutier, J., 454
Boutkan, D. F. H., 573
Bouvier, J.-C., 205
Bouvier, L., 188
Bouvier, M., 145
Bouzy, O., 3
Bova, A. C., 481
Bovara, G., 489
Bovenschen, S., 879
Bowd, S. D., 451
Bowen, B., 102
Bowen, D. J., 557
Bowen, S., 561
Bowers, R., 99
Bowman, F.-P., 167
Bowser-Nott, C., 216
Boyd, H., 404
Boyde, P., 422
Boye, Karin, 822, 836, 837–38
Boyer, H., 204, 205
Boyle, D., 148
Boyrie-Fénié, B., 202
Bozt, D., 359
Braç, M., 201
Bracciolini, Poggio, 431, 440, 441
Braceli, R., 349
Brach, J.-P., 94
Brachmann, J., 757
Brackert, H., 879
Bracops, M., 39
Bradean-Ebinger, N., 569
Braese, S., 754
Braga, C., 547
Braga, M. L., 315
Braga, Rubem, 309
Brahe, Tycho, 516

Braiato, G., 383
Brait, B., 310
Brake, P., 554
Bräker, Ulrich, 659, 675
Bralczyk, J., 851, 854
Brall, H., 8, 604, 607, 611
Brambilla, A., 473, 508
Brami, L., 478
Branca, M., 480
Branca, V., 403, 501
Brancaleoni, F., 494
Brancati, Giovanni, 10
Brancher, D., 108
Brâncuș, G., 537
Brand, P., 468
Brandi, L., 475
Brandstetter, Alois, 719
Brandstetter, G., 698, 739
Brandt, R., 617
Brandt, S., 800
Brandys, Kazimier, 871, 873
Branscombe, P., 714
Brant, H. J., 349
Brant, Sebastian, 633, 636, 647
Brantly, S., 822
Brantôme, Pierre de, 113
Brasch, Thomas, 759
Brattström, E. W., 841
Bratu, F., 159
Bräuer, R., 592
Brault, G. J., 53, 59
Brault, Jacques, 184, 188
Braun, C., 682
Braun, H., 755
Braun, M., 757
Braun, P., 570
Braun, Volker, 755, 759
Braun, W., 650
Brauneck, M., 711
Brauner, V., 263
Braungart, W., 729
Bravo Elizondo, P., 364
Braw, C., 839
Bray, B., 143
Brea, M., 331
Brea, X. R., 338
Bréal, M., 19
Brébeuf, Jean de, 121
Brecelj, M., 550
Brecht, Bertold, 266, 361, 369, 370, 737, 751, 755, 766
Brecht, C., 884
Brecht, M., 643
Bredel, U., 756
Bredel, Willi, 759
Bredero, Gebrand Adriaensz, 783
Bredman, M., 813
Bree, C. van, 573
Breeze, A., 554, 556, 557, 560

Breger, C., 711
Breig, W., 750, 751
Breithaupt, F., 671
Bremer, B., 710
Bremer, Fredrika, 825
Brems, E., 795
Brems, H., 796
Brendel, I., 735
Brenner, Hans Georg, 677
Brentano, Bettina v. Arnim
Brentano, Clemens, 680, 682, 683, 685–86, 710
Bres, J., 38, 39
Breschi, G., 409
Brescia, G., 470, 489
Bresciani, P., 491
Bresciani Califano, M., 499
Breton, André, 179, 265
Bretscher-Gisiger, C., 587
Breuer, D., 654
Breuer, I., 737
Breuilly, J., 705
Breukker, P., 690
Brévart, F. B., 609
Brevini, F., 470, 503, 512
Breysse, L., 209
Breza, E., 859
Brězan, Jurij, 759
Brezu, C., 544
Brie, Germain de, 94
Brieger, C., 722
Briggs, C. F., 8
Brines, Francisco, 264
Bringsvaerd, Tor-Åge, 808
Brink, A., 137
Brink, L., 800
Brink, S., 816
Brinker-von der Heyde, C., 608, 614, 630, 632, 879
Brinkman, H., 779
Brinkmann, Rolf Dieter, 674, 759, 768
Brinon, Jean, 92
Briones, A. I., 284
Brioschi, F., 481
Brissette, P., 193
Brito, A. M., 313
Brito, Duarte de, 247
Britton, C. M., 198, 199
Britton, Rosa M., 361
Brix, M., 156
Brocato, L. M., 242
Brochu, A., 192
Brockes, Barthold Hinrich, 664
Brockhaus, W., 576
Brockmann, S., 752
Broda, M., 761
Brodal, J., 874
Brodin, L., 818
Broek, M. A. van den, 782

Broekmann, T., 622
Brogelli, F., 706
Brogger, F. C., 806
Brömsel, S., 743
Bronfen, E., 699
Broniewski, W., 861
Bronne, C., 544
Bronner, S. E., 175
Brontë (*the sisters*), 111
Bronzini, G. B., 481
Brook, L. C., 51
Brooke, G., 506
Broomans, P., 836
Broomé, S., 840
Brose, M., 525
Brosig, M., 725
Brosio, V., 517
Brossard, Nicole, 184
Brossman, P. W., 44
Brown, A., 184
Brown, A., 423
Brown, C. J., 78, 84, 88
Brown, C., 250
Brown, E. C., 404
Brown, J. A., 347
Brown-Grant, R., 85, 86
Brownlee, K., 88
Bruch, G., 709
Brucker, C., 55
Bruckmüller, E., 713, 716
Brückner, A., 845
Bruckner, M. T., 59, 61
Brude-Firnau, G., 667
Brudin Borg, C., 839
Brugman, Jan, 778
Bruguera, J., 305
Brühl, K. von, 697
Bruijn, P. de, 791
Brun, H., 745
Bruna, Francisco de, 253
Brundin, M., 829
Bruneau, M. F., 191
Brunel, P., 165
Brunet, E., 31
Brunetière, Fernand, 101
Brunetto Latini, 593
Bruni, A., 492
Bruni, F., 373, 405
Bruni, Leonardo, 429, 430
Bruni, M., 469
Brunner, H., 588, 623, 679, 878, 880
Brunner, M. E., 758, 770
Bruno, Giordano, 431, 435–36, 447, 680
Brunori Deigan, F., 421
Brüns, E., 757
Bruscagli, R., 439
Brusegan, R., 66
Brusselmans, Herman, 794

Bruyland, K., 788
Bruyn, E. de, 780
Bruyn, Günter de, 759–61
Bryant-Quinn, M. P., 558
Bryce Echenique, Alfredo, 363
Brynhildsvoll, K., 806, 808
Brynildsen, Aasmund, 808
Bryson, L., 693
Brzękowski, J., 862
Brzozowski, S., 861, 868
Buarque de Holanda, S., 366
Bubenicek, V., 32, 59
Buber, Martin, 742
Bublitz, W., 383
Bucer, Martin, 108, 574, 645
Bucher, A.-L., 56
Büchner, Georg, 677, 707, 712, 715, 719–20, 731
Buck, T., 578, 670
Buczkowski, Leopold, 871, 873
Budde, B., 716
Budde, E., 668
Buddecke, W., 572
Budé, Guillaume, 92
Budzyński, W., 869
Buenaventura, Enrique, 346
Buero Vallejo, Antonio, 278, 294–95
Bufano, L., 511
Buffa, F., 859
Bugajski, J., 847
Bugliani-Knox, F., 405
Buia, E., 525
Buiskool, D. A., 791
Buitrago, F., 355
Bujnicki, T., 868
Bujold, W. M., 192
Bukowski. P., 829
Bulacio, C., 349
Bullivant, K., 753, 772
Bullock, B., 882
Bullough, D. A., 3
Bumke, J., 609, 611
Bunge, G., 625
Bunners, C., 745
Buñuel, Luis, 259, 261, 774
Bunzel, W., 746, 880
Buonaccorsi, Biagio, 450
Burani, C., 378
Burch, S. L., 62
Burchell, D., 423
Burckhardt, Jacob, 423, 720, 730, 743
Burdett, C. F., 510
Burdziej, B., 862
Bürgel, J. C., 744
Burger, R., 642
Burgers, J. W. J., 778
Burgess, G. J. A., 674
Burgkmair, Hans, 648

Burgos, Carmen de, 273
Burgos, Diego de, 246
Burgos, Julia de, 363
Burgwinkle, W., 213
Buridant, C., 31
Burke, J. E., 240
Burke, P., 423
Burkhart von Hohenfels, 619
Burkhart, D., 862
Burkhhardt, A., 569
Burlacu, A., 546
Burman, L., 825
Burmeister, Brigitte, 761
Bürner-Kotzam, R., 711
Burnett, S., 638
Burns, E. J., 61, 216
Burns, N., 346
Burrichter, B., 57
Burscher-Bechter, B., 551
Burt, R. L., 768
Burton, Tim, 699
Burwick, F., 153
Bury, E., 120, 130, 133, 145, 146
Buryła, S., 873
Busby, K., 51, 83
Busch, H., 615
Busch, P., 628
Busch, Wilhelm, 581, 720
Busche, Hermann von dem, 639
Buschinger, D., 75, 880
Buschman, J., 791
Büsen, W., 737
Bushey, B. C., 592
Buss, M., 815
Busschoff, B., 782
Busse, D., 578
Busse, W., 228, 229
Bussmann, A., 685
Busst, A. J. L., 170
Bustarret, C., 152
Bustillo, C., 355
Bustos Guisbert, E., 221
Bustos-Tovar, J. J. de, 228
Busuioceanu, Alexandre, 544
Buszko, J., 715
Butinyà, J., 306
Butler, J., 267
Butler, J., 699
Butor, Michel, 33, 174–75
Butt, W., 830
Büttner, K., 745
Butzer, G., 717
Buurlage, J., 793
Buzogany, D., 645
Buzura, Augustin, 546
Buzzati, Dino, 508
Byock, J. L., 608
Byre, L., 352
Byrne, C., 259
Byrnes, D., 771

Byron, George Gordon, Lord, 405, 482

Cabal, F., 346
Cabal, Fermín, 292
Caballero Bonald, Manuel, 290, 291
Cabana, D. X., 324
Cabanillas, Ramón, 322, 330, 333
Cabasino, F., 384
Cabella, M., 387
Cabo Aseguinolaza, F., 336
Cabral, Cristina, 364
Cabré, M., 213, 301, 302
Cabrera, C., 220
Cabrera Infante, Guillermo, 356
Cacciani, C., 504
Cacciapuoti, F., 481, 495
Cacciari, C., 381
Cacciari, M., 513
Cacheiro, A., 356
Cacho Blecua, J. M., 240, 242
Cadalso, J., 275
Cadalso, José, 256
Cadioli, A., 501
Cadoni, G., 424, 437
Cadonici, R., 478
Cadot, M., 166
Caesar, Julius, 180
Caesar, M., 511, 518
Caesarius of Heisterbach, 8, 605
Caffarelli v. Maiorano
Cagliari, L. C., 312
Cagnat-Deboeuf, C., 163
Caianiello, V., 456
Caie, G. D., 10
Cain, B., 844
Cairns, C., 447
Cajot, J., 569
Calabrese, A., 377, 379
Călăraşu, C., 527
Calder, R., 132
Caldera, E., 239
Calderara, A., 493
Calderón, M., 245
Calderón de la Barca, Pedro, 268
Calderón Calderón, M., 238
Calderón Campos, M., 352
Caldwell, R. C., Jr., 198
Calella, M., 493
Calenda, C., 419
Calero, J. P., 364
Caliceti, G., 505
Calin, W., 74
Călinescu, G., 543
Calis, P., 792
Calkins, P., 728

Callado, Antônio, 366, 371
Callebat, L., 25
Callesen, G., 619
Callot, Jacques, 692
Calmettes, G., 157
Calvet, L.-J., 210
Calvié, L., 735
Calvillo, A. L., 360
Calvin, Jean, 103, 455
Calvino, Italo, 137, 484, 497, 499, 500, 508–09, 563
Calvo Nava, Gloria, 291
Calzabigi, Ranieri de', 463
Calzadilla, J., 345
Calzolari, A., 519
Camacho Delgado, J. M., 350
Camargo, M., 8
Camba, Julio, 259
Cambiano, G., 430
Cambraia, C. N., 311
Cambron, M., 183
Camerino, G. A., 460, 462, 486
Camiciotti, D., 512
Camilleri, Andrea, 509
Camillo della Croce, 438
Camillo, Giulio, 433
Caminero, J., 264
Caminha, Pero Vaz de, 311
Camion, A., 700, 701
Camlong, A., 310
Cammelli, Antonio, 441
Camp, A., 349
Campa, R. de la, 345
Campa, R., 474
Campana, Dino, 500, 502, 503, 509
Campanella, Tommaso, 434, 435
Campbell, J., 130, 131
Campbell, K. A., 55
Campe, J. H., 575
Campe, R., 720
Campello, Myriam, 371
Campensis (Jan van Campen), 108
Campesino, Pilar, 361
Campion, Henri de, 119
Campion, P., 139, 157
Campioni, R., 428
Campomanes, Count of, 254
Campos, Augusto de, 367
Campos, B., 245
Campos, Javier, 353
Campos Fernández-Figueroa, M. M., 270
Campos Souto, M., 248
Camps, A., 481
Camus, Albert, 175
Camus, Jean-Pierre, 133, 135, 143, 144

Canadé Sautman, F., 74
Canals, Antoni, 304
Canaparo, C., 351
Cañas, Dionisio, 290
Canavaggio, J., 240, 878
Cancik, H., 741, 742
Cancik-Lindemaier, H., 742
Cancio Isla, W., 356
Candel Vila, X., 273
Candiani, R., 491
Candolini, A., 473
Candoni, J.-F., 751
Canducci, Lea, 503, 509
Canepa, Francisco, 512
Canepari, L., 376
Canetti, Elias, 718, 734, 743, 761
Canettieri, P., 232
Canfora, D., 431
Cano Aguilar, R., 223
Cano Ballester, J., 261
Cano González, A. M., 27, 202
Canobbio, S., 387
Canone, E., 435
Canova, A., 438
Canova, Antonio, 666
Canova-Green, M.-C., 136
Cánovas, R., 354
Cansinos-Assens, Rafael, 259, 265, 269
Cant, S. E., 174
Cantelmi, M., 476
Cantù, C., 472
Capasso, R. C., 168
Capecchi, G., 494
Capecchi, S., 476
Capécia, Mayotte, 196, 197, 198
Capodaglio, E., 488
Capone, A., 382
Caporali, Cesare, 441-42
Capovilla, G., 480
Cappellini, M. M., 476
Cappello, G. B., 450
Capponi, G., 480
Capra, C., 466
Capra, D., 244
Capriolo, Paola, 509
Caproni, Giorgio, 470, 497, 501, 502, 503, 509-10
Capt-Artaud, M.-C., 32
Capuana, Luigi, 470, 474
Capuano, T. M., 308
Capuccioni, A., 429
Capusso, M. G., 236
Caputo-Mayr, M. L., 764
Caracciolo, Tristano, 430
Caracostea, D., 546
Carafa, Tiberio, 459
Carageani, G., 546, 547
Caragiale, I. L., 541, 546
Caraion, Ion, 546

Carassou, M., 546
Caravaca, A. B., 359
Caravaggio, M. M. da, 141
Caravedo, R., 227
Carballido, Emilio, 347
Carbonell, Pere Miquel, 308
Cardano, Gerolamo, 424, 435
Cardarelli, Vincenzo, 470, 503, 510
Cardenal, Ernesto, 345, 361
Cárdenas, Rafael, 345
Cardinal, J., 195
Cardinal, Marie, 175
Cardinale, U., 375, 878
Cardinaletti, A., 20
Cardona, S. I., 277
Cardoso, S. A. M., 316
Cardoza, M. M., 690
Carducci, Giosuè, 470, 474, 494, 509
Cardwell, R. A., 264
Cardy, M., 194
Carena, C., 494
Careri, M., 214
Caretti, L., 461
Carglio, J., 423
Carifi, Roberto, 510
Carigiet, W., 552
Carigonan (*shaman*), 192
Carl, G. W., 60
Carlini, A., 431
Carlino, A., 435
Carls, W., 635
Carlsbæk, P., 803
Carlson, D. R., 111
Carlson, H. G., 829, 831
Carlyle, Thomas, 275
Carmiggelt, Simon, 795, 796
Carmigiano, Colantonio, 442
Carmona, F., 247
Cârneci, Magda, 542
Carneddog (Richard Griffith), 565
Carnero, G., 255
Carnero, R., 482, 487, 510
Caro, A. del, 743
Caro, Annibal, 104, 451
Caro Baroja, P., 274
Carone, Modesto, 372
Carotenuto, C., 500
Carpelan, Bo, 834
Carpenter, S., 165
Carpentier, Alejo, 196, 346, 356
Carpo, M., 432
Carr, A. D., 556
Carr, G. F., 883
Carr, T. M., 147, 189
Carrai, S., 441, 443, 461, 462, 466, 482, 502, 503, 524
Carraud, V., 149

Carreira, A., 268
Carreño, A., 260
Carrera, A., 483, 484
Carrera, Arturo, 348
Carrera, J., 297
Carreto, C. F. C., 58
Carriazo Ruiz, J. R., 225
Carrier, Roch, 184, 188
Carriere, M., 684
Carril, S. L. del, 349
Carro, X., 334
Carroll, B. A., 84
Carroll, Lewis, 276, 855
Carruthers, J., 35, 39
Carsaniga, G., 468, 483
Carson, A., 762
Carstanjen, E., 724
Cartagena, Alfonso de, 233, 244, 248
Cărtărescu, Mircea, 542
Cartari, V., 427
Carter, H., 555
Carter, T., 426
Carteret, Lord, 255
Carteri, G., 506
Cartier, Jacques, 185
Cartmill, C., 138
Cartwright, J., 558
Carù, P., 506
Carunchio, T., 433
Carvajal, Antonio, 290
Carvajal, Frei Gaspar de, 367
Carvalho França, J. M., 368
Carvallo, S., 347
Cary, H. C., 405
Casadei, A., 487
Casadei, F., 381, 504
Casadio, C., 504
Casadio, P., 385
Casals, Pedro, 284
Casanave, C., 70
Casanova, E., 307
Casanova, Giacomo, 455, 463
Casanova, J.-Y., 210
Casanova, L., 299
Casanova, Sofia, 263
Casapullo, R., 373
Casares, M., 266
Casaretto, F. M., 3
Casas Gómez, M., 24
Casas Rigall, J., 235, 236
Caselli, C., 385
Caselli, D., 405
Caserio, J.-L., 210
Casey, P., 638, 639
Casini, S., 472
Casnodyn, 557
Cason Angelini, E., 549, 882
Casona, Alejandro, 278
Casorri, Ferdinando, 463

Cassan, M., 112
Cassanello, A., 187
Cassano, M., 477
Cassiodorus, 1, 75
Cassola, A., 392
Cassoli, F., 478
Castellani, A., 406
Castellani, Castellano, 446
Castellani, M.-M., 884
Castellano, R., 525
Castellanos, Rosario, 345, 359
Castelli, R., 477
Castelloza, 216
Castellucci, P., 508
Castelnuovo, Enrico, 474
Castelvetro, Lodovico, 440, 451
Castiglione, Baldassare, 120,
    145, 425, 427, 438, 451
Castilho, A. T. de, 309
Castillo, Diego del, 246
Castillo, J. L., 364
Castillo, J., 340
Castillo-Puche, José Luis, 284
Castoldi, M., 482, 484, 494
Castria, R. T., 515
Castro, Consuelo de, 361
Castro, Fidel, 336
Castro, I., 316, 877
Castro, Inés de, 241, 250
Castro, J. A., 260
Castro, Rosalía de, 333–34
Castro-Gómez, S., 345
Castro Rocha, J. C. de, 366
Castronuovo, D., 483
Catach, N., 33
Catalán, D., 235
Catalano, G., 706
Cataldi, P., 525
Catani, R., 437
Cate, C., 741
Cátedra, P. M., 244, 248, 304,
    881
Catherine de' Medici, 93, 100
Catherine de Vaucelles, 79
Cathey, J. E., 602
Cathomas, R., 552
Cathwulf, 3
Cats, Jacob, 782
Cattafi, Bartolo, 503
Catto, M., 458
Catullus, 521
Caudet, F., 276, 282
Cauhapé, Amédée, 203, 208
Caussat, P., 32
Cavaillé, J.-P., 136
Cavalcanti, Guido, 399, 405
Cavalli Pasini, A., 477
Cavallin, J.-C., 154
Cavallini, G., 496, 507
Cavalluzzi, R., 478

Cavarra, A. A., 429
Cavatorta, G., 502
Cavazza, M., 456
Cavazza, S., 464
Cave, C., 152
Cave, T., 96
Cazauran, N., 109
Cazelles, B., 52
Cazorla, H., 295
Cazzato, L., 508
Céard, J., 102
Ceaușescu, Nicolae (*President of
    Romania*), 535, 540
Ceccherini, G., 491
Ceccherini, Santi, 476
Cecchetti, G., 483, 487
Cecchetti, S., 427
Cecchetto, C., 23, 380
Cecere, A., 430
Celan, Paul, 526, 580, 757,
    761–62
Celenza, C. S., 10, 434
Céline, Louis-Ferdinand, 197,
    511
Cellard, B. R., 185
Ceming, K., 625, 687
Cennamo, M., 23, 375
Cenni, Lucantonio, 458
Centi, T. S., 437
Ceolfrith, 2
Cepach, R., 510
Ceppède, Jean de la, 99
Cercignani, F., 730
Cernuda, Luis, 265, 268–69
Cerqueira, D., 372
Cerquiglini, B., 43
Cerquiglini-Toulet, J., 80
Cervantes Saavedra, Miguel de,
    137, 141, 255, 274, 276, 295
Cervelli, I., 453
Cerverí de Girona, 213, 302
Césaire, Aimé, 197
Cesaretti, E., 477
Cesarotti, Melchiore, 486
Ceserani, R., 492
Cessole, Jacques de, 90
Chabbert, R., 209
Chabert, P., 211
Chacel, Rosa, 262, 273, 290
Chae-Kwang, L., 128
Chaillou de Pestain, 90
Chaitin, G. D., 173
Chaline, J.-P., 160
Chaline, O., 144
Challe, Robert, 135, 146, 147
Chamarat-Malandain, G., 158
Chambellan, Peter, 110
Chamberlain, V. A., 281
Chamberlin, R., 615
Chambers, A., 197

Chambon, J., 747
Chambon, J.-P., 46, 202
Chamfort, 701
Chamisso, A. von, 686
Chamoiseau, Patrick, 196, 197
Chamorro, J. M., 219
Champeau, G., 346
Champion, P., 77, 81, 90
Champourcín, Ernestina de, 290
Chantal, St. Jeanne de, 149
Chanut, G., 210
Chanut, Pierre, 147
Chaouat, B., 154
Chaouche, S., 127
Chapelain, Jean, 119, 136
Chapelle, Claude Emmanuel
    Lhuillier, 120
Chapman, C., 582
Chapman, R., 191
Chapotte, Nelly, 209
Chappell, C. L., 133
Chapple, G., 754
Char, René, 510
Charbon, R., 718, 729
Chareyron, N., 83
Charlemagne (*Emperor*), 600, 623
Charles V (*Holy Roman Emperor*),
    104
Charles I (*King of England*), 112
Charles II (*King of Spain*), 254
Charles III (*King of Spain*), 253,
    255
Charles IV (*King of Spain*), 253,
    255
Charles V (*King of France*), 76, 84,
    91
Charles VI (*King of France*), 75, 84
Charles VIII (*King of France*), 73
Charles IX (*King of France*), 93
Charles II (*Duke of Inner Austria*),
    638
Charles d'Orléans, 76, 77, 79
Charles, D., 165
Charles, M., 349, 832
Charles, P., 35
Charles, S., 113
Charles-Wurtz, L., 156, 165
Charlier, R., 693
Charlon, A., 360
Charlotte Elisabeth de Bavière,
    princesse Palatine, 140
Charnay, A., 217
Charnell-White, C. A., 557, 558,
    561
Charnley, J., 121, 147
Charolles, M., 39
Charron, Pierre, 120, 147
Charron, S., 167
Chartier, Alain, 78, 84, 105
Charue, J., 706

Charue-Ferrucci, J., 706, 707
Chas, A., 246
Chassay, J.-F., 187
Chastellain, Georges, 78
Chateaubriand, François-René de, 154–55, 669
Chatrian, A., 477
Chaucer, Geoffrey, 74, 75, 83, 404, 518
Chaudenson, R., 31
Chaurand, J., 31, 45, 205, 878
Chaurette, Normand, 184, 188
Chauveau, J.-P., 122
Chauvet, J.-C., 129
Chauvet, Marie, 198
Chauvier, B., 349
Chciuk, Andrzej, 873
Checa Puerta, J. E., 279
Chédozeau, B., 131, 144
Chemello, A., 503, 509, 512, 878
Chênerie, M.-L., 62
Cherchi, P., 431
Cherubini, F., 471
Cherubini, Luigi, 463
Cherubum, D., 575
Chesak, L. A., 351
Cheshire, J., 327
Chevalier, G., 35
Chevalier, J.-C., 32, 39
Chevallier, C., 837
Chevallier, M., 150
Chevrel, Y., 724
Chiabrera, Gabriello, 442
Chiamenti, M., 413
Chiáppori, Atilio, 348
Chiari, Pietro, 463, 464
Chiarini, G., 479
Chiarini, P., 666
Chiaromonte, Gerardo, 498
Chiavacci Leonardi, A. M., 420
Chiecchi, G., 401
Chigi, A., 437
Chinca, M., 619
Chinchilla, Pedro de, 250
Chiner Gimeno, J. J., 302, 304, 305
Chini, M., 387
Chiodo, C., 475
Chipps Smith, J., 638
Chiriboga, Luz Argentina, 357
Chirinos, E., 344
Chirio, J., 210
Chiromono, Matteo, 402
Chişm T., 542
Chiss, J.-L., 32
Chivallon, C., 197
Chivu, G., 528, 530, 539
Chludzińska-Świątecka, J., 847, 859
Chmielowski, Piotr, 867

Choate, M., 476
Chodorowska-Zdebiak, K., 857
Choinet, Pierre, 85
Choisy, François-Timoléon, abbé de, 136
Chojak, J., 857
Chojnowski, Z., 869
Cholinus, Maternus, 641
Chomsky, N., 13, 21
Choquette, Robert, 189
Chor Maio, M., 371
Chorier, Nicolas, 136
Chotard, L., 158, 170
Chouciño, A., 358
Choulet, P., 743
Chovelon, B., 157
Chrétien de Troyes, 50, 51, 56–58, 60, 61, 62, 612, 613
Christensen, C., 639
Christensen, L., 803
Christensen, R. Z., 810
Christian IV (*King of Denmark*), 652
Christina (*Queen of Sweden*), 147
Christine de Pizan, 34, 73, 74, 75, 77, 84–87, 97, 98, 216, 593
Christoph, N., 357
Christoph, S., 615, 621, 633
Christow, S., 708
Chrząstowska, B., 852
Chuchro, E., 872
Churchill, Winston, 270
Ciampoli, Domenico, 474
Ciardi, M., 456
Ciavolella, M., 439
Ciccarelli, A., 500
Ciccarelli, S., 455
Ciccuto, M., 507
Ciceri, R., 383
Cicero, 10, 75, 120, 432, 470
Cicognara, G., 493
Cidrás Escáneo, F. A., 323
Ciechanowicz, J., 866
Ciechowicz, J., 874
Cienfuegos, Nicasio Álvarez de, 256–57
Ciérbide, R., 220
Cieślak, R., 874
Cieśla-Korytowska, M., 865
Cieślikowa, A., 854
Cifuentes, L., 304
Cigala Casero, Barnaba, 442
Ciliberto, M., 435
Cima, A., 514, 515
Cimarosa, Domenico, 470
Cimarra, L., 390
Cimaz, P., 747
Cincilei, G., 533
Cincotta, R., 522
Cingolani, S. M., 305, 307

Cino da Pistoia, 419, 420
Cinque, G., 380
Cinquini, C., 442
Ciociola, C., 450
Ciolac, M., 539
Cioran, Emil, 544, 548
Ciplijauskaité, B., 279
Ciravegna, B., 210
Cirillio Sirri, T., 308
Cirillo, S., 522
Cisek, I., 544
Cisek, Oscar Walter, 544
Cisneros, Antonio, 362
Cistelecan, A., 548
Cisterna, C., 353
Cisternino, P., 522
Citra, E., 514
Civinini Arrighi, Giulia, 469
Cixous, Hélène, 175
Clair, Honoré, 170
Clajus, Johannes, 574
Clancier, A., 166
Clancy, J. P., 562
Clark, R. L. A., 62, 81
Clark, S. J., 356
Clarke, A. H., 273
Clarke, Jan, 124
Clas, A., 42
Classen, A., 592, 604, 611, 613, 618, 622, 635
Claudian, 97, 653
Claus, Hugo, 781, 794, 795
Claut, P., 430
Clavería Nadal, G., 220
Clay, D., 398
Clemens VIII (*Pope*), 431
Clémens, J., 112
Clément, B., 124, 150, 176
Clément, D., 579
Clément, J.-P., 154
Clément, M., 95
Cleminson, R., 280
Clerici, L., 471
Clerico, G., 31, 96
Cliche, A. E., 187
Clifton, N., 53
Clivio, G., 387
Clossius, Walter Friedrich, 690
Clyne, M., 231, 568
Clynnog, Morus, 561
Cnapius, Gregorius, 864
Coates, S., 3
Cobos Wilkins, Juan, 290
Cocchi, Antonio, 455
Cocco, M. M., 217
Cochón Otero, I., 336
Cocke, E., 168
Coco, A., 454
Coco Davani, M. C., 465
Cocteau, Jean, 138, 173

Cocula, A.-M., 112
Coda, E., 502
Codax, Martin, 331
Codebò, M., 525
Coelestin, Johann Friedrich, 638
Coelho, Paulo, 372
Coelho Neto, Henrique
 Maximiliano, 366
Coen, A., 738
Coetanfao, Florián, 256
Coetzee, J. M., 196
Cogan, M., 409
Coglievina, L., 882
Cohen, M. A., 316
Cohen, R., 773
Cohen, T. M., 367
Cohn, D. N., 344
Colard, J.-M., 96
Colas-Blaise, M., 33
Colborne, R., 138
Colclasure, D. L., 757
Cole, J., 377, 378
Cole, R., 638
Cole Heinowitz, R., 292
Coleridge, Samuel Taylor, 404
Colet, Louise, 168, 170
Coletta, J. M., 48
Colette, 35
Colgrave, B., 3
Colin, J.-P., 42
Colledge, E., 89
Collet, A., 90
Collett, Camilla, 805
Colli, G., 741
Colliander, P., 580, 800, 802
Colliander, Tito, 842
Collin, F., 799
Collodi, 1
Collodi, Carlo (C. Lorenzini),
 474–75
Collomp, D., 69, 70
Colom Mateu, M., 301
Colombi, Marchesa (M. A.
 Torriani), 475
Colombo, A., 479
Colombo, S. M., 344
Colombo, V., 461
Colombo Timelli, M., 73
Colomina, J., 300
Colón, G. [G. Colò], 25, 26, 225,
 302, 878
Colonna, Francesco, 451
Colonna, Vittoria, 442
Colonna Romano, A., 384
Colonne, Guido delle, 306
Colorni, Eugenio, 519
Colucci, A., 437
Coluccia, R., 374
Columni Camerino, M., 510
Colusso, A., 510

Colvin, S., 658, 722
Combarieu du Grès, M. de, 54
Comenius, J. A., 687
Cometa, M., 666
Comfort, K. A., 159
Comi, Siro, 463
Comisso, Giovanni, 510
Commynes, Philippe de, 85
Compagna Perrone, A. M., 302
Compagnon, A., 101
Company, C., 223
Comte, Auguste, 164, 170
Conan, Laure, 184, 189
Conca, M., 304
Conde, Carmen, 284, 290
Conde, J. C., 243
Condé, Maryse, 197, 198
Conermann, K., 652
Confais, J.-P., 579
Confiant, Raphaël, 196, 197,
 198
Conley, T., 883
Connon, D. F., 169
Conrart, Valentin, 120, 136
Conroy, J., 124
Conscience, Hendrik, 786
Consolo, Vincenzo, 497, 499,
 510
Constance de Rabastens, 86
Constant, J.-M., 119
Constantine, D., 673
Constantinescu, I., 545
Constantinescu, M., 544
Constenla, G., 331
Contardi, S., 456
Conte, R., 275
Contessa, K. W. S., 686
Conti, Prince de, 125
Conti, Angelo, 470
Conti, Antonio, 459
Conti, Sigismondo dei, 470
Contini, A., 454
Contini, G., 515, 518
Contorbia, F., 514
Contreras, A. E., 346
Contro, P., 396
Conway, M., 429
Cook, B. R., 284
Cook, L., 770
Cook, R. E., 737
Coomaraswamy, A., 544
Cooper, B. T., 169
Cooper, R., 79, 102
Copeland, R., 883
Copioli, R., 481
Coppola, T., 716
Coquillart, Guillaume, 89
Coray, B., 551
Corbatta, J., 351
Corbechon, Jean, 91

Corbella Díaz, D., 231
Cordus, Euricius, 642
Corella, Joan Roís de, 307
Corfis, I., 240
Corkhill, A., 664, 685
Cormier, M. C., 41
Cormier, Y., 47
Cornago Bernal, Ó., 293, 294
Cornand, S., 152
Cornaro, Alvise, 433
Cornea, P., 547
Corneille, Pierre, 120, 125, 126,
 141, 158, 678
Corneilson, P., 425
Cornette, G., 48
Corngold, S., 695, 742
Cornille, J.-L., 148
Cornish, A., 421
Coromines, Joan (Juan
 Corominas), 299, 301, 324
Corrado, S., 706
Corral, W. H., 358
Corral Díaz, E., 331
Correa Díaz, L., 355
Correia de Oliveira, P. R., 369
Corriente, F., 226
Corsi, S., 500
Corsini, Anna, 469
Corso, Rinaldo, 442
Cortassa, G., 443
Cortázar, Julio, 346, 350
Cortellessa, A., 502
Cortés, S. M., 297
Cortés Oñate, X., 352
Cortezón, Daniel, 334
Corti, M., 500, 515
Corvetto, I. L., 883
Corzani, J., 186, 198
Cosentino, C., 763
Cosi, L., 460
Cosic, A., 706
Cosimo dal Leone, 429
Cospito, G., 488, 489
Cosset, E., 166
Costa, G., 208, 486
Costa, H., 344
Costa, V., 152
Costa Pereira, M. E., 372
Costantini, A. M., 411
Costas González, X. H., 321,
 322
Costello, C., 278
Costelloe, T. M., 466
Coster, Charles de, 776, 781
Costin, Miron, 529
Costineanu, D., 547
Costinescu, M., 528
Cotin, M. L., 579
Cotruş, Aron, 545
Cottille-Foley, N. C., 63, 177

Couceiro, X. L., 332, 880
Coué, S., 624
Coulet, H., 146
Coulet, N., 202, 203
Couperus, Louis, 789
Coupier, J., 209
Courbet, A., 454
Courbet, Gustave, 710
Courcelles, D. de, 97, 243, 302
Courouau, J.-F., 209
Courteau, J., 370
Courteix, R.-A.160 ,
Courtine, J.-F., 695
Courtois, J.-P.,151
Cousin, Victor, 492
Coutinho, Sonia, 370, 371
Couto, H. H., 318
Couttenier, P., 788
Couture, F., 193
Couture, M., 349
Covarrubias Horozco, Sebastián
 de, 316
Coveri, L., 388
Cowal Byrne, K. B., 349
Cowell, A., 615
Cox, F., 174, 179, 180, 878
Coxon, S., 610
Crăciun, G., 548
Craddock, J. R., 13, 18
Crăiniceanu, I., 533
Cramer, J., 802
Cramer, T., 879
Crane, S., 78
Crașoveanu, D., 534
Crasta, M., 426
Creangă, I., 541
Crecente Vega, José, 330
Cremascoli, G., 8
Cremerius, J., 726
Cremona, J., 392
Crépin, A., 75
Crépon, M., 743
Crescentini, F., 491
Crescenzi, Piero de', 429
Crescenzo, R., 121
Crespi, N., 489
Cresti, C., 454
Cretin, Guillaume, 94
Creus, I., 297
Criado, C., 334
Crisolora, Manuele, 431
Crispin, G., 595
Cristea, O., 383
Cristea, V., 541
Cristelli, F., 455
Cristiani, A., 458
Crites, E., 348
Crivelli, T., 883
Croce, Benedetto, 471, 472, 474,
 477, 518

Crocioni, Giovanni, 473
Croizy-Naquet, C., 82
Cromberger, J., 240
Crossnoe, M. E., 9
Crosta, S., 196, 197, 199, 879
Crotti, I., 471, 476
Crotti, I., 524
Croxen, K., 864
Croz, V., 706, 747
Cruickshank, D. W., 880
Crummy, M. I., 168
Cruz-Ferreira, M., 312
Cruz Giráldez, M., 268
Csech, W. V., 687
Cuadra, I. de la, 627
Cuartero, N., 297
Cucchi, Maurizio, 502, 520
Cucu, M., 44
Cucurachi, A., 374
Cudak, R., 873
Cudini, P., 497
Cuesta, M. L., 244, 248
Cuesta Torre, M. L., 240
Cueto-Asín, E., 267
Cugno, M., 547
Culianu, I. P., 544
Culioli, A., 316
Cuna, A., 428
Cuneo, A. M., 353
Cuneo, P., 638
Cunha, A. G. da, 311
Cunha, Euclides da, 371
Cunița, A., 26
Cunnally, J., 432
Cunqueiro, Álvaro, 334
Cuoco, Vincenzo, 456, 459, 463,
 488
Curat, H., 37
Curi, F., 501, 502
Curiel, Juan, 253
Curros Enríquez, Manuel, 334
Curry, R. K., 361
Curschmann, M., 596
Cusatelli, G., 661
Cuthbert (*Saint*), 3
Cutino, D., 461
Cutugno, F., 377
Cuveiro Piñol, Juan, 320
Cuzzani, Agustín, 347
Cybienko, O., 866
Cybulski, M., 864
Cygal-Krupowa, Z., 866
Cygler, F., 631
Cynan (Albert Evans-Jones),
 561, 563, 564
Cynddelw Brydydd Mawr, 557,
 559
Cynfael Lake, A., 557
Cyprianus of Toulon, 3
Cyra, K., 849, 851

Cyrano de Bergerac, Savinien,
 120, 136
Cyrus (*King of Persia*), 104
Cysat, Renwart, 642
Czachowska, J., 870
Czapla, B., 645
Czapla, R. G., 654, 657, 745
Czapliński, P., 872, 873
Czardybon, M., 856
Czepko, Daniel, 656
Czermińska, M., 872
Czigler, P. E., 811
Czurda, Elfriede, 762
Czyż, A., 864
Czyżak, A., 870

Dabke, R., 608
Dabove, J. P., 341
Dąbrowska, A., 847
Dąbrowska-Kamińska, A., 859
Dadson, T. J., 265
Dafydd ap Gwilym, 558
Dagen, J., 133, 139, 146, 879
Dagerman, Stig, 838
D'Agostino, G., 425
Dahan, G., 595
Dahl, Edwin Wolfram, 762
Dahl, Tor Edvin, 809
Dahlbäck, K., 827, 837
Dahlbäck, L., 829
Dahlberg, L., 833
Dahllöf, M., 812
Dahlström, Magnus, 838
Dahmen, W., 528, 536, 539
Dahmer, H., 741
Dahnke, H.-D., 671
Daiber, A., 606
Daiber, J., 681, 692
Daigger, A., 768
Dainat, H., 660
Daladier, A., 36
Dal Bianco, S., 526
Dal Carretto, Galeotto, 442–43
Dalcq, A.-E., 40
Dale, H., 110
D'Alessandro, F., 523
D'Alessio, C., 509
Dali, Salvador, 261, 262, 264,
 269, 271
Dalin, Olof von, 824
Dalla Riva, O., 478
Dall'Asta, M., 647
Dalla Torre, M., 521
Dalla Valle, D., 133
D'Allemand, P., 363
Dall'Oco, S., 431
Dalmas, M., 579
Dalmaso, E., 762
Damborský, J., 856

D'Ambrosio, M., 472, 502, 513
Damian-Grint, P., 67
Damiani, R., 472
Damiano, R., 383
D'Amico, S., 386, 505
Damjanova, L., 347
Damm, S., 688
Damme, R., 633
Damme, S. van, 121
Damoiseau, R., 47
D'Ancona, A., 473
Dandolo, T., 471
Dane, G., 672
Danelon, F., 472
D'Angeli, C., 464
D'Angelo, C., 499
D'Angelo, E., 4
Daniel, R. I., 559
Danielewiczowa, M., 847
Danieli, M., 383
Daniliuc, L., 527
Daniliuc, R., 527
Danini, Pietro, 141
Danna, B., 464
D'Annunzio, Gabriele, 470, 473, 475–77, 501, 506, 514
Dans, Raúl, 334
Dante Alighieri, 69, 74, 87, 175, 181, 306, 374, 394–422, 427, 428, 439, 445, 448, 470, 472, 478, 483, 488, 493, 514, 515, 518, 521, 525, 596, 788, 882, 883
Danton, Louis, 193
D'Antonio, C., 436
Dantzig, Rudi van, 797
Danuser, H., 668
Danzer, G., 718
Da Ponte, Lorenzo, 459, 460, 463
Da Pozzo, G., 445
Darasz, W. J., 851, 856
Darcos, X., 166
Dardel, R. de, 14, 15
Darío, Rubén, 259, 274, 341
Darmon, J.-C., 149
Darms, G., 551
Daroquí, M. J., 345
Darwin, Charles, 517, 718, 743
D'Arzo, Silvio, 510
Dash, J. M., 196
Dasilva, X. M., 333
Dassoucy, Charles Coipeau, 120
Dattero, A., 492
Daumier, Honoré, 737
Dauphine, J., 210
Dauphiné, J., 94, 106
Dauster, F., 361
Dautzenberg, J. A., 791

Dauven-van Knippenberg, C., 629
David, J., 578
David, Laurent-Olivier, 183
Davidis, M., 750
Davidsen-Nielsen, N., 798, 801
Davidsson, B., 837
Davie, M., 431, 439
Davies, A., 285
Davies, G., 564
Davies, H. M., 564
Davies, J., 426
Davies, M. E., 311
Davies, M., 223
Davies, O., 559
Davies, P. V., 200
Davies, Pennar, 563
Davies, W. V., 581
Davis, G. W., 576
Dawes, E., 42, 43
Dawlewicz, M., 853
Day, L., 176
Day, S. A., 361
Dayan, J., 198
Dayan, P., 166
D'Azeglio, Massimo, 477
Dazzi, G., 551
Dazzi, M., 486
Deacon, P., 255
De Amicis, Edmondo, 477
Dean, T., 424
Death, S., 827
Deaver, W., 365
Debaisieux, M., 133, 137, 141, 879
Debergh, G., 795
De Boer, M.,384
Debout, S., 170
Debski, A., 569
Debus, F., 27, 567, 585
De Carolis, Adolfo, 473
Decembrio, Angelo, 430
Decembrio, Pier Candido, 430
De Céspedes, Alba, 510
De Chirico, Giorgio, 522
Décimo, M., 32
Declercq, G., 119
Decleva, E., 501
De Core, F., 523
De Crescenzo, A., 479
De Cristofaro, F., 495
Décultot, E., 669, 679
Decyk, W., 849, 857, 858, 859
Dédéyan, C., 161
Dedner, B., 677, 719
De Donà, B., 470
Defaux, G., 80, 102, 108, 109, 114
Defays, J.-M., 33, 34
Defigier, C., 164

Defoe, Daniel, 181, 861
Defrance, A., 134
Degiovanni, F., 239, 273
DeGraff, M., 28
Deguileville, Guillaume de, 87
Deguy, Michel, 107, 175–76
Dehennin, H., 783
Deisser, A., 415
Dejbord, P. T., 364
DeJean, J., 126
Dejob, C., 495
De Jong-Crane, B., 423
De La Boetie, E., 511
Delacroix, Eugène, 153, 170, 743
Delaperrière, M., 862
Delatour, J., 429
De Laude, S., 519
Delbart, A.-R., 30, 41
Delbecque, N., 35
Del Bianco, N., 455, 472
Delblanc, Sven, 821, 833, 838
Delcorno Branca, D., 402
Deleanu, M. M., 539
Delécluze, Étienne-Jean, 489, 492
Delègue, Y., 100
Delfino, C., 487
Delft, L. van, 138, 145
Delgado Gurriarán, Florencio, 334
Del Giudice, Daniele, 510
De Libero, Libero, 510
Delibes, Miguel, 283, 285
Delicado, Francisco, 451
Delille, M. M. G., 735
De Liso, D., 466
Della Casa, G., 145
Della Casa, Giovanni, 424, 443
Della Chà, L., 463
Della Neva, J., 104
Della Porta, Giambattista, 447
Dell'Aquila, M., 484
Dell'Aquilano, D., 476
Della Serrata, L., 446
Della Terza, D., 416, 472
Del Litto, V., 164
Del Lungo, A., 162
Delmas, J., 200, 206
Del Negro, P., 457, 464
Delon, M., 93, 154, 161
De L'Orme, Philibert, 95, 103
Del Popolo, C., 520
Delporte, M., 156
Del Puppo, D., 482
Del Río Reyes, M., 361
Del Serra, M., 503, 512
Delsing, L.-O., 818
De Luca, Don Giuseppe, 506
De Lucca, R., 435

Delvaux, P., 671
Delvaux, V., 33
Del Vecchio, A., 473
Del Vento, C., 462, 478
Demandt, J., 676
De Marco, A., 382
Demarolle, P., 35
De Martino, D., 501
Dematté, E., 450
De Matteis, S., 518
De Mauro, T., 373, 518
Dembińska-Pawelec, J., 872
Dembowski, P. F., 32, 89, 90
De Meo, P., 166
Demerson, G., 115
Demonet, M.-L., 94, 102
De Mulder, W., 37, 38, 44
Dendale, P., 38, 44
De Nigris, C., 247
Denina, Carlo, 457
Denis, D., 138, 145
Denizot, V., 99
Denke, A., 635
Dennis, N., 264, 265, 266
Denores, Giason, 439
Denser, Márcia, 371
Dentière, Marie, 98
De Pasquale, E., 511
De Pietro, J.-F., 43
De Poli, L., 411
Deppermann, M., 807
Deprez, A., 786
Depuydt, E., 788
Deraldus of Amiens, 5
D'Eramo, Luce, 511
De Rentiis, D., 631
De Rienzo, G., 490
De Robertis, D., 406, 485, 487, 882
De Roberto, Federico, 477
De Rosa, F., 487, 515
De Rosa, G., 436
Deroy-Pineau, F., 191
Derrida, Jacques, 34, 177, 695
Derrien, E., 62
Derungs, K., 688
Désalmand, P., 164
De Sanctis, Francesco, 471, 472, 477
De Santi, G., 521
Desbrière-Nicolas, B., 757
Descartes, René, 145, 146, 147, 148, 150, 479, 487, 492, 682
Deschamps, Eustache, 74, 75, 76, 80
Deschaux, R., 90
Descœdres, G., 625
Desel, J., 727
Desgent, J.-M., 192
Desgraves, L., 152

Deshoulières, V.-A., 165
De Signoribus, Eugenio, 511
Desiles, E., 142
De Simone, R., 456
Desjardins, L., 140
Desmarets de Saint-Sorlin, Jean, 136
De Smedt, M., 791
Desoche, P., 149
De Souza, P., 192
DesRochers, Alfred, 190
Desrosiers-Bonin, D., 97
Dessì, Giuseppe, 511
Dessons, G., 152, 178
Detering, H., 746, 805
Detering, K., 692
Detjens-Montero, W., 357
Dettmering, P., 699
Dettori, A., 392
Deufert, M., 712
Devaux, J., 75
De Vendittis, L., 501
Devescovi, A., 386
De Vita, D., 397
De Vos, A., 791
Devoto, G., 509
Dewi Carno (Davy Jones), 562
Dewitz, J., 713
Deyermond, A., 236, 243, 245
Dezsö, L., 379
D'haen, Christine, 796
Dhervé, Agustín, 253
Dhuoda, 600
Diaconescu-Blumenfeld, R., 511
Diakoffsky, Mascha, 275
Diane de Poitiers, 95, 137
Dias, J. J. A., 311
Dias, M., 735
Diaz, B., 162, 168
Diaz, F., 457
Diaz, J.-L., 161, 162, 172
Díaz, Jorge, 346, 347, 357
Díaz, R. J., 263
Díaz Castro, Xosé María, 334–35
Díaz de Castro, F. J., 267
Díaz y Díaz, M. C., 325
Díaz-Mas, Paloma, 233, 238, 280, 285
Diaz de Mendoza, F., 277
Diaz Quiñones, A., 363
Di Benedetto, A., 444, 462, 471, 501
Di Benedetto, V., 490
Di Berardino, M., 496
Di Biase, C., 517
Dicenta, Joaquín, 259
Dickens, Charles, 494, 807
Dickinson, L. E., 159
Dickson, S., 673

Di Cristo, A., 33
Diderot, Denis, 457
Didier, B., 137, 154, 168
Didon, S., 838
Diederichs, U., 727
Diefenbach, L., 16
Diegmann-Hornig, K., 686
Diego, Eliseo, 356
Diego, Gerardo, 259, 260, 261, 262, 268, 269
Diehl, G., 627
Diekstra, F. N. M., 10
Diem, A., 615
Dienst, K., 645
Dierinck, J., 795
Diesinger, Hans, 654
Dieste, Rafael, 335
Dieterle, R., 726
Diethe, C., 741
Dietl, C., 617
Dietmar von Eist, 619
Dietrich von der Glezze, 632
Dietrich, Veit, 647
Dietrich, W., 379
Dietz, K., 573
Diez, F., 16
Díez Borque, J. M., 251
Diez Canseco, José, 362
Díez Mediavilla, A., 275
Díez de Revenga Torres, P., 220, 229, 230, 242
Diez de Revenga, F. J., 260, 262, 265, 266, 268, 269, 275, 879
DiFranco, R. A., 235
Di Giacomo, Salvatore, 470, 477
Di Girolamo, C., 302
Di Grada, A., 477
Dijk, A. van, 670
Dijk, H. van, 778
Diktonius, Elmer, 832, 838
Di Liscia, D. A., 434
Dill, U., 646
Diller, G. T., 74, 83
Di Marca, P., 505
Di Megalopoli, Cercida, 515
Di Meola, C., 578
Di Mieri, F., 483
Dimitrescu, F., 536
D'Impero, M., 377
Dinescu, Mircea, 541
Dinglinger, W., 668
Dingstad, S., 805, 806
Dini, M., 508
D'Intino, F., 460, 482
Dinzelbacher, P., 587, 592, 625
Dion, R., 184
Dionisotti, C., 438, 442, 473, 879
Dionysus of Halicarnassus, 648
Diop, Birago, 199
Dios, J. F. de, 240, 245

Di Preta, A., 487
Di Sciullo, A.-M., 27
Di Serio, B., 476
Disraeli, Benjamin, 729
Di Stefano, A., 491
Di Stefano, G., 235, 237, 487
Dittmann, J., 569
Dittmar, N., 387
Dittrich,W., 745
Ditvall, C., 534
Djubo, B., 575
Długosz, Jan, 864
Długosz-Kurczabowa, K., 847
Dobarro, X. M., 338
Dobles, Fabián, 355
Döblin, Alfred, 763
Dobrovie Sorin, C., 20, 534
Dodaro, M., 278
Doderer, Heimito von, 763
Doglio, M. L., 447
Dohm, B., 693
Dohm, Hedwig, 705, 745
Doliński, I. M., 858
Doll, E. J., 292
Dölling, B., 717
Dols, N., 297
Domat, J., 146
Dombroski, R., 468
Doménech Rico, F., 278
Domenge, J.-L., 210
Domenichelli, M., 462
Domergue, R., 209
Domínguez, C., 245
Domínguez, F., 303
Dominguez, V., 99
Dominicy, M., 39
Donahue, N. H., 763
Donahue, W. C., 721
Donat, S., 666
Donatello, 431
Donati, Piccarda, 397
Donato, M. P., 457
Dondero, M., 481, 482, 488
Dong, Qiang, 178
Dongowski, G., 677
Donhauser, K., 879
Doni, A. F., 425, 427, 429, 432
Dönike, M., 698
Donnarumma, R., 516
Donne, F. delle, 9
Donoso, José, 345, 346, 353
Dopart, B., 865
Doppler, A., 747
Döring, D., 575
Dorion, G., 188
Dörner, G., 647
Dorosz, B., 870
Doroszewski, J., 854
Dörr, V. C., 758
D'Ors, Eugenio, 273

D'Ors, I., 225
D'Ors Führer, C., 273
Dorschel, A., 673
Dorst, Tankred, 765
Dossi, Carlo, 477–78
Doss-Quinby, E., 65
Dostoevsky, Feodor, 266, 692
Dotoli, G., 133, 145
Dotti, U., 484, 499
Dotzler, B. J., 672
Dougherty, D., 264
Dove, P., 350
Dover, C. R., 58
Dovetto, F., 377, 378
D'Ovidio, Francesco, 493
Dowling, L. H., 360
Downing, E., 748
Doyer, H., 787
Dragonetti, R., 51
Drawert, Kurt, 763
Drebes, K., 770
Drehsen, V., 726
Drescher, M., 48
Drewitz, I., 684
Drewniak, S., 847
Drews, J., 659, 753, 769
Dreymüller, C., 290
Drigani, A., 437
Drob, J. A., 863
Droixhe, D., 41
Dronke, P., 410
Droscher, B., 360
Drost, Aernout, 787
Droste-Hülshoff, Annette von,
    705, 708, 709, 710, 716, 717,
    720–22
Drucaroff, E., 348
Drummond de Andrade, Carlos,
    369
Drux, R., 712, 714
Drużbacka, Elzbiet, 856
Dryden, John, 141
Dubar, M., 724
Du Bartas, Guillaume de
    Salluste, sieur, 92, 94, 99, 106,
    115, 116
Dubatti, J., 352
Dubé, Marcel, 189
Dubé, P. H., 155
Du Bellay, Joachim, 79, 92, 93,
    95, 96, 104, 107, 114, 176
Dubert García, F., 319, 321,
    326, 327
Dubisz, S., 847, 855, 857
Dubois, C.-G., 112, 122
Dubois, J., 43
Dubois, P. H., 792
Dubois, René-Daniel, 184, 189
Dubois-Charlier, F., 43
Dubost, F., 62

Dubost, J.-P., 136
Dubowik, H., 862
Dubu, J., 131
Dubuis, R., 64, 73
Ducharme, Réjean, 185, 189,
    195
Duchesne, A., 42
Duchet-Suchaux, G., 75
Duckworth, D., 612
Ducros, Simon, 136
Duda, H., 859
Dudášová-Kriššáková, J., 859
Dudinzew, Vladimir, 755
Dueñas, Juan de, 244
Dufaud, J., 212
Dufault, R. L., 185, 186
Duffell, M. J., 232
Duffy, J. H., 43, 181
Dufief, A.-S., 163
Dufief, P., 163
Du Fossé, Pierre-Thomas, 144
Dufour, Antoine, 89
Dufournet, J., 68, 85
Duggan, J., 58
Duguet, Jacques Joseph, 454
Duits, H., 777, 782
Dukiens, C. S., 47
Dulac, L., 75, 87
Dulichenko, A. D., 855
Dulk, Albert Friedrich Benno,
    722
Dull, O. A., 81, 98
Dülmen, R. van, 598
Dulong, G., 47
Duma, J., 860
Dumais, M., 187
Dumas, Alexandre (père), 98,
    161, 164–65, 169
Dumas, Alexandre (fils), 161,
    169, 542
Dumbrava, V., 530
Dumistrăcel, S., 548
Dumitrescu, D., 528, 535
Dumont, P., 81, 146
Dunaj, B., 854
Dunajski, A., 857
Duncan, A., 675
Duncan, C., 353
Duncan, Quince, 355
Duncker, M., 748
Duneton, C., 30
Dunn-Lardeau, B., 98, 110
Dunphy, G., 627
Dunphy, R. G., 611
Dupèbe, J., 102
Du Périer, Antoine, 136
Dupláa, C., 288
Dupuy, Claude, 429
Dupuy, T. (P.), 201
Duque Amusco, A., 267

Durán, A., 235
Durán, J., 359
Durán López, F., 258
Durand, C., 30
Duras, Claire de, 130
Duras, Marguerite, 176
Dürer, Albrecht, 642
Durham, Lord, 185
Durrell, M., 573
Dürrenmatt, Friedrich, 763, 765
Dürrenmatt, J., 159
Dürrer, M., 750
Dürscheid, C., 578, 580
Durst-Andersen, P., 800
Du Ryer, Isaac, 124
Du Ryer, Pierre, 124
Durzak, M., 764
Düsing, W., 879
Duso, E. M., 443
Dutourd, J., 30
Dutton, B. D., 148
Dutton, J. L., 177
Duun, Olav, 808
Du Vair, Guillaume, 134, 144
Duval, E. M., 102, 109
Duval, F., 84
Duverneuil, M., 211
Düwel, K., 599, 600
Dvergsdal, A., 804
Dworkin, S. N., 13, 14, 218, 223, 224
Dworkin y Méndez, K. C., 362
Dworschak, H., 626
Dybel, P., 868
Dyer, D., 529, 530
Dyerval Angelini, P., 515
Dysart, D. L., 750
Dyszak, A., 847
Dziadek, A., 870
Dziwirek, K., 848
Dźwigoł, R., 849


Eadmer of Canterbury, 4
East, W. G., 6
Ebbestad Hansen, J.-E., 703
Ebel, E., 690
Ebenbauer, A., 751
Eberenz, R., 224, 225
Eberhard von Cersne, 633
Eberlin von Günzburg, Johann, 642
Ebguy, J.-D., 161
Ebner, J., 568
Ebner-Eschenbach, Marie von, 705, 706, 718, 722, 744
Ebneter, T., 552
Echeverría, Esteban, 341
Eck, J., 93
Ecker, H.-P., 590

Eckermann, Johann Peter, 667
Eckhart (Meister), 591, 624–26, 687
Eckhoff, J., 771
Eco, Umberto, 106, 285, 497, 500, 511, 680
Edelfeldt, Inger, 835
Edelman, L., 285
Eder, J., 879
Edfelt, Johannes, 832
Edison, T. W., 355
Edlund, L.-E., 817
Edmonds, F., 769
Edmonds, J., 20
Edmund of Abingdon (*Saint*), 65
Edmund of Wessex, 556
Edwards, C., 620, 633
Edwards, E., 562
Edwards, G., 271
Edwards, H. M., 558
Edwards, H. T., 564, 879
Edwards, J. M., 562
Edwards, R. E., 404
Eekhout, Jan, 781
Effen, Justus van, 785
Efrén, 271
Egan, L., 359
Egeberg, E., 806
Eggert, H., 709
Egginton, W., 394
Egidio da Viterbo, 427
Eguzkitza, A., 23
Ehlers, W.-W., 646
Ehlert, H., 736
Ehlich, K., 727
Ehnmark, A., 826
Ehrard, J., 152
Ehrhardt, G., 667
Ehrhart, M. J., 77
Ehrich, V., 580
Ehrismann, O., 608, 731, 732
Ehrlich, L., 715
Ehrmann, Marianne, 683
Eich, Günter, 763
Eichendorff, Joseph von, 683, 687, 753
Eichenhofer, W., 551, 552
Eichinger, L. M., 577, 879
Eidecker, M. E., 769
Eielson, J. E., 344
Eigler, F., 705
Eike von Repgow, 595
Eikelmann, M., 619, 628
Eilhart von Oberg, 611
Einhard, 3
Eisenbichler, K., 437
Eisenreich, Herbert, 763
Eisermann, F., 634
Eitschberger, A., 610
Eiximenis, Francesc, 9, 304–05

Ejder, B., 816
Ejskjær, I., 801
Ek, S. R., 837
Eke, N. O., 715, 769
Ekedahl, N., 824
Ekelöf, Gunnar, 832, 834
Ekelund, Vilhelm, 833, 838
Ekholm, C., 836
Eklund, Ragnar, 838
Eklund, T., 828
Eklund Lykull, Anita, 835
Ekman, H.-G., 829
Ekman, Kerstin, 838
Ekman, S., 824
Ekotto, F., 177
Ekstein, N., 124
Elbro, C., 800, 801
Eldredge, L. M., 11
Eley, P., 61, 67
Eliade, Mircea, 543, 544, 547, 548
Elías, M., 356
Elias, N., 424
Eliot, George, 111, 675
Eliot, T. S., 263, 515, 526, 564, 874
Elisabeth (*Queen of Prussia, wife of Frederick William IV*), 725
Elisabeth of Brandenburg, 638
Elisabeth von Nassau-Saarbrücken, 635, 640
Elizaincín, A., 230
Ellis, K., 353
Ellis, L. B., 369
Elm, T., 712
Elmevik, L., 810, 816, 817
Elon, A., 703
Elsaghe, Y. A., 670
Elslande, J.-P. van, 144
Elsner, U., 771
Elson, C., 176
Elsschot, Willem, 791
Eltit, Diamela, 354
Éluard, Paul, 269
Elvers, R., 679
Elvira, J., 221
Elwert, W., 390
Emar, Juan, 354
Embleton, S., 882
Emelina, J., 129, 130
Emiliani Giudici, P., 472
Emiliano, A., 310
Eminescu, Mihai, 544, 545. 547
Eming, J., 617, 635
Emmanuel, Pierre, 173
Emmerich, W., 754, 762
Emmerson, R. K., 82
Encina, Juan del, 244–45, 251
Endermann, H., 574
Enders, J., 51, 82

Endres, J., 700
Enehjelm, Helen af, 842
Enenkel, K., 423
Engammare, M., 96
Engberg, J., 800
Engdahl, E., 812
Engdahl, H., 832
Engel, E. J., 678, 679
Engel, G., 884
Engelbert of Admont, 9
Engelbert, A., 884
Engelhardt, D. von, 703
England, J., 239
Engler, J., 775
Englisch, B., 630
Engström, Albert, 827
Enikel, Jans, 611
Enke, U., 667
Enoksen, L. M., 817
Enquist, Per Olov, 806, 829, 838
Enrique IV (*King of Spain*), 241, 249
Ensenada, Marquis of, 255
Enzensberger, Hans Magnus, 273, 284, 685, 763
Epple, J. A., 353
Erasmus, 431, 639, 640, 642, 644
Erba, Luciano, 493, 502, 507
Erckmann, E., 477
Erdal Jordan, M., 350
Erdélyi, I. T., 690
Erfurt, J., 530
Erhart, W., 660
Erickson, J., 573
Ericson, Stig, 835
Eriksson, U. I., 833, 841
Eriugena, Johannes Scotus, 6
Erler, G., 722, 723
Erler, T., 722
Ermakova, O. P., 859
Ermenrich of Ellwangen, 3
Ermini Polacci, F., 463
Ernaux, Annie, 176–77
Ernst, G., 527
Ernst, Max, 262, 263
Ernst, P., 576, 741, 880
Ernst, U., 589, 610, 614
Eroms, H.-W., 571, 879
Ertel, R., 761
Ertzdorff, X. von, 618
Escartí, V. J., 301, 302, 305
Escartín, J. V., 302
Escher, M. C., 508
Escobar, J., 275
Escobar, Luis, 271
Escofit, Cristina, 352
Escola, M., 138, 140
Escudero, J., 288
Esenwein, J. von, 665
Eshel, A., 753

Eska, J. F., 553
Esmarch, C., 750
Esneval, A. d', 75
Espadaler, A., 302
Espagne, M., 669
Espejo-Saavedra, R., 273, 284
Espigado Tocino, G., 258
Espinal, M. T., 23
Espmark, Kjell, 843
Esposito, A., 374
Esposito, E., 415
Esposito, R., 512
Esposito, V., 483, 485
Esquerro, M., 363
Esquivel, Laura, 360
Essen, G. von, 692, 698
Essen, Gesa von, 707
Esteban, J., 259
Ester, H., 748
Esterhammer, A., 700
Etienne de Bourbon, 628
Eto, H., 571
Etty, E., 796
Etxenike, Luisa, 283
Eugénie, Empress, 163, 168
Eustatievici (Dimitrie Eustatie Brăşoveanul), 528
Eustis, A., 879
Evans, D. E., 553
Evans, M., 7
Evans, O., 752, 760
Evans, R. W., 557
Evdokimova, L., 67, 75
Evelyn, John, 141
Evenäs, C., 821
Eversberg, G., 749, 750
Evstatiev, S., 623
Ewald, P., 576
Ewbank, I.-S., 807, 831
Ewers, H.-H., 717
Ewertowski, J., 702
Eyck, Hubert van, 633
Eyck, Jan van, 633
Eyck, Pieter N. van, 788
Ezawa, K., 580


Fabbri, Valerio, 511
Fabene, K., 455
Fábián, Z., 384
Fabiano, A., 464
Fabianowski, A., 871
Fabre, François-Xavier, 479
Fabre, P., 208
Fabre, V., 172
Fabri, F., 635
Fabricio de Vagad, Gauberto, 249
Fabrizi, A., 461, 515
Fabrizio-Costa, S., 497

Fachinger, P., 764
Fagerberg, Sven, 838–39
Faggella, M., 523
Faggin, G., 550
Faguet, Alberto, 346
Faguet, E., 101
Fagundes Telles, Lygia, 371
Fagundo, Ana Maria, 290, 291
Fahlgren, M., 842
Fahlström, Öyvind, 839
Fahmüller, E.-M., 756
Fahy, C., 428
Faifer, Florin, 548
Faig v. Fay
Fairservice, D., 511
Faitrop Porta, A. C., 506
Faivre, B., 116
Fajardo, S. J., 266
Falaschi, G., 517
Falcandus, Hugo, 5, 6
Falcetto, B., 523
Falcón, Lidia, 292
Falery, G., 350
Falińska, B., 859
Falk, C., 811
Falk, Johannes Daniel, 676
Falkman, Charlotta, 825
Falkner, Gerhard, 763–64
Fallersleben, H. H. von, 591
Falletti di Barolo, Ottavio, 472
Falletti di Barolo, Tancredi, 472
Fallon, P., 338
Falsetti, Giovanni, 511
Fanfani, M., 517
Fangen, Ronald, 808
Fanlo, J.-R., 95, 111
Fanon, Frantz, 197, 198
Farinella, C., 456
Farinella, G., 502, 519
Farinelli, A., 268
Farinelli, Arturo, 544
Farmer, S. A., 434
Farran-Lee, S., 834
Farrar, K., 579
Farrell, J., 511
Farrelley, D. J., 754
Fasano, P., 478, 484, 492
Fasano, P., 500
Fasbender, C., 605, 612
Faschinger, Lilian, 762
Fasey, R., 266
Fassbinder, Rainer Werner, 724
Fassel, H., 548
Fassel, L., 529
Fassò, A., 216, 217
Fattori, M., 487
Fauche, J.-E., 207
Faucher, E., 579, 879
Faulhaber, C., 242
Faulkner, William, 196, 794

Faure, A., 212
Faure, M., 879
Fauriel, Claude, 488, 489
Fauser, M., 738
Faussart, C., 24
Faustich, E., 316
Favà, X., 299
Favaroni, Agostino, 6
Fávero, L. L., 310
Fay, J., 211
Fazan, J., 873
Fazenda, Luisa, 265
Feal, C., 277
Febbraro, P., 503
Febles, J., 343
Federici, C., 483
Federico, Gennaro Antonio, 460
Fehlen, F., 568
Fehn, E.-O., 677
Fehn-Claus, J., 598
Fehrman, C., 821
Feijoo, Benito Jerónimo, 254, 258
Feilchenfeldt, K., 730, 880
Fein, D. A., 72
Feistner, E., 592, 611
Feith, Rhijnvis, 787
Felber, A., 593
Felberg-Levitt, M., 90
Feldman, S. G., 294
Feleszko, K., 858
Félibien, A., 42
Felici, L., 468, 481, 482
Feliciano, Felice, 443
Felinto de Oliveira, E., 368
Felipe, León, 262, 265
Fellous, S., 249
Fellrath, I., 716
Femia, J. V., 452
Fénelon, F. de S. de la M., 119, 137, 146
Fenner, W., 677
Fenoglio, Beppe, 511
Fenves, P., 694
Ferdinand v. Fernando
Ferlampin-Acher, C., 71
Ferlin, Nils, 839
Ferlito, S. F., 491, 492
Fermín Partido, E., 266
Fernández, A. M., 297
Fernandez, C., 167
Fernández, C., 338
Fernandez, D., 165
Fernández, Macedonio, 350
Fernández, S. C., 360
Fernández Castro, X. M., 334
Fernández Cifuentes, L., 257
Fernández Durán, R., 254
Fernández Galiano, L., 264
Fernández de Heredia, Juan, 242

Fernández Jiménez, J., 235
Fernández L'Hoeste, H. D., 351
Fernández de Lizardi, José Joaquín, 341–42
Fernández Moreno, Baldomero, 347
Fernández Moreno, F., 229
Fernández Moreno, M.-C., 229
Fernández Pecha, Fr. P., 220
Fernández de Perico, M., 347
Fernández Prieto, C., 345
Fernández Rei, E., 319, 326
Fernández Rei, F., 322, 328, 333
Fernandez Retamar, R., 349
Fernández Rodríguez, M., 319, 337
Fernández Salgado, B., 878
Fernández Salgado, X. A., 324
Fernández de la Sota, José, 290
Fernández Urtasun, R., 260
Fernández Vega, J., 351
Fernando III (*King of Spain*), 218, 220
Fernando IV (*King of Spain*), 238, 241
Fernando VI (*King of Spain*), 254
Fernberger, Georg Christoph, 642–43
Ferrand, F., 77, 884
Ferrand, N., 133
Ferrando, A., 301, 307
Ferrant, A., 262
Ferrante, J., 399
Ferrara, E., 508
Ferrara, L., 519
Ferraresi, A., 456
Ferrari, A., 214
Ferrari, Américo, 362
Ferrari, O., 348
Ferrari Zumbini, M., 742
Ferraris, A., 487
Ferraro, B., 447, 508, 524
Ferreira, M. P., 331
Ferreira Cury, M. Z., 369
Ferreira-Pinto (Bailey), C., 370, 371
Ferreiro, Celso Emilio, 335
Ferreiro, M., 337
Ferreiro Fente, X. G., 338
Ferreiro Fernández, M. 320
Ferrer Mallol, M. T., 304
Ferrer, Joan, 299
Ferrer, Josep, 299
Ferrer, M. A., 245
Ferrer v. Vincent
Ferretti, G. C., 523
Ferretti, Jacopo, 478
Ferreyrolles, G., 138
Ferrières, Henri de, 75
Ferro, J., 233

Ferro, T., 539
Ferron, Jacques, 184, 189–90
Ferron, Jean, 90
Ferron, M., 186
Ferroni, G., 102, 482, 497, 502
Ferroul, Y., 50
Ferrucci, F., 475, 484, 486
Ferrús, Pero, 244
Ferstl, C., 583
Féry-Hue, F., 88
Fetscher, I., 677
Fetscher, J., 763
Fetten. U., 262
Fetz, B., 713
Feuchtersleben, Ernst Freiherr von, 722
Feuerhake, T.-R., 736
Feyerabend, Sigmund, 643
Ffowc Elis, Islwyn, 564
Fiandra, E., 706, 727
Ficara, G., 463, 484
Fichte, Hubert, 744, 757
Fichte, J. O., 59
Fichte, Johann Gottlieb, 625, 720, 675, 687–88, 694
Fichtner, I., 880
Ficino, Marsilio, 10, 403, 429, 433, 434, 436
Fickert, K., 767
Fidalgo, E., 332
Fido, Calisto, 430, 446
Fido, F., 457, 469
Fidora, A., 303
Fiedler, H., 617
Fiedler, T., 768
Fieguth, R., 866
Fielding, Henry, 367
Figal, G., 742
Figuera, Ángela, 290
Filelfo, Francesco, 443
Fileno Carabba, Enzo, 505
Filgueira Valverde, Xosé, 329, 335
Filho, Antunes, 370
Filipkowska, H., 867
Filipović, R., 819
Filipowicz, H., 866
Filippo di Ser Brunellesco, 449
Finas, L., 162, 175
Finckh, R., 605
Finetti, Bonifazio, 464
Fingerhut, K., 716
Fink, G.-L., 663, 670, 672
Fink, I., 863
Finke, U., 725
Finlay, F., 754
Fioravanti, M., 459
Fiorentino, G., 24, 376
Fioretos, A., 694, 695
Fiori, G., 455

Firchow, E. S., 602
Firpo, L., 462
Fischer, C., 573, 631
Fischer, H., 621, 725
Fischer, K., 579
Fischer, T., 768
Fishenfeld, Janette, 370
Fisiak, J., 880
Fita, S., 867
Fiut, A., 874
Fix, U., 568, 730
Fjelkestam, K., 834
Flachenecker, H., 744
Flament-Boistrancourt, D., 48
Flaminio, Marcantonio, 106
Flaubert, Gustave, 150, 163, 168, 270, 516, 700
Flaux, N., 44
Flechia, G., 383
Fleischer, M., 723
Fleisser, Marieluise, 764
Fleith, B., 630
Fleming, Paul, 656
Flitter, D. W., 265, 329, 337, 877
Flodman, A., 829
Floeck, W., 296
Flöer, M., 601
Flood, J. L., 592, 609, 647
Florea, L.-S., 534
Flores, C., 880
Flores Arroyuelo, F. J., 251
Flori, J., 52
Florin, M., 830
Florit Durán, F., 260, 268
Flühler, S., 627
Flygare-Carlén, Emilie, 825–26
Fo, Dario, 511
Focher, A., 730
Foehr-Janssens, Y., 64, 71, 73
Foersom, S., 800
Fofi, G., 506
Fogazzaro, A., 470, 471, 478
Fogelklou, Emilia, 833
Fohrmann, J., 715
Foigny, Gabriel de, 137
Fokkema, R., 792
Földényi, L., 700
Fole, Anxel, 335
Folengo, T., 438
Foley, J., 18
Folkers, H., 675
Folkerts, M., 736
Folli, R., 380, 883
Föllner, U., 581
Folz, Hans, 595, 629, 634
Fondane (Fundoianu), Benjamin, 546
Fongaro, A., 513
Fontaine, Nicolas, 144, 148
Fontana, A., 452

Fontane, E., 722
Fontane, Theodor, 671, 704, 707, 708, 710, 711, 722–28, 745, 747, 760
Fontanella, L., 483
Fonte, Moderata, 443
Fonteius Primo, Johannes Baptista, 638
Fontenelle, Bernard Le Bovier de, 146
Fontijn, J., 776
Fontoira, L., 333
Fontpertuis, A. C. du V. A., Mme de, 148
Fonyi, A., 165, 166
Foreman, Richard, 294
Forest, P., 181
Forestier, G., 128
Forgione, M., 450
Forlini, A., 483
Formica, M., 458
Formisano, L., 217
Fornasiero, J., 157
Forneiro Pérez, J. L., 337
Forner, W., 388
Fornés, Lluís, 206
Fornet, J., 344
Forni, P. M., 493
Forno, C., 461
Forsås-Scott, H., 844
Forsén, U., 835
Forser, T., 834
Forsgren, M., 39
Forslund, B., 841
Forssell, P., 825
Forssmann, I., 746
Forssmann, J., 682
Forster, Georg, 663, 676
Förster, H., 548
Förster, J., 572
Förster, N., 756
Forster-Hahn, F., 725
Fort Cañellas, M. R., 226
Fortassier, R., 164
Forte, Dieter, 764
Fortelius, B., 816
Forti, M., 502
Fortini, Franco, 497, 511
Foschi, F., 481, 484
Foscolo, Ugo, 462, 470, 471, 473, 478–79, 486, 487, 489, 522, 525
Fosi, I., 424
Fossat, J.-L., 205
Fosse, Jon, 807
Fossier, R., 597
Foster, D. W., 346
Foster, I., 770
Foster, K., 410
Fosvold, A., 808

Foucaud, Hugues, 5
Foucault, Michel, 37, 616, 624, 680
Fouquet, Nicolas, 121, 655
Fourié, J., 200
Fourier, Charles, 170
Fournier, L., 477
Fourquet, J., 880
Fowler Caleada, V., 355
Fox, E. I., 260, 264, 274
Fox, S., 333
Fozzer, G., 511
Fra Domenico, 429
Fraboschi, A. A., 884
Fracci, Carla, 514
Fradejas Lebrero, J., 250
Fradejas Rueda, J. M., 226, 230, 241
Fradelle, Henri-François, 479
Fradin, B., 43
Fraenen, Y. van der, 791
Fraga, E., 369
Frago Gracia, J. A., 224
Fragonard, Jean-Honoré, 457
Fragonard, M.-M., 95, 102
Fraïsse, C., 5
Fraisse, L., 180
France, Anatole, 181
France, P., 131
Francesca da Rimini, 414
Franceschini, R., 382
Francese, J., 518
Franchini, E., 237
Francioni, G., 462
Francis (*Saint*), 397, 420
Francis I (*Emperor*), 470
Francis, T. A., 575
Franck, J., 386
Franck, Sebastian, 640
Francke, R., 723, 736
Franco, B., 700
Franco, Francisco (*President of Spain*), 266, 281, 282, 285, 294
Franco, J., 883
François de Sales (*Saint*), 120, 148, 149
François 1 (*King of France*), 104
François, Louise von, 705
Francomano, E., 350
Frâncu, C., 528
Frank, H., 725
Frank, I., 618
Franke, W., 404
Frankl, Ludwig August, 714
Franko, Iwan, 867
Franqui, C., 356
Franz, K., 584
Franz, T. R., 273
Franzkowiak, A., 724
Franzos, Karl Emil, 728

Frappier-Mazur, L., 167
Frare, P., 478, 489
Frascarelli, M., 378
Frasson, E., 455
Frateschi, Y., 331
Frattini, A., 513
Frau, G., 549
Frauenlob (Heinrich von Meissen), 606, 621
Freccero, J., 410
Freche, K., 612
Frede, C. de, 424
Fredegar, 599
Frederick I (*Barbarossa, Holy Roman Emperor*), 734
Frederick II (*King of Prussia*), 254, 784
Frederick of Austria (*Duke*), 633
Frederick of Habsburg, 418
Frederick, B., 347
Frederiksen, E., 718
Frederiksen, P., 802
Fredriksson, K. G., 839
Fredriksson, L., 839
Fredro, A., 865
Fredsted, E., 802
Freedman, P., 598
Freeman Regalado, N., 79
Freeman, E., 623
Freeman, M. J., 78, 79, 89
Frege, G., 381
Freienhagen-Baumgardt, K., 626
Freiligrath, Ferdinand, 718
Freise, M., 868
Freitag, S., 716
Freixeiro, X. R., 335
Frénaud, André, 510
Frenzel, E., 588
Frenzel, Karl, 712
Fresnán, Rodrigo, 346
Freud, Sigmund, 127, 158, 175, 188, 669, 670, 691, 701, 730, 742, 743, 761
Freund, W., 718, 738
Frevert, U., 699
Frey, H.-J., 695
Frey, J. A., 156
Frey, W., 629, 879
Freyre, Gilberto, 371
Freyre, X., 336
Freyssinet, G., 96
Freytag, Gustav, 728
Freytag, H., 603
Fricke, H., 690, 761
Fridegård, Jan, 839
Fridell, Folke, 839
Fridell, S., 816, 818
Fridner, G., 816
Fried, Erich, 737, 764

Friedemann, M.-M., 36
Friedländer, David, 678
Friedman, M. L., 353
Friedrich III (*Elector of Brandenburg, King of Prussia*), 652
Friedrich III, (*Duke of Schleswig-Holstein*), 652
Friedrich von Hausen, 618, 619
Friedrich Wilhelm (*Great Elector of Brandenburg*), 652
Friedrich, E. L., 61
Friedrich, T., 724
Friedrich, U., 605
Fries, S., 816
Friis, R. J., 360
Frisch, A., 102
Frisch, H., 543, 544
Frisch, Max, 691, 697, 764, 772
Frischmut, Barbara, 746, 764
Fritsch-Rössler, W., 612
Fritsch-Staar, S., 618
Fritz, T., 636
Fröberg, G., 828
Fröding, Gustaf, 827–28
Froebe-Kapteyn, Olga, 544
Fröhlich, H., 708, 879
Fröhlich, M., 769
Fröhling, S., 696
Froio, R., 495
Froissart, Jean, 73, 77, 83, 84
Frölich, H., 681
Frølich, J., 163
Frost, D. T., 351
Frost, Robert, 406
Frostenson, Katarina, 825
Frühwald, W., 883
Fruttero, C., 475
Frýba-Reber, A.-M., 32
Fryc, J. B., 856
Frydel, S., 714
Fuà Fusinato, Erminia, 469
Fuchs, A., 705
Fuchs, Anton, 764
Fuchs, S., 589, 879
Fucini, Renato, 479
Fuente, J. L. de la, 363
Fuente Ballesteros, R. de la, 260, 276
Fuentes, Carlos, 344, 346, 359
Fuertes, Gloria, 290
Fuertes, J. L., 249
Fueyo, Pelayo, 289
Fühmann, Franz, 764
Fuhrmann, H., 1, 571, 769
Fulda, D., 715, 729
Fülleborn, U., 699
Füllner, B., 715
Füllner, M. B., 716
Fulton, H., 560

Fumagalli, M., 217
Fumaroli, M., 154, 880
Fumen, L., 264
Funes, L., 239, 242
Fürbeth, F., 589, 604, 630, 631, 883
Furst, L. R., 154
Furukawa, N., 36
Furuland, L., 833, 880
Füssel, S., 634, 765
Fussenegger, Gertrud, 764
Fustel de Coulanges, Numa D., 170
Fuster, Jeroni, 305
Futoranski, Luisa, 345
Fyler, J. M., 83
Fynsk, C., 695

Gaatone, D., 35, 41
Gabaldón, Luis, 279
Gabaude, F., 169
Gabbrielli, V., 472
Gabolde, J., 166
Gabriel, E., 582
Gabriele, Trifone, 403, 439
Gabrielle de Bourbon, 113
Gabriëls, S. 785
Gabrych-Owsianko, M., 853
Gadda, Carlo Emilio, 470, 489, 511
Gadeanu, S., 569
Gadet, F., 31
Gaebel, U., 615
Gaeta, L., 378
Gaetani, M., 514, 516
Gagen, D., 266
Gaglianone, P., 511
Gagliardi, E., 510
Gagnon, André, 193
Gagnon, C., 194
Gago Rodó, A., 277
Gaier, U., 717
Gaillard, Auger, 116
Gaillard, F., 162
Gaillard Corsi, J., 470
Gaines, J. F., 127, 128, 129
Gaisbauer, S., 583
Gajda, S., 853, 854
Gajeri, E., 500
Gala, C. S. (C. S. Newton) 272, 281
Galaction, G., 545
Galaicu-Păun, E., 548
Galán, E., 294
Galand-Hallyn, P., 94
Galant, J., 870
Galasso, G., 472
Galateo, Antonio, 451
Gałczyńska, A., 851

Gałczyński, K. I., 872
Galderisi, C., 74
Galdi, Matteo Angelo, 459
Galdós, B. Pérez, 273, 274
Galeani Napione, F., 472
Gałecki, Z., 860
Galembeck, P. T., 310
Galen, 138, 433, 435
Galen, H., 721
Galent-Fasseur, V., 70, 215
Galileo Galilei, 106, 148
Galimberti, C., 482, 486, 487
Galimberti, P. M., 427
Galindo, R. M., 354
Gallagher, M., 196, 199
Gallagher, P., 880
Gallays, F., 190
Gallego, I., 363
Gallego, Vicente, 289
Gallichan, G., 190
Gallingani, D., 457
Gallo, A. M., 448
Gallo, D., 426
Gallo, V., 460
Gallot, M., 493
Galloway, A., 4
Gallwitz, E., 689
Gally, M., 98, 99
Galo Sánchez, A., 242
Galves, C., 313
Gálvez, Manuel, 348
Gambarin, G., 478
Gambaro, Griselda, 347, 352
Gambetta, P. D., 512
Gamper, M., 664
Gandolfino da Roreto, 423
Ganeri, M., 468, 477, 504
Ganivet, Ángel, 260, 275–76
Gans, Eduard, 716
Ganter, D., 616
Ganter, F., 693
Gantert, K., 601
Ganz, P., 601, 720
Gaos, José, 282
Gaquin, A., 201
Garampi, Giuseppe, 454
Garasse, François, 92
Garber, J., 663
Garboli, C., 511
García, Álvaro, 289
García, C. J., 286
García, C., 319
García, Eduardo, 289
García, G. V., 267
García, I., 351
García, L. M. V., 238
García, M., 237, 239
García, X. A., 335
García-Abad García, M. T., 272
García Acuña, Fernando, 335

García Barros, Manuel, 335
García-Bermejo, M., 251
García-Bodaño, Salvador, 336
García Bonilla, R., 360
García Calderón, M., 352
García Casado, Pablo, 289
García de la Concha, V., 267
García Corrales, G., 353
Garcia de Enterría, M.-C., 254
García González, J., 226
García-Hernández, B., 26
García López, J., 248
García Lorca, Federico, 232,
    261, 262, 263, 264, 269–72,
    275, 278, 346, 510, 879
García Márquez, Gabriel, 346,
    354, 355
García Martín, J. L., 289
García Martín, J. M., 232
García Mercadal, J., 259
García Monge, Joaquín, 355
García Montero, Luis, 289, 290
García Morales, Adelaida, 285
García Pinto, M., 364
García Ruiz, V., 260, 271
García Turnes, B., 328
García Turza, C., 878
García Valle, A., 222
García Wiederman, E., 231
Garcilaso de la Vega, 243
Gardt, A., 571, 572
Gardy, P., 116, 206, 217
Gardzińska, J., 849
Garfias, C., 263
Garlinger, P. P., 287
Garmendia, Julio, 365
Garmendia, S., 349
Garms, J., 454
Garneau, François-Xavier, 184,
    190
Garneau, Hector de Saint-
    Denys, 184, 190
Garnero, S., 212
Garnerus, G., 613
Garnier, Robert, 117
Garnier, X., 174
Garofalo, P., 483
Garreau, I., 51
Garréta, A. F., 143
Garrisson, J., 138
Garro, Elena, 347, 360
Garros, Pey de, 116, 217
Gärtner, T., 2, 7
Garton, J., 827
Garval, M. D., 168
Garvin, B., 473
Garza, M. L. de la, 361
Gasarian, G., 174
Gasch, S., 262
Gasiglia, R., 210

Gaski, H., 804
Gaspar Porras, S., 330
Gaspari, G., 489
Gasperini, L., 19
Gasquet-Cyrus, M., 210
Gassendi, Pierre, 145, 149
Gates, Henry Louis, 198
Gates Jr., H. L., 397
Gates, L. D., 111, 113
Gather, A., 14, 27
Gatto, A., 485
Gaucher, E., 62, 73
Gaudy, Franz, Freiherr von, 716
Gauger, H.-M., 568
Gaulle, Charles de (*President of
    France*), 37
Gaullier-Bougassas, C., 61, 72,
    87
Gaunt, S., 88, 213, 302
Gaurico, P., 431
Gaus, D., 661
Gauthier, L., 193
Gautier de Châtillon, 55
Gautier de Coinci, 78
Gautier, Théophile, 155–56,
    165, 170–71, 520
Gauvard, C., 881
Gauvin, Lise, 192
Gavara Gomis, R., 225
Gavazzeni, F., 478, 481
Gavel Adams, A.-C. (L.), 829,
    834
Gawełko, M., 14, 848
Gay, P., 149
Gayraud, P., 212
Gebauer, M., 761
Geben, K., 853
Gębka-Wolak, M., 851
Geckeler, H., 44
Gee, Thomas, 564
Geel, M. C., 354
Geeraedts, L., 779, 790
Geest, D. de, 794
Gehl, H., 569, 583
Gehle, H., 735, 758
Geier, B., 608
Geier, R., 570, 765
Geiger, T., 757
Geijer, Erik Gustaf, 826
Geisdorfer Feal, G., 357
Geisler, E., 362
Geisser, M., 626
Geissler, R., 765
Geist, A. L., 344
Geith, K.-E., 625, 629
Geldner, G., 713
Geldrich-Leffman, H., 344
Gellert, Christian Fürchtegott,
    662
Gellner, C., 737

Gelpí, E., 298
Gemert, G. van, 655
Genco, G., 515
Genet, Jean, 177
Genetelli, C., 488
Genette, G., 498
Genevois, E., 475
Gennari, Giuseppe, 455
Gennaro, R., 525, 526
Genot, G., 525
Gensini, S., 481
Gensollen, R., 211
Gentile, G., 435
Gentile, P., 386
Gentile, S., 434
Gentileschi, Artemisia, 141
Genton, F., 716
Gentry, F. G., 591, 593, 612
Geoffrey of Monmouth, 560
Geoffrey of Vinsauf, 8
Geoffroy de Charny, 83
Georg II (*Landgrave of Hessen-Darmstadt*), 652
George, E. E., 693
George, J. W., 1
George, Stefan, 667, 675, 743, 762
Georgescu, M., 545
Gerald of Wales, 6, 7
Geraldini (*the brothers*), 308
Gérard de Vivre, 33
Gérard, A., 170
Gerber, G., 742
Gerbert of Reims (Pope Sylvester II), 7
Gerbi, S., 519
Gerbier, L., 452
Gerhard, A., 677, 678
Gerhardt, C., 610, 629
Gerhardt, D., 621
Gerhardt, Ida, 792
Gerhardt, V., 743
Gerlach, B., 579
Gerlach, H., 665
Gerlach, I., 766
Gerlach, U. H., 730, 732
Gerli, M., 240
Gernert, F., 451
Gersch, H., 677, 719
Gerson, Jean, 90
Gerstäcker, Friedrich, 711, 728
Gervasani, M., 500
Gervasi, L., 491
Gervassi-Navarro, N., 344
Gesse, S., 679
Gessner, Salomon, 676
Gethner, P., 125
Geulincx, A., 149
Geuss, R., 741
Gevrey, F., 137

Gewey, F. X., 741
Gezelle, Guido, 786, 788, 791, 794
Ghachem, M. W., 152
Ghaussy, S., 770
Gheorghiu, G., 547
Gheri, P., 706
Ghica, M., 548
Ghidetti, E., 480, 482
Ghidinelli, S., 523
Ghilardi, M., 512
Ghisi, F., 425
Giacalone Ramat, A., 386, 387
Giachino, M., 519
Giacone, F., 95, 102, 104
Giacopini, V., 498
Giacosa, Giuseppe, 492
Gialdroni, T. M., 460
Giampieri, G., 440
Giannone, Pietro, 464
Giardini, D., 523
Gibbs, M. E., 612
Gibson, I., 270
Gide, André, 35, 269, 508
Gielniowa, W., 864
Gier, A., 59
Gierała, J., 846
Gieri, M., 519
Gierling, D., 534
Gies, D. T., 264
Gigante, C., 445
Giger, B., 729
Giglio, R., 466
Gignoux, A.-C., 180
Gil de Biedma, Jaime, 291
Gil-Albert, Juan, 264, 271, 282
Gilbert, F., 248
Gilder, A., 42
Giles of Rome, 8
Giles, G., 753
Giles, S., 707
Gili Iriarte, M. L., 359
Gilkison, J., 247, 284
Gill, Claes, 808
Gillebert, 7
Gilleir, A., 702, 746
Gilles li Muisis, 90
Gilles, J., 165, 166
Gilles, P., 568
Gillespie, D. F., 831
Gillhoff, Johannes, 745
Gilliams, Maurice, 791
Gilliéron, J., 16, 17, 31
Gillies, W., 881
Gilly, C., 434
Gilman, S. L., 741
Gilson, S., 401, 411, 421
Giménez-Cacho, L., 271
Giménez López, E., 257

Giménez de Urrea, Pedro Manuel, 247
Gimeno Blay, F. M., 304
Gimeno Menéndez, F., 220
Gimferrer, Pere, 292
Ginebra, J., 299
Giner de los Ríos, F., 274
Gingras, F., 56
Gini de Barnatan, M., 229
Ginters, L., 720
Ginzburg, L., 511
Ginzburg, Natalia, 511–12
Gioanola, E., 493
Gioberti, Vincenzo, 479
Giordani, Pietro, 479, 482
Giordano, A., 348
Giordano, E., 483
Giordmaina, J., 425
Giotti, Virgilio, 512
Giotto, 444
Giovannetti, P., 468
Giovanni da Pian di Carpine, 471
Giovanni del Virgilio, 404, 408
Giovanuzzi, S., 504, 521
Giovenardi, Mattia, 458
Giovene di Girasole, Andrea, 512
Giovini, M., 1, 6
Giovio, Paolo, 427
Gir, P., 493
Giraldi dei Cas, N., 364
Giraldi Cinzio, Giovanni Battista, 438, 446, 447–48
Girard, R., 287, 394
Girard, Rodolphe, 190
Girardi, E. N., 431, 474
Girardi, M. T., 445
Girart d'Amiens, 59
Giraud, M., 197
Giraudo, G., 157
Girndt, H., 687
Girodet de Roucy, Anne Louis (Girodet-Trioson), 160
Girolami, P., 482
Girón Alconchel, J. I., 222
Girondo, Oliverio, 347, 348
Giroussens, P., 204
Girshausen, T., 880
Gisolfi, D., 436
Giudice, F., 466
Giudice, G., 522
Giudicelli, C., 341
Giudici, Giovanni, 503, 512
Giunta, C., 400
Giusti, Giuseppe, 480
Giusti, S., 511
Giustinian, Orsatto, 443
Givone, S., 484, 513
Gizbert-Studnicki, T., 852

Gjerden, J. S., 180
Gladding, J., 595
Gladheart, A., 361
Glaser, E., 643
Glassbrenner, Adolf, 715, 728
Glasscoe, M., 559
Glatz, L. F., 759
Glatzel, I., 861
Gleize, J., 162
Glendinning, N., 254
Glenk, E., 766
Glenn, K., 273
Glick, L. B., 585
Glienke, B., 825, 831, 880
Glinz, H., 571
Glissant, Edouard, 196, 197, 198–99
Glockendon, Georg, 648
Glückert, M., 736
Glynn, R., 510
Gnädinger, L., 608
Gnisci, A., 500
Gobbers, W., 786
Gobetti, P., 501
Goblirsch, K. G., 572
Godard, B., 185
Godbout, Jacques, 112, 185, 186
Gödden, W., 720, 721
Godeau, Antoine, 121
Godeau, J., 163
Godebski, Cyprian, 866
Godin, J.-C., 184, 187
Godlewski, M., 858
Godolin, Pierre, 116
Godt, C. G., 490
Godwin, J., 451
Godwin-Jones, R., 729
Goebel, E., 701, 734
Goebel, K., 727
Goebl, H., 549, 550, 880
Goedegebuure, J., 777, 790
Goerlitz, U., 645
Goes, J., 36, 37, 40
Goethe, Christiane, 688
Goethe, Johann Wolfgang von, 478, 575, 653, 659, 662, 664, 665–75, 676, 678, 680, 682, 685, 686, 688, 691, 693, 703, 706, 713, 714, 715, 733, 736, 738, 739, 742, 743, 746, 754
Goetschel, W., 734
Goetz, H.-W., 589, 596
Goffis, C., 478
Goffredo De Robertis, M., 488
Golawski-Braunhart, J., 678
Goldberg, E. J., 600
Goldin, J., 168
Goldoni, Carlo, 457, 459, 464–65
Goldschmidt, G.-A., 735

Goldstein, R. J., 153
Goldwyn, H., 142
Goloboff, M., 350
Golomb, J., 741, 742
Goltz, R., 731
Golz, J., 668, 670, 672
Gombert, T., 709
Gomberville, Marin Le Roy de, 122, 137
Gombrowicz, Witold, 861, 862, 869
Gomes, Alfredo de Freitas Dias, 369
Gomes, M., 343, 344
Gómez, Ricardo, 263
Gómez de Avellaneda, Gertrudis, 340, 342, 356
Gómez Barroso, Pedro (*bishop of Cartagena*), 240
Gómez Bedate, P., 264
Gómez Bravo, A. M., 243
Gómez Clemente, X. M., 324
Gómez de Enterría, J., 225
Gómez Moreno, A., 243
Gómez Ocampo, G., 345
Gómez Ojea, Carmen, 283
Gómez Redondo, F., 237, 238, 241
Gómez de la Serna, Ramón, 259, 261, 263, 272, 273, 278, 335
Gómez Valderrama, Pedro, 355
Gómez Yebra, A. A., 267
Gonçalves, M. F., 309
Gonçalves, P., 317
Gonçalves Dias, Antonio, 368
Goncourt, Edmond de, 153, 170
Goncourt, Jules de, 153, 170
Góngora, Luis de, 260, 268, 270, 404
Gonin, F., 491
Gonnella, P., 440
Gontarski, S. E., 174
González, A., 355, 361
González, F. M., 343
González, G., 350
González, José Luis, 364
González, Juan, 348
González, M. E., 238
González, M., 319, 325, 326
González, S., 346
González Aranda, Y., 224
González de Ávila, M., 286
González Bachiller, F., 878
González Blanco, A., 259
González Casillas, M., 359
González Centeno, G. E., 360
González Cuenca, J., 252
González Fernández, H., 330, 338

González González, M., 319
González Herrán, J. M., 333
González Iglesias, Juan Antonio, 289
González Ollé, F., 219
González Prada, Manuel, 341
González Rodas, P., 346
González Seoane, E. X., 324
González Tuñón, Raúl, 345
Goodbody, A., 707
Goode, W. O., 127
Goodkin, R. E., 127, 129
Goossens, J., 636
Goozé, M. E., 768
Gorani, Giuseppe, 489
Göransson, S., 816
Gordon, B., 645
Gordon, F., 725, 727
Gordon, Geertruyd, 782
Gordon, R., 518
Göritz, M., 766
Gorla, G., 722
Görlach, M., 581, 720
Gorman, M., 3
Görner, E., 689
Görner, R., 739
Gorni, G., 407, 523
Górnicki, Łukasz, 856, 864
Gorostiza, Celestino, 347, 352
Gorris, R., 95
Gorriti, Juana Manuela, 340
Górski, A., 868
Gorski, E. M., 315
Gorys, E., 593
Göschel, J., 586
Gosk, H., 862
Gosselin, L., 37, 38, 39
Gossip, C. J., 125
Goszczyński, S., 856
Got, J., 713
Göttert, K.-H., 677
Gottfried von Franken, 641
Gottfried von Strassburg, 604, 605, 611, 615
Gotthelf, Jeremias (*pseudonym of Bitzius, A.*), 718, 728–30
Gotti, Vincenzo Ludovico, 455
Göttlicher, A., 594
Gottlieb, M., 770
Gottschall, D., 608
Gottschall, Rudolf von, 712
Gottsched, Johann Christoph, 575
Gottwald, H., 747
Gottzmann, C., 730
Götz, T., 766
Götz, U., 601
Götze, K. H., 736
Gotzkowsky, B., 610, 643
Gouiran, G., 213

Gould, E., 168
Gould, K. L., 188
Goullet, M., 6
Gounaridou, K., 121
Goupil, Laval, 184
Gourdon, M.-L., 205
Gourgaud, Y., 206
Gouttebroze, J.-G., 6
Gouveia, M. C. F., 313
Gower, John, 10
Goya y Lucientes, Francisco, 278, 294
Goytisolo, Juan, 276, 281, 285–86
Goytisolo, Luis, 282
Gozlan, L., 163
Gozzano, Guido, 470, 502, 512
Gozzi, Gasparo, 464, 465
Grabbe, Christian Dietrich, 707, 712, 713, 715, 716, 731, 745
Grabe, T., 677
Grab-Kempf, E., 26
Grabow, J., 745
Graça, A. P., 366
Gracia, P., 247
Gracián, B., 698
Gracq, Julien, 177
Graczykowska, T., 855
Grądziel, J., 873
Graeser, A., 696
Graf, G., 770
Grafinger, C. M., 454
Graf-Stuhlhofer, F., 649
Gragnani, E., 408
Gragnolati, M., 513
Graham, D., 112
Graham, R., 367
Graham-Jones, J., 352
Grambow, J., 745, 767
Grammont, M., 32
Gramsci, Antonio, 280, 452, 499, 501, 505, 518
Granata de Egües, G., 270
Granberg, R. J., 223
Grandbois, Alain, 184, 190
Grande, N., 134
Grandes, Almudena, 282
Grandesso, E., 507, 521
Grandi, Ascanio, 443
Grandperrin, N., 56
Granell, E. F., 263
Granero, Manuel (bull-fighter), 263
Granese, A., 459
Grange, J., 161
Granqvist, Willy, 839
Grant, J., 89
Granzow, Klaus, 765
Grass, Günter, 752, 753, 765
Grassin, G., 8

Grathoff, D., 696
Gratius, Ortwin, 643
Grätz, M., 677
Graves, P., 806
Gravina, Gianvincenzo, 457, 459
Grawunder, M. Z., 372
Gray, F., 94
Gray, Thomas, 486
Grayson, C., 430
Graziosi, E., 493
Greco, A., 444
Greco, M.-T., 384
Greco-Kaufmann, H., 642
Green, J., 206
Greenberg, M., 127
Greenblatt, S., 295
Greene, P. V., 259
Greenwald, R., 809
Gregersen, F., 801
Gregori, I., 547
Gregori, M., 491
Gregorio, L. A., 126
Gregorovius, Ferdinand, 730
Gregory the Great (*Saint and Pope*), 9, 586
Gregory of Tours, 15
Gregory, T., 426
Greiffenberg, Catherina Regina von, 656–57
Grein Gamra, U., 614
Greiner, B., 671, 697
Greiner-Mai, M., 710
Greń, Z., 853, 858
Gren-Eklund, G., 810
Grendler, P. F., 426
Gretsch, M., 2
Greule, A., 584, 601, 631
Grevin, Jacques, 94
Grevy, C., 803
Grial, Sergio, 343
Gribnitz, B., 700
Grieg, Nordahl, 808
Griese, S., 629, 634
Griffi, Ambrogio, 427
Griffin, M., 63
Griffith, M., 2
Griffiths, Ann, 562
Griffiths, G., 429
Grifoni, G., 507
Griggio, C., 431
Grignani, M. A., 515
Grigurcu, G., 548
Grilli, G., 303
Grilli, M., 487
Grillparzer, Franz, 706, 707, 712, 713, 714, 715, 716, 730, 744
Grima, D., 349
Grimaldi Pizzorno, P., 415

Grimbert, J. T., 216
Grimm, H., 679
Grimm, Jacob, 590, 617, 682, 684, 688–90
Grimm, S., 675, 714
Grimm, Wilhelm, 590, 617, 682, 684, 688–90
Grimmelshausen, Hans Jacob Christoffel von, 653, 657
Grindea, Miron, 544
Gripe, Maria, 833, 835, 836
Gris, Juan, 269
Grob, N., 749
Gröber, M., 630
Grobet, A., 34
Grocholo-Szczepanek, H., 853
Grochowiak, S., 862, 873
Grochowski, M., 850, 851
Groddeck, W., 741
Groebner, V., 99
Groenenboom-Draai, E., 785
Groesbeck, M. A., 440
Gromadzki, S., 873
Gronau, D., 736
Gronda, G., 457, 459, 460
Grønli, O. B., 807
Groot, Hugo de, 783
Groot, J. de, 789
Grootes, E. K., 777, 783
Gros, G., 80
Grosclaude, M., 207
Gross, A., 631
Gross, M., 551
Grosschmid, P., 227
Grosse, R., 574
Grosse, S., 571, 612
Grossel, M.-G., 54, 64, 67, 69, 75
Grossi, P., 497
Grossi, Tommaso, 384, 480, 489
Grossman, K. M., 165
Grotans, A. A., 602
Grote, Geert, 626
Groth, K. 730–31
Gruber, B., 682, 751
Gruber, J., 214
Grubmüller, K., 589, 590, 634
Gruchała, J. S., 863
Gruffudd ap Cynan, 561
Gruffydd, R. G., 563
Gruffydd, W. J., 559
Grünbein, Durs, 764, 765
Grundmann, H., 732
Grundy Fanelli, J., 425, 460
Grünfeld, M., 347
Grüninger, Bartholomäus, 640
Grüninger, Johannes, 639
Grus, M., 686
Gruszecka, A., 869
Grybosiowa, A., 851

Gryphius, Andreas, 650, 654–55, 658
Grywatsch, J., 720
Grzega, J., 205
Grzegorczykowa, R., 851
Grzesik, R., 864
Grzimek, Waldemar, 736
Gsell, O., 26
Guacci Nobile, Maria Giuseppina, 494
Guadagni, Gaetano, 460
Guadalajara, J., 248
Guagnini, E., 524
Gualdo, L., 469
Guarda, S., 739
Guarini, Battista, 446
Guarracino, V., 484
Guazzo, S., 145, 424, 431, 432
Gubser, M., 728
Gudiksen, A., 800
Gudiri y Alcócer, José Miguel, 342
Guellouz, S., 139
Guenée, B., 82, 84, 85, 881
Guénon, S. M., 130
Guentner, W., 170
Guerci, L., 456
Guernes de Pont-Sainte-Maxence, 64
Guerra, L., 353, 354
Guerra, Tonino, 500
Guerra-Cunningham, L., 355
Guerrero, M., 277
Guerrero Ruiz, P., 266
Guerzoni, G., 486
Guesclin, Bertrand du, 84
Guèvremont, Germaine, 190, 194
Guglielmi, A., 510
Guglielmi, G., 498
Guglielmi, L., 508
Guglielmi, M., 500
Guglielminetti, M., 524
Guia, J., 304, 306
Guibert of Nogent, 3, 605
Guicciardini, Francesco, 424, 437, 450, 451–52
Guichard-Tesson, F., 90
Guichemerre, R., 133
Guida, S., 215
Guidacci, Margherita, 512
Guidot, B., 58
Guidotti, A., 524
Guieysse, G., 32
Guigui-Grabli, C., 229
Guijarro, J., 881
Guilford, J., 36
Guilhem de Saint-Didier, 217
Guilhem Peire de Cazals, 215
Guillard, G., 724

Guillaume (Guilhem) IX de Aquitaine, 213, 214, 216, 217
Guillaume de Lorris, 61, 88
Guillaume, A., 629
Guillaume, G., 38, 41
Guillaume-Alonso, A., 243
Guillaumie, G., 211
Guillemin, H., 159
Guillén, C., 282
Guillén, Jorge, 262, 268
Guillén, Nicolás, 356
Guillén Salaya, F., 262
Guillerm, J.-P., 153
Guillermou, Alain, 544
Guilloton, N., 43
Guillou, Jan, 833
Guimarães, C., 370
Guimarães Rosa, João, 366, 367, 370, 372
Guinizelli, Guido, 399, 415
Guion, B., 139, 145, 150
Guiraud, P., 48
Guitarte, G., 228
Guittone d'Arezzo, 408
Guixeras, D., 304
Guizot, François, 170, 171
Guldmann, F., 799
Gülich, E., 568
Gullberg, Hjalmar, 839
Gulsoy, J., 208
Gumbert, G., 805
Gumkowska, M., 852
Günderrode, Karoline von, 685, 690
Gundolf, F., 738
Gundolf, Friedrich, 674
Günter, M., 717
Guntermann, G., 757
Güntert, G., 399, 414
Günthart, R., 615
Günther, H., 574, 576, 662
Günther, Johann Christian, 656
Günther, M., 745
Gurik, Robert, 190
Gurriarán, R., 334
Gurski, E. T., 288
Gürtler, C., 706
Gusella, A., 491
Gustafson, S. E., 693
Gustafsson, L., 837
Gustafsson, Lars, 833
Gustafsson Rosenqvist, B., 837
Guțu Romalo, V., 528, 537
Gutenberg, Johannes, 428, 634
Gütersloh, Albert Paris, 763
Guth, D., 675
Guthke, K. S., 739
Guthmüller, B., 419, 638
Guthrie, J., 675
Gutiérrez, Eduardo, 342

Gutiérrez, J., 878
Gutiérrez, M. E., 522
Gutiérrez Carou, J., 245
Gutiérrez Cossío, F., 269
Gutiérrez Girardot, R., 349
Gutiérrez-Rexach, J., 881
Gutiérrez Solana, J., 269
Gutowski, W., 867
Gutzen, D., 753
Gutzkow, Karl, 684, 720, 723, 731
Guy, D. J., 346
Guyard v. Marie de L'Incarnation
Guyon du Chesnoy, J. B. de la M., Dame de, 119, 191
Guzmán, Luis, 348
Guzmán, Martín Luis, 358
Gwalchmai ap Meilyr, 556
Gwara, S., 3
Gwenallt (David James Jones), 563
Gwenllïan ferch Gruffudd ap Cynan, 560
Gwilym ap Hywel, 557
Gwosc, D., 760
Gwyn ap Gwilym, 564
Gyllensten, Lars, 839
Gyssels, K., 199

Haag, C., 604
Haag, I., 832
Haagensen, B., 815
Haaland, L. B., 807
Haan, C. de, 778
Haan, Jacob Israël de, 788
Haar, J., 425
Haarman, H., 535
Haas, A. M., 879, 881
Haas, K. B., 57
Haas, M., 630
Haase, A., 654
Haasse, Hella, 796
Habert, Isaac, 115
Habgier-Tuczay, C., 592, 593
Habra, H., 356, 364
Habrajska, G., 851
Hacker, V., 636
Hackländer, F. W., 731
Haddock, B., 459, 479
Hadermann, P., 795
Hadewijch, 625, 779
Hadley, D. M., 619
Haen, C. A., 782
Haferland, H., 618
Haffad, D., 759
Hafis (*Persian poet*), 744, 746
Hafner, U., 325
Hagedorn, A., 712

Hagedorn, Friedrich von, 676
Hagedorn, S. C., 416
Hagemeijer, T., 317
Hagen, A. M., 777
Hagen, K., 644
Hagerup, H., 808, 809
Hagestedt, L., 691
Hahl, W., 729
Hahn, H., 583
Hahn, P. M., 662
Hahn-Hahn, Ida, 710, 731
Haida, P., 712
Haider, U., 626
Haigh, S., 197, 198, 199, 881
Håkansson, N., 813
Halač, N., 611
Halac, Ricardo, 352
Halbach, K. H., 619
Halevi, Jehuda, 762
Halkiewicz-Sojak, G., 867
Hall, R. A., 53
Hall, R.A., Jr., 15
Hallam, T., 557
Haller, Albrecht von, 662, 676
Halle-Wolfssohn, Aaron, 678
Hallmann, Johann Christian,
    650, 658
Hållner, A., 841
Hallström, A., 819
Hallyn, F., 119
Halsema, J. D. F. van, 789
Halub, M., 689
Halvorsen, A., 534
Hamacher, B., 700
Hamann, Johann Georg, 666,
    676
Hamelin, L., 191
Hamilton, B., 597
Hamkało, M., 872
Hamlin, C., 668, 695
Hamlin, F. R., 208
Hamman, A., 359
Hammar, I., 827
Hammond, N., 136
Hamrick, L. C., 155
Hamsun, Knut, 804, 805–07,
    838
Hand, V., 521
Handelsman, M., 357
Handke, K., 850, 851, 855
Handke, Peter, 294, 708, 765,
    771, 772
Händl, C., 609, 880
Handoca, M., 543, 544
Hanke-Schaefer, A., 349
Hankins, J., 430
Hanscom, M., 775
Hansen, E. B., 805
Hansen, E., 799, 800, 801, 803
Hansen, G., 802

Hansen, J. Wildt, 803
Hansen, Maurits, 804
Hansen, S. L., 798
Hansen, Thorkild, 806, 838
Hansen, W., 608
Hanska, Mme Eve, 163
Hanson, K., 232
Hansson, G. D., 826, 827, 828,
    836, 840, 841, 881
Hansson, Ola, 828
Häntzschel, G., 713, 732, 733
Haran, Dewi (David Evans), 561
Harant, P., 621
Harbert, W., 883
Harbsmeier, M., 635
Harden, T., 579, 880
Hardenberg, Friedrich von
    v. Novalis
Harder, A., 390
Harder, M., 768
Hardwick, J., 173
Hareide, J., 805, 809
Harf-Lancner, L., 83
Hargrave, K., 346
Harig, Ludwig, 765, 766
Harkness, N., 167
Harlan, Veit, 749
Harling-Kranck, G., 817
Harms, W., 616, 628, 637, 639
Harney, M., 241
Haro Tecglen, E., 271
Haroche-Bouzinac, G., 134
Harris, D., 265
Harris, Howel, 564
Harris, N., 428, 594, 760
Harris-Northall, R., 218, 221,
    224
Harrison, N., 175
Harrison, T. J., 484
Harry, P., 133
Harsdörffer, Georg Philipp, 653,
    655, 709
Harstad, F., 812
Hart, G. K., 675
Hart, S. M., 340, 344, 362
Hart, S., 342
Hart, T. E., 602
Hart, T. R., 306
Hartfield-Méndez, V., 265
Hartig, J., 731
Härtl, H., 579
Härtling, Peter, 765
Hartmann von Aue, 588, 590,
    604, 605, 611–12, 619
Hartmann, A., 617, 646
Hartmann, Moritz, 715, 716
Hartmann, P., 713
Hartmann, S., 633
Hartwig von Raute, 619
Haruki, Y., 35

Harvey, C. J., 73
Harvey, R., 213, 215
Hasenpflug, K., 686
Haskå, I., 811
Haslach, A. M., 765
Haslé, M., 707
Haspelmath, M., 22
Hasselbach, K., 719
Hassler, G., 881
Hassler, H., 377
Hasty, W., 612
Hätzlerin, C., 622
Hauck, K., 599
Hauf, A., 304, 305, 306, 307
Hauff, W., 683
Haug, A., 592
Haug, C., 709
Haug, W., 603, 610, 612, 616,
    624, 625, 881
Haugwitz, August Adolf von,
    650. 658
Haupt, B., 610
Haupt, M., 591
Haupt, S., 766
Hauptmann, Gerhart, 707, 712,
    758,
Haushofer, Marlen, 765
Hauskeller, M., 596
Häusler, W., 733
Haust, H., 45
Havard de la Montagne, P., 161
Havercroft, B., 194
Havu, E., 41
Hawcroft, M., 118, 130
Hawkins, P. S., 395
Hay, L., 706
Hayden, Gregor, 629
Haye, T., 5, 7
Hayes, D. M., 65
Hayward, P. A., 5
Heath, M., 97
Hebbel, Friedrich, 332, 712, 713,
    715, 716, 731–34
Hebel, Johann Peter, 690–91
Hébert, Anne, 184, 185, 191,
    195
Hébert, F., 183
Hébert, M., 203
Hébert, P., 183, 193
Hecht, S., 539
Hechtfischer, U., 704
Heckel, S., 614
Hecker, K., 447
Hecquet, M., 167
Hedberg, J., 843
Hedberg, Olle, 839
Hedén, B., 834
Hedman, Kaj, 839
Heeresma, Heere, 797
Heeroma, K., 778

Hegel, Georg Wilhelm Friedrich, 139, 687, 696, 720, 727, 739
Heger, A., 809
Hehle, C., 722
Heiberg, Gunnar, 807
Heiberg, Johan Ludvig, 825
Heidegger, Martin, 361, 694, 695, 762
Heidenreich, W., 766
Heidenstam, Verner von, 828
Heijden, T. C. J. van der, 781
Heimböckel, D., 697
Hein, Christoph, 755, 765
Hein, J., 713, 740
Heine, Heinrich, 705, 706, 708, 709, 710, 714, 715, 716, 717, 731, 734–38, 741, 745, 755, 758
Heinemann, E. A., 53
Heinrich (*Prince of Prussia*), 725
Heinrich von Freiberg, 611, 617
Heinrich von Hesler, 605, 627
Heinrich von Meissen
v. Frauenlob
Heinrich von Melk, 605
Heinrich von Morungen, 618, 619
Heinrich von Mügeln, 628, 631, 633
Heinrich von München, 623
Heinrich von Ofterdingen, 621
Heinrich von Sax, 621
Heinrich der Teichner, 631
Heinrich von dem Türlin, 616
Heinrich von Veldeke, 603, 611, 614, 618, 619
Heinrich of Würzburg, 7
Heinz, S., 881
Heinzle, J., 587, 589, 590, 609
Heise, U. K., 350
Heit, A., 596
Hejmej, A., 873
Hektor, Enno, 581
Helander, K., 834
Helbig, H., 767
Helfer, M., 721
Helft, N., 349
Helgeson, P., 837
Heliade-Rădulescu, Ion, 541
Heliodorus, 134
Helland, F., 807, 808
Helland, H. P., 35
Hellberg, L., 817
Hellberg, S., 812
Heller, P., 742
Hellgardt, E., 602, 880
Hellinga, W., 778
Hellsing, Lennart, 834, 835
Helm, D., 584, 623

Helman, Albert (Lou Lichtveld), 793
Helmantel, M., 578
Helmensdorfer, U., 740
Helmkamp, K., 633
Helmreich, C., 669
Helms-Defert, H., 758
Helmstetter, R., 726
Heloise, 5
Heloys du Paraclit, 90
Heltoft, M., 803
Helvétius, Claude-Adrien, 146
Helzel, F., 762
Hemecker, W., 767
Hemmer, B., 806
Hemmerechts, Kristien, 794
Hempel, H., 573
Hénault, Gilles, 191–92
Henderson, J., 814
Henein, E., 135
Henighan, S., 353, 358
Henke, R., 446
Henkel, A.-K., 717
Henkel, G., 744, 745
Henkel, N., 587, 609
Henn, M., 722
Hennequin, J., 149
Hennig, A., 806
Henningsen, B., 703
Henri I de Bourbon, prince de Condé, 113
Henri II de Bourbon, prince de Condé, 115
Henri de Valenciennes, 68
Henrichsen, P. Juel, 800
Henrietta Maria (*Queen*), 777
Henriksen, B., 802
Henrikson, P., 842
Henry VII (*Emperor*), 418
Henry II (*King of France*), 95
Henry III (*King of France*), 100
Henry IV (*King of France*), 112
Henry V (*King of England*), 105
Henry of Orange (*Prince*), 777
Henry of Avranches, 8
Henry, A., 36
Henry, F. G., 155
Henry, G., 165
Hens, G., 758
Hensel, Luise, 686
Henseler, C., 285
Hentschel, E., 580, 880
Hentschel, F., 630
Hentschel, G., 850
Hentschel, U., 659, 676
Henze, K., 231
Heraclitus, 271
Heraut Beyeren (Claes Heynensoon), 778
Herberger, E., 23

Herbers, K., 631, 635
Herbert, K., 619
Herbert, Zbigniew, 856, 861, 871, 873
Herbin, J.-C., 55, 85
Herbjørnsrud, Hans, 808
Herbort von Fritzlar, 611
Herbst, H., 731
Herchert, G., 622
Herder, Johann Gottfried, 590, 667, 696, 865
Heredia, José María de, 340
Heredia, Juan Fernández de, 374
Heringer, H. J., 591
Herling, M., 884
Herling-Grudziński, Gustaw, 862, 873
Herman, J., 14, 45, 153
Herman, M., 214
Hermann von Sachsenheim, 632
Hermann I of Thuringia (*Landgrave*), 603
Hermans, H., 792
Hermans, Willem Frederik, 793
Hermes Trismegistus, 434
Herminghouse, P., 706
Hermlin, Stephan, 765
Hermundstad, G., 806
Hernández, D. L., 348
Hernández, F. J., 218
Hernández, Felisberto, 346, 364
Hernández, José, 340
Hernández, M. I., 245
Hernández, Mario, 271
Hernández, Miguel, 260
Hernández Alonso, C., 877
Hernández-Catá, Alfonso, 280
Hernández de López, A. M., 359
Héroët, A., 94
Herps, Hendrik, 626
Herr, A., 357
Herrad von Hohenburg, 593
Herren, M. W., 2
Herrera, B., 348
Herrera, F., 355
Herrera, M. T., 225, 238
Herrera del Castillo, M. T., 225
Herrera Petere, José, 264, 282
Herrero, Fermín, 290
Herrero Ruiz de Loizaga, F. J., 223
Herrero Vecino, C., 278
Herrlich, M., 688, 689
Herrmann, K., 759
Hersant, I., 99
Herschberg-Pierrot, A., 161
Hershon, C. P., 215
Herslund, M., 22, 36, 801
Hertling, G. H., 747
Hertzberg, F., 834

Herwegh, E., 738
Herwegh, Georg, 715, 716, 718, 738
Herzberger, D. K., 260, 295
Herzig, A., 716
Heselhaus, H., 721
Hesiod, 681
Hesler, Heinrich, 605, 627
Hess, J., 634
Hesse, E., 622
Hesse, Hermann, 707, 837
Hessky, R., 570
Hessler, G., 44
Hess-Lüttich, E. W. B., 570
Hettche, W., 664, 717, 726, 727, 745, 750
Hettinga, P. M., 576
Hetzer, A., 538
Hetzer, T., 757
Heukenkamp, U., 754
Heusch, C., 240
Hewson, J., 14
Hexelschneider, E., 690
Heydebrand, R. von, 717, 881
Heym, Stefan, 752, 766
Heymann, J., 262, 744
Heyndels, R., 120, 881
Heynensoon v. Heraut Beyeren
Heyse, Paul, 708, 738, 738
Hezel, Charlotte von, 677
Hibberd, J., 700
Hicks, E., 61
Hicks, S. V., 727
Hiddleston, J., 168
Hiebel, H. H., 749
Hierro, José, 260, 292
Highfill, J., 283
Higuera Estremera, L. F., 271
Higuero, F. J., 276, 286
Hilary of Arles, 3
Hilbig, Wolfgang, 753
Hildebert, 7
Hildebrand, O., 720, 738
Hildebrandt, H.-H., 681
Hildegard of Bingen, 7, 605, 608
Hildesheimer, F., 217
Hildesheimer, Wolfgang, 766
Hilgersom, A., 796
Hill, D., 679
Hillbom, G., 824
Hille, M., 690
Hillebrand, B., 680
Hillebrand, R., 679, 682, 691
Hillebrand, S., 758
Hillenaar, H., 792
Hillenbrand, R., 703, 738
Hilmes, C., 747
Hilt, A., 803
Hiltgart von Hürnheim, 593
Hilton, John, 24

Hilty, G., 251
Hilzinger, S., 721
Himmerod, Abbot of, 9
Hindley, A., 81
Hinds, L., 139
Hintermayer Wellenberg, M., 585
Hintz, E. R., 593
Hipp, M.-T., 881
Hirdina, K., 760
Hirdt, W., 411, 878
Hirsch, E., 662
Hirschmann, W., 631
Hjorth, E., 803
Hobbes, Thomas, 145
Hobbs, R. G., 645
Hobson, M., 457
Hochgatterer, Paulus, 766
Hochhuth, Rolf, 707
Hockenjos, V., 831
Hodgart, A. B., 447
Hodge, P. J., 295
Hodgson, R. G., 139
Hoell, J., 758
Hoem, K. A., 809
Hoffenburg, J., 155
Hoffer, Klaus, 766
Hoffman, M. S., 8
Hoffman, P., 148
Hoffmann von Fallersleben, August Heinrich, 710, 738
Hoffmann von Hoffmannswaldau, Christian, 655, 656
Hoffmann, E. T. A. (Ernst Theodor Amadeus), 477, 681, 683, 686, 691–93, 697, 703, 714, 730, 758
Hoffmann, H., 5, 668
Hoffmann, L.-F., 169, 186
Hoffmann, M., 701, 742
Hoffmann, T., 591, 633
Hoffmann, W., 878
Hoffmeister, G., 736
Hofmann, Gert, 766
Hofmann, M., 675, 735, 756
Hofmann, W., 663
Hofmo, Gunvor, 808
Hoft-March, E., 175
Hogg, C., 133
Hoheisel, P., 573, 633
Hohendahl, P. U., 715
Hohl, Ludwig, 766
Höhle, T. H., 849
Höhle, T. N., 579
Hohlfeldt, A., 371
Höhn, G., 737
Höhne, S., 717
Holcot, Robert, 627

Hölderlin, Friedrich, 474, 526, 667, 693–96, 723, 865
Holdsworth, Edward, 561
Holgate, Edwin, 189
Holguín, F. V., 357
Holl, H., 705, 768
Hollander, R., 412, 419
Hollender, M., 403
Hollender, U., 403
Holler, Egidio, 455
Höller, H., 712
Höllerer, F., 735
Hollis, A., 760
Hollis, S., 2
Holloway, C., 228, 231
Holm, B., 829
Holm, G., 816
Holm, I., 841
Holm, L., 800
Holmberg, Åke, 839
Holmberg, C.-G., 821
Holmen, A., 802
Holmes, O., 213
Holmgaard, M., 815
Holmström, M., 843
Holmström, R., 827, 841
Hölscher-Lohmeyer, D., 666
Holt, D. E., 219
Holt, M. P., 294
Holtei, Karl von, 738
Höltenschmidt, E., 702
Hölter, A., 883
Holtus, G., 16, 19, 27, 549, 881
Holub, R. C., 734
Holý, J., 870
Homer, 154, 263, 415, 416, 430, 445, 466, 681
Homeyer, S., 637
Honemann, V., 623, 627, 634
Honess, C., 412
Honhold, A., 726
Honigmann, Barbara, 766
Honold, A., 758
Honorius Augustodunensis, 593
Honowska, M., 847
Honvault, R., 33, 43
Hoock-Demarle, M.-C., 735
Hood, E. W., 355
Hood, G. E., 5
Hooft, Willem D., 783
Hoogenboom, H., 168
Hoogvliet, M., 592
Höök, E., 829
Hoornik, E., 796
Hope, Q. M., 141
Hopkins, B. T., 562
Hoppe, R. B., 755, 756
Hora, D. da, 316
Horace, 8, 105, 432, 434, 478

Horace (Horace-Napoléon Raisson), 172
Horasangian, Bedros, 541
Horcajada Diezma, B., 223
Horia, Vintilā, 544
Horic, A., 187
Horkheimer, M., 697
Hormigón, J. A., 293
Horn, Agneta, 824
Horne, M., 811
Horne, P., 447
Horowitz, L. K., 130
Horowitz, M. C., 435
Horsbøl, A., 802
Horst, C. auf der, 736
Hortis, A., 473
Horváth, E., 592
Horváth, Ödön von, 718
Horzen, D. L., 767
Hotchkiss, R., 602
Houdard, S., 120
Houdebine-Gravaud, A.-M., 43
Hourcade, P., 134
Hout, Maria van, 626
Houvenaghel, E., 355
Houwen, L. A. J. R. , 592
Hovasse, O., 147
Howard, P., 460
Howarth, W. D., 130
Howe, P., 744
Howells, R., 139
Howes, G. C., 762
Hoyer, G., 552
Hoyer-Poulain, E., 55, 69
Höyng, P., 771
Hoyos, A. de, 259
Høystad, O. M., 804
Hrabanus Maurus, 3
Hristea, T., 536, 537
Hrotsvitha of Gandersheim, 1, 4, 590
Huayna Capac (*Inca Emperor*), 340
Hubbard Nelson, D., 86
Huber, C., 627
Huber, M., 317
Huber, Therese, 710
Huber-Rebenich, G., 642
Hubert, J. D., 127
Hübner, W., 10
Hubrath, M., 624
Huch, H.-G., 769
Huch, Ricarda, 746
Huchel, Peter, 766
Huchet, J.-C., 214
Huchon, M., 96, 102
Hudon, J.-G., 194
Hudson, A., 10
Hue de Rotelande, 50, 62
Hüe, D., 57

Huélamo Santamaría, A. M., 241
Huelle, P., 873
Huerta Calvo, J., 254
Huertas Vázquez, E., 254
Huet, Pierre-Daniel, 120, 143
Huet-Brichard, M.-C., 157
Hufeisen, B., 571, 884
Hufeland, K., 619
Huffmann, S., 189
Hüffmeier, W., 727
Hug, M., 43
Hugh of Saint-Cher, 307
Hughes, G., 424
Hughes, I., 559
Hughes, S., 569
Hugo von Trimberg, 627, 628
Hugo, Victor, 54, 150, 156–57. 165, 167, 169, 170, 171, 172, 278, 361, 493, 865
Huidobro, Vicente, 353
Huish, L. A., 740
Huizinga, J., 599
Huldén, J., 824
Hulk, A., 24
Hulmes, Keri, 196
Hülsen, Hans von, 744
Hulst, H. van der, 17, 18, 881
Hult, D. F., 78
Hultberg, T., 839
Hulthem, Charles van, 779
Humbeeck, K., 795
Humble, M., 704
Humboldt, Alexander von, 669
Humboldt, Wilhelm von, 682, 696
Hume, David, 275
Huml, A., 757
Hummel, A., 731
Hummel, C., 759
Humpál, M., 805
Hundsbichler, H., 589, 634
Hunger, H., 740
Hunnius, K., 40
Hunt, T., 79
Huon de Mery, 67
Huot, S., 213
Hüpper, D., 630
Huppert, G., 92
Huschenbett, D., 635
Husserl, Edmund, 526
Hutchenson, G. S., 878
Hutcheson, G. S., 249
Hutchinson, P., 704, 741
Hutnikiewicz, A., 870
Hutsebaut, J., 780
Hutter, M., 593
Huws, B. O., 558, 565
Huygens, Constantijn, 783, 785
Hverven, T. E., 807

Hvilshøj, U., 800
Hyltenstam, K., 815
Hyo Suk, Jo, 179
Hyunseon, L., 766
Hywel Dafi (Hywel ap Dafydd ab Ieuan ap Rhys), 557
Hywel Dda, 556

Iacuzzi, P. F., 485, 507
Iancu-Agou, D., 203
Ianes, R., 342, 355
Iannucci, A. A., 412, 415
Ibolya Bitte, V., 542
Ibsen, Henrik, 807, 830, 831
Ibsen, Sigurd, 807
Icle, G., 369
Iehl, D., 707
Iermano, T., 479, 516
Iestyn Daniel, R., 557
Ifans, D., 561
Ifans, R., 559
Ifor ap Glyn, 563
Igel, R., 370
Iglesias Alvarez, A., 328
Iglesias Feijoo, L., 260
Igliński, G., 862, 868
Ignatius de Loyola (*Saint*), 149
Ihring, P., 610, 884
Ilie, C., 539
Iliescu, M., 19, 536
Illg, J., 874
Illiano, A., 483
Illingworth, R. N., 57
Illyricus, Matthias Flacius, 646
Imbert, M.-T., 210
Imbriani, M. T., 472
Imbs, P., 77
Imerslund, K., 808
Imhoff. B., 221
Immermann, Karl, 715, 738
In, S., 740
Infantes, V., 235, 243, 245
Ingegno, A., 435
Ingen, F. van, 658
Inghirami, T., 437
Inglese, F., 424
Inglot, M., 861, 865, 866, 869
Ingres, Jean Auguste, 160
Innamorati, I., 482
Innes, C., 831
Innocent III (*Pope*), 10, 598
Innocenti, O., 482
Insana, Jolanda, 503, 512
Insúa, Alberto, 259
Ioan Pedr (John Peter), 562
Iolo Goch, 558
Ion, D., 55
Ionesco, Eugène, 544
Ionescu-Ruxăndoiu, L., 527

Ioni, A. M., 490
Iordache, R., 532
Iova, M., 543
Ippolito, M., 380
Irandoust, H., 38
Irigoyen, Ramón, 281
Irizarry, E., 335
Irizarry, G. B., 364
Irmscher, H. D., 666, 748
Irving, J., 270
Irwin, J. L., 657
Irwin, R. M., 345
Irwin, R., 359
Isaac de Lattes, 215
Isaac, G. R., 556
Isaacson, José, 348
Isabella (*Queen of Spain*), 243, 249
Isakson Biehl, E., 581
Isaksson, Folke, 839–40
Isaksson, S., 816
Iseghem, J. van, 788
Isella, D., 427, 478, 479, 491, 494, 514, 525
Isidore of Seville (*Saint*), 9, 648
Isla, José-Francisco de, 257
Islwyn, D., 562
Ismael, J., 263
Isotti Rosowski, G., 522
Israel, M., 124
Italia, P., 523
Itzig v. Sarah Levy
Iurilli, A., 350
Iurlani, F., 720
Ivănescu, G., 529
Ivanović, C., 761
Ivars, A.-M., 815
Ivarsson, I., 825
Iverson, G. K., 576
Iwasiów, I., 862
Iwaszkiewicz, Jarosław, 869–70, 871
Izquierdo, J., 305

Jackman, G., 765
Jackson, D., 748, 749
Jackson, T. R., 605
Jackson, W. H., 613, 615
Jacó Monteiro, V., 367
Jacob, F., 121
Jacob, L., 756
Jacob, M., 766
Jacob, Suzanne, 186, 192
Jacob-Friesen, H., 646
Jacobi, Friedrich Heinrich, 678, 682
Jacobi, K., 303
Jacobo de las Leyes, 242
Jacobs, B., 360, 829
Jacobsen, E., 750

Jacobsen, H. Galberg, 798, 800
Jacobsen, Jens Peter, 831
Jacobsen, S. Nonboe, 798
Jacobus de Voragine, 626
Jacobus, L. A., 175
Jacoby, D., 597
Jacoff, R., 410
Jacomuzzi, S., 461
Jacopone da Todi, 443–44
Jacouty, J.-F., 171
Jacques de Baisieux, 611
Jacques, G., 162
Jadacka, H., 847, 852
Jadot, Jean-Nicolas, 454
Jaeger, C. S., 604
Jaeger, M., 674
Jaeggli, O., 13, 21, 881
Jaeschke, W., 682
Jäger, A. M., 735, 737
Jager, M., 805
Jäger, S., 570, 571
Jahn, J.-E., 393
Jahnn, Hans Henny, 766
Jaimes, H., 365
Jajdejski, W., 873
Jakob, K., 575
Jakob, K.-H., 575
Jakobi, C., 720
Jakobi, R., 1, 8
Jakobson, Roman, 368
Jakobsson, L., 843
Jam, J.-L., 152
Jamerey-Duval, Valentin, 454
James I (*King of England*), 115
James (Jaume) I (*King of Aragon*), 303, 305
James, E. D., 147
James, Henry, 520, 525
James, J. W., 559
James, William, 525
James-Raoul, D., 60
Janés, Clara, 282
Janet, P., 525
Janion, M., 861
Janke, W., 688
Jankowska, J., 857
Janota, J., 620, 629
Janowska, B., 853
Janquert, A., 350
Jansen, S., 510
Jansen-Sieben, R., 780
Jansiti, C., 178
Janssen, M., 690
Janssen-Zimmermann, A., 754
Janssens, J., 780
Janssens, M., 794
Jansson, E., 827
Jansson, M., 832
Jansson, S.-B., 822
Jaouen, F., 132

Japp, U., 683
Jaraczewska, E., 863
Jaramillo-Zuluaga, E., 340
Jarauta, F., 457
Järborg, J., 819
Jardiel Poncela, Enrique, 261, 262
Jarl Kerzar, H., 813
Jarnés, Benjamín, 259, 262, 273, 283
Jarosiński, Z., 871
Jarosz-Sienkiewicz, E., 770
Jarry, A., 158
Jarvad, P., 799, 800, 801
Jarvis, B., 562
Jarzębski, J., 870
Jasieński, Bruno, 870
Jasiński, J., 864
Jastal, K., 714, 761
Jaubert, A., 39
Jaume I v. James I
Jauregui, C., 341
Jauss, H. R., 276, 589
Javitch, D., 438
Jean de Bueil, 85
Jean de Croy, 73
Jean de Meun, 59, 61, 87, 88
Jean Paul v. Richter
Jean Renart, 50, 61
Jeandillou, J.-F., 172
Jeanjean, H., 216
Jeanne d'Albret, 97, 112
Jeanne des Anges, Mère, 122
Jeanneret, M., 96, 104, 109
Jeanroy, A., 216
Jeay, M., 76, 86
Jebing, B., 708
Jedin, H., 436
Jeep, J. M., 615
Jelinek, Elfriede, 707, 766
Jenkins, G. H., 563, 881
Jenkins, I., 562
Jenkins, J., 562
Jenkins, K., 562
Jenny, J., 122
Jens, Walter, 643
Jensen, B. L., 802
Jensen, J., 265
Jensen, K. A., 138
Jensen, T. Juel, 800
Jensen, Wilhelm, 745
Jerome (*Saint*), 120, 431
Jerusalem, Wilhelm, 660
Jessing, B., 664, 667
Jeu, A. de, 783
Jeutter, R., 754
Jewers, C. A., 74
Jeziorkowski, K., 697
Jiménez, J. B., 449
Jiménez, J. O., 345

Jiménez, J., 298
Jiménez, Juan Ramón, 259, 262, 265, 266, 272, 275
Jiménez Lozano, José, 286
Jiménez Ríos, E., 225
Jiménez Romero, Alfonso, 294
Jitrik, N., 352
Joachim, S., 191
Joan of Arc, 84
Joan (*Pope?*), 627
Joan-Elia, A., 345
Joch, M., 758
Jodorowsky, Alexandro, 361
Jodra Davó, Carmen, 289
Johanek, P., 597, 603
Johann von Würzburg, 610, 617
Johannes von Tepl, 632
Johansson, A., 836
Johansson, C. O., 830
John the Evangelist (*Saint*), 395
John Chrysostom (*Saint*), 644
John of the Cross (*Saint*), 270
John (*Duke of Burgundy*), 71
John of Garland, 7
John of Salisbury, 631
John of Wales (Juan de Gales), 241
Johnson, A., 366
Johnson, Eyvind, 833, 840
Johnson, G., 98
Johnson, G., 397
Johnson, K., 881
Johnson, L. P., 603, 618
Johnson, R., 264, 275, 277, 361
Johnson, S. D., 251
Johnson, S., 612
Johnson, Uwe, 581, 766–67, 772
Johnston, D., 557
Johnston, P. G., 272
Joinville, Jean de, 82
Jolibert, B., 117
Jolivet, M.-J., 197
Jolivet, Robert, 85
Jolly, A., 431
Jølsen, Ragnhild, 807
Joly, A., 41
Jomelli, Niccolò, 460
Jonard, N., 465, 488
Jonas, M., 569
Jonasson, K., 35, 36
Jonckheere, W., 790
Joncre, J., 864
Jones, A., 565
Jones, A. R., 561
Jones, B., 197
Jones, Bobi, 563
Jones, C. M., 55, 71
Jones, D. Glyn, 561
Jones, D. S., 563
Jones, J., 345

Jones, J. Meirion, 562
Jones, Jeremiah, 562
Jones, John Gwilym, 564
Jones, John Gwynfor, 563
Jones, M. A., 36
Jones, M. H., 612
Jones, N. A., 556, 557
Jones, P. H., 564
Jones, R. Gerallt, 562, 563
Jones, R. M., 556
Jones, R. O., 555
Jones, T. Hughes, 562
Jones, V. R., 490
Jones, W. J., 567
Jonke, Gert, 767
Jönsson, F., 816
Jönsson, L., 814
Jonsson, Tor, 808
Jordaens, Willem, 626
Jordan, P., 584
Jordan, W. C., 65
Jordán-Cólera, C., 25
Jørgensen, B., 803
Jørgensen, J. Normann, 802
Jørgensen, N., 802
Jørgensen, P., 635
Jørgensen, S. A., 729
Jørgensen, S. W., 798
Jori, G., 443
Josefsson, G., 812
Joseph, E., 709, 743
Joseph, J. E., 696, 882
Josephson, Erland, 830
Josephus, Flavius, 115, 250
Joubert, L., 186
Joudoux, R., 203
Jourde, M., 98, 99
Jousset, P., 164
Jouve, Pierre-Jean, 521
Jovellanos, Gaspar Melchor de, 254
Jover, José Luis, 290
Joy, O., 550
Joyce, James, 331, 337, 398, 511, 516, 861
Juan II (*King of Spain*), 251
Juan Manuel, Don, 239–40
Juana Inés de la Cruz (Sor), 216, 356, 359, 361
Jubinville, Y., 194
Jückstock, N., 767
Judge, A., 38
Judkowiak, B., 872
Julián, C. val, 97
Julius Caesar, 560
Jung, Carl Gustav, 396, 544, 743, 767
Jung, Johann Heinrich, 661
Jung, T., 755
Jung, W., 775

Jünger, Ernst, 544, 767
Jungman, M. E. M., 779
Junius, Franciscus, 601
Jürgens, D., 709, 726, 750, 758, 882
Jurgrau, T., 168
Jurieu, Pierre, 150
Jurkevich, G., 274
Jurkowski, M., 845, 856, 859
Jurma, G., 542
Justinian (*Emperor*), 420
Jutrin, M., 546
Juul, H., 799
Juvenal, 1, 511
Juy, Martin, 353

Kabatek, J., 327
Kablitz, A., 419, 596
Kabulis, J. M., 169
Kabus, P., 722
Kaden, C., 596
Kadyjewska, A., 845
Kafka, Franz, 484, 577, 718, 742, 774, 829
Kahn, J., 585
Kahn-Rossi, M., 424
Kaiser, Friedrich, 738, 741
Kaiser, G. A., 23
Kaiser, H., 733
Kaisse, E. M., 17
Kajtoch, W., 854
Kaleta, S., 573
Kalinowska, M., 861
Kalinowski, I., 735
Kalkofen, R., 602
Kallas, K., 848
Kaloyanova-Slavova, L., 745
Kalske, M., 816
Kaltenbach Markey, N., 213
Kaluta, I., 870
Kambly, O. A., 729
Kamieńska, Anna, 856
Kamińska-Szmaj, I., 850
Kaminski, A., 346
Kammler, C., 773
Kampe, J., 639
Kämper, H., 575
Kampits, P., 713
Kandre, Mare, 840
Kane, M., 760
Kant, Immanuel, 275, 675, 687, 702, 758
Kantorowicz, E. H., 400
Kany, W., 585
Kapp, V., 119, 145
Kapuściński, R., 871
Karagyozov, P., 866
Karahka, U.-L., 837
Karant-Nunn, S., 639

Karaś, A., 851
Karaś, H., 853
Karczewska, K., 883
Kåreland, L., 834
Karénine, W., 168
Karge, H., 725
Karker, A., 799
Karl XII (*King of Sweden*), 822
Karl II, (*Elector of the Pfalz*), 652
Karl Ludwig, (*Elector of the Pfalz*), 652
Karlfeldt, Erik Axel, 828
Karlsson, A.-M., 814
Karlsson, D., 834
Karlsson, S., 812
Karlsson, T., 838
Karnowska, B., 874
Karolak, S., 35, 39
Karpiński, A., 863
Karpluk, M., 851, 858
Karrasch, G., 746
Kartheiser, J., 568
Kartschoke, D., 587, 636
Kaschnitz, Marie-Luise, 767
Kasper, E., 754
Kasper, H., 769
Kasperski, E., 866
Kasprowicz, Jan, 862, 868
Kassim, Z., 191
Kastberger, K., 769
Kastelec, M., 850
Kasten, I., 619, 632, 879, 881
Kasten, L., 242
Kästner, H., 603
Kato, M. A., 21
Katritzky, L., 685
Katsikas, S., 570
Kattan, Naïm, 193
Kauder-Steiniger, R., 721
Kauffeld, C. J., 242
Kauffer, M., 575, 578
Kaufholz-Messmer, E., 724
Kaufman, T., 528
Kaufringer, H., 632
Kaukoreit, V., 764
Käutner, H., 739
Kaváfis, Konstantínos Pétrou, 521, 706
Kavanagh, R. J., 882
Kawaguchi, Y., 46
Kay, S., 54, 213, 302
Kayne, R. S., 21, 22
Kayser, W., 832
Kaziara, S., 857
Keck, A., 880
Kędelska, E., 855
Keefe Ugalde, S., 291
Keel, A., 805
Keifer, R., 769
Keil, G., 631

Keisch, C., 724, 725
Keitz, U. von, 749
Kellendonk, Frans, 793
Keller, E., 134
Keller, Gottfried, 704, 709, 711, 718, 730, 733, 738–39
Keller, H., 589, 631, 882
Keller, H. E., 53, 603, 618, 629, 636
Keller, J., 616, 633
Kellermann, K., 631
Kellermann, R., 753
Kellgren, Johan Henrik, 824
Kellner, B., 609
Kelly, D., 50, 83
Kemenade, A. van, 882
Kempen, M. van, 793
Kemper, H.-G., 656
Kemper, T. A., 621
Kendall, K. T., 251
Kenk, F., 743, 761
Kennedy, A., 276
Kennedy, E., 83
Kennis, B., 795
Kent, C. A., 53
Kępa, A., 867
Kępińska, A., 847, 856, 860
Kepler, Johannes, 516
Kerlan, A., 170
Kern, M., 614, 618
Kern, P., 616
Kerner, Justinus, 689, 716
Kernmayer, H., 705
Kerth, S., 628
Kertscher, H.-J., 659
Kessler, E., 434
Kettemann, R., 882
Keun, Irmgard, 767
Kevra, S., 190
Kewitz, B., 585
Kibler, W. W., 54, 83
Kickethier, K., 749
Kiefer, S., 712, 732, 766
Kielland, Alexander, 805, 807
Kielland, Gustava, 805
Kierkegaard, Søren, 275, 395, 757, 839
Kiermeier-Debre, J., 748
Kies, O., 582
Kiesant, K., 766
Kiesler, R., 383
Kihlman, C., 834
Kikawa, M., 725
Kiklewicz, A., 847
Kiklewitsch, A., 579
Kilcher, A. B., 655, 721
Kim, S., 137
Kim, Y. M., 733
Kimmich, D., 605
Kimoto, S., 743

Kimpel, D., 668
Kindt, S., 30
King, C., 529
King, D. S., 51
Kinkel, Gottfried, 739
Kinzel, U., 757
Kiparsky, P., 232
Kipp, S., 231
Kipphardt, Heinar, 768
Kirby, S. D., 238
Kircher, H., 714, 715
Kirchner, Ernst Ludwig, 709
Kirchner, L., 709
Kirchner, V., 755
Kirkbright. S., 722
Kirnberger, J. P., 679
Kirsch, Sarah, 756
Kis, Danilo, 757
Kiślak, E., 861, 874
Kittang, A., 807
Kittelson, J., 639
Kittler, F., 733
Kizwalter, T., 866
Kjaerstad, Jan, 807
Kjersén Edman, L., 835
Klabunde, S., 716
Klanska, M., 715
Kłańska, M., 880
Klare, A., 619
Klassen, N., 57
Klaus, A., 767
Klauser, Konrad, 643
Klausner, D., 561
Klecker, E., 638
Kleedorfer, J., 717
Kleiber, G., 36, 38, 39
Kleiber, W., 631
Klein, C., 769
Klein, D., 615, 623
Klein, H.-G., 679
Klein, K., 607, 627
Klein, T., 607
Klein, T. A.-P., 8
Klein, W. P., 580
Kleine, S., 693
Kleinhans, B., 687
Kleinhenz, C., 399, 412
Kleinschmidt, E., 715
Kleinschmidt, H., 589
Kleist, Heinrich von, 680, 682, 683, 691, 696–700, 707, 745
Klementowicz, M., 190
Klemm, W., 862
Klemperer, V., 570
Klemperer, Victor, 773
Klengel, S., 263
Kleszczowa, K., 847, 850
Klier, W., 770
Kliffer, M. D., 22
Klingebiel, K., 200

Klingenber, P. N., 350
Klinger, F. M., 703
Klinger, J., 603, 611
Klingmann, U., 743
Klinkenberg, J.-M., 14, 31
Klobucka, A., 371
Klock, S. C., 368
Kloek, J., 784
Kloos, Willem, 788, 789
Klopstock, Friedrich Gottlieb, 669, 676, 707
Kłosińska, K., 869
Klosiński, K., 874
Kloss, H., 28
Klug, C., 726
Kluge, Alexander, 768
Klussmann, P. G., 682
Knapp, B. L., 160
Knapp, F. P., 587, 610, 628
Knapp, L., 508
Knappe, G., 2
Knatz, L., 702
Knauer, M., 637
Knauff, B., 137
Knauth, K. L., 502
Knebel, H., 732
Knecht, P., 612
Knecht, R., 112
Knellwolf, U., 728
Knigge, Adolf Franz Friedrich, Freiherr von, 676–77
Knight, K. W., 191
Knights, V., 280
Knittel, A. P., 697
Knoch, W., 631
Knoll, G., 727
Knöll, S., 654
Knorr von Rosenroth, Christian, 655
Knorring, Sophie von, 826
Knott, G., 53
Knudsen, S., 802
Knütel, W., 765
Knutsen, N. M., 806
Knutson, S., 192
Knutsson, Gösta, 835
Kobylińska, J., 853
Kocay, V., 177
Koch, C., 858
Koch, E. R., 132
Koch, J. T., 556
Koch, M., 673
Koch; Martin, 840
Kochan, A., 865
Kochanowski, Jan, 856, 863, 864
Kocher, G., 630
Kochs, T., 600, 601, 626
Kochskämper, B., 600, 601
Koda, Y., 625
Koelle, L., 761

Koepke, W., 879
Koeppen, Wolfgang, 767, 768
Koerner, E. F. K., 13, 14, 15, 19, 23, 27, 882
Kofta, K., 863
Kogan, V., 171
Kogel, J.-D., 678
Köhlmeier, Michael, 768
Köhn, L., 726
Kokott, H., 632
Kolb, R. A., 638, 639
Kolbe, Uwe, 753, 759, 768
Kolbinger, A., 567
Kolinsky, E., 705
Koller, E., 574, 576
Köller, W., 578
Koller-Andorf, I., 732, 733
Kolloen, I. S., 808
Kölner, H., 633
Kolsky, S., 424, 443
Koltés, Bernard-Marie, 294
Køltzow, Liv, 808
Komaromi, A., 865
Komla Aggor, F., 295
Komornicka, M., 863
Komorowski, D., 768
Komrij, Gerrit, 776
Konecka, K., 857
König, C., 671, 707
König, E., 596
König, S., 806
König, W., 576, 582
Könneker, B., 593
Konopnicka, Maria, 856, 867
Konrad von Ammenhausen, 628
Konrad von Megenberg, 630, 631
Konrad von Würzburg, 605, 611, 617, 626
Konsalik, Heinz G., 768
Kontio, R., 804
Kontje, T., 710
Konwicki, Tadeusz, 862, 871, 873
Kooper, E., 83, 882
Koopman, H., 879
Koopmans, J., 79, 81
Kooten, Kees van, 796
Köpf, G., 770
Köpf, U., 643
Kopitz, Sebastian, 640
Kopperschmidt, J., 572
Korczak, J., 862, 870
Kordt, C.-M., 613
Korfanty, S., 78
Kornacka, M., 846
Kornbacher, A., 667
Kornhauser, J., 854
Kornrumpf, G., 624
Korpysz, T., 857

Korte, H., 687, 756
Kortländer, B., 734, 735
Kortüm, H.-H., 4
Kory, P. B., 756
Korytkowska, M., 858
Korzen, H., 801
Korzen, I., 802
Koschorke, A., 672
Kosek, I., 847
Košenina, A., 664, 703
Koseska-Toszewa, V., 858
Kosiński, J., 862
Koskensalo, A., 577
Koski, R., 186
Kosmicki, G., 210
Koss, G., 584
Kossak, W. von, 633
Kosta-Théfaine, J.-F., 76
Köster, J., 770
Kosterman, Letty, 776
Kostkiewiczowa, T., 864
Koterska, J., 863
Kott, J., 871
Kovadoff, S., 352
Kowalewska, D., 867
Kozameh, Alicia, 352
Kozaryn, D., 856
Kozińska, D., 874
Koźmian, K., 861
Kracauer, Siegfried, 768
Kraft, H., 721, 730
Krah, H., 749
Krajenbrink, M., 769
Krakusin, M., 355, 363
Krall, H., 871
Krallmann, M., 773
Kralt, P., 793
Krämer, H., 766
Kramer, J., 15, 530, 536, 540, 549, 550
Kramer, S., 754
Kranz, C., 757
Krasicki, I., 861, 864, 865
Krasiński, Zygmunt, 866
Kraskowska, E., 869
Krass, A., 611, 622
Kraszewski, J. I., 861
Kratz, B., 750
Krätzen, J., 764
Krätzer, J., 759
Kratzsch, K., 713
Kraus, Karl, 718, 737, 742
Krause, B., 882
Krause, E. H., 727
Krause, H.-B., 45
Krause, M., 580
Krause, P. D., 702
Krause, S., 152
Krause, V., 63, 103
Krausnick, M., 738

Krauss, E., 725
Krauss, H., 754, 768
Krebs, G., 724
Krebs, R., 668
Krehl, B., 685
Kreja, B., 847, 856
Kremer, D., 27, 325, 692, 878, 881, 882
Kremer-Marietti, A., 170
Kremnitz, G., 204
Kretschmann, C., 712, 722
Kreutner, R., 746
Kreutz, P., 38
Krieger, H., 576
Kriegleder, W., 680, 710, 711
Krier, F., 569
Krippendorf, E., 673
Kristeva, Julia, 353, 356
Kristiansen, B., 744
Kristiansen, T., 801
Kritzman, L. D., 176
Krochmalnik, D., 679
Kröger, B. J., 577
Kröger, H., 573, 719
Krognes, H. S., 191
Krohn, R., 593
Kröhnke, K., 608
Krol, E., 788
Kroll, F.-L., 764
Kronegger, M., 122, 143, 882
Krooks, D. R., 602
Kroon, A., 814
Kroon, C., 24
Kropotkin, Peter, 772
Krotz, E., 615
Krüger, K. H., 3
Kruif, J. de, 785
Kruijsen, J., 45
Krummacher, A., 880
Krummacher, H.-H., 879
Krupianka, A., 856
Kruse, B.-J., 630
Kruse, J. A., 715, 734, 735
Krusenstjerna, Agnes von, 836
Kruszyński, Z., 871
Krzywon, E. J., 762
Krzywy, R., 864
Kube, L., 760
Kublitz-Kramer, M., 754, 767
Kubok, B., 853
Kucała, M., 851, 853, 854, 856
Kucharczik, K., 571
Kuchenreuther, M. A., 325
Kucher, P.-M., 757
Kuczyńska-Koschana, K., 870
Kuczynski, I., 659
Kuhlmann, A., 715, 771
Kühlmann, W., 638
Kühn, D., 674
Kühn, I., 585

Kühne, A., 577
Kühne, Gustav, 713
Kühne, U., 608
Kühnel, I. S., 622
Kuhnheim, J. S., 348
Kuin, R., 111
Kuiper, W., 776
Kuizenga, D., 144
Kulawik, A., 872
Kulikowski, M., 4
Kullmann, D., 55, 58, 217
Kully, R. M., 631
Kümmel, B., 652
Kundera, Milan, 685
Kuné, C., 629
Kuniczak-Trzcinowicz, A., 868
Kunisch, J., 679
Kunze, K., 585, 627
Kunze, Reiner, 768
Künzig, B., 668, 743
Küper, C., 579
Kuperty-Tsur, N., 112
Kupiec, A., 149
Kupiszewski, W., 855, 857
Küpper, T., 725, 727
Küppers, J., 617
Kupść, A., 849
Kürenberger (Der), 619
Kürnberger, Ferdinand, 681, 705, 711
Kuropka, N., 645
Kuryłowicz, J., 221
Kurz, Isolde, 708
Kurzová, H., 23
Kurzowa, Z., 866
Kushner, E., 173
Kusinowa, I., 865
Kusmenko, J., 818
Kuśniewicz, A., 862, 871
Küster, U., 662
Küsters, R., 596
Kuszmider, B., 39, 49
Kuzniar, A., 701
Kvia, K., 194
Kvillerud, R., 818
Kwaterko, J., 184
Kwon, S.-H., 744, 745
Kyrklund, Willy, 840


Laage, K. E., 750
Laan, J. M. van der, 671
Labanyi, J., 280
Labaye, P., 706
Labbé, A., 53
Labé, Louise, 92, 111
Laberge, Marie, 184, 185
Labisch, A., 736
La Boétie, Etienne de, 92, 113
Labory, G., 82, 85

Labrador Herraiz, J. J., 234, 235
Labraña Barrero, S., 327, 328
Labriola, A., 452
Labrousse, E., 147
La Bruyère, Jean de, 133, 145, 146
La Calprenède, Gautier de Costes de, 124
Lacan, Jacques, 32, 159, 266, 283, 285, 368, 526, 730
Lacarra, M. J., 233, 236
Lacarra Lanz, E., 233, 252
Lacasa, Cristina, 291
Lacassagne, M., 74, 75, 76
La Châtre, E. de, 119
Lachet, C., 82
Lachmann, R., 870
Lacombe, A., 188
Lacoste, C., 155
Lacoste, J., 668, 743
Lacoue-Labarthe, P., 694
Lacour, C., 42
Lacroix, D. W., 215
Lacrosil, Michèle, 197
Lacy, N. J., 80
Ladegaard, H. J., 798
Ladhams, J., 317
Ladron de Guevara Mellado, P. L., 509
Laederach, Jürg, 768
Laenzlinger, C., 23
Laerkesen, I., 804
La Fare-Alais, G., 208
La Fayette, M.-M. P. de la V., comtesse de, 120, 137, 138
La Feria, M., 474
Laferrière, Dany, 177, 192
Lafitte, J., 204, 206, 207, 208
Lafon, D., 184
Lafont, N., 201, 211, 212
Lafont, R., 52, 215
La Fontaine, Jean de, 122, 140
Laforest, M., 48
Laforet, Carmen, 282, 283
Lafrance, G., 190
Lagarde, F., 131
Lagerholm, P., 813
Lagerkvist, Pär, 829, 832, 834, 840
Lagerlöf, Petrus, 819
Lagerlöf, Selma, 806, 822, 826, 829, 835, 837
Lagerström, M., 829
La Gioia, V., 237
Lago, S., 354
Lago Garabatos, J., 41
Lagorgette, D., 88
Lagos, Concha, 291
LaGuardia, D., 72
Lagueunière, F., 41

Lahiri, A., 17
Lai, P., 428
Laidlaw, J., 75
Laitenberger, H., 275
Lalander, A., 829
Laliberté, Y., 190
Lam, A., 870
Lama López, M. X., 329, 334
Laman, B., 768
Lamarque, Vivian, 512
Lamartine, Alphonse de, 157, 169, 170
Lamas Carvajal, Valentín, 336
Lambert, A. T. de M. de C., marquise de, 139
Lambertenghi, L., 473
Lambruschini, R., 472
Lamela Villaravid, C., 329
Lamennais, Félicité de, 167, 170
Lamiroy, B., 22
Lämmert, E., 879
Lamontagne, A., 190
La Mothe le Vayer, François de, 149
La Moussaye, F. de G. de M., baron de, 138
Lamport, F. J., 671
Lamprecht (*Pfaffe*), 607, 610
Lana, G., 441
Lancellotti, G., 476
Lancelot, Claude, 144
Lancetti, Vincenzo, 480
Land, R., 789
Landa, A., 883
Lander, Jeannette, 768
Landes, C., 202
Landfester, U., 717
Landgren, B., 832
Landheer, R., 44
Landi, P., 481
Landi, S., 454
Landini, P., 388
Landolfi, G., 507, 519
Landoni, E., 384, 488
Landqvist, H., 814
Landry, G., 193
Landry, K., 190
Landsberger, F., 663
Landshuter, S., 731
Lanfranc, 4
Lanfranchi, M., 431
Lang, Fritz, 750
Lång, H., 827
Lang, Jürgen, 21
Langås, U., 808
Langdal, J., 806
Langdon, H., 265
Lange, H., 670
Lange, K.-P., 581
Lange, S., 754, 818

Langer, G., 722
Langer, U., 118, 120
Langgässer, Elisabeth, 768
Langille, E., 184
Längle, Ulrike, 768
Langlois, E., 88
Langner, Ilse, 769
Langner, M. M., 732
Langslow, D., 24
Lanly, A., 25
Lanning, R., 142
Lannoy, Juliana Cornelia de, 784, 785
Lanslots, I., 506
Lanson, G., 98
Lanuzza, S., 522
Lanza, A., 396
Lanza Tomasi, G., 483
Lapesa, R., 218
Lapointe, Paul-Marie, 192
La Porta, C., 483
La Porta, F., 505
Laporte, D., 168
Laqueur, T., 601
Lara, la Contessa (E. C. Mancini), 480
Larade, Bertrand, 116
Laragione, Lucía, 352
Laraway, D., 350, 358
Larbaud, Valéry, 331
Lardon, S., 95, 103, 106, 108, 117
Largier, N., 605, 625, 656, 879
Larivaille, P., 439
Larjavaara, M., 39
La Roche, Sophie von, 662, 677, 683, 710
La Rochefoucauld, François, duc de, 119, 120, 138, 139, 145, 146, 698
Larochelle, C., 184
La Roque, G., 34
Larra, Mariano José de, 275
Larraínzar, Enriqueta, 342
Larraínzar, Ernestina, 342
Larrea, Juan, 259, 261, 263, 286, 288
Larrère, C., 152
Larreta, Enrique Rodríguez, 340, 341
Larriba, E., 255
L'Arronge, Adolf, 712
Larsen, A., 97
Larsen, E. Vive, 802
Larsen, F., 801
Larsen, P. S., 826
Larsmo, Ola, 834, 840
Larson, C., 347
Larson, R., 380
Larsson, J., 811, 838

Lartiga, H. [P. Lartigue], 207
La Rubia-Prado, F., 276
Larue, A., 133
LaRue, Monique, 184
Laskowska, M., 866
Lasnier, Rina, 192
Lasocińska, E., 865
Lassabatere, T., 75
Lassailly, Charles, 153
Lassberg, Joseph Freiherr von, 717
Lastarria, José Victorino, 341
Lastraioli, C., 438
Łaszewski, B. T., 866
Lathers, M., 160
La Tour Landry, Geoffroy de, 109
Latrouitte Armstrong, C., 54
Lattarulo, L., 471
Laube, Heinrich, 711
Lauer, G., 754
Laufhütte, H., 730
Laugaa, M., 136
Lauge Jansen, H., 265
Laumonier, P., 104
Launay, M. de, 743
Laurén, C., 815
Laurence of Durham, 7
Laurenson, H., 267
Laurent, F., 156
Laurent, J.-P., 207
Laurent, R., 18, 313
Lauretta, E., 497
Laurey, G., 816
Lauridsen, H., 803
Laurie, I. S., 74, 214
Laurin, M., 189
Lauter-Müller, W., 743
Lauth, R., 687
Lautréamont, Isadore Ducasse, comte de, 179, 263
Lauwers, P., 16, 31
Laux, C., 204, 206, 208
Lavagnoli, Antonio, 465
Lavalade, Y., 211
LaValva, M. P., 445
LaValva, R., 493
Lavater, Johann Caspar, 662
Lavenia, V., 362
Lavocat, F., 143
Lavoie, L., 184
Lawrance, J., 244, 306
Lawton, D., 883
Lazard, M., 98, 112
Lazard, S., 389
Lăzăroiu, A., 531
Lazzarini, L., 486
Lazzerini, L., 216, 421
Lea, A. E., 556
Leanti, Giuseppe, 465

Leão, José Joaquim de Campos v. Qorop-Santo
Léard, J.-M., 41
Le Besgue. J.-C., 115
Leblanc, A., 187
Leblanc, J., 33
LeBlanc, R., 184
Le Brun, Charles, 122
Le Brun, J., 137
Lecco, M., 90
Lechat, D., 75
Lechoń, Jan, 861, 870
Leckius, Ingemar, 840
Le Clerc, Jean, 120, 121
LeClercq, Chrestien, 121
Le Clézio, Jean-Marie, 177–78
Lecoq, J.-F., 145, 146
Lecoy, F., 65
Lecuppre, G., 6
Ledanff, S., 736
Ledda, G., 401
Ledgeway, A., 373, 390
Ledin, P., 814
Le Draoulec, A., 37
Leduc, Violette, 178
Lee Six, A., 287
Lee, M. L., 179
Lee, M., 669
Leemans, I., 784
Leerssen, J., 145
Leeuw, R. H. van der, 21
Leeuwen, Jan van, 626
Lefebvre, A.-M., 160, 161
Lefebvre, C., 47
Lefebvre, J. P., 762
Lefere, R., 362
Lefeuvre, F., 41
Le Fèvre, Jean, 72, 88
Le Fèvre de la Borderie, Guy, 94
Lefèvre d'Etaples, Jacques, 108, 109
Leffler, Anne Charlotte, 829
Le Franc, Martin, 90
Lefter, I. B., 541
Legeżyńska, A., 871, 872
Legg, S., 775
Léglu, C., 213
Legrand, J., 724
Legros, A., 101
Leguay, T., 30, 42
Lehman, K., 340
Lehmann, A. J., 757
Lehmann, W. P., 571, 690
Lehmberg, M., 573, 574
Lehtimäki, P., 816
Leibniz, Gottfried Wilhelm, 146
Leidner, A. C., 677
Leimbach, C., 673
Leiras Pulpeiro, Manuel, 336
Leiren, T., 807

Leisewitz, Johann Anton von, 662
Leisinger, U., 679
Leiss, E., 578
Leistner, A., 670
Leistner, B., 669, 754, 758
Leistner, M.-V., 746
Leite, M. Q., 309, 310
Leitgeb, C., 730
Lejárraga, M. de la O., v. María Martínez de la Sierra
Le Jeune, Paul, 121, 192
Lelouch, C., 142
Lem, S., 871
Lema, J., 884
Lemaire des Belges, Jean, 94, 114
Le Maistre, Antoine, 119
Le Maistre de Sacy, Isaac, 119
Lemebel, Pedro, 346, 354
Lemée, P. Steensbech, 803
Lemke, A. W., 685
Lemnius, Simon, 641
Le Moyne, Pierre, 121, 145
Lenartowicz, Teofil, 866
Lenau, Nikolaus, 707, 709, 713, 739
Lenbach, Franz, 738
Lence-Santar, Eduardo, 336
Lenclos, Ninon de, 139
Lendinara, P., 3
Leñero, Vicente, 347
Lenerz, J., 579
Leng, R., 598
Lengauer, H., 716
Lenk, E., 721
Lenk, U., 383
Lenormand, Henri-René, 279
Le Nôtre, André, 122
Lenz, B., 579
Lenz, Hans, 624
Lenz, Hermann, 769
Lenz, Jakob Michael Reinhold, 677–78, 719
Lenzi, A., 473
Lenzini, L., 507, 511, 517
León, María Teresa, 281, 286
Léonard, J. L., 45
Léonard, M., 162
Leonardi, C., 597
Leonardi, L., 436
Leonardo da Vinci, 471, 476, 479
Leonardy, E., 122
Leonelli, G., 509
Leonzio Pilato, 430
Leopardi, Giacomo, 444, 460, 465, 470, 472, 480–88, 495, 503, 508, 509, 514, 515, 517, 525, 526

Leopold, Jan Hendrik, 789
Lepage, Y. G., 77
Lepage, Y., 190
Lepeley, O., 354
Lepelley, R., 45
Lepschy, G., 373, 882
Lerchner, K., 628
Leri, C., 489
Le Rider, J., 669, 743, 747
Lermen, B., 757
Lerousseau, A., 770
Leroux, Pierre, 171
Leroy-Turcan, I., 16
Léry, Jean de, 94
Lesage, Alain-René, 117
Lesaulnier, J., 119
Lescarbot, Marc, 121, 144, 192
Lesclache, Louis de, 139
Lesfargues, B., 211
Leshock, D. B., 63, 64
Leśmian, Bolesław, 870
Lessa, Bia, 367
Lessing, Gotthold Ephraim, 659, 678, 686, 710
Lestringant, F., 93, 94, 144, 157
Leszczyński, Z., 850, 855
Letaldus, 4
Lettinck, N., 778
Letts, J., 137
Leuchtenberger, K., 767
Leuschner, P.-E., 462
Leuvensteijn, A. van, 783
Levarie, S., 217
Levasseur, J., 186
Lévêque, L., 155
Levi, Carlo, 498, 509, 512
Levi, Primo, 509, 512–13
Levi Momigliano, L., 454
Lévi-Strauss, Claude, 37
Levin, D. J., 716, 750
Levinas, E., 180
Levine, J. M., 141
Levine, M. G., 863
Levine, P., 414
Levy, B. J., 66
Levy, Sarah (Itzig), 679
Lewald, Fanny, 705, 706, 710, 711, 716
Lewan, B., 824
Lewin, A., 870
Lewis, B. L., 363
Lewis, C., 761
Lewis, C. S., 862
Lewis, D. M., 561
Lewis, H. D., 169
Lewis, P., 85
Lewis, Saunders, 563
Lewis, W. R., 564
Leydi, R., 457
Leyenberger, G., 147

Leyser, C., 9
Lezama Lima, José, 356
L'Hérault, P., 189
L'Huillier, M., 35
Lhuyd, Edward, 561
Liala (A. Negretti Cambiasi), 497
Líbano Zumalacárregui, A., 220
Liberatori Prati, E., 421
Liberek, J., 850
Lichański, J. Z., 864
Lichtenberg, Georg Christoph, 662, 678, 685, 770
Lichtveld v. Helman
Liciński, Ludwig Stanisław, 868
Lick, J., 713
Lida, M. R., 247
Lie, Jonas, 804, 807
Lieber, M., 878
Liebregts, P., 423
Liedke Konow, P., 692
Lienert, E., 587, 609
Lieskounig, J., 754
Lifshitz, F., 4
Liliencron, Detlev von, 710
Lilja, E., 811
Lillo Redonet, F., 330
Limorti, P., 306
Linari, F., 511
Lindau, Paul, 712
Lindbach, K., 804
Lindberg, I., 815
Lindberg, U., 834, 838
Lindberger, Ö., 837, 840
Linde, Gunnel, 835
Linde, S. B., 856
Linde, U., 828, 839, 840, 882
Lindegren, Erik, 828, 832
Lindemann, M., 656
Linder, E., 720
Lindgren, Astrid, 834, 835, 836, 840–41
Lindgren, B., 810, 819
Lindner, Albert, 712
Lindner, J. G., 682
Lindon, J. M. A., 459, 468, 479, 487
Lindorm, Erik, 841
Lindquist, H., 820
Lindqvist, K., 821
Lindström, A., 812
Lindström, J., 812
Lindstrom, N., 371
Linell, P., 814
Lines, D. A., 6
Linhart, A., 740
Link, J., 694, 744
Linke, H., 6, 629
Linke, L.-P., 747
Linnaeus, Carl, 821, 824

Linneberg, A., 805
Lipinski, K., 714
Lipold, G., 570
Lipperheide, C., 742
Lippi, E., 427
Lippmann, F., 466
Lipsius, Justus, 657, 783
Lipska, E., 871
Lipski, J. L., 228
Lispector, Clarice, 371
Lispector, Elisa, 370
Littlejohns, R., 681
Littler, M., 706
Liuccio, G., 439
Liutprand of Cremona, 4
Livbjerg, I., 803
Liver, R., 551, 880
Livingston, P., 831
Livy, 142, 248, 430, 452, 648
Lizinski, B., 636
Lizundia, J. L., 207
Ljung, P. E., 838
Ljung Svensson, A.-S., 842
Ljungberg, C. J., 838
Llach, S., 297
Llamazares, Julio, 282
Llandygai (William Williams), 561
Lleucu Llwyd, 557
Llew Llwyfo (Lewis William Lewis), 564
Llorens, I., 355
Llorens, R. F., 274, 883
Lloyd, A. L., 573
Lloyd, D. M., 562
Lloyd, P. M., 13, 218
Lloyd, P., 882
Lloyd, R., 156
Lloyd Edwards, G., 558
Lloyd-Morgan, C., 560
Lluch, E., 254
Llull, Ramon, 301, 303, 304
Llwyd, A., 563
Llwyd, Morgan, 561
Llywelyn Goch ap Meurig Hen, 557
Llywelyn, Robin, 563
Lobsien, E., 682
Locatelli, A., 707
Loch, E., 863
Lochhead, Liz, 722
Locke, John, 145, 486
Locklin, B. S., 351
Loda, R., 445
Lodares, J. R., 219
Lodge, A., 48
Loest, Erich, 756
Löffler, H., 601
Löfgren, M., 843
Lofsvold, L. A., 825

Lohenstein, Daniel Caspar von, 650, 658
Lohmann, G., 701
Loi Corvetto, I., 385, 392
Lollini, M., 483
Lomazzo, G. P., 424
Lombardi, A., 214, 373, 391, 472
Lombardi, M. C., 837
Lombardi, M. M., 481
Lombardo, G., 413
Lombart, N., 95
Lombnaes, A., 804
Lombroso, C., 276
Lomholt, K., 802
Lomiento, L., 514
Lomonaco, F., 488
Lomonosov, M. V., 575
Lonardi, G., 515
Londero, B., 474
Lönegren, H., 827
Long, J., 766
Longa, V. M., 322, 324
Longfellow, Henry, 788
Longhi, S., 523
Longnon, A., 45
Longo, G., 495
Longo, G. O., 498, 511, 522
Longo, M. L., 193
Longoni, A., 506
Lönnroth, L., 821
Lønstad, F., 808
Loosjes, Adriaan, 787
Looy, Jacobus van, 789
Looze, L. de, 239
Lope Blanch, J. M., 231
Lopes, A. C. M., 877
Lopes, R. E. V., 313
López, A., 332, 333, 335
López, C. E., 265, 278
López, E., 334
López, F., 255
López, I. J., 320
López, I. M., 359, 360
López, J. R., 266
López, T., 330
López, Vicente Fidel, 342
López Abente, Gonzalo, 330
López de Ayala, Pero, 220, 238, 241, 242
López de Baian, Afonso, 331
López Bobo, M. J., 221
López-Casanova, Arcadio, 336
López Casas, M. M., 307
López del Castillo, L., 297
López Castro, A., 246, 251
López Cruz, H. J., 356, 361
López Dávalos, Ruy, 244
López Degregori, C., 362
López Estrada, F., 250
López-García, A., 227

López de Gómara, Francisco, 101
López Martínez, M. S., 320, 322, 324
López-Mejía, A., 355
López Mena, S., 359
López Morales, H., 228
López Mozo, Jerónimo, 292, 295
López Nieto, J. C., 246
López Pacheco, Jesús, 282
López Parada, E., 344
López Serrano, F., 278
López Valero, I. M. M., 249
López Varela, E., 334
López-Vega, Martín, 289
López-Vidriero, M.-L., 253
Loporcaro, M., 19, 389
Loranger, Jean-Aubert, 192
Lorant, A., 160, 164
Lorenczuk, A., 686
Lorentzen, L. R., 35
Lorenz, O., 703
Lorenzetti, L., 458
Lorenzini, N., 470, 484, 502
Lorenzo, E., 226
Lorenzo, G., 322
Lorenzo, R., 321, 332, 882
Lorenzo Gradín, P., 331
Lorenzo Suárez, A. M., 882
Lorkowski, P. W., 768
Lorm, Hieronymus, 740
Lorrain, Claude, 122, 743
Los Arcos, Countess of, 257
Losada Goya, José Manuel, 122
Losada Soto, R., 319
Losch, B., 725
Lösel, F., 740
Löser, F., 624, 625, 627
Loskoutoff, Y., 102
Losonsky, M., 696
Losse, D. N., 101
Loster-Schneider, G., 706, 726
Lotichius Secundus, Petrus, 638, 642
Lotko, E., 858
Lotman, Y., 336
Lötmarker, L., 814
Lottes, W., 725
Louis the German (*Emperor*), 600
Louis IX (*King of France, Saint*), 82, 154
Louis XI (*King of France*), 85
Louis XIV (*King of France*), 121, 130, 133, 139, 141, 145
Louis-Philippe I (*King of France*), 160
Louise de Savoie, 98
Loureiro, A.-G., 256
Loutchitskaja, S., 67
Loutchitskaja, S., 7

Louvat, B., 99
Louvois, F. M. le T, marquis de, 142
Loveling, Virginie, 786, 791
Lovinescu, M., 547
Lowe, J., 285
Lowe, K. J. P., 424
Lowsky, M., 749
Loy, Rosetta, 505
Lozano Marco, M. A., 274, 275
Lubar, R. S., 264
Lubaszenska, A., 874
Lubelczyk, Jakub, 864
Lubkiewicz-Urbanowicz, T., 873
Lubomirski, Karl, 769
Lubomirski, Stanisław Herakluisz, 864, 865
Lucamante, S., 521
Lucan, 6, 180, 415
Lucarelli, Carlo, 384
Lucarini, A., 383
Lucebert, 792
Lucena, Juan de, 250
Lucentini, F., 475
Lucía Megías, J. M., 238, 241, 246, 247
Luciani, S., 516
Lucini, Gian Pietro, 512
Lucken, C., 62, 99
Lucretius, 101, 106
Łuczkowski, T., 866
Ludewig, A., 758
Lüdke, H., 35
Ludolphe de Saxe, 89
Ludorowski, L., 868
Lüdtke, H., 15
Ludwig (*prince of Anhalt-Köthen*), 653
Ludwig VI (*Landgrave of Hessen-Darmstadt*), 652
Ludwig, K., 710
Ludwig, Otto, 739
Ludwig, P., 719
Ludwig, W., 638, 643
Luehrs-Kaiser, K., 758
Luengo, E., 354
Luff, R., 593, 619
Lugones, N. A., 236
Lugowska, J., 862
Lugowski, C., 618
Lühe, I. von der, 726
Luján Atienza, Ángel Luis, 290
Lukacher, M., 168
Lukács, Georg, 372, 674
Lukas, V. A., 701
Lulofs, F., 778
Lumsden-Kouvel, A., 268
Luna, Álvaro de, 249

Lunadei, A., 240
Lund, A. K., 803
Lund, J., 799
Lund, K., 802
Lund, Thure Erik, 808
Lundberg, B., 841
Lunden, Eldrid, 808
Lundgren, Max, 835
Lundkvist, Artur, 832, 833
Lunetta, L., 437
Luongo, S., 234
Lupa, Krystian, 758
Luperini, R., 491, 498, 499, 504, 525
Luporini, C., 483, 485
Luque, Aurora, 289
Lurati, O., 382
Luscher, J.-M., 38
Luserke, M., 665, 667
Lusignan, S., 31
Łuskina, E., 863
Luther, Martin, 93, 102, 574, 637, 639, 643–45, 648, 707, 714
Luti, G., 417, 502
Lütteken, L., 679
Lutz, B., 667
Lutz, E. C., 591, 607, 627, 882
Lutze, P. C., 768
Luukkainen, M., 775
Luzi, Mario, 406, 487, 503, 507, 510, 513
Luzio, Alessandro, 482
Lybeck, Mikael, 827, 841
Lyche, C., 47
Lyngfelt, B., 812
Lyons, J. D., 147
Lysander, Per, 836


Maag, K., 645
Maas, N., 787
Maaz, W., 591
Maazaoui, A., 130
Mac- v. also Mc-
MacDonald, A. A., 213
MacDonald, R., 464
Mach, W., 871
Macha, J., 580, 878
Machado, Antonio, 232, 235, 260, 261, 262, 265, 272, 277
Machado, Dyonelio, 372
Machado, M. P., 314
Machado, Manuel, 259
Machado de Assis, Joaquim Maria, 366, 367
Machalski, H., 861
Machaut, Guillaume de, 75, 77
Maché, U., 658

Machiavelli, Niccolò, 85, 100, 424, 436, 437, 448, 452–53, 472, 485, 698
Machner, B., 724
Maciejewski, Z., 861
Mackert, C., 592, 607
Mackie, A., 517
MacLennan, O. C. L., 188
MacLeod, C., 686
Macrì, O., 517
Macrin, Jean Salmon, 105
Macrobius, 3, 87
Mączyński, J., 850
Maddalon, M., 381, 382
Maddox, D., 62, 83
Mádl, A., 718, 739
Madog ap Maredudd, 556
Madroñal Durán, A., 260
Madsen, B. Nistrup, 798, 800
Madsen, K., 809
Mæhlum, B., 801
Maerlant, Jacob van, 779
Maertz, G., 153
Maestro, M. P. del, 276
Maeterlinck, Maurice, 279
Maeztu, Ramón de, 260
Maffei, Clara, 489
Maffei, Scipione, 458, 459, 465
Maffia, D., 521
Magaldi, S., 369
Magalhães Bulhões, M., 370
Magalotti, L., 136
Magdalena Sybilla (*Queen of Denmark*), 652
Maggi, A., 368
Maggi, Carlo Maria, 465
Maggi, Carlos, 364
Maglio, G., 441
Magnan, R., 74
Magni, E., 22
Magny, Olivier de, 94, 105
Magrelli, Valerio, 513
Magrini, G., 487
Magris, C., 500
Magritte, René, 179, 263
Magro, F., 506
Mahal, G., 593
Mahé, N., 115
Maher, M., 736
Maheux-Forcier, L., 186
Mahieu, R., 162, 163
Mahl, B., 670
Mahler, Gustav, 742
Mahler, K., 718
Mai, A.-M., 808
Maia, M., 314
Maiden, M., 27, 374, 527, 532
Maier, C. T., 8
Maier, C., 277
Maillard, J.-F., 95

Maillet, Andrée, 186, 192
Maillet, Antonine, 184, 193
Mainer, J. C., 281
Maiorano, Gaetano (Caffarelli), 460
Maiorescu, T., 527
Mairet, Jean, 123
Maj, B., 490
Majchrowski, Z., 869
Majda, J., 868
Majewska, M., 848, 850
Majkowska, G., 854
Makowiecki, A. Z., 862
Makowski, S., 865, 866, 873
Makward, C. P., 198
Małachowska, M., 852
Mălăcioiu, I., 547
Malato, E., 456, 468
Malchow, T. B., 771
Malczewski, A., 865
Malebranche, Nicolas, 120, 147, 149
Malec, T., 851
Malenínská, J., 584
Maler, A., 717
Malerba, Luigi, 513
Maleuvre, D., 162
Malfitano, A., 426
Malgaretti, G., 522
Malherbe, François de, 141
Malinkowski, B., 762
Malinowska, E., 853, 854
Malipiero, Gian Francesco, 476
Maliszewski, K., 872
Malkiel, Y., 13, 25, 27
Malkin, J. R., 756
Malkin, S., 167
Mallarmé, Stéphane, 502, 692
Mallén, E., 21
Mallet, N., 169
Mall-Grob, B., 701, 747
Mallo, Maruja, 261
Malm, A. F., 809
Malm, M., 811, 823
Malmberg, Stig, 835
Malmgren, S.-G., 813
Malmio, K., 823
Malory, Sir Thomas, 437
Maltese, D., 428
Maltese, E. V., 428
Mälzer, A.-K., 24
Mamede, S., 329
Mamet, David, 294
Mammana, G., 384
Man, Herman de, 790
Man, J. de, 785
Man, Paul de, 695
Mańczak, W., 17, 25, 221, 848, 853, 860
Mańczak-Wohlfeld, E., 858

Mancaş, M., 527
Manche, F., 451
Mancho, M. J., 220
Mancini v. Lara
Mancini, A. N., 439
Mancini, M., 217, 878
Mandach, A. de, 53
Mande, Hendrik, 626
Mandelartz, M., 673
Mandel'štam, Osip, 762
Mandeville, Sir John, 635, 648
Mandolini Pesaresi, M., 482
Mañer, Salvador José, 257
Månesköld-Öberg, I., 828
Manet, Edouard, 166
Mangado Martínez, J., 878
Manganelli, Giorgio, 691, 758
Manghi, M., 462
Man-Ghyu, P., 49
Mangione, A., 443
Mangolini, M., 396
Mangoni, L., 501
Manicom, Jacqueline, 197
Manilla, Antonio, 289
Maninchedda, P., 882
Maniu, Adrian, 541
Mankell, Henning, 833
Mann, E., 750
Mann, N., 432
Mann, S., 148
Mann, Thomas, 668, 674, 686, 743, 744, 746, 750, 751, 767, 837
Mannarino, L., 464
Manno, G., 35, 48
Mannoni, O., 758
Manolescu, F., 547
Manolescu, N., 545, 546, 548
Manoliu, M. M. [M. Manoliu-Manea], 23
Manotta, M., 485, 502
Manrique, J., 346
Manrique, Jorge, 244
Manrique, Pedro, 245
Manrique, Rodrigo, 245
Manso, C., 275
Manso, Leonor, 352
Mantegna, Andrea, 271
Mantero, A., 95
Mantovani, T., 80, 114
Manu, E., 546
Mănucă, D., 545
Manuel Antonio v. Pérez Sánchez
Manuel Comnenus (*Emperor of Constantinople*), 558
Manutius, Aldus, 647
Manza, T., 493
Manzanaro Blasco, J. M., 306
Manzano, F., 46

Manzoni, Alessandro, 384, 477, 478, 480, 488–92, 506
Manzoni. Francesca, 465
Manzo-Robledo, F., 359
Mao Tse Tung, 766
Maolalaigh, R. O., 881
Marabini, C., 493
Maraini, D., 473
Marana, G. P., 139
Maranta, Roberto, 439
Maranzana, E., 18
Marazzi, M., 494
Marazzini, C., 374
Marbán, J., 365
Marcato, G., 388
Marcelli, N., 449
March, Ausiàs, 302, 305, 307
Marchal, M., 140
Marchal, R., 139, 881
Marchal, S., 158
Marchand, J.-J., 500
Marchant, E., 352
Marchant Lazcano, Jorge, 346
Marchegiani, J., 483
Marchello-Nizia, C., 31
Marcheschi, D., 475
Marchessault, Jovette, 186
Marchetti, L. M., 515
Marchi, G. P., 489, 492, 495
Marchi, M., 513
Marchlewitz, I., 767
Marci-Boehncke, G., 739
Marciniak, M., 849
Marco Polo, 471, 635
Marcoin, F., 166
Marcolungo, F. L., 465
Marconi, D., 383
Marcos Álvarez, F. de B., 225
Marcos Marín, F., 219, 237
Marcotte, G., 191
Marcuschi, L. A., 310, 315
Mărdărescu-Teodorescu, M., 531
Marechal, Leopoldo, 348
Marelli, P., 632
Mareş, A., 536
Maresca, Nicolò, 460
Marescalchi, F., 503
Margantin, L., 701
Margaret of Austria, 89
Margaretha Regula, 627
Mărgărit, I., 538
Margarit, Joan, 308
Margetts, J., 612
Margitic, M. R., 126
Margolis, N., 87
Marguerite d'Autriche, 114
Marguerite de Navarre, 92, 97, 98, 109–11, 112, 308
Marguerite de Valois, 98, 113

Maria Elisabeth (*duchess of Schleswig-Holstein*), 652
Mariacher, B., 758
Mariak, L., 856
Mariano, F., 436, 446
Marías, Javier, 286
Mariátegui, José Carlos, 363
Marichal, J., 267
Marichal, P., 45
Marichalar, Antonio, 263
Marichy, C., 208
Marie de France, 50, 57, 63, 64, 86
Marie de l'Incarnation, Mère (Marie Guyard), 120, 191
Marie de' Médici, 98
Marietti, M., 420
Marigold, W. G., 655
Marin, C., 135
Marin, L., 140
Marin, M., 538
Mariner, F., 144
Marinetti, Filippo Tommaso, 513
Marino, A., 548
Marino, E., 437
Mariño, F. M., 632
Marino, G., 136
Mariño Paz, R., 320, 321, 326
Marinoni, M. C., 217
Marinotti, A., 483
Marivaux, Pierre Carlet de Chamblain de, 117, 146, 176
Markefka, M., 585
Marker, F. J., 831
Markgraf, W., 668
Markiewicz, H., 865
Markis, S., 762
Marler, J. C., 89
Marlitt, Eugenie, 705, 710, 711
Mármol, José, 343
Marnette, S., 50, 52
Marol, J.-C., 213
Maron, Monika, 756
Marot, Clément, 80, 92, 94, 105, 107, 108
Marot, Jean, 80, 94, 114
Marotta, G., 18
Marotti, M. O., 506
Marquardt, M., 734
Marque-Pucheu, C., 39
Marquet, J.-F., 170
Márquez, Pedro José, 257
Marquina, Eduardo, 278
Marquis, B., 587
Marres, R., 793
Marri, F., 389
Marsden, R., 2
Marsé, Juan, 286–87
Marsh, L., 103

Marsh Heywood, M., 72
Marshall, C. C., 769
Marshall, J., 732
Marsman, Hendrik, 790, 796
Marson, S., 176
Marsuppini, C., 430
Marszałek, M., 858
Martel, G., 48
Martel, J., 187
Martel, Julián, 340
Martelli, Ludovico, 448
Martelli, M., 396, 449, 478
Martellini, L., 487
Martello, Pier Jacopo, 459
Marth, R., 599
Martí, José, 343.
Marti, M., 474, 484, 486
Martí, S., 303
Martí-Peña, G., 351
Martianus Capella, 5, 602
Martignago, F., 460
Martignoni, C., 506
Martûiz de Resende, Vaasco, 331
Martin le Franc, 32
Martin of Troppau, 623
Martin, A., 677
Martin, C., 63
Martin, Claire, 192
Martin, D., 100, 794
Martin, G., 209
Martin, J., 883
Martin, J. P., 178
Martin, L., 697
Martin, P., 17, 313
Martin, R., 30
Martin-Fugier, A., 153
Martín Gaite, Carmen, 282, 287
Martín González, M. J., 222
Martín Martínez, J., 264
Martín Rodríguez, M., 278
Martín Zorraquino, M. A., 227
Martinazzoli, M., 490
Martineau, A., 72
Martinelli, Vincenzo, 454, 455
Martines, V., 307
Martinet, A., 17, 39, 43
Martinet, J., 43
Martínez, A., 276
Martínez, E. M., 356
Martínez, I., 365
Martínez, J. L., 351
Martínez, M., 588
Martinez, R. L., 418
Martínez, T., 877
Martínez, Z. N., 353
Martínez Aguirre, Carlos, 289, 290
Martínez Alcalde, M. J., 222
Martínez de Ampiés, M., 248
Martínez Bonati, F., 353

Martínez Cachero, J. M., 275
Martínez Carrizales. L., 359
Martínez Celdrán, E., 219
Martínez Estrada, Ezequiel, 340, 346
Martínez-Gil, F., 326, 881, 882
Martínez López, Ramón, 332
Martinez Mata, E., 257
Martínez Mayo, C., 326
Martínez de Olcoz, N., 361
Martínez Pereiro, C. P., 331
Martínez Reverte, Jorge, 284
Martínez Romero, T., 306, 307
Martínez Ruiz, J., 275
Martínez Sierra, G., 278, 279
Martínez de la Sierra, María, 273, 279
Martínez Torrejón, J. M., 250
Marting, D. E., 363
Martinho, F., 314
Martini, Francesco di Giorgio, 432
Martini, M., 444
Martins, C., 310, 877
Martins, F., 317
Martins, Ivan Pedro de, 371
Martinson, Harry, 832, 841
Martinson, Moa, 836, 841
Martorell, Joanot, 305–06, 307
Martos, J. L., 307
Martus, S., 667
Marx, Karl, 477
Marx, W., 560
Mary Stuart (*Queen of Scots*), 124, 137, 722
Maryniakowa, I., 853
März, C., 603, 621
Marzouki, A., 157
Marzys, Z., 30, 32, 34, 46, 882
Masciandoro, F., 448
Maslan, S., 132
Masłowski, M., 869
Masoero, M., 449
Masoliver Ródenas, J. A., 272
Masotti, A., 388
Massarenti, A., 481
Masser, A., 601
Massey, I., 746
Massini-Cagliari, G., 311, 313
Masson, L., 93
Masson, N., 152
Massot, G., 212
Mastretta, Angeles, 360
Mastronardi, M. A., 460
Matala de Mazza, E., 680
Matas, J., 297
Matei, D., 542, 543
Mateo del Pino, A., 354
Mateos, José, 289
Mateus, M. H. M., 312

Matfre Ermengaud, 215
Matheolus, 88
Mathews, H., 268, 269
Mathey-Maille, L., 67
Mathieu, J.-C., 178
Mathieu, M.-J., 43
Mathijsen-Verkooijen, M. T. C., 787
Matilla García del Barrio, Aurelio, 281
Matilla Jimeno, Alfredo, 281
Matilla Jimeno, Aurelio, 281
Matilla Rivas, A., 281
Matos, G., 314
Matos, M. I. S. de, 367
Matossian, C., 171
Matsumura, T., 70
Matt, B. von, 754
Matt, P. von, 729, 734
Mattenklott, G., 666, 668
Matteoni, O., 84
Matter, H., 745
Matthaei, R., 665
Mattheier, K. J., 878
Matthew of Vendôme, 6, 7
Matthew Paris, 8
Matthieu-Castellani, G., 109
Mattioda, E., 459, 461
Mattlar, J., 842
Matto de Turner, Clorinda, 340
Mattsson, P.-O., 840
Mattssons, G., 819
Matuschek, S., 667
Matúsova, J., 584
Matuszewska, P., 864
Matute, Ana María, 282, 287
Mauelshagen, F., 637
Maugham, W. Somerset, 279
Mauguière, B., 185, 186
Maund, K. L., 560
Maupassant, Guy de, 34, 511
Maure Rivas, X., 320
Maurensig, Paolo, 505
Maurer, M., 678
Mauriello, A., 441
Maurizi, F., 244, 251
Mauro, A. M., 530
Mauro, C., 442
Mauro, R., 426
Mauser, P., 583
Mauss, M., 684
Mauthner, F., 742
Max, F. R., 682, 704
Maxence, P., 163
Maximilian I (*Holy Roman Emperor*), 647
Maximilian II (*King of Bavaria*), 713
Maximin, Daniel, 196, 197
May, Karl, 711, 718

Mayans, Gregorio, 254
Mayer, C. A., 108
Mayer, H., 762
Mayer, M., 669, 678
Mayer, R., 571
Mayer, S., 775
Mayhew, J., 289
Mayoral i Marqué, D., 230
Mayr-Harting, H., 597
Mayröcker, Friederike, 769
Mazaheri, J. H., 163
Mazan, A., 858, 874
Mazarin, Jules (cardinal), 134
Mazouer, C., 131
Mazquiarán de Rodríguez, M., 273, 286
Mazur, J., 852
Mazzacurati, G., 438, 468
Mazzarella, Merete, 834, 844
Mazzella, Scipione, 450
Mazzini, Giuseppe, 494
Mazzocchi, G., 265
Mazzoleni, M., 381
Mazzoni, F., 403, 882
Mazzoni, G., 486, 515
Mazzotta, C., 461
Mazzotta, G., 410
Mazzucchelli, P., 500
Mazzucchi, A., 402
Mc- v. also Mac-
McCaffrey, P., 62
McCalla, A., 170
McCash, J. H., 64
McClelland, I. L., 268
McConnell, W., 592, 613
McCracken, P., 58
McCreesh, B., 64
McDonald, W. C., 617
McDonough, C. J., 1, 9
McEachrane, M., 838, 842
McGinn, B., 625
McGinnis, R., 168
McGrath, W. J., 742
McKinley, M. B., 98
McKitterick, R., 597
McLean, K., 168
McLeman-Carnie, J., 157
McManamon, J. M., 431
McMullan, T., 265
McMunn, M. T., 88
McNab, P., 350
McNeer, G., 292
McPherson, K. S., 188
Meacci, G., 517
Mecatti, F., 482
Méchoulan, E., 119, 136
Mechthild von Magdeburg, 624, 625
Mecke, J., 261
Meckelnborg, C., 648

Mecklenburg, N., 714, 723
Meckseper, C., 603
Mecu, N., 546
Meda, G., 489
Mede-Flock, Hanne, 764
Médeiros, M.-T., 85
Medici, Cosimo I de' (*Grand Duke*), 431, 432, 444
Medici, Lorenzo de' (*the Magnificent*), 426, 438
Médicis, Catherine de (*Queen of France*), 137
Medina, A., 290
Medina, R., 358
Medina, V., 260
Medina Granda, R. M., 201
Medina López, J., 227
Medina Urrea, A., 223
Meding, T., 143
Meekins, A. G., 412, 420, 518
Meerbeeck, M. van, 147
Meerhoff, K., 95
Megale, H., 311
Megged, A., 253
Mehl, J. V., 638, 639
Mehlin, H., 838
Mehlin, M., 838
Mehren, Stein, 809
Mehrens, P., 841
Meid, V., 588, 658, 704
Meidal, B., 829, 830, 831, 834
Meier, A., 650, 682, 738
Meier, B., 672
Meier, C., 593, 628, 631, 882
Meier, F., 671
Meier, Gerhard, 769
Meier, J., 572
Meier, M., 751
Meier, N., 720
Meier, S., 688
Meier, T., 587
Meier-Lenz, D. P., 737
Meijer, D., 777
Meilyr ap Gwalchmai, 559
Meilyr Brydydd, 556
Meinderts, A., 796
Meinecke, E., 573
Meinhold, Wilhelm, 718
Meise, H., 652
Meisel, G., 720
Meisl, Karl, 740
Meister, Ernst, 769
Mejía Ruiz, C., 332, 338
Melanchthon, Philipp, 643, 644, 645
Melançon, R., 190
Melander, B., 814
Melani, S., 216
Melani, V., 517
Melberg, A., 695

Melchiori, G.-B., 471
Melchiori, R., 481
Mel'cuk, I., 42
Meldrum Brown, H., 696
Mele, G., 301
Melehy, H., 128
Meléndez, M., 340
Meléndez Valdés, Juan, 268
Melenk, H., 716
Meliga, W., 216
Melis, L., 36
Melkert, H., 633
Mellace, R., 463
Mellet, S., 38
Mellinghoff-Bourgerie, V., 148
Melo Neto, João Cabral de, 367, 368, 369
Melosi, L., 479, 482
Melzi, Francesco, 455
Melzi d'Eril, Francesco, 472
Membrives, Lola, 263
Memmo, F. P., 520
Mena, Juan de, 232, 244
Ménage, G., 16
Ménager, D., 102
Menant, S., 154
Ménard, M., 160
Ménard, P., 89
Menasseh ben Israël (*rabbi*), 777
Mencé-Caster, C., 232
Menchú, Rigoberta, 358
Mendelssohn, Moses, 668, 678–79
Mendes, P. E. L., 316
Mendes-Flohr, P., 742
Méndez, Concha, 278, 290
Méndez, Luz, 347
Méndez, X. A., 326
Méndez Fernández, L., 335
Méndez Ferrín, Xosé Luís, 333, 336
Mendieta, E., 345
Mendiola, P. J., 348
Mendo Ze, C., 47
Mendonça Teles, Gilberto, 369
Mendoza, Íñigo de, v. Santillana
Mendoza, María Luisa, 360
Ménégaldo, S., 77
Meneghetti, M. L., 213, 233, 301
Menéndez Pelayo, M., 232
Menéndez Pidal, R., 16, 27, 218, 234, 235
Mengaldo, P. V., 498
Menges, K., 739, 879
Mengotti-Thouvenin, P., 148
Menichelli, A. M., 428
Menke, H., 636, 779
Menna, M., 426
Mennecke-Haustein, U., 637
Mennel, D. J., 359

Menninghaus, W., 879
Mensa Valls, J., 303
Mentel, J., 574
Mentrup, W., 575
Menzel, T., 848
Mentzel-Reuters, A., 592
Menzer, M. J., 2
Mercado, Tununa, 352
Mercatanti, R., 443
Mercenaro, G., 514
Merceron, J. E., 52, 69
Mercier, A., 189
Merdas, A., 856
Méré, A. G., chevalier de, 139, 146
Merfyn Jones, R., 555
Mérida, R. M., 306
Mérimée, Prosper, 165–66, 271, 278
Merino, Ana, 287, 289, 290
Merino, E. E., 288
Merino, José María, 287
Merisalo, O., 877
Merkel, Inge, 769
Merkù, P., 549
Merlante, R., 410
Merle, R., 206
Merleau-Ponty, M., 499
Merlin, H., 120, 138
Merlin, M., 510
Mermall, T., 264, 273
Mermier, G. R., 215
Mertens, D., 623
Mertens, V., 615, 668
Mesa Gancedo, D., 350
Mesa Toré, José Antonio, 289
Meschinot, Jean, 79
Meschonnic, H., 31, 176
Meshkinfam, S., 99
Messerli. A., 675
Messner, D., 316
Metastasio, Pietro, 457, 460, 463, 465–66
Metge, Bernat, 305, 307
Methuen, C., 434
Métrich, R., 879
Metzeltin, M., 881
Metzger, H.-K., 668
Metzger, V., 178
Metzner, E. E., 602
Mével, J.-P., 42
Mews, C. J., 5
Mews, S., 751
Meyen, Eduard, 746
Meyer, C., 3
Meyer, Conrad Ferdinand, 571, 704, 707, 710, 719, 739
Meyer, E. Y., 728
Meyer, F., 702
Meyer, F., 754

Meyer, H., 592, 594
Meyer, K., 553, 742
Meyer, M., 610
Meyer, S., 745
Meyer, U., 659
Meyer-Drawe, K., 687
Meyer-Lübke, W., 14, 391
Meyern, Johann Wilhelm
  Friedrich von, 679
Meyran, D., 347
Mézières, Philippe de, 75, 76, 83,
  84
Micciché, L., 517
Micha, A., 61
Micha. P., 679
Michael de Leone, 627
Michael, M., 864
Michaelis, L., 696
Michaels, J. E., 766
Michajlov, A. V., 667
Michajłowa, M., 866
Michalik, M., 853
Michalsky, T., 631
Michaud, G., 189
Michaut, Henri, 178
Michaux, Henri, 521
Michel, A., 154, 391
Michel, Jean, 82
Michel, P., 625
Michel-Bechet, A., 209
Michel-Bechet, J., 209
Michelangelo Buonarroti, 412,
  431
Michelet, Jules, 162, 167, 168,
  170, 171
Micheli, Pietro Adamo de', 427
Michelis, A., 514
Michels, S., 35
Michelstaedter, Carlo, 514, 520
Michler, W., 718
Michnik, A., 871
Miciński, Tadeusz, 862, 868
Mickel, E. J., 53, 55
Mickel, Karl, 769
Mickelsen, D. J., 168
Mickiewicz, Adam, 856, 857,
  861, 862, 863, 865, 866–67,
  868, 869
Miconi, A., 517
Middleton, R., 375, 883
Mieczkowska, H., 859
Mieder, W., 746
Miernowski, J., 95
Migliorini Fissi, R., 422
Miglos, D., 262
Miguel Martínez, E. de, 279
Miguel Prendes, S., 250, 308
Míguez, X. A., 335
Míguez Vilas, C., 277
Mihaes, M., 546

Mihăilă, G., 531
Mihm, A., 573, 631
Mihura, Miguel, 279
Mijares, E., 361
Mijnhardt, W., 784
Mikkonen, K., 843
Mikołajczak-Matyja, N., 850
Mikoš, M. J., 856, 864
Milani, F., 465
Milanowski, A., 758
Mileschi, C., 509
Milin, G., 60
Millán, X. M., 332
Milland-Bove, B., 58, 60
Millanes, J. M., 272
Millares, S., 357
Millás, Juan José, 287287
Miller, E., 725, 727
Miller Powell, J., 356
Millet, C., 165
Milli, M., 743
Milli Cassone, Giannina, 469
Milner, M., 162
Miłosz, Czesław, 862, 871, 872,
  873–74
Mimouni, I., 163
Minardi, G., 362
Minde-Poet, G., 697
Minden, M., 704
Mineo, N., 480
Mínguez Arranz, M., 350
Minikowska, T., 850
Minne, Richard, 791
Minogue, V., 180
Minore, R., 484, 486
Minot, L. A., 167
Minulescu, I., 544
Miodek, J., 847, 848, 853
Miodońska-Brookes, E., 868
Miodunka, W. T., 852, 854
Mioni, A., 884
Mioni, M. A., 550
Mioto, C., 313
Mir, Joaquim, 274
Mirabella, M. B., 86
Miralles, C., 307
Miranda, J. G., 263
Miranda Hidalgo, B., 219
Miras, Domingo, 295
Mirianashvili, L., 603
Mirmina, E., 458
Miró, E., 264
Miron, Gaston, 184, 192–93
Miron, P., 544, 547
Mirosław, A., 872
Mirot, L., 45
Mirza, R., 364
Mischì, G., 551
Misiti, N., 381
Missaglia, F., 577

Missinne, L., 790
Misti, N., 383
Mistral, Gabriela, 346, 352, 353
Mitosek, Z., 866
Mitrache, L., 763
Mitterand, H., 161
Mitterer, Felix, 769
Mitu, M., 536
Mitzman, A., 171
Mix, Y.-G., 690, 760
Mizerkiewicz, T., 873
Mizrahi, I., 263, 280, 286
Mjelve, Sigmund, 808, 809
Mjöberg, J., 840
Młynarczyk, E., 850
Moberg, L., 816
Moberg, Vilhelm, 840, 841
Mocciaro, A., 393
Modena, A., 500, 512
Modesti, M., 510, 513
Modiano, Patrick, 178
Modigliani, D., 724
Moeglin, J.-M., 881
Moelleken, W. W., 550
Moering, R., 685
Moeschler, J., 38
Moevs, C., 394
Möhn, D., 581
Mohr-Elfadl, S., 765
Móia, T., 315
Moisan, A., 54
Moisan, P., 154
Moix, Ana María, 282, 284
Molenduk, A., 37
Molière (Jean-Baptiste
  Poquelin), 32, 117, 120, 126,
  127, 133, 511
Molina, Argote de, 241. 242
Molina, C. A., 335
Molina, Silvia, 360
Molina Foix, V., 264
Molina Martínez, J. L., 273
Molina Sánchez, 269
Molinaro, N. L., 289
Molinet, Jean, 78, 79, 80, 94
Molini, Giovanni Claudio, 462
Mölk, U., 202
Moll, A., 299
Molle, J. V., 76
Møller, B., 803
Møller, J., 802
Möller, K.-P., 726
Möller, R., 586
Mollerus, Bernardus, 645
Mollica, M. C. M., 309
Molloy, S., 345, 348
Mommsen, K., 665, 667, 693
Mommsen, M., 667, 693
Mommsen, Theodor, 733
Monachesi, P., 20, 377, 379, 533

Monaco, T., 451
Monaldo, Giuseppe, 471
Moncada, Santiago, 293
Monchard, C., 175, 176
Mondot, J., 668
Mondragón, J. C., 364
Monducci, E., 441
Monette, Madeleine, 193
Monferran, J.-C., 96, 99
Monfrin, J., 82
Mongin, J., 17
Monin, E.-Y., 214
Moniuszko, Stanisław, 856
Monk of Salzburg, 621, 622
Monleón, J. B., 344
Monleón, J., 267
Monluc, Blaise de Lasseran-
    Massencombe, seigneur de,
    112
Monneret, P., 35
Monoliu-Manea, M., 533
Monroe, M., 722
Monson, D., 213
Montagni, B., 468, 469
Montaigne, Michel de, 92, 93,
    97, 99–101, 113, 118, 134,
    141, 144, 146, 150, 681, 698
Montalban, V., 509
Montale, Eugenio, 1, 498, 499,
    500, 501, 502, 503, 514–15,
    517, 522, 526
Montalto, S., 519
Montanari, A., 458
Montaner, A., 234
Montani, A., 510
Montano, A., 435
Montanyà, L., 262
Montbertrand, G., 190
Montbron, Jacquette de, 98
Monteagudo Romero, H., 319,
    320, 321, 327
Monteiro, S., 317
Montemayor, Jorge de, 143
Montenay, Georgette de, 112
Montero, J. M., 361
Montero, Mayra, 358
Montero, Rosa, 280, 288
Montero Cartelle, E., 225
Montero Padilla, J., 275
Monterroso, Augusto, 360
Montersino, M., 495
Montes, C., 351
Montes, S., 34
Montes Huidobro, Matías, 357
Montesquieu, C. de S. de, 146
Montesquieu, Charles Louis,
    151–52
Montfort, C. R., 142
Monti, Vincenzo, 478, 488,
    492–93, 503

Monti Sabia, L., 430
Montmorency, Henri II, duc de,
    136
Montpensier, A.-M.-L.-H.
    d'Orléans, duchesse de, 140
Montrésor, C. de B., comte de,
    119
Montreuil, J.-P., 18
Montreuil, S., 194
Montserrat, A., 299
Moody, M., 354
Moog, Christa, 769
Mora, Constancia de la, 281
Mora, G., 343
Moraes, J. A., 312
Morala Rodríguez, J. R., 220
Moralejo, J. J., 334, 336
Morales, C. J., 343, 353
Morales, T., 259
Morales-Front, A., 882
Morante, Elsa, 497, 515–16
Morardo, Gaspare, 455
Moraru, A., 536
Moravia, Alberto, 497, 516
Morawe, B., 737
Morawiec, A., 873
More, H., 730
Moreau, M.-L., 43
Moreau, T., 42
Moreh, S., 251
Moreira, B., 315
Morel, B. A., 276
Morel, R., 137
Morelli, Francesco, 462
Morelli, G., 457, 512
Morelli Timpanaro, M. A., 454
Morello, A. A., 112, 139
Morello, N., 176
Moren Vesaas, Halldis, 842
Morena Villa, José, 259, 261,
    262, 263
Moreno, Á., 317
Moreno, M., 246
Moreno Turner, F., 364
Morera, M., 226
Moreschini, C., 481
Moret, P., 139
Moretti, D., 501
Moretti, M., 473
Moretti, V., 495
Moretti, Vito, 516
Moretti, W., 519
Morgan ap Rhys, 557
Morgan, L. Z., 69, 83
Morgan, Mihangel, 563
Morgan, Rh., 562
Morgenthaler, E., 579
Morgner, Irmtraud, 769
Mörike, Eduard, 706, 710,
    739–40

Morín, F., 357
Morin, Y.-C., 96
Morinet, C., 34
Moritz, Karl Philipp, 664, 681,
    686, 711, 716, 720
Moritz, R., 771
Mörk, Jacob, 823
Mormando, F., 436, 437
Mornay, Philippe de, 97
Mörnsjö, M., 812
Moro, C., 428
Moroianu, C., 536, 537
Moroncini, F., 482
Morote, H., 362
Morreale, M., 220, 232
Morris, Anne Marie, 333
Morris, B., 823
Morris, C. B., 265, 266, 270
Morris, L., 757
Morris, Lewis, 561
Morris, M. W., 52
Morris, Richard, 561
Morris Jones, B., 553
Morris-Jones, John, 562
Morrison, J., 659, 664
Morrison, Toni, 343
Morselli, Guido, 516
Morsztyn, Hieronimus, 863, 865
Morsztyn, J. A., 864
Morsztyn, Z., 863
Moruzzi, Gaetana, 455
Mosca, G., 452
Moscherosch, Johann Michael,
    657
Moscoso Mato, E. M., 321
Möseneder, K., 651
Moser, F. C. von, 151
Moser, M., 859
Moses de Leon, 94
Moshövel, A., 621
Mosley, J., 93
Mosteiro Louzao, M., 222, 224
Moszyński, L., 850, 855
Mota, C., 238, 244
Motapanyane, V., 534, 878
Motsch, W., 577
Motta, U., 451
Mottausch, K.-H., 572, 573, 582
Motte Fouqué, Friedrich de la,
    686–87, 697
Mouchard, C., 107, 161
Moücke, Francesco di
    Giovacchino, 454
Moudileno, L., 197, 198
Mougeon, F., 48
Moulaison, G., 184
Moulin, B., 209
Moulin-Fankhänel, C., 588
Mouly, C., 208
Moure, J. L., 241

Moure, T., 324
Moustaki, A., 49
Moya Corral, J. A., 231
Mozart, Wolfgang Amadeus, 713
Możejko, E., 873 Mrazek, H., 852
Mrkonjic, T., 431
Mrożek, S., 874
Mucci, Velso, 516
Mucha, B., 867
Mühlbach, Luise (*pseudonym of* Mundt, Clara), 705, 740
Mühlethaler, J.-C., 76, 79
Mühlherr, A., 633
Muhs, R., 722, 725
Mujdei, C., 538
Mujica Láinez, Manuel, 350
Müling, Johannes Adelphus, 640
Mulisch, Harry, 793
Muljačić, Ž., 28
Müllenbrock, H.-J., 727
Müller, A. L., 315
Müller, Adam, 680
Müller, B., 224
Müller, Bodo 25
Muller, C., 35, 41
Müller, D., 730
Müller, F., 603
Müller, G., 668, 675
Müller, H. M., 757
Müller, H., 715
Müller, Heiner, 765, 767, 769–70
Müller, Herta, 708
Müller, J.-D., 591, 618, 619, 883
Müller, Johann Gottwerth, 679
Müller, S., 592, 607
Müller, U., 589, 592, 603, 613, 738
Müller, W., 873
Müller, Wilhelm, 709, 746
Müller-Mertens, E., 597
Müller-Michaels, H., 726
Müller Niebala, D., 675
Müller-Richter, K., 708
Müller-Seidel, W., 675
Müller-Tragin, C., 700
Mulnich, S., 353
Mulsow, M., 660
Mundó, A., 301
Mundt v. also Mühlbach
Mundt, H., 769
Mundt, L., 641, 646
Mundt, Theodor, 713
Muñiz Muñiz, M. de la N., 481
Munk, I., 803
Muñoz, Luis, 289
Muñoz, R., 248
Muñoz Molina, Antonio, 284, 288

Münster, A., 743
Muntaner, Ramon, 305, 306
Munteanu, E., 530, 538
Munteanu, G., 545
Munteanu, I., 547
Mura, A., 162
Mura Porcu, A., 392
Murakawa, C. A. A., 311
Murat, F. de, 212
Muratore, M. J., 130
Muratori, E., 217
Muratori, Ludovico Antonio, 456, 458, 465
Murdocca, A., 513
Murdoch, B., 613
Muresu, G., 463
Muret, H., 495
Murguía, Manuel, 333, 336
Murià, Anna, 281
Murphy, C. J., 177
Murphy, G. R., 602
Murphy, J. J., 10
Murray, P. D., 741
Murrell, A.-L., 842
Murrell, M., 842
Mus, D., 78
Musacchio, J., 424
Musarra, F., 507, 526
Muschg, W., 729
Musgrove, M. W., 404
Musil, Robert, 718, 720
Mussari, M., 808
Musset, Alfred de, 157, 166, 169, 278
Mustè, M., 479
Musumeci, A., 414, 483
Mutis, Alvaro, 355
Muyres, J., 795
Muzii, M., 450
Muzzioli, F., 498, 499
Myers, E. D., 273
Mykle, Agnar, 809
Myśliwski, W., 871, 874

Nabbe, H., 770
Nacci, B., 487
Nachtergaele, V., 781
Nadler, J., 708
Nadler, S., 149
Naess, H., 805
Näf, A., 633
Nagamori, K., 132
Nagel, N., 631
Nägele, R., 695, 832
Nagórko, A., 848, 850
Nagy, J. F., 560
Naiditsch, L., 762
Nail, N., 575, 584, 586
Nałkowska, Z., 863, 869, 870

Nancy, J.-L., 694, 695
Nanni, L., 431
Naogeorgus, Thomas, 638
Napoléon I, Bonaparte (*Emperor*), 154, 488, 681, 687, 866
Napoli, A., 519, 524
Narbona, A., 227
Nardi, G., 492
Nardout-Lafarge, E., 192
Nariòo, Gilabèrt, 200, 207
Naro, A. J., 313
Naro, N. P., 368
Naruszewicz, A., 864
Narzymski, J., 867
Nascimento, S. H. L., 314
Nasiłowska, A., 868
Näslund, H., 812
Nason, P., 461
Nassichuk, J., 106
Nastasi, P., 456
Nasti, P., 407
Natoli, S., 484, 486
Natri, T., 877
Naubert, Yvette, 186
Naudé, Gabriel, 149
Naudet, V., 69
Nauert, C. G., 638
Naumann, B., 382
Naumann, D., 747
Naumann, H., 738
Nava, Pedro, 372
Naval, M. A., 268
Navarro, G., 308
Navarro, J. R., 349
Navarro, J., 276
Navascués, J. de, 350, 351
Navaza, Gonzalo, 336
Navaza Blanco, G., 325, 326
Nazzi, G., 549, 550
Nazzi, L., 549
Neagoe, V., 538
Neaman, E. Y., 767
Neculce, Ion, 529
Nedelciu, Mircea, 542
Nedoma, R., 599
Nedreaas, Torborg, 809
Neef, M., 577
Neefs, J., 161
Neel, C., 600
Néel, G.-J., 207
Neemann, H., 134
Nègre, E., 208
Negretti Cambiasi v. Liala
Negri, A., 71
Negri, A. M. 490
Negrilă, I., 542
Négroni, N., 123
Negruzzi, Iacob, 546
Nehamas, A., 743

Neidhart von Reuenthal, 621–22, 632
Nekula, M., 577
Nelde, P. H., 568, 880
Nelken, Margarita, 273
Nelles, J., 671
Nelligan, Emile, 193
Nellmann, E., 613, 615
Nelson, D., 57, 236
Nelson, M., 798
Nelson Burnett, A., 645
Nemcová, Bozena, 722
Nemeyr, B., 667
Nencioni, G., 480
Nenon, M., 676
Népote-Desmarres, F., 122
Nepveu, P., 184, 185, 192
Neri, F., 427, 500, 502
Neri, Philip (*Saint*), 436, 443
Nerius, D., 576
Neruda, Pablo, 346, 353
Nerval, Gérard de, 153, 156, 157, 158, 171–72, 269, 337, 735, 865
Nesby, L. H., 805
Nesci, C., 162
Nesi, A., 382
Nespor, M., 20
Nester, B., 759
Nestor, 857
Nestroy, Johann Nepomuk, 712, 713, 714, 716, 718, 732, 740–41
Nettervik, I., 821
Neuber, W., 741
Neubert, A., 568
Neudeck, O., 632
Neuger, L., 869
Neuhaus, S., 744
Neuman, Andrés, 289
Neumann, F., 17
Neumann, G., 178, 573, 673
Neumann, H., 624, 683
Neumann, T., 731
Neumann, U., 766
Neumann, W., 686
Neumann-Holzschuh, I., 21
Neumeister, Johann, 428
Neumeister, S., 216
Nevers, Charles de, 77
Neves, M. H. M., 315
Newerley, I., 870, 871
Newton v. Gala
Newton, F., 4
Newton, G., 568, 569
Newton, Isaac, 394, 466
Nez, C., 162
Niang, S., 199
Nica, D., 535
Nicastro, G., 469

Niccolini, E., 450
Nicholas V (*Pope*), 436
Nichols, S. G., 213, 611
Nicholson, E., 98
Nicholson, M., 348
Nicklaus, M., 880
Nicolai, G. M., 471
Nicolai, P., 475
Nicolaisen, W. F. H., 881
Nicolás, C., 263
Nicolás, R., 332
Nicole, Pierre, 125, 144, 150
Nicolescu, A., 537
Nicolescu, L., 546
Nicoletti, G., 480
Niculescu, A., 14, 533
Niderst, A., 129, 142, 147
Niebaum, H., 580
Niederehe, H.-J., 882
Niedermeier, M., 662
Niefanger, D., 884
Niehaus, M., 720
Niehr, T., 570
Nielsen, A. E., 39
Nielsen, B. Jul, 801
Nielsen, J. C., 802
Nielsen, M. Akhøj, 799
Nielsen, M. Femø, 803
Nielsen, M. Lerche, 799
Nielsen, S. Hedegård, 800
Niemcewicz, Julian Ursyn, 865
Niemeyer, K., 340
Nies, F., 131, 675
Niet, M. de, 785
Nieto Ballester, E., 28
Nieto Soria, J. M., 243, 249
Nietzsche, Friedrich, 263, 270, 275, 484, 662, 680, 701, 706, 707, 708, 709, 730, 741–43, 761, 828
Nieukerken, A. van, 871
Nieva, Francisco, 293, 295
Nieves Sánchez, M., 238
Nievo, Ippolito, 493
Niewöhner, F., 637
Nifo, Agostino, 431
Nigro, K. F., 361
Nigro, R., 439
Nigro, Raffaele, 516
Nijhoff, Martinus, 789, 790
Nikiema, E., 47
Niklas von Wyle, 636
Nilsson, A., 838
Nilsson, Å., 844
Nilsson, H., 838
Nilsson, J., 816
Nilsson, Per, 835
Nilsson, T. K., 572
Nimb, S., 800
Nini, A., 158

Nisard, Paul, 276
Nischik, R. M., 726
Nisticò, R., 500, 523
Nizon, Paul, 768
Noacco, C., 57
Noailly, M., 37
Nobel, P., 10
Nobile, N., 700
Nobili, C. S., 498
Noble, P., 68
Nodier, Charles, 172
Noemi, D., 364
Noetinger, E., 165
Noferi, A., 485
Nogerolles, Pierre de, 116
Nogueira, M. X., 330
Noia, C., 331
Noille-Clauzade, C., 137, 138
Noiray, J., 170
Noiset, M.-T., 97
Nolan, B., 66
Nølke, H., 35
Noll, Ingrid, 770
Noll, João Gilberto, 367
Noll, N., 500
Nölle, V., 732
Nolte, J., 743
Nolte, T., 619, 880
Noonan, M., 175
Noozeman, Jillis, 783
Nordau, Max, 276
Nordberg, B., 810, 814, 820
Nordenstam, A., 822
Nordman, M., 811
Nordström, Ludvig, 843
Norén, Lars, 829, 841
Norlyk, B., 802
Norman, B., 121, 128
Norman, L. F., 119
Normand, C., 32
Norrby, C., 814
Norrick, N. R., 504
Norseng, M. K., 807
Northrop, D. A., 451
Northrup, G., 268
Norwid, Cyprian Kamil, 857, 861, 865, 867
Nossack, Hans Erich, 770
Notker der Deutsche, 602
Noto, G., 217
Nouhaud, D., 356, 359
Novalis (Friedrich von Hardenberg), 680, 682, 683, 700–01, 737, 865
Novás Calvo, Lino, 356
Nove, Aldo, 516
Novelli, 181
Nowaczyński, P., 874
Nowak, E., 851
Nowak, S., 600

Nowakowska, A., 856
Noye, I., 137
Nübel. B., 677
Nübler, N., 858
Nucciarelli, S., 436
Nucera, D., 500
Nucio, M., 235
Nunes, N., 311
Núñez, Nicolás, 246
Nunn, R., 142
Nünning, A., 704
Nuño, A., 348
Nutting, S., 188
Nuvoli, G., 478
Nyan, T., 40
Nyblom, C. R., 829
Nycz, R., 862
Nygren, L., 882
Nykrog, P., 883
Nykvist, K., 823, 824
Nyström, C., 814

Oancea, I., 537
Oates, Joyce Carol, 775
Oberlin, Johann Friedrich, 719
Obermaier, S., 618, 621, 634
Obermaier, W., 713, 740
Obernosterer, A., 879
Oberreiter, S., 758
Obey, André, 179
Obhof, U., 641
Obregón, O., 365
Ocampo, Silvina, 350
Ocello, E., 497
Och, G., 678, 716, 744
Ochsenbein, P., 602, 625
Ociepa, G., 770
O'Connell, P. C., 351
O'Connell, P. L., 351
O'Connor, D., 483
O'Connor, P. W., 278, 292
Odasi, Michele, 444
Ødegaard, S., 809
Ödman, C., 842
Odobescu, Alexandre, 547
O'Doherty, P., 737, 755
Odojewski, W., 862, 871
Odorico of Pordenone, 9
Oé, Kenzaburô, 181
Oegema, J., 792
Oehlenschläger, Adam, 826
Oehler, D., 736
Oellers, N., 739
Oergel, M., 750
Oesman, A., 678
Oesterle, G., 668
Oesterle, I., 735
Offenbach, J., 681
Ogando, I., 338

Ogawa, A., 580
Ogier, J., 633
O'Gorman, F., 405
Ogura, H., 132
Ohainski, U., 586
O'Hara, F., 872
Ohlsson, M., 814
Ohly, F., 594
Ohm, L., 685
Öhrberg, A., 813
Ojeda, L. C., 354
Ojetti, U., 473
Okken, L., 612
Olaso, E. de, 349
Olavide, Pablo de, 253
Olcese, S., 465
Oldani, L. J., 446
Olding, F., 564
Olea (bacharel), 326
Olejniczak, J., 870
Olejniczak, M., 848
Oliva, C., 270, 275
Oliva, G., 476, 495
Oliva, K., 858
Oliva, S., 298
Oliván, Lorenzo, 289
Oliveira, Fernão de, 309
Oliveira, M. T. F., 316
Oliver, Federico, 262
Olivera-Williams, M. R., 346
Olivetan, Pierre Robert, 108
Olivetto, G., 240
Ollé, Carmen, 362
Ollén, G., 829
Ollivier, Emile, 193
Olmedo, José Joaquín de, 340
Olmet, Antón del, 273
Olmos, M. A., 272
O'Loughlin, T., 559
Olscamp, M., 189
Olsen, S., 579
Olsen, U. S., 623
Olsson, B., 823
Olsson, Hagar, 841
Olsson, N., 834
Olsson, U., 830, 831
Oltmans, Jan Frederik, 787
Olwitz, R., 736
Omena, N. P. de, 309
O'Neill, M., 332
O'Neill, T., 507, 522
Onetti, Antonio, 295
Onetti, Juan Carlos, 364
Onnes, H. K., 790, 791
Onofri, Arturo, 509, 516
Onofrio (*Saint*), 374
Onorati, F., 471, 478
Onu, L., 537
Oore, I., 188
Oostendorp, Marc van, 776

Oostrom, F. P. van, 779
Oostrum, W. R. D. van, 777, 778
Opitz, A., 659, 735
Opitz, Martin, 650, 652, 655, 656
Oppitz, U.-D., 592, 879
Orazi, V., 227, 305, 308
Orcel, M., 482
Orcibal, J., 137
Orduna, G., 232, 237
Orengo, N., 516
Orgambide, P., 346
Orgeldinger, S., 575
Orizet, J., 106
Orlando, R., 510
Orme, N., 11
Ormerod, B., 197
Ornea, Z., 547, 548
O'Rourke Boyle, M., 434
Orozco, Olga, 344, 348
Orrillo, W., 362
Orska, J., 869, 872
Ørsnæs, B.,799
Ørstavik, Hannl, 808
Ortega, J., 349
Ortega y Gasset, José, 260, 273
Ortese, Anna Maria, 516
Orth, M., 98
Ortiz, A., 357
Ortiz, Alicia Dujovne, 351
Ortiz, J. L., 348
Ortiz, Lourdes, 283, 288
Ortiz Ceberio, C., 357
Ortmann, C., 632
Ortner, H., 571
Ortner, L., 575
Ortuño, S., 877
Orvil, Ernst, 809
Orwell, George, 799
Orzeszkowa, E., 861
Osborne, J., 723
Oschmann, D., 768
Osés Marcaida, C., 220
Osiander, Andreas, 647
Osinski, J., 731
Osmann, G., 745
Ossian, 689
Ossian Gwent (John Davies), 562
Ossola, C., 438, 457, 503
Ostaijen, Paul van, 789, 790, 794
Ostasz, G., 861
Östberg, U., 819
Osten, Suzanne, 836
Østergård, G., 802
Osterkamp, E., 669
Österlund, M., 835
Østerud, E., 831
Östlund-Stjärnegårdh, E., 815

Östman, H., 823
Ostrov, A., 353, 362
Ostrowitzki, A., 9
Ostrowska, B., 862, 863
Ostrowska, M., 853
Oswald von Wolkenstein, 633
Otaka, Y., 32
Otero, Blas de, 291
Otero Pedrayo, Ramón, 331, 336–37
Otfrid von Weissenburg, 601, 602
Ott, M., 699
Ott, N. H., 587, 606, 630, 633
Ott, U., 768
Otter, G., 503
Otter, M., 4
Otto, H., 571, 644
Otto, R., 669
Ottolia, Giovanni, 517
Otto-Peters, Louise, 705
Ouellet, P., 192
Ouellette-Michalska, Madeleine, 191
Ouimette, V., 883
Outeiriño, Manuel, 336
Ouvrard, Hélène, 185, 186
Ovejero, M., 263
Overton, B., 728
Ovid, 1, 6, 7, 8, 106, 114, 115, 154, 302, 306, 395, 398, 404, 419, 432, 615
Oviedo y Pérez de Toledo, M. del R., 340
Owe, J., 816
Owen, Bob, 563
Owen, G. W., 561
Owen, J., 564
Owen, R. J., 755
Owens, B. G., 563
Özdamar, Emine Sevgi, 770
Ozolina, O., 43
Ozwald, T., 166

Paape, Gerrit, 785, 786
Paasch-Beeck, R., 767
Pacheco, José Emilio, 360
Paci, Enzo, 523
Pacifici, S., 357
Pacini, B., 390
Packalén, M. A., 863
Paco, M. de, 270, 275, 287, 295, 879
Padberg, S., 619
Paden, W. D., 216
Padilla, Heberto, 356
Padoan, G., 408, 416, 418, 478
Padorno, Manuel, 290
Padrosa Gorgot, I., 301

Paduano, G., 499
Paepe, C. de, 270
Pagan, M., 464
Pagano, Mario, 374, 456, 459
Pageaux, D.-H., 166
Pagés-Rangel, R., 342
Pagliaro, A., 413
Paige, N., 122
Pailler, C., 341
Paiva, M. C. A., 309
Pajdzińska, A., 856
Pajević, M., 762
Palacio, Pablo, 346, 356
Palacio Sánchez, A., 326
Palacios Fernández, E., 254
Paladini Musitelli, M., 499
Palandri, Enrico, 505
Palatine (*princesse*) v. Charlotte Elisabeth
Palaversich, D., 346
Palazzeschi, Aldo, 517
Palencia, Alfonso Fernández de, 232, 249, 250
Palencia, B., 269
Paleologu, A., 545
Palermo, A., 474, 477
Palermo, G., 451
Palermo, Z., 344
Palés Matos, Luis, 363
Palgrave, Francis, 479
Paliga, S., 533
Palissy, Bernard, 92
Palladio, Andrea, 433, 444
Palladius, 308
Pallady, T., 544
Pallarés, M. A., 249
Pallarès, M. D., 298
Pallavicini, P., 501
Pallesen, B. R., 799
Palm, A., 824
Palma, Clemente, 343
Palmen, Connie, 796
Palmér, A., 815
Palmer, N. F., 883
Palmieri, P., 509
Palmieri, S., 516
Palumbo, M., 472
Pamio, M., 521
Pampaloni, Geno, 503, 507
Pampín, M., 246, 247
Pan, F., 700
Panã Dindelegan, G., 527
Panagl, O., 681
Pancera, M., 476
Pancino, L., 460
Pane, A. 520
Panetta, M., 427
Panikkar, R., 589
Panizza, G., 482
Panizzi, A., 473

Pankow, E., 695
Pankowski, M., 862
Pansuti, Saverio, 459
Pantini, E., 500
Panzeri, F., 505
Panzini, Alfredo, 493
Paoletti Langé, A., 472, 495
Paoli, Betty, 744
Paoli, M., 520
Paolo da Fucecchio, 437
Papadima, L., 546
Papahagi, P., 539
Papàsogli, B., 145, 457
Pape, W., 729, 753
Papenfuss-Gorek, Bert, 763
Papierz, M., 859
Papini, Giovanni, 517
Papini, M. C., 507
Pappalardo, E., 494
Papuli, G., 484
Paracelsus, 594, 618
Parada, A., 360
Paradis, Suzanne, 185
Paraschiva, S., 542
Paravicini, W., 604
Pardo Bazán, Emilia, 320
Pardo de Guevara, E., 233
Paré, Ambroise, 110
Parekh, B., 151
Pareto, V., 452
Parga Valiña, E. M., 328
Pargner, B., 740
Parini, Giuseppe, 466, 478
Paris, G., 216
Parise, Goffredo, 504, 517
Parisi, L., 490, 508
Parisot, H., 522
Parisse, M., 597
Parker, B., 831
Parkes, S., 754
Parkinson, S. R., 312, 331
Parkvall, M., 317
Parmeggiani, F., 520
Parmentier, B., 121, 143, 145
Parnicki, T., 861
Parra, M. A. de la, 347, 354
Parra, Nicanor, 345, 346
Parri, M. G., 454
Parrilla, C., 243, 244, 245, 246, 877, 883
Parronchi, Alessandro, 401, 515, 517
Parry, G., 554
Parry, M., 387
Parry Owen, A., 557
Parry-Williams, T. H., 562, 563
Parsons, D. N., 817
Partida, A., 361
Parussa, G., 34, 76, 86
Pârvulescu, I., 547

Pasaero, D., 387
Pascal, Blaise, 97, 145, 146, 150, 457, 510
Pascal, J.-N., 152
Paschek, C., 587, 674
Pascoli, Giovanni, 470, 482, 484, 493–94
Pascu, E., 770
Pascual, J. A., 219
Pasetto, B., 384
Pasler, R. G., 631
Paso, Fernando del, 360
Pasolini, Pier Paolo, 497, 499, 516, 517–19
Pasquier, Etienne, 92
Pasquier, M.-C., 156
Pasquini, E., 399, 417
Pasquino, P., 402
Passione, L., 517
Passos, J. L., 371
Pasten, A., 358
Pastonchi, Francesco, 519
Pastor, E., 749
Pastor Alonso, M. A., 361
Pastor Cuevas, M. C., 241
Pastour, J., 210
Pastoureau, M., 6
Pastuszek, A., 870
Pataki, T., 203
Paternina, Z., 365
Paterson, L., 213
Pato, H., 356
Patocka, F., 573, 880
Patrizi, G., 424
Patru, Olivier, 143
Patrzałek, T., 852, 861
Patterson, C., 336
Pau, Jeroni, 308
Paul of Tarsus (*Saint*), 2, 411
Paul, Hermann, 591
Paul, J., 596
Paul, J.-M., 707, 730
Paúl, M., 358, 361
Paulin, R., 660, 670, 729
Paulis, G., 392
Pauly, P., 588
Pausch, O., 713, 740
Pauwels, Y., 103
Pavarini, S., 522
Pavel, M., 537
Paver, C. E., 765
Pavese, Cesare, 500, 501, 519
Pavetto, A., 476
Pavlovski, Eduardo, 346
Pavolini, Alessandro, 519
Pawelec, D., 871
Pawlak, D., 848
Pawyza, F., 93
Payá Bernabé, J., 275
Payán Sotomayor, P., 237

Payne, A. A., 432
Paz, Octavio, 346, 358, 371
Paz, Senel, 346
Paz Gago, X. M., 331, 334
Paz Lestón, X., 337
Paz-Soldán, Edmundo, 346, 352
Paziak, P., 855
Pazó González, N., 331
Pazzaglia, M., 493
Peach, T., 115
Pearre, A., 174
Pearson, L., 353
Pech, T., 133
Peckham, R., 79
Pecora, E., 519
Pedersbæk, B., 798, 801
Pedersen, I. L., 801
Pedersen, K. M., 801
Pedoya, P., 207
Pedrero, Paloma, 292
Pedroni, M., 243
Peeters, B., 48
Peeters, L., 778
Peil, D., 594, 637, 883
Peitsch, H., 677
Péladan, G., 204
Peláez Benítez, M. D., 238, 250
Pellarolo, S., 352
Pellegrini, G. B., 549
Pellegrino, C., 465
Pellen, R., 220
Pellettieri, O., 352, 364
Pellikan, Konrad, 645
Pellini, P., 493, 520
Pellizzi, F., 498
Pelosini, N. F., 494
Pelster, T., 765
Peluse di Giulio, M., 291
Pena, X. R., 337
Pénisson, P., 669, 743
Penna, Cornélio, 367
Penna, Sandro, 502, 519
Pennings, L., 498
Pennington, E., 350
Penny, R. J., 28, 218, 220
Penot, C., 154
Pensado, C., 219, 220
Pensado Tomé, J. (X.) L., 225, 325
Pensel, F., 879
Pensom, R., 65, 79
Pepe, L., 456
Pepe, P., 516
Pépin, J., 399
Pepłowski, F., 856
Pepoli, Alessandro, 459
Pepperle, I., 715
Pera, C., 341
Peraldus, Guilelmus, 10, 626
Perale, M., 479

Perarnau Espelt, J., 304, 307
Percival, A., 260
Percopo, E., 441
Perea, M. P., 298
Pereira, M., 303, 304, 416
Pereira, S. G. C., 309, 315
Pereira Bezerra, A., 370
Pereiro, Lois, 337
Pérennec, M., 571
Pérez, Álvaro, 321
Pérez, J., 277, 290, 347
Pérez, M. de, 116
Pérez de Ayala, Ramón, 259, 262
Pérez Ballesteros, José, 337
Pérez Barcala, G., 247
Pérez Bazo, J., 270
Pérez Bonalde, Juan Antonio, 340, 343
Pérez-Bustamante Mourier, A. S., 268
Pérez Castellano, A. J., 235
Pérez Gago. M. del C., 227
Pérez García, N., 288
Pérez López, H. J., 742
Pérez López, M.-M., 257
Pérez Magallón, J., 254, 260, 275, 883
Pérez Martín, A., 242
Pérez Pascual, J. I., 883
Pérez Priego, M. A, 244, 251
Pérez Sánchez, Manuel Antonio (Manuel Antonio), 322, 330, 336
Pérez Torres, Y., 358
Pérez Varela, C., 337
Peri Rossi, Cristina, 290, 346, 364
Perilli, Achille, 520
Perivolaris, J. D., 364
Perk, Jacques, 788, 789
Perli, A., 514, 520
Perlini, L., 509
Perlongher, Néstor, 348
Pernot, M., 140
Perotti, P. A., 491
Perraudin, M., 735
Perrault, Charles, 122, 133, 140
Perregaard, B., 802
Perrella, S., 509
Perriam, C., 264, 280
Perrot, J.-P., 89
Perrot, M., 168, 548
Perry, C., 164
Persson, A., 815
Pertile, L., 399, 408, 412, 417, 439, 468
Pertusa, Francesc de, 305
Perujo Melgar, J. M., 306
Peruzzi, E., 481

Pesca-Cupolo, C., 447
Pescetti, O., 426
Peschke, U., 745
Pestelli, C., 469, 479
Peteghem, M. van, 22
Peter Damian (*Saint*), 350
Peter of Blois, 6
Peter, E., 661
Peters, G., 669, 736
Peters, G. F., 737
Peters, H. G., 750
Peters, J., 136
Peters, P., 734
Peters, U., 589, 606, 632
Petersmann, H., 25, 882
Peterson, Hans, 835
Peterson, K., 40
Petersson, I.-L., 827
Petherick, K., 829, 837
Petit, A., 884
Petit, J., 570
Petitier, P., 165
Petrarch, 74, 105, 111, 148, 423, 424, 428, 438, 442, 443, 473, 479, 482, 488, 596, 788
Petrescu, Radu, 544
Petrescu, V., 542
Petris, L., 109
Petrocchi, G., 421
Petroni, F., 522, 525
Petronio, G., 477, 498
Petrovici, E., 527
Petrovitz, W., 848
Petrucci, G., 512
Petrucci, P., 528
Petrucciani, M., 509
Petry, U., 478, 642
Petter, M. M. T., 317
Pettersson, B., 826
Pettersson, L., 811, 817
Petzoldt, E., 737
Petzoldt, L., 590, 592
Peuger, L., 624, 625
Peurell, E., 822, 839
Peylet, G., 172
Peyrache-Leborgne, D., 165
Peyre, P., 212
Pezatti, E. G., 315
Pezzin, C., 526
Pfabigan, A., 758
Pfau, Ludwig, 716
Pfeffer, W., 217
Pfefferkorn, Johannes, 646, 647
Pfeiffer, A., 547
Pfeiffer, D., 200
Pfeiffer, E., 359
Pfeiffer, Ida, 744
Pfeiffer, J., 619, 631
Pfeiffer, M., 762
Pfersmann, A., 883

Pfister, M., 25
Pfranger, A., 662
Phaedrus, 511
Phalèse, H. de, 155
Pharies, D., 222
Phelan, A., 737
Philip II (*King of Spain*), 218
Philip V (*King of Spain*), 254
Philip the Good (*Duke of Burgundy*), 85, 246
Philippe de Rémi, 61
Philippe de Thaün, 236
Philippi, J., 580
Phillips, U., 863
Philp, C., 798
Phylib of Emlyn, 558
Phylip ap Morgan, 558
Piacentini, Marco, 443
Piaget, A., 78
Pian degli Ontani, Beatrice di, 469
Piasecki, S., 871
Piazza, R., 491
Piazzolla, Marino, 519
Piazzoni, A. M., 623
Pic, F., 200, 217
Picard, A., 358
Picard, A.-M., 191
Picard, R., 128
Picasso, Pablo, 181, 269
Picchi, L., 526
Piccillo, G., 530
Piccione, M.-L., 185, 186, 188
Piccolomini, A., 424, 426
Piccolomini, E. S., 431
Piccolomini, F., 435
Pich, C., 387
Pich, E., 156, 164
Picherit, J.-L., 69
Pickar, G. B., 721
Pickens, R. T., 63, 83
Pico della Mirandola, Gianfrancesco, 437
Pico della Mirandola, Giovanni, 431, 434
Picón-Salas, Mariano, 365
Picone, M., 398, 413, 418, 883
Picono, Francesco Filippo, 455
Piekarczyk, D., 851
Pielmann, E., 667
Pieper, P., 599
Piera, M., 306
Pierangeli, F., 516
Pierazzo, E., 429
Pierce, G. O., 554
Pierce, G., 491
Pieri, D., 524
Pieri, M., 496
Pierrard, M., 35, 36
Pierre de la Cépède, 72

Pierro, Albino, 519
Pierron, A., 42
Pierrot, R., 163
Piersanti, C., 505
Pietri, Arturo Uslar, 365
Pietro del Monte, 436
Pietropaoli, A., 521
Pietrych, K., 870
Pietrzik, D., 624
Piglia, Ricardo, 351
Pigna, Giovan Battista, 444
Pignatti, F., 440, 449
Pigoń, S., 868
Piirainen, E., 581
Piirainen, I. T., 592, 630
Pikulik, L., 700
Pilardi, J.-A., 173
Pilati, Carlantonio, 464
Pillat, I., 544
Pilling, C., 733, 739
Pilot, M., 857
Pimentel, Eleonora de Fonseca, 466
Pimentel, Luís, 337
Pimpão, T. S., 315
Piña, J. A., 354
Pinalie, P., 47
Pinar, Florencia, 246
Pindar, 483, 666, 696
Pindemonte, Giovanni, 459
Pineau, Gisèle, 199
Piñera, Virgilio, 345, 357
Piñero, P. M., 234, 235
Piñeyro, J. C., 349
Pinfold, D., 766
Pinget, Robert, 179
Pinkert, E.-U., 758
Pinnow, J., 584
Pino-Ojeda, W., 360
Pinter, Harold, 294
Pinto, L., 743
Pintoin, Michel, 84
Pintos, Juan Manuel, 337
Piontek, S., 763
Piotti, M., 471
Piotti, Pier Luigi, 519
Piovene, Guido, 519
Piquero, José Luis, 289
Pirandello, Luigi, 275, 448, 469, 470, 472, 477, 497, 498, 505, 519–20, 522, 831
Pirotti, U., 516
Pirson, R., 132
Pîrvu, E., 532
Pîrvulescu, M., 532
Pisa, K., 722
Pisano, D., 493
Pisarek, W., 852, 854
Pisarkowa, K., 851, 856, 858, 863

Piscator, Ernst, 266
Piscator, Hermannus, 645–46
Piscopo, U., 486
Pisowicz, A., 860
Pistiak, A., 736
Pitavy, D., 548
Pitigrilli (Dino Segre), 497
Pitkänen, A. J., 810
Pittaluga, Gustavo, 262
Pittner, K., 580
Pius IV (*Pope*), 438
Pius V (*Pope*), 438
Piwińska, M., 867
Pizarnik, Alejandra, 344, 346, 348
Pizer, J., 711
Pizzamiglio, G., 457
Pizzi, K., 521
Pizzuto, Antonio, 520
Placanica, A., 484, 486
Plachta, B., 721
Planche, A., 76, 77
Plangg, G., 586
Plastow, J., 352
Plate, B., 619
Platen, August Graf von, 683, 706, 708, 744
Platen, M. von, 824, 828
Plato, 272, 403, 414, 429, 431, 432, 433, 525
Platteau, K. M. C., 788
Platter, Thomas, 646
Plazenet-Haut, L., 134
Pleij, H., 776, 777
Plénat, M., 44
Plenzdorf, Ulrich, 760
Plet, F., 60
Plett, B., 726
Plews, J. L., 773
Pliny the Elder, 431
Pliny, 429, 648
Plöger, P., 571
Plotinus, 434
Plouzeau, M., 82
Plumpe, G., 749
Plutarch, 93
Pociña, A., 333
Pociña López, A. X., 333
Podczaszyński, Michał, 867
Poddighe, Grazia Maria, 503
Podracki, J., 852, 854
Podraza-Kwiatkowska, M., 868
Poe, Edgar Allan, 193, 477, 692
Poeta, S. J., 271
Poey, Bernard de, 116
Poggiogalli, D., 374
Pohl, H. D., 585
Pohl, I., 733
Pohl, Peter, 835, 836
Pohorsky, A., 158

Poiret, Pierre, 150
Poirier, P., 189
Poirion, D., 50, 51, 58, 117
Poisson, F., 187
Poisson, G., 165
Poisson, O., 165
Polacco, M., 509
Polachek, D. E., 97
Polenz, P. von, 572
Polheim, K. K., 712, 722, 746
Poli, S., 140
Policarp, 857
Polidoro, V., 429
Polito, P., 802
Poliziano, Angelo, 402, 427, 438, 440, 446
Polizzi, G., 74, 95
Pollmann, L., 347
Pollock, J.-Y., 21
Pomaro, G., 303
Pombo, Pilar, 292, 295–96
Pombo, Rafael, 340
Pomel, F., 60
Pomilio, Mario, 520
Pomp, S., 710
Pompe, H., 684, 685
Ponath, J., 759
Ponce de León, Napoleón Baccino, 364
Poncy, Charles, 168
Pondal, Eduardo, 337
Ponge, Francis, 178, 179
Poniatowska, Elena, 360
Ponnau, G., 166
Pons, A., 145
Pons, R., 208
Pont, J., 233
Pontano, Giovanni, 430
Ponte, G., 493
Pont-Hubert, C., 185
Ponti, P., 501
Ponz, Antonio, 256
Ponza, M., 480
Ponzi, M., 666
Pop, I., 541, 548
Popa, C., 545
Popescu, C. T., 545
Popescu-Marin, M., 536
Popiel, M., 867
Poplack, S., 47
Poplin, F., 76
Popovici, V., 27
Popowska-Taborska, H., 845, 855, 859
Popp, W., 744
Poppe, E., 1
Poppe, R., 757
Pöppel, H., 345
Poprawa, A., 874
Porayski-Pomsta, J., 852, 853

Porcar Miralles, M., 223
Porcelli, B., 407, 509
Porete, Marguerite, 89, 625
Porta, Antonio, 502, 505, 520
Porta, Carlo, 489, 490, 494
Portegies, A., 777
Portela, C., 877
Porter, J. I., 743
Portinari, Beatrice, 397
Portinari, F., 459, 513, 516
Portugal, J. A., 363
Poruciuc, A., 536
Porzio, D., 508
Porzio, F., 424
Poschmann, H., 719
Posner, R., 14, 326, 380
Pospiszylowa, A., 853
Possamaï-Perez, M., 67
Posse, Abel, 348, 351
Possevino, A., 426
Possiedi, P., 483, 484
Post, B., 33
Post, K. D., 879
Postl v. Sealsfield
Postma, A., 780
Pot, O., 112
Potempa, G., 738
Potocki, W., 863
Pottier, B., 39
Pouey-Mounou, A.-P., 98
Pouget, E., 33
Poulin, Jacques, 185, 193–94
Pound, Ezra, 405, 500
Pountain, C. J., 223
Pourcq, I. de, 63
Povlsen, S. K., 809
Powel, N., 561
Powell, D. A., 167
Powell, H., 719
Powell, J. M., 8
Pozo Garza, Luz, 337
Pozuelo Yvancos, J. M., 267
Prado, Benjamín, 289
Prado Bellei, S. L., 368
Prados, Emilio, 265
Praga, E., 469
Prager, B., 703
Prak-Derrington, E., 775
Praloran, M., 440
Prandi, M., 381, 504
Prati, G., 158
Pratolini, Vasco, 520
Pratt, K., 88
Praz, M., 515, 479
Pré, André du, 116
Preda, R., 405
Predoiu, G. L., 773
Préfontaine, C. F. O., sieur de, 134, 140
Preisler, B., 801

Prejs, M., 863
Prescott, L. E., 355
Presley, P. L., 638
Prest, J., 126
Prester John, 558
Prete, A., 481, 485, 486
Preti, D., 309, 310
Pretzel, U., 615
Prévost, l'Abbé (Antoine
    François Prévost d'Exiles), 146
Preyzner, M., 850
Price, A., 563
Price, G., 356, 528, 554, 883
Prichard, Caradog, 563
Prieto, Gregorio, 268, 269
Prieto de Paula, A. L., 275
Prini, P., 492
Probes, C. M., 140
Probst, M., 626
Proust, Marcel, 130, 163, 181,
    277, 394, 515
Providenti, E., 520
Prudentius, 67
Prudon, M., 262
Prüller, F., 713
Prutz, Robert Eduard, 744
Przepiórkowski, A., 849
Przyboś, J., 862, 872
Przybyła, Z., 866, 867
Przybylski, R. K., 861, 867, 874
Przybyszewski, S., 868
Przychodzen, J., 189
Przyczyna, W., 852, 854
Pseudo-Bede, 4
Pseudo-Bernard, 10
Pseudo-Dietmar, 619
Pseudo-Isidore, 1
Puccetti, V., 490
Pucci, E., 437
Puccini, Bastiano, 450
Puccini, Giacomo, 488
Puchades Bataller, R. J., 305
Pückler-Muskau, Hermann
    Ludwig, Prince von, 684, 715,
    744
Puech, C., 32
Puertos, José Luis, 290
Puga, María Luisa, 359, 360
Puget de la Serre, Jean, 124
Pugh, W. W. T., 415
Puig, J. de, 301
Puig, Manuel, 346, 347, 350, 351
Pujadas, J., 299
Pujol, J., 302, 306
Pujol Payet, I., 224, 225
Pułaski, Kazimierz, 865
Pulci, Antonia, 446
Pulci, Luca, 444
Pulci, Luigi, 444
Pulgar, Fernando de, 249

Pulido Tirado, G., 290
Pulsoni, C., 427
Pümpel-Mader, M., 879
Pupier, P., 44
Puppa, P., 469, 505
Puppi, L., 433
Purdela Sitaru, M., 536, 538
Purnelle, G., 34
Pürtz, H., 728
Puşcariu, S., 527
Pustkuchen, Friedrich, 673
Puteanus, Erycius (Honorius
    Vanden Born), 783
Putman, L., 788
Püttmann, Hermann, 709
Putzer, O., 568
Puzynina, J., 845, 851, 852
Pyle, C. M., 446
Pyrard de la Val, F., 41
Pyrczak, R. M., 173
Pythagoras, 434

Qorop-Santo (José Joaquim de
    Campos Leão), 368
Quackenbush, L. H., 347
Quainton, M., 105
Quasimodo, Salvatore, 503,
    520–21
Quast, B., 607
Queizán, María Xosé, 338
Queneau, Raymond, 521
Quenot, Y., 99
Quéreuil, M., 87
Quéruel, D., 71, 72
Quevedo, Francisco de, 268, 275
Quilis Merín, M., 218
Quillet, J., 76
Quinault, Philippe, 128
Quinet, 172
Quinkenstein, L., 765
Quinones, R. J., 410
Quiñones de Benavente, Luis,
    258
Quint, N., 211, 212
Quintana Tejera, L., 260
Quintáns Suárez, M., 329
Quintilian, 75
Quintin, H., 570
Quirino, I., 517
Quiroga, Horacio, 346, 364
Quist, P., 802
Quondam, A., 424

Raabe, A., 757
Raabe, P., 676
Raabe, Wilhelm, 704, 706, 707,
    711, 719, 744–45
Raat, G. F. H., 787

Rabanus v. Hrabanus,
Rabatel, A., 40
Rabelais, François, 32, 76, 92,
    102–04
Rabenstein, C., 627
Rabinovici, Doran, 770
Rabitti, G., 444, 446
Rabizzani, G., 468
Raboni, G., 442, 523
Rabunhal, H., 336
Racevskis, R., 130, 142
Racine, Jean, 125, 128–32, 164,
    675
Racine, R., 184
Radecke, G., 722, 723, 726
Radermacher, J. 781
Radford, A., 385
Radigán, Juan, 354
Radjaie, A., 746
Rädle, F., 637
Rădulescu, A.-R., 36
Raether, M., 737
Rafanell, A., 883
Rafel, J., 298
Raffaeli, M., 522
Ragg-Kirkby, H., 714, 748
Ragone, G., 501
Ragotzky, H., 632
Rahewin, 5
Rahner, T., 765
Răileanu, P., 546
Raimbaut de Vaqueiras, 201
Raimondi, E., 490, 501
Raimondi, G., 88
Raimund, Ferdinand, 712, 732
Rainer, F., 44
Rainier, F., 43
Raitz, W., 879
Rajnik, E., 799
Rajotte, P., 183
Ramadori, A. E., 239
Ramat, S., 507, 517
Rambaud, H., 33
Ramers, K. H., 576, 578
Ramírez, A. G., 231
Ramírez, E., 259
Ramírez-Pimienta, J. C., 342
Ramm, E., 683
Ramondino, Francesca, 521
Ramos, Graciliano, 366, 367,
    370
Ramos, Marcelo, 352
Ramos, R., 247, 248
Ramos Sucre, José Antonio, 365
Ramsay, P., 355
Ramsey, R., 179
Raña, R., 336
Ranawake, S., 620
Rancière, J., 273, 284
Rancoeur, R., 99

Randall, M., 187
Rando, G., 486
Ranelid, Björn, 842
Ranieri, Antonio, 486, 494
Ranieri, I., 426, 443
Ransmayr, Christoph, 563, 770
Ranson, D. L., 219, 882
Rao, A. M., 454, 456
Raoul of Longchamp, 8
Raphael, 160
Rapic, S., 678
Rapin, C., 205, 207
Raposo, E., 21, 314
Rappoport, M., 93
Rasine, Carmen, 271
Rask, K., 800
Rat, M., 42
Ratajska, K., 868
Rathenow, Lutz, 770
Ratkowitsch, C., 7
Ratti, Andrea, 466
Rattner, J., 718
Rău, A., 548
Rauch, I., 883
Rauh, H. D., 696
Raumer, F. von, 699
Rausch, Albert H., 744
Rauseysen, Philipp Ernst, 679
Rautenberg, U., 634
Rauth, H. W., 690
Ravier, X., 203
Rawles, S., 427
Raya, G., 474
Raymond, J.-F. de, 128, 147
Raynaud, C., 83
Raźny, J., 868
Rea, A. M., 167
Rea, V., 469
Real Pérez, B., 320
Real Ramos, E., 306
Reale, M., 884
Reati, F., 345
Rebecchini, G., 427
Rebhun, Paul, 638
Rebora, Clemente, 521
Reboul, A.-M., 166
Recasens, D., 298
Rech, B., 765
Rechtien, R., 761
Recio, R., 248
Reck, A., 733
Recke, Elisa von der, 662
Reckert, S., 369
Rector, M., 676
Reed, L. A., 882
Reed, T. J., 665
Rees, E., 841
Rees, V., 434
Reeve, W. C., 730
Regalado, N. F., 59

Régaldo, M., 152
Regali, M. C., 463
Regener, U., 879
Regio, Raffaele, 10
Regman, C., 548
Regoyos, D. de, 274
Regueira, X. L., 322, 326, 328
Regueiro, J. M., 13
Rehder, B., 803
Rei, F. F., 879
Rei, M., 338
Reich-Ranicki, M, 752, 710
Reichan, J., 854, 859
Reichardt, L., 586
Reichart, Wolfgang, 646
Reichart, Zeno, 646
Reichelt, G., 749
Reichenbach, H., 38
Reichenkron, G., 374, 375
Reichensperger, R., 730
Reichert, F., 9, 610, 634
Reichmann, E., 718, 730
Reid, J. H., 760
Reiffenstein, I., 569
Reigersberch, Maria van, 783
Reilly, M., 131, 132
Reimann, Brigitte, 755, 770
Reimers, E., 810
Reiner, F., 26
Reiner, O., 809
Reinhammar, M., 818
Reinhammar, V., 818
Reinhart, Johann Christian, 675
Reinhart, M., 637, 653
Reinheimer, S., 14
Reinheimer Ripeanu, S., 532
Reininger, A., 730
Reinmar von Hagenau, 619, 620
Reinshagen, G., 722
Reis, M., 579
Reiss, T. J., 130
Reissmann, B., 724
Reitsma, A., 792
Reitter, P., 735
Rej, Mikoła, 863, 864
Rejter, A., 854
Religieux de Saint Denis, 83
Rem, T., 807
Remaud, O., 171
Renales, J., 553
Renberg, Tore, 808
Renedo, X., 301
Renera-Arribas, V. M., 553
Rengifo, César, 365
Renner, R. G., 673
Rensi, Giuseppe, 433, 515
Renz, C., 723
Répaci, Leonida, 521
Répide, Pedro de, 259
Repossi, C., 491

Requeixo, A., 334, 336
Requemora, S., 120
Resende, A., 331
Resina, J. R., 273
Retat, C., 157
Rettelbach, J., 621, 623
Retti, G., 568
Retz, J.-F. P. de G., cardinal de, 140
Reuchlin, Johannes, 638, 646-47
Reudenbach, B., 594, 600
Reuter, Fritz, 745
Reuter, Gabriele, 705, 706, 718, 745-46
Reuter, T., 597
Reutner, R., 738, 740, 741
Reventlow, Franziska von, 746
Reverdy, Pierre, 269
Reverte Bernal, C., 344
Revol, T., 68
Revueltas, José, 359
Rey, J.-C., 209
Rey, J.-M., 176
Rey, P.-L., 175
Reyes, G., 346
Reymont, W., 862
Reynaud, D., 152
Reynouard, F.-J., 16
Rezeanu, A., 537
Rézeau, P., 45
Rezzori, Gregor von, 770
Rhegius, Urbanus, 638
Rhosier Mortimer, 558
Rhygyfarch, 559
Rhys, Morgan John, 564
Rhys, Prosser, 562
Rhys, R., 562
Rhys, Siôn Dafydd, 561
Riaza, Luis, 294
Ribard, J., 80
Ribeiro, Darcy, 366, 371
Ribémont, B., 91
Ribera, José de, 267
Ribera Llopis, J. M., 336
Ribeyro, J. L., 346
Ribeyro, Julio Ramón, 346, 363
Ribich, Eva, 842
Ribot, T., 525
Ricaldone, L., 476
Riccardo of Venosa, 9
Ricchi, Agostino, 448
Ricci, Angelo Maria, 489
Ricci, Michele, 89
Riccò, L., 454
Rice-Defosse, M., 167
Richard I (*King of England*), 82
Richard, R., 586
Richards, E. J., 74, 86
Richards, S. L. F., 171

Richards, Thomas (Doc Tom), 561, 563
Riché, P., 600
Richelet, P., 42
Richelieu, Armand Jean du Plessis, cardinal de, 112, 134, 144, 383
Richer of St Remi, 5
Richter, F., 849
Richter, Jean-Paul Friedrich (Jean Paul), 681, 682, 701, 703, 745, 760
Richter, L., 548
Richter, Ludwig, 709
Richter, M., 151, 524
Richter, S., 664
Richter, T., 684
Ricketts, P. T., 215, 216
Rico, Manuel, 290
Ricoeur, Paul, 266
Ricorda, R., 510
Ricós, A., 224
Ricouart, J., 193
Ricuperati, G., 457
Ridder, K., 611, 614, 617, 629, 630
Ridruejo, E., 221
Riechmann, Jorge, 290
Riecke, A.-B., 648
Riecke, J., 573
Ried, H., 615
Riedel, F. J., 785
Riedel, Gabriel, 690
Riedel, M., 742, 744
Riedel, N., 767
Riedel, V., 668
Riedel, W., 765
Riedl, G., 655
Rieger, D., 214
Rieger, J., 854
Riemen, A., 687
Riemsdijk, H. van, 20, 21, 883
Riendeau, P., 188
Riera, Carme, 283, 288
Riera, M., 298
Ries, H., 720
Riesco, Laura, 363
Rietberg, L., 787
Rieu, J., 97
Rigal, B., 208
Rigau, G., 322
Rigaud, F.(P.), 202
Riggs, L. W., 128, 129
Righini, M., 488
Rigoni, M. A., 481, 482, 485
Riikonen, H. K., 823
Riisager, O. E., 798
Rijghard, R., 777
Riley-Smith, J., 65
Rilke, Rainer Maria, 718, 832

Rimanelli, G., 483
Rimbaud, Arthur, 265, 692
Rimondi, G., 500
Rinaldi, R., 452, 470
Rincón, C., 360
Rindler Schjerve, R., 385
Ringblom, A., 824, 840
Ringnér-Lundgren, Ester, 842
Rini, J., 221
Rinn, M., 45
Rinuccini, Ottavio, 460
Río, A. del, 245
Río Conde, E., 335
Riopérez y Milá, S., 274
Riordan, C., 772
Riordan, S. M., 155
Ríos, M. C., 333
Riou, D., 134, 141
Rioul, R., 35
Riquer, M. de, 301
Risani, G., 506
Rischbieter, H., 880
Rischel, J., 799
Risco, Vicente, 330
Risi, Nelo, 521
Risse, J.-L., 575
Ritrovato, S., 444
Ritte, J., 724
Rittel, T., 856
Ritter, A., 747
Ritter, H. M., 600, 614, 636
Ritter, H., 659
Ritter, J. W., 681
Ritter, N. A., 881
Ritter, Tadeusz, 870
Ritter Santini, L., 457
Ritter-Schaumberg, H., 600
Rittner, Tadeusz, 758
Ritz, G., 863, 871
Ritzer, M., 713, 732, 733
Riva, J., 489, 492
Riva, M., 484
Rivas, A., 247
Rivas, E., 222
Rivas, Manuel, 283
Rivera, S., 269
Rivera Villegas, C. M., 363
Rivers, K., 9
Riviello, T. C., 483
Riwka Erlisch, Sara, 371
Rizek, C., 624
Rizza, C., 120, 131
Rizzetti, Giovanni, 466
Rizzi, L., 314
Rizzo, S., 430
Roa Bastos, Augusto, 362
Robbe-Grillet, Alain, 179
Roberge, Y., 532
Robert de Boron, 60, 67
Robert de Clari, 68

Robert ap Gwilym Ddu (Robert Williams), 563
Robert ap Huw, 561
Robert, Gruffudd, 561
Robert, H., 160
Robert, L., 697
Robert, Louis Léopold (*Swiss painter*), 736
Robert, Ludwig, 716
Roberts, B. F., 561, 562
Roberts, G. M., 564
Roberts, I., 20, 881
Roberts, K. A., 98
Roberts, K., 189, 194
Roberts, L. M., 563
Roberts, Ll. P., 562, 563
Roberts, T., 554, 558
Robertshaw, A., 633, 883
Robey, D., 406
Robin, Régine, 185
Robine, Marie, 86
Robinet, A., 148
Robinson, C., 194
Robinson, D. W., 765
Robinson, M., 827, 829, 831
Robles, A., 304
Robles, L., 274
Robles, M., 362
Robu, I., 530
Robustelli, C., 375
Roca, I. M., 17
Rocatalhada, Joan de, 307
Rocca, L., 402
Roccatagliata Ceccardi, Ceccardo, 521
Rocco, B., 391
Rocco, F., 364
Roch, E., 751
Rocha, C., 312
Roche, C. de, 693
Rocher, D., 622
Roches, Catherine des, 86, 97
Roches, Madeleine des, 86, 97
Rochette, B., 28
Rochon, F., 195
Rochow, C., 733
Rochwert, P., 234
Röcke, W., 587, 589, 633
Rod, E., 495
Roda, V., 493, 495
Rodden, J., 353
Roddewig, M., 419
Rödel, M., 594
Ródenas de Moya, D., 269, 272, 273, 274
Rodenberg, Julius, 745
Rodick, C., 262
Rodlauer, H., 829
Rodó, José Enrique, 340, 341
Rodoreda, Mercè, 282, 283

Rodrigo Díaz, *el Cid*, 234
Rodrigo Lizondo, M., 301
Rodrigues, A. C. de S., 884
Rodrigues, C. V., 313
Rodrigues, F. O., 311
Rodrigues, Nelson, 369
Rodrigues, S., 372
Rodriguez, A., 77
Rodríguez, Francisco Javier, 320
Rodríguez, J., 277
Rodríguez, J. C., 338
Rodríguez, J. L., 332
Rodriguez, J.-F., 524
Rodríguez, Jemma, 361
Rodríguez, M. P., 283
Rodriguez, N., 35, 43
Rodríguez Cacho, L., 245
Rodríguez Castelao, Alfonso Daniel, 321, 338
Rodríguez Espiñeira, M. J., 222
Rodríguez Fer, Claudio, 337, 338
Rodríguez González, O., 335, 336
Rodríguez Juliá, Edgardo, 363, 364
Rodríguez Marcos, Javier, 289
Rodríguez de Montalvo, Garci, 247
Rodríguez del Padrón, Juan, 246, 247, 250
Rodriguez Somolinos, A., 35
Rodríguez Vega, F., 334
Rodríguez Velasco, J. D., 241
Roe, I. F., 713, 714
Roellenbleck, G., 79
Roemer, N., 734, 735
Roesch, Wolfgang, 638
Roetzel, L. C., 702
Roffé, Reina, 351, 360
Roffet, Pierre, 80
Roger of Hovedon, 6
Roger, J., 178
Rogers, M., 714, 819
Rogers, N. E., 167
Rogge, H., 686
Rohart, J. D., 350
Rohdie, S., 518
Rohland de Langbehn, R., 246, 247
Rohmer, E., 744
Rohou, J., 138
Rohr, W. G., 614, 617, 635, 779
Röhrich, L., 688
Rohse, H., 726
Roig, Jaume, 303
Roig, Montserrat, 288
Rojas, Gonzalo, 344, 353
Rojas-Trempe, L., 362
Roland, A. M., 371

Roland Holst, Adriaan, 790, 796
Roldán, A., 275
Rolfe, C. D., 183, 188, 189, 191, 883
Röll, W., 10, 634
Rolle-Risseto, S., 291
Rölleke, H., 672, 688, 883
Rollo, A., 431
Roloff, H.-G., 603, 646
Roloff, V., 262
Romagnani, G. P., 458, 465, 471
Roman, M., 165
Romani, A. R., 487
Romani, A., 257
Romani, V., 454
Romano, A., 439
Romano, Giulio, 423
Romanowski, A., 868
Rombach, A., 836
Romboli, F., 470
Romero, Concha, 292
Romero, J., 351
Romero, M., 332
Romero Cambrón, A., 222
Romero Esteo, Miguel, 294
Romero Ferrer, A., 258
Romeu Figueras, J., 307
Romisch, H., 316
Romo, L. L., 360
Römpp, G., 687
Roncaccia, A., 440
Ronchi, G., 374
Ronconi, G., 486
Ronconi, L., 505
Rondini, A., 515, 525
Ronge, H. H., 819
Ronneberger-Sibold, E., 580
Ronsard, Pierre de, 92, 95, 98, 104–07, 114, 782
Ronzeaud, P., 131
Roolfs, F., 624
Roos, G., 522
Roques, M., 17
Roquetti, A., 547
Rorchi, L., 237
Ros, E., 201, 206
Rosa, G., 471
Rosa, M., 454, 458
Rosa, Salvator, 692
Rosada, B., 526
Rosales Juega, E., 272
Rosales Sequeiros, X., 322, 324
Rosario-Andújar, J. A., 364
Rosarossa, A., 884
Rosellini, J. J., 771
Roselló Selimov, A., 342
Roseman, S. R., 327
Rosenberg, F. J., 347
Rosenberg, P., 457, 569
Rosenberg, R., 660, 715

Rosendal, J., 799
Rosengren, I., 812
Rosenlöcher, Thomas, 759
Rosenplüt, H., 629
Rosenstein, R., 217
Rosenthal, O., 96, 114
Rosenthall, S., 377
Rosier, L., 33, 34, 39
Rosito, M. G., 437
Rösler, D., 569
Rösler, R., 745
Rosmini, Antonio, 491, 492
Ross, C. S., 437
Rossarolli de Brevedan, G., 239
Rossbach, N., 767
Rossbacher, K., 714
Rossel, S. H., 829
Rosselli, Amelia, 521
Rosset, François de, 133, 140
Rossetti, Ana, 290
Rossetti, D., 473
Rossetti, Dante Gabriel, 405
Rossi, F., 384, 489
Rossi, Gian Domenico, 455
Rossi, L. C., 402
Rossi, L., 44, 66
Rossi, Luigi, 470
Rossi, M., 33
Rossi, N., 39
Rossini, A., 483
Rössler, D., 726
Rössner, M., 261
Rosso di San Secondo, Pier Maria, 497
Rost-Roth, M., 580
Rostaing, Charles, 210
Roszko, R., 850
Rot, Leonhard, 647
Rota, Berardino, 439
Rota, P., 485, 486
Roth, C., 627, 633
Roth, D., 9
Roth, Gerhard, 770
Roth, O., 139
Roth, U., 736
Rothenberg, J., 180
Rothwell, W., 46
Rotondi Secchi Tarugi, L., 431
Rotrou, Jean de, 132
Rotsaert, M.-L., 624
Rottem, Ø., 804, 806
Röttger, K., 347
Roudaut, F., 94
Rouillard, L. M., 71
Roukhomovsky, B., 145
Roulin, J.-M., 165
Rousseau, Jean-Jacques, 100, 146, 168, 337, 362, 457, 465, 677, 681, 694, 701, 758
Roussel, B., 108

Roussel, C., 65, 69
Rousset, J., 457
Roussineau, G., 71
Routledge, M., 213
Rouveret, A., 21, 314
Roux v. Ros
Roux, J., 203
Rovatti, Giuseppe, 466
Rovira, J. C., 883
Rowe, W., 362
Rowland, I. D., 437
Rowley, A., 584
Roy, Gabrielle, 185, 186, 194
Roy, P.-E., 185
Royer, Jean, 192, 195
Rozemond, M., 148
Różewicz, Tadeusz, 857, 871, 874
Rózsa, M., 718
Ruano de la Haza, J. M., 260
Ruberg, U., 594, 618, 626
Rubiera Fernández, J., 260
Rubiera Mata, M. J., 306
Rubin, D. L., 123
Rubino, Antonio, 521
Rubinstein, J., 4
Rubinstein, N., 453
Rubio, C., 247, 354
Rubio, I., 266
Rubio, J. E., 305
Rubio Cremades, E., 275
Rubio Jiménez, J., 278, 294
Ruby, D., 720
Rückert, Friedrich, 744, 746
Rückert, Luise, 746
Ruddock, Gilbert, 563
Rudnicki, A., 871
Rudnik-Karwatowa, Z., 859
Rudolf von Ems, 611, 616
Rudolph, A., 732, 733
Rudzki, P., 870
Rueda, A., 276
Rüegg, S., 764
Ruffato, Cesare, 521
Ruffer, J., 868
Ruffini, Giovanni, 493, 494
Ruffino, G., 877
Rufino, R. J., 16
Ruge, Arnold, 715, 746
Ruggeri, P., 191
Ruggiano, M., 484
Ruh, K., 616, 625
Rühmkopf, Peter, 770
Ruhrberg, C., 682
Ruisiñol, S., 274
Ruiter, J. de, 623
Ruiz, B., 360
Ruiz, I., 747
Ruiz, Juan, Arcipreste de Hita, 237

Ruiz Babero, M.,275
Ruiz Mayordomo, M. J., 251
Ruiz-Fornells, Enrique, 275
Ruja, A., 545
Rulfo, Juan, 346, 359
Rulman, Anne de, 209
Rumble, P., 518
Runeberg, Johan Ludvig, 826
Runkehl, J., 570
Runnalls, G., 81
Running, T., 348
Ruoff, A., 582
Rupert of Deutz, 594, 607
Rupolo, W., 521
Rüppel, M., 677
Rus, M., 89
Rusek, J., 573
Rushdie, Salman, 563
Ruskin, John, 405
Russ, C. V. J., 567, 569
Russell, P., 560, 746, 751
Russo, E., 444
Russo, F., 481, 485
Russo, L., 487, 501
Rusterholz, P., 729
Rustichelli, L., 470
Rutebeuf, 66, 67, 68
Rüther, H., 640
Ruthernberg, M. S., 444
Ruthner, C., 754, 765
Ruusbroec, Jan van, 626
Ruy Sánchez, Alberto, 361
Ruzante (A Beolco), 511
Rydberg, Carina, 834
Rydberg, Viktor, 826
Rymkiewicz, Jarosław Mark, 874
Rytel-Kuc, D., 854
Rzepka, W. R., 855, 857
Rzetelska-Feleszko, E., 858, 860
Rzewuska, E. v. Hanska
Rzewuski, Henryk, 857

Saage, R., 662
Saar, Ferdinand von, 746
Saari, M., 816
Saba, G., 123
Saba, Umberto, 502, 503
Sabbadino degli Arienti, G., 426
Sabel, J., 578
Sabourin, L., 158, 159
Sabrizi, L., 350
Sacher-Masoch, Leopold von, 704, 709, 718, 746
Sachs, Hans, 626, 629, 647
Sachs, Michael, 647–48
Sachs, Nelly, 770
Sachs, R. A., 757
Sack, V., 636
Sacotte, M., 199

Sacrobosco, Giovanni, 374
Sacy, S. S. de, 163
Sade, D. A. F., marquis de, 133, 142, 146, 161
Sadecka, M., 857
Sadoleto, J., 426
Sadowsky, T., 659
Saer, Juan José, 351
Safirman, C., 546
Sagard, Gabriel Théodat, 121
Sagarra, E., 705, 713
Sagnier, J., 159
Sahagún, Carlos, 281, 291
Sahlfeld, W., 520
Said, Edward, 175, 282
Saiko, George, 770
Sailer, J. M., 683
Sailer, M., 849
Saint-Amant, Antoine Girard, sieur de, 123
Sainte-Beuve, Charles Augustin, 157, 160, 172
Saint-Evremond, C. de M. de S.-D., seigneur de, 141
Saint-Gérand, J.-P., 31, 158, 161
Saint-Hyacinthe, Thémiseul de, 142
Saint-Jacques, D., 190
Saint-John Perse, 199
Saint-Martin, L., 193, 194
Saint-Sever, Gratianauld de, 116
Saint-Simon, L. de R., duc de; 141
Saítta, S., 348
Sala, E., 158
Sala, L., 878
Sala, M., 25, 226, 228, 230, 528
Sala Di Felice, E., 392, 883
Sala Valldaura, J.-M., 258
Salacrou, Armand, 179
Salaman, C., 434
Salaquarda, J., 743
Salas, A., 268
Salaün, E., 183
Salaün, S., 261, 281
Salazar, P.-J., 119, 120
Salazar-Ferrer, O., 546
Salazar Rincón, J., 270
Salberger, E., 816
Salcedo, Hugo, 361
Saldini, F., 465
Salemans, B., 776
Sales, E., 247
Sales, T., 303
Salfi, Francesco Saverio, 459, 495
Salgado, C. A., 363, 364
Salgado, M. A., 259, 341
Salgado, X. M., 332, 337
Salhi, K., 186, 197

Salinas, C., 244, 250
Salinas, Pedro, 259, 264, 265, 268, 282, 335
Salinas de Marichal, S., 267
Salkjelsvik, K. S., 360
Salkoff, M., 48
Salles, M., 178
Salman, J., 782
Salmons, J. C., 576
Salom, Jaime, 293
Salsano, F., 417
Saltarelli, M., 13, 21, 535, 883
Saludes Amat, A. M., 306
Salutati, Coluccio, 402
Saluzzo, Diodato, 472
Salvadori, F., 403
Salvadori, G., 510
Salvagnoli, Vincenzo, 494
Salvat, J., 208
Salvo Aguilera, B., 358
Samaritani, A., 436
Sambor, J., 851
Sammern-Frankenegg, F. R., 749
Sammons, J. L., 718, 735, 737
Samper Padilla, J. A., 877
Sampson, R. B. K., 18, 311
Samsó, J., 308
Samudio, Adela, 340
Samuelsson, R. S., 827
San José, J., 244
San Pedro, Diego de, 247–48
San Román, G., 364
Sancha, Antonio de, 256
Sanchez, Afonso, 331
Sánchez, C. F., 156
Sánchez, F., 346, 364
Sánchez, M. A., 248
Sánchez, T. A., 237
Sánchez de Arévalo, Rodrigo, 243, 249
Sánchez de Badajoz, Garci, 244
Sánchez-Blanco, F., 254
Sánchez Ferlosio, Rafael, 273
Sánchez Lancis, C., 224
Sánchez López, P., 345
Sánchez Miret, F., 18, 389
Sánchez Palomino, M. D., 320
Sánchez Prieto-Borja, P., 219, 223, 232
Sánchez Rei, X. M., 323
Sánchez de Santa María, José, 320
Sanchis Sinisterra, José, 293, 296
Sanchis Sivera, J., 301
Sancho IV (*King of Spain*), 239
Sancho, P., 299
Sand, George, 157, 166–68, 729, 731
Sandauer, A., 872

Sandbank, S., 762
Sandberg, M., 806
Sande, Jakob, 809
Sandelin, S., 841
Sandemose, Aksel, 809
Sandén, P. E., 838
Sandersen, V., 799
Sandgren, H., 839
Sandmann, A., 313
Sandoval, C. A., 362
Sandqvist, C., 811
Sandras, M., 161, 166
Sandred, K. I., 816
Sanford, G. U., 771
Sanguineti, Edoardo, 483, 503, 521–22
Sanguineti, F., 406
Sani, R., 426
Sankovitch, T., 213
Sannazaro, Jacopo, 438, 446
Sansone, G. E., 78, 408
Sansone, M., 492
Sant Jordi, Jordi de, 302
Santa Ana, Rafael, 279
Santa Cruz, Nicomedes, 362
Santa Fe, Jerónimo de, 249
Santa Fe, Pedro de, 246
Santa Rosa, Santorre di, 495
Santagata, M., 470, 481, 486
Santagiuliana, M., 489
Santamarina Fernández, A., 320, 324, 879
Santana Neto, J. A. de, 311
Santaniello, W., 741
Santano Moreno, J., 201
Santarém, Gil de, 304
Santareno, Bernardo, 272
Santato, G., 461
Santesson, L., 811
Santiago, R., 220, 222
Santiago-Otero, H., 883
Santiáñez, N., 275
Santillana, Íñigo de Mendoza, marqués de, 244
Santina, M. A., 50
Santini, M. C., 515
Santolaria Solano, C., 293
Santoli, C., 476
Santonja, G., 281
Santoro, C. C., 486
Santorsola, A., 469
Santos, A. L., 314
Santos, M. L. dos,. 369
Santos Domínguez, L. A., 226
Santos Noya, M., 643, 644
Santos Rego, M. A., 884
Santos Simões, J., 329
Sanuda, N., 636
Sanvitale, Francesca, 522
Sanz, J., 242, 245

Sanz, M., 23
Sanz Julián, M., 242
Sapa, D., 862
Saphir, Moritz Gottlieb, 705, 746
Sapienza, A., 469
Sappho, 471, 483
Sappler, P., 621
Sarabia, R., 345
Saralegui, C., 228
Saramandu, N., 538
Sarbiewski, M. K., 864
Sargent-Baur, B. N., 61, 79
Sarment, Jean, 279
Sarmiento, Domingo Faustino, 277, 340
Sarmiento, Fr. M., 884
Sarmiento, Martín, 254, 319, 320, 325
Sarnowsky, J., 630
Saro, G., 452
Sarraute, Nathalie, 176, 179–80, 197
Sartori, E., 97
Sartre, Jean-Paul, 150, 173, 177, 197
Sarzyńska, D., 851, 854
Sasaki, S., 60
Sasso, G., 884
Sassoli, Angelo, 478
Sasson, S. J., 735
Satiat, N., 163
Satkiewicz, H., 848, 850, 851, 854
Satta, Salvatore, 522
Sauder, G., 668
Sauer, N., 572
Sauge-Roth, K., 121
Saul, N., 664, 683, 686, 697, 703, 884
Saulini, M., 449
Saunders, A., 427
Saunier, A., 89
Saunier, E., 39
Saur, P. S., 770
Saurma-Jeltsch, L. E., 615
Saussure, F. de, 32
Saussure, L. de, 38, 39
Sauter, S., 351
Sauvadet, M.-R., 212
Savary, Olga, 369
Savater, Fernando, 284
Savelli, G., 491
Savinio, Alberto, 520, 522
Savino, G., 396
Savioli, S., 519
Savoca, G., 481, 484, 509, 515
Savonarola, Girolamo, 429, 437, 743
Savonarola, M., 429

Savy, N., 171
Savy, R., 377
Sawa, Alejandro, 259
Sawicka, G., 851
Sawicki, M., 852
Sayce, O., 618
Sayers, W., 44
Sbarbaro, Camillo, 522
Scafoglio, D., 456
Scaliger, Julius Caesar, 782
Scalvini, B., 466
Scamozzi, Vincenzo, 432, 433
Scannapieco, A., 464
Scantamburlo, L., 317
Scappaticci, T., 470
Scarlătoiu, E., 539
Scarlett, E., 256
Scarpa, D., 508, 517
Scarpa, E. M., 312, 313
Scarpa, Tiziano, 505
Scarpati, C., 515
Scarron, Paul, 133, 134, 141
Scase, W., 883
Scataglini, Franco, 511, 522
Scavo, R., 452
Scève, Maurice, 92
Schack, J., 800
Schade, G., 660
Schaefer, P., 725, 726
Schaefer, U., 592, 600, 611, 630, 884
Schäfer, F., 770
Schäfer, P., 646
Schäfer, W. E., 657
Schäffauer, M. K., 347
Schafroth, E., 33, 379
Schalk, A., 765
Schaller, D., 592
Schaller, K., 687
Schanze, F., 633, 634
Schanze, H., 670, 701
Schapira, C., 44
Schapira, N., 136
Scharff, T., 882
Schatz, A.-K., 712
Schaudig, M., 749
Schausten, M., 608, 611
Scheck, U., 882
Schecker, M., 571
Schede, H.-G., 766
Schedlinski, Rainer, 753
Scheepers, E., 789
Scheffel, M., 588
Schegk, Jakob, 637
Schehr, L., 162
Scheibelreiter, G., 733, 599
Scheichl, S. P., 713, 716, 740
Scheidt, G., 732
Scheifele, S., 697
Scheitler, I., 706

Scheiwiller, V., 515
Schelling, Friedrich Wilhelm Joseph, 682, 687, 701–02, 703, 744
Schellinger, P., 704
Scheltema, Paulus, 690
Schemme, W., 759
Schenck, L., 840
Schenkel, J., 779
Schenkeveld-van der Dussen, M. A., 776
Schenkeveld-van der Dussen, R., 783
Scherpe, K. R., 726, 879
Scherre, M. M. P., 309
Schestag, T., 696
Schettino, E., 456
Scheuer, H. J., 615
Scheuer, J., 801
Scheuermann, B., 581
Scheuringer, H., 583, 635, 880
Schiavoni, G., 775
Schick, C. Gosselin, 156, 187
Schie, Maria van, 785
Schiendorfer, M., 604, 632
Schiewer, H.-J., 587, 592, 883
Schiewer, R. D., 592
Schild, W., 630
Schildt, Runar, 842
Schiller, Friedrich, 664, 667, 669, 675, 685, 712, 715, 743, 767, 859
Schilling, D., 726
Schilling, J., 637
Schilling, M., 637, 883
Schimmel, Hendrik, 787
Schindel, Robert, 770
Schindler, O., 272
Schindler, R., 718
Schings, H.-J., 667, 672, 879
Schininà, A., 706, 771
Schiöler, N., 843
Schipke, R., 612
Schippel, L., 540
Schippers, A., 215, 780
Schirmer, H., 724
Schirmer, L., 724
Schirok, B., 611, 612
Schirrmacher, F., 773
Schirru, C., 385
Schlaffer, H., 684, 690, 725
Schlafman, L., 367
Schlant, E., 754
Schlechtweg-Jahn, R., 632, 635, 649
Schlee, T., 720
Schlegel, August Wilhelm von, 666, 667
Schlegel, Friedrich, 675, 680, 682, 701, 702

Schlegel, Johann Elias, 707
Schlegel-Schelling, Caroline, 702, 754
Schleiermacher, F 683, 684
Schlesinger, Klaus, 759
Schlette, M., 728
Schlieben-Lange, B., 580
Schlimgen, E., 742
Schlingensiepen, F., 735
Schlink, Bernhard, 770
Schlobinski, P., 570
Schlocker, G., 735
Schloenbach, Carl Arnold, 715
Schlögl, Friedrich, 705, 714
Schlögl, G., 740
Schlögl, W., 740
Schlosser, H. D., 601
Schlossman, B., 156
Schlott, M., 660, 677
Schmeltzl, Wolfgang, 638
Schmelzkopf, E., 718
Schmid, E., 610, 616, 630
Schmid, H., 551
Schmid, S., 387
Schmid, W. P., 586
Schmid-Bortenschlager, S., 706
Schmidel, Ulrico, 350
Schmidt, Arno, 745, 747, 770–71
Schmidt, B., 775
Schmidt, C., 569, 575
Schmidt, Christa, 674
Schmidt, H., 704
Schmidt, H.-J., 598
Schmidt, J., 666, 671, 693, 771
Schmidt, K. A. R., 11
Schmidt, K. M., 749
Schmidt, K., 739
Schmidt, M., 727
Schmidt, P. G., 6
Schmidt, R., 255
Schmidt, R., 691, 692
Schmidt, S., 859, 880
Schmidt, T., 767
Schmidt, V., 430
Schmidt-Bergmann, H., 739
Schmidt-Biggemann, W., 676
Schmidt-Rösemann, B., 703
Schmidt-Westman, H., 730
Schmidt-Wiegand, R., 630
Schmidtchen, V., 598
Schmitt, C., 44, 314, 44, 745, 881
Schmitt, K., 617, 633
Schmitt, L., 633
Schmitt, M., 7
Schmitt, M. P., 131
Schmitter, P., 377
Schmitz, C., 722
Schmitz, H., 692

Schmitz, W., 880
Schmitz-Emans, M., 757
Schmuki, K., 602
Schmull, H., 762
Schnaase, Karl, 725
Schnedecker, C., 37, 39. 40
Schneider, B., 636
Schneider, E., 548
Schneider, G. K., 769
Schneider, J., 623, 645, 757
Schneider, K., 591, 626
Schneider, M., 669
Schneider, Robert, 771
Schneider, S. M., 664
Schnell, B., 630
Schnell, R., 594, 602, 604, 618, 626, 627, 715
Schnepp, B., 759
Schnibben, F., 581
Schnitzer, C., 640, 651, 662, 884
Schnitzler, Arthur, 718
Schnucker, R. V., 638
Schnurre, Wolfdietrich, 771
Schnyder, A., 632, 633
Schnyder, F., 729
Schnyder, M., 614
Schnyder, P., 702
Scho, S., 710
Schobess, C., 771
Schoentjes, P., 34
Schoeps, K.-H., 771
Schöfferlin, Bernhard, 648
Schöier, I., 833
Scholz, C., 579
Scholz, L., 353
Scholz, M. G., 619
Scholz, M., 755
Scholz-Hänsel, M., 261
Scholze, D., 759
Schönborn, S., 662, 666
Schönert, J., 660, 748
Schönfeldt, Sybil Gräfin, 723
Schönherr, B., 576, 879
Schoolfield, G. C., 823
Schoonhoven, Jan van, 626
Schopenhauer, Arthur, 744
Schopenhauer, Johanna, 702, 705, 710, 742, 746
Schopf, W., 736, 737
Schottelius, Justus Georg, 653, 657
Schottenius, M., 834
Schottländer, S., 725
Schoultz, Solveig von, 842
Schouten, R., 796
Schrader, H.-J., 666, 719
Schrambke, R., 582
Schreckenberg, H., 595
Schreckenberger, H., 771
Schrenck, G., 112, 115

Schrijver, E. G. L., 734
Schrijver, P., 554
Schröder, E., 615
Schröder, F., 771
Schröder, I., 581
Schröder, J., 712
Schröder, V., 129
Schröder, W., 590, 591, 617
Schröter, U., 690
Schryver, R. de, 776
Schu, C., 616
Schubert, D., 743
Schubert, F., 873
Schubert, Franz, 673, 714
Schubert, M. J., 603, 604, 633
Schuchardt, H., 16, 389
Schück, H., 822, 832
Schuerewegen, F., 162
Schuler, S., 593
Schuller, M., 699
Schultz, H., 685
Schultze, B., 861, 862
Schultze, Johannes, 727
Schulz, Bruno, 869, 870
Schulz, M., 616, 880
Schulz Cruz, B., 356
Schulz-Grobert, J., 604, 632, 639
Schulze, I., 743
Schulze, U., 587, 629
Schulze-Belli, P., 624
Schulze-Busacker, E., 87
Schumacher, M., 594, 631
Schumann, Gerhard, 771
Schumann, H., 723, 727
Schumann, R., 585
Schunk, G., 582
Schupp, V., 574, 582, 880
Schüppen, F., 717, 730, 733, 738, 747
Schurmann, Anna Maria van, 657
Schürmann, M., 745
Schürr, F., 18
Schürr, R., 389
Schuster, J., 739
Schuster, K., 740
Schuster, P.-K., 724
Schütter, B., 754
Schütz, G., 729
Schwab, Gustav, 689, 717, 746
Schwab, U., 599
Schwab, Werner, 771
Schwabach-Albrecht, S., 732
Schwabe, T., 720, 746
Schwalb, C., 353
Schwan, W., 733
Schwardt, D., 771
Schwarz, A., 884
Schwarz, M., 572
Schwarz, R., 366

Schwarz, W., 548
Schwarz-Bart, Simone, 196
Schwarzbauer, F., 721
Schweda, M., 767
Schwedt, G., 674
Schweikert, R., 880
Schweikhart, G., 633
Schweimler, A., 722
Schweitzer, C. E., 706
Schwertck, H., 316
Schwitalla, J., 574
Schwob, A., 633
Schwob, M., 48
Schwob, U. M., 633
Schwöbel, S., 774
Sciascia, Leonardo, 504, 522
Ścibor-Rylski, Aleksandr, 857–58
Scinà, Domenico, 456
Scirocco, A., 472
Scobbie, I., 821
Scognamiglio, G., 472
Scollen-Jimack, C., 76
Scopesi, A., 385
Scotellaro, Rocco, 522
Scott, D., 761
Scott, Gabriel, 809
Scott, J. A., 400, 401, 415
Scott, P., 125
Scott, S., 153
Scott, Walter, 160
Scotto Di Luzio, A., 458
Screech, M. A., 97, 101, 102
Scribner, R., 656
Scrivano, R., 497
Scrofani, F., 383
Scudéry, Georges de, 121, 122, 142
Scudéry, Madeleine de, 120, 122, 133, 139, 142
Scully, T., 75
Scupoli, L., 149
Scurtu, G., 532
Sealsfield, C. (*pseudonym of* Postl, K.), 681, 711, 747
Sears, D., 179
Sebald, W. G., 754
Sébillet, Thomas, 96
Sebregondi, L., 437
Secchieri, F., 522
Sechehaye, A., 32
Sedgwick, A., 144
See, K. von, 590
Seebacher, K., 722
Seelig, G. F., 767
Seferens, H., 767
Segalen, V., 173
Segeberg, H., 748, 750
Segebrecht, H., 710
Segers, G., 781

Seghers, Anna, 771
Segre, C., 336, 438, 492, 503, 519
Segre, Dino v. Pitigrilli
Segù, E., 428
Seguin, J.-P., 31, 152
Seguin, M., 112
Seiber, S., 359
Seibicke, W., 585
Seibt, G., 730
Seidel, Heinrich Wolfgang, 719, 727
Seidel, J., 719
Seidensticker, P., 585
Seimens, W., 344
Seitz, D., 635, 879
Selbmann, R., 710, 733
Selboe, T., 806
Seldeslachts, H., 16
Selejan, A., 544
Selig, M., 203
Sellier, P., 120, 137, 146, 150
Selting, M., 572
Selzer Goldstein, N., 884
Sem Tob de Carrión, 238
Semon, L., 265
Sen, S. K., 573
Senabre, R., 244, 264
Sénac de Meilhan, Gabriel, 146
Señalada Garcia, F. J., 33
Senancour, E. P. de, 172
Senardi, F., 506
Senatore, F., 450
Senault, Jean-François (le Père), 146
Sender, Ramón J., 259, 288
Senderska, J., 864
Seneca, 306
Seng, E.-M., 662
Seng, J., 674
Sengher, Leopold Sedor, 737
Sengle, F., 716
Senkman, L., 348
Senna, M. de, 367
Sennrich-Levi, D., 214
Seoane, I., 329
Seoane, Luis, 338
Sepe, F., 513
Sephiha, H., 228
Seppänen, L., 571
Sequeira, F. J. M., 309
Serantini, Francesco, 522
Serao, Matilde, 495
Şerbănescu, A., 539
Şerça, I., 34
Sereni, Vittorio, 501, 502, 503, 510, 522–23
Sergiusti, Gherardo, 450
Serio, J. N., 406
Serio, Luigi, 466

Serlio, S., 432
Serlo of Wilton, 5
Sermain, J.-P., 141
Serme, J., 45
Serra, G., 482
Serrai, A., 427
Serrano, C., 261
Serrano, J. E., 259
Serrano, M. J., 230
Serrano, Marcela, 354
Serrano, S., 351
Serrano, V., 270
Serrao, G., 471
Serroy, J., 127, 143
Servaes, H., 166
Servin, H., 185
Servoise, R., 164
Settari, Gregorio, 458
Settembrini, L., 472
Seume, Johann Gottfried, 659
Seuse, H., 625
Severino, E., 484
Sévigné, M. de R.-C., marquise de, 142, 149
Seweryn, D., 866
Seybert, G., 167
Seybold, D. C., 681
Seyfarth, S., 574
Sgroi, S., 383, 391
Shakespeare, William, 1, 111, 150, 156, 166, 169, 334, 446, 698, 699, 742
Sharpe, L., 664, 675, 703
Shaul, M., 229
Shaw, D. L., 344, 345
Shaw, D., 128
Shaw, P., 482
Sheingorn, P., 64
Shepard, J., 597
Shepherd, M., 434
Sheppard, P., 278, 822
Sheppard, Sam, 272
Sheridan, G., 264
Sherr, R., 425
Sherwood-Smith, M., 630
Shua, Ana María, 351
Shyldkrot, H. B.-Z., 40
Siatkowska, E., 856, 859
Siatkowski, J., 845
Sibbald, K. M., 259, 263, 266, 268, 275
Sibille, J., 206
Siciliano, E., 507
Sick, F., 130, 132
Sidney, Sir Philip, 111, 557
Siebel, H. P., 731
Siebenmann, G., 270
Siebers, W., 726
Siebert, S., 577
Siebert-Ott, G., 570

Sieffert, R., 174
Siegel, E. M., 715
Siegrist, C., 659
Sienkiewicz, B., 873
Sienkiewicz, Henryk, 868
Sigier of Brabant, 410
Signorelli, F., 551
Signorini, R., 444
Sigrell, A., 813
Siguan, M., 716
Sigüenza, Xulio, 338
Siles, Jaime, 282
Siller, M., 585
Silone, D., 523
Silone, Ignazio, 523
Silva, D. J., 312
Silva, F. S., 316
Silva, G. M. O., 309
Silva, L. A., 310
Silva, M. C. F., 313
Silva, M. C. V., 311
Silva, M., 366
Silva, T. C., 312
Silva, T. S., 315
Silva, V. L. P., 315
Silva-Corvalán, C., 230
Silva Domínguez, C., 323
Silver, S. K., 123
Silverman, L., 770
Silvestri, A., 524
Simeoni, G., 427
Simian-Seisson, N., 209
Simion, E., 545, 547
Simkova, S., 128
Simmel, Johannes Mario, 771
Simmler, F., 577, 601
Simó, L., 246, 250
Simões, A. R. M., 313
Simon von Ruckersburg, 627
Simon, A., 636
Simon, Claude, 180–81
Simon, H.-U., 639
Simon, I., 633
Simon, J., 741
Simon, J.-F., 187
Simoncini, S., 431
Simonetti, C. M., 428
Simoni-Aurembou, M.-R., 31
Simonis, A., 714
Simonius, Simon, 637
Simons, M. A., 173
Simons, P., 61
Simonsen, K. M., 286
Simpson, J., 670
Simrock, Karl, 713
Sinclair, A., 260
Sinclair, F. E., 56
Sinding-Larsen, S., 436
Singh, G., 483
Singler, C., 364

Sinibaldi, M., 511
Sinielnikoff, R., 848
Sinigaglia, Sandro, 523
Sinisgalli, Leonardo, 523
Sinnreich-Levi, D. M., 74
Sinopoli, F., 500
Siôn Cent, 559
Siôn ap Hywel, 557
Sîrbu, Ion D., 546
Sîrbu, N., 542
Siti, W., 518, 519
Sitler, R. K., 358
Sivertson, R., 614
Siwek, G., 852, 854
Siwiec, M., 865
Sixtus V (*Pope*), 424, 431
Sjöberg, Alf, 831
Sjöberg, B., 826
Sjöberg, Birger, 842
Sjöberg, Erik, (Vitalis), 826
Sjoen, Y. T., 791
Sjögren, L., 827
Sjöstedt, G., 818
Sjöström, M., 841
Sjöström, R.-E., 841, 844
Sjöwall, Maj, 833
Skaftun, A., 805, 806, 807
Skalin, L.-Å., 837
Skare, R., 755, 756
Skármeta, Antonio, 353
Skarżyński, M., 854, 855
Skinner, L., 341
Skow-Obenaus, K., 640
Skram, 804
Skrine, P., 705, 729
Skubalanka, T., 857
Skutta, F., 35
Skwara, M., 869
Skytte, G., 802
Skyum-Nielsen, E., 798
Sławski, F., 845, 855, 857
Sleeckx, Domien, 786
Sleeman, P., 35
Slettan, D., 801
Slijper, B., 792
Slings, H., 779
Śliwiński, M., 865
Słowacki, Juliusz, 857, 862, 865, 867, 868
Słucki, Arnold, 874
Smart, S., 651, 652
Smet, I. A. R. de, 93
Smets, A., 66
Śmigielski, T., 870
Smith, C. C., 597
Smith, E. E., 740
Smith, E.C. (III) 160
Smith, G. L., 77
Smith, H. L., 84
Smith, J. C., 19

Smith, M. B., 11
Smith, M., 97
Smith, N., 318
Smith, P. J., 280
Smith, P., 864
Smith, V., 357
Smith, W., 241
Smith Seminet, G., 346
Smitmans-Vajda, B., 742
Smits-Veldt, M. B., 783
Smoje, D., 98
Smolinsky, H., 637
Smółkowa, E., 856
Smółkowa, T., 850
Smorkaloff, P. M., 355
Smotrycki, M., 846
Smulski, J., 861
Snaawaert, E., 363
Snaith, G., 188
Sneddon, C. R., 8
Snopek, J., 864
Soare, A., 125, 130
Sobczyk, A., 64, 76
Sobejano, G., 275
Sobolewska, A., 861, 873
Sobrevilla, D., 341
Sobrino Pérez, M. A., 327
Sobstyl, K., 851
Sochacka, S., 860
Socrates, 272, 275, 434, 743
Sødal, H. K., 807
Söderberg, G., 818
Söderberg, Hjalmar, 843
Södergran, Edith, 832, 834, 843
Söderlund, P., 825
Söderström, W., 827
Söderwall, K., 819
Sodini, C., 454, 455
Soffici, Ardengo, 524
Soglia, E., 477
Sografi, A. S., 478
Söhrman, I., 549, 552
Sokol, M., 39
Sokolski, J., 863, 864
Sola, A. de, 135
Solà, J., 299, 301
Solares-Larrave, F., 341, 359
Solbach, A., 704, 765
Soldani, M., 519
Soldati, Mario, 524
Soldevila Durante, I., 274
Soldini, F., 471
Soler, A., 303
Soler, L., 546
Solera, E., 519
Solla González, A., 336
Sollers, Philippe, 181
Solmi, Sergio, 503
Solms, H.-J., 878
Solms, W., 688

Sologuren, J., 344
Solomon, P., 762
Sołowjow, W., 866
Solstad, Dag, 808, 809
Solterer, H., 87
Sommer, A., 627, 628
Sommer, D., 342, 343
Sommerfeldt, K.-E., 585
Sommi, Leone de', 447
Sønderby, L. B., 806
Sonderegger, S., 589, 602
Sondheim, S., 303
Sonino, C., 738
Sonnevi, Göran, 842
Sonntag, E., 48
Sophia Eleonora (*Landgravin of Hessen-Darmstadt*), 652
Sophocles, 263, 334, 695
Sora, S., 540
Sorano, Domizio Palladio, 444
Sorbin, A., 93
Sørbø, J. I., 808
Sordello, 418
Sorel, Charles, 120, 134
Sørensen, B. A., 703
Sorensen, D., 350
Sørensen, F., 798
Sørensen, J. Kousgård, 799
Sørensen, S., 824
Sorescu, Marin, 544, 547
Sorescu, R., 546, 547
Sorg, A., 624
Sorg, B., 709, 733
Soria, Diego de, 245
Soria Olmedo, A., 270
Soriano, Elena, 283
Soriano, Osvaldo, 351
Sorkin, D., 679
Sornicola, R., 389
Sośnicka, D., 769
Sosa, E., 345
Sosnowski, A., 872
Sosson, J.-P., 877
Sotelo Vázquez, A., 273, 275
Sotelo Vázquez, M., 287
Sötemann, A. L., 792
Soto, F., 356
Soto, J. M., 883
Soulié, M., 97
Soumagne, L., 581
Sourian, E., 167
Sourieau, M.-A., 198
Sournia, J.-C., 112
Sousa Fernández, X. C., 319, 321, 322
Southern, R. W., 5
Southworth, E., 271
Souto Cabo, J. A., 321
Sozzi, L., 457
Spaggiari, B., 304

Spaggiari, W., 466
Spalatin, Georg, 648
Spallici, Aldo, 524
Spangenberg, K., 582
Spangher, L., 549
Spano, G., 392
Sparks, C., 151
Spaziani, Maria Luisa, 514, 524
Spear, T. C., 197
Specchio, M., 513
Speckter, H., 750
Spector, C., 152
Spee (von Langenfeld),
    Friedrich, 657–58
Spegel, Haquin, 824
Speirs, R., 741
Spence, N. C. W., 30, 46
Spence, S., 213
Spencer, C. J., 127, 131
Spengler, Oswald, 336, 742
Sperber, D., 38
Spescha, A., 551
Spetia, L., 65
Spica, A.-E., 146
Spiegel, G. M., 623
Spielberg, Steven, 272
Spielhagen, Friedrich, 707
Spielmann, G., 125
Spies, M., 777, 782
Spiess, Christian Heinrich, 664,
    703
Spiewok, W., 629
Spilling, H., 643
Spillmann, H. O., 884
Spina, S., 383
Spinazzola, V., 501, 504, 516
Spindler, Carl, 716
Spinetti, M., 430
Spinoza, Benedictus de, 667,
    668, 696, 790
Spiridon, C. M., 548
Spivak, Gayatri, 198
Spoerri, B., 605, 625, 641
Spoglianti, O., 486
Sponsler, C., 81
Spörl, U., 664
Sportiche, D., 21
Sprecher, T., 751
Spreckelsen, T., 734
Spreitzer, B., 592
Sprengel, P., 707
Sprenger, Balthasar, 648–49
Sprenger, M., 756
Sprouse, R. A., 28
Spyri, Johanna, 718
Squartini, M., 19
Squillacioti, P., 214
Squires, J. S., 273
Stachurski, E., 856
Stackmann, K., 581, 621, 622

Staden, Hans, 649
Stadler, H., 624
Staël, Mme. G. de, 154, 155
Staff, L., 868
Stagnelius, Erik Johan, 826
Stahl, I., 640
Staiger, M., 671
Staikos, K. S., 428
Stainton, L., 269
Stala, M., 872
Stålmarck, T., 824, 825
Stampa, Gaspara, 216
Stampa, Stefano, 489
Stampacchia, A. A., 170
Stan, I., 538
Stanceva, R., 547
Stanciu-Istrate, M., 545
Stangenberger, R., 719
Stanislaw-Kemenah, A.-K., 76
Stankowska, A., 873
Stanley-Blackwell, L. C., 184
Stanton, A., 358
Staphylus, Friedrich, 637
Stark, Ulf, 836
Starke, M., 20
Starobinski, J., 457
Stary, Z., 880
Starzyński, Stanisław Dol, 867
Stasse, M., 34
Stati, S., 537
Statius, 416
Staubach, N., 627
Stäube, A., 243
Stauffer, H., 654
Stebler, M., 759
Stecchetti, Lorenzo, 502
Stecher-Hansen, M., 806, 838
Steckbauer, S., 231
Steen, U., 750
Steene, B., 807, 830, 831
Steets, A., 771
Ştefănescu, I., 535
Stefani, A., 446
Stefanin, A., 413
Stefanovska, M., 141
Steffens, Henrik, 703
Steffens, R., 631
Stefonio, Bernardino, 448
Stegemann, V., 751
Steger, H., 582
Stehlíková, E., 747
Steiger, J. A., 644
Stein, D., 327
Stein, E., 7
Stein, P., 45, 715
Stein, S. I., 342
Stein, W. W., 363
Steinecke, H., 715
Steinegger, G., 568
Steiner, H., 707

Steingiesser, C., 675
Steinhoff, H.-H., 629
Steinhöwel, Heinrich, 636
Steinitz, R., 578
Steinkamp, F., 702
Steinle, C., 519
Steinmar, 587
Steinmetz, H., 727
Steinmetz, R.-H., 10, 620, 623,
    627, 632
Steinsdorff, S. von, 880
Stella, A., 491, 492
Stella, F., 468, 503, 523
Stellmacher, D., 581, 880
Stellmacher, W., 668
Stempel, W.-D., 201
Stendhal (Henri Marie Beyle),
    153, 159, 161, 164, 482, 487,
    724
Stenström, J., 824, 840
Stepanek, Lilly, 757
Stephan, A., 880
Stephan, R., 724
Stephany, U., 572
Stephens, A., 696
Stephens, M., 558
Stephenson, R. H., 662, 743
Stępnik, K., 863
Steppich, C. J., 614
Sterckx, C., 560
Stern, C., 251
Stern, E. E., 351
Sterne, Laurence, 367, 468, 474,
    475
Sterpos, M., 461
Steube, Johann Caspar, 659
Stevens, A., 612
Stevenson, Robert Louis, 349
Stewart, I. A. D., 343
Stewart, M. A., 281
Stewart, P., 152
Sthioul, B., 38, 39
Stickel, G., 569
Stieg, G., 570, 668, 734, 747
Stiening, G., 719
Stierle, K., 399, 616
Stiernhielm, Georg, 823
Stiernstedt, Marika, 842–43
Stifter, Adalbert, 682, 683, 701,
    704, 706, 707, 709, 716, 718,
    720, 747–48, 758, 874
Stigliani, Tommaso, 427
Stille, P., 817
Stillmark, A., 714
Stip, Kees, 796
Stirner, M., 743
Stirnimann, H., 625
St-Just, Antoine Louis Léon de,
    719
Stock, L., 155, 163, 170

Stock, M., 619
Stocker, G., 730
Stockhorst, S., 633
Stoica, R., 543
Stoichiţiu Ichim, A., 539
Stoiciu, Liviu Ioan, 542
Stojowski, A., 871
Stoke, Melis, 778
Stolk, F. R. W., 789
Stollmann, R., 768
Stolojan, S., 544
Stols, A. A. M., 796
Stoltzfus, B., 179
Stolz, D., 765, 773
Stolzenberg, I., 727
Stone, R., 271
Stoneburner, M., 74
Storck, J. W., 880
Stork, Y., 880
Storm, Theodor, 615, 683, 696, 704, 706, 707, 710, 748–50
Störmer-Caysa, U., 608, 609, 618
Storni, Alfonsina, 347
Storost, J., 881
Storrs, C., 455
Story, J., 3
Stounbjerg, P., 831
Stouten, H., 777
Stow, K. R., 597
Stramiello, C., 884
Strandberg, S., 817
Strapponi, L., 448
Strasser, A., 769
Straten, H. van, 793
Strauch, D., 725
Straumann, R., 729
Strauss, Botho, 753, 771
Strauss, J., 678
Streeruwitz, Marlene, 771
Streiter-Buscher, H., 723, 724
Streng, J. C., 787
Streuber, H., 745
Stricker (Der), 587, 622, 623
Strien, T. van, 777, 782
Strijbosch, C., 6, 624
Strindberg, August, 807, 822, 827, 828, 829–32, 834, 837
Stroh, C., 26
Stroh, H., 212
Strohm, S., 644
Strohschneider, P., 621, 883
Strohschneider-Kohrs, I., 659, 670
Strojkov, T. R., 353
Ström, Carl-Erik, 843
Strömstedt, M., 840
Stronks, E., 782
Stroud, C., 317
Strozzi, Palla, 431

Strozzi, Tito Vespasiano, 441
Strubel, A., 67
Struck, W., 699, 712, 745
Strudsholm, E., 802
Strumiński, B., 845, 854
Stryjkowski, J., 863, 871, 872
Strzelecka, J., 860
Strzyżewski, M., 867
Stuart, J., 783
Studt, B., 623
Stueland. E., 809
Stugu, O. S., 801
Stuhlmann, Adolf, 581
Stuip, R., 62
Stuparich, Giani, 524
Stuparich Criscione, G., 524
Sturm-Maddox, S., 70, 83, 105
Stussi, A., 373, 521
Stynen, L., 791
Suard, F., 884
Suárez, A., 247
Suárez, J. L., 260, 275, 349
Suárez Fernández, M., 222, 224, 225
Suassuna, Ariano, 369
Subrenat, J., 55, 82
Suchtelen, Nico van, 790
Suetonius, 93
Sufleţel Moraianu, R., 537
Sugg, K., 360
Sugiera, M., 873
Suhr, G., 736
Suhrbier, H., 745
Sullivan, H. I., 682
Sulzer, Johann Georg, 659
Sumien, D., 204, 205
Summers, J., 10
Sund, B., 839
Sundberg, B., 831
Sunder, F., 627
Sundgren, E., 814
Sundman, Per Olof, 843
Sundström, Gun-Britt, 843
Sundström, Mikaela, 843
Suntrup, R., 594
Supervielle, Jacques, 521
Supervielle, Jules, 35
Supple, J.-J., 112
Surdich, L., 512
Surin, Jean-Joseph, 121
Sussekind, F., 367
Süsskind von Trimberg, 621
Suszczyńska, M., 852
Sutton, M., 690
Suzuki, S., 602
Svahn, M., 819
Svantesson, J.-O., 811
Svedberg, O., 837
Svedjedal, J., 822, 842
Svensén, B., 822, 832

Svensøy, K. G., 807
Svensson, J., 811
Svensson, S., 835
Svevo, Italo, 524
Swahn, J. H., 834
Swanson, A., 824
Swanson, P., 351
Swart, H. de, 37, 40
Swedenborg, Emanuel, 824–25
Sweedler, U., 844
Sweetser, M.-O., 127, 131
Światlowski, Z., 761
Świdziński, M., 849
Święch, J., 869
Świeczkowska, H., 849
Świetlicki, M., 872
Swiggers, P., 16, 17, 200
Swisher, M., 614
Switten, M., 213
Sydow, C. von, 828
Sydow, C.-O. von, 824
Sylvester v. Gerbert,
Synnes, O., 805
Synowiec, H., 854
Syréhn, G., 825
Syson, L., 432
Szałagan, A., 870
Szarzyński, Sęp, 863, 865
Szczepankowska, I., 854
Szczęsny, S., 864
Szczuka, K., 869
Szemplińska, E., 869
Szerszunowicz, J., 855
Szkilnik, M., 51, 71, 72
Szlengel, W., 863
Szmetan, R., 348
Szondi, P., 832
Szpiczakowska, M., 856
Szpila, G., 851
Szturc, W., 865
Szubert, A., 801
Szulc, A., 880
Szumowski, A., 852
Szumska, D., 849
Szupryczyńska, M., 849
Szymborska, Wisława, 861, 871, 874
Szymonowic, S., 864
Szymutko, S., 861

Tabarelli, Paolo, 450
Tabarelli, Tommaso, 450
Taberner, S., 765, 773
Tabet, E., 154
Tabet, X., 452
Tabori, George, 771
Tabossi, P., 373
Tabouret-Keller, A., 206
Tabucchi, Antonio, 505, 524

Tachouzin, P., 112
Tacitus, 130, 599, 708
Tadini, E., 500
Taeger, B., 602
Taibo II, Paco Ignacio, 360
Taine, Hippolyte, 153
Talamo, G., 472
Talavera, Arcipreste de
  (A. Martínez de Toledo), 250
Talavera, fray Hernando de, 250
Talhaiarn (John Jones), 562
Tallemant des Réaux, Gédéon,
  142
Talvacchia, B., 423
Talvj (Therese Albertine Luise
  von Jakob), 717
Tamalio, R., 427
Tamaro, Susanna, 505
Tambling, J., 410
Tamburri, S., 451
Tammen, B. R., 630
Tamutis, K., 858
Tanaka, R., 158
Tănase, C.-M., 537
Tănase, E., 533
Tandefelt, M., 818, 820
Tannhäuser, 621
Tansey, J., 120, 121
Tańska-Hoffmanowa, K., 863
Tanturli, G., 451
Tanzer, U., 741
Tarakkamäki, J., 843
Taranowski, J., 858
Tarantino, M., 472
Taras, B., 849, 857
Tarayre, M., 11
Tardif, Guillaume, 11
Tardiu, J.-P., 204
Targioni Tozzetti, Fanny, 486
Tarnowski, A., 84
Tarrête, A., 93, 98, 144
Tarrío, A., 336
Tartarotti, Girolamo, 458
Tasmowski, L., 14
Tasmowski-De Ryck, L., 38
Tasso, Torquato, 402, 415, 424,
  438, 444–45, 446, 448–49,
  461
Tastu, Amable, 157
Tatar, M., 684
Tate, B., 249
Tate, D., 759
Tateo, F., 417, 430, 483, 484
Tatlock, L., 656
Tatlock, L., 745
Tato, C., 246
Tato, L., 329, 330
Tato Plaza, F. R., 321, 325
Tatti, M. S., 471
Tatzreiter, H., 880

Taube, Evert, 826
Taupiac, J., 204, 207
Tausch, Franz Borgia, 575
Tautil, G., 206
Tavani, G., 214
Tavares, M. A., 316
Taverna, Giuseppe, 473
Taverna, L., 34
Távora, Franklin, 368
Tawada, Y., 762
Tax, P. W., 612
Taylor, B., 239, 304
Taylor, Edgar, 690
Taylor, J. H. M., 74, 78, 79, 80
Taylor, K. J., 57, 884
Taylor, R., 719
Tcherkaski, J., 352
Tebaldeo, A., 445
Tebben, K., 705, 746
Techtmeier, B., 527, 539
Tegnér, Esaias, 827
Teiller, Jorge, 353
Teirlinck, Herman, 781, 795
Teissier, C., 769
Teitelboim, Volodia, 352
Teixeira Anacleto, M., 143
Teixeira de Pascoaes, Joaquim,
  333
Teja, A. M., 356
Tejedo-Herrero, L. F., 250
Tejera, Nivaria, 357
Teleman, U., 811, 812
Telesio, B., 435
Telli, D., 551
Tellier, C., 24
Tellini, G., 469, 482
Teltow, A., 724
Temperini, T., 451
Tempesti, F., 475
Tenenti, A., 423, 430
Tennant, E. C., 608
Tennyson, Alfred, Lord, 750
Tenzer, E., 869
Teodonio, M., 474
Teodorescu, M., 530
Teodorico dei Borgognoni, 304
Teodorowicz-Hellman, E., 835
Tepeneag, D., 547
Teposu, R. G., 545
Teraoka, T., 720
Termanini, S., 517
Ternaux, J.-C., 99, 117
Terrado Pablo, J., 220
Terrasse-Riou, F., 162
Terreni, L., 762
Terribile, C., 520
Terry, A., 306
Tervooren, H., 620, 878
Terzi, A., 21
Terzoli, M. A., 500, 515

Teschke, Holger, 771
Tessa, Delio, 502, 516, 525
Tessitore, F., 467
Tessitore, G., 494
Testa, E., 503, 510
Testa, F., 468
Testa, M. C., 426
Testori, Giovanni, 516
Teulat, R., 202, 204, 211
Teuscher, S., 631
Tewarson, H. T., 715
Teyssandier, B., 149
Teyssier, P., 310
Thali, J., 627
Thalken, M., 742
Thatcher, N., 40
Thavenius, J., 880
Theisen, B., 698
Thelander, M., 810
Thente, J., 834
Theobald, R., 740
Theocritus, 471
Théoret, France, 187, 194
Thériault, Yves, 194
Thestrup, M., 800
Thevet, André, 101
Thiam, M., 737
Thibault, A., 41, 42, 222
Thibaut de Champagne, 65, 216
Thienel, M., 745
Thiériot, G., 764
Thierling, D., 552
Thierry, A., 112, 114
Thiolier-Méjean, S., 202
Thiollet, C., 142
Thirard, M.-A., 135
Thirouin, L., 125, 138, 146
Thiry, C., 90
Thiry-Stassin, M., 60
Thoma, Ludwig, 713
Thomas Aquinas (*Saint*), 120,
  404, 409, 420, 435, 596
Thomas à Becket (*Saint*), 64
Thomas, 59, 60
Thomas à Kempis, 626
Thomas, Artus, sieur d'Embry,
  121, 124
Thomas, D., 742
Thomas, Gerald, 367
Thomas, J. T. E., 77
Thomas, J. W., 665
Thomas, Johann, 655
Thomas, M. Wynn, 562
Thomas, N., 613
Thomas, P., 788
Thomas, R. S., 564, 766
Thomas Dublé, E., 348
Thomasberger, A., 696
Thomasen, B. B., 803

Thomasin von Zerclaere, 587, 628, 630, 631
Thomason, S. G., 528
Thomé, H., 744
Thomke, H., 729
Thompson, J. J., 87
Thomsen, H. Erdman, 798
Thomsen, H., 732, 733
Thomson, R. M., 5
Thonon, S., 90
Thorau, H., 880
Thoregaard, H., 803
Thoresen, Magdalene, 805
Thorild, Thomas, 825
Thorne, D., 553
Thornton, A., 378
Thorpe, K., 762
Thunecke, J., 775
Thuret, M., 724
Thüring von Ringoltingen, 587, 618
Tiberia, V., 513
Tideström, G., 833
Tieck, Ludwig, 680, 681, 683, 697, 701, 703
Tierney-Tello, M. B., 354, 363
Tietmeyer, Maria-Therese, 689
Tighe, C., 871
Tignosi, Niccolò, 6
Tihanov, G., 674
Tilch, M., 736
Tilkin, F., 33, 34
Timm, Uwe, 771–73
Timofiejew, A., 866
Timpanaro, S., 479, 487
Tingbjörn, G., 810
Tinnefeld, F., 631
Tinnell, R., 264
Tinnemeyer, U., 581
Tinterri, A., 522
Tiraboschi, Girolamo. 457
Tischel, A., 732, 733
Tisnado, C., 363
Tissier, A., 80, 116
Titli, M., 387
Titone, M. S., 406
Titzmann, M., 615
Tjäder, B., 819
Tlusty, B. A., 637
Tobin, R. W., 148
Tobler, E., 627
Tobler, L., 16
Toch, M., 597
Tochard, Y., 210
Tocqueville, Charles Alexis Clérel de, 162
Todorov, T., 101, 616
Toesca, P. M., 475
Togeby, O., 801
Tognoni, G., 494

Tokarczuk, O., 871
Tokarski, R., 854
Toledo, M. P. Marcondes e Ferreira de, 369
Toledo Neto, S. A., 311
Tolstoi, A., 861
Tolstoy, Leo, 727
Toma, E., 537
Toman, R., 682
Tomaryn Bruckner, M., 216
Tomás, Consuelo, 347
Tomasek, T., 614, 615, 621, 628
Tomasello, D., 520
Tomasi di Lampedusa, Giuseppe, 445, 477, 497, 504
Tomasik, W., 872
Tomasin, L., 493
Tomassini, S., 452
Tomeo, Javier, 289
Tomescu, D., 538
Tomkins, C. M., 352
Tomlinson, C., 358
Tomlinson, E., 351
Tommaseo, Niccolò, 495
Tommasi, A., 519
Tommasini, G., 344
Tommasini, O., 452
Tompkins, C. M., 354
Tomuş, M., 546
Tondelli, L., 524
Tondelli, Pier Vittorio, 501, 525
Tone, N., 545
Tönnesen, C., 740
Tophinke, D., 631
Tophoven, E., 724
Torelli, Pomponio, 427
Torelli, Vincenzo, 494
Torgny, O., 824
Törnqvist, E., 830, 831
Törnqvist, Egil, 807
Törnqvist, L., 841
Toro, A. de, 344, 348
Toro, F. de, 344, 346, 348
Toro, M. I., 248
Toro, Suso de, 338
Torraca, F., 472, 473
Torre, Alfonso de la, 248, 301
Torre, Claudio de la, 279
Torre, Guillermo de, 262, 270
Torreblanca, M., 220
Torrente Ballester, Gonzalo, 289
Torres, A., 364
Torres, V., 344
Torres Feijó, E. J., 335
Torres Nebrera, G., 265, 278
Torres-Pou, J., 341
Torres Villarroel, Diego de, 257–58
Torrinha, F. F. de F., 309
Tortel, Jean, 179

Tos, L., 454
Toscana, David, 346
Toscanini, Arturo, 476
Toscano, R., 204, 209
Toscano, T. R., 442
Toso, F., 388, 439, 442
Touriñán López, J. M., 884
Tournier, Michel, 34, 181–82
Tournon, A., 96, 133, 143
Tourtet, E., 204
Toussaint, I., 194
Tovar, P., 356
Tozzi, F., 496
Tozzi, Federigo, 507, 525
Traba, Marta, 351
Trabant, J., 31, 580
Traber, H., 668
Träger, C., 733
Traina, G., 516, 522
Trakl, Georg, 763
Tramón, Marcos, 289
Trancón, S., 293
Tranströmer, Tomas, 843
Trapp, W., 596
Trappen, S., 879
Trautmann, G., 271
Travaini, Eugenio, 525
Travi, E., 489, 490, 492
Trechi, S., 489
Treece, R., 602
Treichel, Hans-Ulrich, 686, 773
Trejo, Nemesio, 352
Tremblay, Michel, 184, 185, 193, 194–95
Tremblay, V.-L., 187
Trémoille, Jean II de la, 113
Tremp, E., 607
Trend, J. B., 263
Trepte, H. C., 862
Trethewey, J., 119, 126
Treviño, E., 13, 884
Triana, José, 346, 347, 357
Tribolet-Aeschlimann, S. de, 626
Trifuoggi, F., 519
Trigueros, Cándido María, 253
Trinquier, P., 205, 209
Trissino, Gian Giorgio, 433, 445
Tristan, Flora, 169
Tristan L'Hermite, François, 122, 124, 133, 142, 143
Trithemius, Johannes, 645
Tritter, J.-L., 31
Trivero, P., 461
Trocchi, A., 500
Tropea, G., 384
Troszyński, M., 867
Trotha, H. von, 663
Trotter, D. A., 32, 215
Trottmann, C., 149
Trouille, M., 166

Trovato, R., 517
Trovato, S., 391
Troya Déniz, M., 877
Trudsø, L., 798
Trujillo, Rafael Leonidas
(*President of the Dominican
Republic*), 357
Trummer, M., 528
Trumper, J., 381, 391
Trunk, T., 724
Trunz, E., 666
Truth Goodman, R., 363
Tschopp, S. S., 729
Tsuchiya, A., 285
Tuccio, Stefano, 449
Tucker, G. H., 93
Tuczay, C., 609, 632
Tuczyński, J., 865
Tudor, A. P., 64
Tudoreanu, R., 546
Tudur Aled, 557
Tufano, L., 466
Ţugui, P., 527
Tully, C., 722
Tulot, J.-L., 138
Tumanov, V., 181
Turchetti, M. F.,463
Turcotte, Elise, 185
Turi, G., 497, 501
Turmeda, Anselm, 305
Turner, Dawson, 479
Turner, Elizabeth, 479
Turoldo, David Maria, 525, 526
Turpin, D., 47
Turrettes, C., 179
Turró, J., 302
Tusquets, Esther, 282
Tuţescu, M., 36
Tutsch, B., 631
Tuzine, A., 317
Tveita, J., 808
Tveito, F., 809
Twardella, J., 673
Twardowski, Jan, 858, 874
Twardowski, S., 864
Twardzik, W. B., 857
Twm o'r Nant (Thomas
Edwards), 561
Tworek, A., 850
Tyers, M., 172
Tynecka-Makowska, S., 869
Tyniecki, J., 867
Tyrmand, Leopold, 861, 874
Tyson, D. B., 84
Tyssens, M., 53
Tzaneva, M., 757


Ubaud, J., 205
Ubertowska, A., 874

Uc de Saint-Circ, 217
Udolph, J., 586
Uecker, H., 805
Ueda, S., 625
Ugarte, M., 281
Ugidos, Silvia, 289
Ugland, E., 807
Ugoni, C., 472
Uhl, P., 216
Uhland, Ludwig, 689, 709, 717
Uhlig, L., 676
Uhmann, S., 579
Ujejski, K., 861
Ukiah, N., 846
Ulacia, M., 358
Ułaszynówna, Z., 862
Ulbricht, W., 766
Ulchur Collazos, I., 354
Ulewicz, T., 855
Uliasz, S., 861, 871
Ulivi, A., 538
Ullrich, H., 682
Ulmschneider, H., 626
Ulrich von Etzenbach, 617
Ulrich von Gutenburg, 618, 619
Ulrich von Liechtenstein, 621
Ulrich von Türheim, 611
Ulrich von dem Türlin, 617
Ulrich von Winterstetten, 621
Ulrich von Zatzikhoven, 615
Ulrich, P. S., 713
Ulrich, R., 768
Ulven, Tor, 809
Umbach, R., 677
Umbral, F., 277
Umbral, Francisco, 281
Unamuno, Miguel de, 259, 260,
261, 273, 276, 277, 278
Undset, Sigrid, 809
Ungaretti, Giuseppe, 502, 516,
525–26, 757, 762
Unger, G., 157
Unsworth, S., 33
Unterburger, K., 687
Unzeitig-Herzog, M., 612, 614
Urbancic, A., 483
Urbańczyk, S., 845
Urbani, P., 427
Urbano, H., 310
Urdizil, Johannes, 747
Ureche, Grigore, 529
Urey, D. F., 274
Urfé, Honoré d', 143
Uría Maqua, I., 237
Uriţescu, D., 531, 538
Ursa, M., 546
Ursini, F., 388
Urso, A., 374
Usener, K., 615
Usk, Thomas, 10

Uther, H.-J., 719
Utz, P., 729
Utz, R., 884
Uxó González, C., 287
Uyttersprot, V., 780
Uz, Johann Peter, 744
Uztáriz, Gerónimo de, 254


Vaamonde, Florencio, 329, 338
Vaartjes, G., 790
Vacante, N., 496
Vaccari, M. G., 425
Vachon, S., 160, 161, 163
Vachon-l'Heureux, P., 43
Vadian, Joachim, 649
Vaessens, T., 789
Vaget, H. R., 750, 751
Vair, Guillaume de, 98
Vaissière, M., 203
Vakareliyska, C., 527
Val, C., 243
Valassina, G., 526
Valcárcel, M., 332
Valchère, Caroline, 153
Valcke, L., 431
Valderrama, Pilar, 290
Valdés, Juan, 260
Valdés, Zoe, 356, 357
Valdivieso, Mercedes, 354
Valdman, A., 47
Valencia Assogna, L., 363
Valenciano, A., 235
Valender, J., 264
Valente, José Ángel, 281, 291
Valentin, P., 579
Valenzuela, Luisa, 346, 350, 351
Valera, Juan, 16, 275
Valeri, D., 486
Valeri, Diego, 526
Valerio, S., 451
Valerio-Holguín, F., 360
Valerius Maximus, 251
Valero, E. M., 363
Valero, M. E., 365
Valéry, Paul, 523
Valette, B., 175
Valette, J.-R., 59
Valgimigli, M., 501
Valis, N., 288
Valla, Lorenzo, 11, 431
Vallaba, E., 272
Valladares, Marcial, 321
Valle, J. del, 16
Valle, José Cecilio del, 341
Valle-Inclán, Ramón del, 259,
261, 263, 277, 278, 294
Vallecalle, J.-C., 70
Vallee, L., 874
Vallejo, César, 346, 362

Valli, L., 395, 396
Vallone, A., 403
Vallvey, Ángela, 289
Valmarin, L., 548
Valori, Filippo, 429
Valperga di Caluso, Tommaso, 454
Valsalobre, P., 883
Van Alphen, Hiëronymus, 785
Van den Avenne, C., 210
Van Baest, M., 779
Van Den Bossche, M., 200
Van den Broek, C., 166
Van Deyck, R., 36, 80
Van Dijk, S., 167
Van Eeden, W., 531
Van Engen, J., 631
Van Eynde, L., 700
Van Hecke, T., 533
Van Hulle, D., 791
Van Peteghem, S., 791
Van Raemdonck, D., 35, 41
Van Sevenant, A., 34
Van Steen, Elda, 371
Van Tieghem, P., 156
Van de Velde, D., 30
Vance, B. S., 14, 28
Vance, S., 140
Vandamme, L., 788
Vanden Born v. Puteanus
Vanden Braembussche, A., 794
Vanderheyden, A., 48
Vanelli, L., 375, 549, 884
Vangelisti, P., 502
Vanhoutte, E., 791
Vanoncini, A., 162
Vantador, E. C., 480
Vaquero, M., 238
Vaquero de Ramírez, M., 228
Varano, Alfonso, 459
Varchi, B., 448
Varela, Diego de, 250
Varela, Lorenzo, 338
Varela Barreiro, X., 322
Varela Cabezas, R., 320
Varela Suanzes-Carpegna, A., 329
Varese, C., 468
Varga, D., 24
Vargas Llosa, Mario, 24, 346, 362, 363
Vargas Ponce, José , 258
Vargas, M., 347
Vârgolici, T., 545
Varnhagen, K. A., 686
Varnhagen, Rahel Levin, 154, 674, 703, 716
Varni, A., 472
Varol-Bornes, M.-C., 228, 229
Varty, K., 79

Vàrvaro, A., 14, 218, 240, 878
Vasari, B., 524
Vasari, Giorgio, 424, 447
Vasconcellos, J. Leite de, 316
Vasiluță, L., 537
Vasoli, C., 403, 433, 437
Vasque de Lucène, 72
Vassant, A., 41
Vasselin, M., 95
Vasvari, L. O., 234
Vatable, François, 108
Vatamaniuc, D., 545
Vatteroni, S., 214
Vaucher Gravili, A. de, 140
Vaugelas, C. F. de, 32
Vautier, M., 185
Vauvenargues, Luc de Clapiers, marquis de, 146, 172
Vázquez, Ruy (Rui Vasques), 321
Vázquez Fernández, L., 268
Vázquez Montalbán, Manuel, 281, 284
Vázquez Souza, E., 338
Vazsonyi, N., 151, 771
Vazzana, S., 413
Veca, S., 490
Veck, B., 179
Vedel, H., 802
Vega, M. J., 245
Vega Carpio, Félix Lope de, 260
Vegetius, 10
Vegio, Maffeo, 426
Vegt, J. van der, 792
Veiga, A., 223
Veisbergs, A., 802
Velasquez, Diego Rodriguez de Silva y, 524
Velcic-Canivez, M., 40
Velde, M. van de, 578
Veldhorst, N., 782
Velguth, M., 190
Venantius Fortunatus, 1
Vendryes, J., 17
Venesoen, C., 130
Venini, F., 478
Vennemann, T., 584
Ventola, E., 383
Ventura, J., 330
Venturelli, A., 743
Venturoli, A., 436
Verani, H. J., 358
Vérard, Antoine, 78
Verberckmoes, J., 781
Verbij-Schillings, J., 777, 778
Verbraeken, R., 42
Vercingetorix, 708
Verdaguer, P., 297
Verdan, D. T., 437
Verdi, Giuseppe, 492

Verdier, G., 879
Verdino, S., 503, 509, 513
Verdirame, R., 496
Verdon, L., 216
Verga, Giovanni, 470, 477, 495–96, 507
Verga, M., 457
Vergani, G., 476
Vergara-Mery, A., 354
Verger, J., 597
Vergerio, Pier Paolo (the Elder), 426, 431
Verheugd, E., 35
Verhulst, S., 486
Verhuyck, P., 78, 79
Verine, B., 39
Veríssimo, Érico, 372
Verna, A., 483
Verne, Jules, 542
Verner, K. A., 576
Vernet, M., 135
Vernieri, S., 368
Vernon, K. N., 264
Vero Saura, C., 506
Veronesi, D., 551
Veronesi, Sandro, 503
Verrault, R., 195
Verri, Alessandro, 459, 466, 473
Verri, Giovanni, 489
Verri, Pietro, 466, 473
Verrier, F., 453
Vervaeck, B., 793
Vesaas, Tarjei, 804, 809, 842
Veselovská, L., 20
Vesòla, J., 203
Vestad, G., 808
Vestdijk, Simon, 793
Vestly, Anne-Cath., 809
Veszprémy, L., 623
Vet, C., 37
Vetters, C., 37, 38
Viala, A., 98, 121
Viallaneix, P., 171
Vianello, V., 420
Viani, Francesco, 489
Vianna, L. H., 366
Vianna Neto, A. R., 189
Viaplana, J., 300
Viard, B., 171
Viau, Théophile de, 120, 123
Viaut, A., 204, 217
Vicario, F., 550
Vicente, Gil, 246, 251
Vicini, E., 500
Vickers, B., 359
Vico, Giambattista, 151, 170, 459, 464, 465, 466–67, 487, 488
Victorin, P., 73
Vicuña, Cecilia, 353

Vida, M. G., 438
Vidal Bolaño, Roberto, 331
Vidal Figueiroa, T., 324, 326, 327
Videsott, P., 551
Vidocq, F., 163
Vidua, Carlo, 472
Viehoff-Kamper, E., 749
Vieira, António, 367
Vieira, H. G., 316
Vieira. N. H., 371
Vieites, M. F., 337
Vienna, Carlo, 470
Viennot, E., 97, 98, 113
Vieregge, W. H., 576
Vierne, S., 167
Vietta, S., 737
Vieusseux, G. P., 472, 479
Vigário, M., 315
Vigeant, L., 194
Vigenère, Blaise de, 121
Vigliocco, G., 386
Vigneault, Gilles, 195
Vignes, J., 99
Vigneulles, Philippe de, 72
Vignoli, C., 549
Vignolo, M., 381
Vigny, Alfred de, 153, 157, 158, 159
Vigolo, M. T., 381
Vigorelli, G., 488, 490
Vikner, C., 798
Vilallonga, M., 308
Vilarem, S., 210
Vilaseca, D., 285, 286
Vilavedra, D., 329, 330, 335, 877
Vilches de Frutos, M. F., 262, 271, 292, 295
Vilhelmsdotter, G., 822
Villa, A., 404, 445
Villa, C., 415
Villafañe, Segundo I., 340
Villalba, Juan Manuel, 289
Villalta, G. M., 526
Villalta, L., 329
Villalta, M., 347
Villalva, A., 316
Villani, A., 695
Villanova, N., 362
Villar Ponte, Antón, 338
Villar, M., 337, 339
Villares Mouteira, F., 330
Villari, P., 463
Villasandino, Alfonso de, 244
Villaurrutia, Xavier, 359
Villaverde, Cirilo, 340, 343
Villebrun, I., 205
Villedieu, Marie-Catherine-Hortense Desjardins, *dite* madame de, 144

Villegas, Alonso de, 248
Villehardouin, G. de, 68
Villemaire, Yolande, 186
Villemur, F., 97, 98
Villena, Enrique de, 250, 308
Villena, Isabel de, 304
Villiers de l'Isle-Adam, Auguste, comte de, 33
Villon, François, 78, 79, 80, 90
Villoresi, M., 428, 441, 515
Villwock, P., 739
Viña Liste, J. M., 241
Vincensini, J.-J., 60, 71, 72
Vincent Ferrer (*Saint*), 248, 301, 304–05
Vincent of Beauvais, 11, 593
Vincent, N., 22, 882
Vincenz, Stanisław, 862, 871, 874
Vinestock, E., 114
Vinet, M.-T., 47
Vinge, L., 821
Vintilă-Rădulescu, I., 16
Violante Picon, I., 526
Viollet, C., 178
Vîrban, F., 530
Virey, C.-E., 115
Virgil, 1, 6, 8, 99, 105, 154, 174, 179, 180, 395, 398, 404, 415, 416, 418, 429, 444, 470, 657, 878
Virmaux, A., 546
Vis, G., 787
Visceglia, M. A., 424
Visch, E., 17
Visconti, G., 426, 446
Viscontini-Dembowski, M., 164
Vişniec, Matei, 542
Visscher, Anna Roemersdr., 783
Visscher, Maria Tesselschade, 783
Visscher, P., 780
Vital de Blois, 76
Vitale, M., 489, 492
Vitello, F., 512
Vitruvius, 432, 433
Vittorini, Elio, 500, 501
Vitz, E. B., 51, 65, 79
Vivaldi, Antonio, 460
Viviani, Cesare, 513
Viviani, Q., 473
Viziteu, C., 545
Vizkelety, A., 627
Vizmuller-Zocco, J., 393
Vlad, Alex, 541
Vlad, Vasile, 541
Vlad-Nedelcoviciu, V., 529
Vliet, H. T. M. van, 790
Vogel, W., 787
Vogeleer, S., 19, 884

Vogl, J., 672
Vogt, M., 733, 751
Vogt, U., 762
Vogüé, S. de, 38, 39
Voiculescu, Vasile, 545
Voigt, S., 771
Voisin, M., 155
Voiture, Vincent, 141
Volceanov, A., 535
Volceanov, G., 535
Volek, E., 349
Völker, H., 16
Vollhardt, F., 660, 677
Vollmann, B. K., 603
Volovici, L., 546
Volpilhac-Auger, C., 152
Volpini, Gaetano, 489
Volponi, Paolo, 499, 526
Volta, Alessandro, 456
Voltaire (François Marie Arouet), 34, 147, 150, 166, 864
Voltmer, E., 596
Vonhoff, G., 709, 722, 751
Voorbij, J. B., 779
Voorn, P., 633
Voorwinden, N., 610
Vordermayer, M., 685
Vordoni, S., 478
Vos, R., 20
Voskuil, J. J., 794
Vosmaer, Carel, 788, 789
Voss, Johann Heinrich, 655
Voss, Richard, 618, 712
Vosskamp, W., 660, 666, 669, 758
Votre, S. J., 313
Vovelle, M., 457
Vries, A. de, 785–86
Vries, Hendrik de, 694, 792
Vuillaume, M., 38, 879
Vuillemin, A., 547
Vuillemin, J.-C., 132, 133
Vuilleumier, F., 119
Vulpe, M., 527, 536


Wace, 56, 67
Wachinger, B., 618
Wackenroder, W. H., 680
Wackernagel, J., 21
Wackers, P., 778
Wade, M., 652
Waerp, H. H., 805, 806
Wägenbaur, T., 721
Wagener, P., 581, 585, 880
Wagner, D., 690
Wägner, Elin, 844
Wagner, F., 591
Wagner, K., 713, 746

Wagner, N., 585, 599, 608
Wagner, Richard, 263, 608, 750–51, 773
Wagner, W., 758
Wagner-Douglas, I., 725
Wagner-Egelhaaf, M., 738
Wagstaff, C., 518
Wahlberg, M., 817
Wåhlin, K., 811
Wahlöö, Per, 833
Wahrenburg, F., 715
Waibel, V. L., 694
Waichel, S. L., 314
Wailes, S., 647
Walczak, B., 847, 854
Walczak, G., 855
Walde, E., 598
Waldemar, T. P., 359
Waldinger, B. M., 168
Waldo (Waldo Williams), 563
Waldon, Johann Carl, 740
Walenski, T., 775
Waligóra, K., 573
Walker, C., 714
Walker, J. S., 673
Walkley, M. J., 90
Walla, F., 740
Wallach, M. K., 717
Wallén, B., 834
Wallenberg, Jacob, 825
Wallich, Paul, 727
Walliczek, W., 880
Wallisch, R., 642
Walschap, Gerard, 795
Walser, Martin, 667, 674, 773
Walser, Robert, 758, 760
Walsh, A. L., 289
Walsh, J. K., 236
Walsh, M. E., 352
Walsh, Rodolfo, 351
Walsh, T. J., 25, 225
Waltenberger, M., 616
Walter Map, 6
Walter, H., 46
Walter, P., 57, 63, 551, 645
Walter, T., 628
Walter, U., 716
Walters, H., 561, 562, 564
Walters, L. J., 58
Walther von Grieven, 609
Walther von der Vogelweide, 619–20, 738
Waltman, F. M., 242
Walusiak, E., 849, 850
Wambsganz, F., 763
Wandhoff, H., 610, 612
Wanegffelen, T., 144
Wang, L. M., 750
Wanicowa, Z., 850
Wańkowicz, M., 874

Wanner, D., 21, 223
Wanning, B., 702
Wanono, A., 210
Wansch, D., 263
Wapnewski, P., 620, 749
Warburg, K., 821
Ward, A., 218, 223, 877
Ward, D., 518
Ward, J., 623, 874
Ward, S., 768
Warminski, A., 695
Warmland, K., 828
Warncke, I., 574, 884
Warner, R., 277
Warning, R., 616
Warren, J., 714
Wartburg, W. von, 28
Wartusch, R., 697
Wąsik, Z., 846
Wasserman, R., 367
Wästberg, Per, 832
Waszakowa, K., 845, 852
Wat, Aleksander, 869, 870
Watanabe-O'Kelly, H., 651, 878
Watthée-Delmotte, M., 33
Wauquelin, Jean, 72, 73
Wauters, K., 786
Wawerla, G., 358
Wawrzyniak, Z., 569
Waxenberger, G., 599
Weaver, B., 355
Weaver, F. E., 148
Webelhuth, G., 579
Weber, A. P., 79
Weber, Friedrich Wilhelm, 716
Weber, H., 578
Weber, P. J., 550
Weber-Maillot, T., 154
Webern, Carl Maria von, 668
Weckmann, André, 773
Weerth, Georg, 715, 751
Wegener, H., 579
Wegera, K.-P., 878
Wegierski, L., 864
Węgłowska, E., 873
Wegner, B., 749
Wegner, W., 605
Wehrmann, H., 737
Weichselbaumer, R., 604
Weidemeier, K.-H., 584
Weidmann, P. H., 591, 631
Weifenbach, B., 634
Weigel, R. G., 766
Weigel, R., 769
Weigel, S., 625, 757
Weigele-Ismael E., 616
Weil, Simone, 564
Weill, I., 69
Weimar, K., 735
Weimayr, M., 605

Weinland, M., 724
Weinreb, F., 793
Weishaupt, Adam, 677
Weiss, H., 583
Weiss, H. F., 699
Weiss, J., 67
Weiss, J., 244
Weiss, J., 351, 357
Weiss, Peter, 773–75, 830, 843
Weissberger, B., 249
Weissenburger, Johann, 641
Weitin, T., 767
Welch, E., 423
Welker, H. A., 579
Welle, J. P., 518
Wellershoff, Dieter, 775
Wellmann, H., 571
Wells, S., 190
Welsink, D., 796
Wendelius, L., 833, 838
Wendler, Z., 39
Wendt, Bo-A., 818
Wengert, T., 645
Weninger, R., 717
Wenker, Georg, 858
Wennstedt, M., 816
Wentzlaff-Eggebert, H., 261, 263, 345
Wenzel, E., 618
Wenzel, H., 603, 883
Wenzel, M., 667
Werberger, A., 762
Werlen, I., 549
Werner, E., 880
Werner, H. G., 715
Werner, Markus, 775
Werner, N., 615
Werner, Richard Maria, 732
Werner, Zacharias, 683, 703
Wertheimer, Jürgen, 762
Wesenberg, A., 725
Wesendonk, Mathilde, 751
Wessely, K., 806
Westerström, J., 832
Westmorland, M., 200, 360
Westö, Kjell, 844
Westphalen, Emilio Adolfo, 344
Westum, A., 818
Wetsel, D., 149, 150
Wetzel, M., 663
Wetzel, R., 624, 633
Wexelsen, Marie, 805
Weydt, H., 880
Wezel, Johann Karl, 679
Wężyk, F., 861
Whaley, J., 665
Wharton, W., 861
Wheeler, M. W., 297
Whethamstede, John, 11
White, H., 288

White, J. J., 754, 760
White, N., 727
White, S. D., 62
Whitfield, P., 63
Whitman, Walt, 475, 476
Whyte, P., 155, 156
Wichter, S., 571
Wickens, H., 569
Widén, G., 833
Widhe, O., 840
Widmann, S., 643
Widmark, G., 816, 819
Wieczorek, J. P., 759
Wiedemann, B., 762
Wieg, Rogi, 796
Wiegandt, E., 871
Wiel, J. R. van der, 786
Wieland, Christoph Martin, 664, 676, 682
Wiemer, B., 859
Wiernikowskaja, T. W., 852
Wierschin, M., 609
Wierzbicki, J. S., 862
Wierzchowski, J., 848
Wiesinger, P., 575, 583, 586, 880
Wiesner-Hanks, M., 638
Wiessner, E., 621
Wik, I.-B., 842
Wiktorowicz, C., 194
Wilbrandt, Adolf von, 712
Wilcox, J., 333
Wilcox, J. C., 265
Wild, F., 133, 142
Wild, G., 635
Wild, I., 667
Wild, J., 631
Wild, R., 669
Wilde, L., 346
Wildemeersch, G., 795
Wilderode, Anton van (Cyriel Coupé), 794
Wildfeuer, A. G., 688
Wiliam, M., 554
Wiliam, U., 563
Wilkerson, T., 167
Wilkin, R. M., 120, 121
Will, C., 789
Willaert, F., 618, 619
Willard, C. C., 84
Willard, S., 84
Willeit, C., 551
Willems, D., 36
Willems, G., 879
William of Malmesbury, 3, 4
William of Ockham, 404
Williams, Gerwyn, 561, 563
Williams, G., 558
Williams, G. A., 558
Williams, G. S., 587, 635
Williams, Glanmor, 561

Williams, I., 558
Williams, M. A., 554
Williams, N. M., 563
Williams, P., 198
Williams, P., 482, 484, 487
Williams, R., 424
Williams, R., 772
Williams, R. L., 345
Williams, Rhydwen, 563
Williams, S. R., 554
Williams-Krapp, W., 633
Williamson, J. B., 76
Wilmet, M., 30, 33, 36, 39, 41, 884
Wilmink, W., 792
Wilske, D., 815
Wilson, C., 151
Wilson, D., 38
Wilson, Robert, 294
Wilson, W. D., 673, 677
Wilson-Chevalier, K., 98
Wilss, W., 577
Wiltshire, C., 18
Wimbauer, T., 767
Wimmer, Herbert J., 775
Wimmer, S., 361
Winckelmann, Johann Joachim, 679, 686
Windisch, R., 528
Winkler, G. B., 6
Winsnes, Hanna, 805, 807
Winter, C., 648
Winter, J., 814
Winter, U., 602
Winterbottom, M., 10
Wireback, K. J., 18, 219
Wirmark, M., 831, 837, 841
Wirnt von Grafenberg, 587, 605
Wirrer, J., 581
Wiśniewska, L., 874
Wistrand, S., 836, 837
Witkacy, Stanisław Ignac, 869, 870
Witkiewicz, Stanisław, 868, 870
Witosz, B., 852
Witt, J., 579
Witte, A. E., 1
Witte, B., 666, 735
Witteman, S., 795
Wittenwiler, Heinrich, 628, 632, 633
Wittern, R., 630
Wittgenstein, Ludwig von, 690
Wittkop, G., 693
Wittlin, C., 248, 306, 307
Wittlin, J., 862, 863
Wivel, H., 829
Woesler, W., 720, 721
Wohmann, Gabriele, 775
Wójcik, T., 869

Wójcikowa, Z., 845
Wojdowski, B., 863
Wojtak, M., 857
Wojtczuk, K., 855
Wolańska, E., 855
Wölck, W., 880
Wolf, A., 591, 605
Wolf, Christa, 752, 761, 775
Wolf, F. J., 235
Wolf, G., 883
Wolf, H., 391, 736, 737
Wolf, H. J., 325
Wolf, J., 622, 623
Wolf, L., 835
Wolf, N. R., 582
Wolf, R., 572
Wolf, T., 673
Wolf-Bonvin, R., 61
Wölfel, K., 744
Wolfert, R., 805
Wolff, Egon, 354
Wolfgang zu Fürstenberg (*Count*), 592
Wolfram von Eschenbach, 587, 591, 603, 604, 605, 606, 612–15
Wolfram, H., 597
Wolfzettel, F., 56, 57, 58, 59, 261, 612, 634, 884
Wołk, M., 873
Wollny, P., 679
Wollschläger, Hans, 746, 770
Wołowiec, G., 872
Wolski, J., 874
Wolski, W., 580, 762
Wolterbeck, M., 216
Wolzogen, Caroline von, 664, 675, 703
Wolzogen, H. D. von, 725
Wood, A., 141
Wood, C. T., 83
Woodford, C., 653
Woodgate, K. B., 692, 693
Woodhouse, J., 476
Woodyard, G., 352
Wooldridge, T. R., 42
Woolf, Virginia, 337, 861
Wörgötter, I., 583
Workman, L. J., 884
Woronowicz, J. P., 864
Worstbrock, F. J., 590
Worth-Stylianou, V., 125
Woshinsky, B. R., 130, 881
Wozonig, K. S., 744
Wrede, J., 821
Wren, Christopher, 141
Wright, C., 484
Wright, J. M., 168
Wright, R. H. P., 15, 218, 882
Wright, S., 524

Wróbel, J., 868
Wroth, Lady Mary, 111
Wruck, P., 724, 725
Wulf, E., 736
Wülfing, W., 715
Wullen, M., 724, 725
Wunberg, G., 884
Wunder, H., 652, 656, 884
Wunderli, Peter, 880
Wunderlich, D., 580
Wunderlich, W., 592, 593, 602, 614, 617, 746
Wuneng, Y., 667
Wünsch, M., 744
Würker, Achim, 691, 697
Wurm, Christian Friedrich, 690
Wurst, K. A., 677
Wuthenow, R.-R., 722, 733, 741
Wuttke, D., 629
Wyatt, D., 560
Wyclif, John, 10, 11
Wydmusch, S., 202
Wydra, W., 855
Wygant, A., 129
Wyka, M., 868
Wykes, S., 286
Wyller, E. A., 807
Wyn Wiliam, D. 561
Wynne, K., 316
Wyspiański, Stanisław, 868
Wyss, A., 457
Wyss, U., 619, 635
Wyszomirski, Jerzy, 870

Xenophon, 485
Ximénez de Sandoval, F., 262
Ximeno, L. M. de, 356
Xirgu, Margarita, 263
Xove Ferreiro, X., 330

Yandell, C., 97
Yanitelli, V. R., 446
Yates, A., 297
Yates, F., 100, 435
Yates, S., 160
Yates, W. E., 713, 714, 740
Yeats, W. B., 270
Yergau, R., 187
Ying Chen, 193
Ynduráin, D., 244
Young, C., 614
Young, Edward, 482
Young-Kyun, Ra, 718
Yourcenar, Marguerite, 182
Yovel, Y., 742
Ysern Lagarda, J.-A., 304
Ysgolan, 557
Yurkievich, S., 360

Zabarella, Giacomo, 435
Zaccaria, G., 487
Zaccaria, V., 486
Zachau, R., 768
Zachrisson, I., 813
Zaderenko, I., 234
Zadura, B., 872
Zaenker, K. A., 657
Zagajewski, Adam, 875
Żagar, M., 806
Zagari, L., 706, 737
Zahareas, A. N., 259
Zajda, A., 850
Zakrzewska, H., 863
Zaldívar, M. I., 351
Załęska, M., 848
Zambelli, Pietro, 474
Zambon, F., 502
Zamboni, A., 15, 549
Zamboni, S., 517
Zambrano, María, 267, 273, 277-78
Zamora, Juan Alfonso de, 235, 251
Zampieri, L., 481
Zanardi, Z., 428
Zanato, T., 440
Zanchin, M., 436
Zane, Giacomo, 446
Zanella, G., 486
Zanetti, G., 500, 503
Zangerl, A., 728
Zangrandi, A., 384, 480
Zanobini, M., 385
Zantop, S. M., 663, 664, 680, 708
Zanzotto, Andrea, 482, 485, 497, 501, 502, 503, 526
Zapata, Luis, 346, 360
Zapata, M. A., 362
Zapata García, Antón, 339
Zapolska, Gabriela, 869
Zapparolli, Z. M., 310
Zapperi, R., 675
Zappoli, S., 525
Zarader, J.-P., 182
Zardoya, Concha, 290
Zarębina, M., 856
Zarifopol, P., 77
Zarka, Y. C., 146
Zaron, Z., 852
Zarucchi, J. M., 140
Zarych, E., 870
Zăstroiu, R., 546
Zatta, J., 64
Zauberga, I., 802
Zauner, Friedrich C., 775
Zaunstöck, H., 660
Zawodniak, M., 872
Żbikowski, Piotr, 861, 862, 864

Zbróg, P., 847
Zebouni, S., 128
Zecher, C., 191
Zedler, J. H., 567
Zegadłowicz, E., 863, 869
Zegher, C. de, 353
Zeh-Glöckler, M., 568
Zehm, E., 668, 675
Zeler, B., 854
Zell, Katharina, 638
Zelle, C., 679,
Zeller, C., 744, 745
Zeller, H., 721, 739
Zeller, R., 655
Zellini, P., 487
Zelter, Karl Friedrich, 667, 668, 675
Zemb, J.-M., 578, 580
Zemke, U., 716
Zemskaja, E. A., 859
Zeno, Apostolo, 458
Zerbolt van Zutphen, Gerard, 626
Żeromski, S., 867
Zesen, Philipp von, 658
Zettersten, A., 803
Zettler, H., 724
Zeuch, U., 661, 747
Zeyen, S., 618
Zeyringer, K., 754
Zgółko, T., 854, 855
Zgółkowa, H., 854
Zhang, L., 883
Zhiri, O., 102
Ziątek, Z., 871, 875
Ziegeler, H.-J., 644
Ziegler, E., 727
Ziegler, J., 303
Ziegler, K.-H., 598
Zielińska, A., 853
Zielińska, M., 765
Zieliński, M., 852, 854
Zigaina, G., 517, 519
Zilberman, R., 371
Zils, H., 690
Zimmer, S., 554
Zimmermann, B., 666, 749
Zimmermann, H., 661, 678
Zimmermann, K., 28-29
Zimmermann, M. C., 262
Zimmermann, R. C., 667
Zimpel, D., 4
Zimra, C., 197
Zinato, E., 526
Zink, M., 65, 83
Ziółkowska-Boehm, A., 874
Ziolkowski, T., 880
Zipes, J. D., 684
Zito, C. A., 349
Zito, M. L., 474

Zittel, C., 743
Zitterer, M., 711
Zitzlsperger, U., 883
Žižek, S., 286
Žmegač, V., 709
Zmichowska, N., 863
Żmigrodzka, M., 861
Żmigrodzki, P., 849, 850, 854, 855
Zobel, Joseph, 196, 199
Zoberman, P., 133
Zoccolotti, P., 386
Zoggia, A., 480
Zola, Emile, 153

Zöller, S., 617
Zöller, W., 736
Żongołłowicz, B., 873
Zoppi Garampi, S., 434
Zoroaster, 436
Zschirnt, C., 662
Zschokke, H., 751
Zuberbühler, R., 723
Zubizarreta, M. L., 380
Zublena, P., 511
Zuccaro, F 424
Zucchetto, G., 214
Zucchi, Marcantonio, 465
Zucco, R., 478

Zugun, P., 536
Zukowski, T., 874
Zuleta Álvarez, E., 260
Zumbusch-Beisteiner, D., 714
Zumloh, T., 710
Żurek, S. J., 874
Zürrer, P., 583
Zutt, H., 611
Zwanenburg, W., 35, 531
Zweig, Stefan, 718
Zwink, E., 643
Zylinski, L., 726